WORLD CONGRESS ON NEURAL NETWORKS- SAN DIEGO

1994 INTERNATIONAL
NEURAL NETWORK SOCIETY
ANNUAL MEETING

TOWN & COUNTRY HOTEL
SAN DIEGO, CALIFORNIA USA
JUNE 5-9, 1994

VOLUME 2

Lawrence Erlbaum Associates, Inc., Publishers
365 Broadway
Hillsdale, New Jersey 07642

ISBN 0-8058-1745-X

WCNN '94 ORGANIZING COMMITTEE

Paul Werbos, Chairman, *National Science Foundation*

Harold Szu, *Naval Surface Warfare Center*

Bernard Widrow, *Stanford University*

WCNN '94 SPECIAL SESSION CHAIRS

BIOMEDICAL APPLICATIONS OF NEURAL NETWORKS
David G. Brown, *Center for Devices and Radiological Health,*
US Food and Drug Administration
John N. Weinstein, *National Cancer Institute, US National Institutes of Health*

**COMMERCIAL AND INDUSTRIAL APPLICATIONS OF
NEURAL NETWORKS**
Bernard Widrow, *Stanford University*

**FINANCIAL AND ECONOMIC APPLICATIONS OF
NEURAL NETWORKS**
Guido J. Deboeck, *World Bank*

**APPLICATION OF NEURAL NETWORKS IN THE
CHEMICAL PROCESS INDUSTRIES**
Thomas McAvoy, *University of Maryland*

MIND, BRAIN, AND CONSCIOUSNESS
John G. Taylor, *King's College London*

WCNN '94 PROGRAM COMMITTEE

Daniel Alkon, *National Institutes of Health*
Shun-ichi Amari, *University of Tokyo*
Richard A. Andersen, *Massachusetts Institute of Technology*
James A. Anderson, *Brown University*
Kaveh Ashenayi, *University of Tulsa*
Andrew Barto, *University of Massachusetts*
Horacio Bouzas, *Geoquest*
David G. Brown, *Center for Devices and Radiological Health, US FDA*
Gail Carpenter, *Boston University*
David Casasent, *Carnegie Mellon University*
Ralph Castain, *Los Alamos National Laboratory*
Chris Darken, *Siemens Corporate Research*
Joel Davis, *Office of Naval Research*
Judith Dayhoff, *University of Maryland*
Guido J. Deboeck, *World Bank*
David Fong, *Photon Dynamics, Inc.*
Judy Franklin, *GTE Laboratories*
Walter J. Freeman, *University of California at Berkeley*
Kunihiko Fukushima, *Osaka University*
Michael Georgiopoulos, *University of Central Florida*
Lee Giles, *NEC Research Institute*
Stephen Grossberg, *Boston University*
Dan Hammerstrom, *Adaptive Solutions, Inc.*
Robert Hecht-Nielsen, *HNC, Inc.*
Robert Jannarone, *University of South Carolina*
Jari Kangas, *Helsinki University of Technology*
Christof Koch, *California Institute of Technology*
Teuvo Kohonen, *Helsinki University of Technology*
Bart Kosko, *Signal and Image Processing Institute*
Clifford Lau, *Office of Naval Research*
Soo-Young Lee, *Korea Advanced Institute of Science and Technology*
George Lendaris, *Accurate Automation Corporation*
Daniel Levine, *University of Texas - Arlington*
Alianna Maren, *Accurate Automation Corporation*
Kenneth Marko, *Ford Motor Company*

WCNN '94 PROGRAM COMMITTEE

Thomas McAvoy, *University of Maryland*
Thomas McKenna, *Office of Naval Research*
Larry Medsker, *American University*
Erkki Oja, *Lappeenranta University of Technology*
Robert Pap, *Accurate Automation Corporation*
Barak Pearlmutter, *Siemens Corporate Research*
Richard Peterson, *Georgia Tech Research Institute*
Gerhardt Roth, *Brain Research Institute*
David Rumelhart, *Stanford University*
Mohammad Sayeh, *Southern Illinois University*
Dejan Sobajic, *Electric Power Research Institute*
Harold Szu, *Naval Surface Warfare Center*
John G. Taylor, *King's College London*
Brain Telfer, *Naval Surface Warfare Center*
Shiro Usui, *Toyohashi University of Technology*
John N. Weinstein, *National Cancer Institute*
Paul Werbos, *National Science Foundation*
Bernard Widrow, *Stanford University*
Takeshi Yamakawa, *Kyushu Institute of Technology*
Lotfi A. Zadeh, *University of California at Berkeley*
Mona Zaghloul, *George Washington University*

CONGRESS SPONSOR

The International Neural Network Society (INNS) is the sponsor of WCNN '94 - San Diego.

PRESIDENT	**Walter J. Freeman**, *University of California at Berkeley*
PRESIDENT-ELECT	**John G. Taylor**, *King's College London*
PAST PRESIDENT	**Harold Szu**, *Naval Surface Warfare Center*
SECRETARY	**Gail Carpenter**, *Boston University*
TREASURER	**Judith Dayhoff**, *University of Maryland*

BOARD OF GOVERNORS:

Shun-ichi Amari, *University of Tokyo*
James A. Anderson, *Brown University*
Andrew Barto, *University of Massachusetts*
David Casasent, *Carnegie Mellon University*
Leon Cooper, *Brown University*
Rolf Eckmiller, *University of Bonn*
Kunihiko Fukushima, *Osaka University*
Stephen Grossberg, *Boston University*
Mitsuo Kawato, *Advanced Telecommunications Research Institute*
Christof Koch, *California Institute of Technology*
Teuvo Kohonen, *Helsinki University of Technology*
Bart Kosko, *University of Southern California*
Christoph von der Malsburg, *University of Southern California*
Alianna Maren, *Accurate Automation Corporation*
Paul Werbos, *National Science Foundation*
Bernard Widrow, *Stanford University*
Lotfi A. Zadeh, *University of California at Berkeley*

ORDER OF APPEARANCE

TECHNICAL AREAS   continued

TABLE OF CONTENTS

Presenting author is listed first.

VOLUME 1

Plenaries

Special Session: Biomedical Applications of Neural Networks

Oral

TABLE OF CONTENTS   continued

Special Session: Commercial and Industrial Applications of Neural Networks

Special Session: Application of Neural Networks in the Chemical Process Industries

Special Session: Mind, Brain, and Consciousness

Oral

Applications

Oral

TABLE OF CONTENTS   continued

xii

Machine Vision

Oral

TABLE OF CONTENTS   continued

Neural Fuzzy Systems

TABLE OF CONTENTS   continued

VOLUME 2

Neurocontrol and Robotics

TABLE OF CONTENTS continued

Prediction and System Identification

Oral

Poster

Mathematical Foundations

Oral

Hardware Implementations

TABLE OF CONTENTS   continued

Biological Neural Networks

Oral

Poster

TABLE OF CONTENTS continued

VOLUME 3

Signal Processing

Oral

Pattern Recognition

Oral

TABLE OF CONTENTS   continued

Supervised Learning

Oral

TABLE OF CONTENTS continued

TABLE OF CONTENTS continued

Associative Memory

TABLE OF CONTENTS continued

Unsupervised Learning

Oral

Biological Vision

TABLE OF CONTENTS continued

Circuits and System Neuroscience

Oral

Links to Cognitive Science & Artificial Intelligence

Oral

Speech and Language

Oral

TABLE OF CONTENTS continued

Cognitive Neuroscience

Oral

Neurodynamics and Chaos

Oral

TABLE OF CONTENTS continued

Neurocontrol and Robotics

Session Chairs: Andrew Barto
Kaveh Ashenayi

ORAL PRESENTATIONS

Neural Networks for the Intelligent Control of Dynamical Systems

Kumpati S. Narendra
Center for Systems Science
Yale University
New Haven, CT 06520

1 Introduction

A control system is one in which some physical quantities are maintained more or less accurately around prescribed values. One of the fundamental contributions of control theory to science is the concept of feedback whose essence is the use of the error between the desired output and the actual output to control the system. Even very advanced control systems essentially use the same concept, but in such systems precisely what information is to be collected and how it is to be used in the control context is generally not evident. Examples of extremely efficient control systems abound in the biological world. The ease with which such systems perform the tasks of processing sensory information and interacting with uncertain environments has, for a long time, inspired engineers to attempt the design of artificial systems with similar capabilities. Most practical systems have multiple inputs and multiple outputs and the coupling that exists between them makes their control more difficult than that of single variable systems. External disturbances and parameter variations add to this difficulty and the problem of control becomes truly formidable when the system is nonlinear. Our objective in this paper is to describe a methodology for the fast, accurate, and stable control of nonlinear multivariable dynamical systems using neural networks.

An intelligent control system can be broadly defined as one which can operate rapidly and accurately in many environments. Hence a prerequisite for the design of intelligent controllers is that techniques be known for the design of effective controllers in each of the environments that the system might encounter. In this paper we consider systems whose characteristics are nonlinear and which have to operate satisfactorily in the presence of sudden variations in parameters, input disturbances and reference trajectories. Hence, we first describe briefly how neural controllers can be trained to accomplish each of the above objectives.

The training of a neural controller for any new situation is a slow process. Since our objective is to obtain fast and accurate response in all the different situations encountered, it seems reasonable to store the parameters of the neural networks trained for different control situations and use the specific control input that is called for at any moment. For example, if the system encounters a finite number of classes of disturbances, the parameters of the corresponding neural controller can be stored for each class. At any given moment, if the class to which the disturbance belongs can be recognized, the corresponding controller can be used to obtain fast and accurate response. The same procedure can also be used for different reference inputs, parameter variations and noise. Since neural networks perform well as pattern recognizers, expert systems, identifiers and controllers, they are ideally suited to deal with all the problems described thus far.

Due to space limitations, only the principal features of the method are included in this paper. The theoretical questions which are currently under investigation are also briefly outlined. For a more detailed treatment of the various ideas contained here, the reader is referred to [1].

2 Adaptive Control

Before proceeding to consider intelligent control we have to deal with the problem of adaptive control *i.e.*, the problem of controlling a plant whose input-output characteristics are not completely known. The adaptive control problem of a discrete time dynamical system may be stated as follows: The system is described by the equations

$$x(k+1) = f[x(k), u(k)] \tag{1}$$

$$y(k) = h[x(k)] \tag{2}$$

where the functions f: $\mathcal{R}^n \times \mathcal{R} \to \mathcal{R}^n$ and h: $\mathcal{R}^n \to \mathcal{R}$ belong to $\mathcal{C}^\infty$ and are unknown. It is further assumed that the state of the system cannot be measured. The objective is to determine a bounded control input $u(k)$ such that $lim_{k \to \infty} \parallel y_d(k) - y(k) \parallel = 0$ where $y_d(k)$ is a desired output.

There is a vast literature on the subject of linear adaptive control [2], but the above problem cannot be solved using such methods because the plant is nonlinear. We, however, attempt to use the indirect method, in which the plant is first identified using an identification model and the latter in turn is used to determine the optimal controller.

2.1 Input-Output Representation

In [3, 4] it has been rigorously shown that under certain conditions the plant (1-2) can be represented by an equation of the form

$$y(k+1) = F[y(k), y(k-1), ..., y(k-n+1), u(k), u(k-1), ..., u(k-n+1)]$$

where F is a general nonlinear function. Neural networks are ideally suited to approximate F and hence we set up a neural network model having the form

$$\hat{y}(k+1) = N_F[y(k), y(k-1), ..., y(k-n+1), u(k), u(k-1), ..., u(k-n+1)]$$

The parameters of the neural network N_F are updated using the error $e_I(k) = \hat{y}(k) - y(k)$.

2.2 Design of the Controller

Once a reasonably good model of the plant is known, we can attempt to control the plant. It has been shown in [4] that a controller G exists whose output $u(k)$ can be expressed as a nonlinear function of the inputs $y(k), y(k-1), ..., y(k-n+1), u(k), u(k-1), ..., u(k-n+1)$ and a reference input $r(k)$ (defined as the desired output $y(k+d)$) i.e.,

$$u(k) = G[y(k), y(k-1), ..., y(k-n+1), u(k), u(k-1), ..., u(k-n+1), r(k)]$$

Once again we attempt to approximate G using a neural network N_G. Since the only observed error is $e_c(k) = y(k) - y_d(k)$, and the plant lies between N_G and $e_c(k)$, the error has to be backpropagated through the model of the plant.

Simulations carried out during the past four years have clearly revealed that the above method performs very well in the adaptive control of a very large class of nonlinear systems. The mathematical requirements for the nonlinear identifier and nonlinear controller to exist have also been investigated in detail. A sufficient condition for this is that the linearized system around the equilibrium state can be controlled adaptively. Since this is true of almost all systems in industry, the outlined procedure has wide applicability.

3 Robust Control

As mentioned earlier, an intelligent controller is one which can operate satisfactorily under a variety of conditions. In this section we consider the extension of the concepts developed earlier to situations where external and internal perturbations are present.

In [5], the concept of indirect adaptive control was extended to cases where external disturbances are present at the input. The disturbance $v(k)$ was assumed to be bounded and governed by a difference equation of the form $v(k+1) = \eta[v(k)]$. It was shown that for a large class of systems, the effect of the disturbance at the output could be compensated by increasing the dimensionality of the controller.

In [6], the concepts of adaptation and disturbance rejection were extended to multivariable systems. The success of the adaptive methods also increased the search for faster and more accurate control. A few years ago this resulted in the concept of using multiple models and switching between them and tuning the appropriate controller. Such an approach proved effective in the presence of external disturbances as well as internal parameter variations.

4 Intelligent Control

The situations in which a controller is expected to perform satisfactorily can be broadly classified as (i) Anticipated Situations and (ii) Unanticipated Situations.

4.1 Anticipated Situations

This category includes those situations which are anticipated and for which adaptive solutions have been determined in the past. These can include disturbances, inputs and parameter variations which we shall jointly refer to as perturbations. Though, in theory, these perturbations can assume arbitrary values, such is not generally the case in real systems. The system is more likely to have perturbations belonging to a finite number of classes. For instance, if parameters of a system can vary due to faults within the system, their values are generally clustered, where each cluster corresponds to one type of fault. If the fault can be detected, the initial value of an adaptive controller can be chosen to correspond to a point within the cluster so that fast and accurate response can be obtained. In a typical case, the fault is detected and the neural networks, used as identifiers and controllers, are initiated at predetermined values and tuned on-line.

Extensive simulations have been carried out in this area at the Center for Systems Science at Yale University and a large body of empirical knowledge has been acquired in recent years. Research is also in progress to determine theoretical conditions for the stability of such nonlinear switching systems.

One of the principal decisions that have to be made is the classification of the different situations that can arise, and how the optimal controller parameters are to be stored and retrieved. If the number of distinctly different situations that can arise is small, this is not of major concern. However, when this number is very large, the organization of the information becomes critical. A hierarchical structure, similar to that used in pattern recognition, can be used for this purpose. For example, the first level of the hierarchy determines whether an observed change in output due to a given input is due to parameter variations or external disturbances or changes in the reference input. The next lower levels of the hierarchy would then correspond to regions in the parameter spaces where the perturbations lie. Specific parameter values are located at the next level. In all cases, pattern recognition (or identification using an appropriate model) can be used to detect the situation that exists and choose the appropriate controller.

4.2 Unanticipated Situations

When none of the existing models approximates the plant to within a desired tolerance, the situation must be classified as an unanticipated one. Identification, adaptation, learning all correspond to unanticipated situations where the approximate parameter values are not known. Once the process is completed and the parameters of the identifier and controller have reached stable values, the latter can be included in the class of anticipated situations.

When unanticipated (or new) situations arise and adaptation or learning is used, performance in the form of speed, accuracy, stability and robustness become important. A new approach, based on the use of multiple models and switching and tuning, has evolved in recent years for improving performance. A a set of models is used to identify the unknown plant and the one which corresponds to the smallest value of an error function is chosen at every instant. The controller corresponding to that model is connected to the plant and both identification model and controller are tuned on-line.

Multiple models can be used to determine the order of the system, the delay (or relative degree) of the system, which of several adaptive gains are to be used and which of different adaptive algorithms are to be preferred. It can also be used to determine the best among a set of models when the plant is nonlinear or to decide between neural networks of different sizes to represent a plant. Simulation studies of all the above cases have conclusively shown that the methodology is a sound one. Indeed, switching and tuning as an abstract concept appears to be steadily gaining ground among both control theorists and control engineers.

4.3 Stability

It is well known that while simple feedback can improve the performance of a system, it can also make the system unstable. Since "switching and tuning" is merely another form of feedback, the possibility of instability exists when we attempt to use it in a practical context to improve performance. Hence, determination of conditions under which switching and tuning systems are asymptotically stable is an extremely important problem. It is worth remembering, that even though adaptive control had been around since the early 1960s it was only after the stability problem of adaptive control was resolved in 1980 that adaptive control became a truly viable one.

5   Conclusion

Work is currently in progress at Yale in different aspects of adaptive control and intelligent control of nonlinear systems using neural networks. Theoretical work on the stability of different types of switching and tuning systems will appear in [7]. The application of methods based on multiple models to robotics will be reported in [8]. The improvement of performance by switching between discrete and continuous time controllers is the subject of [9]. Finally, a detailed discussion of intelligent control methods based on neural networks which address many of the issues raised in this paper can be found in [1] and [7].

References

[1] K. S. Narendra and S. Mukhopadhyay, "Intelligent Control Using Neural Networks", to appear in *Intelligent Control Systems*, M. M. Gupta and N. K. Sinha eds, IEEE Press, 1994.

[2] K. S. Narendra and A. M. Annaswamy, *Stable Adaptive Systems*. Englewood Cliffs, NJ: Prentice Hall, 1989.

[3] I. J. Leontaritis and S. A. Billings, "Input-output parametric models for non-linear systems, Part I: deterministic non-linear systems", *International Journal of Control*, Vol. 41, No. 2, pp. 303-328, 1985.

[4] A. U. Levin and K. S. Narendra, "Control of Non-linear Dynamical Systems Using Neural Networks, Part II: Observability and Identification", Tech. Report 9116, Center for Systems Science, Yale University, New Haven, June 1992.

[5] S. Mukhopadhyay and K. S. Narendra, "Disturbance Rejection in Nonlinear Systems Using Neural Networks", *IEEE Transactions on Neural Networks*, Vol. 4, No. 1, January 1992.

[6] K. S. Narendra and S. Mukhopadhyay, "Adaptive Control of Nonlinear Multivariable Systems Using Neural Networks", to appear in *Neural Networks*.

[7] K. S. Narendra and J. Balakrishnan, "Intelligent Control Using Switching and Tuning", Tech. Report 9312, Center for Systems Science, Yale University, New Haven, 1993.

[8] M. K. Ciliz and K. S. Narendra, "Intelligent Control of Robotic Manipulators Using Multiple Models and Switching", Tech. Report 9313, Center for Systems Science, Yale University, New Haven, 1993.

[9] H. Yang and K. S. Narendra, " Performance improvement in adaptive control systems by switching between continuous and discrete time controllers", in preparation, Center for Systems Science, Yale University, New Haven, 1993.

Radial Basis Function Networks for Mobile Robot Localisation

Neil W. Townsend   Mike J. Brownlow   Lionel Tarassenko

Robotics Research Group, Department of Engineering Science,
Oxford University, Oxford, OX1 3PJ, UK

Abstract

The problem of estimating a robot's $x - y$ position in its environment is considered. A neural network solution is proposed, using an RBF network whose hidden layer is a Kohonen feature map which relies on (optical) range data for its input. The optimisation of such a network is considered and results from such a network are given. It is shown that the network learns to compensate for the discontinuities in input space which are associated with obstacles within the environment. The network gives an average localisation error which is less than the diameter of the robot and is therefore acceptable for robot navigation tasks.

1   Introduction

There is an increasing demand for robots which can perform tasks which involve the motion not only of an object but also of the robot itself. If a robot is to be capable of moving around an environment in a manner which does not require the room to be specially configured (with beacons or wires under the floor, for example) it is necessary for the robot to be capable both of 'learning' the environment and of subsequently using this 'knowledge' to identify its position in the environment (*ie* to localise itself) and plan its next displacement.

The past decade has seen a resurgence of interest in using neural network techniques for solving problems which have yet to be completely solved using classical artificial intelligence techniques. The aim of the work described in this paper is to examine the suitability of neural techniques for solving the robot localisation problem from data acquired from a time-of-flight optical range finder.

The problem of estimating a robot's position from range scan data is exactly the type of problem which the Hough transform is capable of solving. However, the Hough transform is computationally expensive to perform and is restricted to a grid. Indeed, it is even rejected for line fitting to range data because of its unnecessary computational requirements compared to other methods. The other standard approach is to combine odometry with some form of beacon recognition and use triangulation to calculate a position estimate from within a Kalman filter.

Any localiser which relies on any form of odometry, however loosely, loses the ability to calculate an accurate position estimate if the odometry fails or if it doe not receive an initial position estimate from an outside source. One of the advantages of the neural network localiser described here is its independence from these requirements. We describe a localisation method which is based purely on range data.

2   Range sensing for robot localisation

Range sensing has mostly been performed using with sonar devices. Drumheller [4] showed how such data could be used to localise by extracting short line segments from the range data and matching them to a map of known straight lines in the environment. His results were remarkably accurate considering the problem of specular reflections which affects the determination of range using sonar. The main limit of his work, however, is the time taken to acquire and process a 360° range scan which means that the method could not be adapted to work in real time.

Sethi and Yu [15] used a multi-layer feed forward network, derived from an entropy-net solution, to solve the localisation problem. Their work simulated a robot with a ring of idealised sonar range sensors on its circumference. They trained a feed forward network to estimate the robot's position (*ie* to localise) using the range data from the sensors.

One of the earliest people to use a laser range finder to provide data for mobile robot localisation was Cox [2]. Using what could be described as the standard localisation cycle, in which odometry is used to estimate the robot's position and the sensor data is used to improve or correct the estimate, he showed that his sensor could provide useful data for this task. The estimate improvement was achieved by matching sensor data to an environment map and using the error in the match to correct the position. Freund and Dierks [5] pursued the avenue opened up by Cox and improved the accuracy and speed of the localisation by improving the search strategy of the matching.

Kurz [9] uses the same cycle but in a slightly different manner. He uses a Kalman filter to combine the odometry readings and the results from a Radial Basis Function (RBF) network. The RBF network is trained to identify the 'type' of region in the environment in which the robot finds itself, although the definition of 'type' is left to the training process. This information is used to error correct the position estimate given by the odometry and the Kalman filter. As with all Kalman filter based approaches, this is a time-dependent method (*ie* it relies on previous estimates to maintain the accuracy of its current estimate.)

3 The Oxford Infra-Red (I-R) range sensor

The sensor uses a 100% amplitude-modulated light beam at a frequency of 5MHz. The phase shift in the signal which comes back after reflection from a target surface is used to measure the distance to that target surface (the range value). The sensor also also generates an error signal which allows an estimate to be made of the variance for each reading [1]. Figure 1 shows the quality of the scan data for a difficult indoor environment.

4 Selection of input parameters

For this problem it might seem that the choice of input data is obvious: the range readings themselves provide data from which the robot's position in its environment can be estimated. There are, however, two reasons why this data is not used as the input vector to the network. Firstly, it is advantageous to limit the dimensionality of the input vector because it decreases the computational load if the network is implemented serially and because it is obvious that there is a high degree of redundancy in the information content in adjacent rays. Secondly, if the network is to be capable of successfully estimating its position in real time it is important for the input vector to be independent of the orientation of the robot (*ie* rotation invariant.) To satisfy these constraints a feature set, calculated from the range data, is chosen to be used as the input vector to the localisation network.

The final issue which it is important to consider when selecting input features for this problem is how smoothly the feature varies with small displacements of the robot in the x and y directions. For this reason, the number of visible corners is not a good input because it will undergo zero change for the vast majority of possible robot displacements but will change significantly for a (relatively) small number of small displacements. Having considered these factors, we selected the following seven features for out input vector:

- shortest range measurement in the scan
- median range measurement in the scan
- longest range measurement in the scan

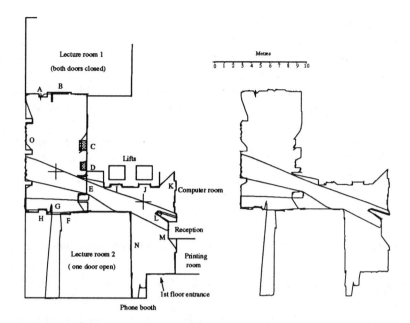

Figure 1: *Typical range scans taken using the Oxford I-R range scanner. On the left is the outline of a room is superimposed on two scans taken from inside that room. On the right the two scans are shown on their own.*

- magnitude of the largest discontinuity in the scan
- magnitude of the second largest discontinuity in the scan
- energy of the scan
- length of the longest wall segment visible to the robot

Intuitively one might expect that this list does contravene in part the requirement for a smoothly varying input vector. However the results in section 7 will show that the discontinuities in input space do not lead to severe discontinuities in the (x, y) output of the trained localisation network.

5 Selection of network

It can be shown, by considering the relation between the walls which make up a room and the path travelled by the I-R beam used to sense range, that the mathematical relationship between the position of a robot in an environment and the range scan data or features derived from that data is uninvertible for any environment other than a simple convex room. Neural networks have been shown to be capable of learning non-linear mappings with a single layer of hidden units [3, 12], with the additional advantage in this case that they do not need a map of the environment either to train or operate. Although they are computationally expensive to *train*, a trained neural network can provide an (x, y) estimate very quickly, especially if implemented in VLSI parallel hardware.

For this localisation problem, an RBF network was chosen because of its known approximating capabilities and because the activities of the hidden units can be visualised using a Kohonen feature map. Previous work has shown how effective and useful this can be [13, 14].

An RBF network has two layers; a non-linear layer followed by a linear layer. Each neuron in the first (non-linear) layer is a basis function whose centre c_j corresponds to a prototype vector in the input space. For a network with N inputs the basis functions are often chosen to be N dimensional Gaussians, with associated covariance matrices $\mathbf{F}_j$:

$$\phi_j = \exp\left(-\frac{1}{2}(\mathbf{x} - \mathbf{c}_j)^T \mathbf{F}_j^{-1}(\mathbf{x} - \mathbf{c}_j)\right) \tag{1}$$

where $\mathbf{x}$ is the input vector (7-dimensional in this case.)

The training of the first layer (*ie* the selection of the prototype vectors) can be performed with any unsupervised clustering algorithm, for example the adaptive K-means procedure [11]. We chose Kohonen's feature map algorithm [7, 8] instead because the topology preservation properties of the feature map allow us to visualise the clustering in a low-dimensional space (2 or 3-D). With the work described in this paper the K centres are positioned on a 2-D grid. After training neurons which are neighbours on the grid have centres which are close in input space in the Euclidean sense. This ensures that if the input changes smoothly over time the grid position of the Gaussian with the closest centre to the input should also vary smoothly. Once the first layer is trained the second (linear) layer is trained by estimating the linear relation between the desired results y_i (the (x, y) coordinates here) and the outputs of the first layer and a bias term:

$$y_i = \sum_{j=1}^{K} w_{ji}\phi_j + w_{oi} \tag{2}$$

This can be done using singular value decomposition or least means squared optimisation.

6 Network training

It is important to have sufficient training data for the number of free parameters in the network representation. For this problem, we found that 10000 points were sufficient: fewer points significantly affected the error rates whilst more did not significantly decrease the rates. It can also be advantageous to consider the distribution of training points: a redistribution such that regions of input space which are hard to learn contain more training points may be beneficial, though we found that it didn't significantly affect Average error rates.

It is also important to have a network of sufficient size for the complexity of the problem being solved. We found that a square Kohonen map of edge length 19 (*ie* 361 neurons) was sufficiently close to optimum, without imposing too heavy a computational burden during training.

During training, a set of training vectors $\{\mathbf{x}\}$ are presented at the input to the feature map. For each presentation the Euclidean distance, d_j, between the vector $\mathbf{x}$ and each centre $\mathbf{c}_j$ is calculated:

$$d_j = \|\mathbf{x} - \mathbf{c}_j\| \tag{3}$$

The centre $\mathbf{c}_{j*}$ which is closest to $\mathbf{x}$ (*ie* the centre which minimises d_j) is found. All the centres inside a neighbourhood $\mathcal{N}$ centred at $\mathbf{c}_{j*}$ are then updated according to the update equation:

$$\mathbf{c}_j(t+1) = \mathbf{c}_j(t) + \alpha(t)\beta(t)\left[\mathbf{x} - \mathbf{c}_j(t)\right] \tag{4}$$

$\alpha(t)$ is a gain parameter which decays exponentially with time, and whose initial value must lie between 0 and 1. $\beta(t)$ is the function which gives the size and type of neighbourhood $\mathcal{N}$ used for training. The neighbourhood is set to be large initially (so that the topological ordering occurs early during training) and decreases in size linearly with time until it contains only one unit or centre. Five values have to be set: $\alpha(0)$, the exponential rate of decay of $\alpha(t)$, the initial size of the neighbourhood $\mathcal{N}(0)$ and its rate of change $\frac{d\mathcal{N}}{dt}$ and the shape of $\beta(\mathcal{N})$. For this work we chose a standard set: $\alpha(0) = 0.5$ and $\mathcal{N}(0)$ was set to include the entire feature map; $\frac{d\mathcal{N}}{dt}$ was set so that $\mathcal{N}$ had shrunk to contain only one unit once half the training iterations had occurred. The decay of α was set to ensure that magnitude of the update became negligible at the end of training. β was chosen to be a triangular function decreasing from its maximum value of 1 at $\mathbf{c}_{j*}$ to a small negative value at the edge of the neighbourhood (*ie* a linear approximation to the Mexican hat function.)

At the end of training the widths of the Gaussian functions associated with each centre were set using the algorithm described by Hartman and Keeler [6] in which each basis function is given a covariance matrix of the form $\mathbf{F}_j = \sigma_j^2\mathbf{I}$ where $\mathbf{I}$ is the identity matrix and σ_j^2 is the squared Euclidean distance (in input space) between $\mathbf{c}_j$ and the nearest centre in input space. It is probable that the use of more complete covariance matrices would improve the accuracy of the results calculated using the (trained) network, though the benefit of these improvements is not likely to be great.

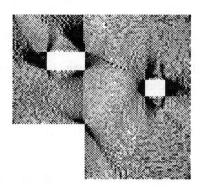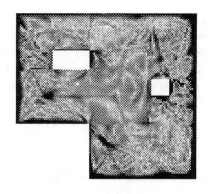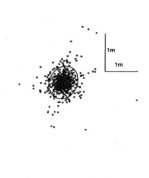

Figure 2: (a) *The left plot shows the change in input for a small change in position.* (b) *The central plot shows the localisation error across the room. In both plots black is high, white is low.* (c) *The plot on the right shows the error vectors for 1000 test points randomly distributed across the room together with the covariance ellipse (assuming a Gaussian distribution).*

7 Results

In section 4 it was stated that a smoothly varying input vector is preferable to one which varies dramatically for a small change in desired output. The effect of such discontinuities on the accuracy of the localisation was examined by calculating the differential of the input vector with respect to a small change in the robot's position at several thousand grid points across an environment. This measure of discontinuity is shown in figure 2a. The accuracy of the localisation from the trained RBF network is shown in figure 2b. The activities in the Kohonen feature map enable us to establish how the discontinuities in input space are transformed in the hidden layer of the RBF network. (In addition we can also follow the trajectories which are generated on the feature map as the robot moves around its environment.)

From these results it can be seen that the network has learnt to cope with the discontinuities in input space which surround the internal obstacles (note that the dark areas around the pillars in figure 2a have mostly gone in figure 2b.) However, in figure 2b, the boundary of the room is dark indicating a large localisation error in this area.

It could be that there is insufficient training data in these regions or that there is much less correlation between changes in input vector and changes in the absolute position of the robot in these regions than in the rest of the room.

To examine the overall accuracy of the network localisation was attempted at 1000 randomly placed test points in the environment. The average error ($\sqrt{(x - \hat{x})^2 + (y - \hat{y})^2}$ where x and y are the actual coordinates and $\hat{x}$ and $\hat{y}$ their estimates from the RBF network using the 7-D input vectors derived from the scan recorded at that position) was calculated for the 1000 results, and the distribution of the $x - y$ errors was approximated to a Gaussian. The average error was just over 23cm (which is well under the diameter of the robot; the major dimensions of the room are $4\frac{1}{2}$m by 5m) and the distribution of the points is shown in figure 2c.

8 Future work

It would be advantageous for the estimates which are generated by the network to have an estimate of the error associated with them. Ideally the (2x2) covariance matrix of the Gaussian probability distribution representing the positional probability density function of the robot would be calculated for each position estimate. Preliminary work indicates that the work of MacKay [10] on the computation of error distributions within multi-layer perceptrons can be extended to calculate error estimates for the output vector of an RBF network.

With this approach it will then be possible to construct the ideal localisation cycle: the combination of a Kalman filter with odometry and a neural localisation routine will allow for real time calculation of position estimates which are accurate, both benefiting from time information whilst being freed from any reliance on it.

The final issue which we will address is the combination of such a method with a strategy for learning the environment in which the robot is to operate. This will remove the restrictions imposed by a once-for-all learning cycle.

References

[1] M. Brownlow. *A time-of-flight optical range sensor for mobile robot navighation.* D.Phil. thesis, Oxford, October 1993.

[2] I.J. Cox. Blanche: Position estimation for an autonomous robot vehicle. In *IEEE/RSJ Internation Workshop on Intelligent Robots and Systems '89*, pages 432–439, September 1989.

[3] G. Cybenko. Approximation by superposition of a sigmoidal function. *Mathematics of Control, Signals and Systems*, 2(4), 1989.

[4] M. Drumheller. Mobile robot localisation using sonar. *IEEE transcripts in Pattern Analysis and Machine Inteligence*, PAMI-9(2):325–332, 1987.

[5] E. Freund and F. Dierks. Laser scanner based free navigation of autonomous vehicles. In *1st IFAC International Workshop on Intelligent Autonomous Vehicles*, pages 229–234, April 1993.

[6] E. Hartman and J.D. Keeler. Predicting the future: advantages of semi-local units. *Neural Computation*, 3, 1992.

[7] T. Kohonen. Self-organised formation of topologically correct feature maps. *Biological Cybernetics*, 43:59–69, 1982.

[8] T. Kohonen. The self-organising map. *IEEE proceedings*, 78:1464–1480, 1990.

[9] A. Kurz. Building maps based on a learned classification of ultrasonic range data. In *1st IFAC International Workshop on Intelligent Autonomous Vehicles*, pages 193–198, April 1993.

[10] D.J.C. MacKay. Bayesian interpolation. *Neural Computation*, 4(3):415–447, 1992.

[11] J. Moody and C.J. Darken. Fast learning in networks of locally-tuned processing units. *Neural Computation*, 1:281–294, 1989.

[12] J. Park and I.W. Sandberg. Universal approximation using radial-basis-function networks. *Neural Computation*, 3:246–257, 1991.

[13] J. Reynolds and L. Tarassenko. Spoken letter recognition with neural networks. *International Journal of Neural Systems*, 3(3):219–235, 1992.

[14] S. Roberts and L.Tarassenko. The analysis of the sleep eeg using a multi-layer network with spatial organisation. *IEE Proceedings-F*, 139(6):420–425, 1992.

[15] I.K. Sethi and G. Yu. A neural network approach to robot localisation using ultrasonic sensors. In *Proceedings of the 5th IEEE International Symposium on Intelligent Control*, pages 513–517, 1990.

Neural Network Control of a Free-Flying Space Robot

Edward Wilson*   Stephen M. Rock[†]

Stanford University
Aerospace Robotics Laboratory
Stanford, California 94305
ed,rock@sun-valley.stanford.edu

Abstract

Recent developments in neural network control at the Stanford Aerospace Robotics Laboratory are presented. A "Fully-Connected Architecture" (FCA) is developed for use with backpropagation (BP). This FCA has functionality beyond that of a layered network, and these capabilities are shown to be particularly beneficial for control tasks. A complexity control method is successfully used to manage the extra connections provided, and prevent over-fitting.

Second, a technique that extends BP learning to discontinuous functions is presented and applied to a difficult on-off thruster control problem. This method has many applications, namely any time a gradient-based optimization is used for systems with discontinuous functions. The modification to BP is very small, simply requiring replacement of discontinuities with continuous approximations and injection of noise on the forward sweep.

The viability of both of these neural network developments is demonstrated by applying them to a thruster mapping problem characteristic of space robots. Real-world applicability is shown via an experimental demonstration on a 2-D laboratory model of a free-flying space robot.

1   Introduction

In our research program in neural network control at the Stanford Aerospace Robotics Laboratory, we have developed some widely-applicable neural network methods during our efforts to apply networks to the control of a free-flying space robot.

In Section 2, the experimental equipment (robot) we have used in this research is described, and the particular thruster mapping problem we address is presented. Controlling the on-off thrusters presents a truly challenging problem for the neural network application. In Section 3, we present a "Fully-Connected Architecture" (FCA) for use with backpropagation (BP), that has greater functionality than a standard layered network. Particular benefits of the FCA, some of which are especially useful for control problems, are outlined. In Section 4, we present a method for using BP learning with systems containing discontinuous functions, such as the on-off thrusters on our robot. The method is a simple modification to standard BP, and extends to multiple layers of hard-limiting neurons or the FCA without modification. The experimental viability of these methods was verified on our robot, and is presented in Section 5.

2   Robot Control Application

The control task that motivated the neural network developments was the control of position and attitude of a free-flying space robot using on-off thrusters. Control using on-off thrusters is an important problem for real spacecraft, and the non-linear and adaptive capabilities of neural networks make them attractive for these problems.

Our experimental equipment consists of a mobile robot that operates in a horizontal plane, using air-cushion technology to simulate the drag-free and zero-g characteristics of space. This robot, shown in Figure 1, is a fully self-contained planar laboratory-prototype of a free-flying space robot complete with on-board gas, thrusters, electrical power, multi-processor computer system, camera, wireless Ethernet data/communications link, and two cooperating manipulators. It exhibits nearly frictionless motion as it floats above a granite surface plate on a 50 micron thick cushion of air [1].

---

*Ph.D. Candidate, Department of Mechanical Engineering. Research partially supported by NASA and AFOSR.

[†]Associate Professor, Department of Aeronautics and Astronautics.

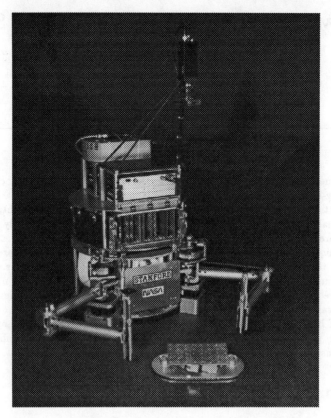

Figure 1: **Stanford Free-Flying Space Robot**

The three degrees of freedom (x, y, θ) of the base are controlled using eight thrusters positioned around its perimeter, as shown in Figure 2. The thruster mapping task to be performed during each sample period is to take an input vector of continuous-valued desired forces, $[F_{xdes}, F_{ydes}, \tau_{\theta des}]$, and find the output vector of discrete-valued (off, on) thruster values, $[T_1, T_2, ..., T_8]$, that minimizes a specified cost function. The on-off nature of the thrusters substantially complicates the control design, due to their discontinuous nature and the fact that each thruster simultaneously produces both a net force and torque. The current base control strategy is shown in Figure 2.

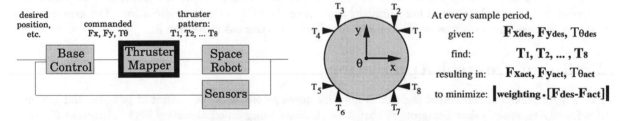

Figure 2: **Base Control Strategy, Thruster Mapping Problem Definition**

Left: the control strategy treats the thrusters as linear actuators. Right: the on-off thrusters and coupling between forces and torque make this problem difficult. The thruster mapper must find the thruster pattern producing a force closest to that requested by the base control module.

In this paper, we focus on developing neural networks for the "Thruster Mapper" component. A subsequent step, made possible by the developments in Section 4, is to merge the base controller and thruster mapper design into a single component, improving performance.

Three different techniques used to solve the thruster mapping problem have been applied as research progressed. They are summarized in Figure 3. The first implementation used an exhaustive search at each sample period to find the thruster pattern minimizing the force error vector [1]. Symmetries are used to

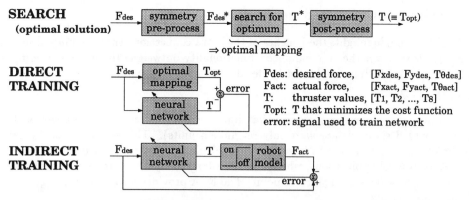

Figure 3: **Thruster Mapping Methods**

reduce the search space, but this method relies on testing every possible thruster pattern to find the one with minimum error. In the second method, a neural network was trained to emulate the optimal mapping produced by the exhaustive search [2]. This work led to the Fully Connected Architecture, presented in Section 3. The third method used a neural network trained to find the optimal solution when presented with a model of the plant, but no optimal teacher. This required back-propagation of error through the discontinuous thrusters, which motivated development of the noise injection method presented in Section 4.

3 Fully-Connected Architecture

3.1 Introduction

We develop a general architecture for feed-forward neural networks that can be trained using backpropagation [3] [4]. This "Fully-Connected Architecture" refers to the structure shown in Figure 4, which was first presented by Werbos [4] [5]. The network's neurons are considered to be ordered, beginning with the first input, ending with the last output, and having hidden units in between, perhaps interspersed among input or output units. Note that there is no longer a concept of layers. Backpropagation restricts information flow to one direction only, so to get maximum interconnections, each neuron takes inputs from all lower-numbered neurons and sends outputs to all higher-numbered neurons.

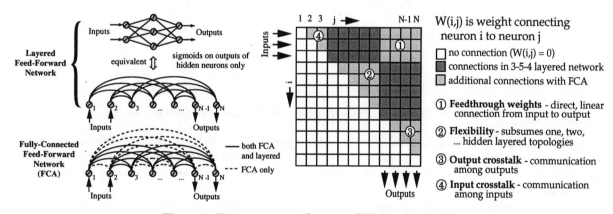

Figure 4: **Extra connections available with FCA**

This general feed-forward architecture subsumes more-familiar single or double-hidden-layer architectures. Here we show that it has all the connections of a single-hidden-layer network, and some extras as well.

3.2 Comparison with layered network

The right side of Figure 4 highlights the benefits of the extra connections that are unused in a single-layered network. The question is whether the enhanced functionality outweighs the increased computational load and susceptibility to over-fitting. This must be decided for each application.

Advantages of the FCA:

- The Feed-through segment is a matrix that implements a direct, linear connection from inputs to outputs (provided sigmoids are used only on hidden units). This provides fast initial learning and allows *direct pre-programming* of a linear solution calculated by some other method. This is particularly important for control applications, where there is a large body of linear control knowledge that can be drawn upon to provide a good starting point. The FCA provides for seamless integration of linear and non-linear components

- Flexibility: since the FCA subsumes any number of hidden layers, when combined with a systematic weight pruning procedure, the network topology (defined by the remaining connections) is set in a systematic manner based on gradient descent.

- Cross-talk among inputs and outputs may be valuable, i.e. one output may excite or inhibit another output, a feature unavailable with layered networks.

Disadvantages:

- Increased complexity: number of weights increases quadratically with the number of hidden units, versus linearly for a layered architecture. The extra weights increase susceptibility to over-fitting.

- Slower hardware implementation: updating must be one neuron at a time, versus one layer at a time for layered networks.

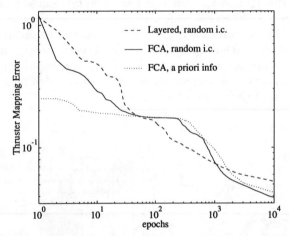

Figure 5: **Training History, FCA versus Layered Networks**

Figure 5 compares learning histories (thruster mapping error on the training set) for the thruster mapping problem outlined in the previous section. The networks, each with 5 hidden neurons, were trained to emulate the optimal mapping (minimizing force error). The figure represents the average performance for ten different sets of initial weights.

Looking at the initial learning performance, the FCA network performs better, due to the weight gradient being instantly available via the direct connection of inputs to outputs. As expected, the FCA network with the *a priori* linear solution built in provides the best early performance.

In the middle region, between 100 and 1000 epochs, the layered performance surpasses that of the FCA, due to the reduced number of parameters, and simplified search space. However, after 1000 epochs, the greater functionality of the FCA network comes into play and performance surpasses that of the layered network.

3.3 Complexity control

The example of Section 3.2 has shown the potential value of the extra connections associated with a fully-connected neural network. However, the high number of parameters, while increasing functionality, makes the network susceptible to over-fitting. Often during training, performance on test and training sets will improve until a certain point, and then test performance will worsen as the network stops generalizing, and begins to fit the particular data set, as seen in Figure 6. Use of a "sufficiently-large" training set can reduce over-fitting problems, but this may not be practical due to a lack of data, or an adaptation speed requirement that requires a faster solution than this brute-force approach.

Many systematic network pruning techniques have been proposed. One we have used successfully involves the addition of a complexity cost term to the total cost function, as first proposed by Weigend and Rumelhart in [6]. Each weight contributes $\lambda \cdot (w_s^2/(w_s^2+1))$ to the total cost function, where $w_s = w/w_0$ is a scaled value of the weight. The scale factor, w_0, effectively sets the cutoff point for weights, and λ selects the relative importance of complexity cost versus performance cost.

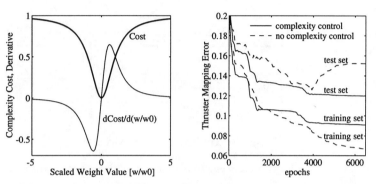

Figure 6: **Complexity Control Function, Effect on Network Performance**

The complexity control function and training histories for a fully-connected network with 5 hidden neurons are plotted in Figure 6. Without complexity control, over-fitting becomes clear at around the 4000th epoch, as the performance on the test set worsens, while performance on the training set improves. With the addition of the complexity term, over-fitting is controlled, as performance histories on test and training sets no longer diverge.

4 Backpropagation for Discontinuous Functions

4.1 Introduction

Optimization methods that us gradient information often converge much faster than those that do not. Use of the backpropagation algorithm to get this gradient information for training neural networks has made them useful in many applications; however, BP's requirement of continuous differentiability, not only for the network itself, but for anything that the error is backpropagated through (e.g. the plant model in a control problem), limits its applicability.

This is a significant limitation since there are many applications where discrete-valued states arise. For example: on-off thrusters commonly used in spacecraft; other systems with discrete-valued inputs and outputs; and NNs built with signums (aka hard-limiters or Heaviside step functions) rather than sigmoids. Signum networks may be preferred to sigmoidal ones due to hardware considerations.

In cases like these, one choice is to use an alternative method not restricted by to continuously differentiable functions, such as unsupervised learning, simulated annealing, or a genetic algorithm, but these are usually significantly slower to train, because they do not use gradient information.

Another option is to approximate the discrete-valued functions with linear functions or smooth sigmoids during the learning phase, and switch to the true discontinuous functions at run-time, as with the original ADALINE [7]. This method works in many cases where the behavior of the system with sigmoids is close enough to that of the real system. However, this assumption is unreliable, and the thruster control problem presented here offers a clear example where this method fails.

In related research aimed at using gradient-based learning for multi-layer signum networks, Bartlett and Downs [8] use weights that are random variables, and develop a training algorithm based on the fact that the resulting probability distribution is continuously differentiable. The algorithm is limited to one hidden layer, requires all inputs to be 1 or -1, and needs extra computation to estimate the gradient.

In this section we present a technique for BP learning for systems with discontinuous functions, and apply it to the on-off thruster control problem described in Section 2.

4.2 Noisy sigmoid training algorithm

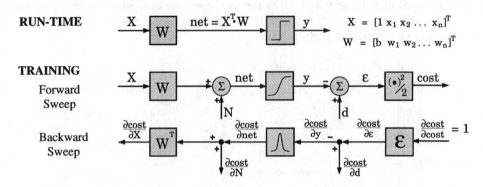

Figure 7: **Training Algorithm**
During training, replace discontinuous signums with sigmoids, and inject noise before the sigmoid on the forward sweep. The backward sweep calculation is the same as standard backpropagation.

We introduce the method of noise injection by applying it to the training of a single hard-limiting neuron, as shown in Figure 7. The first block diagram shows the neuron as it appears at run-time: a dot-product and hard-limiter. The next two diagrams show the neuron during training, where the hard-limit from the top diagram has been replaced by a smooth sigmoid function.

This is almost the same as training a standard neuron with backpropagation – the only difference involves the injection of zero-mean noise, N, immediately before the sigmoid. The noise injection enters just as the desired signal does, and does not corrupt the calculation of $\partial \text{cost}/\partial W$. Using an unmodified backward sweep is not only the simplest thing to do, it does precisely the right calculations for estimating the weight gradient. To summarize, the training algorithm is:

- Replace the hard-limiters with sigmoids during training
- Inject noise immediately before the sigmoids on the forward sweep
- Use the exact same backward sweep as with standard backpropagation

4.3 Intuitive Explanation

Without addition of noise, the network may train using values in the sigmoid transition region (roughly -0.8 to 0.8) that will be unavailable at run-time. Simply rounding off at run-time may introduce significant errors. For example, in a hypothetical cost surface, a value of 0.4 may be optimal, but if forced to choose between -1 and 1, a value of -1 may be better. The goal of noise injection is to move neuron activations away from the transition region, so round-off error will be small when the discontinuous functions are replaced.

An intuitive reason for adding the noise is to throw the neuron off its transition region, and effectively force it to hard-limit at the high or low value. For this reason, the standard deviation of the noise is chosen to be higher than the width of the transition region of the sigmoid. Figure 8 shows how the neuron output distribution changes as the noise level increases. With no noise, only a single output can result, but as noise increases to cover most of the transition region, the output distribution approaches that of a hard-limiting function. Differentiability is maintained, however, so gradient information will be available to speed up learning. Since the noise has pushed the distribution to approximate a hard-limiting non-linearity, when the hard-limiter is re-introduced at run-time the performance degradation will be small.

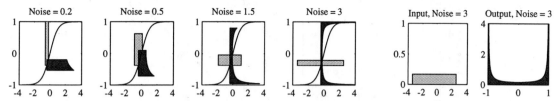

Figure 8: **Effect of Input Noise Level on Sigmoid Output Distribution**

Lightly-shaded region represents the sigmoid input probability distribution (in this case, $-0.3 +$ noise). Darkly-shaded region is the sigmoid output distribution (from -1 to 1), plotted horizontally to correspond to the sigmoid plot. Each distribution has an area of 1. As noise level increases, and the input distribution spreads out, the sigmoid output approaches that of a hard-limiter, while remaining differentiable. At right, input and output distributions are plotted separately.

4.4 Extensions, application considerations

This method has been successfully applied to multiple layers of hard-limiting units with no modification. One concern is the attenuating effect of the derivative-of-sigmoid function. When back-propagated through many layers of near-saturated sigmoids, the error signal is attenuated and may lead to slow learning. To handle this problem, it may be necessary to be gradual in increasing the noise variance - slowly push the outputs from the linear region to the hard-limits, rather than all at once, where the attenuation is high and the network will find it difficult to react.

When using a system with discrete-valued functions that are not Heaviside step functions, the method may work if a continuously differentiable approximating function is used. For example, a function whose output can take on a number of discrete values may be approximated by combining a number of sharp sigmoid functions. This was done for the thruster mapping, replacing the eight (0,1) thrusters with the equivalent set of four (-1,0,1) thrusters.

4.5 Application to space robot

Here, we apply this technique to the thruster mapping, as shown in the third section of Figure 3, where the network finds a solution itself, without the help of an optimal teacher.

Training without this noise-injection technique is not possible. For example if one unit of thrust is requested in the $+x$ direction, during training, the network will set T_4 and T_5 to 0.5, but at run time, for requested forces near 1.0, chances are they will both be 0 or both 1, resulting in a large error.

A good solution results when noise is added because it prevents the network from using a solution that uses non-saturated portions of the sigmoid. Such a solution would give a nearly random output and high error during training. The training algorithm must find a solution that works well *despite* the noise addition. This means the expected value of the output must be well into the saturated region to consistently work well. The results approximate the optimal solution very well, and work when the sigmoids are replaced with signums.

5 Experimental Results

Experiments were performed on the mobile robot described in Section 1 to verify the applicability of these neural network results. The neural network thruster mapping component described in Section 3 is implemented on the on-board Motorola® 68040 processor, as is the rest of the control system (at a 60 Hz. sample rate).

Figure 9 shows robot base position during single-axis and multi-axis maneuvers. For the single-axis maneuver (left), good tracking is obtained from both optimal and neural network thruster mapping components. In the 3-axis maneuver (right), the neural network control system closely follows the 20-second-long straight-line trajectory in (x, y, θ). Tracking error is very small, so to avoid clutter, only the robot's actual (x, y) position is plotted.

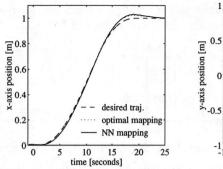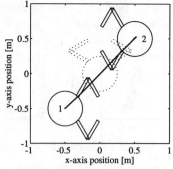

Figure 9: **Experimental Results, Single-Axis Maneuver, Multi-Axis Maneuver**

6 Summary and Conclusions

This paper has described two recent developments in neural network control that grew out of a research program using a laboratory-based prototype of a free-flying space robot. Both advances were motivated by, and developed for, a complex thruster mapping function typical of real spacecraft.

A fully-connected neural network architecture was presented that has connections beyond those provided by a layered network, yet is trainable with backpropagation. Aided by a systematic complexity control scheme, this network was shown to have certain advantages over layered networks, particularly for control problems.

A new technique was developed that extends BP learning to systems involving discontinuities, such as the on-off thrusters used to control our robot. The modification to BP is very small, simply requiring careful injection of noise on the forward sweep.

When tested experimentally on the real robot, all networks provided near-optimal performance during multi-axis trajectories, thus demonstrating the utility of these techniques.

References

[1] M. A. Ullman. *Experiments in Autonomous Navigation and Control of Multi-Manipulator, Free-Flying Space Robots*. PhD thesis, Stanford University, Stanford, CA 94305, March 1993.

[2] E. Wilson and S. M. Rock. Experiments in control of a free-flying space robot using fully-connected neural networks. In *Proceedings of the World Congress on Neural Networks*, Portland OR, July 1993.

[3] D. E. Rumelhart, G. E. Hinton, and R. J. Williams. Learning internal representations by error propagation. In David E. Rumelhart, James L. McClelland, and the PDP Research Group, editors, *Parallel Distributed Processing*, page 318. The MIT Press, Cambridge, MA 02142, 1986.

[4] P. J. Werbos. *Beyond Regression: New Tools for Prediction and Analysis in the Behavioral Sciences*. PhD thesis, Harvard University, Cambridge, MA 02142, August 1974.

[5] P. J. Werbos. Backpropagation through time: What it does and how to do it. *Proceedings of the IEEE*, 78(10):1550–1560, October 1990.

[6] A. S. Weigend, B. A. Huberman, and D. E. Rumelhart. Predicting the future: A connectionist approach. *International Journal of Neural Systems*, 1(3):193–209, 1990.

[7] B. Widrow and R. Winter. Neural nets for adaptive filtering and adaptive pattern recognition. *IEEE Computer*, 21(3):25–39, March 1988.

[8] P.L. Bartlett and T. Downs. Using random weights to train multilayer networks of hard-limiting units. *IEEE Transactions on Neural Networks*, 3(2):202–210, March 1992.

A Neural Network Based Visuosteering Control Algorithm for Autonomous Land Vehicles

Doo-hyun Choi*, Se-Young Oh*, and Kwang-Ick Kim†
*Dept. of Electrical Engineering, †Dept. of Mathematics
Pohang Institute of Science and Technology
Pohang, South Korea 790-600

Abstract

A neural network based navigation algorithm has been developed for the Postech Road Vehicle I (PRV I) to drive on outdoor roads with intersections on campus. The neural net essentially watches a human to drive and remembers driving signals for different road conditions and later on, generalizes this knowledge to similar road conditions. Four neural net modules are used for outdoor driving. The first one detects intersections just by being shown typical intersections. If an intersection is detected, a higher level command selects the proper one among three network outputs, namely the left turn net, the straight-ahead net, and the right turn net. For verification, the whole algorithm has been tested on campus roads and also in simulation of various driving conditions.

I. INTRODUCTION

There has been increasing interest in neural network applications that demonstrate their relative advantages over existing techniques. One application area which can take advantage of neural network's implicit trainability and superior mapping capabilities is autonomous road driving. Research done so far involving outdoor or indoor vehicles include VISOCAR by Frohn et al. [1], Blanche by Cox [2], MAVIN by Baloch[3], NAVLAB I and II by Carnegie Mellon University(CMU) researchers[4][5], VaMoRs by Dickmanns[6], and CONCIC-2 by Cheng et al.[7]. Both the NAVLAB and the VaMoRs demonstrate speedy highway driving. However, these systems require extensive computing power and/or specialized hardware for real time control.

This paper presents a PC-based algorithm based on neural nets to drive on roads with intersections using only camera inputs. Basically, neural nets are trained to implicitly learn the relationship between the input road scenes and the corresponding steering signals by watching a human to drive. Previous navigation research involving neural nets is done by Pomerleau, Baloch, and Cheng of which only Pomerleau has worked with outdoor vehicles. The neural net essentially watches a human to drive and remembers driving signals for different road conditions. But, in order to detect intersections, he relies on other types of sensors such as a laser range finder and an inertial navigation system, whereas only camera data have been used in this paper. Besides, a minimal set of image information (instead of the whole image as in Pomerleau's work) sufficient for vehicle control was input to the net, since the system is based on a PC without any image processing hardware. Four neural net modules are used for outdoor driving. The first one detects intersections just by being shown typical intersections. If an intersection is detected, a higher level command selects the proper one among three network outputs, namely the left turn net, the straight-ahead net, and the right turn net. For verification, the whole algorithm has been tested on campus roads and also in simulation of various driving conditions.

II. Vehicle System Configuration

Fig. 1 shows the vehicle tested PRV I with six wheels altogether, two in the front, two in the middle, and two in the rear. The front and rear pairs are free wheels having no power and the middle pair are driven by two 500 Watt DC motors. The on-board batteries provide power for motors and computers. Eight ultrasonic sensors are attached to the front of the vehicle for emergency stops and obstacle avoidance maneuvering. The vehicle state (forward velocity and steering direction) control command is given either by a remote control pendent for a manual teaching mode or by a program on PC486 for an autonomous mode. This command becomes the set point for the vehicle direction and speed adjusted by the relative difference between the two driving motor speeds and directions. The computer talks to the remote controller through an RS-232C port and also to the vehicle controller board through 80C196 microcontroller's on-chip serial port.

III. Navigation System

A. Neural Network Steering

Fig. 2 illustrates the navigation algorithm in block diagram form. The camera image goes through a very simple preprocessing scheme to be explained in the next subsection. The IDNN (Intersection Detection Neural Network) is trained to recognize road intersections by being shown several examples of them. In case the vehicle has encountered an intersection, the high level path planner, using the road map and the GPS (Global Positioning System) data, decides whether to preceed straight, turn left, or turn right. Depending on the outcome of this decision, the system takes the steering command from a proper output among LTNN (Left-Turn Neural Network), STNN (Straight-going Neural Network), and RTNN (Right-Turn Neural Network). For no-intersection case, it simply takes an output from STNN for straight or curvy maneuvers. The vehicle velocity profile is planned by huristic rules such as "slowly accelerate after start, speed down a little or a lot at intersections(depending on whether to go straight or make turns), and slowly decelerate before stop."

B. Preprocessing of the Driving Scene Image

It is very important for real time control to extract a minimal set of image information sufficient for vehicle control, since the system is based on a PC without any image processing hardware. Out of the frame grabber image of 256×256 pixels in 8-bit B/W gray level, only two narrow horizontal strips of window (each window looking at 8×256 pixels of the road scene) were used. To further reduce data, intensity averaging over a block of 8×8 pixels is used. Therefore, 64 real numbers are generated which then go through the following shifting and scaling operation before being input to the net :

$$x(i) = \bar{I}(i)/c - 1 \tag{1}$$

where $x(i)$ is the input to the network, $\bar{I}(i)$ is the average intensity of the ith block, and c is the normalization factor which simply compensates for some brightness variations. Subtraction of the background intensity will highlight the intensity gradient information.

C. Neural Network Architecture and Its Learning Procedure

The standard backpropagation (BP) multilayer perceptron with a single hidden layer[8] and direct connection between the input and output layers is used to learn the steering commands as well as to recognize intersections. In all steering control networks, training is effected by gathering real world data while actually driving the vehicle with a remote controller. The CCD image which has been preprocessed as described in the previous subsection is input to the neural net and the remote control command becomes the desired output for training the net. In case of

as input to the net. The steering command was generates from the single output node using 4 hidden nodes. The result of a test run at 30 km/h is shown at the bottom of Fig. 3 which may be compared with the result with no learning at all in Fig. 4. Also, to check the algorithm's robustness, test with a slightly different starting position from training has been performed in Fig. 5. The vehicle is shown to move toward the center at it should. As a generalization test, only the first 1/3 of the road (the large block sequence in Fig. 6) was learned and then with learning turned off, the rest (the small block sequence) was test driven with the result shown in Fig. 6.

Finally, the neural navigator was trained on more complicated roads. Let the high level path planner give a command, "Turn left at the first intersection and stop after driving 10 m." The navigation result is shown at Fig. 7. The IDNN detects an intersection at point D and then the vehicle drives as commanded by the LTNN. After a while, the STNN again takes over and continue to run before the vehicle stops. Due to some overlap in road images common to both the LTNN and the STNN, a stable switching characteristic between two differing networks was achieved. The overall simulation performance seems to be quite good and robust.

V. Real Driving Test

The same algorithm as used in simulation was tested with success in real driving on campus roads with intersections and the results were satisfactory according to visual confirmation. It is mentioned however that the real driving results are difficult to present due to some practical problems with vehicle trajectory measurements. All neural nets used 64 input nodes, 4 hidden nodes, and a single output node. The forward processing time of each network was 0.2 seconds. This time involves grabbing an image, memory loading of needed pixels, preprocessing, IDNN forward computation, one of the steering command net's forward computation, and finally sending control commands to the control board's serial port. With 5 Hz of steering updates, a small amount of neural computation errors presents no problem due to the continuing correction efforts. If a real automobile had been used, this image processing speed roughly corresponds to 70 km/h of highway driving, but with PRV I, this speed is not achievable due to the limited motor driving power, not due to the processing speed.

VI. Conclusion and Future Work

The validity and efficiency of using neural networks for autonomous steering control of road vehicles have been positively demonstrated in both simulation and real experiments. Several neural net modules cooperate to generate steering commands for different maneuvers in order to carry out a planned driving path. A significant achievement along the way is the development of both intersection and road driving in a unified framework using neural nets for all. It is also emphasized here that the whole system consists of standard hardware/software components using only an IBM PC486 as host and an 80C196 as the motor controller. Neural nets seems to possess an excellent potential for fast and robust autonomous driving with also great economy in development time and cost. But, still much further work is needed. Continuing investigation is going under way into system stability and robustness under different driving conditions using the simulator and real experiments. The PRV I has recently been equipped with ultrasonic sensors and laser sensors and research on obstacle avoidance and sensor data fusion will also be carried out. Finally, PRV II, the computer controlled van, has been built and will be used for extensive navigation research.

Acknowledgement

This research was fully supported by an ADD grant to the Pohang University of Science and Technology. Also Special thanks are extended to Professors Jin-Soo Lee, Sang-Woo Kim, and Mr. Min-Koo

the intersection detection net, training inputs are the preprocessed intersection/non-intersection images and desired outputs are +1 for an intersection and −1 for a non-intersection.

The steering control nets essentially learn the mapping of "produce this steering when the road looks like this," as done in human driving. Although this relationship cannot be easily put into words even by humans, the neural network can implicitly learn by examples and further, generalize what it learned under similar situations later on. The STNN is trained by looking at scenes while driving through intersections or just following a road. The LTNN is trained while turning left at intersections and the RTNN while turning right. A modest amount of overlap between the LTNN or the RTNN and the STNN is introduced to overcome the subtle switching time error between them. Training patterns are obtained and stored on-line but the neural nets were trained off-line. In practice, initial off-line learning and subsequent on-line modification or fine tuning is recommended.

IV. SIMULATION TEST

A. PRV I Simulator

The PRV I Simulator was built to test the navigation algorithm proposed in Section 3 under various conditions and environments (This might take several months of real experiments just to gather widely varying data). Actually, this simulator used real road images and their shifted and oriented versions. From a 256×256 image taken from the center of the road, the center 200×200 portion of the image was used as input scene in order to handle shifting and rotation. Fig. 3 shows a computer screen of the simulator. Its top portion shows one snapshot of the changing images as the vehicle proceeds with the original image at the left, normalized image at the center, and the network input at the right. The lower portion illustrates the vehicle trajectory on the road.

The original image as well as its left-shifted and right-shifted images were used as training patterns for various driving conditions[5]. After learning, the test image was generated with proper shifts if needed from the selected image prestored in the disk depending on the vehicle's current position. The vehicle position is determined as follows :

$$x_{t+1} = x_t + v_t^V \cos d_t^V \tag{2}$$

$$y_{t+1} = y_t + v_t^V \sin d_t^V \tag{3}$$

where x_t, y_t are the vehicle position components at time t along the road and perpendicular to the road respectively, and v_t^V, d_t^V are the vehicle's actual state and may be different from the input commanded state from the controller. The vehicle and lower level controller dynamics are modeled in simulation as a simple delay :

$$v_t^V = v_{t-1}^C \tag{4}$$

$$d_t^V = d_{t-1}^V + d_{t-1}^C \tag{5}$$

where v_{t-1}^C, d_{t-1}^C are the commands at time $t-1$ given to the vehicle controller.

B. Simulation Results

The first test was on straight roads. 150 images in total obtained at every 50 cm on a road stretch of 80 m long were obtained as the original data base. The training images were selected at every 8 m interval and these along with their transformed images trained the net for 200 iterations. 3 strips of 10×200 pixels with 10×10 block averaging resulted in 60 real values

Kang who have designed and built the hardware/controller for PRV I.

REFERENCES

[1] H. Frohn and W. V. Seelen, "VISOCAR : An Autonomous Industrial Transport Vehicle Guided by Visual Navigation," IEEE Int. Conf. Robotics and Automation, Vol. 2, pp. 1155-1159, 1989.

[2] I. J. Cox, "Blanche : An Autonomous Robot Vehicle for Structured Environments," IEEE Int. Conf. Robotics and Automation, Vol. 2, pp. 978-982, 1988.

[3] A. A. Baloch, "Visual Learning, Adaptive Expectations, and Behavioral Conditioning of the Mobile Robot : MAVIN," Neural Networks, Vol. 4, pp. 271-302, 1991.

[4] C. E. Thorpe, "Vision and Navigation - The Carnegie Mellon Navlab," Kluwer Academic Publishers, 1990.

[5] D. A. Pomerleau, "Neural Network Perception for Mobile Robot Guidance," Ph. D Thesis, Carnegie-Mellon University, Pittsburgh, PA, 1992.

[6] E. D. Dickmanns and B. D. Mysliwetz, "Recursive 3-D Road and Relative Ego-State Recognition," IEEE Trans. Pattern Recognition and Machine Intelligence, Vol. 14, No. 2, Feb. 1992.

[7] R. M. H. Cheng, J. W. Xiao, and S. LeQuec, "Neuromorphic Controller for AGV Steering," IEEE Int. Conf. Robotics and Automation, pp. 2057-2062, May, 1992.

[8] J. A. Freeman and D. M. Skapura, Neural Networks, Addison-Wesley, 1991.

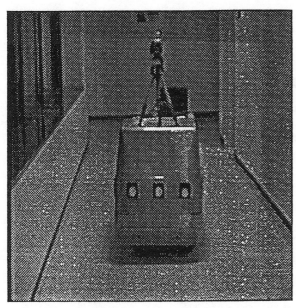

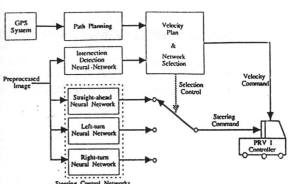

Figure 2. The Neural Net Based Navigation Algorithm.

Figure 1. The Vehicle Testbed PRV I.

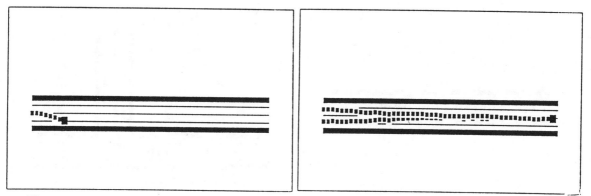

Figure 4. Straight Driving Before Learning.

Figure 5. Straight Driving from Different Starting Position.

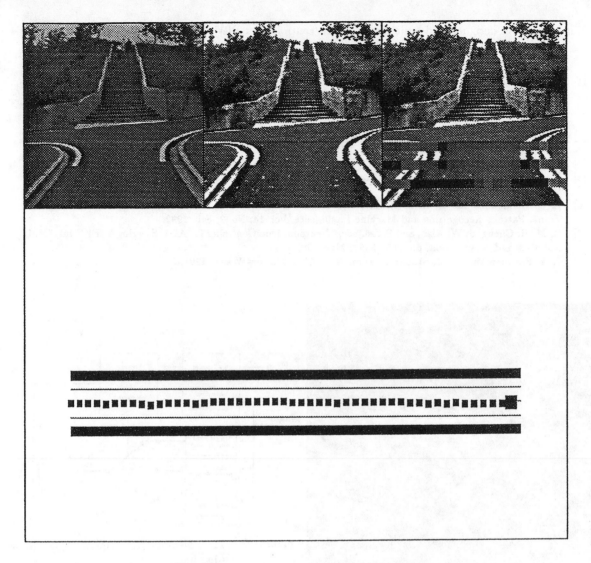

Figure 3. Screen Layout for the PRV I Simulator.
(Also Shows the Result of Straight
Driving after Neural Learning).

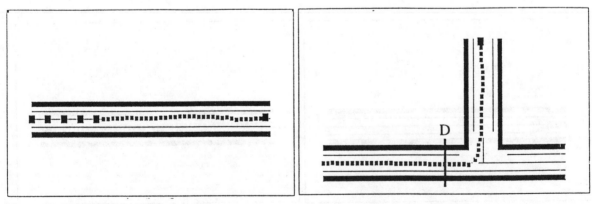

Figure 6. Generalization Test.
(The later 2/3 of the road driving was a
generalization of what it learned to drive
on the first 1/3 of the road).

Figure 7. Test on Intersection Driving.
(Go Straight -> Left Turn -> Go Straight
-> Stop Sequence).

A Robot that Learns an Evaluation Function for Acquiring of Appropriate Motions

Katsunari Shibata and Yoich Okabe
Research Center for Advanced Science and Technology, Univ. of Tokyo
4-6-1 Komaba, Meguro-ku, 153 Tokyo JAPAN
shibata@okabe.rcast.u-tokyo.ac.jp

Summary

An unsupervised learning method of an evaluation function is proposed. By this function, a robot can learn a series of motion to achieve a given purpose. The evaluation function is calculated by a neural network and time derivative of this function is reduced during motions with random trials. We confirmed by simulation that a robot with asymmetric motion feature could obtain an appropriate asymmetric evaluation function and become to achieve a given purpose along an almost optimal path.

1. Introduction

In famous Skinner's experiment, a mouse in Skinner's box becomes to be able to push the button to get a piece of food after some trials as shown in Fig. 1[1]. However, the mouse could not know that it could get a piece of food by pushing the button before the mouse was put into the box. At early stage, the mouse moves randomly, and when it pushes the button unexpectedly, it gets a piece of food. From the experience, the possibility that the mouse pushes the button, slightly becomes large. Then after many experiences, the mouse has an intention to push the button. This means that the mouse in Skinner's experiment did not know only the way to push the button, but also were not given any evaluation functions about getting the food. From this fact, a robot also can obtain an evaluation function through its experiences. Then we assumed a locomotive robot as shown in Fig. 2. The robot has only a purpose to get a target.

The mouse in Skinner's experiment, can learn the evaluation function and motion by the interaction between the mouse and the environment without any supervisors. When we make a robot learn an appropriate series of motion using the interaction, we usually give the robot an evaluation function that we made[2][3]. The evaluation value of the present state is calculated from the sensor signals through the evaluation function. If the robot continues to move towards the gradient direction of the evaluation function, it will be able to achieve the given purpose. For example, in the case of the robot in Fig. 2, an evaluation function can be the inverse of the distance between the robot and the target. As shown in Fig. 3, the robot moves and gets sensor signals. Then the evaluation function makes the supervisor signal for the motion creator from the sensor signals. The motion creator, that is made by a layered type neural network, learns by the supervisor signal, and become to create an appropriate motion signal.

Then we tried to make a robot learn both an evaluation function and a series of motion to achieve a given purpose. We cannot know if the evaluation function, that we give to a robot, is the best for the robot and the environment. Furthermore, if the environment changes, the evaluation function also has to change. For these reasons, the robot has to learn its evaluation function for a good adaptation to the environment.

In this paper, we describe the way to learn the evaluation

fig.1 Skinner's experiment

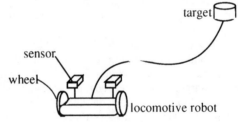

fig. 2 An assumed robot that has a purpose to get a target

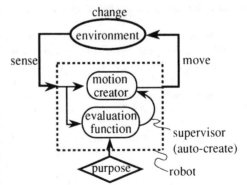

fig. 3 Learning system and interaction to the environment

function without any supervisors, and the way to learn the evaluation function and the motion in parallel. Finally we show the result for comparing which series of motion was closer to the optimal route when the robot was given a fixed evaluation function or when the robot learned the evaluation function by itself.

2. Learning Method of a Series of Motion

Some ways to learn a series of motion from an evaluation function has been already proposed[2][3]. We indicate the way that we employed. Here, the motion signal is calculated by a layered type neural network. Let us suppose the 3 dimensions of space as shown Fig. 4. X, Y axes show sensor signals respectively. The other axis shows the evaluation value. An evaluation value is decided for each set of sensor signals and the surface in this figure is an evaluation function surface. The robot moves according to the sum of the output of a neural network and a small uniform random number as follows,

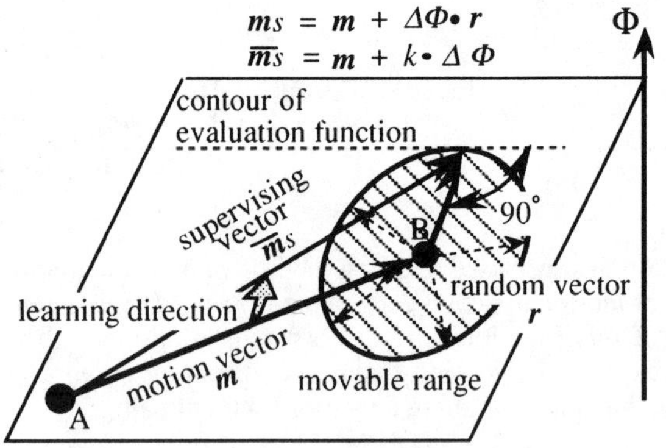

$$M = m + r \qquad (1)$$

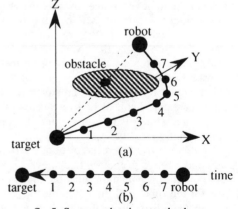

$$m_S = m + \Delta\Phi \bullet r$$
$$\overline{m}_S = m + k \bullet \Delta\Phi$$

fig.4 Motion learning

where M : actual motion vector, m : motion signal vector and r : uniform random number vector. If the robot has two or more actuator, the neural network has two or more output neurons and each output is added by a different random number. The circle filled with oblique line in Fig. 4 shows the movable range of the robot by the random vector r. The robot moves and can get a new evaluation value using the evaluation function. Then the robot makes the following supervisor signal,

$$m_S = m + r\,\Delta\Phi \qquad (2)$$

where m_S : supervisor signal vector for motion signal, $\Phi(t)$: evaluation function and $\Delta\Phi = \Phi(t) - \Phi(t-1)$. The neural network learns at every time unit by this supervisor signal, using a conventional supervised learning algorithm like Back Propagation Method[4]. By the learning through many experiences, the direction of the robot motion vector becomes close to the gradient direction of the evaluation function in average as $\overline{m}_S$ in Fig. 4. Then the robot can learn a series of motion close to the optimal route under the evaluation function.

3. Unsupervised Learning Method of an Evaluation Function

Let us think how should the evaluation function be made. Supposing the 3 dimensions of space in which there is a robot and a target as shown in Fig. 5 (a), we can think of an evaluation method using the distance between the robot and the target. However, how to normalize on each axis cannot be known easily. Furthermore if there is an area that the robot cannot move through, like an obstacle as shown in Fig. 5 (a), it is meaningless to evaluate only by the distance. Then we propose to evaluate by necessary time for arriving at the target. If there is an obstacle, the robot can move beside the area and arrive at the target. If we project the route on the time axis as shown in Fig. 5 (b), we can evaluate under only one criterion and there are no necessity to normalize each axis any longer.

However, if the robot modifies the evaluation function by tracing back the route to the starting point when the robot arrives at the target, the robot must remember all the states it has existed. In order to avoid wasting memory, we propose a real-time learning method of the evaluation function. The evaluation function should be as follows. As shown in Fig. 6, the output of the function is small in an initial state, the output becomes larger as time goes by, and finally the output becomes the largest value when the robot gets the target. Here, the evaluation function is calculated by a layered type neural network and the output function of each neuron is sigmoid between 0.0 and 1.0. The learning method has three phases. When the robot is in an initial state, to decrease the output of the evaluation function, the

fig.5 State evaluation method
(a) evaluation on space
(b) evaluation on time axis

network learns by the supervisor signal as

$$\Phi_s(x(t)) = \Phi(x(t)) - \delta \qquad (3)$$

where $\Phi_s(x(t))$: supervisor signal for the evaluation function and δ : small constant value. Here we employ 0.01 as δ. When the robot arrives at the target, the network learns by the supervisor signal as

$$\Phi_s(x(t)) = \Phi_{max} \qquad (4)$$

where Φ_{max} : the maximum value of the evaluation function (different from the maximum of the output function). Here we employ 0.9 as the maximum value Φ_{max}. Since it is the best state when the robot arrives at the target, the supervisor signal can be a constant value. However, since the initial state is not always the furthest state from the purpose, we cannot set up a constant value, and we set up a slightly small value than the actual output as the supervisor signal. Otherwise from the initial state to the target, in order to increase the output smoothly, the supervisor signal is as

$$\Phi_s(x(t)) = \Phi(x(t)) + \xi \frac{d^2\Phi(x(t))}{dt^2} \qquad (5)$$

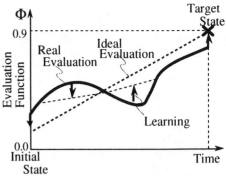

fig.6 Learning method that realizes an evaluation on time

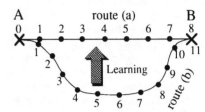

fig.7 An example of optimizing route

where ξ : a smoothing constant. Here we employ 0.5 as the smoothing constant ξ. One thing we have to take care is that the learning is on job learning and the network learns only one iteration using conventional supervised learning algorithm like Back Propagation Method. The output does not become to the value of the supervisor signal, but it becomes closer to the supervisor signal slightly.

Let us assume that a robot moves along the route (b) in Fig. 7 when the robot goes from a point A to a point B. It takes 11 time unit, but if it moves along the route (a) it can arrive at the point B in 8 time unit. By the learning of the evaluation function, it becomes smooth around the route (b). On the other hand, $d\Phi/dt$ along the route (a) is larger than that along the route (b) because the robot can arrive at the point B faster. By the learning of motion, the motion changes to the gradient direction of the evaluation function. The route, that robot moves along, becomes slightly close to the route (a). By repeating the learning of the evaluation function and the learning of motion, the robot becomes to move along the route (a). We can see that the combination of the two learning processes makes the route close to the optimal one.

4. Structure and Flow of the Learning

To realize the combination of the two learning processes, we employ the structure as shown in Fig. 8. The large rectangle shows the robot brain and there are two neural networks. One of them is to calculate the evaluation function and the other is to calculate the motion signal. Each of them calculates the output from the sensor signals, and so we can use only one neural network for both purposes. The robot moves according to the sum of the output of the motion network and a random number. The supervisor signal for the evaluation neural network is usually made from the second order deviation of the output of itself as Eq.(5). The supervisor signal for the motion network is made from the product of the first order deviation of the evaluation output and the random number that was used for creating a motion. Then the each

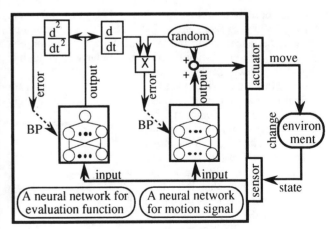

fig.8 Network structure and learning method

network learns only one iteration by the supervisor signal respectively at every time unit. Fig. 9 shows the flow of the learning. First the robot is placed somewhere, and the evaluation network learns by the supervisor signal as Eq.(3). Then the robot repeats a motion as Eq.(1) and learning of both neural networks by the supervisor signals as Eq.(2) and Eq.(5) respectively until it arrives at the target. When it arrives, the estimation network learns by the supervisor signal as Eq.(4). Then the process is repeated many times.

5. Simulation

In this section, we show the simulation result. We assumed the environment as shown in Fig. 10. The locomotive robot has two wheels and can move them independently. The rotate angle of each wheel is decided by the sum of each output of the motion network and a random number. In order to make the environment in which we can make the evaluation function easily, the ratio of the rotation angle against the motion signal is three times larger in the right wheel than in the left wheel. The range of rotating angle of the right wheel is also three times wider that of the left wheel as shown in Fig. 11. The robot also has two sensors. One of them sensed the lateral distance from the robot to the target and the other one sensed the forward distance. Initially a target was placed randomly at the edge of the rectangle except for the edge that the robot existed. It is drawn by a thick line in Fig. 10. The robot moved and if the target went backward passing under the robot, we assumed that the robot could catch the target. If the target went backward passing beside the robot, we assumed that the robot failed to catch the target. In this simulation, when the robot failed to catch the target, the evaluation neural network learned by the supervisor signal 0.1. We defined one experience from placing the target on the initial position to the success or failure to catch the target. However, the robot can move only randomly at first phase and cannot arrive at the target in a finite time. Then we moved the target close to the robot when the robot could not arrive after some time. In order to compare, we do another simulation. We gave the robot an evaluation function that we can think of easily, and make the robot learn only the motion signal.

Then we show the change of the evaluation function in Fig. 12. Each graph in Fig. 12 is drawn on robot centered coordinates. The robot was placed at the center of the coordinates and corresponding evaluation value was plotted on Z axis when the target was placed on each lattice. The contour of the evaluation function is also drawn. Figure 12 (d) shows the evaluation function that we gave the robot in the comparison simulation. Figure 13 shows the contour of the evaluation function and the motion between the robot and the target when the target was placed on each of 5 places. They are also drawn on the robot centered coordinates but on the 2 dimensional surface. Though the robot moved and target did not move actually, the robot was fixed and the target moved in these figures because of the robot centered coordinates. On the locus of the target, the points were plotted at every 10 time unit. In these graphs except for the graph (a), the target moved more when the target was far from the robot and moved to the tangential direction. The reason is that when the robot rotates actually, the target relatively moves according to the product of the rotation angle and the distance on the robot centered coordinates. We also show the loci on the absolute coordinates in Fig. 14. Figure 14(a) shows the comparison between the locus after 5000 experiences and that after 30000 experiences. Figure 14(b) shows the comparison to the case of the fixed evaluation function after 30000 experiences. On the locus of the robot, the points are also plotted at every 10 time unit. After 1000 experiences, the evaluation function did not have an enough expansion of value range and the robot could not get the target as shown in Fig. 13(a).

After 5000 experiences, the evaluation function had a sharp shape and the robot could arrive at the target from any initial positions. The robot got the target at the right half of the robot. The reason is that the right wheel could rotate 3 times more than left wheel and the robot could get the target soon when the target was in the right. After 30000 experiences,

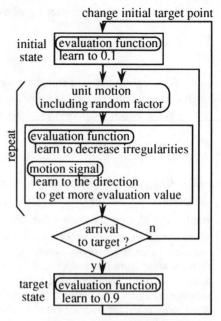

fig.9 Learning procedure

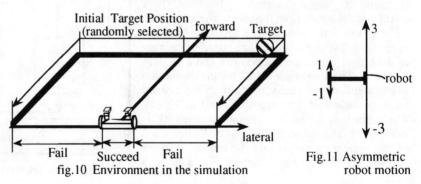

fig.10 Environment in the simulation

Fig.11 Asymmetric robot motion

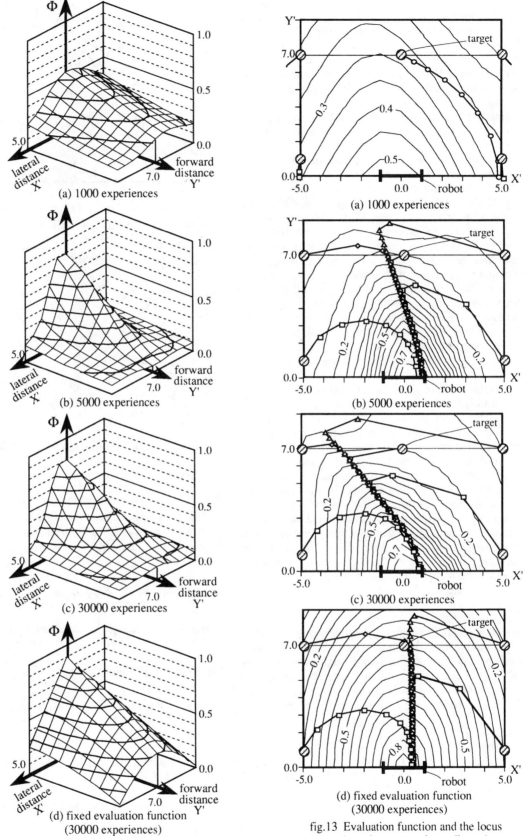

(a) 1000 experiences

(b) 5000 experiences

(c) 30000 experiences

(d) fixed evaluation function
(30000 experiences)

fig.12 Evaluation function (on robot centered coordinates)

(a) 1000 experiences

(b) 5000 experiences

(c) 30000 experiences

(d) fixed evaluation function
(30000 experiences)

fig.13 Evaluation function and the locus
(on robot centered coordinates)

the ridge of the evaluation function moved to the left and the target moved along the ridge. It means that the robot approached the target with looking at it in the left. In the absolute coordinates as shown in Fig. 14(a), the locus of the robot became like an arc after 30000 experiences. Furthermore, the robot went back with rotating itself to the right when the target was seen in the right direction. So, the locus after 5000 experiences seems better than that after 30000 experiences at a glance. However, the necessary time was more after 5000 experiences. The evaluation function and the locus could be reflected the characteristic of the robot. On the other hand, the evaluation function in a comparison simulation is symmetric shape as shown in Fig. 12(d), and the locus of the target expanded in front of the robot as shown in Fig. 13(d). When we see the Fig. 14(b), the locus in the case of fixed evaluation function is close to a straight line and it seems better than that in the case of self-organized evaluation function at a glance. Also in this case, the robot could arrive at the target faster in the case of self-organized evaluation function. Then we show the change of the necessary time for the robot to arrive at the target in Fig. 15. The time is the average of the 12 trials in which the target was placed at a regular interval on the edge of the rectangle. If the robot failed in a trial, the time is set 1000. In this figure, we show the results of 4 simulations. We did two simulations in which the initial weight value in the neural network was different from each other in the case of the fixed evaluation function and in the case of the self-organized evaluation function respectively. We can see that the robot, using the fixed evaluation function, could become to get the target faster than in the case of the self-organized evaluation function in an early stage. The reason is that it took some time to form the evaluation function in the case of the self-organized evaluation function. We can also see from the Fig. 15 that after many experiences the evaluation function and the route of the robot were optimized in the case of the self-organized evaluation function and realized the better route than in the case of the fixed evaluation function.

6. Conclusion

We have proposed an unsupervised learning method by which a machine forms an appropriate evaluation function and a series of motion through its experiences. We confirmed in a simulation that the evaluation function obtained by the learning method was reflected the characteristic of the environment. Then the robot became to be able to move along with the optimal route.

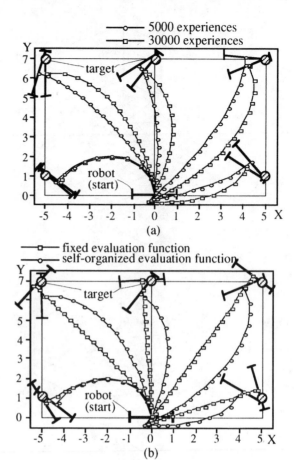

fig.14 Locus of the robot (on absolute coordinates)

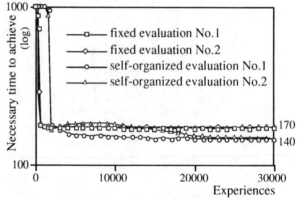

fig. 15 Change of the necessary time to get the target

Reference

[1]Skinner B.F., "Cumulative Record", Appleton-Century-Crofts, 1961

[2]Yoda,H., Miyatake,T. and Matsushima, H., : "A Kinematic Model with a Self-Learning Capability of a Series of Motions Based on Instinctive Incentive", *Trans. of IEICE*, **J73-D-II**, 7,1027-1034, 1990

[3]Nakano, K., Doya, K., SICE'84, S1-3, 1984 (in japanese)

[4]Rumelhart D.E., Hinton G.E. and Williams R.J.: "Learning representations by back-propagating errors", *Nature*, **323**, 9, 533-536, 1986

Learning to Catch a Baseball: A Reinforcement Learning Perspective

Sreerupa Das[†] and Rajarshi Das[‡]

[†]Department of Computer Science, University of Colorado, Boulder, CO 80309-0430

[‡]Computer Science Department, Colorado State University, Fort Collins, CO 80523

Introduction

Scientists have often wondered how baseball outfielders can judge a fly ball by running either forward or backward and arriving at the right point at the right time to catch the ball before it hits the ground [4, 5, 9]. Such a trajectory interception problem is most difficult when the fielder is in the plane of the ball's motion. In this case the fielder does not have a perspective view of the ball's trajectory (Figure 1). Yet, moments after the batter hits the ball, the fielder has to decide if it is a short pop up in front, or a high fly ball over the fielder's head, and run accordingly. Thus, there is an important temporal credit assignment problem in judging a fly ball, since the success or failure signal is obtained long after the actions that lead to that signal are taken. Considerable work in experimental psychology has focused on identifying the perceptual features that a fielder uses to judge a fly ball [8, 9]. Several alternative hypothesis, as to what perceptual features are important in making the decisions, have been postulated. In this paper, we explore the problem in detail using reinforcement learning models. Our experimental results show that one prime hypothesis made earlier about the necessary perceptual features is not sufficiently strong enough to learn the task using reinforcement learning models. We also investigate other perceptual features that help in learning this task. We believe that trying to solve such tasks using reinforcement learning models can provide us with clues that can better guide future research in experimental psychology.

The physics of judging a fly ball

In [5], Chapman analyzed the trajectory interception problem using Newton's laws of motion but neglecting air resistance. For perfect parabolic trajectory, the tangent of the ball's elevation angle ϕ increases at a steady rate with time (i.e. $d(tan\phi)/dt = constant$) over the entire duration of flight, if the fielder stands stationary at the ball's landing point (Figure 2). This simple principle holds true for any initial velocity and launch angle of the ball over a finite range. If the ball is going to fall in front of the fielder, then $tan\phi$ grows at first and then decreases with $d^2(tan\phi)/dt^2 < 0$. On the other hand, if the ball is going to fly over the fielder's head, then $tan\phi$ grows at an increasing rate with $d^2(tan\phi)/dt^2 > 0$.

What happens when a fielder has to run to catch a fly ball? In [3], Brancazio shows that many of the perceptual features available to a fielder (see Table 1) *cannot* provide significant initial cue as to the location

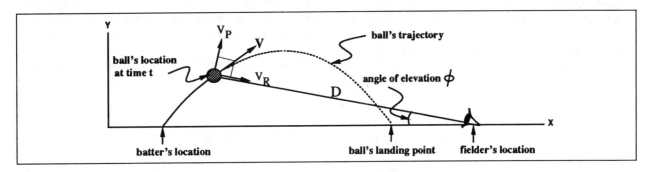

Figure 1: The task of the fielder is to run and intercept the ball at the end of the ball's trajectory.

Brancazio's List of Perceptual Features Available to the Fielder	
Symbol	Feature
ϕ	Angle of Elevation
$d\phi/dt$	Rate of change of ϕ
$d^2\phi/dt^2$	Rate of change of $d\phi/dt$
D	Distance between ball and fielder
dD/dt	Rate of change of D $(= -v_r$, the radial velocity)
v_p	Velocity of ball perpendicular to fielder
dv_p/dt	Rate of change of v_p

Table 1: Brancazio [3] showed that, with the possible exception of $d^2\phi/dt^2$, these features provide no significant initial cue as to the location of the ball's landing point. Note that D is inversely proportional to the apparent size of the ball. Other possible perceptual features include $tan\phi$, $d(tan\phi)/dt$, $d^2(tan\phi)/dt^2$.

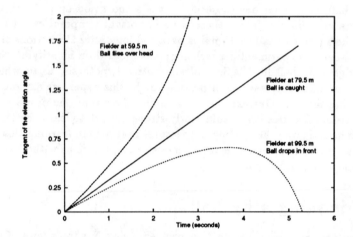

Figure 2: The figure shows the variation in $tan\phi$ as seen by three different fielders standing at 59.5 m, 79.5 m, and 99.5 m from the batter. The initial velocity of the ball is 30 m/s and is hit at a 60° angle. The range of the ball is 79.5 m, and since this simulation ignores air resistance, $tan\phi$ increases at a constant rate only for the fielder standing at 79.5 m.

of the ball's landing point. Recent experimental results obtained by McLeod and Dienes [7] show that an experienced fielder runs such that $d^2(tan\phi)/dt^2$ is maintained close to zero until the very end of the ball's flight. McLeod and Dienes suggest that this is a very robust strategy for the real world, since its outcome is independent of the effects of aerodynamic drag on the ball's trajectory, or the ball following a parabolic path. However little is understood about how human beings *learn* to intercept a free falling ball [7, 8] and what role the $d^2(tan\phi)/dt^2$ information plays in the learning process.

In this paper we use reinforcement learning models to show that $d^2(tan\phi)/dt^2$ information is not sufficient to learn the task. Also, we experimentally determine other perceptual features that appear essential for learning this task.

Using reinforcement learning to catch a baseball

We use Barto, Sutton and Anderson's Multilayer Adaptive Heuristic Critic ($\mathcal{AHC}$) model [1] as well as Watkins' $\mathcal{Q}$-learning model [10] to learn the task. The perceptual features that are available to the fielder while judging a fly ball define the input variables of our system. At any time t, the input to the system are: ϕ, $d^2(tan\phi)/dt^2$, v_f—the velocity of the fielder, and a binary flag which indicates whether $tan\phi$ is greater or less than 90°—that is, whether the ball is spatially in front or behind the fielder. Thus the system receives *no* information about

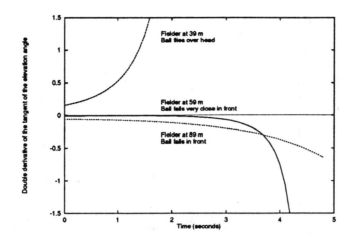

Figure 3: The variation of $d^2(tan\phi)/dt^2$ is shown for three different positions. Aerodynamic drag is taken into consideration here, which decreases the range to 57.5 m for the same initial parameters of the balls as in Figure 2. The ball touches the ground at $t = 4.9$ *seconds*. Note that when the fielder is at 59 m and very close to the ball's landing point, the $d^2(tan\phi)/dt^2$ is close to zero for most of the ball's flight, but it increases dramatically at the end.

the *absolute coordinates of the ball* or *the fielder* at any point in time. Initially, the fielder is positioned at a random distance in front of or behind the ball's landing point. The initial velocity and the initial acceleration of the fielder are both set to zero. The simulation is continued (see Appendix for the equations) until the ball's trajectory is complete and a failure signal is generated. If the ball has hit the ground and the fielder has failed to intercept the ball, the failure signal $f(t)$ is proportional to the fielder's distance from the ball's landing point.

$$f(t) = \begin{cases} 0 & \text{while the ball is in the air,} \\ 0 & \text{if } D(final) \leq \mathcal{R} \text{ (Success!)}, \\ -C \, |D(final)| & \text{if } D(final) > \mathcal{R} \text{ (Failure!)}. \end{cases}$$

where $D(final)$ is the distance between the ball and the fielder when the ball hits the ground, $\mathcal{R}$ is the catching radius, and C is a positive constant. It may be noted here that the information about whether the ball fell in front or behind the fielder is not a part of the reinforcement signal. This information is provided as an input signal (with ϕ) and thus, all through out the ball's trajectory, the fielder knows whether the ball is in front of or behind the fielder.

For the $\mathcal{AHC}$ approach, the action net generates real valued actions similar to that described by Gullapalli [6]. The output of the action network determines the mean, $\mu(t)$, and the output of the evaluation network determines the standard deviation, $\sigma(t)$ of the action space at a particular time.

$$\mu(t) = \text{output of action network}, \quad \sigma(t) = max(\hat{r}(t), 0.0)$$

where $\hat{r}(t)$ is the output of the evaluation network. Assuming a Gaussian distribution Ψ, the action $a(t)$ is computed using $\mu(t)$ and $\sigma(t)$. The action of the network corresponds to the acceleration of the fielder:

$$a(t) \sim \Psi(\mu(t), \sigma(t))$$

The objective function that determines the weight update rules (see [1] for details) is defined as:

$$Error = \begin{cases} f(t) + \gamma\hat{r}(t+1) - \hat{r}(t) & \text{while the ball is in the air,} \\ f(t) - \hat{r}(t) & \text{if the ball has hit the ground.} \end{cases}$$

For the Q-learning model, the network uses a single layer of radial basis hidden units, similar to Anderson [2], to learn the $Q(x, a)$ function. $Q(x, a)$ is a prediction of a weighted sum of future reinforcements given that action a is taken when the system is in state x. For our simulations, the action (fielder's acceleration) is quantized into 20 discrete values equally spaced between ± 2.0 m/s^2. Thus the network has 20 outputs that

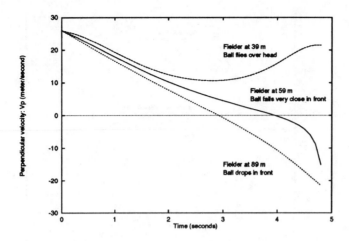

Figure 4: The variation of the perpendicular component of the ball's velocity as seen by the fielder at three different positions. The initial parameters are the same as in Figure 2. The ball touches the ground at $t = 4.9$ *seconds*. Note that the three plots are very close to each other for the first three seconds, and diverge only at the end.

generate Q values corresponding to the 20 possible actions. The action applied to each time step is the one corresponding to the selected winner among the Q values. To introduce exploration, the winner is chosen probabilistically with higher Q values having greater chances of being selected. The failure signal is the same as in $\mathcal{AHC}$. Back-propagation of the following error is used at every time step t, to update the weights as described in [2].

$$Error = \begin{cases} f(t) + \gamma \mathcal{Q}(x_{t+1}, a_{t+1}) - \mathcal{Q}(x_t, a_t) & \text{while the ball is in the air,} \\ f(t) - \mathcal{Q}(x_t, a_t) & \text{if the ball has reached the ground.} \end{cases}$$

Simulation details

The inputs to the network were bounded in the interval [0.0, 1.0] and were computed as follows. The raw inputs, as determined by the system dynamics (defined in the Appendix), were first clipped using the following lower and upper bounds (indicated by $\langle\rangle$): $\langle -10.0, 10.0\rangle m/s$ for the fielder's velocity, v_f; $\langle -5.0, 5.0\rangle m/s^2$ for the fielder's acceleration; $\langle 0^\circ, 180^{circ}\rangle$ for ϕ; $\langle -25.0, 25.0\rangle m/s$ for v_p (referred in the next section); $\langle -0.5, 0.5\rangle s^{-2}$ for $d^2(tan\phi)/dt^2$. The clipped inputs were then scaled to 0.0 and 1.0 and finally presented to the network. Nevertheless, while determining the system dynamics none of the values were either scaled or clipped. The sampling frequency was set to 100 Hz (that is, Δt in the Appendix was set to 0.01s).

During training, each trial began with the fielder positioned randomly in front of the batter. Once the ball was hit, the fielder attempted to catch it by moving forward or backward. The trial ended when the ball hit the ground. In order to account for last moment adjustments made by the fielder (for example, making a final dive at the ball), a catch was considered successful if the ball hit the ground within a region around the fielder's position defined by the catching radius, $\mathcal{R}$. In our simulations, the catching radius was set between $1\ m$ and $2\ m$.

Results

Our results, using both the reinforcement learning methods, show that $d^2(tan\phi)/dt^2$ information by itself is *not* sufficient to learn the task at hand. After an initial learning period, the system surprisingly learns to move the fielder away from the ball's landing point instead of moving towards it. Figure 3 delineates the underlying problem. For a fielder standing at the ball's landing point $d^2(tan\phi)/dt^2$ is always zero. However, if the fielder is only a small distance away from the ball's landing point, $d^2(tan\phi)/dt^2$ is close to zero for most of the ball's flight, until near the end when it increases dramatically. Thus large and small magnitudes of $d^2(tan\phi)/dt^2$ can be associated with both large and small values of negative failure signals. This suggests the need for additional feature(s) that might help in the learning process by removing the ambiguity.

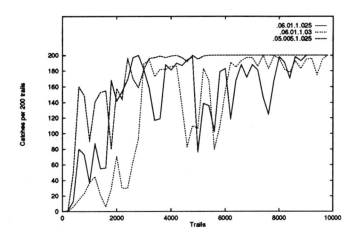

Figure 5: The plots show the number of successful catches every 200 trials as a function of total number of trials for three different sets of learning rates. The initial parameters of the ball are the same as in Figure 2. The fielder's initial position is chosen from a random distribution [47.5m, 67.5m]. The initial velocity and the initial acceleration of the fielder are both set to zero in every trial.

In our second set of simulations we use the perpendicular component of the ball's velocity as seen by the fielder, v_p, as an input along with the other inputs used earlier. Figure 4 plots the variation of v_p as seen by the fielder standing at three different positions. Initially, v_p provides little cue as to the balls landing point, but as the ball's flight comes to an end, v_p is significantly different for the fielders standing at different positions. Interestingly enough, both methods were now able to learn the task, since v_p information adds the necessary discriminating ability in judging fly balls during the latter stages of the ball's flight. Figure 5 shows some typical learning curves using $\mathcal{AHC}$ learning algorithm with fielder starts with a random initial position every trial. Figure 6 shows space-time plots of the fielder's trajectories before and after training for 20 different trials (note that the initial positions of the fielder are set randomly). Plots in Figure 5 and 6 were obtained from the $\mathcal{AHC}$ model (results obtained from the $\mathcal{Q}$ learning were similar in nature).

Conclusion and future work

The above results may be explained as follows. Both $d^2(tan\phi)/dt^2$ and v_p are necessary for learning the task of catching a ball. During the initial part of the ball's flight, the system learns to keep $d^2(tan\phi)/dt^2$ very small, and move in the correct direction. Towards the end of the ball's flight, when $d^2(tan\phi)/dt^2$ increases drastically, the system learns to use v_p to decide whether to run forward or backward.

The goal of this research was to use reinforcement learning models to better understand the perceptual features that actually guides a fielder to learn catch a fly ball. We believe that such findings could help further research in experimental psychology.

References

[1] C.W. Anderson, *Learning and Problem Solving with Multilayer Connectionist Systems*, Doctoral Dissertation, University of Massachusetts, Amherst, 1986.

[2] C.W. Anderson, "Q-Learning with Hidden-Unit Restarting," *Neural Information Processing Systems 5*, 1993, pp. 81-88.

[3] P.J. Brancazio, "Looking into Chapman's homer: The physics of judging a fly ball," *American Journal of Physics*, Vol. 53, No. 9, 1985, pp. 849-855.

[4] V. Bush, *Science is Not Enough*, Wm. Morrow Co., NY, 1967.

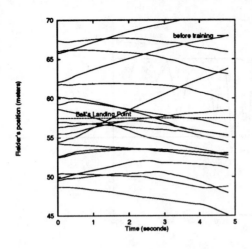
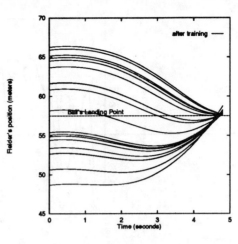

Figure 6: The two space-time plots show the fielder's location in 20 trials, *before* (left) and *after* (right) training for 10000 trials. The initial parameters of the ball are the same as in Figure 2 and the fielder's initial position is chosen from a random distribution [47.5m, 67.5m]. The initial velocity and the initial acceleration of the fielder are both set to zero in every trial. The sampling rate of the dynamics of the ball and the rate at which the fielder's position is updated is the same as the basic simulation rate. i.e. 100 Hz. The ball landing point is at 57.5 m which is reached at $t = 4.9$ *seconds*.

[5] S. Chapman, "Catching a Baseball," *American Journal of Physics*, Vol. 36, No. 10, 1968, pp. 868-870.

[6] V. Gullapalli, "A Stochastic Reinforcement Learning Algorithm for Learning Real-Valued Functions," *Neural Networks*, Vol. 3, 1990, pp. 671-691.

[7] P. McLeod and Z. Dlenes, "Running to catch the ball," *Nature*, Vol. 362, 1993, pp. 23.

[8] K.S. Rosenberg, "Role of Visual Information in Ball Catching," *Journal of Motor Behavior*, Vol. 20, No. 2, 1988, pp. 150-164.

[9] J.T. Todd, "Visual Information About Moving Objects," *Journal of Experimental Psychology: Human Perception and Performance*, Vol. 7, No. 4, 1981, pp. 795-810.

[10] C.J. Watkins, *Learning with Delayed Rewards*, Doctoral dissertation, Psychology Department, Cambridge University, 1989.

APPENDIX: THE EQUATIONS OF MOTION

The equations of motion in two dimensions for a projectile can be expressed as:

$$x'' = -Kvv_x, \qquad y'' = -Kvv_y - g \tag{1}$$

where x'' and y'' are the instantaneous horizontal and vertical accelerations, v_x and v_y are the horizontal and vertical components of the velocity of the ball v, g is the acceleration due to gravity and K is the aerodynamic drag force constant equal to $0.005249\ m^{-1}$ for a baseball [3]. Using a sampling time of Δt second, the above equations are numerically integrated using third derivatives as follows:

$$\Delta x = v_x\Delta t + 0.5x''(\Delta t)^2 + 0.1667x'''(\Delta t)^3, \qquad \Delta y = v_y\Delta t + 0.5y''(\Delta t)^2 + 0.1667y'''(\Delta t)^3, \tag{2}$$

where $x''' = -K(v'v_x + vx'')$, $y''' = -K(v'v_y + vy'')$, and $v' = (v_x x'' + v_y y'')/v$. The velocity components are also updated as:

$$\Delta v_x = x''(\Delta t) + 0.5x'''(\Delta t)^2, \qquad \Delta v_y = x''(\Delta t) + 0.5y'''(\Delta t)^2 \tag{3}$$

Given the current coordinates of the fielder and the ball, and their respective velocities, it is possible to calculate the variables associated with ϕ, and $tan\phi$ including their derivatives using trigonometric equations and calculus.

A State History Queue for Efficient Implementation of a Reinforcement Learning System

Yendo Hu and Ronald D. Fellman

Department of Electrical and Computer Engineering, 0407
University of California at San Diego
December 7, 1993

Abstract - This paper presents a modification to the BOXES-ASE/ACE reinforcement learning algorithm to improve implementation efficiency. We introduce a state history queue (SHQ) to replace the decay variables associated with the states, decoupling the hardware complexity from the number of control states. We analyzed the effectiveness of the SHQ and constructed both a simulation and an actual hardware of a pole-cart balancer. Analysis shows this technique preserves performance, while decimating the required computation time and memory demand of tracking access to each state.

I. INTRODUCTION

The BOXES network, developed by Michie and Chambers [Mich68] and later refined by Barto *et al.* [Bart83], is a reinforcement learning algorithm designed to solve difficult adaptive control problems using associative search elements (ASE) and adaptive critic elements (ACE). The equations of motion of the physical system are not known to the network. Rather, it learns how to respond based upon feedback from past trials. This feedback evaluates system performance from a failure signal occurring when the controlled object reaches an undesired state.

Using the current input state, the ASE acts as a control memory that uses the current system state as its address to look up data, and sends a signal to control the target object, or plant. The resulting action may generate a reinforcement signal, usually negative, that the ASE and ACE receives. On the basis of a first-order linear prediction from past reinforcement signals, the ACE uses this catastrophic reinforcement signal to compute a prediction of the reinforcement signal when the plant produces no actual reinforcement. The ASE updates its control information using both this improved reinforcement signal along with a trace through the previously traversed system states. The effect of a reinforcement signal on a control parameter decreases exponentially with the elapsed time since the system had last entered that state. In [Bart83], a single ASE, along with one ACE, successfully learned to solved the pole balancing problem. Many researchers have also used this pole-cart balancer as a benchmark for evaluating the performance of their algorithms [Bart83][Widr87][Shep88][Ande89].

By monitoring the plant, the ACE adjusts its reinforcement prediction to emphasize learning when the system moves between states. Predicted reinforcement diminishes when the system remains in the same state. It then sends this modified reinforcement signal to the ASE. The ASE, whose output controls the system, learns by adjusting its long-term time-traces of the modified reinforcement signal and its associated time-decaying short-term traces of the control actions given for each state. The ASE assigns a register to hold an output control value for each unique system state. This output register holds the long-term trace that represents both the output action, the trace's sign, and also a confidence level, the trace's magnitude. Thus, high confidence levels are represented by large trace magnitudes. The ASE adjusts only the traces of states that led to the reinforcement event. A second value for each state, the short-term memory trace, tracks the contribution of a state towards producing the current system state. For each state, this short-term trace weighs the reinforcement adjustment of the long-term trace value. This mechanism allows past states to learn from a system failure in proportion to their contribution to the current outcome.

An ASE contains one control output, one reinforcement input, and an input state vector. Each element within the vector represents a unique state within the system. The ASE output, which controls the system, is just the thresholded long term trace selected by the decoded state vector, I(t), as in (1).

$$O(t) = \theta\left(\sum_{j=1}^{N} (I_i(t) \times W_i(t))\right), \theta(a) = 1 \text{ if } a \geq 0, \text{ else } \theta(a) = -1. \tag{1}$$

The following equations recursively relate two internally stored variables: the long term trace, $w_i(t)$, and the short term trace, $e_i(t)$, to each input, i:

$$w_i(t) = w_i(t-1) + \alpha R(t-1) e_i(t-1) \tag{2}$$

$$e_i(t) = \delta e_i(t-1) + (1-\delta) I_i(t-1) O(t-1) \tag{3}$$

where $R(t)$ = reinforcement signal, δ = ASE trace decay rate
             $I(t)$ = state vector, $O(t)$ = output action
             α = positive constant determining rate of change

The ACE contains one modified reinforcement output, one reinforcement input, and a set of inputs equaling the number of outputs from the front end decoder. Two internally stored variables, $\bar{x}_i(t)$, the time decay factor, and $v_i(t)$, the state predictor, recursively update their values each cycle from the current system state. The change in the system predictor, $p(t)$, provides feedback to update the variables, $v_i(t)$ and $\hat{r}(t)$. The following equations describe the operation of the ACE:

$$\bar{x}_i(t) = \lambda \bar{x}_i(t-1) + (1-\lambda) I_i(t-1) \qquad\qquad v_i(t) = v_i(t-1) + \beta \hat{r}(t-1) \bar{x}_i(t-1) \qquad (4)$$

$$p(t) = \sum_{i=1}^{N} (v_i(t) \times I_i(t)) \qquad\qquad \hat{r}(t) = r(t) + \gamma p(t) - p(t-1) \qquad (5)$$

where λ = ACE trace decay rate, N = number of possible input states
             γ = discount factor, β = positive constant determining rate of change

The ACE predicts a reinforcement signal for each input state, based upon past reinforcement signals and their occurrence with respect to input activity. A negative reinforcement signal produces unfavorable prediction values for states with recent signal activity. Positive reinforcement increases the prediction values for recently accessed states. In terms of our notation, positive $\hat{r}$ reinforces actions that move the system into higher v_i, whereas negative $\hat{r}$ discourages actions that move the system toward lower v_i values.

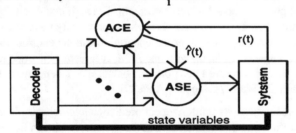

Figure 1. Example of a simple ASE and ACE system.

During operation, the system first quantizes each of four input variables: pole angular velocity, cart position, cart velocity, and the reinforcement feedback. The quantized system parameters then pass through the decoder and activate the unit state vector representing the current system state. The ASE and ACE elements connect as shown in Figure 1. [Bart83] gives detailed experimental results. The ASE/ACE network learned to balance the stick within an average of 70 trials.

II. State History Queue

The short-term trace or eligibility function, $e(t)$, in the ASE, and the state trace, $x(t)$, in the ACE, decay exponentially over time, thus only carry significant values over a limited period. All associated computations involving these variables are influential only during this period. The state history queuing (SHQ) scheme takes advantage of this characteristic to reduce both memory and computation time.

Rather than store a decay value for each system state, the SHQ scheme keeps only a truncated list of all recently traversed input states. Weighting these states by position in the history queue generates an equivalent decay value. By restricting the length of this list, the SHQ scheme, in effect, sets a threshold to truncate insignificant decay values. It ignores weight adjustments of those states whose last visits occurred beyond a time period specified by the list length. Thus for each network update, only variables associated with the states listed in the queue need adjustment. This limited updating algorithm decouples the weight updating time from the input state space size.

The state history queue is just a shift register that keeps track of the past inputs states (Figure 2). The register depth, H, defines the length of the queue. The parameter H sets the time threshold where incremental weight adjustments beyond this point are assumed insignificant, and ignored. The ASE state history queue records the decoded input address and the generated output.

Address	Input State	Output	Decay Scalar
$H_{ase}-1$	$A(t-[H-1])$	$O(t-[H-1])$	k
.	.	.	.
.	.	.	.
.	.	.	.
1	$A(t-1)$	$O(t-1)$	$k(H-1)$
0	$A(t)$	$O(t)$	kH

ASE
State History Queue

Figure 2. The state history queue structure for ASE.

An approximation to the decay function using the queue further reduces the computation time needed for weight adjustments. This is achieved by assigning constant decay scalars to each register within the queue. The approximated decay function for each input state is just the sum of all decay scalars of registers holding the input state. This decay function replaces the decay variables $e(t)$ and $\bar{x}(t)$ in the original algorithm. A linear function to represent the set of constant decay scalars further reduces the complexity of the algorithm. As an example, the approximate decay function for systems that dwell in the same input state is given in equation (6)

$$e(t) = (1 - \delta^t)\, u(t) \approx \sum_{j=1}^{t} (H\kappa - (j-1)\,\kappa) \qquad (6)$$

where δ = trace decay rate, $u(t)$ = step function
            H = length of the state history queue, κ = decay scalar rate of change

The error analysis in the following sub-section and simulations in Section IV confirms the fact that the approximation introduces only a small difference to the overall system performance.

Using the SHQ, equation (2) to update the control weights becomes:

$$w[SHQA[h]]_{new} = w[SHQA[h]]_{old} + R(t)*\alpha * (h+1)* SHQO[h]*\kappa_{ase}$$

where: α = rate of change constant in Barto *et al.* network, h = pointer in SHQ, $0 \leq h < H_{ase} - 1$
              κ_{ase} = change slope between addresses in SHQ, w = weights (addressable memory)

The SHQ algorithm also applies to the ACE, and both ASE and ACE can share the same state history queue. With the SHQ, equation (4) becomes:

$$v[SHQA[h]]_{new} = v[SHQA[h]]_{old} + \beta\,[R(t) + \gamma* p(t) - p(t-1)]\kappa_{ace}$$

where: h = pointer in SHQ, $0 \leq h < H_{ace} - 1$, γ = discount factor (a constant)
              v = prediction values (addressable memory)

Relating the State History Queue to the Time Decay Function

Two parameters control the effective time decay in the SHQ scheme: κ, the decay slope, and H, the register length. Here, we will determine the values of these constants to minimize the average mean squared error between the step responses of these two schemes. Simulations show that as the system stabilizes, it tends to spend most of its time in a particular state or small set of states. Thus, the eligibility function for these states tends to resemble the response to a step input. We therefore match step responses to model this desired system learning behavior.

The original eligibility decay function, $e_i(t)$ of equation (3), is a recursive one-pole infinite impulse response digital filter with an exponential time constant of $\tau = |\ln\delta|^{-1}$. The SHQ simply truncates this impulse response and approximates it as by the sum of all occurrences of a given state within the queue. When only few states are constantly visited, as occurs when the system is beginning to learn, this accumulation can be roughly approximated by the quadratic function given in equation (7) for this typical value of $e_i(t)_{shq}$.

The two functions, $e_i(t)$ and $e_i(t)_{shq}$, should also match at t=0 and t = infinity, giving a constraint on κ and H.

$$e_i(t)_{shq} = \kappa H t - \frac{\kappa t^2}{2} + \frac{\kappa t}{2} \qquad\qquad \kappa = \frac{2}{H^2 + H} \qquad (7)$$

Ideally, we would minimize the mean-squared error between $e_i(t)$ and $e_i(t)_{shq}$ to derive optimal κ and H values that match the SHQ eligibility function to Barto's eligibility function. However, for a simple approximation to find H, we will impose one more condition between the functions $e_i(t)$ and $e_i(t)_{shq}$: the functions should intersect at time τ, the time constant of the step response of $e_i(t)$. From (6), for $t = \tau = |\ln\delta|^{-1}$, $e_i(t) = e_i(t)_{shq} = 1-1/e = 0.632$. Solving (7) for H and setting $t = \tau$ we get:

$$H = \frac{1 + \sqrt{0.367}}{0.632 \,(|\ln\delta|)} = \frac{2.54}{|\ln\delta|} \qquad \kappa \approx \frac{2}{H^2} \qquad (8)$$

The slope, κ, and the SHQ length, H, determine the response of the approximated eligibility function. Equations (7) and (8) fit the SHQ eligibility function $e_i(t)_{shq}$ onto the original eligibility function $e_i(t)$. The step response plot, Figure 3, of the original eligibility decay function and its SHQ equivalent show the difference graphically. For this example, the mean squared error between these two curves is 8%. Our simulations in section IV confirm equivalent learning performance for the SHQ compared to the original algorithm.

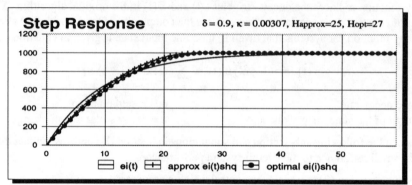

Figure 3. Step response comparison of the original eligibility function and the SHQ decay function.

Effectiveness of the SHQ Scheme

We present two factors to measure the effectiveness of these suggested improvements: TF, the time efficiency factor, and MF, the memory efficiency factor.

$$TF = \frac{\text{time to address memory without modification}}{\text{time to address memory with modification}} \qquad MF = \frac{\text{memory used without modification}}{\text{memory used with modification}} \qquad (9)$$

A large efficiency factor indicates significant improvement achieved by the modifications. We must assess the number of operations per update for the network. The original system without the SHQ would need to update all elements in the e, $\bar{x}$, w, and v array each cycle; whereas the modified network with the SHQ only need update some elements in the array. Figure 4 gives the number of multiplication and addition operations required to update each array.

Operations Per Update

	Without SHQ		With SHQ		
	Multiply Operations	**Addition Operations**	**Multiply Operations**	**Addition Operations**	**Shifting Operations**
e	3M	1M	0	0	H
x	2M	1M	3H	2H	0
w	2M	1M	0	0	H
v	M+2	M+2	H+2	H+2	0

Definition of Variables:
M = total number of possible inputs states
H = Length of State History Queue

Figure 4. Effectiveness of the SHQ measured by the number of operations to update the eligibility array.

In this case, the time efficiency factor becomes:

$$TF_{shq} = \frac{(4M + 2)\,T_a + (M + 2)\,T_m}{2T_s H + (3H + 2)\,T_a + (4H + 2)\,T_m} \qquad (10)$$

where T_s = time to perform one shift operation, T_a = Time to perform one addition operation

T_m = Time to perform one multiply operation.

The memory needed for the original network must be large enough to hold the four arrays: e, $\bar{x}$, w, and v, which gives a total memory demand of 4M. The SHQ modification eliminates the two arrays, e and $\bar{x}$, but adds the state history queue of length H; the SHQ will need 2H memory spaces. The memory efficiency factor is thus:

$$MF_{shq} = \frac{4M}{2H + 2M} \qquad (11)$$

III. SIMULATION RESULTS

Computer simulations of this learning system, both with and without our modifications, measured the improvement in speed, performance, and hardware demand. The original adaptive network by Barto *et al.* offered a reference for comparison. The sequence of experiments presented below evaluates the contribution of each scheme to the network's overall improvement. A NeXT workstation provided the environment to develop the simulations. All programs are written in Objective C and ran under the Unix operating system. We took advantage of the NeXT supplied interface library to generate a graphical user interface that showed the simulated pole-cart system learn in real-time. A hardware implementation using an 8-bit microcontroller (MC68HC11) demonstrated the practical feasibility of such a system.

Recreating Barto's Network and Environment

We recreated the environment and network Barto *et al.* [Bart83] developed. The cart and pole motion equation from their paper defined the physical system. All physical parameters in the network's learning environment remained the same. The simulator used Euler's method to solve the differential motion equation, using a time step of 20 ms. It implemented Barto's network in full, both ACE and ASE algorithms used the same parametric values given by [Bart83]. We measured the performance of the network by observing the number of trails verses elapsed time between failures. The slopes and the peaks of the learn curves reveal the network's learning rate and the control solution's robustness.

Observing the SHQ Effect

We evaluated the SHQ's effects on the learning performance of the modified ASE/ACE network. The SHQ replaced the short-term trace, or 'e' array, in the ASE, and the state trace, or 'x' array, in the ACE. For $\delta = 0.9$, the ASE SHQ length, H_{ase}, was found to be 25 using (8). This result was used to compute $\kappa_{ase} = 0.00307$ from (8). Similarly, for $\lambda = 0.8$, H_{ace} and κ_{ace} were found to be 13 and 0.0109. We computed the average learning curves over ten random seeds using the SHQ as shown in Figure 5. The curves fell within the same range as the Barto's network's

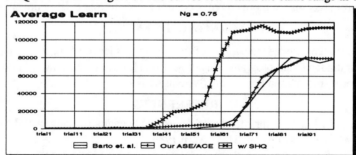

Figure 5. Average learning curve comparing SHQ with original ASE/ACE

learn curve. The different learning rate as seen in Figure 5 using the SHQ algorithm arose as a side effect of the decay truncation in the SHQ scheme and the limited number of noise seeds for the simulation runs. The SHQ approximation to Barto's decay function used only a limited number of past states to compute short-term traces. For all occurrences of a given state within the SHQ, the sum of the constant decay-scalars estimates a short-term trace for that state. This introduced a marked improvement over the original algorithm for this application. The time and memory efficiency gain using the SHQ scheme, defined by TF_{shq} and MF_{shq}, were found to be,

$$\text{TF}_{shq} = \frac{650T_a + 1298T_m}{50T_s + 77T_a + 102T_m} \qquad\qquad \text{MF}_{shq} = \frac{648}{50 + 324} = 1.7326 \qquad (12)$$

IV. HARDWARE IMPLEMENTATION

We constructed a hardware implementation of a reinforcement learning adaptive controller and a pole-cart balancer system that demonstrated the implementation advantages of our modified control network. Its reduced hardware demand enabled us to develop a self contained portable unit capable of performing real time learning.

A low cost 8-bit microcontroller, Motorola 68HC11, implemented most of the algorithm. The reduction in computation time resulting from the State History Queue enabled this 2 MHz processor to update weights in real time, a 50 Hz rate. A Xilinx 3090 programmable gate array augmented the 68HC11 to control external memory and allow implementation of state association. State association would have decreased learning time, but was disabled for these SHQ measurements. The entire network with memory and necessary interface fits onto a 5 in.^{2} board clocked at the 2 MHz controller rate. All 2 kilobytes of firmware code resides within the 68HC11 controller. Computations were performed with 16 bit integer arithmetic and a shift-add multiply routine. The 256 bytes of internal controller RAM held system variables, parameters, and program stack. Less than 1 Kilobyte of external RAM implemented the SHQ, holding values for long-term traces and the ACE's prediction array. For the 68HC11, $\text{TF}_{shq} = 12$.

The non-ideal training environment provided a challenge to the network. Mechanical vibration from the motors reduced the angle sensor's accuracy in determining the stick's state. The stepper motors limited the cart's position resolution. Inconsistency during human supervision when re-centering the stick set different initial states for successive trials. These uncertainties introduced excess noise that reduced system learning rate. Despite this, the system successfully learned to balance the stick for more than 10 minutes after 100 human supervised trials.

V. CONCLUSION

The State History Queue allowed the BOXES-ASE/ACE reinforcement learning algorithm to be effectively implemented using conventional digital technology. This technique scheme not only kept the hardware demand at a practical level, it also improved learning speed. The State History Queue addressed only memory that was significant to the control system, thereby reducing both computation time and memory space.

Algorithmic improvements, such as the state history queue, and leveraging the maturity of digital technology makes possible the implementation of the entire cart-pole controller using a low-cost microcontroller chip. This demonstrated the practical application of associative learning to adaptive control problems. Custom implementation using a VLSI ASIC will further optimize the hardware configuration, rendering a faster and more powerful implementation to perform tasks for the more complex control problems that exist in the physical world.

ACKNOWLEDGEMENT

The authors gratefully acknowledge the support of the National Science Foundation for funding provided through their Research Initiation Grant program. This project was funded by NSF award number MIP-9008839 through the Microelectronic Information Processing Systems division.

REFERENCES

[Ande89]   **Anderson, C. W.,** "Learning to control an inverted pendulum using neural networks," *IEEE Control Systems Magazine*, vol. 9, pp. 31-37 April 1989.

[Ande90]   **Anderson, J. A. and Rosenfeld, E. eds.,** *Neurocomputing*, Cambridge, MA: MIT Press, 1990.

[Bart83]   **Barto, A. G., Sutton, R. S., and Anderson, C. W.,** "Neuronlike adaptive elements that can solve difficult learning control problems," in *IEEE Trans. Syst., Man, Cybern.*, SMC-13, pp. 834-846, 1983.

[Mich68]   **Michie, D. and Chambers, R.A.,** "BOXES: An Experiment in Adaptive Control," in **Machine Intelligence 2**, Editors: E. Dale and D. Michie, Edinburgh: Oliver and Boyd, pp. 137-152, 1968.

[Shep88]   **Shepanski, J. F. and Macy, S. A.,** "Teaching artificial neural systems to drive: Manual training techniques for autonomous systems," in *Proc. of the 1987 Neural Information Processing Systems Conf.*, D. Z. Anderson, ed., Am. Inst. of Physics, New York, pp. 693-700, 1988.

[Widr87]   **Widrow, B.,** "The original adaptive neural net broom-balancer," in *Int. Symp. Circuits and Syst.*, pp. 351-357, May 1987.

Inverse Kinematics via Linear Dynamic Networks

Karl Mathia[*] and **Richard Saeks**[**], Ph.D.

Accurate Automation Corporation
7001 Shallowford Road
Chattanooga, Tennessee 37421

Abstract. **A solution of the inverse kinematics problem in robotics is presented. The usual difficulty of inversion or non–invertability of robot kinematics is circumvented by linearization of the forward kinematics and the design of an appropriate energy function, which then is minimized by linear dynamic networks. The results of the dynamic optimization process are the 'best' joint angle rates which minimize the manipulator's position error. We call the class of networks used *Linear Hopfield Networks*, due to it's similarities with the original Continuous Hopfield Network. A convergence proof for the dynamics of the synchronous Linear Hopfield Network is given. The development of an explicit upper bound on the step size is presented which guarantees convergence and whose values at or near the upper bound provide fast convergence. The simulated tracking control of a trajectory in 3–D Cartesian space with a three–joint robot manipulator demonstrates the performance of this approach.**

1   Introduction

The *forward kinematics* of a robot arm (manipulator) describe the geometry of manipulator motions, i.e. the mapping from given joint angles to the associated position of the manipulator in Cartesian space (or some other space). The *inverse kinematics* problem is to find the joint angles needed to move the end–effector to a desired position, i.e. an inverse mapping from a point in Cartesian space to an associated point in joint angle space must be determined. A closed form solution of the inverse kinematics can be non–trivial to determine or may not even exist, depending on the complexity or redundancy of the robot's forward kinematics.

Initial ideas of circumventing a closed form solution by linearizing the direct kinematics and then defining and minimizing an energy function were presented earlier [2]. The present paper extends the theory and provides simulation results. To find the required joint angles for a desired manipulator position, the inverse kinematics problem is reduced to the numerical solution of a linear system. The linear system is specified and solved for each manipulator position, i.e. for each point on the manipulator's trajectory in Cartesian space, the required associated point in joint angle space is determined via an optimization process.

An appropriate energy function is represented in a form which can be minimized by a linear, fully connected, recurrent network. Due to it's similarities with the original Continuous Hopfield Network (CHN), we call this class of linear dynamic networks *Linear Hopfield Network* (LHN). As opposed to the CHN, which has nonlinear transfer functions and is used as an 'autoassociator' [4], the LHN has linear transfer functions and solves systems of linear equations. A design method for the LHN is presented which guarantees convergence to the optimal solution, here the 'best' joint angle velocity to minimize the manipulator's velocity error. The resulting discrete velocities are integrated to track the preplanned end–effector path. As an example, the simulated control of a three–joint manipulator in 3–D Cartesian space is presented.

* Ph.D. candidate in electrical engineering, Portland State University, Portland/Oregon.
** Vice president of AAC, previously dean of engineering at the Illinois Institute of Technology.
This research is funded by the Office of Naval Research (ONR) under contract N00014–91–C–0268.

2   The Inverse Kinematics Problem

Manipulator kinematics describe the *geometry* of robot arm (manipulator) motions. The end–effector of a manipulator is moved to a target position by controlling the manipulator's joint angles in an appropriate manner. The manipulator's forward kinematics describe this mapping from joint angle space to Cartesian space. Let $x(t)$ be the m–dimensional Cartesian position vector and $\theta(t)$ the n–dimensional joint angle vector, both functions of time. Then the *forward* or *direct kinematic problem* is solved by transforming $\theta(t)$ to $x(t)$:

$$x(t) = f(\theta(t)) , \tag{1}$$
$$f : \mathbb{R}^n \mapsto \mathbb{R}^m, \ \theta \in \mathbb{R}^n, \ x \in \mathbb{R}^m .$$

In general the desired path for the robot manipulator is planned in Cartesian coordinates. Then the *inverse kinematics problem* is to find joint angles $\theta(t)$ (in the robot's control space) such that the manipulator's end–effector is placed at a desired position $x(t)$ in Cartesian space (here the robot's reference space). This inverse mapping is given by

$$\theta(t) = f^{-1}(x(t)) , \tag{2}$$
$$f^{-1} : \mathbb{R}^m \mapsto \mathbb{R}^n ,$$

where unique closed form solutions for the inverse mapping $f^{-1}(.)$ in (2) do not exist for redundant manipulators ($m < n$, fewer equations than unknowns) or may be hard to determine for non–redundant manipulators ($m \geq n$), due to the complexity and nonlinearities of $f(.)$ in (1). Extending initial ideas expressed in [2], this paper proposes a solution of the inverse kinematics problem using 1) linearization of the trajectory $f(\theta(t_k))$ at discrete time instances t_k, 2) the specifications of predesigned energy functions $E(t_k)$, and 3) the numerical solution of the linearized system obtained by optimizing $E(t_k)$. The energy functions $E(t_k)$ are implemented in Linear Hopfield Networks (LHN), which carry out the optimization processes at each discrete point $x(t_k)$ of the end–effector's path.

3   Linearization and Velocities

Difficulties in performing the inverse kinematics (2), introduced by the complexity of $f(.)$ or the redundancy of the system in (1), can be overcome by simplifying the direct kinematics. One approach is to differentiate (1) with respect to time and use the resulting joint angle velocities $\dot{\theta} = d\theta/dt$ and Cartesian velocities $\dot{x} = dx/dt$ as input and output (or reference and control variables) for the manipulator control system. The time derivative of (1) is the velocity equation (3), the inverse is given in (4):

$$\dot{x} = J(\theta) \ \dot{\theta} , \tag{3}$$
$$\dot{\theta} = J^{-1}(\theta) \ \dot{x} , \tag{4}$$

where the Jacobian matrix $J(\theta)$ is defined by

$$J(\theta) = \begin{bmatrix} \dfrac{\delta f_1}{\delta \theta_1} & \cdots & \dfrac{\delta f_n}{\delta \theta_1} \\ \vdots & & \vdots \\ \dfrac{\delta f_1}{\delta \theta_m} & \cdots & \dfrac{\delta f_n}{\delta \theta_m} \end{bmatrix} , \ J \in \mathbb{R}^{nxm} .$$

Given a desired Cartesian velocity profile $\dot{x}_d$, the manipulator joint angles θ are obtained by integrating the joint angle velocities $\dot{\theta}$ obtained by equation (4). When using a digital computer to solve

(4), numerical optimization of an energy function $E(t_k)$ is preferred over the matrix inversion approach for two main reasons: 1) the inversion of J can be numerically unstable, e.g. if the Jacobian is close to singularity (assuming J^{-1} exists), and 2) J may be singular and therefore a unique solution of (4) does not exist, e.g. for redundant manipulators. If J is not invertible, additional constraints can be added to make (4) uniquely solvable. A common way is to apply the Moore–Penrose pseudo–inverse $J^\dagger$, where the additional constraint is given by finding the solution with minimal norm. In the present paper the system in (4) is made invertible in a similar way, and a numerical solution is used where the inverse J^{-1} is not needed at all.

4 Energy Function and Optimization Process

In this paper the inverse kinematics problem for a robot manipulator is converted into an *optimization problem*. The first step is to design an energy function E (cost function, objective function), and then to optimize this performance measure using linear dynamic networks. The primary control objective is to minimize the position error $x_e(t_k) = x(t_k)-x_d(t_k)$ of the manipulator's end–effector. Since in this paper the velocity equation (4) is to be solved, the energy function is expressed in terms of the velocity error $\dot{x}_e(t_k) = \dot{x}(t_k)-\dot{x}_d(t_k)$. As an additional constraint the minimization of necessary joint angle changes, or velocities, $\dot\theta$ is introduced. This additional constraint results in a smoother trajectory in joint angle space (and therefore Cartesian space).

Provided a desired trajectory x_d, the energy function E is defined in terms of the velocity error $\dot{x}_e$ and the joint angle velocity $\dot\theta$ as

$$2E = \|\dot{x}_e\|^2 + \varepsilon \|\dot\theta\|^2 \tag{5}$$
$$= \|\dot{x}-\dot{x}_d\|^2 + \varepsilon \|\dot\theta\|^2$$
$$= (\dot{x}-\dot{x}_d)^T(\dot{x}-\dot{x}_d) + \varepsilon\, \dot\theta^T\dot\theta$$

where ε is an arbitrary non–zero constant (discussed below). The velocity error $\dot{x}_e$ can be expected to increase with ε, which will be demonstrated by simulation results. The factor 2 in (5) is used for later convenience when deriving the energy function for optimization purposes. Equations (3) and (5) result in a representation of the energy function E with joint angle velocity $\dot\theta$ as the optimization variable:

$$2E(\dot\theta) = (J\dot\theta-\dot{x}_d)^T(J\dot\theta-\dot{x}_d) + \varepsilon\, \dot\theta^T\dot\theta$$
$$= \dot\theta^T(\varepsilon\, I + J^TJ)\dot\theta - 2J^T\dot{x}_d\dot\theta + \dot{x}_d^T\dot{x}_d$$
$$= \dot\theta^T A\dot\theta - 2b^T\dot\theta + \dot{x}_d^T\dot{x}_d \quad , \quad A \in \mathbb{R}^{n\times n},\ b \in \mathbb{R}^n, \tag{6}$$

where $A = \varepsilon\, I + J^TJ$ and $b = J^T\dot{x}_d$. The constant ε is used for two purposes: it weights the influence of the angular velocity term on the joint angles (this strategy is common in optimal control methods), and the term εI provides invertability of A for all forms of J and therefore a unique solution of the equation system (6). The energy function E must be minimized at each point along x_d to find the 'best' $\dot\theta = \dot\theta_{opt}$, in order to obtain the 'best' desired velocity $\dot{x}_d$. The derivative of E in (6) with respect to '*iteration time* τ' is (the manipulator moves in physical time t, which 'stays still' during optimization):

$$\frac{dE(\dot\theta)}{d\tau} = \frac{1}{2}\frac{\delta E(\dot\theta)}{\delta\dot\theta}\frac{d\dot\theta}{d\tau}$$

$$\dot E = A\dot\theta - b\,, \tag{7}$$

The energy function settles at $\dot\theta = \dot\theta_{opt}$, i.e. $\dot E(\dot\theta_{opt}) = 0$ (assuming convergence), and consequently minimizing E solves the linear system

$$A\dot\theta = b\,. \tag{8}$$

5   The Linear Hopfield Network

To carry out the optimization process above, the linear system (7) is mapped onto a linear dynamic network. Before the notion of Linear Hopfield Networks (LHN) is introduced, the similarities of equations (6), (7) with the Continuous Hopfield Network (CHN) are pointed out.

Continuous Hopfield Network. In the original paper by Hopfield and Tank [4], the energy function of CHNs (single layer, recurrent) is defined by $2E = -V^T T V - 2I^T V$, with weight matrix T, optimization variable V, constant input vector I, and therefore is similar to the energy function in (6). The derivative of Hopfield's energy function is $\dot E = -TV - I$ and thus almost identical to (7). The CHN is primarily used as an 'autoassociator' and requires sigmoidal transfer functions for it's neurons in order to guarantee convergence of it's dynamics to the nearest minimum of E [3]. If instead a linear transfer function is used, the CHN equation in [4] becomes $\dot V = T^* V + I^*$, with $T^* = -\text{diag}(k_i) + T$ and $I^* = -I$. When converging to the equilibrium ($\dot V = 0$), the linear system $T^* V = -I^*$ is solved, which is a linear system like (8).

Linear Hopfield Network. As shown above, the linear dynamic network defined by (6) and (7) is very similar to the CHN, which also is characterized by a energy function and a differential equation. The main difference between CHN and LHN is the sigmoidal transfer function, which is missing in (6) and (7). This fact leads to our notion of the LHN (single layer, recurrent), which solves the linear system (8), provided convergence to the solution $\dot\theta_{opt}$ with $\dot E(\dot\theta_{opt}) = 0$. A design method for the LHN, which satisfies the convergence requirements, is given below in (9) and (10).

Definition. The Linear Hopfield Network is a single–layer, recurrent network with weight matrix W, constant (clamped) input vector u and linear transfer functions. The dynamics of the continuous–time LHN and the discrete–time LHN by are defined by (9):

$$\frac{d\dot\theta}{d\tau} = -W\dot\theta + u\,, \tag{9a}$$

where τ represents 'iteration time', not physical time t, and

$$W = \alpha A = \alpha\left(\varepsilon\, I + J^T J\right)\,, \quad W \in \mathbb{R}^{n \times n}, \tag{9b}$$

$$u = \alpha b = \alpha J^T \dot x_d\,, \quad u \in \mathbb{R}^n, \tag{9c}$$

and for numerical solutions using digital computers, the discrete time representation of (9a) is

$$\Delta\dot\theta(n) = \dot\theta(n + 1) - \dot\theta(n) = -W\dot\theta(n) + u\,. \tag{9d}$$

In the following we proof that this linear system converges for

$$0 \le \alpha < \frac{1}{\|A\|}\,. \tag{10}$$

The LHN state vector $\dot{\theta}$ is updated in synchronous (simultaneous) mode. Convergence of the continuous–time LHN in (9a) and the discrete–time LHN in (9d) is guaranteed for any initial condition $\dot{\theta}_0$ if the step size α satisfies (10) for some matrix norm $\|A\|$. For fast convergence α should be near it's upper limit. Suitable norms are e.g. the maximum eigenvalue (maximum spectral radius) $\lambda_{max}\{A\}$ or the maximum singular value $\sigma_{max}\{A\}$.

Proof. While the sigmoidal transfer function plays a central role in the convergence proof for the CHN, this proof does not apply to LHNs [3]. Here the defining equations (9) must be 'scaled' with a constant factor α to provide convergence. This is possible due to the fact that the unscaled system (11a) and the scaled system in (11b) have the same solution $\dot{\theta}$, as is shown in (12):

$$A\dot{\theta} = b \tag{11a}$$

$$\alpha A\dot{\theta} = \alpha b \tag{11b}$$

$$\dot{\theta} = A^{-1}b = \frac{1}{\alpha}A^{-1}\alpha b = W^{-1}u . \tag{12}$$

A sufficient condition for the convergence of (11a) as well as for (11b) is (see e.g. [1])

$$\|W\| = \|\alpha A\| = \alpha\|A\| < 1 ,$$

which results in the inequality (10) for some matrix norm $\|A\|$. (q.e.d.)

With a given α and $\Delta\dot{\theta}(n) = \dot{\theta}(n + 1) - \dot{\theta}(n)$ the discrete–time LHN in (9d) can be rewritten as

$$\dot{\theta}(n + 1) = \dot{\theta}(n) - W\dot{\theta}(n) + u \tag{13}$$

$$= \dot{\theta}(n) + \alpha(-A\dot{\theta} - b) \tag{14}$$

$$= \dot{\theta}(n) + \alpha \, \Delta\dot{\theta}(n) . \tag{15}$$

Equation (15) suggests the interpretation of α as a 'step size' (as in the common learning context, here better 'convergence rate'), small enough to guarantee convergence of (15). It is generally known that a greater α provides faster convergence. Equation (10) gives a guideline to chose an upper bound $\alpha = \alpha_{max}$ to achieve the fastest convergence to the solution vector $\dot{\theta}_{opt}$.

6   Practical Considerations and Simulation

For the implementation of the LHN it was intended to keep the required computational power minimal. This is of particular interest because the LHN needs to be specified at each t_k along the desired trajectory, i.e. LHN initialization can require a considerable amount of computational power. A matrix norm $\|A\|$ specifying α for fast convergence may be the maximum singular value $\sigma_{max}\{A\}$, but determining σ_{max} requires a considerable number of floating point operations. Thus the trace$\{A\}$, which is easy to compute, was used for this work as an upper bound of σ_{max}:

$$\sigma_{max}\{A\} \leqq \text{trace}\{A\} = \sum_{i=1}^{n} A_{ii} .$$

According to the Jacobi iteration [1], synchronous (simultaneous) value corrections were used. Successive or asynchronous corrections provide slightly faster convergence, but require more calculations to design W. Also, for simulations it is important to choose appropriate initial conditions $x_d(t_k=0)$: if the initial Jacobian matrix has zero entries $\delta f_i/\delta\theta_j$, the algorithm may not move one or more joints as would be necessary for tracking the desired end–effector path. Zero entries of the Jacobian of course are unlikely in real–world applications, where noise is always present.

Simulation. For simulations an example manipulator, similar to a human arm (Figure 1), and a straight line in 3–D Cartesian space (Figure 7) as desired trajectory were chosen. The manipulator consists of two segments of unit length, two adjustable joint angles θ_1, θ_2 at the shoulder and one adjustable joint angle θ_3 at the elbow. The shoulder is positioned at the origin of the Cartesian reference system. Thus the control system has three reference inputs, three control signals and three control variables: desired Cartesian velocities $\dot{x}_d \in \mathbb{R}^3$, joint angle velocities $\dot{\theta} \in \mathbb{R}^3$ and actual Cartesian velocities $\dot{x} \in \mathbb{R}^3$. The resulting LHN weight matrix is $W \in \mathbb{R}^{3x3}$ (Figure 2).

The desired end–effector path $x_d(t)$ from time $t=0$ to $t=T$ was constructed as follows: Starting and ending point were obtained by (1) with $\theta_d(0)=[\pi/3, \pi/3, \pi/7]^T$, $\theta_d(T)=[2\pi/3, -\pi/3, \pi/5]^T$ to $x_d(0) \approx [0.28, 0.50, 1.87]^T$ and $x_d(T) \approx [-0.70, 1.22, -1.27]^T$. Between these points the selected path x_d is a straight line, consisting of a total of 1000 points, and the velocity curve $\dot{x}_d$ was selected to be bell–shaped. To track the trajectory, the incremental angle velocities $\dot{\theta}(t)$, computed by the LHN, were integrated to obtain the joint angle trajectory (Figure 3). The reader may verify the general shape of $\theta(t)$ by moving his/her hand along a similar virtual line. The position tracking error x_e of the control system increases with increasing ε, although here only the simulation with $\varepsilon=0.05$ is shown. Due to the particular x_d chosen here, the product $J^T J$ is invertible and ε could be set to zero, which also was verified during simulations.

Simulation results are shown in Figures 3 to 7. The three dimensions of the desired and actual Cartesian trajectories are shown in Figures 4 to 6 for $\varepsilon=0.05$. Because the energy function implements a 'compromise' between accurate position and smooth angle velocity curve, the error is not expected to be zero. The 3–D trajectories (desired and actual) for this example are shown in Figure 7. The integrated linearization error can be further reduced by using more points along the desired trajectory. With increasing ε the LHN performance changed towards smoother curves, but with greater position error, as expected.

Conclusion. The presented solution of the inverse kinematics problem, using an appropriate energy function which is minimized by a linear dynamic network (Linear Hopfield Network), shows promising results. It provides a variety of control strategies for a huge number of manipulator kinematics. A drawback of this approach is the required preplanned trajectory with a fixed number of points. From a practical point of view, the upper bound developed for the step size provides a means for confidently operating at a high convergence rate.

Acknowledgement

We would like to thank Chadwick Cox and Professor George G. Lendaris for helpful discussions and suggestions. This research is funded by the Office of Naval Research (ONR) under contract N00014–91–C–0268.

References

[1]   Golub G.H., van Loan C.F. 1989. "Matrix Computations," Johns Hopkins University Press, Baltimore and London.

[2]   Guo J., Cherkassky V. 1989. "A solution to the Inverse Kinematics Problem in Robotics using Neural Network Processing," International Joint Conference on Neural Networks (IJCNN) 1989, Vol. II, pp. 299–304.

[3]   Hertz J., Krogh A., Palmer R.G. 1991. "Introduction to the Theory of Neural Computation," Eddison–Wesley Publishing Company, New York.

[4]   Hopfield J.J., Tank D.W. 1986. "Computing with Neural Circuits: A Model," Science, Vol. 233, August 1986, pp. 625–633.

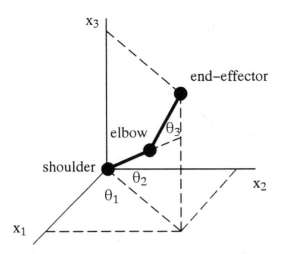

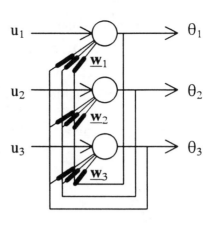

Figure 1: The example manipulator in 3-D Cartesian space.

Figure 2: The 3x3 Linear Hopfield Net for the inverse kinematics example.

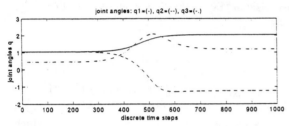

Figure 3: Optimized joint angle vector θ over time for $\varepsilon=0.05$.

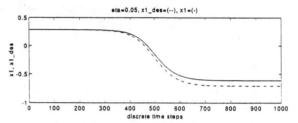

Figure 4: Desired and actual x_1 component of the end-effector trajectory for $\varepsilon=0.05$.

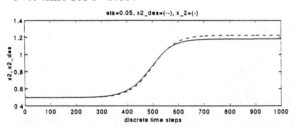

Figure 5: Desired and actual x_2 component of the end-effector trajectory for $\varepsilon=0.05$.

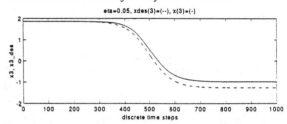

Figure 6: Desired and actual x_3 component of the end-effector trajectory for $\varepsilon=0.05$.

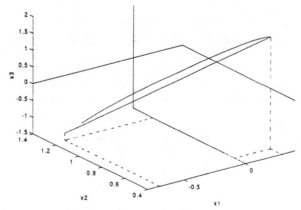

Figure 7: Desired and actual 3-D trajectory in Cartesian space over time for $\varepsilon=0.05$.

Good Fibrations: Canonical Parameterization of Fiber Bundles with Self–organizing Maps

David DeMers   Kenneth Kreutz-Delgado*
Electrical and Computer Engr. 0407
University of California, San Diego
9500 Gilman Dr.
La Jolla, CA 92093-0407

Abstract

A natural parameterization of the redundant degrees of freedom of a robot manipulator is learned from input–output data. A family of direct inverse kinematics functions are constructed by self-organizing maps. As a result, all inverse functions can be computed directly. Optimization of any side function is possible in the low–dimensional space of the natural parameterization, rather than in the full configuration space.

1   Introduction

A naturally arising problem is that of regularizing systems with excess degrees–of–freedom (dof). For example, control of a dextrous robot manipulator with more joints than the minimum necessary to perform its tasks requires "resolving" the redundancy in order to find a unique configuration of joint values which position the manipulator at a desired location.

We consider a system which can be represented as $\mathcal{S} = (\mathcal{B}, \mathcal{W}, f)$

$$f : \mathcal{B} \subset \Theta^n \mapsto \mathcal{W} \subset \mathcal{X}^m$$

($m < n$). Such a function is said to have *excess* or *redundant dof*.

It has been shown that if f is a smooth function and $\mathcal{B}$ (and therefore $\mathcal{W}$) are smooth manifolds[1], $\mathcal{W}$ can be partitioned into disjoint regions $\mathcal{W}_i$ such that the inverse of $\mathcal{W}_i$ consists of a finite number of regions $\mathcal{B}_i^j$ with the property that $(\mathcal{B}_i^j, \mathcal{T}^{n-m}, \mathcal{W}_i, f_i)$ forms a *trivial fiber bundle*, where $\mathcal{T}^{n-m}$ is an $n-m$ dimensional manifold in $\mathcal{B}_i^j$, and f_i is f restricted to $\bigcup_i \mathcal{B}_i^j$ [1], [5]. Each element x of $\mathcal{W}_i$ has as its inverse a unique $n-m$ dimensional submanifold in each $\mathcal{B}_i^j$, homeomorphic to $\mathcal{T}^{n-m}$, [2]. That is, for each $x \in \mathcal{W}_i$ there is a unique "fiber" in $\mathcal{B}_i^j$ which maps to x under f.

The hallmark of a trivial fiber bundle is that there exists a canonical parameterization of the fibers [9]. Any cross section through all the fibers[2] results in a manifold diffeomorphic to $\mathcal{W}_i$. Therefore $\mathcal{B}_i^j$ has a local product space topology equivalent to the product of the topology of $\mathcal{W}_i$ and the topology of the fibers[3], or $\mathcal{X}^m \times \Theta^{n-m}$.

An *inverse function* on $\mathcal{W}_i$ is a (smooth) function $g : x \in \mathcal{W}_i \mapsto \theta \in \Theta^n$ such that $f(g(x)) = x \; \forall x \in \mathcal{W}_i$ [12]. In general, g is not unique, even when $n = m$. For example, let $y = f(x) = x^2$. There are two inverse functions over $W = \mathbb{R}^+$; $g^+(y) = \sqrt{y}$ and $g^-(y) = -\sqrt{y}$. Each region of the workspace, $\mathcal{W}_i$, is invertible

---

*Supported by NSF grant IRI–9202581

[1] A manifold is a space which can be approximated *locally* as a Euclidean space. For example, the surface of a sphere appears locally everywhere as planar, but globally it can not be represented as a plane.

[2] To be more precise, a section through its principal bundle, see [9].

[3] Note that the $\mathcal{W}_i$ may have a simpler topology than $\mathcal{W}$. For example, if $\mathcal{W}$ is S^2, the sphere, and each of two $\mathcal{W}_i$ is a hemisphere, then the $\mathcal{W}_i$ have a topology equivalent to $\mathbb{R}^2$.

(admits an inverse function over the entire region), and there exists independent inverse functions for each $\mathcal{B}_i^j$ of $f^{-1}(\mathcal{W}_i)$ [5]. Each inverse function $g_i^j : \mathcal{W}_i \times T^{n-m} \to \mathcal{B}_i^j$ maps each point $x \in \mathcal{W}_i$ to the fiber in $\mathcal{B}_i^j$, parameterized by the $n-m$ redundant degrees of freedom. Any values for $s \in T^{n-m}$ result in an inverse function; $g(x, s)$ is thus a fully parameterized *family* of inverse functions.

This paper shows that the entire fiber bundle can be approximated with a set of self-organizing maps, such that a natural parameterization of the fibers is constructed. The inverse of f can then be approximated, with the parameterization resulting in $n-m$ free task space variables. If the inverse solution which optimizes a side function is sought, a search through the $n-m$ dimensional space of the redundancy suffices, rather than a search through the full n dimensional configuration space.

2 Self-Organizing Maps

Self-organizing maps have been used to construct inverse functions [10], [11]. However, the redundancy was regularized at training time, resulting in loss of the extra degrees of freedom at runtime. In this section, the basic ideas of using self-organizing maps to identify the *redundancy* are given. As a result, full use of all degrees of freedom is maintained at runtime, thus allowing dextrous use of the manipulator, and ability to change optimization criteria (e.g. between maximum manipulability, $\sqrt{\det(J(\theta)J^T(\theta))}$ and maximum force applicability) without re-training.

The input-output (θ, x) data for f can be partitioned such that the x components of each element of the partition are in the same $\mathcal{W}_i$ [4]. The resulting subsets of data can be further partitioned such that the θ components of each element are in the same $\mathcal{B}_i^j$ [5]. These subsets contain data from a single trivial fiber bundle, corresponding to the map $f : \mathcal{B}_i^j \to \mathcal{W}_i$.

From these input–output data samples we would like to construct a parameterization which is consistent throughout the entire $\mathcal{B}_i^j$ region and thereby construct a canonical parameterization of the complete fiber bundle. This is approximated by constructing self-organizing maps of the same topology as the fibers to a grid of query points in $\mathcal{W}_i$ region. The construction is such that the same parameter value of neighboring fibers corresponds to neighboring points.

Since the topology of the fibers for the case being considered is that of a one–dimensional manifold diffeomorphic to the circle, an appropriate topology preserving map is an elastic network. The Durbin–Willshaw algorithm, [6], applied to a network trained on data samples approximating one of the inverse fibers[4], produces an approximation to the data manifold [11].

The topographic map can be used to parameterize the data by assigning values to the nodes and interpolating between nodes (see, e.g., Figure 3). The network can be constructed to conform to the *a priori* known topology of the data and thus a local parameterization of the data can be generated.

The Durbin–Willshaw algorithm[5] for updating an elastic network is

$$\Delta w_i = \eta(\sum_\mu \Lambda_\mu(i)(d_\mu - w_i) + \kappa(w_{i+1} + w_{i-1} - 2w_i))$$

where d_μ is the location of the μth data point and w_i is the location of the ith node in the network, and $\Lambda_\mu(i)$ is a neighborhood function, here

$$\Lambda_\mu(i) = \frac{e^{|d_\mu - w_i|^2/2\sigma^2}}{\sum_j e^{|d_\mu - w_j|^2/2\sigma^2}}$$

From the data the $\mathcal{W}_i$ space is sampled at a number of locations x_q and data from $\mathcal{B}_i^j$ which approximates the fiber (the inverse of x_q). A self-organizing map is fit to one of these fibers. This map is then used as the initial network to fit to the remaining fibers. We let $w_{q,0}$ represent one of the nodes of the self-organizing map, the canonical zero point. The equivalent node in the next map, $w_{q+1,0}$, can be made to be near to that of its neighbor network by adding the term

$$\alpha(w_{q+1,0}^* - w_{q,0})$$

---

[4] Where the number of data samples is significantly greater than the number of nodes in the elastic network.

[5] We use terminology similar to that in [7].

to its update rule, where w_0^* is the zero position of the initial network and α is an adaptation rate parameter. The adaptation rate parameters, η, κ and α are typically initialized to the same value and annealed in proportion to the number of epochs of data presentation.

3 Manipulators with Redundant Degrees–of–Freedom

In this section an example is shown. The inverse kinematics of a 3–dof robot manipulator operating as a planar positioner is completely regularized and approximated throughout the entire reachable workspace.

The forward kinematics function for the 3–dof planar positioner maps a set of three joint angle values (a *configuration*) to a point (x, y) in the plane. Assuming no joint limits, the topology of an angle space is a unit circle, thus $\mathcal{B}$ is the product of three unit circles, the unit 3–torus. The range space $\mathcal{W}$ is the image of $\mathcal{B}$ under f which is either a disk or an annulus centered at the origin, depending on the lengths of the three links of the manipulator. Generically, $\mathcal{W}$ can be partitioned into either 3 or 4 $\mathcal{W}_i$ regions, [3], such that there are either 2 or 1 associated $\mathcal{B}_i^j$ pre–image regions for each $\mathcal{W}_i$.

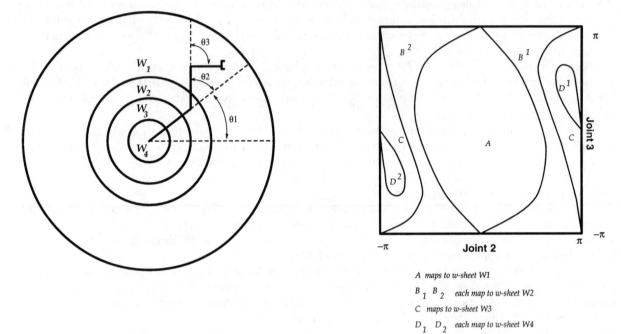

A maps to w-sheet W1

B_1 B_2 each map to w-sheet W2

C maps to w-sheet W3

D_1 D_2 each map to w-sheet W4

Figure 1: **Manipulator Workspace & Joint space** *The range space ("workspace") and the domain space ("configuration space" or "joint space") of the kinematic map for the 3R planar manipulator. The four annular regions are separated by boundaries (called Jacobian Surfaces) which are the image of the singularities of the forward kinematic function. These regions are denoted by $\mathcal{W}_i, i = 1, \ldots, 4$. The configuration space space is the 3-torus, which is shown "cut" and "unfolded" into a cube, and projected to the Joint 2-Joint 3 plane.*

A set of 216,000 data samples are chosen in $\mathcal{B}$ (the *configuration space*) and the end effector location in $\mathcal{W}$ corresponding to each is computed by the forward kinematics function[6]. The workspace $\mathcal{W}$ was partitioned into four regions based on the number and nature of the inverses for 213 query points. Figure 1 shows the partition of the workspace and the inverse regions in the configuration space. Each connected region in the configuration space maps onto one of the four $\mathcal{W}_i$.

In Figure 4 the learned fibration in the configuration space for two of these $\mathcal{W}_i$ (corresponding to the annuli $\mathcal{W}_3$ and $\mathcal{W}_2$ in Figure 1) are shown. The inverse data corresponding to points which map to one of the query points (the fiber) is approximated by individual self-organizing maps. The self-organizing maps

---

[6] Each angle was sampled every 6 degrees over its entire range.

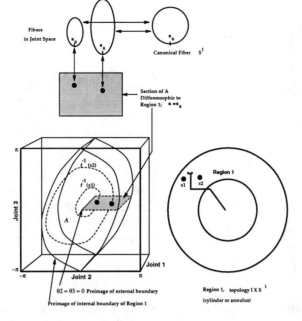

Figure 2: **Fibration of A** $= f^{-1}(\mathcal{W}_1)$. *All points along each of the one–dimensional fibers, $f^{-1}(x_i)$, map to the same point x_i in the range space. Each fiber represents the null–motion of the robot; the manipulator's end–effector remains at the same location in $\mathcal{W}_1$ for all configurations on the fiber. Each fiber is diffeomorphic to the "canonical fiber", S^1. The cross–section shown for $s = s_0$ is $\phi_1^1(\mathcal{W}_1, s_0)$, which is diffeomorphic to $\mathcal{W}_1$.*

can be used to compute a piecewise linear approximation to the fibers. Each fiber is homeomorphic to a circle. The nodes along each map are assigned parameter values based on their normalized distance around the fiber. The parameterization is qualitatively consistent over the set of fibers throughout each region.

4 Regularized Inverse Functions

A function computing the parameter value for any point in $\mathcal{B}_i^j$ can easily be approximated from all of the nodes in all of the elastic nets trained over the region. This function allows the map to be augmented into one which is one–to–one and onto, and thus invertible. That is, we can write $\hat{f} : \theta \in \mathcal{B}_i^j \mapsto (x, s)$ where $x \in \mathcal{W}_i$ and $s \in \mathcal{T}^{n-m}$. Now, given data samples (θ, x) from the original system, we can computed parameter values s for each x and use any nonlinear function approximator to learn the inverse $\hat{f}^{-1} : (x, s) \mapsto \theta$, where $x \in \mathcal{W}_i, s \in \mathcal{T}^{n-m}$ and $\theta \in \mathcal{B}_i^j$. In this way a function which has nontrivial inverse topology can be regularized such that the redundancy is resolved by introduction of free parameters in a canonical way. We have approximated regularized direct inverse functions for the 3–link redundant planar arm over all of its reachable workspace using both feedforward networks and radial basis function (RBF) networks. The average positioning error of each is less than 2% of the diameter of the reachable workspace. The RBF networks are more robust in that when presented with targets outside the reachable workspace, they produce a configuration which is close to that for the nearest reachable location, whereas the feedforward networks do not extrapolate well to unreachable locations.

5 Summary

We have shown that the many–to–one forward kinematics function can be partitioned into regions which have a well–defined topology as a trivial fiber bundle. The redundancy is resolved by introduction of learned free parameters in a canonical way, exploiting the trivial fiber bundle structure of each solution branch $\mathcal{B}_i^j$. A

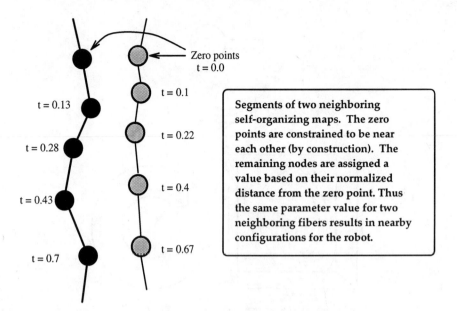

Zero points
t = 0.0

t = 0.1

t = 0.13

t = 0.22

t = 0.28

t = 0.4

t = 0.43

t = 0.67

t = 0.7

Segments of two neighboring self-organizing maps. The zero points are constrained to be near each other (by construction). The remaining nodes are assigned a value based on their normalized distance from the zero point. Thus the same parameter value for two neighboring fibers results in nearby configurations for the robot.

Figure 3: **Interpolated Fibers** *The configurations for two neighboring fibers, corresponding to the inverse solution set for two neighboring points in $\mathcal{W}_i$. The zero points are constructed to be nearby; the remaining nodes in each fiber are parameterized by their normalized distance from the zero point. A configuration for any parameter value is found by interpolation. The entire set of nodes for all fibers form a regularized map between the configuration space and the workspace augmented by a natural representation of the redundancy.*

family of regularized direct inverse functions are constructed over the entire reachable workspace for the 3–link redundant planar arm using self–organizing maps, parameterized by the learned natural representation of the redundancy.

References

[1] Joel Burdick (1988), *Kinematics and Design of Redundant Robot Manipulators*, Stanford Ph.D. Thesis, Dept. of Mechanical Engineering.

[2] Joel Burdick (1989), "On the Inverse Kinematics of Redundant Manipulators: Characterization of the Self–Motion Manifolds", *Proc. 1989 IEEE Int. Conf. Robotics & Automation*, pp. 264–270.

[3] David DeMers & Kenneth Kreutz-Delgado (1993), "Issues in Learning Global Properties of the Robot Kinematics Mapping", *Proc. IEEE Int'l Conf. Robotics & Automation* (Atlanta).

[4] David DeMers & Kenneth Kreutz-Delgado (1993), "Global Regularization of Inverse Kinematics for Redundant Manipulators", in S.J. Hanson, J.D. Cowan, & C.L. Giles, eds, *Advances in Neural Information Processing Systems 5* 255–262 San Mateo: Morgan Kaufmann.

[5] David DeMers (1993), *Learning to Invert Many-to-One Mappings*, Ph.D. Thesis, University of California, San Diego, Dept. of Computer Science & Engineering.

[6] Richard Durbin & David Willshaw (1987), "An Analogue Approach to the Traveling Salesman Problem Using an Elastic Net Method." *Nature* **326**, 689–691.

[7] John Hertz, Anders Krogh & Richard Palmer (1991), *An Introduction to the Theory of Neural Computation.*

[8] Teuvo Kohonen (1982), "Self–Organized Formation of Topologically Correct Feature Maps." *Biological Cybernetics* **43**,59–69.

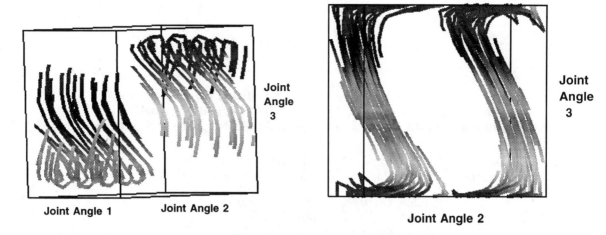

Figure 4: **Inverse fibers.** *(a) Twenty fibers from the inverse image of the next most inner annular region of the workspace of the three–link redundant planar manipulator. (b) Fibers from both inverse regions of the next most outer annular region. Apparent discontinuities are an artifact of the representation of this space (the 3–torus) as a cube — opposite faces of the cube are identified with each other. Greyscale represents an induced parameter value based on normalized distance from a canonical zero point.*

[9] Charles Nash & Siddhartha Sen (1983), *Topology and Geometry for Physicists.*

[10] Helge J. Ritter, Thomas M. Martinetz, & Klaus J. Schulten (1989), "Topology–Conserving Maps for Learning Visuo–Motor–Coordination", *Neural Networks*, Vol. 2, pp. 159–168.

[11] Helge J. Ritter, Thomas M. Martinetz, & Klaus J. Schulten (1992), *Neural Computation and Self-Organizing Maps*, (Addison-Wesley).

[12] Charles W. Wampler II (1988), "The Inverse Function Approach to Kinematic Control of Redundant Manipulators", *Proc. American Control Conference* (Atlanta).

ABSTRACT

Submitted to WCNN'94
June 4-9, 1994

An On-line Adaptive Controller Based on
the Connectionist Normalized Local Spline Neural Network
for the Optimization and Control of a Small-Angle Negative Ion Source

W. C. Mead,[a,b] P. S. Bowling,[c] S. K. Brown,[c] R. D. Jones,[a]
C. W. Barnes,[a] H. E. Gibson,[c] J. R. Goulding,[a,b] and Y. C. Lee[b,d]

[a]*Applied Theoretical Physics Division*
[b]*Center for Nonlinear Studies*
[c]*Accelerator Technology Division*
University of California
Los Alamos National Laboratory, Los Alamos, NM 87545

[d]*Department of Physics and Astronomy*
University of Maryland, College Park, MD 20740

We have developed[1] CTL, an on-line nonlinear adaptive controller, to optimize and control the operation of a repetitively-pulsed negative ion source. The controller processes multiple diagnostics, including the beam current waveform, to determine the ion source operating conditions. A figure of merit is constructed that weights beam current magnitude, noise, and pulse-to-pulse stability. The operating space of the ion source is mapped coarsely using automated scan procedures. Then, CTL, using information derived by fitting the sparse operating-space data using the Connectionist Normalized Local Spline artificial neural network (CNLS-net), interactively adjusts four ion-source control knobs (through regulating control loops) to optimize the figure of merit. Once coarse optimization is achieved using CNLS-net's model of machine parameter space, fine tuning is performed by executing a simplified gradient search algorithm directly on the machine. Beam quality obtained using the neural-net-based adaptive controller is consistently quite good. The search technique has tuned the ion source for near-optimum operation on six cold startups in one to four hours from the time of initial arc.

[1]W. C. Mead, P. S. Bowling, S. K. Brown, R. D. Jones, C. W. Barnes, H. E. Gibson, J. R. Goulding, and Y. C. Lee, *Nucl. Instr. and Meth.* **B72**, 271 (1992).

Neural modeling of non linear systems by systematic state space sampling.

Joan Codina, Josep M. Fuertes, Ricard Villà.

Automatic Control and Computer Engineering Department
Email: jcodina@esaii.upc.es
Universitat Politècnica de Catalunya
Pau Gargallo, 5 E-08028 Barcelona - Spain

Abstract. In non linear systems identification or modeling there is always the problem of finding the best test signal to be used in order to make the identification in a correct way. It's obvious that in linear systems a signal rich in frequencies is good enough but this is not the case for non linear systems. We can state that the best test signal will be the one that is able to make the system evolve through the whole working region of the state space. A method is presented that using artificial neural networks to identify non linear systems is able to optimize its own test signal to be used for system modeling and identification. As the definition of the test signal can not be done without a knowledge of the system behavior, an iterative process uses the partially learned system dynamics to improve the test signal. The same neural network that identifies the system will be used to generate the test signal for the next training phase. At every iteration the state space region already identified grows till it fills the predefined working area.

1. Introduction

One of the problems in modeling non linear, time invariant systems by ANN is related to the design of the correct input signal **u(t)** necessary to obtain a model that works when the inputs are no longer the training ones. This problem is difficult to solve because non linear systems can't, of course, be identified by an impulse signal. The design of the correct signal is related to the system dynamics and non linearities, this means that if we don't know the system dynamics we can't find the optimal input, and if we don't know the optimal input we can't find the optimal model. But from any reasonable input signal we can find some model of the system and from this model of the system we can extract some information to improve the test signal and model.

The research in the field of systems identification by neural networks has produced some models based on feed-forward neural networks. Such models usually take the form given by (1) and use external delay blocks for the inputs and outputs to accomplish the dynamic behavior:

$$y(k) = H [u(k), u(k-1), u(k-2)\dots \quad y(k-1), y(k-2)\dots] \tag{1}$$

In Narendra [1] is presented a very extensive work with such methodology where different configurations are studied. The neuron activation functions used in such work are of sigmoidal type. And input-output simulation of some proposed dynamic systems are carried out.

The use of dynamic neurons or the Hopfield network [2] increases the order of the system to the number of neurons, obstructing the study of the network dynamics.

To allow simpler models for multiple inputs multiple outputs (MIMO) systems we have developed an ANN architecture based on the state space representation of dynamic systems, fig. 1. Such structure allows the application of modern and classical control theories for single input single output and MIMO systems and allow the application of classical techniques. Beginning with linear discrete-time systems, we obtained, Codina [3], a neural network able to learn the matrices of the system state representation from pairs of input-output vector signals. The model was a neural network with three layers: input, state and output. The state and the output layers are connected to the input layer, composed by the actual inputs and state of the system. We used the back-propagation through time learning algorithm Werbos [4], where the error is back-propagated from the actual state to the previous state. With this methodology, and using linear neurons, we can obtain from the system the state space matrices A, B, C and D:

$$x(k+1) = A\, x(k) + B\, u(k)$$
$$y(k) = C\, x(k) + D\, u(k) \qquad (2)$$

This model was expanded in order to deal with non linear systems. But expanding the linear model using sigmoids hinders a theoretical study of the proposed NN model. To solve this drawback we have used a structured neural network based on Fourier series in order to approximate any non linear function, within a bounded interval, by a weighted sum of sines and cosines, Codina [5]. In fig. 2 we can see a neural network that obtains the Fourier coefficients corresponding to a one-dimensional function.

A non linear discrete-time system can be expressed by the following difference equations:

$$x(k+1) = F(\, x(k), u(k))$$
$$y(k) = G(\, x(k), u(k)) \qquad (3)$$

where F and G can be approximated in a bounded interval by a Fourier series.

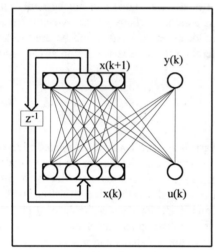

Fig. 1 Proposed linear NN structure   **Fig. 2** Fourier series based model

The use of neural networks with state space system description allows making an exhaustive search through the state space. The same NN which models the sytem is used for generating the inputs to the modeled system so as to improve the identification.

The optimal input signal.

Before beginning to optimize the input signal, we must know which is the attainable optimum, and after that we must search a way to obtain it.

From the state space equations we take only the part referring to the calculation of the next state (3). Applying an input function u(k) to them recursively we can define $\Phi(k)$ as the output after the first k terms of u(k). Assuming an initial state x(0):

$$x(k+1) = \Phi(x(0), u(0) \ldots u(k)) = F(F(\ldots(F(x(0), u(0)), u(1)) \ldots), u(k)) \qquad (4)$$

Then, in a system with n states and m inputs, the optimal input function $\vec{u}(k)$ is the one that, in a bounded working space C of dimension n+m, makes the system evolve through it describing a path that takes all possible values in C once and only once:

$$\vec{u}(k) \quad \text{so that} \quad \forall[\vec{x}_a, \vec{u}_a] \in C \; \exists k_0 \; / \; [\vec{x}(k_o + 1)] = \Phi[\vec{x}(k_0), \vec{u}(k_0)]$$
$$\text{with} \quad \vec{x}(k_0) = \vec{x}_a \quad \text{and} \quad \vec{u}(k_0) = \vec{u}_a \tag{5}$$

This expression gives the optimum, but such an input function does not exist. What is feasible is to have a set of points P, constructed by the cartesian product of P_x, (a regular sampling over the states), and P_u (a regular sampling over the inputs).

$$\vec{u}(k) \quad \text{so that} \quad \forall[\vec{x}_a, \vec{u}_a] \in P \; \exists k_0 \; / \; [\vec{x}(k_o + 1)] = \Phi[\vec{x}(k_0), \vec{u}(k_0)]$$
$$\text{with} \quad \vec{x}(k_0) = \vec{x}_a \quad \text{and} \quad \vec{u}(k_0) = \vec{u}_a \tag{6}$$

It is a very hard condition that the only points the system goes through be in P and to force it to pass through the points once and only once . This condition is very important to guarantee that the learning procedure has the same behavior over all C. To make feasible the search of u(k) we redefine the problem in order to find a set of functions that in a fixed number of steps (controllability is then assumed) bring the system from the initial state to a desired state belonging to the set of points P_x . That is

$$\forall \vec{x}_a \in P_x \; \exists \; \vec{u}_a(k), k_0 \; / \; \vec{x}_a = \Phi[\vec{x}(0), \vec{u}_a(0)..\vec{u}_a(k_0)] \tag{7}$$

Then we can append to each $\vec{u}_a(k)$ succesivally all the values in P_u, so that we can obtain the output corresponding to all the pairs input-state in P:

$$y_{a,b}(k_0 + 1) = G\big(\Phi[\vec{x}(0), \vec{u}_a(0)..\vec{u}_a(k_0)], \vec{u}_b\big) = G(\vec{x}_a, \vec{u}_b) \quad \forall \, \vec{x}_a \in P_x, \; \vec{u}_b \in P_u \tag{8}$$

Now $y_{a,b}(k)$ can be used in order to train the network. But instead of training the network for all k we only do it for $k = k_n + 1$, the last value. Doing so we are training the network for a set of points sampled regularly over the C space. If we use a network with a structure inspired on the Fourier series, Codina [5], then we can assume that the net is calculating Fourier coefficients corresponding to the function F. To get the first N coefficients we need 2N points for each dimentsion in C.

Obtention of $\vec{u}_a(k)$

The problem is now to find $\vec{u}_a(k)$ for all the states in P_x without knowing F. And of course this is not possible. What is possible is to have and approximation of F, obtained by training the neural network with a pair of input-output signals. Thus we obtain an estimation of the state space model and we use it to obtain the approximation to $\vec{u}_a(k)$.

So let's imagine that we have trained the network with a pair of input-output signals, and that the network has learned the system behavior. Let's now suppose that we have a first order, one input system, with F known. We can draw the state trajectory due to the input u(k) , fig. 3. And we assume that if the system has learned to simulate this input-output pair of signals, then it approximates the function F in an area surrounding the trajectory; we call $\tilde{F}_1$ this first approximation. We now use $\tilde{F}_1$ to calculate $\vec{u}_a(k)$ and then we use the resulting outputs of the system to train the network. In this way we obtain the new function $\tilde{F}_2$, which approximates F correctly in a wider area, because the $\vec{u}_a(k)$ were good at least where $\tilde{F}_1$ was good and in some neighbourhood.

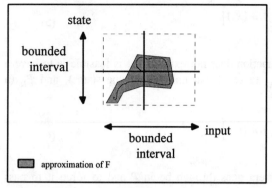

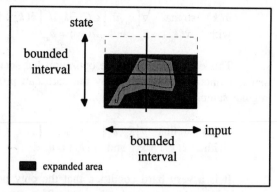

Fig. 3 Area of correct identification   **Fig.4** Expansion of the Area of correct identification

Implementation using neural networks

To obtain $\bar{u}_a(k)$ we use the neural network which has learned the system dynamics. The way to do it is by building the structure of NN shown in figures 5 and 6. There NetSim is the system simulator that implements the function $\tilde{F}_1$, and is used to train the network NetImp. This network is composed of a linear neuron with k_0 inputs, and at each time k only the kth input is activated with a value of 1.0. After k_0 sample times, the state is compared with the desired state and the resulting error is backpropagated. We use the backpropagation through time algorithm to find the way in which each of the inputs influence the output through the state.

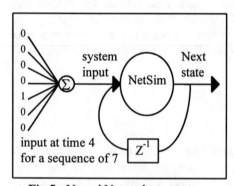 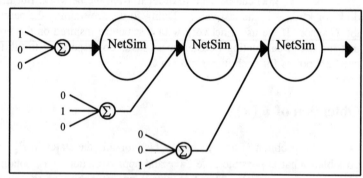

Fig 5   Neural Network structure   **Fig 6**   Learning procedure

After the training is done, the weight of the linear neuron contains the sequence of values that form $\bar{u}_a(k)$. This procedure is inspired in the way used to train NN controllers done by Nguyen [6].

Example

A first order non-linear system has been used to test the NN training procedure:

$$x(k+1) = x(k)u(k) - .5u(k) \tag{9}$$
$$y(k) = e^x + hist(u(k)); \quad hist(x) = x \text{ if } |x| > .4 \tag{10}$$

A signal composed of random steps with noise has been used for the first training iteration. Six Fourier coefficients are used. In fig. 7 it can be seen how the training signal explores the state space. After the first iteration the search in the state space is carried out systematically for the area where the state was reached by the training signal. When we now apply to the system to be identified all the pairs input-state, the system can reach some state outside the searching area. This state will contribute to the expansion of the search area. If no state is outside the searching area then it means that, for the number of Fourier terms considered, this state can not be reached from those initial conditions.

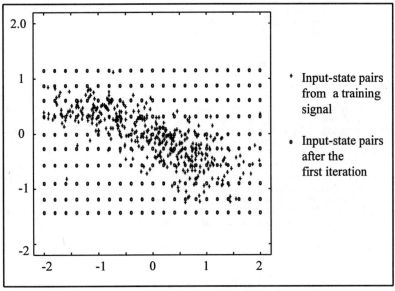

Fig. 7   Area explored by the network during training

Conclusions

In neural modeling of non linear, dynamic, time invariant systems, the selection of the right input-output pair of signals to use is crucial. As there is no prior knowledge of the system to model, there is no possibility to calculate, a priory, the best test signal to be used. A good test signal is that one which makes the system state evolve through all the state space. The use of ANN to optimize the input signal to improve the identification of non linear, dynamic, time invariant systems, is a new subject to be explored. In this paper the basic methodology is presented. The use of ANN has been shown through an example with a first order non linear system. The promising preliminary results indicate the convenience to continue with the theoretical basis development and to test the application to real systems.

References

1. Narendra K.S., Parthasarathy K. Identification and Control of Dynamical Systems Using Neural Networks. IEEE Trans. on Neural Networks. Vol 1. N 1. March 1990.
2. Hopfield, J.J. Neural Netwoks and Physical Systems with Emergent Collective Computational Abilities. Proc. National Academy of Science. 79:2554-2558 (1984).
3. Codina J., Morcego B., Fuertes J.M., Català A. A Novel Neural Network Structure for Control. IEEE Int. Conf. on Systems, Man and Cybernetics. 1339-1344. Chicago, 1992.
4. Werbos P.J. Backpropagation Through Time: What it Does and How to Do it. Proc. of the IEEE. Vol. 78 N. 10 pp. 1550-1560 October 1990.
5. Codina J., Fuertes J.M. Structured Neural Network for Nonlinear Systems Modeling. To be presented at Sicica'94.
6. Nguyen, D.H., Widrow, B. Neural Networks for Self-learning Control Systems. IEEE Control Systems Mag. pp 18-23 April 1990.

A Reinforcement Learning Approach to On-Line Optimal Control

P.E. An, S. Aslam-Mir, M. Brown, C.J. Harris

Advanced Systems Research Group,
Department of Aeronautics and Astronautics,
Southampton University,
Southampton, S09 5NH, UK.

Abstract

This paper presents a hybrid control architecture for solving *on-line* optimal control. In this architecture, the control law is dynamically scheduled between a reinforcement controller and a stabilizing controller so that the closed-loop performance is smoothly transformed from a reactive behavior to one which can predict. Based on a modified Q-learning technique, the reinforcement controller is made of two components: policy and Q functions. The policy function is explicitly incorporated so as to bypass the minimum operator normally required for selecting actions and updating the Q function. This architecture is then applied to a repetitive operation using a second-order linear-time-variant plant with a nonlinear control structure. In this operation, the reinforcement signals are based on set-point errors and the reinforcement controller is generalized using second-order B-Splines networks. This example illustrates how, for a non-optimally tuned stabilizing controller, the closed-loop performance can be bootstrapped with the use of reinforcement learning. Results shows that the set-point performance of the hybrid controller is improved over that of the fixed structure controller by discovering better control strategies which compensate for the non-optimal gains and nonlinear control structure.

1 Introduction

A common objective in closed-loop control tasks is to design suitable control laws such that the systems closely follow their desired trajectories, such as pick and place operations in robotics. The complexity of such control laws vary considerably with the degree of plant nonlinearities. When the plant has an unknown structure, linear or nonlinear modeling techniques are generally incorporated in the design process so that these models adapt to their appropriate representations specific to the *time scale* of their performance objectives. At one extremum of this time scale, the performance objective can be formulated as a supervised learning problem in which the instantaneous cost is minimized. This optimization problem requires that the desired trajectory point be specified in every sampling interval, and constraints of the plants' kinematics and dynamics be satisfied. The controllers essentially adapt to the plant's inverse dynamics such that the closed-loop transfer dynamics is minimized. The standard Least-Mean-Square algorithm or its variants are commonly applied to minimize the instantaneous cost [15].

At the other extremum of the time scale, the performance objective can be formulated as a reinforcement learning problem in which the long-term cumulative costs are minimized. Unlike its supervised learning counterpart, this optimization problem is generally harder because the only information about the desired trajectory is the plant's goal state whereas no other useful action evaluation is fedback to the controller with regard to its transient performance. The controller no longer explicitly models the plant's inverse dynamics, but rather a different representation of knowledge governed by the chosen optimality criteria. By incorporating temporal sequences of the plant's movement throughout the task, this representation generally reveals an additional knowledge on the plant's characteristic, which is ignored in the supervised learning scenarios [11]. The basis of the reinforcement learning control strategy is thus twofold: it is generally diffcult to design an appropriate reference model specific to the choice of the sampling interval and to a plant with an associated degree of uncertainty and nonlinearity so that the constraints of kinematics and dynamics are satisfied; more importantly, this control strategy provides an important channel for designing a particular form of optimality about the long-term plant's behavior. Examples are minimum fuel or minimum time criteria commonly adopted in dynamic programming problems.

Within the context of reinforcement learning control, the problem of pole balancing has been widely studied as a means to explore temporal credit-assignment with delayed reinforcement signals [1, 3]. In this problem, the reinforcement signal is only available to the controller when the pole or the cart falls outside the specified limits. The basis of this reinforcement learning takes on a "trial and error" philosophy in which the underlying control action is stochastic. This facilitates a richer exploratory action throughout the plant states before an optimal control strategy can be estimated. This "trial and error" learning technique, from a control perspective, is *not* justified when the primary concern is the closed-loop stability. One way to resolve this "exploration-stability" tradeoff is to first estimate the control law *off-line* from a set of training data, and later incorporate it into the closed-loop environment. The merit of this control strategy is determined largely by the modeling errors associated with the controller, which results from its structural representation and also its exposure to the *off-line* training experience.

Another way to resolve the "exploration-stability" tradeoff is to perform estimation and control procedures simultaneously [10]. These control architectures incorporate stabilizing controllers to both safeguard closed-loop stability and provide feedback signals to adaptive controllers for parameter estimation. When these controllers are bootstrapped by feedback signals, exploration is generally restricted and the condition of persistent excitation of training inputs is thus critical for proper control [2]. Nevertheless, this resolution is generally preferred to the former one as the control law can be smoothly transformed *on-line* from its purely reactive behavior to one which can predict. This paper proposes a hybrid control architecture for solving *on-line* optimization problems via reinforcement learning. The rest of this paper is organized as follows: The next section reviews the reinforcement learning problem and available techniques that have been proposed to solve the problem. Section 3 presents the hybrid architecture in which the control law is based on a stabilizing controller to ensure closed-loop stability, and a reinforcement controller to provide the long-term performance. This architecture is then applied to a pick-and-place learning operation using a second-order linear plant with a nonlinear control structure. In this operation, the reinforcement controller is generalized using second-order B-Splines networks whereas the stabilizing controller is a fixed gain PID, and the set-point performance results are presented in Section 4. In the final section, the reinforcement learning results are summarized, and practical implementation issues are discussed.

2 Reinforcement Learning

The reinforcement learning problem can be formulated as one which chooses a control policy [1] that minimizes discounted cumulative reinforcements for every possible states. This learning objective provides a potential benefit of resolving temporal credit-assignment issues especially for delayed reinforcement and a long sequence of control actions. Examples are shortest-path planning and pole-balancing control problems [1, 3, 8, 9] where the informative transitional reinforcement occurs infrequently, and is only available upon an arrival of destination/failure. The reinforcement signal for the shortest-path problem can be defined as the number of time steps taken before the goal is reached [8], whereas for the pole-balancing problem it can be defined as the number of failures occurred within a fixed interval [3]. Different definitions in the reinforcement generally result in different forms of optimality in the plant's behavior.

Let x_t and u_t be the current state and action taken at time t. Also, let $J(x_t, x_{t+1}, u_t)$ be its transitional reinforcement when the plant moves to a new state x_{t+1}, and $V_U(x_t)$ be the output of an evaluation function associated with x_t based on some policy U. The learning task can now be described mathematically as estimating an optimal evaluation function $V_{U^*}^*$ which contains minimum cost-to-go values for every states [4], and its policy U^* such that

$$V_{U^*}^*(x_t) < V_U(x_t) \quad \forall x_t \tag{1}$$

where $V_U(x_t)$ is defined as

$$V_U(x_t) = \sum_{k=0}^{m} \gamma^k J(x_{t+k}, x_{t+k+1}, u_{t+k}) \quad \forall x_t \tag{2}$$

m is the number of time steps taken before the goal state is reached. This value generally varies from one trial to another when the adaptation is performed continually. γ is a discount factor which determines the level of influence of future reinforcements on the selection of the current action, and is bounded between 0 to 1. A proper choice of γ generally depends on the length of the task performed, nonstationary characteristics of the plant's dynamics and also the magnitude of the modeling errors introduced when $V_{U^*}^*(x_t)$ is interpolated [13].

To illustrate how the optimal evaluation function and its policy are computed, an example is given in Figure 1 in which the plant takes on discrete states and actions, and has deterministic transitional dynamics. In these sub-figures, S and G are the start and goal state respectively. Each node in the tree represents a state, and associated with each of these states is a set of directional branches that leads to other states under all possible actions. In Figure 1a, the transitional reinforcements are represented by values that are attached to their branches. For example, $J(a \to d) = 4$. Similar to dynamic programming techniques, the computation procedure generally starts from the goal state, and then proceeds backward through the transitional chains under all possible actions, until the start state is located.

---

[1] A control policy is one which maps every states to actions.

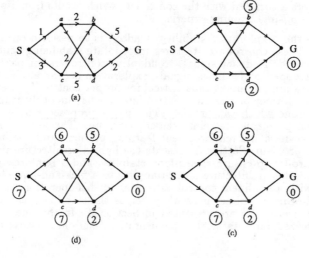

Figure 1: (a) Instantaneous reinforcement assignment. Each node in the tree represents a state, and each branch represents a state transition. Each transition results in an instantaneous cost, as indicated by numerical values. S and G represent the start and goal state respectively. (b) compute minimum cost-to-go values at state b and d, assuming that the goal state has zero cost-to-go value; (c) compute minimum cost-to-go values at state a and c; (d) compute minimum cost-to-go value at S. In (b-d), minimum cost-to-go values are indicated by circles.

In Figure 1b, there is only one possible action taken in either state b or d, and their resulting minimum cost-to-go values are 5 and 2 respectively. To compute $V^*(a)$, two possible cost-to-go values ($\{J(a \to b) + V^*(b)\}$ and $\{J(a \to d) + V^*(d)\}$) are compared, and the minimum cost-to-go value at a is 6. Similar procedures are carried out for state c and S. As soon as the minimum cost-to-go value of the start state is computed, an optimal evaluation function is immediately found, and is given in Figure 1d. The minimum cost-to-go values are indicated by circles, and the optimal policy U^* is ($S \to a \to d \to G$). From a control standpoint, this selection of control actions based on minimizing the cost-to-go values is efficient because it only requires one-step ahead searches of actions to achieve long-term performance. Whereas minimizing only the transitional reinforcement often results in a short-term benefit ($S \to a \to b \to G$), as commonly performed under supervised learning. When the plant has many possible states and actions, the estimation of V^* (or $\hat{V}^*$) can be carried out iteratively so that moderate intermediate solutions can be obtained. Two methods have been proposed to facilitate *on-line* reinforcement learning: Adaptive Heuristic Critic and Q-Learning method. These methods are conceptually similar to the standard dynamic programming (or DP) method for solving nonlinear optimization problems, except that the estimation procedure of the evaluation function is incremental.

2.1   Adaptive Heuristic Critic (AHC)

This method makes use of two separate models, $\hat{V}^*$ and $\hat{U}^*$, to estimate the optimal evaluation function and control policy respectively [2]. These models are functions of the plant's states, and can be implemented in forms of look-up-tables, or connectionist models so that the credit assignment can be generalized spatially. A flow chart of its operation is given in Table 1. At time t, the state x_t is sampled and a stochastic action u_t is computed according to a predefined probability distribution biased by $\hat{U}^*(x_t)$. Consequently, the plant moves from x_t to x_{t+1}. $J(x_t, x_{t+1}, u_t)$ as well as $\hat{V}^*(x_{t+1})$ are computed for the new state. Both models are then adapted such that the temporal-difference error in Step 3 is minimized [11]. One important observation of the AHC is that its action selection and policy update are not based on minimizing the cost-to-go value in every iteration [3]. In the case where the policy is nonstationary (due to step 4), $\hat{V}^*$ often converges to one which is different from V^*.

---

[2] These are referred to as adaptive critic element and adaptive search element respectively in [3]

[3] To be exact, the AHC method only accounts for how the evaluation function is adapted based on the error in step 3, as originally developed in [12].

1. Get → x_t;
2. Apply $u_t = \text{Random}(\hat{U}^*(x_t)) \rightarrow$ get x_{t+1};
3. Compute $TD_{error} = J(x_t, x_{t+1}, u_t) + \gamma \hat{V}^*(x_{t+1}) - \hat{V}^*(x_t)$;
4. Update $\hat{V}^*$ and $\hat{U}^*$ each to minimize TD_{error};
5. Go to 1.

Table 1. A flow chart of the Adaptive Heuristic Critic method.

2.2 Q-Learning

Unlike the AHC, this method makes use of only one model structure: Q function for estimating the cost-to-go values (or $\hat{Q}^*$ values). This function is defined over the state and action spaces, and its action selection and policy update require that these values be minimized among different policies. This function converges to its optimal Q^* when the following condition holds

$$\min_u Q^*(x, u) = V_{U^*}^*(x) \quad \forall x \tag{3}$$

A flow chart of its operation is given in Table 2. At time t, an action u_t is chosen that minimizes immediate $\hat{Q}^*$ values among all possible actions, and consequently the plant moves from x_t to x_{t+1}. $J(x_t, x_{t+1}, u_t)$ and the minimum $\hat{Q}^*(x_{t+1}, u_{t+1})$ are evaluated. The Q model is then updated such that the Q_{error} in step 3 is minimized. Convergence proofs of the Q-function to its optimal Q^* for discrete states and actions have been established [7, 14].

The main difference between these methods stems from the representation of the stored knowledge. In the AHC, the evaluation function estimates the minimum cost-to-go values given that the policy is optimal whereas the Q function estimates the cost-to-go values for different control policies. The convergence of $\hat{Q}^*$ to its optimal solution comes at a price: direct search of actions that minimizes immediate $\hat{Q}^*$ values can be time-consuming, especially when the action space is excessively large. For continuous state and action domains, the Q function must be interpolated and this representation generally results in modeling errors. When the minimum operator is used in the update, the modeling errors often cause the $\hat{Q}^*$ values to be biased [13].

1. Get x_t;
2. Apply $u_t = \text{Random}(\min_{u_t} \hat{Q}^*(x_t, u_t)) \rightarrow$ get x_{t+1};
3. Compute $Q_{error} = J(x_t, x_{t+1}, u_t) + \gamma \min_{u_{t+1}} \hat{Q}^*(x_{t+1}, u_{t+1}) - \hat{Q}^*(x_t, u_t)$
4. Update Q to minimize Q_{error};
5. Go to 1.

Table 2. A flow chart of the Q-Learning method.

3 Hybrid Control Architecture

This section describes a hybrid control architecture which can be used to solve *on-line* optimal control problems. The generation of control actions is dynamically scheduled between a stabilizing controller and a reinforcement controller. Based on a modified Q-learning technique, the reinforcement controller has two components: policy and Q functions, as denoted by $\hat{U}^*$ and $\hat{Q}^*$ respectively. $\hat{U}^*$ estimates the optimal control policy, and is defined with respect to the plant states; whereas $\hat{Q}^*$ estimates the cost-to-go values, and is defined with respect to the state and action spaces. Unlike the Q-learning method, the explicit incorporation of the policy function avoids the minimum operator normally required for selecting actions and updating $\hat{Q}^*$. An overall block diagram of the hybrid architecture is given in Figure 2 and a flow chart of its operation is given in Table 3.

The role of the stabilizing controller is twofold: it ensures that the plant remains bounded within a desired region during a trial and it also bootstraps the reinforcement controller during learning with feedback signals so that the policy and Q functions can be estimated incrementally. This stabilizing controller can be implemented based on any controllers, such as classical PID or H_∞. The Scheduler generates an action according to step 6 in Table 3. α is initially set to 1, and slowly increased as more training experiences are

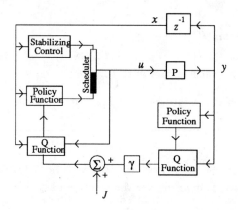

Figure 2: A reinforcement learning control architecture for nonlinear optimal control.

gathered to update the reinforcement controller. This setting allows the control strategy to be smoothly transformed from a reactive type to one which can predict the long-term performance. In addition, the variation in α introduces an extra degree of excitation of training signals for parameter estimation. In the case where the closed-loop performance deteriorates as a result of the control transfer, α can be reset to a small value (≥ 1).

At time t, an action $u(x_t)$ is computed according to step 6, and the plant moves from x_t to x_{t+1}. To update the Q function, u^* is first computed based on $\hat{U}^*(x_{t+1})$ as if this were the optimal action that led to a minimum $\hat{Q}^*(x_{t+1}, u^*)$, or q^*. The Q function is then updated using step 9. To update the policy function, $\hat{Q}^*(x_t, u(x_t))$ and $\hat{Q}^*(x_t, \hat{U}^*(x_t))$ are compared. If the action taken leads to a smaller $\hat{Q}^*$ value, the policy function is then updated using step 11. When a trial is complete, the plant resets to its original state and a new trial begins. Note that α varies only from one trial to another, and stays constant during the trial.

1. Set α to 1; specify the decay constant τ for updating α (see step 11);
2. Do trial l: 1 to n
3. Do time step t: 1 to m
4. Get x_t;
5. Apply $u(x_t) = \frac{1}{\alpha} U_{\text{PID}}(x_t) + (1 - \frac{1}{\alpha}) \hat{U}^*(x_t) \rightarrow$ get x_{t+1};
6. Compute $u^* = \hat{U}^*(x_{t+1})$ and $q^* = \hat{Q}^*(x_{t+1}, u^*)$;
7. Update $\hat{Q}^*(x_t, u(x_t))$ to minimize $Q_{error} = \gamma\, q^* + J(x_t, x_{t+1}, u(x_t)) - \hat{Q}^*(x_t, u(x_t))$;
8. Compute $q' = \hat{Q}^*(x_t, \hat{U}^*(x_t))$;
9. If $\hat{Q}^*(x_t, u(x_t)) < q'$, update $\hat{U}^*(x_t)$ to minimize the control error $= u(x_t) - \hat{U}^*(x_t)$;
10. Go to 4 unless $t = m$;
11. $\alpha = \alpha + \tau$;
12. Go to 3 unless $l = n$;

Table 3. A flow chart of the hybrid control operation.

4 Simulations/Results

In this section, the hybrid control architecture is applied to a pick-and-place operation in which the noiseless plant, unknown to the reinforcement learning controller, has the following characteristics

$$\ddot{y}(t) = -0.5\dot{y}(t) - 5y(t) + 5u(t); \quad |u(t)| \leq 3, \quad |\dot{u}(t)| \leq 1 \tag{4}$$

The second-order dynamics were sampled at a rate of 20Hz, and the stabilizing control was based on a standard PID with its fixed gains chosen to be {0.3 0.3 0.3}. These fixed gains were not tuned to produce an optimal performance for the plant in (4), but rather were chosen to illustrate how this reinforcement control strategy allows the closed-loop performance to gradually improve over that of the PID. The policy and Q functions associated with the reinforcement controller were based on second-order B-Splines networks

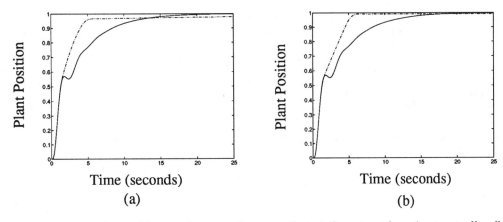

Figure 3: A comparison in tracking performance between the reinforcement learning controller (broken line) and the fixed gain PID controller (solid line). (a) after 2 trials (b) after 10 trials.

in which the univariate basis functions are piecewise linear [4]. These interpolative networks have nonlinear modeling capabilities over a compact input region, and are well suited to *on-line* low-dimensional applications based on their rapid convergence and minimum learning interference properties. Note that for other control problems of high dimensionality, these networks might be undesirable because their memory storage and computational cost grow exponentially with the input dimension. The policy function was defined over $\{y, \dot{y}\}$ whereas the Q function was defined over $\{y, \dot{y}, u\}$. Nine interior knots were uniformly allocated along each of these input axes. Ranges of these network inputs were chosen to be $-1.5 \leq y \leq 1.5$, $-1.5 \leq \dot{y} \leq 1.5$, and $-5 \leq u \leq 5$. Note that additional inputs are generally required when the goal state is non-stationary. The parameters in the policy and Q function were updated using a stochastic approximation version of the normalized LMS algorithm, where the learning rate β_k of the parameter k was defined as

$$\beta_k = \frac{0.5}{1 + \frac{n_k}{50}} \tag{5}$$

where n_k is the number of times the parameter k has been updated. The diminishing learning rate was designed so as to minimize the effect of modeling error/measurement noise, which could deteriorate the cost-to-go value estimation.

The pick-and-place learning task was decomposed into a set of trials, and during each trial, a set of actions was chosen so that the plant moved from its origin state defined by $y_d = 0$ and $\dot{y}_d = 0$ toward its goal state defined by $y_d = 1$ and $\dot{y}_d = 0$ and the reinforcement signal was chosen to be the set-point error, $\left(y_d(t) - y(t)\right)^2 + \left(\dot{y}_d(t) - \dot{y}(t)\right)^2$. After 500 sampling iterations were elapsed, the plant was reset to its origin state, and a new trial repeated. The discount factor γ was chosen to be 0.6 and τ was chosen to be 5, as defined in Table 3. The set-point performance of the hybrid control was compared to that of the PID, and the results are shown in Figure 3a and b after 2 and 10 trials respectively.

5 Discussion

This paper has proposed a hybrid control architecture for solving *on-line* optimal control of partially known dynamical processes. It has been assumed that there exists sufficient prior plant information to select a fixed stabilizing robust controller. In this architecture, the control law is dynamically scheduled between a nonlinear Q function to provide long-term performance and a stabilizing controller to ensure closed-loop stability. While this paper provides a working example based *only* on a linear plant, this hybrid control strategy is generally applicable to many nonlinear plants, such as actuator dynamics and time delay, of which their state variables are observable and transitional behaviors are deterministic. In the case of stochastic plant characteristics, the reinforcement controller must be modified in such a way that the *expected* cost-to-go values are minimized. From the pick-and-place simulation results, the performance appeared to be sensitive to a large γ (near 1). The relatively small γ was thus chosen so as to minimize the modeling errors that were

---

[4] More detail of the model structure and instantaneous learning rule of the B-Splines network is referred to [5, 6].

accumulated when the cost-to-go values were estimated [13] while achieving the long-term performance. The B-Splines model parameters were chosen based on the assumption that the underlying cost-to-go mapping was smooth. τ was chosen so that the reinforcement controller was exposed to reasonably varied feedback signals for cost-to-go function estimation. The reinforcement signal was based on the informative set-point error rather than the binary goal-reaching signal commonly chosen in reinforcement learning literature. In general, this type of learning does not restrict any form of reinforcement signal, and more informative reinforcement signal naturally results in faster learning. While it is a challenging task to design an optimal control law based only on failure signals, incorporating such a critic seems inappropriate when the primary focuses are on closed-loop stability and fast learning convergence.

Acknowledgements   This research has been funded by the European Prometheus Project under Jaguar, Lucas and Pilkington support.

References

[1] Anderson C.W. 1989. *Learning to Control an Inverted Pendulum Using Neural Networks*, IEEE Control Systems Magazine, April, pp.31-37.

[2] Aström K.J., Wittenmark B. 1989. Adaptive Control, Addison Wesley.

[3] Barto A.G., Sutton R.S., Anderson C.W. 1983. *Neuronlike Adaptive Elements That Can Solve Difficult Learning Control Problems*, IEEE Trans. on Systems, Man and Cybernetics, Vol. SMC-13, No. 5, September, pp.834-846.

[4] Barto A.G., Bradtke S.J., Singh S.P. 1993. *Learning to Act Using Real-Time Dynamic Programming*, submitted to AI Journal, special issue on Computational Theories of Interaction and Agency.

[5] Brown M., Harris C.J. 1994. NeuroFuzzy Adaptive Modelling and Control, Prentice-Hall (in press).

[6] Cox M.G. 1990. *Algorithms for Spline Curves and Surfaces*, NPL Report DITC 166/90, 36p.

[7] Jaakkola T., Jordan M. 1993. *On the Convergence of Stochastic Iterative Dynamic Programming Algorithms*, Technical Report 9307, Department of Brain and Cognitive Sciences, Massachusetts Institute of Technology (also submitted to Neural Computation).

[8] Kaelbling L.P. 1993. *Hierarchical Learning in Stochastic Domains: Preliminary Results*, Proc. of the Tenth International Conference on Machine Learning, Boston, Massachusetts, pp.167-173.

[9] Lin L.J. 1992. *Self-Improving Reactive Agents Based on Reinforcement Learning, Planning and Teaching*, Machine Learning, Vol. 8, pp.293-321.

[10] Miller W.T., Glanz F.H., Kraft L.G. 1987. *Application of a General Learning Algorithm to the Control of Robotic Manipulators*, International Journal of Robotics Research, Vol. 6, No.2, Summer.

[11] Sutton R.S. 1988. *Learning to Predict by the Methods of Temporal Differences*, Machine Learning, Vol. 3, pp.9-44.

[12] Sutton R.S. 1984. Temporal Credit Assignment in Reinforcement Learning, PhD Dissertation, Department of Computer and Information Sciences, University of Massachusetts, Amherst.

[13] Thrun S., Schwartz A. 1993. *Issues in Using Function Approximation for Reinforcement Learning*, to appear in the Proc. of the Fourth Connectionist Models Summer School, Lawrence Erlbaum Publisher, Hillsdale, NJ, December.

[14] Watkins C.J.C.H 1989. Learning From Delayed Rewards, Ph.D. Dissertation, Cambridge University, Cambridge, England.

[15] Widrow B., Stearns, S.D. 1985. Adaptive Signal Processing, Englewood Cliffs, NJ: Prentice-Hall.

A PULSE-BASED REINFORCEMENT ALGORITHM FOR LEARNING CONTINUOUS FUNCTIONS

D Gorse
Department of Computer Science
University College, Gower Street, London WC1E 6BT, UK

J G Taylor
Department of Mathematics
T G Clarkson
Department of Electrical and Electronic Engineering
King's College, Strand, London WC2R 2LS, UK

An algorithm is presented which allows continuous functions to be learned by a neural network using spike-based reinforcement learning. Both the mean and the variance of the weights are changed during training; the latter is accomplished by manipulating the lengths of the spike trains used to represent real-valued quantities. The method is here applied to the probabilistic RAM (pRAM) model, but it may be adapted for use with any pulse-based stochastic model in which individual weights behave as random variables.

1. Introduction

Reinforcement learning [1] has many attractions for neural networks; it is more widely applicable than supervised techniques (since target values are not needed for any of the processing nodes), it is biologically plausible, and it is less prone to being trapped in local minima than classical methods like error backpropagation. However standard reinforcement techniques have a major disadvantage in that they were developed to apply to systems with only a finite number of behavioural responses, which makes them unsuitable for learning real-valued functions. In the case of the A_{RP} neural model [1] there are two such responses: output 0 (off, not firing) and output 1 (on, firing). The A_{RP} reinforcement learning rule has the inevitable effect of driving neurons into saturation, changing weight parameters so that neurons will eventually output 0 or 1 with certainty for almost any input pattern. This behaviour is adequate for some control applications, such as the "bang-bang" approach to controlling an inverted pendulum [2], and for classification problems, since the user can define a different binary output code for each pattern class, but not in more general learning situations (such as process control, time series prediction, robot arm movement and so on) for which the desired outputs are continuous functions of the inputs.

The algorithm to be presented here makes use of the noise associated with the representation of real-valued quantities by finite spike trains in order to provide the necessary variation about the mean for weight parameters during training. If a variable x in the interval [0,1] is represented by a spike train of length R, its measured value

$$\hat{x}(R) = \frac{1}{R} \sum_{r=1}^{R} a(r)$$

(where the a(r) are spikes $\in \{0,1\}$, with Prob(a=1) = x) has a variance

$$\sigma^2(x, R) = \frac{x(1-x)}{R} \tag{1}$$

As training progresses, and performance improves, the spike trains representing the weights are lengthened so as to decrease the amount of stochastic variation in their measured values. The advantage of using spike trains in this way, rather than choosing values from a distribution function such as in [3], is that one may then hope for a simple implementation in digital hardware.

2. The pRAM Model

An N-input pRAM [4] has 2^N memory locations, indexed by the N-bit binary vector u = $(u_1, u_2, ... u_N)$. A binary signal i = $(i_1, i_2, ... i_N)$ on the input lines will access just one of these locations, that one for which u = i. The variable stored at this location, α_i, gives the probability that a spike value a=1 will be produced on the output line, given an input i. Thus in this binary input case the mean value of the output is given by α_i. If there is a real-valued signal x = $(x_1, x_2, ... x_N)$ on the input lines each x_j is represented by a stream of pulses i_j in which Prob($i_j = 1$) = x_j. Over $\bar{r}$=1..R time steps a spread of locations (as in general each i(r) will be different) will be accessed and contribute stochastically a spike value a=1 or a=0 to the output stream. In this case the mean value of the output is

$$y = \sum_{\underline{u}} \alpha_{\underline{u}} \prod_{j=1}^{N} [u_j x_j + (1-u_j)(1-x_j)] \equiv \sum_{\underline{u}} \alpha_{\underline{u}} X_{\underline{u}}(\underline{x}) \tag{2}$$

where the variable X_u is the probability location $\underline{u}$ is accessed.

When hardware is used [5] the output of a pRAM is not computed from (2) directly, but as an approximation by averaging over the bits in the output stream:

$$\hat{y}(R) = \frac{1}{R} \sum_{r=1}^{R} a(r) \tag{3}$$

As $R \to \infty$, $\hat{y}(R) \to y$, the mean value of the output. In practice a value of $R = R_{max}$ in the order of hundreds of spikes gives a suitably close approximation to the mean.

The pRAM is not a 'weightless' model; the 2^N variables α_u are the weights of the system. It is not a look-up table, since these variables represent probabilities continuous in the range [0,1] and a pRAM output in general contains spikes that have been contributed by a wide range of locations. The way that noise is introduced into the pRAM model, as an independent random variable for each input channel, is closer to biological reality than models which inject noise only at the threshold; one of the ideas underpinning the pRAM is the biologically realistic synaptically noisy neuron model presented by Taylor in 1972 [6].

3. Reinforcement Learning for pRAM Networks

A binary output version of this algorithm has been described in detail elsewhere [7]. It is a non-linear extension of Barto's A_{RP} rule [1] which can be implemented in self-contained hardware [5]. The learning system interacts with the outside world only through the global reward and penalty signals r and p. The update to an addressed memory location $\underline{u}$ in an N-input pRAM is given by

$$\Delta\alpha_u = \rho[\,(a - \alpha_u)r + \lambda(1 - a - \alpha_u)p\,] \tag{4}$$

The other $2^N - 1$ non-addressed locations do not have their weight parameters updated. The variable a is the spike output of the pRAM on the addressing of location u; r and p have values in [0,1] but may themselves be carried by spike trains. The effect of the rule (4) is to move the addressed memory content α_u in the direction of a 'successful' output if a reward signal is received, to move α_u away from that output value (toward 1-a) if a penalty is received. It is clear that application of (4) will eventually lead to addressed locations containing binary values, since the values toward which the α_u are shifted (a or 1-a) are themselves binary. This is the output saturation problem [3] in the context of the pRAM model.

In order for outputs not to become saturated, the system needs to be able to experiment with values for the α_u which are not binary, but which may be seen to lead to better or worse (encouraged or discouraged) performance. Thus any continuous output reinforcement rule will have the general form

$$\Delta\alpha_u = \rho[\,(\hat{\alpha}_u - \alpha_u)r + \lambda(1 - \hat{\alpha}_u - \alpha_u)p\,]\hat{X}_u \tag{5}$$

In this rule the variable $\hat{\alpha}_u$ is the result of some stochastic experiment performed by the system; it is a 'trial value' for α_u, the effect of which is then assessed by the environment, which delivers appropriate reward and penalty signals. $\hat{X}_u \in [0,1]$, which scales the weight change, reflects the relative contribution of address u during this 'experiment'; it is a random variable which approximates X_u, the address access probability defined in (2).

The variables $\hat{\alpha}_u$ and $\hat{X}_u$ can be defined for a pulse-based simulation (or a hardware implementation) by using counters S_u, A_u to monitor the contributions of individual locations to the R-bit output stream of (3). It is the fact that R is finite (and possibly small) which gives rise to the 'stochastic experiment' needed by a reinforcement training technique, since by (1) real numbers represented by an R-bit pulse stream have a variance inversely proportional to R. Let S_u (an integer from 0 to R) be the total number of times address u is accessed whilst the output $\hat{y}(R)$ is being accumulated according to (3), and let A_u (also an integer from 0 to R) be the number of 1s output by location $\underline{u}$ when accessed during this process. It is evident that

$$\sum_u S_u = R, \quad \frac{1}{R} \sum_u A_u = \hat{y}(R)$$

$\hat{X}_u$, the proportion of times address $\underline{u}$ is accessed, is then defined by

$$\hat{X}_u = \frac{S_u}{R}$$

and the 'trial value' $\hat{\alpha}_u$ by

$$\hat{\alpha}_u = \frac{A_u}{R}, \quad S_u \neq 0$$

In order to avoid the need for special action when $S_u = 0$, it is convenient both for simulation and hardware realisation to write the learning rule (5) in the alternative form

$$\Delta\alpha_u = \frac{\rho}{R}[\,(A_u - \alpha_u S_u)r - \lambda(A_u - (1 - (1 - \hat{\alpha}_u)S_u)p\,] \tag{6}$$

The rule (6) relates to the adaptation of the mean values of the weight parameters; a further rule is required which gives the change in their variance (determined by, and inversely proportional to, the spike train length R) as a function of the performance of the system. This further rule requires in general that R increases when performance improves and decreases when it worsens.

In order to proceed further we will need to define 'performance' more precisely. Although the method described here can be applied in any situation in which it is possible to define a cost or utility function for the purpose of reinforcement, we will from this point on restrict the discussion to the learning of a function from $[0,1]^N$ to $[0,1]^M$, from a set of P training patterns $x_p \in [0,1]^N$ and their corresponding desired outputs $d_p \in [0,1]^M$ (to be learned either by a set of M N-pRAMs or by a multilayer structure, as appropriate). We will use an 'on-line' or pattern-by-pattern updating strategy. A broad overview of the function learning algorithm is as follows:

---

while mean error over training set > tolerance

1.   Pick a pattern p from the training set.
2.   Make an accurate assessment of the performance of the network in classifying this pattern.
3.   Use this measure to update R for the next 'stochastic experiment'.
4.   Make an assessment of the performance of the network during this stochastic procedure.
5.   Use this new measure to calculate reward r and penalty p.
6.   Update weights using r and p.
7.   Go to step 1.

In this case a suitable performance measure is the Euclidean distance D between the actual and desired outputs. Depending on the value of R used in the output computation, this measure may itself show significant stochastic variation. It is best to measure the error as accurately as possible when R is to be updated (step 2.). We define

$$E_p = D(\underline{d}_p, \hat{\underline{y}}_p(R_{max})) \approx D(\underline{d}_p, y_p) \tag{7}$$

where R_{max} is a spike train length sufficiently long that the output $\hat{\underline{y}}_p(R_{max})$ is very close to that which would be obtained by computation using the mean values of the variables (inputs, weights, outputs) of the system. R may then be calculated, for example, from

$$R(E_p) = ceiling \left\lceil \frac{c_R}{E_p^{k_R}} \right\rceil \tag{8}$$

where the 'ceiling' function delivers the smallest integer greater than or equal to its argument, and c_R, k_R are positive real numbers.

In calculating the reward and penalty, the performance measure D will be a random variable whose degree of variation depends on the current (updated by step 3., equation (8)) value of R:

$$E_p = D(\underline{d}_p, \hat{\underline{y}}_p(R)) \tag{9}$$

It is clear that (9), not (7), should be used in the calculation of r and p, since reinforcement should reflect the performance level achieved when $R < R_{max}$ by using 'trial values' α_u of the weight parameters.

The reward and penalty signals can be given in terms of $\hat{E}_p$ by

$$r = 1 - \hat{E}_p^{k_r}, \quad p = \hat{E}_p^{k_p} \tag{10}$$

where k_r, k_p are positive real numbers. It can be shown (see Appendix) that the above algorithm converges provided that

$$k_R + k_r \geq 2, \quad k_p \geq 3, \quad \lambda > 0 \tag{11}$$

These conditions are easy to satisfy and convergence has been observed over a wide region of parameter space.

A construction using Bernstein polynomials can be used to show that any function $F:[0,1] \rightarrow [0,1]$ can be approximated arbitrarily well by a single N-input pRAM of suitably high order. The simulation to be described below shows how the approximation power of a single N-pRAM improves with N. The function to be learned was the chaotic logistic series $x(t+1) = 3.97x(t)(1 - x(t))$; the training set was P = 100 consecutive points of this series, starting from $x(0) = 0.5$. Figure 1 shows how the mean absolute error decreases with epoch (one epoch is a presentation of the complete set of P patterns) for single pRAMs of input dimension N = 4, 6 and 8 (note that in a pulse-based output computation it is necessary to use independent spike trains on the N input lines carrying the single variable x). The parameters used in (8) and (10) were $c_R = 0.25$, $k_R = 1.5$, $k_r = 0.5$, $k_p = 2.0$. The choice $k_R + k_r = 2.0$ gives exponential convergence, and is the optimal choice for a spike train length function given by (8) and reward function given by (10). The penalty parameter λ was 0.01 for each case, but the training rate ρ differed so as to facilitate the plotting of the results on the same scale: for N=4, $\rho = 0.05$; for N=6, $\rho = 0.20$; for N=8, $\rho = 0.50$. It can clearly be seen how the approximation ability improves with input order N.

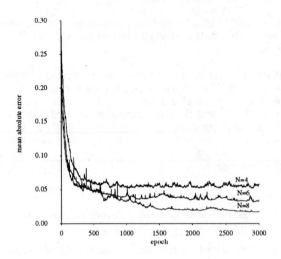

Figure 1

5. Adding Non-linear Output Transforms

Under certain circumstances, in particular when multi-pRAM networks with hidden units are used, it may be desirable to apply a non-linear 'squashing' transformation to the pRAM output function. This greatly extends the functionality of pRAM nets, and leads to more efficient function approximation. By applying a sigmoid-like output transformation a given function can usually be approximated by a more compact network which also uses pRAMs of lower input dimensionality. This reduces the number of free parameters, thereby improving generalisation. The output transform must be applied to the bit stream of (3), integration of which gives an approximation to the polynomial function (2), and applied in such a way as not to disrupt the free flow of pulses from input to final output (performance assessment), on which the stochastic reinforcement algorithm depends. The sigmoid output transform

$$\sigma(y) = \frac{1}{1 + e^{-y})} \tag{12}$$

is designed for models with output activities

$$y = \sum_j w_j x_j \in (-\infty, \infty)$$

not for the current case, where the activity y, as given by (2), is restricted to the interval [0,1]. The transform function

$$s(n, y) = \frac{y^n}{y^n + (1-y)^n} \tag{13}$$

illustrated for various values of n in Figure 2, preserves all the essential features of the sigmoid (12), being steepest (with a gradient equal to n) and closest to linear in its midrange, and with a gradient of zero at the limits of its argument (y = 0, 1 in this case). As well as being a more natural choice than the sigmoid (12) for arguments restricted to [0,1], s(n,y) has the very useful feature that it can be implemented by a simple pulse-based feedback circuit. The output bit stream (mean value y) is tapped and n+1 independently generated bits diverted to a buffer $a_0 a_1 \cdots a_n$. The n spikes $a_1 \cdots a_n$ are input to a recurrent (n+1)-input pRAM with fixed deterministic memory contents

$$\alpha_u = (1-u_0) \prod_{j=1}^{n} u_j + u_0 \left(1 - \prod_{j=1}^{n} (1-u_j) \right)$$

(the 0th input is the self-feedback line). The output of this recurrent pRAM has the mean value (13). By applying an output transform like (13) we are able to effectively increasing the range of the probabilistic weights (the α_u), which are of necessity restricted to the interval [0,1]. However it is commonly observed in the training of conventional neural networks that not all problems require the development of large weights (and the corresponding step-like output function). So the transform we are looking for should be one which can be applied adaptively. It is clear that the parameter n in (13) (the number of external inputs to the recurrent 'squashing' pRAM) is not a good choice for adaptation, since it must necessarily change in discrete (integer) steps, and the effect of such a change can be large (see Figure 2). A much better choice is the interpolation parameter β in the new output function

$$f(\beta, y) = (1 - \beta) y + \beta s(n, y) \tag{14}$$

II-76

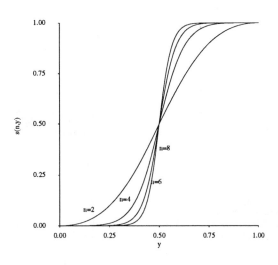

Figure 2

as this function can be accomplished by a 2-input pRAM with memory contents $(0, \beta, 1-\beta, 1)$ and inputs (i) from the untransformed bit stream with mean value y and (ii) from the spike output of the recurrent pRAM whose mean value is given by (13). (It should be noted that a different interpolation pRAM - and hence adaptive β - is to be attached to each pRAM neuron, and that if a single pRAM of high input order is replaced by a pyramidal structure then only the apex pRAM has an output transform circuit.) The variable β in (14) plays a similar role to the 'inverse temperature' parameter in the Boltzmann model. When it is smallest (highest 'temperature', $\beta = 0$) the output function is flattest, when it is largest (lowest 'temperature', $\beta = 1$) the output is most strongly compressed into a step-like form. Of course there will be a limit to the amount of squashing ultimately available which is determined by n. A suitable value for n must therefore be decided by simulation before any hardware is constructed. It appears from work done so far that n does not need to be large; a value between 2 and 4 was adequate for all applications we have investigated. The question remains as to how the interpolation parameter β is to be adapted. In fact all of the machinery is already in place, since this parameter (with its complement, 1-β) is contained in a pRAM and can be learned using the same techniques as were described in Section 3 (with a small amount of additional circuitry to ensure that the sum of the second and third locations in the interpolation pRAM always sum to 1, and that the contents of the first and fourth locations are not adapted). Thus the learning procedure is uniform over all modules; there is only one kind of adaptive circuit required to change both the parameters involved in polynomial fitting (the α_u) and the parameters which allow a non-polynomial 'tuning' of the output behaviour (the βs).

The task chosen to illustrate the use of non-linear output transforms is the same one which was used in Section 3 to show the approximation ability of single N-pRAMs, the chaotic logistic series $x(t+1) = 3.97x(t)(1 - x(t))$, with the same 100-pattern training set. The architecture used in this case had six 2-input pRAMs in the hidden layer and one 6-input pRAM in the output layer (there was no attempt to optimise the archtecture and it is likely that similar results could have been obtained with a somewhat smaller network). Adaptive output transform circuits (with n=2) were attached to all the pRAM neurons. The parameters c_R, k_R, k_r and k_p were set to the same values used in the single pRAM simulation. The α_u had a training rate $\rho_\alpha = 0.025$ and penalty parameter $\lambda_\alpha = 0.01$; the β had a lower training rate $\rho_\beta = 0.0005$ and a higher penalty parameter $\lambda_\beta = 0.1$. The relatively large value chosen for λ_β was needed because training progressed most effectively when the β were initially set to zero, which is an absorbing point when $\lambda_\beta = 0$ [7]. A larger λ_β enables this initial setting to be escaped more easily should this be required. The network begins by trying to fit a polynomial approximation to the data ($\beta = 0$); if this is unsatisfactory the β then begin to increase, otherwise these parameters remain negligible. Figure 3a shows the decrease of mean absolute error with epoch for this example; it should be compared with Figure 1, where the same function is being approximated by single pRAMs of input dimension N = 4, 6 and 8. Notice that although the multilayer net in Figure 3a takes twice as many epochs to converge as the single N-pRAMs in Figure 1, the training rate for the α_u in this case is only 1/8 that used for the 6-pRAM in Figure 1, and 1/20 that used for the 8-pRAM. The final error produced by the multilayer net is significantly less than that produced by the 6-pRAM, and in fact slightly lower than that produced by the 8-pRAM, despite the fact that the multilayer net has only 95 adaptive parameters (88 weights α_u, 7 transform parameters β) compared with the 256 weights of the 8-pRAM.

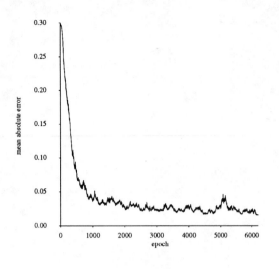

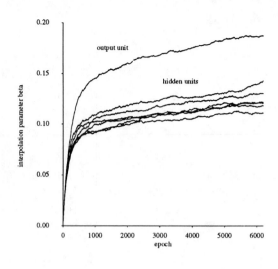

Figure 3a   Figure 3b

Figure 3b shows the evolution of the seven β in the network during training. The top curve is the transform parameter for the output unit, the cluster of six curves below it the βs associated with the hidden units. Notice that all seven β initially show a rapid increase - indicating that the network has discovered that pure polynomial approximation in a network of this architecture is not adequate - but thereafter level off. None of the β achieve a value close to the theoretical maximum of 1, indicating that a transform circuit with n=2 is easily sufficient in this example. However, although the β remain quite small, their presence is crucial to get a result of this quality - with all the β fixed at zero (no output transforms) this network converges to a final error about twice that achieved in Figure 3a.

Discussion

An algorithm has been presented which uses the noise associated with the representation of real-valued quantities by finite spike trains to drive a reinforcement algorithm which can enable a probabilistic RAM (pRAM) net to learn to approximate any function from $[0,1]^N$ to $[0,1]^M$ arbitrarily closely. Because the algorithm can in this way be directly implemented in self-contained hardware, it provides the possibility of embedded neurocircuitry with many applications in areas requiring a real-time learning capability. The underlying ideas are also applicable to any other pulse-based stochastic model in which the weights are treated as random variables.

References

[1]   A G Barto, "Learning by statistical cooperation of self-interested neuron-like computing elements", *Human Neurobiol.* , 4, 229-256 (1985).

[2]   A G Barto, R S Sutton and C W Anderson, "Neuronlike adaptive elements that can solve difficult learning control problems", *IEEE Trans. Syst. Man and Cyb.* , 13, 834-846 (1983).

[3]   V Gullapalli, "A stochastic reinforcement learning algorithm for learning real-valued functions", *Neural Networks* , 3, 671-692 (1990).

[4]   D Gorse and J G Taylor, "An analysis of noisy RAM and neural nets", *Physica* , D34, 90-114 (1989); T G Clarkson, D Gorse and J G Taylor, "From wetware to hardware: reverse engineering using probabilistic RAMs", *Journal of Intelligent Systems* , 2, 11-30 (1992).

[5]   T G Clarkson, C K Ng, D Gorse and J G Taylor, "Learning probabilistic RAM nets using VLSI structures" , *IEEE Transactions on Computers* , 41(12), 1552-1561 (1992).

[6]   J G Taylor, "Spontaneous behaviour in neural networks", *J. Theor. Biol.* , 36, 513-528 (1972).

[7]   D Gorse and J G Taylor, "Universal associative stochastic learning automata", *Neural Network World* , 1, 193-202 (1991).

Neurocontrol and Robotics

Session Chairs: Andrew Barto
Kaveh Ashenayi

POSTER PRESENTATIONS

An Adaptive Heuristic Critic based Architecture for Exploring Mazes with Large Search Spaces

A. G. Pipe, Y. Jin, A. Winfield
Intelligent Autonomous Systems Group
Faculty of Engineering
University of the West of England
Coldharbour Lane, Frenchay, Bristol BS16 1QY
United Kingdom

Abstract

We present a hybrid architecture, called EXP1, which balances exploration and exploitation in order to efficiently solve two dimensional mazes with large state spaces (eg. 262144 states). To achieve this it draws on the strengths of the Genetic Algorithm in search & optimisation, and on the combined strengths of the Radial Basis Function Neural Network and Temporal Difference learning algorithm in approximating continuous functions with strong temporal dependence. The Neural Network acts as an Adaptive Heuristic Critic (AHC). Over successive trials it learns the V-function, a continuous mapping between real numbered positions in the maze and the value of being at those positions. EXP1 solved all the mazes with which we tested it and proved to be quite robust to changes in internal parameters. It also displayed some favourable capabilities in responding to time variant environments.

1. Introduction

In problems with a strong temporal dependence, such as maze solving and manipulator end-effector navigation in uncertain environments, the need for a good balance between exploration of the environment and exploitation of the knowledge gained from that exploration has been well established [Thrun 1992]. In this paper we present the results of an attempt to develop a learning architecture with distinct "exploration" and "exploitation" parts, and strong but structured interaction between the two.

Temporal Difference (TD) reinforcement learning algorithms [Barto et al 1989] such as the Adaptive Heuristic Critic (AHC) [Sutton 1984] [Werbos 1992] and Q-learning [Watkins 1989], both "on-line" approximations to Dynamic Programming [Barto et al 1991], have shown great promise when applied to 2-dimensional maze problems where an agent, such as a mobile robot, attempts to establish an efficient path to a goal state by interaction with its environment. In most maze solving problems presented to date the area covered by the maze is divided into a number of states, usually on an equally spaced 2-dimensional grid [Lin 1993] [Roberts 1993] [Sutton 1991].

Good representative work in this area has been conducted by Long-Ji Lin [Lin 1993]. As part of his PhD thesis he presented an excellent comparison of these two learning algorithms for a class of maze solving problem. He used feedforward and recurrent Multi-Layer Perceptron (MLP) Neural Networks to store information about the states (ie. positions) in the maze. In the case of AHC the Neural Network learns the V-function, an arbitrarily non-linear mapping between state inputs and the value of being at that state. In the case of Q-learning the analogous Q-function learned by the Neural Network represents the multi-output mapping between being at a state and the value of moving to each of the neighbouring states.

Other related work includes the use of a "Holland style" Classifier System [Booker et al 1989] in the creation and reinforcement of rules for navigation in a "grid world" [Roberts 1993] and the use of Genetic Algorithms (GAs) in evolving Neural Network controllers. In the latter case two approaches have been popularly adopted, either each member of the GA population represents a complete Neural Network [Cliff et al 1992], or the GA is used to replace the Neural Network learning algorithm [Belew et al 1990]. Whilst this work is of great interest we will not consider it in detail here.

In all the work referred to above where the learning agent is given a maze to solve the problem domain has been divided into relatively few state spaces, though in some cases there is a large amount of time variance in the environment making the problem much harder. However we are interested in the short term in investigating problems where the maze is finely divided into a very large number of states, and in the long term in investigating those problems where movements in the maze are expressed as real numbers (or at least computer floating point representation), ie. in the limit the concept of a discrete state space entirely disappears.

To test our architecture we restrict our experiments to problems where the maze has 262144 states. The obstacles are relatively sparse in this space. This is not intended as a simplification of the problem, the maze presented is still non-trivial, rather it is an inevitable result of dividing the state space into sufficiently small regions to allow for finely resolved movements whilst still allowing for the traversal of open spaces. These types of environments are representative of real world mobile robot and multi-jointed manipulator navigational problems (in the latter case the state space has three dimensions and is correspondingly huge!).

Large state spaces make the exploration part of the problem much harder. The simple "nearest neighbours" action policy used by many of the methods referred to above would take a very long time to investigate a maze such as that described here, one tiny square at a time.

2.   The EXP1 Architecture

In our architecture a GA is used directly as the exploring part of the agent and a Radial Basis Function (RBF) Neural Network is used to store the knowledge gained from exploration. It acts as an Adaptive Heuristic Critic (AHC), using a Temporal Differences (TD) learning algorithm to learn the V-function as the search progresses.

At each "movement time step" the GA is restarted with a fresh population and searches the entire maze for the "best next movement", any straight line traversal of the maze from the current position. At each generation of the GA Lamarckian interaction with the environment occurs for each population member wherein the position is "tried out" on the maze by making the movement and then returning. If a collision with an obstacle occurs then that population member is modified to be the coordinates of the collision. The fitness function used to rate each member of the GA population is supplied by the RBF Neural Network, which performs a mapping between a given xy-coordinate input and a "value" for that position as its output.

This process continues through the normal process of GA evolution until either the population has converged or a maximum number of generations has been reached. The highest rated population member is then used to make a movement to the next position in the maze. After this has happened a simple variant of the standard Temporal Difference (TD) algorithm [Sutton 1984, Sutton 1991] is executed on the RBF network to change the V-function's shape. It changees the regions of the maze surrounding the movements made so far in the current trial by distributing a discounted reward or punishment back to them. The amount of this reward/punishment is simply derived from the value of the V-function at the new position.

The processes described above are then repeated from the new position in the maze until the goal position is reached. This completes one trial. The RBF Neural Network thus acts as an Adaptive Heuristic Critic (AHC) of the GA's every attempt to explore the maze. It learns a V-function which reflects the true value of being in each position in the maze, refining the accuracy of the function after every movement in every trial of the maze. Knowledge of the maze is embodied in the Neural Network and all that is inherited by EXP1 in successive trials is the new RBF network weight vector.

3.   The Problem to be Solved

Our maze is on a 512 X 512 square grid. Positions in the maze are expressed as 2-D coordinates. Four straight line obstacles form the maze. Although simple it is nonetheless representative of a confounding problem, a sharp "double-back" must be performed in order to find the solution, and after this is negotiated the obvious next moves lead to a "blind alley". EXP1 was applied to mazes with more obstacles, some with more "blind alleys", yielding results consistent with those presented below. This particular maze was chosen simply because the resulting figures illustrating movements are clear enough to print on a small scale in this paper.

In the experiments presented below we wished to simulate an environment wherein the agent knows its absolute position in the maze and where the goal position is at all times, but nothing about the obstacles which will impede its progress until the first trial begins. Since the RBF network is intended to reflect the value of states in the maze it can be off-line trained to reflect this, or indeed any other, *a priori* knowledge. The RBF centres of the Neural Network were off-line trained with a smoothly reducing function of the Euclidean distance from the goal state.

4. Genetic Algorithm

Each GA population member is an 18-bit number made up of a 9-bit x-coordinate and a 9-bit y-coordinate. These are absolute coordinates rather than being relative to the present position purely for computational ease. Though large for maze problems this is quite a small search space for contemporary GAs. A simple implementation was therefore used with a population of 40 individuals. The selection method was "Roulette wheel". Crossover and mutation were both 2-point, one in the x-coordinate and one in the y-coordinate.

To maximise knowledge acquisition from interaction with the environment, when each new GA population member is tested against the maze to evaluate its fitness if a movement results in collision with an obstacle then the population member is truncated to the collision point and returned the fitness value of this position.

5. Neural Network

A Neural Network has a number of advantages over tabular methods for storing the V-function. Firstly it is well known that most classes of real numbered Neural Networks can be designed to perform continuous arbitrarily nonlinear interpolation between known points in the solution space. In our application the exploration strategy may be relatively sparse in the network's input space, good interpolation performance is therefore important so as to extract as much knowledge as possible from the positions visited in the search. More significant in the long term, given the aims expressed above, the function learned is a **continuous** one which will be important when considering real valued search spaces. Secondly a certain amount of data compression can be achieved, though this is variable dependent upon network type.

We chose the local learning Radial Basis Function (RBF) [Sanner & Slotine 1991, Poggio & Girosi 1989] Neural Network rather than the global learning Multi-Layer Perceptron (MLP) used by Long-Ji Lin [Lin 1993] since this class of Neural Network has certain advantages for real time control applications. Firstly since passes of the learning algorithm affect only weights in the local region the problems of "knowledge drift" in other unrelated parts of the input space is avoided. Secondly learning time for these types of networks can be orders of magnitude faster with no local minima to get stuck in. Most importantly however the characteristic of "local generalisation" which this Neural Network type possesses means that changing the V-function mapping at one point in the input space has a tendency to modify the local region to a gradually diminishing degree as distance from this point increases. This property is very useful here in extracting as much knowledge as possible from each movement through the maze. It translates roughly as, for example, "if a position is a good one then the region around it will also be good".

We chose to represent the V-function here rather than the Q-function from Q-learning [Watkins 1989]. In Q-learning the input-output mapping is from state to possible actions from that state. When the possible actions are movements to nearest neighbour states this yields a modest number of Neural Network outputs. In our maze problem the entire maze area is available at every time step, so there are 262144 possible movements from each state. Clearly this is not a practically realisable situation.

The overall feedforward transfer function of the RBF network we used can be defined by the following expression for a given pair of xy coordinates;

$$V = \sum_{i=0}^{maxx} \sum_{j=0}^{maxy} \exp\left(-\frac{(x-cx_i)^2+(y-cy_j)^2}{\sigma^2}\right).w_{ij}$$

Where; V = Neural Network output; i, j = x and y coordinate indexes respectively; maxx, maxy = maximum maze coordinates; cx_i, cy_j = Basis Function centres in x and y dimensions; σ = a suitable measure of RBF width; w_{ij} = weight value for a given neuron.

A critical design consideration is density of the basis functions on each axis. Clearly there is a trade off here between generalizing ability, which could result in fewer explorations being required to solve the problem, against approximation ability in terms of smoothness requirements of the V-function to be learned. If the function centres are too widely separated then EXP1 may fail to investigate small gaps between obstacles. This is clearly a problem dependent factor. However we found experimentally that this is not as limiting as it may at first appear, provided that the centres are above a certain density set by the minimum anticipated gap size in the maze then an over dense network merely results in more painstaking, that is to say unnecessarily localised, learning rather than incorrect behaviour.

6. Temporal Difference Learning

The V-function network was modified after each movement using a simple Temporal Difference (TD) algorithm, according to the following update rules;

$$V_{t-1} = V_{t-1} + TDRATE\ ((V_t - PUNISH) - V_{t-1})$$ for the movement prior to the current one then;

$$V_{t-i} = V_{t-i} + TDRATE\ (V_{t-i+1} - V_{t-i})$$ for i = 2 to HORIZON

Where; V_t = V-function output at time step t; TDRATE = Temporal Difference learning rate between 0 and 1; PUNISH = a small punishment to encourage exploration; HORIZON = TD scope.

The PUNISH factor was included to counteract limit cycles and/or stationary behaviour. Under these circumstances the value of those states will incur a small penalty at each time step, thus resulting in EXP1 eventually breaking out into new areas of the maze. The HORIZON factor limits the effects of the TD learning to a fixed number of backward time steps. This is merely a computational device since, for all TDRATE values used in our experiments, the exponential decline of the effective TDRATE with successive backward steps renders V-function updates negligible by the time HORIZON is reached.

7. Experimental Results

Though many experimental runs have been undertaken we give only a representative set here. The following maze, GA, Neural Network and TD learning parameters pertain to the results given below.

Maze: (1,1) is the starting position (the top left corner in figure 1) and (400,400) is the goal position. Maximum fitness at the goal position is 512. Other off-line trained initial fitnesses calculated by;

$$Fitness_{ij} = 512 \times \left(1 - \left(\frac{\sqrt{(cx_i - goalx)^2 + (cy_j - goaly)^2}}{max.distance}\right)\right)$$

GA: 20 generations executed to determine each movement. Crossover probability = 0.9, mutation = 0.01.
RBF: 64 Basis Function centres on each axis, ie. eight maze positions between each centre. σ was set to 16, ie. 2 X Basis Function separation.
TD: TDRATE = 0.5, PUNISH = 30.0, Horizon = 12

Figure 1 shows the results of the first trial from start to goal position. EXP1 took 121 moves to find the goal position. In the subsequent trial it took 135 moves, mostly investigating areas not covered during the first run. These two trials covered most difficult parts of the maze. In the next 7 runs EXP1 took between 10 and 20 moves, most of these were either spent investigating some small area missed by GA searches in the previous trials or staying still whilst the worth of a position was devalued through the TD learning PUNISH factor. From the 10th trial onwards EXP1's path was stable taking 9 or 10 moves. Figure 2 shows the path taken at the 10th trial.

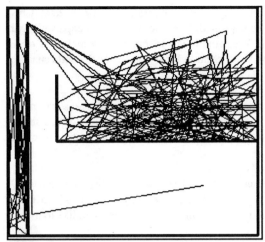

Figure 1

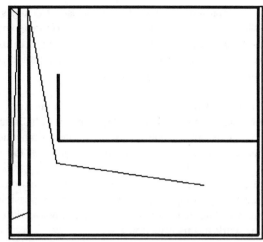

Figure 2

Though there is not space to illustrate it here, from the 10th trial onwards the V-function had a smooth "ridge" along the established path from start to goal position.

We induced a limited form of time variance in the environment by opening up a more direct path as shown in figure 3. In this case EXP1 immediately explores it discovering the quicker route in one trial.

8. Discussion

The limited time variant experiment illustrated in figure 3 represents only the "fortuitous" discovery of the exploration part of EXP1. Once a route is well reinforced through TD learning only the few positions at which EXP1 stops in the maze will continue to be investigated for a better route. If obstacles are removed, or as in this case an opening becomes available near one of EXP1's "stops" then it will immediately

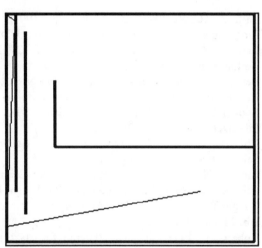

Figure 3

take advantage of it. However if an opening were made in the centre of the second vertical obstacle then EXP1 would "speed" past it. This deeper form of continuous investigation could be brought about by including a "boredom factor" in the TD learning [Sutton 1991], to devalue the established route through time so that search would be reinitiated. However this would inevitably have a detrimental effect on the asymptotic performance for time invariant situations.

We found that EXP1 was fairly robust to changes in value of the many parameters in the system, such as number of RBF centres, TD learning rate, PUNISH & HORIZON values, GA population size & number of generations, mutation and crossover probabilities etc. Most changes induced a more or less efficient search or affected the convergence behaviour over successive trials rather than resulting in incorrect behaviour. For example, as one might expect, lower TD learning rates generally produced a system which established a stable route more slowly, but sometimes found a better route in the end than those systems which converged effectively in one or two trials.

9. Conclusions and Further Work

EXP1 successfully solved all the maze problems with which we presented it within a 512 X 512 state space. However we would like to try the architecture on much bigger search spaces.

It will continue to make fortuitous use of changes in the maze if a better move appears at one of its established "stops", for example the removal of an obstacle will immediately be exploited. However it does not cope well with the more general example of time variance in the environment. We would like to pursue the inclusion of an additional factor in the TD learning which periodically reduces the V-function in local regions of the state space in order to induce re-investigation.

Although EXP1 is relatively robust to internal parameter changes we would like to investigate a means of automatically adjusting the Neural Network's Basis Function centre separation. There is no reason why this should be regular throughout the maze, an interesting concept would be to automatically adjust centre separation to match the resolution required in different regions of the maze.

In EXP1 the RBF network learns the V-function. We are interested in looking at the possibility of a partial Q-function mapping wherein, say, the best 10 possible actions from a given state are learned. Long-Ji Lin [Lin 1993] investigated the use of recurrent Neural Networks to handle so called "hidden" maze states, we would like to extend our work in this direction also.

References

Barto A. G., Bradtke S. J., Singh S. P., 1991, 'Real-Time Learning and Control using Asynchronous Dynamic Programming', Dept. of Computer Science, University of Massachusetts, USA, Technical Report 91-57

Barto A. G., Sutton R. S., Watkins C. J. C. H., 1989, 'Learning and Sequential Decision Making', COINS Technical Report 89-95

Belew R. K., McInerney J., Schraudolph N. N., 1990, 'Evolving Networks: Using the Genetic Algorithm with Connectionist Learning', University of California at San Diego, USA, CSE Technical Report CS90-174

Booker L. B., Goldberg D. E., Holland J. H., 1989, 'Classifier Systems and Genetic Algorithms', Artificial Intelligence 40, pp.235-282

Cliff D., Husbands P., Harvey I., 1992, 'Evolving Visually Guided Robots', University of Sussex, Cognitive Science Research Papers CSRP 220

Lin L., PhD thesis, 1993, 'Reinforcement Learning for Robots using Neural Networks', School of Computer Science, Carnegie Mellon University Pittsburgh, USA

Poggio T., Girosi F., 1989, 'A theory of Networks for Approximation and Learning', MIT Cambridge, MA, AI lab. Memo 1140

Roberts G., 1993, 'Dynamic Planning for Classifier Systems', Proceedings of the 5th International Conference on Genetic Algorithms, pp.231-237

Sanner R. M., Slotine J. E., 1991, 'Gaussian Networks for Direct Adaptive Control', Nonlinear Systems Laboratory, MIT, Cambridge, USA, Technical Report NSL-910503

Sutton R. S., 1984, PhD thesis 'Temporal Credit Assignment in Reinforcement Learning', University of Massachusetts, Dept. of computer and Information Science

Sutton R. S., 1991, 'Reinforcement Learning Architectures for Animats', From Animals to Animats, pp288-296, Editors Meyer, J., Wilson, S., MIT Press

Thrun S. B., 1992, 'The Role of Exploration in Learning', Handbook of Intelligent Control: Neural, Fuzzy, and Adaptive Approaches, Van Nostrand Reinhold, Ed. White D. A., Sofge D. A.

Watkins C. J. C. H., 1989, PhD thesis 'Learning from Delayed Rewards', King's College, Cambridge.

Werbos, P. J., 1992, 'Approximate Dynamic Programming for Real-Time Control and Neural Modelling', Handbook of Intelligent Control: Neural, Fuzzy, and Adaptive Approaches, Van Nostrand Reinhold, Ed. White D. A., Sofge D. A.

A Proposed Hierarchical Neural Network Controller for a Hexapod Leg

A.L. Nel & J.G. Benadé
Laboratory for Cybernetics, Rand Afrikaans University
Johannesburg, *aln@ing1.rau.ac.za*

Abstract

We report on the development of a neural controller for a three degree of freedom leg of a hexapod. Biological systems are considered as motivation to develop the neural control system. Backpropagation training of multilayer perceptrons and a combination of hetrogeneous neurons are used to implement several pattern generators. Previous work [1] shows that a two degree of freedom leg controller cannot compensate for surface irregularities. The proposed controller for the leg is extended to compensate for such surface irregularities. All the components of the proposed controller are biologically feasible. Simulation results that demonstrate the performance of the leg are presented.

1 Introduction

There are two reasons for researching legged robots: viz. a) *mobility* - there is an increasing need for vehicles that can travel on difficult terrain where wheeled vehicles cannot go and b) *understanding* - how humans and animals use their legs for locomotion. Evolved locomotion in animals demonstrates a remarkable mobility, agility and reliability. The use of mathematical computations to simulate such systems is complex and this type of control problem cannot be solved with classical methods in real time, except if very powerful computers are used.

Studies of insect leg control systems, especially the cockroach, have been done by Pearson [2]. Beer *et al* [1], and [3] based their simple artificial leg controller for a leg with two degrees of freedom on these results (Figure 1). Pearson [2] postulated that the coordination of the legs of a hexapod is that of a relaxation oscillator [4], ie. a bistable system that switches from a state A to a state B when a certain internal threshold is reached and back when another threshold is reached.

The legs of the hexapod as described by [1] could only perform simple two degree of freedom motions: viz. lifting the leg and swinging it forward and backward. To compensate for surface irregularities another degree of freedom is needed to enable the leg to maintain the hexapod's body posture in a given state. Our aim was to develop a biologically feasible three degree of freedom leg controller which would perform this task.

2 Proposed Leg Controller

In most mobile robot systems developed a common feature has been the recognition for the need of a hierarchical structure of intelligence and therefore hierarchical decomposition of the task. This is found in lower class animals where motion control is highly decentralized, ie. the higher level (the brain) defines tasks or subgoals for the lower nervous control centers and then monitors their status.

Pearson's model of a motion controller [2] (Figure 2) for a cockroach suggests that these different levels of control. The controller designed by Beer [1] (Figure 1) is extended to three distinct levels of control; viz.

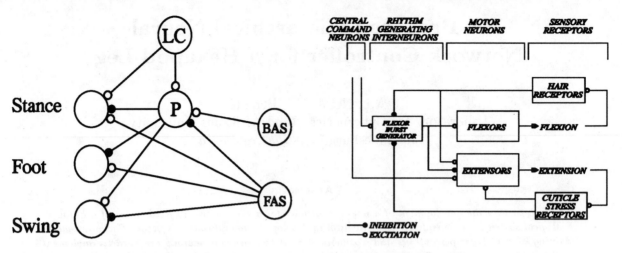

Figure 1: Leg Controller Circuit of Beer

Figure 2: Pearson's Model of Cockroach Locomotion

central pattern control level (CPCL), motion pattern control level (MPCL) and segment control level (SCL) as indicated in Figure 3 in order to control a leg with three degrees of freedom.

There are two different phases that can be distinguished in hexapod walking; a stance and swing phase. The control hierarchy must configure the three joints, ie. the torso, hip, and knee to coordinate the stance and swing phases and so ensure that the hexapod retains its posture.

In Beer's model the central pattern control is activated by a higher level (the brain), causing LC to fire. LC then excites the pacemaker (P) and $Stance$ simultaneously. The excitation of $Stance$ produces the stance phase. Periodically, however, this state is interrupted by a burst from P. This burst excites $Swing$, lifting the foot and swinging the leg forward. When this burst terminates, another stance phase commences, and so the cycle is completed. The rhythmic bursting of P thus results in a basic stance/swing cycle.

To properly synchronise the swing and stance phases as in biological systems, the controller requires some feedback information about the exact position of the three segments of the leg and whether the foot is raised or not. This information is produced by two different sensors which provide the necessary information to the CPCL: viz. the angle (S) and pressure (F) sensors. Angle sensors are used to locate the various leg segment positions. For example, if the leg is at the end of the swing phase, the forward angle neuron (FA) is influenced by the shoulder sensor S_1 causing FA to excite the $Stance$ and inhibit the back angle neuron (BA). The load carried by the leg is determined by the pressure sensor and activates the foot down neuron (FD). FD inhibits P and $Swing$ preventing it from switching to a swing phase. (This sensor corresponds to the hair receptors in the model of Pearson [2].)

A few pattern generators were incorporated into the controller and were implemented in the form of homogeneous neural networks. The use of a pattern generator is consistent with biological evidence [5]. When $Stance$ or $Swing$ are activated, control is passed to the MPCL which consists of a signal processing neuron and a neural pattern generator. The neural networks used for the pattern generators were trained by means of the standard back propagation training algorithm and consisted of one input layer with five neurons, one hidden layer with ten neurons and an output layer with a single output. The training input data is the integrated signal received from the signal processing neuron and the output data is the analytical trajectories calculated using a simulation of the motion of an idealized leg.

Excitation of $Swing$ or $Stance$ causes that neuron to fire, and activates the applicable signal processing neuron. This neuron integrates the incoming signal and transmits the result to the pattern generators which produces the different motor signals for controlling the leg segments.

Biological systems have kinesthetic and vestibular sensors that monitor segment position and loading. Beer [3] argues that such low level feedback control is essential. Most of the information generated by these

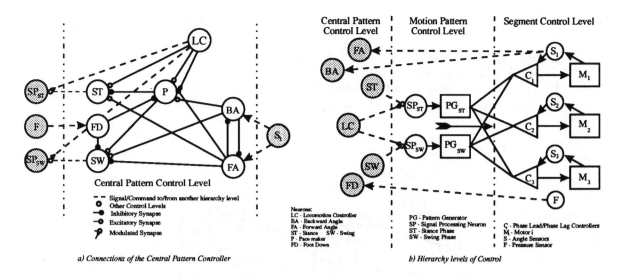

a) Connections of the Central Pattern Controller

b) Hierarchy levels of Control

Figure 3: Hierarchies of the Proposed Controller

sensors is only utilized at the local level, while some of the information is also made available for processing at higher levels. Information from the sensors is utilized in the lower levels for momentary control. This control is accomplished by a strictly local negative feedback closed loop controller.

Instability or oscillations might occor at high input frequencies due to the time constant of the segment which is much smaller than that of the neural controller. The *Renshaw cells* [5] found in most neuron controllers, especially on lower levels reduce the system gain by an inhibitory action on the segment controller at high frequencies. The phase–lead/phase–lag controller in our controller is therfore a type of lower motor control and has the same objective.

The duration of the walking cycle varies inversely with frequency [6]. In other words, higher step frequencies excite *LC* to a higher firing rate. The result is an increased excitation of *Stance* and *P*. The *Stance* is thus continuously activated and deactivated by *LC* and *P*. This is due to the inherent characteristics of the control system. A modulated synapse is implemented between the forward angle sensor neuron and *P*. The result is that *P* is inhibited during the stance over a wide range of frequencies. (Modulated synapses increase/decrease the gain of the affected synapse.) A faster throughput of the pattern is found by using the modulated synapse between the stance and swing neurons and their respective signal processing neurons. This results in an increase in magnitude of increments of the pattern outputs, thereby adjusting the rate at which the leg position is updated.

3 Irregularities in Terrain

How should the proposed controlled be changed to compensate for irregularities in terrain? Figure 5 shows the results of a mathematical simulation for a leg stepping onto an object which varies in height from 5mm to 50mm. Similarity exists between the curves of motor 2 and 3 in that they have the same characteristic of an offset and gain applied to the curve when walking on a horizontal surface. This characteristic is used to derive an equation to enable the controller to adapt to the irregularity in terrain. The equation is the following:

$$\theta_\Delta = \frac{(\theta_{ib} - \theta_{b_{min}} + Gain \times \theta_{b_{min}})\theta_{\Delta_{min}}}{Gain \times \theta_{b_{min}}} \tag{1}$$

where

θ_Δ	Desired angle when foot is at position Δ from horizontal
θ_{ib}	Angle when foot is on horizontal surface
$\theta_{b_{min}}$	Minimum angle of curve when foot is on horizontal surface
$\theta_{\Delta_{min}}$	Minimum angle of curve when foot is at position Δ above horizontal

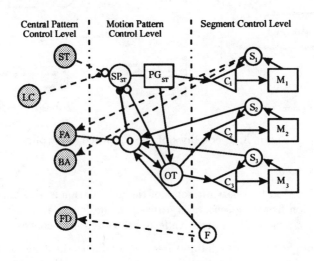

Figure 4: Modified Leg Controller for Irregular Terrain

All the values in the equation above are constant except for θ_{ib} which represents the values of the curve when walking on an horizontal surface. If the constants are known the new curve can be derived. The minimum values, the gain and offset for all the curves in Figure 5 were calculated. A neural network was trained with the motor angles 2 and 3, at positions Δ, as inputs. The gain and minimum values for each curve, when the foot is at position Δ, is obtained as output.

The proposed controller was changed as shown in Figure 4. When the leg has reached the end of the swing phase the FA and the sensor F are activated which then activates the obstacle processing neuron (O). On activation the O inhibits the SP_{ST} neuron to prevent it from firing. The angle values of motor 2 and 3 are sent to O. O uses these signals to generate the gain and offset necessary to change the curve. The result is transmitted to the obstacle trajectory neuron (OT) which then excites the SP_{ST} neuron causing it to fire. The signal received from the SP_{ST} is then changed by OT using Equation 1 and the signals recived from O.

4   Simulation Results

The simulation of a single three degree of freedom leg performed is a full kinematic simulation including the complete neural controller as detailed in Figure 4. The change in inertias of each of the legs as the joints rotate and the standard dc motor model driven by a controlled voltage source is included.

The motor output angles for the walking cycle are shown in Figure 6. A view of the simulated leg positions based on these output angles which are the result of the simulation of the complete neural controller is shown in Figures 7 and 8. These figures are based on a complete kinematic simulation and it can be seen that the motion is not symmetric (the pattern generator is based on a symmetric curve). What can however be seen is that a continuous and realistic power and return stroke has been achieved.

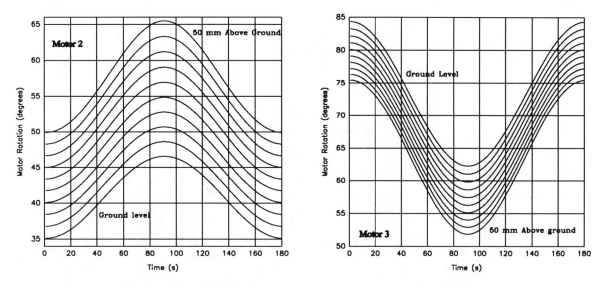

Figure 5: Motor Patterns when Stepping onto an Irregularity

5 Conclusion

As can be seen from the results, a biologically feasible controller for a three degree of freedom leg which consists of a command hierarchy is possible, which divides the general goal into workable sub–commands at each level. Communication between the different levels of the control system is limited to essential neural quantities.

An advantage of the developed controller is that it can be extended to accomplish tasks such as turning without having to redesign the basic structure as has been demonstrated by the extension to incorporate surface irregularities. This is the basis of continuing research.

References

[1] R.D. Beer. *Intelligence as Adaptive Behavior: An Experiment in Computational Neuroethology.* Academic Press Inc., first edition, 1990.

[2] K. Pearson. The control of walking. *Scientific American*, 235:72–86, 1976.

[3] R.D. Beer, R.D. Quinn, H.L. Chiel, and K.S. Espenschied. Robustness of a distributed neural network controller for locomotion in a hexapod robot. *IEEE Trans. Robotics and Automation*, vol.RA-8(3), 1992.

[4] U. Bässler. On the definition of central pattern generator and its sensory control. *Biological Cybernetics*, vol.54:65–69, 1986.

[5] E.W. Kent. *The Brains of Men and Machines.* McGraw-Hill Publishing Co., New York, 1981.

[6] D.M. Wilson. Insect walking. *Annual Review of Entomology*, 11:103–122, 1966.

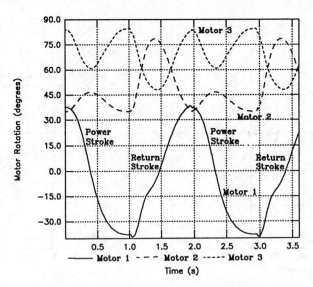

Figure 6: Motor Position during Walking

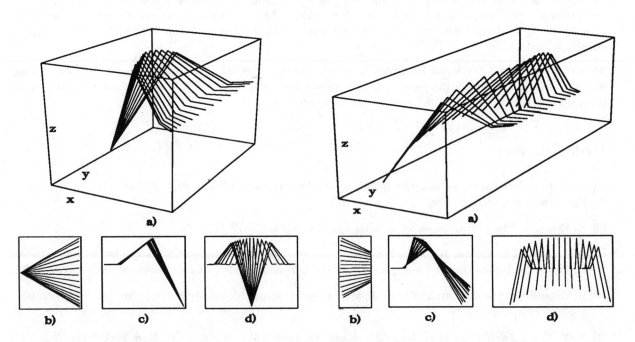

Figure 7: Leg Positions during Stance Phase

Figure 8: Leg Positions during Swing Phase

Hebbian Learning Strategies for Neural Adaptive Control

Chi-Sang Poon

Harvard-MIT Division of Health Sciences and Technology
Massachusetts Institute of Technology
Cambridge, MA 02139

Hebbian associative learning is a common form of neuronal adaptation in the brain. In this paper [1] we show that a Hebbian synapse is an ideal neuronal substrate for adaptive control and other supervised learning tasks. In particular, a homosynaptic Hebbian synapse that exhibits pairing-specific and activity dependent long-term potentiation (LTP) may constitute an adaptive element in a high-gain adaptive control (HGAC) system. Similarly, an associative Hebbian synapse that is conditioned by a heterosynaptic pathway is capable of implementing the delta adaptation rule that is widely used in model-reference adaptive control (MRAC) and error-backpropagation learning schemes.

The peculiar neuronal configuration in a Hebbian synapse suggests that a MRAC adaptation rule based upon Hebbian associative learning must be accompanied by a high-gain (adaptive or non-adaptive) feedback path similar to that of HGAC. The resulting *dual adaptive control* (DAC) system represents a new class of adaptive control scheme that combines the best of HGAC and MRAC. Theoretical and simulation results suggest that DAC is superior to MRAC and HGAC in that: 1) it enjoys the rapid convergence capability of HGAC and zero tracking error capability of MRAC; 2) it shows improved stability for higher-order systems; 3) it is more robust with respect to system uncertainties than is HGAC and MRAC.

Improved robustness is obtained provided the adaptation has leakage or self-decay. In other words, the memory must be short-term. For purpose of neural adaptive control, therefore, short-term synaptic plasticity (e.g., short-term potentiation) is of particular interest because it protects the animal against environmental uncertainties or perturbations. Theoretical analysis shows that a DAC scheme with short-term memory offers the greatest protection against unknown input disturbance and unmodeled system dynamics.

The theoretical results have interesting engineering as well as biological implications. Firstly, the design of physiological control systems is such that different control strategies of reinforcement learning and negative feedback could be simultaneously operative as a result of associative neuronal learning. These complementary strategies may act in concert to enhance the effectiveness and reliability of neural adaptation. Secondly, on the practical side the dual adaptive control scheme that has been inspired by these multi-denominational neuronal strategies may prove to be a useful technique for engineering adaptive control applications.

This work was supported in part by National Science Foundation under Grant BCS-9216419.

Reference
[1] Poon, C.-S. Dual adaptive control by Hebbian associative learning. Technical Report, Industrial Liaison Program, Massachusetts Institute of Technology, Bldg. E38-500, Cambridge, MA 02139.

Neural linearizing control with radial basis function network for chemical processes

Sukjoon Kim[*], Minho Lee[**], Sunwon Park[*], Soo-Young Lee[**], and Cheol Hoon Park[**]

[*]Department of Chemical Engineering
[**]Department of Electrical Engineering
Korea Advanced Institute of Science and Technology
373-1 Kusong-Dong Yusong-Gu,
Taejon 305-701, Korea
Phone : +82-42-869-5431 Fax : +82-42-869-3410
E-mail : mhlee @ kumgang.kaist.ac.kr

Abstract

In this paper a new neural control architecture for chemical processes is proposed, which consists of a PI controller for initial stabilization and a radial basis function(RBF) network for linearization of nonlinear plants. The control input applied to the process is summation of outputs of the PI controller and the RBF network. First, a reference linear model, which defines relationship between the PI controller output and the process output, is determined from the analysis of the past operation data. Initially the PI controller operates the process alone. The RBF network is gradually trained to minimize the difference between outputs of the plant and the linear model. As the training of the RBF network goes on, the dynamics of the nonlinear plant added by the RBF network converges to that of the linear reference model. Then, the overall control problem becomes linear, and the linearized system can be easily controlled by the PI controller with closed-loop architecture, of which parameters can be determined by simple pole-zero assignments. Provided the initial PI controller stabilizes the plant, it remains stable throughout the whole training phase. Computer simulation shows that the proposed control architecture is very effective in controlling nonlinear chemical processes such as continuous stirred tank reactor and pH process.

I. Introduction

Multilayer neural networks have been successfully used for control of unknown nonlinear dynamic systems[1-9]. In these researches, indirect adaptive neural control architecture based on the forward modeling was successfully used for control of the robotic arms[2,8], the truck backer upper problem[1], and nonlinear plants[3,5]. In this indirect approach the neuro-controller was trained by error back-propagation through identifier neural networks. Although this approach gives interesting results, the controller with neural networks only may be inefficient in the real applications because of large computation time, and suffers from local minima[6]. Moreover, the neural identifier for the unknown system must be trained off-line with sufficient input and output data, which are difficult to obtain in many real plants, especially chemical processes[9].

On the other hand, majority of real systems already has conventional controller such as PID controller, and system managers do not want to replace the conventional controller with the advanced one with "yet-to-be-proven" reliability. Therefore, the preferred choice for practical applications may be hybrid control architectures where the neuro-controller increases control performance on existing controller with stability[6,7]. Although the feedback error learning method[7] provides very good control results of robotic manipulators, there still exists question on transient control performances. Also the overall control architecture becomes feedforward in learning phase, and one may suspect robustness above the performance of the linear controller[6].

We propose a new learning control scheme, which maintains the conventional linear controller and increases the control performances by linearization of nonlinear plants. By adding a radial basis function (RBF) network in front of the nonlinear plant, overall system can be made linear. The transient and steady state control performances depend on the linear dynamics and the PI controller gains. Provided the initial linear controller stabilizes the plant the proposed control scheme satisfies the stability criterion during the whole training process and increases the control performances continuously. Computer simulation shows that the proposed control architecture is effective in tracking control of chemical processes such as a continuous stirred tank reactor (CSTR) and a pH process.

II. Radial Basis Function Network

Figure 1 shows the radial basis function(RBF) network. From the regularization theory Green functions may be used as hidden activation functions[10], but Gaussian potential functions are used in this study.

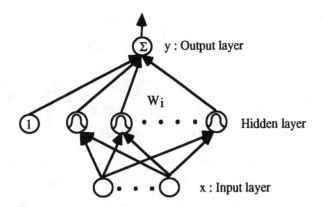

Figure 1. Radial basis function network.

The output of the RBF network is calculated by Eq.(1), where x and y denote the input and output values, and M is the number of hidden neurons. W_i denotes the weight value from the i-th hidden layer neuron to the output, σ_i and c_i denote the standard deviation and the center value of the i-th Gaussian activation for hidden neurons, respectively. Also, $\| \cdot \|$ denotes the Euclidean norm.

$$y(k) = \sum_{i=1}^{M} W_i(k-1) \exp(\frac{\| x(k-1) - c_i(k-1) \|}{\sigma^2_i(k-1)}) \tag{1}$$

The popular learning algorithm of the RBF network consists of the clustering algorithm for determining the center values of hidden activation functions and the least square algorithm for adaptation of weight values, W_i, for minimizing the output error[11,12]. In this study, we adopted the learning algorithm in Ref.[12] to incorporate self-generation of hidden nodes and on-line adaptation of the parameters(c_i and σ_i) for the Gaussian functions. The error $E(k) = (d(k)-y(k))^2/2$ is minimized by gradient descent and error back propagation, where $d(k)$ denotes the desired output values at time k[12].

III. Linearizing Control architecture with Radial Basis Function Network

Fig. 2 shows the proposed control architecture. Basically, by adding the RBF network in front of the plant, we would like to convert the nonlinear plant into a linear system. Then, the linearized system in the dashed box can be easily controlled by the linear PI controller with feedback. The input of the plant is generated by the summation of the outputs from the linear controller and the RBF network. The reference model is chosen as an approximate linear model around the operating point of the process. The training of the RBF network is progressed to minimize the error, i.e., the difference between the output of the preassigned linear model and the output of real plant.

The objective of the RBF network is to make the plant output linearly influence by the linear PI controller output similar to the reference model. To train the RBF network, the training error must be transformed to the output error of the RBF network. In case that the plant dynamics is unknown and the neural identifier does not exist, one may approximate the inverse Jacobian value to simple perturbed sensitivity of input and output values, and the required gradient becomes

$$\frac{\partial E(k)}{\partial v(k-1)} = -(d(k) - y(k))\frac{\partial y(k)}{\partial u_n(k-1)}\frac{\partial u_n(k-1)}{\partial v(k-1)} \quad (2)$$

$$= -(d(k) - y(k))sgn(\frac{\Delta y(k)}{\Delta u_n(k-1)})\frac{\partial u_n(k-1)}{\partial v(k-1)} \,,$$

where the v denotes the RBF parameters, W_i, s_i, and c_i.

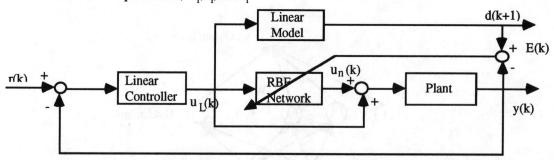

Figure 2. Proposed neural linearizing control architecture using RBF network.

At the initial stage of training, the control performance of the plant mainly depends on the ability of the linear PI controller[6]. As the training of the RBF network progresses, the overall system dynamics of the RBF network and the plant gradually resembles the preassigned linear model. If the overall system dynamics converges to be the preassigned linear dynamics by sufficient training of the RBF network, one can easily design the PI controller of the linearized system for desired poles and zeros. The initial conservative PI controller tuning parameters for stabilization of the process are now changed to these new values, and the overall closed loop system has the desired transient and steady state response. Specific dynamics of the preassigned linear model is not critical to the overall control performance.

IV. Simulation

To investigate its control performance and usefulness the proposed control scheme is applied to two typical chemical processes, i.e., a continuous stirred tank reactor(CSTR) model and a pH process.

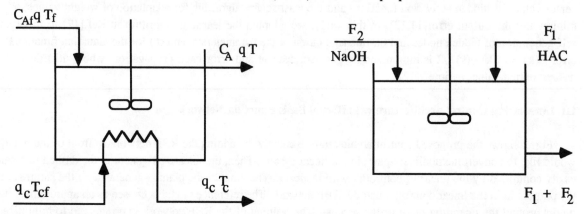

Figure 3. Schematics of CSTR.   Figure 4. Schematics of pH process.

(a) CSTR example

This CSTR model was developed by Henson and Seborg[14], and used for simulation test by Nahas and

Seborg[15]. Fig. 3 shows the schematics of the CSTR. A single irreversible exothermic reaction converts material A to B in the reactor. The process model is shown in Eqs.(3) and (4),

$$\dot{C}_A = \frac{q}{V}(C_{Af} - C_A) - k_0 C_A \exp(-\frac{E}{RT}) \tag{3}$$

$$\dot{T} = \frac{q}{V}(T_f - T) - \frac{(-\Delta H)k_0 C_A}{\rho C_p} \exp(-\frac{E}{RT}) + \frac{\rho C_{pc}}{\rho C_p V} q_c [\; 1 - \exp(-\frac{hA}{q_c \rho_c C_{pc}}) \;] \times (T_{cf} - T) \tag{4}$$

where C_A and C_{Af} are the effluent and the inlet concentration of component A, respectively, T is the reactor temperature and q is the feed flowrate. The nominal operating conditions are shown in Table 1.

$q = 100 \; l \; min^{-1}$	$E/R = 9.95 \times 10^3 \; K$	$v = 1000 \; l$
$C_{Af} = 1 \; mol \; l^{-1}$	$-\Delta H = 2 \times 10^5 \; cal \; mol^{-1}$	$pH = 7$
$T_f = 350 \; K$	$\rho, \rho_c = 1000 \; g \; l^{-1}$	$F_1 = 515 \; l \; min^{-1}$
$T_{cf} = 350 \; K$	$C_p, C_{pc} = 1 \; cal \; g^{-1}K^{-1}$	$F_2 = 81 \; l \; min^{-1}$
$V = 100 \; l$	$q_c = 103.41 \; l \; min^{-1}$	$C_1 = 0.32 \; mol \; l^{-1}$
$hA = 7 \times 10^5 \; cal \; min^{-1}K^{-1}$	$T = 440.2 \; K$	$C_2 = 0.05 \; mol \; l^{-1}$
$k_0 = 7.2$	$C_A = 8.36 \times 10^{-2} \; mol \; l^{-1}$	$[HAC] = 0.0435 \; mol \; l^{-1}$
		$[NaOH] = 0.0432 \; mol \; l^{-1}$

Table 1. Nominal CSTR operating conditions.   Table 2. Nominal pH operating conditions.

In this problem the controlled variable y is C_A and the manipulated variable u is q. The open-loop responses to $\pm 10\%$ step changes in the input are shown in Fig.5. This result shows severe nonlinearity of the process. The initial tuning parameters of the PI controller are set as the proportional gain $k_c = 150$ and the integral gain $t_c = 0.3$. The sampling time Δt is set to 0.1 min. The closed loop response with the PI controller is shown in Fig. 6. The preassigned linear reference model is set as

$$d(k+1) = 0.327y(k) + 0.003u_L(k-1). \tag{5}$$

After training the RBF network and assigning new PI controller gains as $k_c = 293.4$ and $t_c = 0.331$, the closed-loop response is shown in Fig. 7. Obviously the closed loop response of the proposed control architecture is uniform for the different set point changes, and the control performances are improved from the performance shown in Fig. 6.

(b) pH process

The process for the second simulation study is a pH process model reported by McAvoy et al.[16] and studied by Bhat and McAvoy[17]. Its schematic is shown in Fig. 4. The process model is described in Refs.[16,17] and the nominal operating conditions are shown in Table 2. In this problem, the controlled variable y is pH and the manipulated variable u is F_2. The open-loop responses of pH to +2 l/min and -2 l/min step changes in F_2 are shown in Fig.8. There exists very large difference of steady state gains between positive and negative step changes, and it is very difficult to control this process using conventional linear controllers. We use initial parameters of the PI controller as $k_c = 2.5$ and $t_c = 1.5$. Fig. 9 shows the closed loop response of the PI controller. The sampling time Δt is set to 0.5 min. The linear reference model is set as

$$d(k+1) = 0.3796y(k) + 0.7165u_L(k-1). \tag{6}$$

After sufficient training of the RBF network, the closed-loop response with the new PI controller gains, $k_c = 4.0$ and $t_c = 1.5$, is depicted in Fig. 10. In spite of highly nonlinear characteristics of the pH process, the proposed neural linearizing control architecture demonstrates good control performance.

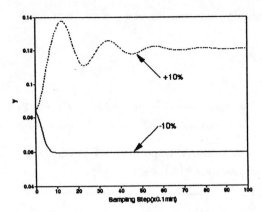

Figure 5. Open loop responses to step input in CSTR process.   ——— : +10% step change
········ : -10% step change

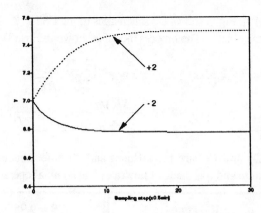

Figure 8. Open loop responses to step input in pH process.   ——— : +10% step change
········ : -10% step change

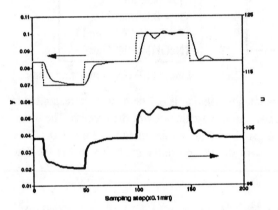

Figure 6. Control response only with PI controller in CSTR process.   ——— : plant output
━━━ : control input
········ : reference trajectory

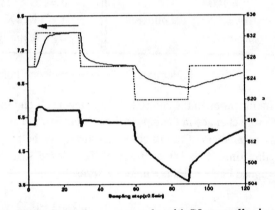

Figure 9. Control response only with PI controller in pH process.   ——— : plant output
━━━ : control input
········ : reference trajectory

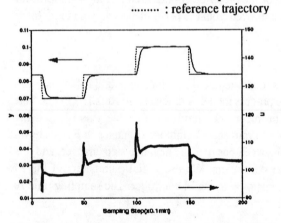

Figure 7. Control response with PI controller and RBF network in CSTR process.
——— : plant output
━━━ : control input
········ : reference trajectory

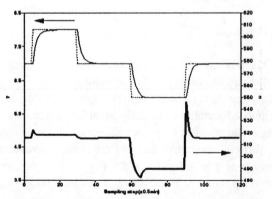

Figure 10. Control response with PI controller and RBF network in pH process.
——— : plant output
━━━ : control input
········ : reference trajectory

V. Conclusion

The proposed neural linearizing control architecture demonstrates good control performances for the continuous stirred tank reactor and a pH process. In this control scheme, a conservative PI controller controls the plant initially and as the training proceeds the RBF network produces the additional control output to linearize the relationship between the linear controller signal and the plant output. Now it becomes a simple linear control problem for the preassigned linear model with PI controller of desired poles and zeros. Provided the initial linear PI controller stabilizes the plant, it becomes stable through out the whole training and following testing phases. An experimental study of implementing the proposed control architecture on a pH chemical process is underway.

References

[1] D.H. Nguyen, and B. Widrow, "Neural networks for self-learning control systems," *IEEE Control Systems Magazine,* vol. 10, no. 3, pp. 18-23, 1990.

[2] M.I. Jordan, D.E. Rumelhart, "Forward models: supervised learning with a distal teacher," preprint.

[3] K.S. Narendra and K. Parthasarathy, "Identification and control of dynamic system using neural network," *IEEE Trans. on Neural Networks,* vol. 1, no. 1, pp. 4-27, 1990.

[4] B. Kosko, *"Neural networks for signal processing,"* The Prentice-Hall international editions, pp.161-187, 1992.

[5] M. Lee, S.Y. Lee, and C.H. Park, "Neural controller of nonlinear dynamic systems using higher order neural networks," *Electronics Letters,* vol. 28, no. 3, pp. 276-277, 1992.

[6] M. Lee, S.Y. Lee, and C.H. Park, "A feedforward/feedback neural control structure and its application to a robotic system," *Procs. of International Joint Conf. on Neural Networks,* vol. 3, pp. 2757-2760, 1993.

[7] M. Kawato, "Feedback-error-learning neural network for trajectory control of a robotic manipulator," *Neural Networks,* vol. 1, pp. 251-265, 1988.

[8] T.Hoshio, M.Kano, and T.Endo, "Optimal control with a recurrent neural network and a priori knowledge of the system," *Procs o2228f International Joint Conf. on Neural Networks,* vol.1, no.3, pp. .226-231, 1991.

[9] M. Lee and S. Park, "A new scheme combining neural feedforward control with model-predictive control," *AICHE Jl,* vol. 38, pp. 193-200, 1992.

[10] T. Poggio and F. Girosi, "A theory of networks for approximation and learning," A.I. Memo No. 1140, Artificial Intelligence Lab., MIT, 1989.

[11] S. Chen, F.N. Cowan and P.M. Grant, "Orthogonal least square learning algorithm for radial basis function networks," *IEEE Tr. on Neural Networks,* vol. 2, pp. 302-309, 1991.

[12] S. Lee and R.M. Kil, "A gaussian potential function network with hierarchically self-organizing learning," *Neural Networks,* vol. 4, pp. 207-224, 1991.

[13] Y. Maeda, H. Yamashita, and Y. Kanada, "Learning rules for multilayer neural networks using a difference approximation," *Procs. of International Joint Conf. on Neural Networks,* vol. 1, pp. 628-633, 1991.

[14] M.A. Henson and D.E. Seborg, "A critique of exact linearization strategies for process control," *AICHE Jl,* vol. 36, pp. 1753-1757, 1990.

[15] E.P. Nahas and D.E. Seborg, "Nonlinear internal model control strategy for neural network models," *Computers Chem. Engng.,* vol. 16, pp. 1039-1057, 1992.

[16] T.J. McAvoy, E. Hsu and S. Lowenthal, "Dynamics of pH in CSTRs," *Ind. Engng. Chem. Process Des. Dev.,* vol. 11, pp. 68-70, 1972.

[17] N.V. Bhat and T.J. McAvoy, "Use of neural nets for dynamic modeling and control of chemical process systems," *Computers Chem. Engng.,* vol. 14, pp. 573-582, 1990.

NEUROCONTROLLER FOR ROBOT BIOLOGICAL JOINT

S. Zein-Sabatto, M. Bodruzzman, and C. Glover*
Center for Neural Engineering
Tennessee State University, Nashville, TN 37209
* Oak Ridge National Laboratory, Oak Rige TN 37831

Abstract

A biologically motivated, Human Like (HL), robot joint is developed and a neurocontroller is designed to provide motor control signals needed by the joint. The main features of biological joints have been translated into electro-mechanical mechanism applying reverse engineering techniques. The proposed servo-mechanism is capable of providing restricted three dimensional motion analogous to that of a human being joint. The developed mechanism is suitable for the design of robot rotational joints. The advantages of a robot arm constructed from a such spherical servo-mechanism are: fast response, high resolution and high force generation per unit volume.

I. Introduction

Description of neurological models vary depending on the objectives for which they are developed. Two approaches exist; the systems anatomical approach and systems scientist approach. In the systems anatomic approach the concern is with the anatomical structure of neural mechanisms and their functions. While from the systems scientist approach the attempt is to describe observed behavior in terms of mathematical models [1]. From anatomical structural point of view most biological joints have spherical shape and produce restricted rotational motion in the three dimensional space. This is proven to be useful and essential for biological systems to accomplish what they do.

II. Biological Joints

A simple observation of a human shoulder movement reveals that biological joints are capable of providing a restricted three degrees of freedom (DOF) motion. This movement is very useful and, if current robots were equipped with smiler biological joint they would be more powerful and extremely flexible. A key element in making the three dimensional motion possible in biological joints is the anatomical structure of such joints. Anatomical studies showed that most biological joints posses spherical shapes, as shown in Figure 1, allowing restricted three dimensional motion [2].

The spherical structure of biological joints will be translated into analogous mechanical structure using reverse engineering technique. This technique will lead to the development of a restricted three degree of freedom servo-mechanism suitable for robot joint design.

III. Human Like Robot Joint

The main features of biological joints are preserved and translated into an electro-mechanical structure. The proposed mechanism is capable of three dimensional rotational motion. It consists of a ball joint and two electrical servomotors coupled through mechanical structure. The two servomotors are positioned along two orthogonal axes. The mechanical coupling structure consists of two arches perpendicular to each other. The two arches provide an opening for a rod connecting the ball joint into the servomotors through the coupling mechanism. A three dimensional visualization of the HL robot joint is shown in Figure 2. On one side of the mechanism a servomotor is attached and on the opposite side a position sensor is mounted to provide additional position feedback signal. The servomotor shaft and the position sensors are both connected together through the coupling structure.

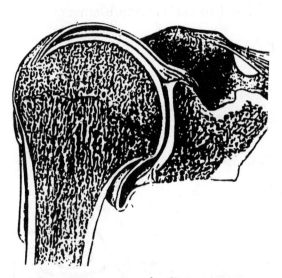

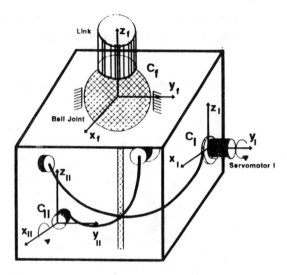

Fig. 1. Anatomic Structure of a Biological Joint

Fig. 2. Visualization of HL Joint with Coordinate Frames

IV. Dynamic Model

A dynamic model of the HL joint is developed. Both the dynamic of the electrical and mechanical parts of the mechanism are considered in the model. First, the model is developed in the form of a transfer function. Then a block diagram is deduced for controller design purpose. All the mechanical frictions and inertia, including the servomotor inertia, are identified in Figure 3.

From Figure 3, the total torque required from each servomotor (assuming only one servomotor is running at a time) is given by the sum of the following torques

$$T_m(t) = (2J_a + J_f)\theta''(t) + (2B_m + 2B_b + B_a + B_f)\theta'(t) + T_l \tag{1}$$

where J_a=servomotor inertia, J_f=ball joint (fixture) inertia, B_m=servomotor friction, B_b=bearing friction, B_f=fixture friction, B_a=arch friction and, T_l=external load. Assuming no load, $T_l = 0$, equation (1) can be written in the Laplace domain as

$$T_m(s) = (J_{eq}s^2 + B_{eq}s)\theta(s) \tag{2}$$

From the electrical circuit of a servomotor the total voltage drops in the armature circuit are equal to the input voltage

$$v_a(t) = L_a \frac{di_a(t)}{dt} + R_a i_a(t) + e_m(t) \tag{3}$$

where the back e.m.f. $e_m(t) = k_e \omega(t)$. The Laplace transform of equation (3) yields

$$V_a(s) - k_e s \theta(s) = (sL_a + R_a)I_a(s) \tag{4}$$

the torque produced by the servomotor is proportional to the armature current $T_e(t) = k_i i_a(t)$. In the Laplace domain

$$T_e(s) = k_i I_a(s) \tag{5}$$

equating equations (2) and (5) gives

$$I_a(s) = \left(\frac{J_{eq}s^2 + B_{eq}s}{k_i}\right)\theta(s) \tag{6}$$

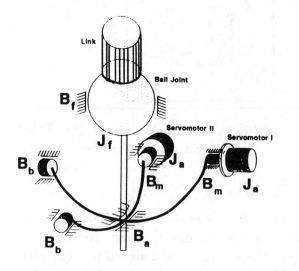

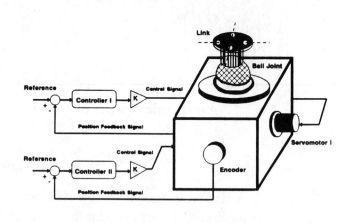

Fig. 3. Inertia and Frictions of HL Joint

Fig. 4. Complete Setup of HL Joint with Controllers

substituting $I_a(s)$ from (6) in equation (4) and simplifying the expression gives a dynamic model of the HL mechanism relating the Laplace transform of the output $\theta(s)$ to the Laplace transform of the servomotor input $V_a(s)$

$$\frac{\theta(s)}{V_a(s)} = \frac{k_i}{s[L_a J_{eq}s^2 + (R_a J_{eq} + L_a B_{eq})s + (R_a B_{eq} + k_e k_i)]} \tag{7}$$

The transfer function dynamic model, equation (7), is transformed into an equivalent block diagram for illustration. Figure 4. shows the dynamic model of the HL joint in the block diagram format.

V. A Classical Controller Design

A general controller transfer function $G_c(s)$ is added to the HL joint dynamic model in a cascade compensation form. Three feedback signals are established to provide input information for the proposed controller. The actual position feedback signal, $\theta_{act}(t)$, is compared with the desired position, represented by a reference input signal $\theta_d(t)$, in order to generate position error signal $e(t)$. The contribution of the velocity and torque feedback signals are to supplement the position error signal and generate a total input for the controller $r(t) = e(t) + \omega(t) + \tau(t)$. Figure 4 shows a complete block diagram including the joint dynamic model, the controller, and the three feedback signals.

Using block diagram reduction techniques Figure 4 was simplified to a single loop feedback system. The closed-loop system characteristic equation is found to be a third-order equation. To simplify the controller design procedure, the servomotor armature inductance is assumed to be small and set equal zero $L_a = 0$. This reduces the characteristic equation into a second-order equation of the following form

$$as^2 + bs + c = 0 \tag{8}$$

where:

$$
\begin{aligned}
a &= R_a J_{eq} - K_t K_i J_{eq} G_c \\
b &= R_a B_{eq}(-K_t K_i B_{eq} + K_e K_i - K_\omega K_i)G_c \\
c &= K_\theta K_i G_c
\end{aligned}
\tag{9}
$$

A desired joint response can be specified by a desired second-order characteristic equation of the form

$$s^2 + 2\zeta\omega_n s + \omega_n^2 = 0 \tag{10}$$

setting equations (8) and (10) equal and comparing term by term to produce the following two equalities

$$2\zeta\omega_n = \frac{b}{a}, \qquad \omega_n^2 = \frac{c}{a} \tag{11}$$

selecting a simple proportional controller $G_c(s) = K_p$ and substituting the terms a, b and c from (9) in equation (11) yields two expressions for the controller gain

$$K_p = \frac{(2\zeta\omega_n J_{eq} - B_{eq})R_a}{(K_e - K_t B_{eq} - K_\omega + 2\zeta\omega_n K_t J_{eq})K_i} \tag{12}$$

or

$$K_p = \frac{\omega_n^2 R_a J_{eq}}{(K_\theta + \omega_n^2 K_t J_{eq})K_i} \tag{13}$$

equations (12) and (13) must be satisfied simultaneously for successful controller design.

A controller was designed under the following conditions; $K_\theta + K_\omega = K_e$, $\omega_n = 2\,rad/sec$ and, $\zeta = 1$ for a response with zero overshoot. The controller gain then can be calculated either from equation (12) or (13). The numerical values of the servomotor parameters and the feedback gains used in the simulation are as follows: $L_a = 0H, R_a = 18\,hom, K_i =$

$0.1Nm/amp, K_e = 9.52V/rad/sec, K_t = 1.0V/Nm, K_\omega = 6.385V/rad/sec$ and, $K_\theta = 2.865V/rad$. Substitution of the above numerical values produced a proportional controller with gain value $K_p = 88.967$. The closed-loop response of the joint to a unit step input is computed. Figure 5 shows this response for different values of the controller gains, $K_p = 88, 84, 80$ and, 76. This Figure also shows that an acceptable joint response with minmum overshoot and settling time is obtained for a value of the controller gain $K_p = 76.0$. The controller respnse with gain $K = 76.0$ was used to train a neurocontroller.

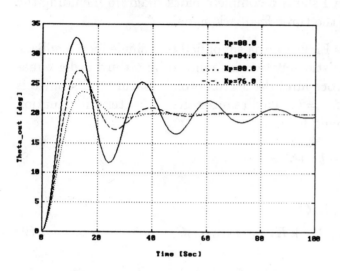

Fig. 5. P-Controller Responses
to a Step Input

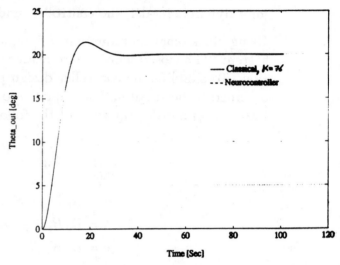

Fig. 6. Neurocontroller Response
to a Step Input

VI. Design of a Neurocontroller

To complete the biological concept of the proposed robot spherical joint a neural network is trained and used to provide motor control signals necessary for the control of the joint. Several neural network architectures and training algorithms are considered. This includes a feedforward neural network with time integration type of neurons and an on-line training algorithm. This neural network paradigm still under investigation and the results will be reported in future work. In this study a feedforward neural network with backpropagation training algorithm is used to build a neurocontroller. The network consists of one hidden layer with five neurons and sigmoid non-linearity. The network is of the single-input single-output type of neural nets. The input-output pairs used to train the neurocontroller are obtained from the input-output pairs of the P-controller driving the joint in response to a step input.

After training is completed the P-controller (teacher) is replaced by the trained neurocontroller and tested on different input signals. Figure 6 shows position response of the joint controlled by the neurocontroller in response to a step input. Similar result are shown in Figure 7 in response to a ramp input. Figure 8 shows the control signal produced by the neurocontroller and that produced by the P-controller. It is clear from Figure 8 that the neurocontroller is superior to the teacher, P-controller, since the former produces lower level control signal for the same task. This can be looked at as if the neurocontroller working as an energy saving device or as an optimal controller with energy performance index. Other teacher controllers, i.e., PD-controller and PI-controller, are also used to train the neurocontroller. The results of such controllers are not presented here for space limitation and will be reported in future work.

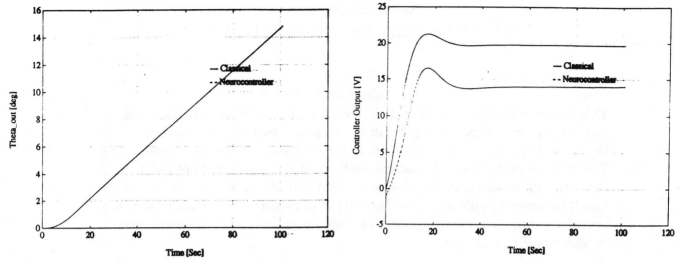

Fig. 7. Neurocontroller Responses
w.r.t a Ramp Input

Fig. 8. Neurocontroller Output
w.r.t. a Ramp Input

VII. Conclusion

A new Human Like robot joint have been suggested and developed. The proposed robot joint have biological motivation and is capable of producing three degrees of rotational motion. The HL robot joint can be used to design flexible robot wrist and/or shoulder making robots more flexible and intelligent. Other application of the developed mechanism is for vision systems providing flexible joint for Camera mount. In active vision systems this provide vision setup similar to a human eye. More complex biologically motivated joints are under research investigation.

Acknowledgement

This work is a part of the research activities conducted in the Center for Neural Engineering (CNE) at Tennessee State University. CNE is supported by the U.S. Navy Grant No. N00014-92-J-1372. The authors wish to thank them for their support for pursuing this research.

References

[1] Linkens, D.A. (Editor) "Biological Systems, Modelling and Control," IEE Control Engineering Series 11, Peter Peregrinus Ltd., New York, 1979.

[2] Taylor, C.L., and Schwartz, R.J. "The Anatomy and Mechanics of the Human Hand," Artificial Limb, Vol. 2, No. 2, pp. 22, 1956.

Neuro-controller via simultaneous perturbation

Yutaka Maeda and Yakichi Kanata

Department of Electrical Engineering, Faculty of Engineering,
Kansai University
3-3-35 Yamate-cho, Suita, Osaka 564 JAPAN

Abstract

This paper proposes a learning rule for a neuro-controller that controls an unknown plant. When we apply a direct control scheme by a neural network, the neural network must learn an inverse system of the unknown plant. Therefore, using a kind of gradient method as a learning rule of the neural network, we must know the sensitivity function of the plant. On the other hand, the learning rule described here does not require information about the sensitivity function. Some numerical simulations for a static plant and a dynamic plant are shown.

1. Introduction

Recently, neural networks (NNs) are well studied and widely used in many field. Also in the field of the control problem, NNs are used as a controller, an identifier or an adjuster that gives some parameters in a conventional controller[1]. Usually, it is very difficult to treat a nonlinear objective in the control theory. However, NNs can handle a nonlinear problem. From this point of view, NNs are promising in the control problem.

There are many schemes to utilize NNs in the control problem. Figure 1 shows a basic arrangement of a neuro-controller (NC). In this arrangement, NC must learn an inverse system of an unknown plant. After the learning process, NC controls an input of the plant directly. This configuration is very simple. However, it is relatively difficult to construct a learning rule of NC without information about the plant.

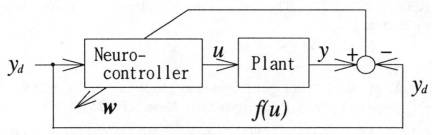

Figure 1 A basic scheme for a neuro-controller.

For convenience, in this chapter, we discuss a case that an input of the plant u and an output of the plant y are both scalar and a characteristic of the plant $y = f(u)$ is static. Moreover, $w = \left(w^1, \cdots, w^n \right)^{\mathrm{T}}$ denotes a weights vector of the NN with n weights. Superscript T is transpose of a vector.

Ordinarily, an error function $J(w)$ is defined by an error between the output of the plant and the desired output for the plant in the arrangement shown in Figure 1. By means of an adjustment of the weights in the NN, the NN must produce an input of the plant that decreases the error. When we use usual gradient method as a learning rule of the NN, we must know the quantity $\partial J(w) / \partial w$.

Define an error function as follows;

$$J(w) = \frac{1}{2} \left(y - y_d \right)^2 \tag{1}$$

where, y_d denotes the desired output of the plant. Then, we have

$$\frac{\partial J(w)}{\partial w} = \frac{\partial J(w)}{\partial y} \frac{\partial y}{\partial u} \frac{\partial u}{\partial w}$$
$$= \left(y - y_d \right) \frac{\partial f(u)}{\partial u} \frac{\partial u}{\partial w} \tag{2}$$

$\left(y - y_d \right)$ is known. Moreover, we can calculate $\partial u / \partial w$ by using so-called back-propagation. However, if we don't know the sensitivity function or, at least, the sign of the sensitivity function of the plant, we can not obtain the quantity $\partial f(w) / \partial u$ or the sign of this quantity. Therefore, it is difficult to use gradient type of learning rule in this arrangement. This is one of difficulties to make use of this arrangement.

Replacing this plant by a NN that learned the characteristic of the plant makes us possible to obtain $\partial f(w) / \partial u$ [1]. On the other hand, we introduce an idea of the difference approximation. In this case, there is no need to know the sensitivity function of the unknown plant.

The difference approximation is a well-known approach to obtain a derivative of a function. We can utilize this kind of technique to our problem.

We add a small perturbation c to the i-th weight, that is, we define w^i as follows;

$$w^i = \left(w^1, \cdots, w^i + c, \cdots, w^n \right)^{\mathrm{T}} \tag{3}$$

Since u, which is the output of the NN, is a function of the weight vector, we obtain

$$\frac{\partial y}{\partial w^i} \approx \frac{f\left(u\left(w^i \right) \right) - f(u(w))}{c} \tag{4}$$

By using Eq.(4), we can apply the gradient method to our scheme.

Similarly, we can employ the difference approximation to obtain $\partial J(w) / \partial w$ overall. That is, by using the following quantity,

$$\frac{\partial J(w)}{\partial w^i} \approx \frac{J\left(w^i \right) - J(w)}{c} \tag{5}$$

We can update the weights of the NN.

Moreover, it is relatively easy to implement this learning rule. M. Jabri, B. Flower and authors fabricated an analog NN circuit with learning ability using the learning rule, independently[2],[3].

This simple idea described above needs much more forward operations of the NN. That is, we must know $J(w^i)$ for all $i = 1, \cdots, n$. Therefore, we can not expect parallel operation of modifying the weights.

The next chapter presents the details of the learning rule using simultaneous perturbation that is an advanced version of the one using simple difference approximation.

2. Learning rule via simultaneous perturbation

First of all, we define the following perturbation vector c_t that gives small disturbance to all weight.

$$c_t = (c_t^1, \cdots, c_t^n)^T \tag{6}$$

where, subscript t denotes iteration.

The perturbation vector c_t has the following properties.

[A1] c_t^i is a uniform random number in an interval $[-c_{max}, c_{max}]$ except an interval $[-c_{min}, c_{min}]$. c_t^i is the i-th element of the vector c_t.

[A2] $E(c_t) = 0$.

[A3] $E(c_t^i c_t^j) = \begin{cases} 0 & \text{if } i \neq j \\ \sigma^2 & \text{if } i = j \end{cases}$

We consider the following learning rule.

$$w_{t+1} = w_t - \alpha \Delta w_t \tag{7}$$

Where, a coefficient α is a positive number that adjusts the magnitude of revision. Moreover, the i-th component of the vector Δw_t is defined as follows;

$$\Delta w_t^i = \frac{J(w_t + c_t) - J(w_t)}{c_t^i} \tag{8}$$

Let's consider the quantity described in Eq.(8). Expanding $J(w_t + c_t)$ in Eq.(8) at w_t, there exists w_{S1} such that

$$\Delta w_t^i = \frac{J(w_t + c_t) - J(w_t)}{c_t^i} = \frac{c_t^T}{c_t^i} \frac{\partial J(w_t)}{\partial w} + \frac{1}{2c_t^i} c_t^T \frac{\partial^2 J(w_{S1})}{\partial w^2} c_t \tag{9}$$

Taking expectation of the above equation, from the assumptions [A1]-[A3] of properties of the perturbation, we have

$$E(\Delta w_t^i) = \frac{\partial J(w_t)}{\partial w^i} + E\left\{\frac{1}{2c_t^i} c_t^T \frac{\partial^2 J(w_{S1})}{\partial w^2} c_t\right\} \tag{10}$$

This means that if the perturbation c_t is sufficiently small, then the right side of Eq.(8) is nearly equal to the derivative of the error function $\partial J(w_t)/\partial w^i$ in the sense of the expected value, because the second term of the right hand side of Eq.(10) is small. Therefore, the learning rule (7) and (8) is a type of stochastic gradient method.

In this learning rule, magnitudes of the perturbation corresponding to all weights are different each other and vary with respect to time t.

As same as the learning rule using the simple difference approximation, this type of learning rules is easy to implement. Author pointed out superiority of these kinds of learning rules for a hardware implementation and fabricated an analog NN circuit using this kind of the learning rule[4]. K.Hirotsu and M.A.Brooke also proposed a similar learning rule and fabricated a NN circuit with their learning rule[5]. From similar point of view, O.Fujita also proposed exhaustive learning rules and insisted on the feasibility of those learning rules[6].

3. Simulation results

In this chapter, we examine effectiveness of the learning rule by using the arrangement shown in Fig.1. A characteristic of each neuron is the usual sigmoid function $1/1+e^{-x}$.

First, we handle a simple static system with a characteristic;

$$f(u) = \sin u \tag{11}$$

Three layered feedforward NN (1-5-1) is used. The NN learns the inverse of $\sin u$ in an interval $(\%_2 \ \pi)$. The number of learning points is ten. The learning points locate on $(\%_2 \ \pi)$ uniformly. An error function $J(w)$ is defined as follows;

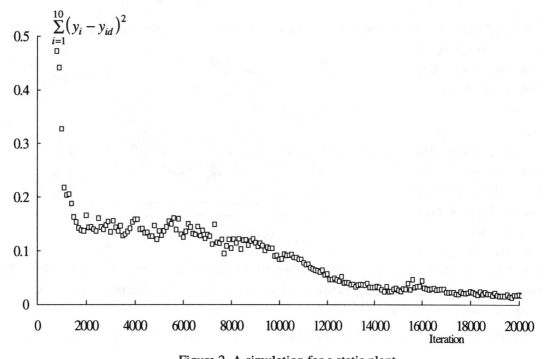

Figure 2 A simulation for a static plant.

$$J(w) = (y_i - y_{id})^2 \tag{12}$$

Where, i denotes a learning point, y_{id} represents a desired value corresponding to y_i. We assume that $\partial f(u)/\partial u$ is completely unknown. In this interval $(\frac{\pi}{2} \quad \pi)$, $\partial f(u)/\partial u$ is negative. Though the learning rate α is positive, we can guarantee the convergence of the learning rule (7) and (8).

Modifications of all weights were performed after a presentation of each learning point. Figure 2 shows simulation results for the learning rule (7), (8). Where, The learning coefficient α is 0.01. c_{max}, which is a maximum value of the absolute value of the perturbation, is 0.01. c_{min}, which is a minimum value of the absolute value of the perturbation is 0.001. These coefficients were determined empirically.

It seemed very difficult to decide an optimal c_{max} and c_{min} theoretically. However, we know that too large perturbation teaches a wrong direction when the weights are updated. This causes that the trial will never converge. At the same time, controlling the magnitude of the perturbation properly, we have a good chance to escape from a so-called local minimum. We need much consideration and analysis about these.

The weights of the NN are randomly initialized in an interval [-10 10]. Fig. 2 shows that the error decreases as iteration increases.

Next, we consider the following dynamic plant characteristic with a non-linear term.

$$y_t = y_{t-1} - 0.5y_{t-2} - 0.1y_{t-2}^2 + u_{t-1} + 0.4u_{t-2} \tag{13}$$

Where, we use a recurrent NN shown in Figure 3. Middle layer has five neurons. Output [0 1] of the NN is linearly converted to [-2.5 2.5]. The error function is defined as follows;

$$J(w) = \sum_{i=1}^{40}(y_i - y_{id})^2$$

That is, the error function is the sum of the squared error between a practical output and a desired output of the plant for every one cycle. One cycle consists of 40 iterations.

We deal with a tracking problem. The desired output of the plant is sinusoidal wave shown in Figure 4 (open circles). Every one cycle, modifications of

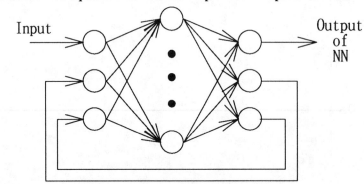

Figure 3 A recurrent neural network

the weights were performed. Output [0 1] of the NN is also linearly converted to [-2.5 2.5]. The initial weights are randomly determined in an interval [-1 1]. The learning rate α is 0.002. Moreover, $c_{max} = 0.05$, $c_{min} = 0.01$.

Triangles in Fig.4 show practical outputs of the above dynamic plant after 50 learning of NC.

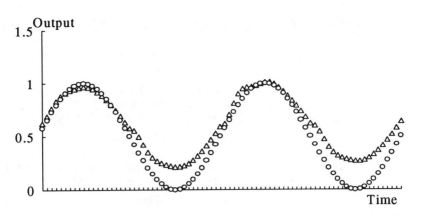

Figure 4 An output of a dynamic plant controlled by NC.

4. Conclusion

In this paper, we described the learning rule for NC. By using the learning rule, we can easily apply the direct control scheme. At the same time, we clarified that the learning rule using simultaneous perturbation is applicable not only to usual feed forward NN but also to recurrent NN. Moreover, the learning rule is relatively easy to implement. From these points of view, the learning rule described here is promising.

References

[1]edited by W.Thomas Miller,III, R.S.Sutton and P.J.Werbos, "Neural Networks for Control", The MIT Press, 1990.

[2]M.Jabri and B.Flower, "Weight perturbation: An optimal architecture and learning technique for analog VLSI feedforward and recurrent multilayer networks", IEEE Trans. Neural Networks, vol. 3, pp.154-157, 1992.

[3]Y.Maeda, H.Yamashita and Y.Kanata, "Learning rules for multilayer neural networks using a difference approximation", in Proc. IJCNN, Singapore, Nov., vol. 1, pp.628-632, 1991.

[4]Y.Maeda, H.Hirano and Y.Kanata, "An analog neural network circuit with a learning rule via simultaneous perturbation", in Proc. IJCNN, Nagoya, Oct., vol.1, pp.853-856, 1993.

[5]K.Hirotsu and M.A.Brooke, "An analog neural network chip with random weight change learning algorithm", in Proc. IJCNN, Nagoya, Oct., vol.3, pp.3031-3034, 1993.

[6]O.Fujita, "Trial-and-error correlation learning", IEEE Trans. Neural Networks, vol 4, pp.720-722, 1993.

Control with Neural Networks Using Minimum Information

A. Navia*, F. Panetsos*, J.M. Zaldívar**

*Laboratorio de Inteligencia Artificial
Universidad Carlos III de Madrid
Avda Mediterráneo 20. 28913 Leganés. Madrid (Spain)
navia@inf.uc3m.es

**Joint Research Center of the Comission of the European Communities
Institute for Safety Engineering Division
21020 Ispra (Italy)

Abstract
A neural network implementation is proposed, such a network uses the least information possible, and is able to learn on-line, adapting its weights in a continuous way using reinforcement learning. At the beginning, the network behaves as a reflex conditioned system, after being vaguely initialized, yielding a rough control signal very similar to bang-bang controllers, but as learning progresses, the response is gradually smoothed. A similar process can be observed in animal behaviour during learning. As an application, the network is used to control a chemical batch reactor. This kind of reactors are difficult to control: they are highly non-linear, they have time varying parameters and no stable state, and the kind of chemical processes and operating conditions change very often.

1.- LEARNING AND EXPERIENCE.

A first approach to human or animal skill learning is that the relation between the mind and the body (thinking and action) is not simply fixed but can be fundamentally changed. At the beginning of the development of a skill, the desired objective is known (goal) but the actions to perform are usually unknown (control signals). As the learning subject interacts with the environment, the connection between intention and act becomes more intense, until the action is correctly performed [16]. Usually, the skill to perform a task is rapidly developed but the quality of the performance is not so good.

Sensory-motor organization in animal subjects relies on the interaction and integration of different sensorial systems. This interaction process can be observed during the learning of voluntary motor gestures. It is also known that reflex responses can be modified by simultaneous activation of other sensorial systems. Depending on the sensorial pathways and the nature of the response (voluntary or reflex), different mechanisms are activated with diverse effects upon the motor response. Motor cortex and cerebellum play an important role in this process, being the latter the most important part in motor coordination. Some kind of hierarchical structure is needed to coordinate all the sensorial pathways. The function of the highest hierarchical levels can be resumed as follows: they join the different sensorial paths in order to select the objectives and make high level decisions. The higher the level is, the less straightforward the relations between stimuli and responses become [6][13].

On the other hand, the spinal reflex lies at the lowest level in the sensor-motor hierarchy. This kind of reflex response makes it possible to produce automatic, fast and simple actions. Such reflex stimulus, nevertheless, is submitted to the control of higher levels, which modify the responses, adapting them in a suitable way to a changing experiential environment or new stimuli.

2.- CONTROL OF NON-LINEAR SYSTEMS.

Several approaches to control are possible within the artificial techniques approach. A possible subdivision can be carried out, yielding two main areas: symbolic techniques (expert systems) and sub-symbolic techniques (artificial neural networks, ANN´s for short). Here we are facing a problem which has no available explicit formulation or this one is too difficult to obtain. Therefore, the latter are best suited to deal with systems of unknown but observable behaviour, and the former can be used in high-level knowledge systems.

When a sufficiently accurate model of the process is available and can be approximated by a linear time-invariant model, one of the conventional control algorithms, like a tuned PID controller, will be able to control the process in a suitable way. In any case, the rational way to deal with nonlinearities is to develop a design theory that takes them into account, using optimal control theory. However, such a design is quite complicated and the resulting control law is complex as well. As mentioned above, artificial neural networks (ANN´s) used in a real-time control environment usually yield good results and are specially adequate for hard-to-control systems exhibiting delayed responses and nonlinearities. Nevertheless, great benefits can be obtained from the combination of ANN´s and classical control systems. For instance, we can use a knowledge-based supervisory system to monitor the ANN´s controllers during operation [8].

Many approaches have been made to control, using ANN´s, but in fact, some topics must be taken into account regardless of the neural model chosen. Usually the actions required to achieve a control objective are unknown, this is, it is not possible to define a gradient function a priori. Instead a gradient surface has to be built interactively. Besides, the goodness of an action can not be determined instantaneously in many cases. This topic has been exhaustively studied in the literature and deals with the temporal correlation between control actions performed at certain instant of time and the results observed later. This delayed behaviour can be experienced in many physical systems and of course, in chemistry. Another main drawback of these methods is that important properties such as stability, convergence and robustness cannot usually be mathematically proved and we have to trust experimental data. A general trade-off between generality and specificity is still present: ANN´s are ill-conditioned when considered as a black-box solution to <u>any</u> problem, instead, specific architectures are needed to achieve a better performance quality.

3.- DESCRIPTION OF THE NEURAL MODEL USED.

The question proposed in this work relates to the minimum amount of information needed to control such non-linear processes in a suitable manner. As proposed in recent studies [7], there are certain non-linear systems that can be easily controlled using linear discriminators and bang-bang control. The main drawback is that this kind of control produces a signal which is highly discontinuous, usually oscillatory between two or more levels. This may not represent an obstacle for problems like the well known inverted pendulum on the cart, but it is impractical for industrial processes in general.

If we try to use as least information as possible we have to deal with two classic topics in control theory: controllability and observability. The former relates to the feasibility of being able to modify the state of our system with the control signals being used. A system is wide sense controllable if it is possible to force every state to an arbitrary target state in a finite number of steps. Nevertheless, this is a sufficient condition but not necessary at all because neither all states are visited during normal functioning nor every state has to be reachable. Only several regions in the state space will be of importance for specific control purposes. A process is observable if every variation in the system state can be detected using the variables under observation. This way, a controller might be able to perform well without knowledge of several state variables. In most practical situations, in fact, not all the state variables are available nor can be easily obtained.

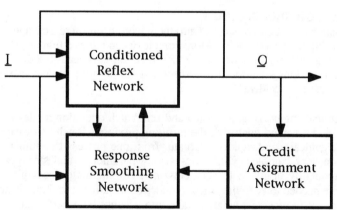

Figure 1: Neural Controller Structure.

The functioning of the proposed system is closely related to animal behaviour, as mentioned above. At the beginning of learning the actions performed to control an unstable system are abrupt and imprecise, usually approaching a bang-bang control. As learning progresses, the responses are gradually smoothed because the system learns to take into account high level interactions and future predictions. It is widely known that continuous force controllers are more robust and more precise than bang-bang controllers, nevertheless, the latter are easier to find as stated in several works. So the scheme proposed seems to be a natural evolution for the controller to achieve a valid configuration

The conditioned reflex network is initialized using data extracted from experimentation, and performs on its own a sort of bang-bang control, such control signalling is not acceptable for real-world chemical processes because the resulting power transitions are highly abrupt and very often such power excursions are impossible to achieve. Nevertheless, it is valuable because it is able to place the reactor in states close to the desired ones, while providing the necessary variability to learn from experience (due to the noisy behaviour). This way, the network can be initially trained on-line using any existent process simulator, even an imprecise one would serve, because the final training will be carried out using a real process.

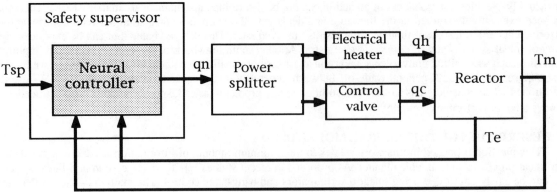

Figure 2: General diagram.

The general framework used for the smoothing network is the well-known topic of reinforcement learning networks dealing with delay between action and reaction [1][2][9][12][15]. It addresses the problem of improving performance as evaluated by *any* measure which values can be supplied to the learning system. This way, the system is not taught with the correct actions, instead, it is told whether or not an action is valuable for the desired purpose. These methods are mainly used because such information is usually unavailable, otherwise a supervised method would be more useful and faster to train. The objective is to map the state of the process into control actions which have to be learnt through experience. Many descriptions of reinforcement learning and delayed critic exist in the l.iterature[1][2][10][12][16], so it will commented no longer. The only difference is that the reinforcement signal used is not only of failure as in the cart-pole problem, but it indicates how the controller is performing, using an empirical criterium based on the measured variables and its first derivative. As mentioned previously, only the input and output data are involved in training the ANN, none of the information about the model is used.

4.- A REVIEW OF CHEMICAL BATCH REACTORS.

The complexity of chemical plants and the diversity of products have been increased due to the rapid development of Chemical Industry during the past decades. More complexity involves a higher risk of accident and also the need for better controlling systems. A poorly controlled reaction may lead to a decrease in final product quality and eventually to a hazardous situation in the reactor, with possible human losses, material damages and environmental impact, in case of accident [3].

From the point of view of chemical engineering, the batch and semibatch operation modes have become very popular due to their versatility and the good quality of the resulting products. Batch processing allows to produce small amounts of special chemicals, and rapidly alternate from one process to another . The main drawback is that batch reactors are very complex, with time-varying parameters and strongly non-linear dynamics and so they are more frequently involved in accidents than continuous process plants (CSTR). Continuous corrections and tuning are needed to keep the reaction under control, because batch reactions have no stable state. In order to optimize such processes, we must take into account both performance and safety although the former has more to do with this work, as a safety monitoring system exists.

The above mentioned discontinuous operating modes (batch and semibatch) are only slightly different. In the former case, the reactor is charged with all the reagents, solvents and catalysts and the control is performed through a heat exchanging process in the cooling-heating circuit while in the latter only a part of those products are fed at the beginning, the rest being provided through a feeding circuit. The semibatch operation is intended for strongly exothermic reactions in which it is not feasible to control the reaction temperature with the heating-cooling circuit alone and the feeding rates have to be controlled as well. Only batch performing is analyzed here.

At the beginning of a typical batch reaction some heat has to be supplied (except in strong exothermic reactions) in order to raise the temperature to a desired value (set point temperature, Tsp) so the reaction can start. When this point is reached, cooling is applied to keep the temperature close to the set point. Towards the end, again aditional heating may be necessary for the reaction to be completed. The power splitting mechanism uses an empirical law to choose between both actuators, but it is not of crucial importance.

A simulator was developed, which is based on the Mettler reaction calorimeter RC1 (which is a computer controlled batch reactor able to carry out isothermal, adiabatic, isoperibolic and temperature programmed experiments) as test bed for small scale reactions (up to 2 litres) [18]. This simulator was used as a "black box" and not as a mathematical model to extract analytical data from, since when the controller is working on real time with a physical reactor, very few parameters will be available (usually only the temperatures T_m, T_c, T_e and T_{sp}). The RC1 simulator was endowed with a control module which treats the process as if it were linear and applies a PID-like algorithm. The heat flow ($q_{removed}$) is proportional to the driving force, i.e. the temperature difference between the reactor and the jacket (T_m-T_e), being the term US the effective heat transfer coefficient:

$$q_{removed} = US \cdot (T_m - T_e) \qquad (1)$$

The base expression is as follows, where e(t) is the time varying error:

$$e(t) = f(T_m\text{-}T_{sp}, T_e\text{-}T_{sp}); \quad u(t) = K \cdot \left[e(t) + \frac{1}{T_i} \cdot \int^t e(t)\, dt + T_d \cdot \frac{d\,e(t)}{dt} \right] \qquad (2)$$

The criteria generally used for early-detection of hazardous states are:

$$\frac{d^2 T_m}{dt^2} > 0 \quad \text{and} \quad \frac{d(T_m\text{-}T_e)}{dt} > 0 \qquad (3)$$

The final results of the neural controller will be compared with that of this PID-like controller.

5- SIMULATION RESULTS

Figure 3 shows the temperature profiles corresponding to PID and neural controller before training. PID control produces very smoothed signals although it exhibits the characteristic offset of this kind of controllers. On the other hand, the neural controller provides a higher accurate following of the path T_m-T_{sp}=0 but due to the initial behaviour as a bang-bang controller, strong variations can be observed in the T_e-T_{sp} curve. In the case of the batch chemical reactor, only temperature and power measures are available, being also of importance such parameters as reacting mass pressure or reagent concentrations. Much effort has been dedicated to design a network with minimum information requirements, but although control is possible with only information about T_m-T_{sp}, another variable T_e has been added to improve performance. In figure 4 the above mentioned behaviour is evident observing the curve of applied power. Although such power profile may not be suitable in a real case, it helps during training.

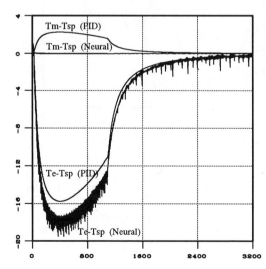

Figure 3: Temperature profiles before learning.

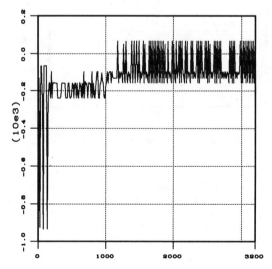

Figure 4 Power applied before learning.

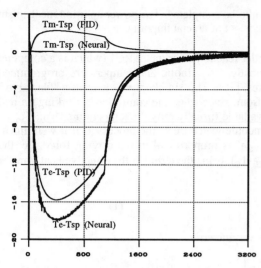

Figure 5: Temperature profiles after learning.

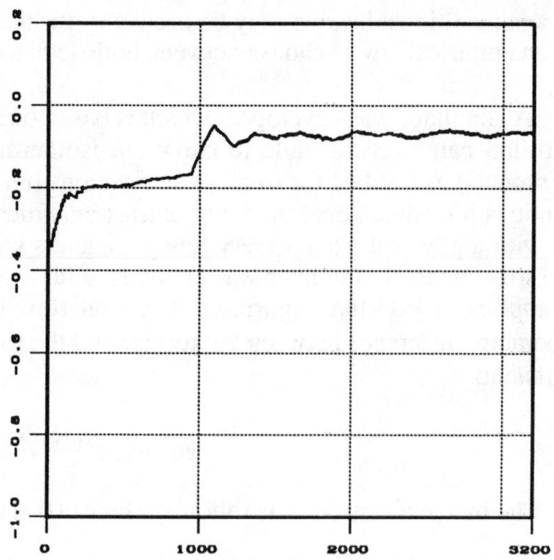

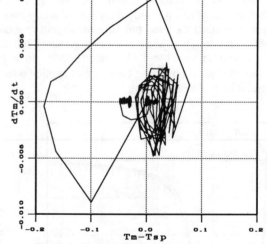

Figure 6: Power applied after learning.

Figure 5 is the counterpart of figure 3 but after learning. The smoothing network has learnt to supervise the reflex network and the resulting power profile (Figure 6) is therefore suitable for a real process. The learning profile is very similar in shape to many other reported in previous researches, but due to the discontinuous nature of these chemical reactions, another measure of performance was used instead of "time to failure". Another result to comment is that an attractor-like pattern can be observed in the states space, very similar to many others obtained when controlling the pole on the cart. This can be regarded as a reminder of the highly unstable nature of the problem, such that only closed loops in the state space, which can also be observed in the cart-pole problem, are the only valid solution for the system to be indefinitely kept under control. The afore mentioned high unstability can also be observed in figure 8, the control was disabled after iteration number 750, and the temperature grows exponentially, showing the strong exothermic nature of the reactions under study (note the modification of the temperature scale).

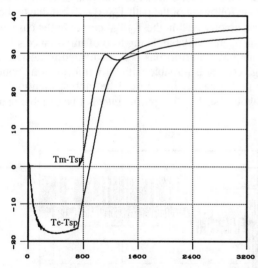

Figure 7: Intentioned exothermic runaway.

Figure 8: Trajectories in state space.

6.- CONCLUSIONS AND FURTHER RESEARCH.

The work presented so far should be regarded as a first step towards a multilevel control network able to deal with different types of reactions while producing a well behaved control signal able to control a real chemical reactor. The analogy between animal skill learning and the proposed scheme gives us much intuition about how to construct such hierarchical control structure. As more variables are taken into account, some kind of reduction in the representation of the state space must be done in order to keep the system between practical limits, while more abilities are added to the controlling system.

7.- REFERENCES.

[1]   Barnard, E. Temporal-Difference Methods and Markov Models. IEEE Transactions on Systems, Man and Cybernetics, Vol23, n°2, March/April, 1993.

[2]   Barto, A. Sutton, R., Anderson, C. : Neuronlike Adaptive Elements that Can Solve Difficult Learning Control Problems. IEEE Transactions on Systems Man and Cybernetics. SMC-13,5, 834-846, 1983.

[3]   Benuzzi, A. and Zaldívar,. J. M. editors. Safety of Chemical Batch Reactors and Storage Tanks. Kluwer Academic Publishers for the Commission of the European Communities. 1991.

[4]   Bingulac, S., VanLandingham, H. F. Algorithms for Computer-Aided Design of Multivariable Control Systems. Marcel Dekker, Inc. 1993.

[5]   Chapman, D. Kaelbling, L. P., Input Generalization in Delayed Reinforcement Learning: An Algorithm And Performance Comparisons.

[6]   Eccles, J. Evolution of the Brain: Creation of the Self. Routledge London and New York. 1989.

[7]   Geva, S., Sitte, J. A Cartpole Experiment Benchmark for Trainable Controllers.

[8]   Gullapalli, V. Barto, A. G. Shaping as a Method for accelerating reinforcement learning. Proceedings of the 1992 IEEE International Symposium on Intelligent Control. Glasgow 1992.

[9]   Handelman, D., A., Lane, S. H., Gelfand, J. J., Integrating Neural Networks and Knowledge-Based Systems for Intelligent Robot Control. IEEE Control Systems Magazine, April 1990.

[10]   Hoskins, J. C., Himmelblau, D. M., Process Control via Artificial Neural Networks and Reinforcement Learning. Computers & Chemical Engineering. Vol 16, April 1992.

[11]   Panetsos F., and Zaldívar J.M.: Batch Chemical Reactors Control and Malfunction Diagnosis Using Neural Networks. Fourth World Congress of Chemical Engineering. Strategies 2000. Karlsruhe/Germany, 16-21 June 1991. 12.1-2 Schön and Wetzel.

[12]   Miller, Sutton, and Werbos, editors. Neural Networks for Control. The MIT Press, 1991.

[13]   Myers, C. Reinforcement Learning When Results are Delayed and Interleaved in Time. INNC Paris, July 1990.

[14]   Schmid, R. Metodi di Analisi dei Sistemi Neurosensoriali. CNR - Gruppo Nazionale di Bioingegneria. Patron Editore, 1986.

[15]   Stephanopoulos, G. Chemical Process Control. PTR Prentice Hall. 1984.

[16]   Sutton, R. S. , Learning to Predict by the Methods of Temporal Differences. Machine Learning 3, Kluwer Academic Publishers, 1988.

[17]   Varela, F. J., Thompson, E., and Rosch, E.The Embodied Mind: Cognitive Science and Human Experience. . MIT Press, 1991.

[18]   Zaldívar, J.M., Hernández, H. and Barcons, C. Development of a Mathematical Model and Numerical Simulator for a Reaction Calorimeter: FISIM, RC1 version, Tech. Note n0. I. 90.109, Joint Research Centre, Commission of the European Communities, Ispra, Italy, 1990.

Rapid Reinforcement Learning for
Reactive Control Policy Design in Autonomous Robots

Andrew H. Fagg[*]
ahfagg@robotics.usc.edu

David Lotspeich[#]
lotspeic@robotics.usc.edu

Joel Hoff[*]
hoffj@robotics.usc.edu

George A. Bekey[*]
bekey@robotics.usc.edu

Center for Neural Engineering
[*]Department of Computer Science and [#]Department of Industrial Systems Engineering
Henry Salvatori Building #300
University of Southern California
Los Angeles, California 90089-0781

Abstract

This paper describes work in progress on a neural-based reinforcement learning architecture for the design of reactive control policies for an autonomous robot. Reinforcement learning techniques allow a programmer to specify the control program at the level of the desired behavior of the robot, rather than at the level of the program that generates the behavior. In this paper, we explicitly begin to address the issue of state representation which can greatly affect the system's ability to learn quickly and to apply what has already been learned to novel situations. Finally, we demonstrate the architecture as applied towards a real robot that is learning to move safely about its environment.

Introduction

Traditional methods of constructing intelligent robotic systems, employing artificial intelligence-based techniques, have met great difficulties in application to real-world problems. Such systems have often required a tremendous amount of computational power in order to make control decisions, and thus have sacrificed the ability to make decisions in real time. In addition, these systems must make many assumptions about the information that is supplied by the sensory processing subcomponents or about the results of actions that are taken. When these assumptions become invalid (which is typically the case when presented with a dynamic environment), these systems become brittle, and ultimately are unable to reliably accomplish their mission.

Reactive or behavior-based control systems have been offered as alternative methods to these more traditional techniques of designing robotic control systems (Arbib, 1989; Arkin, 1990; Bekey & Tomovic, 1986; Brooks, 1986; Brooks, 1991). These approaches embody two key principles. First of all, the control problem is decomposed into a set of simple computing modules, each of which may be designed and implemented separately. Secondly, each module only extracts the information that it needs in order to make a reasonable decision. This approach contrasts significantly with traditional AI approaches, in which the sensing system is used to update a global world model, from which decisions are then made.

However, despite some of the recently reported successes of reactive or behavior-based approaches, hiding behind most successes is a graduate student who spends many hours carefully designing, testing, and redesigning the set of control modules, until the desired behavior is achieved (exceptions to this include (Maes & Brooks, 1990; Mahadevan & Connell, 1992)). One reason that this process is so laborious is that it is typically very difficult for a programmer to put herself *in the shoes of the robot*, and truly understand the information that is being provided by the (often imperfect) sensing subcomponents, as well as understand the range of possible outcomes of actions taken by the robot. In addition, when a robot is picked up and placed into a new environment, there is no guarantee that the control program will continue to function as desired (Verschure & Kröse, 1992).

One possible approach to these difficulties is the application of a reinforcement-based learning technique (Barto & Bradtke, 1991; Barto, Sutton, & Anderson, 1983; Samuel, 1967; Sutton, 1988; Watkins & Dayan, 1992; Williams, 1987). Here, the programmer (or teacher) provides the robot with only an evaluation of its behavior. In our case, this evaluation is a scalar score that is potentially (but not necessarily) given for each control decision that is made by the controller. We refer to the manner in which the reinforcement information is computed as the *reinforcement policy*. Based upon this abstract representation of the desired behavior, the task of the learning system is to infer a reactive control strategy that satisfies the reinforcement policy provided by the teacher.

However, many reinforcement learning techniques suffer from the amount of time required to learn an effective control strategy. This difficulty is due in part to the manner in which states are represented in these systems. Purely localist representations (Barto & Bradtke, 1991; Barto, et al., 1983; Watkins & Dayan, 1992) store the relevant information for each possible state that the system might encounter. Such an approach suffers because it scales poorly with an increasing number of state variables. In addition, neighboring states are not able to share information with one-another, requiring that the system visit all states during the learning process in order to ensure an optimal control policy.

On the other end of the spectrum are the completely distributed representations, such as backpropagation-based techniques (Williams, 1987), where every (hidden) unit participates to some degree in each learned mapping. Although such approaches allow for generalization between states, the very same mechanism that gives us this feature also causes a significant amount of interference between dissimilar states. The result is a rapid slow-down in learning as the state space becomes larger or more complicated. In this work, we seek a state representation that sits somewhere between these two extremes - that allows us to capture some degree of generalization, but is still localist enough such that learning in different regions of the state space will not interfere with one-another.

In the remainder of this paper, we first present a specific neural architecture for the representation of reactive control programs. We next show how this model can be updated in light of reinforcement-based information from a teacher, and how a module that predicts future reinforcement can be used to solve the temporal credit assignment problem. Finally, we illustrate the behavior of the architecture when it is presented with several tasks to be learned.

Problem Description

The Robot

The robotic system used in these experiments is an adapted radio-controlled car. The vehicle is equipped with two tactile bumpers that are mounted on the Front and the Rear of the vehicle. In addition, there are five sonar sensors which are oriented in different directions: Left, Forward, Right, Up (forwards), and Rear.

The Task

The world in which the robot is situated is a standard laboratory environment, with a large variety of obstacles, some of which (such as chair and table legs) are rather difficult to detect, especially with a moving sonar platform. In work to date, we have experimented with three different tasks that the robot is to learn:

1. Avoid collision with obstacles.
2. Environmental exploration.
3. Wall following.

For each different task, the teacher chooses an appropriate reinforcement policy. For example, one possible reinforcement policy for task 1 is to punish the robot when it collides with an obstacle (reinforcement = -1), and otherwise no information is given (reinforcement = 0). From this sparse information, the learning control system must learn a control policy that reliably keeps the robot from receiving the negative reinforcement.

Network Model

The general network architecture is depicted in Figure 1, and has evolved from our work on modeling of primate visual/motor conditional learning (Fagg & Arbib, 1992). The goal of the network is to map current sensory inputs into appropriate actions. Inputs from five sonar units, and two bumpers (I) activate a particular pattern activity across the feature detector units (F). The feature detector units then interact with one-another to contrast-enhance the activity pattern across the vector of feature detectors (G). The feature detector units that continue to be active vote for a favored set of actions at the *action-selection layer* (A). The votes from the set of active feature detector units are gathered together at each action through a summation operation. The one action with the highest activity is chosen to be executed for the current time-step, after which the process is repeated. The six possible actions are movements in the following directions: Left Forward, Straight Forward, Right Forward, Left Reverse, Straight Reverse, and Right Reverse.

In the interest of computational efficiency, the unit dynamics are implemented as a one-pass system. The sensory vector (I) contains one neuron for each bumper sensor (active if touching something), and three neurons each for the sonar inputs (corresponding to Near, Mid, and Far sonar ranges). The mapping from sensors (I) to feature detector units (F) is implemented as a simple matrix-vector

operation:
$$F = W * I + Noise$$
where

I and F are vectors representing the input unit activities and the feature detector inputs.

W is a weight matrix (initially random) that maps from I to F.

Noise is a vector of random signals that are injected into the feature detector units.

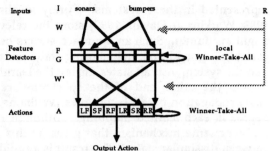

Figure 1: The general network architecture. The sensor inputs activate a set of feature detector units. Those remaining after the local Winner-Take-All competition instantiate votes for one of six actions (LF = left forward, SF = straight forward, ... , RR = right reverse). The one with the highest number of votes is output for execution.

The contrast enhancement function at the feature detector layer is implemented by a *local winner-take-all* operation. Unlike the standard *winner-take-all algorithm*, a particular unit only has an effect over a small neighborhood of the feature detector field. In fact, the interaction between the units is best described as a *mexican-hat connectivity*, with near neighbors supporting the activity of one-another, and neighbors that are further out inhibiting each other.

The interaction amongst the feature-detector units is implemented according to the rule:

$$Winner_i = \begin{cases} 1 & if\ F_i = \underset{i-N \le j \le i+N}{Max}\{F_j\} \\ 0 & otherwise \end{cases}$$

where:

N defines a local neighborhood of feature detectors.

The output activity values (G) are then computed in two steps:

1. $G_i = Winner_i * F_i$
2. If $Winner_i = 0$ and i is a close neighbor of a winner (call it unit j), then :

$G_i = Max(F_i, \gamma F_j)$ where $0 < \gamma < 1$

The Winner vector determines the location of the peaks of activity within the feature detector layer (as implemented by equation 1). Close neighbors of the winning feature detectors are also activated to some degree (equation 2). *Close neighbor* is smaller than the neighborhood size (N), used to compute the Winner vector.

The contrast-enhancement operation serves a vital role in the assignment of credit during the learning process. Through its application, it is guaranteed that only a small number of units in the feature detector layer actually become active at any one time (and thus instantiate their votes at the action selection layer). This is important because when reinforcement information becomes available, identifying those feature detector units that are at fault (so that learning can occur) is a much more precise computation. This will be elaborated further in the Discussion section.

The votes are then collected by the action selection units :

$$A = W' * G + Noise'$$

The action that is output is action i such that:

$$A_i = \underset{j}{Max}\{A_j\}$$

Once the selected action is executed, a new set of sensory inputs is presented to the network and the process of selecting a new action is repeated.

Network Learning

In parallel to the execution process described above, the learning system makes updates to the weight matrices W and W' based on the reinforcement information (R) that is received from the teacher. The sign of this signal indicates the appropriateness (R > 0) or inappropriateness (R < 0) of the *recent behavior* of the robot, and the magnitude of the signal represents the degree of this (in)appropriateness. Inherent in this definition is the fact that an entire sequence of actions may contribute to the final reinforcement signal that is provided by the teacher. Thus, the learning algorithm is faced with propagating current reinforcement information backwards through time in such a way that the recent actions are updated appropriately.

We will first consider the structural credit assignment problem, which states that given some instantaneous state of the network and a reinforcement signal, R, how is blame assigned to the individual weights of W and W'.

Suppose that the execution of the last action yielded a positive reinforcement signal from the teacher. In order to increase the probability of making the same decision the next time the same situation arises, two things must be done. First of all, we must insure that the same set of features are recognized (i.e. the same set of feature detector units are turned on). This may be accomplished by increasing the strengths of the synaptic weights from the currently active input units to the currently active feature detector units. Secondly, given that the same set of features are recognized, the same action must be taken. This is captured by increasing the strength of the synaptic weights from the currently active feature detector units to the selected action.

On the other hand, suppose that a negative reinforcement signal is received from the teacher. The selection of the incorrect action may be due to one of two cases. First of all, the incorrect set of feature detector units may have been selected. If this is the case, then the connection strengths from the currently active input units to the currently active feature detector units should be decreased. The next time that the same situation arises, the total input to these feature detector units will be weaker, giving them less of a chance to win the local winner-take-all competition. In the second case, the set of feature detector units is correct, but the selected action is incorrect. For this case, the connection strength from the active feature detector units to the selected action is decreased, thus reducing its future probability of being selected. The only difficulty is that the system does not know which of the two cases are the correct assessment of blame. Therefore, both sets of weights are updated.

The update rule for both the positive and negative reinforcement cases may be expressed by:

$$\Delta W_{ij} = \alpha R I_i G_j W_{ij}$$

$$\Delta W'_{jk} = \alpha' R G_j \hat{A}_k W'_{jk}$$

where:

α and α' are learning rate constants.

$\hat{A}$ is a vector in which all elements are 0, except for the kth element, where k is the winning action.

$I_i G_j W_{ij}$ and $G_j \hat{A}_k W'_{jk}$ are measures of the participation of specific synapses in the last decision (synapses between input unit i and feature detector j and feature detector j and action unit k, respectively).

In order to approach the problem of temporal credit assignment, we make use of the concept of eligibility, which was first introduced by Klopf (Klopf, 1982) and later used by others, including (Barto, et al., 1983). The eligibility of a weight is defined as a temporal memory of a synapse's participation in recent action decisions, and is computed as follows:

$$\tau \frac{d e_{ij}}{dt} = -e_{ij} + I_i G_j W_{ij}$$

$$\tau' \frac{d e'_{jk}}{dt} = -e'_{jk} + G_j \hat{A}_k W'_{jk}$$

where

e_{ij} and e'_{jk} are the eligibility measures.

τ and τ' determine the temporal width of the memory.

Finally, the weight updates become:

$$\Delta W_{ij} = \alpha R e_{ij}$$

$$\Delta W'_{jk} = \alpha' R e'_{jk}$$

By this definition of eligibility, the assignment of credit or blame for a reinforcement signal is given with the highest weight to the most recent decision that was made, and exponentially decreasing weight for decisions that were made further back in time. One key aspect of this definition of memory is that the number of memory elements does not depend upon the size of the time window over which the memories are stored, and only depends upon the number of synapses in the network.

Reinforcement Prediction

Eligibility provides a simple means by which credit can be assigned to a sequence of control decisions. However, the propagation of reinforcement information is limited to a fixed window of time defined by the decay of the eligibility memory. It is thus possible that a critical decision occurs outside of this window, and therefore would not receive any reinforcement information. As a result, the control network cannot learn to behave properly when an action and the corresponding reinforcement signal are separated by a length of time that is greater than that of the eligibility memory.

This problem is approached in this work through the method of reinforcement prediction (Sutton, 1988). First of all, suppose that we have a prediction network $P(x(t))$ that maps the current state of the system $(x(t))$ into a measure of the expected future reinforcement (relative to a fixed control policy). More explicitly:

$$P(x(t)) = E\left\{\sum_{\tau=t}^{\infty} \lambda^{\tau-t} R(\tau)\right\}$$

where:

$R(t)$ is the reinforcement received at time t.

λ is the discount factor for future reinforcement.

The function $P(x(t))$ can be viewed as the *goodness* of being in state $x(t)$. Now observe that:

$$P(x(t)) = E\left\{\sum_{\tau=t}^{\infty} \lambda^{\tau-t} R(\tau)\right\}$$

$$= E\left\{R(t) + \lambda \sum_{\tau=t+1}^{\infty} \lambda^{\tau-t-1} R(\tau)\right\}$$

$$= E\left\{R(t) + \lambda P(x(t+1))\right\}$$

And define:

$$R'(t) = R(t) + \lambda P(x(t+1)) - P(x(t))$$

$R'(t)$ can be interpreted as a measure of the deviation of the actual reinforcement received from that which was expected by the prediction network (for an individual time-step). In other words, if R' > 0, then the system performed better in the last time-step than it expected to perform; and when R' < 0, the system performed worse than expected. This measure can be used as an internally-generated reinforcement signal, that has the potential for delivering more meaningful reinforcement information at *every instant* that a decision is made, even when the teacher is providing a very sparse reinforcement signal.

It is important to note that the function $P(x(t))$ is also relative to the control policy implemented by the control network. As this control policy adapts through experience, so must this prediction function. In this work, we make use of the method of *Temporal Difference Learning* (Sutton, 1988) to acquire the prediction function. This learning process is performed in parallel with the adaptation of the control network.

The R' that we compute from the non-stationary control policy has several important properties:

• The measure rewards incremental improvements in performance. When the controller discovers an action that leads to a higher level of performance than what was expected, the control network adjusts itself such that the probability of executing the same action given a similar situation is increased. This results in an overall improvement in the system's performance. The prediction network quickly adapts itself such that it expects this new level of performance. At this point, execution of the same action yields a null internal reinforcement signal, and a positive signal is only received if a new action further improves the performance.

• The above implies that even when the teacher only provides negative reinforcement as a way of specifying the desired behavior, the internal reinforcement signal can provide positive reinforcement information for actions that cause the system to receive less negative reinforcement than it was receiving earlier.

• More effective propagation of reinforcement information through time. Consider a controller that has learned for all points in the set A (Figure 2) the correct sequence of actions to drive the system to point p, where it receives positive reinforcement from the teacher. Outside of set A (e.g. point z), however, the system does not know how to get reliably to point p, and in these cases, generates random actions. Once the system has visited the points in set A a number of times, the expected future reinforcement will become that which is received at point p (with some discount in the number of steps required to reach p). Thus, the internal reinforcement for moving from any of these points towards p will effectively be zero.

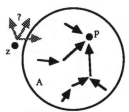

Figure 2: State space representation of a controller's actions. For those points within set A, the controller knows the correct sequence of actions to drive the system to point p, where positive reinforcement is received. However, outside of set A, the system has not yet learned the correct actions. By using R' as the reinforcement signal, the system is able to deliver a large amount of positive reinforcement to network when the boundary is crossed from point z to a point in set A. This is the case even though reinforcement from the teacher is still several time-steps away.

For the case of point z, the expected future reinforcement will be small, if not zero, and expected internal reinforcement will also be zero (because from point z, the system will tend to wander aimlessly outside of the set A). However, there is a some probability that an action chosen at state z will take the system into a point within A - i.e. from a state with low expected future reinforcement to a state with high expected future reinforcement. As a result, the internal reinforcement signal will be high, thus rewarding the action that brought the system into A. This is the case even though the actual reinforcement from the teacher is still several time-steps away.

• Prevention of over-learning. If the external reinforcement signal is used to update the control network, weight updates will continue to be made when positive reinforcement is received, even if the network is already completely committed to the correct action. This can cause problems in terms of unnecessary interference with learning in other nearby regions of the state space. By using R' as the reinforcement signal, the system only adjusts its weights as long it is necessary to ensure commitment to the correct action(s), and then learns no further. Thus, other regions of the state space can be learned more easily, and more neural hardware can be reserved for learning during later experiences.

The updated network architecture is shown in Figure 3. The prediction network is a linear neural network, with the feature detector activity vector (G) serving as the input. The environmental reinforcement signal (R) is now combined with system's prediction of reinforcement to generate an internal reinforcement signal (R'). This signal is not only used to update the connections involved in the action selection process (W and W'), it also serves as an update signal for the prediction network (P).

Experimental Results

In this section, we illustrate the behavior of the system through a series of learning experiments. At this time, we are especially interested in understanding how the reinforcement policy affects the learned behavior.

Experiment 1: Collision Avoidance

Up to this point, the collision avoidance problem has been the primary focus of our experimentation. Several different reinforcement policies have been explored:

1. **Punish running into an obstacle.** When this policy is used, the network has a difficult time determining which action is appropriate, because it is only being told when an action was a bad choice. As a result, the system must spend a significant amount of time searching for the action that will produced the desired behavior.

2. **Reward not running into an obstacle.** The network often quickly discovers a one-move local minimum that satisfies the basic requirements of the behavior. An example of this is always making a forward right turn, causing the robot to move in a circle. However, the network very quickly and completely commits itself to this simple strategy, and when later faced with a new situation (such as an obstacle in the path), it is very difficult for the robot to explore alternative actions.

3. **Punish for running into a wall and reward for not.** Two sub-cases are possible:

3A. |**Punishment**| < |**Reward**|. This type of policy enables the robot to develop short cycles of movements, which result with overall positive reinforcement. When faced with an obstacle, a very common behavior that is learned is one in which the robot moves forward, collides with the obstacle, backs up one step, and then repeats the process. Even though this strategy receives negative reinforcement for the collision, it makes up for it by insuring that it receives a higher degree of positive reinforcement at the next time-step.

3B. |Punishment| > |Reward|. This policy produces control programs that perform the best for the collision avoidance problem. This is due to a balance between policy 1 (from above), where learning requires a long time, and policy 2, where learning happens so quickly that the system does not have adequate opportunity to explore the control space.

Figures 4 and 5 show the learning results of using policy 3B to solve the collision avoidance problem. Figure 4 tabulates a number of the feature detectors that were commonly learned over several experiments, and the actions that these feature detectors supported. In many cases, the input units that activate the feature detectors logically match the preferred actions.

Figure 5 shows the actual and internal reinforcement signals as learning takes place. We see a significant improvement in performance up through about 300 time-steps (as measured by the actual reinforcement curve). Also note that the internal reinforcement begins to deviate from the actual reinforcement curve at about 100 time-steps, demonstrating that the reinforcement predictor has begun to learn something useful. By the 600th time-step, this curve has leveled off, indicating that the predictor has learned to anticipate reinforcement to the best of its ability, and that the controller learning has stopped.

Experiment 2: Environmental Exploration

In this experiment, the goal is to develop a behavior that causes the robot to cover a large area of its environment. The policy reinforces this behavior by rewarding the robot for moving in a straight forward direction, and punishing reverse movements. As it is still important to avoid obstacles, this rule is combined with policy 3B.

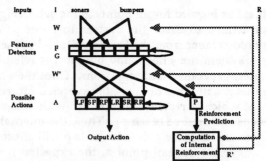

Figure 3: Modified network architecture. The reinforcement information from the teacher is first combined with the output of the Predictor Network to produce an internal reinforcement signal, R'. It is this signal that is used to update the weights in the control network. The Predictor Network (P) is implemented as a linear function of the feature detector outputs (G).

Sensory Inputs	Supported Actions
Mid Range Left Sonar Far Range Left Sonar Far Range Up Sonar	Straight Forward
Front Bumper Near Range Forward Sonar Mid Range Up Sonar Far Range Up Sonar	Straight Reverse
Far Range Up Sonar	Straight Forward
Rear Bumper Far Range Up	Right Forward Left Forward
Near Range Forward Sonar Mid Range Front Sonar Near Range Right Sonar	Left Reverse

Figure 4: Common feature detectors and the actions for which they vote. Over a set of several learning experiments (policy 3B), these rules (with some variation) were consistently learned.

It is possible to assign different weights to each of these two sub-policies to reflect learning priorities. It was observed that the sub-policy given higher priority was learned faster than the other and typically dominated the other.

Experiment 3: Wall Following

A reinforcement policy for this behavior which has been posited is to reward the network when it moves in the straight forward direction while an obstacle is detected in the mid range of the left sonar. This policy is designed to encourage the robot to follow straight sections of walls. It is our belief that the reinforcement predictor network can provide sufficient information to internally reward the robot for properly turning corners when they are encountered. This is the subject of our ongoing experiments.

Discussion

This work has drawn on the results on TD (Temporal Difference) Learning of Sutton (Sutton, 1988), as well as those on Q-Learning (Barto & Bradtke, 1991; Watkins & Dayan, 1992). The primary difference with our algorithm is in its more neural orientation, and in the type of predictive information that is stored at each state. In our case, we only store the expected future discounted reinforcement (Watkin's V() function), as opposed to the expected future reinforcement relative to the next action to be taken (Q-values). The information provided by the Q-values is given to some degree by the activity levels of the output units, in that those actions that have the higher Q-values will tend to acquire higher and higher activity levels as learning progresses.

Our primary contribution is an attempt to identify more efficient coding schemes for state space representation. In this case, efficiency constitutes the amount of experience necessary to yield a competent reactive policy, and the amount of time required to actually learn the policy. For the experiments described above, learning was performed in real time (as the actions were being executed by the robot), and robot was allowed at most 30 minutes to acquire its program (about 1000 time-steps). These results are possible by a combination of the reinforcement predictor (as discussed earlier), and the input state coding scheme used at the feature detector layer.

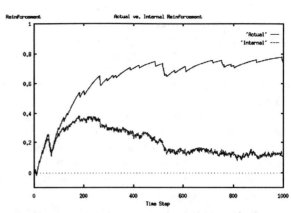

Figure 5: Actual (upper curve) and internal reinforcement (lower) over the course of a single learning collision avoidance experiment.

The local winner-take-all operation at the feature detector layer forces moderately different input activity patterns to activate different sets of feature detector units. As a result, learning that is performed in one region of the state space tends not to interfere with learning in other regions of the space, as is the case with Backpropagation-based reinforcement learning algorithms (Williams, 1987).

One the other hand, local support given by winning feature detectors to nearby neighbors tends to create a topological mapping of the input space (von der Malsburg, 1987). As a result, points that are nearby each other in the input space will activate largely overlapping sets of feature detectors, allowing these points to share their common experiences, yielding some degree of generalization.

State space representation for reinforcement learning as applied to robots has also been addressed in (Mahadevan & Connell, 1992) using statistical clustering techniques.

Conclusions

Reactive or behavior-based systems have been offered as alternative approaches to the more traditional AI-based techniques for the design of intelligent control systems for autonomous robots. Their ability to deal with uncertainties in sensing and in action generation, as well as their limited computational requirements have allowed them to demonstrate some level of success beyond that of AI systems. However, these systems are constructed in a trial-and-error fashion, and can often require long periods of programming time to reliably achieve the desired behavior.

This paper has presented an approach to constructing reactive control systems that allows the programmer (or teacher) to specify only the desired behavior of the program. This specification comes in the form of a reinforcement policy (rewards and punishments for certain behaviors that the robot exhibits), from which the learning algorithm must infer a control policy that attempts to maximize the rewards and minimize the punishments that are received. Specifying programs in this way is useful because the specification happens at a level that is easy for the programmer to express and understand, and yet the programs are evaluated within the environment in which they must ultimately perform.

The problem of programming however has not gone away. It has only shifted from specifying sets of reactive rules to specifying reinforcement policies that lead the learning system to discover sets of rules that accomplish the desired task. As was demonstrated in our experiments described above, this second process is also an iterative one, where the final behavior is observed, the reinforcement policy is adjusted, and the learning process is then repeated.

The current challenge is to construct principles from which reinforcement policies can be designed, such that the time required to learn a desired behavior is minimized. With this goal in mind, two directions are being pursued:

• **Staged Learning** is a technique in which partial solutions to a problem are first taught to the robot before it is expected to solve the entire problem (Lewis, Fagg, & Solidum, 1992; Lin, 1993). This is accomplished by first presenting the robot with a reinforcement policy that encourages the development of the partial solutions. Once the robot has obtained this intermediate level of capability, the reinforcement policy is changed such that the robot is then required to solve the entire problem in order to receive positive reinforcement. This technique can be used to lead the robot along a specific path of learning, significantly reducing the amount of search that is necessary to discover a program that produces the desired behavior. The behavior-based decompositions for the learning system described in (Mahadevan & Connell, 1992) also has some interesting parallels to staged learning.

 • **Learning by Demonstration** is an approach in which motor programs are demonstrated to the robot by the human (Fagg, 1993; Handleman & Lane, 1993; Lin, 1993; Liu & Asada, 1992). The robot first learns to mimic the behavior of the human through a more supervised learning approach. Reinforcement learning is then applied to further refine the learned motor programs such that they are better matched with the robot's own sensory and actuation abilities.

Acknowledgments

The authors would like to thank Dr. Michael Arbib, Gaurav Sukhatme, Mike McHenry, Amanda Bischoff, Nicolas Schweighofer, Tony Lewis, Jason Bagley, Parag Batavia, Anand Ramakrishna, and Mathew Lamb for their comments, suggestions and help during the course of this work. The neural model has been implemented in NSL (Neural Simulation Language (Weitzenfeld, 1991)), which is available via anonymous ftp from yorick.usc.edu. More information may be obtained by contacting Alfredo Weitzenfeld (alfredo@rana.usc.edu). This work has been supported in part by grants from the University of Southern California Graduate School, School of Engineering, and Computer Science Department, and by the Human Frontiers Science Program.

References

Arbib, M. A. (1989). Schemas and Neural Networks for Sixth Generation Computing. Journal of Parallel and Distributed Computing, 6, 185-216.

Arkin, R. C. (1990). Integrating behavioral, perceptual, and world knowledge in reactive navigation. Robotics and Autonomous Systems, 6, 105-122.

Barto, A. G., & Bradtke, S. H. (1991). Real-Time Learning and Control using Asynchronous Dynamic Programming (TR No. 91-57). Department of Computer Science, University of Massachusetts, Amherst.

Barto, A. G., Sutton, R. S., & Anderson, C. W. (1983). Neuronlike Adaptive Elements That Can Solve Difficult Learning Control Problems. IEEE Transactions on Systems, Man, and Cybernetics, SMC-5, 834-46.

Bekey, G. A., & Tomovic, R. (1986). Reflex Control of Robot Actions. In IEEE International Conference on Robotics and Automation, (pp. 240-247). San Francisco.

Brooks, R. A. (1986). A Robust Layered Control System for a Mobile Robot. IEEE J. Robotics and Automation, RA-2(RA-2), 14-23.

Brooks, R. A. (1991). Intelligence Without Reason (A.I. Memo No. 1293). MIT.

Fagg, A. H. (1993). Developmental Robotics: A New Approach to the Specification of Robot Programs. In G. A. Bekey & K. Y. Goldberg (Eds.), Neural Networks in Robotics (pp. 459-86). Norwell, Massachusetts: Kluwer Academic Publishers.

Fagg, A. H., & Arbib, M. A. (1992). A Model of Primate Visual-Motor Conditional Learning. Journal of Adaptive Behavior, 1(1), 3-37.

Handleman, D. A., & Lane, S. H. (1993). Fast Sensorimotor Skill Acquisition Based on Rule-Based Training of Neural Nets. In G. A. Bekey & K. Y. Goldberg (Eds.), Neural Networks in Robotics (pp. 255-70). Norwell, Massachusetts: Kluwer Academic Publishers.

Klopf, A. H. (1982). The Hedonistic Neuron. Washington, D. C.: Hemisphere.

Lewis, M. A., Fagg, A. H., & Solidum, A. (1992). Genetic Programming Approach to the Construction of a Neural Network for Control of a Walking Robot. In Proceedings of the 1992 IEEE Conference on Robotics and Automation, (pp. 2618-23). Nice, France.

Lin, J. J. (1993). Hierarchical Learning of Robot Skills by Reinforcement. In Proceedings of the 1993 IEEE Conference on Neural Networks, (pp. 181-6). San Francisco, California: IEEE.

Liu, S., & Asada, H. (1992). Transferring Manipulative Skills to Robots - Representation and Acquisition of Tool Manipulative Skills Using a Process Dynamic Model. Journal of Dynamic Systems Measurement and Control-Transactions of the ASME, 114(2), 220-8.

Maes, P., & Brooks, R. A. (1990). Learning to Coordinate Behaviors. In AAAI, (pp. 796-802). Boston, MA.

Mahadevan, S., & Connell, J. (1992). Automatic Programming of Behavior-Based Robots Using Reinforcement Learning. Artificial Intelligence, 55, 311-365.

Samuel, A. L. (1967). Some Studies in Machine Learning Using the Game of Checkers. IBM Journal of Research and Development, 11, 601-17.

Sutton, R. S. (1988). Learning to Predict by the Methods of Temporal Differences. In Machine Learning 3 (pp. 9-44). Boston: Kluwer Academic Publishers.

Verschure, P. F. M. J., & Kröse, B. J. A. (1992). Distributed Adaptive Control: The Self-Organization of Structured Behavior. Robotics and Autonomous Systems, 9, 181-196.

von der Malsburg, C. (1987). Ordered Retinotectal Projections and Brain Organization. In F. E. Yates, A. Garfinkel, D. O. Walter, & G. Yates (Eds.), Self-Organizing Systems - The Emergence of Order (pp. 265-78). New York: Plenum Press.

Watkins, C. J. C. H., & Dayan, P. (1992). Q-Learning. Machine Learning, 8(3), 279-92.

Weitzenfeld, A. (1991). NSL - Neural Simulation Language Version 2.1 (TR No. TR 91-05). Center for Neural Engineering, University of Southern California, Los Angeles, CA.

Williams, R. J. (1987). Reinforcement Learning Connectionist Systems (TR No. NU-CCS-87-3). Northeastern University, College of Computer Science.

Visually Guided Motor Control: Adaptive Sensorimotor Mapping with On-line Visual-Error Correction

L. Li[1,2] and H. Öğmen[1]

1 *Department of Electrical Engineering*
University of Houston
Houston, Texas, 77204-4793 USA

2 *Automation and Robotics Division*
NASA/Johnson Space Center
Houston, Texas, 77058 USA

Abstract. *A neural network architecture combining an adaptive sensory-motor mapping and an on-line visual error correction (VEC) mechanism is proposed. The sensory-motor network (SMN) acquires a consistent intermodal mapping through primary circular reactions. During performance, SMN generates feed-forward control commands to the motor networks. This feed-forward command is augmented by VEC which is a feed-back control mechanism. The feedback allows the system to correct immediately during performance, errors that may arise from various sources including intermodal inconsistencies. This dual feed-forward feedback control enables the network to maintain the accuracy of its performance while inconsistencies are resolved through long-term adaptation. We present simulation results that illustrate the long-term learning as well as immediate correction capabilities of the network.*

1 Introduction

Visually guided arm movements constitute an important part of the behavioral repertoire of many biological systems as well as robots. In visually guided reaching, there are four major steps involved: *target selection, sensory-motor transformation, trajectory generation,* and *visual-error correction.* Target selection is, in general, dependent on the the task to be performed. Once the target is selected visually, sensorimotor transformation is required to convert the target's visual activity into the corresponding motor command. This requires that the sensory signals should be converted into *consistent* motor signals so that the trajectory generator moves the arm smoothly to the final position. Often, due to various sources of errors, inconsistencies may arise between the sensory and motor systems. The final arm position may not reach the target, and a visual error may remain even though there may be no motor error. Therefore, a visual-error feedback mechanism is necessary to compensate for such inconsistencies and to correct the arm position.

In this paper, we propose a neural network architecture capable of fast and consistent sensorimotor learning and visual-error correction. The visual-error correction mechanism (VEC) which we developed, does not require the learning of Jacobian matrices. Instead, VEC is an *on-line* visual servoing mechanism as a result of short-term memory (STM) interactions. A major advantage of such an on-line servoing mechanisms is that it allows the system to operate properly even during its learning (re-organization) phase. The resulting motor behavior consists of a mainly two-phase movement observed in many biological systems [1][3]: (i) A feed-forward dominant phase that brings the hand near the target, and (ii) smaller amplitude corrective movements that use visual feedback.

The proposed neural network architecture has a very simple external control interface, and it can be easily integrated with higher-order cognitive networks to fulfill the four steps of visually guided reaching.

2 The Proposed Neural Network

The proposed neural network architecture, shown in Fig. 1, consists of a spatiotopic representation of hand position (Q), target position (U), and a set of three-dimensional (3D) loci where spatiotopic errors are computed (S). Each neuron in S fans-out to motor target position neurons via outstars (W). The outstars encode adaptively a consistent visuo-motor mapping. The network architecture described in this paper is specifically configured for a 3 degrees-of-freedom (DOF) robot with a pair of video cameras for sensory inputs. The architecture, however, can be extended to control a n-DOF robot, as long as the kinematics redundancy can be resolved.

Three *mutually exclusive* signals for mode control are available to external sources: M_B for *babble*, M_P for *performance*, and M_H for *homing*. The babble mode is when the robot learns the sensorimotor mapping from self-generated arm movements (primary circular reactions). The performance mode is when the robot recalls a learned arm posture from the corresponding visual activity of a target. The homing mode is where the robot corrects the arm posture using the visual error. Usually, the homing mode is entered automatically near the end of the performance mode, when the hand is within a certain "spatiotopic radius" of the target.

For each joint on the robot, a motor network is required. Each motor network has five layers of neurons: B, D, T, V, and P. Each layer consists of two neurons representing the two opponent muscle channels: *agonist* and *antagonist*. We incorporated the Adaptive-Vector-Integration-To-Endpoint (AVITE) model developed by Gaudiano and Grossberg [2] as the core of our motor network. The AVITE model is represented by layer T, V and P of Fig. 1.

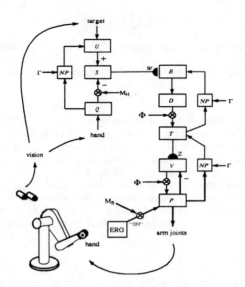

Figure 1: The proposed neural network architecture.

The video cameras are the sensory inputs to the proposed neural network. The activities of the spatiotopic maps, U and Q are computed from the image centroids of the *target* and *hand*, respectively. Activities of U and Q interact in S to produce the appropriate sensory activity for learning, recall, and correction.

Each spatiotopic map is a 3D neuron lattice of dimension $X_u \times Y_u \times Z_u$. The activities of the spatiotopic maps are defined as

$$Q_{ijk} = \left[\frac{1}{\sigma\sqrt{2\pi}} e^{-\frac{(i-i^h)^2+(j-j^h)^2+(k-k^h)^2}{2\pi\sigma^2}} - M_B\theta_t \right]^R, \tag{1}$$

$$U_{ijk} = \frac{\Phi}{\sigma\sqrt{2\pi}} e^{-\frac{(i-i^t)^2+(j-j^t)^2+(k-k^t)^2}{2\pi\sigma^2}} + \Gamma Q_{ijk}, \tag{2}$$

$$S_{ijk} = [U_{ijk} - M_H Q_{ijk}]^R, \tag{3}$$

where $i = 1\ldots X_u$, $j = 1\ldots Y_u$, $k = 1\ldots Z_u$, and $[a]^R = \max(0, a)$. Parameter σ defines the degree of Gaussian spread, θ_t defines the signal threshold, and $\Gamma = M_B(1 - g_p)$ is the *learn* signal. Parameter g_p is the ERG-OFF signal generated by the neural oscillators. Indices (i^h, j^h, k^h) and (i^t, j^t, k^t) are generated from the stereoscopic image coordinates of the hand and target, respectively. The superscripts, 'h' and 't', denote indices of the *hand* and *target*, respectively. The indices for the hand are computed according to

$$i^h = X_L^h/R_x, \quad j^h = Y_L^h/R_y, \quad k^h = \frac{\alpha Z_u}{D_x^h/R_z + \alpha},$$

where R_x, R_y, and R_z are reduction factors for each of the three dimensions. The x-disparity, D_x^h, contains the range information. It is computed as $D_x^h = X_L^h - X_R^h$, where X_L^h and X_R^h are the x-coordinates of the centroids of the hand's left and right image, respectively. Parameter α is simply a positive constant, such that at infinity ($D_x^h = 0$), k^h is bounded by Z_u. The target indices are also computed the same way, except that 'h' is changed to 't'.

A set of *outstar* connections, W, forms the sensorimotor network that bridges the visual space to the motor space. The source nodes of these *outstars* are the neurons in S, and the output nodes are the neurons in B. These outstar networks learn the sensorimotor mapping between the visual and motor modalities according to the following equations:

$$\frac{dB_{ml}}{dt} = -aB_{ml} + b\Phi \sum_{ijk} S_{ijk} W_{ijkml} + c\Gamma T_{ml}, \tag{4}$$

$$\frac{dW_{ijkml}}{dt} = \Gamma S_{ijk}(-\tilde{c}W_{ijkml} + \tilde{e}B_{ml}), \tag{5}$$

where a, b, c, $\tilde{c}$, $\tilde{e}$ are positive constants. Eq. (4) represents the STM dynamics of the output neurons, where $m = 1\ldots3$ is the joint index, and $l \in (+/-)$ denotes *agonist* (+) or *antagonist* (−) muscle channels. Parameter $\Phi = M_P + M_H$ modulates the *outflow* of motor commands so that, during *performance* and *homing*, the outflow paths are enabled. Eq. (5) represents the dynamics of the adaptive connections, where (i, j, k) are the spatiotopic map indices.

One benefit of using the outstars for sensorimotor learning is their abilities to perform both fast and slow learning. This feature is evident in the steady-state solutions of Eqs. (4) and (5) during learning, when $\Phi = 0$ and $\Gamma = 1$. Combining with the steady-state solution of Eq. (4), the steady-state solution of Eq. (5) can be written as $W_{ijkml} = \tilde{\mu}T_{ml}$, where $\tilde{\mu} = (\tilde{e}c)/(\tilde{c}a)$. This shows that W_{ijkml} will encode the motor pattern in T_{ml} during learning. Therefore, *fast learning* can be implemented simply by copying the motor pattern into the appropriate weights. Since the outstars encode the normalized motor patterns [4], the recalled patterns must also be normalized. This is accomplished by the normalizing layer, D, which obeys

$$\frac{dD_{m+}}{dt} = (1 - D_{m+})B_{m+} - D_{m+}B_{m-}. \tag{6}$$

Since each layer in the motor network contains two opponent channels (agonist/antagonist) whose dynamic equations has the same form, only agonist channel equations are shown in this paper. The ability of D to normalize the motor pattern in B is evident from the steady-state solution of Eq. (6).

We used the Endogenous Random Generator (ERG) [2] to synchronize learning during the babble mode. This allows a consistent learning of intermodal and intramodal maps. The theory and equations behind the AVITE and ERG are well-documented by Gaudiano and Grossberg [2]. Therefore, we will not elaborate on this subject.

3 Network Operation

The proposed neural network has three modes of operation: *babble*, *performance* and *homing*. The *babble* mode is further broken down into two phases: *active* and *quiet*. Fig. 2 summarizes the various modes of operation.

During the babble mode ($M_B = 1$), the robot learns from self-generated actions. A random, new arm posture is generated by the ERG-ON channel during the *active phase*, while the hand is visually tracked by Q. At the offset of ERG-ON, the robot will stop moving, and ERG-OFF will become active, and opens all the NP gates to start the *quiet phase*. The *quiet phase* is when the current arm position, P, is printed into T and B, so that simultaneous, consistent, learning of W and Z can take place. In the visual modality, opened NP gate will cause the visual activity of the hand, represented by Q, to be printed into S through U. Note that, during the babble mode, outflow of motor command is blocked ($\Phi = 0$). The active-quiet cycle will repeated indefinitely until M_B is turned off.

The performance mode ($M_P = 1$) is when the robot executes motor patterns recalled from the target's visual activity, U. In this mode, the $Q \to S$ pathway is blocked, leaving U to recall the motor pattern through the $S \to B$ pathway. Also, Φ will open the outflow pathways in the motor network, permitting the embedded AVITE to generate the necessary trajectories.

Due to various sources of errors, the performance mode alone may not place the hand at the target. Therefore, the homing mode ($M_H = 1$) is entered to carry out the VEC mechanism. In our implementation, VEC is activated whenever $d_f \le r_f$, where r_f is a predefined *spatiotopic radius*, and

$$d_f = \sqrt{(i^t - i^h)^2 + (j^t - j^h)^2}. \tag{7}$$

During the homing mode ($M_H = 1$), both $Q \to S$ and $U \to S$ pathways are opened, resulting in a neural computation of $S = [U - Q]^R$. Fig. 3 shows the effects of such a computation. In Fig. 3A, the subtraction between the Gaussian spheres from U and Q creates a *zero plane* where on one side the plane, $S_{ijk} > 0$, and the other side, $S_{ijk} < 0$. With the negative result clipped by the $[.]^R$ operator, as is shown in Fig. 3B, only those $S_{ijk} > 0$ will contribute to the computation of the motor command. According to Eq. (4), the recalled motor command is a weighted average of learned motor patterns associated with nonzero S_{ijk}. Therefore, the result of clipping will cause the arm to move closer toward the target. The closer the hand is to the target, the greater the amount of clipping. Consequently, the arm will continue moving toward the target until Q and U fully overlaps and the hand reached the target.

This visual-error correction (VEC) mechanism has two other desirable features. First, any overshoot of the hand over the target will cause the clipping to appear on the other side, thus causing the arm to move

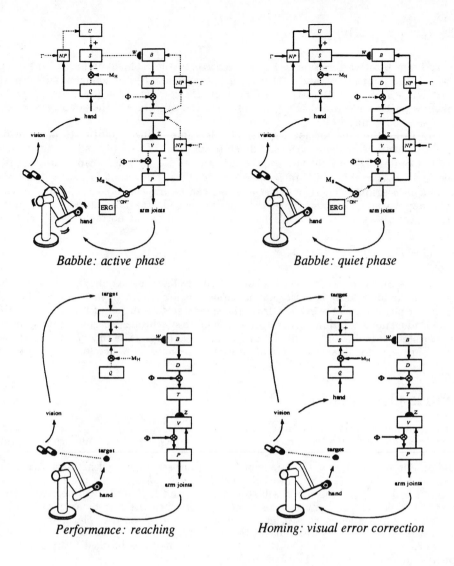

Figure 2: The operating modes of the proposed neural network.

back. Second, the damping of arm movement is automatic, because $\|S\| \to 0$ as the hand moves closer to the target.

To carry out the analysis of this error correction scheme, one needs to relate joint angles to the corresponding spatial coordinates of the tip of the arm, *i.e.*, the kinematics of the arm. To do the analysis independent of the arm structure, we will simply assume that the activation of a set of outstars causes a movement of the arm *towards the spatial point corresponding to the mean, or the "center of gravity" of the activated outstars*. The center of gravity, $\mathcal{G}(\mathbf{x}_t, S)$, is defined as $\mathcal{G}(\mathbf{x}_t, S) = \sum_{\mathbf{x} \in S} G(\mathbf{x}, \mathbf{x}_t) \cdot \mathbf{x}$, where $\mathbf{x} = (i, j, k)$ represents a point in the visual space with coordinates (i, j, k); $\mathbf{x}_t = (i^t, j^t, k^t)$ is the position of the target; $G(\mathbf{x}, \mathbf{x}_t)$ is a Gaussian function defined as

$$ G(\mathbf{x}, \mathbf{x}_t) = \frac{1}{\sigma \sqrt{2\pi}} e^{-\frac{(i-i^t)^2 + (j-j^t)^2 + (k-k^t)^2}{2\pi\sigma^2}}, \tag{8} $$

and $\mathcal{S}$ is the set of "activated" points, *i.e.*, $\mathcal{S} = \{\mathbf{x} = (i, j, k) \mid S_{ijk} > 0\}$.

When $\mathcal{S}$ equals the whole visual space, $\mathcal{G}(\mathbf{x}_t, S) = \mathbf{x}_t$. The center of gravity for a subset, $\mathcal{S}'$, of the visual space may deviate from $\mathbf{x}_t$. Moreover, since AVITE has been analyzed elsewhere [2], we will simply let $P_{ml} = D_{ml}$.

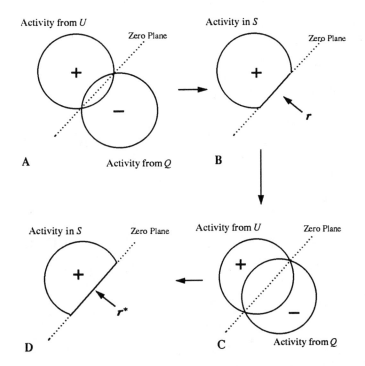

(**A**) *As the hand gets closer to the target, activities of U and Q will overlap.* (**B**) *The result of S computing* $[U - Q]^R$ *will generate a clipped Gaussian sphere that gives a stronger bias to those recalled motor patterns that contribute to moving the hand in the direction* **r**. (**C**) *Arm movement along* **r** *will cause a greater overlap between the activities of U and Q, therefore, a greater amount of clipping will result.* (**D**) *Additional clippings will further strengthen the influence of those motor patterns that contributes to arm movement toward the target until the two spheres completely overlap. If the hand overshoots the target, then the overlap will appear on the other side of the zero plane, and the recalled motor pattern will move the hand back.*

Figure 3: Interactions between spatiotopic maps, U and Q, under the VEC mechanism.

Let $\mathbf{x}_t = (i^t, j^t, k^t)$ be the position of the target and $\mathbf{x}_h = (i^h, j^h, k^h)$ the position of the hand generated by the network in the performance mode (all in the visual space). Usually, one should have $\mathbf{x}_t = \mathbf{x}_h$. But due to various sources of error, $\mathbf{x}_t \neq \mathbf{x}_h$, and a visual error, $\mathbf{e} = \mathbf{x}_t - \mathbf{x}_h$, occurs. When the homing mode is entered, S_{ijk} changes from U_{ijk} to $[U_{ijk} - Q_{ijk}]^R$. As a result, the set, $\mathcal{S}$, is reduced from the whole visual space to a smaller subset.

We will define $\mathbf{x}_m$ as $\mathbf{x}_m = \frac{1}{2}(\mathbf{x}_t + \mathbf{x}_h)$, and let $\mathbf{u}$ and $\mathbf{v}$ be two nonzero linearly independent vectors on the plane passing by $\mathbf{x}_m$ and perpendicular to $\mathbf{e}$. Then $\mathbf{x} \in \mathcal{S}$ if and only if there exist $\tilde{\alpha}, \tilde{\beta}$ and $\tilde{\gamma} > 0$, such that $\mathbf{x} = \mathbf{x}_m + \tilde{\alpha}\mathbf{v} + \tilde{\beta}\mathbf{u} + \tilde{\gamma}\mathbf{e}$. To show this, note that, during the homing mode, $S_{ijk} = [U_{ijk} - Q_{ijk}]^R$, with

$$U_{ijk} = \frac{1}{\sigma\sqrt{2\pi}}e^{-\frac{(i-i^t)^2+(j-j^t)^2+(k-k^t)^2}{2\pi\sigma^2}} \tag{9}$$

and

$$Q_{ijk} = \frac{1}{\sigma\sqrt{2\pi}}e^{-\frac{(i-i^h)^2+(j-j^h)^2+(k-k^h)^2}{2\pi\sigma^2}}. \tag{10}$$

Since the 3D Gaussian function has spherical symmetry, $U_{ijk} = Q_{ijk}$ for points $\mathbf{x} = (i, j, k)$ satisfying the parametric equation,

$$\mathbf{x} = \mathbf{x}_m + \tilde{\alpha}\mathbf{v} + \tilde{\beta}\mathbf{u}. \tag{11}$$

Since the 3D Gaussian function is a decreasing function of the distance from the origin, $U_{ijk} - Q_{ijk} > 0$ for all $\mathbf{x}$ satisfying the parametric equation,

$$\mathbf{x} = \mathbf{x}_m + \tilde{\alpha}\mathbf{v} + \tilde{\beta}\mathbf{u} + \tilde{\gamma}\mathbf{e}, \quad \tilde{\gamma} > 0; \tag{12}$$

and $U_{ijk} - Q_{ijk} < 0$ for all $\mathbf{x}$ satisfying the parametric equation,

$$\mathbf{x} = \mathbf{x}_m + \tilde{\alpha}\mathbf{v} + \tilde{\beta}\mathbf{u} - \tilde{\gamma}\mathbf{e}, \quad \tilde{\gamma} < 0. \tag{13}$$

As a result, $\mathcal{S}$ (denoted by $\mathcal{S}_H$) now consists of points satisfying Eq. (12). This implies that $\mathcal{G}(\mathbf{x}_t, \mathcal{S}_H) = \mathbf{x}_m + \tilde{\alpha}\mathbf{e}$ for some positive constant $\tilde{\alpha}$. Hence, homing mode moves the hand in the direction of the target.

Rewriting Eq. (6) in the form,

$$\frac{dD_{ml}}{dt} = -(\sum_l B_{ml})D_{ml} + B_{ml}, \tag{14}$$

where $l \in (+, -)$, shows that the system will slow down as $\sum_l B_{ml}$ gets smaller. In particular, if we use the steady-state expression of Eq. (4) during recall for B_{ml}, then Eq. (14) becomes

$$\frac{dD_{ml}}{dt} = -\left(\sum_{ijkl} S_{ijk}W_{ijkml}\right)D_{ml} + \sum_{ijk} S_{ijk}W_{ijkml}. \tag{15}$$

This shows that when the arm reaches the target, it will stop, since when $\mathbf{x}_t = \mathbf{x}_h$, $S_{ijk} = 0$ for all i, j, k. and therefore, $\dot{P}_{ml} = \dot{D}_{ml} = 0$.

Oscillations can occur when the learning is insufficient, as illustrated in the following example: Assume that only two outstars are guiding the movement of the hand in the neighborhood of $\mathbf{x}_t$ (this can arise when that region is not sufficiently learned, so that all weights from other outstars are zero). Let the source nodes, $\mathbf{x}^{(1)}$ and $\mathbf{x}^{(2)}$, of these outstars be placed as shown in Fig. 4. When the homing mode starts, $\mathbf{x}^{(1)} \notin S_H$ and

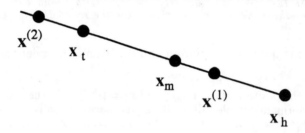

Figure 4: An example of how oscillation can occur when learning is insufficient.

only $\mathbf{x}^{(2)}$ guides the arm. This causes the arm to move towards $\mathbf{x}^{(2)}$; but as soon as the hand crosses to the $\mathbf{x}^{(2)}$ side of the target, $\mathbf{x}^{(1)}$ becomes activated. Consequently, it causes the arm to return to $\mathbf{x}_h$, which yields the original scenario thereby creating an oscillatory pattern.

Various factors, however, will prevent or damp these oscillations. If the trajectory of the hand crosses $\mathbf{x}_t$, the hand will automatically stop on the target. In addition, when the region is sampled more densely, as the hand gets closer to the target, there will be a decrease in $\sum_l B_{ml}$ which, in turn, will slow down significantly the hand near the target.

The particular behavior of the system depends on the structure of the arm as well as the density and distribution of learning samples in a neighborhood. The aforementioned remarks also suggest that the performance will be poorer near the boundaries of the robot's workspace, due to the fact that each of the samples is outside the boundary, so that the distribution of learning samples will be biased.

4   Simulation and Results

The proposed neural network was simulated on an SGI 320VGX graphics workstation running a 3D solid model animation software called Tree Display Manager (TDM). The video cameras were simulated by attaching two view ports on simulated video cameras for display. Frame-grabbing is done by reading the images from the display memory. The neural network equations were integrated using a fourth-order Runge-Kutta solver with an integration step of 0.2. Since the total number of differential equations was very large, we also implemented the fast learning mode.

One of the best ways to evaluate reaching performance is to look at the reach accuracy. For the particular target location, (17, 6, 10), the reach accuracy is recorded in Fig. 5. This plot shows that initially the target and hand are separated by approximately 18 inches from each other. At the instant when the mode changes from perform to homing, the distance is approximately 5.86 inches. After that, the distance decreases to about 1 inch. The small "hump" between $t = 18$ and $t = 25$ (time-steps) is caused by the VEC mechanism, where visual-error feedback are used to compensate an overshoot. The final accuracy achieved for this particular target location is approximately 1 inch (approximately 2% of the robot size), which is within the accuracy allowed by the visual-space quantization limit [5].

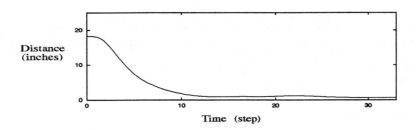

Figure 5: Reach accuracy during performance.

To analyze the network's global performance, we presented the target at 496 different positions for the robot to reach. Out of the 496 target positions, 250 belong to the set of target positions presented to the robot during learning; the other 246 points are generated by commanding the arm to random joint positions while recording the hand's spatial position. The above method of generating target positions ensures that all target positions are *visible* and *reachable* by the robot hand.

To speed up the data gathering process which will otherwise take weeks to compute, we decided to use the target arm position generated by the sensorimotor network directly, without going through the motor networks which, once calibrated, reproduce these positions accurately.

For each target position presented to the robot cameras, an initial move corresponding to the performance mode is carried out. After the initial move, twenty corrective moves corresponding to the homing mode are also carried out to reduce any residual error. The initial move and the follow-on corrective moves are all generated by the sensorimotor network directly, and do not involve the motor network. After the initial and corrective moves are completed, we recorded the relative distance between the target and hand. This process is repeated for the set of 496 target positions.

The above procedure provides a measure of the *global* performance of the neural network after a certain amount of learning. We are interested in seeing how the global performance relates to the amount of learning. So we plotted the average reach-error (over the 496 points) as a function of the number of babbles (*i.e.*, learning trials), and the result is shown in Fig. 6.

The plot shows that after 7000 babbles, the average reach-error remains fairly constant at approximately 1.37 inches, and is slightly higher if the number of babbles is less. Relative to the overall size the robot, which is computed by adding the robot's height and full arm extension (65.4 inches), the average reach-error is only about 2 percent. The lower limit of the error originates mainly from the quantization of the visual space, whose range for $(\Delta x, \Delta y, \Delta z)$ is from (0.6, 0.5, 1), when the arm is at the closest possible position ($Z = 7.3$), to (3.1, 2.5, 15), when the arm is fully extended ($Z = 37.3$). The units of these measurements are in inches.

One of the main benefits of using neural network for robot control is its ability to adapt to plant changes. To evaluate the ability of the proposed neural network in adapting to physical changes, we altered the robot's kinematics by raising the shoulder by 2 inches and by shortening the upper-arm by 3 inches. Then we tested the neural network that was trained by 20000 learning trials (without the robot being altered). One hundred random target positions, which were not part of any previous learning trials, were presented to the robot. The result shows an average reach-error of 1.39 inches (2.13% of the robot size), and a standard deviation of 0.94 inch (1.4% of robot size). It is important to emphasize that this accuracy

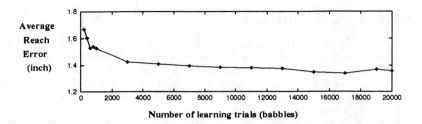

Figure 6: Average error of reach as a function of the number of learning trials.

is obtained without any learning after the modification of the arm only by the corrective effect of VEC.

5 Conclusions

We presented a neural network architecture that shows how a combination of nonlinear feed-forward and feed-back control can yield an efficient learning *and* real-time performance. We showed that the robot can acquire a reach accuracy which is mainly limited by its visual resolution. In addition, we demonstrated that the VEC mechanism can compensate *immediately* for unforeseen perturbations to preserve the accuracy of performance without any learning. It is also important to point out that the proposed mechanism *does not* require the learning of the Jacobian matrix.

Acknowledgements

This material is based in part upon work supported by NASA/JSC and by the Texas Advanced Technology Program under Grant No. 003652023-ATP.

References

[1] W. D. A. Beggs and C. I. Howarth. The accuracy of aiming at a target. *Acta Psychologica*, 36:171–177, 1972.

[2] P. Gaudiano and S. Grossberg. Vector associative maps: Unsupervised real-time error-based learning and control of movement trajectories. *Neural Networks*, 4:147–183, 1991.

[3] A. Georgopolous. On reaching. *Annual Review of Neuroscience*, 9:147–170, 1986.

[4] S. Grossberg. Pattern learning by functional differential neural networks with arbitrary path weights. In K. Schmitt, editor, *Delay and Functional Differential Equations and their Applications*, pages 121–160. Academic Press, New York and London, 1972.

[5] L. Li. Adaptive neural control of visually guided arm movements. Master's thesis, University of Houston, 1993.

PRACTICAL ISSUES IN APPLYING ARTIFICIAL NEURAL NETWORKS FOR IDENTIFICATION IN MODEL BASED PREDICTIVE CONTROL

Joachim Blum, Philippe Villard, Astrid Leuba, Thomas Karjala, and David Himmelblau
Department of Chemical Engineering
The University of Texas, Austin, TX 78712

Abstract

Several investigators have shown that nonparametric model building via artificial neural networks (ANN) can be used with nonlinear programming to implement nonlinear model predictive control (MPC). The use of nonlinear combinations of basis functions in an ANN can often provide models for MPC superior to conventional methods for nonlinear processes. We will discuss how to select an appropriate set of data to be used in training an externally recurrent ANN for modeling nonlinear dynamic processes as well as issues of model validation. In addition, we illustrate the use of an ANN as a process model in an MPC control scheme for parts of the Tennessee Eastman (TE) Test Problem.

1.   Introduction

In this paper we focus on the use of Artificial Neural Networks as models for a model based predictive control strategy.

Most nonlinear control techniques are model based, and thus their success depends substantially on the quality of the model used. This is especially true in the case of model predictive control, where a good dynamic model of the system is essential. Identifying a suitable model is often the major part of the effort necessary to implement model predictive control (MPC). A traditional attempt to develop a model from first principles often proves to be a difficult and costly process because of the large number of variables, poorly understood reaction mechanisms and the overall complexity of the system. Whatever model is developed may well be based on so many simplifying assumptions that its accuracy and utility are degraded.

An alternate approach is to identify the model directly by input/output data collected from the plant. Artificial neural networks (ANN) are one class of nonparameteric identifiers. They have been proven to be capable of approximating any nonlinear function. For this reason they have great potential in nonlinear MPC and have been proposed as process models by several researchers [1, 5, 7, 8, 11].

In following sections we will discuss how an ANN model can be identified and used as a predictor of future system behavior, describe the net architecture implemented for the test problems, and explain how an ANN can be trained effectively for practical applications.

2   Model Identification

To build a predictor, we use a structure capable of predicting an array of N_y measured variables, $y_i(t)$, based on a window of past measurements and of past values of the N_u manipulated variables $u_i(t)$

$$\widehat{y}\left(t\right) = F\left(y\left(t-\Delta t\right),..., y\left(t-T_y\Delta t\right), u\left(t-\Delta t\right),..., u\left(t-T_u\Delta t\right)\right) \tag{1}$$

where u, y, and $\widehat{y}$ are vectors of manipulated variables, measured variables at past time steps (inputs), and predicted variables (outputs), respectively; T_y and T_u set the orders of the model, equal to the number of past values for y and u; and Δt is a uniform time interval. F represent the model and includes a set of adjustable parameters (not shown) that are estimated by minimizing an objective or figure-of-merit function E. E measures the agreement between the data and the predictions of the model. In a conventional maximum likelihood approach we minimize:

$$E = \frac{1}{M_{train}} \sum_{j=1}^{M_{train}} \frac{1}{N_y} \sum_{i=1}^{N_y} \left(\frac{\widehat{y}_{i,j}-y_{i,j}}{\sigma_{i,j}}\right)^2 \tag{2}$$

where $\sigma_{i,j}$ is a weighting factor for variable $y_{i,j}$, and depends on the underlying (generally unknown) distribution of measurement errors. For our purposes it is set to unity. M_{train} is the number of data samples used for identifying the model. N_y is the dimension of y or $\widehat{y}$. To avoid sensitivity to outliers, a more robust objective function based on a Lorentzian distribution would be:

$$E = \frac{1}{M_{train}} \sum_{j=1}^{M_{train}} \frac{1}{N_y} \sum_{i=1}^{N_y} log \left(1 + \frac{1}{2} \left(\widehat{y}_{i,j} - y_{i,j} \right)^2 \right) \tag{3}$$

If we are able to identify a function F well, in application, we can predict $\widehat{y}(t)$ not only one but multiple time steps into the future by successively applying Equation (1) for a moving window of past inputs and outputs. Predicted values $\widehat{y}$ replace measured values of y as the window moves in time along the measurement record. Figure 1 illustrates the "chaining" of a predictor on itself.

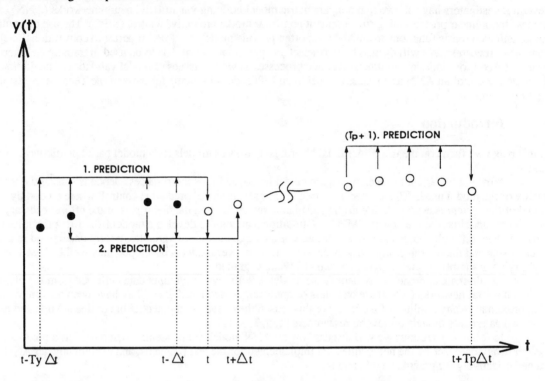

Figure 1: Chaining of a one-step-ahead predictor on itself to obtain multiple-step-ahead predictions: (·) are measured, (○) predicted values of y.

T_p is the number of time steps y is predicted into the future, called the *prediction horizon*. Note that the true values of the manipulated variables $u(t + k\Delta t)$ are assumed to be *known* (or provided by the MPC optimization algorithm— see Section 5), whereas with chaining, the future predictions of y increasingly depend on *prior predicted* values of y as the prediction horizon is extended. This leads to propagation of the prediction error which is also increased as unmeasured disturbances enter the system. The prediction error, therefore, sets a limit on the practical prediction horizon T_p, and requires an error feedback scheme for the strategy to be implemented, as will be explained below.

The predicted trajectories can be used by a model based predictive controller to optimize some system performance objective with respect to the manipulated variables u over the prediction horizon $[t, t+T_p\Delta t]$.

To identify an ANN model, one needs to address the following issues:
- what net architecture will represent the process adequately;
- what training method will estimate the coefficients (weights) of the ANN most efficiently;
- what data must be selected so that the ANN can represent the process adequately in the regions of interest?

Also, during or after training the ANN, one needs to validate / evaluate the performances of the model obtained.

3. The ANN Architecture Used For Modeling

To represent the process model we used an externally recurrent net comprised of one hidden layer of 10 nodes each with sigmoidal activation functions, and an output and input layer each composed of linear activation functions. The input layer received N_y values of y representing delayed output values plus N_u delayed input values. The output layer yielded values of the process output up to N_u future time steps. In the example below there were 45 input nodes representing 3 variables times 15 time steps of u, plus 30 input nodes representing 3 variables times 10 time steps for the delayed outputs. The net had 3 output nodes.

4. Training the Network

The objective function used in this work was Equation (2), hence the training was a minimum squares problem. Ideally, the error index should be the measure of error *while* training the net. In this case, the objective function (2) would be changed to:

$$E = \frac{1}{N_y} \sum_{i=1}^{N_y} \underbrace{\frac{1}{M_{train}} \sum_{j=1}^{M_{train}} \underbrace{\underbrace{\frac{1}{T_p} \sum_{k=1}^{T_p} \left(\hat{y}_i \left(t_j + k\Delta t \right) - y_i \left(t_j + k\Delta t \right) \right)^2}_{\text{mean square error over prediction horizon}}}_{\text{calculated for all sample points in training set}}}_{\text{averaged over all predicted variables}} \tag{4}$$

Referred to as "parallel training," this approach has been suggested as yielding better performance for long-term predictions (e.g. [10], but has not, yet, been implemented in our training scheme yet. Although the goal in training is to create a surface through the training data that minimizes the objective function, it is clear that one could pass an interpolation surface through every sample point in the training set by simply providing a sufficient number of parameters in the ANN such as by increasing the number of hidden nodes or hidden layers. However in fitting the data we really want to create a surface smooth enough to enable good *generalization..* A net possesses good generalization capabilities if it can make good predictions from inputs that were not included in the original training set.

The performance of the net after training and testing is a direct consequence of the quality of the data collected. Usually the training set covers only a sub-space of the entire space of possible measurements. Prediction which involves extrapolation outside of the domain of the data should be considered unreliable, as the network has no apriori information of the underlaying physical phenomena in new regions. Even in regions where data is available, there may not be enough to train the net properly. Furthermore, without an adequate experimental design, measurements in some regions may well have been obtained from steady state operation and consequently do not hold enough information about the dynamic behavior of the system. Without uniformly distributed, or properly weighted, training data, the network's performance will vary greatly across the state space of the predicted variables. Hence, there is clearly a need for building the training and testing sets methodically, not randomly.

If we are simulate a process, we can generate data sets for almost any domain we want. But for a real process, unless designed experiments are possible, we will likely have to work with long data sets of the normal operating record containing mostly steady state data with a relatively small amount of dynamic information caused by perturbations, setpoint changes, etc. Also, the training times for a network with our present hardware become unreasonable if the data sets consist of a few hundred thousand sample points. Consequently, for training and testing we have to either extract subsets of representative data from the recorded process measurements or carry out some form of dimensional reduction, such as principal component analysis, partial least squares, and so on. Another idea would be to apply cluster analysis to the data to provide good coverage of the state space. However, these approaches will not make up for too little dynamic information.

We built a suitable training set via an iterative process based on using the network itself to detect poorly modeled regions of the state space. After the net was trained on a set of data, predictions were made for various other operating conditions, and from the regions in which the predictions were poor, additional data was then added to the training set, and a net with the same architecture trained again on the new training set. The new data can either be taken from a collected data base—but for values not previously used in the training or testing set (as was done in our work), or—if no more data in the critical regions is available—duplicated from the existing data in the training set similar to bootstrapping. This step is equivalent to giving more weight to the sparse data relative to that in the well populated regions.

As to the size of the necessary data sets, for the example below, our first training set contained about 150,000 patterns, and the testing set about 25,000, input/output patterns.

In the example below, we used the NPSOL [6] code in lieu of other codes to train the networks because the training time was less by an order of magnitude compared to BFGS or Conjugate Gradients, it was easy to use, and NPSOL allows for the specification of constraints. This option opens the way for various improvements in the training of networks [11]. We used this feature to put limits on the weights in order to avoid saturation effects in the nodes of the next layer.

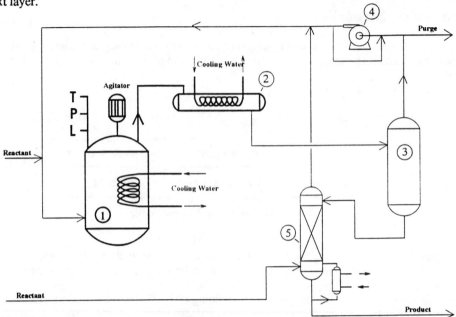

Figure 2: Diagram of Tennessee Eastman Test Problem. (1) Reactor, (2) Condenser, (3) Separator, (4) Compressor, (5) Stripper, (ANN-identified part in bold).

5   The Test Problem

The Tennessee Eastman simulator has been made available to the process control community as a realistic process for the testing of different control strategies [2]. This simulator (coded in FORTRAN) is based on an existing industrial process and is suitable for the study of a wide variety of control issues.

The process makes two products from four reactants. An inert product and a by-product are also present, making a total of eight components. It contains five major unit operations: a reactor, a product condenser, a vapor/liquid separator, a recycle compressor, and a product stripper. A diagram of the whole process is shown in Figure 2.

To provide an example, we identified and controlled the reactor and the condenser unit.
- The predicted and controlled variables were the temperature, the pressure, and the level of the reactor. For each predicted variable, a moving window of 10 measurements was fed to the net input layer. The variables to be manipulated were the reactor cooling water flow, the condenser cooling water flow, and the reactor agitator speed. For each command variable, a moving window of 15 past values was fed to the input layer. Thus, there were 75 input and 3 output nodes altogether.
- To find the optimal number of hidden nodes, the net was initially configured with 10 hidden nodes. During training, additional units were automatically added and subtracted to check whether a changed number of hidden nodes yielded better generalization results on the test set. However, 10 hidden nodes proved to be suitable for this problem.
- The orders of the model with respect to the manipulated and predicted variables, T_u and T_y, respectively, were found by training various nets with different window sizes for both parameters. Figure 3 shows a comparison of four nets each with different window sizes for the manipulated and

predicted variable inputs. Net 3 ($T_u = 15$, $T_y = 10$) was found to have the lowest prediction error of all. This result confirms the rule found for digital filters (IIR) that the filter/model should be of higher order with respect to the command variables to avoid introducing instability into the system (by feeding back the predicted output to the input). Based on an error index, the maximum prediction horizon for the MPC application of the (15/10) net was limited to 500 steps.

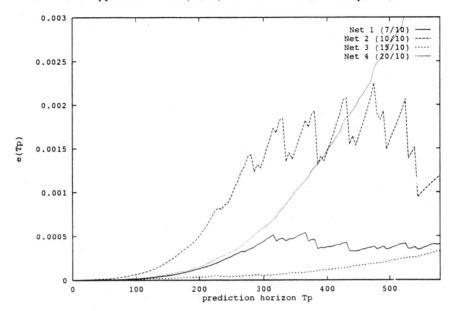

Figure 3. Error indexes for nets with different window sizes (T_u/T_y), trained and tested on the same dta sets.

- In a similar fashion an adequate spacing $\Delta t = t_{j+1} - t_j$ for the input nodes was investigated. Several nets of the same configuration were trained and tested on the same data set with only the time interval between past measurements being different. It was found that $\Delta t = 10s$ gave the best results. There seems to be no general way of determining a suitable Δt; rather the choice will always depend on the inherent dynamics of the modeled system (time constants, dead times, etc.). In our work, with $T_u = 15$ and $\Delta t = 10s$, the input of the net covered a reactor history of 2.5 minutes because of the time-delayed dynamics of the plant's recycle loop.
- The collection of training and testing data was a two-step process. Because of the open-loop instability of the reactor with respect to changes in the manipulated variables (see below), we first generated data corresponding to system responses to step changes of the command variables (simultaneous and/or individual). These runs were of short duration, since the controlled variables quickly went out of control and reached their shutdown limits. With this data on hand we trained a preliminary net that was incorporated into the MPC scheme. The performance of the controller using the poor model was not satisfactory, but allowed us to generate data for a wide range of changes in both manipulated and controlled variables covering a broader region of input space. The final net presented here was trained and tested on this data. In practice, an existing control system could be used to generate the necessary data if open loop data was inadequate.

The reactor exhibited a clear tendency to "run away." It was possible to stabilize the rest of the plant (stripper, separator, compressor) with simple PI-controllers. The reactor, however, could not be made to follow setpoint-changes in temperature and pressure by installing PI loops: Not only was the base case operation mode of the reactor ($p = 2705kPa$, $T = 120.4°C$, $L = 75\%$) highly unstable, but the dynamics of the three controlled variables and the three manipulated variables could not be separated into three independent control loops.

We implemented a MIMO (Multiple Input Multiple Output) control scheme using a model-based predictive controller with the ANN representing the reactor. For a detailed discussion of nonlinear model predictive control, refer to [3] or [9]. Based on predictions of the process model—in this case the trained neural network—a future profile of command variable moves **u** is determined by the controller which will drive the behavior of controlled variables **y** as close as possible to a desired trajectory. This is achieved by solving a minimization problem with the manipulated variables being the independent variables. The objective function represents a measure of the deviations of the predicted from the wanted trajectory of **y**. We also added terms to penalize excessive variations in the control moves to the objective function, i.e., a form of regularization. The profile of **u** on the time interval $[t,t+T_C\Delta t]$, where T_C is the *control horizon*, is usually approximated by a sequence of constant-valued, equal-length segments of **u**.

Theory shows that an infinite horizon control is capable of stabilizing any system, provided that a good model is available. Shorter horizons represent one limitation of applied MPC. The neural net predictor can forecast with a reasonable error on a finite horizon. Choosing a suitable prediction horizon consequently means compromising between a) a horizon long enough to ensure stability of the controlled system, and b) a horizon short enough to avoid instability via accumulating prediction errors. To account for prediction errors and resulting steady-state offsets or for unmeasured disturbances entering the system, an error estimation and feedback scheme is necessary. However, an inappropriate feedback scheme can destabilized the transition from one setpoint to another, so we did not include any feedback of error. Linked to the feedback problem is the question of how frequently the controller should update its output, the optimized profile of command values, **u**. In general, the more often the profile is computed, the better the performance of the controller, but obviously an update at every time step is not feasible because of current computational time requirements both to obtain net responses and execute NPSOL.

Figure 4 shows a successful attempt to drive the reactor temperature from one setpoint (120°C) to another (140°C).

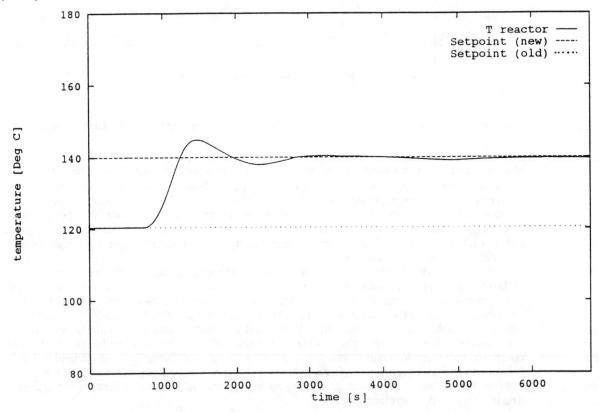

Figure 4: Result of a setpoint change for the reactor temperature; $T_p = 500$, $T_c = 500$.

Figure 5 displays the optimal control profiles of the reactor and condenser coolant flow corresponding to Figure 4.

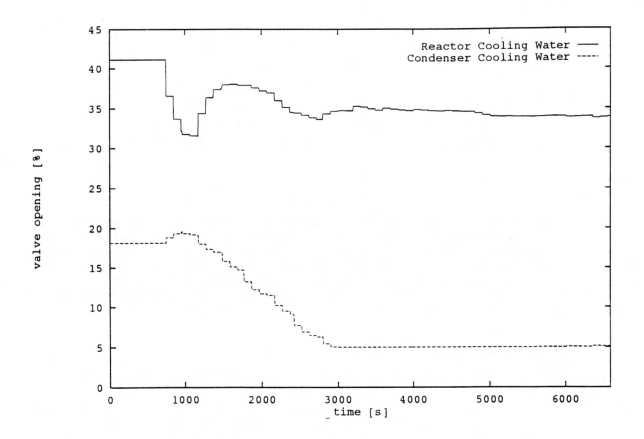

Figure 5: Result of a setpoint change for the reactor temperature: command profile.

References

1   Bhat, N., McAvoy, T., *Use of Neural Nets for Dynamic Modeling and Control of Chemical Process Systems*, Computers and Chemical Engineering, Vol. 14, pp. 573-583, 1990.

2   Downs, J., Vogel, E., *A Plant-Wide Industrial Process Control Problem*, submitted for Computers and Chemical Engineering, 1992.

3   Eaton, J., Rawlings, J., *Feedback Control of Chemical Processes using On-line Optimization Techniques*, Computers and Chemical Engineering, Vol. 14, pp. 469-479, 1990.

4   Gill, P., Murray, W., Saunders, M., and Wright, M., *User's Guide for SOL/NPSOL: A Fortran Package for Nonlinear Programming*, Technical Report SOL 83-12, System Optimization Laboratory, Department of Operations Research, Stanford University, 1983.

5   Haesloop, D., Holt, B., *A Neural Network Structure for System Identification*, 1990 American Automatic Control Conference, Vol. 3.

6   Hsiung, J., Suewatanakul, and Himmelblau, D., *Should Back Propagation Be Replaced By More Effective Optimization Algorithms ?*, Proceedings of IJCNN, Seattle, 1991.

7   Narendra, K., Parthasarathy, K., *Identification and Control of Dynamical Systems Using Neural Networks*, IEEE Transactions on Neural Networks, Vol. 1, March 1990.

8   Saint Donat, J., Bhat, N., and McAvoy, T., *Optimizing Neural Net Based Predictive Control*, 1990 American Automatic Control Conference.

9   Seborg, D., Edgar, T., Mellichamp, D., *Process Dynamics and Control*, John Wiley and Sons, 1989.

10   Su, H., McAvoy, T., *Identification of Chemical Processes Via Parallel Training of Neural Networks*, Ind. Eng. Chem. Res., Vol. 31, pp. 1338-1352, 1992.

11   Ydstie, B., *Forecasting and Control Using Adaptive Connectionist Networks*, Computers and Chemical Engineering, Vol. 14, pp. 583-599, 1990.

Neural Subgoal Generation with Subgoal Graph: An Approach

M. Eldracher *

Fakultät für Informatik, Technische Universität München,
80290 München, Germany, email: eldrache@informatik.tu-muenchen.de

Abstract

Building a world model for manipulators is computationally expensive. If the environment changes over time and no further information is provided, other than that a local misfit has occurred, classical algorithms have to start the model's computation anew. In order to plan complex trajectories, hierarchical planning shows many advantages. In this article we report on an approach, that hierarchically combines sub-trajectories using symbolic graph search techniques and a sub-symbolic neural classification and generalization preprocessing system. We combine a graph of possible subgoals in configuration space with a mapping from configuration space on to this graph.

1 Motivation and Introduction

Trajectory generation for manipulators is a difficult problem, up to now not satisfyingly solved. Despite several classical algorithms are able to construct collision free paths (e.g. (Latombe, 1991)) using only very limited computational resources, there does not exist a general satisfying solution. Typically classical algorithms are based on world models. The construction of a world model takes exponential costs with the number of obstacles to be avoided. Thus feasible solutions for real-world problems can not be provided due to many obstacles. If the environment is slowly changing this problem is aggravated, because a full recomputation must be done after each incremental change.

Glavina (1991) introduces an approach that does not need a world model. In order to construct a path between two points in joint space, the system tries to use a straight trajectory (with a sliding mechanism that is necessary to avoid too many failures). If no straight trajectory can be found, the system successively generates random subgoals. To find a path, all tested straight sub-trajectories between start, generated random subgoals, and goal are stored. A path is then found via graph search methods. Although the algorithm is stochastically complete, the approach in practice suffers from several disadvantages: First the number of subgoals that are tested must be limited (and the search is no more complete). Second the system does in no way optimize the generated trajectories during planning. Third the system does not use knowledge available from prior search.

We want to construct a system that takes the advantages from (Glavina, 1991) but avoids the disadvantages. Following (Glavina, 1991) we plan hierarchically, combining straight trajectories that connect start and goal via subgoals. Opposite to (Glavina, 1991) subgoals are not randomly generated anew for each task, but chosen in order to yield a generally valid subgoal graph for all tasks. This provides the advantage that after construction we can always use the same subgoals without further search.

2 Approach

In order to construct complex collision free trajectories, collision free simpler trajectories are combined. We only use straight trajectories in joint space, but arbitrarily shaped sub-trajectories could be used. If

---

*This work has been funded by the German Ministry for Research and Technology (BMFT) under FKZ FKZ 01 IN 102 B/0. The authors are solely responsible for the contents of this publication.

a straight collision free trajectory exists between two configurations, we call these configurations *directly connected*.

If start and goal are not directly connected, we use subgoals. All sub-trajectories between subgoals in the subgoal graph as well as between subgoals and arbitrary start or goal, have to be directly connected. The idea is to construct a subgoal graph, that allows the following path planning approach: At a first step the closest directly connected *nodes* in the subgoal graph for start and goal are determined. This can be done via testing whether each one of all nodes is directly connected to start or goal. (A different approach is proposed in section 4.) At a second step the subgoal graph is searched for direct connections between subgoals that allow to connect the stored nodes from the first step.

In order to allow the proposed algorithm the subgoal graph has to fulfill the following conditions:

1. Each arbitrary configuration must be directly connected to at least one of the nodes in the subgoal graph.

2. Each two nodes in the subgoal graph must be connected to each other.

To construct the graph, we perform the following procedure. First we chose an arbitrary configuration as first node . Next we choose random configurations to enlarge the subgoal graph. If a random configuration is directly connected to at least one of the nodes graph we check, whether it should be inserted in the set of *candidates* that will probably be inserted into the subgoal graph, soon. If a random configuration is not directly connected any node, we test, whether this configuration is directly connected with the set of candidates. If so, we insert the closest, directly connected candidate into the subgoal graph. This insertion guarantees that the subgoal graph remains connected, as all candidates are directly connected to at least one of the previous nodes. If the random position is not directly connected to the candidate set, we forget about this configuration for the moment and put it into a set of *disconnected* configurations. (Of course we could start a new part of the subgoal graph with this random configuration. It would not be guaranteed any more, that the subgoal graph is connected. Furthermore it is expensive to check whether disconnected parts of a subgoal graph can be reconnected).

If many random configurations are tested, the subgoal graph spans the whole configuration space, if an appropriate heuristics for choosing the candidate set is applied. The simplest technique is to store a fixed number that fulfill the following condition: Of all generated random configurations the candidates are that configurations that have the longest distance to the nearest directly connected node. A technique that yields a better distribution is to use the following criterion: Choose as candidates a fixed number of configurations that have the largest sum of distances between the closest node graph and all other directly connected candidates. If one of the candidates is not directly connected, add a certain maximum distance instead. These heuristics can be further improved, if there are different candidate sets for each node.

After developing the subgoal graph the set of disconnected configurations can be used to test, whether the whole configuration space is directly connected to the subgoal graph. Of course the test could be performed with a new set of random configurations.

3   Results of Graph Construction

For the tests we use two simulation environments for manipulators with two degrees of freedom. Figures 1, 2 and 3, 4 show the environments with their corresponding configuration spaces. In configuration space figures the axes denote the angles of the two joints. White points show configurations that do not collide. Black points show configurations that collide.

Configuration space figures also show three sets of configurations: Black circles mark nodes of the subgoal graph. White circles denote candidates. Black squares label the disconnected. It is interesting, that the disconnected were only disconnected during generation of the subgoal graph, but are directly connected to the nodes graph or at least the candidates after 5000 random configurations were tested. Thus each arbitrary combination of start and goal configurations can be connected using the subgoal graph.

For the environment in Fig. 1 there was only used a common set of ten candidates for all nodes. The insert heuristic for the candidate set was simply "longest distance to the nearest directly connected subgoal graph node". Only three nodes suffice to cover the whole space.

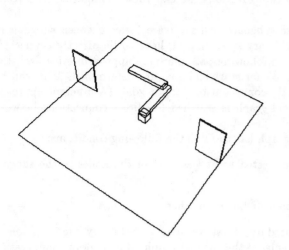

Figure 1: *Two-linked manipulator with two walls as obstacles.*

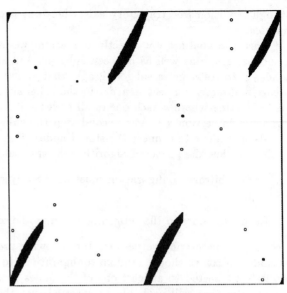

Figure 2: *Configuration space of Fig 1.*

For the environment in Fig. 3 a different candidate set of each ten candidates is used for each node. Furthermore the more complicated heuristics described above is used to insert candidates. Nevertheless using only three candidates in each list and the simple candidate heuristics suffices to produce similar results. The main difference is, that more configurations are temporarily put into the disconnected set, if less candidates are used. Only seventeen nodes suffice to get a one hundred percent task solving ratio within our system.

4 Interlinking the Subgoal Graph with Neural Preprocessing

It is expensive to test all nodes and candidates for all random configurations during construction of the subgoal graph. Neural preprocessing allows to save a lot of computational costs. If a neural network gives the node that is directly connected to previously tested neighboring configurations of the current random configuration, normally only this node has to be tested. If unexpectedly this node is not directly connected, still all other nodes can be tested.

Training of such a neural preprocessor is done straight forward. If a random configuration is directly connected to a node, the neural network is trained using this configuration as input and the directly connected node as output. It is intended to use a CMAC (Albus, 1981) for this neural preprocessor. Compared to backpropagation networks CMAC shows the advantage, that it can be trained incrementally because of its local generalization.

After termination of the subgoal graph construction the neural net has stored the corresponding nodes for every configuration. Thus a search for the next node in the subgoal graph may be omitted by simply asking the neural preprocessor for that node. This considerably speeds up the use of the subgoal graph.

5 Discussion

Our approach shows many advantages over competing algorithms. Opposite to Glavina (1991) there is no need to search anew for subgoals for every task. The subgoal graph has all necessary subgoals for all tasks. That is, knowledge about the configuration space is stored. As a second advantage this knowledge is used in order to save the expensive evaluation of directly connected or not, as this information is inherent in subgoal graph and neural preprocessing. Therefore (after training) the subgoal graph approach is even faster than random search. During subgoal path construction there is furthermore the possibility to incorporate optimization constraints by varying the heuristics for the candidates.

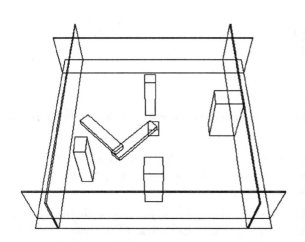

Figure 3: *Two-linked manipulator with four boxes and four walls as obstacles.*

Figure 4: *Configuration space of Fig 3.*

Compared to Eldracher and Baginski (1993b), Eldracher and Baginski (1993a) and Schmidhuber and Wahnsiedler (1992) our approach has the advantage, that an arbitrary number of subgoals is produced depending on the task. Furthermore there is no need to double the input space, as needed for the evaluation function in the articles cited above. Input space doubling hinders application of such subgoal generation systems for manipulators with more than three degrees of freedom (Baginski, 1993).

Compared to classical algorithms (Latombe, 1991) path planning is possible for areas that are already explored, even if no complete model is available. Classical approaches have to compute the whole model first. Furthermore there remains the adaptability of the neural preprocessor. This allows to retrain constantly in order to react on slowly changing environments. Should the change in the environment cause a node to fall into an area that causes collisions, there still remains the possibility to reuse the graph generation process to get an adapted graph. This is computationally cheap as there are only very few nodes in the subgoal graph (opposite to a complete reconstruction of the world model in classical approaches). It could also be thought about moving the nodes according to a Kohonen-like procedure. But this would require a continuous test whether all nodes remain directly connected to other nodes. As this test is the most expensive computation in our approach, it seems not worth to do that.

Regarding the system from a different point, it becomes clear, why it shows so many advantages. The neural preprocessor does something like a cell decomposition. But opposite to classical cell decomposition the mapping onto the subgoal graph gives cells of arbitrary shape. Thus only very few cells suffice to cover the whole free space. Furthermore the combination of symbolic graph search with sub-symbolic preprocessing takes the advantages of both paradigms.

6 Conclusion

It is shown that our approach produces subgoals in order to combine simpler trajectories to complexer ones. Per construction a varying number of subgoals is produced, depending on the task at hand. The approach is not fully implemented yet, but the core, the subgoal graph generation is already tested. Neural preprocessing is a relatively simple classification task and therefore it is not expected, that there will arise any major problems from this part. The subgoal graphs produced show, that very small graphs suffice to yield a path planner that will outperform each of the known planning algorithms with respect to speed, planning success or adaptability.

Reference

Albus, J. S. (Ed.). (1981). *Brains, Behaviour, and Robotics*. Byte Books, Subsidiary of McGraw-Hill. ISBN 0-07-000975-9.

Baginski, B. (1993). Neuronale Generierung von Subzielen für Roboter. Fortgeschrittenenpraktikum. Technische Universität München.

Eldracher, M., & Baginski, B. (1993a). Hierarchical planning using neural subgoal generation. In *Proceedings of IEEE SMC'93*.

Eldracher, M., & Baginski, B. (1993b). Neural subgoal generation using backpropagation. In Lendaris, G. G., Grossberg, S., & Kosko, B. (Eds.), *World Congress on Neural Networks*, pp. III–145–III–148. Lawrence Erlbaum Associates, Inc., Publishers, Hillsdale.

Glavina, B. (1991). *Planung kollisionsfreier Bewegungen für Manipulatoren durch Kombination von zielgerichteter Suche und zufallsgesteuerter Zwischenzielerzeugung. Dissertation.* Ph.D. thesis, Technische Universität München.

Latombe, J.-C. (Ed.). (1991). *Robot Motion Planning* (3 edition). Kluwer Academic Press, Boston.

Schmidhuber, J. H., & Wahnsiedler, R. (1992). Planning simple trajectories using neural subgoal generators. In Meyer, J. A., Roitblat, H., & Wilson, S. (Eds.), *Proc. of the 2nd International Conference on Simulation of Adaptive Behavior*. MIT Press. In press.

A Real Time Controller Based On a Pulse Stream Neural System

M. Chiaberge*, D. Del Corso*, L.M. Reyneri**, L. Zocca*

* Dip. Elettronica, Politecnico di Torino - C.so Duca degli Abruzzi, 24 - 10129 TORINO - ITALY
** Dip. Ingegneria Informazione, Università di Pisa - Via Diotisalvi, 2 - 56126 PISA - ITALY

Abstract

[1] This paper describes a real-time signal processing system based on an Artificial Neural Network chip, which has been developed for and tailored to non-linear control applications. The chip described, which uses Pulse Stream computation principles, has been designed and manufactured using a standard 1.5μm digital CMOS technology. The system can compute up to 140MCPS, with a Nyquist frequency of about 70kHz.

The prototype of a controller board containing one such chip has been developed and fully tested. The board can be directly interfaced to a host computer and the whole system supports neural and cognitive training algorithms. The system is currently being used to assess the performance of these algorithms for real-time control in several applications.

1 Introduction

Several applications of automatic control have very stringent real time requirements. They therefore require a large amount of computing power, which can be obtained only using powerful DSP chips. These have a high cost, they are power hungry and very sensitive to faults. Furthermore they generate a large quantity of electromagnetic interferences.

An interesting alternative to DSPs is the use of silicon Artificial Neural Systems (ANS), which are computing systems based on cognitive approaches [1]. These rely on non-linear correlators which can be implemented in massively parallel arrays using analog and hybrid VLSI analog/digital technologies. They suffer at a lesser extent of the drawbacks of traditional DSP chips. More and more designers are developing specific VLSI circuits using various techniques, ranging from fully digital to fully analog and even optical ones [2, 3].

This paper describes the hardware implementation of a low-power real-time controller based on a VLSI neural chip designed by the authors. Section 2 introduces the system, while sections 3 and 4 describe, respectively, few applications and some training algorithms tailored to the proposed system.

2 Pulse Stream Neural System

Because of the advantages they provide, "Pulse Streams" (PS) [2, 3] are gaining support in the field of hardware implementations of ANS. PS are a class of modulations using "almost periodic" binary signals; continuously-valued information is contained in waveform timing and not in the amplitude. Applying PS to ANS provides high noise immunity, ease of multiplexing, low energy requirements, straightforward interface with external world and it simplifies the design of synapses and neurons.

A PS technique in particular has been used, namely *Coherent Pulse Width Modulation* (**CPWM**, see fig. 1.a), which presents very good performance [3]. With this modulation technique, activation pulses have constant frequency $f_o = \frac{1}{T_o}$, while their width is proportional to an activation value α_i:

$$T_i = T_{max}\alpha_i \tag{1}$$

where $\alpha_i \in [0 \ldots 1]$ and $T_{max} \leq T_o$. All inputs $X_1, \ldots, X_n$ have a phase relationship with the clock signal CCK: waveforms are allowed to be *high* only during the *active phase* of CCK while they are forced *low* during the *idle* phase. In the prototype described here, pulse period is $T_o = 7.2\mu$s, divided into an active and idle phase of $T_{max} = 6.3\mu$s and $T_o - T_{max} = T_{idle} = 0.9\mu$s, respectively, which corresponds to a stream frequency of 139kHz.

[1]This work has been partially supported by the *Italian Research Project: 40% MURST - VLSI Architectures* and the *Inter-University Cooperation "Integrated Neural System for Robotic Applications"* between Italy and Spain.

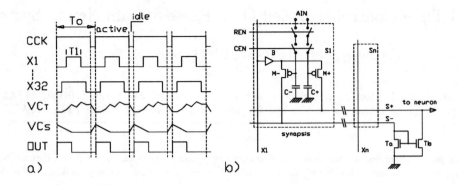

Figure 1: a) Timing of the CPWM system; b) Schematic of a CPWM synapse

2.1 Synapse and neuron architecture

The circuit of a CPWM synapse (figure 1.b) consists of two MOS transistors (M^+ and M^-) that implement a pair of current generators controlled by the voltage stored on two identical capacitors (C^+ and C^-) of about 1pF [3]. The current generators are switched by the incoming CPWM pulse stream (input X_n). At every cycle each synapse injects into the neuron a differential current pulse of duration $T_i = T_{max}\alpha_i$. Provided that the differential voltage on the two capacitors is made proportional to the synaptic weight w_i^j, the total charge injected during one CCK cycle is

$$Q_i^j = K_W T_{max}(w_i^j \alpha_i), \tag{2}$$

where $K_W \approx 2\mu A$ is an appropriate constant depending on technological parameters.

Several synapses are connected to a pair of summing nodes S^+ and S^-, respectively for *excitatory* and *inhibitory* charges. Charges coming from all the synapses are summed up together in the neuron body (not shown), where they either charge or discharge an integration capacitor C_T. The output is reconstructed as a digital CPWM signal through a saturated amplifier (non-linear function) and a sampled voltage-to-time converter.

The voltage on capacitors C^+ and C^- is periodically refreshed from an external digital memory, through a D/A converter using REN and CEN enable signals. Worst case refresh period for an error of 1.5% is higher than 1s.

2.2 Structure and reconfiguration of the prototype chip

A complete general purpose neural network (**NN**) chip with a synaptic array of 1056 synapses ($32 \times 32 + 32$ thresholds) and 32 neurons has been developed and manufactured. As shown in fig. 2.a, the array has 16 inputs coming from the external world (8 digital for direct CPWM signals and 8 analog, internally converted by on-chip A/PS converters [3]) and other 16 inputs internally connected to the outputs of the lower 16 neurons. These can be used as a hidden layer in a multi-layer NN.

Furthermore the weight matrix can be split into different blocks depending on the number of network layers. According to what values are written into the blocks, different networks topologies can be implemented such as, for instance, Hopfield nets, Multi Layer Perceptrons, competitive nets, etc. The chip has 32 digital outputs, including the hidden ones, which are also available outside.

2.3 The Signal Processor Board

A self-standing prototype board has been built to interface the Neural Chip (**NC**) described above to the controlled plant. This board has also been used to test the NC and for performance evaluations. The diagram in fig. 2.b shows the main blocks of the board.

A three phase clock (CCK, ϕ_1, ϕ_2) is obtained from a 2.22MHz quartz oscillator, which controls and synchronizes the whole system.

Refresh of weight capacitors in the neural chip is performed using an external digital RAM plus a refresh counter. Weight values (8 bits) are stored into the RAM and from there periodically transferred into the neural chip via the two DAC converters. RAM size is 8KBytes and it can contain up to four different weight matrices (about 2KBytes per matrix).

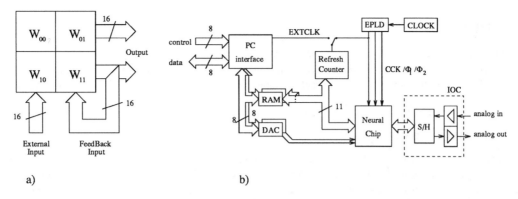

a)   b)

Figure 2: a) Internal organization of the chip; b) Block diagram of the board

The two DACs transform numeric values $[-128 \ldots +127]$ into a differential voltage range $[-1.5V \ldots +1.5V]$. Since refresh is disabled during the active phase, $6.3\mu s$ are available for RAM access and DAC output settling.

The board is interfaced to a host PC via a 16-bit bidirectional parallel port (two 8-bit ports, respectively for data and control signals). The control signals are used for read and write operation between the PS and the digital weight memory (RAM). Weight matrices can only be read or written sequentially under control of the host PC. No random access has been foreseen.

The interface with analog signals (IOC) is composed of few operational amplifiers, with the task of signal conditioning (adapting transducer ranges to the NC input dynamic range, compute signal variations and filtering). One quad sample/hold amplifier is also used for analog signal sampling.

2.4 System implementation and performance

A NC prototype has been designed using a Full Custom approach, manufactured using a $1.5\mu m$ CMOS digital technology and successfully tested. Synapse and neuron size are about $70.000\mu m^2$ and $200.000\mu m^2$, respectively.

The chip computes about 140MCPS with an accuracy better than 1.5% (including inter-neurons spreads), with a total power dissipation of less than 10mW. This corresponds to a computation energy of about 75pJ per connection, which is one of the lowest figures among existing silicon NN implementations [3].

Since the system operates in the discrete time domain, it is appropriate to define its Nyquist frequency $f_N = f_o/2$, which is about 70kHz. This is higher than what can be obtained by most DSP of comparable power consumption. The only drawback is a reduced accuracy, of the order of 7-8 bits, which is yet enough for several practical applications.

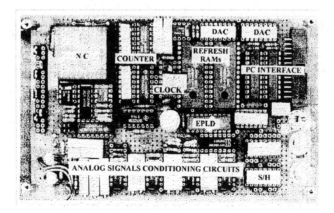

Figure 3: Photograph of the board

3 Applications

The prototype board shown in fig. 3 has been used as a test vehicle to demonstrate how neural networks can be used for control applications. Several applications have been considered and two demonstrators are currently under development: a magnetic suspension and the leg control for a six-legged walking robot.

3.1 Magnetic suspension

The magnetic suspension keeps a steel sphere floating in the air using a magnetic field. This is a simple one-axis magnetic bearing, but the technique developed with this structure will be applied also to more complex bearings, such as those used in vacuum pumps and high speed turbines. Due to the highly non-linear behavior, the design of algorithmic controllers for such systems is very difficult and they are a good test bench for neural networks.

The position of the sphere is sensed by an array of photodiodes, and this signal is conditioned and fed to the analog inputs of the network. The inputs are the sampled position x_k and the differences between current position x_k and previous positions x_{k-1} and x_{k-2}. These values are computed outside the neural chip by the sample/hold circuits. The system is configured as a three-layered 3-5-1 network, and the analog output is amplified to drive the suspension coil. Section 4 describes the training algorithms which have been used for this problem.

3.2 Walking robots

The second application envisaged is the control of leg movements and coordination in a 6-leg walking robot [4]. For this application, an analysis of computational requirements for an analytical (equation solving) approach brought to an estimated processing power comparable with one 80486 processor for each leg. The neural controller makes possible to solve the same problem with a small number of custom NCs, with significant savings in size, power consumption and cost.

The lower layer of leg control, that is the closed loop control of position and speed of leg joints, is handled by conventional control circuitry. Two higher layers use the neural network for:

- leg trajectory control: height from ground of the vehicle and the feet and the trajectory specification are converted into rotation angles for the leg joints.

- leg movements coordination: gaits are executed as instructed from higher "navigation" layers.

Currently, simulations have been performed with several network architectures, and best results have been achieved by either a single four-layers network with 4 inputs, or two separate networks for the different angles of each leg [4]. All these configurations can be realized with one or two NCs with appropriate input and synapse multiplexing.

4 Training algorithms

A crucial point in the design of a critical control system is the selection of an appropriate algorithm. In the magnetic suspension application (section 3.1), the board described has been used to compare traditional solutions (e.g. PID) with modern ones based on *cognitive principles*, in terms of performance, training time and hardware complexity. Actually the board is interfaced with an host PC where the algorithms are executed off-line. Next version of the board will contain the algorithms directly built on chip. In the whole study the constraints of an analog silicon implementation have always been kept in mind: low memory requirements, insensitivity to computation errors and small complexity of the algorithm primitives. The performance of all the methods analyzed is measured in terms of the average position error. The *mean absolute error* (MAE) of the ball has been used:

$$\epsilon_M = \frac{1}{T} \int_T |x| dt, \tag{3}$$

which has also been used as the fitness function for Genetic Algorithms. The following solutions have been considered:

Method	T_C (iterat.)	ϵ_∞ (mm)	Size of population	Memory size (bytes)	Number of trials	Training
PID	-	0.75	1	4	-	on HW
NN	12	0.69	1	38	12	on SW
GA (PID)	8	0.23	50	200	400	on HW
SA (PID)	10	0.68	4	16	80	on HW
GA+SA (PID)	17	0.30	4	16	136	on HW

Table 1: Performance comparison of traditional and cognitive methods

- **Linear PID controller**, which is the reference method. The controller used is a linear PID with a transfer function given by:

$$y_k = K_p x_k + K_d \frac{\Delta x_k}{\Delta t} + K_i \sum_k x_k + K_0 \qquad (4)$$

where K_p, K_d, K_i, K_0 are respectively the proportional, derivative, integral and constant terms of the controller. The PID has been used both alone (with coefficients tuned heuristically) and in conjunction with the other algorithms described further. A PID has a very compact silicon implementation.

- **Neural Network controller (NN)**, that is the same described in section 3.1.

- **Genetic Algorithms (GA)** are powerful optimization methods [5] which can be used within control systems in conjunction with other techniques (e.g. PID, NN, etc.), either to find the best controller parameters (for PID) or the best network topology (for NN). In this work GA has been used to evolve the parameters of a PID and the weights of a NN. In the first case a GA randomly chooses the parameters of a PID within a predefined range. The solution was found after few generations giving good controller performance. In a second case, GA is used to optimize the weights of a NN with the same topology described above (3-5-1). The initial population was composed of neural networks with random weights. Results were bad; barely one network in each generation managed to make the ball rise from the rest position and make it fly for few fractions of a second. This shows that the combination of NN weights that make a good controller is very sparse.

- **Simulated Annealing (SA)** in which the solutions were chosen randomly and evaluated by a fitness function (the same than the GA algorithm) and, if the fitness of the new solution was less than the previous one, it was accepted with a probability of:

$$P(a) = e^{-\frac{\Delta f_k}{T}} \qquad (5)$$

where T is the current "temperature" of the system and $\Delta f_k = (f_k - f_{k-1})$ is the difference between the energy (fitness) of the actual solution and the previous one. With an annealing schedule of T as $1/ln(k)$, the best solution (PID parameters) is obtained after about 10 iterations and with a population of only 4 elements. This approach is slower than the one with GA but this algorithm does not need a large population of possible solutions and in the perspective of a hardware implementation, this is an important factor.

- **Hybrid Approach (GA+SA)** is the combination of a Genetic Algorithm and Simulated Annealing, which keeps the advantages of both methods, namely: lower memory requirements of SA and better performance of GA. A solution better than the one with SA is found in less than 20 iterations, with the same number of genomes as SA (see tab. 1). A hybrid algorithm with just mutations but no crossover has also been tried, as shown in figure 4.

Table 1 compares the different methods in terms of: Number T_C of iterations needed to reach an error close to the asymptotic error e_∞ (namely $\epsilon_M \leq 1.5 e_\infty$); the asymptotic error e_∞, the size of the learning population (i.e. number of *genomes* or *weight sets* needed); size of memory needed (i.e. number of weights or PID coefficients times the size of the population); number of "trials" (i.e. number of times the controlled system is stimulated with different genomes before the controller reaches $\epsilon_M \leq e_\infty$).

The use of the hybrid algorithm GA+SA combines the main properties of the standard GA operators (efficient sampling of the solution space, stochastic hill-climbing, memory of the later stages of search) with those of SA (small population, efficient use of memory, easy hardware implementation).

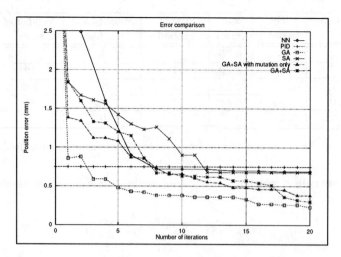

Figure 4: Evolution of the error during training for different cognitive algorithm

5 Conclusion

The paper has described a real-time signal processor based on a Pulse Stream neural chip. That chip has been manufactured, tested and plugged onto the prototype of a neural controller board. The system has been used to assess the feasibility of using cognitive methods for real-world control applications. The board has been interfaced to a PC, for off-line training, on which several traditional and cognitive learning algorithms have been implemented. System performance are better than those of other methods of comparable power dissipation.

6 Acknowledgment

The authors wish to thank Dr. J.J. Merelo and Prof. A. Prieto (Departamento de Electrónica y Tecnología de Computadores, Universidad de Granada, Spain) for the useful cooperation in the development of training algorithms.

References

[1] P.J. Verbos, "An Overview of Neural Networks for Control", *IEEE Trans. on Control Systems*, Vol. 11, No. 1, January 1991, pp. 40-41.

[2] A. F. Murray, D. Del Corso, and L. Tarassenko, "Pulse-Stream VLSI Neural Networks Mixing Analog and Digital Techniques", *IEEE Trans. on Neural Networks*, vol. 2, no. 2, March 1991, pp. 193-204.

[3] L.M. Reyneri, M. Chiaberge, D. Del Corso, "Using Coherent Pulse Width and Edge Modulation in Artificial Neural Systems", to be published on *International Journal on Neural Systems*, Special Issue on Microneuro '93.

[4] D. Bassani, M. Chiaberge, D. Del Corso, G. Genta, F. Zanetti, "Simulation of a Hexapode Walking Machine Controlled by Neural Network", *Proc. of ISMCR 1993*, Torino, September 21-24, 1993

[5] L. Davis, "Handbook of Genetic Algorithms", New York, *Van Nostrand Reinhold*, 1991.

[6] Dan Adler, "Genetic Algorithms and Simulated Annealing: A Marriage Proposal", IEEE International Conference on Neural Networks 1993, San Francisco (CA), March 28- April 1, 1993.

[7] S.W. Mahfoud, D.E. Goldberg, "A Genetic algorithm for parallel simulated annealing", in *Parallel Problem Solving from Nature, 2*, R. Männer, B. Manderick eds., *Elsevier Science Publishers B.V.*, 1992.

Nonlinear Missile Controller Using Memory Neural Networks

Michael P. Fallon, Randy E. Garcia, Murali Tummala
Department of Electrical Engineering
Naval Postgraduate School
Monterey, California 93943, USA

ABSTRACT

Presented is the solution to a nonlinear missile control problem through application of the backpropagation algorithm to a feed-forward artificial neural network that uses *memory neurons*. Memory neuron networks have recently shown promise in identification and adaptive control as the memory neurons allow the network to combine historical values with present backpropagation weights and outputs [1,2]. The learning algorithm employs only locally available information rather than feeding some or all past plant inputs to the network. This solves the memory problem associated with storing all past values of the missile/target system in order to apply a new control to minimize the difference error.

1. Introduction

The practical application of neural networks to such real-world problems has greater possibilities with the advent of increased capabilities of parallel processing architectures. As shown in several previous examples [2-6], neural networks can solve highly nonlinear control problems such as the interception of a target by a missile. Anderson [4] employs reinforcement and temporal-difference learning methods to design a system which balances an inverted pendulum on a cart. His performance measure in training a neural controller is the failure signal delivered by the system output. Nguyen and Widrow [3] apply the estimator/controller cascaded backpropagation scheme in controlling a truck to back up to a loading dock position given a random starting position in a parking lot. Sastry et. al. [2] apply the same technique and suggest a solution for feed-forward controllers and modify it by applying memory neuron networks. In this work, we desire to train a missile to intercept a target with an arbitrary trajectory by applying the latter method, which uses memory neuron networks. A missile *controller* learns to identify given target trajectories and the necessary control required to allow the missile to kill the target successfully. To train the controller, however, we implement another neural network that adequately models the nonlinear plant (transfer function) of the missile system. This neural network is the *estimator*. The purposes of the estimator are to model the plant and allow backpropagation of the error through the entire controller-estimator network. The backpropagated error, in turn, will allow the adjustment of the weights in the controller to provide the learning required to modify control parameters with changing target motion. Training occurs in two phases: estimator first and controller second. The problem is valid in $\mathbf{R}^2$ with obvious extensions to $\mathbf{R}^3$. The result of this work is a memory neuron network missile controller for nonlinear networks involving delay.

2. Problem Definition

The nonlinear plant here is a missile with a $\frac{1}{s^2}$ transfer function. The control input is a bang-bang [7] force input of +u or -u applied to the missile. State variables identifying the missile plant (which will also be used to feed the networks) include:

x_m = missile horizontal position
y_m = missile vertical position
$\dot{x}_m$ = missile horizontal velocity
$\dot{y}_m$ = missile vertical velocity

and the target variables include:

x_t = target horizontal position
y_t = target vertical position
$\dot{x}_t$ = target horizontal velocity
$\dot{y}_t$ = target vertical velocity.

The neural network structure (see figure 1) resembles that used in [2,3]. The variation to the Nguyen and Widrow approach is the addition of memory neurons. The variables that apply to the neural networks are:

L = number of layers in a network
N = network neurons per layer
M = memory neurons per output network neuron
x = input to a network neuron
s = output of a network neuron
w = weight connecting network neurons between layers
f = weight connecting memory neuron to next layer network neuron
α = input weight to a memory neuron
β = weight connecting memory neuron to its output network neuron
g(x) = activation function of a neuron.

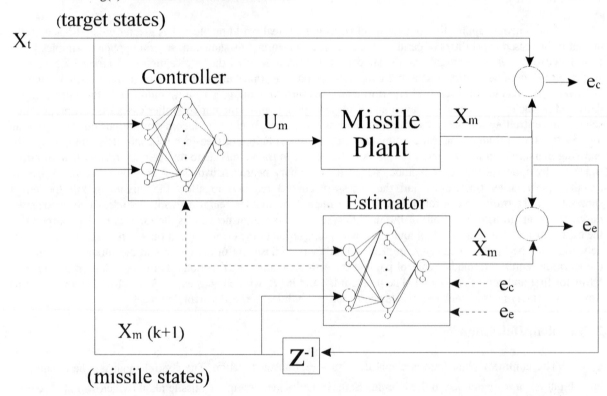

Figure 1. Memory neural network controller architecture.

Details of the design of the memory neurons within the input, hidden, and output layers contained in [2] provide a useful algorithm for updating output values and weights. The difference between memory neural networks and traditional neural networks is in the memory neuron assigned to each network neuron. The memory neuron receives the output of its associated neuron and its own feedback signal to be defined below. The self feedback allows a weighted accumulation of the past neural activity at that processing element. The memory neuron feeds its output to the next layer network neurons in the same manner as its source network neuron.

Traditionally, the input to a hidden or output layer neuron is [3,6]

$$\bar{x}_{i+1} = \bar{s}_i \bar{w}_i$$

where i indicates the layer number. However, with additional outputs from previous layer memory neurons, the input becomes

$$\bar{x}_{i+1} = \bar{w}_i \bar{s}_i + \bar{f}_i \bar{v}_i,$$

and the input to the output layer neuron is further extended by

$$\bar{x}_{i+1} = \bar{w}_i \bar{s}_i + \bar{f}_i \bar{v}_i + \bar{\beta}_i \bar{v}_i.$$

These last two equations show where the effect of the memory neurons take place. Since the output s of any neuron is a function of its input

$$\bar{s}_i = g(\bar{x}_i)$$

each of these additional memory neuron values, which contain historical data of the related network neuron, will affect the output proportionally to the weight derived through learning. The activation functions $g(x)$ chosen for the hidden and output layers [2], respectively, are

$$g_1(\bar{x}) = \frac{c_1}{1 + \exp(-k_1 \bar{x})},$$

$$g_2(\bar{x}) = c_2 \frac{1 - \exp(-k_2 \bar{x})}{1 + \exp(-k_2 \bar{x})}.$$

The beauty of the memory neural network is found in the recursively weighted history seen in the output of the memory neuron whereby

$$\bar{v}_i(k) = \bar{\alpha}_i(k)\bar{s}_i(k-1) + (1 - \bar{\alpha}_i(k))\bar{v}_i(k-1).$$

Time k is included in the notation to isolate which values and weights are dependent on past time quantities. Note that required past values of the total network input and output do not have to be stored in memory as they must be with traditional "look back" smoothing control schemes such as the extended Kalman filter.

With the calculations of neuron input and output values understood, it is now important to determine how the weights are updated in order to perform backpropagation of error. Once the output layer output values are calculated above, the resulting s_i are called the estimates of the plant output. We call this estimate $\hat{\bar{y}}_i$. The squared error between the estimate and the actual plant output is:

$$e = \sum_{j=1}^{N_L} (\hat{\bar{y}}_j - \bar{y}_j)^2$$

where j indicates which neuron's output value (state variable estimate) is being compared to the plant state variable. Backpropagation of this error through the network is now possible. Fortunately, the error backpropagation need not pass through the memory neurons to the network neurons, but solely through the network neurons themselves. Weight updates [2] for time $k+1$ are

$$\bar{w}_i(k+1) = \bar{w}_i(k) - \eta \bar{e}_{i+1}(k)\bar{s}_i(k),$$

$$\bar{f}_i(k+1) = \bar{f}_i(k) - \eta \bar{e}_{i+1}(k)\bar{v}_i(k) .$$

Ostensibly, the ith layer weight depends on the $(i+1)$ layer error that is backpropagated and the previous value of the ith layer weights. Additionally, the past output of the network and memory neuron, respectively, are weighted by a step factor η. The memory neuron weights α and β are updated as well using chain-rule approximations of the differential error with respect to that weight.

3. Results

We chose networks with the characteristics listed in table 1. For this particular control problem, the three-hidden layer zero-memory neuron system failed to adequately train the estimator-controller pair. The six-hidden layer one-memory neuron system the estimator-controller pair. The six-hidden layer one-memory the

	estimator 1	controller 1	estimator 2	controller 2
number of layers L	3	3	3	3
input neurons N_1	5	8	5	8
hidden layer neurons N_2	3	3	6	6
output layer neurons N_3	4	1	4	1
output memory neurons M	0	0	1	1
input values	$\mathbf{u}, \mathbf{x}_m$	$\mathbf{x}_t, \mathbf{x}_m$	$\mathbf{u}, \mathbf{x}_m$	$\mathbf{x}_t, \mathbf{x}_m$
output values	$\mathbf{y}_m$	u	$\mathbf{y}_m$	u

Table 1. Missile controller/estimator architecture.

estimator-controller pair. The six-hidden layer one-memory neuron system gave quite favorable results in the initial estimator training. Estimator training took place for 1000 epochs with a control input of zero, 1000 epochs with a random uniform control input, and 1000 epochs with a sinusoidal control input. State variables were random over the scaled ranges for position and velocity. The altitude varied to 5000 feet (the target at 3000 feet) and the range limit on the horizontal was 30,000 feet. Each epoch trained over a two second interval of sequences spaced by a time step of .01 second. Thus, the estimator reacts to 200 sequences of states and control *each epoch*, for a total of 600,000 time steps. Initially, we gave equal weight to the position and the velocity errors. This caused poor convergence for the position error and good results for the velocity error. We made a key change to favor the position error over the velocity error in the weight updates. Figure 2a shows the position error of the estimator during the first 1000 epochs, and it reflects poor convergence. Figure 2b shows the position error of the estimator after 3000 epochs and considerable training. Figure 3 also shows velocity error improvement.

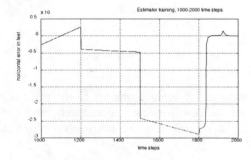

Figure 2a. Early estimator error.

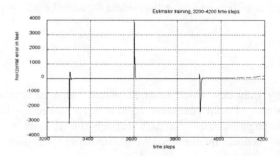

Figure 2b. Estimator error convergence.

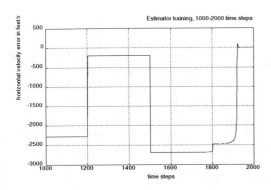 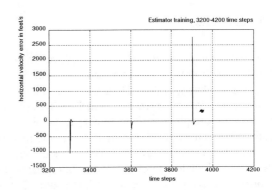

Figure 3a,b. Snapshots of estimator velocity error.

Each initial surge in the convergence plots indicates a new random sequence. The subsequent tapering to zero shows how quickly the estimator minimizes its difference with the actual missile plant. Training the controller off-line decreased the time required to update weights. No adjustment of estimator weights occurs during this phase, and the outputs of the actual missile plant need not be calculated since the estimator should accurately model the plant. Controller training, unlike the estimator, tailors its objective directly to the target intercept problem. The cost function to minimize was the difference between target state and missile state.

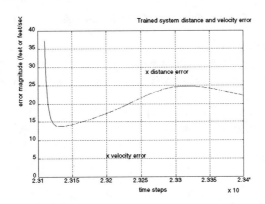

Figure 4. Trained system error magnitude in distance and velocity.

Training the controller on-line allows the estimator to continue learning much like a traditional adaptive controller. A final plot of the trained missile trajectory is shown in Figure 5. Although the trajectories appear to be close, the nearest point of approach was off by 3000 feet.

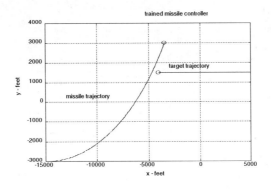

Figure 5. Missile controller trained and employed against target.

4. Conclusions

Estimator training in this system proved to be excellent. The use of memory neurons proved to be a viable method by which to train this two neural network system. Controller training, however, was not optimal in this case. The tendency in the system was to overshoot the trajectory of the missile. The controller net performed much better as a velocity predictor than a position predictor. From this point, there exist two major areas of study which vary in complexity. The first is to emphasize position in our weighting of neural values through the network. This can be performed by lowering the learning coefficient of the control in order to allow the position values and weights to dominate. The other direction of study is to analyze the positive effects of including acceleration. The addition of two more state variables in the target and missile complicate the problem, yet the same principles apply. Only the network structure changes. Similarly, the coefficients associated with acceleration must be fully understood in order to optimize learning and performance of the controller.

5. References

[1] P. Poddar, K. P. Unnikrishnan, "Memory Neuron Networks: a Prolegomenon," *GMR-7493, General Motors R&D Publication,* October 1991.

[2] P. S. Sastry, G. Santharam, K. P. Unnikrishnan, "Memory Neuron Networks for Identification and Control of Dynamical Systems," *GMR-7916, General Motors R & D Publication,* March 1993.

[3] D. Nguyen, B. Widrow, "Neural networks for self-learning control systems," *IEEE Control Sys. Mag.,* April 1990, pp.18-23.

[4] C. W. Anderson, "Learning to Control an Inverted Pendulum Using Neural Networks," *IEEE Control Sys. Mag.,* April 1989, pp.31-37.

[5] A. G. Barto, R. S. Sutton, C. W. Anderson, *IEEE Transactions on Systems, Man, and Cybernetics,"* vol. SMC-13, No. 5, September/October 1983, pp.834-846.

[6] M. Fallon, R. Garcia, "Control of a Nonlinear System Using Neural Networks," EC4900 Course project, NPS, September 1993.

[7] D. E. Kirk, *Optimal Control,* Prentice Hall, 1970, pp. 246-247.

Stable Neural Network Control Systems Using the Multiple-nonlinearity Popov Criterion

S. Kuntanapreeda and R. Fullmer

Center for Self Organizing and Intelligent Systems
College of Engineering
Utah State University, Logan UT, 84322-4130

ABSTRACT

This paper introduces a new concept for training a neural network controller which guarantees Lyapunov stability of a closed loop controlled system. A modified backpropagation algorithm is derived, where the usual minimization problem is constrained to satisfy the multiple-nonlinearity Popov stability condition. The generalized Kalman-Yakubovich condition is used to provide necessary and sufficient conditions for satisfying the Popov criterion.

1. INTRODUCTION

It is well known that the standard backpropagation training rule for a feedforward neural network is a steepest descent solution to a nonlinear least-square minimization problem. Briefly, the rule is obtained by defining the minimization objective function as the sum of n squared terms

$$J(W) = \tfrac{1}{2} \Sigma_{i=1,n} \, \alpha_i \, (x_{di} - x_i(W))^2 \tag{1}$$

where W denotes the weight parameters of a neural network and x_{di} and $x_i(W)$ denote the ith components of the desired and actual response of plant state n-vectors, respectively. The training rule can be written as

$$W_{k+1} = W_k - \delta(\nabla_W J), \tag{2}$$

where δ is known as a training rate and W_k and $\nabla_W J$ are the weights and the gradient at iteration k, respectively.

There are several approaches to train a neural network controller (NNC). For example, it may be possible to train a NNC to emulate the input-output response of some existing non-neural network controller, such as a human operator. Some other possibilities are given in the paper by Nguyen and Widrow[1] and Kuntanapreeda et al.[2], where neural network controller design is independent of existing controllers. Unfortunately, all of those approaches have a major difficulty which prevents their gaining widespread acceptance by the control system community at large. That is, once designed, it is either impossible or prohibitively difficult to prove the stability of the closed loop system. About all that can be done at this stage of neural network control theory is to "demonstrate" the adequacy of closed loop performance through simulation.

This paper introduces a novel modification of the closed loop backpropagation algorithm for training a NNC which guarantees stability (in the Lyapunov sense) of the closed loop neural network controlled system. The idea is to use the multiple-nonlinearity Popov criterion [3,4] as a training constraint. The generalized Kalman-Yakubovich lemma [3] is used as a necessary and sufficient condition for the Popov criterion. Minimization of the constrained objective function is achieved by using an iterative feasible direction method [5,6].

2. DYNAMICAL SYSTEM

Assume the plant is modelled by

$$dx/dt = G(x,u), \tag{3a}$$

where x is the state n-vector of the system and u is an m-vector control input. Without loss of generality, it is assumed that zero is the equilibrium state. Furthermore, it is assumed that the system can be written (by using a Taylor expansion about the equilibrium point) as

$$dx/dt = Ax + Bu + g(x,u), \tag{3b}$$

where A is a real (n × n) matrix and B is a real (n × m) matrix. The nonlinear term g(x,u) is an n-vector function which is assumed sufficiently small when (x,u) is sufficiently close to x = 0, u = 0. The matrix A is assumed to be a Hurwitz matrix and the pair (A,B) to be completely controllable. As usual, assume all of the system states variable are either available for feedback purpose or can be satisfactorily estimated by an observer.

3. NEURAL NETWORK CONTROLLER CONFIGURATION

The NNC of Figure 1 is assumed to be in the form of a single hidden layer network with linear output. The hidden layer consists of p nonlinear neurons whose nonlinear functions satisfy $f(0) = 0$ and $0 \leq f(y)y \leq y^2$. Note that tanh(.) is an example of a function satisfying this requirement. Let W_1 denote the (p × n) weight matrix of the hidden layer and W_2 the (m × p) weight matrix of the output layer.

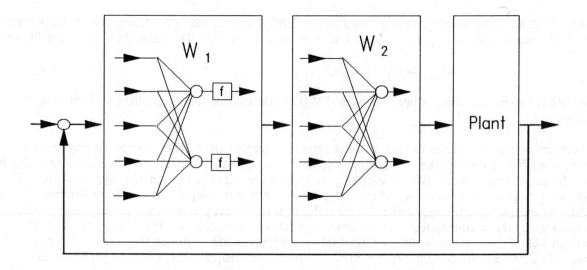

Figure 1. NNC configuration.

4. THE POPOV CRITERION AND THE KALMAN-YAKUBOVICH LEMMA

The following well known theorems will be stated here without proof. They can be found in any number of well known textbooks from control system literature, such as [3] and [4].

Theorem (Popov criterion). *Consider the closed loop system whose state space representation is given by*

$$dx/dt = Fx + Gu$$
$$y = Hx$$
$$u = -\Phi(y), \tag{4}$$

where x, y, and u are the n-state, m-output, and m-control input vectors, respectively. It is assumed for (4) that F is a real $(n \times n)$ Hurwitz matrix; G and H are real $(n \times m)$ and $(m \times n)$ matrices, respectively; (F,G) is completely controllable; and that $\Phi(y)$ is an m-vector function whose i^{th} component ϕ_i is a function of the single variable y_i only, for $i = 1, 2, ..., m$, and where

$$0 \le \phi_i(y_i)y_i \le k_iy_i^2 \text{ and } \phi_i(0) = 0.$$

Then, the equilibrium position $x = 0$ of (4) is asymptotically stable in the sense of Lyapunov if the $(m \times m)$ matrix

$$Z(s) = K^{-1} + H(Is-F)^{-1}G$$

of functions of the complex variable s is positive real, where K is a $(m \times m)$ diagonal matrix with all diagonal elements exactly equal to k_i for $i = 1, 2, .., m$.

Theorem (Kalman-Yakubovich lemma). *Let Γ be a real $(m \times r)$ matrix and F a real $(n \times n)$ Hurwitz matrix. Furthermore, let G and H be real matrices with the dimension of $(n \times m)$ and $(m \times n)$, respectively, and let (F,G) completely controllable. Then, for given $(n \times n)$ symmetric positive semi-definite real matrix Q, a real $(n \times n)$ symmetric positive definite matrix P and a real $(n \times r)$ matrix q satisfying*

$$F^TP + PF = -qq^T - Q$$

and

$$PG - H^T = q\Gamma^T$$

exist if and only if the $(m \times m)$ matrix

$$Z(s) = (\Gamma\Gamma^T/2) + H(Is-F)^{-1}G$$

of functions of the complex variable s is positive real.

5. STABLE NEURAL NETWORK CONTROL

Assume the linearized system (3) is to be controlled by a NNC of the configuration shown in Figure 1. Equation (3) can then be written in the form

$$dx/dt = Ax + Bu$$
$$u = W_2F(h)$$
$$h = W_1x \tag{5}$$

where $F(h)$ is an p-vector function whose i^{th} component ($i = 1, 2, ..., p$) is a function of the single variable h_i, and whose components satisfy

$$0 \le f_i(h_i)h_i \le h_i^2, \text{ and } f_i(0) = 0.$$

Note that the neural network control law can be written as

$$u(x) = W_2F(W_1x). \tag{6}$$

Proposition. *The neural network control system (3) with the control law (6) is at least locally stable if there exists a real ($n \times n$) positive symmetric definite matrix P and a real ($n \times p$) matrix q such that*

$$A^T P + PA = -qq^T - Q \tag{7a}$$

and

$$PBW_2 + (W_1)^T = -q\Gamma^T \tag{7b}$$

where Γ is a real ($p \times p$) diagonal matrix with diagonal elements r_i exactly equal to $r_i = 2^{1/2}$, for each $i = 1, 2, .., p$ and where Q is a real ($n \times n$) positive symmetric semi-definite matrix. Furthermore,

$$V = x^T P x$$

is a Lyapunov function for control system.

Proof. Let the system be given as above and assume P and q satisfy (7). Then

$$-dV/dt = -(dx/dt)^T Px - x^T P(dx/dt).$$

From (5) and (7),

$$-dV/dt = x^T Qx + x^T qq^T x + 2F(h)^T[\Gamma q + W_1]x$$

$$= x^T Qx + x^T qq^T x + 2x^T q\Gamma F(h) + 2F(h)^T h$$

$$= x^T Qx + |x^T q + F(h)^T|_2^2 + 2F(h)^T h - 2F(h)^T F(h).$$

$$\geq 0.$$

Then, V is a Lyapunov function and, therefore, the equilibrium is Lyapunov stable. Q.E.D.

6. TRAINING RULE

In order to train the NNC of Figure 1, it is necessary to minimize the objective function

$$J(W) = \tfrac{1}{2} \Sigma_{i=1,n} \alpha_i (x_{di} - x_i(W))^2, \tag{8}$$

but, in this case, with the added Popov criterion constraints

$$c_1 = A^T P + PA + qq^T + Q = 0$$

$$c_2 = PB(W_2)^T + q^T\Gamma + W_1 = 0. \tag{9}$$

Here A and B are the system matrices of (3); W_1 and W_2 the weight matrices of the NNC; and P and q are defined as in the previous proposition. For convenience, let X_1 be a column vector whose elements are the formed from the consecutive rows of the weight matrices W_1 and W_2, respectively, and X_2 is similarly formed from the rows of P and q. Furthermore, let X and C(X) be defined by $[X_1, X_2]^T$ and $[c_1, c_2]^T$.

Ideally, we need a training rule which minimizes the objective function (8) subjected to the constraints (9). Furthermore, if X_k (X at iteration k) is satisfied, $X_{k+1} = X_k + S_k$ should also be satisfied, i.e.

$$C(X_k) = C(X_k + S_k) = 0. \tag{10}$$

If we expand (10) by using Taylor expansion about the current point X_k, we get

$$C(X_k+S_k) \approx C(X_k) + \Sigma(X_k)S_k, \tag{11}$$

where $\Sigma(X_k)$ is the Jacobian matrix of $C(X)$ corresponding to the current point X_k. Obviously, the local feasible search direction S_k must be in the null space of $\Sigma(X_k)$, i.e. $S_k = Z_k\chi$, where Z_k is a matrix whose columns form a basis for the null space of $\Sigma(X_k)$, i.e. $\Sigma(X_k)Z_k = 0$, and χ is a search direction. Also, let Y_k be a matrix whose columns form a basis for the range space of $\Sigma(X_k)$ when $\Sigma(X_k)Y_k = I$. The matrix (Y_k, Z_k) can be obtained, for example, by QR factorization. Thus an equivalent form of (8) is to minimize the unconstrained objective function

$$\Psi(\chi) = \tfrac{1}{2} \Sigma_{i=1,n} \, \alpha_i \, (x_{di} - x_i(X_k+Z_k\chi))^2. \tag{12}$$

By using the chain rule in $X = X_k+Z_k\chi$, the gradient is given by

$$\nabla_\chi\Psi = Z_k^T(\nabla_X\Psi). \tag{13}$$

Also, $\qquad\qquad \nabla_X\Psi = [\nabla_{X1}J \mid 0] = [\nabla_W J \mid 0]. \tag{14}$

Note that the right hand side term, $\nabla_W J$, of (14) is the same as before, without the Popov criterion constraint. Then the local feasible gradient direction can be written as

$$S_k = -Z_k^T Z_k[\nabla_W J \mid 0] \tag{15}$$

This is called the gradient projection method [6].

The first attempt is to move from X_k to X' in the direction of S_k, i.e.

$$X' = X_k - \delta Z_k^T Z_k[\nabla_W J \mid 0]. \tag{16}$$

for a small positive training rate δ. Since S_k is a local feasible direction, it may lose feasibility. In this case we need some iterative strategy for returning sufficiently close to the feasible region. We seek a point $(X'+p)$ such that $C(X'+p) = 0$. By Taylor expansion, we get

$$0 = C(X'+p) \approx C(X') + \Sigma(X')p,$$

so that

$$\Sigma(X')p \approx -C(X').$$

If we start closed to X_k, we can assume that

$$\Sigma(X_k)p \approx -C(X').$$

Recalling the matrix Y_k ($\Sigma(X_k)Y_k = I$), the equation above can be written as

$$\Sigma(X_k)p \approx -\Sigma(X_k)Y_k C(X'),$$

which implies

$$p = -Y_k C(X'). \tag{17}$$

Next obtain a new point by forming

$$X'(1) = X' - Y_k C(X'). \tag{18}$$

Substituting $X'(1)$ for X' in (18) and successively iterating the process yields a sequence $\{X'(r)\}$

(where r is the iteration index) generated by

$$X'(r+1) = X'(r) - Y_k C(X'(r)).$$ (19)

which, started sufficiently closed to X_k, will converge to a feasible solution X_{k+1}.

Therefore, the learning rule can be written as

$$X_{k+1} = X_k - \delta Z_k^T Z_k [\nabla_W J \mid 0] - Y_k C(X'(r)),$$ (20)

where $X'(r)$ represents the iterative vector in (19).

After training, we get a set of neural network weights which guarantees at least local equilibrium stability of the neural network control system by satisfying the Popov criterion. Furthermore, we also get the matrix P which allows us to establish stability using $V = x^T P x$.

7. CONCLUSION

It has been shown that a NNC can be trained to guarantee the Lyapunov stability of the closed loop controlled system. The method has been successfully applied to training a stable NNC to emulate a non-neural network controller, and also for training a model reference neural network as discussed in [2]. These results, plus a discussion of convergence questions will be presented in a companion paper [7] now in preparation.

ACKNOWLEDGEMENTS

The authors would like to acknowledge support for this work by the Center for Self-Organizing and Intelligent Systems at Utah State University, and for valuable assistance and suggestion provided by its Director, Dr. R.W. Gundersen.

REFERENCES

[1] D.H. Nguyen and B. Widrow, "Neural network for self-learning control system", IEEE Control Syst. Mag., Vol. 10, No.3, April 1990.

[2] S. Kuntanapreeda, R.W. Gunderson, and R. Fullmer, "Neural network model reference control of nonlinear systems", Int. Joint Conf. on Neural Networks, Vol.2, page 94-99, Baltimore, MD, June 1992.

[3] K.S. Narendra and C.P. Neuman, "Stability of continuous time dynamical systems with m-feedback nonlinearities", AIAA Journal, Vol.5, No.11, Nov. 1967.

[4] J.B. Moore and B.D.O. Anderson, "Application of the multivariable Popov criterion", Int. J. Control, Vol.5, No.4, 1967.

[5] R. Flecher, Practical Method of Optimization, John Wiley and Sons Ltd., 1987.

[6] D.G. Luenberger, Linear and Nonlinear Programming, Addison-Wesly Pub., 1989.

[7] S. Kuntanapreeda, R.W. Gunderson, and R. Fullmer, "Results and Convergence of the Stable Neural Network Training Algorithm", in preparation.

Direct Computation of Robot Inverse Kinematic Transformations Using Hopfield Neural Network

D.H. Rao, M.M. Gupta and P.N. Nikiforuk

Intelligent Systems Research Laboratory, College of Engineering
University of Saskatchewan, Saskatoon, Canada, S7N 0W0

Abstract

Computation of inverse kinematic transformations is an important problem in the field of robotics as it must be solved in real-time in order to position the end-effector at the desired position in a given task-space. However, it is a difficult problem for it involves the determination whether or not at least one mathematical set of robot joint angle values exists that will produce the desired coordinate configuration. The mathematical solutions should be checked against the physical constraints associated with the manipulator. The advent of artificial neural networks has made it possible to obtain general learning schemes which can be used to arrive at feasible solutions to inverse kinematics problem in a constrained environment independent of a robotic structure. The intent of this paper is to use the Hopfield neural network for the direct computation of inverse kinematic transformations of two- and three-linked robots, thereby avoiding the off-line training of neural networks.

1. Introduction

1.1   The Problem of Inverse Kinematics in Robotics

The *forward kinematics* problem is concerned with the determination of the configuration (position and orientation) of the end-effector for a given set of the joint variables such as angles and lengths. The joint variables are the angles in the case of rotational joints, and the link extension in the case of prismatic or sliding joints. Thus, the forward kinematics problem uniquely relates the given set of joint variable (the angles between the links θ, and the link lengths L) vector, η, to a set of task-space coordinate vector, X, by a relation $X = \varphi[\eta]$ where φ is a continuously differentiable nonlinear function and $\eta = [\theta, L]^T$. This has a unique solution in the sense that for a given set of joint angles θ and link lengths L, the configuration of the end-effector within the task-space can be uniquely determined. The more difficult problem, which is of primary practical importance in robot manipulation, is the computation of *inverse kinematic transformations*, that is $\eta = \varphi^{-1}[X]$. In other words, the inverse kinematics problem may be stated as follows [1]: Given a desired position and orientation of the end-effector, determine a set of joint variables (angles) that achieve the desired position and orientation.

Equations to determine the robot joint angles are nonlinear in nature because they not only contain the trigonometric functions, but also squared and cross product terms. The periodicity and symmetry of the tangent function and the multiple roots of the squared terms result in an ambiguous determination of the end point location. The problem becomes more severe as the number of links in the robot increases. Therefore, the inverse kinematics problem involves the questions of existence, uniqueness and the method of solution. More specifically, the existence question involves the ability to determine whether or not at least one mathematical set of robot joint angle values exists that will produce a desired configuration. The mathematical solutions that one may arrive at should be checked against the constraints associated with the manipulator in order to determine whether or not they represent physical solutions as well [2].

1.2   Neural Networks in Robotics

Advances in the area of neural networks have given a different direction to robotic control. By virtue of their functional mapping and iterative capabilities, neural networks can be employed for learning coordinate transformations [3 - 6]. The advantage of using the neural approach, over the conventional inverse kinematics algorithms, is that neural networks can avoid time consuming calculations. Furthermore, in a manner that is typical of neural networks, it would be very easy to modify the learned associations upon changes in the structure of the mechanism.

The conventional methodology for computing inverse kinematic transformations involves the training of a multi-layered feedforward neural network off-line for possible data patterns within the robot task space to obtain solutions to the inverse kinematics problem. Because of the generalization property, neural networks can learn the associated patterns and recall the learned patterns. The trained network is then used to achieve the desired end-effector movements. This technique basically involves therefore two modes of operations, namely the training phase and the performing phase. However, the major drawback of this technique is a very long training procedure in addition to the fact that static neural networks do take a very large learning time for a given task.

The emergence of dynamic neural computing (the use of dynamic neural networks) has made it possible to develop learning schemes which can be used to arrive at feasible solutions with relatively small convergence time to complex problems, such as the inverse kinematics problem in robotics. Although the learning of inverse kinematics transformations is a static problem, the use of dynamic neural networks helps to compute the transformations fast compared to static neural networks. The authors used a neural structure called the dynamic neural processor (DNP) for this task [5, 6]. In this paper, the Hopfield neural network is used as an alternative to the slow convergence of static networks and the complexity of DNP for computing inverse kinematic transformations .

Following this introduction, the rest of the paper is organized as follows. A brief description of the Hopfield neural network (HNN) is given in the next section. Computer simulation studies demonstrating the direct computation of inverse kinematic transformations of two- and three-lined robots are discussed in Section 3, followed by the conclusions in the last section.

2. Hopfield Neural Network

The dynamic neural networks, also known as feedback or recurrent neural networks, were first introduced by Hopfield [10, 11]. Unlike the static neural networks, a dynamic neural network employs extensive feedback between the neurons. The node equations in dynamic networks are described by differential or difference equations. Neural architectures with feedback are particularly appropriate for system modeling (identification), control, and filtering applications. From a computational point of view, a dynamic neural structure which contains a state feedback may provide more computational advantage than that of a purely feedforward neural structure. A HNN consists of a single layer network included in a feedback configuration with a time delay, as shown in Fig. 1. This feedback network represents a discrete-time dynamical system and can be described by the following equation

$$y(k+1) = \Psi \left[w(k) \cdot y(k) \right] , \quad x(0) = x_0 \tag{1}$$

where $y(k)$ and $y(k+1)$ represent the states of the neural network at k and k+1 instants of time, x_0 represents the initial value, $w(k)$ denotes the vector of neural weights, and $\Psi[.]$ is the nonlinear activation function. Given an initial value x_0, the above dynamic system evolves to an equilibrium state if $\Psi [.]$ is suitably chosen. The set of initial conditions in the neighborhood of x_0 that converge to the same equilibrium state is then identified with that state. The term "associative memory" is used to describe such systems. The feedback networks with or without constant inputs are merely nonlinear dynamical systems, and the asymptotic behavior of such systems depends on the initial conditions, specific inputs as well as on the nonlinear function. Single-layer HNN consists of n computing elements (neurons) with thresholds w_{0i} as depicted in Fig. 2.

The feedback input to the i-th neuron is equal to the weighted sum of neural outputs y_j, where $j = 1, 2,$ ... , n. Denoting w_{ij} as the weight value connecting the output of the j-th neuron with the input of the i-th neuron, we can express the total input u_i of the i-th neuron as [9]

$$u_i = \sum_{\substack{j=1 \\ j \neq i}}^{n} w_{ij} \, y_j + x_i - w_{0i} \, , \, i = 1, 2, ... , n. \tag{2a}$$

In vector form, Eqn. (2a) can be rewritten as: $u_i = w_i^T y + x_i - w_{0i}$, i = 1, 2, ... , n   (2b)

where $w_i \triangleq [w_{i1}, w_{i2}, ..., w_{in}]^T$ and $y \triangleq [y_1, y_2, ..., y_n]^T$

The linear portion of the recurrent neural network can be described in matrix form as

$$U = W y + X - w_0$$ (3)

where $U \triangleq [u_1, u_2, ..., u_n]^T$, $X \triangleq [x_1, x_2, ..., x_n]^T$ and $w_0 \triangleq [w_{01}, w_{02}, ..., w_{0n}]^T$

The matrix W in Eqn. (3), also called *connectivity matrix*, is an (n X n) matrix. This matrix is symmetrical, i.e., $w_{ij} = w_{ji}$, and with diagonal entries equal to zero, $w_{ii} = 0$ indicating that no connection exists from any neuron back to itself. This condition is equivalent to the lack of self-feedback in the neural structure shown in Fig. 2. The weights of the HNN are updated during the learning process using the following rule

$$w(k + 1) = w(k) + \mu \frac{\partial J}{\partial W(k)}$$ (4)

where $W(k)$ is the estimation of the weight vector at time k, and μ is a step size parameter, that affects the rate of convergence of the weights during learning. The output u_i of the HNN at current time k may be obtained only using the state and input of the network at past time k - 1. The error index, J, should be then defined as

$$J = \frac{1}{2} \sum_{i=1}^{m} [y_{d,i}(k) - y_i(k)]^2 = \frac{1}{2} \sum_{i=1}^{m} e_i^2(k)$$ (5)

where $e_i(k) = y_{d,i}(k) - y_i(k)$ is a learning error between the desired and the observed outputs at time k. For complete details of the learning algorithm, readers are referred to [9].

3.   Computer Simulation Studies

The learning scheme [6] employed for the direct computation of inverse kinematic transformations of two- and three linked robots is shown in Fig. 3. This learning scheme uses a neural network to determine the joint angles for a given set of desired Cartesian coordinates. These estimated joint angles, which act as inputs (after denormalization) to the forward kinematics, are checked against the pre-defined robot task space. This additional level of control makes the robot operate within a specified work-space. The HNN used to compute the inverse kinematic transformations consisted of five neurons configured in a single layer as depicted in Fig. 3. The desired end-effector x-y positions served as inputs to the first two neurons of the HNN. In this section, we discuss the computer simulation results for 2- and 3-linked robots.

3.1 Two-Linked Robot: Consider a 2-linked robot shown in Fig. 4. The point (x,y), the free tip of the second link, also called the 'end point', describes the trajectories based on a Cartesian coordinate system. The origin of the coordinate system is the first joint, which is assumed to be fixed in space, while the end point coordinates (x, y) are located with respect to the two perpendicular axes, X, Y. The relationship between these two angles, defined as θ_1, θ_2 and the end point coordinates, x and y, form the kinematic equations of the 2-linked robot. Specifically, the coordinates x and y are defined as [1]

$$x = L_1 \cos(\theta_1) + L_2 \cos(\theta_1 + \theta_2), \text{ and } y = L_1 \sin(\theta_1) + L_2 \cos(\theta_1 + \theta_2).$$ (6)

The above equations in x and y are the 'forward' kinematic equations of the robot. For the lengths (L_1, L_2), the point coordinates (x, y) of the end-effector are uniquely determined by the two variable joint angles (θ_1, θ_2).

The task at hand is to compute the joint angles (θ_1, θ_2) for a given end-effector Cartesian position without analytically solving Eqn. (6). In the simulation examples discussed below, the lengths of the two links were 0.5 meters.

Example 1: In this example, the desired position of the end-effector was chosen randomly at $x_d = -0.6$ and $y_d = 0.5$. These coordinates served as inputs to the HNN. The weights of the neural networks were adjusted until the output error decreased to a pre-set tolerance limit of ± 0.05. The initial position of the end-effector was arbitrarily set at $x = 0.2$, $y = 0.4$. The desired and the obtained x-y coordinates and the position error trajectories e_x, e_y are shown in Fig. 5. In sequel to this, different desired Cartesian locations were presented to the HNN. The end-effector convergence and the error trajectories are shown in Fig. 6.

Example 2: The adaptive capability of the HNN-based learning scheme is demonstrated by changing the desired end-effector positions during the computational process. Initially, the desired end-effector locations presented to HNN was: $x_d = -0.6$ and $y_d = 0.5$. At time instant $k = 150$, the x,y positions were changed to: $x_d = 0.5$ and $y_d = -0.85$. The simulation results obtained are shown in Fig. 7.

Example 3: In this example, we consider a case where one of the links, L_2, of the robot during the learning process undergoes a stretching effect, for example in a telescopic robot. Due to these dynamic perturbations, the observed end-effector position may not match with that of the desired position which necessitates readjustments in the neural weights. The simulation results are shown in Fig. 8. From these results it may be seen that the HNN could adapt to the change in robot dynamics, thereby demonstrating the robustness of the learning scheme.

Example 4: The successful operation of an intelligent robot depends upon its ability to cope with perturbations that may cause dynamic changes in its structure. To study the performance of neural structures under noisy conditions, the robot dynamics were corrupted with a random signal bounded in the interval [0,1]. Tables 1 and 2 show the targeted and the observed end-effector positions for 20% and 50% noise respectively. These results show that the HNN could compute the robot joint angles fairly accurately even under the presence of noise.

3.2 Three-Linked Robot: A three - linked robot model is illustrated in Fig. 9. The forward kinematic equations of this model are

$$x = L_1 \cos(\theta_1) + L_2 \cos(\theta_1 + \theta_2) + L_3 \cos(\theta_1 + \theta_2 - \theta_3), \text{ and}$$
$$y = L_1 \sin(\theta_1) + L_2 \sin(\theta_1 + \theta_2) + L_3 \cos(\theta_1 + \theta_2 - \theta_3). \tag{7}$$

The lengths of the three links, (L_1, L_2, L_3), were 0.5, 0.5 and 0.2 meters respectively. The proposed neural learning scheme made it unnecessary to derive, from the equations given above, an analytical derivation of the inverse kinematic relations of this three-linked structure. All that was required was the forward kinematic equations given in Eqn. (7), and the output of the third neuron which corresponded to the joint angle θ_3. This shows the ease with which a neural network can be adapted to include a different structure whose inverse transformation needs to be formed. The network outputs were suitably transformed to the Cartesian space using the forward kinematic equations.

Example 1: In this example as in the 2-linked robot case, the desired position of the end-effector was chosen to be $x_d = -0.6$ and $y_d = 0.5$. The weights of the neural networks were adjusted until the output error decreased to a pre-set tolerance limit of ± 0.05. The initial position of the end-effector was arbitrarily set at $x = 0.2$, $y = 0.4$. The desired and the obtained x-y coordinates and the position error trajectories for different desired end-effector positions are shown in Fig. 10.

Example 2: In this example, the desired end-effector positions were changed as follows: $x_d = -0.6$ and $y_d = 0.5$ for $k < 150$, $x_d = 0.5$ and $y_d = -0.85$ for $k \geq 150$. The simulation results obtained are shown in Fig. 11. Extensive simulation studies were carried out for different dynamic perturbations and the computation of inverse kinematic transformations were found to be fairly accurate.

4. Conclusions

In this paper, the Hopfield neural network (HNN)-based learning scheme that could directly compute the inverse kinematic transformations of two- and three-linked robots was described. From the computer simulation results presented in the preceding section, it is clear that the HNN could avoid time consuming analytical calculations in sharp contrast to the conventional inverse kinematics algorithms. Furthermore, in a manner that is typical of neural networks, it would be very easy to modify the learned associations upon changes in the structure of the mechanism as was demonstrated for a three-linked robot.

References

[1]   M.W. Spong and M. Vidyasagar, Robot Dynamics and Control, *John Wiley and Sons*, Inc., 1989.

[2]   W.A. Wolovich, Robotics: Basic Analysis and Design, *Holt, Rinehart and Winston,* New York, 1987.

[3]   A. Guez and Z. Ahmad, "Solution to the Inverse Kinematics Problem in Robotics by Neural Networks", *IEEE Int. Conf. on Neural Networks*, San Diego, Calif., pp. 617-624, March 1988.

[4]   J. Barhen, S. Gulati and M. Zak, "Neural Learning of Constrained Nonlinear Transformations", *IEEE Computer*, pp. 67-76, June 1989.

[5]   M.M. Gupta, D.H. Rao and P.N. Nikiforuk, "Dynamic Neural Network Based Inverse-kinematics Transformation of Two- and Three-Linked Robots", *IFAC Conference*, Sydney, Australia, Vol. 3, pp. 289-296, July 19-23, 1993.

[6]   D.H. Rao, M.M. Gupta and P.N. Nikiforuk, "On-Line Learning of Robot Inverse Kinematic Transformations", *IEEE Joint Conf. on Neural Networks (IJCNN)*, Nagoya, Japan, Oct. 25-29, pp. 2827-2830, 1993.

[7]   J.J. Hopfield, "Neural Networks and Physical Systems with Emergent Collective Computational Abilities", *Proceedings of the National Academy of Sciences*, Vol. 79, pp. 2554 - 2558, 1982.

[8]   J.J. Hopfield, "Neurons with Graded Response Have Collective Computational Properties Like of Those Two-State Neurons", *Proceedings of the National Academy of Sciences*, Vol. 81, pp. 3088-3092, 1984.

[9]   J.M. Zurada, Introduction to Artificial Neural Systems, *West Publishing Company*, St. Paul, MN, 1992.

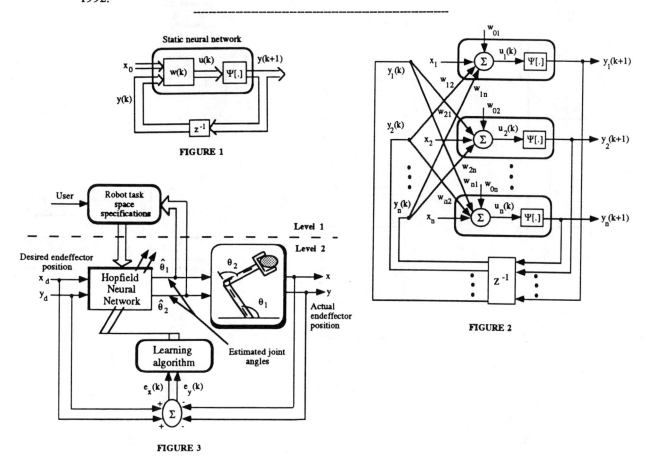

FIGURE 1

FIGURE 2

FIGURE 3

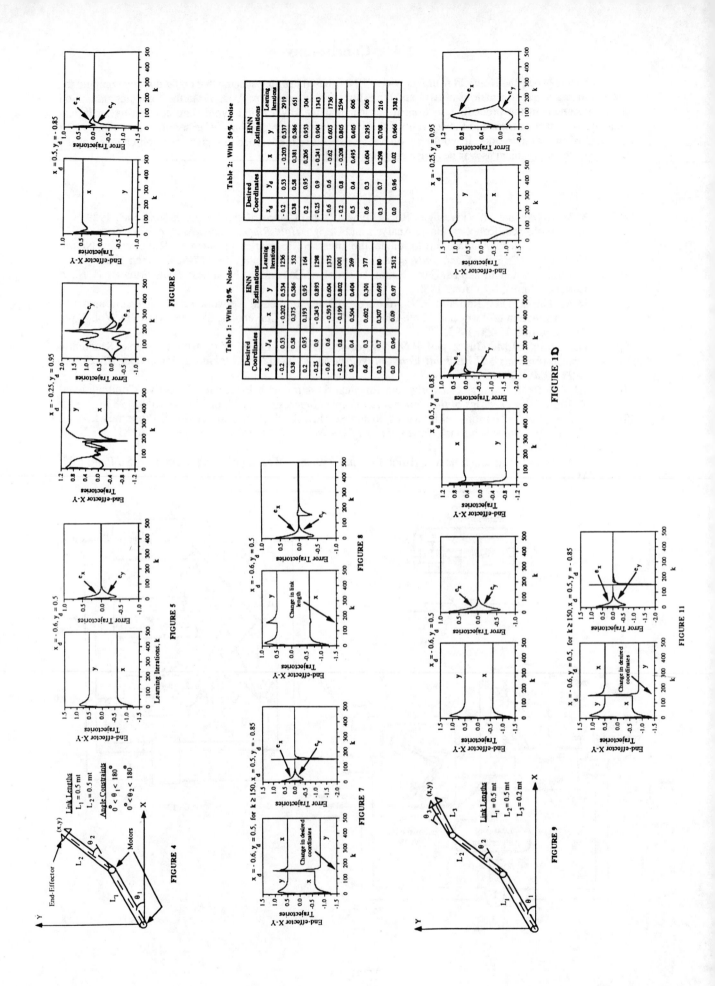

Table 1: With 20% Noise

Desired Coordinates		HNN Estimations		Learning Iterations
x_d	y_d	x	y	
- 0.2	0.53	- 0.202	0.534	1236
0.38	0.58	0.375	0.586	352
0.2	0.95	0.193	0.95	164
- 0.25	0.9	- 0.243	0.893	1298
- 0.6	0.6	- 0.593	0.604	1375
- 0.2	0.8	- 0.199	0.802	1001
0.5	0.4	0.504	0.404	269
0.6	0.3	0.602	0.301	377
0.3	0.7	0.307	0.693	180
0.0	0.96	0.09	0.97	2512

Table 2: With 50% Noise

Desired Coordinate		HNN Estimations		Learning Iterations
x_d	y_d	x	y	
- 0.2	0.53	- 0.203	0.537	2919
0.38	0.58	0.381	0.586	651
0.2	0.95	0.206	0.933	304
- 0.25	0.9	- 0.241	0.904	1343
- 0.6	0.6	- 0.62	0.605	1736
- 0.2	0.8	- 0.208	0.805	2594
0.5	0.4	0.495	0.405	606
0.6	0.3	0.604	0.295	606
0.3	0.7	0.298	0.708	216
0.0	0.96	0.02	0.966	3382

FIGURE 4

FIGURE 5

FIGURE 6

FIGURE 7

FIGURE 8

FIGURE 9

FIGURE 1D

FIGURE 11

Geometry-based Process Control

Jeff Root
c/o Root Associates
55 Whitney Street
P.O. Box 299
Westminster, MA 01473-0299

Abstract

This paper will discuss a straight-forward approach to process control learning and generalization which is based on the geometric mapping of monitored inputs. It will be shown that when output thresholds or goals have been defined and are used as criteria for storing information, unique process shapes are learned. These shapes may be used to automatically derive the appropriate set of control adjustments for each generalized state of the problem.

Introduction: Process Control Framework

The general framework for process control discussed in this paper is shown in figure 1. Controllable process inputs as well as the output state are monitored and used to determine the appropriate feedback to apply to each input.

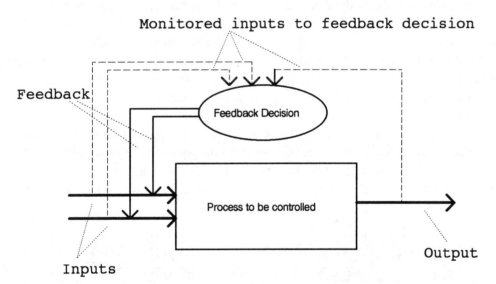

Figure 1: Process Control Framework

There are two unique challenges regarding process control to resolve using connectionist networks. The first is to adaptively generalize similar input sets within an associative memory. The second, more challenging problem has been to provide an adaptive framework for learning solutions to each state of process control problems.

The technique presented here has the ability to learn solutions to a problem as well as providing the input-to-output association capability.

The primary advantages to this approach are:

a)   inputs and outputs are modeled using an editable geometric approach,
b)   output solutions may be determined from the geometry of the inputs using an output threshold or constraint, and
c)   solutions may be assigned from a continuous range of output values.

Serial Proximity Networks

The memory for the geometric mapping approach is provided by serial proximity networks. Serial proximity networks are serial-processing, distributed-memory maps with the following capabilities:
a) pattern recognition
b) generalization
c) instantaneous, unsupervised learning
d) adaptability

They provide a highly dynamic set of associations that enable internal analysis, edit and optimization. This is accomplished by utilizing pre-determined, predictable thresholds of association for each monitored input of a problem. These thresholds, called proximity factors, represent the acceptable range of variability of each input based on a specified monitoring interval. In other words, if we know a particular input varies from one to five units per time interval, we might decide to assign a proximity factor of five in order to associate the highest number of values for this input.

Large proximity factors provide more generalization and require less memory. Smaller proximity factors provide for more specific associations yet require more memory. The architecture of serial proximity networks model each input and output as a separate entity. Input sets are associated to output sets within unique sub-spaces. Figures 2 and 3 depict the architecture of a serial proximity network.

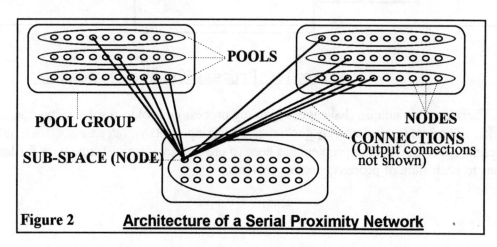

Figure 2   Architecture of a Serial Proximity Network

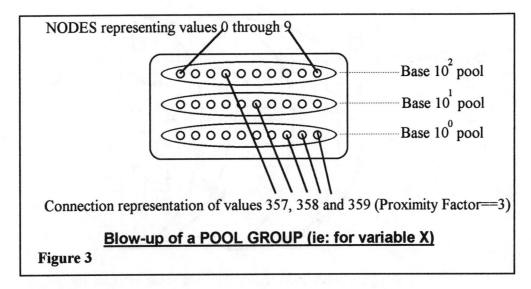

NODES representing values 0 through 9

Base 10^2 pool

Base 10^1 pool

Base 10^0 pool

Connection representation of values 357, 358 and 359 (Proximity Factor==3)

Blow-up of a POOL GROUP (ie: for variable X)

Figure 3

Geometric Maps

Because each input is modeled as a separate entity with a specified range and proximity factor, serial proximity networks actually form a multi-dimensional geometric map of the process. Each input represents one geometric dimension of the problem being modeled. When output boundaries or goals have been defined and are used as a criterion or identifier for storing information within the network, unique process shapes are learned. These shapes may be used to automatically derive the appropriate set of control adjustments for each sub-space.

To illustrate how unique geometric shapes may be learned when storing process data, let us consider the following problem. Let us assume that the process we would like to control could be characterized by the following equation:

$$Z = X^2 - Y^2$$

Let us also assume that the variable ranges for the problem are from 5 to 75 units for X and from -40 to 50 for Y. Also assume that we have determined an upper and lower output control zone for our output Z, based on the following limits:

> *Upper Control Zone*
> > upper limit: 3500 units
> > lower limit: 2200 units

> *Lower Control Zone*
> > upper limit: 1000 units
> > lower limit: 0 units

If we plot these output boundaries over the complete range of input values we would obtain the following approximate geometric shape:

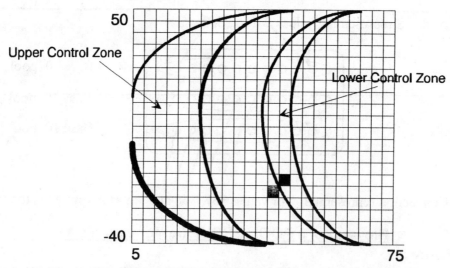

Rough approximation of output control zones mapped using process inputs. Serial proximity sub-space grid shown in background.

When we store sub-spaces within the serial proximity network for this problem we could tag them with an identifier that would associate them with one of two states:

1) Within_Bounds or
2) Out_Of_Bounds

If the state of the output at a particular time interval fell within one of our pre-determined output control zones (black sub-space) we would identify it as being Out_Of_Bounds . Conversely, if the output state during a particular time interval fell between our specified output control zones (shaded sub-space), we could tag it as being Within_Bounds.

Using the Geometric Map to Automatically Derive Feedback

Once we have modeled our process geometrically and tagged our sub-spaces as being either Within_Bounds or Out_Of_Bounds, we have an excellent framework with which to derive our feedback values. Consider the figure above. Look at the black sub-space. What can we determine, visually, regarding corrective measures that might be applied to the black sub-space? We can see that, we should decrease both X and Y via control feedback. What we have just done visually to correct the problem is the fundamental principal behind geometry-based control. In other words, we can determine the solution to a problem by measuring the geometric distance from the current problem state to the closest solution state. Following is a short outline of the geometry-based process control technique.

Outline for geometry-based process control:

1)   Determine limits.

2)   Build a serial proximity network. Tag each new sub-space with a zone identifier based on where this sub-space lies in relation to the pre-determined limits. The tags should represent either of the two conditions:

         Within_Bounds or Out_Of_Bounds

3)   Derive control outputs from the geometry of process. For each Out_Of_Bounds sub-space, associate each input to be controlled with an output value that when added together equals a value that falls within the range of the closest Within_Bounds sub-space. Closeness should be based relative to each input. In other words, when attempting to find the closest Within_Bounds sub-space for calculation of the X output value, the distance should be measured from the current X value to the closest Within_Bounds X value.

Application Results

1) 'Classic' pole balancing problem

Supervised learning via operator actions

A pole-balancing simulator was used to allow an operator to manually balance a 'pole' on a PC screen using a mouse. As the operator balanced the pole the corrections were learned by the network. After a short while, the network was able to balance the pole by itself. This part of the evaluation was developed to demonstrate how well serial proximity networks might provide for rapid supervised learning and generalization. What we found, however, was that the network could easily unlearn all the good corrective moves the operator had taught it if the end of the training suite was filled with poor corrections. We also noted that the set of solutions was fairly brittle. If the operator did not teach the net what to do to correct a particular situation, the pole would fall over.

Unsupervised learning via geometry-based control technique

The pole-balancing simulator was used to map the geometry of the process. Basically the pole was allowed to fall in either direction. As the pole fell the geometry of the process was mapped. The geometry-based process control algorithm was applied to the network. The procedure completed instantaneously. After running the procedure the pole was able to balance itself perfectly. We also tried applying the algorithm after several sloppy manual operator training suites and found that the algorithm fixed the network's solution set such that the pole stayed properly balanced.

2) Multi-dimensional problems

A process control data file was generated from a simulator for a series of non-linear, interactive problem. Inputs and outputs to the problem were provided by the simulator for each time interval of a specified frequency. The file was formatted using TAB delimiters between each process control variable and a carriage return delimiter between each time interval.

A set of output boundaries and control zones were specified prior to building the network. The file was read twice by the geometry-based process control application. The first time the data file was read, each variable's range, minimum value and proximity factor were determined. From this information the input/output network structures (POOL GROUPS, POOLS, NODES) were built. An additional Output Zone POOL GROUP was built to accommodate the process Zone identifier.

The second time the data file was read, pattern data was stored in the network's distributed memory (PATTERN NODES, CONNECTIONS). Each sub-space was tagged with an output zone identifier dependent on where its output value fell in relation to the pre-specified output zones and boundaries.

The process control network was then built from ten thousand lines of process control data in less than 2 seconds. This was achieved using a 80486 chip running at 66Mhz.

The Geometry-based process control algorithm was applied to the network. The procedure completed in less than one second.

The network was then connected to the process simulator such that the simulated inputs were fed into the network while the network outputs provided feedback to the simulator's process controllers.

The maximum activation response time was less than one millisecond and the problem was successfully contained.

Results

In conclusion, it appears that this technique may offer several practical advantages over the current range of adaptive learning methods. Not only does it provide an excellent learning engine for efficient input-to-output association and generalization but it also has the ability to learn solutions to process control problems based on the geometry of the process as it is mapped within the network. It appears that there is much opportunity for applying this technique to many diverse real world process control problems.

References

1. J. Root, (1993) Serial Proximity Networks (Serial Distributed-Memory Processing) - 1993 International Neural Network Society Annual Meeting, VIII
2. J. Root, (1993) The Benefits of Serial Proximity Networks - AI Expert Volume 8, Number 7

NAVITE: A Neural Network System For Sensory-Based Robot Navigation

J. Mario Aguilar[*]

Cognitive and Neural Systems Department
Boston University
111 Cummington St. Rm 240
Boston, MA 02215

José L. Contreras-Vidal[†]

Motor Control Laboratory
Department of Exercise Science and Physical Education
Arizona State University
Tempe, AZ 85287-0404

1 Abstract

A neural network system, NAVITE, for incremental trajectory generation and obstacle avoidance is presented. Unlike other approaches, the system is effective in unstructured environments. Multimodal information from visual and range data is used to improve obstacle detection by eliminating uncertainty in the measurements. This sensory information is then used to generate alternative trajectories which avoid collision. Optimal paths are computed without explicitly optimizing cost functions, therefore reducing computational expenses. Simulations of a planar mobile robot (including the dynamic characteristics of the plant) in obstacle-free and object avoidance trajectories are presented. The system can be extended to incorporate global map information into the local decision-making process.

2 Introduction

The proposed NAVITE system forms a trajectory by instantiating a target position in a synchronous, variable-speed adaptive multijoint controller implemented as a neural network. The target vector is determined by a global path planning algorithm operating at a higher level in the processing hierarchy. Global path planning criteria is utilized to generate a set of these target vectors which define an optimal trajectory based on a-priori knowledge of the environment. The collection of target vectors forms the sequential motor program that drives the trajectory formation network. The nature of this process allows for continuous recalibration of the system's variables and thus permits adaptability to changes in the environment.

The target vector is compared to the present location of the robot and the shortest path is computed incrementally. Navigation begins along this trajectory and if no obstacles are found, the robot's state variables are controlled optimally until the goal is reached. Optimality is obtained through the simultaneous control of state variables to obtain straight and smooth paths. This system is capable of position code invariance so that a trajectory can be generated at several speeds depending on the demands of the task, without altering the path.

On the other hand, the detection of obstacles within a predetermined range will produce a perturbation of the internally generated trajectory which will lead to detour of the robot. Since the original plan remains instantiated, the perturbation is overcome by continuous updating of the trajectory given the present position. Here, the path is no longer the shortest but in exchange, the system is able to simultaneously control the kinematics and dynamics of the robot to avoid unpredicted obstacles, as well as allowing for continuous instantiation of the goal.

Utilization of learned spatial maps (which allow the instantiation of target and present position in allocentric coordinates) and global path planning come into play both when generating the original trajectory and when defining local detours. In this manner, local processing has priority and thus is able to continuously adapt to the environment. However, its configuration and "decision-making" are constantly modulated by the global spatial map. The modulation of local decision processes by global spatial knowledge is the subject of present research. The present implementation assumes that targets instantiated in

[*]Supported in part by ONR (N00014-92-J-1309) and by ARPA (ONR N00014-92-J-4015) darpa (afosr 90-0083) and office of naval research (ONR N00014-92-J-1309).

[†]On leave from Monterrey Institute of Technology (ITESM, México. Supported by a Flinn Foundation Grant). Supported in part by a fellowship from CONACYT (63462)

spatial coordinates which avoid all **known** obstacles (local minima) are available at the input stage of the system.

In the field of path planning for mobile robotics, research has been focused in two different approaches: a) planning within a static environment, and b) planning within an unstructured world. The former has been approached with the assumption that either the environment is known [12] or unknown [10]. In the case of unstructured environments, two main trends can be identified, namely those which emphasize heuristics [7, 8] and those based on perceptual processing [2]. The latter, based on the linking between perception and action has also been called active perception.

Past attempts have shown that the problem of motion planning with multiple non-static objects is intractable using algorithmic approaches [8]. Our approach deals with planning within an unstructured environment utilizing multimodal sensory information. As such, sensory data through perception can trigger adaptive behavior (eg. obstacle avoidance, active target search). Because our method uses incremental planning, it can deal with changing environments.

3   A neural network for trajectory generation

A neural network model that specifies the kinematics of point-to-point arm movements has been proposed in [3]. This model is based on neurophysiology, anatomy, and clinical data concerning the kinematics of synchronous, variable speed multijoint reaching movements. The model, Vector-Integration-To-Endpoint (VITE), produces the typical kinematic signature of most arm movements.

The model provides the position and velocity specification of the desired trajectory from the current position of the arm (Present Position Vector, or PPV) to the target position of the arm (Target Position Vector, or TPV). These vectors can be seen as a pattern of neuronal activation levels distributed across a population of neurons that codes the current and the target position in muscle-length coordinates respectively.

The descending TPV is compared with an ascending "efference copy" of the PPV to produces a difference vector at a stage that specifies the muscle length update (direction and distance vector, DV) required to move the limb from the PPV to the TPV. Before updating the PPV using the DV, a nonspecific speed scalar or GO signal under voluntary control is used to gate multiplicatively the contents of the DV to produce a *desired velocity vector* (Figure 1). Integration of the signal DV times GO to the PPV produces a *desired position vector*. Both the *desired velocity vector* and *desired position vector* comprise the DESIRED-TRAJECTORY which is then used as a command to the plant.

The main features of this GO signal is that before movement, it has a value of zero and then grows faster-than-linearly to a positive value as the movement is developed. In addition, the rate of growth of the GO signal changes the contraction rate synchronously of all muscles contributing to the arm movement, so that all the muscles acting to move the arm have the same onset and offset times. It is hypothesized that in the biological system, the specification of the desired position and velocity vectors by the VITE circuit is used as input to the neuro-muscular system (e.g. the actuator) that actually executes the movement. The structure and neural network implementation of the VITE central controller are depicted in figure 1. The VITE system is specified in terms of nonlinear differential equations as described in [3].

The VITE circuit can also be seen as a proportional + derivative (PD) central controller with time-varying velocity and position gains over the duration of the point-to-point movement. The controller acts as a feedforward controller without sensory feedback, and its outputs generate reciprocal ramp-like descending commands (Present Position Vectors) to antagonist actuators. The duration and amplitude of changes in these PPVs are specified by a GO signal (which affects the time-varying position and velocity gains) and Target Position Vectors. The transient characteristic of this model lies between a perfectly symmetrical smooth movement and a typical skewed PD controller movement.

4   A neural network for navigation control.

We propose to use the VITE system to drive a pair of antagonist (in a push-pull arrangement) DC motors. One of the systems will produce movement along the horizontal axis, and a second system will produce movement along the vertical axis by comparing the magnitude and sign of the differential output of each

Vector Integration To End point (VITE)

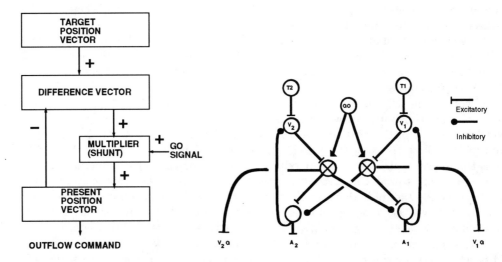

Figure 1: a) Model of trajectory generation based on [3] for synchronous, variable speed multijoint movements. b) Neural network implementation of a two channel, agonist-antagonist, trajectory generator.

VITE system ($A_1 - A_2$). The relative speed of movement between the two DC motors will produce a movement in a given direction.

The uncoupled system of VITE actuators minimizes computational costs by avoiding optimization of cost functions. The algorithm derives the trajectory for a robot of known dynamic capabilities and allows for continuous adaptability.

For reasons of simplicity, the algorithm will be illustrated using an autonomous vehicle with motion being constrained to the XY plane, with bounded distance and velocity. A sample simulation of the trajectory generator system consisting of 2 VITE modules is shown in figure 2a. The trajectories generated by the system in the absence of obstacles are monotonic, in the sense that they display a monotonically decreasing distance to the target position. These trajectories can be performed at different speeds depending on the task or hardware constraints.

This simulation shows the path followed by a mobile robot assuming ideal dynamics. Three goal trajectories (point-to-point) are shown, namely, P0 → P1 → P2 → P3. The velocity profiles for all the trajectories are shown independently for each component in the cartesian space. Note, by the top and bottom flatness on the trajectories, that the robot reaches the pre-established maximum velocity in two of the trajectories. When one of the DC motor reaches this pre-established maximum velocity, the velocity of the other motor is also kept constant (to its current velocity) to allow for straight-line trajectories (e.g. minimum distance) as long as the other actuator moves to maximum velocity. The advantage of this control scheme is that the system will always move towards the target location while tending to maintain the original straight-line path regardless of the structure of the environment, eliminating the need for a parametric search in the space of possible trajectories.

4.1 Obstacle avoidance and DC motor dynamics

The dynamics of a DC motor driving an inertial load are far from the ideal conditions (e.g. 100 % efficiency for all inertial loads), and therefore must be considered. The transfer function of the DC motor controlling motion along the X-axis (or Y-axis) is defined as follows,

$$\begin{bmatrix} \dot{\theta}_x \\ \dot{\omega}_x \end{bmatrix} = \begin{bmatrix} 0 & 1 \\ 0 & -KC \end{bmatrix} \begin{bmatrix} \theta_x \\ \omega_x \end{bmatrix} + \begin{bmatrix} 0 \\ C \end{bmatrix} (A_1 - A_2) \tag{1}$$

where the parameters K and C specify the parameters of the plant (e.g. efficiency and inertial load), and the driving signal $(A_1 - A_2)$ is the output of the VITE module. To transform the coordinate system to the cartesian space, we need to make a change of variables so that $v_x = \omega_x/r$, where r is the radius of the motor wheel, and v_x is the tangential velocity.

Figure 2b shows a simulation of the system including the non-ideal dynamics of the DC motors. Trajectory $P2 \rightarrow P3$ also includes an obstacle as shown. First, note that due to the non-ideal efficiency of the voltage-mechanical energy conversion and the inertial load, the velocity patterns do not reach maximum speed for these trajectories.

In the working model, range data from ultrasonic sensors and vision data (depth) from scene views taken at successive time intervals would be used jointly to guide the mobile robot and avoid collisions. This will be reviewed in the next section. In this simulation, the robot avoids the object by changing momentarily the difference-vector (DV) field in the direction depicted in figure 2b. As described in figure 3, as soon as the robot is outside a safety margin (e.g. force field, d_{safety}) surrounding the obstacle, it turns again toward the target producing a straight path. During the time the robot is avoiding the obstacle, the GO signal is kept constant in both axes. Thus, since the distance to the object is decreasing at rate α, the velocities are effectively decreased as soon as an object is detected at a distance defined by the distance to the obstacle and the safety margin ($d_{object} + d_{safety}$). The rate of deceleration is proportional to the rate of change of the difference, DV, and therefore, it does not matter how far the robot is from the target. The above distance values are tuned so that a safe velocity value can be reached even if the robot is traveling at maximum speed.

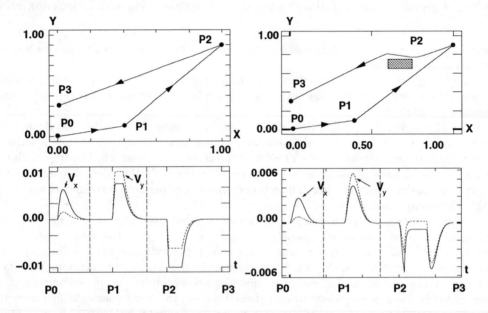

Figure 2: Trajectory formation: a) Ideal trajectory formation without obstacles. b) Trajectory formation with an obstacle and motor dynamics. Two VITE systems generate the position commands driving the DC motors along the X- and Y-axes. Position and velocity for the two systems is shown. *Solid line*: X-direction motor. *Dashed line*: Y-direction motor. *Vertical dashed lines* mark the end of the movement. The rest period indicates that the robot is waiting for the next command.

The flexibility and fine control of the plant arises from the independent control of speed (GO signal) and movement direction (difference vector, DV). The system is tuned so that when the distance between the robot and the obstacle equals the safety margin (d_{safety}), the robot initiates a detour modulated by the characteristics of the sensory data (structure of local environment). Figure 3 depicts the geometry of this formulation. As shown in the figure, in the absence of higher level modulation, the characteristics of the obstacle define the direction which the robot will follow.

As in Brooks' proposal [2], the system uses sensory information to continuously guide the robot when obstacles are found in the desired pathways. This greatly relaxes the constraint commonly introduced by

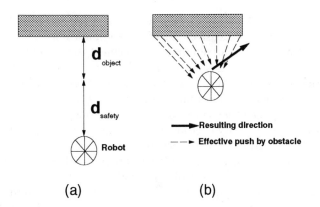

Figure 3: Geometric description of the algorithm used to define the direction and velocity changes of the robot. **a)** The robot detects objects at distance $d_{object} + d_{safety}$ and reduces its velocity. At d_{object}, it initiates a detour determined the characteristics of the obstacle. **b)** The geometry of the obstacle, as determined from sensory data, defines the direction the robot will follow. Each point in the obstacle produces a perturbation in the opposite direction to the reception by the sensors.

other navigation systems which require purely a-priori knowledge of the structure of the environment. In such a circumstance, the sensory data would guide the robot to avoid collision by modulating the GO signal that gates movement and/or by redirecting the robot's path.

5   Multimodal data fusion

In biological systems, multisensory interactions appear to be governed by spatial rules in such a way that coincident multisensory stimuli produce an enhancement of the neuron's firing rate (or reinforcement of the distributed code in a neural population), whereas disparate stimuli provoke either depression or no interaction at all [11].

We propose to use both visual and range data to eliminate uncertainties, noise, and intrinsic errors introduced by the measurements. The sensory data from each modality competes with each other to produce a consistent sensory map of the immediate frontal surrounding.

Multimodal sensory interactions can reduce uncertainty introduced in the sensory representations of stimuli. In particular, the signal-to-noise ratio is improved by combining two or more different modalities of information. In fact, it has been observed that the level of enhancement in the response is greater than the sum of the responses of each modality when the patterns are spatially coincident. On the other hand, spatially-disparate inputs usually depress orienting behavior [11].

The mechanism for data fusion consists of inhibitory feedforward interactions in a neural network with two inputs corresponding to each sensory modality. The sensory inputs are convolved with their respective sensory filters. The results of these convolutions are then combined so that congruent areas in the environment detected by the sensors cooperate while neighboring areas compete and are attenuated by activated neighbors. The details of the data preprocessing are given in [1, 5].

The process of data extraction is performed at successive time intervals along the robot's trajectory. Visual data is pre-processed by a fast segmentation and boundary completion algorithm [4] based on the BCS/FCS system [9], to extract disparity information from motion. This information is then fused with ultrasonic range data to provide a more accurate measure of depth [6].

6   Conclusion

It was noted that path planning algorithms which assume static environments will not be successful in controlling a robot under changing conditions. As an alternative, some algorithms which propose to solve the planning problem under dynamic conditions were reviewed. Their unsuitability to this application was pointed out in terms of the extremely expensive cost of the computations.

Reactive navigation, not as an alternative but as complement to the control scheme, was proposed. A neural network-based reactive navigation system for mobile robotics was presented. The system does not need to optimize any performance index therefore avoiding costly computations. In fact all computations are performed in real time. Additionally, no assumptions are made as to the state of the environment. The system is capable of continuously adapting to changes in the surroundings.

The system is able to autoscale velocity in either axis (or degree of freedom), therefore allowing straight-line trajectories. Since the computation of the trajectory is expressed as a difference vector, the trajectories to the target need not be learned but instead are differentially generated by the network.

The characteristics of the final trajectory evolve through local and possibly global modulation of the current state. Yet, given a detour, the robot resumes along the optimal path from current to target position. The nature of global modulation upon local detour decision making is the focus of current research.

Although the global path planning stage is responsible for defining a path free of local minima, simulations have been run in which the robot escapes typical minima by adding noise or by planned perturbations in the trajectory.

References

[1] Aguilar, M. and Contreras-Vidal, J.L. (1993). An active pattern recognition architecture for mobile robotics. In *Proceedings of the World Conference in Neural Networks 1993*, Portland, OR.

[2] Brooks, R.A. (1987). Intelligence without representation. In *Workshop in Foundations of Artificial Intelligence*. Dedham, MA: Endicott House.

[3] D. Bullock and S. Grossberg, Neural dynamics of planned arm movements: Emergent invariants and speed-accuracy properties during trajectory formation. *Psychological Review*, **95**, pp. 49-90, 1988.

[4] Contreras-Vidal, J.L., and Aguilar, M. (1993). A fast BCS/FCS algorithm for image segmentation. In *Proceedings of the International Conference on Artificial Neural Networks (ICANN-93)*, Amsterdam, September 13-16, 1993.

[5] Contreras-Vidal, J.L., Aguilar, J.M., Lopez-Coronado, J.L., and Zalama, E. (1992). Multimodal real-world mapping and navigation system for autonomous mobile robots based on neural maps. In *Proceedings of the SPIE Conference: Applications of Neural Networks X*. Orlando, Fl.

[6] Elfes, A. (1987). Sonar-based real-world mapping and navigation. *IEEE J. of Robotics and Automation*, **vol. RA-3**, pp. 249-265.

[7] Erdman, M. and Lozano-Perez, T. (1987). On multiple moving objects. *Algorithmica*, **2**, pp. 477-521.

[8] Gil de Lamadrid, J.F. and Gini, M.L. (1990). Path tracking through uncharted moving obstacles. *IEEE Trans. on Systems, Man, and Cybernetics*, **20**, pp. 1408-1422.

[9] Grossberg, S. and Mingolla, E. (1985). Neural dynamics of form perception: Boundary completion, illusory figures, and neon spreading. *Psychological Review*, **92**,173-211.

[10] Lumelsky, V.J. and Stepanov, A.A. (1986). Dynamic path planning for a mobile automaton with limited information on the environment. *IEEE Trans. in Automatic Control.*, **AC-31**, pp. 1058-1063.

[11] Stein, B.E., Meredith, M.A., Huneycutt, W.S., and McDade, L. (1989) Behavioral indices of multisensory integration: orientation to visual cues is affected by auditory stimuli. *J. of Cognitive Neuroscience*, Vol. 1, No. 1, Winter, 1989, pp. 12-24.

[12] Zaharakis, S.C. and Guez, A. (1990). Time optimal robot navigation via the slack set method. *IEEE Trans. on Systems, Man, and Cybernetics.*, **20**, pp. 1396-1407.

Efficient Learning of Generic Grasping Functions using a Set of Local Experts

Medhat A. Moussa and Mohamed S. Kamel

Pattern Analysis and Machine Intelligence Lab.
Department of Systems Design Engineering
University of Waterloo, CANADA

Abstract—In this article, we presented the concept of generic grasping functions that can be used to find grasping choices for arbitrary objects in the environment. Examples of these functions actions can be collected from sensory data and approximated using artificial neural networks. We tested the application of a modular neural architecture to the approximation of some simulated grasping functions. A modified architecture in which the gating network output rule was replaced by a competitive output rule gave better results. We also found that applying an incremental learning process would significantly enhance the learning rate and the approximation accuracy.

1.0 INTRODUCTION

A key measure of success for an autonomous robotic system is to have the ability to grasp an arbitrary object in an uncertain environment. Attaining this ability requires the solution of several complex questions such as what is the object (i.e recognition), how to grasp the object (i.e grasp choice), and which path to take to avoid obstacles present in the environment (i.e. path planning). In this paper, we are interested in the solution of the second question, the grasp choice.

Choosing a grasp for an arbitrary object is a very complex problem. In general, the solution often requires the satisfaction of several constraints such as task requirement, gripper limited capabilities and object geometry. If several solutions are possible, then the chosen grasp is then required to optimize a grasping criteria such as stability. To make the solution tractable, even the most sophisticated grasp model often involves a simplified representation of the grasped object typically treated as smooth, rigid geometric primitives or polyhedra [1]. As a result current grasping models are limited to operate under ideal laboratory conditions. Relaxing geometric simplification is important to allow a robotic system to grasp a wide variety of objects without extensive encoding of object models and with less sensitivity to sensory noise. Tomovic et al. [7] have proposed a grasping model that is based on the representation of target objects of arbitrary shape by one of a small number of geometric primitives. Grasping is then accomplished using a number of standard grasp configurations. Liu et al. [3] have proposed using a BP network to build a multi-dimensional table of object primitives-grasping modes for a multifinger robot hand. Xu et al. [8] applied a modified Hopfield network to find the optimum grasping position for a 2-D arbitrary object.

In [5] we have proposed a neural grasping system that learns the mapping between an object configuration and a gripper configuration at stable grasping points using a BP network. The learned mapping can then be applied to geometrically similar objects irrespective of the complexity of the object geometry itself. While this has relaxed the assumption of simplified representation, learning grasping functions for every conceivable object class through experimentation is impractical due to the large number of training examples needed for each function to be learned accurately. In addition, since multiple solutions can be found for each object configuration, several networks are needed. In this paper we propose a more generic representation of grasping functions which would enable the application of one function learned through grasping experiments on one object to an entirely different object. We will then examine how to train a set of local neural experts to perform an accurate approximation of these functions using a small number of training examples.

2.0 GENERIC GRASPING FUNCTIONS

The orientation and position of an object in the robot work envelope can be described by a 4×4 homogenous transformation matrix, called the object *configuration*, that relates the body attached coordinate frame to a reference coordinate frame. Similarly, the description of the gripper local coordinate frame relative to the reference coordinate frame is called the gripper configuration. To simplify the analysis, we will assume the gripper to be a two finger parallel gripper. Figure 1 illustrates an object that is being grasped. In this figure, the following transformations are defined as:

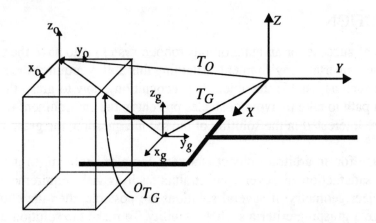

FIGURE 1. Object and gripper configuration during a grasp operation

$T_O \in \mathrm{R}^{4\times4}$ relates the object configuration to the robot base coordinate frame.
$T_G \in \mathrm{R}^{4\times4}$ relates the gripper at a grasping configuration to the robot base coordinate frame. A grasping configuration is defined as the configuration of the gripper when:

- The gripper fingers are in contact with the object faces.
- The object is stable under this grasp.

$^{O}T_G \in \mathrm{R}^{4\times4}$ relates the gripper configuration to the object coordinate frame.

From these definitions T_G can be written as:

$$T_G = T_O \, ^{O}T_G \qquad (1)$$

Evaluating T_O can be done using vision or other sensory information; however, evaluating $^{O}T_G$ represents a grasp choice which is dependent on several variables and even for objects with simple geometrical representation there could be an infinite number of potential grasping configurations [4]. Thus T_G can be written in a general form as

$$T_{Gi} = T_O f_i \text{ (Object geometry, Task requirement, Gripper, Grasping Criteria)} \qquad (2)$$

Where $f_i \in R^{4\times4}$ is a homogenous transformation matrix that represents a grasp choice of the object.

Since no *a priori* encoding of grasping rules will be done, then the question becomes what forms of ^OT_G to learn and how to learn them? Casting the problem in terms of an input-output mapping we first define a generic grasping function as a function $G:R^{4\times4} \rightarrow R^{4\times4}$ such that

$$T_G = G(T_O) \qquad (3)$$

Adopting the roll, pitch and yaw convention for orientation description we then define T_G as

$$T_G = T_G^*(x_g, y_g, z_g, \phi_g, \theta_g, \psi_g) \quad = XYZ\Phi\Theta\Psi \qquad (4)$$

Where $\quad XYZ \equiv \text{Trans }(0,0,x) \text{ Trans}(0,0,y) \text{ Trans}(0,0,z)$

$\Phi\Theta\Psi \equiv \text{Rot }(Z,\phi) \text{ Rot }(Y,\theta) \text{ Rot }(X,\psi)$

$T^* \equiv$ a matrix function $T^*:R^6 \rightarrow R^{4\times4}$ [6]

Similarly T_O can be written as

$$T_O = T_O^*(x, y, z, \phi, \theta, \psi) \qquad (5)$$

Thus equation 3 can be written as

$$T_G = G(T_O^*(x_o, y_o, z_o, \phi_o, \theta_o, \psi_o)) \qquad (6)$$

The mapping can be further simplified by performing a kinematic decoupling. Since $T_O = T_{trans} R_{rotation}$ then we rewrite 1 as

$$Trans_O^{-1} T_G = R_O {}^O T_G \qquad (7)$$

But since $Trans_O$ is a constant that can be evaluated from sensory information, then we rewrite 6 as

$$T_G = G(T_O^*(\phi, \theta, \psi)) \qquad (8)$$

Comparing between equation 2 and equation 8 one can notice that instead of formulating the problem in terms of different objects, different grippers, different tasks and different grasping criteria, the problem now is formulated in terms of three generic rotation angles. That means that a grasping function G could be used to grasp two different objects as illustrated in Figure 2. Two objects with different geometric shapes are both being grasped by a two finger parallel gripper. One can imagine a grasping scenario in which the first object configuration is composed of an initial rotation around the local z-axis with angle ϕ, the gripper has to rotate with the same angle to achieve a correct grasping configuration. But the second object can be grasped by the same grasping function even though they are totally different objects. This observation means that a robot trained to grasp an object can use the same function to grasp another object. However there are still an infinite number of grasping functions that could be learned during grasping a wide variety of objects.

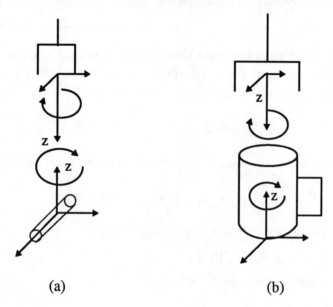

(a)   (b)

FIGURE 2. Two different objects can be grasped using the same grasping function

We can further categorize these generic grasping functions by noticing the degrees of freedom objects normally possess in the environment. R_O has three rotational degrees of freedom; however, in reality most objects have one or two d.o.f only under free standing conditions. This leads to the categorization of generic grasping functions in terms of the object orientation variable of which they could be a function as illustrated in Table 1.

TABLE 1.

Type	Number of variables
Type 0	$T_G = \text{Constant}$
Type 1	$T_G = f(\phi)$ or $f(\theta)$ or $f(\psi)$
Type 2	$T_G = f(\phi,\theta)$ or $f(\theta,\psi)$
Type 3	$T_G = f(\phi,\theta,\psi)$

Categorization of grasping functions makes examining the learning requirements easier and more traceable. However, grasping functions could represent a complex grasping criteria and that could lead to difficulty in learning. At this point the goal is to design an efficient process for learning various types of grasping functions based on examples from experimentation.

3.0 SIMULATION OF GRASPING SCENARIO

Three simple grasping scenarios are considered in this paper. They represent some of the infinite grasp choices that a gripper could have to grasp an object. All three scenarios can be modeled using type 1 grasping functions; however, the complexity of the function could vary. The three scenarios are:

- Grasp 1:

  As illustrated in figure 2a, a constant relationship exists between the object and the gripper.

- Grasp 2:

  This scenario illustrates the same object and gripper but with an objective criteria to reduce the rotation of the manipulator wrist, thus minimize ϕ. This scenario is

  IF $\phi_0 \leq 90°$ THEN $\phi_g = -\phi_0$

  ELSE IF $90° \leq \phi_0 \leq 270°$ THEN $\phi_g = 180 - \phi_0$

  ELSE $\phi_g = 360 - \phi_0$

  This scenario is especially difficult to learn since it contains a function discontinuity at $\phi_0 = 90$ and at $\phi_0 = 270$.

- Grasp 3:

  This scenario illustrates a grasp choice of a cup by the handle. However, the grasp would be done on the cup body if the handle is on the far side of the robot. Thus the scenario is

  IF $0° \leq \phi_0 \leq 120°$ THEN $\phi_g = -\phi_0$

  ELSE IF $300° \leq \phi_0$ THEN $\phi_g = 360 - \phi_0$

  ELSE $\phi_g = 30$

  In addition the gripper experiences translation due to the handle size thus

  IF $90° \leq \phi_0 \leq 270°$ THEN x_g = handle size

  ELSE $x_g = 0$

  Again function discontinuity exists at $\phi_0 = 120°, 300°$

4.0 DESCRIPTION OF LEARNING EXPERIMENTS

In [5] we have reported results on similar simulated grasping functions using a BP network and a modified BP network that increases learning speed. In both cases, long training sessions were noticed along with the need for a large number of training examples. Since we assume that training examples will be obtained through real experimentation, we are interested in using the minimum amount of training data to learn a complex grasping function with a high accuracy. This can be done by using a set of local experts in a modular architecture as proposed by Jacob et al.[2]. In this architecture each local expert is allocated a part of the mapping space which is a less complex mapping than the original mapping, such as linear vs. nonlinear mapping. This uncouples the weights of each expert from other experts weights which makes learning faster and yields better generalization. A gating network divides the space among the local experts using a special error function. The final output of the network, where there are n experts, is

$$y = \sum_{i=1}^{n} g_i y_i \qquad (9)$$

Where g_i is the output of the ith output PE of the gating network

y_i is the output of the ith local expert

We performed four experiments to explore how to design a training process that could yield fast learning using a small training set size.

Experiment 1

In this experiment, we established a benchmark by dividing all grasp scenarios into linear segments and training linear networks on these segments. The size of the training set and the rate of learning represent a benchmark performance that the following networks performance will be measured against. Grasp 1 is already a linear function, while grasp 2 is divided into 3 linear segments: Grasp 2a, 2b, and 2c. However, the first segment is the same function of grasp 1 then only grasp 2b, and 2c are needed. For grasp 3, two linear and a constant segment are possible. Both linear segments are represented by grasp 1 and grasp 2b.

Experiment 2

In this experiment, we presented grasps 2 and 3 to a modular neural network that was constructed using the NeuralWare Professional II simulator. For grasp 2 the network topology has varied considerably starting from 3 experts and up to 6 experts with various internal topologies. The number of PE in the gating network hidden layer also varied from 3 PE and up to 10 PE. Experiments n different topologies were allowed to run for up to 500K before other topologies were explored. For both grasp 2 and grasp 3 *no* reasonable learning was achieved.

Experiment 3

In this experiment, we presented grasps 2 and 3 to a modified modular network in which the output of the gating network was altered after a few thousand epochs from a normalized output

$$g_k = \frac{e^{s_k}}{\sum_{i=1}^{n} e^{s_i}} \qquad (10)$$

where $\mathbf{s} = (s_1,..., s_n)$ is the summation vector of the gating network output layer

To a competitive output defined as

$$g_i = \begin{bmatrix} 1 & if \ s_i > s_l \ \ l = 1...n \\ 0 & otherwise \end{bmatrix} \qquad (11)$$

The effect of this change is eliminating the weighting of the experts output by the gating network output according to equation 9. As a result, the function of the gating network becomes limited to classifying the input pattern to one of the local expert classes without weighting the pattern by how far or close it is to the center of the class.

Experiment 4

In this experiment, we repeated experiments 2 and 3 on a modified training set of grasp 2 in which training cases that follow grasp 1 function were removed, i.e all cases were $\phi_0 \leq 90°$. The idea is that if this function has been learned at grasp 1 then what improvement can result by eliminating all training examples related to it from the learning process of the remaining functions.

5.0 RESULTS AND DISCUSSION

In all experiments an acceptable approximation was achieved when the error on the testing set did not exceed 1° for the angles output and 2 mm for the translation output. Results of the 4 experiments tabulated in tables 2 &3 show the following:

- Learning rate can be significantly increased if we can a priori divide the training set into subsets each representing a less complex mapping. In addition, since learning is localized to one region, excellent generalization is achieved even with very small training sets.

- Using a gating network in experiment 2 and 3 failed to achieve reasonable approximation for grasp 2 and 3. This is due to the fact that the output of the expert network is weighted by the output of the gating network. For a problem such as grasp 2 and 3, where discontinuity could exist in the mapping, the gating network requires a large training set, and takes a longer time to be able to separate between numerically close but quite different inputs.

- The problem of the gating network learning can be rectified by changing the output of the output layer from a normalized output to a competitive output after a reasonable number of training cycles has elapsed. This effectively makes the training process a function of the training of the expert network only, and speeds up training considerably. In addition, during recall high approximation accuracy is achieved even with a small training set size.

- It is recommended while using the modified training procedure to train the network using a small training set rather than a large training set. This allows the gating network to easily separate the adjacent regions, while using competitive learning during recall guarantees good generalization. However, a biased training set might give an opposite effect, this case should be taken into consideration during selection of the training examples.

- Incremental learning where previously learned function actions are removed from the training set greatly enhance the learning process. For grasping, robot experiments can be greatly reduced using previously learned functions to represent a more complex ones.

TABLE 2. Experiment 1

Case	Size of training set	Accuracy mean/max. error	# of epochs
Grasp 1	5	0.4 / 0.9	120
Grasp 2a	5	0.2 / 0.4	100
Grasp 2b	5	0.1 / 0.2	80

TABLE 3. Experiments 2, 3 & 4

Case	Modular Network (Experiment 2)			Modified Modular Network (Experiment 3)		
	Size of training set	Accuracy	# of iterations	Size of training set	Accuracy	# of iterations
Grasp 2	Various sets are used 30 - 180	N/A	Up to 500K	Same as in Experiment 2		
Grasp 3						
Experiment 4						
Grasp 2	23	1.1/90	110K	23	0.02/0.13	11K

6.0 CONCLUSION

Performance of a modular neural architecture is dependant on the performance of the gating network. A modified training process for the gating network proved to be very efficient in both training and recalling. Furthermore, removing previously learned function actions from the training set proved to enhance training speed and reduce the number of trained examples needed to achieve a required accuracy. Future research is directed towards the application of generic grasping functions to multifingered grippers.

ACKNOWLEDGEMENT

This research has been partially funded by the Natural Sciences and Engineering Research Council of Canada.

REFRENCES

[1] Cutkosky, M. R.(1989). "On Grasp Choice, Grasp Models, and the Design of Hands for Manufacturing Tasks", IEEE trans. on Robotics and Automation, Vol. 5, No. 3, pp. 269-279.

[2] Jacobs, R., Jorden, M., Nowlen, S., Hinton, G. (1991) "Adaptive Mixtures of Local Experts", *Neural Computation*, Vol. 3, pp. 79-87.

[3] Liu, H., Iberall, T., Bekay, A. (1989). "Neural Network Architecture for Robot Hand Control", *IEEE Control Systems Magazine*, pp. 38-42.

[4] Lozano-Perez, T., Jones, J.L., Mazer, E., O'Donnell, P.A., Grimson, W.E.L., Tournassoud, P. and Lanusse, A. (1987), "Handy: A Robot System That Recognizes, Plans and Manipulates", *Proceedings IEEE Conference on Robotics and Automation*.

[5] Moussa, M. A., Kamel, S. M. (1993). "Mapping of Complex Grasping Functions using a BP Network", *WCNN*, Vol. 3, pp.

[6] Paul, R. P. (1981). "Robot Manipulators: Mathematics, Programming, and Control", *MIT Press*, Cambridge, Mass.

[7] Tomovic, R., Bekey, G. A., Karplus, W. A. (1987) "A Strategy for Grasp Synthesis for Multifingered Robot Hand," in *Proc. 1987 IEEE Int. Conf. on Robotics and Automation*, Raleigh, pp. 83-89.

[8] Xu, G., Scherrer, H., Schweitser, G. (1990). "Application of Neural Networks on Robot Grippers", *IEEE Int. Conf. on Robotics and Automation*, pp. 337-342.

Computer Recognition of Imprecise Dynamic Arm Gestures of People with Severe Motor Impairment

David M. Roy[1,2], Roman Erenshteyn[1], Marilyn Panayi[3],
William S. Harwin[1], Richard Foulds[1], Robert Fawcus[2]

[1]Applied Science and Engineering Laboratories, A. I. duPont Institute/University of Delaware, USA. [2]City University, London, UK. [3]Educational Consultant, London, UK.

A. I. duPont Institute, Dept. ASEL, P.O. Box 269
Wilmington DE 19899
Email: roy@asel.udel.edu

Tel: 302 651 6830 Fax: 302 651 6895

ABSTRACT

Backpropagation artificial neural networks (ANN) were trained to distinguish two visually similar dynamic arm gestures from a subject with severe speech and motor impairment due to cerebral palsy (SSMICP). Data was collected using a six degree of freedom magnetic position tracker attached to the forearm. The recognition error rates from ANNs trained using both static and motion parameters were compared with static parameters alone and motion parameters alone. Results show that ANNs can be trained to recognize "noisy" arm gestures produced by neuro-motorically impaired individuals. Findings indicate the importance of both static and motion parameters in the machine recognition of such gestures. The results confirm that dynamic gestures can be used to increase the bandwidth of information transfer across the human-machine interface (HMI).

INTRODUCTION

The research into the computer recognition of gesture is part of an overall effort to develop new methods of gestural HMI for people with severe motoric dysfunction. The work is complemented by a concurrent investigation into the human factors of gestural interaction (1,3).

People with SSMICP have limited and imprecise motor control. Each member of this population is likely have an idiosyncratic range of physical abilities. Cerebral palsy is a result of damage to the developing brain usually during or near birth. The damage results in a loss of control over voluntary muscle action together with inappropriate muscle tone (2). If the condition is severe, precise targeting or activities involving fine motor control are very difficult.

This population can often produce a range of imprecise but visually recognizable gestures (3). The machine recognition of such gestures would find applications in the areas of communication through speech synthesis, computer access, interaction in virtual environments, wheelchair, robotic and environmental control.

Although the field of computer recognition of gesture is still in its infancy, research in this area is encouraging. Harwin and Jackson looked at the computer recognition of head gestures from people with cerebral palsy (4). They used the concept of a "virtual head-stick" and hidden Markov models as the recognition method. Their work highlighted the difficulty in automatically segmenting gestures where the movement contains an involuntary component.

Other work into gesture recognition using neural networks (5, 6, 7, 8) has looked at data from hand shapes using the cyberglove or dataglove. However, people with SSMICP commonly exhibit a very spastic clenched fist with limited voluntary control precluding their use of this technology.

APPROACH

The ultimate objective of our work is develop gesture recognition algorithms based on ANNs. Equally important at this stage is the examination of the information content of the gestures themselves. The aim is to use ANNs to:

i) Identify the importance of parameters in the recognition of gestures from people with cerebral palsy.

ii) Examine the value of sensor integration e.g. the combination of EMG and position sensors (9).

iii) Guide the future selection of gesture sub-sets in order to obtain a good feature separation for a high rate of recognition.

Our immediate goal is to determine appropriate feature extraction for this type of dynamic gesture. ANN models are being used both as a tool to understand the problem of gesture recognition and as the means to realize a gestural HMI.

It is possible to consider the voluntary/involuntary components of cerebral palsied motion as a signal/noise model. Unfortunately, knowledge of the mechanisms of human motion in general and cerebral palsied motion in particular is insufficient to enable us to model either signal or noise, or to define how both are interrelated. The ANN approach is well suited to modeling this problem since little a priori knowledge is available.

The well understood simple backpropagation ANN model was chosen for the initial analysis of gestural data.

DATA COLLECTION

The human-factors study looked at twelve subjects aged eight to seventeen years, each with SSMICP. As reported in this study, it was possible to elicit 120 gestures without training. This work proposed that gestural modalities may be an appropriate means of human-machine interactions (1, 3).

Movement and surface EMG data were collected from four of the twelve subjects. The gestures were selected on the basis that they a) reflected the subjects' physical abilities, and b) involved one arm as a principle component of the gesture.

Data was collected using a six degree of freedom magnetic position tracker (the "Bird" from Ascension Technology). The receiver was attached to the right forearm. The data sampling rate was 100 samples/second. The data were stored on the hard disk of a 486 PC. The gestures were produced upon verbal command of the investigator. The time of elicitation was recorded and used to initially segment the data.

The data presented in this paper were collected from one of the subjects, a 17 year old male, with severe spastic-athetoid cerebral palsy. The subject was non-verbal due to severe dysarthria. His method of accessing the environment using assistive technology was limited to pressing up to five large electromechanical switches with various parts of the body including the head, elbow, and knee. This restricted input modality enabled him to communicate using a speech synthesizer and to drive an electric wheelchair. Twenty seven gestures were chosen from the set of 120. The subject performed each the 27 gestures a minimum of 20 times in random sequence (figure 1).

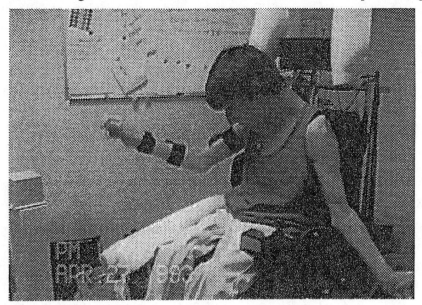

Figure 1. Subject performing dynamic arm gestures

ANALYSIS

The data were animated using an arm model created using Matlab matrix manipulation software. Graphics animation software was developed in-house to render images in real-time on a Silicon Graphics Iris Elan workstation. The software allowed approximate reconstruction of arm motion and was used to view and compare gestures. Gestures were further manually segmented so that the precise onset and finish of controlled motion could be located. These data were used to create training exemplars for the development of gesture recognition algorithms (figure 2).

Gesture (a)   Gesture (b)

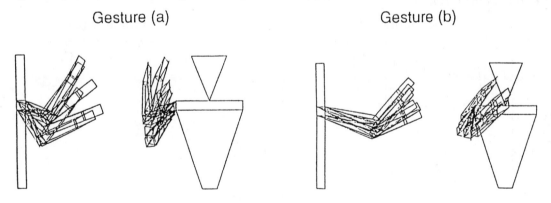

Figure 2. Computer Animation of Dynamic Arm Gestures

To investigate the relative importance of features, two gestures were chosen that looked visually similar. The gestures chosen were a) pretend to play the drums b) pretend to shake hands.

Although there were only 23 elicitations of gesture (a) and 26 of (b), it was possible to increase the number of gestures in each class by considering repetitive gestural segments as individual gestures. Each cycle was manually segmented and then four points automatically extracted from each gesture segment. The resulting data set was divided into two halves, each half containing the same number frames of a particular gesture. These were used as the training set and test set 1 while test set 2 comprised contiguous frames of both gestures (table 1).

Table 1. Size of training and testing data sets

	Gesture (a) (to play the drums)	Gesture (b) (to shake hands)
Training Set	186	118
Test Set 1	186	118
Test Set 2	156	303

Feature Extraction

The data was manipulated using the Matlab matrix manipulation package running on a Sun Sparc 10 workstation. The following features were derived from the raw position and rotation matrix data: Position, velocity, acceleration and Euler angles or $\{x, y, z, \dot{x}, \dot{y}, \dot{z}, \ddot{x}, \ddot{y}, \ddot{z}, \theta, \phi, \rho\}$
These were assembled into the following three feature sets

$$\{x, y, z, \dot{x}, \dot{y}, \dot{z}, \ddot{x}, \ddot{y}, \ddot{z}, \theta, \phi, \rho\} \in F_1 \qquad \{x, y, z, \theta, \phi, \rho\} \in F_2 \qquad \{\dot{x}, \dot{y}, \dot{z}, \ddot{x}, \ddot{y}, \ddot{z}\} \in F_3$$

Neural Network Architecture

The feature sets were presented as the input layer to a back propagation neural network with one hidden layer. The architecture of neural networks is described by: Z1 - Z2 - Z3, where Z1 - number of inputs (6 or 12), Z2 - number of hidden nodes (40) and Z3 - number of outputs (2). Log-sigmoid functions were used as the transfer functions for the hidden and output nodes. Nguyen-Widrow initial weights, momentum and adaptive learning rate were used to improve the training rate. Momentum was used to assist in the learning procedure by taking into account local gradient and trends in the error.

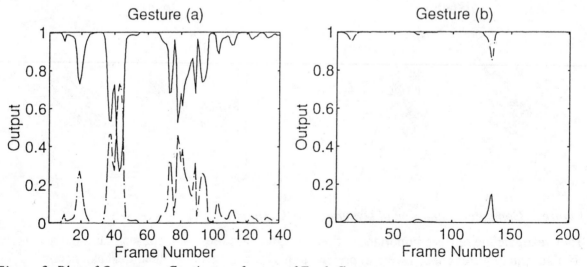

Figure 3. Plot of Output vs. Contiguous frames of Each Gesture

RESULTS AND DISCUSSION

The experimental results are shown in table 2. Recognition error probability was used as a measure of the quality of recognition.

Table 2. Training and testing results.

Problem			Training			Testing 1			Testing 2		
	N_{ep}	E_{sq}	P_1	P_2	P_{av}	P_1	P_2	P_{av}	P_1	P_2	P_{av}
F_1	5000	23.51	0.011	0.076	0.036	0.086	0.347	0.188	0.032	0.066	0.054
F_2	5000	27.96	0.005	0.101	0.043	0.151	0.390	0.243	0.109	0.046	0.068
F_3	5000	82.15	0.215	0.178	0.201	0.312	0.398	0.345	0.256	0.578	0.468

In the table: N_{ep} - maximal number of epochs for training; E_{sq} - sum-squared error; P_1, P_2, P_{av} - recognition error probabilities (for the first gesture, for the second and an average respectively).

Figure 3 shows typical plots of output vs. frame number for test set 2 containing contiguous frame data (using feature set F1). As can be seen from the example graphs, gesture (b) was recognized with more certainty that (a). However, thresholding can be used effectively with very relatively few frame sequences misidentified.

Table 2 shows that although recognition rate was in general higher for F2 (position and orientation only) than for F3 (linear velocity and acceleration only), F1(position, orientation, velocity and acceleration) gave significantly higher results than either F2 or F3. Thus movement parameters contain information that is sufficiently orthogonal relative to position and orientation that they can be used to enhance recognition.

This has significant implications for the computer recognition of the gestures of people with SSMICP. People with SSMICP find precise targeting and tracking in space extremely difficult. However, most assistive devices require either targeting of electromechanical switches which only sense position or operating joysticks which sense path. Thus, the computer recognition of dynamic gestures as a method of human-machine interaction should result in an increase in the bandwidth of information transfer across the HMI in comparison with existing modalities. If bandwidth is used as an objective criterion for the quality of the HMI, then dynamic gestures are clearly an improvement on existing modalities.

CONCLUSIONS

As shown in this study, back propagation NN as a pattern recognition method is very useful for the analysis of feature space taking into account not only output recognition error, but also errors produced in hidden layers. Also, this method can solve complicated meshed class recognition problems which is extremely useful when the topology of the recognized objects is unknown as is the case of imprecise dynamic gestures.

ACKNOWLEDGEMENTS

The authors would like to gratefully acknowledge the financial support of the Nemours Foundation, USA, the Science and Engineering Research Council, UK and the NIDRR, USA.

Special thanks to Dr. Michael Floyd and Professor Ewart Carson of the City University, UK, Dr. Michael Alexander and Dr. Freeman Miller of the A. I. duPont Institute, and Dr. Charles Marler of the University of Delaware, USA for their continued support and encouragement.

Thanks to Dr. Garland Stern, Randy Glass, Marian Cowley for their assistance with the visualization of the data presented in this manuscript. Additional thanks to Cindy Brodoway and Jack Needle of the Medical Photography department of the A. I. duPont Institute.

Particular thanks to student collaborators, their care-givers, and staff of John G. Leach School, A. I. duPont Hospital School, Delaware, HMS School for Children with Cerebral Palsy, and Widener Memorial School, Philadelphia, PA, for their interest and commitment.

REFERENCES

1. Roy, D.M., Harwin, W.S., Fawcus, R. (1993) *The Enhancement of Computer Access for People with Cerebral Palsy through the Computer Recognition of Imprecise Gestures*. Proceedings of ECART2 - European Conference on the Advancement of Rehabilitation Technology, Stockholm, Sweden.

2. Levitt, S. (1992) *Treatment of Cerebral Palsy and Motor Delay, Second Edition*. Blackwell Scientific, Boston MA.

3. Roy, M., Panayi. M., Harwin, W.S., Fawcus, R., (1993) *The Enhancement of Interaction for People with Severe Speech and Physical Impairment through the Computer Recognition of Gesture and Manipulation*. Proceedings of CSUN Conference on Virtual Reality and Persons with Disability, San Francisco.

4. Harwin, W.S., Jackson, R.D. (1990) *Analysis of Intentional Head Gesture to Assist Computer Access by Physically Disabled People*. Journal of Biomedical Engineering, Vol. 12, May, pp 193-198.

5. Murakami, K., and Taguchi, H. (1991) *Gesture Recognition Using Neural Networks*. SIGCHI Proceeding, pp 237-242.

6. Fels, S.S. (1990) *Building Adaptive Interfaces Using Neural Networks: The Glove-Talk Pilot Study*. Technical Report CRG-TR-90-1, University of Toronto, Canada.

7. Briffault, X., and Braffort, A. (1993) *Space, Language and Gesture: A Model of Multimodal Expression of Space*. Proceedings of the Eleventh IASTED International Conference, Annecy, France.

8. Peters, S., Foulds R., (1991) *Interaction and Training Requirements for Machine Recognition of Human Gestures*. Interactive Learning Technology for the Deaf. NATO Advanced Research Workshop, Sint-Michielsgestel, the Netherlands.

9. Roy, D.M., Panayi, M., Harwin, W.S., Fawcus R. (1993) *Advanced Input Methods for People with Cerebral Palsy: A Vision of the Future*. RESNA '93 Conference Proceedings.

NEURAL NETWORKS FOR MANIPULATOR CONTROL:
----METHODOLOGY, STABILITY AND SIMULATIONS

Y. JIN, A .G. PIPE, A. WINFIELD

University of West England, Faculty of Engineering, Frenchay, Bristol BS16 1QY, UK

Abstract: In this paper we discuss how to use neural networks to control robotic manipulators. Two different control structures and neural network on-line learning algorithms are proposed. The reason behind the proposed control structures is also presented. The whole system stability is guaranteed. Neural network off-line learning algorithm is suggested. Off-line learning improves the on-line running performance.

1. INTRODUCTION

Manipulators are coupled multi-input multi-output systems. They are subjected to structured and/or unstructured uncertainties even in a well-structured setting for an industrial use. Structured uncertainties are mainly caused by imprecision in the manipulator link properties, unknown loads, and so on. Unstructured uncertainties are caused by unmodeled dynamics, e.g. nonlinear friction, disturbances, and the high-frequency part of the dynamics.

Despises of complexity and uncertainties, manipulators (n joints) can be modelled in a general form

$$H(q)\ddot{q}+C(q,\dot{q})\dot{q}+g(q)+F(q,\dot{q})=\tau(q, \dot{q}, \ddot{q}) \tag{1}$$

where q is the n×1 vector of joint displacements, τ is the n×1 vector of applied joint torques, $H(q)$ is n×n symmetric positive definite manipulator inertia matrix, $C(q, \dot{q})\dot{q}$ is the n×1 vector of centripetal and Coriolis torques, $\bar{g}(q)$ is the n×1 vector of gravitational torques, and $F(q, \dot{q})$ is the unstructured uncertainties of the dynamics including friction and other disturbances. C is not unique but for one choice $\dot{H}=C+C^{T}$ will hold.

Design of idea controllers for such systems is one of the most challenging tasks in control theory today. PID controllers are simple and easy to implement but their dynamic performance leaves much to be desired. The computed torque method and the adaptive control method (ACM) suffer from three difficulties. First, we must have detailed explicit knowledge of individual manipulators. Second, uncertainties existing in real manipulators seriously devalue the performance of both methods. Although ACM has ability to cope with structured uncertainties, it does not solve the problem of unstructured uncertainties. Third, the computational load of both methods is very high. Since the control sampling period must be in millisecond level, this high computational load requires very powerful computing platforms which result in high cost of implementation.

Neural networks have the potential to overcome all these difficulties experienced by conventional control methods. Because of the universal approximation feature of neural networks, they could be used as general controllers suitable for any manipulator. With their learning ability, neural networks could improve their performance and finally achieve satisfactory results through off-line and/or on-line learning without requiring explicit knowledge of manipulator dynamics. Their parallel computational structure on the other hand could help solve high computational load problems.

Much research effort has been put into the design of neural network applications for manipulator control. Albus (1975) used the cerebellar model articulation controller (CMAC) to control manipulators in 1975. Miller, et al (1990) extended Albus' results and developed neural network learning algorithms. Iiguni, et al (1991) combined manipulator linear optimal control techniques with BackPropagation (BP) neural networks which were used to compensate the nonlinear uncertainty. Kawato, et al (1988) added BP networks in original manipulator PD control systems as feedforward compensators. Although all authors claimed very good simulation or even experiment results, lack of theoretical analysis makes industrists wary of using the results in real industrial environments.

Since 1990 we began involved in this field. A complete set of theories has been established which is presented as the main part of this paper. The results are based on **a conceptual set of neural networks** which is called Linear-Equivalent (L-E) neural network set. Within this set, neural networks have a general form, i.e.

$$y=G(x)^{T}W \tag{2}$$

where y is the neural network output vector, x is the neural network input vector, $G(x)$ is the neural network fixed nonlinear mapping matrix, and W is the neural network weight vector. L-E Neural networks have the universal approximation feature, i.e. neural networks can approximate any continuous function as long as the function input is bounded. The approximation error could be as small as possible by carefully choosing neural network structures (the number of adjustable weights and the fixed nonlinear mapping matrix).

Detailed neural networks in this conceptual set include Radial Basis Function (RBF), Cerebellar Model Articulation Controller (CMAC), and Adaptive Fuzzy Controller (AFC). Therefore the present results stay when one of these type neural networks is used.

2. METHODOLOGY

Considering the general manipulator dynamic form of Equation 1, there are lots of important features which do not depend on individual manipulators. For example, the initial matrix H is positive definite. Since these features are not dependent on detailed manipulator knowledge, they can be used in neural network control design. The details of these important features have been explored in the conventional control theory and are used in our stability proofs.

Neural networks are able to approximate any continuous function (universal approximation feature), so a L-E neural network can be used to approximate manipulator inverse dynamics. Using the L-E neural network general form, we have

$$\tau(q,\dot{q},\ddot{q})=G(q,\dot{q},\ddot{q})^T W+\xi(q,\ \dot{q},\ \ddot{q}) \tag{3}$$

where G is the L-E neural network nonlinear mapping matrix, W is the neural network weights, ξ is the neural network approximation error which satisfies $\|\xi\| \le \varepsilon_m$, ε_m could be as small as possible by carefully choosing the neural network structure. Neural network weights, W, are unknown since the manipulator dynamics are unknown. we shall call W the desired weights and denote the actual neural network weights as $\hat{W}$. In the case where Columbia friction is considered, the manipulator dynamics are no longer continuous functions with $q,\ \dot{q},\ \ddot{q}$. But when $\text{sgn}(\dot{q})$ is considered as function input as well, the manipulator dynamics are continuous functions again. Therefore they can be approximated by a L-E neural network, i.e.

$$\tau(q,\ \dot{q},\ \ddot{q})=G(q,\dot{q},\ddot{q},\text{sgn}(\dot{q}))^T W+\xi(q,\ \dot{q},\ \ddot{q}) \tag{4}$$

For a more general form, we denote x as the joint values which consist of joint displacements, velocities, and/or other variables depended on applications and control structures.

$$\tau(x)=G(x)^T W+\xi(x) \tag{5}$$

In off-line learning, the neural network tries to learn the desired weights as accurately as possible. In other words, the neural network tries to approximate by learning the manipulator inverse dynamics as accurately as possible. Training data are normally discrete sets of manipulator joint driving torques and the corresponding joint values. These sets of data are collected either directly from the manipulator or from simulation software. The off-line learning algorithm must guarantee that the neural network will finally approximate the manipulator inverse dynamics in the sense that **within the training data sets** the neural network outputs the driving torques when its inputs are the corresponding joint values.

In on-line learning, the neural network is used as a control part. Its output is part of control signals which are used to drive the manipulator. The joint values in turn are used to train the neural network on-line. Therefore the on-line learning algorithm must guarantee that these two coupled systems (neural network & manipulator) work in a converging fashion. This is called "**STABILITY**" guarantee in control theory.

If the approximation equation 5 stays, existing results in the conventional adaptive control field may directly be used to design the neural control structure and the neural network on-line learning algorithm. Unfortunately things are not so simple. The neural network universal approximation feature requires that the neural network input must be in a compact set. However, before the whole system stability is proved, the joint values may be unbounded. Therefore the approximation equation is not necessarily true in on-line learning. Two techniques are used to solve this problem. The first technique is to use the desired joint values instead of the actual joint values as the neural network input since the desired joint values are normally bounded. The second technique is to force the joint values into a compact set when they leave away from it. This technique is called "**sliding control**" in the conventional control field and is called "**reflexive stabilizer**" in the learning control field. These two different techniques result in two different control structures. However the neural network learning algorithms in these two different methods are very similar although the neural network input is different.

3. NEURAL NETWORK OFF-LINE LEARNING

In order to use our previous work in Jin et al. (1993) to develop neural network off-line learning algorithm in this application, we rewrite Equation 5 into a scalar form. Let W_i, g_i be the weights and the nonlinear mapping vector for joint i. Then Equation 5 for each joint is

$$\tau_i(x) = g_i(x)^T W_i + \xi_i(x) \qquad i=1,2,\ldots,n \tag{6}$$

where τ_i is the driving torque for joint i, x is the joint values whose actual values depend on control structures and will be specified late, ξ_i is the approximation error and has $|\xi_i| \le \|\xi\| \le \varepsilon_m$, ε_m is the approximation accuracy and could be as small as possible by carefully choosing neural network structures.

Let x^k, τ_i^k be the kth set of training data collected from the actual manipulator or simulation software. During off-line training, x^k is fed into the neural network as inputs. τ_i^k is used to train the neural network. Define $\hat{W}_i^{k-1}$ and $\hat{W}_i^k$ be the actual neural network weights of joint i before and after the kth training date set is used, and y_i is the actual neural network output. We have

$$y_i^k = g_i(x^k)^T \hat{W}_i^{k-1} \tag{7}$$

From Equations 6-7 we obtain

$$\tilde{y}_i^k = g_i(x^k)^T \tilde{W}_i^{k-1} + \xi_i(x^k) \tag{8}$$

where $\tilde{y}_i^k = \tau_i(x^k) - y_i^k$, $\tilde{W}_i^k = W_i - \hat{W}_i^k$. The off-line training algorithm is stated in the following theorem.

Theorem 1: Consider the off-line training algorithm of Equations 9-10. If the two constants, α_i, β_i, are chosen $0 < \alpha_i < \beta_i < 2$, then the neural network weights approach fixed values and the neural network output approaches the manipulator driving torque within the error $e_m = 2\varepsilon_m/(\beta_i - \alpha_i)$.

$$\hat{W}_i^k = \hat{W}_i^{k-1} + \frac{\alpha_i}{1 + g_i(x^k)^T g_i(x^k)} g_i(x^k) e_{\Delta ki} \tag{9}$$

$$e_{\Delta ki} = \begin{cases} \tilde{y}_i^k & \text{if } |\tilde{y}_i^k| > e_m \\ 0 & \text{if } |\tilde{y}_i^k| \le e_m \end{cases} \tag{10}$$

4. CONTROL STRUCTURE AND NEURAL NETWORK ON-LINE LEARNING ALGORITHM---METHOD 1

In this section we present the first control structure and neural network on-line learning algorithm. This method is suitable for any manipulator consisting of only revolute joints. The neural network input i.e. the joint values consist of **the desired joint placement, velocity, acceleration and the sign of the actual joint velocity.** Consider the following function

$$y(q_d, \dot{q}_d, \ddot{q}_d, \text{sgn}(\dot{q})) = H(q_d)\ddot{q}_d + C(q_d, \dot{q}_d)\dot{q}_d + F_c \text{sign}(\dot{q}) + F_v \dot{q}_d + F_1(q_d) + \overline{g}(q) \tag{11}$$

where F_v, F_c are constant positive definite matrices standing for Viscous and Columbia frictions, F_1 stands for unstructured uncertainty whose norm is over bounded, in addition, the norm of $\partial F_1/\partial q$ is over bounded as well. Since the function inputs are bounded and the function is continuous with its inputs, it can be approximated by a L-E neural network with approximation error as small as possible.

$$H(q_d)\ddot{q}_d + C(q_d, \dot{q}_d)\dot{q}_d + F_c \text{sign}(\dot{q}) + F_v \dot{q}_d + F_1(q_d) = G(q_d, \dot{q}_d, \ddot{q}_d, \text{sign}(\dot{q}))^T W + \xi_e(q_d, \dot{q}_d, \ddot{q}_d, \text{sign}(\dot{q})) \tag{12}$$

where G is the L-E neural network hidden layer nonlinear mapping matrix, W is the neural network weights, ξ satisfies $\|\xi\| \le \varepsilon_m$ and ε_m could be as small as possible.

Theorem 2: Consider (1) where $F(q, \dot{q}) = F_c \text{sgn}(\dot{q}) + F_v \dot{q} + F_1(q)$ with the control law

$$\tau = K_p\tilde{q} + K_v\dot{\tilde{q}} + G(q_d, \dot{q}_d, \ddot{q}_d, \text{sgn}(\dot{q}))^T \hat{W} + \varepsilon_m \text{sgn}(\tilde{q} + c\dot{\tilde{q}}) \qquad (13)$$

$$\dot{\hat{W}} = \Gamma G(q_d, \dot{q}_d, \ddot{q}_d, \text{sgn}(\dot{q}))(\dot{\tilde{q}} + c\dot{\tilde{q}}) \qquad (14)$$

where Γ is a constant positive definite matrix called the learning rate. If K_p and K_v are sufficiently large, and c is small enough, then the closed-loop manipulator system is asymptotically stable and $\lim_{t\to\infty}\tilde{q}=0$, $\lim_{t\to\infty}\dot{\tilde{q}}=0$.

Equation 13 defines the control structure and Equation 14 defines the neural network on-line learning algorithm. Set the joint value x be $(q_d^T, \dot{q}_d^T, \ddot{q}_d^T, \text{sgn}(\dot{q}^T))^T$. The off-line learning algorithms in Section 3 can be directly used. Off-line learning in this control structure is very useful. The proof of the theorem uses the Lyapunov method. The

Lyapunov function is $V = \frac{1}{2}\dot{\tilde{q}}^T H(q)\dot{\tilde{q}} + \frac{1}{2}\tilde{q}^T K_p \tilde{q} + \frac{1}{2}c\tilde{q}^T K_v \tilde{q} + c\tilde{q}^T H(q)\dot{\tilde{q}} + \frac{1}{2}\tilde{W}^T\Gamma^{-1}\tilde{W}$. Unlike conventional adaptive control where only a few of the unknown manipulator parameters are adapted, in a neural network controller hundreds of or even thousands of weights are trained. If the neural network has not been trained off-line before on-line running, the initial weight errors will be very large, i.e. the initial Lyapunov function value will be extremely large. This can only result in two possibilities, i.e. either K_v extremely large or c extremely small. Both possibilities are not acceptable in practice. Another problem with a large initial Lyapunov function value is that the joint tracking errors may be very large in transient response since Theorem 2 only guarantees that the tracking errors will asymptotically approach to zero.

Example 1: A two link manipulator discussed in Slotine & Li (1989) is studied here again. The manipulator dynamics have additional terms, i.e. viscous frictions and unmodeled uncertainties. The final dynamics are

$$\begin{bmatrix} a_1 & a_3 c_{21} + a_4 s_{21} \\ a_3 c_{21} + a_4 s_{21} & a_2 \end{bmatrix}\begin{bmatrix} \ddot{q}_1 \\ \ddot{q}_2 \end{bmatrix} + \begin{bmatrix} 0 & a_4 c_{21}\dot{q}_2 - a_3 s_{21}\dot{q}_2 \\ a_3 s_{21}\dot{q}_1 - a_4 c_{21}\dot{q}_1 & 0 \end{bmatrix}\begin{bmatrix} \dot{q}_1 \\ \dot{q}_2 \end{bmatrix} + F = \begin{bmatrix} \tau_1 \\ \tau_2 \end{bmatrix}$$

where $c_{21} = \cos(q_2 - q_1)$, $s_{21} = \sin(q_2 - q_1)$, $a_1 = 0.15$, $a_2 = 0.04$, $a_3 = 0.03$, $a_4 = 0.025$, F includes the viscous frictions and unmodeled uncertainties, i.e.

$$F = \begin{bmatrix} 0.4\dot{q}_1 + 0.8\cos(q_2) \\ 0.2\dot{q}_2 + 0.4\sin(q_1) \end{bmatrix}$$

The manipulator is required to track the following desired joint values

$$\begin{cases} q_{d1} = \dfrac{\pi}{4} + 2(1 - \cos(t)) \\ q_{d2} = \dfrac{\pi}{6} + (1 - \cos(5t/3)) \end{cases}$$

The PD controller parameters are chosen to be $K_d = 2I$ and $K_p = 5I$ where I is an identity matrix with proper dimension. c is chosen to be 1. The L-E neural network is chosen to be a CMAC. Γ is chosen to be $0.8I$. The simulation has been carried out for 80 seconds. The

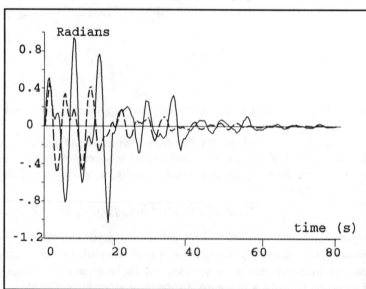

Figure 1: Tracking Errors in Example 1

displacement tracking errors are shown in Figure 1 where the solid line is the joint 1 tracking errors and the dashed line is the joint 2 tracking errors. The tracking errors have asymptotically approached to 0.

5. CONTROL STRUCTURE AND NEURAL NETWORK ON-LINE LEARNING ALGORITHM---METHOD 2

In this section we present the second control structure and neural network on-line learning algorithm. This method is suitable for any manipulator consisting of revolute joints, prismatic joints, or both types of joints. The neural network input i.e. the joint values (x) consists of **the actual joint displacement and velocity, the desired joint velocity and acceleration, and the sign of the actual joint velocity.** A sliding controller is used to force the joint values into a compact set.

For the convenience of the following discussions, define

$$\tilde{q}(t) = q_d(t) - q(t), \qquad \dot{q}_r = \dot{q}_d + \Lambda\tilde{q}, \qquad s = \dot{q}_r - \dot{q} = \dot{\tilde{q}} + \Lambda\tilde{q}$$

where Λ is a positive definite matrix. Let v be $(q^T, \dot{q}^T)^T$ and χ_c be a set $\{v \,|\, \|v\| \le c\}$.

Consider the following function

$$y(q, \dot{q}, \dot{q}_r, \ddot{q}_r, \text{sgn}(\dot{q})) = H(q)\ddot{q}_r + C(q,\dot{q})\dot{q}_r + \bar{g}(q) + F(q,\dot{q})$$

When $v \in \chi_c$, the function inputs are bounded and the outputs are continuous with the inputs therefore the function can be approximated by a L-E neural network with approximation error as small as possible, i.e.

$$
\begin{aligned}
&H(q)\ddot{q}_r + C(q,\dot{q})\dot{q}_r + \bar{g}(q) + F(q,\dot{q}) \\
&= G^T(q, \dot{q}, \dot{q}_r, \ddot{q}_r, \text{sgn}(\dot{q}))W + \xi(q, \dot{q}, \dot{q}_r, \ddot{q}_r, \text{sgn}(\dot{q}))
\end{aligned}
\tag{16}
$$

where W is the desired neural network weights, ξ is the approximation error which satisfies $\|\xi\| \le \varepsilon_m$. ε_m is a constant and is called the approximation accuracy which could be as small as possible.

During the transient response, it is possible that v leaves the set χ_c and, therefore, goes out of the control of the neural network. A technique called **"sliding control"** is used to force v into the set. Let c_d, c_n be constants, which satisfies $c_n > c_d$. c_d is large enough so that $(q_d^T, \dot{q}_d^T)^T$ is always in χ_{c_d}. The whole space of v is divided into three parts, χ_{c_d}, $\varsigma_{c_n} = \chi_{c_n} - \chi_{c_d}$, and $\varsigma_{c_s} = \{v \,|\, \|v\| > c_n\}$. When v is in χ_{c_d}, only the neural controller will be used. When v is in ς_{c_s}, only the sliding controller will be used. When v is in ς_{c_n}, the domination of the control smoothly shifts from neural network into the sliding controller. We define the following dominating factor:

$$\mu(v) = 1 - \text{sat}\left[\frac{\|v\| - c_d}{c_n - c_d}\right] \tag{17}$$

where $\text{sat}(x) = \begin{cases} 1 & \text{if } x \ge 1 \\ x & \text{if } 0 < x < 1 \\ 0 & \text{if } x \le 0 \end{cases}$. Then the above description can be expressed as the following equation:

$$\tau = \mu(v)G^T(q, \dot{q}, \dot{q}_r, \ddot{q}_r, \text{sgn}(\dot{q}))\hat{W} + \varepsilon_m\text{sgn}(s) + K_D(t)s + (1 - \mu(v))u_{sl} \tag{18}$$

where u_{sl} is the sliding control output in Bailey & Arapostathis (1987) and $K_D(t)$ is a uniformly positive definite matrix.

Theorem 3: Consider (1) with the control law of Equation 18. The neural network learning algorithm is

$$\dot{\hat{W}} = \mu(v)\Gamma G(q, \dot{q}, \dot{q}_r, \ddot{q}_r, \text{sgn}(\dot{q}))s \tag{19}$$

Then the closed-loop system is asymptotically stable and $\lim\limits_{t \to \infty}\tilde{q} = 0$, $\lim\limits_{t \to \infty}\dot{\tilde{q}} = 0$.

Set x be $(q, \dot{q}, \dot{q}_r, \ddot{q}_r^T, \text{sgn}(\dot{q}^T))^T$. The off-line learning algorithm in Section 3 can be directly used for this control structure. Off-line learning improves the on-line running performance. Theorem 3 only guarantees asymptotical stability. Large initial weight errors may result in large tracking errors in transient response.

Example 2: The example is a two link manipulator. $H, C, \bar{g}$ are the same as ones in Example 1. $F(q,\dot{q})$ is

$$F=\begin{pmatrix}0.4sign(\dot{q}_1)+0.8\cos(q_1+q_2)\\0.2sign(\dot{q}_2)+0.4\sin(q_1+q_2)\end{pmatrix}$$

The manipulator is asked to track the desired joint position function, i.e.

$$q_{d1}=\frac{\pi}{4}+2(1-\cos(3t)),$$

$q_{d2}=\frac{\pi}{6}+(1-\cos(5t))$. The PD controller is $(\dot{q}_{di}-\dot{q}_i)+8(q_{di}-q_i)$, $i=1,2$. Comparing with Theorem 3, $K_D=I$, $\Lambda=8I$ where I is an identity matrix with proper dimension. A CMAC neural network is used. Γ is chosen to be $0.2I$. Simulation period is 4 seconds. Figures 2a and 2b show the results in the first the tenth trial. The solid line is the joint 1 displacement tracking errors and the dashed line is the joint 2 displacement tracking errors.

6. CONCLUSION

In this paper we present how to use neural networks to control manipulators. Two different control structures and on-learning algorithms are proposed.

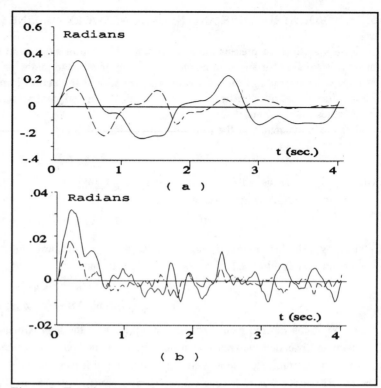

Figure 2: Tracking Errors in Example 2

Stability is guaranteed. Neural network off-line training algorithm is also presented. Off-line training does improve the on-line running performance. The proposed neural network control structures can work together with conventional adaptive control.

There is a difficulty applying the theoretical results, i.e. it is difficult to get the neural network approximation error. The difficulty is overcome in simulations by trial_and_errors.

In on-line learning, neural networks are time-continuous, i.e. the neural network inputs, outputs and weights change time-continuously. Although time-continuous neural networks can be realized by analog circuits, it seems that the implementation of time-continuous neural networks is not so easy as the implementation of time-discrete neural networks which can be realized by current discrete VLSI technology. The results presented in the paper have been extended from using time-continuous neural networks into using time-discrete neural networks.

REFERENCES

[1] J. S. Albus, "A New Approach to Manipulator Control: The Cerebellar Model Articulation Controller (CMAC)", *Journal of Dynamics Systems, Measurement, and Control*, vol.97, pp.220-227, Sept. 1975.

[2] E. Bailey, A. Arapostathis, "Simple Sliding Mode Control Scheme Applied to Robot Manipulators", *Int'l Journal of Control*, Vol.45, pp.1197-1209, 1987.

[3] Y. Iiguni, H. Sakai, and H. Tokumaru, "A Nonlinear Regulator Design in the Presence of System Uncertainties Using Multilayered Neural Networks", *IEEE Trans. on Neural Networks*, vol.2, pp.410-417, July, 1991.

[4] Y. Jin, A. G. Pipe, A. Winfield, "Stable Neural Adaptive Control of Discrete Systems", *World Congress on Neural Networks*, Vol.3, pp.277-280, 1993.

[5] M. Kawato, Y. Uno, M. Isobe, and R. Suzuki, "Hierarchical Neural Network Model for Voluntary Movement with Application to Robotics", *IEEE Control System Magazine*, vol.8, no.2, pp.8-15, April, 1988.

[6] W. T. Miller, R. P. Hewes, F. H. Glanz, L. G. Kraft, "Real-Time Dynamic Control of an Industrial Manipulator Using a Neural-Network-Based Learning Controller", *IEEE Trans. on Robotics and Automation*, vol.6, pp.1-9, Feb. 1990.

[7] J. J. E. Slotine, and W. Li, "Composite Adaptive Control of Robot Manipulators", *Automatica*, vol.25, no.4, pp.509-519, 1989.

Condition Monitoring of Impulsively Loaded Mechanical Equipment using Neural Networks

Travers Snyman
ESKOM – NPTM&C
Germiston – RSA

André Nel
Rand Afrikaans University
Johannesburg – RSA
aln@ing1.rau.ac.za

Abstract

Monitoring of mechanical condition of electro–mechanical circuit breakers as reported in [1], [2] and [3] reflects the necessity of a noninvasive method for predictive maintenance. By far the most common source of malfunction of circuit breakers is due to mechanical faults that are dependant on the number of operations.

In attempting to provide an alternative method for predicting the mechanical condition we have postulated that instead of using spectral information [1] we would simply make use of the original time domain signal. For the pattern recognition process a backpropagation trained multilayer perceptron was implemented.

From results obtained it appears that an accurate classification of the vibration signature of an impulsively loaded mechanical component can be achieved. Not only can faults be detected but a reliable indication of the specific type of abnormality can also be achieved. This type of condition classifier will be very effective in early fault detection and prediction of mechanical failure in large electro-mechanical circuit breakers.

1 Introduction

A regular (ie. planned) schedule of maintenance is followed by most power companies to ensure reliable operation of electro–mechanical circuit breakers. This involves taking the breaker out of service, disassembling the operating mechanism, inspecting the components and adjusting the mechanism to predetermined standards. This is a time consuming and costly operation.

Successful application of non-invasive condition monitoring will lead to early detection of mechanical malfunctions, Such a technique using vibrational signatures is suggested in [1], [2]and [3]. The technique applied is to create an extensive database which combines short-time energy, short-time spectra, event timing extraction techniques and a reference based mechanism for pattern analysis. This *de facto* expert system is then used to determine the condition (*normal* or *abnormal*) of the specific breaker under investigation.

A specific problem with the above approach is that the placing of the transducers on the body of the breaker itself presents a problem in the field. Repeatable placing of the sensor is a requirement for the technique as described in [2]. A further problem is that each different type of breaker leads to the development of new reference features. This makes transfer of experience from one breaker to another virtually impossible. This method only provides a classification between normal and abnormal operation and the specific fault still has to be determined. The reference features also employ time consuming signal processing techniques such as short-time spectra and short-time energy.

In attempting to provide an alternative method for predicting the condition of a circuit breaker we have postulated that instead of using the spectral information, we would prefer to simply make use of the original time domain signal. Inherent in this attempt therefore was the decision to make use of a more standard pattern recognition type approach rather than the direct reference technique described above. For the specific pattern recognition process, a backpropagation trained multilayer perceptron was proposed (described in [4], [5], [6], and [7]).

The problem addressed in this paper is therefore to determine how well a neural network can classify mechanical characteristics of a circuit breaker using vibrational information.

At first a neural network structure (number of input samples, number of hidden neurons and number of hidden layers) was determined experimentally, using only the time domain vibrational information. The classification problem chosen in these experiments was the classification of *close* and *trip* vibrational signals. Finally two similar dc-operated contactors were used to determine the capabilities of a neural network to classify certain mechanical abnormalities using the time domain vibrational signatures of *close* and *trip* operations. Networks were only trained on one of the contactors and tested on both to show that experience can be transferred. The classification capabilities of the neural network was tested when the input consisted of known abnormalities, unknown abnormalities and a variation in the severity of the abnormalities.

2 Experimental Test Setup

The ac-operated and dc-operated circuit breakers used, are small relay operated breakers that are operated from 220 V ac and 110 V dc respectively. These breakers are small enough to be operated under controlled laboratory conditions. In the case of the ac-operated breaker, the acceleraometer was mounted at different points on the baseplate of the breaker using a permanent magnet and in the case of the dc-operated breaker the transducer was mounted with studs on plates connected to the contacts.

The vibrational signals were passed through anti-aliasing filters before being presented to an analog to digital converter. The signals (512 digital samples per signal) are then normalized and presented to the neural network. For perceptron learning to be considered successful, it is essential for the system to perform correct classification of test samples on which the system has not been trained. Sufficient samples must thus be captured to allow for both training and testing.

3 Pattern Recognition

The back-propagation neural network has already been tested with problems related to speech recognition and problems related to visual pattern recognition [5]. The vibration signals yielded by circuit breakers are similar to speech signals and it was felt that a perceptron could be used as a classifier for the mechanical condition monitoring. Small variations will be discounted by the network and it will generalize to such an extent that a single system could be used for monitoring different fault conditions. The generalization capability will also reduce the effect of the sensitivity of the system to transducer mounting positions – a problem experienced in [3]. In contrast to a reference based expert system the perceptron does not require a known set of rules to solve the problem – another problem of the reference based system [3].

4 Neural Network Structure

From a practical point of view there is not much to be gained from distinguishing between a *close* and a *trip* signal. In this case however, this classification was used to determine a successful neural architecture. In the case of the ac-operated contactor, the vibrations are scarcely repeatable. In fact it is sometimes very difficult even for trained opreators to distinguish between a *trip* and a *close* operation by visual inspection. This non–repeatability makes the classification problem non-trivial. The same signal operating the breaker is used for triggering the analog to digital converter and this results in a variable phase in the signal because the triggering does not occur at exactly the same instant in the 50 Hz ac cycle. The variable dc component and the phase variability could be considered as extra parameters which would complicate the classification task. Figure 1 shows an example of *close* and *trip* vibrations.

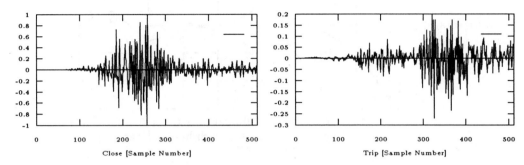

Close [Sample Number]   Trip [Sample Number]

Figure 1: Close and trip vibrations of the ac-operated contactor

The hidden layers of a neural network act as feature extractors in a classification problem. The number of neurons must be large enough to form a decision region that is complex enough to abstract the decision space required for the given problem. In spite of the various attempts to determine stricter bounds on the number of hidden neurons required [9] this is still an open research problem. To determine the number of hidden nodes required by the network for this specific classification problem, the network was trained with the number of neurons varied from 50 to 1000. Only one layer of hidden neurons was used and the number of training samples was held constant at 320. The results are presented in Figure 2.

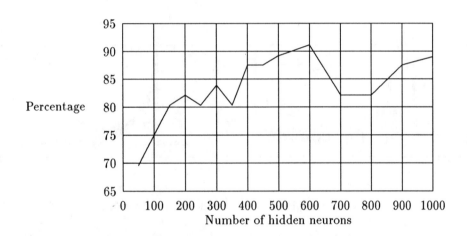

Figure 2: Graph of network performance versus the number of hidden nodes

As pointed out in [5], the neurons of the first hidden layer of a two hidden layer network often function as hyperplanes, that partition a d–dimensional input space into various regions. This together with [6] suggests that multiple hidden layer networks should provide networks that generalize better in some classification problems. Figure 3 shows a graph of network performance as a function of the number of neurons in each hidden layer for networks with multiple hidden layers.

The conclusion to be drawn from the above experiments is that given a finite training set, one way to find a suitable hidden layer structure for the specific classification task is by trial and error. It thus appears that a single hidden layer network with approximately 600 hidden nodes will be sufficient to perform the classification.

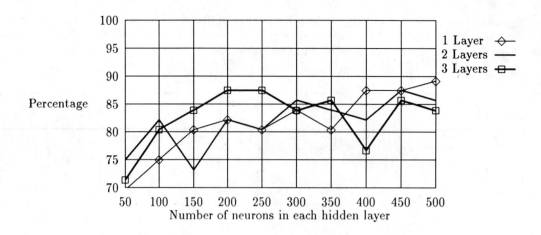

Figure 3: Graph of network performance versus the number of nodes in each hidden layer

5 Fault Classification

The construction of the dc-operated breaker makes it possible to induce the following mechanical abnormalities in a repeatable manner : **Bad Contact**, **Looseness**, and **Bad Spring**. A *bad contact* condition is induced by applying layers of masking tape to the contacts of the breaker. A *bad spring* condition is achieved by replacing one of the springs with one of the same dimensions but reduced stiffness. *Looseness* is achieved by loosening the baseplate screws. Figures 4 and 5 show examples of *close* operations in normal and three abnormal conditions.

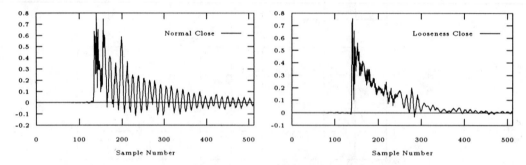

Figure 4: *Close* samples of normal and abnormal conditions

The first step in analyzing the fault classification abilities of the neural network was to determine how well it would perform on input samples that were similar to those on which it was trained. A single hidden layer network with 640 hidden nodes in the hidden layer and 8 output neurons (defining the *trip* and *close* operations of each of the abnormalities) trained to completion and resulted in a 100% correct classification of all the abnormalities. The number of training samples was 640 with an equal number for each of the eight conditions. For test purposes, an equal number of each condition was withheld from training, (160 test samples). If the combination of the *close* and *trip* inputs is considered as a test set this network also resulted in a 100% correct classification of the specific abnormality. The combination of *close* and *trip* inputs is used because the vibrational signals of some abnormalities have a prominent feature in a *close* operation which is sometimes not present in the *trip* operation and vice versa.

Abnormalities do not always occur to the same degree as that on which a network was trained. If the

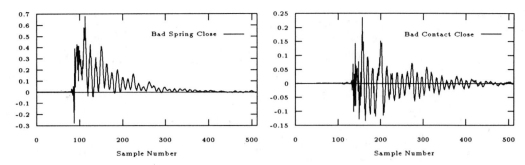

Figure 5: *Close* samples of abnormal conditions

Condition	Number of classifications
Normal	0
Looseness	24
Bad Contact	1
Bad Spring	0
Unknown	5

Table 1: Classification of 30 test sets with both screws slightly loose

trained network should also be used on different degrees of the abnormalities, the classification results are also satisfactory. Tables 1 and 2 show the classification results obtained with varying degrees of looseness. The results obtained from using the network with test sets where the severity of the abnormalities are different from the training set, underlines the generalization capabilities of a neural network. In all of the abnormalities, the network is insensitive to small changes in the feature properties on which it was trained.

In practice there is no certainty that only one abnormality will exist in a contactor when a *trip* or *close* operation is performed. If the trained network is tested on inputs that contain combinations of the abnormalities, abnormal classifications are correctly classified. In all the cases the specific fault is either classified as *unknown* or *bad spring*. It thus seems that the *bad spring* contains a feature that is either easier to detect than the features of the other conditions or which is equivalent to the combination of other features.

When the network is subjected to unknown abnormalities, (eg. some other component in the breaker is loosened), the network still classifies the inputs as abnormal – not necessarily the correct fault but certainly indicating that there is a fault present.

Testing for the ability to transfer experience, the network was also tested on vibrational signals obtained from another breaker of the same type. The results obtained are given in Table 3. The poor classification of the normal conditions can be attributed to the fact that the age of the contactors differed significantly. There is thus some unknown feature in the vibrations of the second breaker when operated under normal conditions. If the network is retrained with some of the normal conditions of the second contactor added to the training set, the poor classification of the normal conditions is corrected while not affecting the fault classification.

Condition	Number of classifications
Normal	2
Looseness	21
Bad Contact	0
Bad Spring	0
Unknown	7

Table 2: Classification of 30 test sets with one screw tight and one screw loose

Condition	Classifications of normal inputs	Classifications looseness inputs	Classification bad-contact inputs	Classification of bad-spring inputs
Normal	6	0	0	0
Looseness	16	10	0	0
Bad Contact	1	0	0	0
Bad Spring	1	0	3	10
Unknown	6	0	7	0
Total tests	30	10	10	10

Table 3: Classification results for a different contactor of the same type

6 Conclusion

The results obtained in this paper indicate that the network classification performance in this application depends strongly on the network architecture and the particular training samples used. It appears that a very accurate classification of the vibration signature of an impulsively loaded mechanical component can be achieved using a very simple neural network classifier. What is particularly interesting is that the results can be achieved in this case only using the time domain data.

It is hoped that these results will assist in making practical recommendations for using neural networks as classifiers of mechanical fault conditions in impulsively loaded mechanical equipment. If successful, this will no doubt be a major step towards cost effective predictive maintenance on large electro–mechanical circuit breakers.

References

[1] V. Demjanenko H. Naidu A. Antur M.K. Tangri R.A. Valtin D.P. Hess S.Y. Park M. Soumekh A. Soom D.M. Benenson S.E. Wright. A noninvasive diagnostic instrument for power circuit breakers. *IEEE Trans. on Power Delivery*, vol.PD-7(2), 1992.

[2] S.Y. Park M.L. Lai C.C. Lin H. Naidu A. Soom A.M. Reinhorn Y.H. Lee V. Demjanenko D.M. Benenson T.T. Soong S.E. Wright. Measurements for noninvasive mechanical diagnostics of power circuit breakers. *Electric Power Systems Research*, 19, 1990.

[3] M.L. Lai S.Y. Park C.C. Lin H. Naidu A. Soom A.M. Reinhorn Y.H. Lee T.T. Soong V. Demjanenko D.M. Benenson S.E. Wright. Mechanical failure detection of circuit breakers. *IEEE Trans. on Power Delivery*, vol.PD-3(4), 1988.

[4] R. Hecht-Nielson. *Neurocomputing*. Addison - Wesley, 1990.

[5] R.P. Lippmann. An introduction to computing with neural nets. *IEEE ASSP Magazine*, pages 4–22, 1987.

[6] J. Stanley. *Introduction to Neural Networks*. California Scientific Software, third edition, 1990.

[7] B. Widrow M.A. Lehr. 30 years of adaptive neural networks. In *Proceedings of the IEEE*, volume 78(10), 1990.

[8] K.G. Mehrotra C.K. Mohan and S. Ranka. Bounds on the number of samples needed for neural learning. *IEEE Transactions on Neural Networks*, 2(6), November 1991.

[9] S-C. Huang Y-F. Huang. Bounds on the number of hidden neurons in multilayer perceptrons. *IEEE Trans Neural Networks*, vol.NN-2(1), 1991.

An Architecture for Learning to Behave

Ashley M. Aitken

AI Laboratory, School of Computer Science and Engineering,
University of New South Wales, Box 1, PO Kensington,
N.S.W., 2033, Australia.
Ph. +61-2-697-3940
Fx. +61-2-663-4576
ashley@cse.unsw.edu.au

Abstract

The SAM architecture is a novel neural network architecture, based on the gross architecture of the cerebral neocortex, for combining unsupervised learning modules. When used as the high-level behavioral mechanism of an agent, the architecture enables the agent to learn the functional semantics of its high-level motor outputs and sensory inputs, and to acquire high-level and complex behavioral sequences by imitating other agents (learning by 'watching', or learning from a coach). This form of learning involves the agent attempting to recreate the sensory sequences it has been repeatedly exposed to. The architecture should scale well to multiple motor and sensory modalities, and to more complex behavioral requirements. Finally, insofar as it is based on the architecture of the cerebral neocortex, the SAM architecture may also help to explain several features of the operation of the cerebral neocortex.

1. Introduction

To survive and thrive in a *realistic environment* (Booker, 1991) agents require a number of different behavioral and learning strategies (Lorenz, 1978; Meyer & Guillot, 1990, September 24-28). Some agents behave predominantly according to *reflexes* or *fixed action patterns* (Beer, 1990; Braintenberg, 1984). Others include more flexible but still *instinctive behavior* or *learning programs* (Gould, 1982). Finally, some agents (in particular those animals with cortical structures) are capable of learning and executing *complex behavioral sequences*. In fact, this ability to *learn to behave* is arguably one of the most important facets of higher intelligence.

If an agent employs a *subsumption architecture* (Brooks, 1986, March) for its control system it is possible to consider the lower level behavioral mechanisms as part of an *extended environment* for a higher level behavioral mechanism (Fig. 1). In this way the precise problem tackled here can be made clear: how can a high level behavioral mechanism, with no *a-priori* control information, learn the functional semantics of its motor outputs and sensory inputs, and acquire and execute complex behavioral sequences? This paper provides a solution to this problem by presenting an architecture based upon the structure and function of the cerebral neocortex (Eccles, 1984; Szentagothai, 1975) which builds upon the hypothesis that "... the cortex is nothing but a mixer of information for the purpose of discovering and recording correlated activity ..." (Braitenberg, 1982).

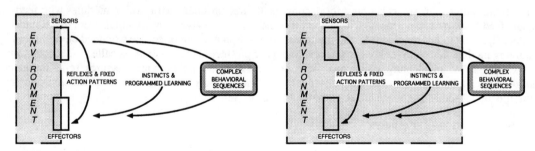

Figure 1. Brooks' creatures employ a range of behavioral mechanisms by way of a subsumption architecture (left). It is possible to consider the lower level behavioral mechanisms as a part of an extended environment for the higher level (right).

Most contemporary neural network architectures are not modular, and use supervised learning rules. However, modularity and unsupervised learning are essential to enable neural networks to scale to larger applications (Murre, 1992). Recent work has sought to find useful modular supervised learning architectures (Jacobs & Jordan, 1991; Nowlan & Hinton, 1991). Regrettably it seems however that little progress has been made on defining general and extendible architectures for combining unsupervised learning modules. The SAM architecture presented in this paper is a general and extendible architecture for combining unsupervised learning modules to learn complex behavioral sequences.

Neural networks for learning behavioral sequences have predominantly used *time-delayed sampling* with standard feed-forward networks, or more complex *recurrent networks* (Elman, 1990) . Although these approaches have been successful they both employ error-backpropagation from desired output states to train the network. For an agent this assumes that the supervisor knows the agent's motor representations. The SAM architecture presented here uses unsupervised learning modules with a coach who repeatedly performs the desired behavioral sequence. The agent 'watches' the coach and, later, attempts to recreate the sensory sequences it was exposed to. In this case, the supervisor and agent need not share similar motor or sensory representations (although some commonality of 'sensory view' and 'motor capability' is assumed).

2. The SAM Architecture

The basic components of the SAM architecture are *unsupervised learning modules*. The modules are required to be capable of detecting and representing correlations in the inputs in a semi-distributed manner, to generalise across input patterns, to have units with stochastic output states, and to be tolerant to noise. However, the SAM architecture is independent of the exact nature of the modules. This research uses extended BCM neurons (Aitken, 1993; Bear & Cooper, 1990) with lateral inhibition amongst neurons to form the unsupervised modules. However, other modules, like CALM (Murre, 1992), Linsker's layers (Linsker, 1988) or even ART (Carpenter & Grossberg, 1988, March), should work just as well.

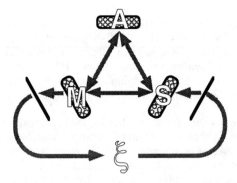

Figure 2 : The basic SAM Architecture - feed-forward and feed-backwrd connections between three unsupervised learning modules - the sensory, the motor and the association module.

The SAM architecture, in its simplest form, consists of three unsupervised learning modules with feed-forward and feed-backward connections. The sensory module (S) also receives sensory inputs from the extended environment (ξ). The motor module (M) also produces motor outputs which effect the extended environment (ξ). The remaining module that receives neither sensory inputs nor produces motor outputs is called the association module (A). The SAM architecture, unlike most other classical or neural network architectures, relies on the *closing of the loop* (Kuperstein, 1988) between motor outputs and sensory inputs by way of the extended environment to define the functional semantics of the motor outputs and sensory inputs.

3. Learning to Act and Perceive

Learning in the SAM architecture commences with random explorations of the motor space due to the stochastic states of the neurons in the modules- much like an infant's random movements or babblings. Initially, as all modules only receive random patterns there is no significant learning. However, when the motor module executes an *effective motor sequence* the sensory module detects and represents the correlation between the motor state and the sensory inputs (Fig. 3). An effective motor sequence is simply a motor sequence that causes a tangible sensory consequence (for example, in mammals compare an ineffective random firing of muscle fibres with a progressive firing of muscle fibres - the former would produce little, if any action, whereas the latter would cause a physical action and sensory consequence). At this stage, the architecture is in effect learning the primitive motor commands and their sensory consequences - it is learning to act and perceive.

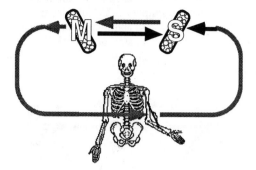

Figure 3 : Closing the loop. Sensory modules detect correlations in the motor outputs and the sensory inputs. Effective motor sequences cause correlated sensory sequences. Clearly, this is a highly schematized diagram - for any reasonable control of an elbow joint a much more complex control system is required.

Significantly then, in the SAM architecture, the sensory modules represent correlations between the motor states and the sensory inputs rather than just sensory inputs. This is in contrast to the traditional view of sensory processing, and in particular to the traditional view of mammalian sensory processing. Traditionally, it has been assumed that the representative units in the sensory areas of mammals directly represented sensory inputs. Interestingly, there may be some physiological evidence for this new view. Nicolelis(Nicolelis, Luiz, & Lin, 1993) has found, when recording simultaneously from up to 23 single thalamic neurons in awake rats, that the receptive fields changed with the motor states (the sweeping of the whiskers). Similar *dynamic receptive fields* would be expected with the SAM architecture as the motor states changes since it also provides input to the sensory module.

4. Learning to Behave

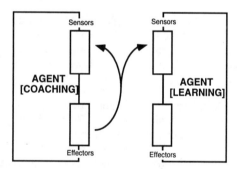

Figure 4 : Learning by Imitation. The teacher (or coach) provides the desired sensory sequences (most commonly as a result of her own motor system). In this way the teacher is not required to know the agent's sensory or motor representations.

It is not feasible to use random exploration of the motor space to learn complex behavioral sequences. Instead, once the SAM architecture has learnt to act and perceive it learns more complex behavioral sequences by imitation[1]. This entails repeated exposure to sequences of sensory inputs - usually the sensory consequences of another agent's motor outputs (Fig. 4). This pushes the sensory module through a sequence of sensory states. As a result of the learnt sensory-motor correlations, the motor module also steps through the appropriate motor sequence for the production of that sensory sequence. With repeated exposure to this sensory sequence, the association module will detect and represent the correlations in the sensory-motor sequence. The association module then becomes the context that

---

[1]Imitation as a form of learning is well known in psychology (Weinsheimer, 1984) but relatively neglected in machine learning.

signals the appropriate motor state for a particular sensory state (and vice-versa, primes the appropriate sensory state for a particular motor state) in a particular behavioral sequence.

The modularity of the SAM architecture allows it to scale well to multiple sensory and motor modalities and more association modules. It is easy to extend the simplest SAM architecture (as described above) by regarding the association module as a higher level "motor module" and adding an extra association model connected to the sensory module and the previous association module (Fig 5.). A similar extension can also be made on the motor side of the sensory-association-motor triangle. With multiple sensory, motor and association modules the system can capture and perform more complex behavioral sequences.

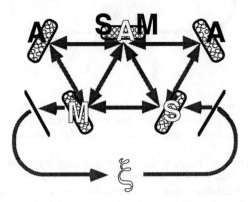

Figure 5 : The Extended SAM Architecture. By considering the standard association module as a higher level "motor module" it is possible to add an extra higher-level associative module on the right-hand side. Similarly, by considering the standard association module as a higher level "sensory module" it is possible to add an extra, higher level, associative module on the left-hand side.

5. Further Discussion

Reinforcement learning (Sutton, 1991) could be included in the SAM architecture by using a critic's evaluation to modify the learning rates of all or some of the modules and hence to direct the learning. Similarly, as the SAM architecture sits on top of a layered architecture (much like the cortex sits on top of the mid- and lower brain in mammal) it operates with and through the lower levels. These lower levels may usefully blinker what the SAM architecture observes and thus learns.

Finally, insofar as the SAM architecture provides a model of the operation of the cerebral neocortex it also hints at possible explanations for a number of clinical findings. Firstly, the way in which higher SAM association modules only form stable representations once the lower modules become correlated is similar to the process of hierarchical learning in young children (Karmiloff-Smith, 1987, April; Karmiloff-Smith, 1992). Secondly, a recent indication that experts tend to use less cortical activity than novices on a similar task (Begley, Wright, Church, & Hager, 1992) may be explained by the SAM architecture as a result of there being more correlated activity in the modules of an expert, compared with the mismatched uncorrelated activity in a novice (where correlations have yet to be detected and represented).

6. Summary and Future Work

In summary, the SAM architecture provides a method for combining unsupervised learning modules to allow an agent to learn the functional semantics of its sensory inputs and motor outputs, and complex behavioral sequences. The SAM architecture learns complex behavioral sequences by a combination of random exploration of the motor space and imitation of observed sensory sequences. As the architecture does not assume any predefine semantics of the agent's inputs and outputs it should make the construction of agents simpler. Also, as a result of learning by 'watching' the coach need not share or know the motor or sensory representations used by the agent. The SAM architecture is inspired by the anatomy and physiology of the cerebral neocortex and as such also provides a model for, and possible explanation of, cortical operation. Future work includes investigation of the relationship between the number of modules, their interconnection, and the complexity of the behavioral sequences that can be learnt.

7. References

Aitken, A. M. (1993). Preliminary Aspects of the SAM theory of the Cerebral Neocortex. In <u>Proceedings of the Second Australian Cognitive Science Conference (CogSci-93)</u> (pp. 104-106).

Bear, M. F., & Cooper, L. N. (1990). Molecular Mechanism for Synaptic Modification in the Visual Cortex: Interaction between Theory and Experiment. In M. A. Gluck & D. E. Rumelhart (Eds.), Neuroscience and Connectionist Theory (pp. 65-94). Hillsdale, N.J.: Lawrebce Erlbaum Associates.

Beer, R. D. (1990). <u>Intelligence as Adaptive Behavior: An Experiment in Computational Neuroethology</u>.

Begley, S., Wright, L., Church, V., & Hager, M. (1992, June 9). Mapping the Brain. <u>Bulletin (with Newsweek),</u> p. 76 - 80.

Booker, L. B. (1991). Instinct as an Inductive Bias for Learning Behavioral Sequences. In J.-A. M. Meyer & S. W. Wilson (Eds.), <u>From Animals to Animats</u> (pp. 230-237). Cambridge, MA: Bradford Book, The MIT Press.

Braintenberg, V. (1984). <u>Vehicles : Experiments in Synthetic Psychology</u>. Cambridge, Massachussetts: The MIT Press.

Braitenberg, V. (1982). Outline of a theory of the cerebral cortex. In L. M. a. S. Ricciardi A.C. (Eds.), <u>Biomathematics in 1980</u> (pp. 127-132). Amsterdam: North-Holland.

Brooks, R. A. (1986, March). A Robust Layered Control System For A Mobile Robot. <u>IEEE Journal Of Robotics And Automation, RA-2</u>(1), 14-23.

Carpenter, G. A., & Grossberg, S. (1988, March). The ART of Adaptive Pattern Recognition by a Self-Organizing Neural Network. <u>IEEE Computer</u>, 77-88.

Eccles, J. C. (1984). The Cerebral Neocortex : A Theory of Its Operation. In E. G. Jones & A. Peters (Eds.), <u>Cerebral Cortex</u> (pp. 1-36). New York, New York: Plenum Press.

Elman, J. L. (1990). Finding Structure in Time. <u>Cognitive Science, 14</u>, 179-211.

Gould, S. J. (1982). Darwinism and the Expansion of Evolutionary Theory. <u>Science, 216</u>, 380.

Jacobs, R. A., & Jordan, M. I. (1991). A competitive modular connectionist architecture. In R. P. Lippmann, J. E. Moody, & D. S. Touretzky (Eds.), <u>Advances in Neural Information Processing Systems 3</u> (pp. 767-73). Morgan Kaufmann Publishers.

Karmiloff-Smith, A. (1987, April). Beyond Modularity: A Developmental Perspective On Human Consciousness. In

Karmiloff-Smith, A. (1992). <u>Abnormal Phenotypes and the Challenges They Pose to Connectionist Models of Development</u> (Technical Report No. PDP.CNS.92.7). MRC Applied Psychology Unit, Cambridge, England.

Kuperstein, M. (1988). Neural Model of Adaptive Hand-Eye Coordination for Single Postures. <u>Science, 239</u>, 1308-1311.

Linsker, R. (1988, March). Self-organization in a perceptual network. <u>IEEE Computer,</u> p. 105-117.

Lorenz, K. Z. (1978). <u>The Foundations of Ethology</u>. New York: Springer-Verlag.

Meyer, J.-A., & Guillot, A. (1990, September 24-28). <u>From animals to animats: everything you wanted to know about the simulation of adaptive behavior</u> No.

Murre, J. M. J. (1992). <u>Learning and categorization in modular neural networks</u>. Hillsdale, NJ: Lawrence Erlbaum.

Nicolelis, M. A. L., Luiz, B. A., & Lin, R. C. S. (1993). Distributed Spatiotemporal Properties of Networks of Neurons in the Ventral Posterior Medial Thalamus of Awake Rats. In J. M. Bower (Ed.), <u>Computation and Neural Systems</u>, . Washington, D.C.

Nowlan, S. J., & Hinton, G. E. (1991). Evaluation of Adaptive Mixtures of Competing Experts. In R. P. Lippmann, J. E. Moody, & D. S. Touretzky (Eds.), <u>Advances in Neural Information Processing Systems 3</u> (pp. 774-80). Morgan Kaufmann Publishers.

Sutton, R. S. (1991). Reinforcement Learning Architectures for Animats. In J.-A. M. Meyer & S. W. Wilson (Eds.), <u>From Animals to Animats</u> (pp. 288-96). Cambridge, MA: Bradford Book, The MIT Press.

Szentagothai, J. (1975). The "Module-Concept" in Cerebral Cortex Architecture. <u>Brain Research, 95</u>, 475-96.

Weinsheimer, J. (1984). Imitation. London: Routledge & Kegan Paul.

APPLICATION OF NEURAL NETWORKS TO
FUZZY CONTROL OF BIOREACTOR

TORSTEN ALVAGER AND ROBERT SHOTWELL

Department of Physics and
Interdisciplinary Center for Cell Products and Technologies
Indiana State University
Terre Haute, Indiana 47809, USA

ABSTRACT

Continuous cell culture in bioreactors is an important tool in cell research. To use it to its full potential a suitable control system must be applied. The objective of this report is to present results from simulation experiments using neural networks to fuzzy control of bioreactors.

INTRODUCTION

Continuous cell culture in bioreactors can provide substantial gains in applications and the method is presently eagerly pursued by a variety of potential users including a group at our laboratory (1). To achieve the maximum benefits of these kind of reactors development of control systems need to be pursued.

Traditional control methods are not well suited for continuous culture bioreactors, often involving nonlinear processes. Fuzzy controllers are possible options especially if on-line biosensors with fluorescence detection techniques are applied.

The objective of this report is to present results from simulation experiments using neural networks to fuzzy control of bioreactors.

PROCESS MODEL

Fig. 1 shows a schematic diagram of a cell culture system with inputs A(1),...,A(n) and an output B. The inputs would, in general, be nutrients while the product B, for instance, could be a useful protein.

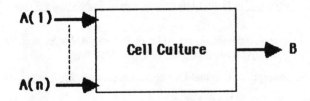

Fig.1 A bioreactor with inputs A(1),...,A(n) and output B.

A given, constant concentration of B (maybe the optimal value) is required. If this concentration for some reason is changed from the desired value the inputs must be changed to compensate for the fluctuation of the B concentration.

The regulation can be achieved by the use of fuzzy control and NN methods which are especially advantageous if the system is nonlinear. For simulation experiments values for B and A are assumed to be related by a function,which will allow us to calculate B from the A-values.

FUZZY CONTROLLER

In the simplest case the concentration (B) of the product and its change (B') depends on one input value only, which we will denote by A. This variable is regulated by a pump, the setting of which will be denoted by u. Table 1 lists the fuzzy control rules for low values (N) of A , for proper level (Z) of A and high values (P) of A respectively.

Table 1

Fuzzy control rules for u when
(N = low level, Z = proper level, P high level)

A = N				A = Z				A = P			
B'/B	N	Z	P	B'/B	N	Z	P	B'/B	N	Z	P
P	N	Z	P	P	Z	P	P	P	P	P	P
Z	N	N	Z	Z	N	Z	P	Z	Z	P	P
N	N	N	N	N	N	N	Z	N	N	Z	P

Using the rules in Table 1 and the standard procedure as outlined by, for example, Kosko (2) for the inverted-pendulum case, we generated the control surfaces of the fuzzy controller for B, B' and u in the intervals [- 0.21 to 0.20], [-1.40 to 0.25], [-6.0 to 6.0] respectively. The result is shown in Fig 2. In the next section a discussion is given of the neural network used for implementation of the fuzzy controller.

NEURAL NETWORK FOR THE IMPLEMENTATION OF FUZZY CONTROLLER

A three-layered neural network system with backpropagation was generated using a NeuralWork (3) software package and data from the fuzzy controller. The output from the neural network system was similar to the result for the fuzzy controller, but the surface was smoother than the one shown in Fig 2.

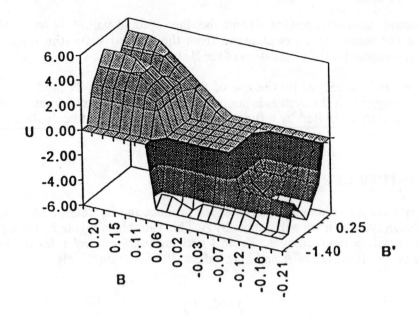

Fig. 2 Fuzzy controller output

CONCLUSION

The performed simulation experiments show the feasibility of the control system. Preliminary experiments with a simple cell culture system confirm this conclusion.

REFERENCES

1. Alvager T, Balcavage W, et al. Applications of fluorescence biosensor to cell culture echnology. Am. Lab. November 1991, pp 21-27
2. Kosko B. Neural Networks and Fuzzy Systems. Prentice Hall, Englewood Cliffs, NJ. 1992
3. Gamble J, Holden D. NeuralWorks Professional II/Plus.AI Exper.1991;6(7),51-9.

Neural Networks in Control: A Practical Perspective Gained from Intelligent Arc Furnace™ Controller Operating Experience

William E. Staib and Santosh K. Ananthraman[1]
Neural Applications Corporation
University of Iowa Oakdale Research Park
2600 Crosspark Road, Coralville, IA 52241-3212

ABSTRACT

Extensive progress has been made in the past half decade or so in the use of neural networks techniques for control [4, 7]. Neural networks offer the ability to approximate nonlinear mappings, and thus, to model nonlinear system dynamics, which is the feature to be most readily exploited in the synthesis of nonlinear controllers. Presented in this paper is a practical perspective on the use of neural networks for control, which the authors have obtained from the operating experience gained out of numerous neural network based Intelligent Arc Furnace™ Controller installations worldwide. A detailed discussion of related issues arising out of such real-world installations has also been provided.

INTRODUCTION

The basic processes involved in the design of a controller for a dynamical system include the mathematical modeling of the system, identification of the system based on experimental data, processing of the outputs, and using them, in turn, to synthesize control inputs to achieve a predetermined system response. The understanding of the fundamental theoretical issues involved in control of nonlinear multivariable systems is still in the initial stages, and the best developed aspects of classical control theory continue to be those related to linear systems.

As control methods have been adapted into standard practice, they have opened the door to a wide spectrum of real-life applications involving complex dynamical systems. Such systems are characterized by poor models, high dimensionality of the decision space, hierarchies, multiple performance criteria, distributed sensors and actuators, high noise levels, and complex information patterns [18]. Hence, there is a need to move away from classical linear control algorithms and look towards novel, intelligent control algorithms, which have the capability to cope with the above mentioned categories of difficulties. The three popular techniques that are used in the context of intelligent control are: **artificial intelligence (AI) based expert systems, fuzzy logic**, and **neural networks** [1].

The manual control of such highly complex systems is more of an art than an exact science. The human (expert) controller controls the system using his or her knowledge base which he or she has formed over years of training on the system. In most cases it becomes extremely hard for the operator to quantify his or her control actions in the form of rules, which are necessary for building AI based expert systems or fuzzy logic based systems. On the other hand, a neural network based system learns the correct control methodology simply by observing training data sets comprised of input-desired output pairs that are generated when the system is in operation. For example, controlling a complex industrial process can be a good task for a neural network, since rules are often difficult to define, historical data is plentiful but noisy, and perfect numerical accuracy is not required [5, 6].

Utilizing their attractive features, neural networks can be shown to be extremely efficient in solving mathematically hard classification, prediction, and process control problems [11, 13]. Presented below is a practical perspective on the use of neural networks for control, which the authors have obtained from operating experience gained out of numerous neural network based Intelligent Arc Furnace™ Controller installations all over the world. An elaborate discussion of related issues arising out of such real-world installations regarding the implementation of neural network based control systems has also been provided.

---

[1] The authors can be reached by email at wes@neural.com or ska@neural.com or by phone at (319) 626-5000

NEURAL NETWORKS: THE HYPE

Phrases such as "neural networks," "fuzzy logic," "artificial intelligence," and "intelligent control" attract a lot of hype. Sentences such as "intelligent control can solve every problem" are often implied in such hyped propaganda from the media/business world and even from some authors of research papers. Some examples of such hype are:

1. "They're fast! They can read! They can generalize! They can do lots of different jobs! They think like you and me. They're neural networks. And if your research facility doesn't have one yet, get ready. Because by the end of the '90s, it will be the rare R&D lab that doesn't use a neural network [16]."

2. "Computer scientists build neural networks by imitating in software or silicon the structure of brain cells and the three-dimensional lattice of connections among them [3]."

Such hype causes concern in two categories of people. **A conventional controls person** considers intelligent control techniques to be non-rigorous, since theoretical or experimental analyses are not performed as has been done in the past for conventional control methods [2, 10]. While such a bias can be attributed partially to the fact that the field is new, it is essentially due to media hype and propaganda from research papers where unjustified comparisons (for example, a backpropagation type neural network based controller compared with a poorly tuned linear controller) are performed. Some authors have even incorrectly portrayed neural networks as a flawless alternative to conventional control theory and statistical methods [17]. Hence, it is up to the neural network (or intelligent) controls community to replace the art in their design by solid engineering practices.

Neural networks can make mistakes as well, since the portion of the dynamics they learn is entirely dependent on the persistence of excitation in the training data. Many users do not understand the implications of the above and wrongly claim to have learned the entire system dynamics; they fail upon trying to operate the system outside the boundary conditions and constraints established by the dynamics reflected by the training data.

When there is time and *a priori* dynamic knowledge, conventional control theory can work very well. Most practical applications probably involve a mix of known and unknown dynamics, so that the ultimate optimum is to combine the conventional and neural control approaches.

A typical process control plant manager whose only exposure to neural networks is through popular magazines (or less in most cases) represents the other category that succumbs to the hype and tends to over expect. One is reminded of the Human-Superhuman Fallacy where a person A says to a person B: "You say your computer is intelligent. Can it write plays like Shakespeare and compose music like Beethoven?". To this B replies: "Can you?". Such over expectations cause drastic problems in the successful functioning of a neural controller in a process control plant.

Hence, it is critical that utmost care be taken to maintain credibility and avoid hype in the presentation of ideas on neural network based control to the real world. Inexpensive, general purpose "any problem, here's the neural network based solution" type software packages do not serve the cause to alleviate the above concern.

THE INTELLIGENT ARC FURNACE™ CONTROLLER

One of Neural Applications Corporation's most successful products has been the Intelligent Arc Furnace™ (IAF™) Neural Network Controller for controlling the operation of electric arc furnaces at steel plants [14, 15]. The IAF™ Controller resides in a sophisticated computing environment which contains an Intel i486 CPU, an Intel i860 40 MHz high performance co-processor, a 400 kHz data acquisition system, and a multi-gigabyte storage subsystem. The IAF™ Controller continually learns to adapt its control of the furnace to correct for changes in scrap makeup, electrode size, system supply voltage, etc. It constantly re-optimizes the control criteria and provides the following major features :

1. It is "three phase aware," in that it takes into account the effect that an electrode positioning signal will have on the correlations among all the three system phases. The three output signals are chosen such that all three phases meet desired operating conditions. This drastically reduces the setpoint hunting observed in traditional controllers.

2. It continually predicts event occurrences 100 to 300 milliseconds in the future, and then sends electrode positioning signals to correct in advance the errors that are anticipated in the future. This causes an unprecedented smoothness in operation.

Figure 1 shows a diagram of an electric arc furnace. Considering only the current flow for phase A, one can see that the current flows from electrode A through the scrap metal and returns through phases B and C. Thus, to control effectively to a setpoint, a controller must account for the interrelationships among the three phases and be "three phase aware" (Figure 2). **A production version of the system has been installed at thirteen different customer locations all over the world,** and the consumption of electric power has been reduced by 5-8% (an average furnace has a capacity of 30 MW or more; enough power for a city of 30,000 people); wear and tear on the furnace and electrodes has been reduced by 20%; and the daily throughput of steel has been increased, often by 10% or more.

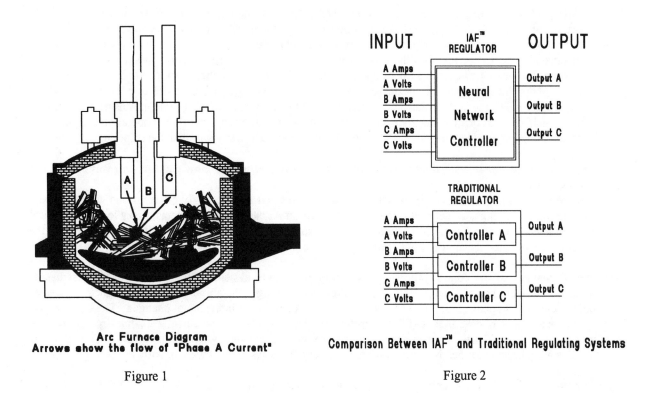

Arc Furnace Diagram
Arrows show the flow of "Phase A Current"

Figure 1

Comparison Between IAF™ and Traditional Regulating Systems

Figure 2

RELATED PRACTICAL ISSUES
A few basic questions are addressed in this section relating to general issues in neural network based control system implementation. These issues have been raised in the context of the installation and the operation of the Intelligent Arc Furnace™ Controller at numerous sites.

1. Need for sophisticated diagnostic procedures within the IAF™ Controller
Because there is a mystique associated with a neural network controller, clients may attribute more intelligence to the IAF™ Controller than it should be credited with. The root of this problem lies in the IAF™s ability to adapt to changes in system characteristics. If a process disruption occurs while running on a **fixed** controller, the client will blame operating practices or maintenance problems. If the same disruption occurs when running under **intelligent, neural adaptive** control, the same client may wonder why the neural controller no longer delivers the performance it did before the disturbance.

To prevent this situation a two-pronged approach is employed. First, the sales department makes sure that the client does not over expect in terms of results (for example, correcting myths such as the neural network's ability to predict scrap cave-ins). Secondly, sophisticated diagnostic procedures incorporated in the system ensure that clients can isolate the exact cause of any anomalies. The IAF™ Controller has a very sophisticated data logging system which logs every control and state variable for every time slice - about 10 MB of data per hour. Since this logging began, the number of hallucinated IAF™ problems has fallen from a few per week to almost zero. A couple of anecdotal examples are given below.

We received a call from a client saying that the neural regulator had suddenly started breaking electrodes. Upon careful analysis of the data we found that the problem was due to a bug in the client's Programmable Logic Controller (PLC). When scrap cave-ins occurred, the client's PLC was incorrectly sending manual override signals to the IAF™ Controller, which, as a result, did not take any corrective action.

The graphite electrodes in an arc furnace wear out as a consequence of the large current flow. When an electrode is too short, the distance between the end of the electrode and the scrap metal is too large for the current setpoint to be maintained. Although the neural regulator outperforms the conventional regulator and handles such situations by increasing the current demand from the other two phases, there is a physical limit to such fault tolerance. Normally when this limit is reached, a furnace operator will notice that an electrode is too short, and will turn off the furnace. This did not occur in one instance and the client stated that the neural regulator had stopped controlling properly since the average current was much below the desired setpoint. Upon analysis of the data files it was immediately obvious that the electrode on one of the phases was too short for reliable operation and that only two of the electrodes were conducting and hence, the three phase average was lower than the setpoint.

2. If the basic process changes, would the control system become obsolete? How can incremental changes in the processes be accommodated ?
Neural network based controllers can be transferred from one process to an entirely different one with relatively moderate amounts of change, unlike controllers that are based on AI based expert systems, fuzzy logic or classical control techniques. However, a boundary conditions and constraints analysis should be performed to ensure that the system operates within the dynamical space learned by the neural controller.

Incremental changes in the control process can be dealt with quite systematically as well. One just has to accommodate the incremental changes into the input/output training system and then go through a process of "retraining" the neural controller in order for the controller to adapt to the incremental changes. The engineers at one of the steel plants wanted their IAF™ Controller to adapt to such an incremental change by adding new hydraulic back pressure inputs. The inputs were simply wired in and the system adapted (on-line) to the new inputs over a short period of time. No changes were necessary in the system hardware or software configurations.

After a successful installation at another steel plant, we discovered another feature of the IAF™ Controller that demonstrated its degree of fault tolerance. Several months after the IAF™ Controller had been successfully operating, the furnace transformer was replaced. The IAF™ Controller ran equally well using the new transformer and was operating for many heats before we temporarily took it off-line for a software update. As soon as the old regulator was put on-line the furnace started breaking electrodes. An investigation revealed that the transformer voltage lines on the secondary winding had been reversed during installation of the new transformer. This caused the classical, old regulator to break electrodes and caused expensive down time. The IAF™ Controller was brought back on-line and continued to run smoothly with the miswiring until the transformer could be correctly wired. The reason the IAF™ Controller was able to compensate for miswiring is because it learns on-line. As problems or changes occur in the process, the neural network will do whatever it can to maintain the current setpoints; the neural network regulator has a very high degree of fault tolerance.

3. Solving a problem in an application domain in which we are not experts ourselves
This is an important issue, since Neural Applications Corporation has diversified its activities by entering process control industries other than steel. In order to prepare for such situations, Neural has established a Scientific Advisory Board which is comprised of leaders in the field of intelligent control. The Neural Applications Group member in charge of a certain project works together with the liaison project engineers at the customer site and

with specialists in the Scientific Advisory Board to accomplish project objectives in the shortest possible developmental time cycle.

There are numerous critical issues that one needs to address when designing a neural network based intelligent control system. Pre-network statistical analysis on the process data to determine best training set (by determining correlation strengths to identify effects of input variables on the output variables), as well as choosing the right architecture and the right control strategy are of supreme importance for successful implementation of the control system [12].

Many neural network companies offer canned software packages as generic solutions to specific problems [8, 9]. They typically offer three-day to week-long classes to the engineers from the customer's plant in order to get them up to speed in the use of their software (and achievement of "neural network expert" status) and implementation of the system. Such packages and courses are really useful to novices trying to solve toy problems in academic laboratories and as a tool to get up to speed in neural networks, or to experts in the field who can indulge in rapid prototyping using powerful software packages to either implement systems or generate data to churn out papers.

But they are of little use to today's average plant engineers who are actually trying to solve a real world problem using such a package simply because of their lack of collective expertise in all three areas - namely, intelligent control, statistical data analysis, and real-world control system implementation. Experience in all these three areas is absolutely critical to the successful design and implementation of a neural network based control system in the real-world. This criticality of expertise became even more obvious during one of our recent projects. In the process of designing a control system for a small-sized MIMO system the system designers came up with seven different control strategies employing combinations of neural/fuzzy/expert system/linear techniques. It was a hard task to pick the one strategy that best optimized the system performance while adhering to prescribed constraints and required considerable intelligent control engineering experience.

The other key issue is the understanding of the underlying principles behind the dynamics of the process before attempting to design the neural network based controller. The degree of persistence of excitation in the training data determines the extent to which the system dynamics can be learned by the neural controller. One has to account for the trade-offs that are involved in such a process and make arrangements within the controller to handle unexpected situations. Failure to do so frequently results in the downfall of a system designed using a canned package.

CONCLUSION

A practical perspective gained by the authors on the use of neural networks in control was presented in this paper. We have learned a lot about the advantages and complications of applying neural network technology to process control, and about the operation of electric arc furnaces. Experienced operators have noticed subtle improvements in furnace operation such as reduced noise, less electrode shaking, and smoother operation, apart from the basic cost-savings and improvement in performance.

Neural networks are extremely powerful **tools** (as are fuzzy, expert system, and classical control techniques) and it is critical that the utmost care be taken to maintain their credibility and avoid hype when presenting ideas in neural network based control to the real world. Depending on the process at hand, a competent control systems engineer should employ the right combination of these tools to achieve the desired system performance.

REFERENCES

[1]   Ananthraman, S., "An Introduction to Neural Network Based Intelligent Systems", *Technical Report*, Neural Applications Corporation, September, (1993).

[2]   Billings, S. A., Jamaluddin, H. B., and Chen, S., "Properties of Neural Networks with Applications to Modeling Non-linear Dynamical Systems", *International Journal of Control*, Vol. 55, No. 1, pp. 193-224, (1992).

[3]   Bylinsky, G., "Computers That Learn By Doing", *Fortune*, pp. 96-102, September, (1993).

[4]   Caudill, M., "The View From Now", *AI Expert*, pp. 24-31, June, (1992).

[5]   Hammerstrom, D., "Neural Networks at Work", *IEEE Spectrum*, pp. 26-32, June, (1993).

[6]   Hammerstrom, D., "Working with Neural Networks", *IEEE Spectrum*, pp. 46-53, July, (1993).

[7]   Hunt, K., Sbarbaro, D., Zbikowski, R., Gawthorp, P. J., "Neural Networks for Control Systems - A Survey", *Automatica*, Vol. 28, No. 6, pp. 1083-1112, (1992).

[8]   Information Technology Special Report, *Fortune*, Autumn, (1993).

[9]   Kaplan, G., "Industrial Electronics: Technology 1994", *IEEE Spectrum*, pp. 74-76, January, (1994).

[10]   Passino, K. M., "Bridging the Gap Between Conventional and Intelligent Control", *IEEE Control Systems Magazine*, pp. 12-18, June, (1993).

[11]   Reinschmidt, K. F., "Neural Networks: Next Step for Simulation and Control", *Power Engineering*, pp. 41-45, November, (1991).

[12]   Ripley, B. D., "Statistical Aspects of Neural Networks", *Invited Lectures for SemStat*, Sandbjerg, Denmark, April 25-30, (1992).

[13]   Shandle, J., "Neural Networks are Ready for Prime Time", *Electronic Design*, pp. 51-58, February, (1993).

[14]   Staib, W. E., "The Intelligent Arc Furnace™: Neural Networks Revolutionize Steelmaking", *World Congress on Neural Networks, Portland*, OR, pp. 466-469, (1993).

[15]   Staib, W. E., and Staib, R. B., "The Intelligent Arc Furnace™ Controller: A Neural Network Electrode Position Optimization System for the Electric Arc Furnace", *International Joint Conference on Neural Networks*, Baltimore, MD, (1992).

[16]   Studt, T., "Neural Networks: Computer Toolbox for the '90s", *R&D Magazine*, September, (1991).

[17]   Werbos, P., "An Overview of Neural Networks for Control", *American Control Conference*, San Diego, CA, May 23-25, (1990).

[18]   White, D. A., and Sofge, D. A., "Handbook of Intelligent Control: Neural, Fuzzy, and Adaptive Approaches", Van Nostrand Reinhold, New York, NY, (1992).

Prediction and System Identification

Session Chairs: Paul Werbos
Guido Deboeck

ORAL PRESENTATIONS

How We Cut Prediction Error in Half
By Using A Different Training Method

Paul J. Werbos
Room 675, National Science Foundation*
Arlington, Virginia, USA 22230

ABSTRACT

Neuroidentification -- the effort to train neural nets to predict or simulate dynamical systems over time -- is a key research priority, because it is crucial to efforts to design brain-like intelligent systems [1,2,3]. Unfortunately, most people treat this task as a simple use of supervised learning [4]: they build networks which take all of their input from a fixed set of observed variables from a fixed window of time before the prediction target. They adapt the weights in the net so as to make the outputs of the net match the prediction target for those fixed inputs, exactly as they would do in any static mapping problem.

With McAvoy and Su, I have compared the long-term prediction errors which result from this procedure versus the errors which result from using a radically different training procedure -- the pure robust method -- to train exactly the same simple feedforward network, with the same inputs and targets. The reduction in average prediction error was 60%, across 11 predicted variables taken from 4 real-world chemical processes. More importantly, error was reduced for all variables, and reduced by a factor of 3 or more for 4 out of the 11 variables [5,p.319]. Followup work by Su[6,p.92] studied 5 more chemical processes (mostly proprietary to major manufacturers), and found that the conventional procedure simply "failed" (relative to the pure robust procedure) in 3 out of 5. This paper describes how we did it; it also tries to correct common misconceptions about recurrent networks, and summarize future research needs.

INTRODUCTION AND GENERAL CONTEXT

Of the hundreds of papers I have seen using artificial neural networks (ANNs) for prediction, all but two (sections 13.5 and 13.6 of [5], and [7]) fit into one or more of three categories:

1. The supervised learning approach, described above.
2. The batch time-series approach. Here, an ANN is adapted by iterating over a fixed time-series database.
3. The forwards propagation approach. Here, an ANN is adapted by a time-forwards variation on backpropagation, published for the general case in 1982[8], and popularized for special cases by Williams and Zipser ("the Williams-Zipser method") and by Narendra ("{dynamic backpropagation").

In the supervised learning approach, some people use simple multilayer perceptrons (MLPs); MLPs for this application are now called "Time-Delay Neural Networks" (TDNNs). In our recent work[5,6], this is what we used. Many other people have used simultaneous-recurrent networks, such as Grossberg-style nets, to learn the exact same static mapping; they often use the term "associative sequence learning." Improved supervised learning designs, in general, are also a priority area for my program at NSF[4]; however, they pose few major design issues unique to prediction as such. Nevertheless, I will begin this paper with a review of this approach, in order to set up notation and make a few observations.

The batch time-series approach to neuroidentification is really just a special case of the general task of "time-series estimation" (as studied in statistics) or of "system identification" (as studied in engineering). Conversely, because of the general approximation capabilities of ANNs, time-series methods applied to neural networks can accomplish virtually anything that the classical approaches can accomplish;

---

*The views herein are the personal views of the author, not the views of NSF.

thus there is no need for complex, unnatural hybrids using "neural" and "nonneural" blocks. (There are two major exceptions to this rule: (1) in special-purpose applications where useful fixed preprocessors or postprocessors are easily available off the shelf, and there is no time to develop something better; (2) in complex neural architectures, which <u>naturally</u> require many components or stages in estimation, where it may be useful to use different kinds of networks -- neural or nonneural -- to fill in different blocks in the design.) The pure robust method is actually a <u>general</u> approach to time-series estimation, developed back in 1974[9], along with backpropagation through time[9,10]. The neural net community could make major contributions to the general problem of time-series estimation, in part because of our interdisciplinary orientation (<u>if</u> we keep extending that orientation!) and in part because computational tools like backpropagation through time are essential to implementing these kinds of designs.

The third approach has sometimes been described as a more brain-like variant of the second approach, because it permits true real-time learning. Unfortunately, the cost per gradient grows as kMNT, where M is the total number of weights in the network, N is the total number of neurons, and T is the total number of time-points. This compares with kMT to calculate the same exact gradient using backpropagation through time [8-10]. In a sense, the time-forwards method is not truly a neural network design, because its costs (and structure) are utterly and grossly implausible for organic brains, where M and N are both huge numbers. Narendra has reported, in a public talk at Yale, that he uses this method less and less, because of its high computational cost, even in medium-sized engineering problems.

The human brain itself does not fit the second approach either, because: (1) it uses real-time learning, rather than batch learning; (2) it may or may not require a <u>stochastic</u> model of its environment, rather than just a <u>forecasting</u> model. In section 13.5 of [5], I specify an error critic design (similar in spirit to [7], but hopefully capable of scaling better to larger systems) which would allow the brain to <u>approximate</u> the best batch time-series designs, in true real-time learning. In section 13.6 of [5], I describe a complex design -- the Stochastic Encoder/Decoder/Predictor (SEDP), building on concepts I published in 1977 [11] -- which learns a true stochastic model of the environment, without making the usual "simplifying" assumption that errors in predicting different targets are unrelated to each other. Earlier, in 1988 [12], I proposed some similar but simpler designs, which include the famous Cottrell design as a special case; however, I have not pursued these simpler designs any further, because of limitations both in performance and in statistical consistency. <u>In most applications today, the usual batch time-series approach is quite adequate; because the error critic is actually just a way to approximate that approach, research directed towards batch time-series issues will still be crucial to the development of effective brain-like systems.</u> After a brief review of supervised learning approaches, the remainder of this paper will focus on the second approach, which includes our recent work with the pure robust method.

The error critic and the SEDP and much of my related work in [5,23] falls under patents pending at BHI[3]. These patents do not limit the use of these ideas in basic research, subject to proper citation and mention of the patents, but revenue-generating applications should be discussed beforehand with BHI.

ISSUES IN SUPERVISED LEARNING FOR PREDICTION

Suppose that we are trying to predict n variables, Y_1 through Y_n, at time t. We may think of these variables as a vector $\underline{Y}(t)$. Suppose that we plan to predict $\underline{Y}(t)$ as a function of earlier values of $\underline{Y}$ in k previous time periods, $\underline{Y}(t-k)$ through $\underline{Y}(t-1)$, and as a function of some other variables, which we may describe as $\underline{X}(t-k)$ through $\underline{X}(t-1)$. (In control applications, the "other variables" are usually the control inputs to the process, denoted as $\underline{u}(t-k)$ through $\underline{u}(t-1)$.) Suppose that the function $\underline{f}$ describes the neural network we are trying to adapt to solve this prediction problem; in other words:

$$\hat{\underline{Y}}(t) = f(\underline{Y}(t-k),..., \underline{Y}(t-1), \underline{X}(t-k),..., \underline{X}(t-1), W) \qquad (1)$$

where W represents the weights in the network and $\hat{\underline{Y}}(t)$ represents the output of the network. In the supervised learning approach, we simply plug in our actual data for $\underline{X}$ and $\underline{Y}$ into $\underline{f}$, and adapt the weights

W to make $\hat{\underline{Y}}(t)$ approximate $\underline{Y}(t)$. <u>Any</u> supervised learning scheme -- from backpropagation through to Hebbian learning -- can be used. Likewise, we could use a simultaneous-recurrent network [4] to widen our choices of functions $\underline{f}$, so as to allow a more powerful function approximation capability[4], <u>so long as we do not confuse</u> "settling down time" (which is internal to the network) with the dynamics of the process we are trying to model.

When we add a simple noise term to equation 1, it becomes what engineers would call a "NARX" model -- a Nonlinear AutoRegressive model with eXogenous variables. (Many authors have mistakenly called this a "NARMAX" model.) Equation 1 also describes what people in signal processing would call Finite Impulse Response (FIR) systems, systems whose "memory" goes back a finite period of time (k).

The next section will describe how the pure robust method may be used to adapt forecasting models like equation 1. The pure robust method is essentially a <u>global</u> modelling technique, like the global techniques for supervised learning described in [4]. However, in [4], I argued that optimal real-time learning requires a special kind of <u>hybrid</u> of local memory-based approaches and global approaches. Perhaps it is premature to stress this issue -- because the relevant kinds of hybrids have yet to be seriously studied even for simple supervised learning -- but it will become a concern sooner or later. As Tan et al point out in this session[13], time sequences have less of a tendency to cluster than do simple snapshots at a fixed time t; in general, the most popular local learning schemes tend to become less workable when the number of inputs grows large, and multiplying the number of inputs by k can be a serious problem. Special designs may be needed to cope with the various issues here.

Many authors also advocate the simple, direct use of Taken's theorem, from chaos theory, to arrive at a choice of k[14]. However, in testing this idea on a variety of real-world time-series, Weigend has found it to be markedly inferior (most of the time) to the more reliable empirical approaches, used for decades by statisticians[15]. This is hardly surprising, because most real-world systems do not emerge as the simple low-dimensional attractors studied by conventional forms of chaos research. (This should not be taken as a criticism, however, of other uses of chaos theory, which are indeed quite promising[16,17].)

The supervised learning approach is inadequate as a model of generalized, brain-like prediction capabilities, for two reasons: (1) It does not lead to a high degree of <u>dynamic robustness,</u> which is crucial to systems like the brain which need to make plans over time periods much larger than their data sampling intervals (circa 0.1 seconds for the neocortex); (2) It does not lead to efficient short-term memory, Kalman-like filtering, adaptation to slow changes in parameters in the external world, or to the ability to learn efficient "relaxation" algorithms (which are crucial in many pattern recognition applications).

This paper will only discuss the first of these problems. The second is discussed at length in [5] and in [10]. A general solution to the second problem is to use <u>time-lagged recurrent networks</u> (TLRNs), networks with real short-term memory. TLRNs represent general NARMAX models. Backpropagation through time -- in its correct, original form [9] -- provides an exact and low-cost technique for adapting such networks, in the general case, for a generalized range of network structures. (It is extremely unfortunate that the term "backpropagation through time" has been misused by some authors to describe alternative inexact or inefficient methods, limited to the MLP case. So far as I know, I was the first person to use this term in any publication [18], and the definition I used in 1990 [10] was extremely specific.) Given an <u>infinite</u> number of parameters or weights -- i.e., an infinite value for k -- any NARMAX model can be represented equivalently by a NARX model; however, the need for additional parameters or weights is devastating to performance in practice, because of the importance of parsimony in determining the generalization capabilities of neural networks [5, chapter 10]. As in statistics, we are far better off by building systems designed to do well in the <u>general case</u>, the NARMAX case, which includes NARX as a special case in a parsimonious manner. The brain itself is, of course, designed to handle the general case.

THE PURE ROBUST METHOD: FOUNDATIONS AND ALTERNATIVES

The easiest way to define the pure robust method is to spell it out as an algorithm. The conventional way to adapt equation 1 is to minimize total error defined by the following calculations:

1. For t = k+1 to T, calculate:

$$\hat{Y}(t) = f(\underline{Y}(t-k),..., \underline{Y}(t-1), \underline{X}(t-k),..., \underline{X}(t-1), W) \qquad (2)$$

$$E(t) = \tfrac{1}{2} \sum (Y_i(t) - \hat{Y}_i(t))^2 \qquad (3)$$

2. Define total error as the sum of E(t) from t=k+1 to t=T.
The usual form of the pure robust method is very similar:
1. Set $\hat{\underline{Y}}(t)$ to $\underline{Y}(t)$ for t=1 to t=k.
2. For t = k+1 to T, calculate:

$$\hat{Y}(t) = f(\hat{\underline{Y}}(t-k),..., \hat{\underline{Y}}(t-1), \underline{X}(t-k),..., \underline{X}(t-1), W) \qquad (4)$$

$$E(t) = \tfrac{1}{2} \sum (Y_i(t) - \hat{Y}_i(t))^2 \qquad (5)$$

3. Define total error as the sum of E(t) from t=k+1 to t=T.
The difference between the two methods may seem very slight at first (i.e., the two extra hats in equation 4 compared to equation 2); however, it has powerful implications. The pure robust method looks even closer to certain methods discussed in adaptive control, where the weights W in equation 4 would be adapted by simple supervised learning; however, in the pure robust method we actually minimize total error accounting for the impact of W in changing $\hat{Y}(t-k)$, for example, all through the dynamics of the process. For each value of W, we calculate total error across the entire time-series, and we try to pick that value of W which minimizes total error.

Intuitively, the pure robust method directly minimizes the long-term stream of errors resulting from using the neural network to predict many periods of time ahead into the future. It makes common sense that this should work better in long-term forecasting, but worse in short-term forecasting. However, this simple piece of common sense is not quite right; the real story is far more complex. Furthermore, the pure robust method is really only the lowest-order member of a family of methods which I first tested out in 1974[9], and improved substantially in 1978[19]. There do exist systems where the pure robust method does worse than the conventional method both in long-term and short-forecasting, but where the next method up in the family does better than the conventional method in both[19]. Section 10.4.6 of [5] describes the next method up and, more importantly, describes some fundamental concepts in statistics which could be used in developing even more powerful methods.

A few words may be in order to sketch out the basic issues, even though they are far too complex to fully explain here. After a careful analysis of what it takes to minimize the error in estimating weights, by adding some kind of externally forced filtering, I arrived at a formula (equation 89 of chapter 10 of [5]) which simply does not reduce to a simple neural network design. The formula suggests that we can adapt a maximally robust, sparse neural network predictor only if we explicitly seek an alternative representation of reality (R) which corresponds to something like the eigenvectors of the dynamics of the external environment. Unfortunately, the eigenvectors of a general matrix are made up of complex numbers, so that the practical implications of this are highly unclear. Intuitively, it would seem that the concepts of "chunking" in artificial intelligence, or the idea of "learning invariants" in biology (see the papers accompanying [2]), may have something very important to tell us, something which goes far beyond the usual foundations (like maximum likelihood theory) which engineers and statisticians rely on almost religiously. A crucial task for future research may be to deepen these concepts, and assimilate them into a more rational time-series framework, building in part on the concepts of section 10.4.6 of [5]. See

[28] for some ideas. In addition, [20] suggests a few further ideas, exploiting the fact that prediction networks are often embedded within control systems (as in the brain).

THE PURE ROBUST METHOD: IMPLEMENTATION AND RESULTS

Both the conventional method and the pure robust method can be adapted by use of backpropagation (or its many variants[4,5]) in batch form, by use of the same traditional approach:
1. Initialize W "at random."
2. Calculate total error for the current value of W.
3. If total error is worse than before, go back to the old W with a smaller learning rate.
4. Calculate F_W, the exact gradient of total error with respect to W.
5. Reset W to W - learning-rate * F_W.
6. If convergence has not been achieved, go back to step 2.

Almost anyone in this field should know how to do this for the conventional method. (If not, see [10].) For the pure robust case, the only possible gap for most readers would be the exact calculation of F_W, which can be done efficiently using backpropagation through time. The equations for this case are given in two different (equivalent) forms, in sections 10.4.1 and 10.9 of [5]; however, these equations all follow quite directly from the chain rule for ordered derivatives, discussed at length both in [1] and in other sections of [5]. (However, the term "+F_Y_2(t+1)*3" should be added to equation 110 in [5].)

As a practical matter, initializing W, tuning the learning rates, and avoiding local minima are all much harder for the pure robust method than for the conventional method. There is a kind of general Murphy's law at work[20], which always makes convergence trickier when the final weight estimates are more accurate. In [5], we used a combination of backpropagation and direct search, because human time was limited. In [6], Su went back to some of the ideas in [5], and proved that he could avoid the need for direct search by an appropriate choice of initial weights. Additional suggestions in [5] may make the learning process still easier in the future. In general, there are many techniques which make later applications easier, <u>after</u> the initial general-purpose computer programs are in place.

The recent results from McAvoy, Su and myself were already summarized and cited in the Abstract. Again, however, the pure robust method was proposed over 20 years ago as a <u>generalized</u> time-series estimation method. In those studies, it outperformed both the conventional method and ARMA models in simulated time-series and in predicting political time-series[9]. In 1978, robust methods reduced error in predicting GNP in Latin America by a factor of 2 [19]. (Error in predicting conflict variables was reduced, but not by as much, because the variables commonly used in predicting conflict at that time had little predictive power; predicting conflict is tricky.) Tests on a simple model of the US economy by Kuh led to similar improvements[19].

The publication of [19] led directly to my employment by the Energy Information Administration (EIA) of DOE, to reevaluate and rebuild major long-term and annual models used by EIA in its official reports to Congress. Backpropagation through time[8,24,25] was important to that effort, as was my <u>understanding</u> of dynamic robustness[25,26]. However, <u>annual</u> modeling in econometrics uses far less data than neural net methods need, and energy use depends heavily on exogenous information about economic growth and population; thus I was able to reach the limits of accuracy here -- 1-1½% error in all demand sectors, but far worse in predicting individual breakthroughs like fuel cell cars -- without <u>explicitly</u> using robust methods. This is another reason why ANN activities -- which often use higher frequency data, like the brain itself or like daily financial data[27] -- are an excellent testbed for robust identification.

The neural net use of these methods was proposed in 1981-7 [8,11,20]. The first step of Kawato's cascade method [21] can be seen as a working example of the pure robust method, though I do not know of any comparisons with conventional methods. Feldkamp of Ford has said that the pure robust method has led to extremely good results in automotive applications this past year; however, because these applications involve key competitive technologies, the details are proprietary. These applications do involve the use of backpropagation through time with true TLRNs. Earlier related work[22] showed that this kind of approach does provide a better basis for dynamic control of the bioreactor benchmark problem in [21] -- a simple but very tricky problem, which has been very useful in sorting out general-purpose designs from the many designs which only work when conditions are simple and the user is extremely lucky.

REFERENCES

1. P.Werbos, *The Roots of Backpropagation: From Ordered derivatives to Neural Networks and Political Forecasting*, Wiley, 1994.
2. P.Werbos, The brain as a neurocontroller, in K.Pribram, ed., *Origins*, Proceedings of the 2nd Appalachian Conference, INNS Press, Erlbaum, 1994.
3. R.Santiago and P.Werbos in *WCNN94 Proceedings*, INNS Press, Erlbaum, 1994.
4. P.Werbos, Supervised learning: Can it escape its local minimum?, *WCNN93 Proceedings*, INNS Press, Erlbaum, 1994
5. D.White and D.Sofge, eds, *Handbook of Intelligent Control: Neural, Fuzzy and Adaptive Approaches*, Van Nostrand, 1992.
6. H.Su, *Dynamic Modeling and Model Predictive Control Using Generalized Perceptron Networks*, PhD thesis, Department of Chemical Engineering, University of Maryland at College Park, 1992.
7. J.Schmidhuber, Recurrent networks adjusted by adaptive critics, *IJCNN90 Proceedings*, Erlbaum, 1990.
8. P.Werbos, Applications of advances in nonlinear sensitivity analysis, in R.Drenick and F.Kozin, eds, *System Modeling and Optimization: IFIP 1981 Proceedings*, Springer-Verlag, reprinted in [1].
9. P.Werbos, *Beyond Regression: New Tools for Prediction and Analysis in the Behavioral Sciences*, Harvard U. PhD thesis, November 1974, reprinted in [1].
10. P.Werbos, Backpropagation through time: What it does and how to do it, *Proc. of the IEEE*, Oct. 1990 issue, updated version reprinted in [1].
11. P.Werbos, Advanced forecasting for global crisis warning and models of intelligence, *General Systems Yearbook*, 1977 issue.
12. P.Werbos, Backpropagation: Past and future, *ICNN88 Proceedings*, IEEE, New York, 1988.
13. S.Tan, J.Hao and J.Vandewalle, Stable and efficient neural network modeling of discrete multi-channel signals, *WCNN94 Proceedings*, INNS Press, Erlbaum, 1994.
14. A.Weigend nd N.Gershenfeld, eds, *Time-Series Prediction*, Santa Fe Series, Addison-Wesley, 1994.
15. G.Box and G.Jenkins, *Time Series Analysis: Forecasting and Control*, Holden-Day, 1970.
16. K.Shimode and W.Freeman, Modeling of chaotic dynamics in the biological system and application to speech recognition, *IJCNN92 Proceedings*, IEEE, New York, 1992.
17. P.Werbos, Self-organization: Reexamining the basics, and an alternative to the big bang, in *Origins*[2].
18. P.Werbos, Backpropagation and neurocontrol, *IJCNN89 Proceedings*, IEEE, New York, 1989.
19. P.Werbos and J.Titus, An empirical test of new forecasting methods derived from a theory of intelligence: the prediction of conflict in Latin America, *IEEE Trans. SMC*, September 1978.
20. P.Werbos, Learning how the world works: specifications for predictive networks in robots and brains, *Proceedings of the SMC Conference*, IEEE, 1987.
21. W.Miller, R.Sutton and P.Werbos, eds, *Neural Networks for Control*, MIT Press, 1990.
22. L.Feldkamp and G.Puskorius, A neural network approach to process control -- the bioreactor benchmark problem, *WCNN93 Proceedings*, INNS Press, Erlbaum, 1993.
23. P.Werbos, Elastic fuzzy logic, *J. of Intelligent and Fuzzy Systems* (Wiley), Vol. 1, No. 4, 1993.
24. P.Werbos, Maximizing gas industry profits...,*IEEE Trans. SMC*, March/April 1989.
25. P.Werbos, Generalization of backpropagation...recurrent gas market model,*Neural Networks*, Oct. 1988.
26. P.Werbos, Econometric techniques: Theory versus practice, *Energy*, March/April 1990.
27. G.DeBoeck, ed, *Trading on the Edge: Neural, Genetic, and Fuzzy Systems for Chaotic Financial Markets*, Wiley, 1994.
28. J.Schmidhuber,Adaptive decomposition of time, *Artificial Neural Networks 1*,North Holland, 1992.

Prediction of Chaotic Time Series and Resolution of Embedding Dynamics with the ATNN*

Daw-Tung Lin[†,‡], Judith E. Dayhoff[‡] and Panos A. Ligomenides[†]
[†]Electrical Engineering Department
and
[‡]Institute for Systems Research
University of Maryland
College Park, MD 20742.

Abstract

Chaotic time series prediction is an essential task of signal processing, physiological analysis and economic forecasting. In this paper, we apply the Adaptive Time-Delay Neural Network ($ATNN$) to study the chaotic Mackey-Glass differential equation prediction problem. We discuss the embedding dynamics, training set size and performance, and prediction over time. We demonstrate this neural network approach to be flexible, to predict the chaotic dynamics, and to achieve good performance.

1 Introduction

How can one predict the future precisely? Prediction of events in temporally changing signals is an important field of research for mathematicians and physicists. Chaotic time series prediction is an essential task of signal processing, physiological analysis and economic diagnosis. One of the significant features of chaotic behavior is that a chaotic signal continually generates new patterns, whereas simpler signals do not. Conventional methodology for probing this problem is to explore mathematical models that describe the physics behind the chaos phenomena and try to solve the parameters of the models by approximation. However, the computation may not converge to explicit solutions due to the high degree of nonlinearity, and resolution of parameters is often impractical.

In neural systems, the relevant information is transformed by distributed neural processing. Therefore, the neural network is regarded as an information processing machine which distributes important information or features through a complex circuit inspired by the function of the human brain. Learning algorithms produce an estimation of the system behavior based on the observation of input-output pairs. These methodologies can be applied to the category of tasks in system identification and prediction. Neural network technology has been found to be useful for universal continuous function approximation [1, 5]. Researchers have exploited neural network technologies such as feedforward networks and radial basis functions for prediction and have demonstrated promising capability [6, 12, 16].

Some neural net paradigms capture temporal dynamics, including the Adaptive Time-Delay Network ($ATNN$) and the Time-Delay Neural Network ($TDNN$), which employ time delay taps on connections. These networks have been successfully implemented for spatiotemporal pattern production and phoneme recognition [7, 8, 9, 14, 15]. In this paper, the $ATNN$ is applied for chaotic time series prediction.

2 Problem Description

The prediction of future variation from past and current system measurements is often an essential task in dynamic systems analysis and control. A dynamic system has time-varying outputs and outputs determined

*This work was supported in part by the Institute for Systems Research, University of Maryland (NSF CDR-88-03012), the Naval Research Laboratory (N00014-90K-2010), and the Applied Physics Laboratory of Johns Hopkins University.

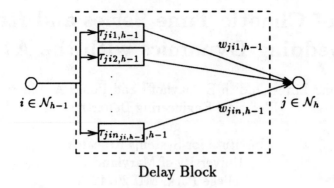

Delay Block

Figure 1: Delay Block: Basic time-delay connections between two processing units (node i of layer $h-1$ and node j of layer h) in $ATNN$, and $n_{ji,h-1}$ is the number of delays applied. Reprinted from Lin et al [7].

by a set of independent parameters. The delay differential equation of the form $\frac{dx(t)}{dt} = F(x(t), x(t-\tau))$ describes a dynamic system in which a stimulus has a delayed response. The time delay factor τ usually determines the nature of the time series. This equation fits many practical examples of physiological control systems, economics, and other fields. The model we will use in this paper is the example proposed by Mackey and Glass which describes the production of white blood cells as following [10]:

$$\frac{dx(t)}{dt} = \frac{ax(t-\tau)}{1+x^c(t-\tau)} - bx(t), \qquad (1)$$

where $x(t)$ denotes the concentration of blood at time t, and τ is a delay time (for leukemia patient, τ is excessively long). The dynamic properties of this differential equation have been addressed extensively by Farmer [4]. The Mackey-Glass system is infinite dimensional, which requires an infinite set of independent real numbers to specify an initial condition [4]. It possesses many dynamic properties such as nonlinearity, limit cycle oscillation, aperiodic wave forms and other dynamic behaviors [4], and the Fourier spectrum is a broad band similar to that of noise. This chaotic time series has become a benchmark for prediction and temporal learning.

3   ATNN for Prediction

Preliminary results from the Adaptive Time-Delay Neural Network ($ATNN$) on system modeling and prediction applications have been shown to be promising [8]. The $ATNN$ architecture and learning paradigm is described briefly in this section. The $ATNN$ model employs modifiable time delays and synapse weights along the interconnections between two processing units, and both time delays and weights are adjusted according to system dynamics in an attempt to achieve the desired optimization. The configuration of multiple interconnections between a single pair of units, each with its own delay, is called a delay block as illustrated in Figure 1. In each delay block, node i of layer $h-1$ is connected to node j of the next layer h, with the connection line having an independent time-delay $\tau_{jik,h-1}$ and synaptic weight $w_{jik,h-1}$. The entire network is constructed by the delay blocks which connect neurons layer by layer [7]. Each node sums up the net inputs from the activation values of the previous neurons, through the corresponding time-delays on each connection line. Then the output of node j is governed by a nondecreasing differential function f of the net input (symmetric sigmoid function is selected in this paper).

The adaptation of the delays and weights are derived based on the gradient descent method to minimize the cost function E during training based on error back-propagation [11]. The mathematical formulas of the weight and time-delay modifications are described below:

$$\Delta w_{jik,h} \equiv -\eta_1 \frac{\partial E(t_n)}{\partial w_{jik,h}}$$

$$\Delta \tau_{jik,h} \equiv -\eta_2 \frac{\partial E(t_n)}{\partial \tau_{jik,h}},$$

where η_1 and η_2 are the learning rates. The training set consists of a sequence of time series and target outputs. The time delay values $\tau_{jik,h}$ can cross one another during learning. Processing units do not receive data through a fixed time window, but gather important information from various time delays which are adapted via the learning procedure. The largest time delay between two units can change during adaptation. With these mechanisms, the network implements dynamic delays along the interconnections of the *ATNN*. The derivation of this learning algorithm was addressed explicitly in [2, 7].

4 Simulations and Results

The *ATNN* implements dynamic delays along the interconnections of an artificial neural network. We applied the *ATNN* architecture to the chaotic time series prediction of Mackey-Glass differential equation as shown in Equation 1. We set $a = 0.2$, $b = 0.1$, $c = 10$ and $\tau = 17$ and the initial value $x = 0.8$. The resulting output is a quasi-cyclic signal with a characteristic time of t_{char}[1] ≈ 50 and with an attractor of fractal dimension ≈ 2.1 [4]. Before collecting the training and test data set, the equation is iterated long enough (after 1000 iterations) to let the transients die out. In our simulation, we use one input unit, three hidden units, and one output unit, four and six delay elements on the first and second connection layer respectively, which is a very economic configuration. In this configuration, the number of delay variables selected on this first connection layer is based on the chaotic series attractor dimension as discussed in Section 4.1, while the choice of delay element number is motivated by the intuition that higher level units should learn to make decision over a wider range in time based on more local abstractions at lower levels [14].

4.1 Resolving Embedding Dynamics

The state at time t of Mackey-Glass differential equation is determined by the function $f(t) = \frac{dx}{dt}$ (Equation 1) at the interval $[t, t - \tau]$. However, the value τ is unknown when only the time series is observed. Then one needs to pick a reasonable delay time $\hat{\tau}$ and model the function according to the information between estimated interval $[t, t - \hat{\tau}]$. This function can be approximated by n samples taken at

$$\Delta \hat{\tau} = \frac{\hat{\tau}}{(n-1)}. \tag{2}$$

These n samples can be thought of as n variables of an n dimensional space vector

$$[x_1, x_2, ..., x_n]^{\mathsf{T}} = [x(t), x(t - \Delta\hat{\tau}), ..., x(t - (n-1)\Delta\hat{\tau})]^{\mathsf{T}}$$

The prediction is accomplished by mapping this n dimensional vector space to a real value. The mapping $f : R^n \longrightarrow R$ maps n measurements of the time series to the value at a future moment $x(t + T)$. Thus, the conventional prediction task was concentrating on finding a function such that $x(t + T) = f(x_1, x_2, ..., x_n)$. The lacking of prior knowledge of choosing embedding n and $\hat{\tau}$ is the obstacle of conventional methods. These parameters are usually chosen by trial and error, although there have been suggestions for choosing n, e.g. $d_a < n < 2d_a + 1$, where d_a is the fractal dimension of the attractor [13]. If $\hat{\tau}$ were too small, the embedding would have incomplete information. If $\hat{\tau}$ were too large, then information is included that is farther in the past than needed. Farmer suggested to weight the delay coordinates before performing the function approximation, in other words, the state vector becomes: $[x(t), \exp^{-hz} x(t - \Delta\hat{\tau}), ..., \exp^{-h(n-1)z} x(t - (n-1)\Delta\hat{\tau})]^{\mathsf{T}}$, however, *a priori* knowledge is still needed to decide h and z [3].

The *ATNN* accomplishes the prediction adaptively in the manner different from the single mapping described above. It employs multiple mappings according to the following procedures in the three layered network case:

1. Distributes the information on the interval $[t, t - \hat{\tau}]$ into j vectors with m dimension, where j is the number of hidden units and m denotes the number of time delay variables employed on

---

[1]t_{char} is the "characteristic time" for the time series estimated as the inverse of the mean frequency in the power spectrum

training set size	epoch	$NRMSE$
200	125	0.1991
300	81	0.1991
400	64	0.1903
500	48	0.1997
600	36	0.2067
700	16	0.2078
800	11	0.2075

Table 1: Experiments of different configurations as the cutoff $RMSE$ is set to 0.02, $T = 1$.

training set size	epoch	$NRMSE$
200	16	0.2515
300	11	0.2418
400	8	0.2371
500	7	0.2713
600	6	0.2701
700	6	0.2701
800	5	0.2775

Table 2: Experiments of different configurations as the cutoff $RMSE$ is set to 0.05, $T = 1$.

the connections between input processor and node j on the hidden layers. Each m dimensional space vector is transformed to a real value y_j by weight vector W_j and squashing function σ which associate with hidden node j.

$$
\begin{aligned}
y_1(t) &= \sigma(W_1^{\mathsf{T}}[x(t - \tau_{11,1}), x(t - \tau_{12,1}), ..., x(t - \tau_{1m,1})]^{\mathsf{T}}) \\
y_2(t) &= \sigma(W_2^{\mathsf{T}}[x(t - \tau_{21,1}), x(t - \tau_{22,1}), ..., x(t - \tau_{2m,1})]^{\mathsf{T}}) \\
&\vdots \\
y_j(t) &= \sigma(W_j^{\mathsf{T}}[x(t - \tau_{j1,1}), x(t - \tau_{j2,1}), ..., x(t - \tau_{jm,1})]^{\mathsf{T}}),
\end{aligned}
$$

where m is the number of time-delays on the first connection layer.

2. These activation values from hidden units are again mapped to a real value which is the prediction target, in a similar manner as described above.

$$
z(t + T) = \sigma(W_2^{\mathsf{T}}[y_1(t - \tau_{11,2}), .., y_1(t - \tau_{1n,2}); ...; y_j(t - \tau_{j1,2}), .., y_j(t - \tau_{jn,2})]^{\mathsf{T}}),
$$

where n is the number of time-delays on the second connection layer.

The time-delay variables and weight parameters of the above functions are adapted as the training proceeds. The appropriate value of $\hat{\tau}$ is obtained from the resulting time-delay parameters ($\hat{\tau} = max(\tau_{jim,1}) + ... + max(\tau_{jim,h}) - 1$), and $\hat{\tau}$ does not have to be sampled at regular intervals as in Equation 2, which gives the potential for better prediction. Therefore, the embedding dynamics is resolved automatically and efficiently from this network paradigm.

4.2   Training Set Size and Performance

We explored the relationship between size of training set, number epochs of training , training $RMSE$ cutoff, and the performance during the system modeling task. In a series of experiments, the size of the training set was varied. The network was trained in batch mode (epochs), with a $RMSE$ cutoff point based on performance on the training set. The performance was measured on the first 4000 time steps of the Mackey-Glass series. Error measure was reported as normalized root-mean-square error[2] ($NRMSE$) over time of the target value and the desired prediction ($\hat{x}(t, T)$), e.g. predicting T steps ahead from observed information. This scheme is equivalent to resolving system modeling of the Mackey-Glass equation when T is equal to one. Note that performance measure $NRMSE$, usually averaged over time, represents a perfect prediction when $NRMSE$ value is equal to zero. If $NRMSE$ approaches one, the performance is no better than a constant predicter. In Table 1, the training $RMSE$ cutoff was 0.02, and in Table 2 the cutoff was 0.05. Each table shows a series of different training set sizes, and reports the number epochs of training needed in each case, and the performance on the 4000 sample test set in each case was denoted in $NRMSE$.

---

[2] $NRMSE = \dfrac{(E[(\hat{x}(t, P) - x(t + P))^2])^{1/2}}{\sigma_x}$ where $x(t)$ is the original signal value and $\hat{x}(t)$ is the network prediction output, and σ_x denotes the standard deviation of the original time series.

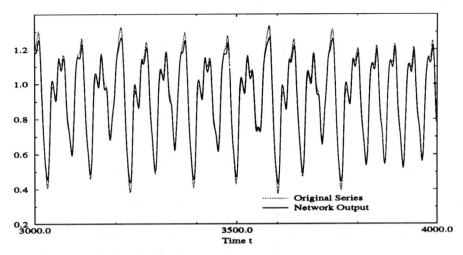

Figure 2: Simulation results of $ATNN$ with Mackey-Glass equation prediction as $T = 1$ and test on $t = 3000$ to 4000 sample data period.

In principle, the larger the training set size is, the longer the network will take to compute on an epoch. Fortunately, from Tables 1 and 2, it is not necessary that the network spends a longer time to converge when a larger set of data is used for training. The number of epochs needed decreases as the training size increases. The performance of the network is excellent, as shown in Figure 2. The network output is plotted in the solid line with the dotted line plotting the original sampling data, these two plots overlap most of the time.

4.3 Prediction Over Time

Usually, prediction error increases over time during the prediction, as in conventional methods without self adjustment. The neural network approach shows advantages. Lapedes's simulation showed that the error measure of conventional methods grow exponentially, while the performance of the neural approach (back-propagation net) continues in a more promising way and is superior to the other traditional techniques, as illustrated in Figure 3. Figure 3 shows $NRMSE$ as a function of prediction time.

In our experimentation, prediction was made iteratively step by step by recursively using the new predicted value to march along further. The results are shown in Figure 4 for various network configurations in which the solid black line A is the result from a network trained on $\hat{x}(t, T = 2)$ with cutoff criteria 0.03. The gray dotted line B and dashed line C are the network performance from $\hat{x}(t, T = 1)$ training with $RMSE$ cutoff at 0.02 and 0.05 respectively. Our results showed that the performance of $ATNN$ prediction on this chaotic time series confirms the high performance of neural networks as observed by Lapedes. Figure 4 demonstrates that when $T = 2$, the network gets better prediction within 300 time steps, while in the long run, the network maintains a more consistent performance for $T = 1$. The performance is better for $T = 1$ and $NRMSE$ does not drift upwards over time.

5 Conclusion

In this paper we have shown that a prediction approach based on $ATNN$ technology is effective and accurate. The beauty of this work is to show this complicated problem, based on the Mackey-Glass time series prediction, can be accomplished by such a simple $ATNN$ architecture, while training can be done with reasonable amounts of data and computing time. Furthermore, the embedding of the system dynamics can be resolved adaptively, unlike exhausting trial and error efforts in conventional methods. We can conclude from this study that the $ATNN$ is a good tool to tackle temporally changing signal processing and prediction problems. The simulation results confirm the performance improvements of the neural network approach, as suggested by Lapedes and Farber [6]. Future work may engage in the examination of numerical comparisons with traditional methods and neural network techniques.

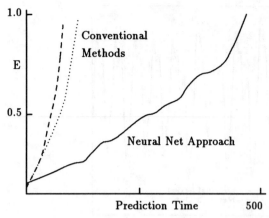

Figure 3: Performance comparison of neural net and conventional methods: relative quantity diagram. Adapted from Lapedes and Farber [6].

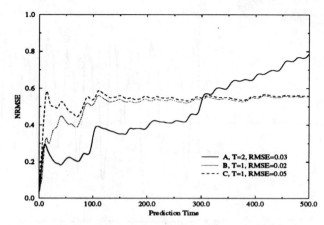

Figure 4: Prediction performance of ATNN on different network configuration with 400 training data.

References

[1] N. E. Cotter and O. N. Mian. A pulsed neural network capable of universal approximation. *IEEE Trans. on Neural Networks*, 3:308–314, March 1992.

[2] S. Day and M. Davenport. Continuous-time temporal back-propagation with adaptive time delays. *IEEE Trans. on Neural Networks*, 4:348–354, March 1993.

[3] D. Farmer and J. Sidorowich. Exploiting chaos to predict the future and reduce noise. In W.C. Lee, editor, *Evolution, Learning, and Cognition*, pages 277–330. World Scientific, Singapore, 1988.

[4] J.D. Farmer. Chaotic attractors of an infinite-dimentional dynamical system. *Physica D*, 4:366–393, 1982.

[5] E.J. Hartman, J.D. Keeler, and J.M. Kowalski. Layered neural networks with gaussian hidden units as universal approximations. *Neural Computation*, 2:210–215, 1990.

[6] A. Lapedes and R. Farber. How neural nets work. In W.C. Lee, editor, *Evolution, Learning, and Cognition*, pages 331–345. World Scientific, Singapore, 1988.

[7] D.-T. Lin, J. E. Dayhoff, and P. A. Ligomenides. Adaptive time-delay neural network for temporal correlation and prediction. In *SPIE Intelligent Robots and Computer Vision XI: Biological, Neural Net, and 3-D Methods*, volume 1826, pages 170–181, Boston, November, 1992.

[8] D.-T. Lin, J. E. Dayhoff, and Panos A. Ligomenides. Learning with the adaptive time-delay neural network. Submitted to Neural Networks, August, 1993.

[9] D.-T. Lin, P. A. Ligomenides, and J. E. Dayhoff. Learning spatiotemporal topology using an adaptive time-delay neural network. In *World Congress on Neural Networks*, volume 1, pages 291–294, Portland, OR, 1993. INNS, New York.

[10] M.C. Mackey and L. Glass. Oscillation and chaos in physiological control systems. *Science*, 197:287, 1977.

[11] J.L. McClelland, D.E. Rumelhart, and the PDP Research Group. *Parallel Distributed Processing: Explorations in the Microstructure of Cognition*, volume 2. MIT Press, Cambridge, 1986.

[12] J. Moody. Fast learning in multi-resolution hierarchies. In D.S. Touretzky, editor, *Advances in Neural Information Processing Systems*, volume 1, pages 29–39, Denver 1989, 1989. Morgan Kaufmann, San Mateo.

[13] N.H. Packard, J.P Crutchfield, J.D. Farmer, and R.S. Shaw. Geometry from a time series. *Physical Review Letters*, 45:712–716, 1980.

[14] A. Waibel, T. Hanazawa, G. Hinton, K. Shikano, and K. Lang. Phoneme recognition using time-delay neural networks. *IEEE Trans. on Acoust., Speech, Signal Processing*, 37:328–339, 1989.

[15] A. Waibel, K. J. Lang, and G. E. Hinton. A time-delay neural network architecture for isolated word recognition. *Neural Networks*, 3:23–43, 1990.

[16] P. J. Werbos. Backpropagation through time: What it does and how to do it. In *Proceedings of the IEEE*, volume 78, pages 1550–1560, October 1990.

A Business Application of Neural Networks[1]

Ilona Jagielska   Ashok Jacob
Monash University, Australia   Tattersall's Australia

A backpropagation neural network was built to predict sales figures for Tattersall's, Australia. The system will be used by the marketing department and will support the marketing managers in making sales forecasts for the lottery products.

Input/Output variables
Past Sales - sales in Million dollars; a sliding window of three immediately past draws each having the following parameters:
Super Draw = (1, 0) where 1 corresponds to "yes" for super draws, *Jackpot* - The number of weeks the division 1 has jackpotted, *Div1Prize* - prize amount in Millions. *Average Weekly Earnings* - AWE figures available from Australian Bureau of Statistics were used. The output consisted of one element corresponding to the sales amount of the current draw.

Training and Testing
The training set consisted of data recorded between July 1989 and December 1991 (130 input/output training vector pairs -   one pair for each week of this period). The trained network was then used to predict weekly sales volumes for the period January 1992 to September 1992 (33 vector pairs).

Analysis of Results
The sales forecasts produced by the network were compared with the actual sales figures as well as the forecasts made by the marketing managers. Some of the results are shown in Figure 1and Figure 2

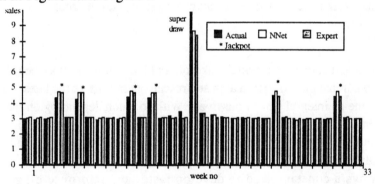

Figure 1. Sales predicted by Neural Network vs. Actual Sales and Experts' Forecasts

Predictions	Correlation	Prediction Error		
		Average	Super draw	Std Error
Neural Net	0.979	3.48%	12%	0.280
Experts	0.977	3.67%	15%	0.316

Figure 2. Comparison of Accuracy of Predictions.

The prediction done by the network compares favourably to the sales forecast of the experts. These studies indicate that neural networks can be successfully applied to this problem.

1. Jagielska I., Ashok J., *A Neural Network Model for Sales Forecasting*, The First New Zealand International Two Stream Conference on Artificial Neural Networks and Expert Systems, ANNES'93, IEEE Computer Society Press.

Search For an Improved Time-Frequency Technique For Neural Network-Based Helicopter Gearbox Fault Detection and Classification

Timothy W. Robinson, Mohammad Bodruzzaman, Mohan Malkani
Center For Neural Engineering
Tennessee State University
Nashville, TN 37209-1561

Robert M. Pap and Kevin L. Priddy
Accurate Automation Corporation
Chattanooga, TN 37406

Both military and civilian helicopters require routine maintenance to prevent problems while they are in flight. One of the most dangerous problems is the failure of gearboxes, which can lead to a catastrophic crash and loss of life. Traditional methods of detecting future problems relied on vibrational analysis models of the gearbox, which were highly complex. Newer techniques focused on applying signal pre-processing techniques, such as the Short-Time Fourier Transform (STFT) or the Wigner-Ville Distribution (WVD) to the vibration time signal and using the results as inputs for neural network training. These methods have all reached a measured level of success. This paper will show that it is possible to have improved neural network learning speed as well as improved fault detection and classification utilizing a new signal pre-processing technique known as Enhanced Time-Frequency Distribution (ETF.) The helicopter gearbox vibration data was supplied by Accurate Automation Corporation and the network architecture used was a two-layer feedforward network using generalized backpropagation learning rule.

1 Introduction

Everyday, thousands of helicopters routinely take-off and land safely around the world. From military reconnaissance and combat missions, to search and rescue operations, to the latest traffic updates, these vehicles have become an integral part of our lives. With so much depending on them, safety becomes a top priority when considering a helicopter as a primary mode of transportation. When an in flight critical failure occurs, such as in a gearbox, landing the craft safely becomes difficult, if not impossible. The result is usually a loss of helicopter and quite possibly the crew.

There is always a constant need to develop faster and improved diagnostic systems for maintenance. Ideally, such systems would be able to analyze a device, detect any flaws or problems, and alert the user in advance so appropriate action could be taken. This would result in two immediate benefits: a decrease in the number of accidents and injuries, and a reduction in overall maintenance costs. The drop in the number of accidents is self-evident; reduced maintenance costs are confirmed by the U.S. Government. A Department of Defense study found that when the gearboxes for one of its series of helicopters were removed for routine maintenance, 47% of them were still in satisfactory operating condition [1].

The first improvements in gearbox fault detection came from analyzing vibrational signatures in terms of its spectral energy content by using the Fast Fourier Transform (FFT). These signatures were obtained from accelerometers, strategically placed in and around the gearbox. A raw accelerometer signal is composed of a failure signal (or a predetermined 'clear signal' if there is no failure), clutter (noise signals that resemble failures) and machinery noise (signals that are unlike failures.) The types of failure signals typically found are those caused by either bearings or gear teeth. For bearings, there are inner and outer race faults, which occur when the raceway becomes spalled and dislodges debris.

There is also a rolling element fault, which occurs when the bearing itself fails. Gear spalls can occur in the teeth due to metal fatigue, which can also lead to a gear fault, where part or all of a tooth breaks off. Clutter arises from shaft imbalances and imprecise gear meshes. Machinery noise is the natural vibrations produced by the system elements. By examining accelerometer signals in the frequency domain, clutter and machinery noise were identified and appropriate filters developed to eliminate them, leaving a signature containing mostly fault information.

The first attempts to classify these faults used spectral templates, which were applied over an FFT-generated spectrum. Spectral components that matched the template criterion were summed together to produce an overall score, which was an indication of spectral energy content. Special rules were then applied to this score to determine whether it matched a previously stored fault in memory [2]. The major flaw with this system was that it neglects the time information, which is crucial to future fault prediction. It relied on the premise that the frequency content of the fault data remained constant during the occurrence of the fault, which is incorrect. In fact, the frequency content (especially the natural frequency) of the helicopter gearbox changes as the fault conditions change over time. Therefore, it is necessary to observe the spectral content as a function of time and frequency.

Newer attempts at fault classification involve a neural network approach. Because of their ease of implementation and execution speed, a properly trained neural network could effectively classify several types of faults. For inputs, the neural network relies on pre-processed fault signal data, which can contain both time and frequency information. There are various time-frequency techniques such as Short-Time Frequency (STFT), Wigner-Ville Distribution (WVD), Wavelet Transform (WT) and Enhanced Time-Frequency Distribution (ETF) that can be used to generate the necessary input data. With enough training examples, a neural network can develop a generalized classification scheme suitable for real-time fault diagnosis. The major problems with using neural networks is getting enough training examples with good features and reducing the training time to produce acceptable training and testing results.

The objectives of this research were to compare three of the above techniques (STFT, WVD, and ETF) and determine which method produced the smallest training error and the lowest amount of classification errors. After pre-processing the fault data with each of the three methods, a neural network is trained from an initial set of weight values. A comparison between the error history training curves as well as results from unseen data classification errors will be used as performance criteria.

2 Signal Pre-Processing

To go from the time domain to the frequency domain, a time signal can be pre-processed with an algorithm that will extract the necessary frequency information. One of the most common methods used to produce a two-dimensional time-frequency (TF) plane is the STFT, which is defined by,

$$S(t,f) = \int_{-\infty}^{\infty} s(\tau)w(t - \tau)e^{-j2\pi f\tau}d\tau \tag{1}$$

where $w(t - \tau)$ represents the selected data window centered at time location τ that is convolved with the time signal $s(t)$. The discrete version at any time instant n is given by,

$$S(n,k) = \sum_{m=-\infty}^{\infty} s(m)w(n - m)e^{-j2\pi km/N} \tag{2}$$

Typically, the data window size is selected to be much shorter than the length of the time signal. There is a trade-off in resolution when using this technique; good time resolution requires a shorter window $w(t)$ and good frequency resolution demands a longer window.

The Wigner-Ville distribution (WVD) is another method that can be used to generate a two-dimensional TF representation. It is an improvement on the original Wigner distribution (WD) algorithm in that no aliasing is created and it does not exhibit low-frequency artifacts typically produced in the real WD [3]. The WVD of a real signal $s(t)$ is defined by,

$$W_S(t,\omega) = \int_{-\infty}^{\infty} z(t + \tau/2)z(t - \tau/2)e^{-j\omega\tau}d\tau \qquad (3)$$

where $z(t)$ is the complex analytic signal associated with the original signal $s(t)$ as follows

$$z(t) = s(t) + jH[s(t)] \qquad (4)$$

and $H[\cdot]$ is the Hilbert Transform. The windowed discrete WD of the signal $s(n)$ is

$$W(n,\omega) = \sum_{m=-L}^{L} w(m)s(n + m)s(n - m)e^{-j2\omega m} \qquad (5)$$

A new technique capable of extracting time-frequency information is Enhanced Time-Frequency distribution (ETF). This method employs computing the FFT of the magnitude spectrum of a time signal, finding the autocorrelation of the resulting signal, then computing the magnitude of the inverse FFT. The result is a TF-like distribution with increased resolution of harmonic frequencies [4]. Mathematically, the procedure for a time signal $s(t)$ is

$$s_I(\omega) = \sqrt{(s(\omega)s^*(\omega))} \qquad \text{where } s(\omega) = FFT[s(t)] \qquad (6)$$

$$a_I(\tau) = a(\tau)a(\tau) \qquad \text{where } a(\tau) = FFT[s_I(\omega)] \qquad (7)$$

$$y_I(\phi) = \sqrt{(y(\phi)y^*(\phi))} \qquad \text{where } y(\phi) = IFFT[a_I(\tau)] \qquad (8)$$

3   Network Architecture

The neural network used was a traditional two-layer feedforward network, with weight updates accomplished using the generalized backpropagation learning rule (70% of previous weight adjustment.) Network input consisted of 1024 points, which was generated by a moving window of 2048 points with 50% overlap for the STFT and WVD data, and a 4096 window with 50% overlap for the ETF. The hidden layer contained 4 nodes and the output layer 2. Continuous bipolar activation was used at all nodes, in addition to a negative bias term.

Three types of gearbox fault data were used: no fault, bearing inner race, and bearing outer race, with a maximum file size of 65,000 points. For training, 60% of the data set was used and the remainder left for testing. Five different randomly generated weight sets were used, to which were applied the three types of TF network inputs for a maximum of 5000 presentations. Two types of training and tests were done: a fault/no fault condition and a comparison of 2 fault types with a no fault condition. For the fault/no fault training and test, bearing outer race fault data was used.

4   Simulation Results

The two best error learning histories are shown for both sets of training conditions (see Fig. 1). For the fault/no fault condition, data that had been processed using the ETF algorithm clearly surpassed the performance of both the STFT and WVD processed data. Each of the weight sets converged to approximately the same level using each respective data type. The WVD data was the second best performer followed by the STFT data.

Training results for all three types of errors again show that overall, the ETF data converges faster than the other two (Fig. 2). In this case, however, we noticed that three of the five ETF curves exhibited a period of oscillations before resuming a smooth training path. Note that with more information used for training, all the network results for the all fault training sessions are surpassed by fault/no fault network training.

In Fig. 3, performance measures are given based on converting a segment of raw data into one input pattern of the respective TF representation. This performance is calculated by taking the following: # of flops ÷ 1 pattern ÷ conversion time. Subsequent performance will be defined as: # of flops ÷ # of patterns ÷ elapsed time. This chart shows that the ETF algorithm used had a very high conversion rate compared to the other two methods. Fig. 4 gives the network training performance for actual sets of patterns. For the ETF/STFT/WVD methods, the corresponding number of patterns are found in Table 1.

Classifications using the training and testing data are shown in Figs. 5 through 8. In Figs. 5 and 6, the criteria level was set to 20% or lower. The results of fault/no fault and all fault classification show ETF as a clear winner for both training and testing, although the all fault tests results were not particularly great. If the criteria are reduced to 10% or lower, Fig. 7 shows that the ETF test results still surpass all others for the fault/no fault condition, but are nearly equivalent to the WVD for the all fault condition.

5 Conclusions

Our research results show promise that training with the ETF distribution algorithm for data analysis is a worthwhile endeavor. The preliminary results reached would seem to indicate that this technique of signal pre-processing is beneficial to this form of fault diagnosis system, with the potential for applications to other types of similar systems. Classifications using this method have matched and/or outperformed comparable techniques. Future areas of research would focus on extending the number of learning cycles and using a richer data set for comparison purposes.

6 Acknowledgment

This work was supported by the U.S. Navy-funded Center for Neural Engineering at Tennessee State University, ONR Grant Number: N00014-92-J-1372. Additional support was supplied by research partner Accurate Automation Corporation of Chattanooga, TN. The authors would like to thank them for their support for pursuing this research.

References

1. Lawrence J. Mertaugh, 'Evaluation of Vibration Analysis Techniques for the Detection of Gear and Bearing Faults in Helicopter Gearboxes,' *Report for Naval Air Test Center, Code RWATD, RW041, Patuxent River, MD 20670-5304*

2. Doug Gore and Glenn Edgar, 'Techniques for the Early Detection of Gear and Bearing Failures in Helicopter Drive Trains,' *Presented at the 40th Annual Forum of the American Helicopter Society, Arlington, VA, May 16-18, 1984*

3. M. Bodruzzaman, S. S. Devgan, 'On-Line Intelligent Health Monitoring Systems for NASP Type Hypersonic Structure,' *Report for Aeronautical Systems Center, Contract No. F33657-90-C-2264, WPAFB, OH 45433-7644*

4. Timothy Robinson, Gee-In Goo, 'Phoneme Detection and Classification as Inputs For Neural Network Speech Recognition,' *Presented at the NSF National Conference on Diversity in the Scientific and Technological Workforce, Washington, DC, September 24-27, 1992*

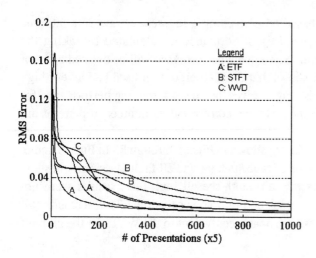

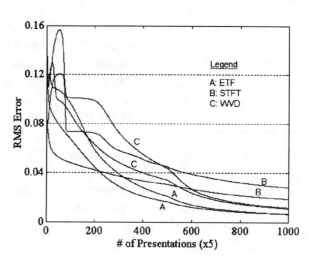

Fig. 1 Error training history using fault/no fault input data.

Fig. 2 Error training history using all fault input data.

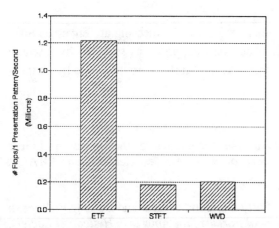

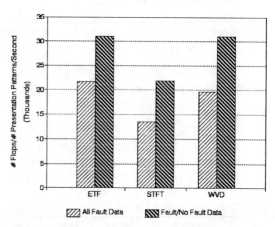

Fig. 3 Performance observed in transforming given input to respective TF representations.

Fig. 4 Performance observed running network using respective inputs.

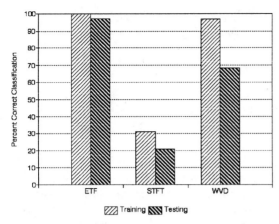

Fig. 5 Classification of errors for fault/no fault data using 20% as correctness criteria.

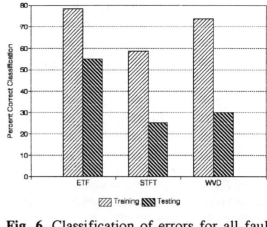

Fig. 6 Classification of errors for all fault data using 20% as correctness criteria.

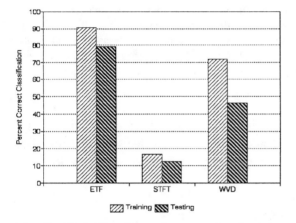

Fig. 7 Classification of errors for fault/no fault data using 10% as correctness criteria.

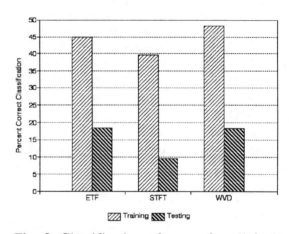

Fig. 8 Classification of errors for all fault data using 10% as correctness criteria.

Table 1

Fault/No Fault Condition				All Fault Condition			
	ETF	STFT	WVD		ETF	STFT	WVD
Input Type	Quantity	Quantity	Quantity	Input Type	Quantity	Quantity	Quantity
Training	54	113	60	Training	78	164	87
Testing	34	72	41	Testing	49	104	60

BINARY RESPONSE FORECASTING: COMPARISON BETWEEN NEURAL NETWORKS AND LOGISTIC REGRESSION ANALYSIS

Mauricio. A. León, MD

Department of Anesthesiology, University of South Florida, College of Medicine,
MDC Box 59, 12901 Bruce B. Downs Blvd., Tampa, Florida 33612

Abstract-Logistic regression models are used to forecast outcomes from binary response events. Examples of such events are patient survival or a blood transfusion. Logistic regression models are calculated using input parameters correlated to the event of interest. The purpose of this research was to compare logistic regression and neural networks forecast performance on simulated data. **Methods:** *Two-615 record data sets were created. Each record included 24 independent and one dependent (outcome) binary variables. In the first data set (probability set), outcome was computed using a probability function. In the second set (rule set), outcome resulted from the application of logic rules. The first 400 records of each set were used for neural network training and logistic regression estimation. The remaining records were used for testing.* **Results:** *Both models estimated correctly 66% of outcomes in the probability set. In the rule set, the neural network predicted outcome significantly better (p<0.0001) than the logistic model (neural network 96% vs. logistic regression 78% correct). Both models estimated outcome significantly better in the rule set than in to the probability set (p<0.0001).* **Conclusion:** *This work compared neural network and logistic regression forecasting performance on two binary data sets. These data sets were selected as extreme examples of cause-effect problems observed in medical research. Our results indicate that neural networks may yield better results that logistic regression. This finding may encourage the use neural networks in problems approached traditionally with logistic regression models.*

1. INTRODUCTION

There are many examples of events that result in only two possible outcomes. This binary response is typical of situations such as patient survival after illness or the decision to transfuse blood. Among statistical methods used to predict binary outcomes or responses, a logistic regression of the form:

$$y = \frac{e^{b_0 + b_1 x_1 + \ldots + b_n x_n}}{1 + e^{b_0 + b_1 x_1 + \ldots + b_n x_n}}$$

is frequently chosen because the output is confined between zero and one. Usually zero and one are assimilated to symbolic concepts such as true or false, yes or no, or pass or fail. The popular mufti-layer back propagation neural network usually generates output responses confined to 0 to 1 or -1 to 1 ranges, thus making this type of neural networks naturally fit for modeling binary response problems. While logistic regression methods are frequently used in bio-medical research (From 1988 to 1993, at least 864 Medline citations report the use of logistic regression models for data analysis), we found no instance of use of neural networks as and addition or alternative to logistic regression analysis. To evaluate the advantages, if any, of using neural networks over logistic regression models for prediction of binary responses, we designed an experiment to compare the forecast performance of the two methods on simulated data sets.

2. METHODS

In order to compare the efficacy of neural networks and logistic regression analysis for forecasting, two data sets were created. Each data set consisted of several independent and a single dependent variable. In the first data set (probability set), the relation between independent and dependent variables was defined by a probability function. In the second data set (rule set), the dependent variable resulted from the application of a fixed number of rules to the independent variables. In both data sets, there were 24 independent and one dependent (outcome) binary variables.

2.1 Assembly of the probability set

A table s of 25 columns and 615 rows was generated in a commercially available spreadsheet. Independent variables s_{ji} were randomly set to zero or 1 for $j = 1,...,615$, $i = 1,...,24$. A table $t = \{t_1,...,t_{24}\}$ was filled with random coefficients normally distributed between -50 and 50. These coefficients determine the initial weight of each on of the independent variables. An additional table $u = \{u_1,...,u_{615}\}$ was filled with random scores normally distributed between zero and 100. These scores were used guarantee that the outcome of each record was a probability function. The outcome variable s_{j25} was calculated using the following equation:

$$s_{j25} = \begin{cases} 0 \text{ if } p_j < u_j \\ 1 \text{ if } p_j \geq u_j \end{cases},$$

where:

$$p_j = b(q_j - a), \quad q_j = \sum_{i=1}^{24} s_{ji} t_i, a = \text{Minimum } (q_j), \text{ and } b = 100 / (\text{ Maximum}(q_j) - a).$$

2.2. Assembly of rule set

A table similar to the one used for the probability set was filled randomly with zeroes and ones. The outcome variable s_{j25} was set to one, if at least one rule (out of six rules) could be applied. The general form of each rule was RULE$_r$ IF [Condition$_1$ AND ... AND Condition$_n$]. Examples of conditions are $\Sigma s_{j0},...,s_{j5} \geq 3$, $s_{j20} = 1$, $s_{j22} = 0$, etc.

After assembly, the first 400 records from each data set were used for calculation of logistic regression coefficients and for training of backpropagation neural networks. The remaining 215 records were used for testing.

2.3. Logistic regression analysis

Multiple logistic regression analysis on both data sets was accomplished using a commercially available statistics package (STATISTICA, Statsoft, CA). The logistic regression option was selected using the quasi-Newton search algorithm. The maximum number of iterations was increased from 100 to 1000. After convergence, coefficients of the multiple regression equations and equation estimates for all training records were saved. Then, using the logistic regression coefficients, a spreadsheet was programmed to forecast the test data outcome.

2.4 Neural Network training

Neural network training was accomplished using a commercially available neural network simulator (DMW, HNC, CA) running on a dedicated accelerator board (BALBOA, HNC, CA) installed in one expansion slot of an AT compatible 486 computer. Neural network training parameters are listed table 1. For each data set, the neural network simulator evaluated 50 different models, varying in the number of hidden layer neurons. The program automatically selected the model yielding the lowest mean squared error and calculated the outcome response for the records set aside for testing.

Table 1
Neural network training parameters

Activation function:	Logistic
No of hidden layers:	1
Learning method:	Smoothing
Max. number of epochs:	1000
Initial weight generation:	Random
Maximum initial weight:	1

3. RESULTS

3.1 Probability set

The probability set-test group consisted of 215 records. One hundred and eleven records had an outcome of one. The outcome of the remaining 104 records was zero. Using optimal cut-off thresholds, 66.5% (n= 143) and 66.9% (n=144) of the test data were estimated accurately by the neural network and the logistic regression models respectively. Cut-off values were 0.33 for the logistic regression and 0.36 for the neural network models.

3.2 Rule set

The rule set-test group consisted of an identical number of records. There were 72 records with an outcome of one, and the outcome of the remaining 143 records was zero. The best cut-off thresholds obtained for the probability set data were 0.44 and 0.39 for the network and logistic models respectively. Using optimal cut-off thresholds, 96%(n=208) and 78% (n=169) of the records were estimated accurately by the network and logistic models respectively. There was a significant difference (p <0.0001) between the correct number of outcomes estimated by the neural network and by the logistic regression model in this group.

3.3. Both methods estimated output significantly better in the rule set group than in the probability set (p<0.0001 for neural network model and p= 0.0068 for logistic regression model)

4. DISCUSSION

Neural networks have been compared to some statistical methods in the medical literature (Watt, 1991). However, we fail to find evidence of any attempt to compare neural networks and logistic regression analysis. The objective of this research was to compare the forecast performance of neural networks and logistic regression models for events having a binary outcome. We selected extreme examples of data groups in which the relation between independent and dependent variables ranged from a highly complex but "stable" (rule set) to a rather "unstable" (probability set) model, in which two records with identical independent variables occasionally resulted in different outcomes. Our results indicate that, at worst, a single hidden-layer back propagation neural network performs as well as a logistic regression model. While this work does not intent to proof mathematically the "superiority" of neural networks, the empirical evidence suggests that neural networks should be considered in research endeavors in which logistic regression analysis has been selected a the main statistical tool.

REFERENCES

Watt R.C. (1991). A comparison of artificial neural networks and classical statistical analysis. *Anesthesiology*, 75, A451

Time Delay Neural Network for Small Time Series Data Sets

Worapoj Kreesuradej, Donald C. Wunsch II, Mark Lane
Texas Tech University
Electrical Engineering Department
Lubbock, TX 79409-3102
nus03@ttacs1.ttu.edu

Abstract

For large data sets neural networks have better time series prediction performance than conventional methods [6]. However, when neural networks are trained with meager data, the problem of overfitting seriously decreases their performance. The objective of this work is set apart from previous neural network approaches by focusing on noisy data of limited record length. Observation of monthly slaughter hog prices from January, 1965 to July, 1987 are used. The work uses two techniques to overcome the problem of overfitting: the validation method and the use of time delay neural networks (TDNN).

Background

Applying neural networks to the problem of time series prediction is not new. Lapedes [3] showed that neural networks are capable of predicting the future values of time series by extracting knowledge from the past. Weigen [6] found that a backpropagation network produced more accurate results than the best mixed autoregressive-moving average (ARMA) model identified so far. Other studies have also concluded that the neural networks perform as well as or better than the conventional methods.

In the general nonlinear time series prediction schemes, the basic framework can be described as

$$\hat{y}(k) = y(k) + e(k) = F(y(k-1), y(k-2), ..., y(k-T)) + e(k) \qquad (1)$$

The estimate of $y(k)$ is given by $\hat{y}(k)$. The error term derived by subtracting $y(k)$ from $\hat{y}(k)$ is assumed to be a white noise.

To approximate a function, $F(.)$, the neural network uses a backpropagation learning process. This constructs the function, $F(.)$, based on the training patterns of data which consist of a current value and lagged values. The network is provided both input patterns and desired outputs. The learning algorithm tries to minimize a cost function, the sum squared error; $e^2(k) = (Y(k) - \hat{Y}(k))^2$, with the goal of making the network respond as desired.

The approximated function, $F(.)$, can also be viewed as a function of the current value and the past values at the input layer and a collection of synaptic weights determined by the training algorithm. Thus, the output of a network is written by

$$F(y(k-1), y(k-2), ..., y(k-T); \mathbf{W}),$$

where $\mathbf{W}$ is a collection of weights. For a general statistical rule of thumb [1], the number of weights should be less than one tenth of the number of training patterns. If a network has a large number of weights, then the bias of the approximated function will be reduced. However, the variance of the function still causes a high mean-squared error[2]. In order to reduce the mean-squared error, the balance between bias and variance of the approximated function must be done. This problem seriously affect on the accuracy of the approximated function when the training set has only a few hundred patterns.

The time delay neural network (TDNN) was proposed by Waible [4] to expand the hidden layer by adding multiple delay-lines. One of its properties, which is suitable for time series prediction, is that TDNNs form an approximated function which has a small number of weights [5]. This reduces the number of free parameters of the network. Therefore, this property help the TDNN reduce bias and variance problems.

During the training process, weights are adjusted in order to fit the features of the data. Therefore, as the training process continues, the degree of bias is decreasing. To keep the balance between bias and variance, the training process must be stop before the network begins to be an unbiased approximator. Thus, the second technique is validation method which is used to avoid overfitting problem.

To train a network with validation technique, the available data are classified into three sets. First, the *training set* is used to determine the values of the weights. Second, the *validation set* is used to monitor the network performance. The training process still continues if the prediction on the validation set improves. When improvement stops, the training process must be terminated. Figure 1 illustrates how if the training process still continues after the end of the improvement in validation set, the network performance begin to degrade. The third, *prediction* or *testing set* is set apart and never used in training.

Error on validation set

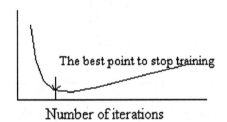

The best point to stop training

Number of iterations

FIGURE 1: Error on validation set is used to decide when to terminate training.

Experiment Result of Hog Price Prediction

The experiment is conducted on the slaughter hog price data. The data series is collected by the Agricultural Marketing Service Group from Jan, 1965 to July, 1987. The data is recorded monthly and is composed of 272 hog prices in total. To train the network, the 272 data points are normalized to (0,1). (We simply divided the data values by 100.) Furthermore, the data are classified into three sets: the *training set*, having 233 points, the *validation set*, which comprises 15 points and the *prediction set*, composed of 24 points.

A TDNN time delay neural network is set up for one-step prediction. The neural network uses a current value and some past values as an input pattern and the next value as a desired output. Then, once the neural network model is set up, it is used to iteratively predict several steps into the future.

The performance of networks is measured by normalized sum squared error, given by

$$nSSE = \frac{\sum\limits_{k=1}^{N} (target_k - prediction_k)^2}{\sum\limits_{k=1}^{N} (target_k - mean)^2} \qquad (2)$$

$$= \frac{1}{\sigma^2 N} \sum\limits_{k=1}^{N} (x_k - \hat{x}_k)^2$$

$x_k, \hat{x}_k$ are the actual value and the prediction value of sequence, respectively. σ^2 is the estimated variance of the actual value sequence and N is the number of data points.

The prediction results for this time series can be found in table1, Figure 2A and figure 3.

Table 1: Normalized sum squared error, nSSE, for predictions of time delay neural network.

Duration	Time Delay Neural Network	
	Single-step Pred. nSSE	Iterated Pred. nSSE
Training Set	0.0211	-
249-253	0.0433	0.3707
249-260	0.0326	0.4585
249-272	0.0489	0.7798

Table 2: Normalized sum squared error, nSSE, for prediction of autoregressive-integrated-moving average (ARIMA)

Duration	$ARIMA(4, 1, 0)(0, 1, 1)_{12}$	
	Single-step Pred. nSSE	Iterated Pred. nSSE
Training Set	0.0482	-
249-254	0.0473	1.4604
249-260	0.0164	0.9485
249-272	0.0214	2.4193

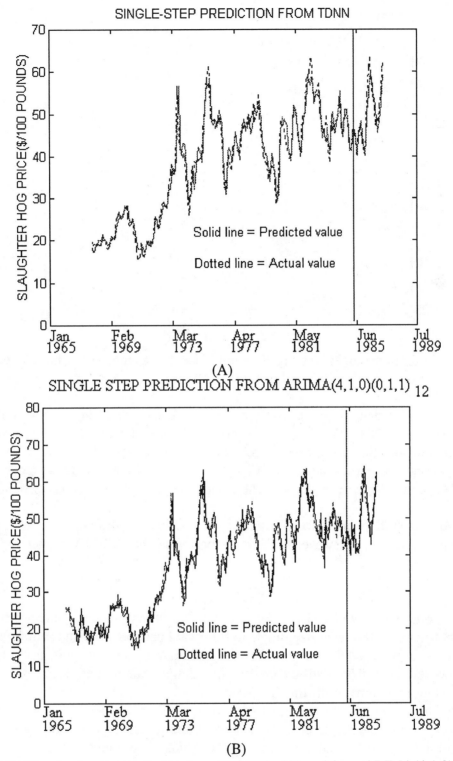

FIGURE 2: The single step prediction from TDNN in (A) and from ARIMA$(4,1,0)(0,1,1)_{12}$ in B. Both models predict on the training set for the data before the vertical line and in the predicted set for the data after the vertical line.

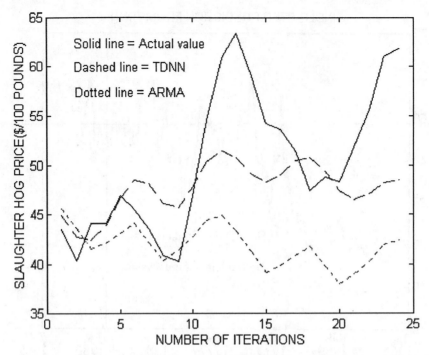

FIGURE 3: Multistep prediction for slaughter hog price data as function of number prediction iterations into the future.

This experiment data set is also used to fit to a linear model in order to compare the results with those of TDNN. The data is transformed to meet stationarity requirements. Then, the autocorrelation and the partial autocorrelation are calculated. From the pattern of the autocorrelations and the partial autocorrelation, the autoregressive integrated moving average model ARIMA $(4,1,0)(0,1,1)_{12}$ is set up. The results are presented in Table 2, figure 2.B and figure 3.

Both models, TDNN and ARIMA, do not show significant difference in performance for the single-step prediction. However, TDNN outperforms the ARIMA model for multistep prediction.

Conclusion

In this work, we show that TDNN can keep more past information, which is necessary for prediction problems, than the same size simple feed forward network. As an example, the TDNN can transform to a static equivalent feedforward which has more weights than the original network. However, the TDNN needs a complex algorithm to train the network. As a result, the network consumes more time for its training process.

Finally, the TDNN is used to predict hog prices, and shows better performance than the ARIMA model. Although effective techniques for learning exist, the appropriate size of the network is still determined by trial and error. This is a time-consuming process. In addition, it rarely produces the network that is optimized for the application. The theoretical analysis and empirical studies related to this issue remain open research subjects. Although research is continuing on the further improvements, the TDNN is already a powerful model for use in time series prediction.

References

1. Eric B. Baum and David Haussler, ",What size net gives valid generalization?", <u>Neural Computation,</u> Vol. 1, 1987, pp 877.
2. Geman, S., Bienstock, E., and Doursat, R. "Neural networks and the Bias/Variance Dilemma." <u>Neural Computation,</u> Vol. 4, No. 1, 1992, pp. 1-58.
3. Lapedes, A.., and Farber, R. "Nonlinear signal processing using neural networks : Prediction and system modeling." <u>Technical report LA - UR - 87 - 2662,</u> Los Almos National Laboratory, 1987.
4. Waibel, A., Hanazawa, T., Hinton, G., Shikamo, K., and Lang, K. " Phoneme Recognition Using Time - Delay Neural Networks." <u>IEEE Transaction Acoust., Speech., and Signal Processing.</u> Vol. 37, No. 3, 1989, pp. 328- 339.
5. Wan, E. "Temporal Backpropagation : An Efficient Algorithm for Finite Impulse Response Neural Networks." <u>Proceeding of The 1990 Connectionist Models Summer School.</u> San Mateo, CA : Morgan Kaufmann, 1990.
6. Weigend, A., Bernado, H., and Rumehart, D. "Predicting the future : A Connectionist Approach." <u>International Journal of Neural Systems,</u> Vol. 1, 1990, pp. 193.

MEMORY NEURAL NETWORKS APPLIED TO

THE PREDICTION OF DAILY ENERGY USAGE

Alvin J. Surkan
Department of Computer Science and Engineering, University of Nebraska
Lincoln, NE 68588-0115   USA   Email: surkan@cse.unl.edu   Fax: 402-272-7767

Alexei N. Skurikhin
Mathematics Department, Institute of Physics and Power Engineering
249020 Obninsk, RUSSIA.   Email: root@ippe.obninsk.su   Fax: + 7 095 230 23 26

Abstract

Daily records of energy consumption make a time series that can be used for predicting demand expected one or more days in the future. A neural network enhanced with memory neurons and called an MNN, has been developed and tested to make approximate time series predictions. At present, the prediction is done without taking external influences into consideration. In an MNN, both inputs and hidden weights are modified by time delay coefficients. Optimized values for the weights and delay coefficients can be learned incrementally from the systematic components of fluctuations extracted from historical data. Currently, the observed time series is the only source of information being used to predict future values. Later, other series of independent predictive data can be used to expand the MNN model. Network training has successfully demonstrated that up to 6000 iterations over the training set can make a ten-fold reduction in the average prediction error. Repeated presentation of hundreds of training patterns in training a network can lead to systematic convergence and the synthesis of a predictive network. Training of the MNN can make the error of prediction fall to be consistently below 20% when averaged over one year of set-aside test patterns.

Problem Context and Internal Delays in Memory Neural Networks

Industrial decision makers need predictions of time series formed from daily energy records. Typically, the time series represent energy used as electrical power and natural gas. Such series are the result of the operation of very complex systems. These systems combine commercial and residential energy consumption over large or extended geographic areas. Data sampling times range over minutes, hours, days, and weeks. The more effective prediction systems must recognize temporal patterns in the historical series of values and environmental factors. Memory elements may be added to layered neural network models to include time-delay variables, implicitly. Memory elements introduce data which implicitly adds another dimension. The effect of including the memory elements is to generate an analog of time-delayed inputs. Differential weighted parts of the time series can effectively account for data that is delayed. The memory elements can help to make predictions for times that are one or more units in the future beyond the last available elements of a series.

Enhancement of Layered Neural Networks by Including Memory Delays

Neural networks with the architectural structure of multiple-layered perceptrons can be augmented so that they learn from time-localized information. This modification is incorporating extra memory neurons. Also, it is suspected that it is advantageous to minimize network size to improve the network's ability to generalize. The parameters of such memory neurons must be learned to optimize their performance as predictors. The MNN proposed by Poddar and Unnikrishnan [1991] has been developed so data from only the current time need be applied at the network's input. In the network, the relative influence of past data effects is represented and stored internally by an adequately trained set of weights. Such a network learns to perform real-time predictions without introducing unacceptable time delays. Excessive delays could diminish or nullify the usefulness of the output values needed for making control decisions.

Effective Convolution Action of Memory Neuron Networks

The contribution to the output from memory neurons is the sequence obtained from a discrete convolution of past outputs of memory neuron and a kernel. This kernel is parameterized by a neuron's single memory coefficient α_j^l where subscript j tags the j-th network neuron of the l-th layer (see Figure 1). Both memory coefficient α_j^l and other weights W_{ji}^l and f_{ji}^l learning is directed by errors accumulated from the difference between the predicted values and the corresponding elements of the target vectors. Such network enhanced with internal memory can be used to identify the system's unknown order and internal delays. Only one input is required because recurrence effects make the output of the MNN depend indirectly on all past inputs introduced while training. The degree of this time-sensitive effect depends on the memory coefficient values that are established by training.

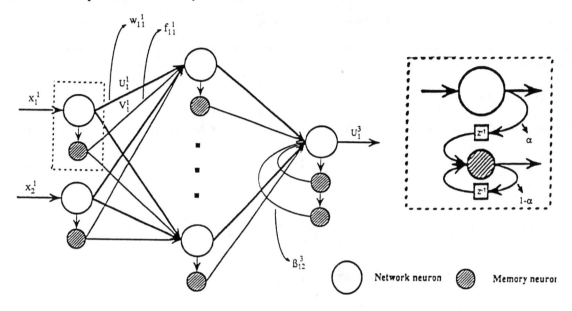

Figure 1. Architecture of a Memory Neuron Network patterned after the sketch of Poddar and Unnikrishnan [1991] showing at right, details of memory neuron associated with the top neuron of the first layer.

Background on Recurrent or Memory Neural Networks

The architecture of an MNN is shown in Figure 1. The larger open circles represent network neurons. Neurons within a layer are not connected to each other, but every network neuron of one layer is connected to every network neuron of the next layer. Corresponding to each network neuron, there is a memory neuron, represented by the smaller shaded circles. These neurons contain information about the past output of the corresponding network neurons. Each network neuron in a layer is connected to all the network neurons and to the memory neurons of the immediately lower layer. There are separate links from a network neuron and its corresponding memory neuron to every network neuron of the upper layer. Corresponding memory neurons can also be provided for the network neurons in the output layer. The net input to the j-th network neuron of layer l, at time t, is given by:

$$X_j^l(t) = \sum_{i=0}^{N_{l-1}} W_{ij}^{l-1} \cdot U_i^{l-1}(t) + \sum_{i=1}^{N_{l-1}} f_{ij}^{l-1} \cdot V_i^{l-1}(t) \tag{1}$$

where N_l is the number of network neurons in the l-th layer.

For the network neurons of the output layer, the net input is given by:

$$X_j^L(t) = \sum_{i=0}^{N_{L-1}} W_{ij}^{L-1} \cdot U_i^{L-1}(t) + \sum_{i=1}^{N_{L-1}} f_{ij}^{L-1}(t) \cdot V_i^{L-1}(t) + \sum_{i=1}^{M_j} \beta_{ij}^L \cdot V_{ij}^L(t) \qquad (2)$$

where M_j is the number of memory neurons associated with the j-th network neuron of the output layer, $U_j^l(t)$ is the output of the network neuron at time t, $V_j^l(t)$ is the output of the corresponding memory neurons at time t, β_{ij}^l is the weight of the connection from the i-th memory neuron of the j-th network neuron to the j-th network neuron in the output layer, memory coefficients W_{ij}^l is the weight connecting from the i-th network neuron to the j-th network neuron of layer (l+1), and f_{ij}^l is the weight of the connection from the corresponding memory neuron to the i-th network neuron of the (l+1) layer, memory coefficients. The output of this network neuron is decided by its transfer function and the net input:

$$U_j^l(t) = g_j^l(X_j^l(t)) \qquad (3)$$

The output of all the memory neurons except for those in the output layer, are derived by

$$V_j^l(t) = \alpha_j^l \cdot U_j^l(t-1) + (1-\alpha_j^l) \cdot V_j^l(t-1) \qquad (4)$$

For memory neurons in the output layer,

$$V_{ij}^L(t) = \alpha_{ij}^L \cdot V_{ij-1}^L(t-1) + (1-\alpha_{ij}^L) \cdot V_{ij}^L(t-1) \qquad \text{where} \qquad V_{i0}^l = U_i^L \qquad (5)$$

To preserve causality, both $U_i^l(t)$ and $V_j^l(t)$ are zero for any $t \leq 0$.

To ensure stability of the network dynamics, the conditions $0 \leq \alpha_{ij}^L,\ \alpha_i^l,\ \beta_{ij}^l \leq 1$ should be satisfied.

Learning by Error Minimization

The external environment of the network is characterized by a sequence of input vectors and the corresponding sequence of target vectors. The squared Euclidean distance was used as the error measure that direct learning.

$$E = \frac{1}{2} \sum_{t=1}^{T} \sum_{j=1}^{N_L} (O_j(t) - U_J^L(t))^2 \qquad (6)$$

The learning process minimizes this error by iteratively modifying the connection strengths W_{ij}^l between network neurons, the connection strength f_{ij}^l between memory neurons and network neurons, and the memory coefficients α_j^l for memory neurons. The original back-propagation learning rule (Rumelhart et al., 1986) was modified by Poddar and Unnikrishnan [1991], Sastry, Santharam and Unnikrishnan, 1993) that include memory neurons.

Each free variable is updated in proportional to the partial derivative of the error with respect to each variable:

$$\frac{\partial E}{\partial w_{ij}^l} = \sum_{t=1}^{T} \delta X_j^{l+1}(t) \cdot U_i^l(t) \; , \qquad \frac{\partial E}{\partial f_j^l} = \sum_{t=1}^{T} \delta X_j^{l+1}(t) \cdot V_i^l(t) \; , \qquad \frac{\partial E}{\partial \alpha_j^l} = \sum_{t=1}^{T} \delta V_j^{l+1}(t) \cdot \alpha_i^l(t)$$

$$(7) \qquad\qquad\qquad\qquad (8) \qquad\qquad\qquad\qquad (9)$$

All the above derivatives can be estimated from only locally available spatial and temporal information. The actual correction term for each variable is obtained by multiplying the corresponding estimate of the derivative by a learning rate. The other novelty in comparison with original back-propagation is that the learning rates for each variable are modified during learning. This speedup in the rate of convergence. The learning rate is modified through a novel heuristic strategy. With this strategy one tests if the partial derivatives along a dimension, in the current and previous iteration, have the same sign. When the sign is the same, then increase the learning rate by taking a larger step along that dimension. Otherwise decrease the learning rate.

Prediction of Daily Energy Consumption

A memory neural network or MNN was trained to predict a time series consisting of daily values of energy demand of a large geographic area. The project began with a program originally developed and supplied by K. P. Unnikrishnan. Some minor errors and bottlenecks were removed and overcome. The results reported here are from a new C program for a MNN. The program runs on both a CYBER 960-32 mainframe and 80386 personal computers. Networks with only one hidden layer and one memory neuron per node in the output layer have been used in these experiments. The number of input and output nodes are determined by the problem's structure. For these predictions only a single neuron was used was used at the network's output. The notation $(n_1{:}n_2)$ is used to denote a network with n_1 input nodes having n_1 corresponding memory neurons and with n_2 hidden network neurons having n_2 corresponding memory neurons.

Functions and Parameters Used for Network Development

The basic network was developed with the following parameters: {momentum factor = 0.48}, {initial range of weights [-0.1,+0.1]}, {rate modifier = 0.01}, {initial learning rate for network-network neuron links = 0.24}, {learning rate for memory-network neuron links = 0.24}, and {initial range for the memory coefficients = 0.1 to 0.9} The activation functions g_1, g_2, g_3, g_4 tested with $c_1 = c_2 = k_1 = k_2 = 1$, had the following definitions:

$$g_1 = \frac{c_1}{1 + e^{-k_1 \cdot X}} \, , \qquad g_2 = c_2 \cdot tahn(k_1 \cdot X) \, , \qquad g_3 = c_2 \cdot \frac{1 - e^{-k_2 \cdot X}}{1 + e^{-k_2 \cdot X}} \, , \qquad g_4 = \sum_{c=1}^{N} input_i$$

A simple linear mapping of the variable's observed extremes to the network's practical operating limits was used to scale data. Data values are mapped either to the range (0.1 to 0.9) or (-0.9 to +0.9) depending on which of the activation functions was in use.

Error Accumulation and Partitions of the Training and Test Data

The learning algorithm used the errors accumulated over batches of input training patterns. Before beginning the training of a network, the historical data records were partitioned into three non-overlapping sets. The first set was used for training. The second was used in selecting of a better trained network. The third set was used for providing the option of choosing a better performing network. The first data gave daily values for the energy consumption over the nine year period from 1981 to 1989. The second set had the daily energy consumption values for the single year 1990. The third set consisted of the same series of values from 1991. This was the original method of data preparation. Later, this method was a modified by limiting the first set of data to only the three years from 1987 to 1989. This modification was made to explore how prediction accuracy reduced with the size of the training set.

Testing of Activation Functions

The effects of different activation functions were tested before completing an extensive series of simulation experiments. Preliminary tests showed that the preferred combination of activation function was a hyperbolic tangent as the nonlinearity for the hidden nodes used in combination with a linear function on the output node. This combination produced the fastest convergence. There was no significant difference in the accuracy of the predictions when a sigmoid replaced the hyperbolic-tangent as the nonlinear activation function. However, the latter choices gave more rapid convergence in learning the mapping. Accordingly, all the results were obtained with the hyperbolic tangent function as the nonlinearity at the hidden nodes while the output node was linear.

Results of Simulation Experiments

For all experiments, the mean prediction errors were monitored by averaging the magnitude of the difference between observed and predicted time series values. Comprehensive simulation studies were made using networks with the structures: (2:2), (2:1), (1:2), (1:10), (2:10). All simulations used the parameter values given earlier in combination with the 3 and 9 year training data sets. Ten trials were implemented for each combination of data and network structure. When two input nodes were used, one of them was scaled the source data signal and the second one was the scaled first difference of the source. One important conclusion from the results of these simulation experiments is that the same accuracy is obtained when using, for input, only one source signal as when the input was both the source signal and its first difference.

In all simulations the process converged in fewer than 5000 iterations. As a rule, most of the accuracy is obtained during the first 100 to 2500 iterations of training. Training with more than 2500 iterations degrades the prediction performance. Another observation is that some trials fail to meet the pre-specified criterion for convergence. Convergence is achievable in the first 200 iterations or near the last 500 iterations of the 6000 iterations. The five previously specified network structures were used to predict 1, 2, or 3 days ahead. Figure 3 provides comparisons of the predicted values and those values known or expected from the test data. The results obtained in predictions for added days ahead were found to degrade as expected with time into the future.

Statistical Test of Errors in the Predicted Values

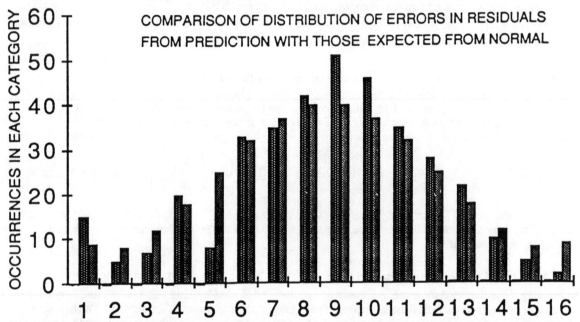

Figure 2 Histograms of the residues in the difference between the observed daily values and those predicted by the memory neuron network MNN over a full year of test data

Observations and Conclusions

An error reduction of 10-fold has been realized by training the network in fewer than 6000 iterations. It is important to discover how the time-delay effects of memory neurons use information from earlier inputs. The main finding was that only one input signal is sufficient when only the single time series data from the energy consumption observations are available. In the limit, one can achieve an average prediction accuracy of 17 to 18 percent. Collectively, the experiments indicate that an MNN using the hyperbolic tangent version as the hidden layer activation function and linear output unit is fastest. The accuracy has little if any dependence on the specific combination of activation functions. Also, a modification of the "QUICKPROP" procedure of S. Fahlman [see Fahlman 1988] obtained a similar result which was no better in either prediction accuracy or in its rate of convergence. Generally, the learning asymptotically approaches a limiting accuracy with a 17-20% level of error.

Figure 2 Graphs comparing final prediction of energy usage by the memory neuron network. The left shows the full year of daily values and at right shows the last 121 days.

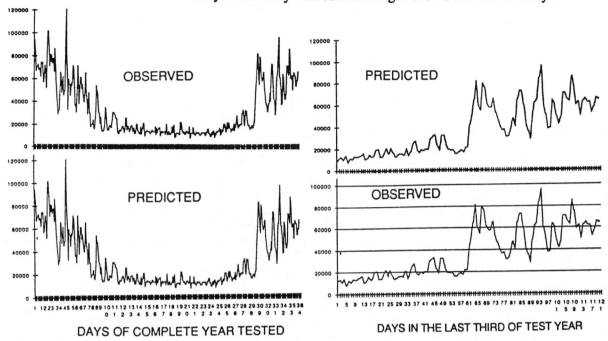

DAYS OF COMPLETE YEAR TESTED   DAYS IN THE LAST THIRD OF TEST YEAR

The accuracy was not improved further by many different modifications of the training process. It would appear that an acceptable pre-specified target accuracy can not be obtained only by additional fine tuning in which one adjusts the number of hidden layers and the number of nodes in these layers or by introducing artificial signals.

Upon completion of the many modifications aimed at improving the MNN, an attempt was made to model the nearly 20% residual noise remaining after the final training of the MNN using the time series data alone. Because this training of the model for the noise was unsuccessful, it is concluded that the residual errors can not be shown to be other than random.(see Figure 2). The chi-square was 32 for 13 degrees of freedom with a significance level of 0.002. It is concluded that the prediction of the time series (on auto-regressive data only) with 17 to 20 percent error may be the best accuracy possible with the available data. Statistical calculations made on the residual errors indicate they are random and devoid of any systematic information content.

Future Directions Suggested by the Experiments

Further enhancement of the structure of the MNN is still desirable. It is proposed to conduct further experiments to explore the following: (1) Possible ways of problem-solving with a two stage algorithm which applies in tandem two stages: global search by a genetic algorithm(GA), and the local search of the memory neuron network (MNN). (2) Interpretation of the obtained link weights to identify the most important factors and to determine the length of the historical record that can play a part in prediction. (3) Applications of more powerful statistical analysis and criteria to compare performance accuracy.

References

Fahlman, S. E. "An empirical study of Learning Speed in back-propagation networks" 1988 Technical Report June 1988 CMU-CS-88-162. Computer Science Department, Carnegie Mellon University, Pittsburgh, PA.

Poddar, Pinaki and Unnikrishnan, K. P. "Memory Neuron Networks: A prolegomenon" R & D Publication GMR-7493, October 21, 1991. NAO Research and Development Center, GM Technical Center, 30500 Mound Road, Box 9055, Warren, Michigan 48090-9055, USA.

Rumelhart, D. E., G. E. Hinton, and R. J. Williams 1986. Learning internal representations by error propagation, In: Parallel Distributed Processing, MIT Press, Volume.1, pp. 318-362.

Sastry, P. S., Santharam, G. and Unnikrishnan, K. P. "Memory neuron networks for identification and control of dynamical systems" R & D Publication GMR-7916, March 9, 1993. (same source as Poddar refernce above).

Experiments using a Group Method Data Handling Neural Network as a predictor in a biotechnical process

D. Tsaptsinos, J.R. Leigh.
Industrial Control Centre, University of Westminster, London W1M 8JS, UK.

Abstract

Present work at the Industrial Control Centre involves the exploration and development of the most suitable techniques for the modelling and control of fermentation processes. Techniques such as Kalman filters, kinetic models and multi-layer perceptrons have been evaluated previously [1,2,3]. In this contribution, work performed for the modelling of an industrial fed-batch fermentation process using the Group Method Data Handling Neural Network (GMDHNN) will be presented [4]. Fermentation processes present the neurocomputing community with a number of challenges due to the non-linearities and dynamics of such processes. The architecture of a GMDHNN is introduced as well as the series of experiments performed using the available data. The experiments address the suitability off the GMDHNN as a selector of inputs, as a one step ahead predictor, and as a long term predictor. Current results seem to be promising. Networks generated for the one step ahead prediction of the residual carbon in the fermentation process provide accurate estimations but the long term prediction presents more problems.

Introduction

The Group Method of Data Handling (GMDH) is an automatic self-organization method introduced in 1970's [5]. The book edited by Farlow [6] presents the initial GMDH algorithm and a number of more recent enhancements. The outcome of the algorithm is a layer-like structure. Each layer contains a number of submodels which are connected to the models of previous and succeeding layers. This paper introduces the GMDH method and reports on the usage and evaluation of a commercial software package (AIM) [7] which implements a version of the algorithm for the modelling of a highly non-linear fermentation process. Additionally, the performance of the AIM generated models as one-step and multiple-step ahead predictors is discussed.

The features of Group Method of Data Handling and AIM models

The GMDH is a modelling technique introduced in the 1970s by A.G. Ivakhenko [1]. The GMDH algorithm creates a model which is based solely on the available data. The generated model has a multi-layered network structure where the first layer simply distributes the inputs and the last layer reports on the generated output. The task of the model is to find the relationship between inputs and the output. Figures 1 and 2 show a typical model structure and a processing element respectively. The output of a processing element is given by the following combination of the 2 inputs:

$$y = \alpha + \beta * x_i + \gamma * x_j + \delta * x_i^2 + \varepsilon * x_j^2 + \varsigma * x_i x_j \qquad (1)$$

A number of methods related to the original GMDH algorithm have been reported in literature. The abductive induction mechanism is implemented by a commercial package (AIM). The package uses what can be considered as a descendant of the GMDH method but with a number of *genes* either missing or being improved.
- The architecture of the AIM-generated model is the same as the one for GMDH depicted in Figure 1.
- The structure of a processing element is as in Figure 2 but 3 inputs are allowed.
- The polynomial is not restricted to just the form shown in equation 1 [5].
- The available data set is not split into training and testing groups. Each model is evaluated using the Predicted squared error criterion [6]. Another benefit is that one does not have to worry about the representativeness of the two groups.

A brief introduction to the fermentation process

Pharmaceutical products are generated by secondary metabolism during the deliberately constrained growth of a micro-organism. The process of organism growth and secondary production depletes the level of carbon and nitrogen in the initial substrate but the levels of these nutrients is maintained by continuous feeding of the reactor with sources of additional carbon and nitrogen. On the commercial scale, standard control is achieved through a normal process management systems but in order to obtain higher levels of performance, process variables, such as secondary product concentration, must be measured in real time and made available to the control system.

Sixteen on-line measurements were made available. These include, temperature, pH, oxygen uptake rate etc. Four state variables need to be estimated but in this paper we will only consider residual carbon. Twenty batches of industrial data were provided with each batch containing the on-line hourly figures and the off-line figures for the state variables. In order to have a complete data set the off-line figures were interpolated. For the estimation of residual carbon, the following on-line measurements were thought by process technologists to be significant: Carbon dioxide evolution rate (RCO2), Carbon source fed in hour (CF), Power input (POWER), and Dissolved oxygen (DOT).

Using AIM as an input selector

All sixteen on-line measurements were employed and AIM was executed for each of the twenty batches in order to compare the selection of the inputs. The main observations were:
- The broth weight (BWT) was the most popular on-line measurement. It appeared on 14 out of 20 networks.
- Head pressure (HP) and Respiratory Quotient (RQ) did not appear in any network.
- Irrespective of the diverse of selected inputs and the polynomial parameters there was a common structure of the generated networks.
- Re-execution of each batch with only the previously selected measurements resulted in identical networks.

It was concluded that the benefits of using GMDH related methods could be obscured by the presence of *bad* data. There were strong indications revealing:
- the sensitivity of the generated models, in terms of polynomial forms and coefficients, towards the training set examples, and
- the reduction of the measurements space is also dependable on what examples are presented.

A review reassessing the available measurements for designing more representative data sets took place. At the end of the reassessment exercise two on-line measurements were dropped. This action was taken because of sensor problems. Five batches were selected to be employed for training.The batches included the normal and the extreme values for each on-line measurement. The generated model is shown in Figure 3.

One step ahead prediction using the AIM model (inputs without memeory)

Figure 4 presents the results obtained using a batch from the training test. Generalization is an important aspect of any modelling exercise. Figure 5 presents the performance of the AIM network with a previously unseen batch. It can be seen that a reasonable fit to the trained and to most of the testing data is obtained but with room for improvement.

One step ahead prediction using AIM (inputs with memory)

In order to improve the performance of the model historical values of the input and output were used. Only the inputs indicated by the previous model were employed, i.e., 5 inputs. Previous unreported work had shown that 2 delayed values were sufficient, hence a total of 17 inputs were used. The generated model is shown in Figure 6. Figures 7 and 8 show the performance of the model using a single batch. The use of historical data was obviously availing.

N-step ahead prediction using AIM (inputs with memory)

It will be advantageous to be able to predict the performance of the residual carbon in multiple steps in the future. For example, a model can be employed to investigate the effect various feed strategies will have to the product concentration and other variables.

For that reason the model was used off-line to test its capabilities for long term prediction. Initially the model was presented with measured values for all inputs and the prediction of the residual carbon was calculated. Then the model was presented with the measured values of the on-line variables, as before, but the residual carbon model prediction replaced the value of the data set. This way, feeding the model's predictions, the errors are being accumulated and it is easier to judge the soundness of the model. Figure 9 shows the performance of the model using two batches.

Conclusions

The employment of GMDHNN in the field of fermentation process seems to be promising. As in any other technique which learns by examples extremely care must be taken for the validation of the process data. The learning data must include the normal and the extreme situations and *bad examples* due to the instrumentation must be identified. Networks generated using AIM can be used for one-step-ahead predictors but more work is required in order to be employed as models of the residual carbon.

A number of decisions are performed automatically by AIM. These decisions they do not become available to the user. In addition to this the manual does not provide enough information about such matters as the type of regression technique employed or the determination of eligible inputs. All in all the user experiences a *black-box* approach and s/he may feel reluctant to use the delivered products.

References

1. Jalel, N.A., Tsaptsinos, D., Mirzai, A.R., Leigh, J.R., and Dixon, K. 5th International Conference on Computer Applications in Fermentation Technology 1992, Keystone, Colorado, USA.
2. Tsaptsinos, D., Jalel, N.A., and Leigh, J.R. Colloquium on the application of neural networks to modelling and control 1992, Liverpool University/ Polytechnic, UK.
3. Tsaptsinos D., and Leigh J.R. Journal of Microcomputer Applications (Special issue on Neural Networks-Techniques and Applications) 1993, Vol. 16, pp. 125-136.
4. Hecht-Nielsen R. `Neurocomputing', Addison-Wesley 1990.
5. Ivankhnenko, A.G. Automatica 1970, Vol 6, 207-219.
6. Farlow, J.S. `Self-organizing Methods in Modelling-GMDH Type Algorithms', Marcel Dekker, New York, 1984.
7. AIM Investigator™ manual, AbTech Corporation, 700 Harris street, Charlottesville, Virginia 22901

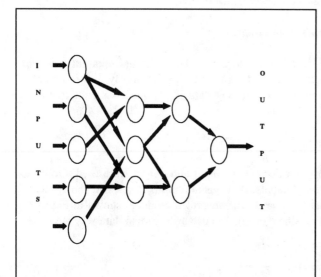

Figure 1: A typical GMDH generated model. A similar model is created by AIM but see text for differences.

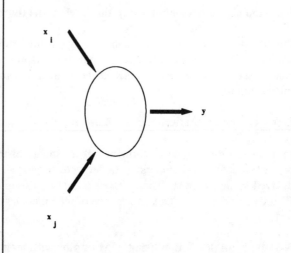

Figure 2: A GMDH processing element. The AIM processing element is the same but with an additional input.

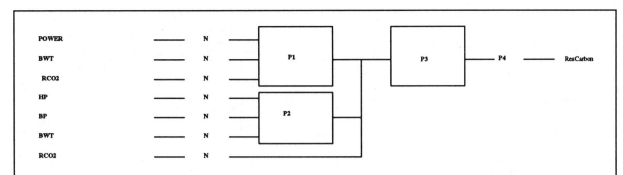

Figure 3: AIM generated network when training data was chosen to span the range of likely operating conditions. The letter N indicates the normaliser function. This function transforms the original input variable into a region with a mean of zero and a variance of one. The letter P stands for polynomials

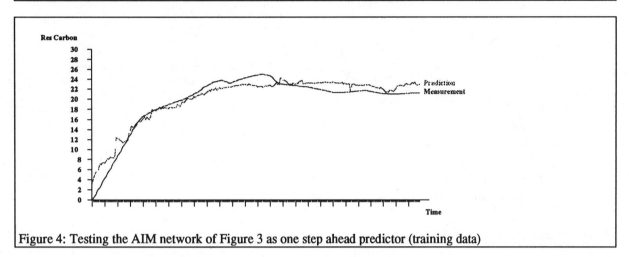

Figure 4: Testing the AIM network of Figure 3 as one step ahead predictor (training data)

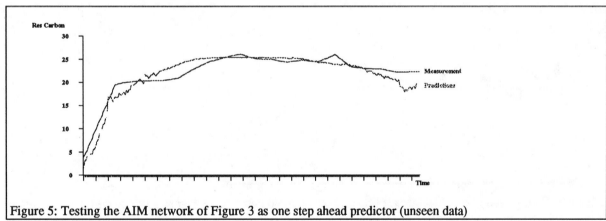

Figure 5: Testing the AIM network of Figure 3 as one step ahead predictor (unseen data)

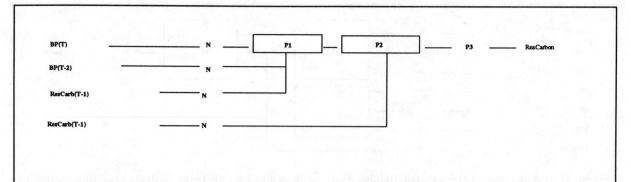

Figure 6: AIM Generated network when training data was chosen to span the range of likely operating conditions and time-delayed measurements were used.

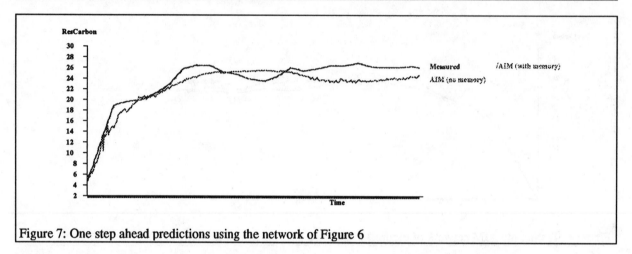

Figure 7: One step ahead predictions using the network of Figure 6

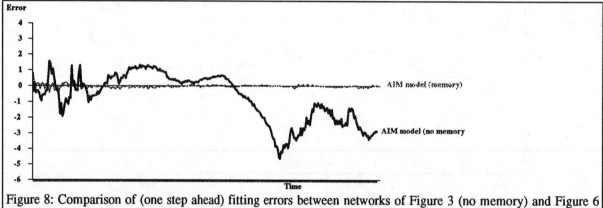

Figure 8: Comparison of (one step ahead) fitting errors between networks of Figure 3 (no memory) and Figure 6 (with memory) for a single batch

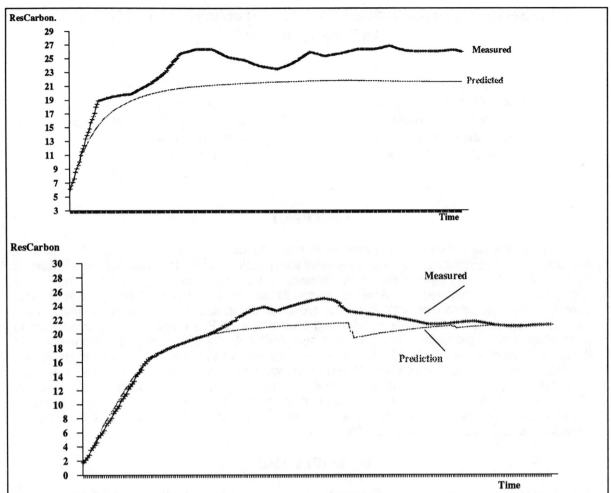

Figure 9: N-step ahead predictions of residual carbon using the feedback version of the network in Figure 6. See text for explanation.

Time Series Prediction Using Minimally-Structured Neural Networks: An Empirical Test[*]

Won Chul Jhee
Dept. of Industrial Engineering
Hong Ik University
72-1 Mapoku Sangsudong
Seoul, 121-791, Korea

Michael J. Shaw
Beckman Institute
Univ. of Illinois at Urbana-Champaign
405 N. Mathew Avenue
Urbana, IL 61801

ABSTRACT

Artificial Neural Networks (ANN) have been much mentioned as a promising new tool for time series analysis and forecasting. However, to answer the question of how to determine the structure of ANN that can effectively capture the characteristics of the time series in a specific forecasting environment, it is still required that ANN be rigorously analyzed, in terms of fitting capability and forecasting accuracy, using real world data that are often contaminated by noise and limited in the number of observations. In this paper, multilayered perceptrons (MLP) are adopted as approximators to time series generating processes. The information from ARIMA modeling is used to determine the input units of MLP so that the designed MLP have minimal structures. The 111 series of Makridakis Competition Data are used to train the MLP and to analyze their performance. A comparative analysis with ARIMA models has been done to determine the factors that affect the forecasting performance of MLP. Examples of these factors are the number of observations, observation intervals, seasonality, trend, and backpropagation learning parameters and procedure. The experimental results are expected to be used as a guideline for designing and training MLP.

INTRODUCTION

ANN have been advocated as an alternative to conventional tools for time series prediction, after Lapedes and Farber [1987] reported that MLP trained by the backpropagation algorithm are better at predicting by orders of magnitude than conventional forecasting methods. For example, there is an argument that well-designed ANN-based forecasting systems proclaim the opening of a new era in the evolution of forecasting and decision support systems. The works of Werbos [1988], Weigend et al [1990, 1991], Tang et al [1991], Sharda and Patil [1992], Foster et al [199], and Hoptroff [1993] support this argument. However, White [1988], Fishwick [1989] and Ripley [1993] reported that standard statistical procedures will often be at least as effective as neural networks when a fair comparison is made. Observing those inconsistent research results from the analyses of socioeconomic data sets, Chatfield [1993] commented that ANN will be able to outperform standard forecasting procedures for at least certain types of situations, but there is little systematic evidence of this as yet. Thus, the purpose of this paper is to provide such evidence using well-known real world data such as M-Competition Data.

Since the success of forecasting methods depends heavily on the properties of the time series to which the methods are applied, especially when the methods are univariate analyses, we first need to address the basic properties of time series from socioeconomic systems. First, most of the series have very limited number of observations. Since the socioeconomic systems are changing their structures and compositions, the addition of data obtained from much earlier observation are often irrelevant or even harmful to the analysis. Furthermore, one cannot generate extra data as needed because they do not allow experiments. Therefore, there are at most 200 observations or so and it is not unusual that there are under 50 observations. Second, the time series are often contaminated by noise from unknown

---

❖ A large part of this work was carried out while professor Jhee was visiting the Beckman Institute, University of Illinois at Urbana-Champaign whose kind hospitality is gratefully acknowledged. He is also grateful to Korea Science and Engineering Foundation (KOSEF) and Hong Ik University who supported the visit.

sources and suffer from high level of measurement errors. This noise and error is not merely added to the series but become embedded in the series. Consequently, there is no reason to believe that the noise follows independent and identically distributed Gaussian random process. Finally, most of the observed series do not satisfy the assumption of stationarity on which most time series analyses rely. There is frequently a clear trend and/or seasonality, -i.e., long memory, in the mean process, and the fluctuations in variance are also often observed. Therefore, differencing and log transformation should be applied through intensive data analysis to transform the data into stationary series. The above three facts partly explain why different analysts have different forecasting results on the same time series, and why simple linear models such as exponential smoothing or the combination of their forecasts are preferred to more complicated methods for practitioners and even M-Competitions.

However, some researchers argue that significant portion of real time series are generated by nonlinear processes and that they can benefit from the recent developments in nonlinear modeling [Tong, 1990; De Gooijer & Kumar, 1992]. Nevertheless, nonlinear models with many parameters are so extremely flexible that they bear the risk of overfitting the time series. That is, the model which provides the best fit to past data does not necessarily provide the best forecasts, especially if there exist noise involved in the series or changes in the generating process. For reasons of conservatism, statisticians have tended to severely restrict the number of free parameters by tolerating some bad results due to underfitting. Since ANN models are at the heart of nonlinear modeling, appropriate parameterization is indispensable to good forecasting performance of ANN. In this sense, the minimally structured neural networks in this paper means that MLP have the proper number of connection weights, which are equivalent to the number of parameters in nonlinear models. To restrict the size of MLP, special attention was paid to determining the number of input units, because the moderate size of input space enables MLP to capture the essential features in a time series without being disturbed by noise. ARIMA model identification results were used as valuable information in determining MLP structures, and our approach was tested using the M-Competition data.

DATA AND METHODS

Makridakis *et al* [1982, 1993] collected time series from real world and held the competitions to determine empirically the post sample accuracy of various univariate methods. Although the results of forecasting competitions are somewhat controversial, the 1001 series provided by the M1-Competition enables us to test a number of interesting questions on forecasting methods. Out of original data base, the 111 series, which consist of 13 annual, 20 quarterly and 68 monthly series, has often been investigated in the previous comparative studies [Sharda & Patil, 1992]. This subset of M1-Competition Data was analyzed in this paper to answer the question of whether the MLP can be an expert under the socioeconomic forecasting environments.

At the time of the first competition, the most recent observations of each series were held out by Makridakis. The numbers of holdout samples were 6, 8, and 18 for annual, quarterly and monthly series, respectively. Forecasting models were fitted to the remaining observations of each series and then used to obtain its prediction values which were compared with the holdout sample values. The performance or error measure was mean absolute percentage error (MAPE) over the forecasting horizons. This evaluation scheme was adopted without any modifications in our comparative analysis between ARIMA models and minimally-structured neural networks.

AUTOREGRESSIVE MOVING AVERAGE MODELS

ARMA models have been served as a benchmark model for creating linear models because of their theoretical elaborateness and accuracy in short-term forecasting. For time series to be modeled $\{Z_t,\ t \in T\}$, transformed if necessary, the general class of ARMA(p,q) model has the following form:

$$\Phi(B)Z_t = C + \Theta(B)a_t,$$

where $\Phi(B) = U(B)\phi(B) = 1 - \Phi_1 B - \Phi_2 B^2 - \cdots - \Phi_p B^p$, $\Theta(B) = 1 - \theta_1 B - \theta_2 B^2 - \cdots - \theta_q B^q$, $U(B) = 1 - U_1 B - \cdots - U_d B^d$, $\phi(B) = 1 - \phi_1 B - \cdots - \phi_{p-d} B^{p-d}$, $BZ_t = Z_{t-1}$, C is a constant, $\{a_t\}$ is a gaussian white noise process. Note that if $U(B) = (1-B)^d$ then ARMA(p,q) model can be expressed as ARIMA(p-d,d,q) in

Box-Jenkins' approach which is the most popular ARMA modeling method. Among the iterative modeling steps in Figure 1, the model identification step which determines the order of p and q is crucial to representing the time series adequately because the resulting model performs poorly if the modeler is prodigal in using the parameters. Therefore, the principle of parsimony is an important modeling philosophy [Box & Jenkins, 1976]. The identification step requires an intensive data analysis where expert judgment must be exercised to interpret some statistics such as ACF and PACF, AIC, etc. because of the difficulties involved in the model identification step, there have been efforts to automate the modeling procedure (for details, refer to Jhee & Lee, 1993). An outgrowth of such efforts is AUTOBOX™ 3.0, whose performance is comparable to human experts. This commercially available software was adopted to secure the objectivity of our comparative analysis. The 111 series of M1-Competition Data was analyzed under the default setting of AUTOBOX™ 3.0, which means the intervention option was not used.

MINIMALLY-STRUCTURED NEURAL NETWORKS

Determining MLP Structures

To predict the future values of time series, the iterative one-step-ahead forecasting procedure was adopted using the following relationship,

$$\hat{Z}_t = \int(Z_{t-1}, Z_{t-2}, \cdots), \quad \cdots\cdots, \quad \hat{Z}_{t+r} = \int\left(\hat{Z}_{t+r-1}, \hat{Z}_{t+r-2}, \cdots, \hat{Z}_{t+1}, Z_t, Z_{t-1}, \cdots\right)$$

where $\left\{\hat{Z}_{t+r}, r \in L\right\}$ are the estimated values for the future observations in forecast horizon L. The function f that is fitted for the past observations will be used to predict one point into the future and simply iterate itself on its own outputs and the past data to predict further into the forecast horizon. In our analysis, this approximation function f was replaced by a multilayered feedforward perceptron which has one output unit and one hidden layer. Therefore, the remaining issue is how to choose right number of hidden and input units, because the size of MLP greatly affects the forecasting performance.

The fact that MLP can be universal approximators [Hornik *et al*, 1989] does not mean that the structures of MLP can be arbitrary chosen. The MLP of large size might promise to extract more information from data, but such MLP also tends to mistake noise for information. As a result, they make more serious errors and rarely yield the gain they promised. This erroneous behavior of MLP tend to be easily magnified in the univariate time series analysis with limited number of observations. Although there has been some research on the optimal design of MLP structures, it is still largely an art to determine the optimal number of hidden units. Furthermore, we can hardly find any research results that reported the impacts of input spaces on the forecasting performance of MLP.

Since the learning paradigm of ANN is learning by examples, an exploratory data analysis before preparing training examples is recommended to increase the performance of learned ANN. This is why we use the results of ARMA model identification, which involves an intensive correlation analysis among data points. In doing so, the starting point is the observation that an ARMA(p,q) process can be put in state space form by defining a state vector of length $m = \max(p, q+1)$ [Harvey, 1984]. Therefore, if the order of time series was identified as ARMA(p,q), we used m as the input space and also as the number of hidden units.

Preliminary Experiment

Before applying our idea to the whole data sets, we tested our idea with 5 time series from the 111 M-competition Data. One of the purposes here is to examine the effects of varying numbers of input and hidden units. Figure 2 - 4 present the typical illustration of our results which were obtained using the S184 series (Figure 2) that follows ARIMA(1,4,4) in terms of Box-Jenkins' or ARMA(5,4). Figure 3 shows the effects of input spaces. When we applied our stopping rule (see the next section for details) the MLP of five input units gave the least MAPE that were measured over the holdout samples and beat the AUTOBOX™ v3.0 of which MAPE is represented by straight line in Figure 3(a). We observe that the large input spaces do more harm than good in predicting the future values, even though they brought better fitting results in terms of R^2, on the past observations. During these preliminary experiments, we traced the performance of each MLP structure as the learning of MLP proceeded, and recorded when the MLP showed the best prediction result. Figure 3(b) shows that five input units is also best for the series

S184. This result may not be always the case. However, we could obtain similar results from the other 4 time series. Figure 4 shows the effects of hidden units when we used 5 and 12 input units. As we expected, the least MAPE's were obtained when we used the same numbers of hidden units as the numbers of input units. Thus, we were very encouraged to utilize the ARMA model identification results in determining the MLP structures. With these favorable experimental results, we analyzed the 111 series of M-Competition Data according to the following training procedure.

Training Procedure

To train MLP on each time series using the backpropagation algorithm, we first adopted the stopping rule as follows: training was terminated if the mean squared error reached 0.0001 before 5,000 training epochs, which was the allowed maximum epochs. This is a very simple rule, but the philosophy behind our stopping rule is "Let MLP learn sufficiently from the given data". Our stopping rule appears to have the risk that MLP overfits the given series, but the risk is not serious as we constrain the size of MLP. If we consider the actual forecasting situations where the future values are not known a priori, our approach can be an easily applicable and sound stopping rule. Before the time series were fed into MLP as training data, each series was linearly transformed into the range between 0.1 and 0.9. We did not consider differencing or deseasonalizing to remove nonstationarity from the time series.

During the preliminary experiments, we also determined learning parameters using twelve time series that were selected equally from four categories. We classified time series into four categories according to time series characteristics, i.e., trend and seasonality. Four combinations of learning rates and coefficients to momentum term, (0.1, 0), (0.1, 0.1), (0.1, 0.9), and (0.3, 0.5), were tried, and the use of (0.1, 0.1) gave slightly better prediction results. We also tested the weight updating interval. In addition to updating connection weights pattern by pattern, we tried two cumulative methods: one updated the weights every five input presentations and the other updated only once during each epoch. Updating the weights at each input presentation outperformed the cumulative methods. Once the MLP learned from time series, the degree of fitness to training data was measured using R^2, and then the learned MLP was tested over the holdout samples of the series. The outputs of the MLP were converted into their original scale and MAPE was computed to measure the prediction ability.

EXPERIMENT RESULTS

Over the 111 series the minimally-structured MLP outperformed ARIMA models in terms of both fitting and forecasting abilities. The pairwise t-tests indicate that performance differences were statistically significant. Some critics on the M-Competition argue that several series in the 111 series are not suitable for forecasting with ARIMA models [Pack & Downing, 1983]. So, we further analyzed the forecasting results from only 72 series as Sharda and Patil [1992] did. Table 1 exhibits the number of series on which MLP performed better than ARIMA and vice versa. Over this reduced data set, the performance differences were also significant. However, the results are grouped according to observation intervals. it is noteworthy that MLP did not perform well on monthly series as they did on yearly or quarterly series. This observation is against our expectation because most of monthly series have more data points than others. Therefore, we rearranged the reduced data set into three categories according to the number of observations. The first category included series having less than 30 data points, and the series in the third category contained more than 100 data points. We subtracted MAPE's of MLP from those of AUTOBOX 3.0. As shown in Figure 5, the performances of two methods were not discriminable in the case of the third category. This analysis confirms the above observation.

To explain this phenomenon, we classified the series into 4 categories according to the characteristics of time series: whether the series has trend or seasonality? Table 2 shows that when the series has the seasonality component MLP did not perform relatively well. This analysis provides us with a cue. In M-Competition Data, the series that have more than 100 data points are all monthly series. If they have seasonality components simultaneously in AR and differencing orders, the MLP in our approach will have large input spaces and overfit the time series to yield poor forecasting performance. At this point, readers need to remember that we did not adopt any data transformations which make the nonstationary series into stationary one. If we use deseasonalized series, the overfitting problems in monthly series will be greatly reduced. Anyway, the minimally-structured neural networks outperform ARIMA models.

CONCLUSIONS

Our experiment provides evidence that artificial neural networks are a promising alternative to conventional forecasting methods. We determined the structure of multilayered feedforward perceptrons using the ARMA model identification results and demonstrated that our design works well for noisy time series of limited number of observations. The approach outlined in this paper can be used as a basis for automating the ANN forecasting procedure. Our experiment also reveals that exploratory data analyses are greatly useful in obtaining better forecasts from MLP.

REFERENCES

[1] AFA Inc., (1991). *AUTOBOX™ 3.0 User's manual.* Hatboro, PA.

[2] Box, G.E.P., & Jenkins, G.M., (1976). *Time series analysis- forecasting and control.* Holden-Day, SF.

[3] De Gooijer, J.G., & Kumar, K., (1992). Some recent developments in non-linear time series modelling, testing, and forecasting. *Int'l Journal of Forecasting,* 8, 135-156.

[4] Foster, W.R., Collopy, F., & Ungar, L.H., (1992). Neural network forecasting of short noisy time series. *Computers and Chemical Engineering,* 16(4), 293-297.

[5] Harvey, A.C., (1984). A Unified View of Statistical Forecasting Procedures. *Journal of Forecasting,* 3, 245-275.

[6] Jhee, W.C., & Lee, K.J., (1993). Performance of neural networks in managerial forecasting. *Intelligent Systems in Accounting, Finance and Management,* 2, 55-71.

[7] Lapedes, A.S. & Farber, R.M., (1987). Nonlinear signal processing using neural networks: prediction and system modeling. Los Alamos Nat'l Lab. Technical Report, LA-UR-87-2662.

[8] Makridakis et al, (1982) The accuracy of extrapolation (time series) methods: results of a forecasting competition. *Journal of Forecasting,* 1, 111-153.

[9] Makridakis et al, (1993). The M2-Competition: A real-time judgmentally based forecasting study. *Int'l Journal of forecasting.* 9, 5-22.

[10] Rumelhart D., & McClelland, J., (1987). *Parallel distributed processing: explorations in the microstructure of cognition.* (eds.), MIT, Cambridge MA.

[11] Sharda, R., & Patil, R.B., (1992). A connectionist approach to time series prediction: an empirical test. *Journal of Intelligent Manufacturing,*

[12] Tang, Z., Almeida, C., & Fishwick, P. (1991). Time series forecasting using neural networks vs. Box-Jenkins methodology. *Simulation,* 57(5), 303-310.

[13] Tong, H., (1990). *Non-linear time series: a dynamical system approach.* Oxford Univ. Press.

[14] Weigend, A.S., Rumelhart, D.E., & Huberman, B.A., (1990). Back-propagation, weight-elimination and time series prediction. in Touretzsky et al (eds), *Connectionist Models: Proc. of the 1990 Summer School,* 105-116.

[15] Werbos, P., (1989). Generalization of back-propagation with application to recurrent gas market model. *Neural Networks,* 1, 339-356.

[16] White, H., (1988). Economic prediction using neural networks: the case of IBM daily stock returns. *IJCNN,* II451-II458.

Table 1. Comparative Prediction Performance classified by Observation Intervals

Unit: No. of Series

Obs. Intervals	YEARLY	QUARTERLY	MONTHLY	Total
MSNN	7	16	30	53
AUTOBOX 3.0	1	2	16	19
Total	8	18	46	72

Table 2. Comparative Prediction Performance classified by the Series Characteristics

Unit: No. of Series

Characteristics	NONE	TREND	SEASONALITY	T + S	Total
MSNN	5	25	15	8	53
AUTOBOX 3.0	1	3	9	6	19
Total	6	28	24	14	72

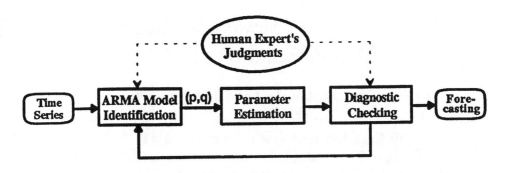

Figure 1. ARMA Modeling Procedure

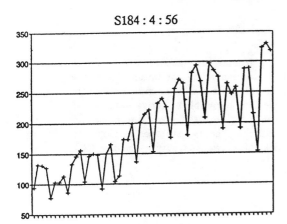

Figure 2. Time Series S184

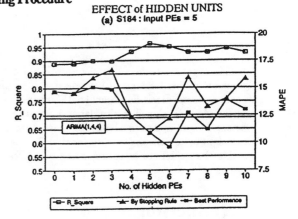

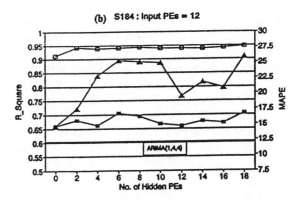

Figure 4. Effect of Hidden Units (S184)

EFFECT of INPUT SPACES

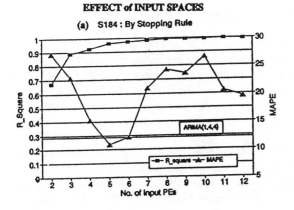

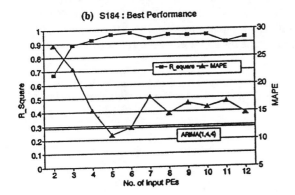

Figure 3. Effects of Input Spaces (s184)

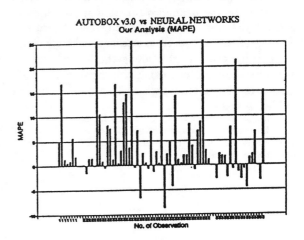

Figure 5. Comparative Forecasting Performance

Stable and Efficient Neural Network Modeling of Discrete Multi-Channel Signals *

Shaohua Tan[†], Jianbin Hao[‡] and Joos Vandewalle[‡]

[†] Dept. E.E., National University of Singapore
10 Kent Ridge Crescent, Singapore 0511
[‡] Dept. E.E., Katholieke Universiteit Leuven
Kardinaal Mercierlaan 94, B-3001 Heverlee, Belgium

Abstract

This paper presents a neural network based recursive modeling scheme that constructs a nonlinear dynamical model for a given discrete multi-channel signal and the corresponding excitation. Using the so-called Radial-Basis-Function (RBF) neural nets as generic discrete-time nonlinear model structure and the ideas developed in the classical adaptive control theory, we have been able to derive a stable and efficient weight updating algorithm that guarantees the convergence for both the prediction error and the weight error. Elements of the spatial Fourier transform and sampling theory have been employed to provide the guidelines in choosing the parameters associated with the network structure and the RBF neurons.

1 Introduction

Neural nets have recently attracted considerable attention for their potential role in offering alternative formulations and solutions for various nonlinear problems [1]. The key feature of neural nets, which is relevant to the modeling problem, is the so-called universal approximation property possessed by classes of feedforward neural nets [3] [4] [5]. More interesting is the fact that such an approximation can sometimes be arrived at using a *finite* sequence of input-output samples only. These interesting features are of particular significance in designing new nonlinear modeling techniques.

The objective of the this paper is to present a discrete-time nonlinear modeling scheme for constructing nonlinear models for multi-channel signals using feedforward neural nets. Three key ideas are important for the development of the new scheme. First of all, the nonlinear model structure is chosen to be that of the so-called RBF neural nets. This choice is made not just because of the universal approximation property associated with this class of feedforward neural nets. More importantly, in the light of the spatial Fourier analysis, RBF nets can be regarded as a general function reconstruction scheme using radial-basis-functions as the interpolating functions for finite number of data samples. This allows rigorous determination of RBF neural net structures for our signal modeling problem. The linear-in-the-weights characteristics of RBF nets also makes possible the derivation of a stable recursive weight updating rule for the nets.

Secondly, the Lyapunov function approach developed in the framework of stable adaptive control theory is employed to derive a simple and efficient recursive algorithm for determining the weights of the RBF nets. This algorithm is proven to guarantee the convergence for both the prediction error and the weight error.

Thirdly, the thoughts along the line of spatial Fourier transform and sampling theory are followed to examine the issue of setting the number of RBF neurons and their parameters as the first stage of the modeling. These analyses lead to a constructive procedure that appears to be effective for common signal modeling tasks.

---

*This research work was partially carried out at the ESAT Laboratory of the Katholieke Universiteit Leuven, in the framework of a Concerted Action Project of the Flemish Community, entitled *Applicable Neural Networks*. The scientific responsibility is assumed by its authors.

2 The modeling scheme

2.1 General idea

Let a discrete-time multi-channel signal $\{y_t\} \in R^m$ $(t = 0, 1, \ldots)$ be generated by an *unknown* discrete-time dynamical system of the following form

$$y_{t+1} = f(y_t, y_{t-1}, \ldots, y_{t-k+1}, u_t, u_{t-1}, \ldots, u_{t-l+1}), \tag{1}$$

where $u_t \in R^q$ is the excitation at time instance t; and $f : R^{km} \times R^{lq} \to R^m$ is a nonlinear vector function which is of course unknown; k, l are two positive integers relating the current sample to k samples and l excitation samples in the past.

The basic idea of our signal modeling scheme is to use RBF nets as a general model structure for the unknown nonlinear function $f(\cdot)$. It follows from the universal approximation property of RBF nets that $f(\cdot)$, defined on a compact set $\mathcal{S}$, can be approximated to a given precision with an appropriate weight matrix and structural parameters. Or more precisely, assuming $x = x_t \overset{\triangle}{=} [y_t, y_{t-1}, \ldots, y_{t-k+1}, u_t, u_{t-1}, \ldots, u_{t-l+1}]^T$ and $y = y_{t+1}$, the universal approximation property asserts the existence of a weight matrix $\bar{W}$ and the structural parameters n (the number of RBF neurons), p_i (center of the RBF neuron) and σ_i (radius of the RBF neuron) such that a given signal $\{y_t\}$ along with its excitation sequence $\{u_t\}$ can be modeled as follows

$$y_{t+1} = \bar{W} z(x_t) \tag{2}$$

where $z(\cdot)$ is Gaussian function. In the preceding equation (2), both the parameters n, p_i, σ_i involved in $z(x)$ and the weight matrix $\bar{W}$ are of course unknown. The central task of the signal modeling is, therefore, to determine n, p_i, σ_i and $\bar{W}$ so that (2) holds.

For the modeling problem to be well-defined, $f(\cdot)$ is required to meet the following two conditions. First, $f(\cdot)$ should be sufficiently smooth on a compact set $\mathcal{S} \in R^{km+lq}$, and have unique solution for any set of initial conditions and any admissible excitation sequence $\{u_t\}$ chosen in $\mathcal{S}$. Secondly, the function $f(\cdot)$ should be time-invariant. As a discrete-time dynamical system, system (1) is also required to be such that any initial condition in $\mathcal{S}$ will result in an output sequence on a compact subset in $\mathcal{S}$. In other words, as long as (1) starts in $\mathcal{S}$, the subsequent dynamical iteration will not bring the output y_t out of $\mathcal{S}$.

2.2 Weight updating rule

The idea for determining $\bar{W}$ is to construct a one-step-ahead recursive predictor which will generate $\hat{y}_t$, the prediction of y_t, using a linear dynamical system. An error model analysis will then yield a stable updating rule for the weight matrix.

To begin with, let $W_t \in R^{m \times n}$ be the weight matrix, and $e_t = \hat{y}_t - y_t \in R^m$ be the prediction error at time t. Upon introducing the so-called auxiliary error vector $\tilde{e}_t \in R^m$

$$\tilde{e}_{t-1} = \frac{C e_{t-1} + W_{t-1} z(x_{t-1}) - y_t}{1 + z^T(x_{t-1}) z(x_{t-1})}, \tag{3}$$

where $C \in R^{m \times m}$ is a constant diagonal matrix to be fixed later, a one-step-ahead predictor can be built as follows

$$\hat{y}_t = A \hat{y}_{t-1} - A y_{t-1} + W_{t-1} z(x_{t-1}) - z^T(x_{t-1}) z(x_{t-1}) \tilde{e}_{t-1}, \tag{4}$$

where $A \in R^{m \times m}$ is a diagonal matrix with all its diagonal elements confined within $(-1, 1)$. Thus, all the eigenvalues of A are strictly inside the unit circle. Subtracting y_t from both sides of (4), and rearranging the terms give rise to the following error equation

$$e_t = A e_{t-1} + W_{t-1} z(x_{t-1}) - y_t - z^T(x_{t-1}) z(x_{t-1}) \tilde{e}_{t-1}. \tag{5}$$

As will be shown shortly, the following weight updating formula

$$W_t = W_{t-1} - \tilde{e}_{t-1} z^T(x_{t-1}) \tag{6}$$

will make both the prediction error vector e_t and the weight error matrix

$$E_t = W_t - \bar{W}$$

converge to zero.

2.3 Convergence analysis

We wish to prove that with appropriate choices for A and C, the preceding modeling scheme will indeed drive both e_t and E_t to zero. For the notational convenience, the ith entry for the vectors $e_t, \tilde{e}_t$ will be denoted by e_t^i, respectively, $\tilde{e}_t^i \in R$, and the ith row of the matrix E_t by E_t^i, where $(E_t^i)^T \in R^n$.

To prove the convergence, let us observe that (5) and (3) can be regarded as constituting a discrete-time mth-order linear system in the following state-space form

$$
\begin{aligned}
e_{t+1} &= Ae_t + Bv_t \\
\tilde{e}_t &= Ce_t + Dv_t,
\end{aligned}
\tag{7}
$$

where the matrices A, C have been introduced in (4), respectively, (3); $B = D = I \in R^{m \times m}$, I is the unit matrix; and $v_t = E_t z(x_t) - z^T(x_t) z(x_t) \tilde{e}_t \in R^m$ representing a closed-loop output feedback term. As all the constant matrices $A, B, C,$ and D involved are diagonal, System (7) with the feedback term v_t can also be treated as a collection of m linear discrete-time first-order single-input and single-output systems of the following form

$$
\begin{aligned}
e_{t+1}^i &= a_{ii} e_t^i + v_t^i \\
\tilde{e}_t^i &= c_{ii} e_t^i + v_t^i,
\end{aligned}
\quad i = 1, 2, \ldots, m,
\tag{8}
$$

where a_{ii}, b_{ii} are the ith diagonal entries for A, respectively, B, with the loop closed by $v_t^i = E_t^i z(x_t) - z^T(x_t) z(x_t) \tilde{e}_t^i$, the the ith entry of the feedback vector v_t.

We first show that if (8) is strictly positive real, then it will be asymptotically stable, consequently, e_t^i and E_t^i will converge to 0 as $t \to \infty$. As (8) is assumed to be strictly positive real, the discrete positive real lemma can be applied, which results in the following set of equations (see, e.g., [2]).

$$
\begin{aligned}
a_{ii}^2 \lambda_i - \lambda_i &= -\rho_i^2 - \gamma_i \\
a_{ii} \lambda_i &= \frac{c_{ii}}{2} + \nu_i \rho_i \\
1 - \lambda_i &= \nu_i^2
\end{aligned}
\tag{9}
$$

where $\lambda_i, \rho_i, \nu_i \in R^+$, and $\rho_i \in R$.

Consider the following scalar function

$$
V_t^i = 2\lambda_i (e_t^i)^2 + E_t^i (E_t^i)^T.
\tag{10}
$$

It is obviously positive and vanishes only at $e_t^i = 0$ and $E_t^i = 0$. The forward difference of V_t^i is easily calculated as

$$
\begin{aligned}
\Delta V_t^i &= V_{t+1}^i - V_t^i \\
&= 2(a_{ii}^2 \lambda_i - \lambda_i)(e_t^i)^2 + 2a_{ii} \lambda_i e_t^i v_t^i + \lambda_i (v_t^i)^2 + E_{t+1} E_{t+1}^T - E_t E_t^T.
\end{aligned}
\tag{11}
$$

Inserting (9) into (11) and rearranging the terms, we have

$$
\Delta V_t^i = -2[\rho_i e_t^i - \nu_i v_t^i]^2 - 2\gamma_i (e_t^i)^2 + 2\tilde{e}_t^i v_t^i + 2E_t^i (\Delta E_t^i)^T + \Delta E_t^i (\Delta E_t^i)^T,
$$

where $\Delta E_t^i = E_{t+1}^i - E_t^i$. Inserting (6) and v_t^i into the last three terms in the above equation

$$
\Delta V_t^i = -2(\rho_i e_t^i - \nu_i v_t^i)^2 - 2\gamma_i (e_t^i)^2 - z^T(x_t) z(x_t)(\tilde{e}_t^i)^2 \le 0.
\tag{12}
$$

The above derivation allows us to conclude that V_t^i is actually a Lyapunov function for (8) with the loop closed by v_t^i.

Returning to (7), consider the following scalar function

$$
V_t = e_t^T P e_t + \text{tr}\left(E_t E_t^T\right),
\tag{13}
$$

where P is a diagonal matrix with the ith diagonal entry being λ_i; $\text{tr}(\cdot)$ denotes the trace of a matrix, which is the sum of the diagonal entries. V_t is obviously positive, and vanishes only at $e_t = 0$ and $E_t = 0$. By noting the following equation

$$
V_t = \sum_{i=1}^{m} V_t^i
$$

and using (12), the forward difference $\Delta V_t = V_{t+1} - V_t$ can be calculated as

$$
\begin{aligned}
\Delta V_t &= \sum_{i=1}^{m} \Delta V_t^i \\
&= \sum_{i=1}^{m} [-2(\rho_i e_t^i - \nu_i v_t^i)^2 - 2\gamma_i (e_t^i)^2 - z^T(x_t) z(x_t)(\tilde{e}_t^i)^2] \\
&= -2 \sum_{i=1}^{m} [(\rho_i e_t^i - \nu_i v_t^i)^2] - 2 \sum_{i=1}^{m} [\gamma_i (e_t^i)^2] - \sum_{i=1}^{m} [z^T(x_t) z(x_t)(\tilde{e}_t^i)^2] \leq 0.
\end{aligned}
$$

We can therefore conclude that V_t is a Lyapunov function for (7), and consequently, the closed-loop system (7) is globally stable. The particular structure of RBF nets can actually allow us to conclude more than the global stability. As $z(x_t)$ can never be zero, ΔV_t will not be zero except at the single point $e_t = 0$ and $E_t = 0$. Consequently, $e_t \to 0$, $E_t \to 0$ $(t \to \infty)$, when the closed-loop system (7) settles down at its equilibrium.

To summarize, starting with finite initial conditions for e_t and E_t, the updating formulae described in the preceding section will guarantee both the prediction error e_t and the weight error E_t to converge to zero. Observe that this convergence property is intimately linked to the positiveness of the functions $z(x_t)$, without which we would not be able to conclude that E_t goes to zero as well.

The preceding proof indicates that both a_{ii} and c_{ii} will have to be chosen to make (8) positive real. Careful analysis shows that as long as a_{ii} stays within -1 and 1, it will not affect the positive realness condition. Thus the task reduces to choosing the parameter c_{ii} to ensure the positive realness of (8). For all the simulation examples to be given in the next section, we have fixed c_{ii} to be $-\frac{1}{2}$ for $i = 1, 2, \ldots, m$. This choice not only guarantees the required positive realness, but also seems to yield good transient response for a wide range of systems we have simulated.

3　Determination of RBF neural net structure

3.1　Heuristic methods and their drawbacks

A commonly used heuristic approach to RBF neural net approximation suggests that n, p_i and σ_i are closely related to the concept of data clusters generated by x_t samples in R^{km+lq}. In this framework, n is interpreted as the number of the data clusters within a pre-defined compact set, and p_i, σ_i as the center, respectively, the radius of the ith data cluster. The central task is, therefore, to devise an effective algorithm that can detect the data clusters given a sequence of data.

The idea of data clustering comes naturally when RBF nets are used for data classification. In this context, given data samples often imply clear separation boundaries among a limited number of data clusters. With prior knowledge about the number of data clusters (usually known from a classification task itself), the centers and the radii of these data clusters can be readily obtained using the well-known k-means clustering algorithm [6].

Our extensive simulation analysis has revealed, however, that the idea of data clusters is not relevant to the structural parameters of a RBF net in the case of nonlinear signal modeling. Generally, a given sequence $\{x_t\}$ is distributed evenly in a compact operation region of the underlying system, thus there are no clearly distinguishable data clusters that emerge from the given data samples. Running the k-means clustering algorithm for the data often results in the supposed centers of clusters wandering around their initial positions aimlessly. Moreover, we can even build $f(\cdot)$ in (1) in such a way that the centers of the constituent Gaussian functions are outside the compact set in which $\{x_t\}$ lies.

Our simulation experiments using $f(\cdot)$ built with the Gaussian functions also show that the approximation error is quite sensitive near the exact RBF centers of the function. A small distance away from the exact centers, the error is far less sensitive to the location of the centers. Thus, there seems to be of little use to fine-tune the centers without knowing exactly where they are, which is always the case for our modeling problem.

3.2　Spatial Fourier theory based structure determination

Note that the nature of the discrete signal modeling problem requires the universal approximation be obtained using the finite number of function samples only. This obviously raises the question as to whether a given set of discrete data can adequately represent a nonlinear function. This is the issue that all the heuristic methods fail to address.

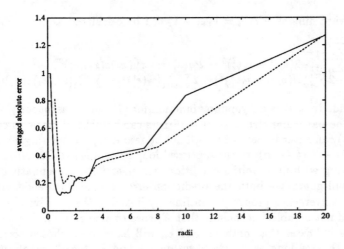

Figure 1: A simulation plot of mean-square modeling error versus the width σ. Solid line: A RBF net with 42 hidden neurons; dashed line: A RBF net with 13 hidden neurons.

Intuitively, all the data will have to be dense enough in a compact region to allow the reconstruction of the function in between the data points. Drawing a similarity with the well-known situation of time signal reconstruction from discrete-time samples, exactly how dense the data samples should be is expected to be made precise using the idea of frequency domain analysis and sampling theory. The only difference is that spatial Fourier analysis should be used instead as the nonlinear functions involved in the signal modeling problem are spatial rather than temporal. Moving along this line, one can further expect that the reconstruction is feasible for a band-limited nonlinear function with spatially sufficiently close data samples. A nonlinear function $f(\cdot)$ in general needs not be Fourier transformable, not to mention band-limited. However, provided that $f(\cdot)$ is sufficiently smooth on a compact set, a suitable truncation can be introduced to limit $f(\cdot)$ to the compact set in such a way that it is band-limited.

These intuitive thoughts are made rigorous in an interesting work reported recently [7]. By confining the approximation to a compact set with a proper truncation, and using a sufficiently fine grid of RBF neurons, [7] shows that the approximation can be arrived at to within a given error bound using only finite number of function samples that determine the weights [7]. This result forms an important theoretical basis for finding the structural parameters of RBF neural nets in the context of nonlinear signal modeling. Thus, instead of trying to rely on heuristics or blind search, the problem of determining RBF neural net structure can be thought of as setting up a sufficiently fine grid of RBF neurons with their centers located at the crossings of the grid, the widths chosen using a simple equation derived from the theory. Such a choice then guarantees the existence of a set of weights so that the approximation meets a pre-specified modeling precision.

In accordance with the theory developed in [7], both Δ and σ can be obtained exactly, given the size of S and a so-called over-sampling parameter. The corresponding error-bound can then be obtained by evaluating some Fourier transform related functions. Our simulation analysis indicates, however, that the recommended theoretical values for Δ and σ do not normally give rise to low mean-square modeling error for the modeling scheme. In particular, the theoretical value for σ appears to be considerably higher than it should be for constructing a more accurate model. Moreover, finding the spatial Fourier transform for a nonlinear function is a time-consuming process, especially for nonlinear functions with many variables, making the error-bound less useful for practical modeling problems.

To be pragmatic yet keeping in line with the theory, we have introduced certain amendments to help determine Δ and σ. The general rule is to set Δ smaller when the modeling error is required to be smaller. An empirical relationship between Δ and σ seems to be

$$\sigma = \frac{2}{3}\Delta \sim \Delta.$$

Seeing from our simulation experiences, this choice of σ appears to bring the mean-square modeling error close to its minimum (see Figure 1).

Let us summarize the preceding discussions into algorithmic steps for the determination of all the structural parameters. Note that the function approximation is confined to be within a compact hypercubic or hyper-rectangular set $S \in R^{mk+lq}$. The existence of S is ensured by the BIBO stability of $f(\cdot)$, and by the bound on the inputs to the system.

Step 1 Use $\{x_t\}$ to determine a compact set S to be the region of operation for an underlying generating system. S should obviously contain the origin of the linear space R^{km+lq}. The size of S can sometimes be fixed by the physical nature of a given signal.

Step 2 Form a uniformly spaced grid in S, which is preferably symmetrical about the origin. The space between two neighboring grid points, denoted by Δ, can be adjusted to change the fineness of the grid, thus the approximation error of the RBF net. Once the grid is set up, the number of RBF neurons n is simply the number of grid points, and their centers p_i's are the coordinates of the grid points.

Step 3 Choose σ to be around $\frac{2}{3}\Delta \sim \Delta$ as the widths for all the RBF neurons. The approximation error is closely related to the width in a way depicted in Figure 1. The optimal σ for a particular modeling problem normally takes a few rounds of trail-and-error to fix.

4   Conclusions

We have presented a discrete-time nonlinear signal modeling scheme based on neural nets. The key motivation is to carry over the essence of the linear ARMA modeling to the nonlinear case with the help of RBF neural nets. In this particular framework, the modeling problem is decomposed into two separate sub-problems of determining the weights and the structural parameters. The theory of spatial sampling and the Fourier analysis helps to find the structural parameters in the light of function approximation. Once the structure is known, a stable recursive algorithm can be readily used to find the weights of the nets. The convergence of the algorithm is relatively easy to establish compared to other types of neural nets where convergence often comes as an accidental by-product of a prolonged training process.

References

[1] K. J. Hunt, D. Sbarbaro, R. Zbikowski and P. J. Gawthrop (1992), "Neural networks for control systems – A survey," *Automatica*, Vol. 28, pp. 1083-1112.

[2] L. Hitz and B.D.O. Anderson (1969), "Discrete positive-real functions and their application to system stability," *Proc. IEE*, pp. 153-155.

[3] J. Park and I. W. Sandberg (1990), "Universal approximation using radial-basis-function networks," *Neural Computation*, Vol.3, pp.246-257.

[4] K. I. Funahashi (1989), "On the approximate realization of continuous mappings by neural networks," *Neural Net.*, Vol.2, pp.183-192.

[5] K. Hornik, M. Stinchcombe and H. White (1989), "Multilayer feedforward networks are universal approximators," *Neural Net.*, Vol.2, pp.359-366.

[6] J. Moody and C. Darken (1989), "Fast learning in networks of locally-tuned processing units," *Neural Computation*, Vol. 1, pp.281-294.

[7] R. M. Sanner and J. E. Slotine (1992), "Gaussian networks for direct adaptive control," *IEEE Trans. Neural Net.*, Vol. 3, pp.837-863.

Forecasting and Decision–Making using Feature Vector Analysis (FEVA)

Alok Kumar
Thayer School of Engineering
Dartmouth College
Hanover, NH 03755
alok@everest.dartmouth.edu

Victor E. McGee
Amos Tuck School of Business Administration
Dartmouth College
Hanover, NH 03755
vmcgee@tuck.dartmouth.edu

Abstract

A multiple set of discrete time series can be visualized as a set of tracks running along together. If the data points are connected by a wire diagram then we have a surface. This surface is *fuzzy* (influenced by error) and *dynamic,* in that interrelationships (transient and permanent) are propogated through time. Our focus is on procedures which can help detect fundmental patterns and time–varying relationships on such a surface. This paper proposes a new approach called *FEVA, feature vector analysis, where the key idea is to replace each scalar data point with a vector of information which represents what the point "sees" around itself.* The main processing unit consists of a *clustering module* to detect patterns in the enhanced (feature vector) data set, and a *neural net simulator* to estimate flexible functional relationships. The cluster analysis results are presented graphically using *pattern–grids* and the neural net simulator builds a *decision surface.* These two visual objects can be used to perform both forecasting and "what-if" analyses. A small but real illustrative example involving stock market information is used to demonstrate the *FEVA* approach.

1 Introduction: Time Series Analysis in Business

In the fields of managerial economics and finance the business environment is measured using a host of variables that can be classified roughly into two sets: (a) those dealing with the capital markets (returns, yields, interest rates, exchange rates, etc.), and (b) those dealing with conditions of the economy (leading indicator variables, production indices, inflation rates, unemployment, etc.). All these time series are discrete, are measured on different time scales (annual, quarterly, monthly, and even minute by minute on the stock exchanges) and often have tricky problems to deal with, such as gaps (no activity over the weekend), unequal chunks (the number of business days in any month varies) and the world time clock (stock markets around the world are open at different times). The traditional approach to analyzing such time series has long been single-linear- equation regression models (e.g., the Fama–French [1989] analysis of the relationship between returns and dividend yields) or multiple-linear-equation econometric models (e.g., the macro-economic models of the national economy or a single state's economy). Time lags are introduced to capture possible forward or backward connections, and the parameter values are determined using global fits to datasets. In other words, the specified linear relationships are assumed to be unchanged over the whole time period.

If time series are examined one at a time then a large number of extrapolative forecasting methods can be applied to them (see Makridakis, Wheelwright & McGee [1983]). The Box-Jenkins ARIMA models are a powerful family of models in this arena, and the Census Bureau performs a universal service using Census X-11 or X-11-ARIMA to create seasonally adjusted series for hundreds of important business series, including the many candidates for leading indicators of economic well- being.

From our point of view there are problems with these traditional approaches. For example, if a simple linear relationship is defined and then tested with a multitude of empirical regression runs the possibility that a nonlinear relationship could do better is never considered. Very often the total time period is separated into time intervals (e.g., to avoid the dramatic volatilities of the great depression or the Black Monday of 1989) and the stability of the hypothesized relationship is tested across intervals. This is a concession to the possibility that relationships can change over time but within each interval the fit is global.

We prefer a method that (a) allows any relationships among variables to reveal themselves, (b) allows relationships to be transient rather than fixed, (c) allows for predictions (i.e., generalizations or forecasts ahead), and (d) allows for "what-if" analysis (i.e., analagous to the use of econometric models to check the impact of specific changes).

2   Problem Definition

Our main objective can be summarized as follows:

> *given a mulyiple set of measurements over time, search for patterns within and across the time series, determine the strength and duration of interrelationships among them, and train a neural net to manage the whole picture.*

From a systems-theoretic point of view we think of each time series as a sub-system and a set of such sub–systems constitutes the environment of interest. We want to know how each time series relates to itself, influences other time series, and is in turn influenced by the other time series. We want to determine the duration of influence within and across subsets of time series. We want to detect lack of interaction too. We do not wish to predetermine the functional form of a relationship nor do we want to prescribe that a relationship is forever.

The key ingredient of our approach is called **FEVA, Feature Vector Analysis,** and will be described in the next section.

After transient patterns have been detected (using classification of the feature vectors) and the functional interconnections have been estimated (using a neural net model), the FEVA model can be used both for forecasting and for performing "what-if" analyses. The study of the effects of changing one (or more) variables on other variables over future time is the standard way of using econometric models. Similarly, in FEVA models, the concept is implemented by perturbing one or more data points at specific time points and examining the influence of the propagating wave so created. All identified transient interconnections (within and across variables) play their roles in the FEVA model output.

3   The Proposed Framework: FEVA

The main idea in FEVA is to replace each data point by a vector of information which represents what that point "sees around it". The vector is called a **feature vector.** It is to be created in such a way as to represent what that single point sees in its local neighborbood, where "local" will be defined in terms of number of time periods (looking into the future and into the past) and the set of other relevant time series in its purview. These are judgment calls and will depend upon subject–matter expertise.

The available dataset (measurements on multiple time series over a range of time) is visualized as a set of side-by-side tracks (as in a running track) and a wire-plot of the data will be seen as a surface. The surface will usually be divided into a *training surface* (a subset on the time scale) and a *test surface* (to check on the validity of the FEVA model projections).

3.1   The Basic Solution Strategy

The overall strategy is summarized by the block–diagram shown in Figure 1. The main steps involved in FEVA are:

1. Replace each data point on the training surface by a feature vector.

2. Perform a cluster analysis to identify similar points and regions on the training surface. Construct pattern grids to display the results.

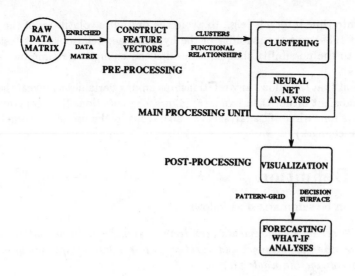

Figure 1: Main processing units in FEVA: the top–level view.

3. Use several multilayered neural nets to estimate functional relationships and to create links between the points on the training surface. The training surface with linked points is given a new name: *decision surface.*

4. Use the decision surface for both forecasting and "what–if" analyses.

3.2 Illustrative Example

Regional stock markets attempt to link their fortunes to those of the big boards and one procedure for doing so used to involve commission splitting. When the SEC ruled that commission splitting had to cease, Business Week reported that this would hurt the regional exchanges. Our example data set involves 35 monthly dollar volumes on the Boston Regional Exchange and the combined NYSE/AMEX markets. The time period covered the SEC ruling and therefore it was expected that some change in the relationship would be evident. See McGee & Carleton [1970]. These data were used to illustrate FEVA.

Given the datasets, the first step of FEVA analysis is to develop a feature vector for each single datum.

3.3 Pre–processing: Constructing Feature Vectors

FEVA converts scalar data points into a vector of information. The basic idea is very simple and makes intuitive sense: a single number cannot give us information about relational measures, i.e., it does not tell us how the point is located with respect to others in the environment. So instead of looking at *one number*, we replace it with a *vector* which holds information about the relative position of the point with respect to other data points in the environment. This vector is known as the *feature vector*. It holds information in a compact form. By introducing additional attributes for each data point, we are effectively increasing the dimensionality of each point, and we expect that with increased dimensionality, the features in the data set will be identified more accurately at local and global levels.

Each data point has three types of vision:

- *Backward vision:* Look at the past history.

- *Forward vision:* Look into the future.

- *Cross vision:* Look at how the neighbors are performing.

II-280

problem.

This approach will be useful for analysis of multiple time series when we have no information about the relationships between them. It will also be useful in cases where we want to find the relationship between *two* time series but we expect interactions from still other series.

4.2 Interaction between different domains

Once the feature vectors are constructed, the next step is to find relationships. It is important to define in mathematical terms what we mean by relationships. Basically, we are looking for similar points, similar regions (sets of points) or similar time series. We are also interested in studying the dynamics of interactions (if any) between these domains. This results in a two step process:

- *Step 1:* Identify *similar domains* in the multidimensional space.

- *Step 2:* Determine if there exists any kind of interaction between the different domains.

In general, a domain can refer to a point (D_p), a region of points (D_r), or an entire time series (D_t). These 3 domains will give rise to 9 possible types of interaction among the domains, for example:

1. $D_p - D_p$ *interaction:* pair–wise interaction.

2. $D_r - D_r$ *interaction:* interaction between two regions (sets) of data points.

3. $D_t - D_t$ *interaction:* interaction between two time–series.

5 The Main Processing Unit

The main processing unit consists of the following:

1. *Clustering Procedure:* for detecting patterns in the data set.

2. *Function Estimator:* for identifying the functional relationships between the time series.

Self–organizing maps are used for making the clusters and a set of neural nets are used to estimate the functional relationships. Based on preliminary analysis of different types of data sets, we felt that self organizing maps (SOM) can be used to perform efficient clustering of any given data set [1].

With all the data points replaced by feature vectors, we define several multilayered neural networks to see if there are relationships among the feature vectors. The first set of neural nets creates links between the points in individual time–series. Forward as well backward links are created. The second set of neural nets estimates the interconnections between the various time–series. The forward connections are used to propagate the effect forward and it is used for forecasting. On the other hand, the cross connections are used to transmit the effect to other time series in the lateral direction.

6 Visualizing the Results from FEVA

The results from the feature vector analysis are:

- A Set of Pattern Grids

- A Decision Surface

Pattern–grids are the output from the clustering module, and the decision surface is used to visualize the results from the neural net simulation. We can visualize the entire system as an elastic sheet where each data point is a *node* on the sheet. The sheet can be used to visualize the dynamics of the system and the interactions between the sub–systems. The decision surface can be used to perform "what if" tests and other kinds of analyses. We can give a small perturbation to one of the data points and observe its effect on the sheet.

---

[1] We would like to thank the team of T. Kohonen, J. Kangas, and J. Laaskonen who developed SOM_PAK; we have used their package for performing cluster analysis.

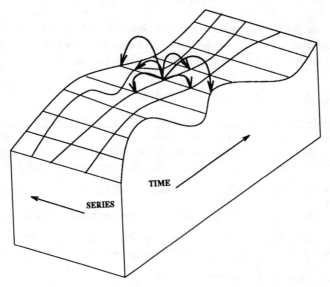

Figure 2: Building the feature vector: looking around and collecting information.

Time Period	Boston SE	NYSE/AMSE
1	7.9	10.6
2	6.9	10.2
3	8.8	13.3
4	7.3	10.7
5	7.9	13.3
6	8.6	12.8

4, 7.3, -1.5, -1.0, 0.7, 1.0, 0.8, 1.1, 10.7, -2.6, -1.0, 2.6, 1.0, 0.8, 1.2

Figure 3: An example of a feature vector with 11 attributes (for Boston–NYSE/AMEX data).

The data point can thus look ahead or behind on its own time series, it can look sideways at the current values of other time series, and it can look ahead or behind at other time series. Just what constitutes a "look" is completely open. Looks can be ordinal ("I am bigger than that datum"), interval ("I am 6 units lower than I was last period"), ratio ("I am 88% of that other variable two periods hence"), comparative ("my change from period $t-1$ to t is less than the change in variable 4 in the interval t to $t+1$"). Figure 2 illustrates the different types of vision and the information gathering step.

Figure 3 shows one example of a feature vector constructed for the Boston–NYSE data. The attributes of the feature vectors are:

4 Defining Relationships

4.1 Interaction among fundamental variables

Any system can be represented by a set of fundamental and derived variables. There are *fundamental* variables which can be measured directly, and there are others which are *derived* from these basic measurements through some kind of transformation. The objective is to use the derived variables to study the interaction between the fundamental variables. But in many instances the derived variables are not able to represent the dynamics among fundamental variables. They change the nature of the

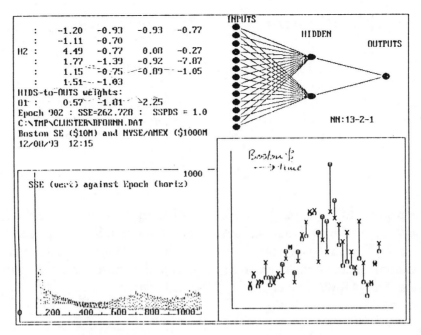

Figure 4: Illustrative Results: using a neural net NN:13–2–1 to fit the Boston dollar volume on the basis of feature vectors shown in Figure 3.

7 Conclusions and Future Work

We have used data sets from stock markets, foreign exchange markets, and other well known data sets to validate the effectiveness of the proposed framework. In addition, we have performed tests on single time–series comparing our results to Box–Jenkins ARIMA models, and we are investigating robustness with respect to small perturbations in the input data. Potential application areas include: real–time financial trading, econometric modeling, forecasts in the marketing field.

References

[1] .F. Fama and K.R. French, "Business Conditions and Expected Returns on Stocks and Bonds," *Journal of Financial Economics*, Vol. 25, No. 23–49, 1989.

[2] K. Knight, "A Gentle Introduction to Subsymbolic Computation: Connectionism for the A.I. Researcher," Technical Report CMU–CS–89–150, School of Computer Science, Carnegie Mellon University, May 1989.

[3] T. Kohonen, J. Kangas, and J. Laaksonen, "SOM_PAK: The Self–Organizing Map Program Package," Version 1.2, November 1992.

[4] T. Kohonen, "The Self–Organizing Map," *Proceedings of the IEEE*, Vol. 78, No. 9, September 1990.

[5] B. Kosko, *Neural Networks and Fuzzy Systems: A Dynamical Systems Approach to Machine Intelligence*, Prentice Hall, Inc., Englewood Cliffs, NJ, 1992.

[6] S. Makridakis, S.C. Wheelwright and V.E. McGee, *Forecasting: Methods and Applications*, John Wiley and Sons, Inc., 1983.

[7] V.E. McGee and W.T. Carleton, "Piecewise Regression," *Journal of the American Statistical Association*, Vol. 65, No. 331, 1109-1124, 1970.

[8] J.W. Sammon, Jr., "A Nonlinear Mapping for Data Structure Analysis," *IEEE Transactions on Computers*, Vol. C–18, No. 5, May 1969.

System Identification with Dynamic Neural networks

Jose C. Principe, Mark A. Motter*

Computational NeuroEngineering Lab
CSE 405 University of Florida
Gainesville, FL32611

* Facility Automated Controls
NASA Langley Research Center
Hampton, Virginia 23681

Abstract

The goal of this paper is to report on the application of several dynamic neural networks to identify the dynamics of a nonlinear dynamical system (wind tunnel). Several focused architectures based on both the TDNN (time delay neural network) and the Gamma model were utilized. We found that the Gamma model outperformed the TDNN architecture for the identification of the system dynamics. An NARMA model provided the best results.

Introduction

The 16 Foot Transonic Tunnel at the NASA Langley Research Center Hampton, Virginia is a closed circuit, single return, continuous flow, atmospheric tunnel with a Mach number capability from 0.2 to 1.30 [1]. The tunnel fans are 34 feet in diameter and driven from 60 to 320 rpm by a 50 MW electric drive system. An air removal system using 30 MW compressor and 10-Foot diameter butterfly valve provides test section plenum suction. The nominal dynamics vary significantly over the operating range. The control input is bang-zero-bang (-1,0,+1), and there is significant transport lag over the operating range. The Mach number computed from pressure measurements is a relatively noisy quantity [2]. Gain scheduled controllers suffer from sluggish performance or limit cycle behavior, so human intervention is frequent.

In this work we study the performance of several dynamic neural networks to identify the dynamics of the tunnel in response to the control input at one given operating condition. A dynamic neural network is a static mapper of the multilayer perceptron (MLP) type extended with a short term memory mechanism. Here we will be comparing the performance of the TDNN type (time delay neural network) [3] with the Gamma model [4]. The Gamma model is based on a time lagged recursive neural network, while the TDNN is purely feedforward [5]. The recurrent parameter of the Gamma model (the Gamma parameter) controls the effective memory depth of the memory structure [5]. A large volume of data showing the system response for several control inputs at different operating points is available. The system output is the wind speed measured in Mach number [2].

System Architecture

The development strategy was to train a dynamic neural network that would produce the same Mach number measured in the tunnel for a given set of control inputs (Figure 1). The input sequence fed to the dynamic artificial neural network (ANN) was the same as the control commands sent to the wind tunnel fan drive system. In this way the ANN will identify the nonlinear relationship between the control input and the Mach number measurements which measure the wind tunnel dynamics at a given operating point.

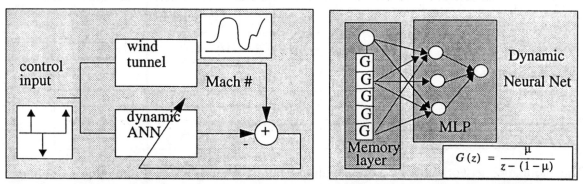

Figure 1. The identification setup, and the architecture of the focused Gamma net.

The output of the ANN was compared to the plant output. The error was fed to the ANN and used to adapt the network weights at each time step, using the backpropagation algorithm [6]. The Gamma parameter was not adapted in this work. However, several different values of the Gamma parameter were utilized in order to vary the memory depth of the input layer [4]. After initial training (20 iterations) all the networks used a *variable learning rate* for the remaining of the training. The rule for changing the step size is very simple: if the mse (mean square error) increased, the learning rate was decreased by 50%. If the mse decreased, the learning rate was increased by 1%.

The training set consisted of three segments totaling 150 points (Figure 2). The first segment with zero control input corresponds to an initial Mach number of 0.54. In this segment the fluctuations due to measurement noise are apparent (samples 0-20 in Figure 2). The second segment corresponds to the control input of -1 (lower) followed by a sequence of zero inputs sufficiently long for settling (samples 25-80). The third sequence had a short sequence of +1 pulses (raise), followed by a sufficient long trailing zeros for settling (samples 85-150). Notice that the network input is mostly (96%) zeros.

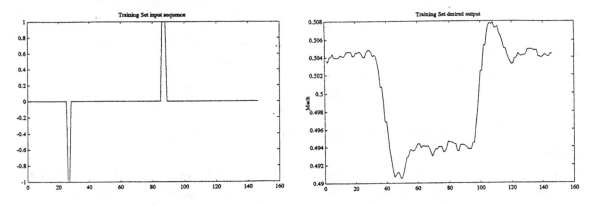

Figure 2. Input Control (left) and Mach number output time series used for training.
Several dynamic architectures based on the MLP were investigated to identify the system dynamics. The focused architectures have two hidden layer with varying number of processing elements.

The input memory structure also varied in size and in characteristics (feedforward or recurrent). Table I summarizes the different topologies

Table 1:

	TDNN #1	TDNN#2	Gamma#1	Gamma#2
input layer	7	64	16	20+20
1st hidden	14	14	14	6
2nd hidden	6	6	6	0
lin. output	1	1	1	1

The Gamma#2 network utilized a double input layer of 20 units each. An integrator (running average of 60 samples) was placed before the second input layer. Notice that the complexity of the input layer was offset by a much smaller number of hidden units. The performance of these two architectures which contain a trade-off in terms of number of inputs/ number of processing elements in the hidden layer convey information regarding the relative importance of mapping abilities and input signal representation.

Results

After training, the networks were tested in a different window of data. Here we will be presenting the results regarding all the topologies in Table 1.

TDNN#1
This ANN never learned the task even after 100,000 iterations (Figure 3). The final mse during training was 0.02. This is to be expected since the memory layer at the input sees zeros for most of the time, and can not relate the change in dynamics with the input. Therefore, the size of the memory layer was substantially increased in TDNN#2.

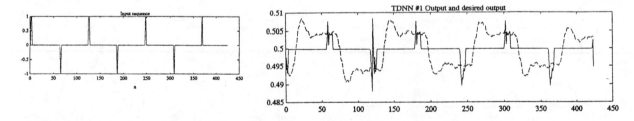

Figure 3. Control input (left) and TDNN#1 output during testing.

TDNN#2
This network has an input memory layer that is able to represent in time the input control until the next control is applied. The network was trained with 10,000 iterations, and although some dynamic capability is noticed in the response (Figure 4), the output is still very different from the system output (mse during training reached 0.004, but oscillated significantly). We conclude that memory depth is not only the determining factor for this network to learn the dynamic behavior.

Since the Mach number measurement is noisy, having a lot of input weights creates confusion in the network, and it never learned the task.

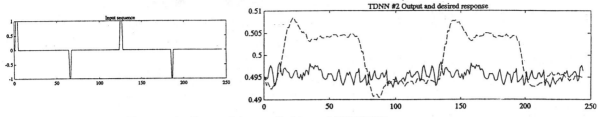

Figure 4. Control input (left) and TDNN#2 output.

Gamma #1

The memory depth parameter was set at 0.2 giving an effective memory depth of 80 samples [4]. The gamma memory is a dispersive memory kernel, so although the depth of the memory is increased the resolution is decreased. The network was trained for 5,000 iterations (mse during training was 0.005 but fast oscillations were noticeable). As Figure 5 shows, some significant features of the input were captured by the Gamma#1 network. The general shape of the variation of the Mach number is apparent in the network output. However, there are still spikes that correspond to the occurrence of the inputs. Variation of the Gamma parameter did not varied appreciably the shape of the network output. The lowpass nature of the Gamma memory seemed to improve the identification. Also, the network architecture is much more parsimonious when compared with the TDNN of the same memory depth.

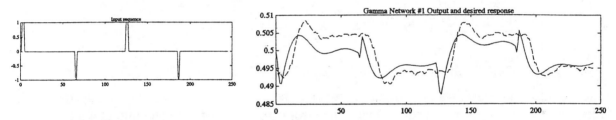

Figure 5. Control input (left) and Gamma#1 output.

Gamma #2

This network utilized not only the control input (20 inputs) but also an integrated input (20 more units). The integrated control input was basically a square wave for this case. The gamma parameter was set at 0.5, creating an effective memory depth of 40 samples. The network trained much faster reaching a mse of 0.003 after 5,000 epochs, basically without oscillations. The output of the gamma net is not very different of the Gamma #1 (Figure 6). However we notice that the steady state values of the of the tunnel can be much more accurately matched. This is attributed to the inclusion of the integrated input, which serves as a direct model of one of the tunnel's response characteristics. We can also conclude that the mapping between input and output can be captured with only 6 hidden PEs.

In order to improve even further the identification capabilities of the network a more sophisticated topology was implemented. The input layer of the network was similar to the network Gamma#2 (Gamma parameter of 0.5), but now another gamma layer with 20 taps (and gamma parameter of

0.5) was placed at the output of the network (Figure 7). These values were then fedback to the hidden layer.

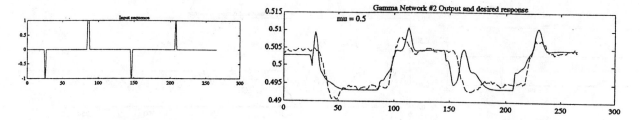

Figure 6. Control input (left) and Gamma#2 output during testing.

The number of hidden layers is kept at 6, with a linear output processing element. This network not only is working with the past values of the input, but also with the past values of the system output. The output of the network was initialized with the value of the first sample of the plant output (Mach number). This avoids transients and simulates the effect of observing the plant for a steady state interval (no noise).

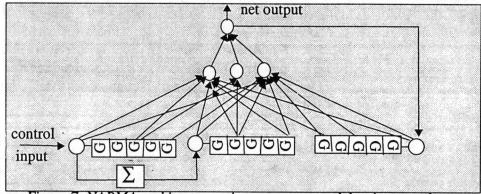

Figure 7. NARMA architecture using a gamma model at input and output.

Another modification that was introduced in this network to boost performance was the change of the cost function. Instead of the mean square error, the error (difference of the plant output with the network output) was passed through the inverse hyperbolic tangent function. Only after it was propagated backwards through the dual of the ANN topology. This procedure resembles an L ∞ norm [7], since larger errors will be emphasized during training, just like the L∞ criterion does. The network was trained for 4,000 iterations and the final mse was 0.001.

This network was able to capture very well the system dynamics as Figure 8 shows. Both the steady state and the rise/decay behavior of the plant are normally well modelled.

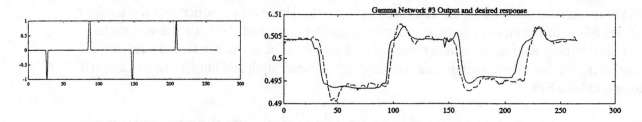

Figure 8. Control input (left) and output of improved NARMA Gamma net.

Conclusions

This study shows that dynamic neural networks can identify the dynamic behavior of complex systems such as the 16 feet transonic wind tunnel at NASA Langley. The system was operated at a single operating point (Mach 0.54). The focused gamma model outperformed the TDNN in this application. We believe that the best compromise memory depth/resolution of the gamma model provides the edge. TDNN must have a lot of delays to represent the control input, but then due to the noisy real world condition, the neural model has too many degrees of freedom (weights) to adapt properly.

Including an integrated input helped in the model performance, which demonstrates that knowledge about the process can be included in the neural model to improve performance. The best model for identifying this plant is a nonlinear autoregressive model (NARMA), where both the past values of the input and output are effectively combined to obtain the network output. With this topology a reasonable identification of the dynamics was achieved.

In this preliminary study a lot of factors were not considered, such as the training of the gamma parameter, and the optimal size of the neural topologies. These aspects affect performance, so they should be handled in the design. It is interesting that the use of a norm resembling the L_∞ norm improved performance, albeit slowing down the training. More research in alternate cost functions for system identification with neural networks should be pursued. Finally we will like to point out that the topology might have benefited from inclusion of measurement updates, incorporating a prediction scheme in the system model. Therefore further work in the prediction with neural models of systems with exogenous inputs will be pursued.

Acknowledgements:

This work was partially supported by NSF grant ECS #920878.

References

1. Peddrew, K.H., "A user's guide to the Langley 16-Foot Transonic Tunnel", NASA Tec. Memorandum 83128, 1981.

2. Mercer, C. E. "Computations for the Langley 16-Foot Transonic Tunnel", NASA Tec. Memorandum 86319, 1984.

3. Waibel, A. Hanazawa T., Hinton G., Shikano K., Lang K., "Phoneme recongition using time delay neural networks", Read. in Speech Recognition, Morgann Kaufmann, 393-404, 1988.

4. deVries B., Principe J., "The gamma model - a new neural model for tewmporal processing", Neural Networks, 5,565-576, 1992.

5. Principe J., deVries B., Oliveira P., "The gamma filter- a new class of adaptive IIR filters with restricted feedback", IEEE Trans. Signal Proc. 42:2, 649-656, 1993.

6. Rumelhart, D., Hinton G., Williams R., "Learning internal representations by error propagation", Chapter 8, Parallel Distributed Processing, vol 1, MIT Press, 1986.

7. Fahlman S. ,"Fast Learning variations on backpropagation: an empirical study", Proc. 1988 Connectionist Model Summer School, Ed. Tourtzky and Hinton, Morgan Kaufmann, 38-51, 1989.

Neural Networks for Predicting Options Volatility

Mary Malliaris
Management Science Department
Loyola University Chicago
820 N. Michigan Ave.
Chicago, IL 60611

Linda Salchenberger
Management Science Department
Loyola University Chicago
820 N. Michigan Ave.
Chicago, IL 60611

Abstract: In this paper, we compare existing methods of estimating the volatility of daily S&P 100 Index for options. The implied volatility, calculated via the Black-Scholes model, is currently the most popular method of estimating volatility and is used by traders in the pricing of options. Historical volatility has been used to predict the implied volatility, but the estimates are poor predictors. A neural network for predicting volatility is shown to be far superior to the historical method.

1. INTRODUCTION

The desire to forecast volatility of financial markets has motivated a large body of research during the past decade (Engle and Rothschild, 1992). Volatility is a measure of price movement often used to ascertain risk. Relationships between volatility and numerous other variables have been studied in an attempt to understand the underlying process so that accurate predictions can be made. The ability to accurately forecast volatility gives the trader a significant advantage in determining options premiums.

Both reseachers and traders use two estimates of option volatility: the historical volatility and the implied volatility. It is almost routinely reported in various publications of exchanges that these two series differ, but no significantly better forecasting model of volatility has emerged. The purpose of this research is to compare these two existing methods of predicting volatility for S&P 100 options with a new approach which uses neural networks. Neural networks, which have been shown to effectively model nonlinear relationships, prove to be a superior approach to predicting options volatility in all cases tested and can be used to develop monthly forecasts.

2. CALCULATING HISTORICAL AND IMPLIED VOLATILITIES

In their seminal work on pricing options, Black and Scholes (1973) assumed that the price of the underlying asset follows an Itô process

$$dS/S = \mu \, dt + \sigma \, dZ \tag{1}$$

where dS/S denotes the rate of return, μ is the instantaneous expected rate of return, σ is the expected instantaneous volatility and Z is a standardized Wiener process ,or dZ is a continuous-time random walk. To simplify their analysis, Black and Scholes assumed that both μ and σ were constants and by using an elegant arbitrage argument, they derived their call option pricing model. Their formula expresses the call price C, as a function of five inputs where S is the current price of the underlying asset, X is the exercise or strike price, T is the time from now to expiration of the option, σ is the expected instantaneous volatility and r is the riskless short term rate of interest.

Observe that the μ of equation (1) does not appear in (2). The mathematical derivation of the call option pricing formula as shown in Malliaris (1982) shows that arbitrage requires that the per unit of risk excess returns between two appropriately designed portfolios must be equal. Making the necessary substitutions in this arbitrage relationship, the term containing μ drops out. With μ now out of the picture and with four of the five remaining variables directly observable, an estimate of the asset's volatility σ in (2) becomes the focal point of attention for both theorists and traders.

There are two main approaches to estimating and predicting the nonconstant σ: the historical approach and the implied volatility approach. The historical approach is the simplest because tomorrow's volatility σ_{t+1} is an estimate obtained from a sample, of a given size, of past prices of the underlying asset. Suppose that the sample size is n and let

$$S_{t-n+1}, \ldots, S_{t-1}, S_t$$

denote daily historical prices for the underlying asset. To get an estimate for σ_{t+1}, first compute daily returns, r_{t-i}, i=0,...,n-2, where $r_{t-i} = \ln(S_{t-i}) - \ln(S_{t-i-1})$.

For a sample of n historical prices, we obtain (n-1) rates of daily return. The annualized standard deviation of these rates of return is defined as the historical volatility and can be used as an estimate of σ_{t+1}. The nearby historical volatility uses 30 days of data, the middle historical volatility uses 45, and the distant historical volatility has 60 daily prices.

An obvious problem with the historical approach is that it assumes that future volatility will not change and that history will exactly repeat itself. Markets, however, are forward looking and numerous illustrations can be presented to show that historical volatility does not always anticipate future volatility and a better estimate comes from the Black-Scholes option pricing model itself (Choi and Wohar, 1992).

Simply stated, supporters of implied volatility claim that tomorrow's volatility σ_{t+1} can only be estimated during trading tomorrow, i. e., in real time. As option prices are being formed by supply and demand considerations, each trader assesses the asset's volatility prior to making his or her bid or ask prices and, accepting the consensus price of a call as a true market price reflecting the corporate opinions of the trading participants, one solves the Black-Scholes model for the volatility that yields the observed call price. When volatility is calculated in this way, it is called the "implied volatility", with the adjective "implied" referring to the volatility estimate obtained from the Black-Scholes pricing formula. Unlike historical volatility, which is backwards looking to past returns, the implied volatility is forward looking to the stock's future returns from now to the time of the expiration of the option. This implied volatility technique has become the standard method of estimating volatility at the moment of trading.

3. NEURAL NETWORKS FOR PREDICTION

While there are dozens of network paradigms, the backpropagation network has frequently been applied to classification, prediction, and pattern recognition problems. Financial applications of neural networks include underwriting (Collins, Ghosh, and Scofield, 1988), bond-rating (Dutta and Shekhar, 1988), predicting thrift institution failure (Salchenberger, Cinar, and Lash, 1992), and estimating option prices (Malliaris and Salchenberger, 1993). The term backpropagation technically refers to the method used to train the network, although it is commonly used to characterize the network architecture. For details of this method, see Rumelhart and McClelland (1986). Currently, a number of variations on this method exist which overcome some of its limitations.

4. DATA AND METHODOLOGY

Data have been collected for the most successful options market: the S&P 100 (OEX), traded at the Chicago Board Options Exchange. Daily closing call and put prices and the associated exercise prices closest to at-the-money, S&P 100 Index prices, call volume, put volume, call open interest and put open interest were collected from the *Wall Street Journal* for the calendar year 1992.

Three estimates for the historical volatilities using Index price samples of sizes 30, 45 and 60 were computed for each trading day in 1992. We also used the Black-Scholes model to calculate implied volatilities for the closest at-the-money call for three contracts: those expiring in the current month, those expiring one month away, and those expiring two months away (nearby, middle, and distant, respectively). Thus, we have approximately 250 observations for six series of volatilities for use in our study.

Comparisons were made between the nearby historical, implied and network volatility estimates. Because the neural network must have sufficient previous data in order to generalize, these estimates were developed using each method for June 22 through December 30, 1992. Trading cycles were used as the prediction periods, with each trading cycle ending on the third Friday of the month.

5. A COMPARISON OF HISTORICAL AND IMPLIED VOLATILITY ESTIMATES

The historical and implied volatility for the nearby contract are graphed together in Figure 1 for June 22 through December 30, 1992. As can be observed, the historical estimate significantly underestimates the volatility used by most traders, i.e., the implied volatility. Since the historical volatility is an average based on returns from 30 preceding days, it is not surprising that the estimate smoothes out the peaks, giving a value for each day which is less variable, and thus less sensitive to daily market fluctuations. The implied volatility for any given day uses only trading information from that day, not a previous time period, to generate a value. Thus, the implied volatility is more reflective of market changes.

The average MAD (mean absolute deviation) and MSE (mean squared error) for the entire forecasting period, from June 22 through Dec. 30 were 0.0331 and 0.0016. The proportion of times which the historical volatility correctly predicted that the implied volatility would increase or decrease are shown in the last column of the table. An overall average of the number of times a change was correctly indicated is .4439, i.e., a little less than half of the time.

Table 1. A Comparision of Historical and Implied Volatilities

Dates of Forecast	MAD	MSE	Correct Directions
Jun 22--Jul 19	.0318	.0012	8/19 = .421
Jul 20--Aug 21	.0292	.0019	11/25 = .440
Aug 24--Sep 18	.0406	.0018	12/18 = .667
Sep 21--Oct 16	.0479	.0027	7/20 = .350
Oct 19--Nov 20	.0213	.0008	14/25 = .560
Nov 23--Dec 18	.0334	.0014	8/18 = .444
Dec 21--Dec 30	.0294	.0009	2/6 = .333

6. DEVELOPMENT OF THE NEURAL NETWORKS

To develop a neural network which is capable of generalizing a relationship between inputs and outputs, the training set selected must contain a sufficient number of examples which are representative of the process which is being modelled. Therefore, the neural network models developed to predict volatility were trained with data sets from historical data from January 1 through July 18 and used to make predictions for six trading cycles beginning with the period July 20 through August 21 and ending with the period from November 23 through December 31. All prior historical data was used when predicting the volatility for the next trading period. Predicting the volatility for the next cycle is a rather rigorous test of the forecasting capabilities of the network since we are asking it to predict volatility for up to 30 days in the future.

There is no well-defined theory to assist with the selection of input variables and generally, one of two heuristic methods is employed. One approach is to include all the variables in the network and perform an analysis of the connection weights or a sensitivity analysis to determine which may be eliminated without reducing predictive accuracy. An alternative is to begin with a small number of variables and add new variables which improve network performance. In this research, the latter was used and variables were selected using existing financial theory, sensitivity analysis, and correlation analysis. Thus, a number of preliminary models were developed to determine which input variables of the group available in the data set would best predict volatility.

The first models were developed with variables representing volatility lagged from 3 to 7 periods to determine an appropriate set of lag variables. Next, other networks were developed and trained to determine which variables were the best predictors of volatility. The final models include the following 13 variables: change in closing price, days to expiration, change in open put volume, the sum of the at-the-money strike price and market price of the option for both calls and puts for the current trading period and the next trading period, daily closing volatility for current period, daily closing volatility for next trading period, and four lagged volatility variables. By including both the time-dependent path of volatility and related contemporaneous variables in our model, we obtained better predictions.

The backpropagation network developed to predict volatility has 13 input nodes representing the independent variables used for prediction, one middle layer consisting of 9 middle nodes, and an output node representing the volatility. The cumulative Delta Rule for training was selected, with an epoch size of 16, and decreasing learning rate initially set at 0.9 and an increasing momentum, initially set at 0.2. The networks were trained using Neuralworks Professional II software from Neuralware.

7. A COMPARISON OF THE NEURAL NETWORK AND IMPLIED VOLATILITY ESTIMATES

Using historical volatility as a benchmark, we evaluated the performance of the neural network by measuring mean absolute deviation, mean squared error, and the number of times the direction of the volatility (up or down) was corrected predicted. These results are shown in Table 2, where comparisons are made between the volatility forecasted by the network and tomorrow's implied volatility. The overall MAD for the entire period was .0116 and the MSE was .0001 as compared to 0.0331 and 0.0016 when the historical was compared to the implied volatility. Furthermore, for each forecasting period, the MAD and MSE were considerably lower, see Tables 1 and 2. In each of the time periods, the proportion of correct predictions of direction made by the neural network was greater than that of historical volatility. The overall proportion of correct direction predictions was 0.794, as compared to .4439 for the historical volatility estimate. This is not surprising since historical volatility smoothes out the estimate because it is an average of 30 values. The correlation between the implied volatility and the volatility predicted by the network is 0.85, as compared with 0.31 for the historical volatility, at the 5% level of significance..

8. DISCUSSION

The results of this comparative study of neural networks and conventional methods for forecasting volatility are encouraging. Because historical estimates are traditionally poor predictors, traders have been forced to rely on formulas like the Black-Scholes which can be solved implicitly for the real-time volatility. But these models are difficult to use and limited since they can only provide estimates to the traders which are valid at that current time. Furthermore, they fail to incorporate knowledge of the history of volatility. The neural network model, on the other hand, employs both short-term historical data and contemporaneous variables to forecast future implied volatility.

The neural network approach has two advantages which make it more useable as a forecasting tool. First, predictions can be made for a full trading cycle, thus avoiding the problems associated with the need for real-time calculations. Secondly, and more importantly, the network forecasts, in the cases we tested, were very accurate estimates of the volatility preferred by traders.

The limitations of neural networks as financial modelling tools are well-documented. Unlike the more familiar analytical models, a trained neural network does not provide information about the underlying model structure. It is often viewed as a black box since there are no theory-based methods available to interpret and analyze network parameters. Neural networks lack systematic procedures for developing network architecture, selecting training and testing sets, and setting network parameters and thus, are difficult to develop. Explicit knowledge of the phenomenon being predicted is required to assist in variable selection.

There are several ways to extend this research. While the performance of these networks in forecasting volatility is superior to the use of historical volatility, improvement may be possible through experimentation with other variables and network architectures. In this paper, we report results for predicting nearby volatility.

However, networks for predicting middle and distant volatility have been developed, using different varialbles and different network architectures.

Table 2. Neural Network and Implied Volatilities

Dates of Forecast	MAD	MSE	Correct Directions
Jun 22--Jul 19	.0148	.0003	16/19 = .842
Jul 20--Aug 21	.0107	.0002	16/25 = .640
Aug 24--Sep 18	.0056	.0001	13/18 = .722
Sep 21--Oct 16	.0127	.0003	19/20 = .950
Oct 19--Nov 20	.0059	.0001	20/25 = .800
Nov 23--Dec 18	.0068	.0001	15/18 = .833
Dec 21--Dec 30	.0039	.0000	5/6 = .833

REFERENCES

F. Black and M. Scholes, The Pricing of Options and Corporate Liabilities, *Journal of Political Economy* 81(1973) 637-654.

]S. Choi and M.E. Wohar, Implied Volatility in Options Markets and Conditional Heteroscedasticity in Stock Markets, *The Financial Review* 27(4)(1992) 503-530.

E. Collins, S. Ghosh, and C. Scofield, An Application of a Multiple Neural-Network Learning System to Emulation of Mortgage Underwriting Judgments, *Proc. of the IEEE International Conference on Neural Networks* (1988) 459-466.

]S. Dutta and S. Shekhar, Bond-rating: A Non-Conservative Application of Neural Networks, *Proc. of the IEEE International Conference on Neural Networks* (1988) 142-150.

R.F. Engle and M. Rothschild, Statistical Models for Financial Volatility, *Journal of Econometrics* 52(1992)1-4.

A.G. Malliaris, *Stochastic Methods in Economics and Finance*, (North Holland Publishing Company, Amsterdam, 1982).

M.E. Malliaris and L. Salchenberger, Beating the Best: A Neural Network Challenges the Black-Scholes Formula, *Proc. of the Ninth Conference on Artificial Intelligence for Aplications* (IEEE Computer Society Press, Los Alamitos, CA, 1993) 445-449.

D.E. Rumelhart and J.L. McClelland, *Parallel DistributedProcessing* (MIT Press, Cambridge, MA, 1986).

L. Salchenberger, E.M. Cinar, and N. Lash, Neural Networks: A New Tool for Predicting Thrift Failures, *Decision Sciences*, 23(4)(1992)899-916.

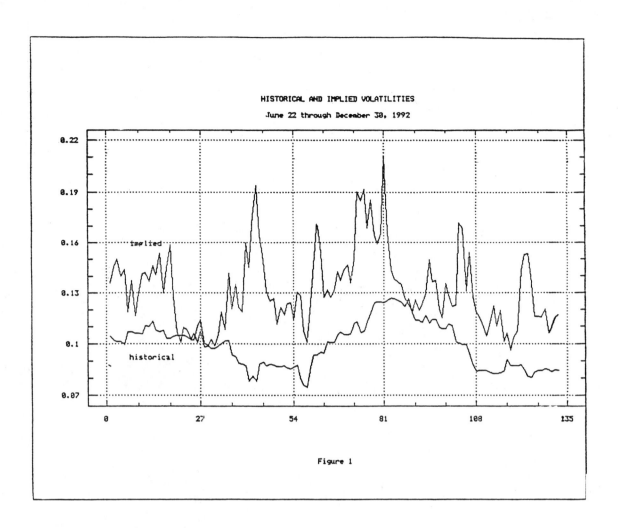

HISTORICAL AND IMPLIED VOLATILITIES

June 22 through December 30, 1992

Figure 1

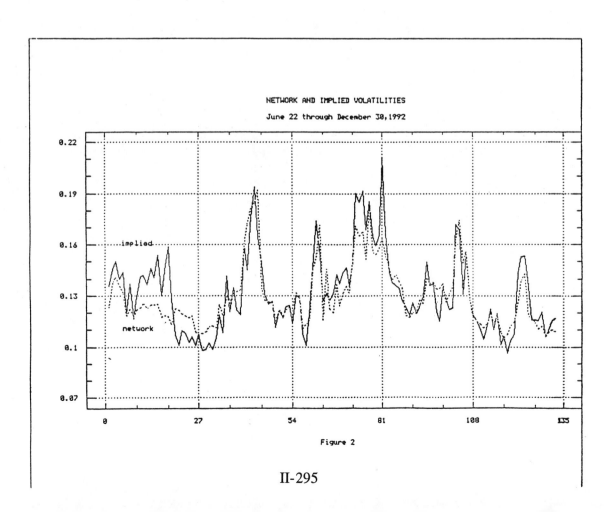

NETWORK AND IMPLIED VOLATILITIES

June 22 through December 30,1992

Figure 2

II-295

Prediction and System Identification

Session Chairs: Paul Werbos
Guido Deboeck

POSTER PRESENTATIONS

A Least-Squares Derivation of Output Error Feedback for Direct State Estimate Correction in Recurrent Neural Networks

David R. Seidl & Robert D. Lorenz
Department of Electrical & Computer Engineering
University of Wisconsin—Madison
1415 Johnson Drive
Madison, WI 53706-1691 USA

Abstract – Iterative least-mean square learning algorithms for recurrent neural networks, such as dynamic backpropagation, have been derived to adapt network weights, but do not directly correct the state estimate. The network estimate of the unknown system's state is propagated without direct compensation. This paper proposes a more general least-mean square problem that produces both dynamic backpropagation weight adjustment and linear output error feedback state estimate correction. The resulting topology is that of an extended Kalman filter with a feedforward network generating the state predictions. The output error feedback eliminates the need to perform state estimate regulation indirectly through weight adjustments.

I. INTRODUCTION

Recurrent neural networks, neural networks with dynamic feedback, are of great interest as a system identification tool because of the general modeling capability afforded, the simplicity of the components, and the computationally-efficient learning algorithms. The learning algorithms use gradient-descent to adapt the network weights to minimize the time-averaged squared-error between the network output and an unknown system. Backpropagation-through-time [1, 2] was the first approximate gradient-descent algorithm. Exact gradient-descent algorithms for fully recurrent networks were introduced in [3, 4]. Dynamic backpropagation, the algorithm for general interconnections of feedforward networks with dynamic linear systems, was derived in [5,6].

Recurrent neural networks coupled with dynamic backpropagation (DBP) directly address two system identification issues: establishing a model for the unknown system and establishing a method for adapting the model parameters. However, the remaining component, determining a system state estimate, is not completely addressed. Both during and after learning, the next network state is a function of the inputs, the weights and the current state. The inputs are known; the weights are adapted through DBP; but no direct correction for error in the current state estimate is made. In practice, even the optimal approximation to the unknown system's state transition function will be imperfect making the creation and propagation of state errors inevitable as discussed in [7]. Consequently, DBP cannot simply find the weights that provide the optimal approximation to the unknown state transition function; it must also vary the weights to indirectly perform state regulation. In our experience modeling control systems, "trained" recurrent neural networks invariably drift once learning is turned off, even if they performed well with learning on. This is because the state regulation is lost.

The problem of optimal state estimation for a known linear system subject to Gaussian noise was solved by the Kalman filter in [8]. The Kalman filter forms an open-loop state estimate using a system model and then forms a closed-loop estimate by adding linear output error feedback scaled by the Kalman gain matrix. A deterministic least-squares optimization problem that yields the same result is reported in [9]. The theoretical framework for closed-loop linear observers was developed in [10]. State estimates for a known nonlinear system can be obtained with the extended Kalman filter (EKF), which uses the nonlinear system model to form the open-loop state estimate as in [11] and many other references. The idea of using a feedforward network to compute the state prediction in an extended Kalman filter was first proposed in [12].

The contribution of this paper is to derive, as a solution to a least-squares state estimation problem, a recurrent neural network with output error feedback state estimate correction added to enhance noise rejection and robustness. A variation of the deterministic Kalman optimization problem in [9] is used to show that a generalization of standard dynamic backpropagation yields the result referred to here as extended Kalman filter/dynamic backpropagation (EKF/DBP). In the continuous learning case covered in this paper, optimizing the state correction term results in output error feedback multiplied by Kalman's gain matrix. Optimizing the weights produces dynamic backpropagation. The resulting topology, shown in Figure 1, is that of an extended Kalman filter with a feedforward network generating the next state predictions.

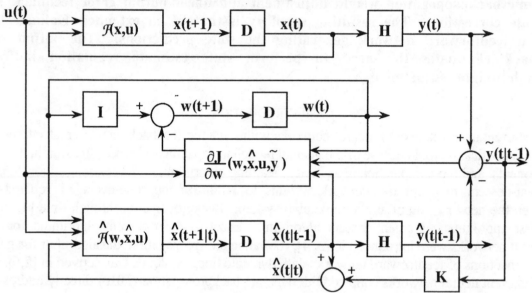

Figure 1: Recurrent Neural Network with Output Error State Correction

II. LEAST-SQUARES PROBLEM FORMULATION

A. Unknown System to be Modeled

The unknown system to be modeled is posed as a nonlinear state equation with a linear output equation. This is the form utilized in Kalman and dynamic backpropagation problem formulations.

$$x(t+1) \quad = \mathcal{F}(x(t),u(t)) \qquad \text{I.C. } x(0) \tag{1a}$$
$$y(t) \quad = \mathcal{H}x(t) \tag{1b}$$

where

$x(t)$	$\in \mathrm{IR}^n$ is the state
$y(t)$	$\in \mathrm{IR}^q$ is the output
$u(t)$	$\in \mathrm{IR}^m$ is the input
$\mathcal{F}(x,u)$	$\in \{g \in \mathrm{IR}^{n+m} \to \mathrm{IR}^n : g \text{ is continuous}\}$ is the state transition function
$\mathcal{H}$	$\in \mathrm{IR}^{q \times n}$ is the output matrix

A. Recurrent Neural Network Model

The recurrent network equations are separated into the state equations (2) and the embedded multilayer feedforward network equations (3). The state update occurs in two steps. First, at time t, the feedforward network $\mathcal{N}$, which approximates the state transition function $\mathcal{F}$, predicts the state at time t+1 in (2a). Second, at time t+1, the state correction term ξ, which may be a function of known values of y(t), is added in (2b). This state correction term has not been included in previous formulations of recurrent networks. When optimized, it provides the desired output error feedback. Note that $\xi(t)$ is designed to be variable with respect to time. The weights W are designed to be constant; their dynamic behavior is an artifact of continuous learning.

1) State recursion equations

$$\hat{x}(t+1|t) = \mathcal{N}(W, \hat{x}(t|t), u(t)) \tag{2a}$$

$$\hat{x}(t+1|t+1) = \hat{x}(t+1|t) + \xi(t+1) \qquad \text{I.C. } \hat{x}(0|-1) \tag{2b}$$

$$\hat{y}(t|t-1) = \mathcal{H}\hat{x}(t|t-1) \tag{2c}$$

$$\hat{y}(t|t) = \mathcal{H}\hat{x}(t|t) \tag{2d}$$

where

$\hat{x}(t+1|t) \in \mathbb{R}^n$ is the open-loop prediction of the state based on $\hat{x}(t|t)$,

$\hat{x}(t|t) \in \mathbb{R}^n$ is the closed-loop corrected state estimate,

$\xi(t) \in \mathbb{R}^n$ is the state correction (or adaptation) term,

$\hat{y}(t|t-1) \in \mathbb{R}^q$ is the open-loop predicted output estimate, and

$\hat{y}(t|t) \in \mathbb{R}^q$ is the closed-loop corrected output estimate.

2) Feedforward Network Equations

$$\mathcal{N}(W, \hat{x}(t|t), u(t)) = W_K a_K \tag{3a}$$

$$a_k = \mathcal{S}_{N_k}\left[W_{k-1}\binom{a_{k-1}}{1} \right] \qquad\qquad a_0 = \begin{pmatrix} \hat{x}(t|t) \\ u(t) \\ 1 \end{pmatrix} \tag{3b}$$

where

N_k = the number of neurons in the kth layer,

$W_k \in \mathbb{R}^{N_{k+1} \times (N_k + 1)}$ is the kth layer weight matrix,

$\mathcal{S}_{N_k}[v]$ applies the sigmoidal nonlinearity to each component of the input vector v

3) Cost Function & Optimization Problem

The quadratic cost function is given in summation (4a) and recursive (4b) forms. The optimization problem in (5) is to minimize $J(W, \xi(\tau), t)$ with respect to W and $\xi(\tau)$ subject to the recurrent network equations (3). The problem reduces to traditional dynamic backpropagation if $\xi(\tau)$ is set to zero for all τ and R is set to the identity matrix. The problem reduces to the deterministic extended Kalman filter problem if the feedforward network is replaced by the state transition function and $R^{-1}(t)$ and $Q^{-1}(t)$ are set to the input and output noise covariance matrices.

When $\xi(\tau)$ is not set to zero, the quadratic state correction term must be included in the cost to penalize its use thus providing the incentive for correct next state prediction. This avoids the problem of allowing perfect output estimation by simply waiting for y(t) then choosing $\hat{x}(t|t)$ to make $y(t) = \hat{y}(t|t) = \mathcal{H}\hat{x}(t|t)$. In continuous learning, $\xi(\tau)$ is part of the "fast" dynamics (as opposed to the slow dynamics of W). Thus, it should be optimized first with the result substituted back into (2) and (4) for the optimization of W.

$$J(W, \xi(\tau), t) = \frac{1}{2} \sum_{\tau=0}^{t} \tilde{y}(\tau|\tau)^T R(\tau)\, \tilde{y}(\tau|\tau) + \frac{1}{2} \sum_{\tau=0}^{t} \xi(\tau)^T Q(\tau)\, \xi(\tau) \tag{4a}$$

$$= J(W, \xi(\tau), t-1) + \frac{1}{2} \tilde{y}(t|t)^T R(t)\, \tilde{y}(t|t) + \frac{1}{2} \xi(t)^T Q(t)\, \xi(t) \tag{4b}$$

where

$\tilde{y}(t|t) = y(t) - \hat{y}(t|t)$ is the output estimate error,

$R(t) \in \mathbb{R}^{q \times q}$ is symmetric, positive semidefinite, and

$Q(t) \in \mathbb{R}^{n \times n}$ is symmetric, positive definite.

$$\min_{W\ \xi(\tau)} J(W, \xi(\tau), t) \qquad \text{subject to (3)} \tag{5}$$

III. Minimization with respect to $\xi(t)$

For brevity, only the filtering problem—τ=t—is considered. In continuous learning, this suffices since it is impossible to alter previous $\xi(\tau)$. However, the smoothing problem, which allows $\xi(\tau)$ to depend on both past and future outputs, may be used in a batch learning situation.

Minimization begins by taking the partial derivatives of the cost with respect to $\xi(t)$. The partial derivative is set to zero and the equation solved to find the optimal $\xi(t)$. (The solutions of this equation are the critical points. All regular points that may be minima can be found among the critical points. In this case, all points are regular points, a minimum is known to exist, and only one critical point exists. It is thus the minimum.) Resort to gradient-descent is thus unnecessary.

The partial derivative of the recursive form of the cost function is shown in (6). The first term in (6) shows that the partial derivative of the cost function inherits a recursive structure. The partial of $\hat{x}(t|t)$ with respect to $\xi(t)$ in (7) can be evaluated using (2) for substitutions. However, $J(W,\xi(\tau),t-1)$ and $\hat{x}(t|t-1)$ are not a functions of $\xi(t)$ so their partial derivatives with respect to $\xi(t)$ are zero in (8). The partial of $\xi(t)$ with respect to itself also in (8) is the nxn identity matrix.

$$\frac{\partial J(W,\xi(\tau),t)}{\partial \xi(t)} = \frac{\partial J(W,\xi(\tau),t-1)}{\partial \xi(t)} - \tilde{y}(t|t)^T R(t)\mathcal{H}\frac{\partial \hat{x}(t|t)}{\partial \xi(t)} + \xi(t)^T Q(t)\frac{\partial \xi(t)}{\partial \xi(t)} \tag{6}$$

$$\frac{\partial \hat{x}(t|t)}{\partial \xi(t)} = \frac{\partial \hat{x}(t|t-1)}{\partial \xi(t)} + \frac{\partial \xi(t)}{\partial \xi(t)} \tag{7}$$

$$\frac{\partial J(W,\xi(\tau),t-1)}{\partial \xi(t)} = 0_{1 \times n} \qquad \frac{\partial \hat{x}(t|t-1)}{\partial \xi(t)} = 0_{n \times n} \qquad \frac{\partial \xi(t)}{\partial \xi(t)} = I_n \tag{8}$$

Substituting (7)-(8) into (6) and setting it to zero yields (9).

$$-\tilde{y}(t|t)^T R(t)\mathcal{H} + \xi(t)^T Q(t) = 0_{1 \times n} \tag{9}$$

Noting that $\tilde{y}(t|t)$ is a function of $\xi(t)$, (2) is used to substitute for $\tilde{y}(t|t)$. This substitution and the required manipulations are done in (10).

$$\xi(t) = Q(t)^{-1}\mathcal{H}^T R(t)\tilde{y}(t|t) \tag{10a}$$

$$= Q(t)^{-1}\mathcal{H}^T R(t)\, (y(t) - \mathcal{H}\hat{x}(t|t-1) - \mathcal{H}\xi(t)) \tag{10b}$$

$$= [I_n + Q(t)^{-1}\mathcal{H}^T R(t)\mathcal{H}]^{-1} Q(t)^{-1}\mathcal{H}^T R(t) \cdot (y(t) - \mathcal{H}\hat{x}(t|t-1)) \tag{10c}$$

$$= K(t) \cdot (y(t) - \hat{y}(t|t-1)) = K(t)\tilde{y}(t|t-1) \tag{10d}$$

Using (10d) to substitute for ξ in (2b) and (4b) yields the modified (2b') and (4b') to be used in optimizing W.

$$\hat{x}(t+1|t+1) = \hat{x}(t+1|t) + K(t+1)\,\tilde{y}(t+1|t) \qquad\qquad \text{I.C. } \hat{x}(0|-1) \qquad\qquad (2b')$$

$$J(W, \xi(\tau), t) = J(W, \xi(\tau), t-1) + \frac{1}{2}\tilde{y}(t|t)^T R(t)\,\tilde{y}(t|t) + \frac{1}{2}(K(t)\tilde{y}(t|t-1))^T Q(t)\,K(t)\tilde{y}(t|t-1) \quad (4b')$$

The recurrent network model (2')-(3) is a deterministic interpretation of the extended Kalman filter and one-step predictor, where the residual is $(y(t) - \mathcal{H}\hat{x}(t|t-1))$ and the Kalman gain matrix $K(t)$ is $[I_n + Q(t)^{-1}\mathcal{H}^T R(t)\mathcal{H}]^{-1}Q(t)^{-1}\mathcal{H}^T R(t)$. When sufficient noise information is not available, a reasonable choice for $R(t)$ and $Q(t)$ is to set the eigenvalues of the linearized system.

III. MINIMIZATION WITH RESPECT TO W

By taking the partial derivatives of the cost and the modified network equations (2')-(4') with respect to the weights and applying gradient-descent, a generalized dynamic backpropagation is obtained. Setting $K(t)=0$ recovers the unaltered dynamic backpropagation. The process begins in (11) by taking the partial derivatives of (4b').

$$\frac{\partial J(W,\xi(\tau),t)}{\partial w_{kij}} = \frac{\partial J(W,\xi(\tau),t-1)}{\partial w_{kij}} - \tilde{y}(t|t)^T R(t)\mathcal{H}\frac{\partial \hat{x}(t|t)}{\partial w_{kij}} - [K(t)\tilde{y}(t|t-1)]^T Q(t)K(t)\mathcal{H}\frac{\partial \hat{x}(t|t-1)}{\partial w_{kij}}$$

$$\text{I.C.: } \frac{\partial J(W,\xi(\tau),0)}{\partial w_{kij}} = 0 \qquad\qquad (11)$$

where w_{kij} is the i,jth element of W_k, the kth layer weight matrix.

The partial derivatives of the state recursions with respect to the weights (12), the partial derivative of the feedforward network with respect to the state (13), and the partial derivative of the feedforward network with respect to the weights (14) follow.

1) Partials of the State Recursions w.r.t. the Weights

$$\frac{\partial \hat{x}(t|t)}{\partial w_{kij}} = \frac{\partial \hat{x}(t|t-1)}{\partial w_{kij}} - K(t)\mathcal{H}\frac{\partial \hat{x}(t|t-1)}{\partial w_{kij}} = [\,I_n - K(t)\mathcal{H}]\frac{\partial \hat{x}(t|t-1)}{\partial w_{kij}} \qquad \text{I.C.: } \frac{\partial \hat{x}(0|-1)}{\partial w_{kij}} = 0_{nx1} \qquad (12a)$$

$$\frac{\partial \hat{x}(t|t-1)}{\partial w_{kij}} = \frac{\partial \mathcal{N}(W,\hat{x}(t-1|t-1),u(t-1))}{\partial \hat{x}(t-1|t-1)}\frac{\partial \hat{x}(t-1|t-1)}{\partial w_{kij}} + \frac{\partial \mathcal{N}(W,\hat{x}(t-1|t-1),u(t-1))}{\partial w_{kij}} \qquad (12b)$$

2) Partials of the Feedforward Network w.r.t. the State

$$\frac{\partial \mathcal{N}(W,\hat{x}(t-1|t-1),u(t-1))}{\partial \hat{x}(t-1|t-1)} = W_K\frac{\partial a_K}{\partial \hat{x}(t-1|t-1)} \qquad (13a)$$

$$\frac{\partial a_k}{\partial \hat{x}(t-1|t-1)} = \frac{\partial a_k}{\partial a_{k-1}}\frac{\partial a_{k-1}}{\partial \hat{x}(t-1|t-1)} \qquad \frac{\partial a_k}{\partial a_{k-1}} = S_{N_k}'\left[W_{k-1}\binom{a_{k-1}}{1}\right]\left(W_{k-1}\binom{I_{N_{k-1}}}{0_{1xN_{k-1}}}\right) \qquad (13b)$$

$$\frac{\partial a_k}{\partial a_{k-1}} = S_{N_k}'\left[W_{k-1}\binom{a_{k-1}}{1}\right]\left(W_{k-1}\binom{I_{N_{k-1}}}{0_{1xN_{k-1}}}\right) \qquad\qquad \frac{\partial a_0}{\partial \hat{x}(t-1|t-1)} = \binom{I_n}{\substack{0_{mxn}\\0_{1xn}}} \qquad (13c)$$

3) Partials of the Feedforward Network w.r.t. the Weights

$$\frac{\partial \mathcal{N}(W,\hat{x}(t-1|t-1),u(t-1))}{\partial w_{kij}} = W_K\frac{\partial a_K}{\partial w_{kij}} + \delta_{k=K}\,1_{(K)ij}\,a_K \qquad (14a)$$

$$\frac{\partial a_k}{\partial w_{kij}} = \frac{\partial a_k}{\partial a_{k-1}}\frac{\partial a_{k-1}}{\partial w_{kij}} + S_{N_k}'\left[W_{k-1}\binom{a_{k-1}}{1}\right]1_{(k-1)ij}\binom{a_{k-1}}{1}\delta_{k=k-1} \qquad (14b)$$

$$\frac{\partial a_k}{\partial a_{k-1}} = S_{N_k}' \left[W_{k-1} \binom{a_{k-1}}{1} \right] \left(W_{k-1} \binom{I_{N_{k-1}}}{0_{1 \times N_{k-1}}} \right) \qquad \frac{\partial a_0}{\partial w_{kij}} = \binom{0_{n \times n}}{\genfrac{}{}{0pt}{}{0_{m \times n}}{0_{1 \times n}}} \tag{14c}$$

where

$1_{(k)ij}$ is the zero matrix with the same dimension as W_k except the ijth element is 1, and

$\delta_{\{cond\}} = \begin{cases} 1 \text{ if } \{cond\}=\text{true} \\ 0 \text{ if } \{cond\}=\text{false} \end{cases}$ is the Kronecker delta.

These partial derivatives are then used in the gradient-descent iteration of (15), which includes momentum, to determine the W_k. The weights must be initialized using structural knowledge or, if no knowledge is available, randomly.

$$w_{kij}(t+1) = w_{kij}(t) - \mu \left(\frac{\partial J(W, \xi(\tau), t)}{\partial w_{kij}} + \lambda \frac{\partial J(W, \xi(\tau), t)}{\partial w_{kij}} \right) \tag{15}$$

CONCLUSION

This paper has shown that a deterministic least-squares optimization problem, that generalizes the dynamic backpropagation formulation, yields a hybrid of the Extended Kalman Filter and Dynamic Backpropagation (EKF/DBP). The new dynamic neural network model includes a state estimate correction term that has the form of the Kalman gain matrix multiplying the output estimation error. This term alters the topology from open-loop to closed-loop state estimator.

ACKNOWLEDGEMENT

The authors thank the Rockwell Foundation whose generous support made this research possible.

REFERENCES

[1]   P. Werbos, "Backpropagation Through Time: What It Does and How to Do It," *Proceedings of the IEEE,* vol. 78, no.10, Oct. 1990, pp. 1550-1560.

[2]   D. Rumelhart, D. Hinton, & G. Williams, "Learning Internal Representations by Error Propagation," D. Rumelhart & F. McClelland, eds., *Parallel Distributed Processing,* vol.1, Cambridge, MA: M.I.T. Press, 1986, pp. 319-362.

[3]   R.J. Williams & D. Zipser, "A Learning Algorithm for Continually Running Fully Recurrent Neural Networks," *Neural Computation,* vol. 1, Cambridge, MA: M.I.T. Press, 1989, pp.270-280.

[4]   B.A. Pearlmutter, "Learning State Space Trajectories in Recurrent Neural Networks," *Proceedings of the International Joint Conference on Neural Networks,* IEEE Press, June 1989, II 365-372.

[5]   K.S. Narendra & K. Parthasarathy, "Identification and Control of Dynamical Systems Using Neural Networks," *IEEE Transactions on Neural Networks,* vol. 1, Mar. 1990, pp. 4-27.

[6]   K.S. Narendra & K. Parthasarathy, "Gradient Methods for the Optimization of Dynamical Systems Containng Neural Networks," *IEEE Transactions on Neural Networks,* vol. 2, no. 2, Mar. 1991, pp. 252-262.

[7]   D.R. Seidl & R.D. Lorenz, "A Structure by which a Recurrent Neural Network Can Approximate a Nonlinear Dynamic System," *Proc. of the International Joint Conference on Neural Networks,* July 1991, II 709-714.

[8]   R.E. Kalman, "A New Approach to Linear Filtering and Prediction Problems," *Transactions of the ASME (Journal of Basic Engineering),* vol. 82D, no. 1, Mar. 1960, pp. 35-45.

[9]   H.W. Sorenson, "Least-Squares Filtering: From Gauss to Kalman," *IEEE Spectrum,* vol. 7, no. 7, July 1970, pp. 63-68.

[10] D.G. Luenberger, "Observers for Multivariable Systems," *IEEE Transactions on Automatic Control,* vol. AC-11, no. 2, Apr. 1966, pp. 190-197.

[11] R.F. Stengel, *Stochastic Optimal Control Theory and Application,* New York, Wiley-Interscience, 1986.

[12] A. Stubberud, H. Wabgaonkar & S. Stubberud, "A Neural-Network-Based System Identification Technique," *Proc. of the 30th Conf. on Decision & Control,* Dec. 1991, pp. 869-870.

Adaptive Inverse Control of Nonlinear Systems Using Dynamic Neural Networks

D.H. Rao, M.M. Gupta and H.C. Wood

Intelligent Systems Research Laboratory, College of Engineering
University of Saskatchewan, Saskatoon, Canada, S7N 0W0

Abstract

It has been demonstrated by many researchers that an unknown dynamic plant can be made to track an input command signal if the plant is preceded by a controller which approximates the inverse of the plant's transfer function. Precascading a plant with its inverse model provides an unity mapping between the input and output signal space. This concept of inverse modeling has been referred to as *adaptive inverse control*. However, the concept of transfer function is limited to linear systems, and the control algorithms developed under this framework can not be extended to nonlinear systems. Due to the functional approximation and learning capabilities, the artificial neural networks can be employed to extend the concept of adaptive inverse control to nonlinear systems. In this paper, two dynamic neural structures, called recurrent neural network and dynamic neural processor, are used to coerce the nonlinear systems to follow the desired trajectories based on the principle of adaptive inverse control. In the process, we compare the performance of these two dynamic neural structures as applied to the inverse control problems.

1. Introduction

Adaptive inverse control is based on the idea of inverse modeling. In this scheme, the inverse model of a plant is estimated and cascaded with the plant, making the overall transfer function of the plant and the inverse model unity [1-12]. If the inverse estimation is good, the error between the targeted and the observed outputs will be very small since the overall transfer function is almost unity. The major concern in adaptive inverse control technique is to accurately obtain the inverse model of an unknown plant. The inverse model is, therefore, not expected to be the exact inverse of the plant but is intended to be a best fit of the reciprocal of the plant transfer function.

The principle of adaptive inverse scheme is commonly employed in the communication field to arrive at feasible solutions to 'intersymbol interference' problems. Sending digital data at high speed through telephone channels, radio channels, and even fiber optic channels often results in a phenomenon called 'intersymbol interference' [7]. Intersymbol interference occurs because of the presence of various frequency components in the source signal, which may experience different amplitude and phase variations as the signal passes through the channel. Filtering the received signal through an approximation of the inverse of the channel model is the principal remedy [7, 13]. Practicalities that may cause time-varying channel dynamics dictate the use of adaptive algorithms for tuning the channel equalizers. Equalization in data modems combats this distortion by filtering incoming signals. A modem's adaptive filter, by adjusting itself to become a channel inverse, can compensate for the irregularities in channel magnitude and phase response [3].

Traditionally, adaptive or self-tuning filters are developed based on finite impulse response (FIR) structures. The FIR filters have the advantage of a very well developed theory with regard to stability and convergence analysis. They have been generally used as they are unconditionally stable and because of the well understood adaptive FIR algorithms. However, the FIR realizations suffer from the problem of indeterminate order when it is necessary to model transfer function poles [14]. In particular, when the poles of the transfer function are close to the unit circle in the z-plane, a high-order FIR filter may be required to meet a particular performance objective [13]. The adaptive inverse control technique proposed by Widrow [1-3] provides only zeros to the controller. He suggested that for proper application, the plant must be stable and the plant zeros should not be extremely close to the $j\omega$-axis in the s-plane or the unit circle in the z-plane. The adaptive inverse control scheme proposed by Widrow involves two modes of operations: (i) the learning phase that estimates an inverse model of the unknown plant, (ii) the control phase that involves implementation of the inverse model to make the plant follow the desired trajectory. In other words, this scheme employs a 'learn-then-control' strategy.

The primary advantage of an infinite impulse response (IIR) filter is that it can perform significantly better than an adaptive FIR filter for the same number of coefficients [15]. This is a consequence of the output feedback which generates an infinite impulse response with only a finite number of parameters. A desired response can be better approximated by a filter that has both poles and zeros (IIR filter) compared to one that has only zeros (FIR filter) [15]. Filters with feedback are particularly appropriate for system modeling (identification), control, and filtering applications.

Despite these advantages, the major obstacle to the use of IIR filters is the lack of well established and well understood adaptive algorithms. This is mainly due to the multimodal nature of their performance. The other major concern is to maintain stability during adaptation so that the poles of the filter do not accidentally move outside the unit circle causing instability. In general, the properties of an adaptive IIR filter are considerably more complex than those of an FIR filter, and it is more difficult to predict the behavior of adaptive IIR algorithms [13, 15]. An inverse control scheme called the inverse-dynamics adaptive controller (IDAC) using an IIR structure for linear systems was proposed in [5, 10].

Most of the adaptive algorithms for FIR and IIR filters reported in the literature are dominated by linear systems theory. There are many problems which require nonlinear dynamics. Artificial neural networks, which are inherently nonlinear, may be considered as a plausible alternative to the existing linear filters to overcome some of the limitations of the latter. The functional approximation, parallelism, fault-tolerance and learning capabilities of neural networks have made them applicable to a diverse set of nonlinear problems. The application of inverse-modeling to robotic trajectory control using a feedforward neural network in the feedback learning scheme is discussed in [6, 16].

Dynamic neural networks can offer great computational advantages over purely static neural networks. In this paper, two such neural structures called the recurrent neural network and the dynamic neural processor (DNP) are employed to extend the concept of adaptive inverse control to nonlinear systems. A brief overview of these neural structures is given in the next section. The computer simulation studies are presented in Section 3, followed by the conclusions in the last section.

2.   Dynamic Neural Networks

2.1 Recurrent Neural Network: The dynamic neural networks, also known as feedback or recurrent neural networks, were first introduced by Hopfield [17, 18]. Unlike the static neural networks, a dynamic neural network employs extensive feedback between the neurons. The node equations in dynamic networks are described by differential or difference equations. Neural architectures with feedback are particularly appropriate for system modeling (identification), control, and filtering applications. A recurrent neural network consists of a single layer network included in a feedback configuration with a time delay. This feedback network represents a discrete-time dynamical system and can be described by the following equation

$$y(k+1) = \Psi \left[w(k) \cdot y(k) \right] , \quad x(0) = x_0 \tag{1}$$

where $y(k)$ and $y(k+1)$ represent the states of the neural network at k and $k+1$ instants of time, x_0 represents the initial value, $w(k)$ denotes the vector of neural weights, and $\Psi[.]$ is the nonlinear activation function. Given an initial value x_0, the above dynamic system evolves to an equilibrium state if $\Psi [.]$ is suitably chosen. The feedback networks with or without constant inputs are merely nonlinear dynamical systems, and the asymptotic behavior of such systems depends on the initial conditions, specific inputs as well as on the nonlinear function. Single-layer recurrent neural networks consists of n computing elements (neurons) with thresholds w_{0i}. The feedback input to the i-th neuron is equal to the weighted sum of neural outputs y_j, where $j = 1, 2, ... , n$. Denoting w_{ij} as the weight value connecting the output of the j-th neuron with the input of the i-th neuron, we can express the total input u_i of the i-th neuron as [19]

$$u_i = \sum_{\substack{j=1 \\ j \neq i}}^{n} w_{ij} \, y_j + x_i - w_{0i} \ , i = 1, 2, ... , n. \tag{2a}$$

In vector form, Eqn. (2a) can be rewritten as: $u_i = w_i^T \, y + x_i - w_{0i} \ , i = 1, 2, ... , n$ $\tag{2b}$

where $w_i \triangleq [w_{i1}, w_{i2}, ..., w_{in}]^T$ and $y \triangleq [y_1, y_2, ..., y_n]^T$. The linear portion of the recurrent neural network can be described in matrix form as

$$U = W y + X - w_0 \qquad (3)$$

where $U \triangleq [u_1, u_2, ..., u_n]^T$, $X \triangleq [x_1, x_2, ..., x_n]^T$ and $w_0 \triangleq [w_{01}, w_{02}, ..., w_{0n}]^T$. The matrix W in Eqn. (3), also called *connectivity matrix*, is an (n X n) matrix. This matrix is symmetrical, i.e., $w_{ij} = w_{ji}$, and with diagonal entries equal to zero, $w_{ii} = 0$ indicating that no connection exists from any neuron back to itself. This condition is equivalent to the lack of self-feedback in the neural structure which guarantees the stability of the network.

2.2 Dynamic Neural Processor: The dynamic neural processor (DNP) is a dynamic neural network developed based on the physiological fact that neural activities any complexity are dependent upon the interaction of antagonistic neural subpopulations namely excitatory and inhibitory. The DNP, thus, comprises of two dynamic neurons called dynamic neural units (DNUs) [9, 20] which are coupled in a flip-flop configuration to function as excitatory and inhibitory neurons. The neural dynamics of the DNU can be expressed in the form of a difference equation as

$$v_1(k) = - b_1 v_1(k-1) - b_2 v_1(k-2) + a_0 s(k) + a_1 s(k-1) + a_2 s(k-2) . \qquad (4)$$

where $s(k) = \left[\sum_{i=1}^{n} w_i s_i - \theta \right]$ is the neural input to the DNU, $s_i \in \mathfrak{R}^n$ are the inputs from other neurons or from sensors, $w_i \in \mathfrak{R}^n$ are the corresponding input weights, θ is an internal threshold, $v_1(k) \in \mathfrak{R}^1$ is the output of the dynamic structure, $u(k) \in \mathfrak{R}^1$ is the neural output, and $a_{ff} = [a_0, a_1, a_2]^T$ and $b_{fb} = [b_1, b_2]^T$ are the vectors of adaptable feedforward and feedback weights respectively. The output of this second-order dynamics, $v_1(k)$, forms an argument to a time-varying sigmoidal function producing the neural output $u(k) = \Psi \left[g_s v_1(k) \right]$, where $\Psi[.]$ is the sigmoidal activation function, and g_s is the somatic gain that controls the slope of the activation function. The DNUs are the basic functional elements in the DNP, shown in Fig. 1, with adaptable feedback connections between the antagonistic subpopulations. The total inputs incident on the excitatory and inhibitory neural units are respectively

$$s_{tE}(k) = w_E s_E(k) + w_{EE} u_E(k-1) - w_{IE} u_I(k-1) - \theta_E , \text{ and} \qquad (5a)$$

$$s_{tI}(k) = w_I s_I(k) - w_{II} u_I(k-1) + w_{EI} u_E(k-1) - \theta_I . \qquad (5b)$$

A direct analytical solution for determining the steady-state and temporal behavior exhibited by the DNP is not possible because of the inherent nonlinearities in the above equations. However, these nonlinear equations can be analyzed qualitatively by obtaining the trajectories in the u_E - u_I phase plane. In this dynamic neural structure, the feedback weights, w_{EE}, w_{IE}, w_{II}, w_{EI}, and the DNU parameters, a_{ff}, b_{fb}, g_s, are the adaptable parameters. The learning algorithm to modify these weights is derived in detail in [21, 22].

3. Computer Simulation Studies

Consider a single-input-single-output (SISO) dynamic plant that has the following input-output relation expressed in a canonical form

$$y(k+1) = f(y(k),...., y(k-n), u(k),...., u(k-m)) = f(x(k), u(k)) \qquad (6)$$

where $x(k) = [y(k),...., y(k-n), u(k-1),...., u(k-m)]^T$ is a state vector, and $f(.)$ is an unknown nonlinear function and satisfies $\partial f(x,u)/\partial u \neq 0$. The canonical form of Eqn. (6) represents a general class of nonlinear systems without internal dynamics. In the adaptive inverse control scheme, the input-output equation of the neural network that produces a control signal to the plant is expressed as

$$u(k) = \Psi(w(.), x(k), r(k)) \qquad (7)$$

where r(k) is the reference (desired) signal, and w(.) is the vector of adaptable weights of the neural network. Using learning algorithms, the nonlinear mapping $\Psi(.)$ can be adapted to approximate the inverse function of the nonlinear system; that is, $\Psi(w, x, s) \rightarrow f_u^{-1}(x, r)$, where $f_u^{-1}(x, r)$ satisfies

$$y(k+1) = f(x(k), u(k)) = f(x(k), f_u^{-1}(x(k), r(k)) = r(k). \qquad (8)$$

From Eqn. (8) it can be seen that an unknown nonlinear plant can be made to track the desired trajectory by making the neural network mapping an inverse of that of the plant. This is the intended behavior of the adaptive inverse control scheme. However, the implicit assumption is that the nonlinear plant under control is invertible. The invertibility of nonlinear systems is addressed in [23], and a sufficient input criterion for designing a neural network to learn the system's inverse was established. In the conventional adaptive inverse control, a multi-layered neural network is trained off-line by comparing the neural network output with the desired system output and the network's output error is computed which is then used to modify the weights. After the neural network is well trained, the input of the neural network is switched to the desired system output. Then, the neural network acts as the inverse of the plant, and its output will drive the system to track the desired trajectory [24]. In this paper, the direct inverse control approach, Fig. 2, is used where the weights of the neural networks are modified based on the system output error.

In this section, we present three simulation examples each one signifying a particular control aspect. The two-layered recurrent neural network, Fig. 3, is used in these simulation studies. The DNP settings were as follows: $w_{EE} = 1.0$, $w_{EI} = 0.5$, $w_{II} = 1.0$, $w_{IE} = 0.5$. The components of the scaling vector w were set to 1.

Example 1: In this example, we consider a general nonlinear plant without internal dynamics represented by the following equation

$$y(k) = u^3(k) + \frac{0.6\, y(k-2) + 0.2\, y(k-1)}{1 + y^2(k-1)}. \qquad (9)$$

The excitation to the system was a unit step input. The weights of the dynamic neural networks were adjusted for a duration of 800 learning iterations. The simulation results are shown in Fig. 4. In Fig. 4a are shown the mappings between the control and input signal space, and the control and plant output space. In the case of the DNP, the unity mapping between the input and the output signal space was achieved very quickly. On the other hand, the convergence of the recurrent neural network was very slow; about 5000 iterations were required to achieve the error tolerance of ± 0.05. The output responses of obtained by the two dynamic neural networks are shown in Fig. 4b.

Example 2: The purpose of this simulation example is to demonstrate the learning and adaptive capabilities of the neural network-based adaptive inverse control scheme. We consider a nonlinear plant described by the following difference equation

$$y(k) = \sum_{i=1}^{2} \alpha_i\, y(k-i) + \sum_{j=0}^{2} \beta_j\, u(k-j) + f[y(k-i),\ u(k-j)] \qquad (10a)$$

with an arbitrary unknown function of the form

$$f[.] = \frac{\left[2 + \cos\left\{7\pi\left(y^2(k-1) + y^2(k-2)\right)\right\}\right] + u^3(k)}{\left[1 + y^2(k-1) + y^2(k-2)\right]} \qquad (10b)$$

with plant parameters $\beta_j = [1.2, 1, 0.8]^T$ and $\alpha_i = [1, 0.9, 0.7]^T$. The input to the system was a unit step input, and the system responses were observed for 800 iterations. The simulation results obtained for this case are shown in Fig. 5. From these results it can be observed that the DNP converged to unity mapping very fast compared to the recurrent neural network which took about 4500 iterations to converge.

Example 3: In this example, a linear plant preceded with an actuator having deadzone characteristics was considered. The plant parameters β_j and α_i were the same as in Example 2. The input to the system was a sinusoidal signal in the interval [-1,1]. The width of the deadzone used in the simulation studies was 0.2. The system responses were observed for 1000 iterations. The simulation results obtained for this case are shown in Fig. 6. In the case of the recurrent neural network, the plant converged to the desired signal after about 7000 iterations.

4. Conclusions

In this paper, the concept of adaptive inverse control was extended to nonlinear systems using the two dynamic neural structures called the recurrent neural network and the dynamic neural processor (DNP). From our initial findings it can be inferred that the principle of adaptive inverse control can be extended to nonlinear systems using neural networks. The DNP was found to be much faster compared a two-layer recurrent neural network. As the weights of these neural networks were adapted based on the system output error, the off-line training of neural networks is avoided. However, further investigations are necessary to study the performance of the neural network-based adaptive inverse control scheme as applied to unstable and non-minimum phase systems.

References

[1]   B. Widrow, D. Shur and S. Shaffer, "On Adaptive Inverse Control", *15th Asilomar Conf. on Circuits, Systems and Computers*, pp. 185-189, Nov. 9-11, 1981.

[2]   B. Widrow, "Adaptive Inverse Control", *IFAC Adaptive Systems in Control and Signal Processing*, Sweden, pp. 1-5, 1986.

[3]   B. Widrow and R. Winter, "Neural Nets for Adaptive Filtering and Adaptive Pattern Recognition", *IEEE Computer*, pp. 25-39, March 1988.

[4]   C.P. Tou, "Inverse Adaptive Modeling of Satellite Communication Channels", *IEEE Pacific Rim Conf. on Communications, Computers and Signal Processing*, pp. 471-474, Victoria, June 1-2, 1989.

[5]   M.M. Gupta, D.H. Rao and H.C. Wood, "Inverse-Dynamics Adaptive Control: A Neural Network Approach", *Proceedings of ISUMA*, Maryland, pp. 189-195, December 3-5, 1990.

[6]   M. Kawato, "Computational Schemes and Neural Network Models for Formation and Control of Multi-Joint Arm Trajectory", in *Neural Networks for Control* , Eds., W.T. Miller, R.S. Sutton and P.J. Werbos, *MIT Press*, 1990.

[7]   C.R. Johnson Jr, "Admissibility in Blind Adaptive Channel Equalization", *IEEE Control Systems Magazine*, pp. 3-15, Jan. 1991.

[8]   K.J. Hunt and D. Sbarbaro, "Neural Networks for Nonlinear Internal Model Control", *IEE Proceedings-D*, Vol. 138, No. 5, pp. 431-438, Sept. 1991.

[9]   M.M. Gupta and D.H. Rao, " Dynamic Neural Units in the Control of Linear and Nonlinear Systems", *The International Joint Conference on Neural Networks (IJCNN)*, pp. 100-105, Baltimore, June 9-12, 1992.

[10]   M.M. Gupta, D.H. Rao and P.N. Nikiforuk, "Neuro-Controller with Dynamic Learning and Adaptation", *Int. J. of Intelligent and Robotic Systems*, Vol. 7, No. 2, pp. 151-173, April 1993.

[11]   D.H. Rao and M.M. Gupta, "Dynamic Neural Adaptive Control Schemes", *American Control Conference*, San Francisco, pp. 1450-1454, June 2-4, 1993.

[12]   D.S. Wang, G.B. Yang and M. Donath, "Non-Collocated Flexible Beam Motion Control Based on a Delayed Adaptive Inverse Control", *American Control Conference*, San Francisco, pp. 552-559, June 2-4, 1993.

[13]   B. Mulgrew and C.F.N. Cowan, Adaptive Filters and Equalizers, *Kluwer Academic Publishers*, Boston, 1988.

[14]   K.J. Hunt, D. Sbarbaro, R. Zbikowski and P.J. Gawthrop, "Neural Networks for Control Systems- A Survey", *Automatica*, Vol. 28, No. 6, pp. 1083-1112, 1992.

[15]   J.J. Shynk, "Adaptive IIR Filtering", *IEEE ASSP Magazine*, pp. 4-21, April 1989.

[16]   R. E. Nordgren and P.H. Meckl, "An Analytical Comparison of a Neural Network and a Model-Based Adaptive Controller", *IEEE Trans. on Neural Networks* , Vol. 4, No. 4, pp. 595-601, July 1993.

[17]   J.J. Hopfield, "Neural Networks and Physical Systems with Emergent Collective Computational Abilities", *Proceedings of the National Academy of Sciences*, Vol. 79, pp. 2554 - 2558, 1982.

[18]   J.J. Hopfield, "Neurons with Graded Response Have Collective Computational Properties Like of Those Two-State Neurons", *Proceedings of the National Academy of Sciences*, Vol. 81, pp. 3088- 3092, 1984.

[19]   J.M. Zurada, Introduction to Artificial Neural Systems, *West Publishing Company*, St. Paul, MN, 1992.

[20]   M.M. Gupta and D.H. Rao, "Dynamic Neural Units With Applications to the Control of Unknown Nonlinear Systems", *The Journal of Intelligent and Fuzzy Systems*, Vol. 1, No. 1, pp. 73-92, Jan. 1993.

[21]   D.H. Rao, M.M. Gupta and P.N. Nikiforuk, "Performance Comparison of Dynamic Neural Processor and Recurrent Neural Networks", The *J. of Neural, Parallel and Scientific Computations*, Invited paper, [In press].

[22]   D.H. Rao and M.M. Gupta, "A Multi-Functional Dynamic Neural Processor for Control Applications", *American Control Conference*, San Francisco, pp. 2902-2906, June 2-4, 1993.

[23]   Y.L. Gu, "On Nonlinear System Invertibility and Learning Approaches by Neural Networks", American Control Conference, Vol. 3, pp. 3013-3017, 1990.

[24]   X. Cui and K.G. Shin, "Direct Control and Coordination Using Neural Networks", *IEEE Trans. SMC*, Vol. 23, No. 3, pp. 686-698, May/June 1993.

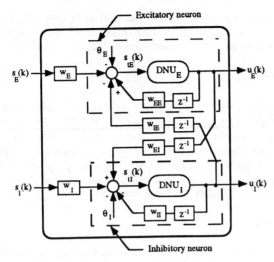

FIGURE 1

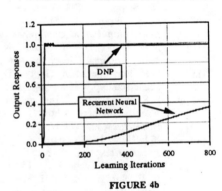

FIGURE 2

FIGURE 3

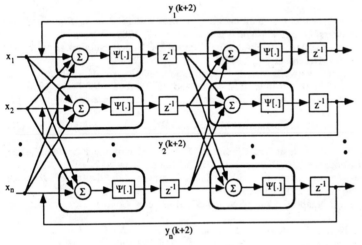

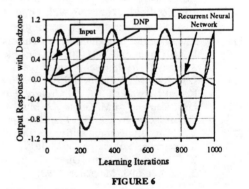

FIGURE 4a

FIGURE 4b

FIGURE 5

FIGURE 6

Computing the Probability Density in Connectionist Regression

Ashok N. Srivastava† and Andreas S. Weigend‡

†Department of Electrical and Computer Engineering
University of Colorado at Boulder
Boulder, CO 80309-0529 USA
srivasan@sebastian.colorado.edu
‡Department of Computer Science and Institute of Cognitive Science
University of Colorado at Boulder
Boulder, CO 80309-0430 USA

We introduce a non-parametric method for determining the degree of uncertainty in prediction and show its use in a regression problem.

1 Problem Statement and Network Architecture

Often, it is not difficult to train a network to generate a number– but what confidence can we have in that number? We would like to compute a probability density whose mean is the target value, and the variance is the confidence.

The problem can be formally expressed in the following manner: given a function $f(\underline{x}):R^n \rightarrow R^1$, we construct a neural network which performs a nonlinear regression on f with a vector of inputs $\underline{x} \in R^n$ whose outputs $\underline{y} \in R^m$ are an estimate of the continuous probability density function $p(\underline{y}|\underline{x})$.

The key idea is to represent a continuum output as a *soft histogram*. The continuos distribution is approximated with m classes. In order to create a training set, we sort the data in ascending order and binned them into m bins with an equal number of points per bin. This approach minimizes quantization errors and shows a method for recasting the function approximation problem as a classification problem by partitioning the range-space of the target function.

The mean and variance of the output distribution can be computed directly via

$$\mu(\underline{x}) = \sum_{i=1}^{m} y_i \zeta_i \tag{1}$$

$$\sigma^2(\underline{x}) = \sum_{i=1}^{m} y_i \zeta_i^2 - [\mu(\underline{x})]^2, \tag{2}$$

where ζ_i is the center of bin i and y_i is the activation of unit i. Figure 1 shows the network and an example of the soft-histogram coding technique (target of 0.24).

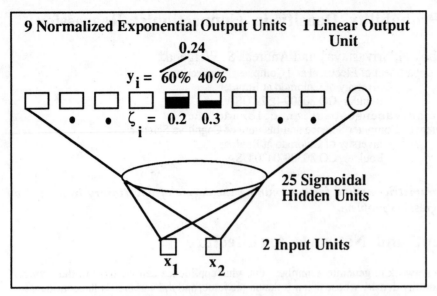

Fig. 1. Network architecture for probability density estimation

The normalized exponential units (also called soft-max) have the functional form

$$p_j = e^{h_j} / \sum_i e^{h_i} .$$ (3)

h_j is the total weighted input received by output unit j, $1...m$ (Rumelhart et al.).

In our experience, learning can be facilitated by having the network perform an additional, easier, task. We added a linear output unit which performs a direct prediction of the mean $\mu(\underline{x})$. This additional output focuses the hidden units to learn the mean. The network has a single hidden layer composed of 25 sigmoidal units, and is trained with backpropagation minimizing the sum-squared error. All units have biases associated with them.

2 An Example

The network's task is to perform a nonlinear regression on a function of the form

$$f(\underline{x}) = g(\underline{x}) + n(\underline{x}).$$ (3)

This function is composed of the target function $g(\underline{x})$ corrupted with additive noise $n(\underline{x})$. The network reconstructs $g(\underline{x})$ and estimates $n(\underline{x})$ from a finite number of samples of $\underline{x}, f(\underline{x})$. The noise estimate can be interpreted as the uncertainty, while the estimate of $g(\underline{x})$ can be thought of as the desired output.

In order to be able to visualize an example, we chose to approximate a mapping $f(\underline{x}):R^2 \to R^1$. The target function, $g(\underline{x})$, which we chose is shown in Fig. 2 and is composed of Gaussians weighted with polynomials (see Matlab User's Guide, 1992, pp. 2-98).

The noise model $n(\underline{x})$ is a Gaussian random variable

$$n(\underline{x}) \sim N(0, \frac{1}{2}(\sqrt{x_1} + x_2))$$ (6).

The variance is bounded between 0 and 1 for values of (x_1, x_2) in the unit square. The training set is composed of 5000 random samples of (x_1, x_2) from the unit square and the corresponding values of f.

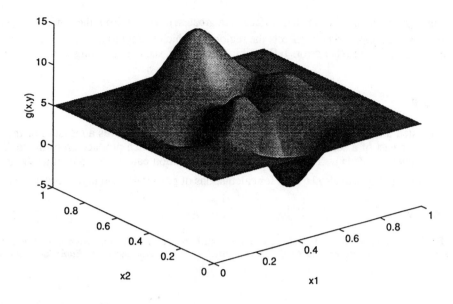

Fig. 2. The target function.

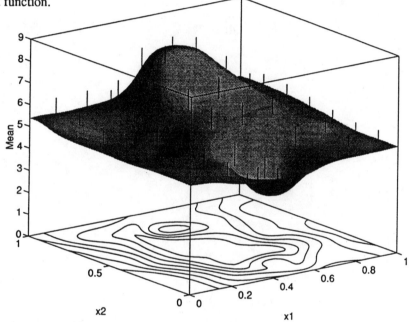

Fig. 3. A surface plot of the mean, a contour plot of the uncertainty surface and error bars.

We trained the neural network with a learning rate of 10^{-5}, which is sufficiently small to avoid artifacts. We used no momentum and trained the network for 850 epochs. The direct-prediction output greatly reduced the training time, and it estimated the mean as expected. The output units are weighed equally in the sum-squared error model since the range of the output units is comparable.

Figure 3 shows a surface plot of the mean of the distribution along with error bars (variance) which indicate the uncertainty in the prediction for evenly distributed pairs of (x_1, x_2) in the unit square. The error bars are symmetric, so only the positive portion of the bars are shown. A contour plot of the uncertainty surface is also shown. It indicates that the uncertainty in the estimate is low near the edges of the surface, but increases toward the center.

II-313

The uncertainty is highest where the estimated surface is in greatest deviation from the function $f(\underline{x})$. Thus, we see that the uncertainty surface appropriately reflects the regions in which the approximation is in error. Apart from the added uncertainty $n(\underline{x})$, there are other errors reflected in the surface, such as sampling error due to the finite sample size.

4 Summary

We designed and tested a neural network which performs a prediction and gives a measure of the precision of the prediction. Outputs consist of a set of normalized exponential units which produce an estimate of the continuous probability density function $p(\underline{y}|\underline{x})$. The variance of this distribution can be interpreted as the uncertainty in the classification. The distribution can also be used for calculations of percentiles and higher order moments.

5 Reference

Rumelhart, D. E., R. Durbin, R. Golden, and Y. Chauvin (still in press), *"Backpropagation: the Basic Theory,"* in *Backpropagation: Theory, Architectures, and Applications, edited by Y. Chauvin and D. E. Rumelhart. Lawrence Erlbaum*

EXPERIENCE WITH USING A NEURAL NETWORK FOR FORECASTING TIME SERIES

Pennagaram D. Devika and Luke E. K. Achenie
Department of Chemical Engineering, U-222
The University of Connecticut
191 Auditorium Road
Storrs, CT 06269

ABSTRACT:

Prediction of future values of time series is an important problem both in engineering and in science. Stochastic model building and forecasting is one of the techniques available for the analysis of discrete time series in the time-domain. Though these models have proven to be accurate for forecasting, they have several important limitations such as an a priori guess of model structure. In this paper, a feed forward neural network implementation is used to predict the future values of different time series by using past knowledge. The network is trained with statistical features such as standard deviation. This hybrid neural network model is shown to be better in prediction than the traditional statistical models.

INTRODUCTION

Prediction of future values of time series is an important problem. The ability to forecast the behavior of time series hinges on two types of knowledge. The first and most powerful one is knowledge of the laws underlying a given phenomenon. When this knowledge is expressed in the form of equations that can, in principle, be solved, the future outcome of a time series can be predicted once the initial conditions are specified. A second, albeit less powerful, method for predicting future values relies on the discovery of strong empirical regularities in observations of the time series.

Neural networks represent one of the approaches to implement intelligent thought processes with a deterministic machine such as a computer. Neural networks have an inherent ability to generalize based only on a set of training data (Rumelhart, 1986 [5]) . An artificial neural network can be trained to recognize a number of patterns. These patterns may be parts of time series, images, etc. If a variation of one of these patterns, corrupted by noise, is presented to a properly trained network, the network can reconstruct the original pattern on which it was trained. In image restoration problems, this technique is used (Timothy Masters, 1993 [6]) with great success. In prediction problems, neural networks have been shown to outperform traditional techniques like ARIMA (Auto Regressive Integrated Moving Average) models (Timothy Masters, 1993 [6]).

In this paper, a feed forward neural network implementation (Achenie, 1993 [1]) is used to predict future values of different time series by using past knowledge. The ARIMA models are fitted using Scientific Computer Associates (SCA) (Liu and Hudak, 1992 [4]) statistical package.

FEED FORWARD NEURAL NETWORK ALGORITHM

In a typical feed forward neural network algorithm, (see for example, Achenie, 1993 [1]), there are s layers of neural elements (an input layer, $s - 2$ layers of neural elements, and one output layer. The jth layer consists of M_j processing elements. W_{k_{j-1},k_j} is the weight associated with the interconnection between the k_{j-1}th element of layer $(j - 1)$ and the k_jth element of layer j. The cumulative input, X is mapped to the output, Y of a processing element by a sigmoidal transfer function.

A generalized transfer function σ proposed by Achenie, 1993 [1] is defined as follows:

$$Y = \sigma(X) = (1 + e^{P(X)})^{-1} - C \qquad (1)$$

where $P(X)$ is a polynomial function of X. The following nonlinear program is solved for the optimal values of Q which is a subset of network parameters, C, W (weights) and parameters associated with $P(X)$ to achieve the network training:

$$\min_{Q} J = \sum_{n=1}^{N} \sum_{k_s=1}^{M_s} \left(Y_{n,k_s} - \hat{Y}_{n,k_s} \right)^2 \tag{2}$$

subject to

$$Y_{n,k_1} = a_{n,k_1}$$
$$Y_{n,k_j} = \sigma(X_{n,k_j}) \tag{3}$$

$$X_{n,k_j} = \sum_{k_{j-1}=1}^{M_{j-1}} W_{k_{j-1},k_j} Y_{n,k_{j-1}} \tag{4}$$

$$Q_{lower} \leq Q \leq Q_{upper} \tag{5}$$

where $a_{n,k_1} = n$-th training data set (input to k_1-th element) and $[Q_{lower}, Q_{upper}]$ are bounds on Q. The performance objective, J is the sum of squares of the deviation of the network output, Y_{n,k_s} from the expected or desired output, $\hat{Y}_{n,k_s}$. At the solution of the nonlinear program, the expected and the desired outputs are close to each other. Achenie, 1993 ([1]) has developed a Successive Programming algorithm for training the feed forward network. In this paper, this algorithm is used to predict the future values of a chaotic time series, a non-stationary time series (Box and Jenkins, 1976 [2]) and a time series collected from a saponification batch reaction.

CHAOTIC TIME SERIES

Ginzberg and Horn [3] considered the following chaotic time series generated by a quadratic map

$$Y_n = 4Y_{n-1}(1 - Y_{n-1}) \tag{6}$$

In this paper, the same example is used to generate a series of 268 values. The first 220 values are used as the training set and the next 48 values are used as the prediction set. The structure of the network is 4-6-1. The output values are scaled between -0.5 and 0.5. The network is tested with different kinds of input sets and the performance of prediction in each case is analyzed.

Case 1: The training set consists of four input elements, namely, $Y_{n-4}, Y_{n-3}, Y_{n-2}$, and Y_{n-1} and one output element Y_n. Network performance on the prediction set is shown in Figure (1).

Case 2: The training set consists of four input elements, namely, $Y_{n-4}, Y_{n-3}, Y_{n-2}$, and $\sigma(Y_{n-3}, Y_{n-2}, Y_{n-1})$. σ is calculated for only the three values in each training set. Figure (2) shows the performance of the network on the prediction set.

Case 3: In this case, the training set consists of the same kinds of input elements as in the second case. However, σ is calculated for all the values starting from the first value until the current three values. Figure (3) shows the network performance in predicting the future values.

Case 4: Finally, the effect of variance is tested. The training set is generated in the same way as in the second case, except the variance of the three values in each training set is used instead of the standard deviation. Figure (4) shows the network performance on the prediction set.

Network performance on prediction is good in all the four cases and very good in Cases (2) and (4) as seen in Figures (2) and (4). In the second and the fourth cases by including the standard deviation and the variance of the observations in the current window, the network has additional useful information about the system. Therefore, the prediction is very good. On the other hand, in the third case, the useful information provided by the standard deviation is degraded by the effect of all past information. Hence, the prediction is not as good as it is in the second and the fourth cases.

NON-STATIONARY TIME SERIES

A non-stationary time series of chemical process concentration (Box and Jenkins, 1976 [2]) is used to test the performance of the feed forward neural network algorithm (Achenie, 1993 [1]) in forecasting the future values. The network is tested with the following different sets of data.

Case 1: The mean is subtracted from the data and the resulting values are used for the analysis. The training and the validation sets contain four inputs, namely, C_{t-2}, C_{t-1}, C_t, and $\sigma(C_{t-2}, C_{t-1}, C_t)$ and one output, C_{t+1}. The original time series is divided into two sets, the first set is used as the training set and the second is used as the prediction set. The structure of the network is 4-10-1. The input and the output values are scaled between -0.5 and 0.5. Figure (5) shows the performance of the network in predicting the future values of the time series.

Case 2: Using the difference method (Box and Jenkins, 1976 [2]), first differences of the original time series are taken and the series is made stationary. This detrended (stationary) series is divided into two sets, training and validation sets respectively. The same kind of inputs and outputs are used as in the first case. Neural network performance on the prediction set is shown in Figure (6).

The statistical model identified for this series is an Integrated Moving Average (IMA) model of order 1.

$$x_t = x_{t-1} + \epsilon_t - (0.714)\epsilon_{t-1} \tag{7}$$

The future values are forecasted using this model and compared with the actual values in Figure (7).

The network predicts well when the series is non-stationary (Figure (5)) due to perhaps the excitation in the series. When compared to the IMA model prediction, network prediction is much better. Since the detrended data is a mixture of cyclical and random fluctuations, it appears that the network could not learn them properly (Figure (6)). However, when compared to the forecasting made by the IMA model (Figure (7)), the network prediction looks better. The IMA model could predict only one value in the future after which it becomes a constant.

TIME SERIES GENERATED BY A SAPONIFICATION BATCH REACTION

The next example used to test the performance of the feed forward neural network algorithm (Achenie, 1993 [1]) is a time series of unreacted $NaOH$ concentration collected by conducting an experimental saponification reaction. This series is divided into two sets. The first set is used to train the feed forward neural network algorithm and the second set is used for validation.

The saponification reaction (a reaction of a fatty acid with an alcohol to form an ester) that is carried out in an isothermal batch reactor is:

Isopropyl Acetate + Sodium Hydroxide $\longrightarrow$ Sodium Acetate + Isopropanol

The neural network is trained with the following kinds of training sets. Each set consists of five input elements and one output namely, t_{n-2}, t_{n-1}, t_n, y_{n-2}, and y_{n-1} where t represents the time and y represents the concentration. The output is y_n. The network structure is (5-10-1). The training file consists of 18 sets. The validation file consists of 15 sets of the same type. The performance of the algorithm in predicting the future values of the series at temperatures 3^0C and 15^0C is shown in Figures (8) and (9) respectively. The comparison is made on both the training set and the validation sets.

The statistical model identified for the series at 3^0C is an Auto Regressive (AR) model of order 3:

$$x_t - (0.3358)x_{t-1} - (0.6665)x_{t-2} - (-0.1365)x_{t-3} = 0.0013 + \epsilon_t \tag{8}$$

For the series collected at 15^0C, the statistical model identified is an Auto Regressive (AR) model of order 1:

$$x_t - (0.8824)x_{t-1} = \epsilon_t \tag{9}$$

Forecasts are made for 17 future values using the above models. The comparisons between the actual values and the forecasted values are shown in Figures (10) and (11) respectively.

In this example, once again, the network's performance in prediction competes with the statistical models predictions favorably. One of the reasons for the poor performance of the statistical model could be the small size of the series. At least 50 or preferably 100 values are needed to fit an adequate statistical ARIMA model. However, the neural network algorithm could predict well even with such a small series.

CONCLUSIONS

The feed forward network algorithm (Achenie, 1993 [1]) seems to forecast the time series used in this paper better than the traditional statistical models. It is found that the introduction of statistical features namely, standard deviation and variance in the network input sets improves the prediction. In addition, the neural network analysis shows that when short term information about the process is available to the network, the prediction is significantly better than when long term information is given. This capablity of the proposed network algorithm in predicting the time series is expected to be very useful for process design, modeling, etc.

References

[1] Achenie, L. E. K. A Quasi Newton Based Approach to the Training of the Feed Forward Neural Network. *Intelligent Engineering Systems Through Artificial Neural Networks*, 3:155–160, 1993.

[2] George E. P. Box and Gwilym M. Jenkins. *Time Series Analysis: Forecasting and Control.* Prentice Hall, 1976.

[3] Ginzberg, I. and Horn, D. Learnability of Time series. *IEEE International Joint Conference on Neural Networks*, pages 2653–2657, 1991.

[4] Lon-Mu Liu, Gregory B. Hudak. *Forecasting and Time Series Analysis using the SCA Statistical System.* Scientific Computer Associates, 1992.

[5] Rumelhart, D. E., Hinton, G. E. and Williams, R. J. Learning Representations by Back-Propagating Errors. *Nature*, 323:533–536, 1986.

[6] Timothy Masters. *Practical Neural Network Recipes in C++.* Academic Press, Inc. Harcourt Brace Jovanovich, 1993.

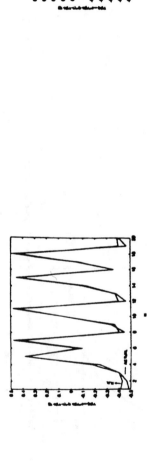

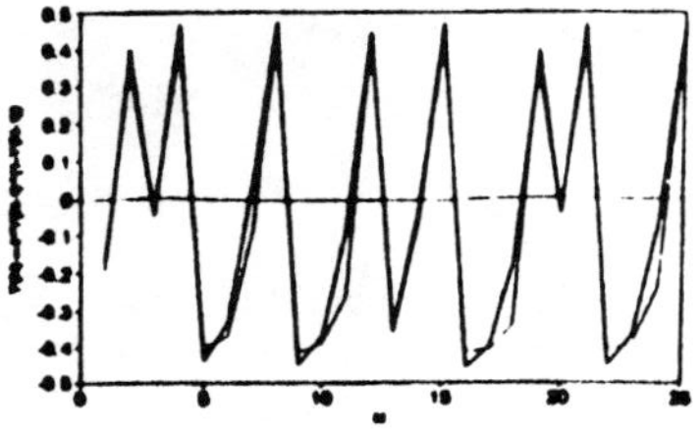

Figure 4: Comparison between N.N. (...) prediction (Case 4) and actual (-) values

Figure 1: Comparison between N.N. prediction (Case 1) and actual values

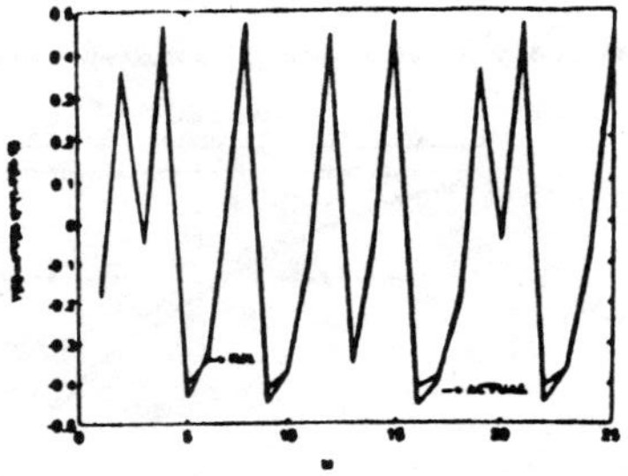

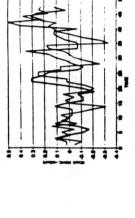

Figure 5: Comparison between N.N. (-) prediction and actual (- -) values

Figure 2: Comparison between N.N. prediction (Case 2) and actual values

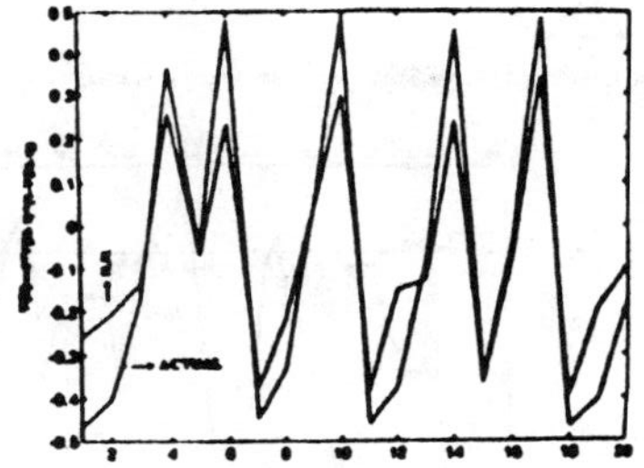

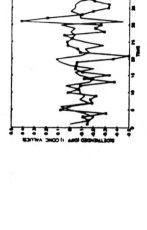

Figure 6: Comparison between N.N. (*) prediction and actual (-) values

Figure 3: Comparison between N.N. prediction (Case 3) and actual values

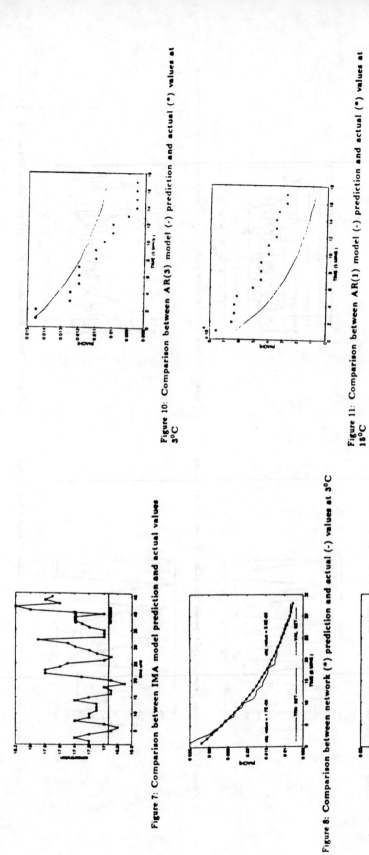

Figure 7: Comparison between IMA model prediction and actual values

Figure 8: Comparison between network (*) prediction and actual (-) values at 3°C

Figure 9: Comparison between network (*) prediction and actual (-) values at 15°C

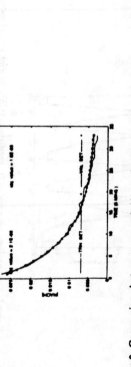

Figure 10: Comparison between AR(3) model (-) prediction and actual (*) values at 3°C

Figure 11: Comparison between AR(1) model (-) prediction and actual (*) values at 15°C

II-320

On-line Learning of a Network with Gaussian Kernel Functions

Rhee M. Kil and Jin Y. Choi
Research Department
Electronics and Telecommunications Research Institute
P.O. Box 8, Daeduk Science Town
Daejeon 305-606, KOREA

Abstract

Most learning algorithms of artificial neural networks are dealing with the efficiency for the teaching patterns only. However, when the trained network is applied to the specific task, the network performance associated with the generalization capacity including the untrained data becomes more important. From this point of view, we consider a new method of on-line learning of a network with Gaussian kernel functions. The suggested approach in this paper has two learning phases, the initial off-line learning phase for the given teaching patterns and the on-line learning phase for the incoming data. At the initial phase of learning, we estimate the necessary number of kernel functions as well as the parameters associated with kernel functions for the given teaching patterns. This process is assumed to be done by the batch process (or off-line learning). After this initial set-up of network structure, on-line learning for the incoming data is done by recruiting the necessary number of kernel functions when the incoming data need to be accommodated to maintain or improve the network performance. To show the effectiveness of our approach, simulation results for the prediction of the Mackey-Glass chaotic time series are presented.

1 Introduction

Most artificial neural networks have focused on training the parameters of a fixed network configuration such as *Multi-Layer Perceptron* (MLP) [1]. However, it may be an extremely powerful tool for constructing an optimal network, if a learning algorithm has a capability of automatically configuring a neural network, in addition to the adjustment of network parameters. Although attempts have been made to apply the idea of self-recruiting neurons to the automatic clustering of input samples [2] and to the identification of class boundaries [3], a major effort needs to be expanded to establish a learning algorithm capable of automatically configuring a network based on the self-recruitment of neurons with a proper type of activation functions. As an effort of such approach, a *Mapping Neural Network* (MNN) [4] using non-sigmoid activation functions, called the "*Potential Function Network* (PFN)" [5, 6, 7] was presented. In PFN, the emphasis is given to the synthesis of a potential field based on a new type of learning called the "*Hierarchically Self-Organizing Learning* (HSOL)" [7]. The distinctive feature of HSOL is its capability of automatically recruiting necessary number of kernel functions. In HSOL, the parameter adaptation was based on *Error-Back-Propagation* (EBP) algorithm [1]. However, EBP algorithm does not guarantee convergence and generally suffers slow learning. In this point of view, a new method of parameter estimation in which linear learning rule is applied between hidden and output layers while nonlinear (piecewise-linear) learning rule is applied between input and hidden layers, has been suggested [8]. The suggested nonparametric estimation provides an efficient way of function approximation from the view point of the number of kernel functions as well as learning speed.

The learning algorithms previewed so far are dealing with the efficiency for the teaching patterns only. However, when the trained network is applied to the specific task, the network performance associated with the generalization capacity including the untrained data becomes more important. From this point of view, on-line adaptation to maintain (or improve) the network performance can be a good strategy for the artificial neural networks. In this paper, we consider a new method of on-line learning algorithm for a network with Gaussian kernel functions. Here, the suggested approach has two learning phases, the initial off-line learning phase for the given teaching patterns and the on-line learning phase for the incoming data. At the initial phase of training this network, we estimate the necessary number of kernel functions as well as the parameters associated with

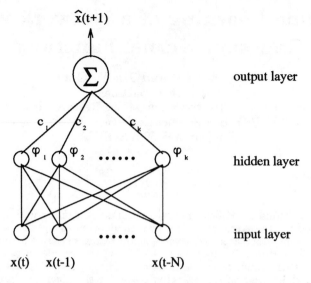

Figure 1: Nonlinear estimation network with Gaussian kernel functions.

kernel functions for the given teaching samples. This process is assumed to be done by the batch process (or off-line learning). After this initial set-up of network structure, on-line learning for the incoming data is done by recruiting the necessary number of kernel functions when the incoming data need to be accommodated to maintain or improve the network performance. To show the effectiveness of our approach, simulation results for the prediction of the Mackey-Glass chaotic time series are presented.

2 Nonlinear Estimation Network Using Gaussian Kernel Functions

The network model proposed here is composed of three types of layers: the input, hidden and output layers. The input and output layers are composed of linear units while the hidden layer is composed of Gaussian kernel functions. The weighted output values of the Gaussian kernel functions are summed by the connection between the hidden layer and the output layer in order to synthesize the desired function. Figure 1 illustrates the schematic diagram of the proposed network. In this network, learning concerns mainly about the determination of minimally necessary number of kernel functions and the estimation of parameters of a network. The strategy to decide the minimally necessary number of kernel functions is to increase the number of kernel functions incrementally whenever a new kernel function needs to be defined for the further improvement of network performance, that is, reducing the network errors for the teaching patterns. Note that, for the network producing multiple outputs, we opt for each output being generated independently by its own set of kernel functions. This makes learning simpler.

2.1 Off-line Learning Algorithm

For the proposed network, the initial off-line learning algorithm is divided into two learning processes. They are the process of recruiting the necessary number of Gaussian kernel functions and the process of parameter estimation associated with Gaussian kernel functions. Each process of learning algorithm is explained as follows:

Recruiting the necessary number of Gaussian kernel functions

The goal of this learning process is to recruit the necessary number of kernel functions. In this process, firstly, for the given input teaching pattern, the actual output of a network is generated and compared with the output teaching pattern. If the error between the actual output and the output teaching pattern is higher than the predefined error criteria, a new kernel function is recruited at the position of the input teaching pattern and the shape of kernel function is decided according to the minimum distance between the position of a newly recruited kernel function and the positions of existing kernel functions. In other words, the mean vector, $\mathbf{m}_{k+1}$ and standard deviation of Gaussian kernel function, σ_{k+1} are determined by

$$\mathbf{m}_{k+1} = \mathbf{x}_n \text{ and} \tag{1}$$

$$\sigma_{k+1} \propto \min_i \| \mathbf{x}_n - \mathbf{m}_i \|, \tag{2}$$

where $\mathbf{x}_n$ represents the training pattern where a new Gaussian kernel function is recruited. In this case, the output weights of kernel functions are adjusted in such a way that the network generates same values with the output teaching patterns at the positions of kernel functions. The estimation of output weights for the exact mapping at the positions of kernel functions is determined as follows:

Let us first define a $k \times k$ matrix, $\mathbf{\Psi}_k$ as

$$\mathbf{\Psi}_k = \begin{bmatrix} \psi_{1,1} & \psi_{1,2} & \cdots & \psi_{1,k} \\ \psi_{2,1} & \psi_{2,2} & \cdots & \psi_{2,k} \\ \vdots & \vdots & & \vdots \\ \psi_{k,1} & \psi_{k,2} & \cdots & \psi_{k,k} \end{bmatrix} \tag{3}$$

where $\psi_{i,j}$ represents the output of the jth kernel function for the ith selected input teaching pattern. That is, $\psi_{i,j} = \exp(\frac{\|\mathbf{x}_i - \mathbf{m}_j\|^2}{2\sigma_i^2})$.

Let us also define a k dimensional vector, $\mathbf{y}_k$ as $\mathbf{y}_k = [y_1, y_2, \cdots, y_k]^T$ where y_i represents the ith selected output teaching pattern. Then the output weight vector, $\mathbf{c}_k = [c_1, c_2, \cdots, c_k]^T$ where c_i represents the output weight of the ith kernel function, is given by

$$\mathbf{c}_k = \mathbf{\Psi}_k^{-1} \mathbf{y}_k \tag{4}$$

since $\mathbf{\Psi}_k \mathbf{c}_k = \mathbf{y}_k$. The $k+1$th matrix of (3) is given by

$$\mathbf{\Psi}_{k+1} = \begin{bmatrix} \mathbf{\Psi}_k & \vdots & \mathbf{u} \\ \cdots & \cdots & \cdots \\ \mathbf{v}^T & \vdots & \psi_{k+1,k+1} \end{bmatrix} \tag{5}$$

where $\mathbf{u}$ is a k dimensional vector defined by $\mathbf{u} = [\psi_{1,k+1}, \psi_{2,k+1}, \cdots, \psi_{k,k+1}]^T$ and $\mathbf{v}$ is a k dimensional vector defined by $\mathbf{v} = [\psi_{k+1,1}, \psi_{k+1,2}, \cdots, \psi_{k+1,k}]^T$.

The inverse matrix of (5) can be represented by the following form:

$$\mathbf{\Psi}_{k+1}^{-1} = \begin{bmatrix} \mathbf{A} & \vdots & \mathbf{b} \\ \cdots & \cdots & \cdots \\ \mathbf{d}^T & \vdots & c \end{bmatrix} \tag{6}$$

Using the recursive formula of inverse matrix, $\mathbf{A}$, $\mathbf{b}$, c and $\mathbf{d}$ can be derived as follows:

$$\mathbf{A} = \mathbf{\Psi}_k^{-1} + \frac{\mathbf{\Psi}_k^{-1} \mathbf{u} \mathbf{v}^T \mathbf{\Psi}_k^{-1}}{\psi_{k+1,k+1} - \mathbf{v}^T \mathbf{\Psi}_k^{-1} \mathbf{u}} \tag{7}$$

$$\mathbf{b} = -\frac{\mathbf{\Psi}_k^{-1} \mathbf{u}}{\psi_{k+1,k+1} - \mathbf{v}^T \mathbf{\Psi}_k^{-1} \mathbf{u}} \tag{8}$$

$$c = +\frac{1}{\psi_{k+1,k+1} - \mathbf{v}^T \mathbf{\Psi}_k^{-1} \mathbf{u}} \text{ and} \tag{9}$$

$$\mathbf{d} = -\frac{\mathbf{v}^T \mathbf{\Psi}_k^{-1}}{\psi_{k+1,k+1} - \mathbf{v}^T \mathbf{\Psi}_k^{-1} \mathbf{u}}. \tag{10}$$

Since
$$c_{k+1} = \Psi_{k+1}^{-1} y_{k+1}, \qquad (11)$$

$c_{k+1} = [c_k^{new}, c_{k+1}]^T$ can be determined by

$$c_k^{new} = c_k^{old} + b e_{k+1} \quad \text{and} \qquad (12)$$
$$c_{k+1} = c e_{k+1} \qquad (13)$$

where e_{k+1} represents the $k+1$th error defined by $e_{k+1} = y_{k+1} - \hat{y}_{k+1}$. Here, y_{k+1} and $\hat{y}_{k+1}$ represent the desired and actual outputs of the network for the $k+1$th teaching pattern respectively.

For the hierarchical recruitment of kernel functions, the error criteria to decide the recruitment of a new kernel function is reduced as the number of learning iterations increases.

Parameter Estimation

After recruiting the necessary number of kernel functions, the positions of kernel functions represent the reference points of the teaching patterns, i.e., the network generates the exact values at the positions of kernel functions. However, this is not so desirable from the view point of interpolation between the positions of kernel functions, and robustness to the noisy teaching patterns. In this sense, the parameters associated with kernel functions are adjusted in such a way to minimize the root mean squared error between the desired and actual outputs so as to increase generalization capability. In this learning process, the parameters of Gaussian kernel functions are adjusted based on piecewise-linear approximation of a network in the space of the parameters of kernel functions. This type of parameter estimation is considered based on the assumption that the parameters of kernel functions are near the optimal values through the recruitment of Gaussian kernel functions which gives coarse approximation of the given teaching patterns. For more detail description of parameter estimation, refer to [8].

2.2 On-line Learning Algorithm

The proposed on-line learning algorithm is composed of two processes. The first process is preparing a new Ψ_k^{-1} matrix of (6) for the calculation of output vector, c_k. This process is required since the Ψ_k matrix of (3) is changed during the process of parameter estimation in the initial off-line learning. The second process is related to the recruitment of kernel functions for the incoming data. This process is similar to the recruitment process of the initial off-line learning. In this process, an additional decision process on the recruitment in which the performances of networks with and without a newly recruited kernel function are compared for the current data (time series), is considered to avoid the overfitting problem. The on-line learning algorithm is described as follows:

Step 1 Initialization of a Ψ_k^{-1} matrix
For the mean vectors of Gaussian kernel functions, i.e., m_i *for* $i = 1, \cdots, M$, where M represents the number of kernel functions, construct a Ψ_k^{-1} matrix of (6).

Step 2 Recruitment of kernel functions
For the incoming data, apply the following procedure:

- Present a new input pattern, x_n to the network.
- Get an actual output of the network, $\hat{y}_n = \phi(x_n)$.
- Calculate an error of the network, $e_n = y_n - \hat{y}_n$.
- Check the condition of recruitment:
  If $e_n > e_c$ (*error criteria*),
  - set-up a new kernel function such that the mean vector, m_{k+1} and the standard deviation, σ_{k+1} satisfy (1) and (2) respectively.
  - adjust c_{k+1} according to (12) and (13).
  - construct $\hat{\hat{y}}$ by including a new kernel function described above.
  - compare the network performances (such as rms errors) of $\hat{y}$ and $\hat{\hat{y}}$ for the recent data.
  - if the performance of $\hat{\hat{y}}$ is bettern than that of $\hat{y}$, a new kernel function is recruited.

In this on-line learning algorithm, two strategies can be considered: one is to maintain the network performance and another is to improve the network performance. In the case of maintaining the network performance, the error criteria needs to be fixed at the desired level during on-line learning process while in the case of improving the network performance, the error criteria needs to be gradually reduced during on-line learning process. However, in the case of improving the network performance, we have to control the error criteria carefully since the rapid reduction of error criteria can cause inefficient recruitment of kernel functions.

3 Simulation

The discrete version of the *Mackey-Glass* (M-G) chaotic time-series [9] is considered for our simulation, that is,

$$x(t+1) = (1-a)x(t) + \frac{bx(t-\tau)}{1+x^{10}(t-\tau)}. \tag{14}$$

By setting $a = 0.1, b = 0.2$, and $\tau = 17$, a chaotic time series with a strange attractor is produced. For the prediction of the M-G chaotic time series, the following form of time-series is considered:

$$x(t+85) = f\Big(x(t),\ x(t-6),\ x(t-12),\ x(t-18)\Big). \tag{15}$$

Similar to the previous work [10], the suggested network were trained with the 500 training data at the initial off-line learning. The training data of M-G chaotic time series are shown in Figure 2. The prediction accuracy for the initial off-line learning is measured with the succeeding 500 data. Here, we consider the prediction accuracy as the normalized root mean squared error[1] to remove the dependency on the dynamic range of data. For the simulation of on-line learning, we consider two cases: the first and second cases are respectively intended to maintain and improve the network performance of the initially trained network during the prediction phase. For the first and second cases, the prediction accuracies after off-line learning are set as 8.94% ($\approx$ rms error of 0.02) with 103 kernel functions and 17.86% ($\approx$ rms error of 0.04) with 31 kernel functions respectively. These results show efficiency in the sense of the number of kernel functions compared to the similar method suggested by Moody and Darken [11].[2]

The error criteria for the first case is fixed at 0.02 while the error criteria for the second case is gradually reduced from 0.18 to 0.01 at the decrement rate of 0.9. For both cases, the performances of networks with and without a new kernel function are compared for the 20 recent data (time series) for the recruitment. In this on-line learning, 14000 data of M-G chaotic time series are presented to the network. The prediction accuracy of a network is measured after the presentation of every 500 data. The results of simulation for the first and second cases are shown in Figures 3 and 4 respectively.

The simulation result of the first case show us that 1) the network with on-line learning has stable level ($\approx$ 6%) and smaller variations of prediction accuracy as the number of incoming data increases as shown in data1 of Figure 3-(a) while 2) the network without on-line learning has larger variations of prediction accuracy as the number of incoming data increases as shown in data2 of Figure 3-(b). In this case, the number of recruited kernel functions increases but becomes saturated as the number of incoming data increases. The simulation result of the second case show us that 1) the prediction accuracy of a network is improved continuously as the number of recruited kernel functions increases as shown in Figure 4-(a), but 2) the increment rate of the number of recruited kernel functions increases also as shown in Figure 4-(b). Hence, in the second case, we better stop reducing the error criteria at the desired level to saturate the number of recruited kernel functions.

---

[1]The normalized root mean squared error is defined by the root mean squared error divided by the standard deviation of the given time-series, $x(\cdot)$.

[2]The prediction accuracy made by Moody and Darken's method is about 15% with 500 kernel functions.

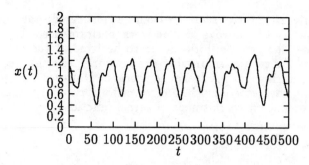

Figure 2: Mackey-Glass chaotic time series for the initial off-line training.

4 Conclusion

In this paper, we have presented a new method of on-line learning of a network with Gaussian kernel functions. The suggested approach has two learning phases, the initial off-line learning phase for the given teaching patterns and the on-line learning phase for the incoming data. At the initial phase of off-line learning, we estimate the necessary number of kernel functions as well as the parameters associated with kernel functions for the given teaching samples. After this initial set-up of network structure, on-line learning for the incoming data is done by recruiting the necessary number of kernel functions when the incoming data need to be accommodated to maintain or improve the network performance. Through simulation on the prediction of the Mackey-Glass chaotic time series, we have found that our approach is effective to maintain or improve the network performance obtained from the initial off-line learning.

References

[1] D. E. Rumelhart, G. E. Hinton, and R. J. Williams. *Parallel Distributed Processing*, volume 1, pages 318–362. MIT Press/Bradford Books, 1986.

[2] G. A. Carpenter and S. Grossberg. Art2: Stable self-organization of pattern recognition codes for analog input patterns. *Applied Optics*, 26:4919–4930, 1987.

[3] D. L. Reilly, L. N. Cooper, and C. Elbaum. A neural model for category learning. *Biological Cybernetics*, 45:35–41, 1982.

[4] R. Hecht-Nielsen. Kolmogorov mapping neural network existence theorem. *IEEE International Conference on Neural Networks*, 3:11–13, 1987.

[5] M. A. Aizerman, E. M. Braverman, and L. I. Rozonoer. Theoretical foundations of the potential function method in pattern recognition learning. *Avtomatika i Telemekhanika*, 25:917–936, 1964.

[6] S. Lee and R. M. Kil. Multilayer feedforward potential function network. *IEEE International Conference on Neural Networks*, 1:161–171, 1988.

[7] S. Lee and R. M. Kil. A gaussian potential function network with hierarchically self-organizing learning. *Neural Networks*, 4(2):207–224, 1991.

[8] R. M. Kil. Function approximation based on a network with kernel functions of bounds and locality: An approach of non-parametric estimation. *ETRI journal*, 15(2):35–51, 1993.

[9] M. Mackey and L. Glass. Oscillation and chaos in physiological control system. *Science*, pages 197–287, 1977.

[10] A. S. Lapedes and R. Farber. Nonlinear signal processing using neural networks: Prediction and system modeling. Technical Report LA-UR-87-2662, Los Alamos National Laboratory, 1987.

[11] J. Moody and C. J. Darken. Fast learning in networks of locally-tuned processing units. *Neural Computation*, 1:281–294, 1989.

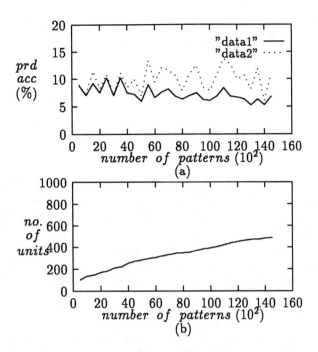

Figure 3: On-line learning to maintain the network performance: (a) represents the prediction accuracy versus the number of teaching patterns presented to the network. Here, data1 and data2 represent the curves of prediction accuracies with and without on-line learning respectively. (b) represents the number of recruited kernel functions versus the number of patterns.

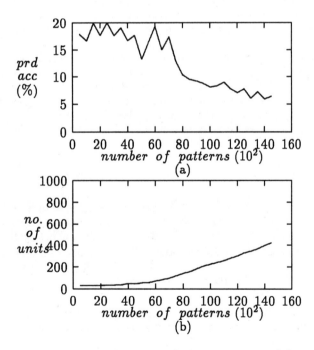

Figure 4: On-line learning to improve the network performance: (a) represents the prediction accuracy versus the number of teaching patterns presented to the network. (b) represents the number of recruited kernel functions versus the number of patterns.

Predicting Prediction: Error Bounds for Feedforward Neural Networks

Stephen Welstead
COLSA Corporation
6726 Odyssey Drive
Huntsville, AL 35801

Abstract

This paper derives an error bound for the output from a three layer feedforward neural network operating on test data from outside of the training set. Three factors influence the size of this bound: accuracy of the neural network model on the training data, distance of the test point from the training set, and *volatility* of the process being modeled and the network model. Volatility is defined as a bound for the derivatives of both the process and the network model. Process derivatives can be estimated from the training data. An example using training and test data generated by the chaotic Henon mapping shows that this error bound can follow actual errors quite closely. For applications such as time series prediction, such an error bound can provide some credibility in advance for the output of a neural network predictor.

1. Introduction

The modeling capabilities of feedforward networks, also known as "backpropagation" networks, are well known. Hornik et al. [Hornik 89] established that three layer feedforward networks are universal approximators. Thus, given a set of training points produced by a well defined deterministic process, we can be reasonably assured of fitting a feedforward network to these points with a high degree of accuracy. Most applications, however, are concerned with the performance of these networks on points not in the training set. For data representing time series, this process is called prediction, or forecasting. Other applications use the term generalization to refer to the ability of a network to fit points outside of the training set. In either case, it would be useful to know in advance how credible the network output is on these points from outside of the training set. Such knowledge would be useful, for example, in financial applications, where networks are trained to provide a look ahead to future market conditions.

The purpose of the present paper is to provide error bounds for the output of feedforward networks operating on test data. This paper is organized into several sections. Section 2 establishes an error bound for general approximation functions. Section 3 derives the particular form of this bound in the case when the approximating function is a three layer feedforward network. In section 4, we will look at a numerical example using data generated by the chaotic Henon mapping. We'll not only see that the expression developed in sections 3 and 4 bounds the error on the test data, but also that this bound is actually quite sharp.

2. Approximation Error

Suppose we wish to approximate a function $f:\mathbf{R}^n \to \mathbf{R}$. For simplicity of notation, we will assume that f is defined on $\mathbf{R}^2$, so that the function expression has the form $f(x,y) = z$. The extension of the results to higher dimensions is straightforward. We assume further that f is defined and has continuous first partial derivatives on a compact convex subset C in $\mathbf{R}^2$. Denote by $T \subset C$ the finite set of training data:

$$T = \{(x_1,y_1), \ldots , (x_N,y_N)\}.$$

Suppose that we have a function $F:\mathbf{R}^2 \to \mathbf{R}$, defined on C, that approximates f at the points of T. F may be a feedforward network, or it may be some other form of approximation, such as a fuzzy system, or a polynomial. Let $\varepsilon > 0$ denote the error bound on T, that is,

$$|F(x_j,y_j) - f(x_j,y_j)| < \varepsilon, \quad j = 1, \ldots , N. \tag{2.1}$$

We assume that F has continuous first partial derivatives on C (this condition is satisfied if F is a feedforward network with a differentiable activation function).

Now consider an arbitrary test point $(x,y) \in C$ (this point may be in T; the more interesting case is when (x,y) is not in T). We wish to establish a bound for $|F(x,y) - f(x,y)|$. Let $(x_j, y_j) \in T$. Then

$$|F(x,y) - f(x,y)| \leq |F(x,y) - F(x_j,y)| + |F(x_j,y) - f(x_j,y)| + |f(x_j,y) - f(x,y)|. \quad (2.2)$$

Also,

$$|F(x,y) - F(x_j,y)| \leq \left| \frac{\partial F}{\partial x}(x',y) \right| |x - x_j|$$

for some x', lying between x and x_j, by the Mean Value Theorem. The convexity of C assures that $(x',y) \in C$. Similarly,

$$|f(x,y) - f(x_j,y)| \leq \left| \frac{\partial f}{\partial x}(x'',y) \right| |x - x_j|$$

for some (different) x'' also lying between x and x_j.

Since $\partial F/\partial x$ and $\partial f/\partial x$ are continuous on C, they are bounded on this compact set. We can rewrite (2.2) as

$$|F(x,y) - f(x,y)| \leq \max\{M_{f,x}, M_{f,x}\} |x - x_j| + |F(x_j,y) - f(x_j,y)| \quad (2.3)$$

where

$$\left| \frac{\partial F}{\partial x}(x,y) \right| \leq M_{F,x}$$

and

$$\left| \frac{\partial f}{\partial x}(x,y) \right| \leq M_{f,x}$$

for (x,y) in C.

The second term in (2.3) can be treated similarly:

$$|F(x_j,y) - f(x_j,y)| \leq |F(x_j,y) - F(x_j,y_j)| + |F(x_j,y_j) - f(x_j,y_j)| + |f(x_j,y_j) - f(x_j,y)|$$

$$\leq \max\{M_{F,y}, M_{f,y}\} |y - y_j| + |F(x_j,y_j) - f(x_j,y_j)|.$$

Here,

$$\left| \frac{\partial F}{\partial y}(x,y) \right| \leq M_{F,y}$$

and

$$\left| \frac{\partial f}{\partial y}(x,y) \right| \leq M_{f,y}$$

for (x,y) in C.

We have thus established the following bound for the error:

$$|F(x,y) - f(x,y)| \leq \min_{(x_j,y_j) \in T} \{ M_x |x - x_j| + M_y |y - y_j| + |F(x_j,y_j) - f(x_j,y_j)| \} \quad (2.4)$$

where

$$M_x = \max \{M_{F,x}, M_{f,x}\}$$

and

$$M_y = \max \{M_{F,y}, M_{f,y}\}.$$

The training error tolerance ε dominates the third term of the expression inside the brackets on the right side of (2.4). As such, this training error tolerance is seen to have only a moderate influence on the total error bound (2.4) (unless, of course, $(x,y) \in T$, in which case the right side of (2.4) reduces to just this single term). Obviously, we want to make this term as small as possible. However, the error can still be quite large even when this term is small. Much more influential are the factors M_x and M_y which we'll call the *volatility factors*. These factors are bounds for the derivatives of f and F. High volatility from either f or F will contribute to large values for M_x and M_y. A highly volatile process f is, not surprisingly, likely to produce large test errors. The system designer cannot control the volatility of f, although it is possible that judicious preprocessing of the data may lessen this effect. Volatility in the model F can contribute to the overall error if this volatility exceeds that of f, and so the system designer should take care not to introduce undue volatility into the model.

Finally, it should be noted that the volatility factors multiply the terms $|x - x_j|$ and $|y - y_j|$ which represent the distance from the test point (x,y) to the training set T. The volatility effect can be mitigated by making these terms small. This can be accomplished by choosing a large training set which covers as much as of the input space as possible.

3. Derivative Bounds for Feedforward Networks

To compute a form of the bound (2.4) in the case when F is a feedforward network, we need to derive expressions for $\partial F / \partial x$ and $\partial F / \partial y$. We assume F is a three layer feedforward network with a single input threshold node and sigmoidal activation function, as shown in Figure 3.1 (according to Hornik et al. [Hornik 89] three layers suffice to provide these networks with universal approximation capability).

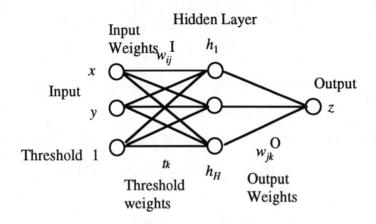

Figure 3.1 Three layer feedforward network.

Thus,

$$z = F(x,y) = \sigma(w_1^O h_1(x,y) + \ldots + w_H^O h_H(x,y))$$

and

$$h_k(x,y) = \sigma(xw_{x,k}^I + yw_{y,k}^I + t_k)$$

where

$$\sigma(x) = \frac{1}{1 + e^{-x}}$$

is the sigmoidal activation function. Using the fact that

$$\sigma'(x) = \sigma(x)(1 - \sigma(x))$$

and setting

$$\alpha = w_1^O h_1(x,y) + \ldots + w_H^O h_H(x,y)$$

we get

$$\left| \frac{\partial F}{\partial x} \right| = \left| \sigma(\alpha)(1 - \sigma(\alpha)) \right| \left| \sum_{k=1}^{H} w_k^O \frac{\partial h_k}{\partial x} \right| \tag{3.1}$$

Note that while $|\sigma(\alpha)|$ and $|1 - \sigma(\alpha)|$ are each bounded by 1, the product $|\sigma(\alpha)(1 - \sigma(\alpha))|$ is actually bounded by 1/4, since that is the maximum value of the function $x(1 - x)$. Thus, (3.1) can be rewritten as

$$\left| \frac{\partial F}{\partial x} \right| \leq \frac{1}{4} \sum_{k=1}^{H} \left| w_k^O \right| \left| \frac{\partial h_k}{\partial x} \right|. \tag{3.2}$$

Similarly,

$$\left| \frac{\partial h_k}{\partial x} \right| = \left| \sigma(\beta)\sigma(1 - \sigma(\beta)) \, w_{x,k}^I \right| \leq \frac{1}{4} \left| w_{x,k}^I \right|$$

where

$$\beta = x \, w_{x,k}^I + y \, w_{y,k}^I + t_k.$$

So (3.2) can be rewritten as

$$\left| \frac{\partial F}{\partial x} \right| \leq \frac{1}{16} \sum_{k=1}^{H} \left| w_k^O \right| \left| w_{x,k}^I \right|. \tag{3.3}$$

Similarly,

$$\left| \frac{\partial F}{\partial y} \right| \leq \frac{1}{16} \sum_{k=1}^{H} \left| w_k^O \right| \left| w_{y,k}^I \right|. \tag{3.4}$$

Note that (3.3) - (3.4) do not depend on the values of x and y, so these are actually global bounds. These bounds contribute to the volatility factors M_x and M_y in the error bound (2.4). Note that the number of hidden nodes H determines the number of terms in (3.3) - (3.4) and so may influence the size of these bounds, and hence the volatility of the network function.

4. An Example: Prediction Error Bounds for the Chaotic Henon Mapping

In practical applications, the usefulness of an error bound is determined by how close the bound fits actual error. A bound that cries "wolf" by consistently overestimating by too much loses its credibility. In this section we'll compute the error bound for a three layer feedforward network trained on data generated by the Henon mapping:

$$f(x,y) = (f_1(x,y), f_2(x,y)), \tag{4.1}$$

where

$$f_1(x,y) = 1 + y - ax^2, \tag{4.2}$$

$$f_2(x,y) = bx.$$

It is well known that many values of the parameters a and b produce chaotic mappings [Welstead 89]. In particular, iteration of the mapping f with parameter values $a = 1.4$, $b = 0.3$ leads to the familiar butterfly shaped strange attractor studied by Henon [Henon 76]. This is the mapping that was used to generate training and test data for the neural network. Starting with the point $(x_1,y_1) = (0,0)$, the point (x_n,y_n), $n > 1$, is generated from:

$$(x_n, y_n) = f(x_{n-1}, y_{n-1}).$$

The first one hundred points generated in this way were used for training, and the next one hundred points were reserved as test points. The network architecture consisted of two hidden layer nodes, with one input threshold node, as shown in Figure 3.1, and two output nodes. The first network output node value is compared with the first output component of the mapping (4.1) for the purpose of computing errors and error bounds. We are not particularly interested here in how well the network models the training data. It is known that this type of network can actually reproduce the strange attractor associated with (4.1) given enough training [Welstead 91]. Rather, we are interested in seeing how the error bound (2.4) compares with the actual error. With this in mind, the network was partially trained, using the 100 training points, so that the error bound could be observed for both large and small errors.

Normalization Issues

In any feedforward network application, training data must be normalized before it is presented to the network. This normalization affects the values of the derivatives used in determining the bound (2.4). For this example, input data values presented to the network are normalized to the range [-5,5], and output data values are normalized to the range [0.05,0.95]. The error bound can be computed either in the original data "X-Y space", in which case the network function derivatives must be adjusted to reflect normalization, or it may be computed in the normalized "network space", in which case normalization changes the value of the original function derivatives. For this example, we'll look at the error and error bound in "network space". Expressions for the derivatives $\partial f_1/\partial x$, $\partial f_1/\partial y$ can easily be derived from the expression (4.2), and maximum values for these expressions over the training data set can be computed. Normalization introduces a linear factor of the form

$$(r_F/R_F)(R_f/r_f)$$

where r_F and r_f are output value ranges for the network and the function, respectively, and R_F and R_f are the corresponding input value ranges.

Volatility Factors

Table 4.1 shows the maximum x and y derivative values computed for the network and the function. These are the values $M_{F,x}$, $M_{F,y}$, $M_{f,x}$, and $M_{f,y}$ of Section 2, with normalization effects taken into account as discussed above. The final line of Table 4.1 shows the volatility factors M_x and M_y. Note that the function derivative contributes to one factor, while the network approximation contributes to the other.

Table 4.1 Derivative bounds and volatility factors
for this example.

	$\partial/\partial x$	$\partial/\partial y$
Network F	0.1042	0.0560
Function f_1	0.3334	0.0285
Max Volatility	0.3354	0.0560

Although here we are using the actual function expression to determine the derivative values in the second line of Table 4.1, in practice this function expression is usually not available. In this case, these derivative values must be estimated by looking at differences computed from the data.

Experimental Results

Figure 4.1 shows a plot of the errors and corresponding error bounds for the 100 test points. The scale for the errors and bounds appears on the left side of this plot. Notice that the error bound, while always greater than the error, follows the actual error quite closely. The magnitude of the difference between the error bound and the error is shown at the bottom of this plot, with a separate scale that is displayed on the right side of the plot. Note that the difference is quite small at times, indicating the bound is fairly sharp. The difference is typically an order of magnitude less than the error bound itself, indicating that the bound supplies useful information about the size of the error.

5. Conclusions

We have derived a bound for the error of a feedforward network operating on test data. Experimental results show that the error bound closely follows actual error values. The error bound provides credibility for the output of a network operating on data not seen during training. This is useful in applications involving prediction, particularly when decisions are based on the output of the network. The system designer may also be able to influence some control over the size of the error bound by reducing volatility in the network approximation, for example by using a minimum number of hidden layer nodes, and also possibly using preprocessing to reduce the volatility of the process being modeled.

References

[Hornik 89] Hornik, K., Stinchcombe, M., and White, H., "Multilayer Feedforward Networks are Universal Approximators", *Neural Networks*, 2, (1989): 359–366.

[Henon 76] Henon, M., "A Two-Dimensional Mapping with a Strange Attractor", *Comm. Math. Phys.* 50, (1976): 69–77.

[Welstead 89] Welstead, S., and Cromer, T., "Coloring Periodicities of Two-Dimensional Mappings", *Computers and Graphics* 13, no. 4 (1989): 539–543.

[Welstead 91] Welstead, S., "Multilayer Feedforward Networks can Learn Strange Attractors", *Proceedings of IJCNN-91-Seattle*, Vol. II, (1991): 139–144.

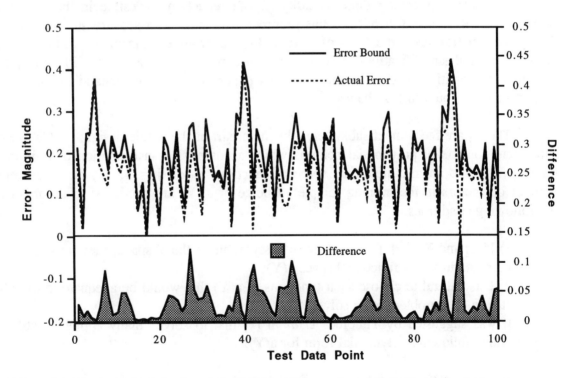

Figure 4.1 The upper graph (scale on left side) shows the error bound (solid line) and actual error (dashed line) for the 100 test points. The lower graph (scale on right side) shows the difference between the error bound and the actual error.

A Threshold Polynomial Neural Network

Danil V. Prokhorov and Donald C. Wunsch II
Texas Tech University
Department of Electrical Engineering
Lubbock, TX 79409-3102

Abstract

Threshold polynomial neural networks offer fast learning of nonlinear mappings. It achieves this by dedicating hidden layer nodes to training patterns and using a polynomial learning algorithm. This paper outlines the architecture and main features of a threshold polynomial network. The functioning of the network and results of simulation are described.

Design

We have m input patterns from p classes to be recognized. We begin by transforming the m input patterns X_j into m vectors $Y_j = \{y_1, y_2, ..., y_n\}_i$. (All Y_j are n-dimensional; the X_j are permitted greater dimensionality if data reduction is desired in the preprocessing step.). We will henceforth refer to this preprocessing stage as a sensory subsystem. (Fig.1.) The transformation takes the form of thresholding, contrast enhancement, scaling, sampling, or other desired simplifications. These topics are well known and we will simply assume binary transformation in the remainder of this paper, with the understanding that the other transformations could instead be used.

The Y_j are fed to next subsystem, the main part of the whole design. This associative subsystem consists of polynomial neurons which accomplish transformation of n-dimensional binary space into an m-dimensional space of functions $a_j(Y)$ (j = 1, ..., m; where m is the number of vectors in the training sample). Choice of $a_j(Y)$ are produced in accordance with the following conditions:

1) If X_i and X_j (i ≠ j) are not linearly separable in the Y space, they must be separated by a hyperplane in a new functional space a(Y);

2) It is natural to choose such functions of a(Y) that would be adequate to the physical representation of a problem to be solved.

It was suggested by Timofeev *et al* in [1] that to solve many applied problems one should utilize following polynomial form for a(Y):

$$a_k(Y_j) = a(Y_j, Y_k) = (y_j^1{}^\wedge y_k^1)\ \&\ (y_j^2{}^\wedge y_k^2)\ \&\ ...\ \&\ (y_j^n{}^\wedge y_k^n),\ k = 1, ..., m, (1),$$

where y_j^1 is the first component of Y_j,

 & is the operation of logical conjunction,

 $^\wedge$ is an operation determined as follows: $0^\wedge 0 = 1, 0^\wedge 1 = 0, 1^\wedge 0 = 1, 1^\wedge 1 = 1$.

The polynomial neurons described by (1) above were used to make up the associative subsystem.

The final part of the network is the decision-making subsystem. Output neurons located there have adjustable weights and a hard-limiting nonlinearity. Each output neuron computes the following function:

$$S_i(Y,u) = F[u_i^1 * a_1(Y) + u_i^2 * a_2(Y) + \ldots + u_i^m * a_m(Y)], \quad i = 1, \ldots, p, \quad (2),$$

where u_i^j is the adjustable weight of the i-th neuron and

$$F[z] = +1, \text{ if } z > 0, \text{ OR } -1, \text{ if } z \leqslant 0.$$

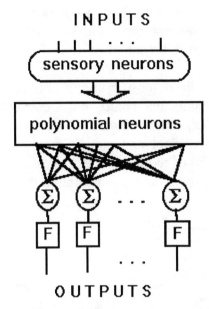

Fig. 1. The threshold-polynomial neural network.

Training and testing

There are two modes of functioning of the network: training and testing.

The threshold polynomial training algorithm converges in one iteration to exactly identify the training set. This is similar to Probabilistic Neural Networks [2] and in marked contrast to backpropagation and various other models [3]. This similarity is not surprizing, since Probabilistic Neural Networks also use one hidden node for each pattern in the training set.

While training, the system arranges the samples in sequence of norm increase (i.e., number of non-zero components in the Y vector). Such ordering gives a possibility to use the following training recursive procedure:

$$u_i^1 = D_i(Y_1), \qquad i = 1, \ldots, p, \; j = 2, \ldots, m, \qquad (3)$$
$$u_i^j = 0, \qquad \text{if } B = D_i(Y_j) * [u_i^1 * a_j(Y_1) + u_i^2 * a_j(Y_2) + \ldots + u_i^{j-1} * a_j(Y_{j-1})] > 0,$$

OR

$$u_i^j = D_i(Y_j) - [u_i^1*a_j(Y_1) + u_i^2*a_j(Y_2) + \ldots + u_i^{j-1}*a_j(Y_{j-1})], \qquad \text{if } B \leqslant 0.$$

The goal of training is to teach all output neurons to adjust actual outputs $S_i(Y,u)$ as close as possible to the desired ones $D_i(Y)$ for every pattern Y in the training sample.

The procedure (3) is straightforward and allows weight computation directly (in a single run). Furthermore, the training algorithm (3) provides a minimum number of non-zero integer-valued weights in (2). After completion of the training process every i-th neuron is active only when the object is from i-th class. Instead of using a separate output neuron for each of the p classes to indicate result of recognition, one may use simple binary coding of output neurons. This allows classification with only $Log_2(p)$ output neurons.

Testing is similiar to training except for weight adjustment. The object to be recognized is applied to the inputs and then some output neurons fire indicating the result.

Fig. 2 shows an example of the fixed (post-training) architecture. It may be easily implemented in an inexpensive reprogrammable board, on a custom-made chip connected through a parallel interface to a computer, or in software. The main parts of this board are AND circuits, summing operational amplifiers and weight memory cells. The cells are simplified due to the integer-valued nature of the weights to be stored. After training, weight values are fed to the board and perform proper circuit switching in the board.

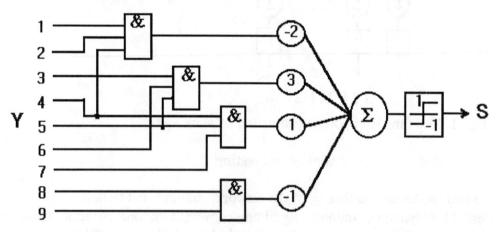

Fig. 2. An example of the fixed network architecture.

Simulation results

The performance of the threshold-polynomial neural net and backpropagation were compared on a benchmark problem given in [4]. The task was to investigate the generalization capability of the nets in problem of reproducing of the following nonlinear function:

$$F = (2/5)*\sin(2*pi*Z) + 1/2, \qquad Z = i/M, \qquad i = 0,\ldots,M, \qquad (4).$$

It was decided to use binary input and output encoding. The piecewise-constant approximation was performed for the function (4), followed by transformation of its values in an integer format. Finally, the ranges of integer-valued Y(Z) and D(F) were from 0 to 127 and from 10 to 89 respectively. The training sample consisted of 64 even pairs (Y,D). The rest (other 64 odd pairs) made up the testing sample.

The threshold-polynomial net showed errorless recognition of the training sample and sum of squares of the errors E = 0.0127 while recognizing the testing set. Backpropagation may be taught to reproduce the nonlinear signal with better precision. However, it takes much more time for training. The training time of the threshold polynomial net was less than ten seconds whereas teaching of the backpropagation net required nearly one hour at the same PC to obtain the equal level of error on the testing sample.

Conclusion

We describe a threshold polynomial neural network architecture. This network is useful in circumstances requiring rapid learning of approximate categories. Future work includes comparison with other models, especially the Probabilistic Neural Networks, which share certain similarities.

References

1   A.V.Timofeev and V.Kh.Pshibikhov, "Algorithms of training and providing minimum complexity for polynomial recognition system", The USSR Science Academy News (Technical Cybernetics), 5, 1974, pp. 214-217 (in Russian).

2.   D.F.Specht, "Probabilistic Neural Networks and the Polynomial   Adaline   as Complementary Techniques   for Classification," *IEEE Trans. Neural Networks*, vol.1, pp. 111-121, Mar.1990

3.   R.P.Lippmann, "An introduction to computing with neural nets", IEEE ASSP Mag., 4, April 1987, pp. 4-22.

4.   S.Nagata, M.Sekiguchi, and K.Asakawa, "Mobile robot control by a structured hierarchical neural network", IEEE Control Systems Magazine, 4, April 1990, pp. 69-76.

LINKING OF AN ARTIFICIAL NEURAL NETWORK WITH THE EEIE EXPERT SYSTEM TO IDENTIFY ENVIRONMENTAL IMPACTS.

Alejandro Pazos. Ph. D. MD.   email: ciapazos@udc.es

Antonino Santos del Riego. Post-graduate student.   email: ciminino@udc.es

Julián Dorado. Post-graduate student.   email: cijulian@udc.es

Laboratory for Biomedical Applications of Artificial Intelligence.

Department of Computer Science. Faculty of Informatic. University of La Coruña. 15071 La Coruña. SPAIN.

ABSTRACT: The reluctance to fully comprehend environmental damage is maintained due to the lack of complete information and admitting that the contingencies that lead to these environmental changes may never be fully known. One way of obtaining conclusions from incomplete information is to identify the environmental rules and the general models. In this paper we describe an Artificial Neural Network (ANN) for the identification of environmental impacts. The ANN inputs have been codificated providing them a format for a better convergence. The results of this identification will be consistent with the Leopold and Battelle methods [1] for the Evaluation of Environmental Impacts (EEI). The impacts identified by the ANN will be incorporated into the group of hypotheses that the expert system EEIE [2] will work with to evaluate these impacts.

INTRODUCTION

The construction of a system to evaluate the environmental impacts produced by the integration of infrastructure and management projects with the environment is hindered by the following two problems:

1.- The amplitude of this domain, due to the large quantity of Environmental Factors (EF) and actions associated with the distinct projects in different environments. The solution to this problem consists of handling the formulated information in a relational data base used by the ANN integrated with the EEIE expert system.

2.- The variability of knowledge in EEI. The appearance of new environmental legislation, as well as the creation of new manufacturing technologies, cleansing, etc, makes precise knowledge in a given moment very subject to changes. The EEIE expert systems structure, organized in four abstraction levels, will allow the easy incorporation of new knowledge into the abstraction level affected, making the rest of the system independent of these changes.

The cases treated by this system are stored in a log file. Then the ANN will be trained with this log file to recognize the hypotheses suggested by the expert system in previous sessions and thus increase its confidence. It will also learn the group of hypotheses that EEIE expert system could not infer by itself but were confirmed by the user.

EEIE expert system solves the problems that were carried forward by the Leopold method:

(a). Non-selectivity: That is, it establishes a line of work without identifying either the impacts or their relationships. The solution to this problem is identifying the main impacts and focusing their objectives.

(b). Non-systematic: This is solved by characterizing the projects impacts in relation to the project, the actions, the EF, expert knowledge and the previous EEI.

EEIE expert system has three knowledge bases. The first characterizes the projects and subprojects that are to be evaluated. The second suggests the posible actions that cause the impact starting out from the subprojects and the actions already established. The third suggests hypotheses of the cause-effect type linking actions from the projects with EF to identify the posible impacts. These links evaluate the effect over the EF starting from the direct measures taken from the environment and suggesting corrective actions that can modify the previous reasoning. The use of this ANN allows the establishment of a more exhaustive group of impacts and adjusts its level of confidence.

THE NEURAL NETWORK MODEL

Due to the problems already mentioned an ANN allows us to recognize standards amongst the great amount of information handled in the EEI facing up to the lack of selectivity in the EEI methods [3].

With this in mind an ANN has been trained in a supervised manner using as input data the projects grouped together by industrial sectors, the principal actions that have caused the impact of these projects, organized by fases, and general characteristics of the environment affected. The ANN output provides an identifying map of posible impacts of the input actions over the EF group and its confidence (see Figure 1). The projects must be evaluated according to the legislation of the European Economic Community (EEC) [4].

In this sense the ANN has a double function, on the one hand, as an identifier and, on the other, as evaluator.

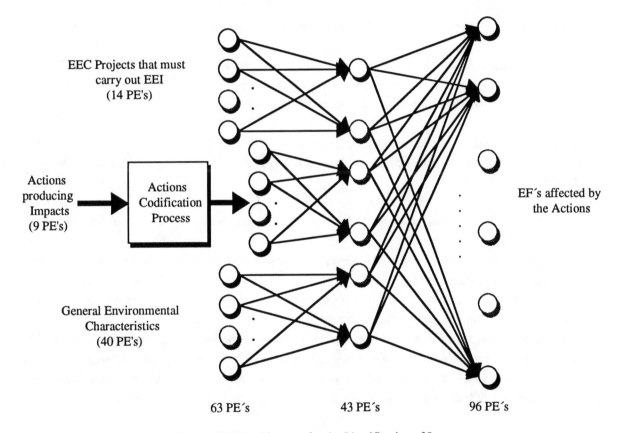

Fig 1.- ANN Architecture for the Identification of Impacts.

Specifically, the objective of the ANN in the system consists in the cuantification of the confidence associated with the identification of each impact. The input into the ANN is divided in three large groups:

II-339

1.- Separate the projects that grouped together by industrial sectors have to carry out EEI according to EEC legislation. The following have been considered:

- Chemical industry (manufacture and treatment of)
    * Sulphuric Acid.
    * Ammonia.
    * Titanium Dioxide.
    * Chlorine, Fluor.
    * Pesticides.
    * Paint, ink, glue and related products.
    * Ethylene, propylene and benzene.
- Paper and wood industry.
    * Cardboard and wood paste plants.
    * Celulose.

- Transport.
    * Airports.
    * Roads.
    * Railway lines.
    * Reservoirs and dams.
    * Electricity lines.

For its representation 14 process elements (PE) have been used with values of (0 or 1).

2.- Actions produced by the introduction of the projects being evaluated. 9 PE have been used to represent 500 actions. Each action is codified with a binary number of 9 bits. This allows a sufficiently low number of input PE. This solution can be adopted as the processing is carried out in one action in each operation of the ANN.

With the aim of facilitating the learning process, a study of hierarchical clustering [5] has been carried out with the aim of grouping together those actions that produce impacts belonging to a similar group. For this the following steps are followed:

(a). Construct a simetrical action*action matrix and represent in each element of the matrix the number of impacts that differentiate the actions involved.

(b). Iteratively, the matrix element with the lowest value is chosen and the actions that form its files and columns are grouped together. Immediately after this the matrix is rebuilt and the new distances are calculated. In this manner the distance between a group and an action is given by the arithmetic mean between the elements of the new group and the rest of the actions, building a hierarchy included in a sole group.

(c). Finally, the actions are codified with 9 bits. To do this in the first place we arrange the actions in a consecutive manner in the order obtained in the hierarchical clustering tree. In second place we assign to each binary codes in such a way that between the codes that correspond to one action and those that correspond to its immediate neighbours we always have a distance of Hamming 1, that is to say, their codes vary in only one bit (See table 1).

3.- Characteristics of the environment affected. It uses 40 PE to represent the most representative characteristics. These characteristics are contained in the following groups:

- Air.   - Water.   - Earth.
- Vegetation.   - Fauna.   - Man.
- Processes from the biotic medium.   - Perception medium.

The inputs of each PE are values of (0 or 1) indicating the absence or presence of these characteristics in the environment under evaluation. The layer of outputs from the ANN is made up of 96 PE representing the 96 EF's taken into account. Each one of these output PE's cuantifies the confidence that the ANN has in considering that the EF in question will be affected by the input action.

These values range from (0 to 1). For the hidden layer 43 PE's have been used as this has been the number of PE's that have best adjusted themselves to the learning process through trial and error techniques.

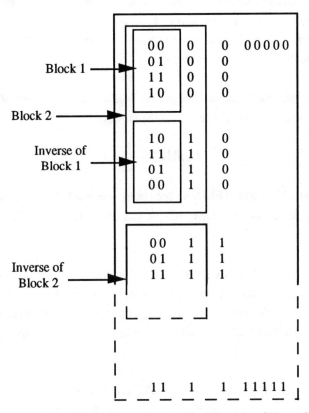

Table 1.- Codification of Actions with a Distance of Hamming 1.

THE FUNCTIONAL CHARACTER OF THE ANN

Its functional character in the complete system lies in its obtaining of confidence values for the group of impacts produced by the input action. These actions are supplied by a presession with the EEIE expert system, which establishes the group of posible actions that can cause impacts for each project under evaluation. The outputs of ANN obtained for each action are used by EEIE, establishing the final group of impact hypotheses for their evaluation starting from a symbolic perspective.

THE ANN'S ARCHITECTURE

The ANN is of the feed-forward type with a back-propagation learning algorithm. The interconnection of the PE's in the three layers is complete. For the learning process the Delta Generalized Rule [6] has been used. The learning coefficient has been established taking into account the classification in clusters of the ANN's inputs [7] (Formula 1).

$$\eta = \frac{1{,}5}{\sqrt{\sum\limits_{1}^{m} n_i^2}}$$

η – learning coefficient
m - number of clusters
n_i - number of actions in the cluster i

Formula 1.- Calculation of the learning coefficient

A value of m = 9 has been established based on experience, as once this number of clusters has been reached they are sufficiently homogeneous. To realize the division in clusters we take as our starting point the root node of the hierarchical tree, taking the two branches as two clusters. From here onwards, and until we reach a total of 9 clusters, the cluster with greatest distance is chosen and is divided in its two clusters.

The sigmoidal transference function has been used due to its suitability for the handling of data with values from (0 to 1), which allow the establishment of confidence levels for the impacts.

RESULTS

For the training of the ANN some 13 studies of EEI have been used, which entails 2403 training cases, due to the fact that each action in an EEI is represented independently from the network, of these some 200 cases have been reserved for the process of network testing.

Once the training process was finished, the ANN added some 13% additional impacts to those that had been detected by the EEIE. Furthermore the great majority of these impacts suggested by the expert system were also suggested by the ANN, increasing in this way its confidence level. The technical parameters of the training can be summarized in: 143000 cycles until a convergence has been achieved with an error level of 0,09. To obtain the convergence a time of 23 minutes was used on a PC-486.

DISCUSSION AND FUTURE WORKS

The ANN presented in this paper deals successfully with the task of identifying the environmental impacts produced by the actions of certain projects. The inherent complexity of this domain has been reduced both in the input and output of the ANN. Initially consideration was given to taking as the input layer all the actions under evaluation and as an output layer the cross matrix formed by Actions-EF. This solution was abandoned due to the huge size of the resulting ANN and above all due to the difficulty in making it converge. Finally the already mentioned solution was opted for and the actions were codified according to their similarities. This codification allows us, on the one hand, to simplify the input, and on the other, provide a format for a better convergence.

In this sense, another possibility has been explored, the use of positional codification, in other words, good results have been obtained using inputs that concentrate the activations of the input layer in one zone for inputs with similar outputs. For example, to obtain the output of two logical functions, these are ordered by similarity (in clusters) and then the following positional codification is used (see Table 2.).

The connectionist approach used in this work, is used for the identification of impacts that are to be evaluated later on through a symbolic approximation. The possibility is therefore left open of training an ANN that will provide as an output an evaluation of each impact for the group of input actions, that is to say, identify it and cuantify it.

In the present system, it is posible to evaluate 14 different types of projects, of the 70 or so that are contemplated in EEC legislation. Actually work is being carried out on the eliciting of knowledge and the collecting together of data to include new types of projects.

$$F1 = (X1 \lor X2) \land X3$$
$$F2 = (X1 \land X2) \lor X3$$

Positional Codification	X1 X2 X3	F1 F2
1 0 0 0 0	0 0 0	0 0
1 1 0 0 0	0 1 0	0 0
1 1 1 0 0	1 0 0	0 0
0 1 1 0 0	0 0 1	0 1
0 0 1 0 0	1 1 0	0 1
0 0 1 1 0	0 1 1	1 1
0 0 1 1 1	1 0 1	1 1
0 0 0 1 1	1 1 1	1 1

Table 2.- Example of positional codification

In summary, this work furnishes new advances, both in EEI, making it more exhaustive and increasing its precision, and in the field of the ANN's, establishing new codifications of the entry data which make the convergence process easier.

REFERENCES

[1]. D. Gómez Orea. "Evaluación de Impacto Ambiental". Ed. Agrícola Española, S.A., 1992. (in Spanish)

[2]. A. Pazos, A. Santos, A. Rivas, V. Maojo & J. Segovia. "EEIE: An Expert System for Environmental Impact Evaluation". Proc. IEEE Eng. Med. Biol. Soc., Vol 2, pp 632-633, 1993.

[3]. J Ríos, A. Pazos, N.R. Brisaboa, S. Caridad. "Estructura, dinámica y aplicaciones de las Redes de Neuronas Artificiales". Ed. Centro de Estudios Ramón Areces, 1991. (in Spanish)

[4]. Salvador González Fernández. "Legislación Ambiental I". Compilaciones, 1989. (in Spanish)

[5]. Domenico Ferrari, Giuseppe Lerazzi, Alessandro Zeigner. "Measurement and Tuning of Computer Systems". Ed. Prentice-Hall, pp 82-90, 1972.

[6]. M. Nelson and W.T. Illingworth. "A practical guide to neural nets". Addison-Wesley Publish. CO., 1992.

[7]. Harry A.C. Eaton & Tracy L. Olivier. "Learning Cofficient Dependence on Training Set Size". Neural Networks, Vol 5, nº 2, Pergamon Press, pp 283-288, 1992.

An Artificial Neural Network Customer Forecasting Model

Mark Cullen, Kh.Eghtesadi and Dai Vu
Advanced Concepts & Technology
Pitney Bowes
35 Waterview Dr, Shelton, CT 06484
USA

1. Abstract

Attributes of more than 7,000 customers of a product for shipping packages were analyzed to develop an automated system for predicting new customers. Critical parameters associated with these customers were identified by principal component analysis. Based upon these parameters and inter-relationships between them, a prediction model was developed to prioritize customer lists for the sales force in the field. An Artificial Neural Network (ANN) was developed to learn and characterize the non-linear model with an output that reflects the likelihood of a product sale in a percentile form. The ANN model was integrated in a user-friendly software package that will be used by the sales force to rank potential new customers. The software was completed and delivered for pilot testing.

2. Introduction

Today's sales and marketing groups have available to them a massive amount of data about both their markets and customers. Without appropriate analysis, however, this data rarely becomes useful information. The more extensive the collected data, the more difficult it can be to process and transform it into usable information about individual prospects and customers. Even if the data processing system is quite sophisticated, at some point its limitations exceed the potential capabilities of traditional modeling techniques. Advanced data processing systems for forecasting and optimization are mathematical and computational challenges. Numerically intensive computing is coming nowadays to the aid in many fields of sales and market forecasting. Advanced modeling, forecasting and decision support systems will become more critical tools in finding the best solutions to sales and marketing problems.

One class of non-linear modeling is Artificial Neural Networks [1]. In its simplified form, an ANN with no hidden layers and linear transfer function approximates the linear regression model common in statistical approaches [2] to target marketing applications. With more processing layers and non-linear transfer function, the ANN can solve a broad range of problems. It has been shown that multilayer feedforward neural networks perform as a class of universal approximators [3]. This means that the ANN can be used to discover functional relationships between input and output parameters. They may apply effectively to database analysis, to model customer characteristics. For problems where the data is clean and the relationships are straight forward and linear, a statistical model will usually provide predictive capabilities. However, such problems are rarely encountered. In a majority of cases, the data is noisy and the relationships have an unknown degree of non-linearity. This can be particularly true of database marketing problems. Under these circumstances, ANN have the advantage of being able to model the relationships and produce reliable predictions.

The objective of this effort was to develop a method for target marketing that can be used to predict the potential sales of products to new customers. Specifically:
1) Develop a method to prioritize a list of new potential customers of a product, based upon features derived from the existing customer database.
2) Develop an ANN model to learn the important feature relationships, and incorporate this model into a software system for use in the field.

3. Data Analysis and Preprocessing
To develop a prediction model for identifying new shipping product customers, attributes of more than 7,000 current customers were analyzed. Customer profile parameters were retrieved from the Dun & Bradstreet database. Distribution of these parameters and their inter-relationships were plotted and analyzed. Based upon this analysis four parameters were identified as primary contributors: *sales, number of employees, company age and employee growth*. Principal component analysis [4] was applied to these variables to determine which have special properties in terms of variances. The analysis transforms the original set of variables into a smaller set of linear combinations that account for most of the variance of the original set. The purpose was to determine factors that contribute to the total variation in the data with as few of these factors as possible. The parameters that were identified by the principal component analysis were normalized to have a gaussian distribution. From the original four parameters, three of them were identified (*sales, number of employees, and company age*) as the principal contributors. To test the relevance of other parameters for classifying or segmenting the customer data, the database was divided into several classes such as: subsidiaries vs. non-subsidiaries, single-buyer vs. multiple-buyers, manufacturing vs. non-manufacturing, and coastal vs. non-coastal business locations. Examining the distributions of *sales, employees, and company age* for each of the aforementioned classes showed that there was no real significance in any of these customer segmentation classes, so these additional parameters were not used. Analysis of the distribution of the three selected variables (*sales, number of employees, and company age*) indicated that they were all skewed to the left in histogram distribution graphs. A common method to cope with this non-normalcy is to apply a non-linear function to the data. The non-linear function simply transforms the original data and uses this output as the new input of the model. Two statistical techniques were used to determine how well the non-linear transfer function normalized the data: the skewness coefficient which measures the distribution symmetry, and the kurtosis coefficient, which measures the "fatness" of the tails and bells of the distribution. Values of -0.5 to 0.5 for the skewness coefficient and -1 to 1 for the kurtosis coefficient were considered

characteristic of normal distributions. Based upon these two tests, the natural logarithm, ln(x), was determined to create the best distribution, as it was the only function to have both skewness and kurtosis values within the desired range for all three variables.

By combining these three parameters a model was developed with an output that reflects the likelihood of a sale, in a percentile form.. From the three selected parameters, a three dimensional surface was generated and a *"Focus Region"* was created (Figure.1) as the "best customer profile". The focus region is defined in terms of the value of the standard deviation a given company's performance is from the mean of each individual parameter. Table I shows the distribution of the focus region and the values of the associated customer focus rating parameter.

Standard Deviation (σ)	Rating Assignment
≤ 0.5	0.9
≤ 1	0.7
≤ 1.5	0.5
> 1.5	0.3

Table I: Focus Rating (FR) Assignments

For the sales data, a 0.9 *focus rating* was assigned if the company's sales parameter was 0.5 standard deviation from the mean; a 0.7 *focus rating* if the parameter was 1.0 standard deviation from the mean; 0.5 *focus rating* if 1.5 standard deviations from the mean, and 0.3 *focus rating* if more than 1.5 standard deviations from the mean. The same process was repeated for both the number of employees data and the company age data.

The three coordinate values of this surface were combined into a function to create a combined Focus Rating parameter as:

$$FR = f(x_1, x_2, x_3)$$

where x_1, x_2, x_3 represents the *sales focus rating*, the number of *employee focus rating* and the *company age focus rating*, respectively.

4. Artificial Neural Network (ANN) Modeling

A three-layer neural network architecture was constructed with three input units, 24 hidden units and one output unit. The three inputs to the neural network model consist of a customer's yearly sales volume, the number of employees, and the number of years the customer has been in business. The output or desired value of the artificial neural network is the focus rating number. The customer database contains 7320 companies with complete information for these selected input and output variables. From this database, 6106 records were selected at random to form a training file, and the remaining 1214 records were collected to form a test file. Figure 2 illustrates the topology of the ANN architecture designed for this application.

5. Results of Training and Testing the ANN Model

The ANN architecture shown in Figure 2 was trained with the training file of 6101 records, using the backpropagation learning algorithm to modify weights in the network. Weight connections between units in the neural network were initialized at random to values between +/- 0.1. The learning parameter was selected to be 0.4 and the momentum parameter was 0.15. Error values at the output of the network were accumulated for 100 presentations of the input data before updating the weighted connections in the network. Input data records were selected at random from the training file, and training continued for 10,000 iterations. The RMS error measured 0.11 following the end of the training cycle.

The ANN was then tested with the test database. An example of the prediction capability of the neural network can be seen in Table II for twenty five records from the test database. In a majority of the cases, the ANN closely predicts the target value expected given the three input variables. For the full test file of 1214 records, the RMS error was calculated to be 0.12. The result for the entire test database is shown graphically in Figure 3. The predicted focus rating output by the neural network clusters well about the target or actual value shown as the heavyset line in the graph. A few results show more than 15% deviations from the target value but overall the results are close to the target value.

6. Conclusion

An ANN model was developed to learn the important features of an existing customer product database. The model may be used by sales force in the field to prioritize potential new customer lists for more effective target marketing. Future applications of ANN in marketing may include analysis of existing product marketing approaches and how to structure new sales and marketing programs to different market segments.

7. References

1. Zurada, J.M., "Introduction to Neural Systems", West Publishing Company, 1992.
2. Hecht-Nielsen, R, "Kolmogorov's Mapping Neural Network Existance Theorem", Proceeding of the International Conference on Neural Networks, Vol III, IEEE Press, 1987, 11-30
3. Hornik, K., Stinchcombe, M., and White, H., "Multilayer Feedforward Networks Are Universal Approximators", Neural Networks 2, 1989, 359-366.
4. Anderson, T.W., "An Introduction to Multivariate Statistical Analysis", John Wiley&Son, 1984.

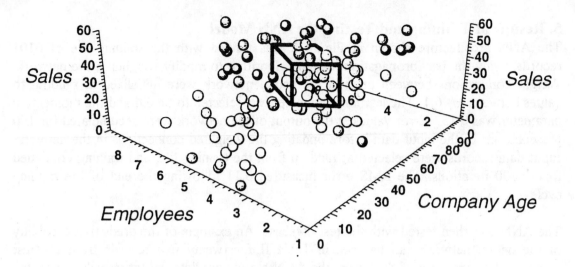

Figure 1: Customer Focus Region Function Diagram

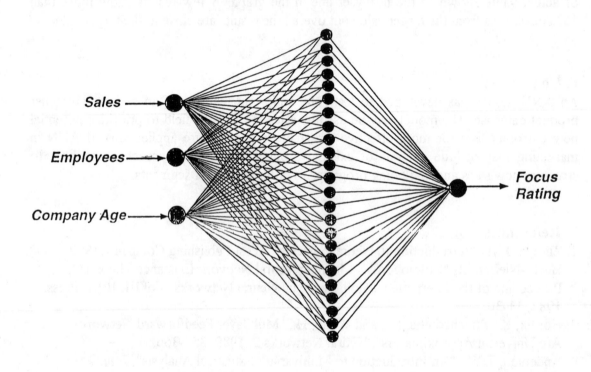

Figure 2: Architecture of Artificial Neural Network

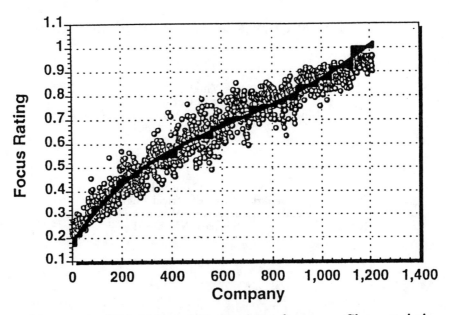

Figure 3: Artificial Neural Network Performance Characteristics
(o - ANN Output, —Target Output)

Customer	X1	X2	X3	Actual Target	ANN Output
1	15.8	4.6	2.5	0.84	0.88
2	15.9	5	3.6	0.71	0.68
3	14.5	2.7	3.3	0.76	0.79
4	17.5	5.4	3.6	0.62	0.59
5	14.4	4.4	3.7	0.62	0.63
6	15.4	3.5	3.1	1	0.97
7	16.3	2.6	3.	0.84	0.93
8	23	5.6	4.7	0.21	0.5
9	17.5	6.1	3.3	0.71	0.64
10	15.8	3.9	3.5	0.86	0.92
11	21.2	2.7	4.2	0.36	0.32
12	16.2	3.6	3.5	0.86	0.94
13	16.8	4.9	3.2	0.84	0.87
14	17.7	6.3	1.9	0.48	0.3
15	19.1	5.1	1.9	0.44	0.3
16	21.4	5.1	3.1	0.5	0.51
17	14.9	3.4	1.6	0.68	0.67
18	16	4.2	2.8	1	0.96
19	14.6	2.5	3	0.76	0.81
20	16.3	3.5	3	1	0.99
21	19.3	2	4.1	0.44	0.24
22	14	3	2.4	0.78	0.77
23	15	3	2.5	0.92	0.91
24	14	2.3	3.3	0.76	0.63
25	13.2	2.4	1.6	0.45	0.28

Table II: Sample test data showing input data, focus rating parameters,
and a focus rating output from the trained ANN output

Fuzzy Curves and System Identification

Yinghua Lin
Department of Computer Science
New Mexico Institute of Mining and Technology
Socorro, NM 87801

George A. Cunningham, III
Department of Electrical Engineering
New Mexico Institute of Mining and Technology
Socorro, NM 87801

Abstract

We introduce "fuzzy curves" and use them to identify significant input variables. Our method is computationally simple and identifies significant input variables easily in complex problems.

1 Introduction

A multilayered neural network can approximate any continuous function on a compact set [4], [6], [9], and a fuzzy system can do this same approximation [8], [13]. Several authors have used neural networks to implement fuzzy models [1], [5], [7] [12]. However, no matter what the modeling approach, the first step is to identify the important input variables for the system.

Sugeno and Yasukawa [10] propose a fuzzy approach to model a system from input-output data. They identify the significant input variables by checking the performance index (e.g. average square error). First, they build a one input fuzzy system for every input candidate, and the input of the fuzzy system corresponding to the lowest performance index is chosen as one significant input. Taking this significant input and every remaining input candidate, they build a set of two input fuzzy systems. The two inputs corresponding to the fuzzy system that gives best performance measure are considered as two important inputs. They keep adding one more input variable until the performance index cannot be improved. For N input candidates the maximum input variable sets to be tested for input variable identification is $\frac{N(N+1)}{2}$.

Takagi and Hayashi [11] propose a neural network driven fuzzy reasoning system to analyze the input-output data. They identify the input variables by eliminating each input variable and checking the performance index. If the performance index is better when one input variable is removed from the system, then that input variable is not significant. They have the same $\frac{N(N+1)}{2}$ problem as in [10].

For a system with hundreds, or thousands, of input candidates N, building $\frac{N(N+1)}{2}$ fuzzy or neural network systems is not practical. To solve this problem, we introduced fuzzy curves. Using the fuzzy curves, we identify the input variables before modeling the system. The time complexity of our method is linear with respect to the number of input candidates.

The paper's second section introduces fuzzy curves and describes how we identify the input variables. The third and fourth sections show examples to demonstrate our model.

No.	x_1	x_2	x_3	y	No.	x_1	x_2	x_3	y
1	14.9	2.0	9.3	3.8	11	6.9	2.3	10.3	3.3
2	16.6	1.7	5.8	3.7	12	7.4	1.9	9.4	2.8
3	21.3	2.1	9.1	3.0	13	11.3	2.0	8.4	3.0
4	24.3	2.9	7.0	4.7	14	17.6	2.0	8.2	2.7
5	26.6	1.7	4.8	4.1	15	19.5	2.4	6.5	3.3
6	23.2	1.3	4.7	3.1	16	21.6	2.5	5.1	4.9
7	22.2	2.5	4.5	3.1	17	26.5	1.9	6.3	4.8
8	18.1	2.5	5.9	2.5	18	26.4	2.2	8.1	4.4
9	13.7	2.8	7.9	3.3	19	23.1	3.8	4.9	2.2
10	7.7	2.6	9.3	2.3	20	21.1	2.5	5.1	1.8

Table 1: Data points used in An Introduction to Fuzzy Curves.

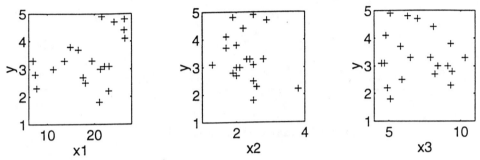

Figure 1: The data points plotted in in x_1–y, x_2–y, and x_3–y spaces.

2 An Introduction to Fuzzy Curves

We consider a multiple-input, single-output system. We wish to find a relationship between each of the input variables and the output variable that we can use to determine the significant inputs. We call the input candidates $x_i\,(i = 1, 2, \ldots, n)$, and the output variable y. Assume that we have m training data points available and that $x_{ik}\,(k = 1, 2, \ldots, m)$ are the ith coordinates of each of the m training points. Table 1 shows an example with $n = 3$ and $m = 20$.

For each input variable x_i, we plot the m data points in x_i–y space. Figure 1 illustrates the data points from Table 1 in the x_1–y, x_2–y, and x_3–y spaces. For every point in x_i–y space, we draw a fuzzy membership function defined by

$$\mu_{ik}(x_i) = \exp\left(-\left(\frac{x_{ik} - x_i}{b}\right)^2\right) \tag{1}$$

We typically take b as about 10% of the length of the input interval of x_i. Figure 2 shows the fuzzy membership functions for the points in Figure 1. In Figure 2, the point where $\mu_{ik} = 1$ coincides with x_{ik}.

We use centroid defuzzification to produce a fuzzy curve c_i for each input variable x_i by

$$c_i = \frac{\sum_k^m \mu_{ik}(x_i) \cdot y_k}{\sum_k^m \mu_{ik}(x_i)} \tag{2}$$

Figure 3 shows the fuzzy curves c_1, c_2, and c_3 for the data in Table 1. If the fuzzy curve for given input is

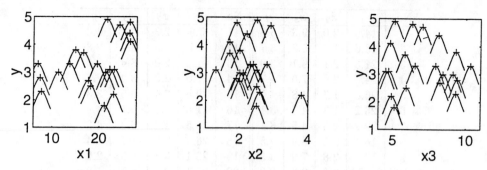

Figure 2: Fuzzy membership functions in x_1–y, x_2–y, and x_3–y spaces.

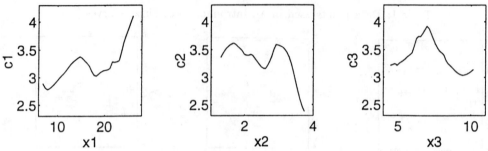

Figure 3: Fuzzy curves c_1, c_2, and c_3.

flat, then this input has little influence in the output data and it is not a significant input. If the range of a fuzzy curve c_i is about the range of the output data y, then the input candidate x_i is important to the output variable. We rank the importance of the input variables x_i according to the range covered by their fuzzy curves c_i. The ranges of fuzzy curves in Figure 3 are 1.32 for c_1, 1.24 for c_2, and 0.89 for c_3. Hence, we deduce that x_1 is most significant input, x_2 is second, and x_3 is third.

3   A Simple Example

We use a nonlinear system with two inputs, x_1 and x_2, and a single output, y, defined by

$$y = \left(1 + x_1^{1.5} - 5\cos(2x_2)\right)^2, \qquad 0 \leq x_1, x_2 \leq 3. \tag{3}$$

We randomly take 100 points from $0 \leq x_1, x_2, x_3, x_4, x_5 \leq 3$. x_1 and x_2 are used by Equation 3 to obtain 100 input-output data, and $x_3, x_4,$ and x_5 are dummy inputs used to illustrate input variable identification.

To identify the significant input variables, we draw the five fuzzy curves $c_1, c_2, c_3, c_4,$ and c_5 for the five input candidates $x_1, x_2, x_3, x_4,$ and x_5. The five fuzzy curves are shown in Figure 4. From Figure 4 we find that the ranges of c_i, for c_1 to c_5, are 43.5, 48.3, 11.7, 14.3, and 11.4, respectively. From this, we easily and correctly identify x_1 and x_2 as the significant input variables for the system.

To test if our model can identify significant inputs for data with noise, we add 10% random noise to x_1, x_2, and y after using Equation 3 to obtain data. The ranges of fuzzy curves (from c_1 to c_5) are 45.9, 55.7, 21.2, 23.8, and 14.0, respectively. So our model can identify input variables within noise.

To test if our model can identify two incorporated variables, we change Equation 3 to

$$y = \left(1 + x_1^{1.5} - 5\cos(2\sqrt{x_2 x_3})\right)^2, \qquad 0 \leq x_1, x_2, x_3 \leq 3 \tag{4}$$

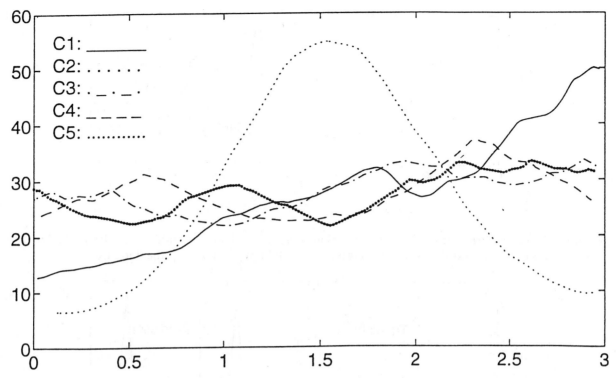

Figure 4: The fuzzy curves for the non-linear system $y = \left(1 + x_1^{1.5} - 5\cos(2x_2)\right)^2$.

and

$$y = \left(1 + (x_1 x_4)^{0.75} - 5\cos(2\sqrt{x_2 x_3})\right)^2, \qquad 0 \le x_1, x_2, x_3, x_4 \le 3 \tag{5}$$

Using the same way as we do for Equation 3, we obtain 100 data from Equations 4 and 5 respectively. The ranges of fuzzy curves(from c_1 to c_5) for Equation 4 are 40.8, 34.6, 30.4, 15.7, and 18.4, respectively, and the ranges of fuzzy curves for Equation 5 are 27.9, 33.3, 32.5, 27.1, and 17.6, respectively. From these ranges of fuzzy curves we find that in both cases, our model identifies the significant inputs successfully.

4 More Examples

We also tested our model with real world problems. The data of Box and Jenkins gas furnace is taken from [2]. The process is a gas furnace with a single input (gas flow rate) $u(t)$ and a single output (CO_2 concentration) $y(t)$. As in [10], we consider the variables $y(t-1), \ldots, y(t-4), u(t-1), \ldots, u(t-6)$ as input candidates. We determine that the significant inputs, listed in order of importance, are $u(t-5), y(t-1), u(t-6), u(t-3),$ and $y(t-2)$. Using these five inputs, we build a four-rule fuzzy-neural system. We use the first 250 data points as the training data and predict the last 40 points. The results are shown in Figure 5.

The example of the Chemical Oxygen Demand in Osaka Bay is originally in [3]. There are 5 input variables: temperature, transparency, oxygen density, salt density, and filtered COD density. There are 45 data points. We find that the salt density variable is not important. We build a four-rule fuzzy-neural system with four inputs. As [11] and [3], we use the first 33 points as training data and check the results with the later 12 points. Our results are shown in Figure 6.

The data on daily stock prices is from [10] for stock A. It has ten input variables $x_1, \ldots, x_{10}$ and 100 data points. We eliminated the variables $x_1, x_6, x_7,$ and x_9. We build a five-rule fuzzy-neural system with six inputs. The first 80 data points are used to build the system and the later 20 points are used to check the model. The results are shown in Figure 7.

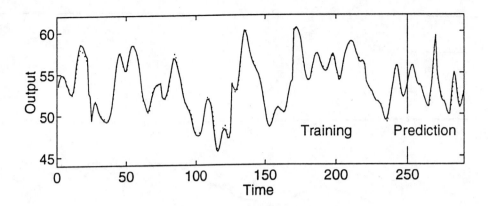

Figure 5: Model performance on the Box and Jenkins gas furnace data. We build the model on the first 250 points and predict the next 40. Actual is shown by the solid line —, model by the dotted line · · ·.

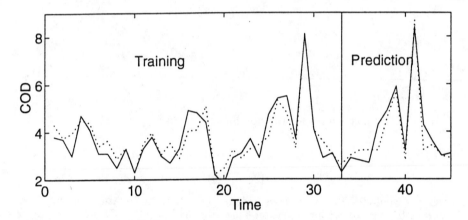

Figure 6: Model performance on the Osaka Bay data. We build the model on the first 33 points and predict the next 12. Actual is shown by the solid line —, model by the dotted line · · ·.

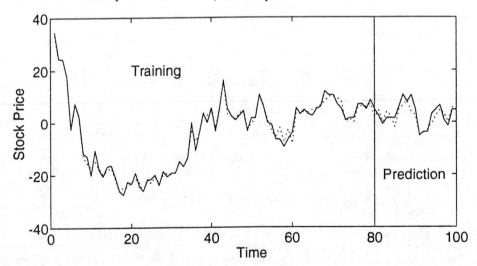

Figure 7: Model performance on the stock price data. We build the model on the first 80 points and predict the next 20. Actual is shown by the solid line —, model by the dotted line · · ·.

5 Conclusions

We introduce the concept of a fuzzy curve and use it to identify the input variables. The time complexity of our model to identify input variables is linear with respect to the number of input candidates. We test our model with several examples and our method quickly and easily identifies the significant input variables.

References

[1] H. R. Berenji and P. Khedkar, "Learning and Tuning Fuzzy Logic Controllers Through Reinforcement," *IEEE Trans. Neural Networks*, vol. 3, no. 5, 1992, p. 724–740,

[2] G. E. P. Box and G. M. Jenkins, *Time Series Analysis, Forecasting and Control*. San Francisco: Holden Day, 1970.

[3] S. Fujita and H. Koi, Application of GMDH to Environmental System Modeling and Management, in *Self-Organizing Methods in Modeling: GMDH Type Algorithms*, (S.J. Farlow, Ed.), Statistics Textbooks Monographs Ser., Vol. 54, Marcel Dekker, New York, 1984, p. 257-275.

[4] K. Funahashi, "On the Approximate Realization of Continuous Mappings by Neural Networks," *Neural Networks*, vol. 2, 1989, p. 183.

[5] S. Horikawa, T. Furuhashi, and Y. Uchikawa, "On Fuzzy Modeling Using Fuzzy Neural Networks with the Back-Propagation Algorithm," *IEEE Trans. Neural Networks*, vol. 3, no. 5, 1992, 801–814.

[6] K. Hornik, M. Stinchcombe, and H. White, "Multilayer Feedforward Networks are Universal Approximators," *Neural Networks*, vol. 2, 1989, 359–366.

[7] J. R. Jang, "Self-Learning Fuzzy Controllers Based on Temporal Back Propagation," *IEEE Trans. Neural Networks*, vol. 3, no. 5, 1992, 714–723.

[8] B. Kosko, "Fuzzy Systems as Universal Approximators." *Proc. 1992 IEEE Int. Conf. on Fuzzy Systems*, San Diego, March 1992, 1153-62.

[9] T. Poggio and F. Girosi, "Networks for Approximation and Learning," *Proc. IEEE*, vol. 78, no. 9, Sept. 1990, 1481-1497.

[10] M. Sugeno and T. Yasukawa, "A Fuzzy-Logic-Based Approach to Qualitative Modeling," *IEEE Trans. Fuzzy Systems*, vol. 1, no. 1, 1993, 7-31.

[11] H. Takagi, I. Hayashi, "NN-Driven Fuzzy Reasoning," *Int'l. J. Approximate Reasoning*, vol. 5, no. 3, 1991, 191-212.

[12] H. Takagi et al., "Neural Networks Designed on Approximate Reasoning Architecture and Their Applications," *IEEE Trans. on Neural Networks*, vol. 3, no. 5, September 1992, 752-760.

[13] L. X. Wang and J. M. Mendel, "On Fuzzy Basis Functions, Universal Approximation, and Orthogonal Least-Squares Learning," *IEEE Trans. on Neural Networks*, vol. 3, no. 5, 807-14, September 1992.

Mathematical Foundations

Session Chairs: Shun-ichi Amari
Daniel Levine

ORAL PRESENTATIONS

Manifolds of Neural Networks and the EM Algorithms

Shun-ichi Amari

Department of Mathematical Engineering and Information Physics

Faculty of Engineering, University of Tokyo

Bunkyo-ku, Tokyo 113, JAPAN

Abstract

In order to realize an input-output relation given by noise-contaminated input-output data, it ie effective to use a stochastic neural network. Such a network includes hidden units whose activation values are not specified nor observed. It is useful to estimate the hidden variables from the observed or specified input-output data. Two algorithms, the *EM*- and *em*-algorithms, have so far been proposed for this purpose. The *EM*-algorithm is an interative statistical technique of using the conditional expectation, and the *em*-algorithm is a geometrical one given by information geometry. The *em*-algorithm iteratively minimizes the Kullback-Leibler divergence in the manifold of neural networks. These two algorithms are equivalent in most cases. The present paper gives a unified information geometrical framework for studying stochastic neural networks, in particular the *EM* and *em* algorithms, showing a condition which gurantees their equivalence. Examples include 1) Boltzmann machines with hidden units, 2) mixtures of experts, 3) stochastic multilayer perceptron, 4) normal mixture model, and others.

The full text of the present paper will appear in *Neural Networks* under the title "Information geometry of the EM and em Algorithms for Neural Networks".

Amari, S. (1985) *Differential Geometrical Methods in Statistics*, Springer Lecture Note in Statistics, 28.

Amari, S. (1991) Dualistic Geometry of the Manifold of Higher-Order Neurons, *Neural Networks*, **4**, pp.443–451.

Amari, S., Kurata, K. and Nagaoka, H. (1992) Information Geometry of Boltzmann Machines, *IEEE Trans. Neural Networks*, **Vol. 3**, No.2, pp.260–271.

Byrne, W. (1992) Alternating Minimization and Boltzmann Machine Learning, *IEEE Trans. Neural Networks*, **3**, pp612–620.

Jordan, M. I. and Jacobs, R. A. (1993) Higherarchical Mixtures of Experts and the *EM*-Algorithm, *Neural Computation*, to appear.

Jacobs, R. A., Jordan, M. I., Nolwan, S. J. and Hinton, G. E. (1991) Adaptive Mixtures of Local Experts, *Neural Computation*, **3**, pp.79–87.

Neal, R. N. and Hinton, G. E. (1993) A New of the EM Algorithm that Justifies Incremental and Other Variants, to appear.

Analysis of the ARTMAP Neural Network Architecture

Michael Georgiopoulos*, Juxin Huang*, Gregory L. Heileman**

Department of Electrical and Computer Engineering
University of Central Florida, Orlando, FL 32816*

Department of Electrical and Computer Engineering
University of New Mexico, Albuquerque, NM 87131**

Abstract

In this paper we analyze the ARTMAP architecture for situations requiring learning of many-to-one maps. Our point of focus is the number of list presentations required by ARTMAP to learn an arbitrary many-to-one map. In particular, it is shown that if ARTMAP is repeatedly presented with a list of input/output pairs, it establishes the required mapping in at most $M_a - 1$ list presentations, where M_a corresponds to the total number of ones in each one of the input patterns. Other useful properties, associated with the learning of the mapping represented by an arbitrary list of input/output pairs, are also examined. These properties reveal some of the characteristics of learning in ARTMAP when it is used as a tool in establishing an arbitrary mapping from a binary input space to a binary output space. The results presented in this paper are valid for the fast learning case, and for small β_a values, where β_a is a parameter associated with the adaptation of bottom-up weights in one of the ART1 modules of ARTMAP.

1 Introduction

A neural network architecture that can be used to learn arbitrary mappings from a binary input space of any dimensionality to a binary output space of any dimensionality was derived by Carpenter et al. ([1]). This architecture was termed ARTMAP in reference to the adaptive resonance theory introduced by Grossberg ([2]). ARTMAP can only learn mappings of arbitrary binary inputs to arbitrary binary outputs.

In this paper we focus on a fast learning ARTMAP architecture, which is specifically designed to establish many-to-one mappings, where many inputs from the input space are mapped to a single output in the output space. This type of mapping is of primary interest in pattern recognition applications. From this point on, when we refer to the word "mapping" we will always imply a "many-to-one" mapping.

One of the contributions of this paper is the derivation of an upper bound for the number of list presentations required by ARTMAP to establish an arbitrary mapping between the inputs and outputs of a list of input/output pairs that is repeatedly presented to ARTMAP. Other useful properties of learning in ARTMAP induced by its internal dynamics are also described. These properties reveal some of the characteristics of ARTMAP as it is trained to learn arbitrary mappings from a binary input space to a binary output space.

2 The ARTMAP Architecture

The ARTMAP neural network architecture is described in detail by Carpenter et al ([1]). In this section we only provide information that is necessary to understand the results developed here. Furthermore, to facilitate the reader we abide by the notational conventions used in [1]. The ARTMAP neural network consists of two ART1 modules designated as ART_a and ART_b, as well as an inter-ART module as shown in Figure 1. Inputs are presented at the ART_a module, while outputs are presented at the ART_b module. The inter-ART module includes a MAP field, whose purpose is to determine whether the mapping between the presented inputs and outputs is the desired one. If $a = (a_1, \ldots, a_{M_a})$ denotes a binary vector, the input to the ART_a module is the binary vector

$$I = (a, a^c) = (a_1, \ldots, a_{M_a}, a_1^c, \ldots, a_{M_a}^c) \tag{1}$$

where

$$a_i^c = 1 - a_i \quad 1 \leq i \leq M_a \tag{2}$$

This type of transformation, called *complement coding*, is necessary for the successful operation of ARTMAP (for more details see [1] page 584). A field of nodes designated as F_0^a receives the input vector a and produces the input I for the ART$_a$ architecture. Hence, F_0^a acts as a preprocessor to the ART$_a$ module. The binary input vector I is subsequently applied at the F_1 field of ART$_a$, designated as F_1^a. No such transformation (i.e., complement coding) is necessary for the output O which is directly applied at the F_1 field of ART$_b$, denoted as F_1^b. Field F_1^a has $2M_a$ nodes, field F_1^b has M_b nodes, the F_2 field of ART$_a$ (F_2^a) has N_a nodes, the F_2 field of ART$_b$ (F_2^b) has N_b nodes, and finally the MAP field F_{ab} has N_b nodes. Fields F_2^a and F_2^b are the fields where compressed representations of the input patterns (the I's) and the output patterns (the O's) are established, respectively.

We use the index i to designate nodes in the F_1^a field, the index j to designate nodes in the F_2^a field, the index k to designate nodes in the MAP field and the F_2^b field, and the index l to designate nodes in the F_1^b field. Hence, $Z_j^a = (Z_{1j}^a, \ldots, Z_{(2M_a)j}^a)$ is the vector of bottom-up weights converging to node j in F_2^a, $z_j^a = (z_{j1}^a, \ldots, z_{j(2M_a)}^a)$ is the vector of top-down weights emanating from node j in F_2^a, $Z_k^b = (Z_{1k}^b, \ldots, Z_{M_b k}^b)$ is the vector of bottom-up weights converging to node k in F_2^b, $z_k^b = (z_{k1}^b, \ldots, z_{k M_b}^b)$ is the vector of top-down weights emanating from node k in F_2^b, and finally $w_j = (w_{j1}, \ldots, w_{jN_b})$ is the vector of weights emanating from node j in F_2^a and converging to the nodes of the MAP field F_{ab}.

For the properties of learning that we intend to develop it is important to understand the role played by the top-down weights emanating from nodes in the F_2^a field. A vector whose components are the top-down weights emanating from a single node in F_2^a is called a template of the ART$_a$ module. Consider now an input I presented to the ART$_a$ module and an arbitrary template of the ART$_a$ module, designated as z^a. A component of an input pattern I is indexed by i if it affects node i in the F_1^a field. Similarly a component of a template z^a is indexed by i if it corresponds to the weight converging to node i in the F_1^a field. Now that we have assigned indices to the components of I and z^a, we can clearly define the set of indices for which the corresponding I or z^a components are one. Based on this definition we can identify two types of learned templates with respect to an input pattern I: *subset templates*, and *mixed templates*. A template z^a is a subset of pattern I if the set of indices for which the z^a components are equal to one is either a subset of, or equal to the set of indices for which the I components are equal to one. A template z^a is a mixed template of pattern I if the set of indices for which the z^a components are equal to one is neither a subset, nor a superset of the set of indices for which the I components are equal to one. Besides the templates defined above, we also define an *uncommitted template* to be the vector of top-down weights associated with a node in F_2^a which has not yet been chosen to represent an input pattern. Each of the components of an uncommitted template is equal to one. With reference to an input pattern I, we also designate nodes in F_2^a as subset, mixed or uncommitted depending on whether their corresponding template is a subset, mixed or uncommitted template with respect to the input pattern I.

We now consider how the ARTMAP architecture is trained to map an input pattern I to an output pattern O. Let us present input pattern I at the F_1^a field, and assume that node J in F_2^a is chosen to represent the input pattern I. Furthermore, suppose that $w_{Jk} = 1$ for $1 \leq k \leq N_b$. Then we say that *node J has no prediction*. On the other hand if $w_{JK} = 1$, $w_{Jk} = 0$ for $k \neq K$, and node K in F_2^b is the compressed representation for the output pattern O, we say that *node J confirms I's prediction*. Finally, if $w_{JK} = 1$, and $w_{Jk} = 0$ for $k \neq K$, and node K in F_2^b is the compressed representation for a different output pattern $\hat{O}$ (i.e., $\hat{O} \neq O$), then we say that node J *disconfirms I's prediction*.

3 Modeling Assumptions

One of the modeling assumptions required for the validity of the results presented in this paper is fast learning. Fast learning implies that the input/output pairs presented to the ARTMAP architecture are held at the network inputs long enough for the network weights to converge to their steady state values. It is worth mentioning that in Carpenter et al. ([1]) only the fast learning scenario is extensively treated. Furthermore, a condition needs to be imposed on the ARTMAP network parameters to guarantee the validity of our results. Before we introduce this condition, let us first discuss the various ARTMAP network parameters.

The network parameters in the ARTMAP architecture are: M_u^a, M_u^b, β_a, β_b, ρ_a, ρ_b, ρ. The parameters M_u^a and β_a are used to define upper bounds for the initial choices of the bottom-up weights in the ART_a module. Similarly, the parameters M_u^b and β_b are used to define upper bounds for the initial choices of the bottom-up weights in the ART_b module. In particular,

$$0 < Z_{ij}^a(0) < \frac{1}{\beta_a + M_u^a} \tag{3}$$

$$0 < Z_{lk}^b(0) < \frac{1}{\beta_b + M_u^b} \tag{4}$$

where the parameter M_u^a should be larger than or equal to the maximum-size input I (i.e., $M_u^a \geq |I|$), and the parameter M_u^b should be larger than or equal to the maximum-size output O (i.e., $M_u^b \geq |O|$). Note that $|I|$ designates the size of the input I, while $|O|$ designates the size of the input O. The size of a binary vector is defined to be the number of its components that are equal to one. For simplicity of the discussion contained in this paper we choose

$$Z_{ij}^a(0) = \alpha_j^a \quad Z_{lk}^b(0) = \alpha_k^b \tag{5}$$

where

$$\alpha_1^a > \alpha_2^a > \ldots > \alpha_{N_a}^a \tag{6}$$

$$\alpha_1^b > \alpha_2^b > \ldots > \alpha_{N_b}^b \tag{7}$$

The above choice of the initial bottom-up weights forces the ART_a module to choose uncommitted nodes in F_2^a in the order, $1, 2, \ldots, N_a$; it also forces the ART_b module to choose uncommitted nodes in F_2^b in the order, $1, 2, \ldots, N_b$. The initial top-down weights in ART_a and ART_b, as well as the initial weights from F_2^a to the MAP field F_{ab} are chosen equal to one.

The network parameters ρ_a, ρ_b and ρ designate the vigilance parameters in the ART_a, ART_b and inter-ART modules, respectively. It is worth pointing out that the vigilance parameter in the ART_a module is allowed to increase during training. In particular, ρ_a starts from a baseline value equal to $\bar{\rho}_a$ and if an incorrect map is established between an input pattern I and an output pattern O, then ρ_a is increased above its baseline value of $\bar{\rho}_a$.

Finally, the network parameters β_a and β_b have an effect on the nodes chosen in F_2^a and F_2^b to represent the input pattern I and the output pattern O, respectively. Specifically, when an input pattern I is applied at the F_1^a field of the ART_a module it produces an input $T_j^a(I)$ at node j in the F_2^a field. This input is given by the following equation:

$$T_j^a(I) = \begin{cases} \alpha_j^a |I| & \text{if node } j \text{ is uncommitted} \\ \frac{|I \cap z_j^a|}{\beta_a + |z_j^a|} & \text{if node } j \text{ is not uncommitted} \end{cases} \tag{8}$$

The ART_a module chooses the node in F_2^a that maximizes $T_j^a(I)$. That is, node J in F_2^a is chosen to represent the input pattern I if $T_J^a(I) = \max_j \{T_j^a(I)\}$. Similar statements are valid regarding the selection of nodes chosen in F_2^b to represent the output patterns O presented at the ART_b module.

The parameter M_u^a may assume values in the interval $[M_a, \infty)$, while M_u^b may assume values in the interval $[M_b, \infty)$. The parameters β_a and β_b may take values in the interval $(0, \infty)$. The baseline vigilance parameter $\bar{\rho}_a$ may assume values in the interval $[0, 1]$; which implies that ρ_a takes values in the interval $[\bar{\rho}_a, 1]$. Since we are only focusing on many-to-one maps the value of the vigilance parameter ρ_b is taken to be equal to one. Finally the inter-ART vigilance parameter ρ takes values in the interval $(0, 1]$. Our results are valid for any set of the parameter values in the aforementioned ranges with the exception of the parameter β_a, which needs to be constrained further to satisfy the following assumption:

Assumption 1:
In the fast learning ARTMAP case, an input pattern I that is presented to the ART_a module chooses subset nodes first, prior to choosing any mixed nodes.

It is shown in [3] that if β_a satisfies the following constraint, then Assumption 1 is valid.

$$\beta_a \leq \max \left\{ M_a^{-1}, \ \frac{\bar{\rho}_a}{1 - \bar{\rho}_a} \right\} \tag{9}$$

In review, the results presented in this paper are valid for a fast learning ARTMAP architecture with parameters M_u^a, M_u^b, β_b, $\bar{\rho}_a$, ρ_a, ρ_b, and ρ with values in the ranges prescribed above, and small β_a parameter values.

Small β_a parameter values correspond to β_a values that satisfy inequality (9), and consequently satisfy Assumption 1. Before we proceed with the presentation of the results it is important to modify slightly the rules of the ARTMAP architecture.

4   A Modification of the ARTMAP Rules

The results described in the next section are valid under the modeling assumptions of Section 3 and for the following scenario: We have a collection of input/output pairs designated as (I^1, O^1), (I^2, O^2), $\ldots, (I^N, O^N)$ that we refer to as the input list. We want to train the ARTMAP architecture to learn the following mapping: I^1 to O^1, I^2 to O^2, and eventually I^N to O^N. To do so, we present the input list repeatedly to the ARTMAP architecture. That is, we present I^1 to ART_a and O^1 to ART_b, then I^2 to ART_a and O^2 to ART_b, and eventually I^N to ART_a and O^N to ART_b; this corresponds to one list presentation. We present the input list to ARTMAP as many times as it is necessary for the architecture to learn the desired map. The order of presentation of the input pairs within the list is not essential, as long as all the pairs in the list are presented within every list presentation. It is important, for the aforementioned scenario, to be able to determine when the learning process is completed. Hence, for the ARTMAP architecture and the aforementioned scenario we have:

Definition 1:
When a list of input/output pairs is repeatedly presented to an ARTMAP architecture, the learning process is declared complete if every input pattern from the list chooses a node in the F_2^a field that satisfies the direct-access, no-learning conditions. A node j in F_2^a chosen by a pattern I satisfies the direct-access, no-learning conditions if (a) node j is the first node chosen in F_2^a by pattern I, (b) node j is not reset, and (c) the weights corresponding to node j (i.e., Z_j^a's, z_j^a's, and w_j^a's) are not modified. Conditions (a) and (b) are the direct access conditions and condition (c) is the no-learning condition.

In the sequel, we present the ARTMAP rule that causes a confusion as to when the learning process is complete. Furthermore, we state a modification of this rule, denoted as Modification 1, which clarifies this confusion (for more details regarding this issue see [3]).

ARTMAP rule:
If an input pattern I is applied at the F_1^a field, the initial choice in F_2^a is the one node with index J satisfying

$$T_J^a = \max_j (T_j^a)$$

If more than one nodes is maximal, choose one of these nodes randomly.

Modification 1:
If an input pattern I is applied at the F_1^a field, the initial choice in F_2^a is the one node with index J satisfying

$$T_J^a = \max_j (T_j^a)$$

If more than one nodes is maximal, choose the node with the lower index.

It is worth pointing out that Modification 1 of the ARTMAP rules does not alter the capabilities of ARTMAP to achieve any mapping between a binary input space and a binary output space. However, if we follow the ARTMAP rules with Modification 1 the categories produced will be different than those formed if we follow the original ARTMAP rules. From this point on, whenever we refer to ARTMAP we will assume that the original ARTMAP rules are followed, with the incorporation of Modification 1.

5 Results for ARTMAP

The scenario under which the results presented here are valid was described at the beginning of Section 4, and the modeling assumptions under which these results are true were mentioned in Section 3. The proof of the results presented below can be found in [3].

Result 1:
Consider a list of input/output pairs, which is repeatedly presented to an ARTMAP architecture. Under the modeling assumptions of Section 3, and in list presentations $\geq x$, where $2 \leq x \leq M_a$

- **a:** *If an input pattern I chooses a node in F_2^a with corresponding template size $\leq x - 2$, then this node confirms I's prediction.*

- **b:** *Size-$(x-1)$ templates can not be created in the ART_a module.*

- **c:** *Size-x templates can not be destroyed in the ART_a module.*

Based on Result 1 we can show that in ARTMAP, under the assumptions of Section 3, learning is completed by the end of the $(M_a - 1)$-th list presentation. We state this result below, and we name it Result 2.

Result 2:
Consider a list of input/output pairs, which is repeatedly presented to an ARTMAP architecture. Under the modeling assumptions of Section 3, learning in ARTMAP will be completed by the end of the $(M_a - 1)$-th list presentation.

If we are dealing with an ARTMAP architecture, whose baseline vigilance parameter $\bar{\rho}_a$ is such that $\lceil M_a \bar{\rho}_a \rceil > 1$ ($\lceil y \rceil$ designates the smallest integer greater than or equal to y), then we can prove results that are stronger than Results 1 and 2. We state these results below as Results 3 and 4.

Result 3:
Consider a list of input/output pairs, which is repeatedly presented to an ARTMAP architecture with baseline vigilance parameter $\bar{\rho}_a$, such that $\lceil M_a \bar{\rho}_a \rceil > 1$. Under the modeling assumptions of Section 3, and in list presentations $\geq x$, where $2 \leq x \leq M_a + 1 - \lceil M_a \bar{\rho}_a \rceil$

- **a:** *If an input pattern I chooses a node in F_2^a with corresponding template size $\leq \lceil M_a \bar{\rho}_a \rceil - 1 + x - 2$, then this node confirms I's choice.*

- **b:** *Size-$(\lceil M_a \bar{\rho}_a \rceil - 1 + x - 1)$ templates can not be created in the ART_a module.*

- **c:** *Size-$(\lceil M_a \bar{\rho}_a \rceil - 1 + x)$ templates can not be destroyed in the ART_a module.*

Result 4:
Consider a list of input/output pairs, which is repeatedly presented to an ARTMAP architecture with baseline vigilance parameter $\bar{\rho}_a$, such that $\lceil M_a \bar{\rho}_a \rceil > 1$. Under the modeling assumptions of Section 3, learning in ARTMAP will be completed by the end of the $(M_a - \lceil M_a \bar{\rho}_a \rceil)$-th list presentation.

6 Conclusions

In this paper we considered the ARTMAP architecture for the fast learning case, and under the assumption that subset nodes are chosen prior to mixed nodes in the ART_a module. Furthermore, the original ARTMAP rules were slightly modified in order for us to define, in a meaningful way, the "end of the learning process" in ARTMAP. Finally, the type of mappings that we focused on were many-to-one mappings, which are of interest in pattern recognition applications.

The most important result proven was Result 2. Result 2 states that in ARTMAP, and under the above conditions, learning of the mapping implied by a list of input/output pairs, repeatedly presented to the architecture, will be completed in at most $M_a - 1$ list presentations. The parameter M_a corresponds to the number of components of the input patterns that are equal to one. For the case where the baseline vigilance parameter $\bar{\rho}_a$ is such that $\lceil M_a \bar{\rho}_a \rceil > 1$, a result stronger than Result 2 (i.e., Result 4) was proven. In particular, for large M_a values and $\bar{\rho}_a$ values close to one, Result 4 is much more powerful than Result 2. More specifically, if $M_a = 1000$ and $\bar{\rho}_a = 0.8$, then Result 2 predicts an upper bound for the completion of learning a list of input/output pairs equal to 999 list presentations, while Result 4 predicts an upper bound for the completion of learning a list of input/output pairs equal to 200 list presentations.

Acknowledgments: This research was supported in part by a grant from the Florida High Technology and Industry Council, in part by a grant from the Division of Sponsored Research at the University of Central Florida, and in part by a grant from Boeing Computer Services under contract W-300445.

References

[1] G. A. Carpenter, S. Grossberg, and J. H. Reynolds, "ARTMAP: Supervised Real-Time Learning and Classification of Non-Stationary Data by a Self-Organizing Neural Network," *Neural Networks*, Vol. 4, No. 5, pp. 565-588, 1991.

[2] S. Grossberg, "Adaptive Pattern Recognition and Universal Recoding II: Feedback, Expectation, Olfaction, and Illusions," *Biological Cybernetics*, Vol. 23, pp. 187-206, 1976.

[3] M. Georgiopoulos, J. Huang, and G. L. Heileman, "Properties of Learning in ARTMAP," *Neural Networks*; to appear.

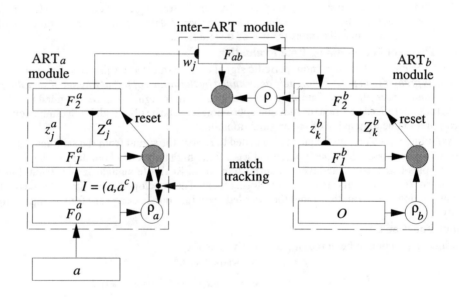

Figure 1: A block diagram of the ARTMAP architecture

Minimal Training Set Size Estimation For Sampled-Data Function Encoding

Aleksander Malinowski, Jacek M. Zurada

Department of Electrical Engineering,

University of Louisville, Louisville, KY 40292, USA

e-mail: a0mali01@starbase.spd.louisville.edu, jmzura02@ulkyvx.louisville.edu

Abstract: A new approach to the problem of n-dimensional function approximation using two-layer neural network is presented. The generalized Nyquist theorem is introduced to solve for the optimum number of learning patterns in n-dimensional input space. Choosing the smallest but still sufficient set of training vectors results in the reduced number of hidden neurons and learning time for the network. Analytical formulas and algorithm for training set size reduction are developed and illustrated by two-dimensional data examples.

1. Introduction

Neural networks as approximators of input/output relationships among many variables are currently under intense investigation, with emphasis on their approximation capabilities and performance for different network architectures and learning conditions [1]. Generalization and approximation without specifying equations and coefficients are indeed very promising features of neural networks, particularly in cases where the unknown model describing a plant is complex and training data abundant. Due to their ability of generalization, multilayer feedforward neural networks (MFNN) are commonly used for this purpose [2], [3].

Papers on the subject of approximation using MFNN were published lately [4], [5]; however, they do not focus on the size minimization of the training data set. The frequency-based analysis approach for training set pruning is proposed in [6], with the emphasis on choosing the neuron transfer function such that its frequency spectrum is similar to that of an approximated function, and no conclusion for sufficiency of reduced training data set size is derived. Preliminary heuristic solutions of this problem along with single variable function examples have been published in [7] and [8].

This paper offers a generalization of an analytical approach for multidimensional input space. An analytical approach based on the generalization of the sampling theorem is applied to function approximation using MFNN. An analogy between time-dependent functions and single variable functions is made and then expanded into multidimensional space. An estimated minimum sampling frequency for MFNN training can then be found for a required approximation accuracy. The results can be used for reducing the number of data required in a neural network training set. The experimental part of the paper illustrates the use of this method.

2. Sample Data Theorem For Sampling Rate Evaluation

The well-known Sampling Theorem (non-periodic signal case) states that : *A function f(x) which contains no frequency components greater than f_0 Hz is uniquely determined by the values of f(x) at any set of sampling points spaced at most $1/(2f_0)$ seconds apart* [9], [10]. Sampling rates defined for time signals can be extended to other independent variables so that the generalized theorem for function approximation can be obtained. Each dimension of the transform will then correspond to one dimension of the original domain.

Obviously, sampling with a certain frequency is needed to restore the signal from the samples taken. However, the theorem refers to the ideal case where the input signal has a finite high frequency boundary so that it can be accurately restored from samples taken using the inverse Fourier transform. Real-life signals are not band-limited, and other mechanisms than Fourier transforms are used for restoring them. The developed algorithm is based on the assumption that only certain fraction of information about the sampled-data function is necessary for the approximation with required accuracy.

2.1. Continuous Function Case

Let the continuous function to be approximated be given as f(x),

$$f(x) : \mathfrak{D} \to \mathfrak{R}, \text{ where } \mathfrak{D} \subset \mathfrak{R}^N$$

$$\mathfrak{D} \doteq (x_{MIN1} .. x_{MAX1}) \times (x_{MIN2} .. x_{MAX2}) \times ... \times (x_{MINN} .. x_{MAXN}) \qquad (1)$$

$$x \doteq [x_1, x_2, ..., x_N]$$

and let B_i be the range of the i-th variable x_i:

$$B_i \doteq x_{MAXi} - x_{MINi} \qquad (2)$$

The multidimensional Fourier transform of f(x) is defined in following way as

$$F(\Omega) \doteq \frac{1}{(2\pi j)^N} \int_{x_{MIN1}}^{x_{MAX1}} \int_{x_{MIN2}}^{x_{MAX2}} ... \int_{x_{MINN}}^{x_{MAXN}} f(x_1, x_2, ..., x_N) e^{2\pi j x_1 \omega_1} e^{2\pi j x_2 \omega_2} ... e^{2\pi j x_N \omega_N} dx_1 dx_2 ... dx_N \qquad (3)$$

$$\text{where} \quad \Omega \doteq [\omega_1, \omega_2, ..., \omega_N]$$

The criterion for minimum sampling frequency estimation can be formulated in a number of ways. First, the basic formula for optimization should be defined as a norm evaluating the information density at particular frequencies. This norm as defined in (4) has a meaning of generalized energy density.

$$E_d(\Omega) \doteq |F(\Omega)|^2 \tag{4}$$

We also use function (5) for evaluating the amount of information enclosed by the frequency band Ω. In case of a multi-dimensional band-limited function, the energy, $E(\Omega)$, can be computed by integrating the generalized energy density (4) in the frequency domain in spherical [11], or more precisely, ellipsoidal coordinates within an N-dimensional ellipsoid. For example, in the simplest case assuming that function F has isotropic properties in each dimension ($\omega = \omega_1 = \omega_2 = ... = \omega_N$), this yields

$$E(\omega) \doteq \int_{r=0}^{1} \int_{\phi_1=0}^{2\pi} \int_{\phi_2=0}^{2\pi} ... \int_{\phi_{N-1}=0}^{2\pi} |F(\omega r \cos\phi_1 \cos\phi_2 ... \cos\phi_{N-1}, \omega r \sin\phi_1 \cos\phi_2 ... \cos\phi_{N-1}, ..., \omega r \sin\phi_1 \sin\phi_2 ... \sin\phi_{N-1})|^2 J(.) d\phi_1 d\phi_2 ... d\phi_{N-1} dr \tag{5}$$

where $J(r, \phi_1, \phi_2, ..., \phi_N)$ is a term resulting from the change of the integration coordinates from cubic to spheric [12]. However, in general it cannot be assumed that the approximated function will have isotropic properties. It may then be reasonable to choose smaller sampling densities in some dimension. The function (5) becomes more complex due to different boundaries in each dimension

$$E(\Omega) \doteq \int_{r=0}^{1} \int_{\phi_1=0}^{2\pi} \int_{\phi_2=0}^{2\pi} ... \int_{\phi_{N-1}=0}^{2\pi} |F(\omega_1 r \cos\phi_1 \cos\phi_2 ... \cos\phi_{N-1}, \omega_2 r \sin\phi_1 \cos\phi_2 ... \cos\phi_{N-1}, ..., \omega_N r \sin\phi_1 \sin\phi_2 ... \sin\phi_{N-1})|^2 J(.) d\phi_1 d\phi_2 ... d\phi_{N-1} dr \tag{6}$$

where $J(r, \Omega, \phi_1, \phi_2, ..., \phi_N)$ is a term obtained as previously from the change of the integration coordinates from cubic to spheric.

Let C_{INFO} called the *information rate factor* be the fraction describing the required minimum energy content of the signal sampled with frequency Ω, divided by the energy E_{TOT} of the original function (or function sampled with very high frequency). The information rate factor is a theoretical measure of the information amount needed to approximate a function with a required accuracy. Function $f(x)$ needs to be sampled with frequency Ω satisfying condition (7).

$$\frac{E(\Omega)}{E(\Omega_{MAX})} \geq C_{INFO} \tag{7}$$

where the frequency $\Omega_{MAX} \doteq [\omega_1, \omega_2, ..., \omega_N]_{MAX}$ is high enough, so that

$$|F(\Omega_{MAX})|^2 \approx 0 \text{ and } E(\Omega_{MAX}) \approx E_{TOT} \tag{8}$$

Let us now express the total number of samples in the training set. The number of samples taken per dimension, M_{Li}, is equal to

$$M_{Li}(\omega_i) \doteq (2B_i\omega_i + 1) \tag{9}$$

The total number of sampled data, M_L, can be expressed as

$$M_L(\omega_1, \omega_2, ..., \omega_N) \doteq \prod_{i=1}^{N} M_{Li}(\omega_i) \tag{10}$$

The objective is to search among vectors Ω which satisfy the condition (7) and minimize the value of M_L defined in (10). The vector $\Omega_{OPT} \doteq [\omega_1, \omega_2, ..., \omega_N]_{OPT}$ which is the solution to the given optimization problem contains the minimum sufficient sampling frequencies in the new training data set. The final sampling interval, Δx_i, is different for each dimension depending on the chosen frequency ω_i.

$$\Delta x_i = \frac{1}{2\omega_{OPTi}} \tag{11}$$

2.2. Sampled Data Function Case

Let us consider data acquired by measuring or sampling a plant characteristic for which no closed form formula exists. Assume that data is collected with intervals $\delta x \doteq [\delta x_1, \delta x_2, ..., \delta x_N]$ on $\mathcal{D}$, so that there is a given data set $\mathcal{S}$ for estimation

$$\mathcal{S} \doteq \left\{ ((x_{1k_1}, x_{2k_2}, ..., x_{Nk_N}), y_{k_1, k_2, ..., k_N}), \quad k_1 = 0..K_1, \ k_2 = 0..K_2, \ ..., \ k_N = 0..K_N \right\} \tag{12}$$

where

$$x_{ik_i} = x_{MINi} + \delta x_i k_i \text{ and } K_i = \left[\frac{B_i}{\delta x_i} \right] \tag{13}$$

The set $\mathcal{S}$ contains the entire information available about the function to be approximated. The final training set after calculations of minimum sufficient sampling density will be its subset.

Let us redefine the results for continuous functions for discrete data sets. Now the information about the frequency domain can be obtained using the discrete Fourier transform (DFT) as follows:

$$F(l) \doteq T \sum_{k_1=1}^{K_1} \sum_{k_2=1}^{K_2} \cdots \sum_{k_N=1}^{K_N} y_{k_1 k_2 \dots kN} \, e^{2\pi j \left(\frac{k_1 l_1}{M_1} + \frac{k_2 l_2}{M_2} + \dots + \frac{k_N l_N}{M_N} \right)} \tag{14}$$

where the vector l is the multidimensional discrete frequency equal to

$$l = [l_1, \, l_2, \, \dots, \, l_N] \quad \text{and} \quad l_i = -\frac{K_i}{2} \dots \frac{K_i}{2} - 1 \tag{15}$$

The set $\mathcal{S}$ contains the band–limited spectrum of the approximated function due to the finite sampling density in the data available. Therefore, no information about higher frequency components exist. For this reason, initial sampling rates Ω_{MAX} should be chosen carefully. The value Ω_{MAX} corresponds to L_{MAX}, where $L_{MAX} \doteq [l_1, l_2, \dots, l_N]_{MAX}$ is the maximum discrete frequency in the DFT domain.

$$L_{MAX_i} \doteq \frac{K_i}{2} - 1 \tag{16}$$

The norm for information density for discrete functions can be defined as in (17)

$$E_d(l) \doteq |F(l)|^2 \tag{17}$$

The amount of information which remains after narrowing the sampling boundary is evaluated by (18), where the summation is performed over the samples from the interior of the multidimensional ellipsoid and corresponds to equation (6) for continuous data sets.

$$E(l) \doteq \sum_{k \in \mathcal{K}(l)} |F(k)|^2 \tag{18}$$

In (18),

$$\mathcal{K}(l) \doteq \left\{ [k] : \frac{k_1^2}{l_1^2} + \frac{k_2^2}{l_2^2} + \dots + \frac{k_N^2}{l_N^2} \le 1 \ \wedge \ k_1^2 + k_2^2 + \dots + k_N^2 > 0 \right\} \tag{19}$$

Let us note that l_i is an integer number, and it corresponds to the sampling frequency

$$\omega_i \doteq l_i \Delta \omega_i \tag{20}$$

where

$$\Delta \omega_i \doteq \frac{1}{2 \delta x_i L_{MAX_i}} \quad \text{and} \quad \omega_{MAX_i} \doteq \frac{1}{2 \delta x_i} \tag{21}$$

and to the final number of samples per dimension, M_{Li}.

$$M_{Li} \doteq \frac{B_i}{\delta x_i L_{MAX_i}} l_i + 1 \tag{22}$$

The term M_L in (10), which is the number of sampled data tabularized for training, can be evaluated as

$$M_L(\Omega) \doteq \prod_{i=1}^{N} \left(\frac{B_i}{\delta x_i L_{MAX_i}} l_i + 1 \right) \tag{23}$$

The optimization problem is formulated in a similar way as previously in (10) with constraints (7)

$$\frac{E(l)}{E(L_{MAX})} \ge C_{INFO} \tag{24}$$

and reduces to the minimization of M_L in (23) while satisfying the condition (24). One of solutions is proposed in the following section.

2.3. Simplified Approach for Estimating Minimum Sufficient Sampling Rates

Equation (18) provides the exact result for the amount of information present in frequency components lower than $l_1, l_2, \dots l_N$. However, it takes a lot of computational effort to evaluate this function. Therefore, a simplified expression is shown in (25) below for the multidimensional rectangle inscribed into the multidimensional ellipsoid as is also proposed in [11].

$$G(l) = \sum_{k_1=1}^{l_1} \sum_{k_2=1}^{l_2} \cdots \sum_{k_N=1}^{l_N} |F(k)|^2 \tag{25}$$

The requirement for sufficient information replacing now (7) and valid after narrowing the frequency boundary reduces to

$$\frac{G(l)}{G(L_{MAX})} \ge C_{INFO} \tag{26}$$

Function G(l) produces values higher than E(l) because summation is performed over a larger volume. However, the difference is not significant because the energy value below the frequency boundary are usually small, and the additional energy calculated using (25) instead of (18) is not significant. However, if the condition

$$|F(\Omega_{OPT})|^2 \approx 0 \qquad (27)$$

is not satisfied, then the power spectrum has to be evaluated using formula (18).

3. Algorithm For Estimation Of The Information Rate Factor

The last constant which has to be estimated is C_{INFO} from equations (7), (24) and (26). This constant defines the minimum sufficient amount of information after narrowing the function frequency spectrum in terms of its energy.

Let us define mean square average error of approximation, MSE, as

$$MSE \doteq \sqrt{\frac{\sum_{p=1}^{P}(d^{(p)} - o^{(p)})^2}{P}} \qquad (28)$$

where P is the number of data entries, $d^{(p)}$ is the known function value for input vector $x^{(p)}$, and $o^{(p)}$ is the value computed by the neural network. Error defined in the sense of (28) is based on the energetic distance between the original and the approximated function and is also useful for expressing the training termination condition. In order to determine the value of MSE, it is necessary to know the average power of the original function, P_{TOT}. P_{TOT} can be calculated from the Fourier power spectrum in the frequency domain either in the x domain using formula (29) for the continuous case, or (30) in case of discrete data.

$$P_{TOT} = \frac{\int_{x_{MIN1}}^{x_{MAX1}} \int_{x_{MIN2}}^{x_{MAX2}} \cdots \int_{x_{MINN}}^{x_{MAXN}} f(x_1, x_2, \ldots x_N)^2 dx_1 dx_2 \ldots dx_N}{\prod_{i=1}^{N} B_i} \qquad (29)$$

$$P_{TOT} = \frac{\sum_{p=1}^{P}(d^{(p)})^2}{P} \qquad (30)$$

The terms of integration in equation (29) or summation in (30) evaluate the same energy, which is used in the denominators of conditions (7), (24) and (26).

The required approximation accuracy Ψ links together MSE and P_{TOT}.

$$\Psi = \frac{MSE}{\sqrt{P_{TOT}}} \qquad (31)$$

The reason for normalizing the variables defined in (28) and (30) is to allow easy comparison of results of training and to evaluate the quality of the approximation without considering the number of patterns used each time. Finally we have the relation

$$C_{INFO} = 1 - \Psi \qquad (32)$$

which links the final condition for training (28) with equations (7), (24) and (26).

4. Algorithm For Finding Minimum Sufficient Sampling Rates

The following algorithm can be used for finding the minimum sufficient sampling rates is based on the theoretical assumptions presented above:

STEP 1. Sample given function or measure plant characteristics with certain input data step with excessively sampling to sufficient allow for generalization. $f(x) \blacklozenge f(k)$ (δx is a vector of sampling intervals).

STEP 2. Compute DFT of the sampled function. $f(k) \blacklozenge F(l)$
Note that the upper boundary of the Fourier transform depends on the sampling interval δx. Condition (8) has to be satisfied. Therefore, if the sampling interval is too long, the significant part of the frequency response is lost.

STEP 3. If the frequency response is not small enough at the highest frequency in comparison to lower ones, i.e. (8) is not satisfied, first two steps must be repeated for 5 to 10 times more frequent sampling in the appropriate dimensions.

STEP 4. Complete the information measurement function $G(l)$ as in (25) and normalize it so that its maximum is equal to 1. $F(l) \blacklozenge G(l)$

STEP 5. Evaluate C_{INFO} and MSE for particular requirements of approximation accuracy Ψ using (32).

STEP 6. Check for what frequencies function $E(l)$ from (26) reaches the levels evaluated in the STEP 5. $\{l\} \blacklozenge \{ l : E(l) \geq C_{INFO} E_{TOT}\}$

STEP 7. Solve for l which produces minimum M_L in (23) using the set of $\{l\}$ satisfying condition from STEP 6. $l_{OPT} \blacklozenge l : M_L(l) = \min\{M_L(l)\}$ over all $l \in \{l\}$.

STEP 8. Choose the sampling steps slightly higher than those corresponding closely to frequencies computed in STEP 7.
STOP.

If there are problems with convergence, the MFNN architecture should be changed or the learning constants decreased. If the approximation error after completed training is excessive, sampling steps should be decreased by choosing more severe constraints than given in (32).

5. Experimental Results

A series of experiments were conducted to confirm the theoretical results and to test the heuristic guidelines proposed for sampling rates. A MFNN with one hidden layer has been used for a single–variable function approximation. The experiments were performed for approximating one– [7–8], and two–dimensional functions using neural network architectures with different numbers of hidden neurons and for different final error conditions which provide more insight into the practical use of the method.

To prevent saturation of neurons and to provide similar conditions for each test, the scaling of input data was performed so that normalized input variables varied form 0 to 1. Since bipolar continuous neurons were used, it was necessary to scale functions to be approximated to the range between –1 and 1. Standard and modified (lambda learning [13]) error backpropagation algorithms were used for learning. Functions were first sampled with very high density for evaluating the discrete Fourier transform and for evaluating the approximation accuracy after completing training. Before each training with a new sampling step, a new learning data set was created and network weights were initialized once again. Each training was performed until it reached the MSE error set previously.

Theoretical estimations were compared with frequencies obtained from experiments. As anticipated, **there exists an optimal number of learning points for a given approximation accuracy. This number of points can be evaluated from the integral of its Fourier transform (25).**

Fig. 1a shows an example function used for approximation. Fig. 1b depicts one quadrant of the frequency domain

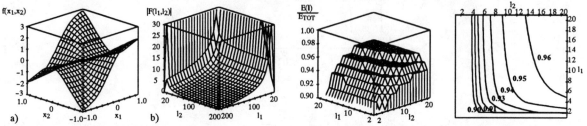

Fig. 1. Approximated function f(x) as in (33) (a), and its Fourier transform (b). $P_{TOT}=1.12$.

Fig. 2. Amount of energy $E_{NORM}(l)$ covered by bounded frequency spectrum. f(x) as in (33). Profiles for $E_{NORM}>0.90$.

of the magnitude of its discrete Fourier transform. Function values were generated using formula (33) with the sampling interval $\delta x_i=0.005$ in each dimension ($K_1=K_2=400$ samples).

$$f(x) = \frac{x_1^2 x_2 + 5x_1 x_2^2}{x_1^2 + x_2^2 + 0.1} \ , \ x_1 = -1..1, \ x_2 = -1..1 \qquad (33)$$

The normalized energy function of f(x) given by (33) covered by the frequency l is shown in Fig. 2. The normalized energy has been computed from the left side of condition (24).

The average power, P_{TOT}, was calculated for the given function using the formula (30); it is of value $P_{TOT}=1.12$. A MFNNs with 2 inputs, and 20 hidden neurons was trained to the error MSE=0.08 as defined by the formula (28). Ψ and C_{INFO} were then calculated using formulas (31) and (32), giving the values: $\Psi=0.07$, and $C_{INFO}=0.93$. The optimum number of samples for each dimension has been found from Fig. 3 by finding the minimum of M_L over fre-

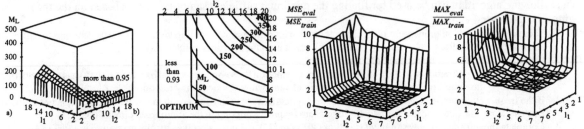

Fig. 3. Number of samples in learning set in area of normalized $E(l_1,l_2)>C_{INFO}$. f(x) as in (33). Profiles for $0.95 \geq C_{INFO} \geq 0.93$ (a), and $C_{INFO} \geq 0.93$ (b).

Fig. 4. Neural network performance (MSE) after training in versus sampling frequencies. MSE=0.08. f(x) as in (33).

Fig. 5. Neural network performance (MAX) after training versus sampling frequencies l. MSE=0.08. f(x) as in (33).

quencies satisfying condition (26) which gives the contour line bounding the domain of solution. This figure shows the contours for the number of data entries in the training set, M_L, for different l_1 and l_2 which satisfy the condition (26). The minimum of M_L can be seen at $l_1=4$ and $l_2=8$. It can be evaluated from equation (22). This corresponds to 9 samples for variable x_1 and 17 samples for variable x_2.

MFNNs with architectures described above were trained for different numbers of samples in each dimension to verify the theoretical results. The results of training are illustrated in Figs. 4–8. Fig. 4 and Fig. 5 show the quality of training in terms of MSE and the maximum error achieved during approximation verification based on a very large testing set (500x500 samples). It can be seen that the error decreases dramatically when $l_1 \geq 2$ and $l_2 \geq 3$. This corresponds to 5 and 7, respectively, samples per dimensions.

Fig. 6 shows the number of training steps required for the learning process, while Fig. 7 shows only the number of

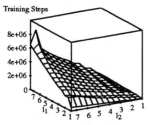

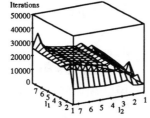

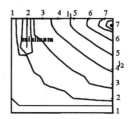

Fig. 6. Number of training steps versus sampling frequencies; f(**x**) as in (33).

Fig. 7. Number of iterations versus sampling frequencies; f(**x**) as in (33).

Fig. 8. Number of training steps versus sampling frequencies for area of sufficient learning; f(**x**) as in (33).

iterations (cycles). After achieving certain frequencies of sampling the function to build a training set, the number of iterations does not increase or increases only slowly, while the overall number of steps still increases due to the growing number of data entries.

Fig. 8 summarizes the computational experiment. The number of iterations for the sampling frequencies **l** providing accurate learning is displayed. Local minima can be observed for the frequencies $l_1=2$ and $l_2=5$ for the first MFNN and for $l_1=2$ and $l_2=6$ for the second. This corresponds to five and eleven, and five and thirteen samples per dimension, respectively. This is in agreement with four and eight samples per appropriate dimension. The obtained results are close enough to those evaluated previously using the derived theoretical algorithm and displayed in Fig. 3.

6. Conclusions

The results of the computational experiments and theoretical studies show that the generalized sampling theorem can be applied to the approximation problem of a sampled–data function using neural networks. The smallest, but still large enough for the sake of accuracy data set should be selected, and then network model can be found through training [14–15]. Our results indicate that least training sets with only some data from the large measured real–life data sets are required to obtain successfully trained neural networks capable of accurate approximation of sampled–data functions.

7. References

[1]   E. J. Hartman, J. D. Keeler, J. M. Kowalski, "Layered Neural Networks with Gaussian Hidden Units as Universal Approximations," *Neural Computation II,* 1990, pp. 210–215.

[2]   S. Shekhar, M. B. Amin, "Generalization by Neural Networks," *IEEE Trans. on Knowledge and Data Eng.,* vol. 4, no. 2, April 1992, pp. 177–185.

[3]   Y. Shin, J. Ghost, "Approximation of Multivariate Functions Using Ridge Polynomial Networks," *Proc. of International Joint Conference of Neural Networks,* Baltimore, Maryland, June 7–11, 1992, vol. 2, pp. 380 – 385.

[4]   R. M. Sanner, J–J. E. Slotine, "Gaussian Network for Direct Adaptive Control," *IEEE Trans. on Neural Networks,* vol. 3, no. 6, November 1992, pp. 837–863.

[5]   C.–H Choi, J. Y. Choi, "Construction of Neural Networks for Piecewise Approximation of Continuous Functions," *Proc. of the IEEE International Conference on Neural Networks,* San Francisco, CA, March 28–31, 1993, vol. 1, pp.428–433.

[6]   B. E. Segee, "Using Spectral Techniques for Improved Performance in Artificial Neural Networks," *Proc. of the IEEE International Conference on Neural Networks,* San Francisco, CA, March 28–31, 1993, vol.1, pp. 500–505.

[7]   J. M. Zurada, A. Malinowski, "Sampling Rate for Information Encoding Using Multilayer Neural Networks," *Proc. of International Joint Conference on Neural Networks,* Nagoya, Japan, October 25–29, 1993.

[8]   A. Malinowski, J. M. Zurada, "Minimal Training Set Size for Neural Network–based Function Encoding," *Proc. of the Conference Artificial Neural Networks in Engineering,* St. Louis, Missouri, November 14–17, 1993, pp. 149–154.

[9]   A. D. Poularikas, S. Seely, *Elements of Signals and Systems,* PWS–KENT Publishing Company, Boston, 1992.

[10]   C. L. Philips, H. T. Nagle, *Digital Control Systems - Analysis and Design,* Prentice Hall Inc., New Jersey 1990.

[11]   H. C. Andrews, W. K. Pratt, K. Caspari, *Computer Techniques in Image Processing,* Academic Press Inc. Ltd., London, 1970, pp. 157–161.

[12]   T. M. Apostol, Mathematical Analysis, *A Modern Approach to Advanced Calculus,* Addison–Wesley Publishing Company, London 1957, pp. 270–275.

[13]   J. M. Zurada, "Lambda Learning Rule," *Proc. of the IEEE International Conference on Neural Networks,* San Francisco, CA, March 28–31, 1993, pp. 1808–1811.

[14]   J. M. Zurada, *Introduction to Artificial Neural Systems,* West Publishing Company, St. Paul, Minn., 1992.

[15]   J. Hertz, A. Krogh, R. G. Palmer, *Introduction to the Theory of Neural Computation,* Addison–Wesley Publishing Company, 1990.

Constructive Uniform Approximation of Differentiable Vector-Functions by Neural Network Methods

Moshe Shoam, Mark Meltser
Faculty of Mechanical Engineering
Technion-Israel Institute of Technology
Haifa, Israel

and

Larry M. Manevitz
University of Haifa Polytechnic University
Haifa, Israel New York, NY

Abstract

A method for constructively approximating any twice differentiable function in the uniform (i.e. maximal error) norm by successive changes in the weights and number of neurons in a neural network is developed. This is a realization of the approximation results of Cybenko, White, Gallant, Loshno and others. The constructive approximation in the uniform norm is more appropriate for, e.g. certain robotic applications, and stands in contrast with more standard methods, such as back-propagation which approximate only in the average error norm.

Introduction

It is now known that an appropriate neural network can approximate to arbitrary accuracy almost any reasonable function. On the other hand, learning methods, most notably "back-propagation" give a gradient descent method to find the parameters of the network based on examples. However, these two results are not symmetric; the first result (existence) guarantees arbitrary approximation in the *maximal* error norm; while the second result (constructive) finds an answer by doing gradient descent in the *average* error norm.

The reason for this, of course, is that the average error is a differentiable function; so the chain rule, etc. can be used to derive the back-propagation algorithm. Trying gradient descent on the maximal error function seems a priori impossible because the function is non-differentiable. However, note that if it could be done, for many applications one might expect the approximation to be superior using the maximal error norm. For example, in many robotics applications, it is not sufficient that on the average the performance is accurate; one requires that the maximal deviation be within certain (e.g. safety) bounds.

In this work, we derive a constructive methodology for approximating in the maximal error norm; thereby in principle solving this problem. To do this, we apply a somewhat more sophisticated theory of differentiation due to Danskin, developed in the context of game theory. So in fact, we are able to do a form of gradient descent on a function since it is differentiable in this more general sense.

We also approach the question of the appropriate architecture for a problem, by showing how to increase the number of neurons in the hidden layer in such a way as to decrease the maximal error.

The establishment of these results suggests the following mechanism. One starts with a given network with a relatively small number of hidden neurons. One then uses our result to follow a gradient descent until a local minimum on the maximal error function is found. If this error is not sufficiently small, one then uses the other result to increase the dimension and change the weights in such a way that the maximal error decreses. One can then continue with the gradient descent again to reach a local minimum, again increase the dimension, etc.

Actually, there are other possibilities opened by these results. Since we are in a gradient descent situation, one can apply analogues of simulated annealing, or of multiple searches from different starting points. One can imagine mixing methods that allow some combination of searches for good local minima together with jumps in dimension. (We have another result giving another suggestion for increasing dimension.) On the other hand, the current results do not address the issues of speed of convergence, and of robustness. That is, one has to address the feasibility of following the recipe given by theorem 5 when one is not precisely at a local minimum. Experiments are also needed to decide on the proper mix of continuing to a local minimum in a given dimension and jumping to a higher one.

Note that this method is *not* a variant of back-propagation, but a different gradient descent method. One deals with *all* of the weights in the network (from all levels) at once and calculates a direction to decrease the maximal error directly from the known inputs that currently give the largest error. So the change in the weights is not done recursively by levels, but all at once. (In this paper, we developed the formulas for one hidden level, but they are directly extendible for an arbitrary number of levels.)

We also point out that we are simultaneously arranging to minimize the maximal error of each of the derivatives. However, our approach here is somewhat different than that of either [3] or [4] because we do not try to obtain the approximation of the derivative as the derivative of the neural network approximation; but rather as a direct approximation using additional outputs of the neural network. In this case, a major virtue of this approach is its simplicity; there is no need to deal with an analogue of Sobolev spaces appropriate for the maximal error norm. On the other hand, one needs to know all the derivatives at the sample data points.

The only result presented here which requires differentiability of the function being approximated (in fact twice differentiability) is Theorem 5 which depends on Lemma 2 where the hypothesis is used. In particular the gradient descent method holds without this hypothesis

Since the proofs of the results are somewhat intricate and lengthy, in this short paper, we omit them and simply state the results. The full paper [7] should appear shortly.

Our work proceeds as follows: Theorem 1 is just a restatement of Cybenko's theorem [1]. We then define and prove a slight variant of Danskin's theorem (Theorem 2) which establishes the necessary generalized directional derivatives that are needed. Theorem 3 is a technical result establishing how to constructively calculate the gradient. Theorem 4 is included for completeness, and shows how one can always increase the gradient even if one is not at a local minimum by increasing the dimension. Theorem 5 shows (using the result of Theorem 3) how to increase the dimension so that the error always decreases.

Results

Let M_n be a compact connected subset of R^n. Suppose g is a function from M_n to R^m. If F is another function on the same domain and range, we can consider F as an approximation to g and measure the quality of approximation by one of several metrics. One possibility is the Hilbert norm $\|g - F\|_h^2 = \int_{M_n} \sum_{i=1}^m [g_i(x) - F_i(x)]^2 dx$.

However this norm measures the *average* error and, as was discussed in the introduction, one might want to measure the quality of the *maximal* error. This is given by the uniform norm $\|g - F\|_1 = \max_{x \in M_n} \sum_{i=1}^m |g_i(x) - F_i(x)|$.

We now specialize to our specific interest, i.e. we assume that g is continuous and that F is generated by a neural network (NN-method). To be specific, let us suppose that F is given by a three level neural network with n neurons on the first layer and m neurons on the third layer and l neurons on the "hidden" layer. We assume that each neuron in the hidden layer responds by a simple sigmoidal $f(t) = \frac{1}{1+e^{-t}}$. We can denote the weights by the matrices $W^{(1)}$ (a $l \times n$ matrix) for the weights between the first and second layer and $W^{(2)}$ (an $m \times l$ matrix) for the weights between the second and the third layer and by an $l-$ length vector β the thresholds of the second layer.

Thus our function $F = (F_1, ... F_m)$ is given by the formula

$F_s(x, y) = \sum_{t=1}^l W_{s,t}^{(2)} f(u_t(x, y))$,

where $u_t(x, y) = \sum_{j=1}^n W_{t,j}^{(1)} x_j + \beta_t$.

The following vector valued version of the theorem of Cybenko [Cy] guarantees that arbitrary good approximations of this sort exist for any continuous function in the uniform norm . (We note that this is also known to hold for larger classes of functions in the Hilbert norm by the results of [8] and [2] , etc.)

Theorem 1 (Cybenko) *For any continuous vector function $g : M_n \to R^m$ and for any small $\epsilon > 0$ there exists a function F generated by the NN-method such that $\|g - F\|_1 < \epsilon$.*

Our goal is to effectivize Cybenko's theorem , i.e. to show how to construct such approximation in the *uniform* norm. We repeat that previous constructive methods have worked in the Hilbert norm.

Thus, given a positive ϵ, we need to determine the free variables W^1, W^2, and β so that with these values the approximation is within ϵ.

We now denote by the vector y all of these free parameters; thus the parameters y are chosen from the space $R^{(m+n+1)l}$, i.e. $y = (y_1, \ldots, y_{(m+n+1)l})$. Note that the dimension of y is a function of l; i.e. we allow for the possibility that the number of hidden neurons changes.

We denote by $\Phi(x, y)$ and $\phi(y)$ the functions
$\Phi(x, y) = \sum_{s=1}^{m} [g_s(x) - F_s(x, y)]^2$ and $\phi(y) = \max_{x \in M_n} \Phi(x, y)$.

Thus, the problem is to find y, minimizing ϕ. (Since it is easy to see that there are positive constants C_1, C_2 such that $C_1 \|g - F\|_1 \le \phi(y) \le C_2 \|g - F\|_1$ it follows that ϕ as a norm is equivalent to the uniform norm.)

Theorem 1 shows that there exist choices of the parameter y (including the choice of l) so that $\phi(y)$ is arbitrarily small. The rest of this paper is devoted to showing how to *constructively* find the y.

The construction of y is by a form of gradient descent. That is, given a y^1 we find a y^2 with $\phi(y^2) < \phi(y^1)$. However, note that since $\phi(y)$ is *not* differentiable the standard gradient does not exist, and therefore none of the usual mechanisms (e.g. back-propagation) are available to us.

To handle this problem, we follow the analysis originally introduced by J. Danskin [5] in the theory of max-min. Let γ be a direction (i.e. a unit vector) in the space $R^{(m+n+1)l}$. We define what we call the Danskin operator in the direction γ.

Definition: The *Danskin operator* in direction γ of $\phi(y)$, $(D_\gamma \phi)(y)$, is

$$(D_\gamma \phi)(y) = \lim_{\alpha \to 0+} \frac{1}{\alpha} [\phi(y + \alpha\gamma) - \phi(y)]$$

Theorem 2 (Danskin) *Properties of the Danskin operator :*
   (i) If $(D_\gamma \phi)(y)$ is negative at y^1, then $\phi(y)$ decreases in direction γ .
   (ii) For each point y and each direction γ $(D_\gamma \phi)(y)$ exists.
   (iii) $(D_\gamma \phi)(y)$ has the value

$$(D_\gamma \phi)(y) = \max_{z \in X(y)} < \Phi_y(z, y), \gamma > .$$

[Here $X(y) = \{x \in M_n : \Phi(x, y) = \phi(y)\}$ is the set of maximal points of the function $\Phi(x, y)$,

$\Phi_y(z, y) = (\Phi_{y_1}(z, y), \ldots, \Phi_{y_{(m+n+1)l}}(z, y)) \in R^{(m+n+1)l}$ is a vector of partial derivatives $\Phi_{y_i}(z, y) = \frac{\partial \Phi}{\partial y_i}(z, y)$, and

$< \Phi_y(z, y), \gamma > = \sum_{i=1}^{(m+n+1)l} \Phi_{y_i}(z, y)\gamma_i$ is a scalar product in the space $R^{(m+n+1)l}$.]

We will need the following corollary as well.

Corollary 1 *The Danskin operator $(D_\gamma \phi)(y)$ is a continuous function on the variables γ and y.*

The following theorem provides the constructive rule for our version of gradient descent.

Theorem 3 *Let y^1 be an arbitrary point in $R^{(m+n+1)l}$ with $\phi(y^1) > 0$ and let*
$$r_i = \max_{z \in X(y^1)} \Phi_{y_i}(z, y^1) \, , \, q_i = \min_{z \in X(y^1)} \Phi_{y_i}(z, y^1) \, ,$$
$$\sigma_1 = \sqrt{\sum_{r_i \leq 0} q_i^2 + \sum_{q_i \geq 0} r_i^2}$$
and $\sigma_2 = \sqrt{\sum_{r_i \leq 0} r_i^2 + \sum_{q_i \geq 0} q_i^2}$

Then exactly one of the following holds:

(i) y^1 is a local minimum point of $\phi(y)$;

(ii) the function $\phi(y)$ decreases in a direction γ^0 (we call it an antigradient of $\phi(y)$ in the point y^1), which is defined by coordinates

$$\gamma_i^0 = \begin{cases} -\frac{q_i}{\sigma_1} & \text{if } r_i \leq 0 \\ -\frac{r_i}{\sigma_1} & \text{if } q_i \geq 0 \\ 0 & \text{if } q_i < 0 < r_i \end{cases}$$

Theorem 3 allows us to perform our version of gradient descent constructively, but always keeping the same number of neurons. The next two theorems tell us how to change the weights when the number of hidden neurons is increased by one.

Theorem 4 *Suppose y^1 isn't a local minimum point of $\phi(y)$ in the space $R^{(m+n+1)l}$, and γ^0 is an antigradient from the point y^1 . There exists a direction $\gamma^1 \in R^{(m+n+1)(l+1)}$ such that $(D_{\gamma^1}\phi)(y^1) < (D_{\gamma^0}\phi)(y^1)$. (This direction can be found constructively.)*

In order to consider the correct passage from a local minimum to a better approximation with an increase in the hidden layer, we need to strengthen the hypothesis on g to assume that g is in fact twice differentiable. We then approximate not only g, but also its partial derivatives simultaneously. (This is necessary for the proof of Lemma 2.)

II-376

Since the previous theorems of course hold in this case, this means that we will have a constructive method for the simultaneous approximation in the uniform norm of both the function and its partial derivatives; under the assumption that the function is twice differentiable. (For a different kind of approximation to the function and its partial derivative see the papers [3] and [4].)

So we now assume that g is actually of the form $g = (h_1, \cdots, h_p, \frac{\partial h_1}{\partial x_1}, \ldots, \frac{\partial h_1}{\partial x_n}, \frac{\partial h_2}{\partial x_1}, \ldots, \frac{\partial h_p}{\partial x_n})$ where $h = (h_1, \ldots, h_p)$ is a twice differentiable function.

We now add some notation:

$A_s(x,y) = g_s(x) - \sum_{t=1}^{l} W_{s,t}^{(2)} f(u_t(x,y)) \ (s = 1, \ldots, m)$,

$B_t(x,y) = \sum_{s=1}^{m} A_s(x,y) W_{s,t}^{(2)} f'(u_t(x,y)) \ (t = 1, \ldots, l)$. Then $\Phi(x,y) = \sum_{s=1}^{m} A_s^2(x,y)$ and

$$\Phi_{y_i}(x,y) = \begin{cases} -2A_s(x,y)f(u_t(x,y)) & \text{if } i = (s-1)t \\ -2B_t(x,y)x_j & \text{if } i = ml + (t-1)n + j \\ -2B_t(x,y) & \text{if } i = (m+n)l + t \end{cases}$$

Lemma 1 *If y^1 is a local minimum point in the space $R^{(m+n+1)l}$ and $\phi(y^1) > 0$, then the set of maximal points $X(y^1)$ does not include an open subset .*

Theorem 5 *Let a vector y^1 be a local minimum point of the function $\phi(y)$ in the space $R^{(m+n+1)l}$ and let $\phi(y^1) > 0$. Then there exists a parameter $\mu > 0$, vectors $\vec{B} = (B_1, \ldots, B_l) \in R^l$ with $B_i \geq 0$, $\vec{\lambda} = (\lambda_1, \ldots, \lambda_m) \in R^m$ with $\|\vec{\lambda}\| = 1$, and $\vec{P} = (P_1, \ldots, P_{n+1}) \in R^{n+1}$ such that a vector $\hat{y} \in R^{(m+n+1)(l+1)}$ with coordinates*

$$\hat{y}_i = \begin{cases} y_{i-s+1}^1 - B_t\lambda_s & \text{if } i = (s-1)l + t \\ \mu\lambda_s & \text{if } i = s(l+1) \\ y_{i-m}^1 & \text{if } i = m(l+1) + (n-1)t + j \\ P_j & \text{if } i = (m+n-1)(l+1) + j \\ y_{i-m-n}^1 & \text{if } i = (m+n)(l+1) + t \\ P_{n+1} & \text{if } i = (m+n+1)(l+1) \end{cases}$$

satisfies the inequality $\phi(\hat{y}) < \phi(y^1)$.

In other words the new weights are given by

$$\hat{W}_{s,t}^{(2)} = \begin{cases} W_{s,t}^{(2)} - B_t\lambda_s & (s = 1, \ldots, m; t = 1, \ldots, l) \\ \mu\lambda_s & (s = 1, \ldots, m; t = l+1) \end{cases}$$

$$\hat{W}_{t,j}^{(1)} = \begin{cases} W_{t,j}^{(1)} & (t = 1, \ldots, l; j = 1, \ldots, n) \\ P_j & (t = l+1; j = 1, \ldots, n) \end{cases}$$

$$\hat{\beta}_t = \begin{cases} \beta_t & (t = 1, \ldots, l) \\ P_{n+1} & (t = l+1) \end{cases}$$

From the preceding theorems we obtain a method for the construction of an optimal vector of parameters y . Let y be a vector of parameters in the space $R^{(m+n+1)l}$. If y is a local minimum point of $\phi(y)$ then apply theorem 5 to take the next update of y a vector in $R^{(m+n+1)(l+1)}$. If y is not a local minimum point one can either use theorem 3 to move y to a local minimum point of $\phi(y)$ in $R^{(m+n+1)l}$, or use theorem 4 to choose the new y in $R^{(m+n+1)(l+1)}$ (perhaps by checking if this choice is better than that via theorem 3 , since theorem 4 does not guarantee a decrease in the value of $\phi(y)$) .

In more detail assuming y is not a local minimum point one can apply theorem 3 to construct an antigradient γ^0 . Then letting $y(\alpha) = y + \alpha\gamma^0$ one can choose α_0 so that $\phi(y(\alpha_0)) = \min\phi(y(\alpha))$. Then let the new y be $y(\alpha_0)$.

If one uses theorem 4 then one sets a direction γ^1 in $R^{(m+n+1)(l+1)}$. Let $\hat{y}$ be

$$\hat{y} = \begin{cases} y & \text{on } R^{(m+n+1)l} \\ 0 & \text{on } R^{(m+n+1)(l+1)} \end{cases}$$

Now we define $\hat{y}(\alpha) = \hat{y} + \alpha\gamma^1$ and find α_1 such that $\phi(\hat{y}(\alpha_1)) = \min\phi(\hat{y}(\alpha))$

Then one chooses the new y to be $\hat{y}(\alpha_1)$ (in the space $R^{(m+n+1)(l+1)}$) or $y(\alpha_0)$ (in the space $R^{(m+n+1)l}$) according as $\phi(\hat{y}(\alpha_1))$ or $\phi(y(\alpha_0))$ is smallest .

Now we can prove the following theorem .

Theorem 6 *The above method gives a constructive solution of our problem .*

BIBLIOGRAPHY

1 . G. Cybenko , " Approximation by superpositions of a sigmoidal function " , Mathematics of Control Signals and Systems , vol. 2 , pp 303 - 314 , 1989.

2 . K. Hornik , M. Stinchcombe , H. White , " Multilayer Feedforward Networks are Universal Approximation " , Neural Networks , 2 , pp 359 - 366 , 1989 .

3 . K. Hornik , M. Stinchcombe , H. White , " Universal Approximation of an Unknown Mapping and its Derivatives " , Neural Networks , 3 , pp 551 - 560 , 1990 .

4 . A. R. Galant , H. White , " On Learning the Derivatives on an Unknown Mapping with Multilayer Feedforward Networks " ,Neural Networks , 5 , pp 129 - 138 , 1992 .

5 . J. Danskin , " The Theory of Max - Min " , Springer - Verlag , New - York , 1967 .

6. M. Shoham, C. Li, Y. Hacham and E. Kreindler, "Neural Network Control of Robot Arm", CIRP Annals, 41/1, 1992.

7. M. Shoham, M. Meltser and L. Manevitz, "Constructive Uniform Approximation of Deifferentiable Vector-Functions by Neural Networks", preprint, U. Haifa 1993.

Training of Elliptical Basis Function NN

M. Kokol,[*] I. Grabec[†]

Faculty of Mechanical Engineering

Ljubljana, Slovenia

Abstract

The radial basis function neural network (RBF NN) is extended to the elliptical receptive fields of neurons. It is shown that an optimal response function of the elliptical basis function neural network (EBF NN) is the conditional average of the dependent variable with respect to the independent one. An analytical form of the conditional average is calculated for a special case when the probability density function (p.d.f.) is represented as a sum of K multidimensional Gaussian functions.

Learning algorithms are derived from relative entropy discrepancy measure between representative and empirical p.d.f. The training is done in batch and adaptive mode.

Two-dimensional examples of approximated regression curves are presented and a comparison between radial and elliptical basis function NN is made.

1 Introduction

The idea of a localized basis function neural network was introduced by (Moody et.al., 1989). The network provides a mapping of an independent variable x to a dependent one y. The topology of RBF NN can be represented as a three-layer neural network with input, hidden and output layer. Neurons in the input layer distribute input signals x to the neurons in hidden layer. A response function of network with K neurons in a hidden layer is

$$\widehat{y}(x) = \sum_{i=1}^{K} A_i \mathcal{R}_i \left(\frac{x - q_i}{\sigma_i} \right) \tag{1}$$

The localization stems from limited receptive fields of neurons in the hidden layer. Commonly used is the radial Gaussian basis function

$$\mathcal{R}_i \left(\frac{x - q_i}{\sigma_i} \right) = \frac{\exp -\|x - q_i\|^2 / 2\sigma_i^2}{\sum_{j=1}^{K} \exp -\|x - q_j\|^2 / 2\sigma_j^2}$$

Here the vector q_i and the scalar parameter σ_i describe the center and the width of the receptive field of the i-th neuron. In contrast to this, the output neurons have linear activation functions. Vector $\|A_1^{(i)}, A_2^{(i)}, ..., A_K^{(i)}\|^T$ represents the weights of the i-th output neuron. The performance of the estimator (1) has been improved heuristically by introducing a linear term (Stokbro et.al.,1990)

$$\widehat{y}(x) = \sum_{i=1}^{K} \left(A_i + \underline{B}_i \cdot (x - q_i) \right) \mathcal{R}_i \left(\frac{x - q_i}{\sigma_i} \right) \tag{2}$$

The main intention of this article is to show how a similar improvement can be introduced by a mathematically more strict procedure of network performance optimization.

---

[*]Email: miran.kokol@fs.uni-lj.si

[†]Email: igor.grabec@uni-lj.si

2 Regression model

The estimators mentioned above are special cases of a more general estimator based on localized basis functions. Thus, our approach generalizes this estimator to the class of elliptical basis functions, including the Moody-Darken circle estimator as a special case. Accordingly, to introduce it, we consider the joint-probability density function $p(x, y)$. The optimal, non-parametric mean-square estimator of a dependent vector variable is the conditional average (Grabec et.al., 1991)

$$\widehat{y}(x) = E[y|x]. \tag{3}$$

Here, the joint vector $z \in \Re^{m+n}$

$$z = x \oplus y = \left\| \begin{array}{c} x \\ y \end{array} \right\|$$

is defined so as to distinguish the given input from the estimated output variables. The joint p.d.f $p(z)$ has to be estimated from a finite number of samples $\{z_1, z_2, ..., z_N\}$ by appropriate smoothing. Rather than the commonly-used spherical filter function, we utilize here an elliptical, multi-variate Gaussian basis function, which significantly improves the estimation of the p.d.f. as well as the conditional average estimators derived form it. The joint p.d.f. is represented by

$$p_r(z, Q, \underline{B}, U) = \frac{1}{(2\pi)^{d/2}} \sum_{j=1}^{K} U_j \sqrt{|\underline{B}_j|} \exp\left(-\frac{1}{2}(z - Q_j)^T \underline{B}_j(z - Q_j)\right). \tag{4}$$

The vector Q_i is the position-vector of the center, or briefly, center-vector. The matrix $\underline{B}_i$ determines the receptive field, and the amplitude U_i corresponds to the excitability of the i-th neuron. The matrices $\underline{B}_i$ have to be symmetric and positive definite. We split the center-vectors and the matrices into input and output parts

$$Q_j = \left\| \begin{array}{c} Q_{(x)j} \\ Q_{(y)j} \end{array} \right\| \tag{5}$$

$$\underline{\Sigma}_j = \underline{B}_j^{-1} = \left\| \begin{array}{cc} \underline{\Sigma}_{(xx)j} & \underline{\Sigma}_{(xy)j} \\ \underline{\Sigma}_{(yx)j} & \underline{\Sigma}_{(yy)j} \end{array} \right\|. \tag{6}$$

By inserting the parametric p.d.f. $p_r(z)$ into the conditional average (3), we obtain, after some cumbersome, algebraic manipulations (Taylor, 1974), the estimator

$$\widehat{y}(x) = \sum_{j=1}^{K} \left(Q_{(y)j} + \underline{\Sigma}_{(yx)j} \underline{\Sigma}_{(xx)j}^{-1}(x - Q_{(x)j}) \right) \mathcal{R}_j(x), \tag{7}$$

where the functions $\mathcal{R}_i(x)$ have the form

$$\mathcal{R}_i(x) = \frac{U_i |\underline{\Sigma}_{(xx)i}|^{-1/2} \exp\left(-\frac{1}{2}(x - Q_{(x)i})^T \underline{\Sigma}_{(xx)i}^{-1}(x - Q_{(x)i})\right)}{\sum_{j=1}^{K} U_j |\underline{\Sigma}_{(xx)j}|^{-1/2} \exp\left(-\frac{1}{2}(x - Q_{(x)j})^T \underline{\Sigma}_{(xx)j}^{-1}(x - Q_{(x)j})\right)} \tag{8}$$

This estimator is similar to the one introduced before heuristically (2), but it is derived from very basic statistical concepts. It is reduced to the form (1) if the matrices $\underline{B}_i$ are diagonal: $\underline{B}_i = \sigma_i \underline{Id}$. A particular elliptic receptive field is oriented in the direction of the greatest concentration of empirical samples in the vicinity of the basis function center. Accordingly, a network with hidden neurons having activation functions of the form (8) is called an *elliptical basis function neural network* (EBF NN).

3 The learning rule

Let us consider a sample of N measured pairs of independent and dependent variables (x_i, y_i); $i = 1, 2, 3 \ldots, N$. Using this sample the parameters in estimator $\hat{y}(x, \zeta)$ must be determined during the training phase. The vector ζ merges all parameters in the estimator. The radial basis function neural network is usually learned either by a supervised or by a hybrid method. In the supervised learning scheme, a mean squared error is defined

$$\mathcal{N} = \sum_{i=1}^{N} [y_i - \hat{y}(x_i, \zeta_k)]^2$$

and minimized on all included parameters ζ_k; $k = 1, 2, 3, \ldots$. Optimization is done by solving a system of nonlinear equations

$$\frac{\partial \mathcal{N}}{\partial \zeta_k} = 0$$

either in batch or adaptive manner. It is obvious that such minimization leads to a very difficult numerical problem even in the case of estimator (1). Therefore, an unsupervised learning method is used for training the EBF NN. This method is based on estimation of the joint p.d.f. $p_r(z, U_i, Q_i, \underline{B}_i)$ on the empirical sample z_i; $i = 1, 2, \ldots, N$. For the estimation of the empirical p.d.f. a Parzen window estimate is utilized. It is denoted by $p_e(z)$

$$p_e(z) = \frac{1}{N} \sum_{i=1}^{N} \frac{1}{(2\pi)^{(n+m)/2} \sigma^{(n+m)}} \exp - \frac{(z - z_i)^T (z - z_i)}{2 \sigma^2}. \tag{9}$$

Accordingly, two p.d.f.'s are spanned over the sample space which are denoted the empirical p.d.f. $p_e(z, z_i)$ and the representative p.d.f. $p_r(z, \zeta)$. They should be as close as possible to the true p.d.f. which is, of course, unknown to us. However, if the empirical p.d.f. is well defined than it reflects the major statistical features of the sample space. To guarantee that the representative p.d.f. would reflect these features too, the two p.d.f.'s should be similar to each other. Therefore, some measure of discrepancy between p.d.f.'s is to be used. Different measures are elaborated in detail elsewhere (Kokol, 1993). In this place, a natural measure between p.d.f.'s is applied based upon information entropy. This measure is *relative entropy*[1] which is defined by the expression

$$\mathcal{N} = \int_{-\infty}^{\infty} p_e(z) \ln \frac{p_e(z)}{p_r(z)} d^{(n+m)} z. \tag{10}$$

It is not the first time that relative entropy has been used in the theory of neural networks. The learning of Boltzmann Machines and the learning of the Haken synergetic neural network is also based on a relative entropy criterion (Hertz et.al., 1991; Haken, 1990). To give the $p_r(z, \zeta)$ a meaning of p.d.f., a normalization constraint has to be imposed on excitability parameters

$$\sum_{i=1}^{K} U_i = 1$$

The complete relative entropy discrepancy measure is then

$$\mathcal{N} = \int_{-\infty}^{\infty} p_e(z) \ln \frac{p_e(z)}{p_r(z)} d^{(n+m)} z + \lambda (1 - \sum_{i=1}^{K} U_i) \tag{11}$$

---

[1] It is called sometimes *Kullback information* or *information gain*.

The constant λ is the Lagrangian multiplier. Under the assumption that N is a large number, the relative entropy measure can be simplified to maximum likelihood criterion

$$\mathcal{N} = \frac{1}{N} \sum_{i=1}^{N} \ln p_r(\boldsymbol{z}_i) + \lambda \left(1 - \sum_{j=1}^{K} U_j\right). \tag{12}$$

We further utilize optimization procedures which require the evaluation of the gradients $\frac{\partial \mathcal{N}}{\partial \zeta_k}$. However, all mathematical steps are not needed here and the interested reader should refer to (Duda, 1973).

To write results of optimization procedure in concise form, a new function $\rho(\boldsymbol{z}, \boldsymbol{Q}_l, \underline{\boldsymbol{B}}_l, U_l)$ is first introduced by

$$\rho(\boldsymbol{z}, \boldsymbol{Q}_l, \underline{\boldsymbol{B}}_l, U_l) = \frac{U_l \sqrt{|\underline{\boldsymbol{B}}_l|} \exp\left(-\frac{1}{2}(\boldsymbol{z} - \boldsymbol{Q}_l)^T \underline{\boldsymbol{B}}_l (\boldsymbol{z} - \boldsymbol{Q}_l)\right)}{\sum_{j=1}^{K} U_j \sqrt{|\underline{\boldsymbol{B}}_j|} \exp\left(-\frac{1}{2}(\boldsymbol{z} - \boldsymbol{Q}_j)^T \underline{\boldsymbol{B}}_j (\boldsymbol{z} - \boldsymbol{Q}_j)\right)}.$$

By using this function, convenient batch equations for unknown parameters are obtained

$$U_l(t+1) = \frac{1}{N} \sum_{i=1}^{N} \rho(\boldsymbol{z}_i, \boldsymbol{Q}_l, \underline{\boldsymbol{B}}_l, U_l)$$

$$\boldsymbol{Q}_l(t+1) = \frac{\sum_{i=1}^{N} \boldsymbol{z}_i \, \rho(\boldsymbol{z}_i, \boldsymbol{Q}_l, \underline{\boldsymbol{B}}_l, U_l)}{\sum_{i=1}^{N} \rho(\boldsymbol{z}_i, \boldsymbol{Q}_l, \underline{\boldsymbol{B}}_l, U_l)}$$

$$\underline{\boldsymbol{B}}_l^{-1}(t+1) = \frac{\sum_{i=1}^{N} (\boldsymbol{z}_i - \boldsymbol{Q}_l)(\boldsymbol{z}_i - \boldsymbol{Q}_l)^T \, \rho(\boldsymbol{z}_i, \boldsymbol{Q}_l, \underline{\boldsymbol{B}}_l, U_l)}{\sum_{i=1}^{N} \rho(\boldsymbol{z}_i, \boldsymbol{Q}_l, \underline{\boldsymbol{B}}_l, U_l)}$$

The training is a stochastic gradient descent procedure, so it can be done in an adaptive manner. Using the Robinson-Monro stochastic approximation procedure we get adaptive equations

$$\boldsymbol{Q}_l(t+1) = \boldsymbol{Q}_l(t) + \alpha(t) \, \rho(\boldsymbol{z}_{t+1}, \boldsymbol{Q}_l, \underline{\boldsymbol{B}}_l, U_l) \, \underline{\boldsymbol{B}}_l (\boldsymbol{z}_{t+1} - \boldsymbol{Q}_l)$$

$$\underline{\boldsymbol{B}}_l(t+1) = \underline{\boldsymbol{B}}_l(t) + \alpha(t) \, \rho(\boldsymbol{z}_{t+1}, \boldsymbol{Q}_l, \underline{\boldsymbol{B}}_l, U_l) \left(\underline{\boldsymbol{B}}_l^{-1} - (\boldsymbol{z}_{t+1} - \boldsymbol{Q}_l)(\boldsymbol{z}_{t+1} - \boldsymbol{Q}_l)^T\right)$$

$$U_l(t+1) = U_l(t) + \alpha(t) \left(\frac{\rho(\boldsymbol{z}_{t+1}, \boldsymbol{Q}_l, \underline{\boldsymbol{B}}_l, U_l)}{U_l} - \frac{1}{K} \sum_{k=1}^{K} \frac{\rho(\boldsymbol{z}_{t+1}, \boldsymbol{Q}_k, \underline{\boldsymbol{B}}_k, U_k)}{U_k}\right)$$

The function $\alpha(t)$ depends on a number of iteration steps and must be appropriately selected to ensure convergence. A simple discussion on how to choose this function can be found in (Traven, 1991).

4 Examples

The localized basis function NN has been trained on simulated samples generated by different functions, with random noise added. In the examples presented, 500 training points were used. Small dots in the figures denote training samples, whereas small circles show centers of basis functions. Large ellipses or circles represent the range of receptive fields of neurons. The regression curves calculated from (3) are drawn as thick lines. Fig. 1 shows the approximation of a linear

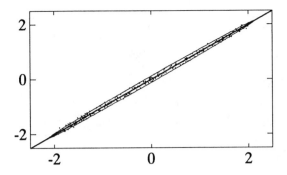

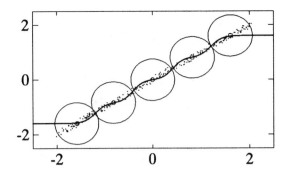

Figure 1: Linear function approximated by 1 elliptical basis function.

Figure 2: Linear function approximated by 5 radial basis functions.

function by just one elliptical neuron. The initial state of training was chosen randomly, and the training was run on 5 batch iterations. The same function as in Fig. 1 is approximated by 5 radial basis functions in Fig. 2. Satisfactory interpolation behaviour of approximation is observed, but this is not valid for extrapolation mapping properties. Generally, a large extrapolation error is characteristic of all approximations with radial basis functions. A more complicated example is shown in Fig. 3. A parabolic distribution is approximated by six elliptical basis functions. The picture is the result of 20 batch iterations from a random initial state. For the sake of comparison, the same distribution is represented by radial basis functions, as shown in Fig. 4. The widths were determined by a supervised method based on the minimization of regression error. The regression curves in Fig. 5 and Fig. 6 are trained on 1000 points. It is obvious that good approximation curves for different nonlinear functions can be obtained even with very a low number of elliptical basis functions.

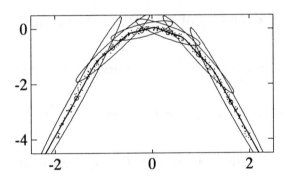

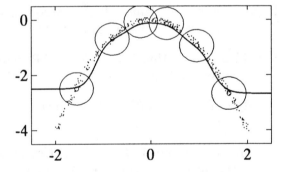

Figure 3: Quadratic function approximated by 6 elliptical basis functions.

Figure 4: Quadratic function approximated by 6 radial basis functions.

5 Conclusions

Comparison of the figures reveals that the performance of the RBF NN can be improved significantly by introducing elliptical receptive fields of neurons. The probability density function is represented better between the sample points, and therefore the regression error is reduced, when estimating the

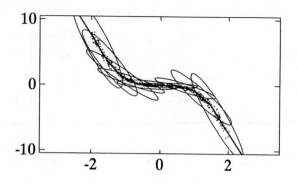

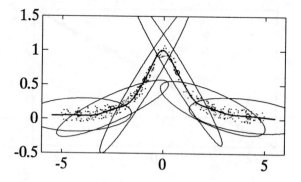

Figure 5: Cubic function approximated by 10 elliptical basis functions.

Figure 6: Cauchy function approximated by 6 elliptical basis functions.

conditional average from the elliptical basis functions. However, the method is then computationally more demanding, especially on account of matrix inversion.

6 References

Duda R.O., Hart P.E.: **Pattern Classification and Scene Analysis.**
John Wiley & Sons, New York, 1973.

Grabec I., Sachse W. (1991): *Automatic Modeling of Physical Phenomena.* Journal of Applied Physics, **69**, (6233-6244)

Haken H.: **Synergetic Computers and Cognition**
Springer-Verlag, Springer Series in Synergetics: Vol 50, Berlin, 1990.

Hertz J., Krogh A., Palmer R.G.: **Introduction to the Theory of Neural Computation**
Addison-Wesley, Redwood City CA, 1991.

Kokol M. (1993): *Modeling of Physical Phenomena by Regression Neural Network.* M.Sc. Thesis, University of Ljubljana - Department of Physics, Ljubljana (In Slovene)

Moody J., Darken C. (1989): *Fast Learning in Networks of Locally-Tuned Processing Units.* Neural Computation, **1**, (281-294)

Stokbro K., Umberger D.K., Hertz J.A. (1990): *Exploiting Neurons with Localized Receptive Fields to Learn Chaos.* Complex Systems 4, (603-622)

Taylor D.L.: **Probability and Mathematical Statistics**
Harper & Row, New York, 1974

Traven H.G.C.: **A Neural Network Approach to Statistical Pattern Classification by Semiparametric Estimation of Probability Density Functions**
IEEE Trans. on Neural Networks, NN-2, (366-377), 1991

Counting the Number of Functions Realizable with Two Hidden Layer Networks

Akito SAKURAI

Advanced Research Laboratory, Hitachi, Ltd.

Hatoyama, Saitama 350-03, JAPAN

E-mail: sakurai@harℓ.hitachi.co.jp

Abstract. We investigate the number of dichotomies realizable with multi-layer neural networks. For n-real-input two-hidden-layer neural networks with h_1 units in the first hidden layer and h_2 in the second ($h \equiv h_1 + h_2$), where the units use the linear threshold function (Heaviside function), we show that the networks can implement between $\sum_{i=0}^{(h_1 h_2 + n h_2)/2} \binom{N}{i}$ and $\sum_{i=0}^{(h_1 h_2 + n h)(\log h + 2 \log \log h)} \binom{N}{i}$ dichotomies for almost any set of N input points but they can implement between $2 \sum_{i=0}^{h_1 h_2 + n h_2} \binom{N-1}{i}$ and $2 \sum_{i=0}^{h_1 h_2 + 2nh} \binom{N-1}{i}$ dichotomies for some set of N input points with infinite Lebesgue measure.

1. Introduction

One problem we confront when we applying neural networks to certain classification tasks is how to ensure the networks' generalization capabilities. Valiant's PAC (Probably Approximately Correct) framework provides bounds using the VC-dimension ([3],[4]). We obtained the VC-dimensions of multi-layer neural networks of fixed number of or unrestricted number of hidden layers with fixed number of hidden units ([10],[11], [12]) and conducted experiments on the one-hidden-layer case to determine the validity of the theoretical results. Suppose that one hidden layer network with h hidden units (linear threshold function units) is trained by a backpropagation-like learning algorithm for randomly given input points. We found that, although the VC-dimension and, consequently, the theoretically ensured generalization capability is a function of $nh \log h$, they behaved as a function of h with slower growth. We imagine that the reason is that, for a large portion of sets of $N < d$ input points where d is the VC-dimension of the set of neural networks, the number of realizable dichotomies is far less than 2^N, and this makes the solution space small so that many possible solution exist close to the true one. This stimulated our research on the number of dichotomies of N input points realizable by a set of networks.

When Cover defined the capacity of single n-input threshold (linear or nonlinear) unit networks (*i.e.*, the set of a threshold unit with varying weights and thresholds) as the maximal N such that for any set of N input points in general position in $\mathcal{R}^n$, the network can implement some half of all the dichotomies of the pointset, he obtained the number of realizable dichotomies as exactly $2 \sum_{i=0}^{n} \binom{N-1}{i}$ for any pointset in general position and less than that for any pointset not in general position. Note that the number is independent of the geometrical position of input points.

For the multi-layer network case, the relative positions of input points are important, since the number of realizable dichotomies of N points is now not only a function of N but also a function of the geometrical arrangement of the points. Suppose, for example, that we consider the set of all the n input networks of one hidden layer with h hidden units and let $N_1 = (1/2)(nh)(\log_2 h)(1 - O(\log \log h / \log h) - O((\log h)/n))$ For some set of N_1 points, at least $2^{N_1} \approx h^{(1/2)nh}$ dichotomies are realizable ([10]), but for another set of N_1 points, only $2 \sum_{i=0}^{nh} \binom{N-1}{i} < ((1/2)e \log_2 h)^{nh}$ dichotomies are realizable ([6],[10]).

In this paper, we summarize the one-hidden-layer case and show new results on the two-hidden-layer case, which are improvements on the results given by Kowalczyk ([6]) where only the first hidden layer units are taken into account.

2. Notations

A *linear threshold element*, hereafter referred to simply as an *element* or *unit*, is an element with k inputs $(x_1, x_2, \ldots, x_k)$, 1 output, and $k + 1$ parameters $(w_1, w_2, \ldots, w_k), and \theta$ which outputs $\text{sgn}(\sum_{i=1}^{k} w_i x_i - \theta)$, where $\text{sgn}(x)$ is the sign function. We consider only a feedforward network composed of threshold elements, and all the networks we deal with in this paper have only one binary output. The inputs to the network or the output from the network are called *external inputs* or *external output* to distinguish them from intra-network inputs and outputs. The *depth* of a network is the length of the longest path from its external inputs to its external output, where the length is the number of the elements on the path. We can naturally assign the *depth* to each element in a network as the length of the longest path from the output of the element to the external input, where the length is the number of the elements on the path. The depth of the external output element is the depth of the network. A *hidden layer* is a set of elements with the same depth except for the external element. A point x in $\mathcal{R}^n$ is on the *output value boundary* of a network when in any of its neighborhoods there exists a point for which the network outputs 1 and another point 0.

A *0-1vector* is a vector whose elements are 0's and/or 1's. $\mathbf{a} \cdot \mathbf{b}$ is the inner product of two vectors $\mathbf{a}$ and $\mathbf{b}$. An *N-pointset* is a pointset whose cardinality is N, and $\#(P)$ or $|P|$ represents the cardinality of a set P.

An N-tuple S of N points in $\mathcal{R}^n$ is in the *0-th order general position* or just in *general position* if there exists only a non-trivial solution $\mathbf{w} = \mathbf{0}$, $w_0 = 0$ for the simultaneous equation $\mathbf{w} \cdot \mathbf{x}_i = w_0$ $(1 \le i \le n+1)$ for any $\{\mathbf{x}_1, \ldots, \mathbf{x}_{n+1}\} \subset S$ (where S is interpreted as a pointset). It is in the *first order general position* if there exists only a non-trivial solution $\mathbf{w} = \mathbf{0}$, $w_0 = 0$, $w_1 = 0$ for the simultaneous equation $\mathbf{w} \cdot \mathbf{x}_i = w_0$ $(1 \le i \le n)$, $\mathbf{w} \cdot \mathbf{x}_{n+1} = w_0 + w_1$ and $\mathbf{w} \cdot \mathbf{x}_{n+2} = w_0 + w_1$ for any $\{\mathbf{x}_1, \ldots, \mathbf{x}_{n+2}\} \subset S$. The set $\mathcal{GP}_i(n, N) \subset (\mathcal{R}^n)^N$ of all the N-tuples in the i-th general position is open and dense, so that almost all N-tuples are in the i-th general position. The above definition of $\mathcal{GP}_0$ is an extension of one in [6].

A *dichotomy* of a pointset or tuple S is a $\{0,1\}$-valued function defined on S. A *counting function* $\Pi_{\mathcal{F}}(S)$ is the number of dichotomies of S realizable by a function set (or a network set) $\mathcal{F}$.

The following property of $\mathcal{GP}_1$, similar to the $\mathcal{GP}_0$ ([6]) case, holds.

Theorem 2.1. Suppose $\mathcal{F}_2$ is a set of n-input 1-output two-hidden-layer networks with h_1 units in the first hidden layer and h_2 in the second. Then $\Pi_{\mathcal{F}_2}(P)$ as a function of P is constant on every connected component of $\mathcal{GP}_1(n, |P|)$.

3. Statement of main results

For the one-hidden-layer case, that is, the case when $\mathcal{F}_1$ is a set of n-input 1-output one-hidden-layer networks with h hidden units, the upper and lower bounds of the counting function $\Pi_{\mathcal{F}_1}(S)$ are easily obtained from our previous results ([8],[10], [6]).

Theorem 3.1. Suppose h is even. For any pointset S in general position,

$$\Pi_{\mathcal{F}_1}(S) \le \sum_{i=0}^{nh(\log h + 2\log\log h)} \binom{|S|}{i},$$

$$\Pi_{\mathcal{F}_1}(S) \ge 2 \sum_{i=0}^{\min\{nh/2, |S|/2\}} \binom{|S|}{i}.$$

Theorem 3.2. For some pointset S in general position,

$$\Pi_{\mathcal{F}_1}(S) = 2 \sum_{i=0}^{nh} \binom{|S| - 1}{i}.$$

What we are going to present here is the two-hidden-layer network version of the above theorems. Suppose that $\mathcal{F}_2$ is a set of n-input 1-output two-hidden-layer networks with h_1 units in the first hidden layer and h_2 in the second.

Theorem 3.3. Suppose h_1 and h_2 are even. For any pointset S in the first order general position,

$$\Pi_{\mathcal{F}_2}(S) \le \sum_{i=0}^{(h_1 h_2 + nh)(\log h + 2\log\log h)} \binom{|S|}{i},$$

$$\Pi_{\mathcal{F}_2}(S) \ge 2 \sum_{i=0}^{\min\{(h_1 h_2 + nh_2)/2, |S|/2\}} \binom{|S|}{i}.$$

Theorem 3.4. For some pointset S in the first order general position,

$$\Pi_{\mathcal{F}_2}(S) \le 2 \sum_{i=0}^{h_1 h_2 + 2nh} \binom{|S|-1}{i},$$

$$\Pi_{\mathcal{F}_2}(S) \ge 2 \sum_{i=0}^{h_1 h_2 + nh_2} \binom{|S|-1}{i}.$$

In the next two sections we give proof sketches of the above theorems. Before going to our proof, we just briefly describe some implications of the results. Since a network in $\mathcal{F}_2$ contains $W = (n+1)h_1 + (n+h_1+1)h_2 + (h_1+h_2+1) \approx h_1 h_2 + n(h_1+h_2)$ weights and thresholds, the above theorem statements may be thought as implying the following.

1. For almost all pointsets of up to W points, we can find a network to realize any of their dichotomies.
2. For some pointset of up to $2W$ points, we can find a network to realize any dichotomy in some half of their dichotomies.

From the results for one linear threshold case, we imagine that we can store about two patterns per connection (in probability $1/2$), that is, we expect that

3. For almost all pointsets of up to $2W$ points, we can find a network to realize any in some half of their dichotomies.

holds, but we still have no evidence to support or to reject it.

4. Counting function for almost all cases

We briefly exhibit ideas for our proof of Theorem 3.3. The basic technique used in the proof is similar to the one used for the one-hidden-layer case in [8]. We are going to confine points whose assigned category is 1 by pairs of hyperplanes. The only complication is that we have to utilize two hidden layers to effectively generate $h_1 h_2$ confinements of a single point using $h_1 + h_2$ hyperplanes. Intuitively, this is done as follows:

1. Divide the input space $\mathcal{R}^n$ with h_1 parallel hyperplanes into $h_1 + 1$ subspaces. One subspace contains $nh_2/2$ points, and each of the other subspaces contains $h_2/2$ points.
2. Use $h_2/2$ pairs of hyperplanes to confine $nh_2/2$ points in the first subspace by confining n points by every hyperplane pair.
3. Use $h_2/2$ pairs of hyperplanes to confine $h_2/2$ points in each of the remaining subspaces by confining a single point by every pair.

Suppose that we are given a pointset P in $\mathcal{GP}_1(n, N)$ where $|P| = N$ and a dichotomy of $P = P_1 \cup P_0$. P_1 is a set of points which, when input to a network, should produce 1 as its external output. Let us call points in P_1 1-output points. Without loss of generality, we assume $|P_0| \ge |P_1| = (h_1 h_2 + nh_2)/2$. In the following, we show a way to find weights and thresholds for units $g_1^1, g_2^1, \ldots, g_{h_1}^1$ in the first hidden layer (the layer closer to the external input) and units $g_1^2, g_2^2, \ldots, g_{h_1}^2$ in the second hidden layer (the layer closer to the external output). The weights and thresholds are only implicitly expressed in this paper in terms of hyperplanes.

When an $(n-1)$-dimensional hyperplane H is $\{\mathbf{x} : \mathbf{w} \cdot \mathbf{x} = d\}$ for some $\mathbf{w}$, a hyperplane $H + c$ means $\{\mathbf{x} : \mathbf{w} \cdot \mathbf{x} = d + c\}$. The positive side of the hyperplane is expressed by H^+, that is, $H^+ = \{\mathbf{x}; \mathbf{w} \cdot \mathbf{x} - d > 0\}$, and the negative side H^-. $< H, L >$ is a strip $H^+ \cap L^-$.

(Step 1) Define h_1 parallel hyperplanes $H_0, H_0 + \rho_1, \ldots, H_0 + \rho_{h_1-1}$ to satisfy the following conditions where $\rho_0 = 0$ and $\rho_i < \rho_{i+1}$:

· $nh_2/2$ 1-output points are in H_0^-,

· $< H_0 + \rho_{i-1}, H_0 + \rho_i >$ contains $h_2/2$ 1-output points for $1 \le i \le h_1 - 1$.

· H_i's do not contain any points in P.

Let us name these strips $S_0 = H_0^-$, $S_i = < H_0 + \rho_{i_1}, H_0 + \rho_i >$ and $S_{h_1} = (H_0 + \rho_{h_1-1})^+$.

(Step 2) Define $h_2/2$ hyperplanes $H_1, \ldots, H_{h_2/2}$, so that each contains exactly n points in S_0 without duplication.

(Step 3) Suppose that $1 \le i \le h_1$ and $1 \le j \le h_2/2$. Define $\rho_{i,j}$ so that a hyperplane $H_j + \rho_{i,j}$ contains one 1-output point in S_i without duplication. This is possible because of the first-order general-position condition.

(Step 4) The ϵ which appears in the following is taken to be small enough that a pair of hyperplanes designated by g_{2j-1}^2 and g_{2j}^2 does not confine any points in P other than those specified.

    4.1. Let connection weights from external inputs to g_i^1 be such that g_i^1 designates $H_0 + \rho_{i-1}$.

    4.2. Let connection weights from external inputs to g_{2j-1}^2 be such that g_{2j-1}^2 designates $H_j - \epsilon$, and those to g_{2j}^2 be such that g_{2j}^2 designates $H_j + \epsilon$.

    4.3. Let a connection weight from g_i^1 to g_{2j-1}^2 be such that in S_i, g_{2j-1}^2 designates $H_j + \rho_{i,j} - \epsilon$, and a weight g_i^1 to g_{2j}^2 be such that in S_i, g_{2j}^2 designates $H_j + \rho_{i,j} + \epsilon$. This can be done by setting both of the weights as $-\rho_{i,j} + \rho_{i-1,j}$.

(Step 5) The connection weights from g_i^1 to the external output unit are 0, and that from g_j^2 is $(-1)^{j+1}$. The threshold of the external output unit is $+0.5$.

This completes the construction of a network (*i.e.*, assignment of weights and thresholds). Since the functions of units in the network is intuitively clear, we omit the proof of the intended function of the network.

5. Counting function for some special case

In this section, we prove Theorem 3.4, using a very useful algebraic curve we used in [8], which also plays an important role in [6]. The curve is represented in a parametric form as $\mathbf{c}(t) = (t, t^2, \ldots, t^n)$ in $\mathcal{R}^n$, which has the following advantageous property.

Theorem 5.1. Any set of points on the curve $\mathbf{c}(t)$ is in the first order general position.

Let t_i be real numbers such that $t_1 < t_2 < \cdots < t_N$. and $P = \{\mathbf{c}(t_i) : 1 \le i \le N\}$. A *transition* of a dichotomy $P = P_1 \cup P_0$ is an index i such that $\mathbf{c}(t_i)$ and $\mathbf{c}(t_{i+1})$ belong to different categories under the dichotomy.

We prove the next theorem using the above property and the technique similar to the one in the proof of Theorem 3.3.

Theorem 5.2. Any dichotomy of $P = P_1 \cup P_0$ is realizable by a network in $\mathcal{F}_2$ if the number of transitions of the dichotomy is less than or equal to $h_1 h_2 + n h_2$.

(Proof sketch) We may suppose, without loss of generality, that the transitions are $\{i_1, \ldots, i_\tau\}$ where $\tau = h_1 h_2 + n h_2$ and $t_1 \in P_0$. We have two cases for n, namely, even n and odd n. Suppose first that n is odd. The construction procedure is:

(Step 0) Find arbitrary points $p_{i,j}$ between t_{i_j} and t_{i_j+1} for $1 \le j \le \tau$.

(Step 1) Find $H_0, H_0 + \rho_1, \ldots, H_0 + \rho_{h_1-1}$ (where $\rho_0 = 0$ and $\rho_i < \rho_{i+1}$) such that

    · $H_0 + \rho_i$ intersects $\mathbf{c}(t)$ at only one point and $\mathbf{c}(\infty) \in H_0^+$.

    · nh_2 transitions are in H_0^-,

    · $< H_0 + \rho_{i-1}, H_0 + \rho_i >$ contains h_2 transitions for $1 \le i \le h_1 - 1$.

Let us name these areas $S_0 = H_0^-$, $S_i = < H_0 + \rho_{i-1}, H_0 + \rho_i >$ and $S_{h_1} = (H_0 + \rho_{h_1-1})^+$.

(Step 2) Find hyperplanes $H_1, \ldots, H_{h_2}$ such that

    · H_k contains $\mathbf{c}(p_{i_{(k-1)n+1}}), \ldots, \mathbf{c}(p_{i_{kn}})$ for $1 \le k \le h_2$.

The direction of H_{2l-1} and H_{2l} (where $1 \le l \le h_2/2$) is defined so that $< H_{2l-1}, H_{2l} >$ contains points of category 1, that is, $\mathbf{c}(t_i) \in P_1$ iff $\mathbf{c}(t_i) \in H_{2l-1}^+$ and $\mathbf{c}(t_i) \in H_{2l}^-$ for $i_{(2l-2)n} \le i \le i_{2ln+1}$.

It is easily observed that H_k^+ contains $\mathbf{c}(\infty)$.

(Step 3) Suppose that $1 \le i \le h_1$ and $1 \le j \le h_2$. Define $\rho_{i,j}$ so that a hyperplane $H_j + \rho_{i,j}$ contains one transition point $p_{i_{nh_2+(i-1)h_2+j}}$ ($\in S_i$). Clearly $H_j + \rho_{i,j}$ contains no other point of the curve $\mathbf{c}(t)$ in S_i. This is because the first-order general-position property holds for any pointset on the curve $\mathbf{c}(t)$. Note that for the adjacent points $\mathbf{c}(t_{i_{nh_2+(i-1)h_2+j}})$ and $\mathbf{c}(t_{i_{nh_2+(i-1)h_2+j}+1})$, if j is odd, the fact that $\mathbf{c}(t_{i_{nh_2+(i-1)h_2+j}}) \in (H_j+\rho_{i,j})^-$ and $\mathbf{c}(t_{i_{nh_2+(i-1)h_2+j}+1}) \in (H_j+\rho_{i,j})^+$ corresponds to the category assignment

$c(t_{i_{nh_2+(i-1)h_2+j}}) \in P_0$ and $c(t_{i_{nh_2+(i-1)h_2+j}+1}) \in P_1$; if j is even, the fact that $c(t_{i_{nh_2+(i-1)h_2+j}}) \in (H_j + \rho_{i,j})^+$ and $c(t_{i_{nh_2+(i-1)h_2+j}+1}) \in (H_j + \rho_{i,j})^-$ corresponds to the category assignment $c(t_{i_{nh_2+(i-1)h_2+j}}) \in P_1$ and $c(t_{i_{nh_2+(i-1)h_2+j}+1}) \in P_0$.

(Step 4)   Define weights and thresholds as follows:

   4.1. Let connection weights from external inputs to g_i^1 be such that g_i^1 designates $H_0 + \rho_{i-1}$.

   4.2. Let connection weights from external inputs to g_j^2 be such that g_j^2 designates H_j.

   4.3. Let a connection weight from g_i^1 to g_j^2 be such that in S_i, g_j^2 designates $H_j + \rho_{i,j}$. This can be done by setting the weight as $-\rho_{i,j} + \rho_{i-1,j}$.

(Step 5)   The connection weights from g_i^1 to the external output unit are 0, and those from g_j^2 are $(-1)^{j+1}$. The threshold of the external output unit is $+0.5$.

This completes the construction of a network (*i.e.*, assignment of weights and thresholds) for the case when n is odd. Since the function of the units in the network is intuitively clear, we omit the proof of the intended function of the network.

For the even-n case, we make pairs of units in the second hidden layer. The largest difference between the proofs lies in Step 2. The new step is as follows:

(Step 2)   Find hyperplanes $H_1, \ldots, H_{h_2}$ such that

· for odd k $(1 \le k \le h_2 - 1)$, H_k contains

$$c(p_{i_{(k-1)n+1}}), c(p_{i_{(k-1)n+4}}), c(p_{i_{(k-1)n+5}}), c(p_{i_{(k-1)n+8}}), \ldots, c(p_{i_{(k+1)n-3}}), c(p_{i_{(k+1)n}}),$$

· for even k $(2 \le k \le h_2)$, H_k contains

$$c(p_{i_{(k-2)n+2}}), c(p_{i_{(k-2)n+3}}), c(p_{i_{(k-2)n+6}}), c(p_{i_{(k-2)n+7}}), \ldots, c(p_{i_{kn-2}}), c(p_{i_{kn-1}}).$$

The direction of H_{2l-1} and H_{2l} (where $1 \le l \le h_2/2$) is defined so that $< H_{2l-1}, H_{2l} >$ contains points of category 1, that is, $c(t_i) \in P_1$ iff $c(t_i) \in H_{2l-1}^+$ and $c(t_i) \in H_{2l}^+$. for $i_{(2l-1)n+1} \le i \le i_{2ln}$.

It is easily observed that H_k^+ contains $c(\infty)$.

Other constructions are done in the same way, so they are omitted here. (End of proof)

For a proof of our upper bound, we take very specific points on the curve $\mathbf{c}$, in contrast to the way we took in [8] where points were taken arbitrarily. Let $t_i = \gamma^{i-1}$, where $\gamma = 2^{n+2} N (N + 2n)!$ and $P = \{c(t_i) : 1 \le i \le N\}$. Then the following properties hold:

Lemma 5.3.   Suppose that $\mathbf{z}$ is a 0-1 vector of length h. If we vary $\mathbf{z}$, we get at most 2^h hyperplanes

$$\mathbf{w} \cdot \mathbf{x} + \mathbf{z} \cdot \begin{pmatrix} w_1 \\ \vdots \\ w_h \end{pmatrix} = 0.$$

Then these hyperplanes intersect with at most $h + 2(n-1)$ of the total of $N - 1$ arcs $\widehat{c(t_i)c(t_{i+1})}$ on the curve $\mathbf{c}(t)$.

This lemma can be proved using Lemmas 5.4, 5.5 and 5.6. Lemma 5.4 is proved through a lengthy calculation of the van der Monde matrix, although proofs for the lemmas are omitted for lack of space.

Lemma 5.4.   Let R_n be an $n \times n$ matrix whose (i, j) entry is $(1 + (\epsilon_{ij})^j)(x_i)^j$. If $\forall i$ $0 < x_i < (1/K)x_{i+1}$ and $\forall i \forall j$ $|\epsilon_{ij}| < (2^{n+1}(1+1/K)^{n(n-1)})^{-1}$ for some $K > 0$, then $\det R_n \ne 0$.

Lemma 5.5.   If $h \times h$ 0-1 matrix K is regular, $1 \le |\det K| < h!$.

Lemma 5.6.   Suppose that $\mathbf{z}_1, \ldots, \mathbf{z}_{h+1}$ are 0-1 vectors of length h. If $\mathbf{z}_1, \ldots, \mathbf{z}_h$ are linearly independent and $\mathbf{z}_{h+1} = \sum_{i=1}^{h} a_i \mathbf{z}_i$, then $|a_i| < h!$.

Theorem 3.4 is now obvious. Let the transitions be $\{i_1, \ldots, i_\tau\}$. By Lemma 5.3, $\tau \le nh_1 + h_2(h_1 + 2(n-1)) < h_1 h_2 + 2nh$. Therefore, any dichotomy realizable by $\mathcal{F}_2$ has at most $h_1 h_2 + 2nh$ transitions, that is,

$$\Pi_{\mathcal{F}_2}(P) \le 2 \sum_{i=0}^{\tau} \binom{|P|-1}{i} \le 2 \sum_{i=0}^{h_1 h_2 + 2nh} \binom{|P|-1}{i}.$$

This completes the proof for the upper bound.

6. Discussion

This paper, obviously an extension of Cover's ([5]) work, is also an improvement on Kowalczyk's work([6]). While Kowalczyk considered only the first hidden layer units, we have taken into account all the units in two hidden layers. Using Bartlett's proof (??) of his lower bound of VC-dimension of the two hidden layer neural networks, we can derive a lower bound of the counting function which is similar to but weaker than ours shown in Theorem 3.4. Note that the networks he considered do not have connections which skip hidden layers, to which our methods cannot be applied.

A great discrepancy between Cover's case and ours appears clearly in the results summarized in Section 3. Cover's one-unit case is simple and clear in two points:

· The counting function does not depend on the geometrical arrangements of input points.

· The counting argument itself is constructive, so that upper bounds and lower bounds coincide automatically.

One weak point in our results is that Theorem 3.2 and Theorem 3.4 hold only for "some pointsets" of input points. If we could show that the claims hold for "almost all pointsets" of input points, then we could say that "for almost all pointsets of input points, we can realize half of all the dichotomies". This remains to be proven.

7. References

[1] Bartlett, Peter I.: The sample size necessary for learning in multi-layer networks, *Proceedings of ACNN'93*, 14-17 (1993).

[2] Baum, E. B.: On the capabilities of multilayer perceptrons, *Journal of Complexity*, vol. 4, 193-215 (1988).

[3] Baum, E.B., and D. Haussler: What size net gives valid generalization?, *Neural Computation*, vol.1, 151-160 (1989).

[4] Blumer, A., A. Ehrenfeucht, D. Haussler, and M. K. Warmuth: Learnability and the Vapnik-Chervonenkis Dimension, *Journal of the ACM*, vol.36, no.4, 929-965 (Oct. 1989).

[5] Cover, T. M.: Geometrical and statistical properties of systems of linear inequalities with applications in pattern recognition, *IEEE Transactions on Electronic Computers*, vol. 14, 326-334 (1965).

[6] Kowalczyk, A.: Counting function theorem for multi-layer networks, to be presented at *NIPS*93* (1993).

[7] Mitchison, G. J., and R.M. Durbin: Bounds on the learning capacity of some multi-layer networks, *Biological Cybernetics*, vol. 60, 345-356 (1989).

[8] Sakurai, A.: n–h–1 networks store no less n·h+1 examples but sometimes no more, *Proceedings of IJCNN92*, vol.III, 936-941 (June 1992).

[9] Sakurai, A., and M. Yamasaki: On the capacity of n–h–s networks, *Artificial Neural Networks,2* , Elsevier Science Publishers, 237-240 (1992).

[10] Sakurai, A.: Tighter Bounds of the VC-Dimension of Three-layer Networks, *Proceedings of WCNN93*, vol.III, 540-543 (1993).

[11] Sakurai, A.: On the VC-dimension of Depth Four Threshold Circuits and the Complexity of Boolean-valued Functions, *Proceedings of ALT'93*, LNAI 744, Springer Verlag, 251-264 (1993).

[12] Sakurai, A.: On the VC-dimension of Neural Networks with a Large Number of Hidden Layers, to be presented at NOLTA'93 (1993).

[13] Vapnik, V.: *Estimation of Dependences Based on Empirical Data*, Springer-Verlag (1982).

On the Mappings of Optimization Problems to Neural Networks

Arun Jagota, Max Garzon

Department of Mathematical Sciences, Memphis State University
Memphis, Tennessee 38152 USA
{jagota,garzonm}@hermes.msci.memst.edu

In the past, neural networks have often performed poorly on optimization problems, often because the mappings are deficient (see [11, 1] for example). This work is motivated by the need to study better the mappings of optimization problems to neural networks, and builds on some early work in this area [17]. Its technical roots are in the topic of approximation-preserving reductions in computational complexity theory.

1 Basic Definitions

Definition 1 A function f is called *polynomial time computable* if the time to evaluate f on any input is at most polynomial in the size of the description of that input.

The following definition is derived from [15, 5].

Definition 2 An (NP) optimization problem is a three-tuple $A = \langle I_A, F_A, c_A \rangle$ where I_A is the set of *instances* of the problem, $F_A(i_a)$ is the set of *feasible solutions* of instance i_a, and $c_A(i_a, f_a) \in \Re$ is the *cost* of feasible solution $f_a \in F_A(i_a)$ in instance i_a. c_A is a polynomial time computable function.

The goal is to find a feasible solution of minimum cost in a given instance i_a of problem A.

Throughout this paper, i_x denotes an instance of problem X, and f_x a feasible solution in i_x.

Example. The Maximum Clique problem (MC) may be informally formulated as an (NP) optimization problem as follows. We will use this definition throughout the paper.

INSTANCE: Graph
FEASIBLE SOLUTION: A maximal (not necessarily maximum) subset of the vertices of G that form a clique (every pair of vertices is adjacent)
COST OF A FEASIBLE SOLUTION: -1 times the cardinality of the clique

Definition 3 A reduction of an optimization problem $A = \langle I_A, F_A, c_A \rangle$ to an optimization problem $B = \langle I_B, F_B, c_B \rangle$ is a pair of polynomial time computable functions $\langle f, g \rangle$ where $f : I_A \to I_B$ maps instances of A to instances of B and g is a *partial* function that maps a feasible solution $f_b \in F_B(f(i_a))$ to a feasible solution $f_a \in F_A(i_a)$. By partial we mean that g is not necessarily defined for every feasible solution of $f(i_a)$. We write the reduction as $A \xrightarrow{f,g} B$. We write $g(i_a, f_b)$ to denote the feasible solution in i_a that the feasible solution f_b in $f(i_a)$ maps to. We write $\mathrm{dom}(g(i_a))$ as the set of feasible solutions of $f(i_a)$ on which g is defined and $\mathrm{Im}(g(i_a))$ as the image of g on $\mathrm{dom}(g(i_a))$.

Computationally, to obtain a feasible solution of an instance i_a of problem A, i_a may first be reduced to instance $f(i_a)$ of problem B by using f, a feasible solution f_b may then be found in $f(i_a)$ by using some algorithm for B, which may then be used to obtain a feasible solution $g(f_b)$ of A by using g. f and g are polynomial time computable to keep this composite algorithm tractable. B may be a neural network using an energy-minimizing algorithm for example.

In all the two-argument functions such as c_A, g and others to be defined later, we suppress the first argument i_a when it is clear from the context.

2 Properties of Reductions

In the following definitions, the term reduction denotes $A \xrightarrow{f,g} B$. For all properties P defined in this section and later, a reduction satisfies P only if every instance $i_a \in I_A$ satisfies P.

Definition 4 ([17]) A reduction is called *total* if g is a total function, that is, g is defined on every feasible solution in the instance $f(i_a)$ of B.

A reduction that is not total has some feasible solutions in $f(i_a)$ that cannot be converted back to i_a.

Definition 5 A reduction is called *onto* if g is an onto function, that is, g maps onto every feasible solution of instance i_a of A.

A reduction that is not onto does not represent every feasible solution of i_a in $f(i_a)$. Perhaps not even the optimal is represented.

Definition 6 is a slight modification of the one in [17].

Definition 6 A reduction is called *order-preserving* if, for every distinct pair f_b', f_b'' of feasible solutions in $f(i_a)$ on which g is defined, $c_B(f_b') < c_B(f_b'') \Longrightarrow c_A(g(f_b')) < c_A(g(f_b''))$.

Definition 7 A reduction is called *order-reversing* if, for every distinct pair f_b', f_b'' of feasible solutions in $f(i_a)$ on which g is defined, $c_B(f_b') < c_B(f_b'') \Longrightarrow c_A(g(f_b')) > c_A(g(f_b''))$.

Order-preserving and order-reversing are mutually exclusive in that no reduction can simultaneously be both.

Definition 8 A reduction is called *equality-preserving* if, for every distinct pair f_b', f_b'' of feasible solutions in $f(i_a)$ on which g is defined, $c_B(f_b') = c_B(f_b'') \Longrightarrow c_A(g(f_b')) = c_A(g(f_b''))$.

A reduction that is order-preserving and equality-preserving guarantees that if we "improve" upon a feasible solution in $f(i_a)$ we always get an "improved" feasible solution in i_a. If we replace order-preserving by order-reversing then if we "worsen" a feasible solution in $f(i_a)$ we always get an "improved" feasible solution in i_a. Thus, for an order-reversing reduction, we need an algorithm whose objective is to find the poorest feasible solution in $f(i_a)$, not the best.

Definition 9 A reduction is called *k-cost-preserving* if every feasible solution in i_a of cost $\leq k$ is contained in $\text{Im}(g(f(i_a)))$.

In particular, if we can reduce the size of an instance i_a while preserving all its solutions of cost $\leq k$, then we have a k-cost-preserving reduction of A to itself which also potentially makes the instance relatively easier to solve because of its size reduction. Section 7 presents one such reduction.

Definition 10 A reduction $A \xrightarrow{f,g} B$ is called *invertible* if there exists a polynomial time inverse f^{-1} of f and a polynomial time inverse g^{-1} of g such that $B \xrightarrow{f^{-1},g^{-1}} A$ is a reduction. $B \xrightarrow{f^{-1},g^{-1}} A$ is called an *inverse* of $A \xrightarrow{f,g} B$ and is not necessarily unique.

In the above definition, the invertibility of a given f is a central issue. Since f^{-1} is required to be total, an f that is not onto, for example, is not invertible. Every g on the other hand is invertible because we do not insist that g^{-1} be total. Furthermore, g^{-1} is not necessarily unique as for a given $f_a \in Im(g)$, $g^{-1}(f_a)$ may be chosen as any f_b such that $g(f_b) = f_a$. The second issue is whether the inverses are polynomial time. Here also it turns out that for most commonly used reductions, a polynomial time inverse g^{-1} of g exists.

Let $F_A(i_a, k) \subseteq F_A(i_a)$ denote the set of feasible solutions in instance i_a having cost k. Let $E_A(i_a) = \sum_k k|F_A(i_a, k)|/|F_A(i_a)|$ denote the expected cost of a feasible solution in instance i_a under the uniform distribution on its set of feasible solutions $F_A(i_a)$.

Let $F_B(i_a, k) = \{f_b \in F_B(f(i_a))|c_A(g(f_b)) = k\}$ denote the set of feasible solutions in instance $f(i_a)$ of B that correspond to feasible solutions in instance i_a of cost k. Let $E_B(i_a) = \sum_k k|F_B(i_a, k)|/|F_B(f(i_a))|$ denote the expected cost of a feasible solution in instance i_a under the uniform distribution on the set of feasible solutions in $f(i_a)$.

Definition 11 A reduction is called *expected-cost-decreasing* if $E_B(i_a) < E_A(i_a)$.

If a reduction is expected-cost-decreasing then an algorithm that samples a feasible solution f_b of $f(i_a)$ uniformly at random from $F_B(f(i_a))$ will return on average a better feasible solution $g(f_b)$ of i_a than an algorithm that samples a feasible solution f_a of i_a uniformly at random from $F_A(i_a)$. Even if no such algorithms exist, we can at least say that the reduction improves the distribution of costs of feasible solutions of i_a as measured by the expectations as defined above. Section 7 presents one reduction that is motivated by this definition.

3 Reductions from Computational Complexity Theory

The notion of approximation-preserving reductions in computational complexity theory is one technical ancestor of the reduction properties in this paper. Here we list these early definitions in our terminology, noting that our problems are always minimization ones. We list them for completeness sake and to facilitate comparisons. Readers may skip this section as later sections do not depend on it. The approximation-preserving reductions in complexity theory all require that g be total and never discuss whether g is onto or not.

A *reencoding* [16] is a reduction that is **total, onto, invertible**, and for all $f_b \in F_B(f(i_a))$, $c_A(g(f_b)) = c_B(f_b)$.

Let m be an approximation measure defined as follows. When applied to feasible solution f_a of instance i_a of problem A, $m_A(i_a, f_a)$ measures how good an approximation $c_A(f_a)$ is to $c_A(f_a^*)$, the cost of an optimal solution f_a^*. m_A must satisfy $m_A(f_a) \geq 0$ and $m_A(f_a) = 0$ if and only if $c_A(f_a) = c_A(f_a^*)$. A *strict reduction* [19] is a reduction that is **total** and for any approximation measure m, for all $f_b \in F_B(f(i_a))$, $m_A(g(f_b)) \leq m_B(f_b)$. That is, with respect to the measure m, $c_A(g(f_b))$ is at least as good an approximation to $c_A(f_a^*)$ as is $c_B(f_b)$ to $c_B(f_b^*)$.

Let m^r be the approximation measure called *relative error*, defined as $m_A^r(i_a, f_a) = |c_A(f_a^*) - c_A(f_a)|/c_A(f_a^*)$. A *bounded reduction* [19] is a reduction that is **total** and for all $f_b \in F_B(f(i_a))$, $m_B^r(f_b) \leq \epsilon \Longrightarrow m_A^r(g(f_b)) \leq k(\epsilon)$ where $k : Q^+ \longrightarrow Q^+$ is a computable function. A bounded reduction bounds the relative error by a function k. The *continuous reduction* [19] and F-reduction [5] are stronger variants of bounded reduction.

An *L-reduction* [20] is a reduction that is **total** and for some positive constants α and β, $c_B(f_b^*) \leq \alpha c_A(f_a^*)$, and for all $f_b \in F_B(f(i_a))$, $|c_A(f_a^*) - c_A(g(f_b))| \leq \beta |c_B(f_b^*) - c_B(f_b)|$.

Define a *performance ratio* as $R_A(i_a, f_a) = c_A(f_a)/c_A(f_a^*)$. A *ratio preserving reduction* [22] is a reduction which is **total**, and for some constant $k = k_1 k_2$, for all $f_b \in F_B(f(i_a))$, $R_A(g(f_b)) \leq k R_B(f_b)$.

Let $c_A(f_a^{max})$ denote the maximum cost of a solution f_a^{max} of i_a. Let the *structure* of an instance i_a be $\text{struct}_A(i_a) = \langle a_0, \ldots, a_k \rangle$ where $k = c_A(f_a^{max}) - c_A(f_a^*)$ and $a_i = |\{f_a \in F_A(i_a)|c_A(f_a^{max}) - c_A(f_a^*) = i\}|$. A *structure preserving reduction* [2], with only its main aspect specified here, is one in which $\text{struct}_A(i_a) = \text{struct}_B(f(i_a))$. As defined in [2] however, it is not a reduction in our sense because it does not include a function g to map a feasible solution of $f(i_a)$ to one of i_a.

All of the above complexity theory definitions employ approximation measures of one kind or another as they are motivated mainly by approximability (relative to the optimum) considerations. None of our definitions in this paper employ approximation measures as they are motivated by more basic considerations of whether the reductions preserve certain feasible solutions and their properties. Our considerations are less important from the complexity theory point of view but perhaps more important for practical problem solving by reduction (such as by reduction to neural networks).

4 Reductions to Illustrate our Properties

In this section, we illustrate our simpler properties by describing or citing some reductions on which they do or do not hold. All of these reductions have been used as intermediate ones in mapping certain optimization problems to neural networks [13, 12].

MVC reduction to MIS. Consider the *minimum vertex cover* problem (MVC), define its feasible solutions as the vertex sets $V' \subseteq V(G)$ of a given graph G that form a cover (each edge of G is incident on at least one vertex of V'), and the cost of a feasible solution as its cardinality. The *maximum independent set* (MIS) problem on G is the maximum clique problem, defined earlier, on its complement graph G_c in which the edges of G are replaced by non-edges and vice-versa. Consider the following reduction of MVC to MIS. Given a graph G, construct its line graph H by converting every edge $\{v_i, v_j\}$ of G into a vertex v_{ij} of H. Two vertices v_{ij}, v_{kl} are adjacent in H if and only if the corresponding edges e_{ij} and e_{kl} share a common vertex in G. It can be shown that a maximal independent set $\{v_{i_1 j_1}, \ldots, v_{i_k j_k}\}$ of H represents the vertex-set $\{v_{i_1}, v_{j_1}, \ldots, v_{i_k}, v_{j_k}\}$ of G which is a vertex cover. Thus this reduction is **total, equality-preserving,** and **order-reversing.** It is not **onto,** however, since only vertex covers with even number of vertices are representable as maximal independent sets of H. For example, in the graph $G = (V, E)$, $V = \{v_1, v_2\}$, and $E = \{\{v_1, v_2\}\}$, the vertex cover $\{v_1\}$ is not representable as a maximal independent set of H. This reduction is not **invertible** as not every graph is a line graph of some graph.

MAXSAT reduction to MC. Consider the *maximum satisfiability* problem (MAXSAT) on conjunctive form boolean formulae, define its feasible solutions as a set of clauses satisfiable by some value assignment to the boolean variables of a given formula, and the cost of a feasible solution as negative its cardinality. Consider an approximation-preserving reduction of MAXSAT to MC, described in [4]. We do not describe the reduction here but illustrate the end result on the following example. Let the formula be $\Phi = (u_1 + u_2)(\bar{u}_1 + u_2)$, containing two clauses c_1 and c_2. The feasible solutions of Φ may be easily checked to be $\{c_1\}$, $\{c_2\}$, and $\{c_1, c_2\}$. Upon reduction, the graph $G_\Phi = (V, E)$ turns out to have the following structure: $V = \{c_1 u_1, c_1 \bar{u}_2, c_2 \bar{u}_1, c_2 u_2\}$ and $E = \{\{c_1 u_1, c_2 u_2\}, \{c_1 \bar{u}_2 c_2 \bar{u}_1\}\}$. E is also the set of feasible solutions (maximal cliques) of MC on G_Φ. For the reduction of any instance of MAXSAT to MC in the above way, only partly illustrated in the above example, if we strip away the u symbols from a feasible solution of MC (maximal clique), it can be shown that we get a feasible solution of MAXSAT (set of satisfiable clauses). Note that the cardinality of the set remains unchanged by this stripping process. (In the above example, for instance, the maximal clique $\{c_1 \bar{u}_2, c_2 \bar{u}_1\}$ represents the set of satisfiable clauses $\{c_1, c_2\}$.) Thus this reduction is **total, order-preserving,** and **equality-preserving.** On the other hand, the feasible solution $\{c_1\}$ of the SAT instance in the above example is not represented as a feasible solution (maximal clique) of its reduced MC instance. Hence this reduction is not **onto.**

GC reduction to MIS. Consider the *graph coloring* problem (GC) on a graph G, define its feasible solution as a coloring of the vertices such that for all v_i, v_j: $\{v_i, v_j\} \in E(G) \Longrightarrow \mathrm{color}(v_i) \neq \mathrm{color}(v_j)$, and the cost of a feasible solution as the number of distinct colors it uses. Consider the following reduction of GC to MIS. Let $\Delta(G)$ denote the maximum degree of a vertex in G. Given an n-vertex graph G, construct a graph H containing $n \times (\Delta(G) + 1)$ vertices, partitioned into n disjoint sets $V_1, \ldots, V_n$ respectively. $V_i = \{c_1 v_i, \ldots, c_{\Delta(G)+1} v_i\}$ is the vertex-set of partition i. Vertex $c_l v_i$ in H represents the assignment of color c_l to vertex v_i in G. Each V_i is viewed as a vertical column. H may also be viewed as composed of $\Delta(G) + 1$ horizontal layers $L_1, \ldots, L_{\Delta(G)+1}$. $L_i = \{c_i v_1, \ldots, c_i v_n\}$ is the vertex-set of layer i. We now add the edges to H. For $i = 1, \ldots, n$, V_i is made a clique. For $i = 1, \ldots, \Delta(G) + 1$, $H[L_i]$, the subgraph of H restricted to the vertices L_i, is made equal to G. It can be shown that this reduction is **total** and **onto.** It is not **equality-preserving** as it can be shown that all feasible solutions (maximal independent sets) in the MIS instance have the same size n (hence cost $-n$) [3, 17, 14], whereas the corresponding feasible solutions in the GC instance may have differing cost (number of colors used). It is vacuously **order-preserving.**

5   Transitivity of Reductions

It is sometimes useful to reduce an optimization problem to another (such as to a neural network) through a sequence of reductions. For example, in [14] we map some optimization problems in telecommunications to neural networks this way. It is then useful to know whether properties that hold for individual reductions in a sequence also hold for the reduction represented by the sequence.

It is clear that if $A \xrightarrow{f_{ab},g_{ab}} B$ and $B \xrightarrow{f_{bc},g_{bc}} C$ are reductions, then so is $A \xrightarrow{f_{bc}(f_{ab}),g_{ab}(g_{bc})} C$. We now consider the question of the transitivity of their properties. The following facts are easy to show.

1. If $A \xrightarrow{f_{ab},g_{ab}} B$ and $B \xrightarrow{f_{bc},g_{bc}} C$ are total then so is $A \xrightarrow{f_{bc}(f_{ab}),g_{ab}(g_{bc})} C$, with $\mathrm{Im}(g_{ab}(g_{bc})) \subseteq \mathrm{Im}(g_{ab})$ and equality holding when g_{bc} is onto.

2. If $A \xrightarrow{f_{ab},g_{ab}} B$ and $B \xrightarrow{f_{bc},g_{bc}} C$ are onto then so is $A \xrightarrow{f_{bc}(f_{ab}),g_{ab}(g_{bc})} C$, with $\mathrm{dom}(g_{ab}(g_{bc})) \subseteq \mathrm{dom}(g_{bc})$ and equality holding *only* when g_{ab} is total.

3. If $A \xrightarrow{f_{ab},g_{ab}} B$ and $B \xrightarrow{f_{bc},g_{bc}} C$ are total and onto then so is $A \xrightarrow{f_{bc}(f_{ab}),g_{ab}(g_{bc})} C$, with $\mathrm{Im}(g_{ab}(g_{bc})) = \mathrm{Im}(g_{ab})$ and $\mathrm{dom}(g_{ab}(g_{bc})) = \mathrm{dom}(g_{bc})$.

4. If $A \xrightarrow{f_{ab},g_{ab}} B$ and $B \xrightarrow{f_{bc},g_{bc}} C$ are order-preserving (equality-preserving) then $A \xrightarrow{f_{bc}(f_{ab}),g_{ab}(g_{bc})} C$ is also order-preserving (equality-preserving), with $\mathrm{dom}(g_{ab}(g_{bc})) \subseteq \mathrm{dom}(g_{bc})$ and equality holding when g_{ab} is total.

6   Reductions to Neural Networks

The Discrete Hopfield Network (DHN) [10] is structurally a fully-connected graph with symmetric weights w_{ij} connecting units i and j, and a bias I_i associated with unit i. We assume that the state S_i of a unit is 0 or 1. For more details, see [9]. In this section, we examine some well-known encodings of optimization problems in DHN, and evaluate their properties in terms of the above definitions. By viewing DHN as the following (NP) optimization problem, such encodings may be viewed as reductions.

INSTANCE: A DHN instance given by number of units N, weight matrix W, bias vector I
FEASIBLE SOLUTION: A network state $S \in \{0,1\}^N$ that is a local minimum of $E(S) = -1/2 S^T W S - S^T I$
COST OF A FEASIBLE SOLUTION: The value of $E(S)$ for local minimum S

TSP reduction to DHN. It is well known that the original encoding of the travelling salesperson problem to DHN [11] is not **total** and this is one main reason why it has not worked well [1].

Maximum Clique reduction to DHN. The following encoding or essentially equivalent ones are from [3, 7, 17, 21, 8]. Given an N-vertex graph G, construct an N-unit DHN instance, unit i associated with vertex v_i. $w_{ij} = -1$ if $i \neq j$ and $\{v_i, v_j\} \notin E(G)$, $w_{ij} = 0$ otherwise. $I_i = 0.5$. This reduction is **total** and **order-preserving** [17]. It is also easy to check that it is **onto** and **equality-preserving**.

Graph Bipartitioning Reduction to DHN. The *graph bipartitioning problem* may be defined as follows.

INSTANCE: A graph $G = (V, E)$ with even number of vertices
FEASIBLE SOLUTION: A partition of V into two equal sets

We use the reduction of graph bipartitioning to DHN in [9], attributed to [6]. This reduction employs $-1/1$ units. Given an N-vertex graph G, construct an N-unit DHN instance, unit i associated with vertex v_i. For all i, $I_i = w_{ii} = 0$. For $i \neq j$, $w_{ij} = 1 - 2\mu$ if $\{v_i, v_j\} \in E(G)$, $w_{ij} = -2\mu$ otherwise. A local minimum corresponds to the partition (V_1, V_2) of V where $V_1 = \{v_i | S_i = 1\}$ and $V_2 = \{v_i | S_i = -1\}$.

Proposition 1 *For $0 < \mu < 1$, this reduction is neither **total** nor **onto**.*

Proof: Consider the 4-vertex graph with $E = \{\{v_1, v_2\}, \{v_2, v_3\}, \{v_1, v_3\}\}$. Note that v_4 is isolated. It is easy to check that $(1, 1, 1, -1)$ is a local minimum of the network obtained from reduction. This minimum corresponds to the partition $(\{v_1, v_2, v_3\}, \{v_4\})$ which is not a feasible solution. Consider the feasible solution $f = (\{v_1, v_2\}, \{v_3, v_4\})$ in the same example. Neither $(1, 1, -1, -1)$ nor $(-1, -1, 1, 1)$ is a local minimum so f is not represented as a feasible solution of DHN $\square$.

Shortest Paths reduction to HN. The *shortest paths* problem may be defined as follows.

INSTANCE: A directed graph $G = (V, E)$ with weights d_{ij} on the edges (v_i, v_j) and two vertices s and d
FEASIBLE SOLUTION: A vertex-disjoint path from s to d

We use the reduction of shortest paths to DHN in [18] which is used to solve routing problems in computer networks modeled as shortest paths problems. Given an N-vertex directed graph $G = (V, E)$, construct a $2\binom{N}{2} + 1$-unit DHN instance with 0/1 units. Unit v_{ij} represents directed edge (v_i, v_j) of G. We add a *distinguished* unit v_{ds}^*. For v_{ds}^*, $I_{ds} = \epsilon > 0$. For all other v_{ij}, $I_{ij} = -d_{ij}$. For all v_{ij}, v_{kl}, $w_{ij,kl} = a$ if $i = l$ or $j = k$; $w_{ij,kl} = -a$ if $i = k$ or $j = l$; $w_{ij,kl} = 0$ otherwise.

The following proposition has a non-trivial proof, which is omitted. Let $d_{max} \equiv \max_{(i,j)}(d_{ij})$ denote the maximum weight of an edge in G.

Proposition 2 *For $a > d_{max}/4$, this reduction is onto.*

It is not clear whether this reduction is total or not.

7   Design of Reductions

In this section we present some new reductions whose design was guided by some of the properties defined in this paper.

Consider the following reduction of Maximum Clique to itself. Given G and a positive integer k, construct H as follows:

$H \leftarrow G$
while $\exists v \in V(H) : \deg(v) < k - 1$ do
$\quad H \leftarrow H \backslash \{v\}$
end

It is clear that all the maximal cliques of G of size $\geq k$ are preserved in H. Hence this reduction is $(-k)$-cost-preserving. When $V(H) \subset V(G)$, this reduction may be useful because the size of the problem is reduced while all its maximal cliques of size $\geq k$ are preserved. This reduction may be conveniently realized in a DHN encoding of Maximum Clique by clamping the units in $V(G) \backslash V(H)$ to zero.

The following reduction is motivated by the property *expected-cost-decreasing*. The idea is to attempt to increase the number of good feasible solutions more than the number of poor ones.

Maximum Clique Self-reduction. Given an N-vertex graph $G = (V, E)$ construct a graph $G^2 = (V^2, E^2)$ where $V^2 = V \times V$ and $E^2 = \{\{(v_i, v_j), (v_k, v_l)\} | \{v_i, v_k\}, \{v_j, v_l\} \in E(G)\}$. Let the feasible solutions of Maximum Clique be cliques, not maximal cliques as defined earlier. Define a k-clique as a clique of size k. It is clear that if $\{(v_{i_1}, v_{j_1}), (v_{i_2}, v_{j_2}), \ldots, (v_{i_k}, v_{j_k})\}$ is a k-clique in G^2 then $\{v_{i_1}, v_{i_2}, \ldots, v_{i_k}\}$ and $\{v_{j_1}, v_{j_2}, \ldots, v_{j_k}\}$ are k-cliques in G. Arbitrarily, let us associate the first such k-clique in G with the k-clique in G^2. It is easy to see that this reduction is **total**, **onto**, **order-preserving**, and **equality-preserving**. Let n_k denote the number of k-cliques in G. We state the following without proof, which is easy.

Proposition 3 *The number of k-cliques in G^2 is $k!(n_k)^2$.*

It is an interesting question how

$$E_{\text{MC}}(G) = -\sum_k k n_k / \sum_k n_k$$

relates to

$$E_{\text{MC}}(G^2) = -\sum_k k k! (n_k)^2 / \sum_k k! (n_k)^2$$

We can construct individual instances of MC for which $E_{\mathrm{MC}}(G^2) < E_{\mathrm{MC}}(G)$. Consider the 4-vertex graph $G = (V, E)$ where $E = \{\{v_1, v_2\}, \{v_2, v_3\}, \{v_3, v_4\}, \{v_2, v_4\}\}$. It can be checked that $E_{\mathrm{MC}}(G^2) = -1.81$ and $E_{\mathrm{MC}}(G) = -1.66$. The larger question however remains open.

We consider a restriction of this question when G is a random graph (an edge slot contains an edge, independent of other slots, with some constant probability p). On such graphs, $E[n_k] = \binom{N}{2} p^{\binom{k}{2}}$. Table 1 calculates some approximate numerical results for $E_{\mathrm{MC}}(G)$ and $E_{\mathrm{MC}}(G^2)$, where G is a random graph, by substituting $E[n_k]$ for n_k in $E_{\mathrm{MC}}(G)$ and $E_{\mathrm{MC}}(G^2)$.

Table 1: Approximate expected clique size in random graphs and their reduced graphs

N	p	$E_{MC}[G]$	$E_{MC}[G^2]$
100	0.5	4.72	5.75
1000	0.5	7.47	8.84
100	0.9	16.05	25.90
1000	0.9	32.58	47.26

The results of Table 1 suggest that $E_{\mathrm{MC}}(G^2)$ is less than $E_{\mathrm{MC}}(G)$, especially for large p (dense graphs). This suggests that if G is a random graph, an algorithm that samples cliques from the uniform distribution on cliques will find a larger clique on average on G^2 than on G. Unfortunately, it is not clear if such an algorithm exists for the MC problem. We conjecture nevertheless that some simple algorithms, such as those that can be implemented in neural networks, will find larger cliques in G^2 than in G. Even if so, this has to be weighed against the size increase of G^2. In a neural network encoding of MC, G requires N units and $\binom{N}{2}$ connections, G^2 requires N^2 units and $\binom{N^2}{2}$ connections. (Many of the connection strengths may be 0.) Perhaps in future implementations of neural networks the size increase will be less of an issue than the necessity for the neural network to emulate a simple algorithm in which case such a reduction would be potentially useful if such a simple algorithm works better on G^2.

8   Summary and Discussion

This paper is motivated by the need to closely study the mappings of optimization problems to neural networks. We have proposed certain properties for the characterization of mappings. We have shown how these properties relate to approximation-preserving reductions from computational complexity theory. We have examined certain reductions, including those to neural networks, and shown which properties hold for them and which do not. Finally, guided by some of the properties, we have designed two new reductions.

We hope that this paper will stimulate further work on this topic. There are many other mappings of optimization problems to neural networks in the literature that can be examined in terms of these properties, to give some indication of how well they are expected to work. Some of our properties may also be useful, as we have seen in Section 7, for the design of new mappings of optimization problems to neural networks.

References

[1] S.V.B. Aiyer, M. Niranjan, and F. Fallside. A theoretical investigation into the performance of the Hopfield model. *IEEE Transactions on Neural Networks*, 1(2):204–215, 1990.

[2] G. Ausiello, A. D'Atri, and M. Protasi. Structure preserving reductions among convex optimization problems. *Journal of Computer and System Sciences*, 21:136–153, 1980.

[3] D.H. Ballard, P.C. Gardner, and M.A. Srinivas. Graph problems and connectionist architectures. Technical report, Department of Computer Science, University of Rochester, Rochester, NY, 1987.

[4] P. Crescenzi, C. Fiorini, and R. Silvestri. A note on the approximation of the maxclique problem. *Information Processing Letters*, 40(1):1–5, October 1991.

[5] P. Crescenzi and A. Panconesi. Completeness in approximation classes. *Information and Computation*, 93(2):241–262, 1991.

[6] Y. Fu and P.W. Anderson. Application of statistical mechanics to NP-complete problems in combinatorial optimization. *Journal of Physics A*, 19:1605–1620, 1986.

[7] G.H. Godbeer, J. Lipscomb, and M. Luby. On the computational complexity of finding stable state vectors in connectionist models (Hopfield nets). Technical report, Department of Computer Science, University of Toronto, Toronto, Ontario, 1988.

[8] T. Grossman and A. Jagota. On the equivalence of two Hopfield-type networks. In *IEEE International Conference on Neural Networks*, pages 1063–1068. IEEE, 1993.

[9] J. Hertz, A. Krogh, and R.G. Palmer. *Introduction to the Theory of Neural Computation*. Addison-Wesley, 1991.

[10] J.J. Hopfield. Neural networks and physical systems with emergent collective computational abilities. *Proceedings of the National Academy of Sciences, USA*, 79, 1982.

[11] J.J. Hopfield and D.W. Tank. "Neural" computation of decisions in optimization problems. *Biological Cybernetics*, 52:141–152, 1985.

[12] A. Jagota. Graph coloring using the hopfield-clique network. In *World Congress on Neural Networks*, New York, July 1993. Portland, IEEE.

[13] A. Jagota. Optimization by reduction to maximum clique. In *IEEE International Conference on Neural Networks*, pages 1526–1531, New York, March 1993. San Francisco, IEEE.

[14] A. Jagota. Scheduling problems in radio networks using hopfield networks. In J. Alspector, R. Goodman, and T. Brown, editors, *Proceedings of the International Workshop on Applications of Neural Networks to Telecommunications*, pages 67–76. Lawrence Erlbaum Associates, 1993.

[15] D.S. Johnson. Approximation algorithms for combinatorial problems. *Journal of Computer and System Sciences*, 9:256–278, 1974.

[16] V. Kann. *On the approximability of NP-complete optimization problems*. PhD thesis, Royal Institute of Technology, Stockholm, Sweden, 1992.

[17] J.H.M. Korst and E.H.L. Aarts. Combinatorial optimization on a Boltzmann machine. *Journal of Parallel and Distributed Computing*, 6:331–357, 1989.

[18] S. Neuhauser. Hopfield optimization techniques applied to routing in computer networks. In J. Alspector, R. Goodman, and T. Brown, editors, *Proceedings of the International Workshop on Applications of Neural Networks to Telecommunications*, pages 203–209. Lawrence Erlbaum Associates, 1993.

[19] P. Orponen and H. Mannila. On approximation preserving reductions: complete problems and robust measures. Technical Report C-1987-28, Department of Computer Science, University of Helsinki, 1987.

[20] C.H. Papadimitriou and M. Yannakakis. Optimization, approximation, and complexity classes. *Journal of Computer and System Sciences*, 43:425–440, 1991.

[21] Y. Shrivastava, S. Dasgupta, and S.M. Reddy. Neural network solutions to a graph theoretic problem. In *Proceedings of IEEE International Symposium on Circuits and Systems*, pages 2528–2531, New York, 1990. IEEE.

[22] H.U. Simon. On approximate solutions for combinatorial optimization problems. *SIAM Journal on Discrete Mathematics*, 3(2):294–310, 1990.

Combinatorial Optimization Neural Nets Based on
A Hybrid of Lagrange and Transformation Approaches

Lei Xu

Dept of Computer Science, The Chinese University of Hong Kong, Shatin,NT, Hong Kong

Abstract *A novel scheme for combinatorial optimization is suggested via analog constrained optimization. The constraints are separated into two parts. One is relieved by Lagrange approach, and the other by penalty or barrier function. In comparison with the existing Hopfield type networks, the new scheme has several new features. It is applicable to nonquadratic energy functions, and has reduced needs on externally controlling artificial weighting parameters. It also provides new potential for improving convergence and performance. In addition, it supplies a general combinatorial optimization scheme with its special cases being closely related to statistical physics method, EM algorithm, elastic net and robust PCA.*

1. Introduction

Combinatorial optimization takes very important roles in many fields such as computer science and operational research. Unfortunately, many problems of combinatorial optimization are NP- hard. Since Hopfield and Tank (1985) proposed to use neural networks for combinatorial optimization, a lot of efforts have been made along this direction. The detailed reviews of these efforts can be found in many recently published textbooks, e.g., Hertz, Krogh& Palmer(1991) and Cichocki and Unbehaunen (1993).

Roughly speaking , the existing combinatorial optimization networks share two common features. One is that they will finally become a unconstrained analog optimization of a *quadratic* energy function by a Hopfield type networks. The other is that they transform the constraints into *quadratic* penalty functions as a part of the resulted unconstrained energy function. Because these algorithms are either implemented by Hopfield network or its variants, we use *Hopfield Scheme* to refer them. This paper propose a novel general scheme which is no longer confined to the two features. It solves constrained optimization by a hybrid of *Lagrange and Transformation* approaches. It separates the constraints into two parts, namely linear-constant-sum constraints and binary constraints. The linear-constant-sum constraints are treated by Lagrange approach, and the binary constraints are transformed into *penalty or barrier* functions. The new scheme has several advantages. First, it can be used for *nonquadratic* energy functions, while *Hopfield Scheme* applies only to *quadratic* energy functions. Second, it has eliminated those artificially controlled parameters that are needed in Hopfield scheme for linear-constant-sum constraints. In other words, the new scheme ensures the linear-constant-sum constraints satisfied exactly without an approximate treatment by penalty functions weighted by parameters controlled heuristically and externally; as a result, its performance and convergence can be improved. Third, it provides a general scheme which can include *Statistical Physics* methods (Yuille & Kosowsky, 1993) as special cases. In addition, its certain special case is also closely related to clustering by finite mixture model with EM algorithm (Xu&Jordan,1993a&b; Xu, Jordan& Hinton, 1993), as well as to robust PCA (Xu& Yuille, 1993) and elastic nets (Durbin& Willshaw, 1987).

2. Combinatorial Optimizations As Constrained Optimizations

Many combinatorial optimization problems can be usually formulated into the following types of constrained optimization problems

- Type I

$$\min_{\vec{v}} E_I(\vec{v}) = \min_{v_1,\cdots,v_N} E_I(v_1, \cdots, v_N),$$

$$subject \ to \quad C_s : \quad \sum_{i=1}^{N} v_i = D, \tag{1}$$

$$C_b : v_i \ is \ binary, \ i.e., v_i = 1 \ or \ v_i = 0 \ for \ each \ v_i. \tag{2}$$

with D being a given constant. For example, for the graph bipartition problem (Cichocki and Unbehaunen, 1993), $E_I(\vec{v})$ and C_s become

$$E_I(\vec{v}) = \sum_{i=1}^{N} \sum_{j=1}^{N} w_{ij}(v_i + v_j - 2v_i v_j), \quad C_s : \quad \sum_{i=1}^{N} v_i = N/2, \tag{3}$$

with N being an even integer number and w_{ij} are known parameters.

- Type II

$$\min_{V} E_{II}(V), \ V = \{v_{ij}, i = 1, \cdots, N, j = 1, \cdots, M\},$$

$$\text{subject to} \quad C_s^{col} : \quad \sum_{i=1}^{N} v_{ij} = D_j^{col}, j = 1, \cdots, M, \quad C_s^{row} : \quad \sum_{j=1}^{M} v_{ij} = D_i^{row}, i = 1, \cdots, N;$$

$$C_b : v_{ij} = 1 \text{ or } v_{ij} = 0 \text{ for each } v_{ij}. \tag{4}$$

with $D_j^{col}, j = 1, \cdots, M$ and $D_i^{row}, i = 1, \cdots, N$ being given constants.

We observe some typical examples. The first is the traveling salesman problem with $N = M$ and

$$E_{II}(\vec{v}) = \sum_{x=1}^{N} \sum_{y \neq x}^{N} \sum_{i=1}^{N} d_{xy} v_{xi} (v_{y,i+1} + v_{y,i-1}),$$

$$C_s^{col} : \quad \sum_{i=1}^{N} v_{ij} = 1, j = 1, \cdots N, \quad C_s^{row} : \quad \sum_{j=1}^{N} v_{ij} = 1, j = 1, \cdots, N. \tag{5}$$

where d_{xy} are known parameters. The second is the standard linear assignment problem (Cichocki and Unbehaunen, 1993), for which we have

$$E_{II}(\vec{v}) = \sum_{i=1}^{N} \sum_{j=1}^{M} c_{ij} v_{ij},$$

$$C_s^{col} : \quad \sum_{i=1}^{N} v_{ij} = 1, j = 1, \cdots, M, \quad C_s^{row} : \quad \sum_{j=1}^{M} v_{ij} = 1, i = 1, \cdots, N. \tag{6}$$

with c_{ij} being known parameters. The third one is the graph K-partition problem (Cichocki and Unbehaunen, 1993) with $M = K$ and

$$E_{II}(\vec{v}) = \sum_{i=1}^{N} \sum_{j \neq i}^{N} \sum_{k=1}^{K} \sum_{l \neq k} w_{ij} v_{ik} v_{jl},$$

$$C_s^{col} : \quad \sum_{i=1}^{N} v_{ij} = N/K, j = 1, \cdots, M, \quad C_s^{row} : \quad \sum_{j=1}^{N} v_{ij} = 1, i = 1, \cdots, N, \tag{7}$$

with $N = mK$ and m being an integer.

For each type, we observe that the constraints, that the minimization is subject to, consist of two parts. One is the linear equality constraints which ensure that the sums of the specific subsets of variables are equal to given constants. We denote this kind of constraints by C_s or C_s^{col} & C_s^{row}, and call them by the linear-constant-sum constraints. The other requires that each variable takes only binary value 0 or 1. We denote this constraint by C_b and call it the *binary constraint*.

3. Constrained Optimizations By A Hybrid of Lagrange and Transformation

To solve the constrained optimizations eq.(2) & eq.(4), the usual way is to change them into unconstrained optimization problems. For the exitisting optimization neural networks of *Hopfield Scheme*, the binary constraint C_b is considered directly by the sigmoid function $v_i = 0.5[1 + tanh(\frac{u_i}{T})]$ or $v_{ij} = 0.5[1 + tanh(\frac{u_{ij}}{T})]$ with u, u_{ij} being dummy variables. The linear-constant-sum constraints C_s or C_s^{col} & C_s^{row} are transformed into some *quadratic* penalty functions, for examples (Cichocki and Unbehaunen, 1993):

- For the graph bipartition problem, the linear-constant-sum constraint is transformed into the 2nd term of the following unconstrained energy:

$$E(\vec{v}) = \sum_{i=1}^{N} \sum_{j=1}^{N} w_{ij}(v_i + v_j - 2v_i v_j) + \frac{\kappa}{2}(\sum_{j=1}^{N} v_i - \frac{N}{2}). \tag{8}$$

- For the traveling salesman problem, the linear-constant-sum constraints are transformed into the 2nd, the third and the 4th terms of the following unconstrained energy:

$$E_{II}(\vec{v}) = \sum_{x=1}^{N} \sum_{y \neq x}^{N} \sum_{i=1}^{N} d_{xy} v_{xi}(v_{y,i+1} + v_{y,i-1}) + \frac{\kappa_A}{2} \sum_{i=1}^{N} [\sum_{x=1}^{N} v_{xi} - 1]^2 + \frac{\kappa_B}{2} \sum_{x=1}^{N} [\sum_{i=1}^{N} v_{xi} - 1]^2. \tag{9}$$

In both eq.(8) and eq.(9), $\kappa, \kappa_A, \kappa_B$ are positive scalars externally and heuristically selected for the amount of penalty to the cases that the linear-constant-sum constraints are broken. Their values will directly influence the performance, and the appropriate selection of the parameters is usually a difficult task.

Here, we propose a novel scheme for the constrained optimizations eq.(2) & eq.(4). We tackle the linear-constant-sum constraints C_s or C_s^{col} & C_s^{row} by Lagrange approach instead of penalty functions. Furthermore, we transform the binary constraints C_b into either *penalty* or *barrier* functions instead of directly introducing the nonlinear $tanh(.)$ function. In other words, we transform the problems eq.(2) & eq.(4) into the minimization of the following unconstrained energies:

$$E(\vec{v}) = E_I(\vec{v}) + \lambda(\sum_{i=1}^{N} v_i - D) + \frac{1}{\beta}\sum_{i=1}^{N} P(v_i)$$

$$E(V) = E_{II}(V) + \sum_{j=1}^{M} \lambda_j^{col}[\sum_{i=1}^{N} v_{ij} - D_j^{col}] + \sum_{i=1}^{N} \lambda_i^{row}[\sum_{j=1}^{M} v_{ij} - D_i^{row}] + \frac{1}{\beta}\sum_{i=1}^{N}\sum_{j=1}^{M} P(v_{ij}); \quad (10)$$

where $\lambda, \lambda_i^{row}, \lambda_j^{col}$ are Lagrange coefficients which will be determined later. $P(v)$ is a penalty function. It reaches its minimums at $v = 0$ or $v = 1$.

β is a positive scalar for controlling the penalty. The smaller is β, the heavier is the penalty for v deviating from binary values. A set of examples for penalty function are given by

$$P_2(v) = |v|^p|1 - v|^q, \quad p > 0, q > 0. \quad (11)$$

The above is a hybrid of Lagrange approach and penalty function approach. Similarly, we can combine Lagrange approach and barrier function approach, which leads us to

$$E(\vec{v}) = E_I(\vec{v}) + \lambda(\sum_{i=1}^{N} v_i - D) + \beta\sum_{i=1}^{N} B(v_i)$$

$$E(V) = E_{II}(V) + \sum_{j=1}^{M} \lambda_j^{col}[\sum_{i=1}^{N} v_{ij} - D_j^{col}] + \sum_{i=1}^{N} \lambda_i^{row}[\sum_{j=1}^{M} v_{ij} - D_i^{row}] + \beta\sum_{i=1}^{N}\sum_{j=1}^{M} B(v_{ij}); \quad (12)$$

where the parameters are similar to those in eq.(10), and $B(.)$ is a barrier function that is either ∞ or undefined beyond the interval $[0,1]$. Now, β controls the barriers in such a way that the larger its value is, the more difficult it is for v to reach its boundary values 0 or 1; when β reduces, v is gradually able to reache its boundaries. A set of examples for barrier function are as follows

$$B_1(v) = 1/(|v|^p|1 - v|^q), \quad B_2(v) = \ln[v^p(1 - v)^q], \quad p > 0, q \geq 0. \quad (13)$$

Both $B_1(v), B_2(v)$ set up barriers at $v = 0, 1$. $B_2(v)$ further forces v defined only on the open interval $(0,1)$. One may notice that in eq.(13) we allow $q = 0$. It seems in this case that only a barrier at $v = 0$ is set up and v is seemly free to go beyond $v = 1$. However, for the cases that $D = D^{row} = 1$ as in eqs.(5)(6)&(7), the cooperation of the barrier functions and the constraints C_s will implicitly prevent v to go beyond $v = 1$.

One disadvantage for the barriers functions eq(13) is that v is not defined at the two end points $v = 1$ and $v = 0$, while our original combinatorial problems require $v = 1$ or $v = 0$. To overcome this pitfall, we make integral on $B_2(v)$ to rule out the divergence at 0 and 1

$$B_3(v) = \int_0^v \ln[v^p(1 - v)^q]dv, \quad p > 0, q \geq 0. \quad (14)$$

One can check that this generalized integral is well defined at 0 and 1, and is defined only within the closed interval $[0,1]$. A more interesting point is that $B_3(v)$ is monotonously decreasing from 0 to 1 and reaches its minimum at $v = 1$. we see that $B_3(v)$ not only supplies the barriers at two end points, but also penalizes the deviations from $v = 1$. For the cases that $D = D^{row} = 1$ as in eqs.(5)(6)&(7), the constraints $C_s, C_s^{row}, C_s^{col}$ will prevent all the v_i or v_{ij} towards 1 and drive most of them towards zeros. Therefore, this new function combines the features of penalty and barrier functions together.

We further consider how to solve the problems eq.(10) and eq.(12). We only discuss the solution with the energy $E(V)$ since $E(\vec{v})$ can be regarded as a special case of $E(V)$ and it can be solved exactly in the same way. We propose to solve the problems via the following two steps:

- Calculate

$$\frac{\partial E(V)}{\partial v_{ij}} = \frac{\partial E_{II}(V)}{\partial v_{ij}} + \lambda_j^{col} + \lambda_i^{row} + \beta \frac{d\Phi(v_{ij})}{dv_{ij}} \tag{15}$$

where $\Phi(v_{ij})$ can be $P(v_{ij})$ or $B(v_{ij})$. From $\frac{\partial E(V)}{\partial v_{ij}} = 0$, we try to get an equation of the form

$$v_{ij} = M_p(V, \lambda_i^{row}, \lambda_j^{col}, \beta), \tag{16}$$

with $M_p(.)$ being a mapping function such that $\frac{\partial M_p(V, \lambda_i^{row}, \lambda_j^{col}, \beta)}{\partial v_{ij}} \neq 1$.

For example, when $\Phi(.) = B_3(.)$, eq.(15) becomes

$$\frac{\partial E(V)}{\partial v_{ij}} = \frac{\partial E_{II}(V)}{\partial v_{ij}} + \lambda_j^{col} + \lambda_i^{row} + \beta \ln[v_{ij}^p (1 - v_{ij})^q] \tag{17}$$

and a possible choice for eq.(16) is

$$v_{ij} = \frac{a_i b_j}{(1 - v_{ij})^{q/p}} exp(-\frac{1}{p\beta} \frac{\partial E_{II}(V)}{\partial v_{ij}}) \tag{18}$$

where $a_i = exp(-\frac{\lambda_i^{row}}{p\beta})$ and $b_j = exp(\frac{-\lambda_j^{col}}{p\beta})$.

- From $\sum_{i=1}^{N} v_{ij} = D_j^{col}$ and $\sum_{j=1}^{M} v_{ij} = D_i^{row}$, we get two equations

$$D_j^{col} = \sum_{i=1}^{N} M_p(V, \lambda_i^{row}, \lambda_j^{col}, \beta), \quad D_i^{row} = \sum_{j=1}^{M} M_p(V, \lambda_i^{row}, \lambda_j^{col}, \beta) \tag{19}$$

and we solve them to get

$$\lambda_i^{row} = \Lambda_i^{row}(V, \beta, D_i^{row}, D_j^{col}, \{\lambda_j^{col}\}_1^M), \quad \lambda_j^{col} = \Lambda_j^{col}(V, \beta, D_i^{row}, D_j^{col}, \{\lambda_i^{row}\}_1^N), \tag{20}$$

with $\Lambda_i^{row}(.), \Lambda_j^{col}(.)$ being certain functions.

For example, when $\Phi(.) = B_3(.)$, eq.(19) becomes

$$b_j = D_j^{col}/\{\sum_{i=1}^{N} a_i (1 - v_{ij})^{-q/p} exp(-\frac{1}{p\beta} \frac{\partial E_{II}(V)}{\partial v_{ij}})\},$$

$$a_i = D_i^{row}/\{\sum_{j=1}^{M} b_j (1 - v_{ij})^{-q/p} exp(-\frac{1}{p\beta} \frac{\partial E_{II}(V)}{\partial v_{ij}})\}. \tag{21}$$

with $\lambda_i^{row} = -p\beta \ln a_i$, and $\lambda_j^{col} = -p\beta \ln b_j$.

- Given p, q, β, and initialize a set of $N \times M$ array of neurons $\{v_{ij}^{(0)}\}$ randomly by taking values between $[0, 1]$. Moreover, initialize $N + M$ dummy variables $^{(0)}\lambda_i^{row}, ^{(0)}\lambda_j^{col}$. Next, we start an iterative process by eqs.(16)& (20)

$$^{(k+1)}\lambda_i^{row} = \Lambda_i^{row}(V^{(k)}, \beta, D_i^{row}, D_j^{col}, \{^{(k)}\lambda_j^{col}\}_1^M),$$
$$^{(k+1)}\lambda_j^{col} = \Lambda_j^{col}(V^{(k)}, \beta, D_i^{row}, D_j^{col}, \{^{(k)}\lambda_i^{row}\}_1^N),$$
$$v_{ij}^{(k+1)} = M_p(V^{(k)}, {}^{(k+1)}\lambda_i^{row}, {}^{(k+1)}\lambda_j^{col}, \beta), \tag{22}$$

For example, when $\Phi(.) = B_3(.)$ we initialize $M+N$ dummy variables $a_i^{(0)}, b_j^{(0)}$ instead of $^{(0)}\lambda_i^{row}, ^{(0)}\lambda_j^{col}$, and use the following recursive equations to replace those in eq.(22):

$$b_j^{(k+1)} = D_j^{col}/\{\sum_{i=1}^{N} a_i^{(k)} (1 - v_{ij}^{(k)})^{-q/p} exp(-\frac{1}{p\beta} \frac{\partial E_{II}(V^{(k)})}{\partial v_{ij}})\},$$

$$a_i^{(k+1)} = D_i^{row} / \{\sum_{j=1}^{M} b_j^{(k)} (1 - v_{ij}^{(k)})^{-q/p} exp(-\frac{1}{p\beta} \frac{\partial E_{II}(V^{(k)})}{\partial v_{ij}})\},$$

$$v_{ij}^{(k+1)} = a_i^{(k+1)} b_j^{(k+1)} (1 - v_{ij}^{(k)})^{-q/p} exp(-\frac{1}{p\beta} \frac{\partial E_{II}(V^{(k)})}{\partial v_{ij}}). \tag{23}$$

In addition, during the above iteration we can let $\beta^{(k)}$ to start at a large enough value and then gradually reduce so that the constraints $C_s, C_s^{row}, C_s^{col}$ will be more and more easier to drive most of neurons towards zeros.

Eq.(22) or eq.(23) define a recurrent optimization network. It is an $N \times M$ array of neurons $\{v_{ij}\}$, and the interactions of these neurons are made through nonlinear connections specified by the mapping function M_p. The analog dynamic equations of the network are given by

$$\frac{d\lambda_i^{row}}{dt} = \Lambda_i^{row}(V, \beta, D_i^{row}, D_j^{col}, \{\lambda_j^{col}\}_1^M) - \lambda_i^{row},$$

$$\frac{d\lambda_j^{col}}{dt} = \Lambda_j^{col}(V, \beta, D_i^{row}, D_j^{col}, \{\lambda_i^{row}\}_1^N) - \lambda_j^{col},$$

$$\frac{dv_{ij}}{dt} = M_p(V, \lambda_i^{row}, \lambda_j^{col}, \beta) - v_{ij},$$

$$\frac{db_j}{dt} = -b_j + D_j^{col} / \{\sum_{i=1}^{N} a_i (1 - v_{ij})^{-q/p} exp(-\frac{1}{p\beta} \frac{\partial E_{II}(V)}{\partial v_{ij}})\},$$

$$\frac{da_i}{dt} = -a_i + D_i^{row} / \{\sum_{j=1}^{M} b_j (1 - v_{ij})^{-q/p} exp(-\frac{1}{p\beta} \frac{\partial E_{II}(V)}{\partial v_{ij}})\},$$

$$\frac{dv_{ij}}{dt} = a_i b_j (1 - v_{ij})^{-q/p} exp(-\frac{1}{p\beta} \frac{\partial E_{II}(V)}{\partial v_{ij}}) - v_{ij}. \tag{24}$$

A useful variant of eq.(23) can be obtained by ignoring the constraint C_s^{row} or cooperating its transformed penalty function into $E_{II}(V)$, i.e., $E_{II}'(V) = E_{II}(V) + \kappa(\sum_{j=1}^{M} v_{ij} - D_i^{row})^2$, such that eqs.(10)&(12) become

$$E(V) = E_{II}'(V) + \sum_{j=1}^{M} \lambda_j^{col}[\sum_{i=1}^{N} v_{ij} - D_j^{col}] + \beta \sum_{i=1}^{N} \sum_{j=1}^{M} B_3(v_{ij}) \tag{25}$$

with $\lambda_i^{row} = 0, i = 1, \cdots, N$. In this case, we have $a_i = 1, i = 1, \cdots, N$ and eq.(23) is simplified into

$$v_{ij}^{(k+1)} = D_j^{col} \frac{(1 - v_{ij}^{(k)})^{-q/p} exp(-\frac{1}{p\beta} \frac{\partial E_{II}(V^{(k)})}{\partial v_{ij}})}{\sum_{i=1}^{N} (1 - v_{ij}^{(k)})^{-q/p} exp(-\frac{1}{p\beta} \frac{\partial E_{II}(V^{(k)})}{\partial v_{ij}})}. \tag{26}$$

Here, we have no iteration for Lagrange coefficients since in each step they can be solved explicitly.

From constrained optimization theory (Gill & Murray, 1974), the penalty function approach and barrier function methods are together called the *transformation* approach. So we use a scheme of *Hybrid Lagrange and Transformation* to denote the above proposed approach.

In order to let the above proposed scheme work, there are two key points to be satisfied: (1) The selection of $\Phi(v_{ij})$ should enable us to get eq.(16). For some $\Phi(v_{ij})$, we may be not able to get eq.(16); (2) Eq.(16) should be designed such that $M_p(.)$ becomes a contracting mapping operator. Otherwise the above iteration may not converge. The two points are closely related to specific task and the selection of Φ.

Before closing this section, we observe the proposed methods for two very common combinatorial problems.

For the linear assignment problem eq.(6), we have $\frac{\partial E_{II}(V)}{\partial v_{ij}} = c_{ij}$, and thus eq.(23) becomes

$$b_j^{(k+1)} = D_j^{col} / \{\sum_{i=1}^{N} a_i^{(k)} (1 - v_{ij}^{(k)})^{-q/p} exp(-\frac{c_{ij}}{p\beta})\},$$

$$a_i^{(k+1)} = D_i^{row} / \{\sum_{j=1}^{M} b_j^{(k)} (1 - v_{ij}^{(k)})^{-q/p} exp(-\frac{c_{ij}}{p\beta})\},$$

$$v_{ij}^{(k+1)} = a_i^{(k+1)} b_j^{(k+1)} (1 - v_{ij}^{(k)})^{-q/p} exp(-\frac{c_{ij}}{p\beta}). \tag{27}$$

For the Traveling Salesman Problem eq.(5), we have $\frac{\partial E_{II}(V)}{\partial v_{ij}} = \sum_{k \neq i} d_{ik}(v_{k,j+1} + v_{k,j-1})$, and thus eq.(23) becomes

$$b_j^{(k+1)} = D_j^{col}/\{\sum_{i=1}^{N} a_i^{(k)} (1 - v_{ij}^{(k)})^{-q/p} exp(-\frac{1}{p\beta} \sum_{k \neq i} d_{ik}(v_{k,j+1} + v_{k,j-1}))\},$$

$$a_i^{(k+1)} = D_i^{row}/\{\sum_{j=1}^{M} b_j^{(k)} (1 - v_{ij}^{(k)})^{-q/p} exp(-\frac{1}{p\beta} \sum_{k \neq i} d_{ik}(v_{k,j+1} + v_{k,j-1}))\},$$

$$v_{ij}^{(k+1)} = a_i^{(k+1)} b_j^{(k+1)} (1 - v_{ij}^{(k)})^{-q/p} exp(-\frac{1}{p\beta} \sum_{k \neq i} d_{ik}(v_{k,j+1} + v_{k,j-1})). \tag{28}$$

4. Remarks

Due to limited space, we leave further theoretical and experimental analyses on convergence and performance of the proposed approach elsewhere (Xu, 1994). Here, we briefly mention the relations of the proposed approach to some existing ones.

We consider the case that $\Phi(.) = B_3(.)$ with $q = 0, p = 1$. In this case, we have $B_3(v_{ij}) = \int_0^{v_{ij}} \ln v_{ij} dv_{ij} = v_{ij} \ln v_{ij} - v_{ij}$. Putting it into eq.(12), we get

$$E(V) = E_{II}(V) + \sum_{j=1}^{M} \lambda_j^{col}[\sum_{i=1}^{N} v_{ij} - D_j^{col}] + \sum_{i=1}^{N} \lambda_i^{row}[\sum_{j=1}^{M} v_{ij} - D_i^{row}] + \beta \sum_{i=1}^{N} \sum_{j=1}^{M} v_{ij} \ln v_{ij} - \beta \sum_{i=1}^{N} \sum_{j=1}^{M} v_{ij}$$

This formula is very similar to eq.(13) in Yuille & Kosowsky (1992), obtained from statistical physics. The only exception is an extra term $\beta \sum_{i=1}^{N} \sum_{j=1}^{M} v_{ij}$. However, when the constraints C_s^{row}, C_s^{col} are satisfied, this extra term becomes constant, and has no influence on the original problem. So we see that the scheme proposed in this paper includes statistical physics method as a special case.

Next, if we replace $E'_{II}(V)$ in eq.(25) by $\sum_{j=1}^{M} \sum_{i=1}^{N} v_{ij} \|x_i - m_j\|^2$, and let $\Phi(.) = B_3(.)$ with $q = 0, p = 1$. Then we can show that the optimization of $E(V)$ will result in clustering of $\{x_i\}_1^N$ into M clusters with centers $m_j, j = 1, \cdots, M$. This clustering is very similar to clustering by finite mixture model with EM algorithm (Xu&Jordan,1993a&b; Xu, Jordan& Hinton, 1993). Therefore, the cases of $\Phi(.) = B_3(.)$ with $q \neq 0$ actually provide new algorithms for clustering analysis. Moreover, the proposed scheme also provides new algorithms for robust PCA (Xu& Yuille, 1993) and elastic nets (Durbin& Willshaw, 1987) since the two approachs are closely related to EM algorithm and statistical physics approach. The detailed discussions are given in (Xu, 1994).

Acknowledgment   I would like to thank the support from CUHK by a DIRECT GRANT for Research 93-94.

References

Cichocki.A. & Unbehaunen, R.(1993), *Neural Networks for Optimization and Signal processing*, Wiley, Pub.

Durbin, R. & Willshaw, D. (1987), *Nature, vol. 326*, pp689-691.

Gill, P.E., and Murray, W. (1974), *Numerical Methods for constrained Optimization*, Academic Press.

Hertz, J., Krogh, A, & Palmer, R.G.(1991), *Introduction to Theory of Neural Computation*, Addison-Wesley Pub.

Hopfield, J.J, & Tank, D.W, (1985), *Biological Cybernetics, Vol.52*, pp141-152.

Xu, L., Jordan, M. I. & Hinton, G.E.(1993), " A modified gating network for the mixtures of experts architecture", submitted to WCNN'94, San Diego, CA.

Xu, L.& Jordan, M. I. (1993a), Proc. WCNN'93, Portland, OR, Vol. II, 1993, 431-434.

Xu, L.& Jordan, M. I.(1993b), "Theoretical and Experimental Studies of The EM Algorithm for Unsupervised Learning Based on Finite Gaussian Mixtures", MIT Computational Cognitive Science, Tech. Rep. 9301, MIT, USA.

Xu, L. & Yuille, A.L. (1993), in S.J. Hanson, J.D. Cowan, and C.L. Giles (Eds.), *Advances in NIPS 5*. Morgan Kaufmann, San Mateo, CA, 467-474.

Xu,L.(1993), "Multisets Modeling Learning: An Unified Theory for Supervised and Unsupervised Learning", to appear on Proc. IEEE ICNN'94, invited paper.

Xu,L(1994), "A Novel Approach for Combinatorial Problems: Analog Constrained Optimization, Parallel Computing and Neural Network Implementation", Tech. Rep., Dept. of Computer Science, CUHK.

Yuille, A.L. & Kosowsky, J.J., (1992), "Statistical physics algorithms that converge", Harvard Robotics Lab., Tech Rep. No. 92-7. to appear on *Neural Computations*.

A Modified Gating Network for the Mixtures of Experts Architecture[1]

Lei Xu[1], Michael I. Jordan[1] and Geoffrey E. Hinton[2]

1. Dept of Brain and Cognitive Sciences, MIT, USA

2. Dept of Computer Science, Univ. of Toronto, Canada

Abstract   *We modify the mixtures-of-experts model by utilizing a different parametric form for the gating network. The modified model is trained by an EM algorithm. In comparison with earlier models— trained by either EM or gradient ascent—there is no need to select a learning stepsize to guarantee the convergence of the learning procedure. We report simulation experiments that show that the new architecture yields significantly faster convergence. We also utilize the new model to perform piecewise nonlinear function approximation with polynomial, trigonometric, or other prespecified basis functions.*

1. Mixtures-of-experts and EM learning

The *mixtures of experts* model is a modular neural network architecture (Jacobs, Jordan, Nowlan & Hinton, 1991) that solves function approximation problems by adaptively dividing the input space into regions and fitting separate functions within each region. The model is based on the following following conditional mixture density:

$$
\begin{aligned}
P(y|x,\Theta) &= \sum_{j=1}^{K} g_j(x,\nu)P(y|x,\theta_j), \\
P(y|x,\theta_j) &= (2\pi det\Gamma_j)^{-\frac{1}{2}} \exp\{-\frac{1}{2}[y - f_j(x,w_j)]^T \Gamma_j^{-1}[y - f_j(x,w_j)]\}.
\end{aligned}
\tag{1}
$$

where Θ consists of $\nu, \{\theta_j\}_1^K$, and θ_j consists of $\{w_j\}_1^K, \{\Gamma_j\}_1^K$. The vector $f_j(x,w_j)$ is the output of the j-th expert net. The scalar $g_j(x,\nu), j = 1, \cdots, K$ is given by the *softmax* function:

$$
g_j(x,\nu) = e^{\beta_j(x,\nu)} / \sum_i e^{\beta_i(x,\nu)}.
\tag{2}
$$

In this equation, $\beta_j(x,\nu), j = 1, \cdots, K$ are the outputs of a single feedforward network referred to as a *gating network*. In the probability model, the gating net can be viewed as a stochastic gate (switch) which selects the output of the j-th expert net with probability $P(j|x) = g_j(x,\nu)$.

The outputs of the expert networks in a mixture-of-experts architecture can be utilized in one of the following three modes:

$$
\begin{aligned}
o(x) &= E(y|x,\Theta) = \sum_j g_j(x,\nu)E(y|x,\theta_j), \quad \text{[regression function]}, \\
o(x) &= E(y|x,\theta_{j*}), \text{ with } P(j* = j) = g_j(x,\nu), \quad \text{[stochastic switching]}, \\
o(x) &= E(y|x,\theta_{j*}), \text{ with } j* = \arg\max_j g_j(x,\nu). \quad \text{[winner take all]}
\end{aligned}
\tag{3}
$$

The *regression function* mode is commonly used. Recently, Ghahramani & Jordan (1993) have discussed the use of the latter two modes for problems involving one-to-many mappings.

The parameter vector Θ is estimated by Maximum Likelihood (ML). That is, given a training set $\{y^{(t)}, x^{(t)}\}_{t=1}^N$, we find a Θ^* which maximizes the following likelihood function:

$$
L = \sum_t \ln P(y^{(t)}|x^{(t)}, \Theta).
\tag{4}
$$

Jacobs, Jordan, Nowlan & Hinton (1991) proposed a gradient ascent algorithm to maximize L. Recently Jordan & Jacobs (in press) have proposed an Expectation-Maximization (EM) algorithm (Dempster, Laird & Rubin, 1977) for maximizing eq.(4). They found that EM yielded a considerably improved rate of convergence when compared to gradient ascent. The readers are referred to Jordan & Xu (1993) and Xu & Jordan (1993) for a detailed discussion of EM and some new theoretical results.

---

[1]The correspondence address: Dr. Lei Xu, Dept. of Computer Sciences, HSH ENG Bldg, Room 1006, The Chinese University of Hong Kong, Shatin, Hong Kong, Fax 852 603 5024, Email lxu@cs.cuhk.hk

Given the current estimate $\Theta^{(k)}$, the EM procedure for maximizing eq.(4) consists of two steps.
(1) E-step. First, for each pair $\{x^{(t)}, y^{(t)}\}$, we compute:

$$h_j^{(k)}(y^{(t)}|x^{(t)}) = P(j|x^{(t)}, y^{(t)}) = \frac{g_j(x^{(t)}, \nu^{(k)})P(y^{(t)}|x^{(t)}, \theta_j^{(k)})}{\sum_i g_i(x^{(t)}, \nu^{(k)})P(y^{(t)}|x^{(t)}, \theta_j^{(k)})}; \qquad (5)$$

Then we form a set of new set of objective functions:

$$\begin{aligned} Q_j^e(\theta_j) &= \sum_t h_j^{(k)}(y^{(t)}|x^{(t)}) \ln P(y^{(t)}|x^{(t)}, \theta_j), \quad j = 1, \cdots, K; \\ Q^g(\nu) &= \sum_t \sum_j h_j^{(k)}(y^{(t)}|x^{(t)}) \ln g_j^{(k)}(x^{(t)}, \nu^{(k)}). \end{aligned} \qquad (6)$$

(2). M-step. Find a new estimate $\Theta^{(k+1)} = \{\{\theta_j^{(k+1)}\}_{j=1}^K, \nu^{(k+1)}\}$ with:

$$\theta_j^{(k+1)} = \arg\max_{\theta_j} Q_j^e(\theta_j), j = 1, \cdots, K; \quad \nu^{(k+1)} = \arg\max_{\nu} Q^g(\nu). \qquad (7)$$

In certain cases, the maximization in eq.(7) will be able to be performed analytically. In particular, when $f_j(x, w_j)$ is linear with respect to θ_j (e.g., $f_j(x, w_j) = w_j^T[x, 1]$), $\max_{\theta_j} Q_j^e(\theta_j)$ can be solved by solving $\partial Q_j^e / \partial \theta_j = 0$. When $f_j(x, w_j)$ is nonlinear with respect to w_j, however, the maximization can not be performed analytically. Moreover, due to the nonlinearity of the softmax function in eq.(2), the maximization $\max_{\nu} Q^g(\nu)$ cannot be solved analytically in any case. For these nonlinear optimization problems, two possibilities present themselves. One is to make use of a conventional iterative optimization technique (e.g., gradient ascent) in an inner-loop iteration that performs the maximization. The other possibility is to abandon the attempt to maximize the function and to simply find a new estimate such that

$$Q_j^e(\theta_j^{(k+1)}) \geq Q_j^e(\theta_j^{(k)}), j = 1, \cdots, K; \quad Q^g(\nu^{(k+1)}) \geq Q^g(\nu^{(k)}). \qquad (8)$$

Dempster, Laird and Rubin (1977) refer to algorithms that perform a full maximization during the M step as "EM" algorithms, and algorithms that simply increase the Q function during the M step as "GEM" ("Generalized EM") algorithms. In this paper we will further distinguish between EM algorithms that require an iterative inner loop and algorithms that do not require an iterative inner loop, calling the former *single-loop EM* and the latter *double-loop EM*.

Jordan and Jacobs (in press) considered the case of linear $\beta_j(x, \nu) = \nu_j^T[x, 1]$ with $\nu = [\nu_1, \cdots, \nu_K]$ and semi-linear $f_j(w_j^T[x, 1])$ with nonlinear $f_j(.)$. They proposed a double-loop EM algorithm by using the *Iterative Recursive Least Square (IRLS)* method to implement the inner-loop iteration. For more general nonlinear $\beta_j(x, \nu)$ and $f_j(x, \theta_j)$, Jordan & Xu (1993) showed that an extended IRLS can be used for this inner loop. Actually, it can be shown that IRLS and the extension are equivalent to solving eq.(6) by the so-called *Fisher Scoring* method.

2. A modified gating net and an alternative EM algorithm

For the original model discussed above, the nonlinearity of *softmax* makes the analytical solution of $\max_{\nu} Q^g(\nu)$ impossible even for the simple and useful cases in which $\beta_j(x, \nu) = \nu_j^T[x, 1]$ and $f_j(x^{(t)}, w_j) = w_j^T[x, 1]$. That is, we do not have a single-loop EM algorithm for training this model even when all the maximizations related to the expert nets are analytical solvable. We need to use either double-loop EM or GEM. Although it was shown by Dempster, Laird and Rubin (1977) that both EM (including single and double loop variants) and GEM will converge monotonically in likelihood, the convergence rates and computing costs can be quite different. For single-loop EM, convergence is guaranteed automatically without setting any parameters or restricting the initial conditions. For double-loop EM—e.g., the IRLS loop of Jordan & Jacobs (in press)—inner-loop iteration can increase the computational costs considerably. Moreover, in order to guarantee the convergence of the inner loop, safeguard measures (e.g., appropriate choice of a step size) are required. This can also increase computing costs. For a GEM algorithm, a new estimate that satisfies eq.(7) is generally obtained by a nonlinear optimization technique. In general, the use of nonlinear optimization techniques requires external control or extra search to guarantee the satisfaction of eq.(7); this can slow convergence.

To overcome this disadvantage of the softmax-based gating net, we propose the following modified gating network:

$$g_j(x, \nu) = \alpha_j P(x|\nu_j) / \sum_i \alpha_i P(x|\nu_i), \quad \sum_j \alpha_j = 1, \alpha_j \geq 0$$
$$P(x|\nu_j) = a_j(\nu_j)^{-1} b_j(x) \exp\{c_j(\nu_j)^T t_j(x)\}, \quad b_j(x) \geq 0, \quad a_j(\nu_j) = \int b_j(x) \exp\{c_j(\nu_j)^T t_j(x)\} dx \quad (9)$$

where $\nu = \{\alpha_j, \nu_j, j = 1, \cdots, K\}$. $P(x, \nu_j)$'s are density functions from the exponential family. $a_j(.), b_j(.), c_j(.), t_j(.)$ are prespecified functions. $t_j(x)$ is a sufficient statistic. The exponential family covers most of the density functions that are useful in practice. The commonly such density is the Gaussian density:

$$P(x|\nu_j) = (2\pi \det \Sigma_j)^{-\frac{1}{2}} \exp\{-\frac{1}{2}(x - m_j)^T \Sigma_j^{-1}(x - m_j)\}, \quad (10)$$

with ν_j consisting of m_j and Σ_j.

In eq.(9), $g_j(x, \nu)$ is actually the posteriori probability $P(j|x)$ that x is assigned to the partition corresponding to the j-th expert net, obtained from Bayes' rule:

$$g_j(x, \nu) = P(j|x) = \alpha_j P(x|\nu_j)/P(x, \nu), \quad P(x, \nu) = \sum_i \alpha_i P(x|\nu_i). \quad (11)$$

Inserting this $g_j(x, \nu)$ into the model eq.(1), we get

$$P(y|x, \Theta) = \sum_j \frac{\alpha_j P(x|\nu_j)}{P(x, \nu)} P(y|x, \theta_j). \quad (12)$$

If we directly substitute this $P(y|x, \Theta)$ into eq.(4) and derive an EM algorithm, we again find that the maximization $\max_\nu Q^g(\nu)$ cannot be solved analytically. To avoid this difficulty, we rewrite eq.(12) into an equivalent form:

$$P(y, x) = P(y|x, \Theta)P(x, \nu) = \sum_j \alpha_j P(x|\nu_j)P(y|x, \theta_j). \quad (13)$$

Assume that the parameters $\{\alpha_j\}_1^K, \{\nu_j\}_1^K, \{\theta_j\}_1^K$ are already known, then by taking integral over y on the both sides of eq.(13), we have $P(x, \nu) = \sum_j \alpha_j P(x|\nu_j)$. This suggests that we can easily obtain the model eq.(12) from eq.(13)—an asymmetrical representation of joint density.

Therefore, we accordingly modify eq.(4) as follows:

$$L' = \sum_t \ln P(y^{(t)}, x^{(t)}) = \sum_t \ln\{\sum_j \alpha_j P(x^{(t)}|\nu_j)P(y^{(t)}|x^{(t)}, \theta_j)\}. \quad (14)$$

After some derivations, we obtain the following two steps of the EM procedure for this ML problem:

(1) E-step.

$$h_j^{(k)}(y^{(t)}|x^{(t)}) = \frac{\alpha_j^{(k)} P(x^{(t)}|\nu_j^{(k)})P(y^{(t)}|x^{(t)}, \theta_j^{(k)})}{\sum_i \alpha_i^{(k)} P(x^{(t)}|\nu_i^{(k)})P(y^{(t)}|x^{(t)}, \theta_j^{(k)})}; \quad (15)$$

By letting both the numerator and denominator of eq.(15) be divided by $P(x)$ and utilizing eq.(11), we find that eq.(15) is identical to eq.(5). In addition, the objective functions $Q_j^e(\theta_j), j = 1, \cdots, K$ are the same as given in eq.(6). Moreover the objective function $Q^g(\nu)$ can be further decomposed into

$$Q_j^g(\nu_j) = \sum_t h_j^{(k)}(y^{(t)}|x^{(t)}) \ln P(x^{(t)}|\nu_j), \quad j = 1, \cdots, K;$$
$$Q^\alpha = \sum_t \sum_j h_j^{(k)}(y^{(t)}|x^{(t)}) \ln \alpha_j, \quad with \ \alpha = \{\alpha_1, \cdots, \alpha_K\}. \quad (16)$$

(2). M-step. Find a new estimate with

$$\theta_j^{(k+1)} = \arg\max_{\theta_j} Q_j^e(\theta_j), j = 1, \cdots, K;$$

$$\nu_j^{(k+1)} = \arg\max_{\nu_j} Q_j^g(\nu_j), j = 1, \cdots, K;$$

$$\alpha^{(k+1)} = \arg\max_{\alpha} Q^\alpha, \ s.t. \ \sum_j \alpha_j = 1. \tag{17}$$

The maximization for the expert nets is the same as in eq.(7). However, for the gating net the maximizations now become analytically solvable as long as $P(x|\nu_j)$ is from the exponential family. That is, we have:

$$\nu_j^{(k+1)} = \frac{1}{\sum_t h_j^{(k)}(y^{(t)}|x^{(t)})} \sum_t h_j^{(k)}(y^{(t)}|x^{(t)}) t_j(x^{(t)}),$$

$$\alpha_j^{(k+1)} = \frac{1}{N} \sum_t h_j^{(k)}(y^{(t)}|x^{(t)}). \tag{18}$$

In particular, when $P(x|\nu_j)$ is a Gaussian density, the update becomes:

$$m_j^{(k+1)} = \frac{1}{\sum_t h_j^{(k)}(y^{(t)}|x^{(t)})} \sum_t h_j^{(k)}(y^{(t)}|x^{(t)}) x^{(t)},$$

$$\Sigma_j^{(k+1)} = \frac{1}{\sum_t h_j^{(k)}(y^{(t)}|x^{(t)})} \sum_t h_j^{(k)}(y^{(t)}|x^{(t)})[x^{(t)} - m_j^{(k)}][x^{(t)} - m_j^{(k)}]^T. \tag{19}$$

3. Simulation results

To compare the EM algorithm for the modified model to the original model, we conducted a simulation in which data were generated from a univariate function consisting of two linear segments (see Fig.1a). We used 1000 data points and considered mixture-of-experts architectures with $K = 2$ expert networks. For the expert nets, we modeled each $P(y|x, \theta_j)$ by a Gaussian with linear $f_j(x, w_j) = w_j^T[x, 1]$. For the modified gating net, the $P(x, \nu_j)$ in eq.(9) is Gaussian as given by eq.(10). For the original gating net in eq.(2), we used the parameterization $\beta_1(x, \nu) = 0$ and $\beta_2(x, \nu) = \nu^T[x, 1]$.

The two lines in the scatter plot in Fig.1(a) are the fits of the two expert nets. The fits obtained by the modified and the original models are almost the same. However, the learning speeds are significantly different. As shown in Fig.1(b), the modified algorithm requires k=15 iterations for the log-likelihood to converge to the value of -1271.8. These iterations require $1, 351, 383$ $flops$ (each operation of real addition, subtraction, multiplication and division is one $flop$). For the original model, we use the IRLS algorithm given in Jordan and Jacobs (in press) for the inner loop. In pilot experiments, we found that it usually took a large number of iterations for the inner loop to converge. To save computations, we limit the maximum number of iterations by $\tau_{max} = 10$. (This does not influence the final performance.) In Fig.1(b), we see that the outer loop converges in around 16 iterations. Each inner loop requires $290, 498$ $flops$ and the entire process takes $5, 312, 695$ $flops$. So we see that the modified algorithm converges approximately 3.9 times faster than the original algorithm based on IRLS. In fig.1(b), one can observe that the final value of the likelihood for the original model is slightly better than the modified model; the reason being that eq.(14) is not exactly equivalent to eq.(13) for a finite training set.

An advantage of the modified algorithm is the lack of any free parameters. Although the original algorithm also has no free parameters, we found that the inner loop of IRLS can diverge without a step size. In our experiments, we found that a small step size of 0.01 was required.

One disadvantage of the modified gating net is that the number of parameters is $K(1 + d/2 + d^2/2)$ in comparison with $(K - 1)d$ required by the original gating net, where d is the dimension of x.

4. Piecewise Nonlinear Function Approximation

For a single-loop EM algorithm, we need to ensure that the maximization $\max_{\theta_j} Q_j^e(\theta_j), j = 1, \cdots, K$ given in eq.(6) is solvable analytically. One such case involves linear experts of the form $f_j(x, w_j) = w_j^T[x, 1]$, in which case the mixture-of-experts as a whole implements a smoothed version of piecewise linear approximation of a nonlinear function. This model can be generalized by allowing the experts to be linear in the parameters but nonlinear in the input—single-loop EM still applies to this case. Assume the following model:

$$f_j(x, w_j) = \sum_i w_{i,j}\phi_{i,j}(x) + w_{0,j} = w_j^T[\phi_j(x), 1], \tag{20}$$

with $\phi_{i,j}(x)$ being prespecified functions of x. The resulting maximization problems for $\max_{\theta_j} Q_j^e(\theta_j), j = 1, \cdots, K$ in eq.(6) are weighted least square problems that can be solved analytically.

A useful special case is the one in which $\phi_{i,j}(x)$ are canonical polynomial terms $x_1^{r_1} \cdots x_d^{r_d}$, $r_i \geq 0$. In this case, the mixture-of-experts model implements smoothed piecewise polynomial approximations. Another useful case is the case in which $\phi_{i,j}(x)$ is $\prod_i \sin_i^r(j\pi x_1) \cos_i^r(j\pi x_1), r_i \geq 0$. In this case, the mixture-of- experts will implement smoothed piecewise trigonometric approximations. We can also use hybrids of polynomial, trigonometric, and other basis functions in different expert nets.

Figs.2(a)&(b) show the results of a computer experiment that studied piecewise polynomial approximation. The modified model with the EM algorithm proposed in the previous section was used. As shown in Fig.2(a), we used 1000 training points sampled from a univariate function which consists of two pieces of third degree polynomials. We consider a mixture-of-experts model with $K = 2$. For the expert nets, each $P(y|x, \theta_j)$ is Gaussian with $f_j(x, w_j) = w_{3,j}x^3 + w_{2,j}x^2 + w_{1,j}x + w_{0,j}$. In the modified gating net each $P(x, \nu_j)$ is again Gaussian.

The two curves in the scatter plot in Fig.2(a) are the estimated fits of the two expert nets. As shown in Fig.2(b), the log-likelihood converges to the value of -608.3 after about $k = 5$ iterations. The converged parameters for two experts nets are $w_1 = [w_{3,1}, w_{2,1}, w_{1,1}, w_{0,1}] = [0.7639, 0.0422, 0.4321, 0.1932]$ and $w_2 = [w_{3,2}, w_{2,2}, w_{1,2}, w_{0,2}] = [-0.014, -0.6751, 0.4321, 0.1932]$. We see from these values and from Fig.2(b) that the high order nonlinear regression has been fit quite well.

Figs.3(a)& (b) show the results of an experiment with the same data using the modified model with linear $f_j(x, w_j) = w_j^T[x, 1]$. From the fits in Fig.3(a) or the converged likelihood value, we see that the approximation is obviously worse than the results obtained in Figs.2(a) & 2(b).

This project was supported in part by a grant from the McDonnell-Pew Foundation, by a grant from the ATR Human Information Processing Laboratories, by a grant from Siemens Corporation, by grant IRI-9013991 from the National Science Foundation, and by grant N00014-90-J-1942 from the Office of Naval Research. Jordan is NSF Presidential Young Investigator. Hinton is a fellow of the Canadian Institute for Advanced Research.

References

[1] Dempster, A.P., Laird, N.M., and Rubin, D.B. (1977), Maximum-likelihood from incomplete data via the EM algorithm, *J. of Royal Statistical Society, B39*, pp. 1-38.

[2] Ghahramani, Z, and Jordan, M.I. (1993), Function approximation via density estimation using the EM approach, MIT Computational Cognitive Science Tech. Rep. 9304, Dept. of Brain and Cognitive Sciences, MIT.

[3] Jacobs, R.A., Jordan, M.I., Nowlan, S.J., and Hinton, G.E., (1991), Adaptive mixtures of local experts, *Neural Computation, 3*, pp. 79-87.

[4] Jordan, M.I. and Jacobs, R.A. (1992), Hierarchies of adaptive experts, *Advances in Neural Information Processing System 4*, J.E. Moody, S. Hanson and R.P. Lippmann, (eds.), San Mateo: Morgan Kaufmann Pub., pp. 985-992.

[5] Jordan, M.I. and Jacobs, R.A. (in press), Hierarchical mixtures of experts and the EM algorithm, *Neural Computation*.

[6] Jordan, M.I. and Xu, L. (1993), Convergence properties of the EM approach to learning in mixture-of-experts architectures, MIT Computational Cognitive Science Tech. Rep. 9302, Dept. of Brain and Cognitive Sciences, MIT.

[7] Xu, L., and Jordan, M.I. (1993), Theoretical and experimental studies of the EM algorithm for unsupervised learning based on finite gaussian mixtures, MIT Computational Cognitive Science Tech. Rep. 9301, Dept. of Brain and Cognitive Sciences, MIT.

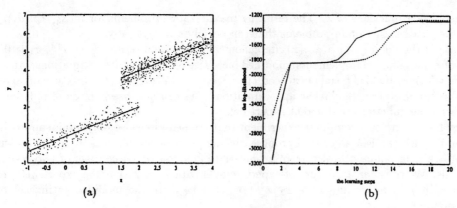

(a)   (b)

Figure 1: (a) 1000 samples from $y = a_1 x + a_2 + \varepsilon$, $a_1 = 0.8$, $a_2 = 0.4$, $x \in [-1, 1.5]$ with prior $\alpha_1 = 0.25$ and $y = a_1' x + a_2' + \varepsilon$, $a_1' = 0.8$, $a_2' =' 2.4$, $x \in [1, 4]$ with prior $\alpha_2 = 0.75$, where x is uniform random variable and z is from Gaussian $N(0, 0.3)$. The two lines through the clouds are the estimated models of two expert nets. The ones obtained by the two learning are almost the same. (b) The changes of the log-likelihood as the iteration goes. The solid line is for the modified learning. The dotted line is for the original learning (the outer-loop iteration

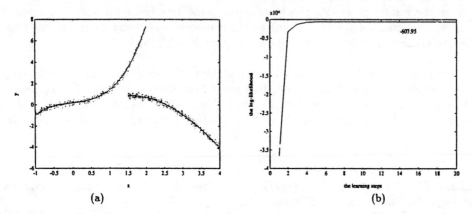

(a)   (b)

Figure 2: Piecewise 3rd polynomial approximation. (a) 1000 samples from $y = a_1 x^3 + a_3 x + a_4 + \varepsilon$, $x \in [-1, 1.5]$ with prior $\alpha_1 = 0.4$ and $y = a_2' x^2 + a_3' x^2 + a_4' + \varepsilon$, $x \in [1, 4]$ with prior $\alpha_2 = 0.6$, where x is uniform random variable and z is from Gaussian $N(0, 0.15)$. The two curves through the clouds are the estimated models of two expert nets. (b) The changes of the log-likelihood as the iteration goes.

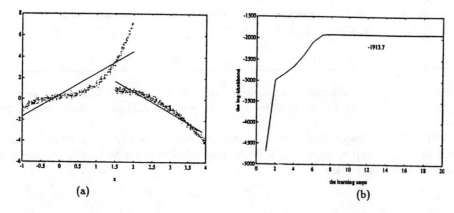

(a)   (b)

Figure 3: Piecewise linear approximation. (a) The two lines estimated for two expert nets. (b) The changes of the log-likelihood as the iteration goes.

Spatial Variation of the Weights of Recurrent Synapses During Equilibrium

Antônio C. Roque-da-Silva-Filho
Departamento de Geologia, Física e Matemática
FFCLRP, Universidade de São Paulo, Campus de Ribeirão Preto
Ribeirão Preto-SP 14040-901
Brazil
E-Mail: antonior@biomag.ffclrp.usp.br

Abstract

A generalized version of Amari's field-theoretic approach to neural networks is used to model a situation in which the weights of the recurrent synapses across a two-dimensional neural field vary with time according to a Hebbian type law. Assuming equilibrium, an equation relating the synaptic weight function to the neuronal receptive field overlap is derived. It is studied in a simple case in which the weights are isotropic and symmetric.

1 Introduction

An interesting problem which can be tackled by a neural network modeler is the one of mathematically deriving possible shapes for the recurrent synaptic weight function, i.e. the function which embodies the properties and characteristics of the lateral connections between neurons along a given cortical layer. Most neural network modelers assume the lateral weights to be fixed in time: obeying a Mexican hat type function in the case in which neurons can be both excitatory and inhibitory at the same time (von der Malsburg 1973; Amari 1977; Hertz *et al* 1989); or decaying exponentially and isotropicaly with distance in the case in which neurons can be either exclusively excitatory or exclusively inhibitory (Wilson and Cowan 1973; Idiart and Abbott 1993). In all cases it is tacitly assumed that: i) the weights of the synapses made by a neuron have, on the average, larger values closer to the neuron than far away from it; and ii) the synaptic weight function tends to zero at great distances. Although being very reasonable, and expected to reproduce qualitatively the behaviour of real synaptic efficacies these assumptions are imposed *ad hoc* to the models. However, this does not need to be so. An opposite point of view would be to take other assumptions as the basis for a theoretical model, and use this model to derive possible forms of spatial variation for the synaptic weight function. The possible forms obtained could then be adopted in other models, or motivate experiments to test their validity.

The second point of view mentioned above is adopted in this work. Starting from no *a priori* assumption about the shape of the recurrent synapses, an equation for the spatial behaviour of those synapses is derived from other assumptions regarding neural dynamics.

2 The Model

In this work, Amari's field-theoretic approach to neural networks (Amari 1983; Amari 1990) is applied to a situation in which the weights of connections between neurons in the same neural field (recurrent connections) vary with time according to a Hebbian type law (Hebb 1949). The neural field is assumed to be two-dimensional, and made of either exclusively excitatory neurons or exclusively inhibitory neurons. An external excitatory input coming from a signal space is applied to the neurons in the field for a time much longer than the relaxation times of both the excitatory and the inhibitory neurons, but much shorter than the respective time constants of synaptic modification. One can then assume that a near-equilibrium regime is reached a short time after the external input is applied, and consider the dynamical variables of the model as constant until the cessation of the signal (Caianiello 1962; Amari 1983).

The equilibrium value of the recurrent synaptic weight function is given by the equation

$$\omega(\vec{x},\vec{x}') = c \int p(\theta) f[U(\vec{x},\theta)] f[U(\vec{x}',\theta)] d\theta, \tag{1}$$

where $\omega(\vec{x},\vec{x}')$ is the weight of the synapses made by neurons at $\vec{x}'$ with neurons at $\vec{x}$; c is a constant having value +1 for a field made of excitatory neurons, and value -1 for a field made of inhibitory neurons; $p(\theta)$ gives the probability distribution for the inputs applied from the signal space, which is parametrized by n coordinates represented here as θ for short; $f[U(\vec{x},\theta)]$ is the equilibrium firing rate of neurons at $\vec{x}$ when signal θ is applied ($f[U]$ is a nonlinear function of the equilibrium membrane potential U); and the integral is to be performed over the whole signal space. Equation (1) allows the obtaintion of analytic expressions for $\omega(\vec{x},\vec{x}')$ from assumptions about the form of function $f[U]$ and the structures of the equilibrium receptive fields of neurons at $\vec{x}$ and $\vec{x}'$.

3 An Analytic Expression for the Synaptic Weight Function

Let us assume that the signal space is two-dimensional as the neural field. Let us also assume that neurons at $\vec{x}$ in the neural field have circular receptive fields of radius $R(\vec{x})$. The receptive field of a neuron is defined here as the region of the signal space whose signals are capable of driving the neuron's equilibrium firing rate to its maxim value, assumed to be $f[U] = 1$. It is also assumed that signals outside a neuron's receptive field cannot excite it to significant levels of equilibrium activity, so that one can consider $f[U] = 0$ when they are applied. These assumptions make (1) read

$$\omega(\vec{x},\vec{x}') = c \int_{RF(\vec{x}) \cap RF(\vec{x}')} p(\theta) d\theta, \tag{2}$$

where the integral is performed over the region of intersection between the receptive fields of neurons at $\vec{x}$ and $\vec{x}'$, denoted by $RF(\vec{x}) \cap RF(\vec{x}')$.

For a special case in which $p(\theta) = p = const.$, equation (2) implies that $\omega(\vec{x},\vec{x}')$ is proportional to the area of the receptive overlap of neurons at $\vec{x}$ and $\vec{x}'$. This overlap is schematically represented at Figure 1. For this case equation (2) implies that

$$\omega(\vec{x},\vec{x}') = cp\left[R_1^2 \arccos\left(\frac{D^2 + R_1^2 - R_2^2}{2R_1 D}\right) + \right.$$

$$\left. R_2^2 \arccos\left(\frac{D^2 + R_2^2 - R_1^2}{2R_2 D}\right) - \frac{1}{2}\sqrt{4R_1^2 D - (D^2 + R_1^2 - R_2^2)^2} \right], \tag{3}$$

where $R_1 \equiv R(\vec{x})$, $R_2 \equiv R(\vec{x}')$, and D is the distance separating the centers of the two receptive fields. This equation can be used to calculate the weight of the synaptic connection between any two neurons in the neural field, one at $\vec{x}$ and the other at $\vec{x}'$, from assumptions about the sizes of $R(\vec{x})$ and of $R(\vec{x}')$, and the distance between the centers of these two receptive fields.

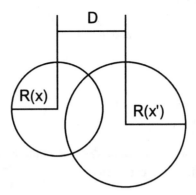

Figure 1. A scheme of the receptive fields of neurons at $\vec{x}$ and $\vec{x}'$. The respective radii are indicated by $R(x)$ and $R(x')$, and the centers are separated by a distance D.

4 An Isotropic and Symmetric Weight Function

In this section we will assume that all the receptive fields have the same radius R, and that the distance between the centers of any two receptive fields depends only on the distance between the respective neurons along the neural field, i.e.

$$D = g\big(\left|\vec{x}' - \vec{x}\right|\big), \tag{4}$$

where g is any well behaved function relating distances in the two spaces: the signal space and the neural field. The above assumptions turn (3) into

$$\omega(x) = cp\left[2R^2 \arccos\big(D\!\big/\!2R\big) - \frac{D}{2}\sqrt{4R^2 - D^2}\,\right], \tag{5}$$

where the origin of coordinates in the neural field was placed at $\vec{x}$, and $x = \left|\vec{x}'\right|$ is the distance from origin. In this case $\omega(\vec{x}, \vec{x}')$ is isotropic (depends only on the distance $\left|\vec{x} - \vec{x}'\right|$) and symmetric, i.e. $\omega(\vec{x}, \vec{x}') = \omega(\vec{x}', \vec{x})$. It also is the same function, apart from the signal of c, for the excitatory and inhibitory neurons, because the radius R was chosen as the same for both types of neuron. Obviuosly, this is not the most general case but it ilustrates some of the basic features of a general synaptic weight function.

Equations (4) and (5) allow one to determine the spatial structure of the synaptic weight function during equilibrium. The hypothesis behind equation (4) is that there is a mapping from points in the signal space to points in the neural field. This hypothesis is supported by experimental evidence (Kaas 1987; Knudsen *et al* 1987). An important property of these so called cortical maps is that they are topographic: neighbouring cortical cells respond to neighbouring stimuli. This implies that function g must be a growing function of its argument, i.e. the greater the value of x the greater the value of g, and therefore of D.

We will assume that the relation between points in the signal space and points in the neural field is topographic, so that D is a growing function of x. Furthermore, in order to simplify the discussion of this section, we also will assume that

$$D = x \text{ and } R \equiv 1,$$ (6)

which implies that (5) reads

$$\omega(x) = cp\left[2\arccos\left(\frac{x}{2}\right) - \frac{x}{2}\sqrt{4-x^2}\right].$$ (7)

A plot of (7) is given below, where the product cp was made equal to 1, and only the region for which both x and $\omega(x)$ are positive was considered.

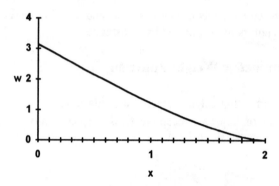

Figure 2. Graph of equation (7) for $cp = 1$.

The above figure gives the shape of the equilibrium synaptic weight function for the simple case considered in this section. It shows a function decaying from a maximum value at the origin towards zero at some point, which defines the maximum range of variation for the function (we are only interested here in positive values of ω). Thus, although simple, the equation derived here displays all the basic features of the recurrent synaptic weight functions assumed by other authors. The difference is that in this case an equation has been derived for it, instead of being imposed. This derived equation could be used in other models, as an alternative to the more commonly used exponential, to represent the time invariant recurrent synaptic weight function

5 Conclusions

The work of Amari and others on the field-theoretic approach to neural networks has been used to study neural maps and their properties from a theoretical point of view (Amari 1990; Zhang 1991; Roque da Silva Filho 1992). The present paper offers a contribution to this effort, by showing how the continuous model can be used to derive possible expressions for the equilibrium recurrent synaptic weight function. A general equation — equation (2) — has been obtained relating this weight function to the receptive field overlap between neurons at two different positions in the neural field. This equation has been explored here for the simple case in which the recurrent synaptic weights are isotropic and symmetric: a solution has been obtained showing decay with distance and a maximum range beyond which the synaptic weight is null. This is in accordance with what is expected for recurrent synapses, and with the general properties of recurrent synaptic functions postulated by other authors in their works.

The derivation of the synaptic weight equation was based on certain assumptions, the most important of them being: i) the assumption that an equilibrium state is invariably reached a short time after the application of an external stimulus; and ii) the assumption that the map from signal space to neural field is topographic. The former allows the obtaintion of an analytically tractable equation, while the latter guarantees the spatially decaying behaviour of $\omega(x)$. An assumption other than the topography of the mapping would lead to a different synaptic weight function, which could describe a non-decaying spatial behaviour.

Equation (2) might have further implications not studied here, mainly in connection with the so called *percent overlap rule* (Sur *et al* 1980) observed in cortical somatotopy, according to which the degree of receptive field overlap is linearly related to the horizontal distance between two cortical recording sites. The integral in the right hand side of (2) is related to the receptive field overlap, and the synaptic weight function $\omega(\bar{x}, \bar{x}')$ is a function of the distance between two points in the neural field. Equation (2) could then be used to study the relationship between these two quantities, and the conditions under which it is linear. This will be explored in a further work. Finally, we would like to point out that this work has shown a possible way of determining equilibrium values for recurrent synaptic weights from information about receptive fields. In particular, one could use experimental data to determine these weights, establishing thus a bridge between experiment and theory.

References

Amari S (1977) "Dynamics of Pattern Formation in Lateral-Inhibition Type Neural Fields." *Biol. Cybern.*, **27**:77-87.

Amari S (1983) "Field Theory of Self-Organizing Neural Nets." *IEEE Trans. Syst. Man Cybern.*, **13**:741-748.

Amari S (1990) "Formation of Cortical Cognitive Map by Self-Organization." *Computational Neuroscience*, EL Schwartz (ed.), chapter 21. MIT Press, Cambridge, Mass.

Caianiello ER (1961) "Outline of a Theory of Thought Processes and Thinking Machines." *J. Theor. Biol.*, **1**:204-235.

Hebb D (1949) *The Organization of Behavior*. Wiley, New York.

Hertz J, Krogh A, Palmer RG (1991) *Introduction to the Theory of Neural Computation*. Addison-Wesley, Redwood City, CA.

Idiart MAP, Abbott LF (1993) "Propagation of Excitation in Neural Network Models." *Network*, **4**:285-294.

Kaas JH (1987) "The Organization of Neocortex in Mammals: Implications for Theories of Brain Function." *Ann. Rev. Psychol.*, **38**:129-151.

Knudsen EI, du Lac S, Esterly SD (1987) "Computational Maps in the Brain." *Ann. Rev. Neurosci.*, **10**:41-65.

von der Malsburg C (1973) "Self-Organization of Orientation Sensitive Cells in the Striate Cortex." *Kybernetik*, **14**:85-100.

Roque da Silva Filho AC (1992) "Analysis of Equilibrium Properties of a Continuous Neural Network Made of Excitatory and Inhibitory Neurons." *Network*, **3**:303-321.

Sur M, Merzenich MM, Kaas JH (1980) "Magnification, Receptive-Field Area and Hypercolumn Size in Owl Monkeys." *J. Neurophysiol.*, **44**:295-311.

Wilson HR, Cowan JD (1973) "A Mathematical Theory of the Functional Dynamics of Cortical and Thalamic Nervous Tissue." *Kybernetik*, **13**:55-80.

Zhang J (1991) "Dynamics and Formation of Self-Organizing Maps." *Neural Computation*, **3**:54-66.

Competitive Activation, Bayesian Networks, and ART

Frank E. McFadden

Department of Computer Science

University of Maryland

College Park, Maryland 20742

Winner-takes-all (WTA) behavior in a competitive system has been central to theories of computational map formation in the brain because WTA behavior makes it possible for a distributed system to make choices. Competitive models have generally relied on direct lateral inhibition, which requires a very high proportion of inhibitory connections, whereas the cerebral cortex is dominated by excitatory connections. This article introduces new theoretical analysis of a competitive model proposed by [Reggia, 1985] as an alternative to direct lateral inhibition. This model, based on competitive activation with virtual lateral inhibition (CAVLI), is seen to be based on iterative Bayesian updating, with architectural outlines that closely resemble ART1, but with no bottom-up weights and with rational (multiplicative) error adjustment. CAVLI and ART1 are compared with respect to inhibitory mechanisms, biological plausibility, and scaling.

1 Introduction

The class of neural models described in [Carpenter and Grossberg, 1987] and the paradigm introduced by [Reggia, 1985] both involve competition among neurons in a field, during a short term memory phase (STM) while the network approaches equilibrium. In both cases, the activation dynamics during the STM phase features competition that may result in WTA behavior. Competition in Grossberg's models occurs by direct lateral inhibition, as typified by population models of mutually predatory species, whereas competition in Reggia's models occurs by "virtual lateral inhibition," typical of competition among firms producing similar goods. The latter class of models will therefore be referred to as Competitive Activation based on Virtual Lateral Inhibition, or CAVLI, to distinguish it from the class of models based on competitive activation with direct lateral inhibition, of which ART is the best known example. It will be shown that the CAVLI models are closely related to probabilistic models such as Bayesian networks used in diagnostic modeling. Because the ART model is well-known, it will not be reviewed here, but the CAVLI model will be described and analyzed from a new theoretical point of view. The two models will then be compared and contrasted.

2 Theory of CAVLI

2.1 Basic Theory

The central formula in CAVLI models has been one that computes connection strengths indirectly, by way of a "weight matrix." In order to make the formulation clear, the model shall be stated in terms of a two layer feedforward CAVLI network, with activations in the first layer denoted by the m-vector x and activations in the second layer denoted by the n-vector y. Further, denote the input to node i by I_i, and let w_{ij} represent the connection strength for impulses transmitted from node j (in the first layer) to node i (in the second layer). As in many neural network models, the input is summed linearly:

$$I_i = \sum_{j=1}^{m} w_{ij} x_j. \tag{1}$$

The basic formula that distinguishes the CAVLI models is that used to compute w_{ij}

$$w_{ij} = \frac{v_{ij} y_i(t)}{\sum_k v_{kj} y_k(t)}, \tag{2}$$

where v_{ij} is the parameter matrix.[1] While variations on this basic theme have appeared, the essence of the CAVLI notion is contained within the basic model defined by equations (1) and (2). Equation (2) is formally identical to Bayes rule, and the matrix of weights, v_{ij}, plays a role that is very similar to that of the topdown weights in the ART1 model, but there are no independently parametrized bottom-up weights in the CAVLI model.

An interpretation clarifies the formal identification of the CAVLI model with a simple Bayesian diagnostic model. The y layer can be interpreted as prior probabilities on a set of mutually exclusive "disorders", and the x layer as the distribution on a set of "manifestations." Let Y_i denote the event that disorder i is present, and X_j the event that manifestation j is present. v_{ij} is the conditional probability, $P(X_j|Y_i)$, that manifestation X_j will be observed when disorder Y_i is present (exclusively). It is also assumed that manifestations are mutually exclusive, and occur in the population with probabilities $x_j = P(X_j)$.

It can be seen by substitution that

$$\begin{aligned} w_{ij} &= \frac{P(Y_i) \ P(X_j|Y_i)}{\sum_k P(X_j|Y_k) P(Y_k)} \\ &= P(Y_i|X_j), \end{aligned}$$

according to the usual derivation of Bayes rule, which holds under the assumption that the disorders Y_k are a disjoint partition of the probability space. Thus the forward coefficient w_{ij} is the conditional probability that disorder i is present when manifestation j is observed.

Overall, the model can be regarded as a Markov process in which the $y(t)$ vector is modified, depending on what manifestation is observed at time t, where manifestation j occurs with probability x_j. A sequence of input data, $\xi(t)$ is observed, and the update rule is used to modify the y values. The data vector $\xi(t)$ is an indicator variable that equals 1 in the component corresponding to the observed manifestation, and 0 in all other components. Thus

$$y_i(t+1) = I_i(y(t), \xi(t)), \tag{3}$$

and the expectation of $y(t+1)$ conditional on $y(t)$, over the population distribution of manifestations is given by

$$E(y_i(t+1)) = \sum_{j=1}^{m} I_i(y(t), e_j) x_j, \tag{4}$$

where e_j is the jth standard basis vector.

Equation (4) is the update equation for the basic CAVLI model, and an invariant distribution of the process defined by equation (3) corresponds precisely to an equilibrium point of the basic CAVLI model. That is,

$$E(y(t+1)) = y(t), \tag{5}$$

in equation (4) is equivalent to the convergence criterion for the basic CAVLI model defined by equations (1) and (2), with updates given by

$$y_i(t+1) = I_i(t). \tag{6}$$

The activation dynamics of a basic CAVLI model are generally characterized as a Markov process based on updating of a simple Bayesian diagnostic model, with the process continued until it reaches an invariant distribution.

---

[1] The letter V is used for this matrix of topdown weight parameters because it suggests "Vorgestalt".

2.2 Rational Error Adjustment

A unique feature of the CAVLI models is their implicit use of a ratio-based error adjustment criterion. In the basic CAVLI model defined by equations (1) and (2), with updates given by equation (6), we have

$$y_i(t+1) = \sum_{j=1}^{m} \frac{y_i(t)v_{ij}}{\mathcal{D}_j(t)} x_j, \tag{7}$$

where, for convenience, we have defined

$$\mathcal{D}_i = \sum_k y_k v_{ki}. \tag{8}$$

Equation (7) implies

$$\frac{y_i(t+1)}{y_i(t)} = \sum_{j=1}^{m} v_{ij} \frac{x_j}{\mathcal{D}_j(t)}. \tag{9}$$

In this equation, we define

$$\rho_i = \frac{x_i}{\mathcal{D}_i}, \tag{10}$$

and

$$R(t+1) = V\rho(t), \tag{11}$$

where V is the matrix with entries v_{ij}. $\rho(t)$ is the error ratio vector observed at the input layer and $R(t+1)$ is the correction ratio propagated up to the output layer of the network, so that the update rule, by examination of equation (9), can be expressed in the ratio form

$$y_i(t+1) = R_i(t)y_i(t). \tag{12}$$

In the interpretation of the basic CAVLI model as a diagnostic model, $\mathcal{D}$ is the distribution on the set of manifestations that would be consistent with the prior probability distribution on the set of disorders and the fixed conditional probabilities coded in the V matrix. The estimate, $\mathcal{D}$, is compared with the observed x and an error ratio is computed. The error ratio is then gated through the weight matrix V up to the output layer, where it becomes the correction ratio R that is applied to the y vector until the system reaches STM equilibrium with $R = 1$ in each component.[2] This is a form of resonance between a topdown transformation of the prior distribution and the observed distribution at the input layer of the network. As with the ART1 model, the underlying philosophy is that the mental perception is dynamically modified during STM dynamics up to the point when it reaches sufficient agreement with the observed data.

3 CAVLI Compared with ART1

3.1 Basic Design

Both CAVLI and ART1 are based on resonance between a stored topdown pattern that is communicated from the output layer to the input layer, and the pattern observed at the input layer. In both cases, the objective is to minimize the error observed at the input level, and in both cases, a kind of feedback is involved, explicit in the case of the ART1 model and implicit in the dynamics of the CAVLI model. In this section, the two mechanisms for achieving resonance will be compared, then they will be compared in terms of the biological plausibility of their handling of inhibition and scaling properties.

The most unusual characteristic of the CAVLI model is its use of a rational error signal. *The STM adjustments of the CAVLI model are essentially multiplicative, whereas dynamics are additive for most neural network paradigms.* This provides CAVLI with the capability of replicating psychophysical experiments such as those of [Land, 1986] that established discounting of the illuminant in visual perception. This is because the basic equations are affected only by the relative intensities of the input components.

---

[2] A precise analysis of convergence is included in [McFadden, 1993].

An obvious difference between the two models is that the ART1 uses twice as many gating parameters. Bottom-up weights an topdown weights are both fully represented, with one entry for a forwards connection and another for a backwards connection between the same node. In CAVLI models, by contrast, all of the weight parameters function in a topdown fashion, while the connections are nevertheless treated as feedforward connections. The addition of bottom-up parameters in the ART1 model undoubtedly has advantages for the stability of the model, and is consistent with the presence of bidirectional connections in biological systems, but applications of the CAVLI model, such as those of [Sutton, 1992], do not appear to suffer unduly from the absence of bottom-up parameters.

3.2 Extent of Inhibitory Connections

One of the potential drawbacks of ART1 as a biological model, and of other models based on direct lateral inhibition, is the large number of inhibitory connections required to enforce direct lateral inhibition. Anatomical data from [Beaulieu and Colonnier, 1983] indicate that roughly 16% of all cortical synapses are symmetrical, and this can be taken as a rough estimate of the proportion of inhibitory synapses. The pattern storage capacity of a basic ART1 module will be estimated, subject to the restriction that the proportion of inhibitory connections is limited to 16% of all connections present in the module.

In the ART1 model, denote the number of nodes in the F1 and F2 layers by m and n respectively. The F2 layer has n^2 mutually inhibitory connections, including those for self-inhibition. In one realization of the basic model,[3] the F1 layer sends m inhibitory connections to the novelty detector, and the nodes of F1 have m inhibitory connections for self-inhibition. Excitatory connections include $2mn$ for both the topdown and the bottom-up gates, plus m from the gain control to the F1 nodes, plus n from the F2 layer to the gain control, m from the input to the novelty detector, and m from the input to the F1 layer.

Under this counting scheme, the total number of inhibitory connections is $n^2 + 2m$ and the total number of excitatory connections is $2mn + 3m + 2n$. We consider the ratio $r = n/m$ when the proportion of inhibitory connections is limited to 16%, as in the study by Beaulieu and Colonnier. Based on our realization of the ART1 model, the proportion of total connections that are inhibitory is given by

$$\frac{r^2m^2 + 2m}{r^2m^2 + 2rm^2 + 5m + 2rm} = \frac{r^2m + 2}{r^2m + 2rm + 5 + 2r} = .16. \tag{13}$$

In a system with a large number of neurons, such as the brain, it is reasonable to consider m to be large, so that we can take the limit as $m \rightarrow \infty$ in (13) to arrive at the equation

$$\frac{r^2}{r^2 + 2r} = .16,$$

which implies that $r \approx .38$.

In summary, it has been shown, based on reasonable assumptions, that if the number of inhibitory connections in the ART1 module were limited to 16% of the total number of connections, consistent with the currently known data concerning the proportion of inhibitory connections in the cortex, then the pattern storage capacity of the F1 layer would be limited to a number of patterns that is roughly 38% of the size of the F2 layer.

CAVLI models are not subject to a similar restriction because explicit inhibitory connections are not used in these models. The drawback of the CAVLI formulation is that virtual inhibition has been achieved indirectly, by way of an allocative mechanism similar to that used in competitive learning. It is unclear what biological mechanisms might be involved in this process. The CAVLI formula solves the problem of excessive inhibitory connections, but raises difficult questions of biological plausibility.

3.3 Scaling

Priciples established in psychophysics imply that a perceptual model should scale properly, that is, that its response should not saturate at very high or very low intensity levels. Data in [Wyszecki and Stiles, 1982],

---

[3] ART1 is often described in more general terms, according to which distributed representations at the F2 layer would be possible, but mutual lateral inhibition is generally assumed in order to make decisions possible for pattern classification.

for example, show that a Weber-Fechner law holds rather well for photopic (cone) vision in normal ranges of intensity, without saturation.

For the basic CAVLI model, analysis of scaling is straightforward, since the model with the update rule $y_i(t+1) = I_i(t)$ is linear in the intensity of the external input. This is not in full agreement with Fechner's law, which hypothesizes that the response is proportional to the *log* of the stimulus, but saturation, in any case, is not a problem.

For the activation rule used in [Reggia et al., 1992], however, saturation is a problem. This rule is

$$\dot{y}_i(t) = I_i(M - y_i(t)) + c_s y_i(t), \tag{14}$$

where y_i is the activation of the ith cortical node, in_i is input to the node, c_s is inhibitory self-decay, and M is the maximum activation that a node can have. The analysis is similar to that of [Grossberg and Levine, 1975]. Assuming that the dependence of I_i on the y vector can be temporarily ignored, then the equilibrium equation is seen to be

$$\bar{y}_i = \frac{M \, in_i}{I_i - c_s},$$

which clearly saturates as I_i grows without limit, with

$$\lim_{I_i \to \infty} \bar{y}_i = -\frac{M}{c_s}.$$

These effects are analyzed in greater detail in [McFadden, 1993], using implicit partial differentiation in order to analyze the response pattern of the model for a variety of parameter values.

3.4 Other Points of Comparison

There are several other ways in which the ART1 models differ from the currently known variations of CAVLI models. Contrast enhancement behavior in the ART models is generally effected by the use of direct lateral inhibition, and achieved largely by the dynamics within the F2 layer. For the CAVLI model, contrast enhancement is only meaningful when the transformation of one layer into another is considered. This is a profound difference, and it is unclear whether this systemic contrast enhancement or the intra-layer contrast enhancement of models such as ART is more plausible biologically. These effects are analyzed in detail for small networks in [McFadden, 1993], where it is pointed out that Hebbian learning effects may perturb contrast enhancement properties.

The novelty detector in the ART module is part of the solution to the stability-plasticity dilemma. This extra node was used to determine whether a new input was sufficiently similar the the existing set of patterns, or whether it was necessary to form a new pattern. Novelty detection has not yet been considered for CAVLI networks, but there is no reason why similar mechanisms could not be tried.

Finally, the handling of input formats is significantly different between the two models. The ART1 model applied to binary inputs, whereas the basic CAVLI model is not restricted to binary input. The CAVLI formalism introduces a plausible way of handling continuous input data in a relatively straightforward way.

4 Conclusions

1. CAVLI models, essentially, perform interative Bayesian updating in order to resonate with the output pattern node most likely to explain an input pattern.

2. The CAVLI mechanism contrasts with ART1 by implictly using a rational error adjustment procedure, and by using only the topdown weight parameters (without bottom-up parameters).

3. Because CAVLI models do not assume direct lateral inhibition, they are not subject to capacity limitations that would be imposed on the ART1 model if it were limited to the proportion of inhibitory connections

estimated for the cerebral cortex; nevertheless, it remains to be seen whether the CAVLI mechanism could occur biologically.

4. Because the basic CAVLI model is based on a rational error adjustment process, it scales very naturally, but the scaling property cannot be taken for granted in extensions of the CAVLI model.

5. CAVLI models are in most respects addressing the same questions that are addressed by the ART models, and in a similar way. The CAVLI formulation of an unsupervised learning network has enough strong points to make it an alternative to ART.

REFERENCES

Beaulieu, C. and Colonnier, M. (1983), The number of neurons in the different laminae of the binocular and monocular regions of area 17 of the cat. *Journal of Comparative Neurology,* **217**, 337-344.

Carpenter, G. and Grossberg, S. (1987) A Massively Parallel Architecture for a Self-Organizing Neural Pattern Recognition Machine. *Computer Vision, Graphics, and Image Processing*, 37, 54-115.

Grossberg, S. and Levine, D. (1975), Some Developmental and Attentional Biases in the Contrast Enhancement and Short Term Memory of Recurrent Neural Networks. *Journal of Theoretical Biology* **53**, 341-380.

Land, E. (1986), Recent advances in retinex theory. *Vision Research,* **26**, 7-21.

McFadden, F. 1993, *Competitive Learning and Competitive Activation in Cortical Map Formation*, Ph.D. thesis, University of Maryland, College Park.

Reggia, J., D'Autrechy, C., Sutton, G., and Weinrich, M. 1992, A competitive distribution theory of neocortical dynamics. *Neural Comp.*, **4**, 287-317.

Reggia, J. (1985). Virtual Lateral Inhibition in Parallel Activation Models of Associative Memory. **Proceedings of the Ninth International Joint Conference on Artificial Intelligence, Vol. 1**. Los Angeles, CA, 244-248.

Sutton, G. (1992), *Competitive Learning and Map Formation in Artificial Neural Networks using Competitive Activation Mechanisms*, Ph.D. thesis, University of Maryland, College Park.

Wyszecki, G. and Stiles, W. (1982), **Color Science: Concepts and Methods, Quantitative Data and Formulae.** Wiley, NY.

Robustness of Neural Networks

K. KrishnaKumar

Dept. of Aerospace Engineering, The University of Alabama, Tuscaloosa, AL 35487-0280
e-mail: kkrishna@ua1vm.ua.edu

Abstract

This paper analyzes the robustness characteristics of Neural Networks (NN) using linear systems theory. Robustness is defined as the ability of a neural network to map untrained data (data not used during training) within an error tolerance. An induced Euclidean matrix norm is used to derive error bounds for NN with activation functions that predominantly exhibit linear behavior. Lyapunov stability theory is used to derive bounds on the non-linear variations in NN with activation functions that exhibit non-linear behavior. A Monte Carlo simulation analysis is conducted to examine the robustness characteristics of fully and sparsely connected networks. The following conclusions are drawn based on the above analysis: (a) sparsity in the NN connection topology is highly desirable to achieve robustness; (b) two hidden layer networks with equal number of neurons in each layer exhibit very poor robustness; (c) a fully forward-connected network with sparsity is the most robust and accurate for a given number of neurons; and (d) for NN with many neurons, highly non-linear activation functions exhibit very poor robustness.

1. Introduction

Robustness of neural networks (NN), defined as their ability to generalize, is an important characteristic for many applications ranging from simple function mapping to more complicated non-linear process control problems. Most popular neural networks in use today use multi-layered feed-forward networks with connections going from one layer to the next. Several investigators have shown the approximating capabilities of these networks (for example, see Reference 1). Another type of network that has received some attention is the fully-forward connected network [2,3]. KrishnaKumar [3] has shown using empirical results that if this type of network is made sparse, the networks are more accurate and robust for a given number of neurons. Many other researchers have shown similar empirical results using sparse multi-layered feed-forward networks (Mozer et al. [4], Rumelhart et al. [5], and Sietsma et al [6]).

In this paper, we address the general question of how to define relative robustness of different neural network structures. We assume that the network has been trained to provide a desired accuracy for the training data set. The question then is simply one of how to relate the given NN structure to certain bounds on its mapping error for untrained data. We first define robustness given a NN structure and then examine the robustness of layered networks, fully-forward connected networks, and sparse networks.

The paper is organized as follows. We begin with the definitions of NN structures that are discussed in this paper. Next, we state the linear systems theory results that will be used to define robustness. We then present an interpretation of NN equations in terms of the linear systems theory and present a Monte Carlo simulation analysis to examine the robustness characteristics. The following conclusions are drawn based on the above analysis: (a) sparsity in the NN connection topology is highly desirable to achieve robustness; (b) two hidden layer networks with equal number of neurons in each layer exhibit very poor robustness; (c) a fully forward-connected network with sparsity is the most robust and accurate for a given number of neurons.

2. Neural Network Preliminaries

In this paper, without loss of generality, we will assume one input, one output neural networks with *N-2* sigmoidal hidden neurons. The hidden neurons could be arranged either in a layered form or in a fully-forward connected form (Figure 1). A fully-forward connected NN could be seen as a layered NN as shown in Figure 2. Also, a fully-forward connected NN with the proper connections removed can be made to look like a traditional single or double layered networks. Since our main concern is one of generalization and not accuracy in mapping, it is assumed that the user has made a choice of the NN weights via some learning scheme. The equation for a fully-forward connected NN is given as:

$$x_i = \phi_i \left(\sum_{j=1}^{i-1} w_{ij} \, x_j \right), \qquad y_i = x_i \, , \qquad 2 \leq i \leq N \qquad (1)$$

$$x_N = \text{NN output}$$

$$x_1 = \text{NN input and the input neuron is a linear neuron}$$

where

y_i = output of the ith neuron

w_{ij} = weight connecting the ith neuron to the jth neuron.

$\phi_i (\ )$ = non-linear neuronal activation function.

Equation 1 can be used to arrive at layered networks by simply zeroing out appropriate elements of the weight matrix. This will be illustrated in section 4.

3. Mathematical Preliminaries

3.1 Vector Norm

For any vector $x \ \epsilon \ R^n$, the Frobenius (Euclidean) norm is given as

$$\|x\|_F = \|x\|_2 = + \sqrt{\sum_j |x_j|^2} \qquad (2)$$

3.2 Spectral Matrix Norm

A spectral matrix norm $\|G\|_s$ of matrix $G \ \epsilon \ R^{n \times n}$ is a matrix norm induced by the Euclidean vector norm and is given as:

$$\|G\|_s = + \sqrt{\lambda_{max}[G^T G]} = \sigma_{max}[G] \qquad (3)$$

i.e., the spectral norm equals the largest singular value of matrix G. Based on the above definitions and using Holder's inequality [7], we have for a given $y = Gx$

$$\|y\| \leq \|G\| \|x\| \quad \rightarrow \quad \|y\| \leq \sigma_{max}[G] \|x\| \qquad (4)$$

Examining the above equations we see that the $\sigma_{max}[G]$ represents the least upper bound for the ratio of the output and input norms.

3.3 Lyapunov Stability Theory

Let a non-linear perturbed discrete system be

$$x(k+1) = \Phi x(k) + h[k, \, x(k)] \qquad (5)$$

where $\Phi \ \epsilon \ R^{n \times n}$ is the state transition matrix, $x(k)$ is the state vector at time step k, and $h[k, x(k)]$ is the non-linear perturbation in the system. Let the non-linear perturbation be bounded by

$$\|h[k, \, x(k)]\| \leq \xi \|x(k)\|, \ \xi > 0. \qquad (6)$$

i.e., the norm of h does not exceed the norm of x multiplied with a fixed gain ξ. The system given in equation 5 is exponentially stable if the solution $x(k)$ satisfies the condition [7]

$$\|x(k)\|_F \leq \beta \|x(0)\|_F \exp(k \ \ln \ \rho_s) = \beta \|x(0)\|_F \ \rho_s^k \, , \quad \beta > 0 \quad 0 \leq \rho_s < 1 \qquad (7)$$

where β is some positive constant and ρ_s is the degree of stability. An estimate of ρ_s can be derived for the non-linearly perturbed system using norm-like Lyapunov functions in terms of the non-linear perturbation bound ξ [7] as

$$\xi < \xi_N = 1 - \hat{\rho}_s = \frac{1.0}{\sigma_{max}[P] + \sqrt{\sigma_{max}[P]\sigma_{max}[P-I_n]}} \tag{8}$$

where $\hat{\rho}_s$ is the estimate of ρ_s, I_n is the identity matrix, and $P \in R^{nxn}$ satisfies the Lyapunov equation [7]

$$\Phi^T P \Phi - P = -I_n \tag{9}$$

The above equations imply that the stability margin of the non-linearly perturbed system is governed by the system matrix Φ and the gain ξ_N. Larger ξ_N (smaller $\hat{\rho}_s$) implies greater stability.

4. Robustness Analysis of Neural Networks

The neural network equation presented in equation 1 can be interpreted as a non-linear system with x_i representing the inputs to the system and y_i representing the outputs of the system. Now, let $\tilde{X}$ be a vector corresponding to inputs not used during the training. Then the corresponding outputs are given by

$$\tilde{y}_i = \phi_i \left(\sum_{j=1}^{i-1} w_{ij} \tilde{x}_j \right) \qquad 1 \leq i \leq N \tag{10}$$

Now, let y_i^* be the desired output and x_i^* be the input such that

$$y_i^* = \phi_i \left(\sum_{j=1}^{i-1} w_{ij} x_j^* \right) \qquad 1 \leq i \leq N \tag{11}$$

Expanding the right hand side of equation (10) in a Taylor's series form about X^*, we get the vector equation

$$\tilde{Y} - Y^* = A(\tilde{X} - X^*) + h[\tilde{X} - X^*] \tag{12}$$

where

$h[\tilde{X} - X^*] =$ the higher order non-linear terms.

It is clear from equation 12 that if $\|\tilde{Y} - Y^*\|$ is small for a given $\|\tilde{X} - X^*\|$, the NN will be considered robust. Also, in the above equation, A is the first order derivative matrix. Depending on the type of NN structure, the matrix will have different entries. Given below are examples of three first order derivative matrices for three types of NN structures. In the matrices given below, $\phi' = \dfrac{\partial \phi(\ )}{\partial (\ )}$. It is noted here that the sparsity in these matrices can be created either by zeroing the weights or the slope of the activation functions.

First order derivative matrix for a fully connected NN (1 input, 7 hidden neurons, and 1 output

$$
\begin{bmatrix}
0.00 & 0.00 & 0.00 & 0.00 & 0.00 & 0.00 & 0.00 & 0.00 & 0.00 \\
\phi'W_{21} & 0.00 & 0.00 & 0.00 & 0.00 & 0.00 & 0.00 & 0.00 & 0.00 \\
\phi'W_{31} & \phi'W_{32} & 0.00 & 0.00 & 0.00 & 0.00 & 0.00 & 0.00 & 0.00 \\
\phi'W_{41} & \phi'W_{42} & \phi'W_{43} & 0.00 & 0.00 & 0.00 & 0.00 & 0.00 & 0.00 \\
\phi'W_{51} & \phi'W_{52} & \phi'W_{53} & \phi'W_{54} & 0.00 & 0.00 & 0.00 & 0.00 & 0.00 \\
\phi'W_{61} & \phi'W_{62} & \phi'W_{63} & \phi'W_{64} & \phi'W_{65} & 0.00 & 0.00 & 0.00 & 0.00 \\
\phi'W_{71} & \phi'W_{72} & \phi'W_{73} & \phi'W_{74} & \phi'W_{75} & \phi'W_{76} & 0.00 & 0.00 & 0.00 \\
\phi'W_{81} & \phi'W_{82} & \phi'W_{83} & \phi'W_{84} & \phi'W_{85} & \phi'W_{86} & \phi'W_{87} & 0.00 & 0.00 \\
\phi'W_{91} & \phi'W_{92} & \phi'W_{93} & \phi'W_{94} & \phi'W_{95} & \phi'W_{96} & \phi'W_{97} & \phi'W_{98} & 0.00
\end{bmatrix}
$$

First order derivative matrix for a single hidden layer NN (1 input, 7 neurons in the hidden layer, and 1 output)

$$
\begin{bmatrix}
0.00 & 0.00 & 0.00 & 0.00 & 0.00 & 0.00 & 0.00 & 0.00 & 0.00 \\
\phi' W_{21} & 0.00 & 0.00 & 0.00 & 0.00 & 0.00 & 0.00 & 0.00 & 0.00 \\
\phi' W_{31} & 0.00 & 0.00 & 0.00 & 0.00 & 0.00 & 0.00 & 0.00 & 0.00 \\
\phi' W_{41} & 0.00 & 0.00 & 0.00 & 0.00 & 0.00 & 0.00 & 0.00 & 0.00 \\
\phi' W_{51} & 0.00 & 0.00 & 0.00 & 0.00 & 0.00 & 0.00 & 0.00 & 0.00 \\
\phi' W_{61} & 0.00 & 0.00 & 0.00 & 0.00 & 0.00 & 0.00 & 0.00 & 0.00 \\
\phi' W_{71} & 0.00 & 0.00 & 0.00 & 0.00 & 0.00 & 0.00 & 0.00 & 0.00 \\
\phi' W_{81} & 0.00 & 0.00 & 0.00 & 0.00 & 0.00 & 0.00 & 0.00 & 0.00 \\
0.00 & \phi' W_{92} & \phi' W_{93} & \phi' W_{94} & \phi' W_{95} & \phi' W_{96} & \phi' W_{97} & \phi' W_{98} & 0.00
\end{bmatrix}
$$

First order derivative matrix for a two-hidden layer NN (1 input, 4 neurons in the first hidden layer, 3 neurons in the second hidden layer, and 1 output)

$$
\begin{bmatrix}
0.00 & 0.00 & 0.00 & 0.00 & 0.00 & 0.00 & 0.00 & 0.00 & 0.00 \\
\phi' W_{21} & 0.00 & 0.00 & 0.00 & 0.00 & 0.00 & 0.00 & 0.00 & 0.00 \\
\phi' W_{31} & 0.00 & 0.00 & 0.00 & 0.00 & 0.00 & 0.00 & 0.00 & 0.00 \\
\phi' W_{41} & 0.00 & 0.00 & 0.00 & 0.00 & 0.00 & 0.00 & 0.00 & 0.00 \\
\phi' W_{51} & 0.00 & 0.00 & 0.00 & 0.00 & 0.00 & 0.00 & 0.00 & 0.00 \\
0.00 & \phi' W_{62} & \phi' W_{63} & \phi' W_{64} & \phi' W_{65} & 0.00 & 0.00 & 0.00 & 0.00 \\
0.00 & \phi' W_{72} & \phi' W_{73} & \phi' W_{74} & \phi' W_{75} & 0.00 & 0.00 & 0.00 & 0.00 \\
0.00 & \phi' W_{82} & \phi' W_{83} & \phi' W_{84} & \phi' W_{85} & 0.00 & 0.00 & 0.00 & 0.00 \\
0.00 & 0.00 & 0.00 & 0.00 & 0.00 & \phi' W_{96} & \phi' W_{97} & \phi' W_{98} & 0.00
\end{bmatrix}
$$

Letting $\bar{Y} - Y^* = \delta Y \quad and \quad \bar{X} - X^* = \delta X$, we get from equation (12)

$$\delta Y = A \; \delta X + h[\delta X] \tag{13}$$

CASE 1: Predominantly linear activations

If $h[\delta X]$ is small, we can approximate equation 13 as $\delta Y = A \; \delta X$. Recalling the Holder's inequality for vector and matrix norms [7], we have

$$\|\delta Y\|_F \leq \|A\|_S \; \|\delta X\|_F. \tag{14}$$

For an Euclidean norm, $\|A\|_S = \sigma_{max}[A] = \rho$. This implies that if ρ is small, the output error will be a small proportion of the input deviations. In essence, the numerical value of the norm of A defines the robustness of the mapping and smaller ρ implies better robustness. Figure 4 presents results of a Monte Carlo simulation conducted for various types of neural network structures. The entries of matrix A were chosen randomly to lie between -1 and +1. In all, 500 samples were generated for each type of NN structure. Sparsity in the network was created by randomly zeroing out the non-zero elements of the A matrix. Figures 4 and 5 present the mean and standard deviation of the robustness measure ρ. Figure 6 presents the number of connections (or non-zero elements in the weight matrix) for different NN structures used in this study. The following observations are made from Figures 4,5, and 6:

(1) The standard deviation of the robustness measure is small and remains a constant for low sparsity networks. This implies that the mean of the robustness measure is a good indicator of robustness regardless of the choice of the NN weights.
(2) As the number of neurons increases, robustness decreases.
(3) Two hidden layer networks with equal number of neurons in each layer exhibit very poor robustness.
(4) Examining Figures 4, 5, and 6 it can be concluded that the fully-forward connected NN with sparsity

is the best in terms of both accuracy of mapping (due to higher number of available free parameter or weights. See Figure 6.) and robustness for a given number of neurons. This result was stated in reference 3 using empirical data.

<u>CASE 2: Non-linear activations</u>

Most of the neuronal activation functions in use today exhibit locally linear behavior. For example, the sigmoidal network has three distinctly linear regions as shown in Figure 7. The analysis conducted above should be applicable to the three linear regions shown in Figure 7. In the case where the non-linearity cannot be ignored, we have the following situation:

$$h[\delta X] \neq 0, \text{ but bounded as } \quad \|h[\delta X]\| \leq \xi \|\delta X\| \tag{15}$$

Now combining equations 13, 14, and 15, we get

$$\|\delta Y\| \leq \|A\| \ \|\delta X\| + \xi \|\delta X\| \tag{16}$$

From equation 16 it is obvious that smaller ξ implies better robustness. Since our interest is to compare robustness between different neural networks with non-linear behavior, we define robustness in terms of an upper limit on the allowable non-linear variations, i.e., an upper limit for ξ. Here we use the Lyapunov stability condition presented in section 3.3 and define an acceptable upper bound for ξ as

$$\xi < \xi_N = 1 - \rho_s = \frac{1.0}{\sigma_{max}[P_A] + \sqrt{\sigma_{max}[P_A]\sigma_{max}[P_A - I_n]}} \tag{17}$$

and from equation 7, with k=1, we have

$$\|\delta Y\|_F \leq \beta \|\delta x\|_F \exp(\ln \rho_s) = \beta \|\delta x\|_F \ \rho_s \quad where \quad \beta > 0 \quad 0 \leq \rho_s \leq 1.0 \tag{18}$$

In the above equation I_n is the identity matrix and P_A satisfies the Lyapunov equation

$$A^T P_A A - P_A = -I_n \tag{19}$$

From equations 17 and 18 it is clear that ξ_N is a good measure of robustness for the non-linear mapping as it relates to the bounds on the NN output presented in equation 13. It is also noted that higher ξ_N (lower ρ_s) implies greater robustness. Figures 8 and 9 present the mean and standard deviation of the robustness measure ξ_N. From these figures it is seen that the robustness to non-linear variations in the activation functions is very similar to the linear case, i.e., sparsity is important for robustness and the two-hidden layer exhibits very poor robustness. In addition it is seen that as the number of neurons increases, both the mean and the standard deviation of ξ_N approach zero. This suggests that for large NN, highly non-linear activation functions are not well suited for robustness.

5. Conclusions

Simple robustness measures for neural networks with linear and non-linear behavior were presented. Using these measures, robustness of several neural networks were examined using a Monte Carlo simulation with 500 samples for each type of neural network structure. The results of the analysis reinforces the need for sparsity and the need to use fully-forward connected NN with sparsity instead of the traditional multilayered neural networks. Also, two hidden layer neural networks were shown to be the least robust among the popular structures currently in use. Another interesting result is that for neural networks with large number of neurons, non-linear activation functions are not the best for robustness.

ACKNOWLEDGEMENT

This material is based upon work supported by the National Science Foundation under Grant No. ECS-9113283 and the University of Alabama Research Grants Commission under Grant No. 1641.

REFERENCES

[1]   K. Hornik, Approximation Capabilities of Multi-layer Feedforward Networks, *Neural Networks,* 4, (1991) 251-257.

[2]   P. J. Werbos, Back-propagation Through Time: What It Does and How To Do It. *Proceedings of the IEEE,* 78 (10) (1990) 1550-1560.

[3]   K. KrishnaKumar, Optimization of the Neural Net Connectivity Pattern Using a Back-propagation Algorithm, *Journal of Neurocomputing,* 5, (1993) 1-14.

[4]   M. C. Mozer and P. Smolensky, *Skeletonization: A Technique for trimming the fat from a network via Relevance Assessment,* Tech. Rpt. CU-CS-421-89, Department of Computer Science and Institute of Cognitive Science, University of Colorado, Boulder, Co, 1989.

[5]   D. E. Rumelhart, J. L. McClelland, and the PDP Research Group, *Parallel Distributed Processing: Explorations in the Microstructure of Cognition. Volume 1: Foundations,* (MIT Press, Cambridge, 1986).

[6]   J. Sietsma and R. J. F. Dow, Creating Artificial Neural Networks that Generalize, Neural Networks, 4 (1991) 67-79.

[7]   A. Weinmann, Uncertainty Models and Robust Control, Springer-Verlag Wien, New York, 1991.

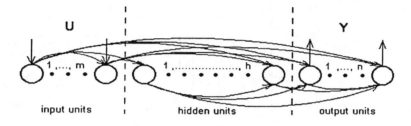

Fig 1. A fully-forward connected NN

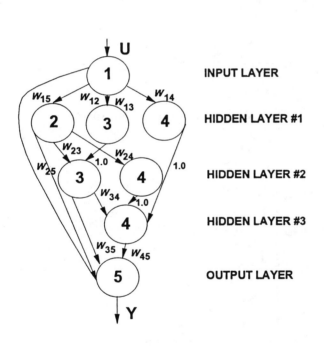

Fig 2. A fully-forward connected NN seen as a multi-layered NN

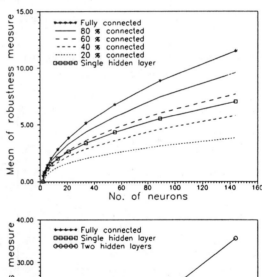

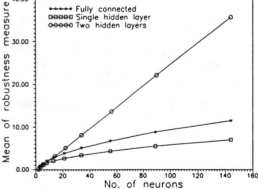

Fig 3. Mean of ρ for various NN structures

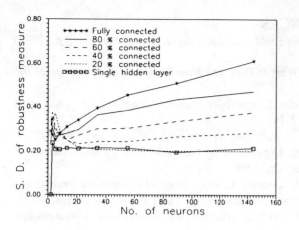

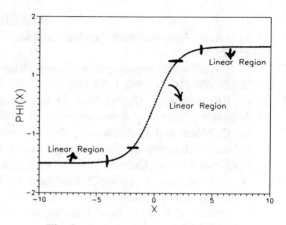

Fig 6. Sigmoidal activation function

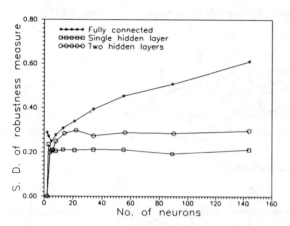

Fig 4. Standard deviation of ρ for various NN structures

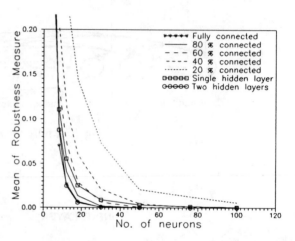

Fig 7. Mean of ξ_N for various NN structures

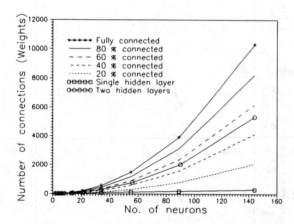

Fig 5. Number of connections (or weights) for various NN structures

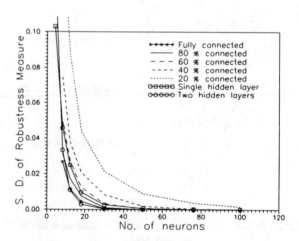

Fig 8. Standard deviation of ξ_N for various NN structures

Mathematical Foundations

Session Chairs: Shun-ichi Amari
Daniel Levine

POSTER PRESENTATIONS

PERFORMING DIFFERENTIAL AND INTEGRAL CALCULUS USING RADIAL-GAUSSIAN NEURAL NETWORKS

Ian Flood
Department of Civil Engineering
University of Maryland
College Park,
MD 20742

Abstract - The paper describes a novel means of performing calculus using networks of radial-Gaussian neurons. The network architecture and training algorithm used for this purpose is described briefly. Once trained, a network can be converted into a form that provides the differential or integral of the learned function, by a simple substitution of the type of activation function used at the hidden neurons. A range of substitute activation functions, for conversion to first and second order partial differential and integral forms of the network, are derived. Following this, the technique is tested on a selection of calculus operations. The converted networks produced in these experiments provide accurate models of the actual differentials and integrals of the function the original networks had been taught. A method of improving the accuracy of results by training the original network beyond the region in which the converted networks operate, is described. The paper concludes by identifying some areas for further development of the technique.

INTRODUCTION

Feedforward artificial neural networks with synchronously operating neurons can be represented in a functional form that enables manipulation by a variety of mathematical operations, including rotation, differentiation (see for example Hornik et al. [1990]) and integration. Often, the function resulting from the operation can itself be represented in the form of a neural network. In the case of differential and integral calculus operations, the subject of this paper, the conversion from the original network can be effected by a simple substitution of the type of activation function used at the hidden neurons.

The technique can be applied no matter how many output or input neurons comprise the network. In the former case, the differential or integral of the function generated at each output neuron will be provided. In the latter case, the partial differential or integral will be provided with respect to whichever input required. Moreover, by selecting an appropriate substitute activation function, second and higher order differentials and integrals can be achieved. It would seem, therefore, that neural networks offer a powerful automated method for performing calculus. In particular, the technique could be useful when (i) an analytical solution to the differential/integral of a function is not available, or (ii) a set of points, suitable for training a network, is all that is known about the function for which the differential/integral is required.

However, it should be remembered that a converted network will provide the differential/integral of the function performed by the original network rather than the differential/integral of the function the original network had attempted to learn. Consequently, there is no guarantee that the converted network will provide a valid model of the true differential/integral.

A second issue arises from the desire to limit the network to a single layer of hidden neurons. If more than one hidden layer exists then the differential/integral function becomes unwieldy and difficult to implement using a simple substitution of activation functions. Ideally, therefore, the chosen type of network should be capable of providing an accurate model of the original function with just one layer of hidden neurons.

In principle, the popular backpropagation system [Rumelhart et al, 1986] could be used as a mechanism for performing calculus operations. However, although a proof exists that these devices can model any function of interest using a single layer of sigmoidal hidden neurons [Hecht-Nielsen, 1989], there are many functions that, in practice, require at least two hidden layers [Lippmann, 1987]. To overcome this problem, the radial-Gaussian network architecture and training algorithm proposed by Flood [1991] was adopted. This system never requires more than one hidden layer of neurons to model a function and demonstrates a number of other characteristics well suited to the task at hand. In particular, it is capable of providing highly accurate models of a function, does not become stuck during training, learns rapidly, and determines automatically the number of hidden neurons required to achieve a given level of accuracy for a set of training data.

RADIAL GAUSSIAN NETWORKING SYSTEM

The following provides an overview of the radial-Gaussian network architecture and training algorithm as relevant to this paper. For a more detailed description of this system the reader is referred to Flood [1991]. The structure of these networks, illustrated in Figure 1, comprises a layer of input neurons that perform a normalizing function, a single layer of hidden neurons each of which implements a radial Gaussian function, and a layer of output neurons that act as simple summers of incoming values. The operation of these networks can be formalized by the following system of five equations:

Activation at the *y-th* output neuron is given by:

$$o_y = \sum_{n=1}^{N} v_{n,y} h_n \tag{1}$$

where $v_{n,y}$ are weights on the links to the output neuron.

Activation at the *n-th* hidden neuron is given by:

$$h_n = g(s_n, \tau_n) \tag{2}$$

$$\tau_n = \sum_{x=1}^{X} (\overset{\circ}{i}_x - c_{x,n})^2 \tag{3}$$

where s_n is a squeezing parameter; $c_{x,n}$ are offsets on the connections to the hidden neuron; and $g()$ is the following Gaussian function:

$$g() = e^{-s_n \tau_n} \tag{4}$$

Activation at the *x-th* input neuron is given by:

$$\overset{\circ}{i}_x = \alpha_x i_x \tag{5}$$

where α_x is a normalizing parameter; and i_x is the value input to the neuron.

In its simplest form, training proceeds by developing one hidden neuron at a time. Each successive hidden neuron is trained on the component of the problem its predecessors failed to learn, using an error gradient descent technique. Typically, neurons are added as such until the error in the network (measured on either the training patterns or a set of test patterns) reaches an acceptable level. The system includes a smoothing technique, adopted in the experiments reported in this paper, based on training the network on three variations of the problem and taking the average output.

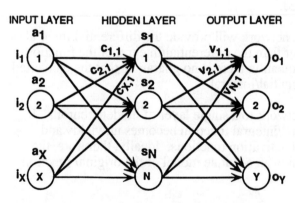

Fig 1: Radial-Gaussian Network Architecture

DIFFERENTIATION

To convert a trained radial-Gaussian network into its first differential form, all that is required is to change the activation function used at the hidden neurons (given by Equation 4) to the following:

$$g'() = -2s_n\alpha_\xi\delta_{\xi,n}e^{-s_n\tau_n} \tag{6}$$

where ξ is the index of the respective input for the partial differential; and $\delta_{\xi,n} = (\alpha_\xi i_\xi - c_{\xi,n})$.

To confirm this, consider the following functional representation of the radial Gaussian network:

$$o_y = \sum_{n=1}^{N} v_{n,y}e^{-s_n\sum_{x=1}^{X}(\alpha_x i_x - c_{x,n})^2} \tag{7}$$

Differentiating this expression gives:

$$\frac{\partial o_y}{\partial o_\xi} = -\sum_{n=1}^{N} v_{n,y}2s_n\alpha_\xi(\alpha_\xi i_\xi - c_{\xi,n})e^{-s_n\sum_{x=1}^{X}(\alpha_x i_x - c_{x,n})^2} \tag{8}$$

which is the same as the original network expression except that it embraces the extra term $-2s_n\alpha_\xi(\alpha_\xi i_\xi - c_{\xi,n})$. Conveniently, this term can be made part of the activation function of the hidden neurons as indicated in Equation 6, leaving the rest of the network unchanged.

Through a similar argument, it can be shown that the second differential of this type of network can be obtained by changing the activation function used at the hidden neurons to the following:

$$g''() = \alpha_\xi^2((2s_n\delta_{\xi,n})^2 - 2s_n)e^{-s_n\tau_n} \tag{9}$$

Similarly, third and subsequent differentials can be obtained by substituting the activation function used in the original network.

The first problem chosen to demonstrate the technique was that of determining the first and second differentials of two periods of the sine function. A set of 100 example patterns, evenly spaced between the limits 0 and 4π along the input, was established to train the network. Training was allowed to continue until 50 hidden neurons had been added to the network giving an average absolute error $\bar{\varepsilon}$ of 0.00023 for 1,000 randomly selected test patterns. Figures 2.a and 2.b plot the output from the first and second differential forms of this network between the 0 and 4π limits. From these it can be seen that the differential networks provide accurate approximations to the true differentials (the cosine and negative sine functions respectively) except for some perturbations near the limits of the training domain (the region in input space where the training patterns are located). These perturbations are greater for the second differential network and would become worse in subsequent differentials. Both the first and second differential networks were tested on 1,000 randomly selected test patterns and found to have an average absolute error $\bar{\varepsilon}$ of 0.0028 and 0.0753 respectively. One way of reducing the error would be to train the network with an extended set of training patterns that goes a short way beyond the domain for which the differential of the function is required. Such an approach is considered in the next example.

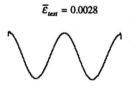

$\bar{\varepsilon}_{test} = 0.0028$

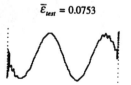

$\bar{\varepsilon}_{test} = 0.0753$

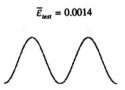

$\bar{\varepsilon}_{test} = 0.0014$

(a) First Differential   (b) Second Differential   (c) First Integral

Fig 2: Output from Differential and Integral Forms of a Network Taught the Sine Function

To illustrate partial differentiation, a network was taught the cowboy hat function, $t = \text{sine}\left(\sqrt{i_1^2 + i_2^2}\right)$, for i_1 and i_2 ranging between -5.0 and 5.0 as shown in Figure 3.a. A set of 121 training patterns was set-up for this purpose, marking the points indicated by the intersections of the grid lines in Figure 3.a, and the network was trained until it comprised 100 hidden neurons. The network was then converted to its first partial differential with respect to i_2. Figure 3.b shows the actual partial differential of the function:

$$\frac{\partial t}{\partial i_2} = i_2 \cos\left(\sqrt{\left(i_1^2 + i_2^2\right)}\right) \Big/ \sqrt{\left(i_1^2 + i_2^2\right)} \tag{10}$$

and Figure 3.c shows the output from the partial differential network for i_1 ranged between 0.0 and 5.0 and i_2 ranged between -5.0 and 5.0. Just half of the function over the training domain was plotted to reveal the discontinuity in the function at the origin. The network has provided a good approximation to the partial differential including its discontinuity (having an average absolute error $\bar{\varepsilon}$ of 0.0185 for 1,000 randomly selected test patterns). However, there are once again significant perturbations in the function near the boundaries of the training domain. A second network was trained on the same problem, this occasion using an extended training domain covering the limits ±6.0 for both i_1 and i_2. The output from the first partial differential of the network, for i_1 ranged between 0.0 and 5.0 and i_2 ranged between -5.0 and 5.0, is shown in Figure 3.d. It can be seen from this that extending the training domain has reduced the perturbations at the boundaries of the plot significantly. The average absolute error $\bar{\varepsilon}$ between the ±5.0 limits for the same set of 1,000 test patterns, was reduced slightly to 0.0175.

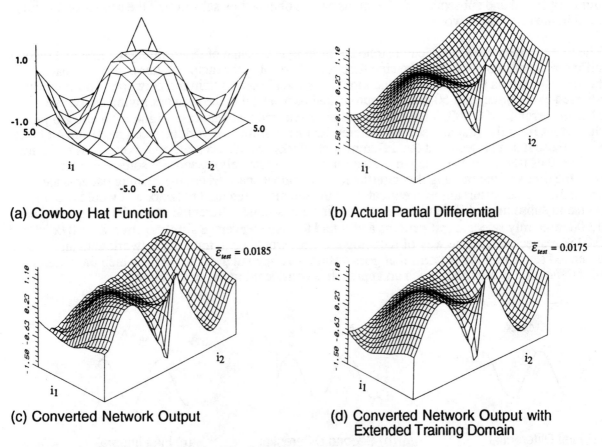

(a) Cowboy Hat Function

(b) Actual Partial Differential

(c) Converted Network Output

(d) Converted Network Output with Extended Training Domain

Fig 3: Examples of Partial Differentiation of the Cowboy Hat Function

INTEGRATION

As with differentiation, the integral of a network can be obtained by simply changing the activation function used at the hidden neurons. For networks that operate in accordance with Equations 1 to 5, the substitute activation function for the first integral becomes:

$$g^I() = \frac{e^{-s_n \Delta_{\xi,n}}}{\alpha_\xi} (\delta_{\xi,n} - \frac{s_n \delta_{\xi,n}^3}{3(1!)} + \frac{s_n^2 \delta_{\xi,n}^5}{5(2!)} - \frac{s_n^3 \delta_{\xi,n}^7}{7(3!)} ...) \tag{11}$$

where:

$$\Delta_{\xi,n} = \tau_n - \delta_{\xi,n}^2 = \sum_{x=1}^{X, x \neq \xi} (\alpha_x i_x - c_{x,n})^2 \tag{12}$$

The derivation of the activation function first requires the functional representation of the network (given in Equation 7) to be reorganized as follows:

$$o_y = \sum_{n=1}^{N} v_{n,y} e^{-s_n \Delta_{\xi,n}} e^{-s_n (\alpha_\xi i_\xi - c_{\xi,n})^2} \tag{13}$$

The first step in integrating this expression with respect to i_ξ results in:

$$\int_{-\infty}^{i_\xi} (o_y) \partial i_\xi = \sum_{n=1}^{N} v_{n,y} e^{-s_n \Delta_{\xi,n}} \int_{-\infty}^{i_\xi} (e^{-s_n (\alpha_\xi i_\xi - c_{\xi,n})^2}) \partial i_\xi \tag{14}$$

The integral term to the right can then be expanded to the following:

$$\int_{-\infty}^{i_\xi} (e^{-s_n (\alpha_\xi i_\xi - c_{\xi,n})^2}) \partial i_\xi = \int_{-\infty}^{c_{\xi,n}} (e^{-s_n (\alpha_\xi i_\xi - c_{\xi,n})^2}) \partial i_\xi + \int_{c_{\xi,n}}^{i_\xi} (e^{-s_n (\alpha_\xi i_\xi - c_{\xi,n})^2}) \partial i_\xi \tag{15}$$

It is generally not valid to use a neural network to extrapolate far outside the training domain [Flood 1991], and thus integration should be made between two limits within or close to this region. To achieve this, the two values representing the limits of the integration (both of which should fall on a line parallel to the direction of integration) must be put through the integral network in turn, and the difference in the results calculated. Consequently, the first integral term on the right of Equation 15 will cancel and can therefore be ignored. The second integral term on the right of the equation can be solved by first substituting the following series:

$$e^{-s_n (\alpha_\xi i_\xi - c_{\xi,n})^2} = 1 - \frac{s_n (\alpha_\xi i_\xi - c_{\xi,n})^2}{1!} + \frac{s_n^2 (\alpha_\xi i_\xi - c_{\xi,n})^4}{2!} - \frac{s_n^3 (\alpha_\xi i_\xi - c_{\xi,n})^6}{3!} ... \tag{16}$$

which when integrated gives:

$$\int_{c_{\xi,n}}^{i_\xi} (e^{-s_n (\alpha_\xi i_\xi - c_{\xi,n})}) \partial i_\xi$$

$$= \frac{(\alpha_\xi i_\xi - c_{\xi,n})}{\alpha_\xi} - \frac{s_n (\alpha_\xi i_\xi - c_{\xi,n})^3}{3\alpha_\xi (1!)} + \frac{s_n^2 (\alpha_\xi i_\xi - c_{\xi,n})^5}{5\alpha_\xi (2!)} - \frac{s_n^3 (\alpha_\xi i_\xi - c_{\xi,n})^7}{7\alpha_\xi (3!)} ... \tag{17}$$

Substituting this into Equation 14 allows the activation function of Equation 11 to be extracted.

Depending on the values $\delta_{\xi,n}$ and s_n, the expansion term in Equation 11 may not converge. Fortunately, this occurs at a point where $\delta_{\xi,n}$ is sufficiently large that extending beyond it would lead to little further change in the value of the integral. Consequently, a limiting value for $\delta_{\xi,n}$ can be adopted to avoid the problem. For the experiments presented here, $\delta_{\xi,n}$ was limited to a value where the activation of the hidden neuron before conversion to its integral form is equal to 0.001, giving $\delta_{\xi,n}^{max} = \sqrt{-\ln(0.001)/s_n}$. An alternative approach might be to replace the expansion term with a look-up table.

To demonstrate integration, the network taught the sine function problem considered in the previous section was converted into its first integral form. Plotting output from this network for limits of integration between a and b, where a=0 and b ranges from 0 to 4π, results in the curve shown in Figure 2.c. From this it can be seen that the network provides a smooth approximation of the actual integral (the negative cosine plus one). The average absolute error $\bar{\varepsilon}$ for 1,000 randomly selected test patterns was found to be 0.0014.

As a final example, the problem of integrating the function given by Equation 10 (see Figure 3.b) was considered, demonstrating the application of the technique to problems comprising more than one independent variable. Integrating this function from $i_2 = -5$ to $i_2 = 5$ should result in the function shown in Figure 3.a except for differences due to the exclusion of the term $\int_{i_2=-\infty}^{-5.0} (o_y)\partial i_2$. A set of 121 training patterns was set-up on a square grid between the limits ± 5.0 and the network was trained up to 100 hidden neurons. The output from the integral network, plotted in Figure 4, was found to have an average absolute error $\bar{\varepsilon}$ of 0.0069 for 1,000 randomly selected test patterns, clearly demonstrating the validity of the technique.

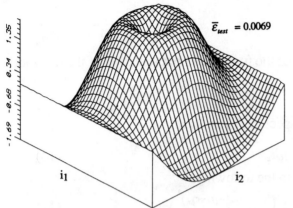

Fig 4: Output from Partial Integral Network

CONCLUSIONS

The paper has demonstrated the use of radial-Gaussian networks as an automated mechanism for performing calculus. The technique is straightforward and has been shown capable of providing accurate results for a variety of operations including first and second order partial differentiation and integration. Moreover, it is possible to rotate the function performed by the original network, in the input plane, by simply adjusting the values of the offsets, $c_{x,n}$, and so the differential or integral of the function can be found readily in any direction, not just parallel to the input axes.

Further work is required to assess the potential of the system when the data used to train the original network is unevenly distributed in the input plane and/or includes errors, as might be expected in many real-world applications of the technique. Consideration should also be given to the use of an alternative Gaussian-like activation function for the hidden neurons that provides a more convenient substitute activation function for integration operations.

REFERENCES

Flood, I. (1991). "A Gaussian-Based Feedforward Network Architecture and Complementary Training Algorithm", Proc. Int. Joint Conf. on Neural Networks, IEEE and INNS, Vol. 1, Singapore, pp. 171-176.

Hecht-Nielsen, R. (1989). "Theory of the backpropogation neural network." Proc. Int. Joint Conf. on Neural Networks, Washington DC, Vol. I, pp. 593-605.

Hornik, K., Stinchcombe, M. and White, H. (1990). "Universal Approximation of an Unknown Mapping and its Derivatives Using Multilayer Feedforward Networks", *Neural Networks,* Vol. 3, pp. 551-560.

Lippmann, R. P. (1987). "An Introduction to Computing with Neural Nets"' IEEE ASSP Magazine, pp. 4-22.

Rumelhart, D. E., Hinton, G. E. and Williams, R. J. (1986). "Learning Internal Representations by Error Propagation", in *Parallel Distributed Processing,* Vol. 1, Rumelhart, D. and McClelland, J. Eds. Cambridge, MA: M.I.T. Press.

Path Integrals for Stochastic Neurodynamics

Toru Ohira
Sony Computer Science Laboratory
3-14-13 Higashi-gotanda, Shinagawa, Tokyo 141, Japan

Jack D. Cowan
Department of Mathematics, The University of Chicago,
Chicago, IL 60637

Abstract

We present here a method for the study of stochastic neurodynamics in the framework of the "Neural Network Master Equation" proposed by Cowan. We consider a model neural network composed of two–state neurons subject to simple stochastic kinetics. We introduce a method based on a spin choerent state path integral to compute the moment generating function of such a network. A formal construction of the path integral is presented and the general expression for many neuron networks is obtained. We show explicitly that the method enables us to obtain the exact moment generating function for a single neuron case. Possible directions for the analysis of many neuron networks as well as an alternative path integral formulation are discussed.

I. Introduction

The "Neural Network Master Equation" (NNME) was recently introduced by Cowan to describe stochastic neural networks[1]. The NNME is a master equation [2] for neural networks based on the formalism of "second quantization" for classical many–body systems [3][4]. This formulation of the master equation enables us to use techniques developed in quantum field theory. Two directions of analysis have been investigated in previous works. A hierarchy of moment equations is derived and used to obtain time dependent description of statistical parameters of simple networks[5]. A Feynman diagram representation of the moment generating function (MGF) of a neural network described by the NNME has also been proposed [6]. The purpose of this paper is to present another approach with the NNME. We construct a path integral for the MGF using spin coherent states. The formal expression of such a path integral for a many neuron network is obtained and the exact MGF is recovered for a single neuron with self-excitation. Possible directions for the analysis of networks with many neurons, including results from alternative path integral formulation, are discussed.

II. Neural Network Master Equation

We first review the Neural Network Master Equation. We assume that neurons at each site, say ith site, can be in one of two states, either "active" or "quiescent", denoted by two dimensional basis vectors using the Dirac notation $|1_i >$ and $|0_i >$ respectively.

$$|0_i >= \begin{pmatrix} 0 \\ 1 \end{pmatrix}_i, \quad |1_i >= \begin{pmatrix} 1 \\ 0 \end{pmatrix}_i \qquad (1)$$

We define the inner product of these states as

$$< 1_i|1_i> = < 0_i|0_i> = 1, \quad < 0_i|1_i> = < 1_i|0_i> = 0. \tag{2}$$

The transition rate of the ith neuron from one state to the other is given as follows:

$$|1_i> \overset{\alpha}{\to} |0_i>, \qquad |0_i> \overset{\phi(V_i)}{\to} |1_i>, \tag{3}$$

where α is a uniform "decay rate", V_i is the weighted sum of all inputs from active neurons connected to the ith neuron, and ϕ is the "activation rate" function. In general, ϕ is nonlinear and is assumed to have the standard sigmoid shape[7].

Let the states (or configurations) of the network be represented by $\{|\Omega>\}$, the direct product space of each neuron in the network.

$$|\Omega> = |v_1> |v_2> \ldots |v_N>, \qquad v_i = 0 \ or \ 1. \tag{4}$$

Let $P[\Omega, t]$ be the probability of finding the network in a particular state Ω at time t. We introduce the "neural state vector" for N neurons in a network as

$$|\Phi(t)> = \sum_{\{\Omega\}} P[\Omega, t]|\Omega>, \tag{5}$$

where the sum is taken over all possible network states.

With these definitions, we can write the NNME for a network with the transition rates given by (3), using the "creation" and "annihilation" operators, σ_i^+ and σ_j^- in the Pauli spin formalism.

$$\sigma_i^+ = \begin{pmatrix} 0 & 1 \\ 0 & 0 \end{pmatrix}_i, \quad \sigma_j^- = \begin{pmatrix} 0 & 0 \\ 1 & 0 \end{pmatrix}_j \tag{6}$$

These operators anti-commute at the same site ($i = j$) to satisfy the physical assumption of single occupancy, and commute for differing sites ($i \neq j$). The NNME then takes the form of an evolution equation:

$$-\frac{\partial}{\partial t}|\Phi(t)> = \mathbf{L}|\Phi(t)> \tag{7}$$

with the network "Liouvillian" $\mathbf{L}$ given by:

$$\mathbf{L} = \alpha \sum_{i=1}^{N} (\sigma_i^+ - 1)\sigma_i^- + \sum_{i=1}^{N} (\sigma_i^- - 1)\sigma_i^+ \phi(\frac{1}{n}\sum_{j=1}^{N} w_{ij}\sigma_j^+\sigma_j^-) \tag{8}$$

where n is an average number of connections to each neuron, and w_{ij} is the "weight" from the jth to the ith neuron. Thus the weights are normalized with respect to the average number n of connections per neuron.

We can derive an equation for the MGF of the network from the NNME using the "spin-coherent states"[8]:

$$< \vec{Z}| = < 0||Exp[\sum_{i=1}^{N} Z_i\sigma_i^-] = \prod_{i=1}^{N}(< 0_i| + Z_i < 1_i|), \tag{9}$$

where the product is taken as a direct product, Z_i are complex parameters, and

$$< 0|| = < 0_1| < 0_2| < 0_3| \ldots < 0_N|. \tag{10}$$

Introducing one-point and multiple-point moments as

$$\ll v_i(t)\gg = \sum_{\{\Omega\}} v_i P[\Omega,\ t], \qquad \ll v_i v_j \ldots (t)\gg = \sum_{\{\Omega\}} (v_i v_j \ldots) P[\Omega,\ t], \tag{11}$$

it can be shown that the moment generating function $G(\vec{Z},t)$ is given as

$$G(\vec{Z},t) = < \vec{Z}|\Phi(t) > \tag{12}$$

from which we can recover the moments as

$$\ll v_i(t)\gg = \frac{\partial}{\partial Z_i} G(\vec{Z},t)|_{\vec{Z}=1}, \qquad \ll v_i v_j \ldots (t)\gg = \frac{\partial}{\partial Z_i}\frac{\partial}{\partial Z_j} \ldots G(\vec{Z},t)|_{\vec{Z}=1} \tag{13}$$

We obtain the equation for $G(\vec{Z},t)$ by simply projecting the NNME onto the spin-coherent states:

$$-\frac{\partial}{\partial t} G(\vec{Z},t) = < \vec{Z}|\mathbf{L}|\Phi(t) > \tag{14}$$

III. Construction of a Path Integral

We now describe a path integral representation of the MGF. From Eqs. (7) and (12), we obtain the following expression for the MGF:

$$G(\vec{Z},t_f - t_i) = \langle \vec{Z}|e^{-\mathbf{L}(t_f - t_i)}|\Phi(t=0)\rangle \tag{15}$$

It can be shown that with suitable initial conditions and normalization, the MGF $G(\vec{Z},t)$ equals the "transition element" T given by [9]

$$T = \langle \vec{Z^f}|Exp[-\mathbf{L}(t_f - t_i)]|\vec{Z^i}\rangle. \tag{16}$$

We express the transition element T in path integral form using the resolution of identity:

$$1 = \frac{2}{\pi}\int_c \prod_i^N \frac{d^2 Z_i}{(1 + Z_i^* Z_i)^3}|\vec{Z}\rangle\langle\vec{Z}| \equiv \int_c d\mu(\vec{Z})|\vec{Z}\rangle\langle\vec{Z}|, \tag{17}$$

where the integration is taken over the entire complex plane of Z_i. The construction of a path integral follows closely the derivation in [10].

We first factorize the operator $e^{-\mathbf{L}(t_f - t_i)}$ into the product of the short time operators:

$$e^{-\mathbf{L}(t_f - t_i)} = \prod_{i=1}^M e^{-\mathbf{L}\epsilon} \tag{18}$$

with $\epsilon = (t_f - t_i)/M$. We now insert the resolution of identity M times between each of the factors to obtain:

$$T = \int (\prod_{s=1}^M d\mu(\vec{Z}_s))\langle \vec{Z^f}|\vec{Z^M}\rangle\langle \vec{Z^M}|e^{-\mathbf{L}\epsilon}|\vec{Z^{M-1}}\rangle \ldots \langle \vec{Z^s}|e^{-\mathbf{L}\epsilon}|\vec{Z^{s-1}}\rangle \ldots \langle \vec{Z^1}|e^{-\mathbf{L}\epsilon}|\vec{Z^i}\rangle. \tag{19}$$

In the limit of $M \to \infty$ and $\epsilon \to 0$, we obtain:

$$\langle \vec{Z^s}|e^{-\mathbf{L}\epsilon}|\vec{Z^{s-1}}\rangle = \langle \vec{Z^s}|\vec{Z^{s-1}}\rangle[1 - \epsilon\frac{\langle \vec{Z^s}|\mathbf{L}|\vec{Z^{s-1}}\rangle}{\langle \vec{Z^s}|\vec{Z^{s-1}}\rangle}] = \langle \vec{Z^s}|\vec{Z^{s-1}}\rangle Exp[-\epsilon\frac{\langle \vec{Z^s}|\mathbf{L}|\vec{Z^{s-1}}\rangle}{\langle \vec{Z^s}|\vec{Z^{s-1}}\rangle}]. \tag{20}$$

Hence, we obtain the expression

$$T = \lim_{M \to \infty} \int \prod_{s=1}^{M} d\mu(\vec{Z}^s) \prod_{s=0}^{M} \langle \vec{Z}^{s+1} | \vec{Z}^s \rangle \, Exp[-\epsilon \sum_{s=0}^{M-1} \frac{\langle \vec{Z}^{s+1} | \mathbf{L} | \vec{Z}^s \rangle}{\langle \vec{Z}^{s+1} | \vec{Z}^s \rangle}], \qquad (21)$$

where $|\vec{Z}^0\rangle = |\vec{Z}^i\rangle$ and $\langle \vec{Z}^{N+1} | = \langle \vec{Z}^f |$. We now let $|\delta \vec{Z}^{s+1}\rangle = |\vec{Z}^{s+1}\rangle - |\vec{Z}^s\rangle$, then

$$T = \lim_{M \to \infty} \int \prod_{s=1}^{M} [d\mu(\vec{Z}^s) \langle \vec{Z}^s | \vec{Z}^s \rangle] \langle \vec{Z}^f | \vec{Z}^M \rangle [\prod_{s=1}^{M}(1 - \frac{\langle \vec{Z}^s | \delta \vec{Z}^s \rangle}{\langle \vec{Z}^s | \vec{Z}^s \rangle})] Exp[-\epsilon \sum_{s=0}^{M-1} \frac{\langle \vec{Z}^{s+1} | \mathbf{L} | \vec{Z}^s \rangle}{\langle \vec{Z}^{s+1} | \vec{Z}^s \rangle}]. \quad (22)$$

We now assume that the major contribution to the integral comes from those paths for which $|\delta\vec{Z}^s\rangle$ is of order ϵ. Setting $\frac{d}{dt}|\vec{Z}\rangle = \frac{1}{\epsilon}|\delta\vec{Z}\rangle$, and using Eq. (22), we obtain the continuous expression:

$$T = \int \prod_{i=1}^{N} (\frac{2}{\pi} \frac{d^2 Z_i}{(1 + Z_i^* Z_i)^2}) Exp[\mathbf{S}], \qquad (23)$$

where the action $\mathbf{S}$ is given as

$$\mathbf{S} = -\int_{t_i}^{t_f} d\tau [\sum_{i=1}^{N} (\frac{1}{1 + Z_i^* Z_i}) Z_i^* \frac{dZ_i}{dt} + \frac{\langle \vec{Z} | \mathbf{L} | \vec{Z} \rangle}{\langle \vec{Z} | \vec{Z} \rangle}] + ln[\langle \vec{Z}^f | \vec{Z}(t_f) \rangle]. \qquad (24)$$

The boundary conditions are:

$$|\vec{Z}(t_i)\rangle = |\vec{Z}^i\rangle, \quad \langle \vec{Z}(t_f) | = \langle \vec{Z}^f |. \qquad (25)$$

Eq. (24) can be put into a more symmetric form via integrating by parts to yield the following:

$$\mathbf{S} = -\int_{t_i}^{t_f} d\tau [\frac{1}{2} \sum_{i=1}^{N} \frac{1}{(1 + Z_i^* Z_i)} (Z_i^* \frac{dZ_i}{dt} - Z_i \frac{dZ_i^*}{dt}) + \frac{\langle \vec{Z} | \mathbf{L} | \vec{Z} \rangle}{\langle \vec{Z} | \vec{Z} \rangle}] + \frac{1}{2} ln[\langle \vec{Z}(t_i) | \vec{Z}^i \rangle \langle \vec{Z}^f | \vec{Z}(t_f) \rangle]. \quad (26)$$

These equations define the path integral form of the transition element T or, equivalently, the moment generating function G.

IV. Single Neuron Case

We first consider the case of a single neuron with self-excitation. The Liouville operator is given as follows:

$$\mathbf{L} = \alpha(\sigma^+ - 1)\sigma^- + \rho(\sigma^- - 1)\sigma^+. \qquad (27)$$

The action in this case is:

$$\mathbf{S} = -\int_{t_i}^{t_f} \frac{1}{(1 + Z^* Z)} [\frac{1}{2}(Z^* \frac{dZ}{dt} - Z \frac{dZ^*}{dt}) + \alpha(Z^* - 1)Z + \rho(1 - Z^*)] dt$$

$$+ \frac{1}{2} ln[(1 + Z^*(t_i) Z^i)(1 + Z^{f*} Z(t_f))]. \qquad (28)$$

In this case, we can calculate T exactly using the classical approximation or saddle-point evaluation [11] of the path integral, in a fashion similar to the free particle in quantum mechanics. The classical approximation to the path integral with the action given by (28) yields:

$$\frac{\partial \tilde{\mathbf{L}}}{\partial Z} = \frac{d}{dt} \frac{\partial \tilde{\mathbf{L}}}{\partial \dot{Z}}, \qquad \frac{\partial \tilde{\mathbf{L}}}{\partial Z^*} = \frac{d}{dt} \frac{\partial \tilde{\mathbf{L}}}{\partial \dot{Z}^*} \qquad (29)$$

with

$$\tilde{\mathbf{L}} \equiv -\frac{1}{(1+Z^*Z)}[\frac{1}{2}\{(Z^*\frac{dZ}{dt} - \frac{dZ^*}{dt}Z)\} + \alpha(Z^*-1)Z + \rho(1-Z^*)]. \tag{30}$$

This classical equation of motion leads to equations for Z and Z^*:

$$\frac{dZ}{dt} = (-\alpha Z + \rho)(Z+1), \qquad \frac{dZ^*}{dt} = (\alpha - \rho Z^*)(Z^*-1). \tag{31}$$

with the boundary conditions: $Z(t_i) = Z^i$, $Z^*(t_f) = Z^{f*}$. Substitution of (31) into (28) leads to the classical action in the simple form:

$$\mathbf{S_{CL}} = \int_{t_i}^{t_f} dt\{-\rho + \frac{1}{2}[\alpha Z(t) + \rho Z^*(t)]\} + +\frac{1}{2}ln[(1 + Z^*(t_i)Z^i)(1 + Z^{f*}Z(t_f))] \tag{32}$$

We can finally show, via a tedious but straightforward calculation of explicitly solving the classical equation of motion and of the classical action, the transition element given by $T = Exp[\mathbf{S_{CL}}]$ with the following identification

$$\frac{Z^i}{(1+Z^i)} \to P_+, \quad Z^{f*} \to Z. \tag{33}$$

(P_+ is the probability of being in the active state at time t_i.) gives the exact moment generating function:

$$G(Z, t_f - t_i) = (1 - P(t_f - t_i)) + ZP(t_f - t_i), \tag{34}$$

where

$$P(t) = (\frac{\rho}{\alpha + \rho}) + ((\frac{\rho}{\alpha + \rho}) - P_+)e^{-(\alpha + \rho)t}. \tag{35}$$

We note here that the end point factors appearing in the path integral play a role in obtaining this solution.

V. Many Neuron Case

We now consider the many neuron case with $\mathbf{L}$ given by Eq. (8). The path integral representation is given by (26) with

$$\frac{\langle \vec{Z}|\mathbf{L}|\vec{Z}\rangle}{\langle \vec{Z}|\vec{Z}\rangle} = \sum_{i=1}^{N}[\alpha\frac{(Z_i^*-1)Z_i}{(1+Z_i^*Z_i)}] + \frac{1}{\langle \vec{Z}|\vec{Z}\rangle}\langle \vec{Z}|(\sum_{i=1}^{N}(\sigma_i^- - 1)\sigma_i^+\phi(\frac{1}{n}\sum_{j=1}^{N}w_{ij}\sigma_j^+\sigma_j^-)|\vec{Z}\rangle. \tag{36}$$

The second term requires a Taylor expansion for ϕ, and cannot be written in a concise form. Here, we proceed with the case $\phi(x) = x$ (the linear case without self-activation). Then

$$\frac{\langle \vec{Z}|\mathbf{L}|\vec{Z}\rangle}{\langle \vec{Z}|\vec{Z}\rangle} = \sum_{i=1}^{N}[\alpha\frac{(Z_i^*-1)Z_i}{(1+Z_i^*Z_i)}] + \frac{1}{n}\sum_{i=1,j=1}^{N}[w_{ij}\frac{(1-Z_i^*)}{(1+Z_i^*Z_i)}\frac{(Z_i^*Z_i)}{(1+Z_i^*Z_i)}]. \tag{37}$$

Eqs. (26) and (37) formally define the path integral for the linear case. We note that this path integral is defined on a curved surface with non-linear factors $1/(1 + Z_i^*Z_i)$. Because of this, the algebraic manipulations required to deal with the many neuron case are rather complicated [12].

VI. Discussion

We now wish to discuss what can be done with these formal derivations of the spin coherent state path integral for the NNME. In principle, even for the many neuron case, we can proceed with saddle point approximations and other approximation schemes developed for path integrals. The difficulty associated with a curved surface complicates such calculations. It turns out that we can alternatively formulate an equivalent path integral using boson coherent states, which circumvents this difficulty at the expense of using twice as many variables. In such formulation, we have shown that we can obtain an equivalent of the mean field approximation via a saddle point approximation to such a path integral. The corresponding derivation with the spin coherent state path integral presented here as well as higher order approximation to both formulations of path integrals are currently being investigated.

References

[1] J.D.Cowan, in *Advances in Neural Information Processing Systems 3*, edited by R. P. Lippman, J. E. Moody, and D. S. Touretzky (Morgan Kaufmann Publishers, San Mateo, 1991), p.62.

[2] N.van Kampen, *Stochastic Processes in Physics and Chemistry*(North Holland, Amsterdam, 1981)

[3] M.Doi, J.Phys.A 9,1465 (1976)

[4] P. Grassberger and M .Scheunert, Fortachritte der Physik **28**, 547, (1980)

[5] T.Ohira and J.D.Cowan, Phys.Rev.E **48**, 2259, (1993)

[6] T.Ohira and J.D.Cowan, to be published in *Proceedings of Fifth Australian Conference of Neural Networks, 1994*

[7] J. D. Cowan, in *Neural Networks*, edited by E. R .Caianiello(Springer, New York 1968), p. 181.

[8] A. Perelomov, *Generalized Coherent States and Their Applications* (Springer, New York, 1986)

[9] M.Doi, J.Phys.A 9,1479 (1976)

[10] J.Blaizot and G.Ripka, *Quantum Theory of Finite Systems*(The MIT Press, Cambridge, 1986)

[11] M. Swanson, *Path integrals and quantum processes*, Academic Press, San Diego,, 1992.

[12] H. Kuratsuji, *Path integrals in the SU(2) coherent state representation and related topics*, Path Integrals and Coherent States of SU(2) and SU(1,1) (Singapore) (A. Inomata, H. Kuratsuji, and C. C. Gerry, eds.), World Scientific, Singapore, 1992.

Positional Sharpening in the Boundary Contour System[*]

Lothar Wieske

University of Hamburg
Department of Computer Science
Bodenstedtstr. 16
D-22765 Hamburg (Germany)

wieske@informatik.uni-hamburg.de

Abstract

This work builds upon the proposal of the Boundary Contour System proposed in [GrossbergMingolla85] and [GrossbergMingolla87] as a subsystem of the FACADE architecture introduced in [Grossberg90]. We analyse the positional sharpening capabilities of the competitive layers in the competitive cooperative loop. Positional sharpening as set up by Grossberg and Mingolla may be seen as a two-stage process, where a threshold-linear signal function transforms the input and drives the subsequent positional competition stage. We draw the conclusion that positional sharpening is enforced by thresholding rather than by positional competition.

1   Introduction and Motivation

A large part of human and mammal brains is dedicated to visual perception and the combination of locally ambiguous visual information into a globally consistent and unambiguous representation of the visual environment. So the question arises, how multiple sources of visual information like texture, stereo, and motion cooperate to generate a visual percept.

One of the key ideas for the development of the FACADE by Stephen Grossberg and coworkers is the conviction that modular approaches with special purpose procedures are not very useful for an understanding of real-world vision. The working hypothesis of the FACADE architecture is, that every stage of visual processing multiplexes together several key properties of the scenic representation.

The FACADE architecture aims at an explanation of how the visual system is able to detect relatively invariant surface colours under variable illumination conditions, to detect relatively invariant object boundaries under occlusion conditions, and to recognize familar objects or events in the environment. More elaborated versions of the FACADE architecture include processing of stereo and motion. We deal here with the simplified variant defined in [Grossberg90], where the Feature Contour System (FCS), Boundary Contour System (BCS), and the Object Recognition System (ORS) are designed in correspondence to the above processing goals of the overal architecture.

Processing of the visual input in retina and LGN relies on local measurements which introduce some amount of uncertainty into the representation at the corresponding processing stages. The FACADE architecture sets up parallel and hierarchical interaction schemes that can resolve these uncertainties by means of several processing stages.

---

[*]This work was funded by the German Federal Ministry of Science and Technology (NAMOS/413-4001-01 IN 101 C 1)

The following diagramm visualizes the dataflow bewteen the subsystems of the FACADE architecture and within the Boundary Contour System and its competitive and cooperative layers.

FACADE   **Boundary Contour System**

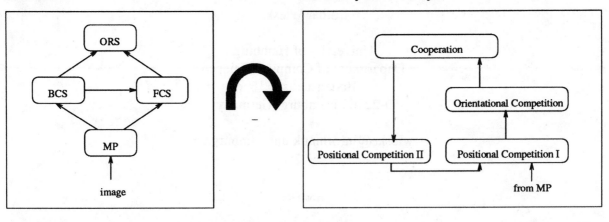

The MP stage defines oriented receptive fields for each perceptual location which are sensitive to local contrast in the intensity function in accordance to the hypercolumn model of the primary visual cortex by Hubel and Wiesel. The local contrast detectors feed into the competitive-cooperative loop of the Boundary Contour System which generates an emergent segmentation of boundaries in the scene by means of spatially short-range competitive interactions and spatially long-range cooperative interactions. Two successive stages of spatially short-range competitive interactions feed into a cooperative stage with in turn feeds back inbtwo the first competitive stage via an intermediate competitive stage. Preattentive processing in the Boundary Contour System does not rely on memorized templates or expectancies but is purely data-driven. Emergent segmentation provides a way to generate boundaries which have no direct physical correlate in the intensity function but are perceived by human subjects in psychophysical experiments. The Kanizsa square and the Ehrenstein illusion are prominent examples used in those experiments. The proposal of the Boundary Contour System aims at an explanation of how those *illusory contours* are generated by the visual system.

In the first competitive layer a cell of prescribed orientation excites like oriented cells at the same location and inhibits like-oriented cells at nearby positions. This on-center off-surround organization of like-oriented cells exists around every perceptual location. In the second competitive layer cells compete that represent different orientations — notably perpendicular ones — at the same perceptual location. An additional net effect of the first and second competitive layer is to generate end-cuts. The competitive layers feed into the cooperative stage which defines spatially long-range interactions for boundary completion. The output of the cooperative stage is enhanced by a further competitive layer and fed back into the first competitive layer. This feedback allows for the discontinuous completion of continuous boundaries. (For details see [GrossbergMingolla85],[GrossbergMingolla87].)

2 Positional Sharpening and Positional Competition

In [GrossbergMingolla85] and [GrossbergMingolla87] the authors define the following process for the second positional competition layer to realize the postulate of positional sharpening

$$v_{ijk} = \frac{h(z_{ijk})}{1 + \sum_{(p,q)} h(z_{pqk}) \cdot W_{pqij}}$$

with a circular inhibitory weighting kernel and a threshold-linear signal function.

$$W_{pqij} = \begin{cases} W & \text{if} \quad (p-i)^2 + (q-j)^2 \leq W_0^2 \\ 0 & \text{otherwise} \end{cases} \qquad \text{and} \qquad h(z) = L \cdot [z - M]^+$$

The variables z and v denote the output of the cooperative stage and the subsequent competitive stage. The incdices i,j, and k have the following meaning. The pair $<i,j>$ indexes a perceptual location whereas k is an index to an orientation band. Since there are no interactions between different orientation bands, we will leave out the index k in our further considerations. The definition of the first competitive stage is quite similar and uses the same mechanism, but is not so well suited for an analysis of positional sharpening since it mixes two inputs.

"Functionall, the $z_{ijk} \rightarrow v_{ijk}$ transformation enables the most favored cooperations to enhance their preferred positions and orientations as they suppress nearby positions with the same orientation."

3 Analysis of Positional Competition

For an analysis of the positional competition stage and its relation to the postulate of positional sharpening we first state that the transformation defined in the preceeding section may by seen as a two stage process, i.e. the transformation given by

$$\{T(I)\}(x,y) = \frac{\{h(I)\}(x,y)}{1 + \{h(I) \star W\}(x,y)}$$

may be rewritten as the concatenation of two transformations where a point operation (thresholding) is followed by a positional competition transformation:

$$T(I) = T_2(T_1(I)) \quad \text{with} \quad \{T_1(I)\}(x,y) = h(I(x,y)) \quad \text{and} \quad \{T_2(I)\}(x,y) = \frac{I(x,y)}{1 + \{I \star W\}(x,y)}$$

Before we can analyze positional sharpening we have to clarify our understanding of this notion. We want to relate two one-dimensional stimuli I_1 and I_2 where I_2 is a transformed version of stimulus I_1. We assume that I_1 and I_2 are positive unimodal functions having their maximum in $t = 0$. Defining the meaning of I_2 is *sharper* than I_1 is a debatable issue. We start with the definition of the opposite.

Definition 1: Given two positive unimodal functions I_1 und I_2 having their maximum in $t = 0$, we say that I_2 is **broader** than I_1, if

$$\frac{I_2(t)}{I_2(0)} = \overline{I_2(t)} > \overline{I_1(t)} = \frac{I_1(t)}{I_1(0)} \quad \text{for} \quad t \neq 0$$

The intuition behind this definition is that the function I_2 is something like a cheese cover of the same height for the function I_1, if I_2 is *broader* than I_1. (See the illustration after proposition 1.) One alternative for the definition of "*sharper*" is the inversion of the above inequality. Other possible definition include the reduction of the full-width-at-half-height or the reduction of the area under the normalized function. There is no need for a final decision since our further investigations will show that the transformation T_2 as defined above will essentially broaden the input. So all of the broadening-effect of the overall transformation T is due to the threshold operation T_1 for a large class of inputs and inhibitory kernels.

We establish our results as follows. In proposition 1 we investigate the behaviour of the transformation T_2 for the one-dimensional case with a Gaussian input and a boxed weighting kernel. We extend this result to the two-dimensional case and study the transformation of a Gaussian activity distribution under positional competition with the inhibitory weighting kernel proposed by Grossberg and Mingolla. This extension leads us to a useful lemma which allows us to draw more general conclusions on the *broadening* behaviour for the one-dimensional and two-dimensional positional competition transformation in proposition 3 and proposition 4.

Proposition 1: Given a Gaussian input I ($\sigma > 0$) and a boxed weighting kernel K ($h > 0$ and $w > 0$)

$$I(t) = G_\sigma(t) = \frac{1}{\sigma\sqrt{2\pi}} \exp(-\frac{t^2}{2\sigma^2}) \qquad K(t) = \begin{cases} h & |t| \leq w \\ 0 & \text{otherwise} \end{cases}$$

the positional competition transformation $\mathcal{T}_K$ broadens I, i.e. $\mathcal{T}_K(I)$ is *broader* than I.

$$\{\mathcal{T}_K(f)\}(t) = \frac{f(t)}{1 + \{f \star K\}(t)}$$

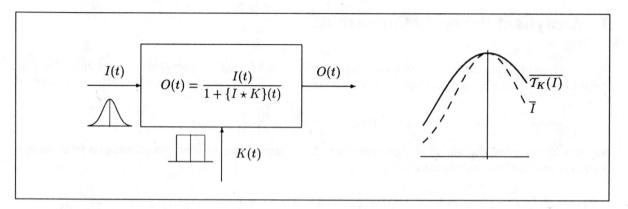

Proof of Proposition 1: We have to show, that

$$\frac{\overline{\{\mathcal{T}_K(I)\}(t)}}{\overline{I(t)}} = \frac{1 + \{I \star K\}(0)}{1 + \{I \star K\}(t)} > 1 \quad \text{if } |t| > 0.$$

and we see that $\{I \star K\}(0) > \{I \star K\}(t)$ has to be shown for $|t| > 0$. With

$$\{I \star K\}(t) = \frac{1}{2} \cdot \left(\text{erf}(\frac{t + w}{2\sqrt{2}}) - \text{erf}(\frac{t - w}{2\sqrt{2}}) \right)$$

we find that this function has a global maximum at $t = 0$ by differentiating

$$\frac{\partial}{\partial t} \left(\text{erf}(\frac{t + w}{2\sqrt{2}}) - \text{erf}(\frac{t - w}{2\sqrt{2}}) \right) = G_\sigma(t + w) - G_\sigma(t - w)$$

The first derivative vanishes and the second derivative is negative for at $t = 0$, but the first derivative does not vanish for $t \neq 0$, which completes the proof. ✓

Proposition 2: For a Gaussian-shaped input I with $\sigma > 0$ and a circular weighting kernel K with $h > 0$ and $w > 0$

$$I(x,y) = I(x) = G_\sigma(x) \qquad K(x,y) = \begin{cases} h & x^2 + y^2 \leq w^2 \\ 0 & \text{otherwise} \end{cases}$$

the positional competition transformation $\mathcal{T}_K$ broadens I, i.e. $\{\mathcal{T}_K(I)\}(x,y) = \{\mathcal{T}_K(I)\}(x)$ is *broader* than $I(x,y) = I(x)$.

$$\{\mathcal{T}_K(f)\}(x,y) = \frac{f(x,y)}{1 + \{f \star K\}(x,y)}$$

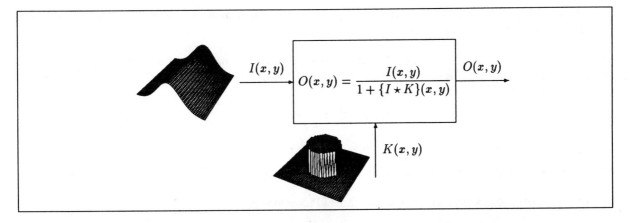

We postpone the proof of proposition 2 and motivate a useful lemma by simplifying the convolution integral

$$\{I \star K\}(x, y) = \int_{-w}^{w} I(x - u) \cdot \left[\int_{-\sqrt{w^2 - u^2}}^{\sqrt{w^2 - u^2}} h \, dv\right] du = \int_{-w}^{w} I(x - u) \cdot \left[2 \cdot h \cdot \sqrt{w^2 - u^2}\right] du$$

The last integral indicates that the two dimensional transformation with the proposed circular weighting kernel may be seen as the one-dimensional transformation with a monotone decreasing kernel given by

$$K(t) = \begin{cases} 2 \cdot h \cdot \sqrt{w^2 - t^2} & |t| \leq w \\ 0 & \text{otherwise} \end{cases}$$

The extension to the 2D case motivates an extension of the 1D case studied in proposition 1. We may ask whether more general inhibitory weighting kernels also yield broadening of the input by the corresponding positional competition.. We prepare these generalization by the following lemma.

Lemma 1: Let f and g be positive, even functions which are montone decreasing with distance from the origin. we require f to be strictly decreasing such that

$$
\begin{aligned}
f &\in C^\infty & g &\in W^{1,1} \\
f(t) &> 0 & g(t) &\geq 0 \\
f(t) &= f(-t) & g(t) &= g(-t) \\
f(t_1) &> f(t_2) & g(t_1) &\geq g(t_2) \quad 0 \leq t_1 < t_2 \\
& & \int_0^\infty \Phi(t) \cdot g'(t) \, dt &< 0 \quad \forall \Phi \in C^\infty, \Phi(t) > 0
\end{aligned}
$$

Then their convolution product

$$\{f \star g\}(t) = \int_{-\infty}^{\infty} f(u) \cdot g(t - u) du$$

takes its maximum in $t = 0$.

Proof of Lemma 1: We show that $\{f \star g\}(0) - \{f \star g\}(t)$ takes a global minimum in $t = 0$. So

$$\{f \star g\}(0) - \{f \star g\}(t) = \int_{-\infty}^{\infty} f(u) \cdot (g(u) - g(t - u)) \, du$$

Now

$$\frac{\partial}{\partial t} \left(\{f \star g\}(0) - \{f \star g\}(t)\right) = \int_0^\infty (f(t - u) - f(t + u)) \cdot g'(u) \, du$$

The sign of this derivative directly depends on the sign of $f(t-u) - f(t+u)$. For $t > 0$ we have $f(t-u) - f(t+u) > 0$ since f is even and strict decreasing with distance from the origin. If $t = 0$ the difference is 0. For negative t we conclude that the difference is negative because of the identity $f(t - u) - f(t + u) = -(f(|t| - u) - f(|t| + u))$.

So the function $\{f \star g\}(0) - \{f \star g\}(t)$ has an extremum in $t = 0$, and is strictly monotone decreasing with distance from the origin, which finishes the proof. ✓

Proposition 3: Let the stimulus $I(t)$ fulfill the conditions of the function f in lemma 1, and the inhibitory weighting kernel $K(t)$ fulfill the conditions of the function g. Then the positional competition transformation $\mathcal{T}_K$ broadens I, i.e. $\mathcal{T}_K(I)$ is *broader* than I.

$$\{\mathcal{T}_K(f)\}(t) = \frac{f(t)}{1 + \{f \star K\}(t)}$$

•

Proof of Proposition 3: We verify the inequality $\{I \star K\}(0) > \{I \star K\}(t)$ for $t \neq 0$ by invoking lemma 1. ✓

Proof of Proposition 2: Proposition 2 is a special case of Proposition 3. ✓

Proposition 4: Let the stimulus $I(x, y) = I(x)$ fulfill the conditions of the function f in lemma 1, and the inhibitory weighting kernel $K(x, y) = K(\sqrt{x^2 + y^2})$ fulfill the conditions of the function g. Then the positional competition transformation $\mathcal{T}_K$ broadens I, i.e. $\{\mathcal{T}_K(I)\}(x, y) = \{\mathcal{T}_K(I)\}(x)$ is *broader* than $I(x, y) = I(x)$.

$$\{\mathcal{T}_K(f)\}(x, y) = \frac{f(x, y)}{1 + \{f \star K\}(x, y)}$$

•

Proof of Proposition 4: Transforming th convolution integral

$$\{I \star K\}(x, y) = \int_\infty^\infty I(x - u) \cdot \left[\int_\infty^\infty K(u, v) \right] du$$

we see that the bracketed integral is a function of u which fulfills the properties of the one-dimensional kernel $K(t)$ in proposition 3 and may use the result reported there. ✓

4   Conclusion

We have analyzed the positional sharpening capabilities of the Boundary Contour System as a subsystem of the FACADE architecture. Positional sharpening as set up by Grossberg and Mingolla may be seen as a two-stage process, where a threshold-linear signal functions transforms the input and drives the subsequent positional competition stage. We come to the conclusion that the sharpening effect of the positional sharpening process is due to the transformation by the threshold-linear signal function. A similar analysis has been given in [ElliasGrossberg75] several for other types of shunting equations.

Acknowledgement. I would like to thank O. Ludwig and R. Sprengel for fruitful and stimulating discussions.

References

[ElliasGrossberg75]   S.A. Ellias and S. Grossberg. Pattern formation, contrast control, and oscillations in the short term memory of shunting on-center off-surround networks. *Biological Cybernetics*, 20:69–98, 1975.

[Grossberg90]   S. Grossberg. Neural facades: Visual representations of static and moving form-and-color-and-depth. *Mind & Language*, 5:411–456, 1990.

[GrossbergMingolla85]   S. Grossberg and E. Mingolla. Neural dynamics of perceptual grouping: Textures, boundaries, and emergent segmentation. *Perception and Psychophysics*, 38:141–171, 1985.

[GrossbergMingolla87]   S. Grossberg and E. Mingolla. Neural dynamics of surface perception: Boundary webs, illuminants, and shape-from-shading. *Computer Vision, Graphics, and Image Processing*, 37:116–165, 1987.

Psychological Laws of Choice (the Generalized Matching Law), Psychophysical Perception (Steven's Law) and Absolute Rate (Herrnstein's Equation) Can be Derived from Stochastic Networks

Larrie V. Hutton, Ph.D.
RobiNets Homuncular Solutions
2114 Bank Street
Baltimore, MD 21231
410-327-5765 or e-mail: lvh@connect.win.net

A stochastic neural network, using the ordinary laws of thermodynamics, can develop a representation of what might be called a state of cognitive equilibrium (Hutton, 1991). If it is assumed that there is a quantal nature to behavior (and hence cognition) and that inputs are logarithmically transformed, three important and not obviously related psychological laws, usually treated as empirical generalizations, can be derived from first principles. Steven's Law relates the subjective impression of a stimulus to its objective magnitude. Herrnstein's equation relates absolute response rate to absolute reinforcement rate. The generalized matching law makes quantitative predictions about choice by assuming that a power law describes the relationship between behavioral states and relative value of alternatives. Assume a neural net with symmetric weights and a stochastic update rule. This results in relative output probabilities that are determined by a Boltzmann distribution. If inputs are logarithmically transformed, then the generalized matching law and Steven's Law can be derived from the network equations. Assuming limited capacity, Herrnstein's equation falls out. The results suggest heretofore unreported links between some apparently unrelated psychological laws, and show the importance of thermodynamic principles to states of cognitive/behavioral equilibria. They also show a plausible mechanism for the emergence of power law relationships that is not in any way restricted to treatments of cognitive and other behavioral states.

Behavioral Laws Can Be Derived from Thermodynamic Laws

A neural network model of behavior should be able to reproduce experimentally verified relationships between input and output in either human or subhuman organisms. It is here shown how three laws, themselves empirical generalizations, can develop from a very simple neural network that is based on the First and Second Laws of thermodynamics. The three laws are the generalized matching law, Steven's Law, and Herrnstein's equation.

The generalized matching law (Baum, 1973) relates the relative probability of responding to two alternatives (B_1/B_2) to the relative rate of reinforcement (r_1/r_2). When the relative rates are displayed on a log-log plot and the resultant linear equation is exponentiated, one obtains

$$\frac{B_1}{B_2} = k\left(\frac{r_1}{r_2}\right)^a, \tag{1}$$

which is the generalized matching law. The constant k is a bias term reflecting, for example, a position or color preference. The exponent a, usually 1 or less, can be regarded as a measure of discrimination; e.g., a value of 0 would reflect indifference to the relative value of the inputs. The model presented here assumes that entropy-preserving transformations tend to push the system toward values of 1.

Steven's Law (Krueger, 1989) is of similar form, but it relates the perceived magnitude of a stimulus to its objective intensity. Steven's Law is

$$\Psi = iS^\beta \tag{2}$$

in which ψ is perceived value and S is objective stimulus magnitude. The constant i is a scaling factor, and β is an index of sensitivity to a specific sensory modality.

Herrnstein's (1970) equation gives predictions for absolute response rates given the absolute reinforcement rate on a variable interval schedule of reinforcement. Like the other two laws, it requires fitting two free parameters (j and r_o) for each organism:

$$B_1 = \frac{jr_1}{r_1 + r_0} \qquad (3)$$

in which B_1 is the absolute response rate, r_1 is the scheduled reinforcement rate, j is a presumed asymptotic rate, and r_0 reflects reinforcement from sources not under direct experimental control.

(Equation 3 provides quantitative predictions that at first appear counterintuitive. For example, response rate increases if value injected into the system is response contingent, which increases r_1, but it decreases if the events of value are noncontingent, which increases r_2 [Rachlin and Baum, 1972]. An analysis based on superstitious reinforcement would predict increased responding in both cases. An analysis not taking hypothetical reinforcers into account would falsely predict a response rate that is independent of reinforcement rate. Nor does a linear association between response and reinforcer produce the veridical hyperbolic relationship.)

All three equations can be derived from assumptions that are consistent with certain neural networks. Assume that the inputs are logarithmically transformed (Cornsweet, 1970; Mead and Mahowald, 1988; Hoffman, 1987). This is equivalent to a system that extracts information about input magnitude (Norwich, 1989), and is also consistent with Fechner's Law (Krueger, 1989).

Assume further that we have a neural network as shown below in Figure 1. A and B are input nodes, C and D are output nodes, and E and F are bias nodes. w_1 through w_5 are symmetric weights connecting the nodes shown. We assume that w_1 and w_2 are equal to the logarithms of the reinforcement rates, r_1 and r_2. We might assume that the weights are scaled in such a way that the threshold stimulus has a value of 1 (and hence a log of 0), to avoid negative weights. Although this is more physiologically plausible, it will not make any difference mathematically. Assume the minimum conductance, or weight, is zero, corresponding to an absolute threshold of detection.

The system described is intended to be a stochastic system at temperature T. The probability that any node will stay

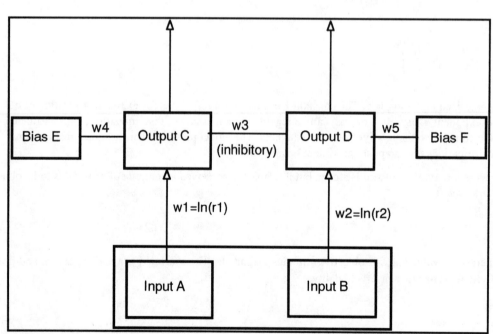

Figure 1. A simple neural net that will produce outputs consistent with the generalized matching law, Herrnstein's equation, and Steven's Law. Nodes A, B, E, and F are clamped.

or flip to the "on" position is given by

$$p(o_j = ON) = \frac{1}{1 + e^{\frac{a_j}{T}}} \tag{4}$$

from Hinton and Sejnowski (1986). Because the bias nodes, E and F, and the input nodes, A and B, are clamped, there are only four possible states of the system (all combinations of C and D on and off). The energies for these four states are shown in Table 1.

State	Node C	Node D	Energy
A	Off	Off	0
B	On	Off	$(w_1+w_4)/T$
C	Off	On	$(w_2+w_5)/T$
D	On	On	$(w_1+w_2+w_4+w_5-w_3)/T$

Table 1. Energy of the four possible states on a Concurrent VI Schedule

The last state, state D, is unlikely because w_3 is strongly inhibitory; in realistic situations, this inhibitory role is played by a changeover delay (COD) between reinforcers (Silberberg and Fantino, 1970). Similarly, state A is improbable if w_1 and w_2 are relatively large (recall that w_1 and w_2 must be at least 1). For example, if $w_1 = w_2 = 3$, $w_4 = w_5 = 0$, and $w_3 = 6$, the system will spend about 95% of its time in state B or state C.

Of particular concern is the relative probability of states B and C. Although the system is not designed to be a Boltzmann machine, it does satisfy the requirements for one at thermal equilibrium. Hence, the relative probability follows a Boltzmann distribution, and we have

$$\frac{p_B}{p_C} = e^{[(w_1+w_4)-(w_2+w_5)]/T}, \tag{5}$$

which corresponds to a negentropy interpretation of information. It follows that

$$\frac{P_B}{P_C} = \frac{e^{\frac{w_1+w_4}{T}}}{e^{\frac{w_2+w_5}{T}}} \tag{6}$$

$$= \left(\frac{e^{w_4/T}}{e^{w_5/T}}\right) * \left(\frac{e^{w_1}}{e^{w_2}}\right)^{\frac{1}{T}} \tag{7}$$

$$= k\left(\frac{e^{\ln r_1}}{e^{\ln r_2}}\right)^{\frac{1}{T}}. \tag{8}$$

$$= k\left(\frac{r_B}{r_C}\right)^{a}, \quad a = \frac{1}{T}. \tag{9}$$

Thus, we have derived the generalized matching law. Steven's Law follows if we assume that r_C is some (perhaps internal) fixed stimulus, which would make P_C constant, so that

$$\frac{P_B}{P_C} = \frac{r_B^a}{r_C^a}, \tag{10}$$

and

$$P_B = \left(\frac{P_C}{r_C^a}\right) r_B^a \tag{11}$$

$$= i r_B^a, \tag{12}$$

which is the form required for Steven's Law. From this point, it is a simple matter to derive Herrnstein's equation. Assume that the measured output of the system P_B and P_C, reflects the "cognitive state" of a system with limited capacity. Let P_B be the target of interest and P_C be attentional behavior controlled by all sources other than r_B, with constant sum. Thus,

$$\frac{P_B}{P_C} = \frac{r_B}{r_C}, \quad a = 1/T = 1 \tag{13}$$

or

$$\frac{P_B}{P_B + P_C} = \frac{r_B}{r_B + r_C}, \tag{14}$$

and

$$P_B = k \frac{r_B}{r_B + r_C}, \quad (P_B + P_C) = \text{constant}, \quad (15)$$

which is Herrnstein's equation. The derivation, however, follows for strictly cognitive states at thermal equilibrium and need not be restricted to overt behavioral measures.

References

Baum, W. M. (1973). On two types of deviation from the matching law: Bias and undermatching. *Journal of the Experimental Analysis of Behavior*, **22**, 231-242.

Davison, M., and Kerr, A. (1989). Sensitivity of time allocation to an overall reinforcement rate feedback function in concurrent interval schedules. *Journal of the Experimental Analysis of Behavior*, **51**, 215-231.

Cornsweet, T. N. (1970). *Visual Perception*. New York: Academic Press.

Herrnstein, R. J. (1970). On the law of effect. *Journal of the Experimental Analysis of Behavior*, **13**, 109-282.

Hinton, G. E. & Sejnowski, T. J. (1986). Learning and relearning in Boltzmann machines. In D. E. Rumelhart and J. L. McClelland (Eds.), Parallel Distributed Processing (pp. 282-317). MIT Press: Cambridge.

Hoffman, J. E. (1987). *The psychology of perception*. In J. E. LeDoux & W. Hirst (Eds.), Mind and Brain: Dialogues in Cognitive Neuroscience (pp. 7-32). Cambridge: Cambridge.

Hutton, L. V. (1991). The matching law and Boltzmann distributions. *JHU/APL Technical Report, RMI-91-019*, Mathematics and Information Science Group, Research Center, The JHU Applied Physics Laboratory, Laurel, MD 20723.

Krueger, L. E. (1989). Reconciling Fechner and Stevens: Toward a unified psychophysical law. *Behavioral and Brain Sciences*, **12**, 251-320.

Mead, C. A. & Mahowald, M. A. (1988). A silicon model of early visual processing. *Neural Networks*, **1**, 91-97.

Norwich, K. H. (1989). The Fechner-Stevens law is the law of transmission of information. *Behavioral and Brain Sciences*, **12**, 285.

Rachlin, H. & Baum, W. M. (1972). Effects of alternative reinforcement: does the source matter? *Journal of the Experimental Analysis of Behavior*, **18**, 231-241.

Silberberg, A. & Fantino, E. (1970). Choice, rate of reinforcement and the changeover delay. *Journal of the Experimental Analysis of Behavior*, **13**, 187-198.

Neural networks for short term pattern storage

Gregory Francis[1]

Purdue University
Department of Psychological Sciences
1364 Psychological Sciences Building
West Lafayette, IN 47907-1364

Abstract

An analysis of long-term memory processes indicates a need for short-term mechanisms that store arbitrary spatial patterns of neural activity for substantial lengths of time. This paper analyzes the short-term pattern storage properties of generalized on-center, off-surround neural networks. Except for special cases, such networks cannot store patterns for arbitrarily long lengths of time (to equilibrium). However, bounds of pattern degradation show that networks close (in a precise sense) to these special cases may store arbitrary spatial patterns of activity for substantial lengths of time with good accuracy.

1 Introduction

Most neural networks code information by a spatial distribution of neural activity and store spatial patterns of neural activity for long periods of time by control of connection weights (e.g., Grossberg, 1968; Anderson, Silverstein, Ritz, & Jones, 1977; McClelland & Rumelhart, 1981; Hopfield, 1982). Learning these patterns requires sampling the current neural pattern and modifying weight strength so that the network can replay the same pattern in the future.

A network embedded in a real-time environment requires a careful analysis of the interplay between short-term and long-term dynamics. Learning in many real time environments and networks requires a short-term memory (STM) process that stores an item before long-term memory (LTM) mechanisms encode it. The following situations (at least) require short-term storage:

- When LTM weights change slowly they may not learn the item during its brief physical presence. In this case a STM process prolongs the spatial pattern coding the item and allows longer LTM sampling.

- A decision to code an item in LTM may not occur until after the item has disappeared in the environment (e.g., in a reinforcement learning experiment, Grossberg, 1982; or perhaps during the hypothesis searches of ART systems, Carpenter & Grossberg, 1987). A STM process stores the spatial pattern coding the item until other processes reach a decision.

These cases apply to many real-time neural network models, thus there is a need to investigate neural networks that function as STM processes. This paper extends some of the results discovered by Grossberg (1973) concerning the pattern storage abilities of on-center, off-surround neural networks. An analysis of generalized on-center, off-surround networks reveals the duration of accurate pattern storage for a large class of neural networks that could act as STM processes.

2 On-center, off-surround networks

Grossberg (1973) analyzed on-center, off-surround networks where each cell feeds back onto itself with an excitatory connection and receives inhibition from every other cell in the network. Grossberg (1973) suggested that each cell activity obeys a shunting equation of the form:

$$\frac{dx_i}{dt} = -Ax_i + (B - x_i)f(x_i) - x_i \sum_{k \neq i} f(x_k),\tag{1}$$

---

[1]This material is based upon work supported under a National Science Foundation Graduate Fellowship.

where $f(w)$ is a strictly monotone increasing function bound on $[0, B]$. The parameter B, referred to as the cell's carrying capacity, represents the number of available receptors on a single cell. The value of x_i models the number of filled receptors; and the term $(B - x_i)f(x_i)$ models how positive feedback fills the receptors through mass action. The term $-Ax_i$ models a process that passively empties filled receptors. The term $-x_i \sum_{k \neq i} f(x_k)$ models a process that actively empties filled receptors by mass action.

Grossberg showed that depending on the type of signal function, $f(w)$, the network transforms an initial set of activations $(x_1(0), x_2(0), ..., x_n(0))$ into different equilibrium activations $(x_1(\infty), x_2(\infty), ..., x_n(\infty))$. If $f(w)$ is faster than linear (i.e., $f(w) = wg(w)$ such that $g(w)$ is strictly increasing), then at equilibrium all activities except those with the largest initial activity equal zero. If only one cell has the largest activity the limiting distribution is called *0-1*, if more than one cell shares the largest activity, it is called *locally uniform*; the network is usually referred to as a choice network since it "chooses" to preserve the largest initial activity. When $f(w)$ is slower than linear (i.e., $f(w) = wg(w)$ such that $g(w)$ is strictly decreasing), then at equilibrium all activities are identical. Such a network produces a *uniform* distribution since the the limiting distribution ignores the initial differences between activities.

On the other hand, if $f(w)$ is a linear function (i.e., $f(w) = Cw$), then pattern variables $X_i(t) = x_i(t)/\sum_{j=1}^{n} x_j(t)$ remain constant for all time. That is, $X_i(t) = X_i(0)$ for all i and for all time t. Such a network produces a *fair* distribution since no activity loses its strength relative to other activities. Finally, Grossberg (1973) showed that when $f(w)$ was a sigmoid containing a linear part, the network parameters could be set so that some activities stay in the linear region and exhibit fair pattern storage, while the faster than linear region squashes smaller initial activities. This type of network removes weak activations (noise) and stores strong activations (signal). Significantly, if the sigmoid does not contain a linear part, each cell activity must converge to one of three values (Grossberg, 1973).

Grossberg (1973, 1982, 1987) uses networks with choice and fair limiting distributions (including those with sigmoid output functions) in many neural models. In particular, a network with a fair distribution stores any spatial pattern of initial activity for arbitrarily long lengths of time and therefore, acts as an ideal STM process.

Although Grossberg (1973) uses equation (1) to describe an on-center, off-surround shunting network, other architectures may have the same mathematical properties. For example, an on-center, off-surround network of cells with activities obeying the equations

$$\frac{dx_i}{dt} = -Ax_i + Bf(x_i) - x_i \sum_{k=1}^{n} f(x_k) \tag{2}$$

has additive excitation and shunting inhibition (Sperling & Sondhi, 1968) and is mathematically identical to equation (1). The following section describes generalized on-center, off-surround networks.

3 Adaptation level systems

The equations for an adaptation level system are:

$$\frac{dx_i}{dt} = a_i(x_1, x_2, ..., x_n)[b_i(x_i) - c(x_1, x_2, ..., x_n)], \tag{3}$$

where each self-excitation function $b_i(x_i)$ is compared to an inhibitory state-dependent adaptation level $c(\ )$. As a generalized on-center, off-surround network, $a_i(\ )b_i(x_i)$ is the on-center input and $a_i(\ )c(\ )$ is the off-surround input. With mild constraints on $a_i(\ )$ and $b_i(x_i)$ and by requiring the system to be competitive, $\partial c/\partial x_i > 0$, Grossberg (1978) proved that the system always approaches a stable fixed point in state space. Such strong stability properties are highly desirable because an adaptation level system will not undergo oscillations or chaotic behavior as it changes parameters. Grossberg (1988) and Hirsch (1989) review the stability of these and other neural networks.

Adaptation level systems include networks obeying equations (1, 2) as special cases by setting $a_i(\ ) = x_i$, $b_i(x_i) = f(x_i)/x_i$, and $c(\ ) = \sum_{k=1}^{n} f(x_k)$. Grossberg and his colleagues have investigated some variations of equation (1) in detail. Grossberg & Levine (1975) analyzed networks that obey equations of the form:

$$\frac{dx_i}{dt} = -Ax_i + (B_i - x_i)f(x_i) - x_i \sum_{j \neq i} f(x_j), \tag{4}$$

where each cell has a distinct carrying capacity B_i. When the output function $f(w)$ is linear, Grossberg & Levine (1975) found a closed-form solution for the equations and showed that only the cell (or cells) with the largest B_i parameter remained non-zero at equilibrium. For pattern storage, this result implies that slight deviations in carrying capacity across cells in the network of equation (1) destroy the network's ability to accurately store arbitrary spatial patterns for arbitrary lengths of time. Similar properties exist for many adaptation level systems, as the following theorem proves.

Theorem 1 (Generalization of Grossberg & Levine (1975), Theorem 7.) *If an adaptation level system defined by the equations*

$$\frac{dx_i}{dt} = x_i[B_i - c(x_1, x_2, ..., x_n)] \tag{5}$$

with an initial state $(x_1(0), x_2(0), ..., x_n(0))$, *has a non-zero, bounded limiting distribution and some* B_i *are different, then the nonzero values of* $x_i(\infty)$ *correspond to the equations with the largest* B_i *term.*

Proof: Without loss of generality assume all initial activities are positive. If $x_i(\infty) \neq 0 \neq x_j(\infty)$, then solving equation (5) with $dx_i(\infty)/dt = 0$ shows that $B_i = B_j$. Thus all nonzero limits have the same B_i term. To prove, by contradiction, that this term corresponds to the maximal B_i, suppose $B_i < B_j$ and $x_i(\infty) > 0 = x_j(\infty)$ so that $x_i(\infty)x_j^{-1}(\infty) = \infty$. Define variables

$$R_{ij}(t) = \ln\left(\frac{x_i(t)}{x_j(t)}\right), \tag{6}$$

and compute the change in $R_{ij}(t)$ over time as,

$$\frac{dR_{ij}}{dt} = B_i - B_j < 0, \tag{7}$$

which implies that $R_{ij}(\infty) < R_{ij}(0) < \infty$. But this contradicts $x_i(\infty)x_j^{-1}(\infty) = \infty$. Thus only the cells with the largest B_i can take nonzero activities in the limit. •

In the case studied by Grossberg & Levine (1975), the B_i terms in equation (4) correspond exactly to the B_i terms in equation (5). Theorem 1 generalizes their result by allowing $c(\ )$ to be any function that produces a limiting distribution.

Ellias & Grossberg (1975) investigated another variation of equation (1) of the form:

$$\frac{dx_i}{dt} = -Ax + (B - x_i)Cx_i - x_i \sum_{j \neq i} Dx_j, \tag{8}$$

where the on-center function Cw is different from the off-surround function Dw. When the two functions are identical, the network produces a fair limiting distribution. Ellias & Grossberg (1975) proved that when $C \neq D$, the network becomes either a choice network ($C < D$) or a uniformizing network ($C > D$). Thus small deviations in the cell output pathways destroy the network's ability to store a pattern of neural activity for arbitrary lengths of time. A similar theorem exists for some adaptation level systems.

Theorem 2 (Generalization of Ellias & Grossberg (1975), Theorem 1.) *If an adaptation level system defined by the equations*

$$\frac{dx_i}{dt} = x_i[b(x_i) - c(x_1, x_2, ..., x_n)] \tag{9}$$

with an initial state $(x_1(0), x_2(0), ..., x_n(0))$, *has a non-zero, bounded limiting distribution, then the following is true:*

(i) If $b(w)$ *is strictly increasing then the limiting distribution is 0-1 or locally uniform.*
(ii) If $b(w)$ *is strictly decreasing then the limiting distribution is uniform.*

(iii) If $b(w)$ is a constant then the limiting distribution is fair.

Proof: Without loss of generality assume that the initial activities are all positive and can be ordered as $x_1(0) \leq x_2(0) \leq ... \leq x_n(0)$. The network dynamics preserve this ordering since if $x_i(t) = x_j(t)$, then $dx_i/dt = dx_j/dt$. From equation (6)

$$\frac{dR_{ij}}{dt} = b(x_i) - b(x_j). \tag{10}$$

Note that due to the ordering property, dR_{ij}/dt never changes sign if $b(w)$ is monotone. When $|R_{ij}(\infty)| < \infty$ then $dR_{ij}(\infty)/dt = 0$, so at equilibrium $b(x_i) = b(x_j)$ and when $b(w)$ is strictly monotone $x_i(\infty) = x_j(\infty)$.

(i) Suppose $b(w)$ is strictly increasing and $x_n(0) > x_i(0)$. By equations (6) and (10), $R_{ni}(t)$ is positive and monotone increasing. To prove, by contradiction, that $R_{ni}(\infty) = \infty$, suppose $R_{ni}(\infty) < \infty$, and write it as $R_{ni}(\infty) = \ln(1+r)$, $0 < r < \infty$, and write

$$\lim_{t \to \infty} \left[\frac{x_n(t)}{x_i(t)} - e^{R_{ni}(\infty)} \right] = 0 \tag{11}$$

as

$$\lim_{t \to \infty} \frac{x_n(t) - x_i(t)}{x_i(t)} = r. \tag{12}$$

Now, if $0 < R_{ni}(\infty) < \infty$ then $x_n(\infty) - x_i(\infty) = 0$, so for the limit in equation (12) to be greater than zero, $x_i(\infty) = 0$ and then $x_n(\infty) = 0$ as well. But the theorem statement assumes $x_n(\infty) \neq 0$, thus it must be that $R_{ni}(\infty) = \infty$. Following the above argument, $r = \infty$ and $x_n(\infty) - x_i(\infty) > 0$ but bounded. Hence, $x_i(\infty) = 0$ and $x_n(\infty) > 0$. If there are m, $1 \leq m \leq n$, indices i such that $x_i(0) = x_n(0)$ then the limiting distribution is $0 - 1$ or locally uniform depending on whether $m = 1$ or $m > 1$.

(ii) Suppose $b(w)$ is strictly decreasing and $x_i(0) \geq x_j(0)$, then $dR_{ij}/dt < 0$ and $R_{ij}(0) \geq 0$. Hence, $R_{ij}(t)$ decreases to $R_{ij}(\infty) \geq 0$; in particular $|R_{ij}(\infty)| \leq |R_{ij}(0)| < \infty$. Therefore, $x_i(\infty) = x_j(\infty)$. This argument applies to all i, j so the limiting distribution is uniform.

(iii) Suppose $b(w)$ is a constant, then $dR_{ij}/dt = 0$, which implies $R_{ij}(t) = \ln(x_i(0)/x_j(0))$ for all time. Thus, $x_i(t)/x_j(t) = x_i(0)/x_j(0)$ for all time. Summing over i and inverting each term produces $X_j(t) = X_j(0)$. •

In the case studied by Ellias & Grossberg (1975) in equation (8), $b(w) = BC - A + (D - C)w$, which is strictly increasing if $C < D$ and is strictly decreasing if $C > D$. Application of Theorem 2 produces the results found by Ellias & Grossberg (1975). Theorem 2 also generalizes some of the proofs in Grossberg (1973).

The analysis of adaptation level systems suggests that the ability to store arbitrary spatial patterns of neural activity for arbitrarily long lengths of time is possible only for a small subset of adaptation level systems. In particular, perfect pattern storage is achieved only when the cell activities stay within a range where the on-center term $wb_i(w)$ is linear, and when all cells have the same parameters ($b_i(w) = b_j(w)$). Physically realistic networks, where the on-center functions are nonlinear or where they differ slightly across cells, lose perfect pattern storage. The following section bounds the rate of pattern degradation.

4   Dynamics of short-term pattern storage

In a biological neural system, each cell has unique parameters that determine the cell's activity. If the differential equations governing cell activities fit adaptation level system equations, the above theorems indicate that small differences in parameter values prevent the network from accurately storing a spatial pattern of activity for arbitrary lengths of time (to equilibrium).

As the Introduction indicates, however, the STM process only needs to store the neural code of an item long enough for long-term memory mechanisms to encode it. Thus, if the network dynamics do not degrade the spatial pattern of initial activity too much too quickly, the network can function as a STM process that meets the demands of the LTM process. The following theorem provides bounds on pattern degradation in some adaptation level systems.

Theorem 3 (Bounds on pattern change) *In an adaptation level system defined by:*

$$\frac{dx_i}{dt} = x_i[b_i(x_i) - c(x_1, x_2, ..., x_n)], \tag{13}$$

with an initial state $(x_1(0), x_2(0), ..., x_n(0))$, *let* $\gamma = \max_{i,x_i} b_i(x_i) - \min_{i,x_i} b_i(x_i)$. *Then any pattern variable* $X_j(t)$ *is bound by* $X_j(0)e^{\gamma t} \geq X_j(t) \geq X_j(0)e^{-\gamma t}$.

Proof: Define $R_{ij}(t)$ as above. Equation (10) becomes

$$\frac{dR_{ij}}{dt} = b_i(x_i) - b_j(x_j). \tag{14}$$

and it obeys the bounds:

$$-\gamma \leq \frac{dR_{ij}}{dt} \leq \gamma. \tag{15}$$

This implies that at time t the following bounds also hold:

$$-\gamma t + R_{ij}(0) \leq R_{ij}(t) \leq \gamma t + R_{ij}(0). \tag{16}$$

Taking the exponential of each term produces

$$\frac{x_i(0)}{x_j(0)} \exp(-\gamma t) \leq \frac{x_i(t)}{x_j(t)} \leq \frac{x_i(0)}{x_j(0)} \exp(\gamma t); \tag{17}$$

summing over index i, and inverting each term produces:

$$X_j(0) \exp(\gamma t) \geq X_j(t) \geq X_j(0) \exp(-\gamma t). \bullet \tag{18}$$

Thus, each pattern variable changes over time at a rate no faster than γ, which indicates deviations within the $b_i(x_i)$ terms either within a cell or between cells. Theorem 3 shows that if the network is not too deviant (γ small) from the special cases that exhibit perfect pattern storage ($\gamma = 0$), then the system provides good pattern storage for a long length of time. Note that this result holds even if the activities $x_i(t)$ change dramatically, as might occur if the network normalizes total activity (Grossberg, 1973).

5   Conclusions

The theorems in this paper characterize the short-term pattern storage properties of a large class of on-center, off-surround neural networks. In physically unrealistic special cases, such networks can store arbitrary spatial patterns of activity for arbitrarily long lengths of time. Physically realistic variations on these special cases have weaker storage properties that exhibit pattern degradation. Networks with small deviations from the special cases can store arbitrary spatial patterns of activity with little degradation for long lengths of time. Such networks may be able to act as STM processes that satisfy the requirements of learning systems in a real-time environment.

References

[1] Anderson, J., Silverstein, J., Ritz, S., & Jones, R. (1977). Distinctive features, categorical perception, and probability learning: Some applications of a neural model. *Psychological Review, 84*, 413-451.

[2] Carpenter, G. & Grossberg, S. (1987). A massively parallel architecture for a self-organizing neural pattern recognition machine. *Computer vision, graphics and image processing, 37*, 59-115.

[3] Ellias, S. & Grossberg, S. (1975). Pattern formation, contrast control, and oscillations in the short term memory of shunting on-center off-surround networks. *Biological Cybernetics, 20*, 69-98.

[4] Grossberg, S. (1968). Some nonlinear networks capable of learning a spatial pattern of arbitrary complexity. *Proceedings of the National Academy of Sciences, 59*, 368-372.

[5] Grossberg, S. (1973). Contour enhancement, short term memory, and constancies in reverberating neural networks. *Studies in Applied Mathematics, LII*, 213-257.

[6] Grossberg, S. (1978). Competition, decision, and consensus. *Journal of Mathematical Analysis and Applications, 66*, 470-493.

[7] Grossberg, S. (1982). A psychophysiological theory of reinforcement, drive, motivation, and attention. *Journal of Theoretical Neurobiology, 1*, 268-369.

[8] Grossberg, S. (1987). Competitive learning: From interactive activation to adaptive resonance. *Cognitive Science, 11*, 23-63.

[9] Grossberg, S. (1988). Nonlinear neural networks: Principles, mechanisms, and architectures. *Neural Networks, 1*, 17-61.

[10] Grossberg, S. & Levine, D. (1975). Some developmental and attentional biases in the contrast enhancement and short term memory of recurrent neural networks. *Journal of Theoretical Biology, B53*, 341-380.

[11] Hirsch, M. (1989). Convergent activation dynamics in continuous time networks. *Neural Networks, 2*, 331-349.

[12] Hopfield, J. (1982). Neural networks and physical systems with emergent collective computation abilities. *Proceedings of the National Academy of Sciences, 78*, 2554-2558.

[13] McClelland, J. & Rumelhart, D. (1981). An interactive activation model of context effects in letter perception: Part 1. An account of basic findings. *Psychological Review, 88*, 375-407.

[14] Sperling, G. & Sondhi, M. (1968). Model for visual luminance discrimination and flicker detection. *Journal of the Optical Society of America, 58*, 1133-1145.

Study on the Kinds of Training Difficulty in Feedforward Neural Networks

Xun Liang[2,1]   and Shaowei Xia[1]

1. *Department of Automation, Tsinghua University, Beijing 100084, P.R.China*
2. *Computer Research Center, Peking University, Beijing 100871, P.R.China*

Abstract: Training difficulty in feedforward neural networks has been studied since the resurge of the Back Propagation technique. By a new way in which symmetry group and Pólya Theorem are used, this paper discusses how many different kinds of training difficulty (DKTD) are there to the maximum if the training patterns are binary. The results for the case of $N \leqslant 3$ are given where N is the dimension of input patterns. We find that the above numbers are much smaller than those we usually think intuitively and the ratios of them decrease greatly as N increases, i.e., 0.444, 0.1605, 0.0236 $\cdots$.
Key Words: Feedforward neural networks, training sets, different kinds of training difficulty

1. Introduction

In feedforward neural networks, we assume that the training pattern pairs are binary and let the input dimension be N and the output dimension be 1. Thus in the input space, there are 2^N vertices. Each vertex can be valued 0 or 1 or -1, where 0, 1 and -1 are the output pattern values in the training pattern pairs, and -1 denotes that there is no this pattern pair. Thus it seems that there exsit 3^{2^N} kinds of training difficulty (see Fig.1). But, two "different" kinds of training difficulty may be identified with each other after one training set "rotates" in the N dimensional space (see Fig.1(c) and (g), or (f) and (h); also see Fig.2(c)$\sim$ (f), or (g)$\sim$ (j)). That is to say, in the 3^{2^N} kinds of training difficulty, some are the same in the meaning of rotation. Hence the number of DKTD is less than 3^{2^N}. So in Section 3, the DKTD for the case of $N = 1$ and 2 are discussed, both intuitively and mathematically, and the two methods lead to the same results. In Section 4, we deduce the DKTD for the case of $N = 3$ only mathematically since it is hard to enumerate the DKTD intuitively. In order to be read conveniently, Section 2 gives some mathematical preparations about symmetry groups (Weissbluth, 1978; Elliot & Dawber, 1979) and Pólya Theorem (Pólya, 1937; Graver & Warkins, 1977; Pólya & Read, 1987). Finally, Section 5 summarizes the whole paper and suggests the further work.

2. Mathematical Preparation

2.1. Point Group and Symmetry Operations

In Section 3 and 4, point group and symmetry operations will be used. Hence in this section, they will be reviewed briefly.

A point group is defined as a group consisting of elements whose axes and planes of symmetry have at least one common point of intersection. All possible symmetry operations for point groups can be represented as a combination of (a) a rotation through a definite angle about some axes and (b) a reflection in some planes.

There are the following symmetry operations which will be used in Section 3 and 4.

E :   identity transformation.

C_n :   a rotation through an angle $\dfrac{2\pi}{n}$ about a given axis; $n = 1,2,3, \cdots$. When $n = 1$, the angle of rotation is 2π (or 0) which is simply an identity transformation E. C_n^2, C_n^3, $\cdots$ are rotations through $2(\frac{2\pi}{n})$, $3(\frac{2\pi}{n})$, $\cdots$. Also, $C_n^n = E$.

σ : reflection in a plane, $\sigma^2 = E$.

2.2. Pólya Theorem

Here the formation of Pólya Theorem is changed for applying conveniently to working out the DKTD.

Let $G = \{a_1, ..., a_g\}$ be the permutation group operating on the p vertices. If these vertices are painted in q colors, then the different coloring schemes are:

$$\frac{1}{|G|} \sum_{i \in G} \prod_{j=1}^{p} (\sum_{k=1}^{q} b_k^j)^{d_j(a_i)} ,$$

where

b_k is the kth color,

$d_j(a_i)$ is the repetend number which is equal to j with regard to

the permutation a_i, $i \in G$.   □

3. Different Kinds of Training Difficulty for the Case of $N = 1$ and 2

Since the purpose of training is to find some hyperplanes to separate the input training patterns which belong to different classes (i.e., output patterns 0 or 1). From this standpoint, there is no difference while we are training the training pattern sets which can become the same by rotation operation or can be identified with each other if 0 and 1 are exchanged in one set.

For the case of $N = 1$, obviously the training sets shown in Fig.1(b) and (d), or (a) and (e) have the same training difficulty, and training (a) is easier than training (b) since the separated hyperplane in (a) is easier to be found than does in (b). Therefore we obtain that the number of DKTD for the case of $N = 1$ is 4 (see Fig.3).

For the case of $N = 2$, by the rotation whose axis is perpendicular to the paper plane and through the center of the square, Fig.2(a) can become (b), so do the (c)$\sim$(f) and (g)$\sim$(j). Besides rotation, inversion, reflection and rotary reflection are also operations on the training sets which can lead to finding the same kind of training difficulty. These point operations will be seen more clearly in the case of $N = 3$, and in fact compose O_h group in the theory of symmetry group. In addition, in the situation of this paper, if 0 and 1 are exchanged in one training set, which results in that it becomes another, we should also consider that the training difficulty of the two sets are the same. For example, Fig.2(c) and (g) should be the same kind, which results in that (c)$\sim$(j) have the same training difficulty. Therefore, we obtain that there are 13 DKTD (see Fig.4) for the case of $N = 2$ rather than $3^{2^2} = 81$.

In the above, we achieved 4 and 13 intuitively. Now we calculate the two numbers mathematically by symmetry operations and Pólya Theorem.

To work out the number of DKTD, we have to obtain the concrecte coloring schemes; then consider that the two sets are the same if exchanging 0 and 1 in one set results in that it becomes another; finally enumerate the coefficients of the terms in the polynomial to achieve the number of DKTD.

For the case of $N = 1$ (see Fig.5), there are operations E and σ which can also be expressed by the permutations (1)(2) and (1 2) because both groups are isomorphic, provided that we assign the two vertices the numbers 1 and 2 repectively. It follows that these operations can be represented by the formations $(1)^2$ and $(2)^1$ respectively, where in $(u)^v$, u is the repetend length and v the repetend number which is equal to u.

Denote 0 by b (blue), 1 by r (red), -1 by y (yellow), and we have the following coloring schemes:

$$\frac{1}{2} [(r+b+y)^2 + (r^2+b^2+y^2)] = (r^2+b^2+y^2) + (br+ry+by).$$

We regard r as b, remove the repeated terms, and have: $(b^2+y^2)+(br+by)$,
where b^2 represents that the two vertices are all valued 0, y^2 represents that the two vertices are all no pattern pair, br represents that one vertex is valued 0 and one valued 1, by represents that one vertex is valued 0 and one has no pattern pair (see Fig.3).

We enumerate the coefficients of the above polynomial and also obtain that the number of DKTD is 4 for the case of $N=1$.

For the case of $N=2$ (see Fig.6), there are operations E, $2C_4$, C_2, $2\sigma_1$, $2\sigma_2$, where σ_1 is a plane through the middle points of the two opposite edges of the square, σ_2 is a plane through the two opposite vertices of the square. They are also denoted by the permutations:

one (1)(2)(3)(4), two (1 2 3 4), one (1 3)(2 4), two (1 4)(2 3), two (1)(3)(2 4).

These operations can be represented by the formations:

one $(1)^4$, two $(4)^1$, three $(2)^2$, two $(1)^2(2)^1$.

Hence the coloring schemes are:

$$\frac{1}{8} [(r+b+y)^4 + 2(y^4+b^4+r^4) + 3(r^2+b^2+y^2)^2 + 2(y+b+r)^2(y^2+b^2+r^2)]$$

$$= (y^4+b^4+r^4) + 2(b^2y^2+y^2r^2+b^2r^2) + (by^3+y^3r+b^3r+r^3b+r^3y+b^3y)$$

$$+ 2(bry^2+yrb^2+byr^2).$$

We regard r as b, remove the repeated terms, and have:

$$(y^4+b^4) + 2(b^2y^2+b^2r^2) + (by^3+b^3r+b^3y) + 2(bry^2+yrb^2).$$

We enumerate the coefficients of the polynomial and also obtain that the number of DKTD is 13 for the case of $N=2$.

4. Different Kinds of Training Difficulty for the Case of $N=3$

It is very complex to enumerate the DKTD for the case of $N=3$ intuitively because the symmetry group is not so evident at this time as before. Therefore we apply the symmetry group theory and Pólya Theorem.

First of all, we briefly review groups O and O_h (Weissbluth, 1978; Elliot & Dawber, 1979).

O group is the symmetry group of proper rotations of a cube. There are 24 elements in O group (see Fig.7).

E : identity.
$8C_3$: rotations of $\pm 120°$ about the four body diagonals.
$3C_2$: rotations of $\pm 180°$ about the C_2.
$6C'_2$: rotations of $\pm 180°$ about the six axes C'_2.
$6C_4$: rotations of $\pm 90°$ about the C_4.

Group O_h is the full symmetry group of the cube. It is composed of the elements of O plus those obtained by multiplication with I. The 48 elements are E, $8C_3$, $3C_2$, $6C'_2$, $6C_4$, I, $8S_6$, $3\sigma_h$, $6\sigma_v$, $6S_4$, where

σ_h : reflection in a horizontal plane which is through the middle points of opposite four edges of the cube and perpendicular to the C_4(see Fig.8);

σ_v : reflection in a vertical plane which is containing the opposite edges of the cube (see Fig.8);

I : inversion in the origin;

S_n : rotary reflection. This is a rotation through an angle of $\dfrac{2\pi}{n}$ together with reflection in a plane perpendicular to the axis. S_n is also called an improper rotation. $S_2 = I$, $S_n = C_n\sigma_h = \sigma_h C_n$; also $I\sigma_h = C_2$, $IC_2 = \sigma_h$.

We note that σ_h and C_n commute; other operations that commute are two rotations about the same axis, two reflections in percendicular planes.

Thus, we know that the formations of the operations are:
one $(1)^8$, eight $(1)^2(3)^4$, three $(2)^4$, six $(2)^4$, six $(4)^2$,
one $(2)^4$, eight $(2)^1(6)^1$, three $(2)^4$, six $(1)^4(2)^2$, six $(4)^2$.

Finally, we calculate the number of DKTD for the case of $N = 3$.

From the above, the schemes are obtained as follows:

$$\frac{1}{48}\,[(b+r+y)^8 + 8(b+r+y)^2(b^3+r^3+y^3)^2 + 13(b^2+r^2+y^2)^4$$

$$+ 12(b^4+r^4+y^4)^2 + 6(b+r+y)^4(b^2+r^2+y^2)^2 + 8(b^2+r^2+y^2)(b^6+r^6+y^6)]$$

$$= [(y^8 + b^8 + r^8) + (y^7b + y^7r + b^7r + b^7y + r^7y + r^7b)$$

$$+ 3(b^2y^6 + r^2y^6 + y^2r^6 + b^2r^6 + y^2b^6 + r^2b^6)$$

$$+ 3(b^3y^5 + r^3y^5 + y^3r^5 + b^3r^5 + y^3b^5 + r^3b^5)$$

$$+ 6(b^4y^4 + b^4r^4 + y^4r^4)] + [3(br^6y + b^6ry + bry^6)$$

$$+ 6(br^2y^5 + rb^2y^5 + yr^2b^5 + ry^2b^5 + yb^2r^5 + by^2r^5)$$

$$+ 10(br^3y^4 + rb^3y^4 + ry^3b^4 + yr^3b^4 + yb^3r^4 + by^3r^4)$$

$$+ 16(b^2r^2y^4 + b^2y^2r^4 + y^2r^2b^4) + 17(b^3r^3y^2 + b^3y^3r^2 + y^3r^3b^2)].$$

We regard r as b , remove the repeated ones, and have:

$$[(y^8 + b^8) + (y^7b + b^7r + b^7r) + 3(b^2y^6 + y^2b^6 + r^2b^6) + 3(b^3y^5 + y^3b^5 + r^3b^5)$$

$$+ 6(b^4y^4 + b^4r^4)] + [3(br^6y + bry^6) + 6(rb^2y^5 + ry^2b^5 + yr^2b^5)$$

$$+ 10(rb^3y^4 + ry^3b^4 + yr^3b^4) + 16(b^2r^2y^4 + y^2r^2b^4) + 17(b^3y^3r^2 + y^2r^3b^3)].$$

We enumerate the coefficients of the polynomial and obtain that the number of DKTD is 155 for the case of $N = 3$.

5. Conclusions and Further Work

In this paper, a new method of estimating the number of different kinds of training difficulty for the case of $N = 1,2,3$ is given, under the condition that the input dimension is N and output dimension is 1. These results can be easily extended to the multi−output cases. The achieved numbers are much smaller than those we usually think intuitively, and the ratioes decrease greatly as N increases. In summary, we have Table 1.

Unfortunately, we can only give the results for the case of $N \leqslant 3$, which means that it is far from the engineering applications. Therefore further work includes working out the number of different kinds of training difficulty for the case of $N \geqslant 4$ and clarifying further applied meanings in practice.

N	1	2	3	4	5	...
3^{2^N}	9	81	6561	43046721	1853020188851841	...
L	4	13	155	...	...	...
$\dfrac{L}{3^{2^N}}$	0.4444	0.1605	0.0236	...	...	...

Table 1. Summary of the numbers of different kinds of training difficulty. The ratios of those numbers to those we usually think intuitively decrease greatly as N increases.

Acknowledgements

This work was supported by Laboratory of Management, Decision and Information Systems, Academia Sinica and National Nature Science Foundation 69375003. Thanks are also owed to Ms. J. Xie for drawing all the figures.

References

Elliott, J. P. & Dawber, G. P. (1979). *Symmetry in Pgysics*. London: The Macmillan Press Ltd.

Graver, J. E. & Watkins, M. E. (1977). *Combinatorics with Emphasis on the on the Theory of Graphs*. New York: Springer–Verlag.

Pólya, G. (1937). Kombinatorische anzahlbestimmunge für gruppen, graphen und chemische verbindungen. *Acta Math*. vol.68, pp.145–254.

Pólya, G. & Read, R. C. (1987). *Combinatorial Enumeration of Groups, Graphs, and Chemical Compounds*. New York: Springer–Verlag.

Weissbluth, M. (1978). *Atoms and Molecules*. London: Academic Press.

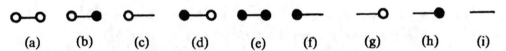

Fig.1. All the nine training pattern sets for the case of $N = 1$, where $\bigcirc$ denotes 0, $\bullet$ denotes 1, neither $\bigcirc$ nor $\bullet$ denotes that there is no this pattern pair in the training pattern set. Hence (a) denotes the training patterns set {(0,0), (1,0)}; (b) denotes {(0,0), (1,1)}; (c) denotes {(0,0)}; (d) denotes {(0,1), (1,0)}; (i) denotes φ; etc.

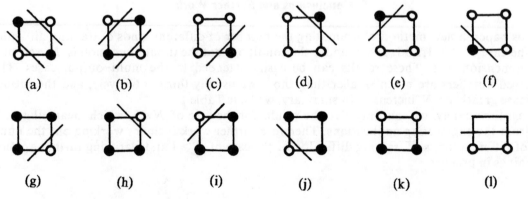

Fig.2. Some examples of different or identical kinds of training difficulty.

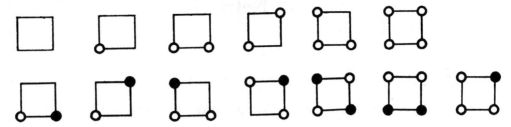

Fig.3. Different kinds of training difficulty for the case of $N = 1$.

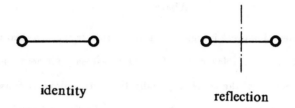

Fig.4. Different kinds of training difficulty for the case of $N = 2$.

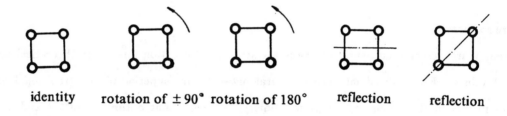

identity   reflection

Fig.5. Symmetry group for the case of $N = 1$.

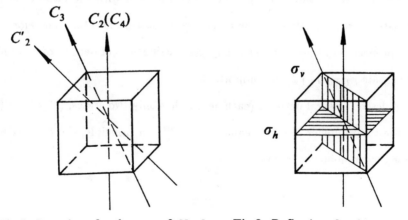

identity   rotation of $\pm 90°$ rotation of $180°$ reflection   reflection

Fig.6. Symmetry group for the case of $N = 2$.

Fig.7. Rotations for the case of $N = 3$.   Fig.8. Reflections for the case of $N = 3$.

On The Properties of The State Space of Discrete Neural Network

Zhang Cheng-fu

Department of Physics, Peking University, Beijing 100871, China

Abstract

The state space of neural network is high dimensional descrete space, a clear understanding of the space and simple formulas of relevant calculation are nescesary for neural network research. In this paper, the properties of the space, especially the distributions of density of state $\rho(x)$ and conditional density of state $\rho_2(x_0, x_1 \mid x)$, are discussed. Simple formulas to calculate the volume of sphere, shell, basin attraction and etc. are given in the paper.

1.Introduction

Recent years, research on neural networks attracts much attention due to its theoretical and practical values. For artificial inteligence, neural networks are superior to the traditional approaches mainly in three aspects: associate memory[1-3], constraint optimization[4-5] and non-linear mapping[6]. In all of these aspects, the key points are fault-tolerance, generalization and the probability to find some given states. They are closely connected with the basin of attraction, the distribution of state densities relative to one or two given states and etc.. Therefore, a clear understanding of the properties of the space, especially the distributions of density of state $\rho(x)$ and conditional density of state $\rho_2(x_0, x_1 \mid x)$, are important.

The state space of descrete neural network (each neuron has only two states, (-1,+1) or (0,1)) is descrete and finite, the total number of states equals $\Omega_0 = 2^N$. In principle, the properties of the space can be expressed by combination number

$$C_N^{\ddot{} } \equiv \frac{N!}{(N - d)!d!} \tag{1}$$

and its summation and/or multiplication. For example, for a given attractor the basin of attraction is

$$B_s = \sum_{d=1}^{N} P(d)C_N^d. \tag{2}$$

Here $P(d)$ is the probability of the states (with Hamming distance d) which belong to the basin. $P(d)$ could be determined thoretically or by numerical sampling. But practically, the numerical calculation is very difficult because: 1. For large N, C_N^d is a huge number. 2. C_N^d is a steeply increased function of d. 3. The terms of summation is large.

In this paper, we'll show that the distribution of state densities, the volume of sphere, shell, basin and etc. can be calculated simply. Based on the formulas, the properties of the state space are analysed and discussed clearly.

2. The density of state and the volume of sphere

Given a state, the number of states which apart from the state with Hamming distance d, equals the number of combination C_N^d. The volume of sphere with radius d, i.e. the total number of states which apart from the given state $\leq d$, is given by the summation of C_N^i

$$V(d) = \sum_{i=0}^{d} C_N^i \tag{3}$$

As mentioned above, in fact the calculation of $V(d)$ is difficult. We take following procedures to simplify the calculation and to show the distribution of density of state clearly.

First, all quantities are expressed by reduced ones. The number of states is normarized by the total number of space $\Omega_0 = V(N) = 2^N$. For large network, Ω_0 is a huge number (e.g. if N=100, $\Omega_0 \approx 2^{30}$). Therefore, there are often the cases that the absolute number of states or the basin of attraction are very large but in fact the efficiencies of the networks are extremely small. The reduced volume of sphere or basin of attraction not only reflects the efficiency of the network but also shows the probability to find the sphere or the basin starting from random initial condition. The distance is reduced by N, i.e. $x = d/N$. The reduced volume of sphere is

$$V(x) = \frac{1}{\Omega_0} \sum_{i=0}^{Nx} C_N^i.$$
$$V(1) = 1.$$

Second, for large m, the factorial $m!$ can be expressed by Stirling formula, neglect the terms of $o(1/m)$, we have[7]

$$m! \approx S(m) = \sqrt{2\pi m} m^m \exp\{-m\}. \tag{4}$$

In fact S(m) is a good approximation only if $m \geq 1$ as shown in Tab.1.

Table 1.

m	1	2	3	$\cdots$	10
$\dfrac{S(m)}{m!}$	0.922	0.960	0.973	$\cdots$	0.992

With equation (4), the number of combination can be expressed as

$$C_N^d \approx C(N,x) = \frac{1}{\sqrt{2\pi N x(1-x)}}(1-x)^{-N}(x^{-1}-1)^{Nx}. \tag{5}$$

Tab.2 shows that the difference between C_N^{Nx} and $C(N,x)$ is small only if $x \geq 1/N$ (i.e. $d \geq 1$). In the following we know that the main contribution of volume is come from larger x, therefore equation (5) is a very good approximation.

Table 2.

x	1/N	2/N	3/N	4/N	$\cdots$
$\dfrac{C(N,x)}{C_N^{Nx}}$	1.084	1.042	1.029	1.021	$\cdots$

Thirdly, for large N, the descreteness of x is unimportant. We take x as a continue number, the summation is substituted by integration, i.e.

$$\sum_{i=1}^{d} \rightarrow N \int_{1/N}^{d/N} dx$$

Therefore the volume of sphere is

$$V(x) = \int_{1/N}^{x} \rho(x')dx'.$$

$$\rho(x) = \frac{N}{\Omega_0}C(N,x) = \sqrt{\frac{N}{2\pi x(1-x)}}2^{-N}(1-x)^{-N}(x^{-1}-1)^{Nx}. \tag{6}$$

Here $\rho(x)$ is the reduced density of states. From the definitions of $\rho(x)$ and $V(x)$, it is shown clearly that they have following simple properties:

1. $\rho(x) = \rho(1-x)$ because $C_N^d = C_N^{N-d}$.

2. $V(0.5) = 0.5$, $V(1) = 1$.

3. $V(0.5+y) = 1 - V(0.5-y)$.

Therefore in the following it is enough to restrict the regine of x as $N^{-1} \leq x \leq 0.5$.

To show the properties of $\rho(x)$ clearly, equation (6) can be expressed as

$$\rho(x) = \sqrt{N} a(x) \exp\{-N b(x)\}. \tag{7}$$

Here

$$a(x) = \frac{1}{\sqrt{2\pi x(1-x)}}.$$
$$b(x) = \ln 2(1-x) - x \ln(x^{-1} - 1). \tag{8}$$

The variations of a(x) and b(x) with x are shown in Fig.1, it is shown that except the point of x=0 (in the point a(x) approaches infinity), they are *normal* monotonous decendent functions, i.e. the variations of a(x) and b(x) are small if dx is small, the Taylor expansion is available for them. This is very important in the following calculations.

But for large N, $\rho(x)$ is a very steeply increased function of x, it increases with x exponentially, while x=0.5 it approaches maximum value $\rho(0.5) = \sqrt{2N/\pi}$.

The behavior of $\rho(x)$ near x=0.5 can be obtained as following. Let $x = 0.5 + y$ with $y \ll 1$, make Taylor expasion of a(0.5+y) and b(0.5+y) and keep to y^2 terms, we have

$$\rho(0.5 \pm y) = \frac{1}{\sqrt{2\pi \Delta_c^2(1 - 4y^2)}} \exp\{-\frac{y^2}{2\Delta_c^2}\}. \tag{9}$$

Here $\Delta_c = \frac{1}{2\sqrt{N}}$. It means that $\rho(x)$ is approximately Gaussian around x=0.5 with width $\Delta_c \sim 1/\sqrt{N} \ll 1$. The larger the N, the narrower the width. Almost all of the states are concentrated in the thin layer of width $\sim \frac{1}{\sqrt{N}}$ near x=0.5. Apart from the layer, the $\rho(x)$ is exponentially small.

The fast variation of $\rho(x)$ with x in the region of $x < 0.5$ can be seen as following. Let

$$\rho(x + \delta x) = 2\rho(x). \tag{10}$$

Direct expansion of $\rho(x + \delta x)$ is impossible but the Taylor expansion of a(x) and b(x) is possible. Due to Eqs.(7) and (8), we have

$$\delta x = D(x)/N.$$
$$D(x) = \frac{\ln 2}{\ln(x^{-1} - 1)}. \tag{11}$$

The variation of D(x) with x is shown in Fig.2, it is a number of order of one. Therefore $\rho(x)$ double its value within a small range $\delta x \sim 1/N \ll 1$.

Due to the fast variation of $\rho(x)$, the usual numerical integration involving $\rho(x)$ is difficult. A slmple method to calculate the volume of sphere or shell is nescesary.

For calculation the volume of sphere, let

$$V(x) = \int_{1/N}^{x} \rho(x')dx' = \rho(x)\Delta_B(x). \tag{12}$$

Differentiate equation (12), we got the equation of $\Delta_B(x)$

$$\frac{dV(x)}{dx} = \rho(x) = \frac{\rho(x)}{dx}\Delta_B(x) + \rho(x)\frac{\Delta_B(x)}{dx}. \tag{13}$$

Substitute into equation (7), we have

$$\frac{\Delta_B(x)}{dx} + N\Delta_B(x)\left[\ln(x^{-1} - 1) + \frac{2x - 1}{Nx(1 - x)}\right] = 1. \tag{14}$$

For large N, the second term in bracket can be neglected. If $|\frac{d\Delta_B}{dx}| \ll 1$, the first term in equation (14) also can be neglected, therefore we have

$$\Delta_B(x) = [N\ln(x^{-1} - 1)]^{-1}. \tag{15}$$

For check the condition, we have

$$\frac{d\Delta_B(x)}{dx} = \frac{E(x)}{N}. \tag{16}$$

Here $E(x) = [x(1-x)]^{-1}[\ln(x^{-1} - 1)]^{-2}$, its variation with x is given in Fig.2. It shown that for large N and $x \leq 0.4$, the condition of $|\frac{d\Delta_B}{dx}| \ll 1$ is satisfied. Therefore the volume of sphere is simply given by Eqs.(12) and (15). It means that the volume of sphere of radius x is almost concentrated in the thin outer layer, the width of the layer equals $\Delta_B(x) \sim 1/N \ll 1$, the inner regine of the sphere is *almost empty* . This property is quite similar with the one of high dimensional Euclidian space. The volume of sphere in Euclidian space is $V_E(r) = C_N r^N$, i.e.

$$V_E(r) = \int_0^r \rho(r')dr' = \rho(r)\Delta_E(r).$$

$$\rho(r) = C_N N r^{N-1},$$

$$\Delta_E(r) = r/N \propto 1/N. \tag{17}$$

Compared with the descrete space, $\Delta_B(x)/\Delta_E(x) = F(x) = [x\ln(x^{-1} - 1)]^{-1}$, it is a slow varied function of x and $F(x) \sim 3.6 - 6.8$ as shown in Fig.2.

As for the sphere volume of x near 0.5, let $x = 0.5 - y$, $y \ll 1$, from equation (9) we have

$$V(x) = V(0.5) - \int_x^{0.5} \rho(x')dx' = 0.5 - \int_0^y \rho(0.5 - y')dy' = [1 - erf(\frac{y}{\sqrt{2}\Delta_c})]/2. \tag{18}$$

Here erf(x) is the error function.

3. The calculation of basin of attraction

The basin of attraction of any given attractors of neural network (reduced by Ω_0) is given by

$$V_B = \int_{1/N}^{x_0} P(x)\rho(x)dx. \tag{19}$$

Here $P(x)$ is the probability with which the states of distance x belong to the attractor. Usually $P(x)$ is a slow varied function of x, and can be estimated theoretically or numerically. The upper limit of integration x_0 is determined by $P(x_0) \approx 0$. Usually we have $x_0 < 0.5$.

Owing to the fast variation of $\rho(x)$, the direct integration of (19) is difficult. Noticing the slow variation of $P(x)$, equation (19) can be expressed by summation of finite terms. Separate the sphere into n shells, x_i, $i = 1, 2, \cdots, n$, $x_1 = 1/N, x_n = x_0$. Therefore

$$V_B = \sum_{i=1}^{n-1} P(x_i)V_s(x_i, x_{i+1}). \tag{20}$$

Here $V_s(x_i, x_{i+1})$ is volume of the shell from x_i to x_{i+1}, it equals

$$V_s(x_i, x_{i+1}) = V(x_{i+1}) - V(x_i) = \rho(x_{i+1})\Delta_B(x_{i+1}) - \rho(x_i)\Delta_B(x_i). \tag{21}$$

Substitute (21) into (20), we have

$$V_B = \sum_{i=1}^{n-1} [P(x_i) - P(x_{i+1})]V(x_i). \tag{22}$$

Owing to $V(x_i)$ increases with x_i exponentially, the main contribution of V_B come from the tail part of $P(x)$ (but $P(x) > 0$).

It should be pointed out that, for convenience of calculation, the statistics theory of neural network often assumes thermodynamical limit case, i.e. $N \to \infty, M/N$ is finite (here M is the number of storage samples). Theoretical calculation shows that each sample attractor has finite radius of attraction R. It means that the sample attractors have fairly large basins of attraction. But as discussed above, if $x_0 < 0.5$ (by definition, $R = 2x_0$, i.e. $R < 1$, it is always the case), the sphere volume is exponentially small. Therefore the reduced basin of attraction of sample attractor, or the efficiency of network, is exponentially small. The larger the N, the lower the efficiency. For simple estimate, assume $P(x) = 1$ if $x \leq x_0$ and otherwise $P(x) = 0$. Therefore

$$V_B = \rho(x_0)\Delta_B(x_0) = \frac{a(x_0)}{\sqrt{N}\ln{(x_0^{-1} - 1)}} \exp\{-Nb(x_0)\}. \qquad (23)$$

For example, according the paper of Krauth et al[8], as $\alpha = M/N = 0.5$, the radius of attraction $R \approx 0.2$, i.e. $x_0 \approx 0.1$, the total basins of attraction (reduced by Ω_0) of sample attractors MV_B are given in Table 3. It shows that the sample attractors and its basins only occupy a tiny minority of state space, there are exponentially large number of spurious attractors and almost all of space is occupied by them and its basins. Therefore, from the point of view of practical purpose, unnescesary increasing the scale of network is uneconomic.

Table 3.

N	50	100	200	500
MV_B	4.3×10^{-10}	3.4×10^{-18}	2.3×10^{-34}	1.6×10^{-82}

4. The conditional density of state

In practical application, it is often useful to know some conditional density of state, e.g. the density of state relative two given states. Given two states A and B, the distance between them is d_0, what is the distribution of states which distance with A is d_1 (fixed) and the distance with B is d (variable)? This is the definition of $\rho_2(x_0, x_1 \mid x)$. Here $x_0 = d_0/N$, $x_1 = d_1/N$, $x = d/N$ are reduced distances, x_0 and x_1 are as parameters, x is as variable. In the following we deduce the explicit expression of ρ_2 and discuss its properties.

Separate the N neurons into two subset $(d_0, N - d_0)$. The first subset consists of the neurons which states are same for A and B, the second subset consists of the neurons which states are different for A and B. A new state can be constructed as following: starting from state A, flip n_1 neurons of first subset and flip n_2 neurons of second subset. The n_1 and n_2 should satisfy following conditions

$$n_1 + n_2 = d_1.$$

$$(d_0 - n_1) + n_2 = d. \qquad (24)$$

Therefore we have

$$n_1 = \frac{1}{2}(d_0 + d_1 - d),$$

$$n_2 = \frac{1}{2}(d + d_1 - d_0). \tag{25}$$

From the condition $d_0 \geq n_1 \geq 0$ and $N - d_0 \geq n_2 \geq 0$, we know that d_0, d_1 and d must satisfy following conditions:

$$d_0 + d_1 \geq d \geq |d_0 - d_1|,$$

$$d_0 + d_1 + d \leq 2N.$$

Therefore, the reduced conditional density of state can be expressed as

$$\rho_2(x_0, x_1 \mid x) = \frac{N}{\Omega_0} C_{d_0}^{n_1} C_{N-d_0}^{N_2}. \tag{26}$$

Combined with (7),(8) and (25), we have

$$\rho_2(x_0, x_1 \mid x) = a(X_1)a(X_2) \exp\{-NB(x)\}. \tag{27}$$

here

$$X_1 = (x_0 + x_1 - x)/2x_0,$$

$$X_2 = (x + x_1 - x_0)/2(1 - x_0),$$

$$B(x) = x_0 b(X_1) + (1 - x_0)b(X_2). \tag{28}$$

It shows that $\rho_2(x)$ is also a steeply varied function of x. The location of maximum $\rho_2(x)$ is determined by equation $\frac{dB(x)}{dx} = 0$. It gives that as $x = x_m = x_0 + x_1 - 2x_0 x_1$ (while $X_1 = X_2 = x_1$), $\rho_2(x)$ approaches maximum

$$\rho_2(x_0, x_1 \mid x_m) = \frac{1}{2\pi x_1(1 - x_1)} exp\{-Nb(x_1)\} = \frac{1}{\sqrt{2\pi x_1(1 - x_1)}} \rho(x_1). \tag{29}$$

Now lets calculate the distribution of ρ_2 near the x_m. Let $x = x_m + y$, $|y| \ll 1$, make Taylor expansion of $B(x_m + y)$ for y and keep to y^2 terms, it gives

$$\rho_2(x_0, x_1 \mid x_m + y) = \frac{1}{\sqrt{2\pi x_1(1 - x_1)}} \exp\{-\frac{y^2}{2\Delta_2^2}\} \rho(x_1). \tag{30}$$

Here

$$\Delta_2 = \sqrt{\frac{4x_0(1 - x_0)x_1(1 - x_1)}{N}} \sim \frac{1}{\sqrt{N}} \ll 1.$$

It means that around x_m, $\rho_2(x)$ is Gaussian with width Δ_2, apart from the regine, $\rho_2(x)$ is exponentially small.

If $0 \leq x_0, x_1 \leq 0.5$, then the position x_m of maximum ρ_2 satisfies

$$0.5 \geq x_m \geq max(x_0, x_1). \tag{31}$$

As a sample of possible application of above properties, we discuss the selection of initial condition of TSP (the Traveling Salesman Problem)[4,5]. For descrete TSP network of n-cities, $N = n^2$, the distances of all states of tour (include the shortest tour) from the state $(0,0,\cdots,0)$ are $x_0 = n/N = 1/n$. If we select initial condition randomly, i.e. $x_1 \approx 0.5$, therefore the distance between initial state and the tour state is most possibly $x \approx x_m = 0.5$. It is very difficult to enter the tour state because it requires the tour attractor has a very large basin of attraction. If we select the initial condition randomly but with restriction $x_1 \leq 1/n$, then the distance between initial state and the tour state is most possibly $x \approx x_m \approx 2/n$. Therefore it is much easier to enter the tour state.

5. The basin of attraction of complex network

Here is a another sample of possible application. Consider a complex network, it consists of two subnets of N_1 and N_2. Assume there is no coupling between two subnets. Given a attractor, its basin of attraction in two subnets are known as $P_1(N_1, x)$ and $P_2(N_2, x)$ respectively, what about its basin of attraction in the complex network? $(N = N_1 + N_2)$.

According the definition, we have

$$P(N, x) = \frac{1}{C_N^{Nx}} \sum_{i=0}^{i_{max}} C_{N_1}^i C_{N_2}^{Nx-i} P_1(N_1, i/N_1) P_2(N_2, (Nx - N_1 x_1)/N_2). \tag{32}$$

Here $i_{max} = \min\{N_1, Nx\}$. Expressed by integration

$$P(N, x) = \int_0^{i_{max}/N_1} g(N_1, N_2, x_1, x) P_1(N_1, x_1) P_2(N_2, (Nx - N_1 x_1)/N_2) dx.$$

$$g(N_1, N_2, x_1, x) = N_1 C_{N_1}^{N_1 x_1} C_{N_2}^{(Nx - N_1 x_1)/N_2} / C_N^{Nx}. \tag{33}$$

From Eqs.(6)–(8), function g can be expressed as

$$g(N_1, N_2, x_1, x) = \sqrt{\frac{NN_1 x(1-x)}{2\pi N_2 x_1(1-x_1)(x+d_1)(1-x-d_1)}} \exp\{-NB_1(x, x_1)\}. \tag{34}$$

here $d_1 = (x - x_1)N_1/N_2$ and

$$B_1(x, x_1) = \frac{N_1}{N}[b(x_1) - b(x)] + \frac{N_2}{N}[b(x+d_1) - b(x)]. \tag{35}$$

It can be see clearly that g is a steeply varied function of x_1. As $x_1 = x$, $B_1(x, x_1) = 0$, g approaches maxmum. Near the maxmum, let $x_1 = x + y$, $|y| \ll 1$, make Taylor expansion of $B_1(x, x + y)$ for y and keep to y^2 terms, we have

$$g(N_1, N_2, x + y, x) \approx \frac{1}{\sqrt{2\pi\Delta_3^2}} \exp\{-\frac{y^2}{2\Delta_3^2}\}. \tag{36}$$

Here

$$\Delta_3 = \sqrt{\frac{x(1-x)}{N}} \sim \frac{1}{\sqrt{N}} \ll 1.$$

Therefore we have

$$P(N, x) \approx P_1(N_1, x)P_2(N_2, x) + \frac{1}{2}[P_1(N_1, x)P_2''(N_2, x) + P_1''(N_1, x)P_2(N_2, x) - 2P_1'(N_1, x)P_2'(N_2, x)]\Delta_3^2. \tag{37}$$

It means that the main term of P(N,x) is $P_1(N_1, x)P_2(N_2, x)$, the second term is a small quatity proportional to 1/N. Therefore

$$P(N, x) \leq max\{P_1(N_1, x), P_2(N_2, x)\}$$

i.e. the distribution of fault-tolerance of complex network is always smaller than the ones of subnets.

Conclusion

In high dimensional descrete space of neural network, the distributions of state densities $\rho(x)$ and $\rho_2(x_0, x_1 \mid x)$ are steeply varied functions of x, its calculation with usaual numerical methods is difficult. It is shown that they are highly concentrated near Gaussian maximum with width $\propto 1/\sqrt{N} \ll 1$. Apart from this thin layer they are exponentially small. The volume of a sphere with radius $x \leq 0.5$ is concentrated in a thin boundary layer, its inner regine is *almost empty*. Simple formulas to calculate the volume of sphere, shell, basin attraction and ect. are given in the paper.

References

[1] T.Kohonon, Self-organization and Associative Memory. Springer-Verlag, Berlin(1984).

[2] J.J.Hopfield, Proc. Natl. Acad. Sci. U.S.A. Vol. 79(1982), pp.2554.

[3] J.J.Hopfield, Proc. Natl. Acad. Sci. U.S.A. Vol. 81(1984), pp.3088.

[4] J.J.Hopfield and D.W.Tank, Biol. Cybern. Vol. 52,(1985),pp.141.

[5] D.W.Tank and J.J.Hopfield, IEEE Trans. CAS, Vol.CAS **33**(5), (1986), pp.533.

[6] D.T.Rumelhart et. al., Parallel Distributed Processing: Exploration in the Microstructure of Cognition, MIT Press, Cambridge, MA(1986).

[7] R.S.Burington, Handbook of Mathematical Tables and Formulas, McGraw-hill, Inc.(1973).

[8] W.Krauth, J.P.Nadal and M.Mezard, J. Phys. A **21**(1988), pp.2995.

The work is supported by NSFC and by Doctorial Program Foundation of Institution of Higher Education of China.

Fig. 1.

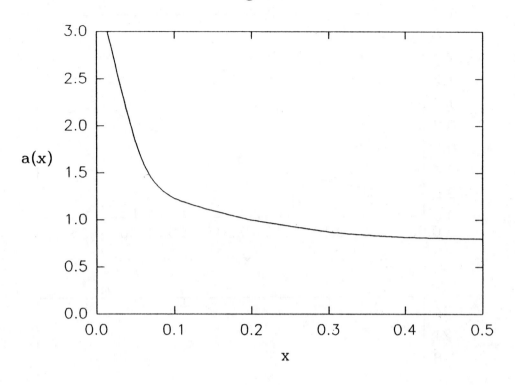

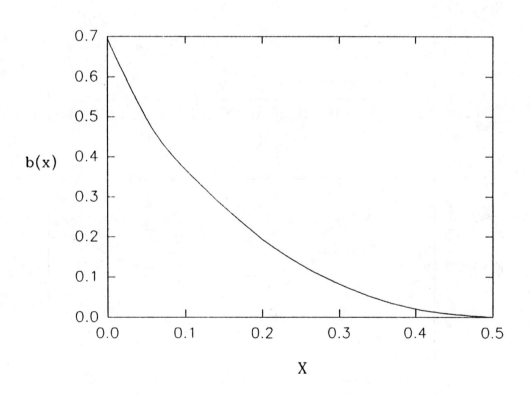

Fig.2

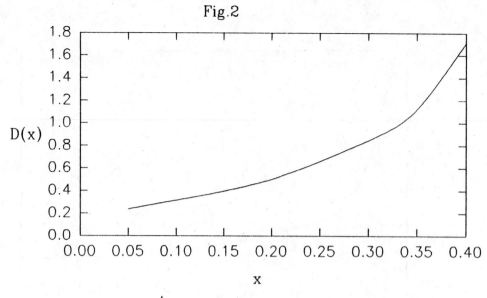

x

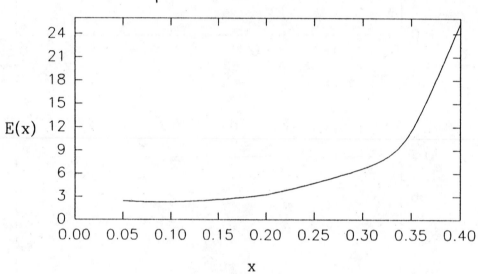

x

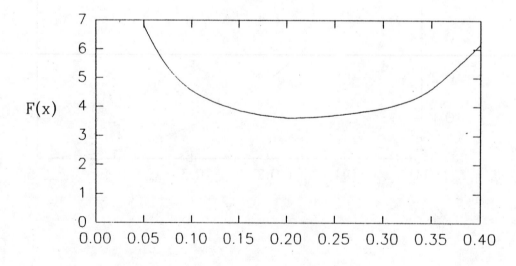

x

Representation of Number:
A Theory of Mathematical Modeling

John Cristofano
933 Greendale Ave.
Needham, Ma. 02192
Compuserve: 71302,1235
Internet: omo@park.bu.edu

Abstract: *In order for mathematics to be used in the modeling of physical events there must exist a definable mapping between number, which is a mental construction, and dimension, which is a property of a physical object. In most instances this is trivial. However, in competitive dynamical systems, such as most neural networks that are used to model biological systems, it is possible for the system to require a different mathematical representation of number at each time step if there is no a priori way for the system itself to have an absolute and invariant representation of 'number'. This situation occurs when a change in the value of a mathematical variable implies, not only a change in the value of some physical dimension but also a change in the systems ability to measure information and hence its representation of number. Computer simulations of biological competitive systems are also subject to this criticism because a computer has an absolute and invariant representation of number, as does the mathematics it simulates; but the biological system to which the analogy is then made does not necessarily have this same invariance. In biological systems it is very likely that the state of the system affects its ability to interpret information.*

Introduction

Number and Dimension

When mathematics is applied to the description of a real world event the ontological status of 'number' must be considered in order for a mathematical analysis to be valid. That is, there must be some correspondence, or mapping, between the symbols on a piece of paper, which represent numbers and operations between numbers, and a measured occurrence in the world. A correspondence is then established so that symbolic manipulations in an equation represent changes, or predictions of changes, in a modeled environment.

To clarify the mathematical-physical mapping the applied mathematician must address two questions for any given context: 1) what does a number represent in the mathematical symbolism and 2) what is the representation of number in the system being modeled. In brief, a number represents some quantity in the physical world provided that this number is concatenated with the proper dimension. In contrast to this, the representation of number describes how a person, or computing machine, intrinsically represents 'number' so that a claim such as "there are 10 units" is representable. If a computing machine is doing the calculations there is a very precise definition or representation of what the number means; namely, a certain number of memory locations with a certain potential. If a person is performing the computations the representation of number is much more complex and leads one into number theory. This is excursion is not necessary for the present argument[1].

The question of how much stuff is being sent is related to what a number represents. For example, if an object receives 10 volts then '10' represents a quantity; namely, it represents how many volts are being received. The question of what kind is related to the question "what is a volt". If an object receives 10 volts there must be some intrinsic mechanism in the object for knowing that it is a 'volt' that it has received and not some other kind of thing, and secondly that it has received '10' of these 'volts'.

In general, mathematics deals with the quantitative aspect of measurement and leaves the qualitative, what kind, question as an a priori assumption. For most mathematical modeling this is sufficient. However, this a priori

---

[1] See Carnap, *The Logical Syntax of Language* for a more formal description of the differenece between number and the representation of number.

assumption is not valid for mathematical modeling of a large class of systems known as competitive systems; examples of which are predator prey problems and competitive neural networks. In systems of this type the state of the system affects the system's ability to measure and recognize the information being sent and received. This will be the case unless there is an absolute and invariant mechanism for information recognition and measurement at each sending and receiving node in the system. Thus, when the object is in a very elevated state the reception of a unit of input may have a different meaning then when the object is in a very depressed state and receives the same input. This is a dimensional phenomena that should not be confused with the non-linearity of the system, which is a numerical phenomena.

What does a number represent?

When mathematics is applied to an object there is always measurement of some property. In any system which describes the physical world there are about a half dozen basic physical units in use from which all other dimensions or properties, are derived. Which members actually belong to the primitive properties of objects may be disputed but there is no dispute about accepting the concept that objects have properties which can be modeled mathematically. These dimensions are covered in most any introductory physics book.

In any system of measurement the basic units of dimension are axiomatic. Although the dimensions are arbitrary in the sense that there is an infinite number of fundamental propositions, every system must have some unjustifiable, fundamental measuring stick against which all other measurement is made. The basic units of dimension are axiomatic definitions of the concept '1 unit' of a particular kind. For example, 1 kilogram is defined as the mass of a specific platinum-iridium alloy cylinder kept at the International Bureau of Weights and Measures at Sevres, France; one second is the time required for a cesium-133 atom to undergo 9,192,631,770 vibrations, etc. Within these definitions the quality of the thing, the 'unitness', is described as well as what is meant to say that one has *1* of such a unit. '1 kilogram' is an axiomatic statement, '1 second' is an axiomatic statement, etc. There is an infinite number of ways of defining '1 second' or '1 kilogram'. To produce any physical results one must state these axioms and then proceed.

Within this context a number represents a ratio of the thing measured to some primitive dimension or combinations of dimension. For example, a measurement of 2.5 meters is a statement that the thing being measured is 2.5 times longer than the axiom (definition) '1 meter'. All cardinal measurements are ratios of some combination of the fundamental units. If the measurement being taken is ordinal, that is, the objects under consideration are being enumerated such as in a frequency measurement, then there is no dimension per se but merely a social understanding of what "1 member of a given category" is to be. For example there is a generally accepted notion of 'a book' or 'a dog' and in general of what represents 1 unit of such things. '1 member of a given category' is a socially dependent axiom for enumeration. A person can then, within the limits of normal experimental error, simple enumerate the number of things under observation. Whether one enumerates or takes a ratio measurement there is always a dimension. In an applied mathematical equation a number represents a ratio relative to a dimensional axiom.

What is the representation of number?

Any time mathematics is used in the physical world 'number' is defined either explicitly or tacitly. Most often little attention is given to how the system itself could model 'number'. However, if one begins to explicitly define 'number' for any system being modeled certain inconsistencies may be shown[2].

Consider a simply example of modeling the communication between two individuals. Each person is able to send, receive, and process information about simple mathematical strings. One person may say the phrase "3 + 2" and the other person would respond with the result, "5". On the surface of it this is an extremely simple model that can be described mathematically in the following way:

Object	Information Sent	Information Received
Person A	two numbers	utterance from B
Person B	one number	utterance from A

---

[2] An example of a definition of 'number' is given by Russell in *Principia Mathematica* as the class of all those classes that can be put into one-to-one correspondence to a given class (the number).

Person A utters two numbers and person B utters the sum. This is modeled quite simply as $x + y = z$. Given any number x and y the output from person B is known. Although painfully simply at first glance there is a very strong axiomatic assumption which is required for $x + y = z$ to be sufficient: Each person must have an exact and invariant *representation of number* in the same way that the mathematics used by the modeler does. In the case of 2 people communicating 'number' has acquired a representation through a social and/or cognitive process so that person A and person B never need to inquire of the other if their representations are the same. The modeler of this system interprets the mathematics in a way that number is represented exactly as it is represented in person A and person B because the modeler himself who performs the mapping from symbols to system.

Mathematical representation of number is number theory. The physical representation of number is a case by case, system specific issue. These two must correspond in order for a system to be mathematically modeled.

Measuring Objects

Situations analogous to this present themselves in many other types of systems. For example, any time a measurement is made there must be some mechanism that performs the measurement and reads this number from the measuring instrument. Usually the mechanism that takes the measurement is the experimenter. The process of taking the measurement is quite complex and based on a the process of socialization in which the individual comes to understand what a number is in a commonsense way that reflects the same understanding of number as others in the community.

If I measure 1.5 inches and I convey this information to another person, this person does not ask me what my notion of 1.5 is. There is a tacit assumption that each of us has an invariant concept of 1.5 and therefore when I transfer my information - that I measured 1.5 units - to this other person, he or she will then be able to use this information exactly as I because our representation of number is identical. This infers that the measurer must have an a priori concept of number that allows him to read the measurement.

In the case of a person reading an instrument there is a well established, completely consistent notion of number. This concept, however it may end up being rigorously defined, acts as an axiom in the system of measure and is a necessary part of mathematical modeling.

Suppose that there is no human around to read the measuring device, but only some primitive biological process; and that the results of the measurement are then passed on to other parts of the system for further processing. Further suppose that the modeler only has access to the system's input, output and structure but not to the state of the internal parts of the system. The crucial question that the modeler must address is how this biological process has come to determine what the unit is being sent to it and how much of this unit there is any given time.

This is particularly true of models of competitive biological systems such as neural networks, or models of cognitive processes. The idea in these systems is that the structure is defined, the input is defined and the initial state of the network is set; a switch is flipped and the system is allowed to run and then at some point the state of the system is read again. But the mathematics will only work if the biological mechanism has an invariance in the representation of number similar to that in the mathematical equation.

As an example consider an experimenter who is alone in a room and who has no interaction with other Homo Sapiens. He is measuring the effects of a substance on his body when taken internally. To keep track of the amount of substance he is taking he uses part of his body as a measuring mechanism. So, for example, he may take a volume of substance equal to the volume of his little finger. He then goes about charting the change in his body in relation to the amount of substance taken. What if the substance is growth hormone so that in essence the measuring stick changes at each step of the way?

The notion of 'a fingerfull' changes from day to day because the measuring ability of the system changes and so the representation of number as 'a fingerfull' changes as well. In other words the notion of '1 unit' changes so that what was once '1 unit' of measure on one day may only be equivalent to '.9 units' on another day; yet the experimenter will still believe that the dimensional axiom, i.e., 'a fingerfull' has not changed. The unit of measure from the experimenter's perspective can be called '1 interpreted unit' and from an absolute perspective simple '1 unit'. The man in the room measuring the effects of growth hormone is always working with the notion of '1 interpreted unit', whereas the observer outside the room is always using the notion of '1 unit'. The crucial question when modeling a physical system is to decide if the concepts '1 unit' and '1 interpreted unit' are always commensurable.

The idea that the state of the system changes the ability of the system to interpret information it sends and receives is novel in many areas of mathematical modeling but it is a concept several decades old which is encompassed in the special theory of relativity.

Changes in the Representation of Number and Dimension

Our physical knowledge of any system, which can be mathematically modeled, can only come from some type of measurement of the system. The act of measuring must be a describable process. If the measuring process is only implicitly and tacitly assumed and cannot be explicated then the mathematical description lacks justification and therefore may simply be false even though predictive. Since all measurement is based upon dimensional axioms any event that alters the axioms, either literally or through lack of unfiltered access to the axioms, cannot be described using the ordinary mappings between numerical symbols and physical events.

Let X_p be the state of a system as represented or predicted by a mathematical equation. All symbols X_p contain a numerical part, X_p^n, and a dimensional part, X_p^d. Every addend in any equation must have the same dimension d. This is the fundamental hypothesis of dimensional analysis (you cannot add feet and seconds). Let '&' represent a concatenation operator for concatenating items such as strings. Thus, for any addend X_p,

1) $$X_p = X_p^n \, {}_\& \, X_p^d$$

Let X_m be a measured value. X_m cannot be broken down into a numerical and dimensional part because there is no sense in which the result of a measurement can be a pure number or a pure dimension, e.g., one cannot measure '3' and one cannot measure 'volt' but only '3 volts' or in general a ratio relative to a dimensional axiom.

In order for the symbols on paper to have any relevance to the measured values there must be a mapping

2) $$X_P \Rightarrow X_m$$

which is equivalent to

$$X_p^n \, {}_\& \, X_p^d \Rightarrow X_m.$$

A mathematical simulation of a physical event is a mapping between the concatenation of a number and a dimension to the measurement of the simulated event or object in the physical world. This mapping is assured because both the measured values and the mathematical predicted values are based upon the same set of dimensional axioms. This is the case because we assume that every competent experimenter shares the same understanding of the dimensional axioms and the same representation of number.

Consider the process that an experimenter goes through to determine the state of a dynamical system at a particular time. Let S_P be the predicted state of the system at the time interval T_p and let S_m be the measured state of the system at the measured time interval T_m. To demonstrate the validity of a mathematical model a prediction of the system's state is made; time T_p is inserted into the mathematical description of the system and from this is determined the expected state of the system S_P, that is, $f(T_p) = S_P$. To determine how well the mathematical model works, measurements of the systems state S_m is taken at time T_m using appropriate measuring devices.

For example, if one writes '3 seconds' then '3' would be represented by T_p^n and 'seconds' would be represented by T_p^d, where T represents the a description of a time event.

This need for a numerical/dimensional distinction becomes obvious when using transcendental operators. For example, consider expressions of the type e^{t} where t is time. If $\mathbf{t}$ = '1 second' then $\mathbf{t}$ is composed of the numerical part '1' and the dimensional part 'second' It is only a coincidence that, in most cases, one can bifurcate the number and the dimension from the initial time measurement and operate on the number alone with e and then append the dimension 'second' after the operation and have a suitable answer. One cannot write $e^{t\ seconds}$ but only e^{t} seconds where it is understood that the concatenation operator '&' is implied, i.e., e^{t} & seconds.

The measured value $\mathbf{X}_m$ cannot be further divided into numerical and dimensional components because $\mathbf{X}_m$ is a ratio based upon an axiomatic description of a certain amount (number) of a particular quality (dimension). It makes no sense to measure some amount of a certain property.

There are three ways in which a mathematical description of a physical event can become inconsistent: 1) $\mathbf{X}_p^n$ changes which implies that the representation of number changes and therefore numerical symbols are treated differently at different times, 2) $\mathbf{X}_p^d$ changes which implies that the recognition of a dimension is not the same at all times, and 3) $\mathbf{X}_m$ changes which means that the dimensional axiom upon which all measurements, dimensional ratios, are based changes.

Consider an experimenter who is determining a relationship between a mathematical model of simple harmonic motion and the motion of a spring. The goal is to show that measured length of the spring $\mathbf{L}_m$ at any given time matches the value $\mathbf{L}_p$ predicted value by the equation. Throughout all states of the system the experimenter's concepts of number $\mathbf{L}_p^n$ and dimension $\mathbf{L}_p^d$ never change. No rigorous account of what length is or how numbers are represented is needed. It is assumed that the experimenter will never make a categorical error and measure some dimension other then length or use the symbols for numbers inconsistently. The system itself never requires an internal representation of number or dimension because the experimenter plays this role and plays it invariantly. The experimenter acts as a link between the mathematics and the physical world; it is the experimenter who is represented by the mapping function $\Rightarrow$.

It is an error to assume that all mathematical models have an invariance similar to the 'experimenter as measurer' approach above. This is usually the underlying assumption but on closer examination these assumptions are inconsistent with the purported structure of the system. The quintessential example is the self-organizing system because all appeals to number and dimension are internal to the system. That is, in the formal description of such systems there is the tacit assumption that for all states of the system any $\mathbf{X}_m$, which is a measurement of information sent or received, is absolutely invariant in regard to the categorical representation of number and the categorical representation of dimension. This assumption, however, must be stated explicitly because it is quite possible that it is not the case.

In a self-organizing system the measurement of information $\mathbf{X}_m$ cannot be based upon an external dimensional axiom. That is, when information is transferred in such a system the amount and type of information is measured and recognized by an internal process in the system. It is this internal process of recognition that must be included in the mathematical model of such a system if the mathematics is to be justified. The mapping operator $\Rightarrow$ becomes a physical process when the experimenter is removed from the model.

Computer Simulations

Suppose A and B represent computers which are connected in such a way that information can be exchanged between them. Every computer has an absolute and invariant measure of the axiom '1 unit' so that the transfer of information is always of the same kind and always in a ratio to the fundamental dimension. It is necessary to recognize that it is only humans who operate with pure numbers, the action of a computer is a physical event and therefore must have an internal measuring process for the transfer of all information.

In the case of digital computers the *kind* of information which the system understands is called the 'bit'. The bit acts as a dimensional axiom in the same way that the dimensions of physics act as axioms. The invariant mechanism for recognition of this *kind* of dimension is simply a threshold voltage potential. Regardless of the state of the computer the information being transferred, the means of recognition and measurement are invariant.

In the case of an eight bit architecture the dimension can be noted as 00000001 so that the axiom '1 unit' can be represented symbolically as '1 0000001'. (The initial '1' can be dropped since it is understood that every dimensional axiom represents the unit quantity of the unit). 2 bits is represented as '2 & 0000001' where 2 is the numerical part, X_p^n, and '0000001' is the dimensional part, X_p^d.

Although we may generally think of the computer as working with pure numbers it is a physical process and therefore every represented number has a dimension. When a computer is to simulate an event all dimensions are mapped to the dimension 'bit', e.g., 1 volt is represented as 1 bit, 4 meters is represented as 4 bits. This mapping is acceptable because the enumerative dimension 'bit' and the physical dimensional axioms are invariant so there is essentially a one-one mapping between all physical dimensions and the bit. However, when the computer model is used to predict a physical event, especially a competitive system, the bit must map to an absolute and invariant dimensional axiom in the system for the simulation to be justified. Unless this is done the computer model is merely a simulation of a mathematical equation.

If A and B are biological systems, such as neurons, then the internal representation of number is a subtle but crucial point to consider. Suppose that the fundamental unit of measure in such a system is '1 volt', and '1 volt' in this system is represented as some biological process that has the capacity to create a potential difference. Without knowing the specifics of this process there are certain conclusions that can be drawn. First, if the equation is successful as a means of prediction then there must be an absolute internal representation for number in the biological system that is independent of the state of the system in the same way that the internal representation of number in the computer is invariant regardless of the state of the computer. If such a mechanism cannot be found or reasonably postulated then one is likely to find that the representation for number will have a functional relation to the state of the cell. In this case '1 unit' will need to be redefined through time in the biologic system. Mathematically this results in a recursion in which the dimensional part of each addend contains the operation of the entire equation. This will be further explicated in a forth coming paper.

Conclusion

The above arguments are not relevant to the mathematical systems themselves but only with the conclusions that are drawn from them about physical systems. This paper does not make arguments for or against the validity of any particular model; it is only concerned with the justification for using symbols on paper to map to physical events. When computer simulations are used to match or predict measured data it is particularly alluring to assume that this is a partial proof for the correctness of a particular model. However, this alone is simply not sufficient. Epistemic principles require that any statement about the world requires some sort of justification in order for that statement to be considered as an increase in knowledge about the world. To simply say "the model matches the data" is not sufficient justification.

Bibliography

Barenblatt, G. I., *Dimensional Analysis*, Gordon and Breach, New York, New York, 1987.
Bhaskar, R. and Nigam, Anil, Qualitative Physics Using Dimensional Analysis, *Artificial Intelligence*, **45** (1990) 73-111.
Bridgman, P.W.; *Dimensional Analysis*, Yale University Press, Hew Haven, CT., 1922.
Carnap, Rudolf. *The Logical Syntax of Language* 1937. Translaterd by Amethe Smeaton.
Grossberg, S., *Studies of Mind and Brain*, D. Reidel Publishing Co., Boston, 1982.
Rumelhart, David E, and McClelland, James L., *Parallel Distributed Processing*, MIT Press, Cambridge, Ma. 1988.
Russell and Whitehead, *Principia Mathematica* (1927).

An Ecological Approach to Cognition

Paul S. Prueitt
Department of Natural Science and Mathematics
Saint Paul's College, Lawrenceville, VA
prueitt@nnrf.georgetown.edu

Abstract

The human mind recognizes natural kind in its environment and accommodates cultural experiences through observations on these natural kind. Information on the things of the world are gathered, we suppose, by feature extraction and clustering. However, perceptions of natural kind are products of complex interactions between the observer and its external world. Thus, as a principle of considerable importance, we cannot reasonably isolate learning behavior from the social ecosystem. Using today's advanced computers, we can model many levels of activity and integrate these levels together, resulting in an ecological approach to cognition. The foundation for this approach is provided by specifying the evolution equations for transient neuronal and subneuronal compartments operating within a complex electromagnetic subspace. This network architecture must also be constrained by quantum field dynamics, as proposed by neuroscientist Karl Pribram. A framework is suggested to accomplish this hybrid field/network architecture. Of interest to the author are the dynamics responsible for acquired cognitive disability. To accomplish an ecological model of acquired cognitive disability, the classical mathematical theory of conditioning is extended by embedding neural and immune network architectures into a complex dissipative system.

The study of temporal and spatial boundaries in biological systems reveals informational interfaces that distinguish animate and inanimate systems. Of considerable importance is the observation that, in ecosystems, transient structures exist at multiple levels of a hierarchy. A mathematical theory of process hierarchies is needed to capture this observation. The organization of the process hierarchy in neural systems depends on physiology, protein and chemical interaction as well as phase coherence in the electromagnetic (EM) spectrum. EM phase coherence produces transient structures that play active roles in energy manipulation. Potential manifolds, similar in nature to Hopfield optimizers (Hopfield, 1984) and the associational layers of parallel distributed processing, also play an active role. In each level, each structure maintains boundaries between constituents and with environments. Stratification by time scale is also fundamental to the expression of functional kinetic structures that depend on phase coherence and/or kinematic constraints; i.e., surfaces colliding with surfaces.

What is transient phenomena for one level of organization are the atoms from which another level is constructed. At the level of social behavior, it transient phenomena arise from the activity of an individual in his or her environment. Kugler & Turvey's (1987) thermodynamical treatment of self-organizing information systems was anticipated by J.J. Gibson (1979) in his analysis of perceptual structures that arise in animal optical flow. The school of ecological psychology, initiated by Gibson, has explored the viewpoint that interaction of information sensitive systems cannot be completely rendered as (complex) collisions between atoms. This school supports the view that logical entailment; i.e., inference, is not (solely) a product of computational grammars and that physical entailment; i.e., causality, is not (solely) a product of discrete interactions.

Ecological psychology makes the observation that information is the primary means through which biological systems influence systems of similar type. Furthermore, it is argued that selection and intersystem interaction result in the production of structured signals and mechanisms for interpreting these signals. Pattee (1971), for example, frames the discussion between living and non-living matter in exactly these terms, and points out that the exceptional coherence of structural units within a community implies an ubiquity of language-type structures. These structures transfer information, not data, between units within hierarchical strata segmented by dynamical time scales. The study of artificial and non-human language structure has motivated a specialized use of linguistic terms to supplant computational grammars. The use of syntax, semantics and pragmatics in the discussion of science has an interesting history; which we will defer to others (Pattee, 1977,

Carello et al, 1987; Rosen, 1985; Kugler et al, 1990.)

The ecological approach has a wide scope that includes generic behavioral phenomena, not just signaling behavior. For example, the generic nature of perception-action cycles is examined in the context of language (Kugler et al, 1990.) For Kugler and his colleagues, the question of signal origin is answered in the language of non-equilibrium thermodynamics. Emergent structure is seen to have relations (affordances) to the immediate environment from which it forms, and thus semantics and syntax arise in the physical entailment of the structure's existence. There are good reasons for supposing that semantic and syntactic forms are set in the transition forces that create and then break symmetries prior to the creation of emergent structure. Once created, such forms would be lawful within a finite period of time and act within a closed compartment, thus models may be amenable to closed form evolution equations with addition and multiplication. However, the expression of this lawful behavior by individual organisms has repercussions to the ecosystem and to the organism and this may require elements of catastrophe theory to explain further.

Semantics and syntax arise and exist within the context of temporal phenomena representable as a <u>process compartment</u>. In common parlance, a representational account has a pragmatics axis when reflecting the true relationship between a specific behavior and a supporting set of external circumstances. At transition points a pragmatic dimension becomes operational allowing a restructuring that reflects the characteristics of the environment. The pragmatics dimension is therefore critically dependent on time and circumstance, not only because living systems behave through a cyclic expression arising from internal dynamics but also because the world itself is non-stationary. The formation of symbolic constructs enters at exactly the same point that intentionality can be most efficiently expressed. Intentionality involves the prediction of the future as a function of expectation and behavioral expression. With intentionality comes expectation and the top down stabilization of otherwise chaotic systems. It pulls us away from the pragmatic axis while at the same time producing symbols and assigning meaning to them. These symbolic structures are a bi-product of the conflict between a self-organized compartment and its environment.

Semantics captures the meaning of internal representations by an appeal to universal types as experienced by the interpreter. The process of capture is a function of the interface; i.e., pragmatic in nature. Once captured; however, the semantic value is maintained as part of episodic phenomena and is dependent on the endophysics of the transient structure. It is thus likely that both observation and intention are expressed at the temporal interface where structure emerges; i.e., on the edge of chaos (Kaulfman, 1992.)

Commonality in dynamical behavior observed in stratified and compartmentalized systems arises from elementary interaction principles, reflecting the underlying organization of stratified and compartmentalized systems. These principles are reflected in network architectures and corresponding differential and difference equations (Nigrin, 1993.) *Associative learning* enables the strengthening or weakening of connections between subsystems based on contiguity. *Lateral inhibition* enables choices between competing percepts, drives, categorization, plans or behaviors. Lateral inhibition has the ability to automatically transform order relations from a microscopic scale to a macro scale and thus is used to "read" information from encoded states (as in ART architectures of Carpenter and Grossberg.) *Opponent processing* enables search processes to discard evaluated categories and to address novel stimulus. *Neuromodulation* enables contextual refinement of attention based on the systemic needs of a community of local systems (compartments.) *Interlevel resonant feedback* enables reality testing of tentative classification or goal setting. An extended discussion of these principles is given in Levine, Parks and Prueitt (1993) and in Prueitt, 1993. Also see the introductory text, Levine (1991.)

Neuronal connectivity is only part of the necessary information required to understand how higher functions arise from the brain. There is organizational complexity both in functional/structural relations between brain regions and across processing strata where time scale verses event occurrence delineates levels. Refinements of the "neuronal model" of cognitive process are possible by detailing additional biological processes as computational models and by incorporating advanced theory (Eccles (1993), Edelman (1987), Pribram (1991), Houk and Barto (1991), Changeux & Dehaene (1989), Hameroff (1987) and Freeman (1991).) Edelman's work is cited for its derivation neuronal group selection (Edelman, 1987) from the theory of clonal selection (Burnet, 1958) and natural selection (Darwin, 1859.) Pribram's work is cited for his early work in neuropsychology (1973) and his more recent work in quantum neurodynamics (1991, 1993.) Houk and Barto (1991) is cited for the synthesis of a theory of neurodynamics for *in vitro* networks, particularly those involved in the expression of motor intentions (i.e., motor programs.) Changeux's work is cited for his description of indirect (allosteric) dynamics and for suggesting that a generator of diversity is essential to understanding normal cell function. Freeman's work has placed the mathematical theory of chaos into a now well established role in basic pattern recognition research. Hameroff's work allows us to find basement strata; microtubulin, protein metastable states and quantum fluctuations, to the dynamics of neuronal processes (Hameroff et al, 1993.) Eccles is cited for demarking a specific mechanism that creates symmetry at the sub-synaptic level and stating what is now called the quantum metaphor in clarification of the mind-body problem, Eccles (1993.)

The ecological study of learning behavior explores the nature of learning by examining both the self and its environment. Immune network research has addressed the self/not-self recognition issue via the notion of self concept supported by regulatory circuits and thus represents a different approach than that taken by mainstream artifical intelligence and neural network research. Self concept regulation is defined in terms of help-suppression circuits (Jerne, 1955; Richter, 1978; Eisenfeld & Prueitt, 1989.) In recent decades, the dynamic circuits of both immune and neural response have been found to involve several orders of complexity. By the late 1960s, a series of research publications identified that two classes of lymphocytes, T cells produced in the thalmus and B cells produced in bone marrow, cooperate to produce the generic antibody response. A review of this early literature on T and B determinants (see Tada, 1984) reveals that the immunological complementation between T and B lymphocytes is a synergism arising as a result of antigen (or anti-idiotypic reagent) perturbation of virtual equilibrium. Virtual equilibria are manifest, in real time, by dynamic circuit responses involving lymphocyte production and differentiation, field distributions of chemical agents, and EM events.

In the examination of specific factors involved in T and B cell interaction, Tada's analysis depends on the analogies between self and not-self and between help and suppression. This analogy uncovers a richer discussion of the regulator effects of major histocompatibility complex (MCH) encoded structure on T cell selection and B cell differentiation. Help and suppression in interaction induces a self-organization of field kinetics, and structural mechanics (kinematics) to produce an endophysics that occurs within closed compartments, but which also create initial conditions for state transitions at critical points such as birth and death of emergent forms.

Response models based on help-supression, circuit based response mechanisms develop three types of equilibria. Each of the equilibria define the functional properties of a compartmental model of immune response when stimulated. In the first compartmental model, immunological memory of antigen challenges allow a quick response to any future encounter of an agent that shares the same idiotype. This response is called a memory response. A different type of response develops when the system is not able to develop a memory response. In this second case, the mechanism involved in stimulus response has <u>acquired an active inability to respond</u>. This inability to respond is called <u>tolerance</u>. Tolerance responses develop when a series of low doses of antigen, doses below a certain threshold, are encountered (low zone tolerance, LZT) or where the system is paralyzed by a series or very high doses (high zone tolerance, HZT); (Burnet 1958), (Dresser and Michison, 1968) and (Richter 1979). Both tolerance equilibria are often portrayed as the product of the immune system's need to recognize self-antigens.

Learned helplessness is often considered to be a global phenomena, influencing every aspect of a person's life; however, some argue that learned helplessness can become specific to one aspect of self concept and not to others. The traditional problems with self concept research have to do with a disinclination by some researchers to trace environmental stimulus to an effect on internal states. There is support for an ecological approach to self concept. Gorrell & Bandura (1977) and Gorrell (1990) point out that self-efficacy has a role in changing specific beliefs about specific areas of one's life. Our question is about how stimulus is accommodated via message production and interpretation.

On close examination, an analogy linking all forms of acquired cognitive disability can be derived from theoretical principles embodied in natural selection (Darwin, 1859), clonal selection (Jerne, 1955; Burnet, 1959), and neuronal group selection (Edelman, 1987.) Interaction between a system and its environment corrolates with the emergence of localized phenomena and thus is related to the system's ability (or not) to choose between options. From this exotic theory comes a very practical result. A major remediation principle, for non-response syndromes, is an enhancement of behavioral choice as related to behaviorally relevant tasks seen as novel to the individual. The present model suggests that we identify a pragmatic (three way) interface between internal states of self image, local computation from subspace expression, and environmental constraints. This interface arises during the birth and death of compartmental phenomena formed through local symmetry mechanisms.

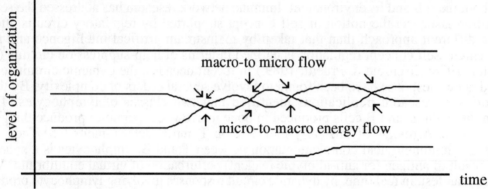

Figure 1: Compartmental formation in stratified systems. Pragmatic, syntax and semantics come together when the constraints of an environment work against the behavioral subspace to produce a new set of observables in semantics space.

A compartment is thermodynamically defined as a system with distinct inside and outside; i.e., it is closed to energy exchanges. Compartments may even become functionally isolated, causing a temporary violation of classical thermodynamics. This violation is observed as variations of the probability distribution of likely outcomes (Eccles 1993; Werbos, 1993.) This is a central issue for theoretical physics and mathematics. Prigogine's theory of dissipative structures provides considerable insight on the dynamics of interfaces, internal physics and compartmental expression in an external world (Pribram, 1993 Appalachian Conference proceedings, in progress.) As would be expected, the discussion by Pribram's group has been centered around the questions of measurement and observation (Rosen, 1985.)

Several network based computational systems have been combined to define an immune network/dipole compartment with appropriate gradient fields. Each compartment acts as a constraint within a dissipative system. The dissipative system has the form:

$$H(\underline{x}, d\underline{x}/dt) = 1/2 \ m \ d\underline{x}/dt^2 + V(\underline{x}) + D(d\underline{x}/dt) + E(\underline{x}) \tag{1}$$

where the first term is an energy function, the second corresponding to architectural constraints, and the last two terms correspond to flows of energy originating from outside the compartment. Architectural constraints are modeled as connectivity between regional process centers with a traditional connectionist layered network as well as with non-layered associative connection (as within a single Grossberg type gated dipole.) Higher order terms, existent at transitions, may be modeled with: $$H(\underline{x}, d\underline{x}/dt) = 1/2\ m\ d\underline{x}/dt^2 + V(\underline{x}) + p(\underline{x}, d\underline{x}/dt) \qquad (2)$$

where p is a polynomial in x and dx/dt. Additional descriptions of the relationship between the manifolds of an embedding dissipative system will be forthcoming. A discussion of the change in dimension of the observable x is given in Prueitt & Levine (in progress.)

H is an operator whose domain set is the cross product of a vector representation, $\underline{x} = ($ x_1, $x_2, ... , x_{n(t)})$, of determinant viability and their time rates of production, $d\underline{x}/dt$. The term n(t) is an integer depending on a specific episode and level in the process hierarchy. In the simplest case H is the harmonic oscillator. Compartments arise in the process hierarchy that themselves are dissipative systems constrained by micro/macro influences. A temporally stratified process hierarchy has m subsystems $\{S_k\}$ where m is an integer dependent on time and observation. Each S_k has the form of equation (2) but with time variable t_k where $t_k = a_k\ t_1$, and $\{a_k\}$ is a finite positive monotone decreasing sequence with a_1 less than 1. The resulting computational model relies on the selection of a manifold topology, at t_a that is stable only within a finite period; e.g., within the corresponding episode. The span of the manifold is measured by the continuum of time, $t\ \varepsilon\ [t_a , t_b]$. This representation is degenerate; i.e., one to many, at t_a and t_b and deterministic within the compartment. This feature of initial degeneracy allows for a dynamic restructuring of the observation space at the beginning of each episode.

If a number of concepts have been encoded and associated together and the stimulation of those concepts are controlled by a help-suppression ensemble in a tolerant state, then a sufficiently novel concept will remain unaffected by a general tolerance of the conceptual type. There will be no response to stimulation. However, a new attractor subsystem, with a memory equilibrum, can be created with novel stimulation. As this attractor system is developed, the help-suppression ensemble controlling the subsystems may achieve a new memory equilibrium rather than remain linked to the tolerant equilibrium. This is then followed by a global restructuring of the temporal hierarchy and the accommodation of environmental stimulus.

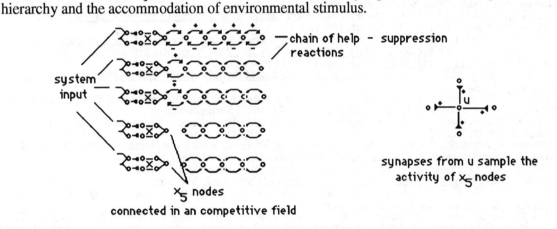

Figure 2. System input excites one side of a number of dipoles. The pattern of input is then processed through the dipoles and into a competitive field that is under the influence of a reward center. Each of the x5 nodes excite a chain of help-suppression reactions that in turn suppresses the x5 node. The chain has stable states that cause characteristic memory recall behavior.

The possibility of creating a new attractor basin for concepts that share some commonality also creates the possibility of reorganizing the way in which memory is maintained. A "flash of insight" may be a sensory indication of such reorganization. This suggest the design of clinical trials to delineate the phenomena of Acquired Cognitive Disability (ACD.) We have conjectured that a sensation comes from an electromagnetic induced resetting of help-suppression ensembles as part of the process of accommodating new information. The correlation of jerk reflexes with memory reorganization may lead to experimental confirmation of the existence of a help-suppression mechanism involved in memory maintenance and self concept.

References:

Bandura, A (1977.) Self-Efficacy: Toward a unifying theory of behavioral change. Psy. Review, 84, 191-215.

Berger, D.H, Pribram, K,H,, Wild, H; Bridges, C. (1990.) An analysis of neural spike-train distribution: determinants of the response of visual cortex neurons to changes in orientation and spatial frequency. *Experimental Brain Research.* **80** 128-134.

Burnet, Macfarlane (1958). The Clonal Selection Theory of Acquired Immunity, Vanderbilt .

Bulsara, A.R. & Maren, A.J. (1993.) Coupled Neural-Dendritic Processes: Cooperative Stochastic Effects and the Analysis of Spike Trains, in K. Pribram (Ed) Rethinking Neural Networks: Quantum Fields and Biological Data Hillsdale, NJ, LEA

Carello, Claudia, Turvey, M.T. Kugler, Peter, and Shaw, Robert (1984). Inadequacies of the Computer Metaphor, in M. Gazzaniza (Ed), Handbook of cognitive neuroscience. pp 229-248. Menlo Park: Benjamin Cummings.

Changeux, J.P. & Dehaene, S, (1989.) Neuronal models of cognitive function, *Cognition* 3, 63-1

Darwin, c. (1895.) On the origin of species. London: Murry.

Dresser, D. W. and Michison, N.A. (1968). The mechanism of immunological paralysis. Adv. Immunol, 31, 23-43.

Eccles, John (1993.) Evolution of Complexity of the Brain with the Emergence of Consciousness, in K. Pribram (Ed) Rethinking Neural Networks: Quantum Fields and Biological Data, Hillsdale, NJ, LEA

Edelman, G. (1987). Neural Darwinism, New York: Basic Books.

Eisenfeld J. and Prueitt P. (1988). Systematic Approach to Modeling Immune Response, Proc. Santa Fe Institute on Theoretical Immunology (A. Perelson, ed.) Addison-Wesley.

Freeman, W (1993) The Emergence of Chaotic Dynamics as a Basis for Comprehending Intentionality in Experimental Subjects, in K. Pribram (Ed) Rethinking Neural Networks.

Gibson, J.J. (1979.) *The ecological approach to visual perception*. Boston: Houghton-Mifflin.

Gorrell, J. (1990.) Some Contributions of Self-Efficacy Research to Self-Concept Theory. *Journal of Research and Development in Education* 23, **2,**

Hameroff, Stuart (1987.) Ultimate Computing: Biomolecular Consciousness and Nanotechnology, North-Holland, Amsterdam.

Hameroff, S., Dayhoff, J. Lahoz-Beltra, R, Rasmussen, S, Insinna, E, and Koruga, D. (1993.) Nanoneurology and the Cytoskeleton: Quantum Signaling and Protein Conformational Dynamics as Cognitive Substrate, in K. Pribram (Ed) Rethinking Neural Networks: Quantum Fields and Biological Data, Hillsdale, NJ, LEA

Hopfield, J.J., (1984). Neurons with graded response have collective computational properties like those of two-state neurons. Proc. Natl. Acad. Sci., **81**, 3088-3092.

Houk, J. C. & Barto, A.G. (1991.) Distributed Sensorimotor Learning, in Tutorial in Motor Behavior II, edited by G.E. Stelmach and J. Requin. Amsterdam: Elsevier.

Jerne, N.K. (1967.) Antibodies and learning: Selection verses instruction. In, The neurosciences: A study program, ed G.C. Quarton, T. Melnechuk, and F.O. Schmitt. pp 200-205. New York: Rockefeller Univ. Press.

Kauffman, S.A (1993.) The Origins of Order Oxford: Oxford Press,

Kugler , P.N. & Turvey, M.T. (1987.) Information, natural law, and the self-assembly of rhythmic movements. Hillsdale, NJ: LEA.

Kugler, Peter, N., Shaw, Robert E., Vincente, Kim, J., and Kinsella-Shaw, Jeffery (1990.) Inquiry into intentional systems I: Issues in ecological physics, *Psychological Research*, Springer-Verlag

Levine, D.S. and Prueitt (1989). Modeling Some Effects of Frontal Lobe Damage - Novelty and Perseveration. *Neural Networks*, Vol. 2.

Levine D;Parks,R.; & Prueitt, P.S. (1993.) Methodological and Theoretical Issues in Neural Network Models of Frontal Cognitive Functions. *International Journal of Neuroscience* **72** 209-233

Levine, Daniel (1991.) Introduction to neural and cognitive modeling. Hillsdale, NJ: ERA

Nigrin, Albert (1993.) Neural Networks for Pattern Recognition, Cambridge: MIT Press.

Pattee, H.H. (1971). The nature of hierarchical controls in living matter. In R. Rosen (Ed.) Textbook of Mathematical Biology. New York: Academic press.

Pattee, H.H. (1977) Dynamic and linguistic modes of complex systems, *Inter.Jour. of General Systems.* **3** 259-266.

Pribram, K. H. (1973.) Languages of the Brain, experimental paradoxes and principles in neuropsychology, Prentice Hall, New Jersey.

Pribram, K. H. (1991). Holonomic Brain Theory, Erlbaum, Hillsdale, N.J.

Pribram, Karl (1993) (Ed) Rethinking Neural Networks: Quantum Fields and Biological Data, Hillsdale, NJ, LEA

Pribram, Karl (in progress). Second Appalachian Conference Proceedings.

Prueitt Paul S. & Levine, Daniel (in progress). An Ecological Approach to Learning Behavior.

Prueitt, Paul S. (1993a) Network Models in Behavioral and Computational Neuroscience, invited chapter in Non-animal Models in Biomedical & Psychological Research, Testing and Education, New Gloucester: PsyETA.

Richter, Peter H. (1979). Pattern Formation in the Immune System, Lectures on Mathematics in the Life Science, Vol 11. 89-107.?

Rosen, Robert (1985). Anticipatory Systems. Philosophical, mathematical and methodological foundations. New York:Pergamon

Tada, Tomio (1984.) Help, Suppression, and Specific Factors, in William E. Paul (Ed) Fundamental Immunology, Raven

Werbos (1993) Quantum Theory and Neural Systems: Alternative Approaches and a New Design, in K. Pribram (Ed) Rethinking Neural Networks: Quantum Fields and Biological Data, Hillsdale, NJ, LEA

Necessary and Sufficient Condition for the Existence of Neural Network Models for Logic Circuits

Zhong Zhang and Ruwei Dai

National Research Center for Intelligent Computing Systems,
Institute of Automation, Academia Sinica

Abstract

In this paper, a new approach for logic circuit modeling using neural networks is proposed. Using the Hopfield model, the constrained energy equations are established based on the truth table of a logic device. Using linear equations theory, the necessary and sufficient condition for the existence of its neural network is derived, from which the general neural parameter expression for a basic logic gate is obtained.

I. Introduction

Neural networks have strong potential for applications in many different fields. It is quite attractive that the parallel computing power of neural networks is used to solve some problems on logic circuits, such as function verification, test generation and so on. Therefore, it is very important to establish effective neural network models for logic circuits.

Early in 1986, Abu-Mostafa[1] proposed a simple neural network model for logic circuits in which each basic logic gate is represented by one neuron and the network has no effective feedback. This neural model can be used to simulate the logic function of any combinational circuit. In 1988, Chakradhar et al.[2], using the Hopfield model[4], derived *a necessary condition* for the existence of a logic circuit neural network model by introducing the concept of the neural decision hyperplane from which the bidirectional neural network for the logic circuit is established. This neural network model can be used in the test generation problem. After that, Fujiwara[4] improved Chakradhar's model by using a three-valued model to replace the binary model, and proved that it is more efficient.

In this paper, using the Hopfield model, the constrained energy equations are established based on the truth table of a logic device. Using linear equations theory, *the necessary and sufficient condition* for the existence of its neural network is derived, from which the general neural parameter expression for any logic gate is obtained. The results show that our approach is very effective.

This paper is organized as follows. Section II gives an outline of the Hopfield neural network model and the neural representation for logic circuits. Section III gives the existence theorem for the logic circuit neural network. Section IV describes the neural network for basic logic gates. Discussion is provided and conclusions are drawn in Section V.

II. Hopfield Model and Logic Circuit Neural Networks

In this paper, we adopt Hopfield's binary model. A neural network is composed of interconnected neurons and its behavior is completely deterimined by the specification of the interconnection. Let $V_i(t)$ denote the state of neuron i at moment t, i.e., $V_i(t) \in \{0,1\}$ for $i = 1, 2, \ldots, N$, where N is the number of neurons in the network, and each neuron updates its state stochastically at a mean rate W using the following rule:

$$V_i(t + i) = step[\sum_{j=1}^{N} T_{ij}V_j(t) + I_i] \tag{1}$$

where *step* is defined as

$$step(x) = \begin{cases} 1 & x > 0 \\ 0 & x \leq 0 \end{cases}$$

and T_{ij} is the link weight between neuron i and neuron j, and I_i is the external input of neuron i. The energy function for the neural network is

$$E = -\frac{1}{2}\sum_{i=1}^{N}\sum_{j=1}^{N} T_{ij}V_iV_j - \sum_{i=1}^{N} I_iV_i + K \tag{2}$$

where K is a constant. Hopfield has shown[4] that if $T_{ij} = T_{ji}$ and $T_{ii} = 0$ for all i, neurons always change their states in such a manner that the network converges to a stable state and the energy function for the network is minimized locally at a stable point.

In a logic circuit, every node (signal line) is represented by a neuron and the value on the node is the state value (0 or 1) of the neuron. Each gate is independently represented by a neural network and the interconnections between the gates are used to combine the individual gate neural networks into the entire neural network representing the circuit. The energy function for the logic circuit has global minima if and only if the neuron states are consistent with the function of all gates in the circuit, and the energy function has higher energy for all states that are inconsistent with the function of the gates in the circuit.

III. Existence of Neural Networks for Logic Circuits

A logic device with N terminals (as shown in Fig.1) realizes a logic function as shown in the truth table in Table.1, in which $x_i \in \{0,1\}$ and $m = 2^{N-1}$. The energy function surface for its neural network is shown in Table.2.

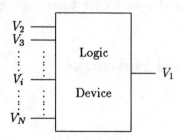

Figure 1: A logic device

V_2	V_3	.	.	.	V_i	.	.	.	V_N	V_1
1	0	0	.	.	.	.	.	.	0	x_1
0	1	0	.	.	.	.	.	.	0	x_2
				.		.				.
				.		.				x_i
				.		.				.
1	1	1	.	.	.	.	.	.	1	x_m

Table 1: Truth table for a logic device

$V_1, V_2, \ldots, V_N$ are state values of neurons corresponding to the terminals of the logic device. When the state values satisfy the truth table they are called *consistent states*, otherwise they are called *inconsistent states*. If $V_1, V_2, \ldots, V_N$ are consistent states, the energy function $E = 0$. If they are inconsistent states, the energy function E is a positive constant $A_i (i = 1, 2, \ldots, m)$.

Substituting the values of Table.2 in (2), we get a group of nonhomogenous linear equations as folllows:

$$\begin{cases} -\frac{1}{2} \sum_{i=1}^{N} \sum_{j=1}^{N} (V_i^1 V_j^1) T_{ij} - \sum_{i=1}^{N} V_i^1 I_i + K = E_1 \\ -\frac{1}{2} \sum_{i=1}^{N} \sum_{j=1}^{N} (V_i^2 V_j^2) T_{ij} - \sum_{i=1}^{N} V_i^2 I_i + K = E_2 \\ \qquad \cdots\cdots \\ -\frac{1}{2} \sum_{i=1}^{N} \sum_{j=1}^{N} (V_i^n V_j^n) T_{ij} - \sum_{i=1}^{N} V_i^n I_i + K = E_n \end{cases} \tag{3}$$

These equations are called *constrained energy equations*. There are $n = 2^N$ equations. The link weight matrix of a neural network in the Hopfield model is a symmetric matrix with zero diagonal elements (*i.e.*, $T_{ij} = T_{ji}, T_{ii} = 0$), in which the number of T_{ij} is $\frac{1}{2} N(N-1)$, the number of I_i is N, and there is one K. So the total number of unknown quantities is $\frac{1}{2} N(N+1) + 1$. If these unknown quantities can be solved by the 2^N equations in (3), then the neural network is obtained. Therefore, we get the following theorem about the existence of a neural network for a logic device.

Theorem 1 *If the constrained energy equations given in (3) are solvable, then the corresponding neural network exists, and the solution of the equations in (3) gives the fundamental parameters of the neural network.*

From linear equations theory, we know that the necessary and sufficient condition for a set of nonhomogeous linear equations to have a solution is that the rank of the coefficient matrix of the equations is equal to the rank of its extended matrix. Thus, we obtain the result that *the necessary and sufficient condition for the existence of the neural network of a logic device is that the rank of the coefficient matrix of the constrained energy equations is equal to the rank of its corresponding extended matrix.*

IV. Neural Networks for Basic Logic Gates

On the basis of the existence theorem, we can derive neural networks for the basic logic gates. Consider a 2-input basic logic gate (as shown in Fig.2), whose logic function is given in the truth table in Table.3, where $f_G^k \in \{0, 1\}(k = 00, 01, 10, 11)$ is *the function term* for logic gate G. Also, logic gate G has input symmetry, i.e., $f_G^{10} = f_G^{01}$. Its neural network is shown in Fig.3, the corresponding energy surface is shown in Table.4, where $V_i (i = 1, 2, 3)$ is the state value of the neuron corresponding to the line x_i in gate G, and $\overline{f_G^k} = 1 - f_G^k$.

V_1	V_2	V_3	$\cdots$	$\cdot$	V_i	$\cdots$	$\cdot$	V_N	E
1	0	0	$\cdot\,\cdot$	$\cdot$	$\cdot\,\cdot$	$\cdot$	$\cdot$	0	E_1
0	1	0	$\cdot\,\cdot$	$\cdot$	$\cdot\,\cdot$	$\cdot$	$\cdot$	0	E_2
			$\cdot$	$\cdot$	$\cdot$	$\cdot$	$\cdot$		$\cdot$
			$\cdot$	$\cdot$	$\cdot$	$\cdot$	$\cdot$		$\cdot$
			$\cdot$	$\cdot$	$\cdot$	$\cdot$	$\cdot$		E_i
			$\cdot$	$\cdot$	$\cdot$	$\cdot$	$\cdot$		$\cdot$
			$\cdot$	$\cdot$	$\cdot$	$\cdot$	$\cdot$		$\cdot$
1	1	1	$\cdot\,\cdot$	$\cdot$	$\cdot\,\cdot$	$\cdot$	$\cdot$	1	E_n

Table 2: Energy surface for a logic device

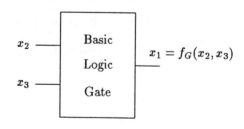

Figure 2: A basic logic gate

When the state values satisfy the truth table, the energy function takes a minimal value of $E = 0$, otherwise the energy function has a higher energy value which is a positive constant $E_G^j (j = 1, 2, 3)$.

x_2	x_3	$x_1 = f_G(x_2, x_3)$
0	0	$f_G^{00} = f(0, 0)$
1	0	$f_G^{10} = f(1, 0)$
0	1	$f_G^{01} = f(0, 1)$
1	1	$f_G^{11} = f(1, 1)$

Table 3: Truth table for a basic gate

V_1	V_2	V_3	E_G
f_G^{00}	0	0	0
f_G^{00}	0	0	E_G^1
f_G^{10}	1	0	0
f_G^{10}	0	1	0
f_G^{10}	1	0	E_G^2
f_G^{10}	0	1	E_G^2
f_G^{11}	1	1	0
f_G^{11}	1	1	E_G^3

Table 4: Energy surface for a basic gate

On the substitution of the state values of Table.4 in the equations of (3), we get the constrained energy equations for gate G as follows:

$$
\begin{pmatrix}
1 & -f_G^{00} & 0 & 0 & 0 & 0 & 0 \\
1 & -(1-f_G^{00}) & 0 & 0 & 0 & 0 & 0 \\
1 & -f_G^{10} & -1 & 0 & -f_G^{10} & 0 & 0 \\
1 & -f_G^{10} & 0 & -1 & 0 & -f_G^{10} & 0 \\
1 & -(1-f_G^{10}) & -1 & 0 & -(1-f_G^{10}) & 0 & 0 \\
1 & -(1-f_G^{10}) & 0 & -1 & 0 & -(1-f_G^{10}) & 0 \\
1 & -f_G^{11} & -1 & -1 & -f_G^{11} & -f_G^{11} & -1 \\
1 & -(1-f_G^{11}) & -1 & -1 & -(1-f_G^{11}) & -(1-f_G^{11}) & -1
\end{pmatrix}
\begin{pmatrix}
K \\ I_1 \\ I_2 \\ I_3 \\ T_{12} \\ T_{13} \\ T_{23}
\end{pmatrix}
=
\begin{pmatrix}
0 \\ E_G^1 \\ 0 \\ 0 \\ E_G^2 \\ E_G^2 \\ 0 \\ E_G^3
\end{pmatrix}
\tag{4}
$$

Through a sequence of elementary transformations, the coefficient matrix and the extended matrix are

$$
\begin{pmatrix}
1 & 0 & 0 & 0 & 0 & 0 & 0 & : & \frac{f_G^{00}}{2f_G^{00}-1} E_G^1 \\
0 & 1 & 0 & 0 & 0 & 0 & 0 & : & \frac{1}{2f_G^{00}-1} E_G^1 \\
0 & 0 & 1 & 0 & 0 & 0 & 0 & : & \frac{f_G^{00}}{2f_G^{00}-1} E_G^1 - \frac{f_G^{10}}{2f_G^{10}-1} E_G^2 \\
0 & 0 & 0 & 1 & 0 & 0 & 0 & : & \frac{f_G^{00}}{2f_G^{00}-1} E_G^1 - \frac{f_G^{10}}{2f_G^{10}-1} E_G^2 \\
0 & 0 & 0 & 0 & 1 & 0 & 0 & : & \frac{-1}{2f_G^{00}-1} E_G^1 + \frac{1}{2f_G^{10}-1} E_G^2 \\
0 & 0 & 0 & 0 & 0 & 1 & 0 & : & \frac{-1}{2f_G^{00}-1} E_G^1 + \frac{1}{2f_G^{10}-1} E_G^2 \\
0 & 0 & 0 & 0 & 0 & 0 & 1 & : & E_G^2 - \frac{1}{2}(E_G^1 + E_G^3) \\
0 & 0 & 0 & 0 & 0 & 0 & 0 & : & \frac{2f_G^{11}-1}{2f_G^{00}-1} E_G^1 - \frac{2(2f_G^{11}-1)}{2f_G^{10}-1} E_G^2 + E_G^3
\end{pmatrix}
\tag{5}
$$

The rank of the coefficient matrix is equal to the rank of its extended matrix. The last row gives:

$$
\frac{2f_G^{11}-1}{2f_G^{00}-1} E_G^1 - \frac{2(2f_G^{11}-1)}{2f_G^{10}-1} E_G^2 + E_G^3 = 0
\tag{6}
$$

in which, $E_G^i > 0, (i = 1, 2, 3)$. Equation (6) is the necessary and sufficient condition for the existence of this neural network. If equation (6) is satisfied, then the rank of the coefficient matrix is equal to the rank of its extended matrix. That is, $r = 7 < n = 8$ (n is the order of the linear equations). Thus, the homogeous linear equations have only the zero solution. From the equations in (5), we get the solution of the nonhomogeneous linear equations in (4):

$$
\begin{cases}
K = \frac{f_G^{00}}{2f_G^{00}-1} E_G^1 \\
I_1 = \frac{1}{2f_G^{00}-1} E_G^1 \\
I_2 = I_3 = \frac{f_G^{00}}{2f_G^{00}-1} E_G^1 - \frac{f_G^{10}}{2f_G^{10}-1} E_G^2 \\
T_{12} = T_{13} = \frac{-1}{2f_G^{00}-1} E_G^1 + \frac{1}{2f_G^{10}-1} E_G^2 \\
T_{23} = E_G^2 - \frac{1}{2}(E_G^1 + E_G^3)
\end{cases}
\tag{7}
$$

The equations in (7) are a general solution of the neural network for the basic logic gate with 2-inputs. For a specific logic gate, we use its logic function to determine the corresponding function terms f_G^k, then substitute them into the equations in (7) to obtain the basic parameters for the neural network. For example, for a 2-input AND gate, $f_{AND}^{00} = f_{AND}^{10} = 0, f_{AND}^{11} = 1$. Substituting this into equation (6), gives

$$
- E_{AND}^1 + 2E_{AND}^2 + E_{AND}^3 = 0
\tag{8}
$$

This is the constrained condition that the neural network has to satisfy. This may be used to reduce one of constants $E_{AND}^i (i = 1, 2, 3)$. From the equations in (7) we obtain the neural parameters for the AND gate as follows

$$
\begin{cases}
K = 0 \\
I_1 = -E_{AND}^1 \\
I_2 = I_3 = 0 \\
T_{12} = T_{13} = E_{AND}^1 - E_{AND}^2 \\
T_{23} = E_{AND}^2 - \frac{1}{2}(E_{AND}^1 + E_{AND}^3)
\end{cases}
\tag{9}
$$

Suppose $E_{AND}^2 = A, E_{AND}^3 = B$. Equation (8) gives $E_{AND}^1 = 2A + B$, which is the same as Charkradhar's result[2].

In a similar manner, we can get the neural parameters for 2-input OR, NAND and NOR gates. However, the cases for XOR and XNOR gates are quite different. For a 2-input XOR gate, $f_{XOR}^{00} = f_{XOR}^{11} = 0, f_{XOR}^{10} = 1$. Substituting into equation (6) gives

$$
E_{XOR}^1 + 2E_{XOR}^2 + E_{XOR}^3 = 0
\tag{10}
$$

Because $E_{XOR}^i > 0 (i = 1, 2, 3)$, equation (10) can not be satisfied. Thus, there is not a neural network with three neurons representing a 2-input XOR gate.

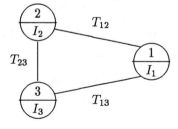

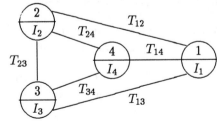

Figure 3: Neural network for a basic gate   Figure 4: XOR gate neural network

Adding a hidden neuron, x_4, we try to construct a neural network with four neurons representing a 2-input XOR gate (as shown in Fig.4). This hidden neuron has an activation value of 1 when both inputs to the gate are 1. In a similar manner, the necessary and sufficient condition for the existence of the neural network gives the set of constained equations. And then, we can get the neural parameters for the XOR gate.

V. Discussion and Conclusion

As shown above, we use the Hopfield model to obtain the energy surface and its constrained energy equations based on the truth table of a logic device. Using linear equations theory, we achieve the necessary and sufficient condition for the existence of its neural network, from which the general neural parameter expression for any logic gate is obtained. From equation (6), we can see that the logic function terms f_G^k affect the existence of the neural network model.

Chakradhar[2] classified the consistent state sets for neurons as three classes:P_{i_on}, P_{i_off}, P_{i_other}, and introduced the neuron decision hyperplane to derive *a necessary condition* for the existence of the neural network of a logic device. In this paper, on the basis of the truth table, we classify the neural network states as *consistent states* and *inconsistent states*. Then, we introduce the constrained energy equations, use linear equations theory to derive *the necessary and sufficient condition* for the existence of a neural network for a logic device, from which we obtain the general neural parameter expression for a basic logic gate. Chakradhar's result is merely a special case of our work.

We have used the method proposed in this paper to implement the logic circuit neural network simulation system on a SUN 3/260 workstation in C language. The preliminary experimental results show that our method is feasible, and predict its success[6].

The approach in this paper may be extended to the three-value neural network model[8] for logic circuits as well as the neural network model for functional level logic circuits.

References

[1] Y.S.Abu-Mostafa, "Neural networks for computing ? ", *Neural Networks for Computing(Snowbird), Ed. J.S.Denker, New York: American Institute of Physics*, pp.1-6, 1986

[2] S.T.Chakradhar, M.L.Bushnell and V.D.Agrawal "Automatic test generation using neural networks", *Proc. Int. Conf. on CAD*, pp.416-419, Nov. 1988

[3] S.T.Chakradhar, V.D.Agrawal and M.L.Bushnell "Neural net and Boolean satisfiability models of logic circuits", *IEEE Design & Test of Computers*, pp.54-57, Oct. 1990

[4] J.J.Hopfield, "Neural computation of decisions in optimization problems", *Biological Cybernetics*, Vol. 52, pp.141-152, 1985

[5] H.Fujiwara, "Three-Valued neural networks for test generation", *Proc. 20th Fault-Tolerant Computing Symposium*, pp.64-71, 1990

[6] Zhong Zhang, "Simulation of logic circuit neural network and its experimental results", *Journal of Computer Science & Technology*, (to be published)

Hardware Implementations

Session Chairs: Clifford Lau
Ralph Castain
Mohammad Sayeh

ORAL PRESENTATIONS

Challenges in Neurocomputers

Clifford G. Lau
Office of Naval Research
800 N. Quincy Street
Arlington, VA 22217

ABSTRACT

In the last decade, renewed interest in developing computational models of the brain, coupled with advances in VLSI technology, has created many opportunities to realize these computational models in silicon. Along with these biologically motivated neural chips, artificial neural networks (ANN) have also re-emerged as massively parallel solutions to previous adaptive learning algorithms. The advantage of ANN over adaptive algorithms is in terms of much faster computation and learning. However, to realize that computational power, ANNs must be realized in VLSI hardware. When algorithms are put on silicon, many issues have to be addressed, such as what is the circuit architecture, analog or digital implementations, voltage mode or current mode, general or special applications, size of the network, learning algorithms, and weight storage. Several challenges are particularly important to realize the computational power of neurocomputers, which in the broad sense of the word can mean any computer architectures based on neural network paradigms. Many neural network chips and boards, including digital ones, have been shown to be able to perform extremely fast computations. But, input/output interfaces are still very important to bring the data in and out of the chips/boards. Another issue is packaging. Because of the massively parallel nature of neural network architectures, three-dimensional (3-D) packaging may be necessary to avoid serial data interfaces. Circuit and computational architecture is another important factor in realizing high performance neurocomputers. In this paper, the latest research efforts in neurocomputers, and the challenges facing this community, will be discussed.

Subthreshold MOS Fuzzy Max/Min Neuron Circuits

Coskun Baysoy and Larry L. Kinney

Department of Electrical Engineering
University of Minnesota
Minneapolis, MN 55455

Abstract— We propose simple feedforward neuron circuits in *subthreshold MOS technology* that implement multi-variable, soft *max/min* functions for analog fuzzy neural VLSI. The circuits have several advantages: extremely low power consumption, small silicon complexity, fine *max/min* approximation, and relatively large signal dynamic ranges. The performances of the circuits are discussed. The effects of parameter mismatches and temperature changes are analyzed. SPICE simulations are given.

1. Introduction

This work was motivated by a particular neuron model that replaces the *sum* function of the well-known weighted summation neuron with *max / min* functions while keeping its basic structure intact. Such neurons are fundamental primitives extensively used in *neural* systems such as in pattern recognition applications [1] and in *fuzzy* systems as (weighted) fuzzy set aggregators [2], [9]. A large volume of work has been reported on miscellaneous summation neuron hardware. Surprisingly, however, only a few multi-input *max / min* circuits [3]-[5] and to our knowledge only one [4] in subthreshold MOS circuit regime [6]-[8] have been designed with analog fuzzy neural VLSI systems in mind. Typically, fuzzy neural information is processed in parallel on a vast network of densely interconnected neurons. Bare implementability at the neuron level is therefore is not sufficient; the challenge is in monolithic integration of tens of thousands of neurons, each with equally large number of synapses. Accordingly, efficiency of integration and the possibility of even achieving such neuron densities on a single chip need to be addressed.

We propose *subthreshold* MOS, *feedforward*, n-input *max / min* neuron circuits containing as low as $n+3$ transistors. The characteristics of the circuits are independent of device geometries. Considering this property along with their small transistor counts, the circuits are suitable for VLSI where limited area is one of the primary design constraints. Achievable integration density in a given area is also limited by the power dissipated by each device. This is exactly where subthreshold regime operations become precious because, in this regime, a MOS transistor operates in its *off* state and consumes practically no power [6]. The circuits exploit the robustness under imprecision, uncertainty, and noise property of fuzzy neural computing which makes the known impediments of analog circuits such as inaccuracy less of an inferiority. Fuzzy neural computing is deliberately an *approximation*, hence allowing rough definitions of system primitives by overlooking their actual, detailed characteristics. The proposed circuits, to fine approximations to *max / min* functions, essentially implement the $p-norm$ operator

$$\|u\|_p = (u_1^p + u_2^p + \ldots + u_n^p)^{1/p} \tag{0}$$

defined on non-negative inputs u_k by using *only e^x and $ln(x)$* functions. This transformation defines novel soft *max / min* aggregators that yield sharp approximations for surprisingly small $p \geq 0$ values, and as demonstrated, result in simple structures in silicon. The constant parameter p may be set to a desired value from a certain interval.

2. Subthreshold MOS Device Model

The subthreshold region of a MOS transistor (Fig. 1) has been well studied by others, e.g., [6]-[8] and the relevant NMOS equations are given below. With the proper changes in signs, the equations are also valid for a PMOS device.

Subthreshold MOS transistors use *diffusion* currents due to spatial density gradients of carrier particles (in contrast to strong inversion currents due to particle *drift* under an external electric field). Particles travel voluntarily according to Boltzman law, resulting in the subthreshold drain current modeled by

$$I_D = I_o \, e^{\frac{\kappa V_{GS}}{V_t}} (1 - e^{-\frac{V_{DS}}{V_t}}) \qquad V_{GS} < V_{Th} \tag{1}$$

where V_{GS} is gate-to-source voltage, V_{DS} is drain-to-source voltage; $V_t = kT/q$ ($V_t \approx 25.9 \, mV$ at $27°C$) is thermal voltage, T is temperature, q is the charge of an electron, k is Boltzman's constant; κ is the so-called subthreshold coefficient; and I_o is a process, geometry, and temperature dependent constant: $I_o = (\mu W / \kappa L) C_{ox} V_t^2 e^{\kappa V_{Th}/V_t}$

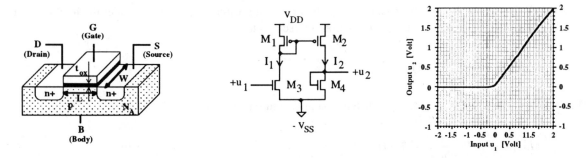

Figure 1 A typical NMOS transistor.   **Figure 2** A single-input *max* neuron and its simulated DC characteristic.

where μ is carrier mobility; W and L are channel width and length, respectively; V_{Th} is the threshold voltage; and $C_{ox} = \varepsilon_{ox} / t_{ox}$ is the gate oxide capacitance where ε_{ox} is the permittivity of oxide and t_{ox} is the gate oxide thickness.

The subthreshold drain current exhibits a strong exponential dependence to V_{GS}. The *subthreshold slope* ω of $I_D - V_{GS}$ curve is conveniently defined and given by

$$\omega = \frac{\partial (ln I_D)}{\partial V_{GS}} = \frac{\kappa}{V_t} \tag{2}$$

The dependence of the subthreshold current to V_{DS} is, however, significant only when $V_{DS} \approx 0\,V$. For V_{DS} values exceeding a few $V_t \approx 25.9\ mV$, (1) with the substitution of (2) can be simplified to

$$I_D = I_o\, e^{\omega V_{GS}} \qquad V_{GS} < V_{Th} \tag{3}$$

which is valid for drain currents roughly satisfying $I_D \leq \mu \varepsilon_{ox} W V_t^2 / t_{ox} L$. From the circuit design point of view, (3) provides a clean exponential function with essentially two parameters: I_o and ω. The value of I_o (typically, $10^{-19}\,A \leq I_o \leq 10^{-16}\,A$) is not tightly-controlled during fabrication, and therefore, is not useful in circuit synthesis. In contrast, the subthreshold slope ω is almost constant in neighboring transistors with similar body-to-source voltages and is available as an adjustable design parameter. In terms of the physical parameters ω is given by

$$\omega = \frac{\kappa}{V_t} \approx \frac{q}{kT} \frac{1}{1 + t_{ox} N_{eff}^{1/2} \sqrt{\dfrac{\varepsilon_{si} q}{2\varepsilon_{ox}^2 (\Phi_s - V_{BS})}}} \tag{4}$$

Typical values of κ range from 0.67 to 0.90 with less than 5% spread [6], [8]. This translates to subthreshold slope range $25.5 \leq \omega \leq 35.1$ at room temperature with a similar spread. As will be seen later, large values of ω is desirable. From (4), the theoretical maximum of ω occurs at $\omega = q / kT \approx 38.61$ at room temperature. This limit may be approached by *decreasing* gate oxide thickness t_{ox}, or channel doping N_{eff}, or body-to-source voltage V_{BS}, or the temperature T. Scaling down t_{ox} to the minimum value allowed by oxide reliability constraints also decrease subthreshold voltage mismatch and minimize short-channel effects while maximizing the saturation current. The surface potential Φ_s may be replaced by an average value $\Phi_s = 0.5\,V$.

3. Single-input *Max* Neuron (Soft *Max*{*x*, *0*} Function)

Subthreshold MOS transistors can be combined to synthesis a large class of two-port circuits having linear and nonlinear transfer characteristics. A trivial example of such circuits is the half-wave rectifier circuit (Fig. 2) given by the constitutive relationship $u_2 = Max\{u_1, 0\}$. The subcircuit containing PMOS transistors M_1 and M_2 is the identity circuit (current mirror) which satisfies $I_1 = I_2$ ideally. Supposing $V_{SS} = 0\,V$ for simplicity, it follows from (1) that constitutive relations of M_3 and M_4 are $I_1 = I_o e^{\omega u_1}$ and $I_2 = I_o e^{\omega u_2}(1 - e^{-(1/V_t)u_2})$, respectively. Assuming matched I_o and ω for M_3 and M_4, u_2 relates to u_1 as $u_2 = (1 / \omega) ln(e^{\omega u_1} + e^{[\omega - (1/V_t)]u_2})$ provided that the identity circuit is ideal. Recall that $\omega = \kappa / V_T$ where κ can be very close to 1 but it cannot exceed it. Consider the limit case where $\kappa \to 1$ so that $\omega \to 1/V_t$, for which $u_2 - u_1$ relationship reduces to

$$u_2(u_1, \omega) = \frac{1}{\omega} ln(e^{\omega u_1} + 1) \tag{5}$$

This is an approximation to $u_2 = Max\{u_1, 0\}$ function in the sense that

$$Max\{u_1, 0\} = \lim_{\omega \to \infty} \frac{1}{\omega} ln(e^{\omega u_1} + 1) \tag{6}$$

For a finite ω, $u_2(u_1, \omega)$ is then a soft $Max\{u_1, 0\}$ function such that $u_2(u_1, \omega) > Max\{u_1, 0\} \geq 0$. Fig. 2 shows the $u_2 - u_1$ plot obtained from a SPICE simulation of the circuit, where ω was about 25.7 for NMOS transistors.

4. Two-input *Max / Min* Neurons

Using the scalar function $f(x) = Max\{x, 0\}$, two-variable *Max* and *Min* functions can be given as

$$u_{max} = Max\{u_1, u_2\} = u_1 + Max\{u_2 - u_1, 0\} \tag{8}$$
$$u_{min} = Min\{u_1, u_2\} = u_1 - Max\{u_1 - u_2, 0\} \tag{9}$$

With the substitution of (6) using the proper arguments, (8) and (9) can be expressed alternatively as

$$Max\{u_1, u_2\} = \lim_{\omega \to \infty} \frac{1}{\omega} ln(e^{\omega u_1} + e^{\omega u_2}) \tag{10}$$

$$Min\{u_1, u_2\} = \lim_{\omega \to \infty} -\frac{1}{\omega} ln(e^{-\omega u_1} + e^{-\omega u_2}) \tag{11}$$

An advantage offered by (10) and (11) is that extensions to n-variable cases are quite straightforward through direct substitutions which again result in simple expressions due to the convenient order of e^x and $ln(x)$ functions.

5. Multiple-input *Max / Min* Neurons

Figs. 3 and 4 show n-input *max* and *min* neuron circuits implementing the generalizations of (10) and (11) to n-variable cases, respectively. Notice first the similarity of their structures: One is obtained from the other through PMOS for NMOS, and vice versa, transistor substitution and exchanging the supply rails. The circuits consist of n parallel-connected input transistors, each associated with a variable from the input set $\{u_1, u_2, ..., u_n\}$. It is assumed that $u_k \geq 0 \ \forall k$. As will be seen later, input transistors provide exponential functions and M_3 provide the logarithm function. M_1 and M_2 form an identity circuit which may or may not operate in subthreshold circuit regime. Notice that if M_4 is short-circuited, the multiple-input circuits have the same basic structure as the single-input *max* neuron

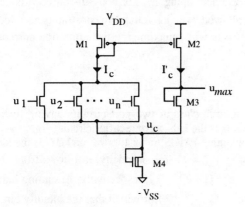

Figure 3 n-input *max* neuron circuit.

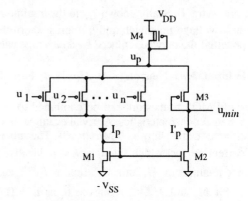

Figure 4 n-input *min* neuron circuit.

circuit of Sec. 3 in that a new input transistor is added for each additional variable (e.g., compare Figs. 2 and 3). M_4 circuitry may contain one or more diode-connected series transistors; or it may be a short-circuit. It is added to simultaneously extend the voltage dynamic ranges of the input transistors and also M_3.

Consider the analysis of the *max* neuron circuit. Suppose for simplicity that $Max\{u_1, u_2, ..., u_n\} >> V_t$ and $V_{SS} = 0\,V$. Assume that all NMOS transistors match and the identity circuit is ideal, i.e., $I_c = I_c'$, and that the output current withdrawn from the circuit is negligible compared to the drain current of M_3. Then, the *max* neuron circuit satisfies

$$I_o e^{\omega(u_{max} - u_c)} = I_o \sum_{k=1}^{n} e^{\omega(u_k - u_c)} \tag{12}$$

or by solving (12) for u_{max}, we obtain

$$u_{max} = \frac{1}{\omega} ln(\sum_{k=1}^{n} e^{\omega u_k}) \tag{13}$$

provided that *all* NMOS devices necessarily operate in their subthreshold regions. The right-hand side of (13) is a multi-variable soft *max* operator in the sense: Given a set of non-negative real numbers $\{u_1, u_2, ..., u_n\}$, we have

$$u_{max}^* = Max\{u_1, u_2, ..., u_n\} = \lim_{\omega \to \infty} \frac{1}{\omega} ln(\sum_{k=1}^{n} e^{\omega u_k}) \tag{14}$$

Proof: Eq. (14) can be written equivalently as

$$u_{max}^* = \lim_{\omega \to \infty} \frac{\sum_k u_k e^{\omega u_k}}{\sum_k e^{\omega u_k}} = \lim_{\omega \to \infty} \sum_k \left(\frac{u_k}{m + \sum_{i \in N} e^{\omega(u_i - u_k)}} \right) \tag{15}$$

where $N = \{i \mid u_i \neq u_k \ \forall i\}$ and $m \geq 1$ is the number of u_i such that $u_i = u_k$, $\forall i$. As $\omega \to \infty$, the *i*th exponential term of the inner summation becomes either 0 or ∞. In the former case, no contribution is made to the inner summation, and in the latter, the entire *k*th term of the outer summation is 0. Hence the result follows.

Similarly, the *min* neuron circuit satisfies

$$u_{min} = -\frac{1}{\omega} ln(\sum_{k=1}^{n} e^{-\omega u_k}) \tag{16}$$

which approximates $u_{min}^* = Min\{u_1, u_2, ..., u_n\}$ for a set of non-negative real numbers $\{u_1, u_2, ..., u_n\}$ in the sense that

$$u_{min}^* = \lim_{\omega \to \infty} -\frac{1}{\omega} ln(\sum_{k=1}^{n} e^{-\omega u_k}) \tag{17}$$

The outputs of the circuits always satisfy $u_{max} > u_{max}^* \geq 0$ and $0 \leq u_{min} < u_{min}^*$. For the simplest *max/min* neuron circuit (where M_4 is a short-circuit), input voltages are limited to the rough interval $[0, V_{Th}]$ due to the subthreshold regime requirement $V_{GS} < V_{Th}$. As mentioned before, voltage dynamic ranges can be increased by adding one or more diode-connected, serial transistors to M_4. Each added transistor concurrently modulates both input and output voltages by the same amount, widening their useful ranges arithmetically. If M_4 has $r - 1$ devices and $V_{SS} = 0\,V$, the useful voltage range extends roughly to $[0, rV_{Th}]$ for the *max* neuron and to $[V_{DD} - rV_{Th}, V_{DD}]$ for the *min* neuron. This extension has no effect on the *max/min* approximations since Eqs. (13) and (16) are free of r.

Fig. 5 shows the SPICE DC simulation results of a 6-input *max* neuron circuit with $r = 4$ and a 3-input *min* neuron circuit with $r = 2$, respectively. In the simulations, all but one input were held at fixed voltages and the remaining input was continuously increased from 0 to V_{DD}. The bold curves correspond to the output voltages. The DC characteristics agree well with the theoretical anticipations over a wide portion of the supply voltage range. The success of the circuits in terms of the closeness of approximations is due to the steep nonlinearity of the e^x function.

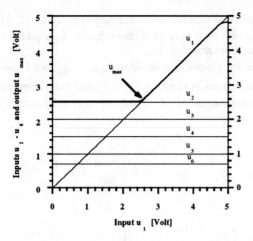 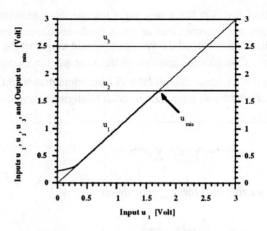

Figure 5 Simulated DC characteristics of **(a)** a 6-input *max* neuron ($V_{DD} = 5V$, $V_{SS} = 0V$) and **(b)** a 3-input *min* neuron ($V_{DD} = 3V$, $V_{SS} = 0V$). [For PMOS: $W/L = 4/4$, $t_{ox} = 39.8\ nm$, $N_{sub} = 9.28 \times 10^{15}\ 1/cm^3$, $V_{Th} = -0.85\ V$, $\gamma = 0.697\ V^{1/2}$; for NMOS: $W/L = 4/4$, $t_{ox} = 39.8\ nm$, $N_{sub} = 6.82 \times 10^{14}\ 1/cm^3$, $V_{Th} = 0.769\ V$, $\gamma = 0.1734\ V^{1/2}$.]

5.1 Performance Analysis

Closed form formulations (13) and (16) reduce the *max/min* computation effort to a simple [feedforward] algebraic calculation. But, so-calculated *max/min* is only an approximation since exact values are obtained *only* in the limit as $\omega \to \infty$. This is important because, in terms of the circuits, ω is a physical parameter and its range is limited. Also, we deliberately assumed matched devices in the derivations of (13) and (16); but physical devices never match. In the following, we investigate the influence of finite ω values and the effects of parameter mismatches and the temperature changes on the operation of the circuits.

A) **Influence of finite** ω: The relative difference ε between $u_{max}(\omega)$ calculated from (13) and the precise value $u_{max}^* = u_{max}(\omega \to \infty)$ is defined and given by

$$\varepsilon = \frac{u_{max} - u_{max}^*}{u_{max}} = 1 / \left[1 + \frac{\omega u_{max}^*}{\ln(m + \sum\limits_{u_i \neq u_{max}^*} e^{-\omega(u_{max}^* - u_i)})} \right] \tag{18}$$

where $m \geq 1$ is the number of u_i such that $u_i = u_{max}^*$, $\forall i$. From (18), the relative difference clearly depends on the values of input set elements as well as the value of ω. Particularly, the difference becomes significant *only* when two or more inputs share the same value u_{max}^*. The *worst-case* corresponds to the case where *all* set elements are *equal* to each other, for which (18) simplifies to

$$\varepsilon_{worst} = \frac{1}{1 + \dfrac{\omega u_{max}^*}{\ln(n)}} \tag{19}$$

where n is the cardinality of the input set $\{u_1, u_2, \ldots, u_n\}$. Likewise, the worst-case relative difference for the n-input *min* neuron circuit is obtained as

$$\varepsilon_{worst} = \frac{1}{\dfrac{\omega u_{min}^*}{\ln(n)} - 1} \tag{20}$$

For a finite ω, one therefore obtains better approximations on relatively smaller input sets having larger values. The dependence on n through $\ln(.)$ function is however weak. Thus, the set size is not really a limitation. On the other hand, for increased precision the upper portion of available input voltage range should be utilized.

II-504

B) Influence of parameter mismatches: The following analysis is given for the *max* neuron circuit only. Consider the case where ω is perfectly matched in all NMOS transistors but I_o shows the worst-case mismatch ΔI_o from the nominal resulting in the output voltage $u_{(I)max} = u_{max} + \Delta u_{max}$. Then, the *absolute* mismatch Δu_{max} can be shown to be always less than or equal to

$$\Delta u_{max} = \frac{1}{\omega} ln(\frac{1+\delta_o}{1-\delta_o}) \tag{21}$$

where $\delta_o = \Delta I_o / I_o$. For example, if $\delta_o = 0.4$ (about its maximum in standard MOS processes), absolute mismatch in u_{max} for $\omega = 35$ should be below $\Delta u_{max} = 0.024$. Even though the value of I_o is not well-controlled over silicon processes, the circuit suppresses the I_o mismatch effect through $ln(.)$ function of (21). Moreover, increasing ω not only increases the output precision but also reduces the effect of I_o mismatch. Next consider the case in which I_o is matched perfectly while ω exhibits $\Delta\omega$ worst-case mismatch causing the output to change from u_{max} to $u_{(\omega)max}$. To simplify the task without loosing the generality, let us consider this mismatch in the limit as $\omega \rightarrow \infty$ and when $u_k = u^*_{max}$ for all k. The worst-case *relative* mismatch for the case considered is then given by

$$\varepsilon_\omega = \frac{u_{(\omega)max} - u_{max}}{u_{(\omega)max}} = \frac{2\delta_\omega}{1+\delta_\omega} \tag{22}$$

where $\delta_\omega = \Delta\omega / \omega$. For example, for $\delta_\omega = 0.04$ and $\delta_\omega = 0.01$, ε_ω is about 7.6% and 1.9%, respectively. The effect of ω mismatch is more pronounced than that of I_o mismatch. However, as mentioned previously, unlike I_o, the value of ω is well-controlled over processes. For constant temperatures, ω values are reported [6] to be quite constant among devices in a single fabrication batch (δ_ω can be well below 5%.) The effect of the mismatches in the identity circuit is similar to that of I_o mismatch. Finally, the known methods for improving matching can be utilized. These include making larger devices of the same size and shape that have similar surrounding structures, etc..

C) Influence of temperature changes and the body-effect: The relative change $\delta_T = \Delta\omega_T / \omega_T$ due to a change $\Delta T / T$ in temperature is $\delta_T = -\Delta T / T$, i.e., even the smallest changes in T is reflected directly onto ω. However, T may be assumed constant for clusters of transistors in a sufficiently small neighborhood. This is particularly true if power dissipated on chip is very low. Also, the circuits have the property that there is no so-called body-effect on the quality of approximations due to identical modulation of source voltages of input transistors and M_3 by M_4.

6. Concluding Remarks

We presented n-synapse, fuzzy *max/min* neuron circuits in subthreshold MOS technology. The proposed circuits have small silicon complexities ($O(n)$) and consume very little power—attributes that are essential for high-density integration. But, they are slower compared to binary standards due to small currents (dis)charging regular device and layout capacitances. While this trade-off seems apparent, the speed evaluation should, nevertheless, not be attempted at the neuron level because of the collective and analog nature of fuzzy neural computing at the system level.

REFERENCES

[1] T. Watanabe, M. Matsumoto, M. Enokida, and T. Hasegawa, "A Design of Multiple-Valued Logic Neuron," in Proc. 20th IEEE Int. Symp. on Multiple-Valued Logic, pp. 418-425, May 1990.

[2] R. R. Yager "Toward a Unified Approach to Aggregation in Fuzzy and Neural Systems," Proc. WCNN'93, Vol. II, pp. 619-622, Portland, July 1993.

[3] T. Yamakawa, T. Miki, and F. Ueno, "The Design and Fabrication of the Current Mode Fuzzy Logic Semi-Custom IC in the Standard CMOS IC Technology," Proc. 15th IEEE Int. Symp. MVL, pp. 76-82, May 1985.

[4] C. Baysoy and L. L. Kinney, "Asymmetric Feedback Max/Min Circuits of O(n) Complexities for Analog VLSI Neural, Multiple-Valued, and Fuzzy Logic Systems," Proc. WCNN'93, Vol. II, pp. 97-101, Portland, July 1993.

[5] M. Sasaki, T. Inoue, Y. Shirai, and F. Ueno, "Fuzzy Multiple-Input Maximum and Minimum Circuits in Current Mode and Their Analyses Using Bounded-Difference Equations," IEEE Trans. Computers, Vol. 39, No. 6, pp. 768-774, June 1990.

[6] C. A. Mead, *Analog VLSI and Neural Systems*, Addison-Wesley, NY, 1989.

[7] T. Grothjohn and B. Hoefflinger, "A Parametric Short-Channel MOS Transistor Model for Subthreshold and Strong Inversion Current," IEEE J. Solid-State Circuits, Vol. SC-19, No. 1, pp. 100-112, Feb. 1984.

[8] E. Vittoz and J. Fellrath, "CMOS Analog Integrated Circuits Based on Weak Inversion Operation," IEEE J. Solid-State Circuits, Vol. SC-12, No. 3, pp. 224-231, June 1977.

[9] D. Dubois and H. Parade, "A Review of Fuzzy Set Aggregation Connectives," Information Sciences, **36**, pp. 85-121, 1985.

RESULTS FROM A NEURAL NETWORK APPLICATION IN HIGH-ENERGY PHYSICS USING THE ETANN CHIP

C. Baldanza, F. Bisi, A. Cotta-Ramusino, I. D'Antone,
L. Malferrari, P. Mazzanti, F. Odorici, R. Odorico, M. Zuffa
INFN/Bologna, Via Irnerio 46, 40126 Bologna, Italy
E-mail: odorico@bo.infn.it

C. Bruschini, P. Musico, P. Novelli
INFN/Genoa, Via Dodecaneso 33, 16146 Genoa, Italy

M. Passaseo
CERN, 1211 Geneva 23, Switzerland

ABSTRACT

A neural trigger module for fast classification of high-energy physics events, based on the analog neural microprocessor ETANN by Intel, has been realized. It has been employed in the experiment WA92 at CERN. Task of the neural trigger is to send events to be analyzed with high priority on a special data stream, the Fast Stream. Its response time is less than 10 microseconds. The limited precision of the ETANN chip affects the choice of the neural net architecture, as it is discussed in some detail. Results from the experimental run are presented.

1. Introduction

High-energy physics offers special challenges to neural network applications (Odorico, 1982; Odorico, 1992). Response times are required to be very short, typically less than 10 µs. Output from the experimental apparatus can be very complex, of the order of several hundred independent channels. A most often considered task for neural networks is triggering. Conditions for the particle beam intensity and density of the target may be set up so that several million collision events occur per second. But only a fraction of them are interesting to record. The trigger is a device that by making a quick elaboration of the detector output is able to decide whether the event is worth recording or not. Neural networks can be used as part of the trigger device: they can contribute to the trigger decision by making a pattern recognition of the detector output. Neural networks become essential in this task when a significant discrimination of the interesting events, i.e. the signal, from the background can only be attained by exploiting correlations among the various components of the detector output which are characteristic of the signal.

The neural trigger module, whose realization and on-line running results are presented here, consists of a VME crate utilizing the analog neural chip ETANN by Intel (80170NX, 1991) which has operated within the WA92 experiment at CERN (Adamovich et al., 1990) during the 1993 run. WA92 is an experiment looking for the production of beauty particles by a π^- beam at 350 GeV/c impinging on a Cu target. Interactions are triggered if a secondary vertex signature is detected by a specially designed hardware processor (the BCP, see below). Only interactions where this signature is accompanied either by a lepton or by a particle with high transverse momentum (relative to beam direction) are written onto tape. Task of the neural trigger is to send events to be analyzed with high priority on a special data stream, the Fast Stream. Target of the neural trigger are events which in addiction to the primary production vertex also contain secondary C3 vertices, i.e. branching into three particle tracks with sum of the electric charges equal to ±1. The latter may be originated by the decay of unstable heavy flavor particles, i.e. carrying the charm or beauty quantum numbers. At the time of running only the ETANN part of the crate was operational. The training of the ETANN chip was done using 1993 WA92 data, with C3 events certified by the Trident event reconstruction program. Input to the neural crate was provided by the Beauty Contiguity Processor (BCP) of Darbo and Rossi (Darbo et al., 1990), which determined tracks and their impact parameters on-line, using data from the silicon microstrip Vertex Detector. The BCP data, arranged in 5x64-bit hit-maps, were preprocessed within the neural crate to yield 16 input variables for the neural chips.

2. WA92 Trigger Apparatus

The part of the WA92 trigger detector relevant for the input to the neural chips consists of 6 silicon-microstrip planes of the Vertex Detector (VD), measuring the z coordinates of tracks, where the z axis has the direction of the magnetic field (bottom-up direction). The last plane is positioned at about 41 cm downstream of the target and has a square shape with a 5 cm side, centered around the beam. The hit information from the 6 planes is processed by the Beauty Contiguity Processor (BCP) developed by Darbo and Rossi (Darbo et al., 1990), which reconstructs tracks and their impact parameters (IP), with a global response time of about 40 μs (Bruschini et al., 1992). IP is defined as the signed difference between the z value of the track extrapolated back to the target-center plane and the beam z position. The BCP supplies to the Neural Trigger (NT) 5 words of 64-bit each, plus a standard go-ahead termination word. Each one of the 5 words directly represents the hit-map of tracks on the last (6th) VD layer, divided in 64 bins, for tracks falling within a given IP window. The BCP could supply up to 8 hit-maps, with a resolution which can reach 256 bits. Data transfer times would be correspondingly increased. Simulation has shown that the arrangement we eventually employed is adequate for the task and does not lead to any significant loss of performance.

The BCP also makes a first level decision about accepting the event. Defining as secondary tracks those with $|IP| >$ 100 μm and as primary the other tracks, the Standard Non-Leptonic Trigger (SNLT) requires the presence of 3 primary tracks, 2 secondary tracks and 1 track in the Butterfly Hodoscope with high p_T (defined in a detector dependent mode, roughly corresponding to > 0.6 GeV/c along the z axis). The Neural Trigger considers only events which have already been accepted by the SNLT.

3. Neural Trigger Hardware

The Neural Trigger module consists of an Extended VME crate (VME9U boards). Its overall structure is shown in Fig. 1. There are 9 boards in the crate:

- one VIC 8250 module by CES, interfacing the VME Bus to an IBM-compatible personal computer;
- one Input Interface Board, interfacing to the WA92 apparatus;
- 4 Preprocessing Boards, with 2 Preprocessing Units each, each unit calculating variables for a given IP window;
- 2 MA16 Boards, with one MA16 chip per board; they will be not discussed here;
- one ETANN Board, hosting two independent ETANN chips.

All inputs from the WA92 apparatus enter through connectors in the front panel of the Input Interface Board. Outputs to the WA92 trigger logic and data acquisition exit through connectors in the front panels of the MA16 and ETANN Boards.

The VIC 8250 board by CES connects the VME Bus to a VBAT 8218 card, also by CES, installed in the PC. Specific C++ programs have been developed for configuring, testing and monitoring the crate from the PC. Also, programs have been developed for simulating on-line running conditions, and having recorded experimental inputs or simulated inputs passed through the crate with collection of the corresponding outputs.

There are 4 printed-circuit Preprocessing Boards, each one hosting 2 independent Preprocessing Units. Each Preprocessing Units outputs the input variables to the neural chips for a given IP window. With 5 IP windows, only 5 such units are actually used. Determination of the input variables is done by calculating them from the 64-bit hit-maps by means of Look Up Tables (LUT's) implemented on EPROM's. A total of 16 input variables to the neural chips are obtained in this way. The configuration which was finally adopted for them turned out to be the optimal one among several attempted in the preliminary studies.

The ETANN chip can operate in 1-layer mode, accepting a maximum of 128 input variables, and in 2-layer mode with a clocked-back feedback operation, accepting a maximum of 64 input variables. In both cases, it has 64 independent outputs (thus, a maximum of 64 hidden layer nodes in the 2-layer mode). Precision of the chip is quoted (80170NX, 1991) as being equivalent to 6-7 bits. Operatively, with our set-up, after conversion of the output to a 8-bit digital number (range 0-255), we have found during the experimental run a maximum deviation of 4 units for a high response, around or above the threshold value of about 146 for triggering, and a maximum deviation of 6 units for a lower response (likely due to the larger degree of cancellations), when routinely sending a prefixed set of test patterns chosen so as to uniformly cover the output range. ETANN was serviced by a voltage regulator, stabilizing its power voltage to within $\Delta V \leq 5$ mV, and a temperature controller stabilizing its temperature at 18 °C within $\Delta T \leq 1$ °C.

Input variables from the Preprocessing Boards are converted to analog signals for ETANN by Digital to Analog Converters (DAC's). The range of the input variables is 0-16, therefore 8-bit input precision is sufficient. 32 variables can be accepted by the ETANN board, but we found that 16 variables were enough in our application and we used just them also to save on trasfer time. The 8-bit input is converted to an analog signal from 1.6 to 3.2 V, with zero corresponding to $V_{REFI} = 1.6$ V, as required by ETANN. The output from ETANN, ranging from 0 to 3.2 V, is converted by Analog to Digital Converters (ADC's) to an 8-bit digital number in the range 0 to 255. The parameter controlling the transfer function slope has been set at $V_{GAIN} = 4.0$ V. In the iNNTS trainer (iNNTS, 1992), we have set the zero reference value for the output at $V_{REFO} = 1.6$ V.

Adding to the response time from the chips the time spent in the Interface and Preprocessing Boards and data transfer (i.e. including the loading time of DAC's), which is 3.2 μs, one has a total response time for the Neural Trigger module of 5.8 μs for the single-layer net we have actually used. That would grow to 9.3 μs for a 2-layer net.

NEURAL VME CRATE

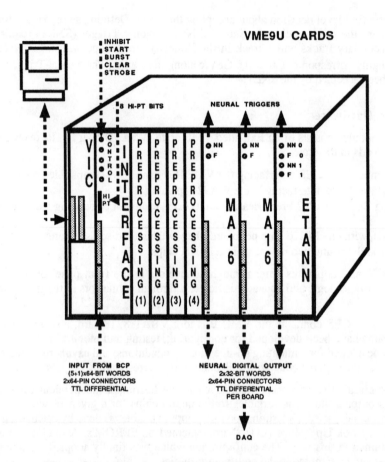

Fig. 1. Schematic view of the Neural Trigger VME crate.

4. Neural Network Architecture and Training

In principle, we could have set as target for the Neural Trigger the direct recognition of beauty particle decays, defined by simulated events obtained by an event generator with added GEANT simulation of the WA92 apparatus. However, we refrained from doing that mainly for two reasons: i) although such simulated events were available, they were suitable for off-line studies, after some event selection, and were not appropriate for quantitative tuning of a neural trigger, also because of the general dependence of event generators on model assumptions which are especially critical for the relatively low mass beauty particles and for a complex nuclear target like copper; ii) the necessity of depending on graphical scanning, with the long waiting times involved, to have indications on the actual performance of the neural trigger.

Taking into account the effective necessities of the experiment, which required the analysis of many tens of millions of events to extract the few thousands affordable by graphic scanning, we rather focused on the enrichment in events which are selected for that sake. Especially interesting, from this point of view, are events with C3 secondary vertices, branching into three tracks with sum of electric charges equal to ± 1. A C3 vertex is a signature for $D \rightarrow K\pi\pi$ decay, and thus a non-leptonic signature for beauty particles. Certification of these events comes from the Trident event reconstruction program. By applying the event reconstruction program to real data obtained with a given experimental set-up, one gets the necessary event training samples to tune the Neural Trigger for enrichment in C3 events with the same experimental set-up. In this way one avoids altogether dependence on theoretical modeling and only relies on the event reconstruction program. This is the target we have chosen for the Neural Trigger. In doing that the Neural Trigger does not act alone, but in conjunction with the first level Standard Non-Leptonic Trigger (SNLT, see Section 2): only events already accepted by the SNLT are worked out by the Neural Trigger. By concentrating on SNLT events only, the Neural Trigger can better focus on correlations present within the events which discriminate signal from background. The SNLT&NT non-leptonic signature has been used to send events to be analyzed with high priority on a special data stream, the Fast Stream, where they lay together with events selected by semi-leptonic signatures.

Only input variables simple to calculate with the available hardware were taken into consideration. The basic strategy in devising them was to have them convey multi-scale information on the hit maps provided by the BCP. We first considered the maximum resolution made available by the BCP: 256 bits. By directly studying the corresponding hit maps for a set of events, however, we saw that 64-bit hit maps were enough. Using such a resolution had the advantage of reducing transfer times. We then considered variables counting the number of hits with 1-bit, 4-bit, 8-bit, 16-bit, 32-bit resolutions. We submitted them to significance tests based on Fisher discrimination (Kendall et al., 1983; Mazzanti et al., 1993). It turned out that the significant variables were those associated with 1-bit and 16-bit resolutions. The study was made by varying the IP window segmentation. Eventually, we found that an adequate IP window segmentation was the following one (the BCP allows for a maximum of 8 IP windows): -200 < IP < 200, 200 < IP < 400, -400 < IP < -200, 400 < IP < 900, -900 < IP < -400. We found that 16 input variables were adequate according to significance tests based on Fisher discrimination. Input variables were built by dividing each 64-bit map in 4x16-bit groups, ordered bottom-up in z, and calculating the following quantities on them:

K16MAP(i)   = #hits in group i = 1-4   (range: 0-16)

K16   = #groups hit   (range: 0-4)

KDW16   = #groups in bottom half hit   (range: 0-2)

KUP16   = #groups in top half hit   (range: 0-2)

A set of 16 variables extracted from this pool was found to be adequate for the problem at hand.

One can argue against reliance on significance tests based on Fisher discrimination for choosing the input variables, regarding them as appropriate when discussing the separation of the bulk of the event class distributions but too insensitive to the tail structure of these distributions, which is in principle relevant in high enrichment applications. Being aware of that, in our preliminary neural net studies we made several tries with larger samples of input variables, taken from the wide original pool. But we got no significant improvement of the results.

For the neural net architecture we considered the two options offered by ETANN: a 2-layer or a 1-layer net, the latter being equivalent to a Fisher discriminant. As discussed at some length in (Mazzanti et al., 1993), the optimal type of neural net totally depends on the problem at hand. If the two class distributions one has to discriminate have a gaussian shape with similar correlation matrices, no classifier can outperform the Fisher discriminant. We made preliminary software studies simulating some of the ETANN restrictions, as represented by the software handling the iNNTS development system. Specifically, weights and thresholds were requested to stay between -2.5 and 2.5 with input variables limited to ± 1. No useful way was found to simulate the limited weight precision. After training by standard back-propagation, the 2-layer net gave results slightly better (of the order of 20%) than a 1-layer net. But, after loading the nets on ETANN and having made some chip-in-loop training of the 2-layer net (that is not necessary for a 1-layer net), we found that the small margin in favor of the 2-layer net evaporated. Looking in detail at how event patterns were processed in the 2-layer net, we realized that the net had organized itself so that discrimination between the two event classes was largely due to small differences between the responses of the first layer which entered cancellations performed by the second layer node. Thus, weight precision had a large incidence on the results. We found no way of forcing back-propagation to direct the organization of the net to a structure less sensitive to weight precision. (Procedures to compensate for the limited weight precision by separately changing the transfer function slopes of nodes (Hoehfeld et al., 1992) are not applicable to ETANN, which has a single parameter,

V$_{GAIN}$, to control all the, nominally, equal slopes.) We had other reasons pressing us toward a 1-layer architecture: i) simplicity of training, since a 1-layer net, i.e. a Fisher discriminant, requires only inversion of the pooled-over-classes correlation matrix for that sake; ii) avoidance of chip-in-loop training, which may burn out nodes in ETANN, the latter being required essentially because of the variance of the transfer functions of nodes, which becomes irrelevant for a 1-layer net with one output node; iii) increased robustness towards changes in the operating conditions of the trigger detector, e.g. due to temperature excursions which can change alignments and the level of electronic noise, since the net is less fine-tuned to details of the shapes of the event class distributions; iv) shortening of the response time of the Neural Trigger.

In conclusion, we adopted a 1-layer net architecture with one output node. Its weights (i.e. the Fisher vector components) were determined on a conventional workstation by a simple matrix inversion operation and then loaded on ETANN by means of iNNTS. The procedure was fast and straightforward, in compliance with the strict time restrictions we had to meet during the experimental run. The training event samples we used consisted of 3000 C3 events and 10000 non-C3 events, accepted by the SNLT. The collection of the C3 event sample required the running of the Trident event reconstruction program for about 4 days on 3 alphavaxes 3000/400.

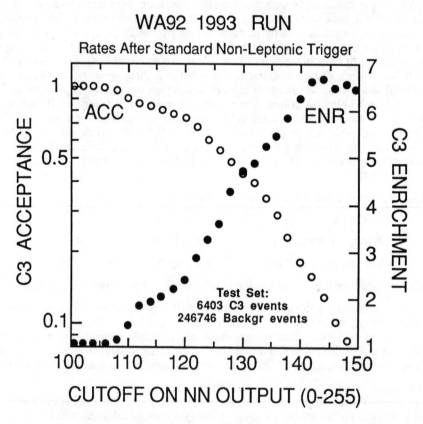

Fig. 2. C3 event enrichment and acceptance obtained when varying the lower cutoff on the Neural Trigger output (range 0-255), for the WA92 1993 data.

5. Results from the Experimental Run

The Neural Trigger, after its training was completed, operated for two continuous weeks within the apparatus of WA92. The results we present are based on a sample of events collected about two weeks after the acquisition of events used for training. It consists of 6403 C3 events and 246746 non-C3 events accepted by the SNLT and certified by the Trident reconstruction program. Fig. 2 shows the values of C3 event acceptance and enrichment obtained by the Neural Trigger when varying the lower cutoff on the neural net output, ranging from 0 to 255 (8-bit output). The results refer to the output from one of the ETANN chips, the other ETANN chip giving consistent results.

Above a certain value the C3 enrichment flattens out when increasing the cutoff on the neural net output. Setting the cutoff to a value corresponding to the beginning of the plateau, one obtains for a C3 event acceptance of 18% a C3 event enrichment of about 6.5, corresponding to a rejection factor for the background of about 36. The enrichment obtained by the Neural Trigger should be multiplied by that provided by the SNLT, which is somewhat larger than an order of magnitude, to get the total enrichment for C3 events given by the SNLT&NT trigger.

5. Conclusions

A Neural Trigger device based on the ETANN chip has been demonstrated by two weeks of continuous running in the experiment WA92. Task of the neural trigger was to send events to be analyzed with high priority on a special data stream, the Fast Stream. That represents the first example of an actual application of neural network technology to triggering in a high-energy physics experiment. Effects of the limited precision of the analog chip, also associated with dependence of its response on power voltage and temperature, had to be duly taken into account when designing the architecture of the neural network.

Acknowledgements

The WA92 Collaboration is gratefully acknowledged for support. A. Benvenuti has suggested the idea of demonstrating neural network techniques within experiment WA92, and has contributed, together with D. Bollini and F.L. Navarria, at the early stages of this project. The MA16 project is being made possible by the continuous support of J. Beichter, N. Brüls and U. Ramacher, of Siemens AG, Munich. C. Lindsey has made us familiar with a number of features of ETANN. F. Degli Esposti, M. Lolli, P. Palchetti and G. Sola, of the INFN Electronics Laboratory of Bologna, have given relevant contributions to the hardware development. M.L. Luvisetto, F. Ortolani and E. Ugolini have helped us in sorting out a number of problems with C++ programming. One of us, R.O., acknowledges useful conversations with R. Battiti about neural net training procedures.

References

Adamovich M. et al. (1990), WA92 Collaboration, CERN/SPSC 90-10 (1990), Nucl. Phys. (Proc. Suppl.) B 27 (1992) 251.

Bruschini C. et al. (1992), 1992 Nuclear Science Symposium, Orlando, Florida, 1992, Conf. Record p. 320.

Darbo G., and Rossi L. (1990), Nucl. Instr. and Meth. A 289 (1990) 584.

Fisher R.A. (1936), Annals Eugenics 7 (1936) 179.

Hoehfeld M., and Fahlman S. E. (1992), IEEE Trans. Neural Networks 3 (1992) 602.

Kendall M., Stuart A., and Ord J.K. (1983), The Advanced Theory of Statistics, Vol. 3, 4th ed. (C. Griffin &Co. Ltd., London).

iNNTS Neural Network Training System User's Guide (1992), Intel Corp..

Mazzanti P., and Odorico R. (1993), Zeitschrift f Physik C59 (1993) 273.

Odorico R. (1982), Proc. of the 1982 DPF Summer Study on Elementary Particle Physics and Future Facilities, Snowmass, Colorado, 1982, p. 478; Odorico R., Phys. Lett. 120B (1983) 219; Ballocchi G., and Odorico R., Nucl. Phys. B229 (1983) 1.

Odorico R. (1992), Invited Talk at the 1992 Nuclear Science Symposium, Orlando, Florida, 1992, Conf. Record p. 822; IEEE Transactions on Nuclear Science 40 (1993) 705.

80170NX Electrically Trainable Analog Neural Network Data Booklet (1991), Intel Corp. 2250 Mission College Boulevard, Santa Clara, CA 95052-8125, USA.

VLSI Implementation of a Pulse-Coded Winner-Take-All Network

Jack L. Meador and Paul D. Hylander
School of Electrical Engineering and Computer Science
Washington State University, Pullman WA, 99161-2752

Abstract

This paper presents a pulse-coded winner-take-all (PWTA) network which employs a unique combination of presynaptic and lateral inhibition that can be efficiently implemented in VLSI. The manner in which the network not only selects the winner but also indicates the weight of the decision made is unique among established winner-take-all networks. A combination of all-or-nothing and graded responses is encoded as a variable rate pulse train appearing only at the output of the winning unit. The mechanism used is closely related to the presynaptic inhibition approach introduced in [Yuille 88] with the exception that it is self-resetting and has properties which make it well suited for electronic realizations using asynchronous pulse-coded circuitry.

Winner-Take-All Functions and Competitive Neural Networks

The winner-take-all (WTA) function plays a central role in competitive neural networks and is related to recurrent on-center off-surround models of natural neural systems [Grossberg 73]. The WTA function can be computed sequentially using numerical comparisons, or in parallel using a Hopfield network [Majani 88] or MOS current conveyors [Lazzaro 88, Andreou 91].

The WTA function is useful because it is an essential component of well established neural networks such as ART, self organizing feature maps, and counterpropagation networks [Zurada 92]. It also finds use in applications such as vector quantization and coding, statistical data clustering, and optimization [Hertz 91].

In simple competitive networks, connection weight vectors (or "prototype vectors") are updated to move toward closely related input vectors. The function of the WTA subnetwork is to determine which of the prototypes is nearest by some distance measure. A simple competitive learning rule based on the inner product distance measure can be expressed concisely in terms of a randomly distributed input vector and a set of prototype vectors associated with unit outputs:

$$Y_i = \begin{cases} 1 & \text{if } W^T_i X > W^T_j X \ \forall \ j \neq i \\ 0 & \text{otherwise} \end{cases}$$

$$\Delta W_i = \eta Y_i (X - W_i)$$

(1)

where W_i and X correspond to the prototype vector for unit i and the input vector respectively. Here, only unit output Y_i is active, so only row i of W is adapted in proportion to learning rate constant η. In competitive networks the inner product computation and winning unit computation are distributed across two distinct subnetworks as illustrated in Figure 1. The focus of this paper is upon the implementation of the winning unit computation independent of others associated with distance measures and adaptation.

One characteristic of particular importance to the VLSI implementation of WTA networks is area complexity. WTAs using the Hopfield network organization (Figure 1a) are less practical for VLSI than those using an "inhibitory interneuron" approach (Figure 1b) since winning unit feedback requires a more complex interconnect. The Hopfield net approach has $O(N^2)$ area complexity while the use of an inhibitory interneuron requires only $O(N)$ area for N units. The architecture of the WTA network introduced here uses the more space-efficient inhibitory interneuron approach.

Computation In The Pulse Probability Domain

Asynchronous pulse coded processing units similar to the axosomal circuits first described in [Meador 91] are the basic elements of the WTA network to be presented here. The functional organization of a simple axosomal circuit is shown in Figure 2.

The axosomal circuit operates by cyclically charging and discharging the integrating capacitor C at a rate in proportion to the instantaneous magnitude of the synaptic current Inet. During the integration phase of circuit operation, S1 is closed and S2 is open. In this state weighted synaptic currents are summed via Kirchoff's current law to form the input current Inet which is integrated over time on C. With increasing time, the voltage across C increases, eventually reaching the upper threshold of the Schmitt trigger. At this threshold the output of the Schmitt trigger toggles, causing S1 to open and S2 to close causing C to discharge through R and S2. When the capacitor

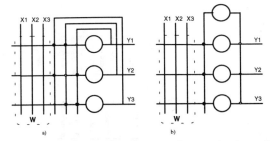

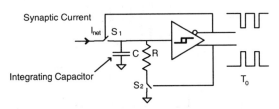

Figure 1. Winner-take-all network organization within a simple competitive network: a) Hopfield network approach and b) the use of a recurrent inhibitory interneuron. Inner product distance computations are computed in the distinct W subnetwork, independent of the WTA implementation.

Figure 2. Functional structure of an "axosomal circuit" for asychronous pulse stream processing. Pulses having a fixed width of T0 are generated at a rate determined by the magnitude of the synaptic current Inet.

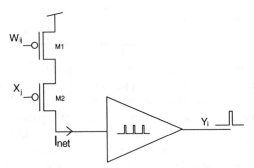

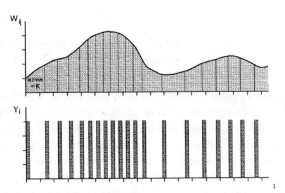

Figure 3. The axosomal circuit of Figure 2 controlled by a simple fixed synapse circuit. The rate at which output pulses are generated varies in direct proportion to with the connection weight (which increases with decreasing voltage Wij in this case) and increasing pulse frequency on Xj.

Figure 4. Output pulses generated from a continuously varying weight with a fixed input having firing probability one (continuously firing). The integral of the resulting pulse stream varies in direct proportion to the input signal integral.

voltage reaches the lower Schmitt threshold, the circuit reverts to the integration state. The width of the output pulse is dictated by the time constant of the RC circuit, while the rate at which pulses occur depends upon the magnitude of the synaptic current. The axosomal circuit is effectively a current controlled oscillator exhibiting several orders of magnitude of dynamic range and essentially mimics the basic firing cycle of most natural neurons [Guyton 86]. In fact, the term "axosomal" is inspired by nature in the sense that the locus of action potential generation typically lies in the axon hillock region of the neuron soma.

The axosomal circuit of Figure 2 can be used to compute a scaled and weighted summation of pulse probabilities. When used in conjunction with certain pulse stream multipliers or "synapse circuits," the probability that the output pulse stream is generating an action potential or is "firing" is proportional to the weighted summation of the probabilities that input pulse streams are in the action potential state. This is best understood by examining axosomal circuit behavior in conjunction with a simple fixed synapse circuit such as that diagrammed in Figure 3. In the figure, Wij is a voltage which represents the weight of the synapse. This voltage is maintained such that M1 approximates an ideal current source that is gated by transistor M2. Several orders of weight magnitude are available if Wij is maintained in the weak inversion region of M1 [Meador 91]. Since transistor M2 in turn is controlled by the pulse stream input signal Xj, the more frequently (inverted) pulses arrive at Xj, the longer M2 remains on, transferring more charge to the axosomal circuit. Similarly, with increasing weights (decreasing weight voltage in this case), more charge per pulse will flow. If a continuously varying Wij and a fixed Xj having firing probability one (is continuously firing) is presented to the circuit the response will be the integral pulse frequency modulation (IPFM) of Wij [Bayly 69, Gestri 71, Sanderson 80] as illustrated in Figure 4.

IPFM yields a pulse stream having a repetition rate which varies in proportion to the integral of the weight

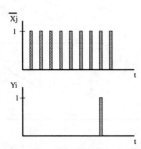

Figure 5. Pulse stream firing probability scaling with binary pulse stream input Xj. Wij is fixed and a variable rate pulse stream applied to Xj. The output firing probability varies in direct proportion with that of the input.

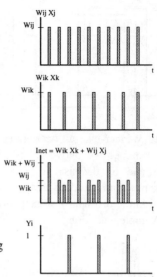

Figure 6. Weighted summation of pulse stream firing probability for two inputs Xj and Xk.

modulating signal. Since each individual output pulse has constant width and magnitude, the integral of the output pulse stream varies in direct proportion to the integral of the input. A new constant area pulse is generated each time the signal integral reaches a multiple of a constant determined by axosomal circuit parameters (equivalent to the area K in Figure 4). Given this and also that the integral of a binary pulse stream per unit time estimates pulse firing probability, it is a simple matter to demonstrate that the axosomal circuit can be used to scale pulse stream firing probabilities, as for example is shown in Figure 5. In this figure, the connection weight Wij is assumed fixed (or slowly varying) and a variable rate pulse train is applied to Xj. Firing probability scaling can be succinctly expressed as:

$$\Pr(Y_i = 1) = K^{-1} w_{ij} \Pr(X_j = 1) \tag{2}$$

where the firing probabilities are sampled over identical time intervals independent of circuit state. K depends upon C and the Schmitt threshold voltages. It is proportional to the quantity of charge required to raise C's terminal voltage to the firing threshold voltage.

The extension of this result to a weighted summation of several inputs is straightforward. Parallel synapse circuits yield a summation of individual weighted inputs via Kirchoff's current law. The firing probability of the result is simply a scaled, weighted sum of input pulse probabilities:

$$\Pr(Y_i = 1) = K^{-1} \sum_j w_{ij} \Pr(X_j = 1) \tag{3}$$

This result is presented graphically for two pulse stream inputs in Figure 6. It is important to note that this result proceeds asynchronously independent of signal timing. This means that under certain conditions a relative phase shift between the two signals will yield only a minor variation in the overall result. Any deviation from the ideal sum due to a phase shift is bounded by the accuracy limits established by pulse width and the signal observation interval.

Although the traditional sigmoidal output function is not explicitly represented in Equation (3), it is implied by the probabilistic signal representation. Just as probabilities are bound by 0 and 1, the response of an asynchronous pulse coded neuron circuit consisting of the axosomal and synapse circuits presented here saturates at zero and some maximum firing rate determined by the pulse width T0. A small T0 yields a large dynamic range for pulse repetition rates, increasing the accuracy of the signal representation for constant obervation intervals.

An Experimental CMOS PWTA

This section presents a CMOS PWTA along with experimental measurements verifying its functionality. A simple variation of the axosomal circuit of Figure 2 is used in combination with 3-bit digitally programmable synapse circuits in a simple competitive neural network. Test results show that the network correctly matches 4-element input vectors with their stored prototypes.

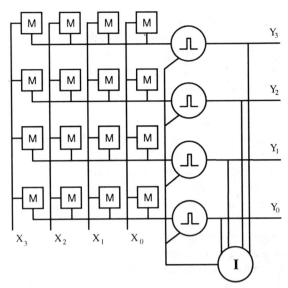

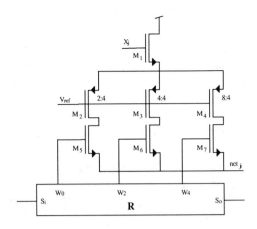

Figure 7. Pulse coded winner-take-all system organization.

Figure 8. The programmable synapse circuit consists of a 3-bit programmable MDAC. Eight synaptic weight levels are available for testing PWTA response. Minimum size devices are used unless noted otherwise in the diagram.

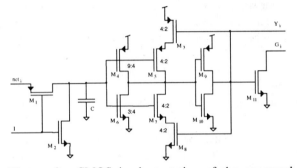

Figure 9. CMOS implementation of the axosomal circuit.

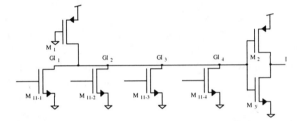

Figure 10. Global inhibition circuitry. One weak pullup transistor and an inverter are needed for the network with transistor M11 is repeated for each axosomal circuit.

CMOS Circuits

Figure 7 shows a block diagram of the experimental system. The Pulse coded inputs X0 through X3 are weighted by the programmable synapse circuit array and distributed to the axosomal circuits. The outputs (Y0 through Y3) control a global inhibition generator, I. The global inhibition signal feeds back to all the neurons in the network using an O(n) architecture like that of Figure 1 a).

The programmable synapse circuits are simple 3-bit MDACS controlled by serial-in-parallel-out registers (Figure 8). These registers are chained together in a bit-serial fashion for simplified interfacing to host hardware. Although this simple weight I/O organization would not likely be used in more complex systems requiring synapse adaptation, it does provide a straightforward method for examining the functionality of experimental PWTA circuits. Input signal Xi gates supply current to M2 - M4 via M1. Vref is selected for subthreshold operation with transistor aspect ratios increasing in powers of two for binary weighting. Dynamic SIPO register **R** controls which branches are active to establish eight synaptic weight levels. A layout organization consisting of mirrored pairs of the circuit has dimensions 318 x 198 microns.

In the axosomal circuit shown in Figure 9, M1 and M2 correspond to S1 and S2 and M3-M8 form the Schmitt trigger of Figure 2. In this implementation, the integration capacitance primarily consists of the gate-bulk capacitance of transistors M4-M7. With the aspect ratios given, the threshold voltages of the Schmitt trigger are 1.5 V and 3.0 V for Vtl and Vth respectively. M11 forms the local branch of the global inhibition generator. Each axosomal circuit layout has dimensions of 186 x 48 microns.

The global inhibition signal **I** controls the switching between integration and firing phases of the axosomal circuits. Figure 10 shows how the transistors corresponding to M11 from network axosomal circuits connect together to compute the OR global inhibition function. When the output of one neuron fires, the **I** inputs of all axosomal circuits will be forced high. This will in turn cause all of them to enter the network firing phase, simultaneously discharging all the integrating capacitors and effecting their simultaneous inhibition.

Network Initialization

Certain initialization conditions must be adhered to for a PWTA network to correctly indicate a winning input [Meador 92]. In practical implementation terms, these constraints mean that the activation of the winning unit (voltage across the integration capacitor) should decay toward some value less than V_{tl} while the activation of all losing units should decay toward V_{tl} precisely. Furthermore, the losing unit decay rate should exceed that of the winning unit so that it has converged upon V_{tl} to a reasonable degree of accuracy when the network exits the firing phase. Meeting these conditions in the ideal case guarantees that transition boundaries between winning units can be made arbitrarily precise.

In actual circuits however, a number of error sources conspire against this ideal goal. Variation in threshold voltages, time delays, and discharge rates between fabricated axosomal circuits means that erroneous decisions can be made in the region of ideal transition boundaries. Functional simulations have previously shown that two nonideal effects, namely vascillation and hysteresis can be observed in transition regions where two inputs are too close to resolve [Meador 92]. Absolute precision is an unreasonable design goal for obvious reasons, so an alternate design criterion must be developed.

In the case of the network presented here, consistent behavior within transition regions is considered to be more important than absolute precision. Specifically, the network here has been designed to consistently exhibit hysteresis within indeterminate transition regions. This behavior occurs rather naturally with a relatively simple circuit since both winning and losing units approach ground simultaneously, with the losers by definition starting at a lower activation level than the winner. When the winning activation reaches V_{tl} the losing activations all are significantly smaller since the decay rates are large. Thus the current winner will begin the following integration phase with a higher activation, and will continue to win until some other input reaches a significantly larger value.

IC Test Results

A MOSIS 2-micron CMOS Tiny Chip was used to test an experimental PWTA implementation. The resulting measurements were obtained using a Tektronix DAS9200 / LV500 digital tester in combination with a Phillips PM3580 logic analyzer. The tester was programmed to deliver variable duty cycle pulse trains to each of the four system inputs while the logic analyzer recorded system responses. The network was first programmed bit-serially with the four prototype vectors [1 7 3 5], [7 1 3 5], [1 7 5 3], and [1 3 5 7] respectively. The vectors were chosen to have equal magnitude so that true Euclidean distance would form the basis for all comparisons. Pulse trains were applied to the network inputs having duty cycles corresponding to these four vectors and the system responses recorded (Figure 11). In the figure, it can be seen that the unit programmed with the matching prototype vector is the only one to be activated. Another observation made is that although each winning unit fires with about the same probability for the same winning input magnitude (about 3-5 pulses per 90 uS), the firing is irregular - a consistent, fixed firing period is not observed. This result most likely arises from parasitic capacitance in the synaptic summing junction on the axosomal input. Charge continues to accumulate in the summing junction during the network firing phase, independent of the integrating capacitor within the axosomal circuit. At the begining of the next network integration phase, the accumulated charge is redistributed onto the integration capacitor, resulting in an apparent instantaneous increase in net input current. Since all units re-enter the integration phase simultaneously and the accumulated charge will be greater for the winner than all other units, this will not affect the winning outcome unless the parasitic capacitance is somewhat larger than the axosomal integrating capacitance. One reasonable way to avoid such error is to simply use a larger axosomal integrating capacitance. A second, more scalable approach would be to distribute the switches S1 and S2 (Figure 2) throughout the synaptic array, thereby maintaining a constant ratio between parasitic and integrating capacitors.

Discussion

The PWTA system presented in this chapter has several interesting features which distinguish it from other previous WTA implementations. One of those is the ability to indicate the strength of input data upon which a decision is based. Saturating WTA algorithms such as those described in [Majani 88] effectively filter out such

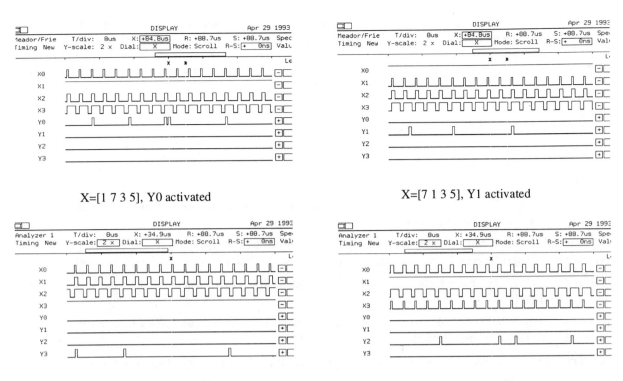

X=[1 7 3 5], Y0 activated

X=[7 1 3 5], Y1 activated

X=[1 7 5 3], Y2 activated

X=[1 3 5 7], Y3 activated

Figure 11. Fabricated IC response to matching inputs. In each example the input vector X matches one of the four stored prototype vectors. In each case, the unit associated with the stored prototype is the

information. In the presynaptic inhibition algorithm [Yuille 88] the rate at which system state changes is directly related to input signal strengths. The time required to arrive at a decision can be considered an indicator of the importance or "weight" carried by the inputs. A larger input signal is interpreted as "significant" so a decision is made rapidly. If all inputs are small, more time is taken to gather evidence before a final decision is made. The PWTA algorithm inherits this property from its presynaptic predecessor, but instead indicates input signal strength by winning unit firing rate.

The PWTA algorithm also inherits a useful input averaging property from the presynaptic inhibition algorithm. Unit dynamics are such that activation increases monotonically with a filtered average of the input signal. In electronic implementation terms, this makes it possible to directly process the kind of pulsed input signals employed in asynchronous-pulse-coded ICs [Meador 91, DeYong 92, Hamilton 92, Moon 92, Watola 92]. Although a combination of the original O(N) WTA circuit [Lazzaro 1988] with Mead's self-resetting neuron circuit [Mead 1989] would yield a system that generates pulses, it would not properly process input pulse trains since the current-mode WTA expects data represented as continuous input currents.

One interesting property of this network is that most power is dissipated only when pulses are generated. With low input currents (low output firing rates), most of the power is dissipated as Vc approaches Vth during the transition into the firing phase. Less power is dissipated during the firing phase since much less time is spent resetting the network than integrating input signals. At higher input currents, the average dissipation of the axosomal circuits increases with the winning unit firing rate. At zero input current, the inherent charge leakage of MOSFET source/drain connections will cause Vc to tend away from Vth. As a result, the network dissipates very little power when inputs become quiescent, yet responds instantaneously when nonzero inputs become available, dynamically adjusting power requirements to suit the input processing needs. This differs significantly from the self-resetting neuron circuits originally described by Mead [Mead 1989] where continuous power dissipation results from operating a fixed-threshold inverter in its high gain region.

In conclusion, the pulse coded winner take all system which has been presented in this chapter not only possesses useful physical properties that are well-suited for VLSI implementation, but also novel functional properties. Low-order system layout complexity, compact cell implementations, and dynamic power dissipation combine with the ability to encode decision strength to yield a flexible and efficient implementation of an important neural network function.

References

[Andreou 91]   Andreou, A.G., Boahen, K.A., Pouliquen, P.O., Pavasovic, A., Jenkins, R.E. and Strohbehn, K., "Current-Mode Subthreshold MOS Circuits for Analog VLSI Neural Systems," *IEEE Trans. on Neural Networks*, V.2, 215-213, 1991.

[Bayly 69]   Bayly, E., "Spectral Analysis of Pulse Frequency Modulation in the Nervous System," *IEEE Transactions on Bio-Medical Engineering*, V.15, pp. 257-265, 1969.

[DeYong 92]   DeYong, M.R., Findley, R.L. and Fields, C., "The Design, Fabrication, and Test of a New VLSI Hybrid Analog-Digital Neural Processing Element," *IEEE Trans. on Neural Networks*, V.3, 363-374, 1992.

[Gestri 71]   Gestri, G. "Pulse Frequency Modulation in Neural Systems, a Random Model," *Biophysics Journal*, V.11, pp. 98-109, 1971.

[Grossberg 73]Grossberg, S., "Contour enhancement, short term memory, and constancies in reverberating neural networks," *Studies in Applied Mathematics*, V.12, 213-257, 1973.

[Guyton 86]   Guyton, A.C., *Textbook of Medical Physiology*, 7th ed., Saunders, Philadelphia, 1986.

[Hamilton 92] Hamilton, A., Murray, A.F., Baxter, D.J., Churcher, S., Reekie, H.M., and Tarassenko, L., "Integrated Pulse Stream Neural Networks: Results, Issues, and Pointers," *IEEE Trans. on Neural Networks*, V.3, 385-393, 1992.

[Lazzaro 88]   Lazzaro, J., Ryckebusch, S., Mahowald, M.A., and Mead, C.A., "Winner take all networks of O(n) complexity," *Advances in Neural Information Processing Systems 1*, 703-711. Morgan Kaufmann, 1988.

[Majani 88]   Majani, E., Erlanson, R., and Abu-Mostafa, Y., "On the K-winners-take-all network," *Advances in Neural Information Processing Systems 1*, 635-642. Morgan Kaufmann, 1988.

[Murray 91]   Murray, A.F., Del Corso, D. and Tarassenko, L., "Pulse-Stream VLSI Neural Networks Mixing Analog and Digital Techniques," *IEEE Trans. Neural Networks*, 193-204, 1991.

[Mead 89]   Mead, C.A., *Analog VLSI and Neural Systems*, 193-204. Addison-Wesley, 1989.

[Meador 91]   Meador, J.L., Wu, A., Cole, C., Nintunze, N., and Chintrakulchai, P., "Programmable Impulse Neural Circuits," *IEEE Trans. on Neural Networks*, V.2, 101-109, 1991.

[Meador 92]   Meador, J., "Finite precision effects on dynamic behavior in a pulse-coded winner-take-all mechanism," *Proc. Int. J. Conf. on Neural Networks*, V.III, 432-437, 1992.

[Moon 92]   Moon, G., Zaghloul, M.E., and Newcomb, R.W., "VLSI Implementation of Synaptic Weighting and Summing in Pulse-Coded Neural-Type Cells," *IEEE Trans. on Neural Networks*,V.3, 394-403, 1992.

[Sanderson 80] Sanderson, A., "Input-Output Analysis of an IPFM Neural Model: Effects of Spike Regularity and Record Length," *IEEE Transactions on Biomedical Engineering*, V.27, pp. 120-131, 1980.

[Watola 92]   Watola, D. and J. Meador, "Competitive Learning in Asynchronous-Pulse-Density Integrated Circuits," *Analog Integrated Circuits and Signal Processing*,V.2, 61-82, 1992.

[Yuille 89]   Yuille, A.L., and Grzywacz N., "A Winner-Take-All Mechanism Based on Presynaptic Inhibition Feedback," *Neural Computation 1*, 335-347, 1989.

[Zurada 92]   Zurada, J. M., *Artificial Neural Systems,* Webb Publishing, 1992.

A Theoretical Study of Training Set Parallelism for Backpropagation Networks on a Transputer Array

Foo Shou King, P Saratchandran (INNS Member), N Sundararajan

School of Electrical and Electronic Engineering
Nanyang Technological University
Nanyang Avenue, Singapore 2263
E-mail: ESKFOO@NTUVAX.NTU.AC.SG

Abstract

Training set parallelism and network based parallelism are two popular paradigms for parallelising a feedforward (artificial) neural network. Training set parallelism is particularly suited to feedforward neural networks with backpropagation learning where the size of the training set is large in relation to the size of the network. This study analyses training set parallelism for feedforward neural networks when implemented on a transputer array configured in a pipelined ring topology. Analytical expression for the training time per epoch (iteration) is derived. Given a fixed neural network and a fixed number of training samples, using this expression, one can find out the optimal number of transputers needed to minimise the training time per epoch without actually performing the simulations. An expression for speed up is also derived. This expression shows that the speed up is a function of the number of patterns per processor, communication overhead per epoch and the total number of processors in the topology.

1. Introduction

Backpropagation [1] is one of the most widely used training algorithm for multilayer neural networks. However, training a network using this algorithm usually takes large amount of processing time on a serial machine. To speed up the training time, this algorithm is parallelised. There are mainly two paradigms for mapping a neural network; viz. network based parallelism and training set parallelism [2]. This study analyses the communication and computing times, which constitute the training time per epoch, for a neural network simulated on a transputer array using training set parallelism. Training set parallelism involves distributing the training examples over the processors, i.e. slice the training set and assign one slice to each processor while keeping a complete copy of the whole neural network in each processor node. In this analysis, analytical expressions for both the computation and communication times in an epoch and the optimal number of processors (i.e. transputers) to minimise the epoch time are derived. This analysis is useful because the derived training time per epoch can be used to predict the overall benefits of parallelisation. Besides, given a fixed network and a fixed number of training samples, an estimate may be computed for the optimal number of transputers that minimises the training time per epoch. This will enable the user to use the correct number of transputers even before getting involved in the simulations. Experimental results which verify the above analytical expressions are also presented.

2. Transputer Network Topology

In this study the transputers (T805-20) are connected in a pipelined ring topology as shown in Figure 1. The ring topology is a widely used transputer topology for neural network implementations [4]. In our pipelined ring topology there is one root or administrative processor and four pipe processors. The root processor is connected to a host machine (a 486-33 personal computer).

The main concept of a pipeline is that each pipe receives intermediate results or data from its upstream processor, processes the data, and then sends them down to the next downstream processor. After receiving and re-transmitting the data destined for other downstream tasks, each downstream task will then process upon its own data set. Results are propagated down the stream and eventually to the administrator for updating and comparison. This process continues until a certain criterion is met.

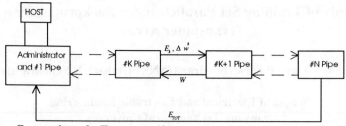

Figure 1:   Pipeline Connection of a Transputer Array

3.   Time Components in a Pipeline Implementation

In a transputer network the processors have to perform both calculations and data transfer. The total time spent on an epoch is thus made up of two parts; viz. communication time and computation time. The time spent on a single communication T_{comm} consists of a constant part T_{init} and a variable part T_{trf}. T_{init} is the time taken to initiate a communication process and for our transputer network we measured it as 9μ seconds. T_{trf} is the time taken to transfer (send or receive) the data over a link and is directly proportional to the size of data. i.e.

$$T_{trf} = r * d * (No._-of_-data_-element)$$

where r the number of bytes in a single data element and d is the time needed to send (or receive) one byte. We measured $r * d$ for our transputer array as 2.25μ seconds.

The time spent on computation T_{comp} also has a constant part T_{con} and a variable part T_{cal}. T_{con} is the time spent on such things like initialising the variables (e.g. weight changes) at the start of an iteration and T_{cal} is the time taken to perform the training calculations. Increasing the number of processors in a network, for instance, would lead to a decrease in T_{cal} but not in T_{con}.

4.   Parallelising Backpropagation

In training set parallelism each processor has to simulate the same neural work over a different subset of the training set and the weights are updated after each epoch (batch learning). When the training algorithm is parallelised this way, each processor has its own copy of the entire network and also a copy of the training patterns allocated to it.

The following steps are involved in executing one epoch of the backpropagation algorithm.

1.   The weight changes and bias changes for the current epoch are initialised to zero at the start.

2.   After initialisation, the forward pass and the backward pass of the backpropagation algorithm [1] are performed for each training pattern assigned to the processor. The forward pass involves calculation of the product sums of weights and activations and sigmoid operations at each neuron in the network. The quadratic error between the desired and actual output is also calculated. In the backward pass the weight change due to each pattern is calculated.

3.   The total weight change and error due to all the patterns assigned to the transputer are calculated by accumulating the weight change and error calculated for individual patterns in step 2.

4.   The first pipe processor sends its accumulated weight change and error to its down stream (right) neighbour that adds its own accumulated weight change and errors and sends the updated sums to its right neighbour which in turn updates the sums and sends to its right neighbour and so on. The last pipe processor would thus receive the accumulations of all the processors to its left, adds its own weight change and error and obtains the total weight change and error for the epoch. It then adds the weight change to the to the existing weight values and obtains new values for all weights in the neural network. The new weight values are then passed upstream by each pipe processor except the first. In an n transputer network, there will be $n-1$ transfers of weight change and error and another $n-1$ transfers of weights.

5.   At the same time as the weights are updated, the last processor sends the total error to the root processor that checks whether convergence is reached.

Assuming that there are only 4 processors present, the timing diagram for one epoch when the same number of patterns are allocated to each processor is shown in Figure 2.

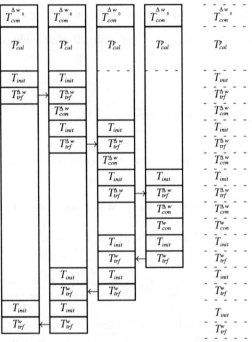

Figure 2:   Timing diagram when the training set is equally distributed amongst the processors

The various notations in Figure 2 are explained below.

$T_{con}^{\Delta w_0}$:   Time for initialising the weight changes and error.

T_{cal}^{p}:   Time for the forward and backward pass of backpropagation for all the assigned patterns in the processor.

$T_{trf}^{\Delta w}$:   Time for sending the weight changes and error.

$T_{con}^{\Delta w}$:   Time for accumulating the weight changes and errors.

T_{con}^{w} :   Time for updating the weight values in the last pipe processor.

T_{trf}^{w}:   Time for sending the updated weights.

5. Optimal Number of Processors

To find the optimal number of transputers to minimise the epoch time, we initially need to obtain an expression for the time for one epoch.

From the timing diagram of Figure 2 the time for an epoch can be written as

$$T_{epoch}^n = T_{con}^{\Delta w} + T_{cal}^p + (n-1)[T_{init} + T_{trf}^{\Delta w}] + (n-1)T_{con}^{\Delta w} + T_{con}^w + (n-1)[T_{init} + T_{trf}^w]$$

Since the number of weight changes in a neural network equals number of weights, $T_{trf}^{\Delta w} = T_{trf}^w$. T_{cal}^p can be expressed as $T_{cal}^p = pT_c$.

where T_c is the time to taken to perform the forward and backward pass for a single pattern and p patterns are assigned to the processor. Assuming the training set P is equally divided amongst the n processors $p = P/n$. The equation for T_{epoch}^n can be rewritten as

$$T_{epoch}^n = 2(n-1)[T_{init} + T_{trf}] + T_{con}^{\Delta w_0} + T_{con}^w + (n-1)T_{con}^{\Delta w} + (\tfrac{P}{n})T_c \tag{1}$$

where T_{trf} is the time taken to send all the weights (or weight changes) from one processor to its neighbour.

The time required for each term in equation (1) is analysed and an expression for T_{epoch}^n is obtained in terms of primitive machine operation times. The resulting expression for T_{epoch}^n is given as,

$$T_{epoch}^n = \underbrace{2(n-1)[T_{init} + r*d*N_{wb}]}_{comm} + \underbrace{(\tfrac{P}{n})T_c + N_{wb}(2t_{ASSIGN} + t_M + t_A + t_{AA} + (n-1)*t_{AAS})}_{comp} + (n-1)*t_{AAS} \tag{2}$$

where N_{wb} is the total number of weights and biases in the neural network. $t_{ASSIGN}, t_M, t_A, t_{AA}, t_{AAS}$ are the times for an assignment, multiply, add, compound add, and add & assign operation. The actual derivations can be found in [3].

Optimal number of processors $\hat{n}$ can be now found by taking the first derivative of equation (2) with respect to n and setting it equal to zero.

$$\hat{n} = \sqrt{\frac{PT_c}{2T_{init} + (2rd + t_{AAS})N_{wb} + t_{AAS}}} \tag{3}$$

To verify equation (2) above, experiments were conducted based on the encoder problem. The processor network in the experiment had four T805-20 transputers each with 1MByte of external memory. Figure 3 shows the analytically calculated (from equation (2)) and experimentally obtained values for T_{epoch}^n for a 64-6-64 encoder with varying training set sizes. The difference in the epoch time in the experimental result is mainly due to using two dimensional array timings throughout the analytical calculations.

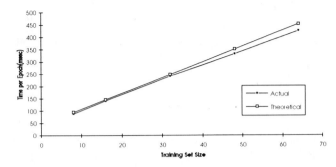

Figure 3:   Time per Epoch Comparison for a 64-6-64 Encoder Problem

From equations (2) and (3), we note that given a certain number of training patterns and a certain network size, there is always an optimal number of transputers needed for minimising the time per epoch during training. This result implies that we cannot go on increasing the number of transputers in order to achieve speed up. There will always come a time when the communication overhead will actually exceed the computation time causing it to be inefficient to run on a bigger transputer array. The degradation in performance (D) of not using the optimum number of transputers is given by the following equation (expressed in percentage and normalised to the optimal

time per epoch for each encoder configuration): $D = \left[(T^n_{epoch} - T^{\hat{n}}_{epoch}) / T^{\hat{n}}_{epoch} \right] \%$

where T^n_{epoch} is the training time per epoch achieved using n number of transputers

$T^{\hat{n}}_{epoch}$ is the training time per epoch achieved using the optimal number of transputers $\hat{n}$

i.e. when the training time per epoch is minimised

It can be observed from this figure that the slope of the curve is steep before it hits the optimal transputer value and shallow after this optimal value. Due to the steep change in gradient before the optimal transputer value, a large improvement in the time per epoch is expected for every additional transputer added to the pipeline system.

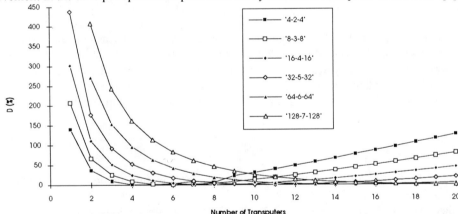

Figure 4:   Percentage Change in the time per epoch for a varying number of transputers

5.   Speed up

Speed (S) up is the ratio between the epoch time on a single processor, and that on a multiprocessor network. The time for an epoch on single processor can be obtained by putting $n = 1$ and ignoring the communication time component in equation (2).

II-523

$$S = \frac{PT_c + N_{wb}(2t_{ASSIGN} + t_M + t_A + t_{AA})}{2(n-1)[T_{init} + rdN_{wd}] + (\frac{P}{n})T_c + N_{wb}(2t_{ASSIGN} + t_M + t_A + t_{AA} + (n-1)t_{AAS}) + (n-1)t_{AAS}} \qquad (4)$$

The maximum achievable speed up on a fixed size transputer network can be found by letting P in equation (2) become very large. In the limit, $\lim_{P \to \infty} S = n$.

Thus for neural networks with large training set the achievable speed up is proportional to the size of the transputer network. Equation (4) can be used calculate the speed up for any neural network as long its size (i.e. number of weights and neurons) and the training set size are given. Figure 5 shows the experimental and analytical speedup comparisons for varying neural network sizes. As shown from this figure, when the training set becomes larger the speed up approaches n (4 in this case).

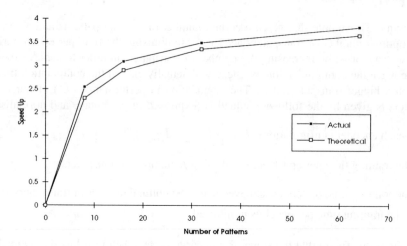

Figure 5:   Speedup Comparison for varying neural network size

Conclusion

The Backpropagation Algorithm has been implemented on an array of transputers connected in a pipeline architecture. Training set partition is used in parallelising the algorithm. A model to predict the training time per epoch has been formulated. The analytical expressions for the time per epoch as well as the speed up have been derived and verified experimentally. With this formulation, given a neural network size and its training set, we can predict the optimal number of transputers needed for minimising the time per epoch without actually carrying out the simulations.

References

[1]   Rumelhart, D. E., Hinton, G. E., and Williams, R. J., "Learning internal Representations by error propagation," *Nature*, Vol. 323, pp. 533-536, 1986
[2]   K. Wojtek Przytula, Viktor K. Prasanna, "Parallel Digital Implementations of Neural Networks," Prentice Hall, 1993
[3]   S. K. Foo, P. Saratchandran and N. Sundararajan, "A Mathematical Analysis on A Transputer Based Implementation of Backpropagation Neural Networks," Technical Report EEE/CSP/9302, Centre for Signal Processing, School of Electrical and Electronic Engineering, Nanyang Technological University, Singapore, 1993
[4]   Weidong Pan and Peter K. Sharpe, "A Simulation of Multilayer Perceptrons Exploiting Training Set Parallelism," *Proceedings of the International Joint Conference of Neural Networks*, Vol. 1, pp 183-188, Beijing, 1992

PRACTICAL APPROACH
TO IMPLEMENTATION OF NEURAL NETS
AT THE MOLECULAR LEVEL.

Nikolay G. Rambidi

International Research Institute for Management Sciencies

9, Prospect 60-let Oktyabria, 117312 Moscow, Russia

Potentialities for implementing simple neural net information processing devices based on chemical and biochemical dynamic media are discussed. This approach gives an opportunity to construct efficient systems capable of performing some primitive operations important for image processing.

Nowadays the general way to design neurochips is to use the wide-spread traditional semiconductor circuitry and technology. Nevertheless applications of this approaches to the practical elaboration of neural net devices face considerable complications (such as nightmare of inter-connections and so on).

Therefore attempts seem to be natural to implement neural nets based on media fundamentally different from discrete semiconductor primitives. Rather promising among them are the distributed nondiscrete dynamic media showing a high behavioral complexity.

There are known many different simple biological and biomolecular systems functioning in different nonlinear dynamic regimes. Between them at different levels of organization are [1] :

- neural net activity in miocardium (body tissue level),

- dynamics of biological population evolution (cell level),

- biochemical reactions in cells and membranes (supramolecular system level),

- complicated chemical reactions (molecular level).

It is known that the dynamics of the distributed nonlinear system showing sufficiently complicated behaviour can be described by the set of nonlinear differential equations of the type :

$$U_i(\bar{r},t) = F[U_1(\bar{r},t), U_2(\bar{r},t), ...U_N(\bar{r},t)] + \sum_{k=1}^{N} \nabla [D_{ik} \nabla U_k(\bar{r},t)] \ ,$$

where U_i is the concentration of i-th component of reactions proceeding in the system, A is a key parameter, D_{ik} are diffusion coefficients.

The complicated behaviour of this system is determined by a nonlinear kinetics of reactions described by the function F.

On the other hand, the dynamic media functioning on the basis of nonlinear processes can be considered as realizations of neural nets where :

- each point of the medium can be considered as a primitive micro-processor,
- sufficiently complicated responces to external excitations (optical, chemical, and some other) are typical, including stepwise reactions,
- short-range local interactions between primitive processors are displayed (more exactly, in principle each microvolume is coupled with all others by diffusion, but because of a rather low speed of spreading these interactions proceed with a delay proportional to the distance between microvolumes).

In the most general form homogeneous neural nets can be described by the system of integro-differential equations of the type [2] :

$$U_i(r,t) = - \frac{U_i(\bar{r},t)}{\tau_i} + G[-T_i - A + Z_i] = - \frac{U_i(\bar{r},t)}{\tau_i} + G\{-T_i - A +$$

$$+ \sum_{m=1}^{N} \int \phi_m[\bar{r}, \bar{x}, t, U_1, U_2,...U_N] U_m(\bar{x},t)\, dx\}$$

Here G_i is the response function for elements of i-th type on activating signal Z_i , T_i is the shift of G_i function, ϕ_m is the function of spatial coupling between active elements.

These equations can't be represented in general case by the system of differential equations. Nevertheless, under some conditions these two models happen to be sufficiently adequate.

It is important that media under consideration (they are known as excitable media) can be in several stable states.

As is known the responces of the molecular excitable media to the local elementary excitation can represent :

- travelling wavefront of switching from one stable state into another,
- travelling pulse of excitation,
- formation of time-stable spatial dissipative structures,
- synchronous oscillations between two states.

Chemical reactions of Belousov-Zhabotinsky type were chosen for the implementation of complicated nonlinear dynamics. The Belousov-Zhabotinsky type media are complex enough to demonstrate rather complicated behaviour. At the same time they are simple enough to be investigated by contemporary physical methods.

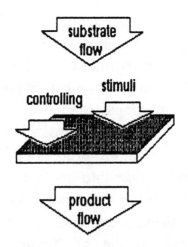

Figure 1. Simplified model
of a biochemical information processing device.

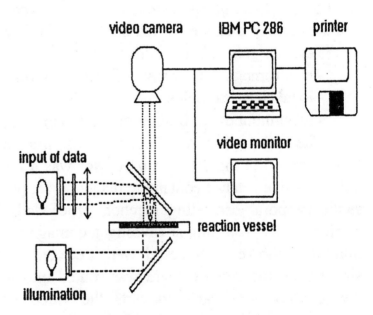

Figure 2.Schematic representation of the pilot "hardware"
model of an information processing device based on
Belousov-Zhabotinsky reaction.

The Belousov-Zhabotinsky reaction is a catalytic oxidation of malonic acid (or some other organic substance) by potassium bromate or some other oxidizing agent. The mechanism of this reaction is very complex. The most known and simplified model (the so-called Field-Korosh-Noyes approximation) consists of five coupled intermediate stages.

The Belousov-Zhabotinsky reaction is convenient for the investigation purposes. The catalyst in the process of a reaction, when the medium comes from one stable dynamic state into another, changes its electronic state. As a consequence the reagent changes its colour (from red to blue or vice versa). That's why it is easy to visualize the evolution of dynamic processes.

Excitable media of Belousov-Zhabotinsky type give an opportunity to construct various in their structure versions of neural nets. For instance, it is possible to use three-dimensional network of elementary processors combined into integral system (a restricted volume of Belousov-Zhabotinsky reagent). But the control of the system and the input-output of information proved to be in this case too complicated a problem.

That's why pseudo two-dimensional system, representing thin layer of Belousov-Zhabotinsky reagent, was chosen as molecular dynamic processor (see Fig.1). The flow of reaction substrates is the power supply for the processor ; reaction products being removed from the system. The control of the processor and the input of data are carried out by physical or physico-chemical stimula acting on the system. It is rather effective to use :
    - electromagnetic, mostly visible light, radiation,
    - local electrical fields,
    - local input of controlling molecules or ions, and so on.

The pilot "hardware" model of information processing system was constructed (see Fig.2). The processor was a thin (0.5 to 1.5 mm) non-stirred, light-sensitive catalyst containing reagent layer placed in a reaction vessel in which spatio-temporal oscillating reaction proceeded. The input of information was carried out by projecting an investigated image onto the reaction layer surface. The images of the reaction vessel were detected by video camera. The total video signal from the video camera was routed into the monitor and to the analog to digital converter which converts the video signal to digital form. The TV equipment was integrated into a recording and controlling system based on the personal computer IBM PC AT-286.

It was found out as results of the experiments performed [3] that in general case the input of a light radiation (an image) into active medium functioning in

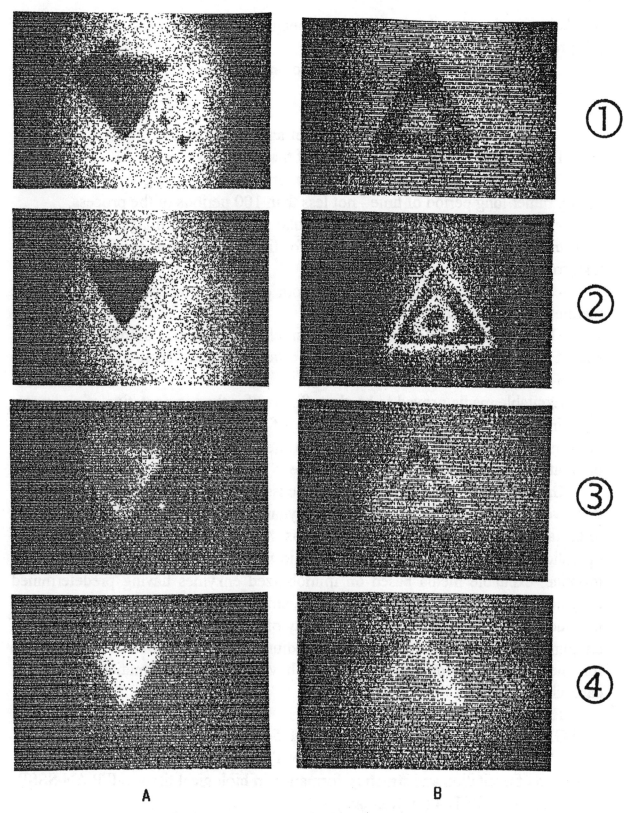

Figure 3. Computer records of processes of :
noises removing (A) and contour enhancement (B),
by active Belousov-Zhabotinsky media
(1-4 are consecutive steps of the process temporal evolution).

oscillating mode proved to give rise to specific periodic process. Each period of this process is a sequence of :

- the emerging of the negative image of an input picture,
- the extraction of its contour,
- temporal evolution of the contour,
- the emerging of the positive image of an input picture.

The important information features of these processes are :

- the functioning of the media as memory devices, storing input information during rather long period of time - not less than 100 periods of the process,
- the disappearance of small non-regular features of an image at some stages of its temporal evolution that can be used for filtration of the image from statistical high frequency noises,
- appreciable dependence of the contour evolution process on the state of the medium and characteristics of an image.

The processes of disappearance of small non-regular features of an image and of contour enhancement that are important image processing operations are shown in Fig.3.

Excitable media proved to be also effective for the segmentation of an image, repairing defects, and the implementation of Blum type algorithms. Operations performed by these media are invariant to the size of the investigated image, its orientation, and displacement on the surface.

Given experimental investigations discussed above it is possible to conclude that even very simple in their structure dynamic media are capable to perform important information processing operations. And what is more the complexity of operations carried out by nonlinear dynamic media can be greatly increased. For instance, excitable media based on immobilized enzymes having predetermined enzyme distribution on the solid surface seem to be rather promising. They may provide both the high behavioral complexity of system dynamics and selectivity of coupling between chosen points of the medium. These features are indispensable for the implementation of neural nets having broad information processing capabilities.

References :

1. N.G.Rambidi, Computer, v.25, No 11, 51-54, 1992.
2. A.V.Masterov, M.I.Rabinovich, V.N.Tolkov, V.G.Yakhno, Cooperative dynamics of excitation and structure formation in biological tissues, IFP AN SSSR, Gorky, 1989, P. 89-104 (in Russian).
3.N.G.Rambidi, A.V.Maximychev, A.V.Usatov, Advanced Materials for Optics and Electronics (in press).

HIGH-PERFORMANCE DIGITAL NEURAL NETWORKS:
THE USE OF REDUNDANT BINARY REPRESENTATION FOR CONCURRENT ERROR DETECTION

Vincenzo PIURI, Simone BETTOLA

Department of Electronics and Information, Politecnico di Milano
piazza L. da Vinci 32, I-20133 Milano, Italy

Abstract

Efficient implementation of neural networks requires high-performance architectures and data representations, while practical VLSI realization must include fault-tolerance techniques. Contemporaneous solution of such problems has not yet been completely afforded in the literature. This paper focuses on data representation to support high-performance neural computation and on error detection to provide the basic information for any fault-tolerance strategy. To achieve massively-parallel performances and to guarantee the early verification of computation correctness, we propose the use of redundant binary representation with a three-rail logic implementation. Costs and performances are evaluated for different architectural solutions, referring to multi-layered feed-forward networks.

1. Introduction

Artificial neural networks are an attractive solution in several application areas, requiring massively-parallel computation, when no algorithmic approach is known or when it cannot be easily formalized (e.g., in signal and image processing and in real-time control). Wide interest is supported by the availability of reasonably-cheap digital implementations due to the recent advances in integration technologies and architectural design.

Problems related to defect and fault tolerance are important for VLSI/WSI implementations and in mission-critical areas. Many authors considered these problems in relation with specific implementations. Intrinsic robustness of the neural paradigm has been considered in [1], by adopting a behavioral error model and by evaluating the errors' effects onto the neural computation. In [2], redistribution of the computation and information has been discussed to minimize the influence of faults onto the computation by exploiting the intrinsic fault tolerance of the network. Error detection and fault localization are the preliminary steps of any defect/fault tolerance technique: for continuous result correctness, concurrent error detection techniques are required, in particular when high system credibility is mandatory. An algorithmic approach to error detection has been presented in [3] for some DSP applications; AN+B [4] and residue [5] codes were considered for data coding. While algorithmic techniques are application-specific, AN+B and residue codes are general, but costs may be high and performances similar to those of architectures without fault tolerance. Moreover, they usually consider single-bit errors to limit the additional circuit complexity.

In the present paper, we present the use of *redundant binary representation* [6] realized by means of a *three-rail logic* implementation [7], as an effective approach for high-speed computation and concurrent error detection at the same time. This approach allows in fact to improve the computation parallelism by avoiding carry propagation within the arithmetic units, while it guarantees that the whole system is strongly fault secure with respect to all unidirectional stuck-at faults on multiple gate input and/or output lines [6, 7, 8] (i.e., multiple-bit errors are considered). These additional features are achieved at a reasonable (but not neglectable) cost in terms of circuit complexity: however, the massive increase of computational capability with respect to traditional solution and the very high detection capabilities may justify such a complexity increase in several applications.

A very simple model is adopted for the individual neuron: its behavioral description is defined by $x_i = f_i(\sigma_i - \vartheta_i) = f_i(\sum_j w_{ij}x_j - \vartheta_i)$, where x_i is the output signal of the neuron, $\sigma_i = \sum_j w_{ij}x_j$ is the sum of the weighted inputs, ϑ_i is a threshold value, and $f_i(.)$ is an arbitrary non-linear evaluation function.

A direct implementation of such equation implies one-to-one mapping of operators onto digital components; for large networks, time-multiplexing of some components may be used to reduce the circuit complexity for the current VLSI/WSI integration techniques. Even though we do not make any specific assumption on the technological implementation, we restrict our analysis to systems adopting fixed-point bit-parallel arithmetics. Without loss of generality, effectiveness of our technique is discussed for the case of multi-layered feed-forward networks; our results can be extended to any kind of acyclic network and, with some constraints, to cyclic networks.

Section 2 introduces the coding technique and the arithmetic units for the neural network implementation. Section 3 discusses and evaluates different architectures with concurrent error detection both for one-to-one mapping and for time-multiplexed systems.

2. The Fault and Error Models and the Coding Technique

In our research we consider the traditional fault models at gate level [9] both for permanent, transient and intermittent faults in all components of the neural architecture. In particular, we consider stuck-at faults, stuck-on and stuck-open faults. Related to such model, we adopt a traditional error model at gate and functional levels [9]: physical faults appear as wrong bits in the result of the considered unit, if they are not masked by the actual input data. No restriction is imposed on the bit multeplicity of the error.

The wide classes of faults that we consider may be reduced to *unidirectional* stuck-at faults on multiple gate output lines [8], i.e., to faults in which wrong bits are of the same type (all *0* or all *1*). Let F be the set of faults: any fault $f_j \in F$ sticks multiple gate output lines at the same value (*0* or *1*). We assume that faults arise one at a time; $\varphi = $ $<f_1, f_2, \ldots, f_n>$ is the sequence of faults $f_j \in F$ occurring from the initial observation time till the current time. Since, generally, $U_{j=1}^{k} f_j$ of unidirectional faults is not a unidirectional fault, we assume that any fault cannot change the value which has already been stuck by a previous fault.

Each digital component G of the architecture implementing the neural network is *fault secure* with respect to the set of faults F, if the output is either correct or is a non-codeword for all faults in F and for all codeword inputs. G is *self-testing* with respect to F, if there is at least one codeword input that produces a non-codeword output for all faults in F; G is *totally self-checking* with respect to F, if it is fault secure and self-testing with respect to F. G is *code disjoint*, if it maps codeword inputs into codeword outputs and non-codeword inputs into non-codeword outputs when it is fault free. A circuit is a totally self-checking checker with respect to F, if it is totally self-checking with respect to F and code disjoint when it is fault free. G is *strongly fault secure* with respect to a fault sequence φ with $f_j \in F$, if the output is either correct or is a non-codeword for any subsequence $\varphi_k = <f_1, f_2, \ldots, f_k>$, with $k \leq n$, and for all codeword inputs. G is *strongly fault secure* with respect to F, if it is strongly fault secure with respect to all fault sequences whose elements belongs to F. Every totally self-checking circuit is strongly fault secure, while a strongly fault secure circuit is either totally self-checking or can be easily converted into such a circuit [8]. In [6, 7] it was proved that arithmetic circuits can be easily designed to be strongly fault secure and totally self-checking by using the *redundant binary representation* and the *three-rail logic implementation*. In particular, in [7] it was proved that *essentially inverter-free* circuits (i.e., circuits without inverters but in encoders) with *unordered output code space* (i.e., any codeword has not at least one *1* where another codeword has) are strongly fault secure with respect to unidirectional stuck-at faults on multiple gate input and/or output lines. These reasons suggest to use such codes for an effective error detection even in the presence of multiple-bit errors and fault sequences.

The *redundant binary representation* [6] is a signed-digit number representation in the fixed radix 2 with a digit set $\{-1, 0, 1\}$. A n-digit redundant binary integer y is represented by $[y_{n-1} y_{n-2} \ldots y_0]$, where $y_i \in \{-1, 0, 1\}$; its value in the decimal representation is $\sum_{i=0}^{n-1} y_i 2^i$. From these definitions, it follows that an integer can be represented in several ways: multiple representation allows to avoid carry propagation in arithmetic units and to achieve very high performances. The above representation and remarks can be immediately extended to the case of fixed-point real numbers in the full-fractional notation since there is a one-to-one correspondence between such numbers and integers; therefore, from now on, we will consider only the case of integer data.

To provide error detection capabilities within the redundant binary representation, we adopt the *three-rail logic* approach for each digit. It is a traditional 1-out-of-3 code which allows to detect the presence of an error in each digit, separately from the others. Independent checking on each digit is directed to support the maximization of the computational parallelism introduced by the redundant binary representation. In this approach, we encode each digit y_i by means of three bits: we assign the codeword *100*, *010*, and *001* to the digit values -1, 0, and 1, respectively. An output digit is correct if it is one of the above codewords; otherwise, a fault occurred in circuits which generate it. The result of any neural operator is correct if all output digits computed by such an operator are correct.

Neither the redundant binary representation nor the three-rail logic require any modification of the neural computation, i.e., they do not affect the neural characteristics of the network (learning, recall, generalization) with respect to the theoretical definitions. They map the nominal data into the codeword space: in such a space, the neural computation is performed by applying the modified arithmetic and non-linear operators, suitable for the codeword space. Results are obtained in the codeword space and, possibly, transformed back into the nominal output space.

Let's consider *addition*. When two redundant binary integers y and z must be added [6, 7], an intermediate selector $t_i \in \{-1, 0\}$ is evaluated for each position i: t_i is -1 if y_i or z_i is equal to -1, otherwise it is 0. Then, an intermediate carry $c_i \in \{0,1\}$ and an intermediate sum $r_i \in \{-1,0\}$ are computed for the i-th bit, by applying the equation: $2c_i + r_i = y_i + z_i - 2t_i + t_{i-1}$. Finally, the sum digit $s_i \in \{-1,0,1\}$ is obtained by adding r_i and c_{i-1}, without propagating any carry. Parallel addition can be performed in constant time, independently from the operand length.

In *multiplication*, the partial products are generated from the n-bit input data: n n-bit numbers are produced [6,7]. Then, they are added together to obtain the final result, by using a cascade of n-1 adders; since the computational time of partial product generation and the computational time of each addition are constant and independent from the operand length, the total multiplication time is $O(n)$. For high computation speed, a binary tree of adders can be adopted [7]; the computational time of the multiplication is reduced to $O(\lceil \log_2 n \rceil)$.

An implementation of the above operations is given in [7]; the arithmetic units presented in such paper are strongly fault secure with respect to unidirectional stuck-at faults on multiple gate input and/or output lines. In fact, they are essentially inverter free and their output code space is unordered.

In [10], it has been shown that it is possible to connect strongly fault-secure adders and multipliers in any cascaded structure by preserving such a property for each arithmetic unit and by granting it to the whole cascaded system. Whenever no intermediate inverter is introduced in the cascade, conditions granting the strongly fault-secure property still hold. The use of the above data coding and arithmetic units allows to compute the *weighted summation* of the neuron's inputs by means of a circuit which is strongly fault secure with respect to all unidirectional stuck-at faults on multiple gate input and/or output lines.

As the *non-linear evaluation function* is concerned, the strongly fault-secure property is strictly related to the specific function and to the specific implementation. For this functional unit, it is therefore necessary to adopt a design strategy which guarantees the conditions granting the strongly fault-secure property in order to obtain a strongly fault-secure implementation of the whole neural architecture. Otherwise, correctness of the computation must be checked only at the outputs of circuits generating the weighted summation by using the redundant binary representation with the three-rail implementation; for the non-linear functional unit, a specific solution should be adopted, possibly without any regard to the coding approach adopted for the linear part.

Each *encoder* of the nominal neural inputs transforms the binary representation in the corresponding redundant binary representation: it receives n-bit inputs (each bit x_i belongs to $\{0,1\}$) and generates the corresponding 1-out-of-3 codewords. The encoder circuit is composed of n inverters (the only ones allowed in the whole network). Conversion time is constant and independent from the input length.

Each results computed in the codeword space can be transformed back into the nominal output space of the neural network by means of a *decoder*: it generates the nominal output by reducing the multiple representation into the corresponding unique binary representation. This operation implies propagation of carries through the decoder itself. To guarantee the strongly fault-secure property in the whole system, also the decoder must be totally self-checking. An example is given in [7]; it transforms the 1-out-of-3 neural result into a 1-out-of-2 code representation: the set of the first bit of each output digit is the final result, while the set of the second bit of the output digits is the one's complement of the final result. The second set can be used to verify the decoder correctness. It is possible to show that decoding needs a $O(n^2)$ computational time.

Error checking implies verification that the units' outputs belong to the corresponding codeword space. In the case of adders and multipliers, result's checking may be reduced to correctness verification for each individual digit of the redundant binary representation, i.e., to verify that each three-bit digit belongs to the 1-out-of-3 code. Similarly, checking of the decoder's outputs can be obtained by verifying that the each two-bit digit of the decoder's result belongs to the 1-out-of-2 code. In the literature (e.g., [11]), several totally self-checking checkers have been presented for m-out-of-n codes: by using such kind of checkers, it is possible to guarantee that the whole neural architecture is strongly fault secure with respect to with respect to all unidirectional stuck-at faults on multiple gate input and/or output lines. The computational time of all this checkers is constant and independent from the input length.

3. The Application to Neural Network Architectures

The use of redundant binary representation with three-rail logic implementation in digital neural networks is based on the functional units introduced in the previous section to perform the nominal neural computation in the codeword space; the general structure is presented in fig. 1. Nominal input data presented at the input layer of the network are transformed into the coded representation by encoders; no encoder is required within the network since all computation checking can be performed on codewords, directly. Codeword outputs generated by the network's output layer can be transformed back into the nominal output space by decoders; no decoder is required within the network since the whole neural computation is performed in the same codeword space. Internal organization of neurons is based on adders and multipliers discussed in section 2; the detailed topology depends on the characteristics of data presentation, i.e., on the possible use of time-multiplexing of some functional units to reduce the circuit complexity (despite of the computational time). Error checking is performed by checkers placed in the neural architecture according to the strongly fault-secure characteristics of the non-linear functional units and to the fault localization features required in the overall structure; checkers are connected also to each output decoder to guarantee the self-checking property of decoders themselves. In this section we present different architectural solutions that can be designed by taking into account time-multiplexing, the strongly fault-secure characteristics, and fault localization.

Consider first the basic architecture with one-to-one mapping of the neural operators onto functional units; in each neuron, we introduce one multiplier for each synaptic product, one register to store each encoded weights, a tree of adders to compute the weighted input summation, and one non-linear unit for the evaluation function.

If the non-linear function unit is not strongly fault secure, we can check the computation correctness by using the redundant binary representation and the three-rail logic only for the evaluation of the weighted input summation (see fig. 2). This checker generates an active error signal whenever the weighted input summation structure produces a non-codeword output. Let's assume that no error occurred in the weighted summation while it arises in the non-linear evaluator. If the evaluator output is a non-codeword, the error is detected in the cascaded neurons since the non-codeword is propagated to the adjacent layer; otherwise, the error is not detected by our technique. To avoid this drawback, dedicated error detection techniques may be used to protect the evaluator itself, according to the adopted evaluator implementation; the dotted circuit in fig. 2 allows to generate the neuron's error signal.

If the non-linear evaluation function is strongly fault secure, we can move the checking circuit at the evaluator output (see fig.3): this checker detects all error in the whole neuron's structure and generates the neuron's error signal.

Localization of the faulty neuron within the neural architecture can be achieved by observing the neuron's error signals produced by the *local error detection* technique. To reduce the internal wiring among neurons for error signal propagation, a dedicated interconnection network can be designed as shown in fig. 4; localization can be performed by means of a triangularization technique: a faulty neuron belongs to the layer corresponding to the leftmost vertical error signal which is active and, in such a layer, it is identified by an active horizontal error signal.

In the case of strongly fault-secure non-linear evaluators, we can avoid the checker within each neuron to reduce the circuit complexity. No checking is therefore executed on the computation performed by each individual neuron. Computation is checked only at the network's outputs by checkers connected at the decoders by adopting a *global error detection* approach. This does not reduce the error detection capabilities of the network since the detection properties are preserved in the whole architecture. Conversely, fault localization is not possible, since no enough information is contained in error signals generated at network's outputs; these signals state only if there is an error.

Consider now the case of time multiplexing to reduce the overall circuit complexity. In the literature, several approaches have been presented to multiplex (partially or totally) the synaptic multipliers and, consequently, the weighted summation adders. In these cases, only one multiplier is used in each neuron: synaptic weights are stored in suited registers and are presented sequentially to the multiplier, synchronously with the corresponding neuron input. One two-input adder is used to generate the partial sum of weighted inputs: the intermediate result is stored in a register for the subsequent iterations. The interconnection network between adjacent layers must provide the neuron inputs in the proper order, according to the neural operation.

As in the one-to-one mapping case, verification of the computation can be performed by means of *local error detection*. If the non-linear evaluation unit is not strongly fault secure, we can protect only the weighted input summation by using the redundant binary representation with the three-rail logic implementation (see fig. 5). A checker is attached to the adder output to observe summation correctness at each intermediate step. Since an error in the weighted input summation must be detected when an error occurred at least in one partial summation, and since error masking may occur due to the re-using of arithmetic units and registers, the error signal related to the weighted input summation must be generated by OR-ing the error signals produced at each iteration. Note that also errors in the partial summation register are detected.

Dedicated checking of the non-linear evaluator can be introduced to detect errors occurred in such a unit. In this case, the neuron's error signal is generated by the dotted circuits in fig. 5, connected at the evaluator output.

If the non-linear evaluation unit is strongly fault secure, error checking can be completely performed in the codeword space. Only one checker is required at the evaluator output to verify if the neuron's output belongs to the redundant binary representation with the three-rail notation adopted in this paper (see fig. 6). Checking must be executed at each iteration of the input addition to avoid error masking due to component re-using. Therefore, the non-linear evaluation function must be computed at each iteration to provide the datum for error checking; obviously, only the non-linear output corresponding to the complete weighted input summation (i.e., the output after completion of all synaptic iteration) must be delivered to the subsequent layer as neuron's output.

In the case of strongly fault-secure non-linear evaluators, we can avoid the checker within each neuron to reduce the circuit complexity. A *global error detection* strategy is adopted to check the computation only at the network's outputs by using the checkers connected at decoders. With this approach, error detecting capabilities are partially reduced due to possible error masking related to reconvergent paths; besides, fault localization is not possible, since no enough information is contained in error signals generated at network's outputs.

As in other approaches to concurrent error detection with multiplexed components (e.g., [4, 5]), control circuits for time-multiplexed buses providing data propagation cannot usually be protected by the coding technique, i.e., they are the hard-core fo the system.

If the non-linear evaluation function unit is multiplexed, the same design strategies can be adopted. The resulting structures are similar to those described above for the different cases of the non-linear evaluator, and have the same characteristic constraints, since the same properties hold to provide strongly fault security.

Experimental evaluation of the computational performances and of the circuit complexity have shown that the use of the redundant binary representation with a three-rail logic implementation for concurrent error detection in digital neural networks is effective and practically realizable.

The detection capability of the coding technique is complete for all faults discussed in section 2, but in the case of global error detection with a time-multiplexed, strongly fault-secure non-linear evaluation unit (in this case, some simulations have shown that error detection may be reduced till 95%).

The additional circuit complexity depends on the specific solution adopted and on the operand length. Experimental implementations at gate level have shown that the number of logic gates (a typical measure of the circuit complexity) is approximately 75-85% higher than in the nominal architecture with carry propagation within each arithmetic unit; roughly, we can consider that only 50% is required by the error detection capabilities, while the remaining circuits are related to the parallelization of the computation at digit level.

As computational time is concerned, experiments have shown that it can be greatly reduced by 50-60% with respect to the carry-propagating architecture. Therefore, also the computational power (i.e., the product of the circuit complexity by the square of the computational time) is reduced by 45-55%.

4. References

1. V. Piuri, M. Sami, R. Stefanelli: "Fault tolerance in neural networks: theoretical analisys and simulation results", *IEEE Proc. Compeuro 1991*, Bologna, Italy, May 1991

2. C. Neti, M.H. Schneider, E.D. Young: "Maximally fault tolerant neural networks", *IEEE Trans. Neural Networks*, Jan. 1992

3. V. Piuri: "An algorithmic approach to concurrent error detection in artificial neural networks", *IEEE Proc. VLSI Signal Processing*, Napa, CA, Oct. 1992

4. V. Piuri, M.G. Sami, R. Stefanelli: "Arithmetic codes for concurrent error detection in artificial neural networks: the case of AN+B codes", *IEEE Proc. Defect and Fault Tolerance*, Dallas, TX, Nov. 1992

5. V. Piuri, M.G. Villa: "The use of residue codes for concurrent error detection in artificial neural networks", *Proc. WCNN93*, Portland, OR, July 1993

6. A. Avizienis: "Signed-digit number representations for fast parallel arithmetic", *IRE Trans. Electron. Comput.*, vol. EC-10, Sept. 1961

7. N. Takagi, S. Yajima: "On-line error-detectable high-speed multiplier using redundant binary representation and three-rail logic", *IEEE Trans. on Computer*, vol. C-36, Nov. 1987

8. J.E. Smith, G. Metze: "Strongly fault secure logic networks", *IEEE Trans. on Computer*, vol. 27, June 1978

9. J. Abraham, W.K. Fuchs: "Fault and error models for VLSI", *IEEE Proceedings*, May 1986

10. V. Piuri, R. Stefanelli: "Use of redundant binary representation for fault-tolerant arithmetic array processors", *IEEE Proc. ICCD'88*, Rye Brook, NY, Oct. 1988

11. A.M. Paschalis, D. Nikolos, C. Halatsis: "Efficient modular design of TSC checkers for m-out-of-n codes", *IEEE Trans. on Computer*, vol.C-37, Mar. 1988

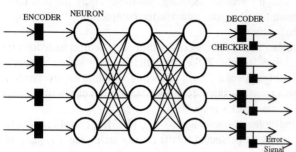

Fig. 1 - The overall neural architecture with the strongly fault-secure property

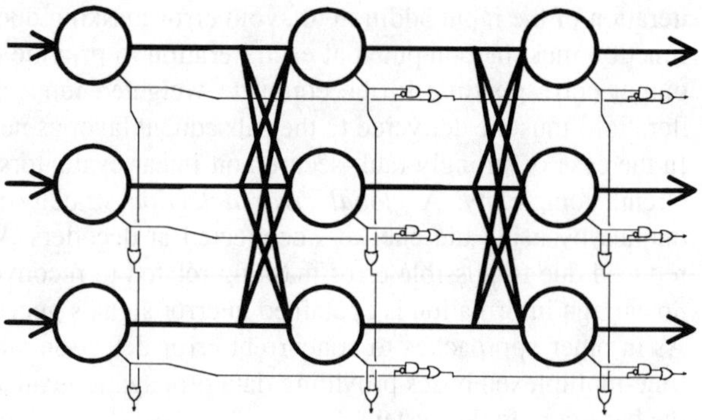

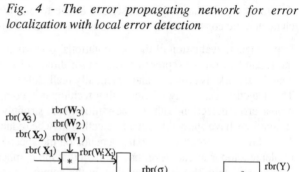

Fig. 4 - The error propagating network for error localization with local error detection

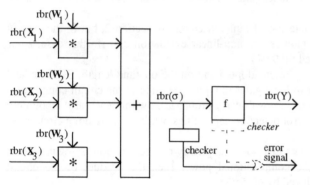

Fig. 2 - The neuron's architecture with local error detection: only the weighted input summation is protected by the redundant binary representation with the three-rail logic implementation

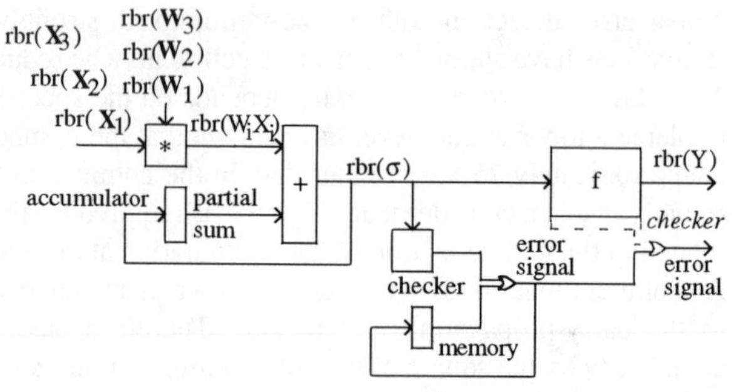

Fig. 5 - The neuron's architecture with global error detection: only the weighted input summation is protected by the redundant binary representation with the three-rail logic implementation

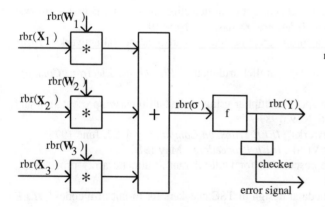

Fig. 3 - The neuron's architecture with local error detection based on the redundant binary representation with the three-rail logic implementation

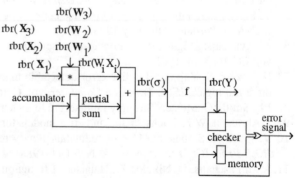

Fig. 6 - The neuron's architecture with global error detection based on the redundant binary representation with the three-rail logic implementation

The impact of finite precision in the VLSI implementation of Neural Architectures for image processing

Cesare Alippi[1,2]   *Luciano Briozzo[3]*

[1]Dipartimento di Elettronica, Politecnico di Milano, P.za L. Da Vinci 32, Milano, Italy
[2]Department of Computer Science-University College London, Gower Street, WC1E 6BT, London,U,K.
[3]SGS-THOMSON Microelectronics, Via Olivetti 2, Agrate brianza, Milano, Italy

Abstract: *In this paper the sensitivity of a feed-forward neural network to weights and inputs perturbations is studied at a behavioural level. By modelling inputs and perturbations we construct a stochastic frame which provides a measure of the loss in performance at the network outputs. A suitable definition for the signal to noise ratio applied to the output neural signal and to the perturbation, here induced by a finite precision representation of neural values, provides precision requirements for inputs and weights. Results are then tailored to image processing and applied to two real-time demanding applications: ship identification in radar images and defect identification in machined parts of mechanical objects, the second being realised with a dedicated digital VLSI chip.*

1. Introduction

Performance degradation caused by finite precision realisations is a critical issue in developing dedicated neural VLSI devices for real-time demanding applications (such as the ones involving image processing). In general, a compromise between the hardware compactness (in terms of a reduced number of bits to represent neural values for digital implementations) and the induced loss in performance at the network outputs is required.
A careful analysis must be performed to achieve a fine-tuned architecture.
Only the relaxation phase of a neural network is considered, learning is carried out on a host computer and only when the appropriate weights have been determined they are loaded into the final dedicated neural device. Sometimes, digital hardware emulations are envisaged to determine precision requirements and consider, during learning, some finite-precision constraints. In such emulations learning trajectories in the weight space are constrained by neural values quantization; they divert from the nominal one (ideally obtainable with infinite precision devices) and may lead to poor weight configurations i.e., impairing the generalisation ability of the network. Evaluation limited to hardware emulation does not generally provide a meaningful measure for the loss in performance caused by neural values quantization; this issue is tackled by sensitivity analyses. Therefore, both hardware emulations and sensitivity analysis should be taken into account to build the final hardware architecture.
Validation of the final hardware configuration requires the analysis of two inter-dependent aspects: network sensitivity and performance distortion. The problem of network sensitivity has been tackled by several authors. In particular, the sensitivity of madalines to weights and inputs perturbations has been considered in [Ste90]. There, results were limited to binary inputs and hard limited activation functions. Results were partly extended in [Pic93] to cover the sensitivity of the outputs of a neural network to errors in its weights. Sensitivity of inputs and weights perturbations to some class of perturbations can be finally found in [Ali93a], [Ali93b] where stochastic models for the error generation and propagation are presented. The second aspect, namely performance distortion, relies on the definition of a suitable figure of merit able to correctly measure the loss in performance due to neural parameter perturbations, caused, in the context, by finite precision representations. Such figures of merit generally rely on signal to noise definitions and are based either on the ratio of signal to noise variances ratio such as in [Pic93], or on the ratio of average powers as suggested in [Dur93].

In the present paper, results cover perturbations influencing both weights and inputs and are tailored to image processing applications.

In particular, section 2 provides a statistical framework for modelling perturbations and their behaviour, while the analysis of the induced and consequent loss of performance is presented in section 3. In section 4 the theoretical frame is then applied to two real world image processing applications: classification of ships in radar images and defect identification in machined parts of mechanical objects.

2. The error perturbation model

Let us consider a single neuron, whose neural computation involves the scalar product evaluation between the n-dimensional vectors $\mathbf{I}$ (inputs) and $\mathbf{W}$ (weights) followed by the activation function mapping to produce the neuron's output. Let moreover ϕ be the bias variable contributing to the final neural activation x. Let δy denote the perturbation influencing the generic y variable which leads to the perturbed variable y_p. With the same notation, by perturbing the bias, the input and the weight vectors, the neural activation may be expressed as:

$$x = (W, I) + \phi = \left(W_p + \delta W, I_p + \delta I\right) + \phi_p + \delta\phi \tag{1}$$

Let δx be the perturbed value at the neuron's activation and defined as:

$$\delta x = x - x_p = (W, I) - \left(W_p, I_p\right) + \phi - \phi_p = \left(W_p, \delta I\right) + (\delta W, I) + \delta\phi \tag{2}$$

Expectation value E[δx] and variance Var[δx] of the perturbed activation values may be computed by modelling the input and the input perturbation distributions. Remember that ϕ, W, Wp and δW are fixed entities (learning is terminated and the δW perturbation fixed) and that there exists a linear relationship in (2) between weight and input vectors. In particular, each component of the δW vector, as for $\delta\phi$, can be seen as a random variable uniformly extracted from a symmetrical interval [-α,α]. This model is justified by the fact that errors generated by quantization techniques such as truncation and rounding are modellable as a random variable with samples uniformly extracted from the $\left[-2^k, 2^k\right]$ interval, being k the index of the truncated or rounded bit [Hol93].

Let us define $\Gamma(y)$ as the distribution associated with the random variable y of mean μ_y and variance σ^2_y, and assume that each component of the I and δI vectors are, within the specific vector, independent random variables having $\Gamma(I)$ and $\Gamma(\delta I)$ distributions, respectively. The expectation value E[δx] may be simply obtained by applying the mean operator E[·] to (2):

$$E[\delta x] = \left(\delta W, J(\mu_I)\right) + \delta\phi = \mu_I \sum_{i=1}^{n} \delta w_i + \delta\phi \tag{3}$$

while its variance is:

$$Var[\delta x] = E\left[\left[\left(W_p, \delta I\right) + (\delta W, I) - \left(\delta W, J(\mu_I)\right)\right]^2\right] + Var[\delta\phi] =$$

$$= E\left[\left[\left(W_p, \delta I\right) + \left(\delta W, I - J(\mu_I)\right)\right]^2\right] + Var[\delta\phi] = E\left[\left[\left(W_p, \delta I\right) + (\delta W, \Psi)\right]^2\right] + Var[\delta\phi] \tag{4}$$

Being $J(x)$ the n-dimensional vector having all the vector components equal to x. The Ψ vector is consequently the unbiased input vector. By introducing the Cauchy-Schwarz inequality expression (4) can be rewritten as:

$$Var[\delta x] \leq E\left[(W_p, \delta I)^2\right] + E\left[(\delta W, \Psi)^2\right] + 2\sqrt{E\left[(W_p, \delta I)^2\right] E\left[(\delta W, \Psi)^2\right]} + Var[\delta \phi] \qquad (5)$$

Under the independence assumption between the δI and Ψ components, (5) becomes

$$\left|W_p\right|^2 \sigma_{\delta I}^2 + \left|\delta W\right|^2 \sigma_\Psi^2 + 2\sqrt{\left|W_p\right|^2 \left|\delta W\right|^2 \sigma_{\delta I}^2 \sigma_\Psi^2} + \sigma_{\delta \phi}^2 = \left(\left|W_p\right| \sigma_{\delta I} + \left|\delta W\right| \sigma_\Psi\right)^2 + \sigma_{\delta \phi}^2 \qquad (6)$$

In particular, expression (6) may be specialised to cover two interesting real cases where the distribution for the input errors is always uniform (as we said in the introduction this is the appropriate model for truncation and rounding quantization techniques) while the input distribution may either be uniform or a sum of independent gaussian.

1. Both δI and Ψ have components extracted from an uniform distribution defined over the symmetrical intervals bounded by $\alpha_{\delta I}$ and α_Ψ, respectively: $\delta I = U\left(0, \alpha_{\delta I}^2 / 3\right)$ and $\Psi = U\left(0, \alpha_\Psi^2 / 3\right)$. The variance of (6) becomes:

$$Var[\delta x] \leq \frac{1}{3}\left(\left|W_p\right| \alpha_{\delta I} + \left|\delta W\right| \alpha_\Psi\right)^2 + \sigma_{\delta \phi}^2 \qquad (7)$$

2. The input error has uniform distribution while the input histogram is gaussian: $\delta I = U\left(0, \alpha_{\delta I}^2 / 3\right)$ and $\Psi = N\left(0, \sigma_{N,\Psi}^2\right)$. In this case the variance becomes:

$$Var[\delta x] \leq \left(\left|W_p\right| \frac{\alpha_{\delta I}}{\sqrt{3}} + \left|\delta W\right| \sigma_{N,\Psi}\right)^2 + \sigma_{\delta \phi}^2 \qquad (8)$$

Expression (8) may be generalised to cover the relevant case related to image processing, in which the luminance histogram of the image is composed of a set of independent gaussians. In such case we suppose each component of the input vector extracted from a random variable whose distribution is the weighted sum of m gaussian distributions having their own mean values and variances. These requirements can be modelled as

$$\Gamma(I) = \sum_{i=1}^m \xi_i G(\mu_i, \sigma_i^2) \quad \text{where} \quad \sum_{i=1}^m \xi_i = 1$$

being ξ the weighting term.
The expectation and the variance can be easily derived:

$$E[\delta x] = \sum_{i=1}^m \xi_i \mu_i \sum_{j=1}^n \delta W_j \qquad Var[\delta x] \leq \left(\left|W_p\right| \frac{\alpha_{\delta I}}{\sqrt{3}} + \left|\delta W\right| \sqrt{\sum_{j=1}^m \xi_j \sigma_{N,\Psi_j}^2}\right)^2 + \sigma_{\delta \phi}^2 \qquad (8')$$

The uniform or gaussian distribution hypothesis for the neuron's inputs assumes each component of the input vector to be real.

Nevertheless, when images are taken into account, input neurons will receive integer inputs, generally defined over a byte and bounded between 0 and 255. In this case, the uniform distribution is defined over a discrete set of elements. Let us thus compute the associated mean and variance values. Let us consider a discrete random variable z whose elements are uniformly sampled from an integer set containing the first n_z+1 elements (elements range from 0 to n_z).

The expectation value and the variance of z can be easily computed and lead to

$$\mu_z = \frac{n_z}{2} \qquad \sigma_z^2 = \frac{n_z(n_z+2)}{12} \tag{9}$$

These values should be substituted in expressions (7), (8) and (8'). Results thus derived are discussed in the next section.

3. The Signal to Noise Ratio

In several applications of neural networks to image processing the final neural architecture reduces to a single neuron that can be seen as a convolver whose optimal weights are identified via learning [Ali93c]. Classification abilities can be functionally implemented with a non linear activation function or with more classical techniques which, generally, involve definition of a suitable functional or metric to realise classification. The transformed image via the neuron's convolution already contains fundamental image features, which will be exploited in the subsequent classification phase (see section 4). The loss in performance can then be evaluated at the neuron's activation level. By extending Pichè's results [Pic93] to our purpose we define the signal to noise ratio SNR at the neural activation level as the ratio of variance of the signal (the activation value) and the variance of the noise (the perturbation at the activation level):

$$SNR = \frac{Var[x]}{Var[\delta x]} = \frac{\sigma_x^2}{\sigma_{\delta x}^2} \tag{10}$$

Expressions for noise's variance, to be inserted in (10), can be derived from (7), (8) or (8'), integrated by (9), when image processing is taken into account (real variances are close to their theoretical bounds); we have then to evaluate the variance for the activation signal x.

From now on we consider inputs coming from an image and assuming the first n_z+1 integer values. We suppose two distributions for the neuron's activation value: uniform $x = U(0, \sigma_{U,x}^2)$ and unknown. For both models we have to determine the variance.

Moreover, we will suppose, as it happens in most of real applications, a low dimensionality for the input and weight space. If n is small (reduced fan in for the neuron) the central limit theorem cannot be successfully applied; the x distribution is consequently not modellable as gaussian and other tools need to be investigated.

1. If the input distribution is uniform, from (9) we have $I = U(\mu_I, \sigma_I^2)$. We obtain that the x dynamic is bounded by

$$W_m \, n_z = Min(\sum_{W_i<0} W_i, 0) \, n_z \leq x \leq Max(\sum_{W_i>0} W_i, 0) \, n_z = W_M \, n_z \tag{11}$$

and therefore the variance, because of the uniform distribution hypothesis, becomes:

$$Var[x_U] = \frac{(W_M - W_m)^2 n_z^2}{12} \qquad (12)$$

Finally, the signal to noise ratio, in the case of uniform distributions for inputs and scalar product (see expressions (6) and (9)) can be express as:

$$SNR_U = \frac{\sigma_{U,x}^2}{\sigma_{\delta x}^2} = \frac{\dfrac{(W_M - W_m)^2 n_z^2}{12}}{\left(|W_p|\sigma_{\delta I} + |\delta W|\sqrt{\dfrac{n_z(n_z+2)}{12}}\right)^2 + \sigma_{\delta \phi}^2} \qquad (13)$$

2. When the neural activation distribution is unknown, the final variance cannot be estimated by exploiting this feature. To solve the problem we can apply the law of the variance propagation to the (1) and the variance on x becomes

$$Var[x] = |W|^2 \sigma_I^2 \qquad (14)$$

where σ_I^2 is the input variance.

4. From SNR to precision requirements in image processing applications

In this section we will make use of former results to determine precision requirements in two real-time demanding image processing applications: identification of ships in radar images and defects identification in machined parts of mechanical objects.

- *Ships' identification in radar images*

The problem is that of identification of ships sailing in instrumental weather conditions with radar images (164x241 pixels grid defined over a 255 grey level scale). It has been proved that single tuned neurons, grouped in a single layer, suffice to solve the application [Ali93c]. Weights are determined on a host computer and need to be quantized while it is required all the 8 bits to represent inputs (and therefore no errors will be introduced by input quantization). We will focus on the clear weather condition case. The input frequency histogram can be successfully modelled as a gaussian [Ali93c] where the mean value coincides with the clutter one (the sea and its turbulences).

The signal to noise ratio (10) may be used to determine weights precision. The x distribution is unknown (and therefore expression (14) will be utilised for the signal variance) while expression (8) will be used since the input distribution is gaussian.

The signal to noise ratio becomes:

$$SNR = \frac{|W|^2 \sigma_I^2}{|\delta W|^2 \sigma_{N,\psi}^2 + \sigma_{\delta \phi}^2} \cong \frac{|W|^2 \sigma_I^2}{1/3 \; n \; 2^{2nb} \sigma_I^2 + 1/3 \; 2^{2nb}} = \frac{3|W|^2 \sigma_I^2}{(n \; \sigma_I^2 + 1)2^{2nb}} \cong \frac{3|W|^2}{n \; 2^{2nb}} \qquad (15)$$

having assumed a truncation quantization technique, the same precision for bias and weights and substituting the expectation value of $|\delta W|^2$ to the real value. In this application n (the neuron fan-in) is 9, while the squared weight magnitude is 6.38. As suggested in [Pic93] given a SNR=20db (the variance of the signal 100 times the variance of the noise) 2 bits (from (15)) suffice to represent the decimal part of weights, 3 bits for the integer one and one bit for the sign for a total of 6 bits resolution to represent weights.

- *Defects identification in machined parts of mechanical objects*

In this application weights are determined off line, on a host computer. No constraints are set on weights which can be represented with arbitrary precision. This implies that weights are given and no weight perturbation terms need to be considered. We want to determine the appropriate number of bits to represent inputs. Inputs can be modelled as an uniform distribution where $n_z=255$. The neuron's activation distribution is not uniform and therefore expression (14) is used to compute the signal variance. The SNR becomes:

$$SNR = \frac{|W|^2 \sigma_I^2}{\dfrac{|W|^2 \alpha^2_{sI}}{3}} = \frac{3\sigma_I^2}{\alpha^2_{sI}} = \frac{n_z(n_z+2)}{4 \, 2^{2nb}} \qquad (16)$$

Given SNR= 20db we obtain nb=4 bits to represent inputs. In our specific application learning was carried out in a partial emulation which considered 6 bits to represent input data. In such case, assuming a SNR=20db we obtain nb=4. The input resolution can therefore be further decreased to 4 bits making feasible an higher input parallelism degree of the chip. In fact, by reducing the input dynamic from 8 to 4 bits, and considering fixed the number of chip's pins, more data per input cycle can be inputted into the neural device.

Conclusions

In this paper a stochastic frame which models generation and subsequent propagation of quantization errors in neural computation is provided. Here quantization errors are supposed to be generated by digital quantization techniques such as truncation and rounding. By introducing a suitable signal to noise definition, we obtain a technique to set precision requirements for inputs and weights. Results are given at a behavioural level, are then tailored to a digital technology and applied to two image processing applications: identification of ships in radar images and defects identification in machined parts of mechanical objects, the latter being realized in digital VLSI hardware.

References

[Ali93a] C.Alippi, *Sensitivity of Artificial Neurons to weights and input quantization: 1. the input neurons case*, In Proc. of WCNN93, Portland, Oregon, July 1993.

[Ali93b] C.Alippi, *Sensitivity of Artificial Neurons to weights and input quantization: 2. the hidden neurons case*, In Proc. of WCNN93, Portland, Oregon, July 1993.

[Ali93c] C.Alippi, *Filtering and Clutter/signal classification of ships' radar images with Neural Networks*, In Proc. of WCNN93, Portland, Oregon, July 1993.

[Dur93] J.Durham, E.VonColln, *A measure of Signal to Noise ratio for multilayer perceptrons trained as 0-1 classifiers*, In Proc. of WCNN93, Portland, Oregon, July 1993.

[Hol93] J.Holt, J. Hwang, *Finite precision error analysis of neural network hardware implementations*, In the IEEE Transaction on Computers, Vol 42, No 3, March 1993.

[Pic93] S.Pichè, *The effects of Weight errors in Neural Networks*, In Proc. WCNN93, Portland, Oregon, July 1993.

[Ste90] M.Stevenson, R.Winter, B. Widrow, *Sensitivity of Feedforward neural networks to weights errors*, In IEEE Transaction on Neural Networks, Vol 1, No 1, March 1990.

Analog VLSI Neuromorph with Spatially Extensive Dendritic Tree

John G. Elias and David P. M. Northmore

Electrical Engineering &
Neuroscience Program
University of Delaware
Newark, DE. 19716

Abstract

The architecture of an analog VLSI neuromorph which can receive and process large numbers of pulsatile inputs via a spatially extensive artificial dendritic tree is described. The artificial dendritic tree is a hybrid VLSI circuit which has distributed over its length synapses of three types: hyperpolarizing, depolarizing, and shunting. Because of the distributed nature of the circuit and its natural dynamics, input signals are segregated both spatially and temporally. In addition, neuromorph dynamics is programmable over a wide range which permits one to match neuromorph dynamical response with application dynamics. Experimental results are presented that show "membrane" response of a directionally selective neuromorph preserved over four orders of magnitude in target speed as neuromorph dynamics is correspondingly changed.

Introduction

Our neuromorphs are VLSI circuits that comprise a spatially extensive artificial dendritic tree [1]-[2], a spike generating soma, and many spike output pathways, each of which imparts a programmable delay to the spikes traveling on it. Figure 1a is a simplified circuit diagram of a short, five-compartment section of silicon dendrite. Each compartment has a capacitor, C_m, representing a membrane capacitance, two programmable resistors, R_m and R_a, representing a membrane resistance and a cytoplasmic resistance, and several MOS field effect transistors that simulate synapses by enabling transient inward or outward transmembrane current. The resulting potential appearing at the soma, point S in Figure 1b, determines the rate of output spike firing. P-channel transistors (upper) produce excitatory effects on spike firing by increasing the membrane potential. Inhibition is mediated by two interleaved populations of n-channel transistors (lower). Half have their source terminals connected to ground and exert inhibitory effects by lowering membrane potential; the other half have their source terminals connected to a programmable "shunt" voltage and exert inhibitory effects by pulling the membrane potential towards this voltage. When this voltage is set near the membrane resting voltage these transistors behave like shunting or silent inhibitory synapses [3]-[5].

The synapse transistors are turned on (activated) for 50-100 nsec by an impulse signal applied to their gate terminals. The resultant transmembrane current, which depends on the conductance of the transistor in the on state, the duration of the gate terminal impulse signal, and the potential difference across the transistor, produces an impulse response at the soma that may last nine orders of magnitude longer than the impulse signal. The temporal behavior of the impulse response depends primarily on dendritic dynamics which is programmable over a range of six orders of magnitude [6]. In most of our VLSI implementations, the dendritic branches have sixteen compartments (32 synapses) which are connected together to form artificial dendritic trees (ADTs) like that shown in Figure 1b.

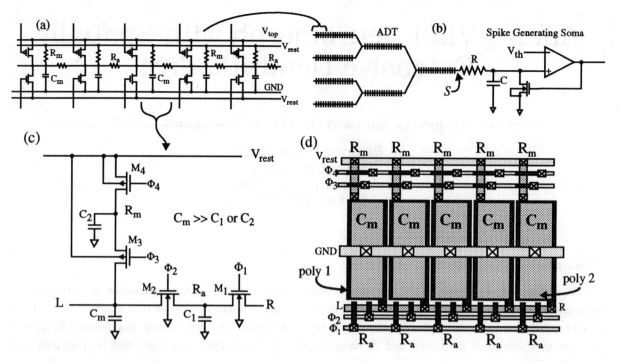

FIGURE 1. a) Five compartment segment of artificial dendrite. b) Diagram of VLSI neuromorph comprising a spatially extensive artificial dendritic tree (ADT), a spike generating soma, and a programmable number of spike output pathways that connect to synapses on ADTs. Each pathway has independent programmable delay. The crosses on the ADT represent synapse locations. c) Switched-capacitor implementation of compartmental resistances. Transistors M_3, M_4 and capacitor C_2 emulate R_m. Transistors M_1, M_2, and capacitor C_1 emulate R_a. Clock signals, ϕ_1, ϕ_2, ϕ_3, ϕ_4, permit adjustment of resistance over a wide range. V_{rest} establishes the resting voltage (typically 2.5V). d) Basic VLSI layout. Five compartments are abutted together to form a short dendrite branch section (synapse circuitry not shown). The compartmental capacitor, C_m, is implemented with poly1/poly2 plates and varies between 0.1-2.0 pF, depending on the particular chip design. Construction of ADTs is done by placing compartments side-by-side until the desired branch length is reached. Branches are then connected via metal or poly wires to form trees. The spacing between compartments is 2 μm, and they are aligned such that the inputs of one compartment connect to the outputs of the previous compartment.

VLSI Implementation

Figure 1c shows the circuit diagram for the programmable axial and membrane resistors in our dendrite compartment. Switched-capacitors are used to emulate the resistors and provide a means to easily change the effective resistances. Capacitor C_1 switched by transistors M_1 and M_2 emulates the axial resistor, R_a, while C_2, switched by M_3 and M_4 emulates the membrane resistor, R_m. The switches, M_1, M_2, M_3, and M_4, in the open state have a resistance of about $10^{12} \Omega$, and in the closed state their resistance is about 30 KΩ. The gate signals, Φ_1/ Φ_2 and Φ_3/ Φ_4 do not overlap in the logic 1 state, ensuring that only one switch of each pair is closed at a time. Figure 1d illustrates the basic integrated circuit layout of a five compartment VLSI dendrite section, excluding the synapse circuitry.

The analog output voltage of each ADT is processed by a spike-generating artificial soma whose output spikes are delayed by programmable amounts of time before they reach their destination synapses. Our VLSI soma, shown schematically in figure 1b, is a simple voltage controlled oscillator with programmable gain and threshold. Whenever the soma produces a spike, the synapses that it connects to are activated after a programmable delay which is specified for each efferent connection. In our present system, each efferent spike can be individually delayed with one millisecond resolution, from zero to 256 msec.

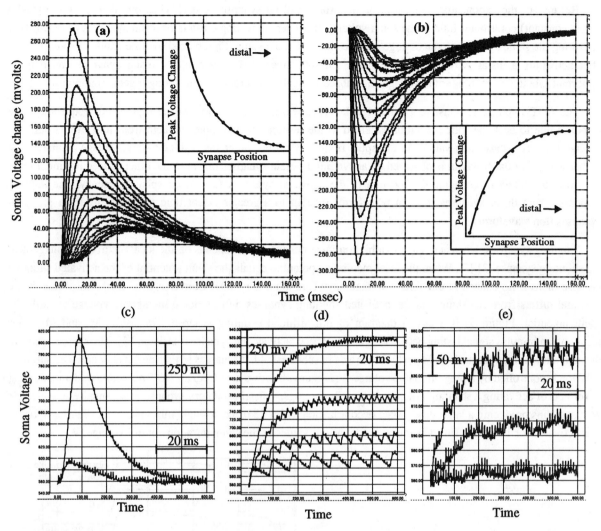

FIGURE 2. Experimental results from ADT-neuromorph to afferent stimulation. a, b) Measured impulse responses at soma (point S, Fig. 1b) due to activating a single synapse at different locations for 100 nsec. Left plot shows excitatory results; right is inhibitory. Note that the response lasts over 1,000,000 times longer than the signal that caused it. Insets show the peak voltage change as a function of synapse position. c) Response from the most distal synapses on a two-branch neuromorph. Lower curve is single activation. Larger response is from ten activations spaced 0.5 ms apart. d) Response from closely spaced afferent spikes on a mid-branch synapse. Higher spike densities produce larger voltage changes at soma. e) response from various synapses to fixed afferent spike frequency. Impulse responses from more distal synapses overlap to a greater extent.

ADT Basic Electrical Response - Single Synapse Activation

The measured impulse responses after activating a single excitatory or inhibitory synapse at 15 different locations on an ADT are shown in Figures 2a,b (voltages measured at soma, point S in Figure 1b). Although the synapse transistor is turned on for only 100 nsec, the resulting impulse response may last up to nine orders of magnitude longer. The duration of the impulse response depends on the ADT dynamics. The peak amplitude of the response is largest for synaptic activation nearest the soma and diminishes rapidly for sites farther away, while the latency to peak increases with distance from the soma. These effects of synapse position mimic those occurring in passive dendrites of biological neurons [7]-[8]. They also illustrate how the ADT structure inherently accords different weights to synapses: pulsatile afferent signals exert effects in time and amplitude that depend upon synapse position.

Because of the exponential attenuation in dendrites, a distal synapse by itself (i.e., one that is well beyond a length constant) contributes little to the soma voltage. However, activating clusters of distal synapses or repetitively activating the same synapse produces large voltage changes at the soma. Figure 2c shows the resultant soma voltage after activating a distal ADT synapse once and multiple times. This suggests that distal synapses can play an important role in determining soma voltage and subsequent spike generation when acting together temporally.

The ADT's voltage response to a burst of spikes is shown in Figure 2d for several input spike frequencies. The response due to each synaptic activation is added to the resultant branch point voltage from past events until the voltage reaches a maximum value. As the spike frequency grows larger the resultant soma voltage saturates at a higher value. Similar behavior is observed by activating different synapses one after the other spaced in time. Figure 2e shows the effect of changing the location of the activated synapses for a fixed spike frequency. The impulse responses from distal synapses (bottom waveform) overlap to a greater extent than those arising from proximal synapses (top waveform).

Shunting synapses, when activated, exhibit nonlinear behavior that depends on the local membrane voltage near the shunting synapse [3]-[5]. When the local membrane potential equals the shunt potential of the activated shunting synapse there is no change in membrane voltage anywhere along the ADT. Conversely, when the local membrane potential differs from the shunt voltage, activated shunting synapses pull the local membrane voltage towards the shunt potential. Figure 3a is a circuit diagram of our artificial shunting synapse. Transistors M_1 and M_2, after receiving an impulse signal lasting between 50 and 100 nsec, activate the synapse transistor, M_4. The synapse stays in the activated state until transistor M_3, which operates in subthreshold, discharges M_4's gate capacitance. The shunting duration is controlled by a programmable voltage, V_s. Figure 3b shows data from an ADT-neuromorph demonstrating the effects of activating a shunting synapse. In these recordings, a distal excitatory synapse was tonically activated for 74 msec, thus producing a large steady state depolarization. After 25 msec, a single more proximal shunting synapse was activated for 100 nsec. This was repeated for various values of the shunt duration control voltage, V_s.

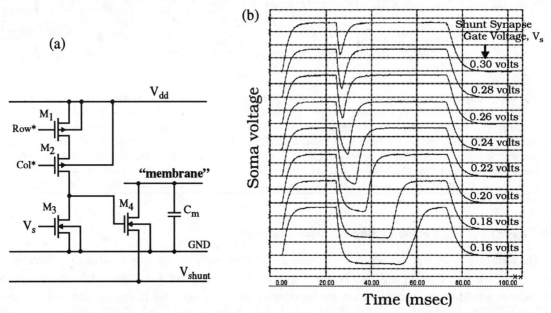

FIGURE 3. a) Circuit diagram of a shunting synapse. M_3 operates in subthreshold region to discharge M_4's gate voltage whenever it is activated by M_1 and M_2. The shunt transistor, M_4, pulls "membrane" voltage towards V_{shunt}. b) Experimental recordings from a neuromorph in which an excitatory synapse was tonically activated to produce a steady state depolarization. After 25 msec, a more proximal shunting synapse was activated. Shunt duration depends on control voltage, V_s, and temperature.

Multiple Synapse Activation and Variable Dynamics

The activation of an arbitrary set of synapses, both excitatory and inhibitory, in a temporal sequence gives rise to a complex waveform at the soma representing the summation (not necessarily linear) of individual impulse responses. The waveform shape depends on the dynamics, the spatial locations of activated synapses, and the temporal spacing of afferent impulses. If the same pattern of synapses is activated at different temporal rates the response waveforms exhibit very different behavior. However, variable dynamics allows a synaptic pattern activated at different rates to generate soma voltage waveforms that are essentially identical in shape over widely different time scales, analogous to wavelet dilation and contraction. Figures 4a-d illustrates this principle with a directionally selective neuromorph [9]. In these experiments, a target traversed a one-dimensional sensor array at a constant speed first in one direction and later in the opposite direction. The directionally selective neuromorph responds by producing different peak soma voltages for the two directions. The larger voltage is produced in the so called preferred direction. The waveforms are nearly identical in shape; the main difference is that they span widely different time scales. Figure 4a corresponds to a target speed of 1000 pixels/sec and Figure 4d is for a target speed of 1 pixel/sec. The same VLSI neuromorph with exactly the same synaptic connections produced all four waveforms; the only difference was its dynamics.

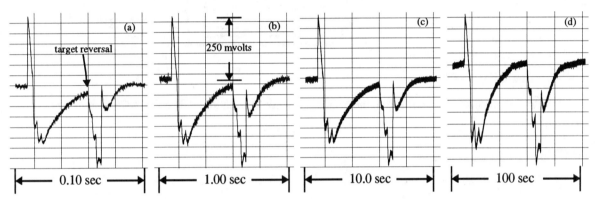

FIGURE 4. Measured soma voltage from directionally selective neuromorph [9] during period in which a target of constant velocity first moves across a one-dimensional sensor array in the preferred direction and later reverses direction and moves back across the sensor array with same speed as in the preferred direction. The four recordings correspond to four different target speeds with a comparable change in dynamics obtained by changing the switching rate of the switched-capacitors. All synaptic connections between sensor array and neuromorph were identical for each recording. Nothing was changed between the recordings except for target speed and neuromorph dynamics. a) target speed: 1000 pixels/sec. b) 100 pixels/sec. c) 10 pixels/sec. d) 1 pixel/sec.

Activating Synapses through Virtual Wires

To overcome package I/O limitations, we make use of a multiplexing scheme that we refer to as virtual wires [1]. In this scheme, the outputs of active neurons and sensors (i.e. those that are currently producing a spike or impulse) cause the synapses that they connect with to become activated after a delay that is specific for each efferent connection. The process of reading an active output causes that output to return to the inactive (i.e. nonspiking) state. Virtual wires are formed using three circuits: synapse Row and Column Address Decoding, State Machine, which determines neuromorph output states, and Connection List, which specifies the locations of synapses and the delay associated with each connection. Address Decoding is on-chip; the Connection List and State Machine are off-chip. Figure 5 is a simplified block diagram of our experimental system, which has been implemented on a 6U VME board connected to either a Sparc Station or, through an adapter, to a PC. Each board accommodates sixteen neuromorph chips in DIP-40 packages.

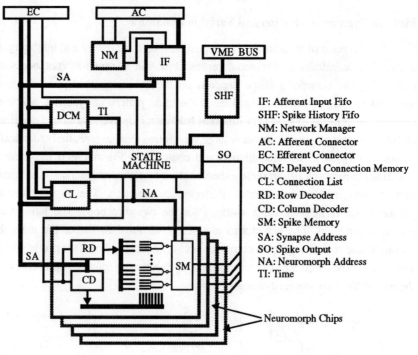

FIGURE 5. Simplified block diagram of experimental system implemented on VME 6U board. State Machine detects the occurrence of neuromorph spiking and makes connection from spike source to destination synapses by looking up connections in the Connection List. Those connections to be delayed are temporarily stored in the Delayed Connection Memory until their time has expired, after which they connect to their destination synapses. Afferent spikes generated by other boards enter through the Afferent Input Fifo. All spikes occurring on a board and the time at which they occurred are stored in a Spike History Fifo which is read by the Sparc Station processor.

IF: Afferent Input Fifo
SHF: Spike History Fifo
NM: Network Manager
AC: Afferent Connector
EC: Efferent Connector
DCM: Delayed Connection Memory
CL: Connection List
RD: Row Decoder
CD: Column Decoder
SM: Spike Memory
SA: Synapse Address
SO: Spike Output
NA: Neuromorph Address
TI: Time

ACKNOWLEDGEMENTS

This work was supported by grants from the National Science Foundation (# BCS-9315879) and the University of Delaware.

REFERENCES

[1]   J. G. Elias, "Artificial dendritic trees," *Neural Computation,* vol. 5, pp. 648-664, 1993.

[2]   J. G. Elias, "Silicon dendritic trees," to appear in *Silicon Implementation of Pulse-Coded Neural Networks,* ed. J. Meador, Chap. 2, 1994, Kluwer Academic Press, Norwell, Mass.

[3]   V. Torre and T. Poggio, "A synaptic mechanism possibly underlying directional selectivity to motion," *Proc. R. Soc. Lond.* B. vol 202, pp. 409-416, 1978.

[4]   C. Koch and T. Poggio, "Biophysics of computation: neurons, synapses, and membranes," in *Synaptic Function* edited by G.M. Edelman, W.E. Gall, W.M. Cowan. Wiley-Liss, New York, pp. 637-697, 1987.

[5]   C. Koch, T. Poggio, and V. Torre, "Nonlinear interactions in a dendritic tree: Localization, timing and role in information processing," *Proc. Natl. Acad. Sci.* vol. 80 pp. 2799-2802.

[6]   J. G. Elias and D. P. M. Northmore, "Neuromorphs implemented with switched-capacitors achieve wide-range variable dynamics," submitted

[7]   W. Rall, "Theoretical significance of dendritic trees for neuronal input-output relations," in *Neural Theory and Modeling*, R. F. Reiss, Ed., Stanford University Press, pp. 73-79, 1964.

[8]   G. M. Shepherd and C. Koch, "Dendritic electrotonus and synaptic integration", in *The Synaptic Organization of the Brain*, ed. G. M. Shepherd, Oxford University Press, appendix, 1990.

[9]   D. P. M. Northmore and J. G. Elias, "Directionally selective artificial dendritic trees," *Proceedings of the World Conference on Neural Networks, Portland,* 1993, vol. IV, pp. 503-508

A Quick Search of Optimal Solutions for Cellular Neural Networks

Sa H. Bang and Bing J. Sheu

Department of Electrical Engineering,
and Signal and Image Processing Institute,
University of Southern California, Los Angeles, CA 90089-0271
sheu@pacific.usc.edu, shbang@okada.usc.edu

ABSTRACT

Hardware annealing, which is a paralleled version of mean-field annealing in analog networks, is an efficient method of finding the optimal solutions for cellular neural networks. It does not require any stochastic procedure and henceforth can be very fast. Once the energy of the network is increased, the hardware annealing searches for the globally minimum energy state by gradually increasing the gain of neurons. In typical non-optimization problems, it also provides enough energy to frozen neurons caused by ill-conditioned initial states.

1. Introduction

A cellular neural network (CNN) [1,2] is a massively parallel, locally connected, nonlinear dynamic system. The ability to seek a stable point in a multidimensional space, at which the generalized energy function of the network is minimized, makes it possible to use the CNNs in many optimization-oriented applications such as image or signal processing. Under the mild conditions [1], the CNN is always stable and finds an optimum output in the steady state. However, the final result may not be a globally optimal solution in terms of generalized network energy, because there may exist multiple minima at which the energy is minimized locally. This might, in turn, cause undesired network operations as long as the objective is to map the input signal in one space to the output in another space by minimizing the cost function involved.

2. Optimizing Neural Networks

In optimization-oriented applications like nonlinear system optimization problems and feature recognition tasks, a quick search of optimal solution is highly desirable. It is important to avoid any local minimum which can result in a sub-optimum solution or completely unwanted result. Existence of local minima is common in many optimization-oriented artificial neural networks such as perceptrons and Hoplield's networks. There has been various suggested procedures for performing the hill-climbing necessary for avoiding getting stuck in the local minima. Frequently used schemes are simulated annealing and mean field annealing [3] on digital computers. Simulated annealing is a stochastic optimization method. The Boltzmann-machine technique with the addition of intentional noises or the simulated annealing technique is quite capable of escaping the local minima. The mean-field learning method uses a set of deterministic equations instead of extensive calculation of probabilities at each temperature in the Boltzmann machine. The hardware annealing is an efficient electronic version of mean-field annealing in which the temperature of the network is increased to a predetermined high value and then decreased gradually down to a critical low temperature. In fact, the local minima in recurrent associative networks such as binary or multilevel Hopfield networks [4,5] and cellular neural networks can be successfully eliminated by applying the hardware annealing directly to the analog neural networks. It does not include any stochastic procedure. Once the energy of the network is increased by reducing the gain of neurons, the hardware annealing quickly searches for the globally minimum energy state.

3. Local Minima in CNN

Figure 1 shows an $n \times m$ CNN where n and m are the numbers of rows and columns, respectively. The Lyapunov function of an $n \times m$ CNN is given as [1]

$$E(t) = -\frac{1}{2} \sum_{i,j} \sum_{k,l} A(i,j;k,l) v_{yij}(t) v_{ykl}(t) + \frac{1}{2R_x} \sum_{i,j} \left[v_{yij}(t) \right]^2$$
$$- \sum_{i,j} \sum_{k,l} B(i,j;k,l) v_{yij}(t) v_{ukl} - \sum_{i,j} I v_{yij}(t) \qquad (1)$$

where $A(i,j;k,l)$ and $B(i,j;k,l)$ are the feedback and control operators between neuron cell $C(i,j)$ and its r-th neighborhood cells $C(k,l) \in N_r(i,j)$, $\forall i,j$, respectively. In a simplified form using vector and matrix notations,

$$E = -\frac{1}{2} \mathbf{v}_y^T \mathbf{A} \mathbf{v}_y + \frac{1}{2R_x} \mathbf{v}_y^T \mathbf{v}_y - \mathbf{v}_y^T \mathbf{B} \mathbf{v}_u - I \mathbf{v}_y^T \mathbf{u}$$
$$= -\frac{1}{2} \mathbf{v}_y^T \left[\mathbf{A} - \frac{1}{R_x} \mathbf{I} \right] \mathbf{v}_y + \mathbf{v}_y^T [-\mathbf{B} \mathbf{v}_u - I \mathbf{u}] \equiv -\frac{1}{2} \mathbf{v}_y^T \mathbf{M} \mathbf{v}_y + \mathbf{v}_y^T \mathbf{b} \qquad (2)$$

where $\mathbf{v}_y = [\mathbf{v}_{y1} \mid \mathbf{v}_{y2} \mid \cdots \mid \mathbf{v}_{yn}]^T$, $\mathbf{v}_{yk} = [v_{yk1} \; v_{yk2} \; \cdots \; v_{ykm}]$, $\mathbf{u} = [1 \; 1 \; \cdots \; 1]^T$, and $\mathbf{A}$ is an $n \cdot m \times n \cdot m$ real, symmetric matrix defined as

$$\mathbf{A} = \begin{bmatrix} \mathbf{A}_0 & \mathbf{A}_1 & & & \mathbf{0} \\ \mathbf{A}_1 & \mathbf{A}_0 & \mathbf{A}_1 & & \\ & \mathbf{A}_1 & \mathbf{A}_0 & \ddots & \\ & & \ddots & \ddots & \mathbf{A}_1 \\ \mathbf{0} & & & \mathbf{A}_1 & \mathbf{A}_0 \end{bmatrix}. \qquad (3)$$

In (3), $\mathbf{A}_0$ and $\mathbf{A}_1$ are two $m \times m$ Toeplitz matrices with elements determined by given cloning template. $\mathbf{A}_0 = Toeplitz(c_{A0}, c_{A1})$ and $\mathbf{A}_1 = Toeplitz(c_{A1}, c_{A2})$, where $Toeplitz(a,b)$ is defined as the Toeplitz matrix with all a's in the main diagonal, and all b's in above and below the main diagonal. The input vector $\mathbf{v}_u$ and the matrix $\mathbf{B}$ can be defined similarly. Note that the matrix $\mathbf{A}$ or $\mathbf{B}$ is not Toeplitz, but always real, symmetric as long as the cloning templates are space-invariant. To see how the Lyapunov function of (1) is affected by given cloning templates, initial state, and input, assume that $\mathbf{b} = 0$ for simplicity and the matrix $\mathbf{M}$ is diagonalized by an orthonormal set of eigenvectors as $\mathbf{M} = \mathbf{E}^T \mathbf{\Lambda} \mathbf{E}$ where $\mathbf{\Lambda}$ is a diagonal matrix with eigenvalues of $\mathbf{M}$ on the diagonal and $\mathbf{E}$ is an orthonormal matrix with the corresponding eigenvectors as columns. Then the equation (2) becomes

$$E = -\frac{1}{2}\mathbf{v}_y^T \mathbf{M}\mathbf{v}_y = -\frac{1}{2}(\mathbf{E}\mathbf{v}_y)^T \mathbf{\Lambda}(\mathbf{E}\mathbf{v}_y) = -\frac{1}{2}\sum_{k=1}^{n \cdot m}\lambda_k(v_{yk})^2. \qquad (4)$$

If $\lambda_k > 0$, $\forall k$, then $\mathbf{M}$ is positive definite and $E \leq 0$ for all $\mathbf{v}_y \in [-1,+1]^{n \times m}$, where the equality holds only at the origin $\mathbf{v}_y = \mathbf{0}$. Thus the energy surface denoted by $E(\mathbf{v}_y)$ is a convex with the maximum value $E_{max} = E(0) = 0$. Since $|v_{yk}| = 1$, $1 \leq k \leq nm$, in the steady-state, all corners of the $n \times m$ dimensional hypercube are possible minima having the same energy value

$$E(+\infty) = -\frac{1}{2}\sum_{k=1}^{n \cdot m}\lambda_k = -\frac{n \times m}{2}\left[A(i,j;i,j) - \frac{1}{R_x}\right]. \qquad (5)$$

If $\mathbf{b} \neq \mathbf{0}$, the energy $E(t)$ is maximized at $\mathbf{v}_y = \mathbf{v}_{y0}$ where $\mathbf{v}_{y0}$ is the solution of the equation $\mathbf{M}\mathbf{v}_y = \mathbf{b}$. Because $\mathbf{M}$ is nonsingular when $A(i,j;i,j) > 1/R_x$, this equation has a unique solution

$$\mathbf{v}_{y0} = \mathbf{M}^{-1}\mathbf{b} = \sum_{k=1}^{nm}\frac{\mathbf{e}_k^T \mathbf{b}}{\lambda_k}\mathbf{e}_k \qquad (6)$$

where $\mathbf{e}_k$ is the eigenvector of $\mathbf{M}$ associated with the eigenvalue λ_k. If the location of E_{max} is inside the hypercube, i.e., $\mathbf{v}_{y0} \in [-1,+1]^{n \times m}$, then all corners are possible minima as in the case when $\mathbf{b} = \mathbf{0}$. However, due to the nonzero value of $\mathbf{b}$ the energy value at each corner is distinct in general. If $\mathbf{v}_{y0} \notin [-1,+1]^{n \times m}$, then some of the corners are not equilibrium points. Secondly, let us consider the case when some of the eigenvalues of $\mathbf{M}$ are negative even when the condition

$$\sum_{k=1}^{n \cdot m}\lambda_k = \sum_{k=1}^{n \cdot m}\mathbf{M}(k,k) = n \cdot m \cdot \left[A(i,j;i,j) - \frac{1}{R_x}\right] > 0 \qquad (7)$$

is satisfied. In this case, the matrix $\mathbf{M}$ is indefinite, and the energy surface is convex in some directions and is concave in others. This can be readily checked by assuming that only one eigenvalue, say λ_l, is negative and $v_{yk} = 0$, $\forall k \neq l$. However, the indefiniteness exists only in a limited region of the hypercube along the axes of $v_{yk} = 0$ for some k. It does not occur at the corners of the cube and, when $\mathbf{b} = \mathbf{0}$ the energy is still given by Eq. (5) in the equilibrium. The saddle-point occurs at the origin $\mathbf{v}_y = \mathbf{0}$ when no input is present. From the above analysis, when the forcing function $\mathbf{b}$ is not zero, there exists as many as $n \times m$ minima at the corners of the space $[-1,+1]^{n \times m}$. Furthermore, when the sigmoid function is used as a neuron nonlinearity, the magnitude of neuron outputs are not exactly equal to one because there always exists a maximum value of neuron state in the steady state such that $1 \leq |v_{xij}(+\infty)| \leq |v_{x\max}|$ [1]. In this case, the local minima are still present even when no external inputs or bias are present. Given input $\mathbf{v}_u$ and initial state $\mathbf{v}_x(0)$, the output vector $\mathbf{v}_y$ moves toward the closest stable point in the boundary $\mathbf{v}_y \in [-1,+1]^{n \times m}$ and stays there. Because the network always operates toward a direction so that the energy is decreased as time elapses, the inequality $E(+\infty) \leq E(0)$ must be satisfied where

$$E(0) = -\frac{1}{2}\mathbf{v}_x(0)^t\left[\mathbf{A} - \frac{1}{R_x}\right]\mathbf{v}_x(0) - \mathbf{v}_x'(0)[\mathbf{B}\mathbf{v}_u - I\mathbf{e}] \qquad (8.a)$$

and

$$E(+\infty) = -\frac{1}{2}\mathbf{v}_y{}'\left[\mathbf{A} - \frac{1}{R_x}\right]\mathbf{v}_y - \mathbf{v}_y{}'\left[\mathbf{B}\,\mathbf{v}_u - I\,\mathbf{e}\right]. \tag{8.b}$$

Here, the constraint conditions $\left|v_{xij}(0)\right| \le 1, \forall i, j$, is used. In other words, $\mathbf{v}_y(0) = \mathbf{v}_x(0)$ for the neuron with a piecewise linear transfer function. If $E(0) \ge E(+\infty)$ with more than one elements in the set $\{\mathbf{v}_y\}$, then there exists the same number of local minima that the network can stay in the steady state.

Another way to examine the existence of multiple minima in the CNN is shown in Fig. 2 (a) & (b). In Fig. 2 (a), the x-, y-, and z-axis represent the outputs of neuron $C(2,2)$ and $C(2,3)$, and the corresponding network energy, respectively, in a 4×4 cellular neural network with $R_x = 10^3\,\Omega$, $I = 0$ and the cloning templates

$$\mathbf{T}_A = 10^{-3} \times \begin{bmatrix} 1 & 1 & 1 \\ 1 & 2 & 1 \\ 1 & 1 & 1 \end{bmatrix} \text{ and } \mathbf{T}_B = 10^{-3} \times \begin{bmatrix} 0 & 0 & 0 \\ 0 & 1 & 0 \\ 0 & 0 & 0 \end{bmatrix}. \tag{9}$$

Here, all neurons other than $C(2,2)$ and $C(2,3)$ have fixed outputs of -1 or +1. Notice that there are three minima $[v_{y22}, v_{y23}] = [-1,-1]$, $[+1,-1]$, and $[+1,+1]$. Depending on the values of $\mathbf{v}_x(0)$ and/or $\mathbf{v}_u$, the output $[v_{y22}, v_{y23}]$ will be among $[-1,-1]$, $[+1,-1]$, and $[+1,+1]$ in the steady state. The point $[v_{y22}, v_{y23}] = [+1,+1]$ is obviously the global minimum with the lowest energy value. Figure 2 (b) shows the contours of the energy function and the trajectory of the output values for the initial state marked by X. The output $[v_{y22}, v_{y23}]$ is attracted to the point $[-1,-1]$, which is one of the local minima.

4. Hardware Annealing

The hardware annealing is performed by increasing the neuron gain $g(t)$, which is assumed to be the same for all neurons throughout the network. The initial gain at time $t = 0$ can be set to an arbitrarily small, positive value such that $0 \le g(0) \ll 1$, and after the annealing process for t_A seconds the final gain $g(t_A) = 1$ is maintained until the next operation. Figure 3 shows the result of hardware annealing for the network and conditions given in Figs. 2 (a) & (b) and $g(t) = \alpha t$ where α is a constant. In Figure 3 (a), the local minima corresponding to the output $[v_{y22}, v_{y23}]$ have been removed and the output $[+1,+1]$ which was the global minimum before annealing, became the only minimum that can exist after annealing. The decrease in the energy by the hardware annealing is shown in Figure 4 for three different cooling schedules $g(t) = \alpha_1 t^2$ (A), $\alpha_2 t$ (B), and $\alpha_3 \sqrt{t}$ (C) for constant α_1, α_2, and α_3. In Figure 5, the corresponding waveforms for neuron states and outputs are plotted. In both figures, the annealing begins at the normalized time $t = 1$. Figure 6 shows the edge detection results of a 64-by-64 CNN for un-annealed and annealed conditions. Figure 6 (a) shows the original gray-scale image. The sigmoid function is used as the neuron nonlinearity and the same cloning templates as in [2, Fig. 18] are used. Figures 6 (b) and (c) show the CNN outputs due to the annealing effect. Here, the image is applied to the input only and $\mathbf{v}_x(0) = \mathbf{0}$. Two networks resulted in the same, correct outputs.

When the image is applied to both the input and initial state, the output is not correct as shown in Figure 6 (d). Figure 6 (e) shows the correct output when the annealing operation is applied to the condition described in Fig. 6 (d). In Figures 6 (f) and (g), the constraint condition $\left| v_{xij}(0) \right| \leq 1$, $\forall i,j$, is removed and random values of the initial state between 1 and 5 are used. As a result, the output in Figure 6 (f) contains many neurons that are not able to toggle the states. However, as shown in Figure 6 (g), the hardware annealing provides enough energy to such frozen neurons caused by ill-conditioned initial states.

Despite of the time-varying nature of the hardware annealing, the stability of the network is still maintained. The time derivative of the energy function for any neurons with bounded, differentiable, nondecreasing nonlinearity is given by

$$\frac{dE(t)}{dt} = -\sum_{i,j} C \frac{dv_{yij}}{dv_{xij}} \left[\frac{dv_{xij}(t)}{dt} \right]^2 . \qquad (10)$$

Equation (10) indicates that the network is always stable as long as the neuron transfer function dv_{yij}/dv_{xij} is nonnegative. When applying the hardware annealing method to the CNN, the quantity (dv_{yij}/dv_{xij}) is also nonnegative although it is a function of time during the annealing process. Therefore, the hardware annealing does not alter the stability requirements.

5. Conclusions

The hardware annealing is a very effective method of overcoming local minima in the CNN. Instead of using stochastic optimization as in simulated annealing, or Boltzmann machine, the proposed method continuously reconfigures the energy surface of the network so that the network state easily finds the global minimum. In applications other than optimization, the hardware annealing is also useful. For instance, the constraint condition $\left| v_{xij}(0) \right| \leq 1$ [1] is not required in the CNN with the hardware annealing because the annealing provides enough energy to frozen neurons caused by ill-conditioned initial state.

References

[1] L. O. Chua, L. Yang, "Cellular neural network: Theory," *IEEE Trans. Circuits Syst.*, vol. 35, pp. 1257-1272, Oct. 1988.

[2] L. O. Chua, L. Yang, "Cellular neural network: Applications," *IEEE Trans. Circuits Syst.*, vol. 35, pp. 1273-1290, Oct. 1988.

[3] C. Peterson, J. R. Anderson, "A mean field theory learning algorithm for neural networks," *Complex Systems*, vol. 1, no. 5, pp. 995-1019, 1987.

[4] B. W. Lee, B. J. Sheu, "An investigation of local minima of Hopfield network for optimization circuits," in *IEEE Int. Conf. Neural Networks*, San Diego, CA, vol. I, pp. 45-51, July 1988.

[5] B. W. Lee, B. J. Sheu, *Hardware Annealing in Analog VLSI Neurocomputing*, Norwell, MA: Kluwer Academic Publishers, 1991.

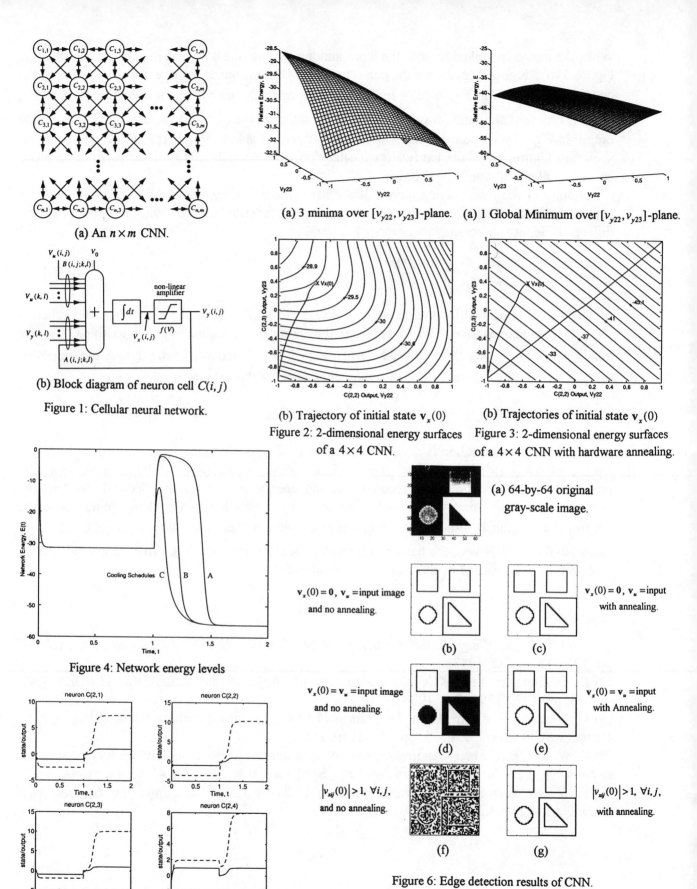

(a) An $n \times m$ CNN.

(b) Block diagram of neuron cell $C(i,j)$

Figure 1: Cellular neural network.

(a) 3 minima over $[v_{y22}, v_{y23}]$-plane.

(a) 1 Global Minimum over $[v_{y22}, v_{y23}]$-plane.

(b) Trajectory of initial state $\mathbf{v}_x(0)$

(b) Trajectories of initial state $\mathbf{v}_x(0)$

Figure 2: 2-dimensional energy surfaces of a 4×4 CNN.

Figure 3: 2-dimensional energy surfaces of a 4×4 CNN with hardware annealing.

Figure 4: Network energy levels

Figure 5: Neuron states & outputs

(a) 64-by-64 original gray-scale image.

$\mathbf{v}_x(0) = \mathbf{0}$, $\mathbf{v}_u =$ input image and no annealing.

$\mathbf{v}_x(0) = \mathbf{0}$, $\mathbf{v}_u =$ input with annealing.

(b)

(c)

$\mathbf{v}_x(0) = \mathbf{v}_u =$ input image and no annealing.

$\mathbf{v}_x(0) = \mathbf{v}_u =$ input with Annealing.

(d)

(e)

$\left| v_{xij}(0) \right| > 1$, $\forall i, j$, and no annealing.

$\left| v_{xij}(0) \right| > 1$, $\forall i, j$, with annealing.

(f)

(g)

Figure 6: Edge detection results of CNN.

An Improved Programmable Neural Network and VLSI Architecture Using BiCMOS Building Blocks

D. Zhang, R. Gu and M.I. Elmasry

VLSI Research Group, Department of Electrical and Computer Engineering
University of Waterloo, Waterloo, Ontario, Canada N2L 3G1

Abstract

A typical programmable neural network (PNN) implementation based on mixed analog / digital design have been proposed in [1]. In this paper, we analyze its basic circuits, including synapse and neuron, and improve their performance using BiCMOS technology. The corresponding PNN architecture in VLSI are developed and two kinds of building blocks, which are simpler since digital signals can be directly applied as programmable weights, are used in the architecture. Compared with the previous design, simulation results show that this PNN architecture can provide more accurate weight currents up to 30 times, and less silicon area and more driving capability by the factor of 2 and 3, respectively.

1. Introduction

Research into neural networks has not only embraced modeling and algorithms, but has also dealt with corresponding architectures and implementations [2-3]. There have been a variety of implementation approaches for neural networks, including software and hardware, electronic and optical implementations, etc. [4-6]. The real promise for applications of neural networks currently lies in specialized hardware, in particular VLSI implementations [7-8].

VLSI technology can provide full exploitation of the massively paralleled computing power of neural networks. The analog VLSI approach is quite attractive in terms of hardware size, power consumption, and speed. With increasing size, however, designing large integrated analog circuits in VLSI, is a difficult task. On the other hand digital processing, which appears to be inferior to analog processing in terms of computational density, has advantages of flexibility in terms of programming for a variety of architectures and learning strategies, as well as simplifying the task of memory retention. Therefore, a mixed analog / digital approach is a right choice in the implementation of electronic neural systems.

In this approach, local data computation is executed by analog circuitry to achieve full parallelism and to conserve power consumption. Inter-processor communication is carried out in the digital format to maintain strong signal strength and to achieve direct scalability in neural network size. Based on this mixed analog / digital approach, a compact and general purpose neural network with electrically programmable connection weights for each new problem statement, called programmable neural networks (PNN), can be obtained.

Various PNN implementations have been reported in [9-10]. A typical PNN design, i.e., the binary-weighted MOSFET analog multiplier approach, was presented by Hollis and Paulos [1]. The technique given makes it possible to achieve low power levels with moderate device width-to-length ratios, and to avoid the use of components that waste chip area or require special processing. However, our analysis and simulation have demonstrated that there are some problems in such a PNN implementation, including low accuracy, small driving capability and large area in VLSI.

In this paper, we will improve the performance of this programmable neural network by BiCMOS technology, and build the corresponding PNN architecture with our goal as implementation efficiency. The organization of the paper is as follows: In Section 2 we investigate the model of the PNN design. The PNN architecture, including BiCMOS circuit building blocks and their connection network, are discussed in Section 3. Section 4 shows the simulation results and analyzes the performances of the architecture. In Section 5 we summarize the conclusions of the paper.

2. Analysis and Design for PNN

The PNN design in [1] is to use MOSFET analog multipliers to construct weighted sums, and to permit asynchronous analog operation from fully programmable digital weights to neurons, as shown in Fig.1. Digitally programmable weights are installed with a parallel set of switchable NMOSFETs and they satisfy $(W / L)_{i,j} = 2 (W / L)_{i,j-1}$, where $(W / L)_{i,j}$ represents the binary weighted width-to-length ratio in the jth bit at the wight i ($i = 1, 2, ..., N$; $j = 0, 1, ..., n$). These independent weights are easily programmable and can be stored in RAM. The analog neuron model in the PNN can be described in the following two steps:

Step 1: The Input Voltage $\Rightarrow$ The Weight Current

$$I_{D1} - I_{D2} = \frac{K}{2} V_{IN} \sqrt{\frac{4I_0}{K} - (V_{IN})^2}$$

$$\text{for } |V_{IN}| = |V_{G1} - V_{G2}| < \sqrt{\frac{2I_0}{K}} \tag{1}$$

Here $K = \mu_0 C_{0x} W/L$, where μ_0 is the carrier mobility in the channel, C_{0x} is the gate oxide capacitance per unit area; $I_0 (= I_{D1} + I_{D2})$ is the programmed weight current, where $I_D = \frac{K}{2}(V_{GS} - V_T)^2$; V_{IN} is the differential input voltage of the current-steering transistor pair. This means that the differential output current is proportional to the square root of the weight current rather than to the weight current directly.

Step 2: The Weight Current $\Rightarrow$ The Output Voltage

$$V_0^+ - V_0^- = R_L \sum_j (I_{D1} - I_{D2})_j \tag{2}$$

where R_L is a linear load resistance. It is shown that the model can achieve low power consumption with moderate device area.

Analyzing the model given, we can find some problems in the circuit. The most important problem is suffer from the perturbation of threshold voltage. This is because that in order to save power, $V_{gs} - V_t$ should be set to 0.2v such that the switchable weight currents in the model are designed as small as possible. In this case, the currents of lower-bit binary weights may be comparable with the error current of high-bit weights. It can be analyzed in a schematic figure of current source of switchable NMOSFETs (See Fig.2(a)). Assuming that Q_{n1} is operated in the saturation, Q_{n2} is in the linear region and V_{02} is less than 0.2v. The current I passing the two NMOS transistors is

$$I = K(V_{in2} - V_{tn})V_{02} - 0.5KV_{02}^2$$
$$= 0.5K(V_{in1} - V_{02} - V_{tn})^2 \tag{3}$$

we assume the two transistors have the same K. If differentiating the above equations with the threshold voltage V_{tn}, and choosing $V_{in2} = 2v$, $V_{in1} = 1.3v$, $V_{tn} = 0.8v$ and $V_{02} = 0.2v$, the error current is

$$\delta I = -0.3K\delta V_{tn} \tag{4}$$

The current decreases when the threshold voltage increases and vice versa. Assuming there are 6 bits binary weights such that $K_6 = 32K_1$. If $\delta V_{tn} = 0.02v$, which is reasonable assumption for the current VLSI technology, the error current of the 6th bit is equal to $0.006K_6 = 0.192K_1$. According to [1], the gate voltage of switchable NMOSFET is set to small in order to reduce power. In this case, the current of the first bit is equal to $0.5K_1(V_{in1} - V_{02} - V_{tn})^2 = 0.045K_1$. Obviously, the error current in the high bit is larger than the weight current in the low bit. The problem is especially serious when the gate voltage is small and the weight circuits are far apart in the same chip. This circuit can not work if the perturbation of threshold voltage exists. We briefly summary the problems in the following:

a. The threshold voltage variations may cause inaccuracy of binary-weighted

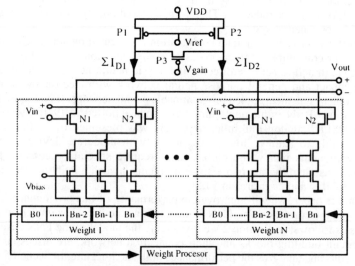

Fig.1 A programmable analog neuron model

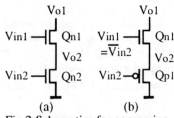

(a)   (b)

Fig.2 Schematics for comparing the effect of V_t perturbation

current source such that reduce the importance of the existence of th lower-bits.

b. In order to reduce the power, the control signals of switchable NMOSFETs weights is not fully digital signal. Thus, the outside circuit complexity is increased.

c. Silicon area consumption is still a major concern in the circuit design. In order to get reasonable swing at output, the W/L ratio of PMOS P1 and P2 should be similar to the sum of W/L ratio of NMOS N1 and N2. In the real application, there are hundreds or thousands synapse circuits parallel linked. Thus, P1 and P2 should be very large.

Next, we will propose a BiCMOS circuit to overcome these problems. A significant improvement by using PMOSFETs instead of NMOSFETs can be found in Fig.2(b), where Q_{p1} is a current source controller, and Q_{n1} is a resistance compensator to keep the node V_{o2} at a stable voltage. These two MOS transistors are both operated in the saturation region. Choosing the suitable W/L ratio, V_{o2} is forced to around 1.3v. In our case, $(W/L)_{p1} = 8(W/L)_{n1}$. V_{in1} and V_{in2} are inverted signals. Given $V_{in2} = 0$ and $V_{in1} = 4v$, the current I passing the two MOS transistors is

$$I = 0.5K(V_{o2} - V_{tp})^2(1 + \lambda V_{o2})$$
$$= 0.5K((V_{in1} - V_{tn} - V_{o2})^2(1 + \lambda(V_{o1} - V_{o2})) \tag{5}$$

Differentiating the above equation and for small λ, we got

$$\delta I = K(V_{o1} - V_{tp})(\delta V_{o1} - \delta V_{tp}) \tag{6}$$

We can represent R and R' as the resistor of PMOS and NMOS, respectively. Choosing R' = 4R, $V_{o1} = 1.3v$, and noting that V_{tp} will increase to 1.1v as substrate bias increases, we got

$$\delta I = 0.01K\delta V_{tp} \tag{7}$$

Compared with Eq.(4), we find that the proposed circuit is 30 times accurate than the previous circuit. The current tends to remain same if threshold voltage varies. Because of small R / R' ratio, higher-bit tend to operate more accurately than lower-bit. The physical explanation is: If V_{tp} increases, the resistor of the PMOSFET, R = 1 / $\lambda K(V_{o2} - V_{tp})^2$, tends to increase. Hence, the ratio of R / R' increases causes V_{o2} increases. Thus, the current I = $0.5K(V_{o2} - V_{tp})^2$ remain the same. The perturbation of V_{tp} and V_{tn} do not affect the accuracy of current source. Power consumption is also reduced due to the low mobility of PMOSFETs, i.e., current is only half if the same layout patterns are kept.

In order to save energy, the gate voltage of the switchable NMOSFETs in Fig.2(a) is kept around 1.3v. In this case, the gate voltage swing is from 0 to 1.3v. The gate voltage of the switchable weights is difficult to adjust. Because we keep the source voltage of the switchable PMOSFETs at 1.3v, full digital signals (0-5v) can be applied to the binary weights.

3. PNN Architecture

VLSI technology offers a highly advanced implementation medium both at the fabrication and the CAD level if efficient PNN architecture to be used. In this section, we will develop such a PNN architecture using BiCMOS building blocks.

Synapse Building Block

The programmable synapse building block, as shown in Fig.3(a), is designed by a simple PMOS / NMOS analog multiplier instead of the NMOS one in Fig.1, where complete digital weights are used to obtain high precision and analog summing to maintain high speed. Using this PMOS / NMOS structure, a small current source at very small gate voltage can be obtained to provide more accurate weight current. Each weight value, Bk (k = 0, 1,..., n), can be, in serial, received (or sent out) by the ports, Win / Wout. The binary weight for each bit is stored in the corresponding register, which two opposite outputs, 0 and 1, provide the input signals to the NMOSFET and the PMOSFET, respectively. As a symbol representation of the synapse circuit, an input pair (V_{in}^+ / V_{in}^-), an output pair (I_{out}^+ / I_{out}^-) and a weight pair (Win / Wout) are used in Fig.3(b).

Neuron Building Block

The neuron building block is composed of a differential input amplifier and two cascade BiCMOS inverters (See Fig.4(a)). The analog output signals from the synapse circuits are applied to two inputs, U1 and U2, respectively. The inputs of the neuron circuit are connected to Bipolar PNPs which replace PMOSFETs (P1 and P2) in Fig.1 to save area and increase the drive. The BiCMOS inverters are used to achieve sigmoid functions and their outputs can be also as the feedback signals to the synapse circuits. Major advantage of using BiCMOS inverters as the output units is to increase the drive because the load capacitance may

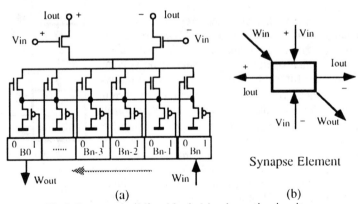

Synapse Element

(a)   (b)

Fig.3 Synapse building block (a) schematic circuit and (b) its symbol representation

be very heavy in large scale PNN implementation. Its symbol representation is given in Fig.4(b).

Using these two kinds of building blocks, synapse and neuron, a regular connection network, built by M neuron blocks and N x M synapse blocks, can be easily obtained in Fig.5. There are three connecting paths in the network, i.e.,

(a) x_i (the ith signal input) $\Rightarrow$ Vin (all synapse blocks at ith row);

(b) Iout(j) (all synapse blocks at jth column) $\Rightarrow$ U(j) (the jth neuron block);

(c) W_{IN} (weight input) $\Rightarrow$ W_{ij} (all synapse blocks) $\Rightarrow$ W_{OUT}.

where i = 1, 2, ..., N and j = 1, 2, ..., M. It is evident that the connection network can satisfy the following function:

$$Y_j = F (u_j)$$
$$u_j = \sum_i w_{ij}x_i + \theta_j \qquad (8)$$

where F is represented as sigmoid function and u (See Fig.4(a)) is a linear weighted sum plus a constant bias term, θ.

The connection network can be used in some PNN applications. As two examples, Hopfield network is implemented by such a single network, where each output of the neuron blocks is connected with all inputs of m synapse blocks; However, multilayer network with BP learning is by using such a network as a processing layer p (= 1, 2, ..., S) and connecting each layer in the defined rule, just as shown in Fig.6, where Layer S is the output layer, δ is the error signal, and Dj is the required output of the jth neuron block at the output layer.

4. Experimental Results

In order to evaluate the effectiveness of the PNN architecture, we ran many experiments by using 0.8μm BiCMOS technology and compared its performance with that of the previous PNN. The results show that the PMOS / NMOS structure in Fig.3(a) can act as a small self-calibrated current source which operates at very small gate voltage. When the threshold voltages (V_{tp} and V_{tn}) are varied, they do not affect the accuracy of current source. The results also show that V_{o2} varies within 1% in all round digital weighting operations. The proposed weight current source is accurate enough for 6-bit digital programming.

The advantages of using PNP in Fig.4(a) are to save the area and increase the drive. As mentioned before, the PMOSFETs (P1 and P2) in Fig.1 should be designed very large in order to match the output resistance. Their W / L ratio should be similar to hundreds or thousands times W / L ratios of single NMOS

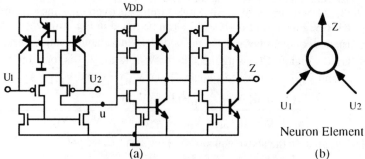

(a)

Neuron Element

(b)

Fig.4 Neuron building block (a) schematic circuit and (b) its symbol representation

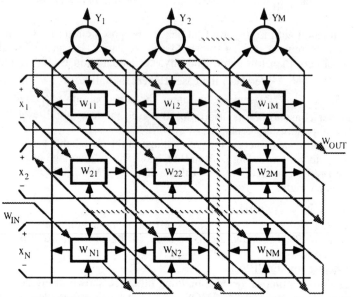

Fig.5 Connection network using the building blocks

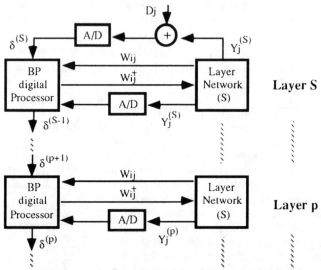

Fig.6 Multilayer network implementation using BP algorithm

N1 and N2. The very large PMOSFETs not only cost area, but also transfer delayed signal from the drain to the source, resulting in slow operating speed. Because of the smaller output resistance of PNP transistors, we use PNPs instead of PMOSFETs to save area. The simulation results with 40 weight units show that the output voltage almost stays at the lowest voltage when the switchable current does not reach its maximum with the 20 times minimum size PMOSFET driving 40 weight units, as shown in Fig.7. If one to one relation of current versus output voltage waveform is required, the size of PMOSFETs should be chosen around 30 times its minimum size. HSPICE simulation results show that one minimum size PNP to do the same job. According to the layout rules, area cost of one minimum size PNP is equal to that of 16 x PMOSFETs. This means that the area cost is reduce by a factor of 2. The design rules also set the maximum size is 45 times minimum for PNPs and 500 times for PMOSFETs. Thus, one maximum size PNP can drive 1,800 weights, but one maximum PMOS drive 650 weights. The voltage versus current transfer characteristics is plotted in Fig.8. For the input voltage different larger than 0.9v, the output voltages is linear to weight currents. When the input voltage is full a digital signal, an accurate linear relation between output voltage and weight current is obtained. As the input / output result of the neuron, a sigmoid function is given in Fig.9.

5. Conclusion

In this paper, we explore a typical PNN implementation based on mixed analog / digital design. The basic circuits, including synapse and neuron, are analyzed and some performances are improved by using BiCMOS technology. The corresponding PNN architecture in VLSI are developed and two kinds of building blocks, which are simpler since digital signals can be directly applied as programmable weights, are used in the architecture. Compared with the previous design, simulation results show that this PNN architecture can provide more accurate weight currents up to 30 times, and less silicon area and more driving capability by the factor of 2 and 3, respectively.

6. References

[1] P.W. Hollis and J.J. Paulos, 1990, "Artificial neural networks using MOS analog multipliers," IEEE Journal of Solid-State Circuits 25, 3, 849-855.

[2] P. Antognetti and V. Milutinovic (eds.), 1991, Neural networks: concepts, applications, and implementations, Prentice Hall, Englewood Cliffs, New Jersey.

[3] E. Sanchez-Sinencio and C. Lau, (eds.), 1992, Artificial neural networks: paradigms, applications, and hardware implementations, New York: IEEE Press.

[4] J.M.J. Murre, 1993, "Transputers and neural networks: an analysis of implementation constraints and performance," IEEE Trans. on Neural Networks 4, 2, 284-292.

[5] R.H. Nielsen, 1986, "Performance limits of optical, electro-optical, and electronic neurocomputers," Proc. SPIE, 634, 277-306.

[6] B.W. Lee and B.J. Sheu, 1991, Hardware annealing in electronic neural networks, Boston, MA: Kluwer Academic.

[7] B.A. White and M.I Elmasry, 1992, "The digi-neucognitron: a digital neocognitron neursl network model for VLSI, " IEEE Trans. on Neural Networs 3, 1, 73-84.

[8] Y. He, U. Cilingiroglu, and E. Sanchez-Sinencio, 1993, "A high-density and low-power charge-based hamming network," IEEE Trans. on Very Large Scale Integration (VLSI) Systems 1, 1, 56-62.

[9] B.W. Lee and B.J. Sheu, 1990, "A compact and general purpose neural chip with electrically programmable synapses," Proc. of IEEE Custom Integrated Circuits Conf., 26.6.1-4, Boston, MA.

[10] S. Bibyk and M. Isnail, 1989, "Issuues in analog VLSI and MOS techniques for neural computing, " in Analog VLSI Implementation of Neural Systems, C. Mead and M. Ismail (eds.), Kluwer Academic Publishers: Boston, MA.

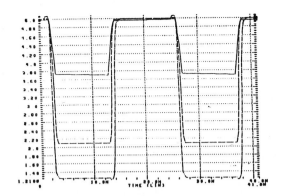

Fig.7 Simulated result of synapse blocks

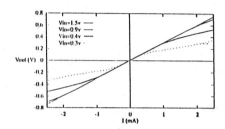

Fig.8 Measured results of programmable synapse

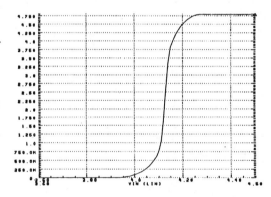

Fig.9 The input / output voltage of the neuron

Hardware Implementations

Session Chairs: Clifford Lau
Ralph Castain
Mohammad Sayeh

POSTER PRESENTATIONS

A Parallel Algorithm for Neural Computing

Q.M. Malluhi, M.A. Bayoumi, and T.R.N. Rao

The Center for Advanced Computer Studies

University of Southwestern Louisiana, Lafayette, LA 70504

Abstract: *This paper presents a high-performance technique for implementing artificial neural networks (ANNs) on hypercube-based general-purpose massively parallel machines. The paper synthesizes a tree-based parallel structure which is embedded into the hypercube topology. This structure is referred to as mesh-of-appendixed-sheered-trees (MAST). Both the recall and the learning phases of the multilayer with backpropagation ANN model are mapped on the MAST architecture. Unlike other techniques presented in the literature which require $O(N)$ time, where N is the size of the largest layer, our implementation requires only $O(\log N)$ time. Moreover, it allows pipelining of more than one input pattern and thus further improves the performance.*

I. Introduction

The area of Artificial Neural Networks (ANNs) is currently experiencing exceptional research efforts in investigating alternative computing models for real-life applications. A basic ANN computation model has several characteristics that favor massively parallel digital implementation. These include highly parallel operations, simple processing units (neurons), small local memory per neuron (distributed memory), and fault tolerance to connection or neuron malfunctioning [Ghos89]. Therefore, a highly parallel computing system of thousands of simple processing elements is a typical target architecture for implementing ANNs.

Mapping ANNs on general-purpose massively parallel machines has several advantages over special-purpose ANN architectures. Massively parallel machines provide a fast and flexible medium for experimenting with various neural computing models and for tuning network parameters for a specific application. Moreover, In many cases, they provide adequate performance for the application at hand. Cost effective use of hardware is another advantage since instead of having a dedicated special-purpose ANN hardware, the same parallel system can be shared by very wide band of users working in various areas.

Several mapping schemes have been reported to implement neural network algorithms on parallel architectures. Examples can be found in [Brow87, Kung88, Tomb88, Hwan89, Kim89, Zhan89, Wah90, Lin91, Chu92]. In this paper, we present a technique to implement the multilayer feedforward with backpropagation learning (FFBP) on hypercube massively parallel machines. A major advantage of this technique is high performance. The proposed mapping scheme takes $O(logN)$ time whereas all other techniques presented in the literature require $O(N)$time, where N is the size of the largest layer. Another important feature of this method is that it allows pipelining of more than one input pattern and thus further improves the performance.

The paper is organized as follows. Section II provides some basic definitions and terminology to be used throughout the paper. Section III explains the mapping procedure and discusses the issue of pipelining multiple patterns. Section IV compares our technique with other techniques proposed in the literature. Finally, Section V concludes the paper.

II. Preliminaries and Terminology

In this section we are going to introduce some basic concepts and definitions. In addition we are going to establish the terminology of the paper. A basic ANN model of computation consists of a large number of neurons connected to each other by connection weights. Each neuron, say neuron i, has an activation value a_i. Associated with each connection from neuron j to neuron i, is a synaptic weight (or simply, a weight) w_{ij}. The ANN computation can be divided into two phases: recall phase and learning phase. The recall phase updates the outputs (activation values) of neurons based on the system dynamics to produce the derived ANN output as a

The authors acknowledge the support of the National Science Foundation and State of Louisiana grant NSF/LEQSF (1992–96)-ADP-04.

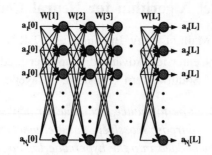

Figure 1: *An L layers feedforward network.*

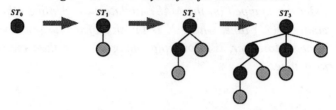

Figure 2: *Recursive construction of sheered trees.*

response for an input (test pattern). The learning phase performs an iterative updating of the synaptic weights based upon the adopted learning algorithm. In this paper we mainly deal with feedforward with backpropagation learning neural networks which is central to much of the work going on in the field nowadays.

A Multilayer (L layers) feedforward network has the general form shown in Figure 1. The network interconnection is such that each node (neuron) in a layer receives input from every node of the previous layer. This interconnection topology implies that for every layer, say layer l, there is a weight matrix $W[l]$ of synaptic weights for the links between layers l and l-1. We will use the index between brackets to indicate the layer number and a superscript to denote the test pattern number. For example $w_{ij}[l]$ represents the element in the ith row and the jth column of the weight matrix $W[l]$ of the lth layer and $a_i^p[l]$ represents the activation value for the ith neuron in the lth layer for the pth input pattern I^p. We will use N_i to denote the number of neurons in layer i. For notational convenience, the input terminals will be considered as layer number 0. Therefore, N_0 will represent the number of input terminals.

For input pattern $I^p = \left(I_1^p, I_2^p, \ldots, I_{N_0}^p\right)$, system dynamics for the recall phase is given by,

$$a_i[0] = I_i^p$$

$$a_i[l] = f(h_i[l]) = f\left(\sum_j w_{ij}[l]a_j[l-1]\right). \tag{1}$$

Each neuron i computes the weighted sum h_i of its inputs and then applies a nonlinear function $f(h_i)$ producing an activation value (output) a_i for this neuron. For each input I^p, there is a target (desired) output t^p. The backpropagation (BP) learning algorithm proceeds along the following iterative equations for $l = L, L-1, \ldots, 2$,

$$\delta_i^p[L] = f'(h_i^p[L])(t_i^p - a_i^p[L])$$

$$\delta_i^p[l-1] = f'(h_i^p[l-1])\sum_j w_{ji}[l]\delta_j^p[l]$$

$$\Delta w_{ij}[l] = \eta\delta_i^p[l]a_j^p[l-1] \tag{2}$$

$$w_{ij}^{new}[l] = w_{ij}^{old}[l] + \Delta w_{ij}[l].$$

Definition 1: The zero dimensional hypercube 0–HC is the one node graph. The address (label) of this node is the null string. The $(n+1)$-HC can be defined using two identical n-HCs as follows: relabel each node a of the first n-HC as $0a$ and each node of the second n-HC as $1a$. Connect each node oa in the first n-HC to the node $1a$ in the second.

In other words, the n-HC consists of 2^n nodes each is given an n-bit label (or address). Two nodes a and b are adjacent if and only if their labels differ by exactly one bit.

Definition 2: A sheered tree ST_k is a tree of 2^k nodes defined as follows: ST_0 is the one node tree. ST_k is constructed from ST_{k-1} by adding a right-most child to each node in ST_{k-1}.

Figure 2 illustrates the recursive construction of sheered trees. Notice that the depth of ST_k is k. Moreover, notice that sheered trees can be grasped in a different wise. Lemma 1 provides a different recursive definition of sheered trees.

Lemma 1: ST_k for $k > 0$, can be constructed from two copies T_1 and T_2 of ST_{k-1} by (1) taking the root of T_1 as the ST_k root and (2) making the root of T_2 the leftmost child of the root of T_1.

The above result can be seen from the construction process specified in Definition 2. When we go to larger trees starting at ST_1, we are actually constructing two identical sheered trees rooted at the two ST_1 nodes. This paper makes use of sheered trees in two manners. First, sheered trees are used to broadcast a value from the root to all the leaves. Second, sheered trees are utilized to sum values in its leaves and produce the result in the root. Notice that both of these operations can be performed in such a way that a node interacts with exactly one neighbor at a time. Observe also that for ST_k, each of these operations requires exactly k time steps.

III. Mapping Procedure

In this section we develop a mapping on what we call the MAST architecture. The MAST structure is shown to be embedded into the hypercube topology. Therefore, the algorithms developed for the MAST can be directly carried out on the hypercube. The mapping procedure is developed in stages. We start the discussion by describing the procedure for mapping the recall phase of a single layer on a MAST. After that, doses of complexity are gradually added by discussing more complex situations and by showing how to enhance the performance of the given mapping algorithm through processing more than one pattern in a pipelined fashion.

III.1. Mapping the Recall Phase

As a first step, consider the recall phase and concentrate only on the operations of one layer, say layer l. That is, we consider only the computation of layer l activation values $(a_i[l] \mid 1 \leq i \leq N_l)$, from the activation values $(a_i[l-1] \mid 1 \leq i \leq N_{l-1})$ of the preceding layer. Equation (1) hints that the operations involved in the computation are as follows:

1. Distribute $a_j[l-1]$ to all the elements of column j in the weight matrix $W[l]$. This is done for all $1 \leq j \leq N_{l-1}$.
2. Multiply $a_j[l-1]$ and w_{ij} for all $1 \leq i \leq N_l$ and $1 \leq j \leq N_{l-1}$.
3. Sum the results of multiplications of step 2 along each row of $W[l]$ to compute the weighted sums $(h_i[l] \mid 1 \leq i \leq N_l)$.
4. Apply the activation function $f(h_i[l])$ for all $1 \leq i \leq N_l$.

To start with, we suppose that each weight $w_{ij}[l]$ is stored in a distinct processor WP_{ij} (Weight Processor). In addition, we assume that each of the activation values $a_j[l-1]$ of layer $l-1$ is stored in processor CAP_j (Column Appendix Processor). An output activation value of layer l, $a_i[l]$, will be produced in processor RAP_i (Row Appendix Processor).

Steps 1 through 4 constitute the skeleton of our implementation. As we will see, step 1 can be performed in $O(\log N_l)$ time units using a sheered tree structure. All the multiplications of step 2 can be done in parallel in the various weight processors, and therefore, step 2 will only take one time unit. The summation of step 3 can be computed in $O(\log N_{l-1})$ time units via a sheered tree structure. Finally, the function f is applied concurrently on all the h_i values in the different $RAPs$.

The above discussion implies an architecture illustrated in Figure 3. This architecture is referred to as Mesh-of-Appendixed-Sheered-Trees (MAST). The $N \times M$ MAST, where $N = 2^n$ and $M = 2^m$, is constructed from a grid of $N \times M$ processors. Each row of this grid constitutes a set of leaves for a sheered tree called RAST (Row-Appendixed-Sheered-Tree). Similarly, each column of this grid forms a set of leaves for a sheered tree called CAST (Column-Appendixed-Sheered-Tree). For each RAST/CAST, there is an appendix RAP/CAP connected to the root of the tree. Each of the N RASTs has $2M + 1$ nodes and each of the M CASTs has $2N + 1$ nodes. Summing up and subtracting the grid size, since the grid processors are members of both RASTs and CASTs, we get the total number of nodes in a MAST $= N(2M + 1) + M(2N + 1) - NM = 3NM + N + M$.

The algorithm to map the operations of layer l is given in Figure 4. For this purpose we use an $N_l \times N_{l-1}$ MAST. We suppose that matrix $W[l]$ is pre-entered into the grid processors (weight processors) so that processor WP_{ij} stores $w_{ij}[l]$ in its local memory. Moreover, the activation values of layer $l-1$ are assumed to be placed into the $CAPs$ so that $a_j[l-1]$ is kept in the local memory of processor CAP_j. We make use of two procedures. Procedure

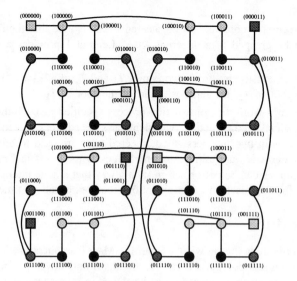

Figure 3: *4×4 MAST.*

AST-Bcst(T, v) broadcasts the value v from the appendix of the appendixed sheered tree T to all its leaves. Procedure *AST-SumLeaves(T, v, s)* finds the sum of variable v values in the leaves of T and produces the result in its appendix.

In Step 1 of the algorithm in Figure 4, CAP_j, $1 \leq j \leq N_{l-1}$, broadcasts $a_j[l-1]$ through $CAST_j$ so that, WP_{ij} $1 \leq i \leq N_l$ receives $a_j[l-1]$. Then, each WP_{ij} finds the product $w_{ij}[l]a_j[l-1]$. After that, $RAST_i$, $1 \leq i \leq N_l$, is used to sum the product values in its leaves and the result $h_i[l]$ is produced in RAP_i. Finally, The set of RAPs compute $(a_i[l] = f(h_i[l]) \mid 1 \leq i \leq N_l)$. Step 1 of the algorithm takes $log\,N_l + 2$ time steps because the depth of the CASTs is $log\,N_l + 2$. Likewise, step 3 takes $log\,N_{l-1} + 2$. We assume that computing the product in step 2 takes a single unit of time. In addition, we assume that computation of the function f in step 4 requires one time unit only. As a result, the total time for the computation of layer l, $T_l = log\,N_l + log\,N_{l-1} + 6$.

Thus far, we have seen the implementation of one layer. Now we will generalize the above discussion for a multilayer network. We start at layer 1 and compute $(a_i[1] \mid 1 \leq i \leq N_1)$ from $(a_i[0] \mid 1 \leq i \leq N_0)$. The RAPs will contain the result of computation. In order to continue the processing for the second layer, we need to place $(a_i[1] \mid 1 \leq i \leq N_1)$ into the CAPs. However, we can alleviate the need for this step by storing the transpose of $W[2]$ rather than $W[2]$ itself into the grid of WPs and repeating the operations of the algorithm backwards starting from the RAPs and getting the results $(a_i[2] \mid 1 \leq i \leq N_2)$ in the CAPs. For the third layer, $W[3]$ is stored in the WPs and we start at the CAPs and get the resultant activation values at the RAPs as we did for layer 1. We continue this way going back and forth from CAPs to RAPs and from RAPs to CAPs until we reach the output layer L.

Thereof, we use an $N_d{\times}N_e$ MAT where, e and d are the largest even and odd layers respectively. Let $N = max(N_e, N_d)$ and $M = min(N_e, N_d)$. We initialize the local memories of the WPs by storing $W[1], W^t[2], W[3], W^t[4], ...$ in the upper left corner of the WPs grid, that is, if l is odd, $w_{ij}[l]$ is stored into the local memory of WP_{ij}, otherwise, $w_{ij}[l]$ is kept into the local memory of WP_{ji}. The CAPs local memories are initialized to have the ANN input values $(I_i \mid 1 \leq i \leq N_0)$. After the initialization is complete, we proceed according to Algorithm 1 (Figure 4).

Taking L as a constant, Lemma 2 below shows that we can process the recall phase in a time complexity which is logarithmic in terms of the size N of the largest layer. This is achieved at the expense of using a maximum of $3N^2 + 2N$ processing units corresponding to an $N \times N$ MAST.

Lemma 2: Algorithm 1 takes less than or equal $2L(log\,N + 3)$ time steps.

Proof: Let T_{Recall} be the total time for computing the output. We have,

$$T_{Recall} = \sum_{l=1}^{L} T_l = \sum_{l=1}^{L} (log\,N_l + log\,N_{l-1} + 6)$$

$$= \sum_{l=1}^{L} (log\,N_e + log\,N_d + 6)$$

$$\leq 2L\,log\,N + 6L = 2L(log\,N + 3). \qquad \square$$

Algorithm 1: {RECALL PHASE}
for *l*=1 **to** *L* **do** *RECALL-LAYER(l)* **endfor.**

procedure *RECALL-LAYER(l)*
    if *l* is odd **then**
1.   **for all** $1 \leq j \leq N_{l-1}$ **do parbegin** *AST-Bcst*(CAST$_j$, $a_j[l-1]$) **parend**
2.   **for all** $1 \leq i \leq N_l$, $1 \leq j \leq N_{l-1}$ **do parbegin** *WP$_{ij}$* finds the product $p = w_{ij}[l]a_j[l-1]$ **parend**
3.   **for all** $1 \leq i \leq N_l$ **do parbegin** *AST-SumLeaves*(RAST$_i$, p, $h_i[l]$) **parend**
4.   **for all** $1 \leq i \leq N_l$ **do parbegin** *RAP$_i$* applies the function $f(h_i[l])$ **parend**
    else {*l* is even}
            Same as Steps 1, 2, 3 and 4 but replace CAST, RAST, *RAP* and *WP$_{ij}$* by RAST, CAST, *CAP* and *WP$_{ji}$* respectively
    endif
endprocedure.

Figure 4: *Algorithm for the recall phase of an L layers ANN.*

So far, we have seen how to implement FFBP ANNs on MASTs. Theorem 1 shows that MAST algorithms can be directly carried out on the hypercube. The proof of Theorem 1 provides an easy procedure to embed MASTs into hypercubes.

Theorem 1: The $2^x \times 2^y$ MAST where, $x, y > 0$, can be embedded into the $(x + y + 2)$-HC.

Proof: We will prove this result by assigning $(x + y + 2)$-bit names (or addresses) to the nodes of an $2^x \times 2^y$ MAST in such away that two adjacent nodes are given addresses that differ in exactly one bit position (see Definition 1). The proof is an inductive proof that depends on a recursive procedure to construct MASTs. We will divide the address of a node into three components (*class, rowadd, coladd*). The component *class* is a two-bit binary number identifying the type of a node. The different values for *class*; 00, 01, 10, or 11 indicate whether the node is an appendix, a row tree node, a column tree node, or a mesh (weight) node respectively. The components *rowadd* and *coladd* specify the row and column numbers of the node. In fact, restricting ourselves to these addressing conventions is not necessary for the proof. However, it is useful for practical implementation.

We use induction on x and y. The basis is true for $x = y = 1$. The basis is shown in Figure 5(a). Suppose that the $2^x \times 2^{y-1}$ MAST is named as required, we have to show how to expand the MAST along the rows and assign proper names for the nodes the $2^x \times 2^y$ MAST. Consider two copies C_1 and C_2 of a $2^x \times 2^{y-1}$ MAST. Rename each node (s, r, c) of C_1 as $(s, r, 0c)$ and each node (s, r, c) of C_2 as $(s, r, 1c)$. Connect the root of the ith row in C_1 to the root of the ith row in C_2 for $0 \leq i < 2^x$. Recall the result of Lemma 1 which indicates that connecting the roots of two 2^{y-1} nodes sheered trees produces a larger sheered tree of 2^y nodes. Now, for each row, choose one of the two original roots as the root of the newly constructed row sheered tree and ignore the appendix of the other root. The above construction and naming procedure is illustrated in Figure 5(b). Thus far, we have shown the expansion along the rows. For the proof to be complete, we have to show the expansion procedure along the columns which is very analogous. Figure 5(c) illustrates MAST expansion along the columns. □

III.2. Mapping the Learning Phase

The learning phase is composed of two parts: forward propagation part and backpropagation part. The forward part is identical to the recall phase whose implementation is provided in Algorithm 1. However, some values in Algorithm 1 have to be given special attention as they will be needed later during the BP part. When an appendix CAP_i/RAP_i receives a weighted sum h_i from the root of its tree RAST$_i$/CAST$_i$, it should apply the function $f(h_i)$ and then save h_i for future use (see Equation (2)). Similarly, when a *WP* receives an activation value a_i it multiplies it by the corresponding weight and then saves it because it will be used in the calculation of Δw in the BP part (check Equation (2)). The BP part is performed in a manner similar to the forward propagation part, going the other way around. The BP part starts from the appendices CAP_i/RAP_i containing the computed values $(a_i[L] \mid 1 \leq i \leq N_L)$ after the forward part and goes backwards. It is not difficult to show that the BP phase can be performed in $< 2L(\log N + 5)$ units of time.

III.3. Pipelining Patterns

In this subsection, we introduce an improvement to the above algorithm by showing how to process more than one input pattern in parallel. This is done by pipelining up to $2\log M + 4$ input patterns. Our ability to pipeline patterns depends on the assumption that links are full duplex, that is, links can carry data in both directions

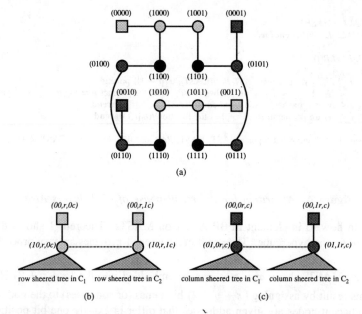

Figure 5: *(a) Embedding the 2×2 Mast into the 4–HC, (b)*
Row-wise expansion of MASTs, (c) Column-wise expansion of MASTs.

simultaneously. In pipelining input patterns we have to be careful not to assign more than one computation to a single processor during any moment of time. We exploit processors of RASTs/CASTs that are broadcasting activation values downwards but performing no computation. At the same time, we will be having another pattern being processed by these processors in the other direction. This, of course, increases processor utilization.

Consider the following scenario: CAP_i passes $a_i^1[0]$ downward to the root of $CAST_i$ starting a recall phase computation. In the second time step, $a_i^1[0]$ will move further down in $CAST_i$. At that moment CAP_i sends $a_i^2[0]$ of the second pattern to the root of $CAST_i$ starting the recall phase of the second pattern. In the following time step, we initiate the broadcasting of $a_i^3[0]$ to start the recall phase of the third pattern. The process continues in this manner. However, there is a limit to the number of patterns that can be concurrently placed in the pipeline. This limit is governed by the constraint that no processor should ever be doing more than one computation at a time. Such a situation occurs when $a_i^1[1]$ reaches WP_{ij} coming down $RAST_i$ (while performing the computations of layer 2) at the same time when $a_j^p[0]$ reaches WP_{ij} while going down $CAST_j$ (while performing the computation of the first layer for pattern p). In the very next time step WP_{ij} is required to perform two computations. The first is to multiply $a_i^1[1]$ by $w_{ji}[2]$ and the second is to multiply $a_j^p[0]$ by $w_{ij}[1]$. We can prove that $p \geq 2logM + 5$ (proof is omitted due to lack of space). Therefore, the maximum number of patterns that can be pipelined is $2logM + 4$.

IV. Evaluation and Comparison with Previous Work

In this section we compare the characteristics of our mapping technique with three major techniques in the literature. The first of these techniques was introduced by [Kung88, Hwan89]. It maps ANNs on the systolic ring architecture. Extensive work in the literature has since depended on this technique. The second technique [Sham90] is an extension of Kung's method in order to make it possible to pipeline M input patterns. The target machine for this mapping scheme is a two-dimensional SIMD processor array. The third technique [Lin91] implements ANNs on fine grain mesh-connected SIMD machines. The mapping is established based on a set of congestion-free routing procedures. Four characteristics are considered; the number of processors used, the time for precessing one pattern, the power of pipelining patterns, and finally the time to process k input patterns in a pipelined manner. The comparison is furnished in the table of Figure 6.

V. Conclusions

This paper has presented a high-performance scheme for implementing both the recall and the learning phases of the FFBP ANN model on hypercube massively parallel machines. This scheme requires a time complexity of

Mapping scheme	Architecture	no. of processors	time for one pattern	pipelining?	time for k Patterns (pipelined)
[Kung88]	systolic ring	$O(N)$	$O(N)$	NO	$O(kN)$
[Sham90]	SIMD 2D mesh	$O(MN)$	$O(N)$	YES	$O(kN / M)$
[Lin91]	SIMD 2D mesh	$O(N^2)$	$O(N)$	NO	$O(kN)$
Our approach	Hypercube	$O(N^2)$	$O(\log N)$	YES	$O(kN / \log N)$

Figure 6: *Comparison with other mapping schemes.*

$O(log N)$, where N is the number of neurons in the largest layer. The technique further promotes the performance by offering the capability to process input patterns in a pipelined fashion. We should note here that even though the technique has been only illustrated for the FFBP ANN model, the idea can be extended to accommodate other models such as the Hopfield model, the self-organizing feature maps, and the Boltzmann machine.

References

[Brow87] Brown, J. R. and S. F. Vanable, "Artificial Neural Network on a SIMD Architecture," *Proceedings of the 2nd Symposium on the Frontiers of Massively Parallel Computation*, pp. 127–136, 1987.

[Chu92] Chu L. C., B. W. Wah, "Optimal Mapping of Neural-Network Learning on Message-Passing Multicomputers," *Journal of Parallel and Distributed Computing* 14, pp 319–339, 1992.

[Ghos89] Ghosh, J. and K. Hwang, "Mapping Neural Networks onto Message-Passing Multicomputers," *Journal of Parallel and Distributed Computing*, 6, pp. 291–330, 1989.

[Hwan89] Hwang, J. N. and Kung, S. Y., "Parallel Algorithms/Architectures for Neural Networks," *Journal of VLSI Signal Processing*, 1989.

[Kim89] Kim, K. and Kumar K. P., "Efficient Implementation of Neural Networks on Hypercube SIMD Arrays," *International Joint Conference on Neural Networks*, 1989.

[Kung88] Kung, S. Y., "Parallel Architectures for Artificial Neural Nets," *International Conference on Systolic Arrays*, pp. 163–174, 1988.

[Lin91] Lin W., V. K. Prasanna and K. W. Przytula, "Algorithmic Mapping of Neural Network Models onto Parallel SIMD Machines," *IEEE Transactions on Computers*, 1991.

[Sham90] Shams S. and W. Przutula, "Mapping of Neural Networks onto Programmable Parallel Machines," *IEEE International Symposium on Circuits and Systems*, New Orleans, LA, May 1990.

[Tomb88] Tomboulian, Sherryl, "Overview and Extensions of a System for Routing Directed Graphs on SIMD Architectures," *Frontiers of Massively Parallel Processing*, 1988.

[Wah90] Wah B. W. and L. Chu, "Efficient Mapping of Neural Networks on Multicomputers," *Int. Conf. on Parallel Processing*, Pennsylvania State Univ. Press, Vol. I, pp. 234–241, 1990.

[Zhan89] Zhang, X., et. al., "An Efficient Implementation of the Back Propagation Algorithm on the Connection Machine CM-2," *Neural Information Processing Systems 2*, pp. 801–809, 1989.

Programmable Synapse and Neuron Circuits in VLSI for Perceptions and Cellular Neural Networks

Joongho Choi, Bing J. Sheu, Josephine C.-F. Chang

Department of Electrical Engineering (Electrophysics and Systems)
University of Southern California, Los Angeles, CA 90089-0271

Abstract

Although neural networks have the intrinsic property of parallel operations, the traditional computers cannot fully exploit it because of serial hardware. By using analog circuit design techniques, large amount of parallel functional units can be accommodated in a small silicon area, and at the same time, the precision requirement for neural operations can be achieved. A synapse circuit which can perform four-quadrant multiplication has been designed. Dynamically refreshed weight value storage provides programmable capability. An input-neuron circuit which performs as a fast buffer and an output-neuron circuit with gain-adjustable capability are also designed. A prototype system using the designed components has been successfully trained by the Generalized Delta Rule.

I. Introduction

Very large scale integration (VLSI) technologies are now maturing with emphasis towards submicron structures and sophisticated applications combining tremendous amount of analog and digital circuits on a single chip. Examples are found on today's advanced systems for telecommunications, robotics, automotive electronics, image processing, intelligent sensors, etc [1-10]. To process large number of data obtained from the real world in real time requires a sequential digital machine to operate at a speed of more than 10^{18} floating point operations per second. Nowadays, researches on digital machines have focused on increasing processing speeds of functional units and efficiency of hardware utilization by using special techniques such as superscaler and superpipeline [11]. Communication overheads of multiple data and control paths would seriously reduce the computing power of a digital system when the number of functional units becomes large. On the other hand, an analog VLSI hardware with intrinsic capability of massively parallel processing and compact silicon area provides a method for implementing adaptive systems based on neural models [12]. As a result, analog VLSI has been recognized as a major technology for future information processing.

With massively parallel processing capabilities, artificial neural networks can be used to solve many engineering and scientific complex and time-consuming problems. The optimized data structure in a neural network can be realized by an analog neural hardware. A desirable general-purpose machine to implement a biological neural system must provide some key features such as neuron thresholds and transfer functions, programmable synaptic weight values and time constants either externally or by the machine itself. In an analog design, the neuron functions can be approximated by transistor characteristics inherently as opposed to table-look-up or iterative computations in a digital machine. Synaptic weight values can be either DRAM-type stored and refreshed [4,6] or EEPROM-style stored [5,13]. The DRAM-type synapse can be quite compact, and designed without having to access special technology, but an off-chip controller is needed to continuously update the weights. The EEPROM-style synapse provides the highest possible density, but learning is relatively slow, and a special technology is need. In this paper, possible VLSI design of neural components for general neural operations are described and experimental results are also given.

II. General Architecture

The generic neural operation in a perceptron and a cellular neural network consists of a weighted summation and nonlinear function, which are summarized as,

$$v_j = f_s \left(\sum_i w_{j,i} v_i \right) \tag{1}$$

where v_i and v_j are the i-th neuron output and the j-th neuron output, respectively. The synapse value between the i-th and the j-th neurons is represented by $w_{j,i}$ and f_s is the nonlinear function, which is usually a sigmoid function. This operation describes a feedforward or retrieving process in the artificial neural network algorithms. Figure 1 shows the block diagram of a multi-layered neuroprocessor chip. It consists of an array of input neurons, an array of output neurons, and the synapse matrix. In order to support the feedback or learning process, the weight value can be programmable — it can be efficiently updated and reliable maintained. Synapse value computation can be done by a host processor core or by some dedicated on-chip learning circuitry.

There have been many researchers for analog VLSI neural networks implementation using various design technologies [5-10]. Significant numbers of synapses and neurons are included in order to achieve a high computational throughput by using fully massive parallelism.

III. Major Components

Compact analog components are suitable for exploiting the property of massive processing in an artificial neural network. In this section, analog circuit design techniques for implementing a general-purpose neural chip will be discussed.

A. Programmable Synapses

Since the number of synapse cells dominates that of neurons, characteristics of an analog multiplier used to realize the synapse cell determine the overall accuracy, silicon area, and power consumption of the neuroprocessor chip. Several design issues should be considered for performance optimization of the synapse cell.

In order to implement a linear multiplication between the input voltage and the stored synapse weight voltage, the Gilbert multiplier circuit can be used. All transistors operate in the saturation region. Figure 2 shows the complete circuit schematic of the multiplier used for the synapse cell [10]. PMOS differential pairs are used to achieve large operational range by reducing the number of transistors stacked between two power supply lines. The output current is obtained from the difference of two currents, I^+ and I^-. The input voltage $V_{IN,i}$ is applied to the NMOS differential pair of M_1-M_2, while the synapse weight value $W_{j,i}$ is applied to the PMOS pairs of M_6-M_7 and M_9-M_{10}. The differential input and weight values ensure the balanced-operations of the positive and negative signals as well as can achieve the common-mode rejection. The differential output current is converted into the single-ended current through the cascode current-mirror stage consisting of transistors M_{12} through M_{21}. The synapse output current can be determined as

$$I_{j,i} = K\sqrt{\frac{1}{2}\beta_P\beta_N}(V_{IN,i}^+ - V_{IN,i}^-)(W_{j,i}^+ - W_{j,i}^-) = G_m V_{IN,i} W_{j,i} \;, \tag{2}$$

where K is the current gain from transistor $M_{12(14)}$ to transistor $M_{13(15)}$. Here β_P and β_N are transconductance parameters of a PMOS transistor and an NMOS transistor in the differential pairs, respectively. The sizes of all transistors in a prototype design are also listed in Fig. 2.

The learning algorithms can be performed in the host computer or the companion digital signal processing (DSP) core and the synapse values are stored in the digital memory. Every synapse value is converted into the analog voltage and loaded into the capacitor of the synapse cell. The synapse value is dynamically stored on the capacitance which are contributed by the MOS transistor and possibly augmented by the additional capacitor. Address decoders are used to direct the common signal line to the desired synapse site. Periodic refresh is required to maintain the accurate synapse weight values [4]. For a given leakage current of 10 pA, refreshing in every 1 *msec* is sufficient to maintain the 8-bit accuracy.

B. Input Neurons

The input neuron buffers the input signal and provides the high-speed driving capability for a large capacitive load. An input neuron can be constructed by an operational amplifier configured as the unity-gain buffer. Since there is a large number of synapse cells to be driven by one input neuron, the equivalent load capacitance to the input neuron might be quite large. Thus, a fast settling response of the input neuron needs careful design. It is desirable to let the input neuron occupy a compact silicon area and dissipate very low power. Figure 3 shows the circuit schematic diagram of the designed input neuron which provides the differential input to the synapse cells. In order to reduce the power consumption in the output branch while maintaining the speed, the class-AB output stage is used [14].

C. Output Neurons

The output neuron converts the summed current into the voltage and performs one of several types of functions such as the thresholding, linear amplification, and sigmoid function. The detailed circuit schematic of the output neuron is shown in Fig. 4 [10]. Summation of the weighted products is naturally done by hard-wiring according to the Kirchoff's current law. Current-to-voltage conversion is performed by the transresistance amplifier consisting of an operational amplifier and a feedback resistor. Since the output impedance of the synapse cell is finite, the synapse current is dependent on the output voltage, which is the input node voltage of the output neuron. In the proposed design, this node is connected to the virtual ground of the operational amplifier to eliminate the synapse current variation.

Since the current summation results from a large array of synapse cells, the transresistance amplifier should have a sufficient capability to handle a large magnitude of the current for proper linear conversion. Thus, the operational amplifier includes the source follower as an output stage as shown in Fig. 4(a). In addition, six transistors are used to implement the active feedback resistor, which can achieve higher accuracy in the wide operational range and less silicon area [15]. The summed current is converted into the voltage according to the following expression,

$$V_{LIN,\,j} = R_{eq} \cdot \sum_{i=1}^{M} I_{j,\,i} = \sum_{i=1}^{M} I_{j,\,i} \, / \, 2\beta_R (V_{RF} - V_{thp}) \,, \tag{3}$$

where V_{RF} is the control voltage to tune the equivalent feedback resistance value R_{eq}. Here β_R and V_{thp} are the transconductance parameter and the threshold voltage of transistors $M_{RF\,1(2)}$, respectively.

Sigmoid function generation is required for performing the back-propagation learning algorithm. The sigmoid function is effectively realized by cascading simple inverting amplifiers with the input and feedback resistors as shown in Fig. 4(b). The voltage gain of the sigmoid function is determined as

$$\frac{V_{SIG,\,j}}{V_{LIN,\,j}} = \left[\frac{R_{eq,\,2} \, / \, R_{eq,\,1}}{1 + (1 + R_{eq,\,2} \, / \, R_{eq,\,1}) \, / \, A} \right]^2 \,, \tag{4}$$

where A is the voltage gain of the inverting amplifier. Since the resistors are realized by transistors biased in the triode region, their equivalent resistance values can be controlled,

$$R_{eq,\,1(2)} = 1 \, / \, \beta(V_{R\,1(2)} - V_{th}) \,, \tag{5}$$

where β, V_{th} are transconductance parameter and the effective threshold voltage of the transistors, respectively. The control voltages, V_{TH_P} and V_{TH_N} are used to reduce the offset voltage of the sigmoid function generator due to process-induced nonideal device characteristics. Their values can be set during the chip-initializing phase. The entire gain of the output neuron are controlled by the gate voltages of the PMOS transistors of the feedback resistor in the transresistance amplifier (V_{RF} in (3)) and the voltages of the input and the feedback resistors in the sigmoid function generator (V_{R1} and V_{R2} in (5)).

IV. System-Level Considerations and Experimental Results

In our design, the digital synapse weight information in the system memory is periodically converted by the digital-to-analog converter and written into the analog memory site to maintain the accuracy of the stored data. If there are M synapse cells in the entire system, the time to write the computed weight value into the synapse storage, T_{update}, consists of the following item,

$$T_{update} = M \cdot (T_{data} + T_{DAC} + 6R_{on} C_W) \,, \tag{6}$$

where T_{data} is the amount of time for fetching the digital data from the system memory, T_{DAC} is the digital-to-analog conversion time, R_{on} is the ON-resistance of the switch transistor, and C_W is the effective storage capacitance. The amount of time for the synapse value to experience a change equivalent to the 1/2-bit resolution, ΔT, must be greater than T_{update} to fulfill the timing requirement of the system for a reliable refreshing scheme. Figure 5 shows the numerical examples of the size and accuracy relationship of the synapse matrix for different values of the storage capacitances.

A prototyping general-purpose neural network chip consisting of an array of the input neurons, an array of the output neurons, and the synapse matrix was fabricated in a 2-μm double-polysilicon CMOS technology from the MOSIS Service of USC/Information Science Institute [16]. Figure 6 shows the measured DC characteristics of a synapse cell performing linear multiplication. The cell can be arbitrarily accessed by the row/column address decoders from the synapse matrix. The differential synapse values in Fig. 6(a), and the input voltage in Fig. 6(b) ranges from -2.0 V to 2.0 V in a step size of 0.5 V. The operation ranges for the input signal and the synapse weight value corresponding to a linearity error of less than 1% is -1.75 V to 1.75 V. The small offset current can easily be compensated through the modification of synapse weight value and/or the use of an additional synapse weight connecting with the output neuron.

Fig. 7 shows the measured dynamic synapse weight value changes as a function of time due to the leakage current. The rate of the output current change is about 12.5 nA/sec. For the conductance value of the synapse cell of 5 uA/V, the voltage change rate is 2.5 mV/sec, which corresponds to the time elapse of about 4 seconds for the 1-bit resolution change of the synapse weight value in 8-bit operations.

The measured dynamic range of the input neuron is from -3.0 V to 3.0 V, which is sufficient to drive the synapse cell. The settling time with 1% error is about 300 nsec for the capacitive load of 7 pF. Measured result of the linear current-to-voltage converter as a part of the output neuron is shown in Fig. 8(a). This converter can handle the input current level of more than 250 μA. In the measurement, the active feedback resistance was set to 4 kΩ. The measured sigmoid function with various voltage gains of 6.5, 2.8, 0.8 are shown in Fig. 8(b). The achievable maximum voltage gain is around 2,000.

The system-level experiments were conducted with the fabricated synapse cells in our laboratory in order to investigate the feasibility of neuroprocessing system implementation. Figure 9 shows the schematic diagram of the measurement setup, which consists of four synapse cells and a linear current-to-voltage converter as a simple output neuron. Here, the sigmoid function is not included in the simple learning. The host processor executes the learning algorithms. An analog-to-digital converter was used to interface the output voltage of the network. Update of the synapse values was performed sequentially by the digital-to-analog converter and the address control signals. An additional digital-to-analog converter was used for determining the analog input voltages.

The primary goal of the learning experiment is to compensate the bias which was intentionally added so that the desired output voltage will return to zero. The bias current was provided by the constant voltage source V_{bias} and the resistor R_{bias}. The Generalized Delta Rule [17] was used to train the network. Figure 10 shows the measurement results. In the initialization phase (marked A), four weight values were set to be quite small random numbers. Thus, the summation current is -57.5 μA and the output voltage is 1.12 V. After the learning proceeded for a sufficiently long period, the summation current became 0.1 μA, and the output voltage became -1.95 mV which is close to the desired output value.

VI. Conclusion

The design techniques and considerations for implementing VLSI neural components which are suitable for perceptrons and cellular neural networks have been addressed. The synapse circuit is capable of performing four-quadrant multiplication, and the output neuron is gain-adjustable. Our on-going effort is to use these components to implement a large scale neural system.

References

[1]   Y. Arima, K. Mashito, K. Okada, T. Yamada, A. Maeda, H. Notani, H. Kondou, and S. Kayano, "A 336-neuron 28k-synapse, self-learning neural network chip with branch-neuron-unit architecture," *IEEE Jour. of Solid-State Circuits,* vol. 27, pp. 1637-1644, Nov. 1991.

[2]   T. Watanabe, K. Kimura, M. Aoki, T. Sakata, and K. Itoh, "A single 1.5-V digital chip for a 10^6-synapse neural networks," *Proc. IEEE/INNS Inter. Joint Conf. of Neural Networks,* vol. 2, pp. 7-12, Baltimore, MD, June 1992.

[3]   C.-F. Chang and B. J. Sheu, "Digital VLSI multiprocessor design for neurocomputers," *Proc. of IEEE/INNS Inter. Joint Conf. of Neural Networks,* vol. 2, pp. 1-6, Baltimore, MD, June 1992.

[4]   B. W. Lee and B. J. Sheu, *Hardware Annealing in Analog VLSI Neurocomputing,* Kluwer Academic Publishers: Boston, MA, 1991.

[5]   M. Holler, S. Tam, H. Castro, and R. Benson, "An electrically trainable artificial neural network (ETANN) with 10240 floating gate synapses," *Proc. of IEEE/INNS Inter. Joint Conf. of Neural Networks,* vol. 2, pp. 191-196, 1989.

[6]   C.-F. Chang, B. J. Sheu, W.-C. Fang, and J. Choi, "A trainable analog neural chip for image compression," *Proc. of IEEE Custom Integrated Circuits Conf.*, pp. 16.1.1-16.1.4, San Diego, CA, May 1991.

[7]   P. W. Hollis and J. J. Paulos, "Artificial neural networks using MOS analog multiplier," *IEEE Jour. of Solid-State Circuits*, vol. 25, pp. 849-855, June 1990.

[8]   B. Boser, E. Säckinger, J. Bromley, Y. LeCun, and L. D. Jackel, "An analog neural network processor with programmable topology," *IEEE Jour. of Solid-State Circuits*, vol. 26, pp. 2017-2025, Dec. 1991.

[9]   S. Satyanarayana, Y. P. Tsividis, and H. P. Graf, "A reconfigurable VLSI neural network," *IEEE Jour. of Solid-State Circuits*, vol. 27, pp. 67-81, Jan. 1992.

[10]   J. Choi and B. J. Sheu, "VLSI design of compact and high-precision analog neural network processors," *Proc. of IEEE/INNS Inter. Joint Conf. of Neural Networks*, vol. 2, pp. 637-641, Baltimore, MD, July 1992.

[11]   K. Hwang, *Advanced Computer Architecture: Parallelism, Scalability, Programmability*, McGraw-Hill, Inc.: New York, NY, 1993.

[12]   *Analog VLSI Implementation of Neural Systems*, Edited by C. Mead, Mohammed Ismail, Kluwer Academic Publishers: Boston, MA, 1989.

[13]   B. W. Lee, H. Yang, and B. J. Sheu, "Analog floating-gate synapses for general-purpose VLSI neural computation," *IEEE Trans. on Circuits and Systems*, vol. 38, pp. 654-658, June 1991.

[14]   R. Gregorian and G. C. Temes, *Analog MOS Integrated Circuits for Signal Processing*, John Wiley and Sons: New York, NY, 1986.

[15]   M. Banu and Y. Tsividis, "Floating voltage-controlled resistors in CMOS technology," *Electronic Lett.*, vol. 18, pp. 678-679, 1982.

[16]   C. Tomovich, "MOSIS-a gate way to silicon," *IEEE Circuit and Device Mag.*, vol. 4, pp. 22-23, Mar. 1988.

[17]   D. E. Rumelhart, J. L. McClelland, and the PDP Research Group, *Parallel Distributed Processing*, vol. 1, The MIT Press: Cambridge, MA, 1989.

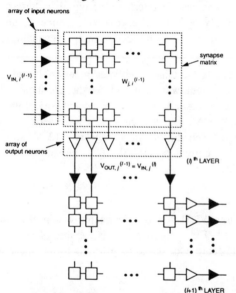

Fig. 1   Block diagram of a multi-layered neural network.

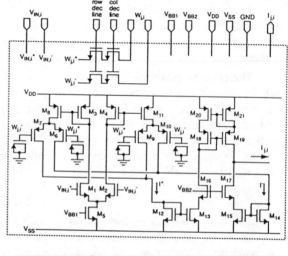

Fig. 2   Circuit schematic of a synapse cell based on the wide-range Gilbert multiplier.

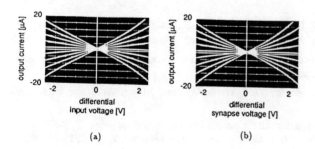

(a)   (b)

Fig. 6   Measured results on the multiplication operation of the synapse cell. (a) Synapse current versus input voltage. (b) Synapse current versus weight voltage.

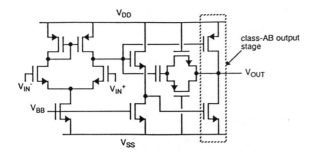

Fig. 3 Circuit schematic of an input neuron.

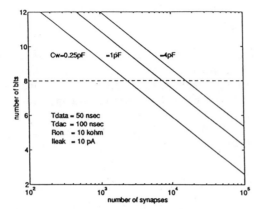

Fig. 5 Synapse weight accuracy versus the number of synapses connected to one common signal line.

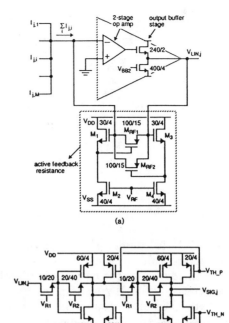

(a)

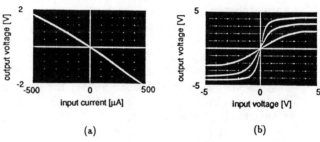

(b)

Fig. 4 Circuit schematic of an output neuron.
(a) Linear current-to-voltage converter.
(b) Sigmoid function generation circuit.

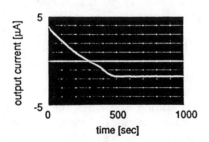

Fig. 7 Measured results of the synapse weight retention characteristics.

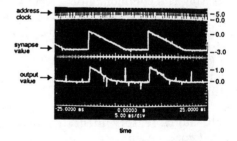

(a)   (b)

Fig. 8 Measured results of the output neuron.
(a) Linear current-to-voltage conversion. (b) Sigmoid function generation.

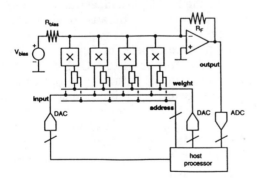

Fig. 9 Measurement setup for system-level experiments.

Fig. 10 The intentionally added bias term can be removed by the learning process. The output value has been flipped in the figure so that a more negative value appear on top of the ground value.

An Asynchronous Inter-Processor Communication Based, Input Recycling Parallel Architecture for Large Scale Neural Network Simulation

Myung Won Kim, Jong Moon Kim, Yoonseon Song, Youngjik Lee, and Hoon Bock Lee

Research Department, ETRI

P.O. Box 8, Taedok Science Town, Taejon, Korea

Abstract

The SIMD is currently a common architecture for neurocomputers, however, it suffers from the limited scalability for simulating large scale neural networks in real-time. In this paper we investigate an asynchronous communication based, scalable parallel architecture called the wavefront array processor (WAP). We compare the scalabilities of two architectures for simulating multi-layer perceptrons. We also propose input recycling for a significant reduction of communication time for the WAP. In addition we describe the architecture of the DNP-II, the unit processor for our neurocomputer EMIND-II, based on the WAP architecture.

I. Introduction

Attempts have been made to implement digital neurocomputers by means of the network of processors (PEs) each of which perform basic functions such as multiplication, addition for synapse computation and inter-processor communication for signal transfer between neurons[2, 3, 4, 6, 10]. This approach generally exploits a high degree of regularity and locality intrinsic to neural network computations, which well maps into the processor network architecture. The entire computational task of a neural network is divided into subtasks which are distributed to and executed by PEs in parallel. It is important that neural computation often needs no complicated scheduling and control of the subtasks. By exploiting such characteristics of neural computation, it is desirable to implement a cost-effective neurocomputer for simulating large scale neural networks.

The current, most common parallel architectures for digital neurocomputers are the SIMD and its variants such as systolic array. The SIMD architecture is simple and suits the regularity and locality of neural computations. However, it lacks scalability due to clock skew and broadcasting time constraint which prohibit from expanding the system for performance enhancement beyond a certain limit. The clock skew is the maximum delay between the clock signals that control adjacent PEs. It is caused by the differences in resistivity and capacitance, and the physical lengths of the clock lines. Significantly large clock skew may cause inter-PE communication failure. In spite that broadcasting is a common, global communication scheme of the SIMD, broadcasting time increases as the processor array grows and it often results performance saturation. Because of such problems, the SIMD architecture is significantly limited in scalability.

For continuous speech recognition, however, the computation speed of 10^9 connections per second (CPS) and the storage of 10^6 connections are required. More than 10^{10} CPS and 10^9 words of weight memory are necessary for dynamic image processing. In the future, a large size network consisting of several tens or hundreds of thousand PEs will be required to simulate neural networks in real-time for complex tasks such as continuous speech recognition, dynamic image processing, and multi-modal sensory integrated recognition and control. Adaptive control applications based on neural networks often need on-line learning for real-time adjustment of control parameters, which requires a high performance of neural network computation. In addition, it is often the case that training neural networks takes endurably a long time. A high performance neurocomputer is also needed for fast training of neural networks so that, for a given problem, the user can design an optimal architecture by way of testing various neural network architectures. In conclusion, however, the SIMD architecture should not be efficient for simulating large-scale neural networks because of its limited scalability.

In our research we investigate a scalable parallel architecture based on asynchronous inter-processor communication called the wavefront array processor (WAP) for simulating large scale neural networks. The WAP is considered a systolic array incorporated with data-driven computing. In the WAP each PE is independently programmed and it communicates with its neighbors in an asynchronous manner. Unlike the SIMD the wavefront array needs no global clock for controlling the entire network of proccessors and each PE can even be clocked differently: the clock skew becomes no longer a problem. Thus, it is possible to construct a massively parallel network consisting of many PEs.

In this paper we describe the WAP as a scalable architecture for neural network simulation. In Section II, we compare the scalabilities of the SIMD and the WAP for simulating multi-layer perceptrons. We also propose input recycling which significantly reduces the amount of inter-processor communications for neural computation in the WAP. In Section III, we describe an implementation of the DNP-II (Digital Neural Processor), our unit processor and the EMIND-II (ETRI Machine Imitating NeuroDynamics), our neurocomputer based on the WAP architecture.

II. Scalability Comparison of the WAP and the SIMD

In this section we compare the scalabilities of both architectures for simulating multi-layer percep-trons(MLPs). We consider, as a SIMD configuration, a linear ring of PEs employing the broadcast bus and the ring bus for communication as in the CNAPS[2]. We also consider, as a WAP config-uration, an nxn 2-D toroidal mesh of PEs each of which communicates with its four adjacent PEs in an asynchronous manner.

For simulating a neural network, the SIMD architecture generally employs node parallelism. In this scheme neural network nodes are distributed to and computed by PEs (a node is computed by a single PE at a time) in parallel as input values are broadcast. Time-multiplexing is used for computing more than one node by a PE. The outputs of nodes of a layer, in turn, are broadcast as the input values to the next layer nodes. Different layers are computed in a time-multiplexing way.

In the WAP mapping, the weight matrix for a layer is divided into subblocks, which are dis-tributed to PEs. Unlike the SIMD, the WAP adopts node and weight parallelism. A node is computed by a row (column) of PEs and each PE in the row shares weighted summation for the node. In this configuration PEs can be divided into two groups of different functions: the synapse processors(SP) and the cell processors(CP). The SPs compute weighted sums while the CPs com-pute the outputs of nodes. Partial weighted sums for a node computed by the SPs in a row are accumulated to the CP in the same row, which then computes the output of the node. Each row of PEs computes a node in parallel and more than one nodes can be computed by time-multiplexing. The outputs of a layer computed by the CPs, in turn, are fed into the adjacent PEs for computing the next layer. Fig. 1 shows mapping of a network layer into the SIMD and the WAP architectures and Fig. 2 illustrates data flows for computing an MLP layer in the WAP.

2.1 Performance and Scalability

Consider a multi-layer perceptron consisting of L layers each of which has N_l nodes. The total computing time for the SIMD in the number of clock cycles approximately is

$$T_S = \sum_{l=1}^{L-1} t_s N_l \left[\frac{N_{l+1}}{p} \right], \tag{1}$$

while the time for the WAP is

$$T_W = \sum_{l=1}^{L-1} \left\{ \left[\frac{N_{l+1}}{n} \right] \left(t_w \left[\frac{N_l}{n} \right] + t' \right) + t'n \right\}. \tag{2}$$

Here, t_s and t_w are the unit times for computing a synapse (a multiplication followed by an addition) in the SIMD and in the WAP, respectively. And t' is the unit time for accumulation of partial weighted sums of the adjacent SPs in the WAP. The last term of equation (2) is the time for a row (column) accumulation of partial weighted sums for a node computed by SPs in a row; it is necessary to be considered for time-multiplexing layers in the WAP. Also, $n^2 = p$ (the number of PEs) and $\lceil x \rceil$ represents the smallest integer not less than x. We ignore the time for sigmoid transformations for outputs because it is relatively small and we assume that pipelining is adopted for a synapse computation including communication for both architectures. Now, we can generally assume that

$$t_s = max(t_{s,cm}, t_{s,cp}), \quad \text{and} \quad t_w = max(t_{w,cm}, t_{w,cp}) \tag{3}$$

where $t_{s,cm}$ and $t_{s,cp}$ represent the unit times for a data broadcasting and for an internal synapse computation (the maximum of non-communication "multiply and accumulate" pipeline stages), respectively. Similarly, $t_{w,cm}$ and $t_{w,cp}$ represent the unit times for a data communication and a synapse computation in the WAP, respectively. Because of clock skew and broadcast time constraint in the SIMD, t_s depends on the size of the processor array while t_w does not. Since $t_{s,cm}$ is proportional to the size of the SIMD array, we can have $t_{s,cm} = \alpha p$, where α is determined from chip design and fabrication factors. If we let $p_0 = t_{s,cp}/\alpha$, p_0 specifies the number of processors of the SIMD array for $t_{s,cm} = t_{s,cp}$. In other words, if the size of the processor array exceeds p_0, t_s is determined by

$$t_s = \frac{p}{p_0}. \tag{4}$$

Fig. 3(a) shows the performances of the SIMD and the WAP for simulating a 3-layer perceptron of 256 input nodes, 100 hidden nodes, and 42 output nodes, which we have designed for phoneme recognition. Here, we have $t_s = 1$, $t_w = 2$, and $t' = 1$, as complying with our implementation. Fig. 3(b) illustrates the performance behavior of the SIMD and the WAP for simulating large scale neural networks. Here, we simulate an artificial 3-layer perceptron of 1280x500x210, which is, in the number of nodes, a five times scale-up of the phoneme recognition network. The figures clearly show the limited scalability of the SIMD array compared to the WAP. The performance of the SIMD reduces significantly when the size of the array exceeds p_0, while that of the WAP keeps improved as the array size grows.

Moreover, if the size of the target neural network is sufficiently large compared to the size of the processor array, from equations (1) and (2), and $\lceil x \rceil \simeq x$ for large x, we obtain

$$T_S \simeq t_s \frac{c}{p} \quad \text{and} \quad T_W \simeq t_w \frac{c}{p}, \tag{5}$$

where c is the total number of connections of the neural network. From this, we further have the following asymptotic performance ratio $\rho(T_S/T_W)$ of the WAP to the SIMD:

$$\rho \simeq \frac{t_s}{t_w} \text{ if } p \leq p_0 \quad \text{and} \quad \rho \simeq \frac{p}{t_w p_0} \text{ if } p > p_0. \tag{6}$$

So far we assume the same clock rate for both architectures, however, for the WAP, we can use a faster clock rate than that for the SIMD. Different clock rates for two architectures can be taken into account by appropriately determining the p_0 value. For example, reducing p_0 by half is equivalent to using for the WAP twice faster a clock rate than that for the SIMD. Fig. 5 shows the asymtotic performance ratio when the size of the target neural network is sufficiently large and simulation results comply with our approximation. In this simulation we use linear scale-ups of the phoneme recognition network.

2.2 Input Recycling

Because of handshaking overhead associated with asynchronous communication, it is often the case that a significant communication cost should be paid for computing neural networks in the WAP. In the above we consider the WAP architecture in which each time of a synapse computation a

PE needs an input value sent from one of its adjacent PEs and it causes a significant performance reduction of the WAP. In this section, however, we describe input recycling which significantly reduces communication time by exploiting a characteristic of neural computation that an input value can be used repeatedly for computing nodes by a PE. In input recycling, each PE stores a set of input data into its separate storage called "input memory" and it recycles the data as many times as needed for neural computation. In this way a PE can efficiently compute weighted sums by pipelining and parallel access of the input data and the weight data. For example, if a set of input data of length l is recycled m times by a PE, the total time for computing the weighted sum is $lt_{w,cm} + lmt_{w,cp}$. The performance ratio η of input recycling to no input recycling is given by

$$\eta = \frac{rm}{m + r}, \quad \text{where} \quad r = \frac{t_{w,cp}}{t_{w,cm}}. \tag{7}$$

For the WAP with input recycling, equation (2) is rewritten into

$$T_W = \sum_{l=1}^{L-1} \left\{ \left[\frac{N_{l+1}}{n} \right] \left(t_{w,cp} \left[\frac{N_l}{n} \right] + t' \right) + t_{w,cm} \left[\frac{N_l}{n} \right] + t'n \right\}. \tag{8}$$

And we also have

$$\rho = \frac{rp}{t_w p_0}, \tag{9}$$

for sufficiently large neural networks. In Fig. 3 performance for input recycling is shown in thick solid lines. It should be noticed that for a sufficiently large neural network the performance of the WAP with input recycling is very close to the best performance in dotted line (Fig. 3(b)). As we can see, performance gain increases as m and r increase. In other words, input recycling is useful when the size of the target neural network is relatively large compared to the size of the processor array. In this case the necessary communication overhead for asynchronous communication is negligible. Performance gain for input recycling approaches r when m is large (Fig. 4).

For implementing input recycling a PE needs only a separate memory for input storage. As we notice in the above, since the performance for input recycling is independent of the size of input data, the input memory not necessarily be large.

So far, we have discussed feed-forward computation of MLPs. EBP training generally consists of three, connection involved, most time-consuming stages: forward recall, error back-propagation, and weight updates. In the SIMD, error back-propagation is executed using the ring bus, which implements the transpose of the weight matrix. In the WAP, error back-propagation is similar to forward recall except data flow direction reversed. Weight updates executed in a similar way to synapse computation in both architectures. Considering these, we still have the similar performance and scalability behaviors for both architectures.

For simulating other neural network models, we also have a similar scalability characteristic to that of MLPs. For example, as far as we are concerned with performance, we can consider a Hopfield network as a 2-layer perceptron with the same number of input and output nodes.

III. Implementation

3.1 DNP-II

DSPs and transputers have been used as the PEs for neural network simulators. Such processors should not necessarily be cost-effective for computing neural networks because they are originally designed for different types of computational tasks from neural computation. It is highly desirable to design a processor well tailored to neural processing. Processor architectures for digital neural processing have been implemented or proposed including the X1 of Adaptive Solutions[2], the MA-16 of Siemens[8], and the SPERT of the University of California at Berkeley[9]. However, they are all processors for the SIMD (or systolic) architecture.

The DNP-II is a unit processor for our WAP neurocomputer; it is the second generation of the DNP which has been designed for our first neurocomputer EMIND[5]. The DNP-II is considered similar to the DSP in architecture and function, however, its functions are simpler and more tailored to neural computation than the DSP. It also facilitates efficient asynchronous communication exploiting the regularity and locality of neural computation. Its key features include: 1) 40 MHz operating clock; 2) a 16x16 bit parallel pipelined multiplier; 3) four-way 16 bit parallel, asynchronous communication; 4) 256 words(16 bits a word) of program memory; 5) 128 words of input memory; 6) 512 words of weight memory. It is also devised with instruction prefetch and subroutine call capability. Fig. 6 shows an overall architecture of DNP-II. It consists of four major functional blocks: 1) memory block, 2) control block, 3) arithmetic block, and 4) I/O interface block. The memory block consists of 512 words of data memory and 128 words of input memory. The data memory is used for storing weights, intermediate results, tables, and initial parameters. It also has an adder for address generation for flexible data access. There is a separate register(ICR) containing four sets of increments/decrements for address generation. Each instruction involving memory access needs to specify one of these sets. The input memory is used to temporarily store data read in through the communication channel for recycling them.

The control block consists of a separate program memory of 256 words of 16 bits and an instruction decoder. It contains a counter which specifies the number of repetitions to execute repeatable instructions. The arithmetic block consists of a multiplier, an arithmetic/logic unit(ALU), and general purpose registers. The ALU performs addition, subtraction, shifting, and bitwise logic functions. The communication block consists of four asynchronous parallel I/O communication units. The block also has a special register(IOPR) which contains four pairs of I/O port numbers. Each instruction involving I/O communication should specify one of these pairs.

The DNP-II takes a single clock cycle for executing most instructions but two clock cycles for I/O communication. The instruction set of the DNP-II is optimized for various neural network models and learning algorithms. The instructions are largely of the RISC type except a few pipeline instructions. The DNP-II operates basically in 16 bits for arithmetic and logic operations. The two-stage pipeline multiplier produces a 16 bit product of two 16 bit, fixed-point integers. It also has a three-stage pipelined instruction of "multiply and accumulate" which multiplies an input value from the input memory and a from the weight memory, then accumulate the result into the accumulator.

3.2 DNP-II Array Architecture

The DNP-II array as the parallel architecture for our neurocomputer EMIND-II, consists of 1024 DNP-II interconnected in a 2-D toroidal mesh. It corresponds to the maximum 512K connection weights and the peak performance is estimated to be 40 GCPS.

The whole array is composed of four boards each of which mounts 256 DNP-IIs (equivalently, 8x8 DNP-II chips). It is like the whole 2-D array four-folded. In this case connections between boards are important because inter-board latency may cause a significant communication overhead and optical interconnection is considered for the problem. The DNP-II array board, in turn, will be connected to a host computer via a data interface which provides efficient data transfer to and from the host. One of the useful features of our architecture is the capability of parallel memory loading. When data are loaded into the array, data are written into columns (rows) of PEs in parallel, like a high bandwidth memory with multiple buses. According to our estimation it takes 0.8 ms to load 512K words, the entire memory capacity of the DNP-II array. This allows simulation of neural networks exceeding the array memory capacity.

We are currently undertaking revision of our first design of the DNP-II to incorporate input recycling. We plan to integrate four DNP-IIs into a chip, using 0.8μ CMOS standard cell technology. According to our plan, fabrication of the DNP-II chip will be completed in April, 1994 and the EMIND-II system will be completed in October, 1994.

VI. Conclusions

Computing neural networks for real world problems which involves voluminous, noisy, and ambiguous data needs a massively parallel architecture of $10^4 \sim 10^6$ PEs at the speed of hundreds of billion connections per second. However, the network of processors of such a size may cause various problems such as clock skew, broadcasting time constraint, power dissipation, interconnection latency, and low utilization.

In this paper we describe a wavefront array processor architecture for real-time simulation of large scale neural networks. We have shown that the WAP exhibits a high degree of scalability. We also have proposed input recycling for a significant reduction of communication time. In addition, the WAP has a great flexibility for mapping neural networks, which often results enhanced performance. Fujimoto, et al. has proposed a parallel architecture similar to ours and a load balancing algorithm for almost linear speed-up with the number of PEs[1].

Further investigation should be made to develop a more efficient communication structure such as a tree of WAPs. The WAP architecture integration using the WSI technology, would provide a cost-effective solution to the problems of the SIMD, currently a common neurocomputer architecture.

References

[1] Yoshiji Fujimoto, Naoyuki Fukuda, and Toshio Akabane, Massively parallel architecture for large scale neural network simulations, *IEEE Transactions on Neural Networks*, Vol. 3, No. 6, pp. 876-888, Nov. 1992.

[2] Dan Hammerstrom, A VLSI architecture for high-performance, low-cost, on-chip learning *Proc. of IJCNN*, Washington, DC, Vol. 2, pp. 537-544, 1990.

[3] A. Hiraiwa, *et al.*, A two level pipeline RISC processor array for ANN, *Proc. of IJCNN*, Washington, DC, Vol. 2, pp. 137-140, 1990.

[4] H. Kato, *et al.*, A parallel neurocomputer architecture towards billion connection updates per second, *Proc. of IJCNN*, Washington, DC, Vol. 2, pp. 47-50, 1990.

[5] Myung Won Kim, *et al.*, E-MIND: An implementation of a digital neurocomputer and its application to handwritten digit recognition, *Proc. of IJCNN*, Beijing, Vol. III, pp. 258-263, 1992.

[6] J. R. Nicholls, The design of the MasPar MP-1: A cost effective massively parallel computer, *Proc. of COMPCON Spring 90*, San Francisco, pp. 25-28, 1990.

[7] Tomas Nordstrom and Bertil Svensson, Using and designing massively parallel computers for artificial neural networks, *Journal of Parallel and Distributed Computing 14*, pp. 260-285, 1992.

[8] Ulrich Ramacher, SYNAPSE - a neurocomputer that synthesizes neural algorithms on a parallel systolic engine, *Journal of Parallel and Distributed Computing 14*, pp. 306-318, 1992.

[9] J. Wawrzynek, K. Asanovic, and N. Morgan, The design of a neuro-microprocessor, *IEEE Transactions on Neural Networks*, Vol. 4, No. 3, pp. 394-399, 1993.

[10] Moritoshi Yasunaga, *et al.*, A self-learning neural network composed of 1152 digital neurons in wafer-scale LSIs, *Proc. of IJCNN*, Singapore, Vol. 3, pp. 1844-1849, 1991.

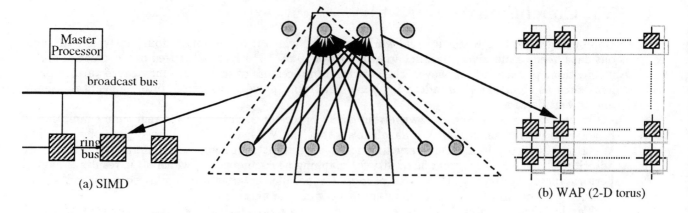

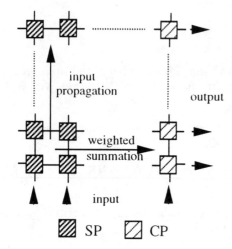

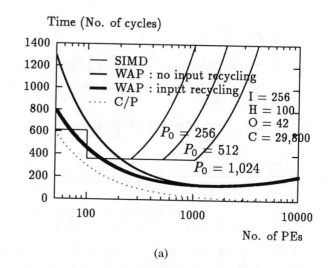

Fig. 1: Parallel Architectures and MLP layer mapping

Fig. 2: Data Flow for an MLP Layer
In the WAP

(a)

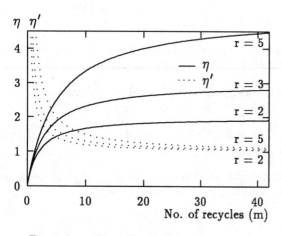

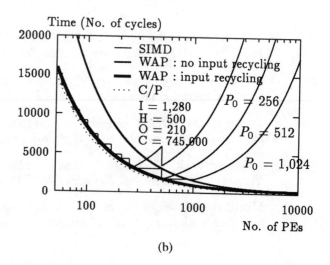

Fig. 4: Input Recycling Efficiency

Fig. 3: Performance Comparison

(b)

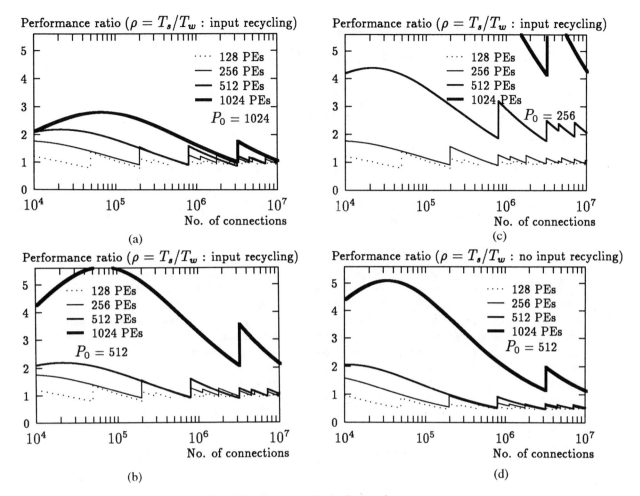

Fig. 5: Performance Ratio Comparison

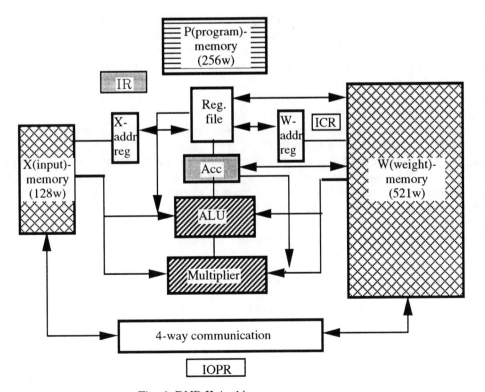

Fig. 6: DNP-II Architecture

Placing Feedforward Neural Networks Among Several Circuit Complexity Classes[1]

Valeriu Beiu[†,‡], Jan A. Peperstraete[†], Joos Vandewalle[†] and
Rudy Lauwereins[†,2]

[†] Katholieke Universiteit Leuven, Department of Electrical Engineering, Division ESAT
Kardinaal Mercierlaan 94, B-3001 Heverlee, Belgium

[‡] on leave of absence from "Politehnica" University of Bucharest, Computer Science Department
Spl. Independentei 313, 77206 Bucharest, Romånia

Abstract – This paper examines the circuit complexity of feedforward neural networks having sigmoid activation function. The starting point is the complexity class NN^k defined in [18]. First two additional complexity classes NN_Δ^k and $NN_{\Delta,\varepsilon}^k$ having less restrictive conditions (than NN^k) concerning fan-in and accuracy are defined. We then prove several relations among these three classes and well established circuit complexity classes. All the proofs are constructive as being built around binary adders. By relaxing the fan-in condition from logarithmic [18] to (almost) polynomial, the results show that substantially larger classes of sigmoid activation feedforward neural networks can be implemented in polynomial size Boolean circuits. This is done on the expense of a logarithmic factor increase in the number of layers, but having constant fan-in (of 2). The main conclusion is that there are interesting fan-in dependent depth-size tradeoffs when trying to digitally implement sigmoid activation neural networks.

Keywords – neural networks, threshold gate circuits, Boolean circuits, circuit complexity.

1. Introduction

In this paper a *network* will be considered an acyclic graph. It has several input nodes (*inputs*) and some (at least one) output nodes (*outputs*). The nodes of the network are characterized by *fan-in* (the number of incoming edges) and *fan-out* (the number of outgoing edges), while the network has a certain *size* (the number of nodes) and *depth* (the number of edges on the longest input to output path). If with each edge a synaptic *weight* is associated and each node computes the weighted sum of its inputs to which a nonlinear activation function is then applied (*artificial neuron*), the network is a *neural network* (NN). A particular case which has been intensively studied is represented by the threshold activation function; now the artificial neurons are in fact *threshold gates* (TGs), while the neural network is nothing else than a *threshold gate circuit* (TGC). Similarly, a *Boolean circuit* (BC) is a network of gates implementing elementary Boolean functions (BFs).

The paper starts by presenting known circuit complexity results and also by defining two new complexity classes for NNs in Section 2. Two lemmas about adding *m* words of β bits, one for BCs and the other one for TGCs are proved in Section 3. These results are used in Section 4 to determine relations among the two newly defined NN complexity classes on one hand, and several of the complexity classes which have also been mentioned, on the other hand. The main idea of these proofs is to replace the third conversion step (from [18]) by one of the "tree of adders" defined in Section 3. Several conclusions and open question end the paper.

[1] This research work was partly carried out in the framework of a **Concerted Research Action** of the Flemish Community, entitled: ***"Applicable Neural Networks"***. The scientific responsibility is assumed by the authors.

[2] Senior Research Associate of the Belgian National Fund for Scientific Research.

2. Circuit Complexity

The *circuit complexity* of a function is the size complexity of the family of minimal BCs, or TGCs, that compute that function of n inputs [23, 24]. Several well known classes are:

- AC^k (NC^k) represents the class of BFs computed by BCs of polynomial size AND and OR unbounded (constant) fan-in gates and depth $O(\log^k n)$;
- TC^k represents the family of BFs realized by polynomial size TGCs with unbounded fan-in and depth limited by $O(\log^k n)$;
- LT_k ($\hat{LT}_k$) is the class of BFs computed by polynomial size TGCs with arbitrary real weights (bounded by a polynomial in the number of inputs n) and depth k [8, 19];
- MAJ_k is the class of BFs computed by polynomial size, depth k circuits of MAJORITY gates (TGs having ± 1 weights) [2, 15]; clearly $MAJ_k \subset \hat{LT}_k$ (is a subclass of $\hat{LT}_k$).

While many results concerning TGCs have been lately discovered or improved [8, 9, 19, 20] and their complexity discussed [2, 5, 15, 17, 26], little is known for the case of *sigmoid activation functions*. For placing NNs in the context of BC complexity the class NN^k has been defined [18] to be those BFs *"which can be computed by a family of polynomially sized neural networks with weights and activation values determined to b bits of accuracy, fan-in equal to Δ and depth h, satisfying* $\log(\Delta) = O(\sqrt{\log n})$, $b\log\Delta = O(\log n)$ *and* $h\log\Delta = O(\log^k n)$*"* and:

$$NC^k \subset NN^k \subseteq AC^k \tag{1}$$

has been proven. If $NC^k \subset NN^k$ follows easily by directly converting the AND and OR gates to equivalent TGs, the second part $NN^k \subseteq AC^k$ is proven in three steps (see [18] for more details):

- negative weights are eliminated, increasing the size by at most a factor of 2;
- the NN with positive weights is converted to a TGC by taking 2^b copies of each node; it has the same depth, the size and the fan-in being increased by 2^b, while the accuracy has been doubled $2b$;
- using techniques of communication complexity [12], the conversion of a linear TG to an equivalent BC, having depth $2\log\Delta$, fan-in $2^{b+\log\Delta}$ and size at most $2\Delta^{b+\log\Delta+1}$, is performed.

The overall result is that a NN of size N, depth h, maximum fan-in Δ and accuracy of b bits can be converted to an equivalent BC with depth $h(2\log\Delta+1)$, fan-in $2^{2b+\log\Delta}$ and size $2 \cdot N \cdot 2^b \cdot (2\Delta)^{2b+\log\Delta+1}$ at most.

Relaxing the fan-in and the accuracy condition, we define:

- NN_Δ^k is the family of polynomial size NNs ($N = O[poly(n)]$) and depth $h = O(\log^k n)$ which has polynomial fan-in ($\Delta = O[poly(n)]$) and logarithmic accuracy $b = O(\log n)$;
- $NN_{\Delta,\varepsilon}^k$ is the family of polynomial size NNs and depth $h = O(\log^k n)$ which satisfies slightly more restricting conditions for fan-in and accuracy: $\log\Delta = O(\log^{1-\varepsilon} n)$ and $b = O(\log^{1-\varepsilon} n)$ for $\varepsilon > 0$ a small constant.

Due to the imposed restrictions on fan-in and accuracy the following holds:

$$NN^k \subset NN_{\Delta,\varepsilon}^k \subset NN_\Delta^k. \tag{2}$$

For proving relations with other complexity classes we shall use the first two steps from [18], but change the third step by using plain addition to replace the TGs, thus making the proofs constructive.

3. ADDITION

Some of the adders build of AND-OR bounded fan-in logic gates have (we use *delay* instead of depth, and *gates* instead of size, like in the original articles):

- $2n-1$ *delay*   and $5n-3$ *gates*   (school method);
- $4\log n$ *delay*   and $35n-6$ *gates*   (carry-lookahead adders [10]);
- $4\log n$ *delay*   and $14n-\log n-10$ *gates*   [7];
- $3\log n$ *delay*   and $3n\log n+12.5n-8$ *gates*   (conditional sum adders [13]);
- $(2+\varepsilon)\log n$ *delay*   and $(2+\varepsilon)n\log n+5n$ *gates*   [25];
- $2\log n+1$ *delay*   and $3n\log n+10n-6$ *gates*   (conditional sum adder [24]);
- $2\log n$ *delay*   and $2.5n\log n+5n-1$ *gates*   [13];
- $2\log n+2k+2$ *delay*   and $n(8+6/2^k)$ *gates*   (prefix algorithms [14]); for $0 \le k \le \log n$
- $\log n+7\sqrt{2\log n}+16$ *delay*   and $9n$ *gates*   (Krapchenko [24]).

Lemma 1 *Adding m words of β bits each can be done by a fan-in 2 BC having size $O(m\beta)$ and depth $O[\log m (\log \beta + \log\log m)]$.*

Proof We use a binary tree of adders having size $O(\beta)$ and depth $O(\log\beta)$: $m/2$ adders of size $\lambda\beta$ and depth $\mu\log\beta$ in the first layer, followed by $m/4$ adders of size $\lambda(\beta+1)$ and depth $\mu\log(\beta+1)$ in the second layer and so on until the last (the $\log m^{th}$) layer having one adder of size $\lambda(\beta+\log m-1)$ and depth $\mu\log(\beta+\log m-1)$. Here λ and μ are constants depending on the adder one has chosen (e.g. $\lambda = 14$ and $\mu = 4$ for the Brent and Kung adder [7]). By computing the size we have:

$$\text{size}(m,\beta) = \lambda \sum_{i=1}^{\log m} \frac{m(\beta+i-1)}{2^i} \qquad = \lambda m\beta \sum_{i=1}^{\log m} \frac{1}{2^i} + \lambda m \sum_{i=1}^{\log m} \frac{i-1}{2^i} =$$

$$= \lambda m\beta \frac{m-1}{m} + \lambda m \sum_{i=2}^{\log m}\left(\sum_{j=i}^{\log m} \frac{1}{2^j}\right) \quad = \lambda\beta(m-1) + \lambda m \sum_{i=2}^{\log m}\frac{m-2^{i-1}}{m \cdot 2^{i-1}} =$$

$$= \lambda\beta(m-1) + \lambda m \frac{m-\log m-1}{m} \qquad = O(\beta m). \tag{3}$$

The depth is:

$$\text{depth}(m,\beta) = \mu \sum_{i=1}^{\log m} \log(\beta+i-1) \qquad < \mu\left[\log\beta + \sum_{i=1}^{\log m-1}(\log\beta + \log i)\right] =$$

$$= \mu\log\beta\log m + \mu \sum_{i=1}^{\log m-1}\log i \qquad = \mu\log\beta\log m + \mu\log[(\log m-1)!]$$

and using Stirling's formula $k! = \sqrt{2\pi k}\,(k/e)^k e^{\theta/12k}$ (where $0 < \theta < 1$):

$$\text{depth}(m,\beta) < \mu\log\beta\log m + \mu\log\left[\sqrt{2\pi\log m}\left(\frac{\log m}{e}\right)^{\log m} e^{\frac{1}{12\log m}}\right] =$$

$$= \mu\log\beta\log m + \mu\left[\frac{\log 2\pi + \log\log m}{2} + \log m(\log\log m - \log e) + \frac{\log e}{12\log m}\right] =$$

$$= O[\log m(\log\beta + \log\log m)]. \tag{4}$$

which concludes the proof. $\qquad\qquad\qquad\qquad\qquad\qquad\qquad\qquad\qquad\qquad\qquad\qquad$ ❑

Based on the knowledge that: (i) *at least* on the order of K^2 TGs of fan-in 2 are needed to replace one fan-in K TG [1], and (ii) the needed accuracy for the weights of a fan-in K TG is on the order of $K\log K$ bits [11, 16], we can take $m = K$ and $\beta = K\log K$, which makes the size $O(K^2\log K)$, being just a logarithmic factor larger than the theoretical lower bound $\Omega(K^2)$ [1].

Lemma 2 *Adding m words of β bits each can be done by a fan-in Δ TGC having:*

$$\text{size}(m,\beta) = O\left(\frac{\log^2 m(\log\beta + \log m/\beta)}{\log\Delta}\right) \quad \text{and} \quad \text{depth}(m,\beta) = O\left(\frac{\log m(\log\beta + \log\log m)}{\log\Delta}\right).$$

Proof The proof is based on a TG adder [5, 6] of size $O(\beta\log\beta/\log\Delta)$ and depth $O(\log\beta/\log\Delta)$. It has been shown that for $\Delta \leq O(\log^k n)$ the weights are polynomially bounded (i.e. the TGC belongs to $\hat{L}T_{\log\beta/\log\Delta}$ [5]; for $\Delta > O(\log^k n)$ the weights are unbounded (superpolynomial or exponential). The proof follows the line of Lemma 1 by building a tree of TG adders:

$$\text{size}(m,\beta) = \lambda \sum_{i=1}^{\log m} \frac{(\beta + i - 1)\log(\beta + i - 1)}{\log \Delta} < \frac{\lambda}{\log \Delta} \sum_{i=0}^{\log m - 1} (\beta + i)\left(\log \beta + \frac{i}{\beta}\right) <$$

$$< \frac{\lambda}{\log \Delta}\left(\log \beta \log^2 m + \frac{\log^3 m}{3\beta}\right) = O\left(\frac{\log^2 m \,(\log \beta + {}^{\log m}\!/\beta)}{\log \Delta}\right). \tag{5}$$

The depth is computed as in equation (4):

$$\text{depth}(m,\beta) = \mu \sum_{i=1}^{\log m} \frac{\log(\beta + i - 1)}{\log \Delta} = O\left(\frac{\log m \,(\log \beta + \log\log m)}{\log \Delta}\right) \tag{6}$$

which concludes the proof. ❏

4. Neural Network Conversion

As a linear threshold gate does in fact a summation of (some of) the incoming weights, such adders, having fan-in $m = 2^b \Delta$ and accuracy $\beta = 2b$, can be used in the third step of the conversion from [18].

Theorem 1 $NN_\Delta^k \begin{cases} \subset MAJ_{\log^{k+2} n} \subset \hat{LT}_{\log^{k+2} n} \\ \subset NC^{k+2} \end{cases}$ \hfill (7)

Proof   We use Lemma 1 to convert the TGC resulting after applying the first two steps of the conversion [18]. The TGC has size $2 \cdot N \cdot 2^b$, depth h, maximum fan-in $2^b \cdot \Delta$ and accuracy of $2b$ bits. The equivalent fan-in 2 BC will have size at most (see equation (3)):

$$2 \cdot N \cdot 2^b \cdot \lambda\left[2b\,2^b\Delta - 2b + 2^b\Delta - \log(2^b\Delta) - 1\right] < \lambda N\, 2^{2b+1}\Delta\,(2b+1). \tag{8}$$

Taking logarithms of equation (8), we can see that the BC is polynomially sized:

$$\log N + 2b + \log \Delta + \log(2b+1) + \lambda + 1 = O\,(\log n) \tag{9}$$

if the conditions of NN_Δ^k are met: $N = O\,[poly(n)]$, $\Delta = O\,[poly(n)]$ and $b = O\,(\log n)$. The depth of this BC is (see equation (4)):

$$h\,\mu\left[\log(2b)\log(2^b\Delta) + \log(2^b\Delta)\,\log\log(2^b\Delta) + ...\right] \tag{10}$$

which for the same conditions makes the parenthesis $O\,(\log n \log\log n)$. As $h = O\,(\log^k n)$ we have the proof that the depth is $O\,(\log^{k+2} n)$.
This proves that $NN_\Delta^k \subset MAJ_{\log^{k+2} n}$ and $NN_\Delta^k \subset NC^{k+2}$. ❏

Theorem 2 $NN_{\Delta,\varepsilon}^k \begin{cases} \subset MAJ_{\log^{k+1} n} \subset \hat{LT}_{\log^{k+1} n} \\ \subset NC^{k+1} \end{cases}$ \hfill (11)

Proof   The beginning of the proof is identical with the proof of Theorem 1. The size of the equivalent BC will still be polynomial (equation (9)), but due to the more restrictive conditions imposed by $NN_{\Delta,\varepsilon}^k$ the parenthesis from equation (10) will be bounded by $O\,(\log^{1-\varepsilon} n \log\log n)$, which proves that the depth of the BC is only $O\,(\log^{k+1} n)$.
The result that $NN_{\Delta,\varepsilon}^k \subset MAJ_{\log^{k+1} n}$ and $NN_{\Delta,\varepsilon}^k \subset NC^{k+1}$ follows. ❏

Theorem 3 $NN_\Delta^k \subset \hat{LT}_{\log^{k+1} n}$ \hfill (12)

Proof   We use Lemma 2 with $\Delta \leq O\,(\log^k n)$ (the weights being polynomially bounded). The size of the resulting TGC is (see equation (5)):

$$2 \cdot N \cdot 2^b \cdot \frac{\lambda}{\log\Delta} \left[(b + \log\Delta)^2 \log b + \frac{(b + \log\Delta)^3}{6b} \right] = \lambda N \, 2^{2b+1} (b + \log\Delta)^2 \left(\log b + \frac{\log\Delta}{b} \right). \quad (13)$$

By taking logarithms and considering $\Delta = O\,(\log^k n)$ the previous equation becomes:

$$\log N + 2b + 2\log(b + k\log\log n) + \log\left(\log b + \frac{k\log\log n}{b} \right) \quad (14)$$

showing that the size is polynomially bounded if $b = O\,(\log n)$. The next step is to compute the depth of this TGC (see equations (4), (6) and (10)):

$$h\,\mu\, \frac{\log(2^b\Delta)\,\log(2b) + \log(2^b\Delta)\,\log\log(2^b\Delta) + \dots}{\log\Delta} \approx h\mu\, \frac{(b + \log\Delta)\,[\log b + \log(b + \log\Delta)]}{\log\Delta} \quad (15)$$

which for $\Delta = \log n$ and $b = O\,(\log n)$ makes the fraction $O\,(\log n)$.
The weights being polynomially bounded the claim $NN_\Delta^k \subset \hat{LT}_{\log^{k+1} n}$ follows ($h = O\,(\log^k n)$). $\qquad \square$

Theorem 4 $\quad NN_\Delta^k \subset LT_{\log^{k+\varepsilon} n}$

> **Proof** From Theorem 3 we know that the size is polynomially bounded (equation (14)) for $b = O\,(\log n)$. If now $\Delta = O\,(n)$ the depth from equation (15) will be bounded by $O\,(\log\log n)$.
> Now the weights are no more bounded so $NN_\Delta^k \subset LT_{\log^{k+\varepsilon} n}$ $\qquad \square$

Putting all these results together and adding some others already known or considered obvious, the following tree of inclusions is obtained:

$$NC^k \subset NN^k \begin{cases} \subseteq AC^k & & (16) \\[4pt] \subset TC^k & & \\[4pt] NC^{k+1} & \subset & NC^{k+2} \\[2pt] \cup & & \cup \\[2pt] \subset NN_{\Delta,\varepsilon}^k \begin{cases} \subset LT_{\log^{k+\varepsilon}} & & \\[4pt] & \subset NN_\Delta^k & \subset \hat{LT}_{\log^{k+1} n} \end{cases} \\[4pt] \cap & & \cap \\[2pt] MAJ_{\log^{k+1} n} & \subset & MAJ_{\log^{k+2} n} \\[2pt] \cap & & \cap \\[2pt] \hat{LT}_{\log^{k+1} n} & \subset & \hat{LT}_{\log^{k+2} n} \end{cases}$$

5. Conclusions

The paper has examined the circuit complexity of feedforward neural networks and presented a constructive proof on the lines of [18], by *relaxing the logarithmic fan-in condition to a polynomial (or almost polynomial) fan-in one*. The class of sigmoid activation feedforward neural networks which can be implemented in polynomial *size* Boolean circuits is thus substantially enlarged, on the expense of more layers, but with a constant fan-in of 2.

It can be observed that *there are interesting fan-in dependent depth-size tradeoffs* when trying to digitally implement sigmoid NNs (see also [22]) which should be related to the depth-size tradeoffs TGCs [3, 4, 5, 21].

Still many questions remain open:

- Is it possible to constructively reach the $\Omega\,(K^2)$ lower bound from [1], or to lower the $O\,(K^2 \log K)$ size of the tree of adders? This would improve our results by lowering the depth of the circuits.
- Are there any other ways to lower the depth?
- Can the results for BCs be improved by increasing the fan-in? All the results for BCs have been obtained with gates having the fan-in just 2.

References

[1] Y. Abu-Mostafa "Complexity in Neural Systems". In C.A. Mead: *Analog VLSI and Neural Systems*, Addison Wesley, Reading, 353-358, 1989.

[2] A. Albrecht "On Bounded-Depth Threshold Circuits for Pattern Functions". *Proc. ICANN'92* (Brighton, UK), Elsevier Science, Amsterdam, 135-138, September 1992.

[3] V. Beiu, J.A. Peperstraete, J. Vandewalle, and R. Lauwereins "Efficient Decomposition of COMPARISON and Its Applications". *Proc. ESANN'93* (Brussels, Belgium), Dfacto, Brussels, 45-50, April 1993.

[4] V. Beiu, J.A. Peperstraete, J. Vandewalle, and R. Lauwereins "Overview of Some Efficient Threshold Gate Decomposition Algorithms". *Proc. CSCS'93* (Bucharest, Românía), vol. 1, 458-469, May 1993.

[5] V. Beiu, J.A. Peperstraete, J. Vandewalle, and R. Lauwereins "Area-Time Performances of Some Neural Computations". Submitted for publication.

[6] V. Beiu, J.A. Peperstraete, J. Vandewalle, and R. Lauwereins "Optimal Parallel ADDITION Means Constant Fan-In Threshold Gates". Submitted for publication.

[7] R.P. Brent, and H.T. Kung "A Regular Layout for Parallel Adders". *IEEE Trans. Comp.*, C-31(3), 260-264, 1982.

[8] J. Bruck "Harmonic Analysis of Polynomial Threshold Functions". *SIAM J. on Disc. Math.*, 3(2), 168-177, 1990.

[9] J. Bruck, and R. Smolensky "Polynomial Threshold Functions, AC^0 Functions and Spectral Norms". *SIAM J. Comput.*, 21(1), 33-42, 1992.

[10] P.K. Chang, M.D.F. Schlag, C.D. Thomborson, and V.G. Oklobdzija "Delay Optimization of Carry-Skip Adders and Block Carry-Lookahead Adders Using Multidimensional Programing". *IEEE Trans. on Comp.*, C-41(8), 920-930, 1992.

[11] J. Hong "On Connectionist Models". *Tech. Rep.* 87-012, Dept. CS, Univ. of Chicago, 1987.

[12] M. Karchmer, and A. Widgerson "Monotone Circuits for Connectivity Require Super-Logarithmic Depth". *Proc. ACM Symp. on Theory of Computing*, 20, 539-550, 1988.

[13] T.P. Kelliher, R.M. Owens, M.J. Irwin, and T.-T. Hwang "ELM A Fast Addition Algorithm Discovered by a Program". *IEEE Trans. on Comp.*, C-41(9), 1181-1184, 1992.

[14] R.E. Ladner, and M.J. Fischer "Parallel Prefix Computations". *J. ACM*, 27(4), 831-838, 1980.

[15] E. Mayoraz "On the Power of Networks of Majority Functions". *Proc. IWANN'91* (Grenade, Spain), Springer-Verlag, 78-85, June 1991.

[16] P. Raghavan "Learning in Threshold Networks: A Computational Model and Applications". *Tech. Rep.* RC-13859, IBM Research, 1988.

[17] V.P. Roychowdhury, K.-Y. Siu, A. Orlitsky, and T. Kailath "On the Circuit Complexity of Neural Networks". *Proc. NIPS'90* (Denver, USA), Morgan Kaufmann, San Mateo, 953-959, 1991.

[18] J.S. Shawe-Taylor, M.H.G. Anthony, and W. Kern "Classes of Feedforward Neural Nets and Their Circuit Complexity". *Neural Networks*, 5(6), 971-977, 1992.

[19] K.-Y. Siu, and J. Bruck "Neural Computation of Arithmetic Functions". *Proc. IEEE*, 78(10), 1669-1675, 1990.

[20] K.-Y. Siu, and J. Bruck "On the Power of Threshold Circuits with Small Weights". *SIAM J. on Disc. Math.*, 4(3), 423-435, 1991.

[21] K.-Y. Siu, V. Roychowdhury, and T. Kailath "Depth-Size Tradeoffs for Neural Computations". *IEEE Trans. on Comp.*, C-40(12), 1402-1412, 1991.

[22] K.-Y. Siu "On the Complexity of Neural Networks with Sigmoid Units". *Proc. IEEE-SP Workshop NNSP-92* (Helsingoer, Denmark), IEEE Press, 23-28, August 1992.

[23] R. Smolensky "Algebraic Methods in the Theory of Lower Bounds for Boolean Circuit Complexity". *Proc. ACM Symp. on Theory of Computing*, 19, 77-82, 1987.

[24] I. Wegener *The Complexity of Boolean Functions*. Wiley-Teubner, Chichester, 1987.

[25] B.W.Y. Wei, and C.D. Thompson "Area-Time Optimal Adder Design". *IEEE Trans. on Comp.*, C-39(5), 666-675, 1990.

[26] R.C. Williamson "ε-Entropy and the Complexity of Feedforward Neural Networks". *Proc. NIPS'90* (Denver, USA), Morgan Kaufmann, San Mateo, 946-952, 1991.

On the Design of an MIMD Neural Network Processor

R. Saeks and K. Priddy
Accurate Automation Corp.
7001 Shallowford Rd.
Chattanooga, TN 37421

K. Schnieder
Telebyte Technologies Inc.
270 E. Pulaski Rd.
Greenlawn, NY 11740

S. Stowell
I.D.E.A.
520 Main St., Ste. 104
Waltham, MA 02154

Abstract

The design of a unique MIMD Neural Network Processor is described. The MIMD parallel processing architecture chosen facilitates the implementation of a wide variety of neural network paradigms with maximum efficiency. This efficiency is achieved by using an instruction set which is optimized for neural network processing allowing one to compute a neuron activation without arranging the weight matrix into linear arrays and/or inserting "artificial zero weighted connections", using an MIMD parallel processing architecture to permit neurons with totally different input topologies to be updated simultaneously without loss of efficiency, and using dual neuron memories to virtually eliminate memory contention and maintain absolute memory coherence.

1 INTRODUCTION

Although a myriad of neural network applications ranging from financial analysis to signal processing and robotics have been demonstrated neural network hardware designs have been aimed almost exclusively at image and speech processing applications [Carson, 1993; Chiang, 1993; Faggin and Meade, 1990; Lazzaro and Meade, 1991; Lyon and Meade, 1988; Meade, 1989; Owechko and Soffer, 1990 & 1993] typically assuming a classical SIMD matrix / vector multiplication architecture [Hammerstrom, 1990; May, 1989; Morton, 1991; Rudnick and Hammerstrom, 1989] a dedicated two dimensional multilevel feedforward neural network architecture, or an analog implementation [Holler, 1989; Kub 1991] The purpose of the present paper is to outline an alternative **MIMD Neural Network Processor architecture** which was designed to *implement a wide variety neural network paradigms; including Hopfield and recurrent networks, functional links, and feedforward networks with sparse and / or non-uniform topologies; with the maximum efficiency in either a single processor and multiprocessor environment*.

To achieve the desired efficiency we have adopted a design which:

♦ uses an *instruction set which is optimized for neural network processing* allowing one to compute a neuron activation without arranging the weight matrix into linear arrays and/or inserting "artificial zero weighted connections",

♦ uses an *MIMD (multiple instruction multiple data) parallel processing architecture* to permit neurons with totally different input topologies to be updated simultaneously without loss of efficiency, and

♦ uses <u>dual neuron memories</u> to virtually *eliminate memory contention* and *maintain absolute memory coherence*.

This architecture allows us to implement a relatively simple single processor NNP module stringing together multiple NNP modules along a dedicated Interprocessor Bus with *computational power (and cost) increasing "almost" linearly with the number of modules.*

This architecture facilitates the design of a Neural Network Processor which:

♦ can *implement multiple interconnected neural networks of differing architecture simultaneously* using *16 bit twos complement binary fixed point arithmetic* with up to <u>*8k total neurons*</u> and <u>*32k connection weights*</u> per module, and

♦ is capable of running at *133,000,000 to 160,000,000 connections* (byte wide multiply / additions) per second per module for a total of a **billion plus connections per second in an 8 processor array,**

Each processor in an NNP array is controlled by a separate program written in a *"RISC-like" instruction set* supported by a complete software development system including a dedicated "neural network assembly language".

2 FUNCTIONAL OVERVIEW
2.1 Single Processor Operation
A simplified schematic diagram of the MIMD Neural Network Processor is shown in Figure 1. The key functional components are the 32k by 16 bit *Program* and *Weight Memories* (PM

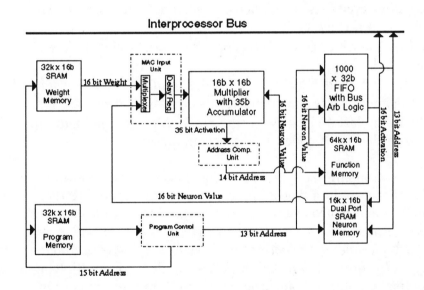

Figure 1. Schematic Diagram of MIMD Neural Network Processor.

and WM), the 64k by 16 bit *Function Memory* (FM), the 16k by 16 bit *dual ported Neuron Memory* (NM), and the *Multiplier / Accumulator* (MAC). During normal processor operation the *PM and WM are configured as a single 32k by 32 bit Program / Weight Memory* or PWM, the NM is linearly subdivided into an *8k neuron memory*, and an *8k buffer memory*, while the FM is linearly subdivided into *4 16k function memories* used to store neuron transfer functions.

The instruction set for the processor is made up *4 arithmetic instructions*; three *multiply / accumulate instructions* used to compute neuron activations, an instruction to pass a neuron activation (stored in the accumulator) through a *transfer function and store the resultant neuron value*; and 5 *control instructions*.

The most commonly used instructions are the *multiply / accumulate instructions* which multiply a neuron value, a_j, by a connection weight, w_{ij} (or the neuron value, a_k, fetched by the previous instruction). Since a neural network connection weight is fixed while a neuron value is a variable w_{ij} *is included in the multiple / accumulate instructions in immediate form* while a_j *is indirectly addressed* by including its address in the NM's neuron memory in the instruction. The connection weight is passed directly to the MAC (with an appropriate delay) while the neuron value is fetched from the NM and then passed to the MAC. The MAC then computes the product of the weight and the neuron value and adds the result to the accumulator (with or without first clearing the accumulator) to obtain the desired neuron activation.

The *multiply / accumulate instructions are pipelined over ten clock cycles* with a new instruction executed each clock cycle. As such, once the pipeline is filled an n term neuron activation may be computed in n clock cycles.

♦ In the first 3 clock cycle the *instruction is fetched* from the program / weight memory and decoded.

♦ In the 4th, 5th and 6th clock cycles the required *neuron value is fetched* from the neuron memory while the connection weight is held in a buffer.

♦ Finally, in the last 4 clock cycles the *product is computed* and pipelined through the MAC with the result added to the accumulator.

It is instructive to compare the type of multiply / accumulate operation used in the MIMD processor with that used in a typical matrix / vector multiplier. Rather, than including the connection weight and neuron value address in the instruction such architectures typically *set pointers to the location of the desired weight and neuron value* and then execute an instruction which *pipelines a sequence of multiply / accumulate instructions using <u>sequentially stored weights and neuron values</u>*. Although this is ideal for multiplying a full matrix by a vector, computing a Fourier Transform, or convolution, *in the case of a neural network if there is any topological non-uniformity one typically must insert artificial "zero weighted connections" to fill-in the gaps in the stored weight sequence*. This, in turn, results in *wasted multiplications by zero* with its associated reduction in processor efficiency. Indeed, the problem is further exacerbated when one desires to compute several neuron activations in parallel and must fill-in enough zeros to produce a rectangular weight array. To the contrary *with our indirect addressing architecture one can deal with arbitrarily interconnected networks without loss of efficiency or pipeline interruptions*, even in a parallel processing environment.

Our remaining arithmetic instruction is used to *pass a neuron activation stored in the accumulator through a transfer function and store the result in the NM's buffer memory.* The instruction includes the address where the resultant neuron value is to be stored and the number of the desired transfer function stored in the FM and is *pipelined over eight clock cycles.*

- ♦ In the first 3 clock cycle the *instruction is fetched* from the program / weight memory and decoded.
- ♦ In the 4th, 5th and 6th clock cycles the address of the new *neuron value is computed and fetched* from the function memory while the storage address is loaded into the FIFO.
- ♦ Finally, in the last 2 clock cycles the new neuron value is loaded into the FIFO..

Note, for single processor operation the FIFO is extraneous and simply loads the new neuron value into the buffer memory. The *FIFO is, however, required in a multiprocessor configuration* where it holds the neuron value until it can obtain access to the Interprocessor Bus (IB) after which it loads the neuron value into the specified address in the buffer memories of all modules on the bus simultaneously. In either case the FIFO outputs the neuron value to the buffer memory (memories) *asynchronously* and this data is not required by any other instructions until the *memory interchange / synchronization (inbm) instruction* is executed (usual after all of the neuron values on a given level have been evaluated). As such, the fact that the pipeline for the *"load buffer ..."* is shorter than that of the multiply / accumulate instructions does not introduce any pipeline delays.

Finally, it is instructive to comment on the *role of the buffer memory.* In a single processor environment its role is to *guarantee that the neuron values in the neuron memory are not changed until all neurons have been updated.* Although this normally does not cause a problem in a feedforward network in a recurrent network the original value of a neuron value may still be required to update additional neurons after its own neuron value has been updated. As such, one stores the new neuron value in the buffer memory until all neurons have been updated and then executes an *instruction which interchanges the neuron and buffer memories* after which the next iteration of the process is initiated using the new neuron values. Moreover, in the multiprocessor case this process guarantees that the *local neuron memories in each processor will remain perfectly coherent*; i.e., be identical at all times.

In addition to the arithmetic instructions the MIMD Neural Network Processor has *5 control instructions* for looping, terminating a program, etc. *I/O is handled externally* via the Interprocessor Bus by a "partial I/O processor" or off-line via the Memory Bus MB.

2.2 Multiprocessor Operation
The key to running the MIMD Neural Network Processor in a multiprocessor mode is the FIFO and buffer memories. First one must initialize all processors with identical neuron memories and buffer memories. Then the *processors run autonomously each with their own programming and weight set*, reading neuron values from their local neuron memory which is guaranteed to remain coherent with the other processors since it operates in a read-only

mode. When any processor updates a neuron value it is loaded into its FIFO which requests access to the Interprocessor Bus and *loads the new neuron value into <u>all</u> of the buffer memories simultaneously* via their second port. As such, the buffer memories remain coherent at all times.

The only point in the process where the parallel NNP's have to wait for each other is when an iteration has been completed or a neural network layer updated and an *instruction to interchange the neuron and buffer memories is executed*. In this case, to guarantee coherency; i.e., that all processors operate on the same data; *each processor must wait until all processors have executed an interchange instruction* at which point the buffer and neuron memories in all processors are interchanged simultaneously.

3 Instruction Set

The MIMD Neural Network Processor has 9 instructions, each coded into a 32 bit words stored in the Program / Weight Memory. These include 4 arithmetic instructions for computing the required activations and neuron values and 5 control instructions.

3.1 Arithmetic Instructions

mula activ_addr, weight: Multiplies the neuron value stored in the neuron memory at address *activ_addr* by the connection weight, *weight*, and adds the resultant product to the contents of the accumulator.

mull activ_addr, weight: Multiplies the neuron value stored in the neuron memory at address *activ_addr* by the connection weight, *weight*, and loads the resultant product into the accumulator.

mulap activ_addr: Multiplies the neuron value stored in the neuron memory at address *activ_addr* by the neuron activation fetched by the previous (*mula, mull,* or *mulap*) instruction

lbtf buff_addr, tf: Passes the contents of the accumulator through the transfer function stored in function memory *tf* and loads the resultant neuron value into the buffer memory at address *buff_addr*.

3.2 Control Instructions

inbm: Signals the other processors in the system that this processor is ready to interchange its neuron and buffer memories, waits until all other processors in the system have also executed an inbm instruction, and then interchanges the memories.

llc count: Load the loop counter with *count*.

djnz label: Decrements the loop counter and if the result is non-zero jumps to address, *label*, in the program weight memory.

nop: No operation.

stop: Stop processing

4 REFERENCES

Carson, J.C., (1993). " 'Silicon Neuron' Seeker: The Application of 3D Artificial Neural Network (3DANN) to Kinetic Energy Interceptor Mission", GOMAC 1993 Digest, New Orleans, Nov. 1993, pp. 253-256.

Chiang, A.M., (1993). "CCDD Neural Net VME Board for Pattern Recognition", GOMAC 1993 Digest, New Orleans, Nov. 1993, pp. 277-280.

Faggin, F., and C. Meade, (1990). "VLSI Implementation of Neural Networks", in An Introduction to Neural and Electronic Networks, (ed. Zornetzer, S.F., Davis, J.L., and C. Lau). San Diego, Academic Press. pp. 275-292.

Hammerstrom, D., (1990). "A VLSI Architecture for High Performance, Low-Cost On-Chip Learning", Proc. of the Inter. Joint Conf. on Neural Networks, San Diego, pp. II-537-ii-542.

Holler, M., Tam, S., Castro, A., and R. Benson, (1989). "An Electronically Trainable Artificial Neural Network (ETANN)", Proc. of the Inter. Joint Conf. on Neural Networks, Washington, pp. II-191-II-196.

Kub, F.J., K.K. Marn, and J.A. Modulo, (1991). "Analog Programmable Chips for Implementing ANN's using Capacitive Weight Storage", Proc. of the Inter. Joint Conf. on Neural Networks, Seattle, pp. I-487-I-492.

Lazzaro, J., and C. Meade, (1990). "A Silicon Model of Auditory Localization", in An Introduction to Neural and Electronic Networks, (ed. Zornetzer, S.F., Davis, J.L., and C. Lau). San Diego, Academic Press. pp. 155-173.

Lyon, R.F., and C. Meade, (1988). "An Analog Electronic Cochlea", IEEE Trans. on Acoustics, Speech, and Signal Processing, Vol. ASSP-36, pp. 1119-1134.

May, N., (1988). "Fault Simulation of a Wafer-Scale Integrated Neurocomputer, Report CS/E-88-020, Oregon Graduate Center, Beaverton.

Mead, C. (1989). Analog VLSI and Neural Systems, Reading, Addison-Wesley.

Morton, S., (1991). "Advance Data Sheet for the 'A236 Neural Network Module'", Oxford Computer Inc., Oxford, (July 1991).

Owechko, Y, and B.H. Soffer, (1990). "Optical Interconnection Method for Neural Networks using Self-Pumped Phase Conjugate Mirrors", Opt. Lett., Vol. 16, pp. 675-677.

Owechko, Y, and B.H. Soffer, (1993). "Optical Neurocomputer Based on Multiple Grating Holography", GOMAC 1`993 Digest, New Orleans, Nov. 1993, pp. 265-268.

Rudnick, M., and D. Hammerstrom, (1988). "An Interconnection Structure for Wafer Scale Neurocomputers", Proc. of the Connectionist Models Summer School, (ed. Touretzky, D., Hintin, G., and T. Sejnowski), San Meteo, Kaufmann.

Neurocomputer Taxonomies

Kjetil Nørvåg

NNNR

Moholt Alle 8-14, 7035 Trondheim, Norway

November 29, 1993

Abstract

To be able to compare, classify, and develop better neurocomputers, a good taxonomy is important. This paper presents earlier approaches to neurocomputer classification, and presents a new one, more suitable both for neurocomputers of today and for the future. This taxonomy is based on taxonomies for existing computer architectures and Philip Treleaven's taxonomy presented in 1989.

1   Introduction

To be able to compare and easier understand a set of related objects, it is useful to classify them, according to a taxonomy.

Several taxonomies exists for conventional computer architectures, with Flynn's taxonomy and the Erlangen taxonomy [6] as the most well-known. While both of them are able to successfully describe control driven computers, they give us little help when it comes to neurocomputers. The main problem is that we can no longer talk about instructions, data and arithmetic logic units. Therefore, we need another kind of classification. Ideally, it should be possible to use the same classification schema on all computer system architectures, but, at least for the moment, this seems impossible.

2   Previous Neurocomputer Taxonomies

Several neurocomputer taxonomies have been proposed, but only one (or rather modified versions of it) is in common use: Treleaven's taxonomy [9]. Treleaven saw the neurocomputer as a parallel computer architecture, just as control flow, dataflow, and cellular arrays are parallel computer architectures. Neurocomputers were further divided into subclasses, as shown on figure 1. Treleaven's taxonomy is the most common in use, and it is suitable for comparison of neurocomputers vs. other computer architectures. Comparing neurocomputers is

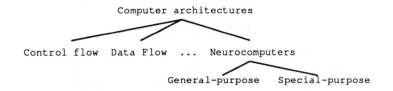

Figure 1: Treleaven's taxonomy.

often difficult with this taxonomy. It often gives unprecise classifications, making comparison more difficult.

3 A Modified Taxonomy

In my taxonomy, neurocomputers are subgroups, or rather applications, of different computer architectures. This is different from Treleaven's where neurocomputers are seen as an architecture on its own. As with Treleaven, this taxonomy also divides neurocomputers into general-purpose and special-purpose neurocomputers, but with an additional group: Partially special-purpose neurocomputers.

3.1 General-Purpose Neurocomputers

General-purpose neurocomputers can be divided into standard computers and co-processors. Standard computers are computers made for *general-purpose computing*, and can be further divided into sequential and parallel standard computers.

Standard computers are flexible, but the flexibility has its cost, both in economy and performance. With co-processors it is possible to get low-cost high-performance neurocomputers. Standard computers connected to the co-processors take care of input and output.

Co-processors are divided by their architectures: Accelerator cards, control driven co-processors, data driven co-processors, systolic arrays, and reconfigurable logic (see figure 2 and table 1). Control driven co-processors can be naturally subdivided from the interconnection networks of the processor elements: Bus, ring/linear array, mesh, hypercube and reconfigurable topology.

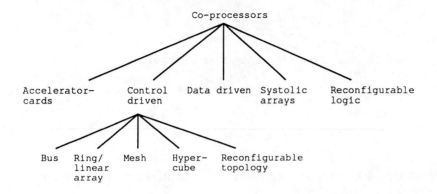

Figure 2: Co-processors.

Subclass	Example of neurocomputer
Accelerator cards	Numerical co-processors
Control driven, bus	TRW Mark III [5]
Control driven, ring	CNAPS[1]
Control driven, mesh	AAP2 [10] and TI NETSIM [4]
Control driven, hypercube	nCube/n, Intel iPPSC/860
Control driven, reconfig.	RENNS [7]
Data Driven	Q-v 1 [2]
Systolic arrays	Warp [3]
Reconfigurable logic	Perle-0 [8]

Table 1: Co-prosessor classes, with examples.

3.2 Partially Special-Purpose Neurocomputers

Partially special neurocomputers[1] are neurocomputers capable of simulating *a class of neural networks*.

Partially special-purpose neurocomputers are often made from special chips – neurochips. These chips can be either digital or analog, and are most often specialized for dotproduct neurons.

3.3 Special-purpose Neurocomputers

Special-purpose neurocomputers are divided by their implementation technology, just as in Treleaven's original taxonomy: Electronic, optical and molecular neurocomputers. To include earlier neurocomputers, groups for electro-mechanical and electro-chemical computers could be added.

Until now, most special-purpose computers have been based on optics. Most electronic implementations have been general-purpose or partially special-purpose, but a few special-purpose neurocomputers based on electronics exists. Examples are the WISARD [9].

4 Conclusions

I have now presented a neurocomputer taxonomy, well suited for classifying neurocomputers of today, and hopefully also tomorrows neurocomputers.

The taxonomy is developed from an *implementors* point of view, other taxonomies might be better desciding neurocomputers for other purposes. For some purposes an taxonomy even more focused on implementation technology could be useful.

References

[1] Adaptive Solutions, Inc. *CNAPS Server — Preliminary Data Sheet*, 1993.

[2] Ali M. Alhaj and Hiroaki Terada. A data-driven implementation of back propagation learning algorithm. In *International Joint Conference on Neural Networks*, 1992.

[3] M. Annatarone, E. Arnould, T. Gross, H.T. Kung, M. Lam, O. Menzilcioglu, and J. A. Webb. The Warp computer: Architecture, implementation and performance. *IEEE Transactions on Computers*, C-36(December):1523–1538, 1987.

---

[1] In other taxonomies these neurocomputers are often classified together with the general-purpose neurocomputers

[4] Simon C J Garth. A chipset for high speed simulation of neural network systems. In *IEEE International Conference on Neural Networks*, 1987.

[5] Robert Hecht-Nielsen. *Neurocomputing*. Addison-Wesley Publishing Company Inc., 1990.

[6] Wolfgang Hädler. The impact of classification schemes on computer architecture. In *International Conference on Parallel Processing*, 1977.

[7] Olav Landsverk, Jarle Greipsland, Jon Gunnar Solheim, Jan Anders Mathisen, Håkon Dahle, and Lisbet Utne. RENNS — a REconfigurable Neural Network Server. In *International Conference on Artificial Neural Networks*. Elsevier Science, 1992.

[8] Marcin Skubiszewski. A hardware emulator for binary neural networks. Technical report, DEC PRL, 1990.

[9] Philip Treleaven. Neurocomputers. Technical Report 89/8, UCL, London, 1989.

[10] Takumi Watanabe, Yoshi Sugiyama, Toshio Kondo, and Yoshihiro Kitamura. Neural network simulation on a massively parallel cellular array processor: AAP-2. In *International Joint Conference on Neural Networks*, 1989.

Temporal Binding in Analog VLSI

Stephen R. Deiss

Applied Neurodynamics, 345 Via Montanosa, Encinitas, CA 92024 (deiss@cerf.net)

Abstract - Binding together perceptions, cognitions and consciousness with time requires a very clear notion of simultaneity. In aVLSI systems signals are multiplexed for efficiency reasons. Multiplexed channels skew events in time and add jitter. Neurons responding to those events may act differently than biological neurons unless simultaneity can be represented. Herein is examined the concept of simultaneity as it applies in neural networks and how it can be represented. In doing so a paradigm for understanding neurons is suggested called *Relativistic Neurodynamics*.

I. Introduction

Temporal Binding is currently a leading theoretical construct for understanding conscious events including perception, memory, attention, and cognition [1]. It has been proposed as the mechanism by which wholes arise from parts in cognition [1,6,16]. Temporal binding has been observed within the limits of multichannel recording technology today and is a very active area of experimentation [6,7].

Analog VLSI systems (aVLSI) seek to model real biological networks in their relevant information processing details, although there is not total agreement on what is relevant [4,5,12,13,14]. Insofar as consciousness is not merely an epiphenomenon of brain activity, but rather may correspond with the highest levels of coding and system state at any moment, then aVLSI has to address the problem of how to model this too. This means that we need to model temporal binding in neuromorphic systems, and we have to be able to detect it and, preferably, also measure it.

This is not a straightforward task. The technology of interconnect will not permit use of point to point axon like communication channels in any cost effective configuration. There are packaging limitations, routing limits, and connection density limits. We are forced to use time division multiplexed access (TDMA) channels, and there are a thousand varieties to start from [consider 3,8,9,10,11,15,18]. This creates a problem for the representation of time bound signals that are linked through some phase relationship, whether a fleeting synchronization or an enduring oscillation. TDMA channels are, by nature, not real time. Signals are forced to walk the channel single file, thus, skewing their time of arrival at their destination(s) by a variable amount compared to what it would be on a dedicated channel.

This gives rise to a *bandwidth-synchrony dilemma* explored elsewhere [2]. For a given neural integration time constant, low speed TDMA channels have a tendency to desynchronize multiplexed signals, and high speed channels bunch signals in time making them tend to synchronize. This interferes with the representation of temporal binding, and even with the very basic notion of correlated inputs for a neuron. Possible solutions are explored in [2].

To better understand this problem so that one might better recognize a solution, it is worthwhile to explore the concept of simultaneity. In the following section an informal analysis is presented.

II. Simultaneity

Clearly this concept is intertwined with our notions of time and space. Much has been written about time and space both from the standpoint of our ordinary language concepts and from the standpoint of the physicist's space-time [17]. Here the notions of time and space are taken as primitives.

The first observation is that simultaneity is a relative thing in the sense that it depends upon who is the observer (or what object or process is affected) and the context in which it is being asserted or denied. For two events to occur simultaneously they have to fall within the same temporal window. This is something that has to be measured, and no real act of measurement is exact to an unlimited number of decimal places. The size of the temporal window is established by the context of the measurement. For example, in some high speed digital circuits, two events might be considered simultaneous 'for all practical purposes' if they occur within a nanosecond of each other. However, in a high energy physics data acquisition experiment events might be distinguishable on a femtosecond interval through a long chain of observations and inferences. At the other extreme, two congressmen who introduced related legislation within the same month or even the same year might be considered to have acted simultaneously on beaurocratic time scales.

What is the proper time scale for neural event messages? The first answer is 'which messages and who receives them?' One can look at this question from numerous perspectives. From the perspective of an ionic channel, one time scale applies. At the level of a neuron, more specifically, an axon hillock, a different time scale of post synaptic potential integration applies. At the level of a modifiable synapse, another time scale might be more relevant in detecting correlation between release of transmitter packet and feedback from the postsynaptic neuron regarding any state change or any global change in state of reinforcement.

All these neurobiological processes are based upon neurochemical mechanisms that have time constants which operate in relatively narrow ranges governed by electrochemical feedback. These narrow ranges force a kind of consistency to the behavior of the system as a dynamical system. There is no multiplexing here. In biological systems time truely is its own representation. Things take as long as they take as participants in causal chains, and the underlying physical processes are consistent thanks to the basic uniformity of nature.

All these things suggest that two neural action potentials can be judged as simultaneous if they both arrive within the neural integration time for the recipient neuron which is listening to the inputs. Another neuron may view the simultaneity of those action potentials differently because of different delays along the axonal pathways feeding it. In fact it might be more accurate to say that a neuron is not tuned to action potentials. Rather it is tuned to the synaptic current flows that arise from the action potentials. It has no direct global information about distances traveled along axons. That global connectivity information directly affects simultaneity from a higher level perspective, but from the low level local neural perspective, its just the location and timing of inputs along dendrites and the cell body itself. Simultaneity is relative among neurons, but its fairly consistent over time. At least that is true from our higher vantage point that includes a clock.

An interesting thought experiment asks what would happen if the brain's neurons were interconnected by parallel broadcast optics instead of axon delay lines. In such a small volume of tissue, and given the speed of optical transmission (c), every connected neuron would feel the effects of a particular action potential virtually simultaneously (from our point of view). The receptive field of each neuron would be tremendously altered unknown to the neuron itself. It is not clear what effect this would have on the information processing aspects of a neural network, especially on the network system's ability to detect, remember and respond to causal relationships.

The receptive field of a neuron involves projections from other neural areas. Unlike the optical system in the thought experiment, action potentials take appreciable time to propagate relative to the time scale of neural integration. The propagation time is fairly invariant for any given axonal pathway. The receptive field, therefore, is not just a 3D spatial map. It is a space-time map with a geometry all its own. Anything that changes the timing along those pathways by adding skew or jitter would be just as disruptive to the system behavior as it would be if the synapses along the dendritic tree were allowed to make and break contact at random. Fortunately, this timing jitter does not occur in real neural systems. However, it can happen in neuromorphic systems with TDMA communication channels.

Assuming that the important thing about temporal binding is the timing relationship between action potentials, then it should not matter how the action potentials get communicated as long as their relative timing is communicated with consistency, the time span of the ordering is wide enough to allow resolving time differences with a neural mechanism, and the mapping itself is not moving around.

III. Observability

How can we observe simultaneity in a network to confirm that it is forming temporal bindings? The first method involves detecting synchronizations just as brains do, with tuned neurons attached to effectors. This would allow for a large variety of behaviorist style experiments to be done on artificial networks that are just impossible now in natural networks. However, this is an expensive solution. One would have to know in advance what bindings were being sought, train or program the network to detect them, and connect it up so that the detectors could report their occurance. This approach is not unlike multichannel recording used experimentally today.

A step back would be to monitor network activity on a color monitor using the experimentor's own recognition ability to try and capture regularities. However, this would no doubt be a high vigilance task requiring significant time and training. The reports of observed bindings would be subjective and hard to support if challenged unless they were very dramatic and tape recorded.

A third and superior approach would be to devise a system that makes time explicit in neural event messages, filter for events falling within a common widow of phase or oscillation, and record the activity for offline analysis and display. With explicit time stamps, it should be fairly straightforward to devise such a binding filter. Once a binding has been detected and recorded, data presentation can be greatly enhanced and possibly displayed in delayed real time. Since the data can be recorded, it might also be possible to perform post processing to study the chain of events that lead up to the binding code.

IV. Coding and Communicating Neural Messages

A family of related encoding schemes falls under the general heading of space-time-attribute or STA codes [2,5,12]. When an axon potential occurs the space-time location is broadcast along with optional attributes further defining the event. Some of the advantages of such a code are 1) ease of routing of events through a network using a geometric definition of source location and for destination receptive fields, 2) use of network transit time and geometric distance from source to calculate an axon delay after receipt at the destination so the event can be properly queued, 3) ability to utilize technology's bandwidth advantage to overcome the interconnection disadvantage, 4) ability to devise solutions to the observability problem, and 5) compatibility with a number of digital communication media. See [2] for a more detailed description of these features. In this section the focus will be on how STA coding helps one encode and observe bindings in aVLSI.

When STA events are tagged with a time stamp as well as their geometric origin, this information can be used to represent axon delays. When a message arrives at a destination board or chip, it is passed through by virtue of having an address that matches a receptive field of one or more neurons on the other side of the gate. This same message can be delayed in time to represent the axon pathway delay adjusted by the time already lost in transit over the communication link. As long as there is sufficient bandwidth in the network to ensure that events always arrive at or ahead of their expected real arrival time counting axon delay, there is no loss of timing information. Since the delay value is calculated from the geometry, there is no need for a large amount of storage for these delays. If several neurons inside a chip all receive projections from a neuron coming from another chip or another board, they each might best be served by different representations of the axon delay. This can be done either by extending the above method to the chip level which might be expensive in terms of silicon, or by associating with each analog synapse an analog one shot timing circuit to insert the proper delay for the axon path to that synapse. Such a lumped representation of delay incurs a silicon penalty that can be traded off against loss of the finer representation of time accuracy.

With STA coding the observability of binding in the aVLSI system is a tractable problem. The simplest method would be to record all event traffic as it flows. This data can then be analyzed offline. If there is a single common bus or channel serving the entire system, the data could possibly be examined, filtered and binding data displayed online. The filtering logic would maintain an ordered list representing a span of recent event history from which bindings could be selected out and displayed when they meet the criterion for simultaneity which is that both occur within a system specified time window. When more than one channel is involved, the data have to be converged at some point to detect bindings in this manner.

With this kind of data collection and analysis capability in the neuromorphic system, it should produce a fruitful interplay between theory and experiment. No where else is it possible to obtain correlation statistics over such a range of neural activities to arbitrary levels of precision, nor possible to unwind the clock and look at actual causal sequences, if necessary.

V. Conclusion

There appears to be no limits to what abstractions human intelligence is capable of encoding and modeling all the way from quarks to quasars. Perhaps this is in part because human intelligence is rooted in that same physical world and governed by the same dynamical system principles. It is suggested here that some of the notions used to understand physical space-time such as relative simultaneity may also have a place in understanding neurodynamics.

There is lots to be learned in this search for a Relativistic Neurodynamics not least of which is to identify what the invariances are in nervous systems. It is the author's hope that this proves to be much more than an overextended analogy.

VI. Acknowledgements

The author thanks the following members of the 'Idyllwild Collaboration' for their continued interest and feedback as these ideas develop: Rodney Douglas, Mike Fisher, Christof Koch, John Lazzaro, Misha Mahowald and Tony Matthews.

References

1. Crick F., Koch C., "Towards a Neurobiological Theory of Consciousness," *Seminars in the Neurosciences*, 2:263-275, 1990

2. Deiss S., "Connectionism without the Connections", in press, ICNN, IEEE, 1994.

3. Deiss S. et. al., "Neural Systems Interface (IEEE MSC Study Group Report)," request from author, Encinitas, CA, 1989.

4. Douglas R., Mahowald M., "A Constructor Set for Silicon Neurons," in press, MRC, Oxford, UK, 1993.

5. Douglas R. et. al., "Neuromorphic Analog VLSI," in press, MRC, Oxford, UK, 1994.

6. Eckhorn R. et. al., "Coherent Oscillations: a mechanism of feature linking in the visual cortex," *Biol. Cybern.*, 60:121-130, 1988.

7. Gray C.M., Singer W., "Stimulus-specific neuronal oscillations in orientation columns of cat visual cortex," *PNAS* 86:1698-1702.

8. *IEEE Standards for Local and Metropolitan Area Networks: Overview and Architecture*, IEEE, 802-1990.

9. *IEEE Standard for Scalable Coherent Interface (SCI)*, IEEE 1596-1992

10. *IEEE RamLink, IEEE P1596.4 Draft*, IEEE, 1994.

11. *IEEE Standard Backplane Bus Specification for Multiprocessor Architectures: Futurebus+*, IEEE 896.2-1991.

12. Lazzaro J. et. al., "Silicon Auditory Processors as Computer Peripherals," *NIPS 5*, Morgan Kaufmann, 1993.

13. Mahowald M., *VLSI Analogs of Neuronal Visual Processing: A Synthesis of Form and Function*, Dissertation, Caltech-CS-TR-92-15, 1992.

14. Mead C., *Analog VLSI and Neural Systems*, Addison Wesley, 1989.

15. Rambus Inc., *Rambus Technology Guide, Rev .90 - Preliminary*, Rambus, Mountain View, CA, 1992.

16. Shastri L., Ajjanagadde V., "From simple associations to systematic reasoning: A connectionist representation of rules, variables and dynamic bindings using temporal synchrony," *Beh. Brain Sci.*, 16:417-494, 1993.

17. Taylor E., Wheeler J., *Spacetime Physics*, Freeman, 1963.

18. *VME64 Draft Specification*, 1993, VITA, Scottsdale, AZ.

High Performance Compressor Building Blocks
for Digital Neural Network Implementation

D. Zhang and M.I. Elmasry

VLSI Research Group, Department of Electrical and Computer Engineering
University of Waterloo, Waterloo, Ontario, Canada N2L 3G1

Abstract

In this paper, a digital neural networks (DNN) implementation approach based on complex complementary pass-transistor logic (C^2PL) is presented. Some types of 3-2 compressor designs in C^2PL are discussed and a number of experiments are conducted to optimize their performance. Based on the 3-2 compressors, two typical building blocks in DNN implementation, i.e., 4-2 and 7-3 compressor, are developed. Example of the application is given to illustrate the effectiveness of the approach.

1. Introduction

There have been a variety of implementation approaches for neural networks, including software and hardware, electronic and optical, discrete component realizations, and so on. The real promise for applications of neural networks currently lies in specialized hardware, in particular VLSI or WSI implementations that achieve high levels of computational performance with modest development effort [1-3].

Typically, the high interconnectivity and relatively low precision needed for signals in neural networks are well tailored to an analog approach [4-5]. With increasing neural networks size, however, designing large integrated analog circuits, based on VLSI implementation, is a difficult task. On the other hand digital processing, which appears to be inferior to analog processing in terms of computational density, has advantages of flexibility in terms of programming for a variety of architectures and learning strategies, as well as simplifying the task of memory retention. There is still a development tendency to implement neural networks in VLSI using digital technology [6-7].

Numerous studies have shown that the complexity of DNN does not stem from the complexity of its nodes but rather from the multitude of ways in which a large collection of these nodes can interact [7]. As an example, for a fully connected layered network with two layers and n neurons per layer, each neuron is required to form an inner product of n elements using 1-bit binary input lines and m-bit weights (e.g., m=16), where carry propagation is an expensive operation in digital arithmetic of the inner product. Thus, a key problem for implementing high performance, high capacity DNN is to build effective compressors to reduce the impact of carry propagation.

CMOS digital circuits can be used in such data compressor building block implementation due to high noise immunity, operation at a wide range of power supply voltages, low power dissipation, relatively high speed, and compatibility to other logic families [8]. There are many logic design styles to choose from in implementing CMOS digital circuits. Some typical logic design styles are preudo-NMOS CMOS logic, CMOS non-threshold logic (NTL), cascode voltage switch logic (CVSL), differential cascode voltage switch logic (DCVS), differential split-level logic (DSL), and Zipper CMOS logic [8]. These logic styles achieve different tradeoffs in speed power, and area. The highest speed logic families also tend to consume the most power. The most compact tend to be slow.

Complementary pass-transistor logic (CPL) proposed by K. Yano, et al. in [9] seems to offer modest performance, is compact, and low power. The CPL circuit is twice as fast as conventional CMOS because of lower input capacitance and higher logic functionality. However, CPL design needs more area in silicon like conventional CMOS one due to the mixed interconnection, as well as CPL implementation must take into account noise margin and speed degradation caused by mismatched input signal level and the logic threshold voltage of the CMOS driver, both fluctuating independently with process variations [10].

In this paper, a new member of CPL family, called complex complementary pass-transistor logic (C^2PL), will be presented for implementing compressor building blocks in DNN. The basic C^2PL model is defined in Section 2. Applying this model to 3-2 compressor design, Section 3 discusses some typical C^2PL circuits and their performances. Section 4 provides two types of building blocks, 4-2 compressor and 7-3 compressor, in DNN application. In Section 5 we summarize the conclusions of the paper.

2. C^2PL Model

A basic CPL schematic structure consists of complementary inputs / outputs, an NMOS pass transistor logic network, and CMOS output inverters, as shown in Fig.1, where complementary input space is defined as: $\mathcal{R} = \mathcal{R}^{(G)} + \mathcal{R}^{(D)}$, i.e., gate input space $\mathcal{R}^{(G)} = \{ \alpha, \alpha', ..., \omega, \omega' \}$ and drain input space $\mathcal{R}^{(D)} = \{ a, a', ..., z, z' \}$, and complementary output space as $Q = \{ A, A', ..., Z, Z' \}$. The pass transistors function as pull-down and pull-up devices. Thus PMOS latch can be eliminated, allowing the advantage of the differential circuits to be fully utilized. However, the output inverters are necessary because of amplifying the output signals, shifting the logic threshold voltage and driving the capacitive load [9].

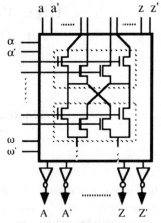

Fig.1 Basic CPL structure

Note that the NMOS pass transistor logic network is built by some logic layers shown in Fig.1, where each achieves a given logic function. Assuming that these logic layers are symbolized as L_i (i = 1, 2, ..., n), and n is the number of the layers in the network. CPL structure is limited in the following: (1) Only the NMOS pass transistor logic network is used; (2) All complementary gate inputs receive data from the input space $\mathcal{R}^{(G)}$; (3) The complementary drain inputs of each layer receive data from previous layer except for L_1. Obviously, these limit CPL to design flexibly in various applications.

The basic concept of C^{2}PL is to regard each logic layer in a network as an independent layer which they can be built by NMOS or PMOS/NMOS pass transistor logic, and eliminate the limit conditions in CPL. This means that both complementary drain and gate input for logic layer L_i may receive data from either $\mathcal{R}$ or previous layer L_{i-1}, and the complementary outputs of each layer can be connected to its next layer directly or the corresponding output units, CMOS or BiCMOS driver. It is evident that CPL is a special example of C^{2}PL.

3. 3-2 Compressor Design

3-2 compressor is a basic arithmetic unit in DNN implementation. We can separate it into two parts: the logic design part and the output driver part. Their designs in C^{2}PL are discussed in the following:

<u>1. Logic Design</u>

Let the complementary input space $\mathcal{R} = \{ a, a', b, b', c, c' \}$, and the complementary output space $Q = \{ S, S', C, C' \}$. S (sum) and C (carry) for a 3-2 compressor can be represented as

$$S = (a \ominus c) b' + (a \ominus c)' b \qquad (1)$$
$$C = (a \ominus c) b + (a \ominus c)' c \qquad (2)$$

where $\ominus$ is a XOR operator. We can extract two basic cells, $(a \ominus c)$ and $(a \ominus c)'$, from Eq.(1)-(2). Let $F = a \ominus c$. Thus, the equations can be rewritten as $S = F b' + F' b$ and $C = F b + F' c$.

Using C^{2}PL to design such a 3-2 compressor, a simple logic structure can be obtained in Fig.2(a). Note that in the structure two logic layers are needed, where their input / output spaces are $\mathcal{R}1 = \{a, a', c, c'\} / Q1 = \{ F, F' \}$ and $\mathcal{R}2 = \{F, F', b, b', c, c'\} / Q2 = \{ S, S', C, C' \}$, respectively. Only two types of logic cells, i.e. $\Psi = \alpha\beta' + \alpha'\beta$ and $\Omega = \alpha\beta + \alpha'\chi$, are used in the design (See Fig.2(b)). Analyzing the logic structure in Fig.2(a), two useful features can be obtained in the following:

I. Only two complementary inputs in $\mathcal{R}$ are required in the first logic layer. This feature is superior in multi-layer design. It can be proved in Section 4.

II. The complementary output space Q1 of the first logic layer are directly used as the gate input space $\mathcal{R}2^{(G)}$ to the next layer. Obviously, this causes noise margin and speed degradation by mismatched inputs.

To reduce the effect generated by the last feature and improve the performance of the compressor, some effective approaches in CMOS circuit design should be adopted to provide current paths for any full-down or pull-up operation. As an example, two typical C^{2}PL 3-2 compressors, called C^{2}PL(1) and C^{2}PL(2), are given in Fig.3, where their second logic layers are the same, but PMOS latch and PMOS/NMOS device approaches are used in the first layer,

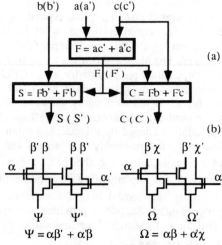

Fig.2 (a) 3-2 compressor logic structure and (b) its two basic cells

respectively. If we take CMOS driver as their output unit, the entire 22 and 24 transistors are required in each compressor.

A number of experiments using 0.8μm BiCMOS technology have been achieved to optimize these compressors, and some useful results are :

(i) The optimum gate width ratio between logic layers, $\zeta = W_{up} / W_{down}$, is at the ratio of about 2, as shown in Fig.4.

(ii) The optimum gate width ratio between PMOS and NMOS in output driver, $\phi = W_p / W_n$, exists at the ratio of about 1.25 (See Fig.5).

Note that the ratios given above are different from CPL and ordinary CMOS drivers in [9] because we adopt a power-delay product as our measurement, which is more reasonable than a single delay time.

2. Output Driver Design

An output driver buffers the complementary outputs generated in the logic design to drive the capacitive load. Depending upon the interconnection wiring capacitance in practice, we can use one of the following three ways in output part: (1) Directly drive the load without any buffer (Note that in this case two PMOS latches must be attached to the last logic layer); (2) Use a CMOS buffer as a driver, as shown in Fig.6(a); (3) Use a BiCMOS buffer as a driver for large capacitive load. (See Fig.6(b))

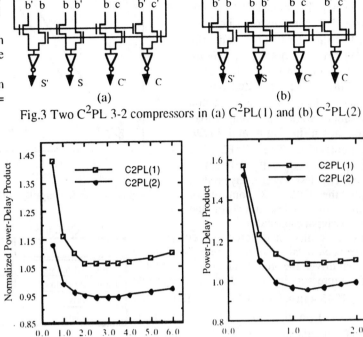

Fig.3 Two C^2PL 3-2 compressors in (a) $C^2PL(1)$ and (b) $C^2PL(2)$

Fig.4 The gate width ratio, $\zeta = W_{up}/W_{down}$

Fig.5 The gate width ratio, $\phi = W_p / W_n$

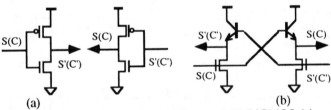

Fig.6 The output units (a) CMOS driver and (b) BiCMOS driver

To compare the performance between the CPL 3-2 compressor in [9] and the C^2PL 3-2 compressor in Fig.3, generally, area, power and delay estimations given by the design are three most important measures. In this section, we will analyze these measures and some experimental results are given, where the CMOS drivers are used in both C^2PL and CPL 3-2 compressors.

The circuit simulations are performed using the 0.8μ device parameters at a supply voltage of 5V. The worst delay time, T, refers to situations where the inputs are such that circuit operation is slowest and the dynamic power, P, resulting from charging and discharging the capacitances in the circuits is given as

Based on the types of drivers given (e.g., none, CMOS driver and BiCMOS driver), some simulation results for different loads, e.g., the worst delay time and power dissipation, can be obtained. Considering their product, i.e., power-delay, as shown in Fig.7, a 3-2 compressor with no buffer is available when the output load is less about 0.25pf, but one with BiCMOS driver can be selected for large load.

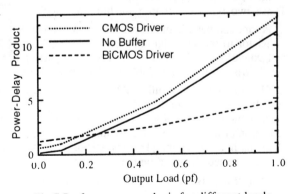

Fig.7 Performances analysis for different loads

$$\mathcal{P} = C_{load} \cdot (V_{cc})^2 \cdot f \qquad (3)$$

where C_{load} is the total capacitance in the circuit, V_{cc} is the supply voltage and f is the operating frequency. The simulated $\mathcal{T}$ ($\mathcal{P}$) of three 3-2 compressors, i.e., the CPL, the $C^2PL(1)$ and the $C^2PL(2)$, are 0.56ns (1.95mw), 0.58ns (1.89mw) and 0.55ns (1.78mw). The simulated power-delay product, $\mathcal{T} \times \mathcal{P}$, as a function of supply voltage and output load are shown in Fig.8 and Fig.9, respectively. The C^2PL 3-2 compressor, especially $C^2PL(2)$, is about 10% less power-delay product than the CPL 3-2 compressor mainly due to less transistor and smaller input capacitance.

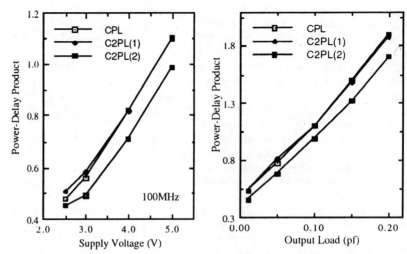

Fig.8 Simulation for supply voltages   Fig.9 Simulation for output loads

Layout results for different 3-2 compressors have been obtained in our group. Without the output driver, the areas required for these types of compressors based on the 0.8μ design rule are 1245.44μm² for CPL, 865.18μm² for $C^2PL(1)$ and 867.57μm² $C^2PL(2)$. Obviously, the area of C^2PL 3-2 compressors can be reduced by about one-thirds.

The results mentioned above are summarized in Table 1. It is shown that C^2PL 3-2 compressor have the lower area complexity in silicon and the smaller power while maintaining the same high computing speed.

Table 1 Comparison of 3-2 compressors between CPL and C^2PL

	CPL	$C^2PL(1)$	$C^2PL(2)$
# of transistors	28	22	24
the worst delay time	0.56ns	0.58ns	0.55ns
power	1.95mw	1.89mw	1.78mw
area	1245.44μm²	865.18μm²	867.57μm²

4. Typical Building Blocks in DNN

Using C^2PL 3-2 compressor as a basic cell, two typical building blocks in implementing DNN, i.e., 4-2 compressor and 7-3 compressor, can be designed in Fig.10, where some output drivers between the layers can be saves, and the longest data flow paths in the blocks are shown in dash line. Based on the feature obtained in the previous section, the numbers of the required logic layers to pass the longest data flow paths are 3 for 4-2 and 5 for 7-3, respectively.

These two types of compressor building blocks in C^2PL are comparable in power, delay and number of transistor to the same building blocks in both CPL and conventional logic [11-12]. Their comparisons are shown in Table 2 and Table 3, respectively. Here,

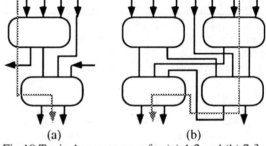

(a)   (b)

Fig.10 Typical compressors for (a) 4-2 and (b) 7-3

Table 2 Comparison of 4-2 compressors

	Power	Delay	# Tran.
$C^2PL(3)$	1.83mw	0.73n	60
$C^2PL(2)$	1.97mw	0.70n	46
CPL	2.66mw	1.07n	56
IEEE paper [11]	2.1mw	1.70n	58

$C^2PL(3)$ is built using full PMOS/NMOS device approach. The results show us that the building blocks in C^2PL can offer the highest performance in VLSI design.

As an example in DNN application, we assume that a perceptron sums the 1010 data inputs, each with one bit. A reduction process is to use 7-3 compressor to reduce the initial 1010 row matrix to a matrix with no more than three elements in each column [13]. The whole process is shown in Fig.11, where 252 7-3 compressors and 6 processing stages are needed. Based on the different logic designs in Table 3, the required parameters (i.e., power, delay and number of transistor) are: 0.66w, 9.3n and 27,216 ($C^2PL(3)$); 1.14w, 10.44n and 28,224 (CPL), and 0.69w, 18n and

28,224 (Conventional Logic (CL)). This means that power and delay in C^2PL are only about half as much as one in CPL and in CL, respectively.

5. Conclusion

In this paper, we present a DNN implementation approach based on a new logic design style, called complex complementary pass-transistor logic (C^2PL). Applying the C^2PL model to compressor designs, some types of 3-2 compressor are developed and a number of experiments are conducted to optimize their performance. As an example of DNN application, two typical building blocks, i.e., 4-2 and 7-3 compressor, are discussed. Compared with CPL and conventional logic, our simulation results show that the C^2PL compressors in DNN have the best performance in power, delay and number of transistor.

6. References

[1] J.M.J. Murre, 1993, "Transputers and Neural Networks: An Analysis of Implementation Constraints and Performance," IEEE Trans. on Neural Networks 4, 2, 284-292.

[2] R. H. Nielsen, 1986, "Performance Limits of Optical, Electro-Optical, and Electronic Neurocomputers," Proc. SPIE, 634, 277-306.

[3] B.W. Lee and B.J. Sheu, 1991, Hardware Annealing in Electronic Neural Networks, Boston, MA: Kluwer Academic.

[4] C. Mead and M. Ismail, 1989, Analog VLSI Implementation of Neural Systems, Kluwer Academic Publishers, Boston / Dordrecht / London.

[5] P.W. Hollis and J.J. Paulos, 1990, "Artificial Neural Networks Using MOS Analog Multipliers," IEEE Journal of Solid-State Circuits 25, 3, 849-855.

[6] B.A.White and M.I.Elmasry, 1992, "The Digi-Neocognitron: A Digital Neocognitron Neural Network Model for VLSI", IEEE Trans. on Neural Networks 3, 1, 73-85.

[7] J.B. Burr, 1991, "Digital Neural Network Implementation", in Neural Networks, Concepts, Applications, and Implementations, Prentice Hall, 237-285.

[8] M.I. Elmasry (ed.), 1992, "Digital MOS Integrated Circuits II with Applications to Processors and Memory Design", New York: IEEE Press.

[9] K. Yano, et al., 1990, "A 3.8-ns CMOS 16x16-b Multiplier Using Complementary Pass-Transistor Logic", IEEE Journal of Solid-State Circuits 25, 2, 388-395.

[10] A.P. Chandrakasan, S. Sheng and R.W. Brodesen, 1992, "Low-Power CMOS Digital Design", Ibid, 27, 4, 473-483.

[11] J. Mori, et al., 1991, "A 10-ns 54x54-b Parallel Structured Full Array Multiplier with 0.5-mm CMOS Technology", Ibid, 26, 4, 600-605.

[12] E. Hokenek, R.K. Montoye and P.W. Cook, 1990, "Second-Generation RISC Floating Point with Multiply-Add Fused", Ibid, 25, 5, 1207-1213.

[13] D. Zhang, G.A. Jullien, W.C. Miller and E. Swartzlander, 1991, "Arithmetic for Digital Neural Networks", 10th IEEE Symposium on Computer Arithmetic, Grenoble, France, 58-63.

Table 3 Comparison of 7-3 compressors

	Power	Delay	# Tran.
$C^2PL(3)$	2.61mw	1.55n	108
$C^2PL(2)$	3.37mw	1.45n	94
CPL	4.54mw	1.74n	112
IEEE paper [12]	2.74mw	3.0n	112

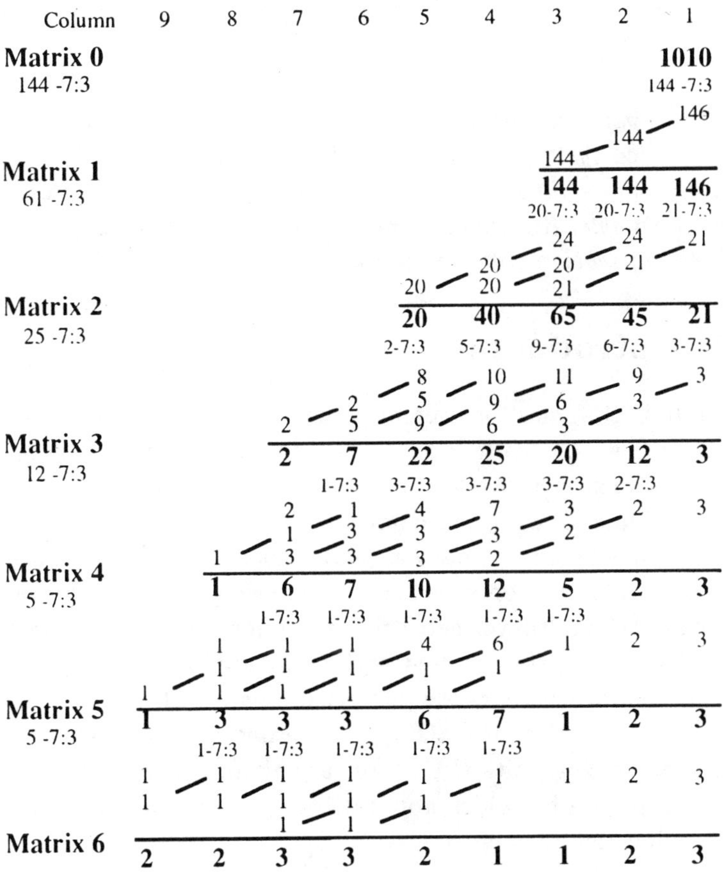

Fig.11 Reduction process in the bit matrix

Coprocessors for special neural networks
KOKOS and KOBOLD

H. Speckmann, P. Thole, M. Bogdan, W. Rosenstiel
University of Tübingen
72076 Tübingen, Sand 13, Germany

Abstract

In this paper we present a system for accelerating special kinds of neural networks. It is a hardware supported system consisting of different parts. A special-purpose neural coprocessor is connected to a personal computer (PC) by a special, asynchronous interface. Two different neural coprocessors are available, KOKOS, a coprocessor for Kohonen's selforganizing map, and KOBOLD, accelerating backpropagation with online learning.

1   Introduction

Large CPU-times for training large data sets to neural networks and the impossibility of real-time evaluation constitute a serious obstacle for practical applications of neural networks. Software simulations on MIMD-computers, e.g. transputer networks [15], or on SIMD-computers (we are using MasPar with the language Parallaxis [1]), bring up the performance. For some general concepts which have many applications specialized hardware may further improve the performance. Two of these concepts are the selforganizing map (SOM) which has been introduced by T. Kohonen [8] and the multilayer network with online learning backpropagation introduced by Rosenblatt [12].

These networks are used with many applications, requiring different architectures. So in multilayer neural networks the number of neurons, layers and connections depend on the special applications. As far as the SOM is concerned the topology of the net and the number of components and processing-units (PUs) are varying and there is no satisfying theory saying which parameters are to choose for which application. So a system implementing the SOM should include tools for verifying the learning results.

2   The system configuration

The whole system consists of three main parts. A neural coprocessor (KOKOS, KOBOLD) is connected to a personal computer (PC) by a special interface. The coprocessor calculates the parallel parts of the neural algorithm, has a modular structure and is scalable for the different applications. In addition to the asynchronous communication the interface has the ability to interpret complex commands and controls the neural coprocessor to simplify the programming of the neural coprocessor. The PC holds the software implementation of the serial parts of the neural algorithms, controls the neural coprocessor and evaluates the learning results.

2.1   KOKOS: A coprocessor for Kohonen's selforganizing map

For our implementations we use a modified version of Kohonen's algorithm [14]. The concept of the SOM is to map a high dimensional space to a lower dimensional space while preserving the topology of the high dimensional input space. This describes the SOM's algorithm for 2-dimensional output space, but higher dimensional output spaces are possible. Our hardware realisation is not restricted to any dimension of the input or the output space because the structure of the map is not hardwired.

The hardware implemented learning in KOKOS works as follows: The PC determines randomly an input vector from the input data set and delivers it to the neural coprocessor which rapidly finds the position of the processing unit (PU) with the minimum euclidean distance to the input vector. With the coordinates of the nearest PU the PC calculates the excitation matrix for the map holding the adaptation factor for each PU and the coprocessor calculates the adaption of each PU.

In [13] we discussed the two possibilities of parallizing the SOM, neuron parallelism, leading to the architecture of an array processor and synapse parallelism, leading to the architecture of the vector processor. Weighting up the pros and cons of the two concepts we choose the last concept because it is easier to control, has less effort of hardware and the search for the minimum distance is avoided.

As you see in figure 1, the neural coprocessor consists of the following parts, n so called 'Memory-and-Arithmetic-Boards' (MAB), $\lceil \log n \rceil$ stage adder tree and the controller of the coprocessor. In our prototype we use eight MABs and a three stage adder. Each MAB holds the arithmetic and memory necessary for learning one input vector component. So you can process one input vector for one PU in parallel and store the weights of the whole SOM with the neural coprocessor. The arithmetic of the MAB is pipelined.

To determine the PU with the minimum euclidean distance to the input vector you calculate the partial distances in the MAB arithmetic SUB-MULT pipelines. The outputs of the pipelines are added to the whole distance by the adder tree, which is organized as a three stage pipeline. For adaption the adaptation factor is loaded into every MAB and according to equation (2) we calculate adaptation using the MAB's SUB-MULT-ADD pipeline.

For many applications eight components are not sufficient. But with the coprocessor's ability of time multiplexing every number of vector components can be handled. The only restriction is the finite memory size of the MAB's. The restriction is that the number of PU's multiplied by the degree of time multiplex must not exceed 2^{16}.

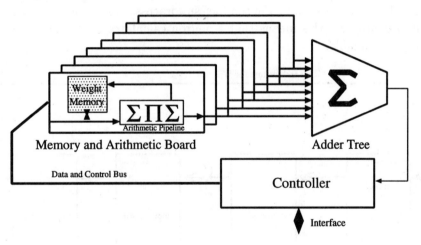

Figure 1: The architecture of KOKOS

2.2   KOBOLD: A neural coprocessor for backpropagation with online learning

In contrast to other implementations [10, 11] our concept allows different extensions and has a special communication structure. The neural coprocessor consists of several subprocessors (SP). As shown in figure 2 each SP represents one column of the neural network. Using several subprocessors in linear order we can build a network of an arbitrary size. In the actual version the number of SPs is limited to 128. Although most applications don't use more than four layers we implement eight layers per subprocessor [3]. This gives the ability to construct recursive nets or 4 layer networks with 256 neurons per layer.

The SPs are connected by an optimized ring bus structure shown in figure 3. Generally needed

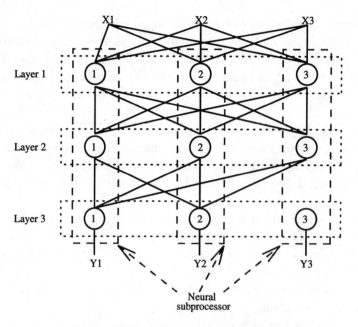

Figure 2: The topology of the coprocessor

data, forward propagation of the output X_j of the previous layer and the backpropagation of the error δ_j, is distributed by using a synchronous global bus. Additionally a local bus connects each SP with its direct neighbours. This bus is used for distributing the connection weights w_{ij} in forward and backward mode. The data turns around in a ring in one direction. Each data has included its target adress. So each subprocessor checks the incoming data for its adress. If it is relevant it is stored. Otherwise the data will be sent to the next subprocessor. Own results will be inserted into the dataflow. If a data returns to the sending subprocessor an error signal occurs. The whole system is dataflow controlled, this means that a neuron calculates its weighted sum as soon as all necessary inputs are available.

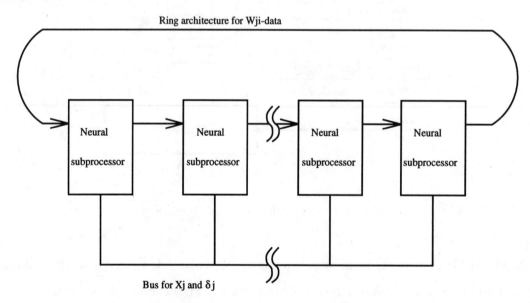

Figure 3: The topology of the busses

The SP's arithmetic is optimized and pipelined. According to [7] 16 bit precision is needed. Though 8 bit precision is sufficient for forward propagation, backpropagation's convergence is guaranteed with 16 bit resolution. In [6] it is shown that the limited precision of integer performs calculations in most applications as well as floating point. So we choose integer arithmetic because it can be implemented faster and easier. The sigmoid function and its derivation is implemented

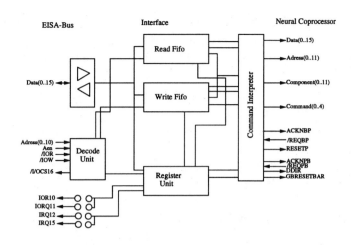

Figure 4: The architecture of the asynchronous interface

by a lookup table.

2.3 The special interface

The asynchronous interface reduces the communication requirement as follows. Data is buffered in 2 FIFOs, one for reading data from the PC and one for the opposite direction. The flow of control is reduced by connecting the neural coprocessor to a command interpreter interpreting complex PC commands to easier commands understandable by the coprocessor. The interface is connected to the PC-EISA bus (IEEE B996). As you can see in figure 4 the interface consists of 5 main parts. The command interpreter demultiplexes the 16 bit data from the PC to 45 bit data for the neural coprocessor. The read and write FIFO consist of a RAM where the adress is generated by a counter. The decode unit and the register unit control the communication of PC and interface, like connection to the PC boards and interrupts.

3 Hardware implementation

For the implementation of the coprocessor and the special interface we use off-the-shelf elements and FPGAs. Off-the-shelf elements were used for building fast arithmetic like multiplier and the adder tree. Irregular structures like a subtractor with different datapaths for calculating the euclidean distance and adaptation necessary for KOKOS, controller and command interpreter, were implemented with XILINX FPGAs. This concept yields to a fast and flexible prototype.

4 Results and conclusion

We compared KOKOS to a software implementation running on a SISD-computer (SUN 4). The virtual selforganizing map consists of 60x60 PUs learning 10000 vectors with 8 components. The following table shows the results we obtained:

Implementation	MCUPS
Sun Sparc 2	1
MasPar MP 1 (16 K)	11 (best case)
KOKOS (4 MABs)	16 (clock frequency 10 MHz)

The algorithm written in C achieves a learning rate of nearly 1 MCUPS. The MasPar MP 1 with 16 K processors achieves 11 MCUPS [2] in best case. Our implementation achieves about 16 MCUPS for the same application running with a clock frequency of 10 MHz.

In the next table different concepts of different online backpropagation concepts are compared concerning their performance, two software simulations on SISD computers, one on a SIMD computer (MasPar) [9], one neurocomputer (CNAPS [5]), and one net of digital signal processors (MUSIC [4]).

Hardwareimplementierung	MCUPS
PC	0.47
Sun Sparc 10	0.146
MasPar MP 1 (16 K)	176 (best case)
CNAPS (512 PNs)	1900
MUSIC (60 DSPs)	246
KOBOLD (128 SPs)	122 (worst case)

So KOBOLD is factor 260 faster as a PC and factor 835 faster as a SUN. Although our system will be cheaper than MUSIC 20 or MasPar it is much faster.

Therefore both coprocessors KOKOS and KOBOLD are useful for learning and for fast, online evaluation. The hardware implementation with programmable gate arrays ensures the system's flexibility to different requirements of the various applications.

References

[1] I. Barth, T. Bräunl, S. Engelhardt, und F. Sembach. Parallaxis version 2 user manual. Technical Report 2/91, University of Stuttgart, 1991.

[2] H. Bayer. Massiv parallele Simulation der selbstorganisierenden Karten von Kohonen auf einem SIMD-Rechner. Diplomarbeit, Universität Stuttgart, 1991.

[3] M. Bogdan. Kobold, a neural coprocessor for backpropagation with online learning. Diplomarbeit, University of Tübingen, 1993.

[4] A. Gunzinger, U. Müller, W. Scott, B. Bäumle, P. Kohler, H. von der Mühll, F. Müller-Plathe, W. von Gunsteren, und W. Guggenbühl. Achieving supercomputer performance with a DSP array processor. In *International Conference on Supercomputing, Minneapolis*, 1992.

[5] D. Hammerstrom. A VLSI Architecture for high-performance, low-cost, on-chip learning . In *IJCNN Seattle*, 1991.

[6] J. Holt und T. Baker. Backpropagation simulations using limited precision calculations. In *IJCNN Seattle*, 1991.

[7] J. Holt und J. Hwang. Finite precision error analysis of neural network electronic hardware implementations. In *IJCNN Seattle*, 1991.

[8] T. Kohonen. *Selforganization and associative memory*. Springer Verlag Heidelberg New York Tokyo, 1984.

[9] N. Mache. Entwicklung eines parallelen Simulatorkernes für neuronale Netze auf der MasPar MP-1. Diplomarbeit, Universität Stuttgart, 1991.

[10] S. Mackie. A parallel vector processing chip architecture for neural networks. In *Micro Neuro*, 1993.

[11] D. Naylor, S. Jones, D. Myers, und J. Vincent. Design and application of a real-time neural network based image processing system. In *Micro Neuro*, 1993.

[12] F. Rosenblatt. *Principles of neurodynamics*. Spartan Books, Washington DC, 1962.

[13] H. Speckmann, P. Thole, und W. Rosenstiel. Hardware implementations of Kohonen's selforganizing feature map. In *IJCNN Bejing, China*, Seiten III 183–187, 1992.

[14] V. Tryba. *Selbstorganisierende Karten: Theorie, Anwendung und VLSI-Implementierung*. VDI Verlag, 1992.

[15] A. Ultsch und H. P. Siemon. Exploratory Data Analysis: Using Kohonen networks on transputers. Technical report, Universität Dortmund, 1989.

Circuit Implementation of the Multivalued Exponential Recurrent Associative Memory

Ren-Jiun Huang and Tzi-Dar Chiueh

Department of Electrical Engineering, Room 511
National Taiwan University
Taipei, Taiwan 10617

Abstract

In this paper we describe a circuit implementation of the multivalued exponential recurrent associative memory (MERAM) proposed previously. Major components of the new model, including a similarity-measure computation circuit and a weighted average circuit, are developed. These components as well as a weight-storage capacitor are arranged in a basic building block, called MERAM cell. HSPICE simulation results of the MERAM model storing three patterns confirm the functionality of the propose circuits.

1 Introduction

Many VLSI implementations of the Hopfield model with either programmable or fixed synapse weights have been proposed. However, it is also known that the Hopfield model, as an associative memory, has a storage capacity of $0.15N$. Successful attempts to greatly increase the storage capacity have been developed previously [1]-[2]. Furthermore, a high-capacity associative memory that processes multivalued patterns, called multivalued exponential recurrent associative memory (MERAM), was also proposed [3]. In this paper, we present a CMOS circuit implementation for MERAM.

Assume that $\mathbf{S}^u, u = 1, 2, \cdots, P$ are M-component patterns stored in a MERAM, the motion equation is given by

$$S_i(t + 1) = \frac{\sum_{u=1}^{P} a^{\psi(\mathbf{S}^u, \mathbf{S}(t))} S_i^u}{\sum_{u=1}^{P} a^{\psi(\mathbf{S}^u, \mathbf{S}(t))}}, \tag{1}$$

where $\psi(\mathbf{S}^u, \mathbf{S}(t))$ denotes a similarity measure between a memory pattern, $\mathbf{S}^u$, and the current state, $\mathbf{S}(t)$, and $\mathbf{S}(t + 1)$ is the next state. Major operations in Equation (1) include similarity-measure computation between two M-component vectors, weighted average computation of P inputs, and a nonlinear component, a^ψ. In the following section, we shall present circuits that implement these functions.

2 The Basic Building Block of The MERAM Model

The block diagram of the MERAM model is shown in Figure 1. A similarity computation block is used to find all similarity between the current state (input) and the P memory vectors. This is followed by a module that compute weighted average of these memory vector, using the exponential of the corresponding similarities as weights. In order for easy VLSI implementation, a repeatable MERAM cell is designed. This basic building block contains three elementary circuits to be discussed in the following.

2.1 Similarity Computation Circuit

To compute the similarity-measure between the input pattern and stored patterns, a similarity computation circuit as in Figure 2 is designed. This circuit is derived from the "bump" circuit proposed by Delbück [4]. When V_{out} is much smaller than V_1 and V_2 and the absolute magnitude of the differential input voltage V_{in} is small, both $M1$ and $M2$ operate in the linear region. The output current I_{out} is given by

$$I_{out} = \frac{1}{2}(I_{SS} - \frac{\sqrt{2}}{2}KV_{id}^2). \tag{2}$$

Equation (2) actually computes a similarity measure that is based on the Euclidean distance between two components. If M copy of these circuits are joined at the output nodes, a similarity measure that is proportional to a constant minus the squared Euclidean distance between two M-component vectors can be computed.

2.2 Weighted Average circuit

Figure 3 shows a weighted average circuit [5] composed of simple transconductance amplifiers. Each amplifier supplies a current proportional to the difference between the two input voltages. The contribution of each input to the output voltage is weighted by the transconductance of the corresponding amplifier. The output voltage is given by

$$V_{out} = \frac{\sum_{i=1}^{n} G_i V_i}{\sum_{i=1}^{n} G_i}$$

where G_i is the transconductance of the ith amplifier. In weak-inversion region, G_i depends exponentially on the bias voltage of the current source transistor. Therefore, the actual weights are exponentials of whatever the bias voltages are. If the bias voltage is made proportional to the similarity measure current, then the exponential function as well as the weighted average process is achieved by this circuit alone.

2.3 Current-To-Voltage Converter

Figure 4 illustrates an I-V converter previously proposed [6], which transforms similarity measure currents to bias voltages used in the weighted-average circuit. The transfer function of the I-V converter is

$$R = \frac{V_{out}}{I_{in}} = \frac{1}{K\{V_{DD} + mV_c/(2-m) - 2V_{Tn}/(2-m)\}}$$

where m is a constant typically in the range 1.1 to 1.35. By adjusting control voltage V_b, we get different V_c and hence different resistances to accommodate varying pattern width.

2.4 MERAM cell

Figure 5 shows the basic building block of the MERAM circuit, which includes a similarity computation cell, a transconductance amplifier for weighted average, and a weight storage capacitor and its access switch. Figure 6 illustrates a layout plot of the MERAM cell. The complete MERAM structure including an address decoder and an off-chip weight-refresh structure is depicted in Figure 7.

3 Simulation Results

Suppose that the patterns stored in the MERAM are

$$\left\{ \begin{array}{lll} Pattern\ 1 & : & (\quad 1 \quad\quad 1 \quad\ 1) \\ Pattern\ 2 & : & (-1 \quad\quad 0 \quad\ 1) \\ Pattern\ 3 & : & (\quad 1 \quad -1 \quad\ 0) \end{array} \right\}.$$

HSPICE simulation results of this MERAM circuit are shown in Figure 8. Initial state, $(V_{i1}\ V_{i2}\ V_{i3}) = (0.5V\ 0.5V\ 0.5V)$, is applied to the circuit. At time $5\mu s$, the input switches are closed and the MERAM is allowed to run. In $6\mu s$, the MERAM settles to the correct pattern, the first memory pattern (1 1 1).

4 Conclusion

In this paper, an expandable basic building block of the multivalued exponential recurrent associative memory is presented. This basic building block contains three simple subcircuits. Regular structure and low transistor count characteristics made this design amenable to VLSI implementation for a high-capacity multivalued neural associative memory.

Acknowledgement
This work is supported in part by the National Science Council, Taiwan, ROC under Grant No. NSC83-0404-E-002-060.

References

[1] T. D. Chiueh and R. M. Goodman, "High-capacity exponential associative memory," in *Proc. IEEE Int. Conf. Neural Networks*, San Diego, CA, vol. I, 1988, pp. 153–160

[2] T. D. Chiueh and R. M. Goodman, "Recurrent correlation associative memories," *IEEE Trans. Neural Network*, vol. 2, pp. 275–284, Mar. 1991.

[3] T. D. Chiueh and H. K. Tsai, "Multivalued associative memories based on recurrent networks," *IEEE Trans. Neural Network*, vol. 4, no. 2, pp. 364–366, Mar. 1993.

[4] T. Delbück, ""Bump" circuits for computing similarity and dissimilarity of analog voltage," *Proc. of the International Neural Network Society*, Seattle, Washington, 1991.

[5] C. Mead, *Analog VLSI and neural systems*. Addison-Wesley, Reading MA, 1989.

[6] Z. Wang, "Current-controlled linear MOS earthed and floating resistors and their application," *IEE Proceeding*, Pt. G, vol. 137, no. 6, pp. 479–481, Dec. 1990.

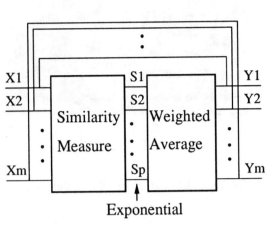

Figure 1: Block diagram of the MERAM model.

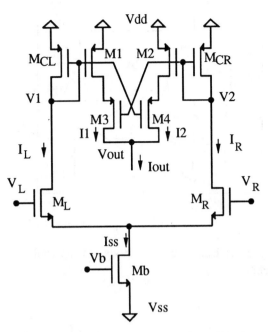

Figure 2: Similarity computation circuit.

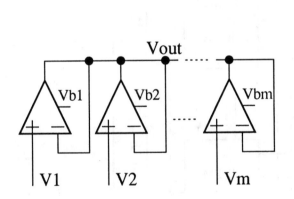

Figure 3: Weighted average circuit.

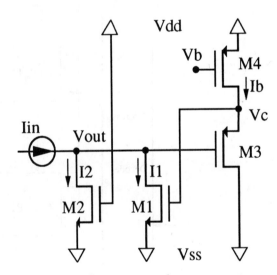

Figure 4: Current-to-voltage converter.

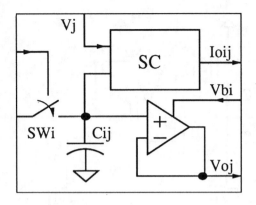

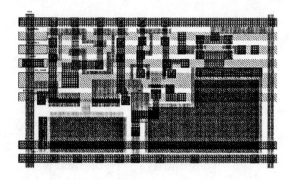

Figure 5: Basic building block of the MERAM circuit.

Figure 6: Layout of the basic building block.

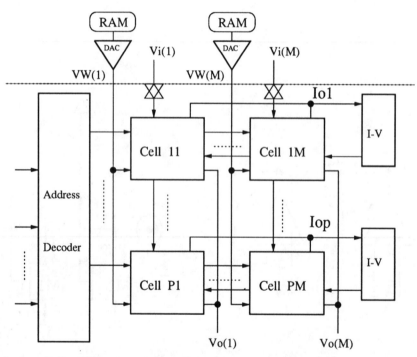

Figure 7: Architecture of the MERAM chip.

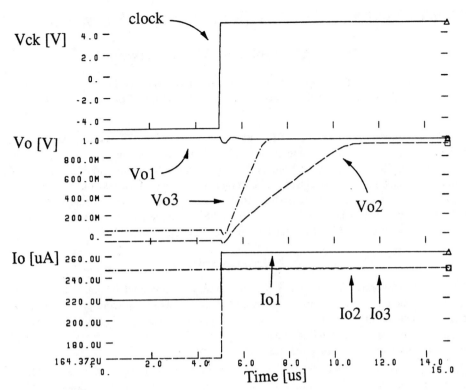

Figure 8: Simulation results of a MERAM with three patterns, each with three components.

Hybrid Chip Set for Artificial Neural Network Systems

B. A. Alhalabi and M. A. Bayoumi

The Center for Advanced Computer Studies
University of Southwestern Louisiana, Lafayette, Louisiana 70504

Abstract: This paper proposes a complete self-contained chip set for ANN systems based on back-propagation model with on-chip learning. We mixed both technologies, digital and analog, as to combine the best of the two worlds. Our system which is constructed from two distinct chips, SynChip and NeuChip, performs the entire neural computations in analog mode. Interface and communications with host and I/O systems is totally digital. A representative system of 3 layers and 100K analog (16–level) synapses per layer would require 300 SynChips and 40 NeuChips and sustain a performance of 31.46 x 10^{15} CPS. Moreover, such a system acquires direct input and output ports with a bandwidth of 12800 digital bits or 3200 analog channels.

I. Introduction

Artificial neural networks, ANNs, have demonstrated an unparalleled potential for tackling nonlinear applications such as vision, recognition, optimization and speech. This magnificent processing power is manifested from the attempt to emulate the brain structure whose recognition capability (distinguishing Steve from Dave) far surpasses the computation capability (adding piles of numbers). The success in neural networks field is substantially bounded by the efficiency of performing the basic ANN computations.

An artificial neural network is a collection of a large number of neurons and their associative weights and the interconnect. Different models develop from different interconnect topologies, the characteristics of the constituent elements and the learning algorithm. Nevertheless, All ANNs share a basic characteristic; They are parallel in nature and for any ANN implementation or algorithm to be meaningful, a large number of processing elements must be utilized. The following is the most experimented neural model.

1. Feed-Forward Network with Back-Propagation Learning

This network consists of L layers and each layer has N neurons. (N may vary from layer to another.) Typically, each neuron receive inputs from all neurons in the preceding layer. Each input is multiplied by the corresponding weight and all the products are added up. Then, a nonlinear function (activation function) is applied to the sum to generate the neuron output (activation value). These activation values are the inputs to the following layer. If the computed output differs from the desired one (precomputed), an error vector is calculated and back propagated through the network in reverse order. On the way, weight are updated gradually in such a way to minimize the error vector as it reaches the input layer. A recursive procedure that uses a set of test inputs and their predetermined outputs is called a training session. For our chip set design, we will utilize the feed forward neural networks model with back learning due to its widespread applications and implementations [9..Nord92].

We will use the index between brackets to indicate the layer number and a superscript to denote the test pattern number. For example $w_{ij}[l]$ represents the element in the ith row and the jth column of the weight matrix $W[l]$ of the lth layer and $a_i^p[l]$ represents the activation value for the ith neuron in the lth layer for the pth input pattern I^p. We will use N_i to denote the number of neurons in layer i. For notation convenience, the input terminals will be considered as layer number 0, thus, N_0 will represent the number of input terminals.

For input pattern $I^p = (I_1^p, I_2^p, \ldots, I_{N_0}^p)$, the system dynamics for the recall phase is given by,

$$a_i[0] = I_i^p \qquad \text{eq. 1}$$

$$a_i[l] = f(h_i[l]) = f\left(\sum_j w_{ij}[l]a_j[l-1]\right). \qquad \text{eq. 2}$$

Each neuron i computes the weighted sum h_i of its inputs and then applies a nonlinear function $f(h_i)$ producing an activation value (output) a_i for this neuron. The function f is usually a sigmoid function.

The authors acknowledge the support of the National Science Foundation and State of Louisiana grant NSF/LEQSF (1992–96)-ADP-04.

For each input I^p, there is a target (desired) output t^p. The backpropagation (BP) learning algorithm gives a prescription for changing the synaptic weights in any feedforward network to learn a training set of input-target pairs. This type of learning is usually referred to as "supervised learning" or "learning by teacher". The learning phase involves two steps. In the first step, the input is presented at the input terminals and is processed by the ANN according to the recall phase equations. In the second step, the produced output is compared to the target and an error measurement value is propagated backward (from the output layer to the first layer) and appropriate changes of weights are made. The second step proceeds along the following iterative equations:

$$\delta_i^p[L] = f'(h_i^p[L])(t_i^p - a_i^p[L]) \qquad\qquad \text{eq. 3}$$

$$\delta_i^p[l] = f'(h_i^p[l]) \sum_j \delta_j^p[l+1]w_{ji}[l+1] \quad \text{for} \quad l = L-1, ..., 2, 1 \qquad\qquad \text{eq. 4}$$

$$\Delta w_{ij}[l] = \eta \delta_i^p[l]a_j^p[l-1] \qquad\qquad \text{eq. 5}$$

$$w_{ij}^{new}[l] = w_{ij}[l] + \Delta w_{ij}[l]. \qquad\qquad \text{eq. 6}$$

2. Analog and Digital Design Issues

Researchers have undertaken two technological disciplines to build or map their ANN implementations: Digital and analog. In digital paradigm, early researchers' emphasis was the efficiency of new algorithm to map ANN into general purpose huge digital machines with massive parallelism power such as the Connection Machine and MassPar. The more enthusiastic digital researchers focussed on building custom VLSI chips to implement ANNs that offer competitive performance and yet much less cost than the giant counterparts. These two digital directions have been extensively studied and compared and many references for representative proposals are enumerated in [9..Nord92]. Whereas, in analog paradigm, researchers claim that digital implementations with both expensive general-purpose machines and specialized custom chips are still too slow for many real-time applications [13..Spie92]. To achieve the reasonably-comparable high speed and small size of the brain, many researchers have concluded that ANNs should be implemented with analog building blocks [11..Schn91].

In spite of the advantages of digital systems such as programming flexibility, computational accuracy, and noise immunity, their inherit drawbacks due to their sequential nature [13..Spie92] make them far less emulative to the brain parallel power than analog counterparts [12..Shim92]. For example to sum 1024 numbers using the fastest tree adders will still take ten time units. In contrast, analog systems with their natural temporal processing capabilities can sum all these numbers in one time unit using one current-summation Op Amp. Another example is the sigmoid function which can be implemented by an integrating Op Amp with an equivalent area size of a digital flip flop. Whereas, in digital systems a huge look-up table is required which is too costly to be replicated for each neuron [11..Schn91].

Analog architectures however, have some drawbacks, the greatest of which is storing the weight coefficients and maintaining their analog level [5..Hasl91]. Many researchers have already devised efficient architectures to overcome these inherent analog difficulties [10..Saty92] [2..Barr92] [12..Shim92] [13..Spie92]. Several of these proposed analog architectures have been already fabricated and tested and fascinating results were obtained [3..Bose91] [1..Arim92] [12..Shim92].

Moreover, the classical problems of the analog components have been progressively solved due to the latest advances in VLSI technology and research. For instance, to maintain the charge value on a capacitor representing a synaptic weight, researchers have developed several methods for refreshing [7..Lee92] [4..Eber89] [6..Holl89] [1..Arim92]. Also, the limited accuracy of analog elements is not problematic due to the fact that neural networks are tolerant to the errors of the individual elements. That is because the network output is the aggregate response of too many constituent elements to and it is less likely to be distorted by minor element degradation [3..Bose91] [11..Schn91] [8..Mont92]. In the past three years, several researchers have proposed analog neural networks occupying a total silicon area of few square inches with performance equivalent to digital systems with 10^{12}–10^{13} FLOPS processing power [13..Spie92].

II. Hybrid Systems and an Optimal ANN Chip Set

The hybrid system, we are proposing, is a complete self-contained ANN system for back propagation model. We mixed both technologies, digital and analog, as to combine the best of the two worlds. During the discussion of the system components, the following points must be kept in mined. In the figures, the solid lines represent digital signals, whereas the doted lines represent analog signals. Moreover, all directive clauses such as horizontally, vertically, left to right, and top-down, are relatively in tact when you look at a particular layer of the system such that SynChip, NeuChip, SynMod, and NeuMod labels are read straight.

1. General Organization

The proposed architecture is based on two distinct chips: SynChip and NeuChip. These two chips may be cascaded in a regular-grid fashion to build an ANN of any arbitrary input, output, and layer sizes as illustrated in Fig. 1. The example of Fig.1 shows a network of two layers the first of which consists of 3x2 SynChips and 2 NeuChips and the second of 2x2 SynChips and 2 NeuChips. Layer 0 has only NeuChips (in this example 3). To expand the input bandwidth of the network, more columns (1 NeuChip and 2 SynChips) may be appended to the left side of the network and with each new column, 128 digital (32 analog) direct inputs are added. Same analogy applies to the expansion of the output bandwidth at the right side of the network. Moreover, with the input and output bandwidth remains the same, the network can be expanded vertically to increase the size of the synaptic weight matrix for higher accuracy and greater memorization capacity. This is done by appending more rows (1 NeuChip and 5 SynChips) to the bottom of the network.

The chips are connected side to side for simple Printed Circuit Board or Multi Chip Module fabrication. Furthermore, the SynChip is necessarily square as to appropriate the side-to-side connection with the NeuChips from both top and right sides as shown in Fig.1. Expansion with this simplicity and readiness would have been impossible in digital systems as will be elaborated on latter.

2. SynChip and NeuChip

The block diagrams of the SynChip and NeuChip and their interconnection relationships are depicted in Fig.2 which is a close look of a SynChip and its neighbor NeuChip of Layer1 of the network of Fig.1. The digital host bus (DataAdd) runs between the chips to pass the necessary signals to all NeuChips and SynChips in the same row. These bus lines are the only exception to the localization of the system interchip connectivity. Note that the top side of the SynChip (Fig.2) mates directly to the bottom side of another SynChip and to the right side of the NeuChip. Also, the right side of SynChip mates directly to the left side of another SynChip and to the left side of the NeuChip.

The NeuChip (Fig.2) consists of 32 analog neuron modules, NeuMod (Fig.4), and a digital control block, NeuLogic. The SynChip consists of an array of 32x32 analog synapse modules, SynMod (Fig.3), a digital control block, SynLogic, a voltage reference of 16 levels, and 32 refreshing blocks, RefMod. The circuitries of SynLogic and NeuLogic (white blocks in Fig.2) are pure digital, whereas, all other blocks are mostly analog. This mixture of technologies allowed us to integrate the small size of analog functional units with the convenient control and interface of conventional digital host computers. The following is a detailed description of these two chips and their constituent building blocks.

Through the right side and from the host bus (DataAdd), the SynChip receives some digital signals (solid lines) such as address and data. These signals are used by the SynLogic block and passed to the adjacent SynChip through the left side. Also (looking at Fig.2), the SynChip receives horizontal control lines (HorCont) from the NeuChip of the same layer and vertical control lines (VerCont) from the NeuChip of the previous layer. Note that the HorCont and VerCont lines respectively propagate horizontally and vertically throughout the entire matrix of SynChips within the same layer. Derived from these signals, DataAdd, HorCont, and VerCont, the SynLogic of every SynChip generates and stores all local and global addressing signals, configuration parameters, and modes of operation. The outputs of the SynLogic block (Fig.2) are the RefCont bus and a set of 32 SynCont busses. The RefCont signals connect to all 32 vertical refreshing modules (RefMod) to provide the proper refreshing control. Each RefMod is responsible for refreshing the synapses of the 32 SynMods to its left. Each SynCont bus connects to the 32 SynMods in the same column.

Besides the digital control signals, the SynChip has two sets of analog lines (dotted lines in Fig.2): 32 horizontal analog lines (HAL1–i–32) and 32 vertical analog lines (VAL1–j–32). The HALs are all physical analog wires which run horizontally across each SynChip from left to right and from one SynChip to another till they mate directly to the left side of the NeuChip within the same layer. Same thing for the VALs except that they run vertically to mate directly to the right side of NeuChip of the previous layer. Both HALs and VALs are bidirectional analog lines which either collect current signals from SynMods and inject them into the NeuMods, or take voltage signals form NeuMods and distribute them to SynMods.

The NeuChip comprises the NeuLogic and the 32 NeuMod blocks as depicted in Fig.2. The NeuLogic which encapsulates all digital control circuitries receives DataAdd signals from the host bus as well as a special signal (ScanIn) from the NeuChip of the previous layer. The NeuLogic blocks are responsible for the generation of all addressing signals; They generate the HorCont busses from the left side to control all the rows within the same layer, and the VerCont busses from the right side to control all the columns of the next layer. Note that one NeuChip controls one complete row of SynChips within the same layer and one complete column of SynChips of the next layer. In addition to the HorCont and VerCont addressing signals, the NeuLogic generates a special signal (ScanOut) which connects to the ScanIn line of the succeeding NeuChip. This ScanIn/ScanOut sequence from one NeuChip to another within the same layer and from one layer to another is our new technique for sequential initialization of all the layers in the system (see the hair line connecting all NeuChips in the 2-layer system of Fig.1). As will be detailed latter, this technique eliminates the need for an off-chip global addressing hardware.

3. NeuLogic and SynLogic

The NeuLogic of the NeuChip encapsulates the digital control of the system initialization, interchip addressing, and various modes of operation. System Initialization is a sequence of host operations which, for each NeuChip, downloads a unique identification label to a dedicated register called LAY-ROWCOL. The 3-bit LAY part of this register identifies the number of the layer to which this NeuChip belongs. The 8-bit ROWCOL part of the identification register holds one number that serves two purposes. On one hand, it identifies within the same layer, the row number of the SynChips matrix to which this particular NeuChip is associated. On the other hand, it identifies the column number within the next layer. These two numbers, LAY and ROWCOL, once loaded in the initialization sequence, remain unchanged throughout the entire system operation until the system is reset. During all modes of operation, they are used for chip address decoding purposes. For the network of Fig.1, the addresses are:

$L, N_0, N_1, N_2 = 2,3,2,2,$

and the LAY-ROWCOL binary values are:

000-00000001, 000-000000010, 000-00000011
001-00000001, 001-000000010
010-00000001, 010-000000010.

Have all the LAY-ROWCOL registers been initialized, every SynChip of the system is now uniquely addressable. Note that the maximum system configuration is 8 layers and 256x256 SynChips per layer (64Meg synapses per layer). The host accesses any SynChip by placing the layer, row, and column numbers on address lines A23-21, A20-13, and A12-5, respectively. The least significant five bits of the host address, A4-0, are used to identify a column of SynMods within the SynChip. This would enable the host to load/unload data to/from 32 synapses at a time. A SynChip requires 32 bus cycles to complete the weight load/unload process.

The CONFIG register is used to hold the system configuration information such as setting the NeuChips of any layer to act as input, intermediate, or output stage, or to accept/produce analog or digital direct inputs/outputs. Moreover, the CONFIG register holds the information which identifies the mode of operation such as Recall, Learn, Load, Unload and others. When A25A24=10 , the host can write to the CONFIG register of all NeuChips of one layer identified by A23-21, but when A25A24=11, it writes to all CONFIG registers of all NeuChips of the system. All these configuration informations are decoded to generate the neuron control bus, NeuCont, which is passed to all the NeuMods of the NeuChip (Fig.2). The control signals, NeuCont and SynCont, orchestrate the switches inside the NeuMods and SynMods and the final settings of all switches determine the state of the ANN system. The system can be configured for ten different neural operations

The CONFIG register of the SynLogic of the SynChip is just a copy of that of the NeuLogic and it is loaded in the same fashion. The Addressing Logic block takes the VerCont and HorCont busses, the low address lines (A4-0), and the configuration bits (CONFIG register) to generate the necessary control signals inside the SynChip. The Refreshing Logic block generates the sequential refreshing control signals fed to the DEC blocks. The RefCont bus signals generated by decoder DEC, identically control the switches in all RefMods (Fig.2). Similarly each SynCont bus generated by decoder DECj, identically control the switches in all SynMods of column j.

4. SynMod, Synapse Module

The synapse module is illustrated in Fig.3. The solid hexagons labeled SS1-8 (synapse switches) are all unidirectional (except SS1 and SS4) passive analog switches each of which is controlled by a dedicated digital control signal (not shown in the figure for clarity) from the Switches Control block. These digital control signals are level-sensitive (high=on and low=off).

The VALj line (Fig.3) carries the activation value $a_j[l-1]$ as a voltage level from the previous layer and passes it vertically to all SynMods$_{(1j-32j)}$ in all SynChips within the same layer. This activation value and the weight value w_{ij}, stored in capacitor Cw, are presented by SS7 and SS2, respectively, to the voltage multiplier $a_j w_{ij}$ (Fig.3). The multiplier acts as a current source and its output whose value is proportional to the inputs voltage levels passes to the HALi line via switch SS6. The HALi line horizontally collects all current contributions $\{a_j[l-1]w_{ij}[l]\}$ from all SynMods$_{(i32-i1)}$ of all SynChips (Fig.1) within the same layer and present the accumulated current to the corresponding NeuMod which is a current-summing OpAmp (Fig.4). Thus, in the recall mode of operation, SS2, SS6, and SS7 are on and the data flows into the SynChips as voltages via the VAL lines and flows out as currents via the HAL lines.

In the learning mode of operation, SS5 and SS8 are on instead of SS6 and SS7 as to allow data to flow backward; Error signals $\delta_i[l]$ (Fig.3), coming from the NeuChips of the same layer, flow into the SynChips as voltages via the HAL lines, get manipulated, and flow out as currents $\{\delta_i[l]w_{ij}[l]\}$ via the VAL lines. These currents which are the product outputs of the individual $\delta_i w_{ij}$ voltage multipliers accumulate vertically on the VAL lines and finally get added up in the NeuChips of the previous layer. (See the current input at the right side of the NeuMod in Fig.4.) The third voltage multiplier in the SynMod calculates the weight update value $\Delta w_{ij} = a_j \delta_i \eta$ which is the product of the activation value of previous layer, error value, and learning factor. The product output is added (by the Adder Block) to the original value of the weight and the new weight value is determined. Then, switch SS3 comes on to update the Cw voltage level. (Note that SS3 inhibitively turns SS2 off.)

The triangular block labeled Buff is a voltage buffer which helps the weight capacitor Cw retains its voltage level against charge sharing with other functional units. The η block represents the learning factor which is a constant generated at the SynChip level and distributed to all SynMods in the SynChip. Capacitor Ca is utilized to temporarily store the last activation value when the mode of operation is switched to learning. Switch SS4 and the RefVolt horizontal line are utilized by the refreshing mechanism to refresh the synaptic weights as will be explored latter. Finally, SS1 is provided to load/unload the weight value to/from capacitor Cw.

If the system has been previously trained and all synaptic weights are known, they may by downloaded from the host to the SynChips and stored in the analog capacitors. Note that the subscript of the weights (e.g. $w_{(32r-31)(32c+s-1)}[l]$) represent the weight index in the weigh matrix of layer [l] as a whole. For example, $w_{278\ 517}[2]$ will be downloaded to Cw of SynMod$_{ij}$ = SynMod$_{22\ 5}$ (Fig.2) of the SynChip in row r=9 and column c=17 of layer 2.

5. NeuMod, Neuron Module

The neuron module, NeuMod, is illustrated in Fig.4. Note that in contrast to the SynMod, the HAL and VAL lines of the NeuMod do not pass throughout the module from side to side; They are two different signals. The summation block $h_i = \sum_j a_j w_{ij}$ is a current-summing OpAmp which adds up all currents $\{a_j[l-1]w_{ij}[l]\}$ accumulated on the HALi line. The sum is passed through the nonlinear function block $f(h_i)$ to compute the activation value $a_i[1]$ for the next layer. This activation value is presented as a voltage level on the VALi line via switch NS8 (Fig.4). Therefore, in a normal recall mode, only NS1 and NS8 are turned on. However, if there is a desire to monitor the activation values of any layer [l] by the host, switch NS6 may be turned on and the analog value $a_i[1]$ is digitized by the ADC block and its 4-bit representation is read off the 4-bit data lines D(4i-4)–(4i-1). Note that the data bus of the host is 128-bit wide allowing the host to read all of the 32 4-bit activation values from the 32 NeuMods in one NeuChip in one bus cycle. (See the data lines at the left side of the NeuChip of Fig.2.) Moreover, in some cases, it might be desired to obtain the activation value $a_i[1]$ through NS6, ADC, DAC, and NS10 instead of directly via NS8.

In the learning operation the data flow is reversed as the error signals propagated backwards: at every VALi line, a set of currents $\{\delta_j[l+1]w_{ji}[l+1]\}$ accumulate and pass to the summation block $\sigma_i = \sum_j \delta_j w_{ji}$ via NS12. The sum, then, passes NS11 to the multiplier $\delta_i = f'(h_i)\sigma_i$ to generate the error $\delta_i[l]$ which is outputted at HALi via NS2. Note that the multiplier obtains the value $f'(h_i)$ from the $f'(h_i)$ block whose input value h_i was temporarily stored in capacitor Ch during the recall phase. Switch NS3 turns off in the learning phase to retain the Ch voltage level.

Loading/unloading the synaptic weights to/from the capacitors from/to the host is done via the HAL line and switches NS4 and NS5. The ADC and DAC are connected back to back through the 4-bit register, LATCH, which is connected to the host data bus. Switches NS7 and NS9 are provided to monitor and control the values of the error signals.

III. Conclusions

In this proposal, we adopted analog technology in developing algorithms and architectures for a self-contained neural processor. The entire ANN computations within the proposed modules are performed in analog. These analog operations of the processor core provide a natural implementation of neural models as it loosely emulates the information flow of the brain. Moreover, digital circuits are employed to facilitate the interface and communications with conventional digital hosts. Combining both technologies provided the optimal chip set design for neural systems. The main features of the system are:

- Complete system-level integration for feed-forward model with back-propagation algorithm.

- System based on two distinct chips, synapse and neuron chips. The chips are especially laid out and sized for cascading on regular grid to readily form networks of any size including a whole-wafer level.

- The synapse chip has 1k analog synapses with automatic host-invisible macroscopic refreshing scheme.

- The neuron chip has 32 analog neurons with special hardware to support back propagation learning signals.

- All ANN computations (multiplications, additions, and sigmoid functions) are done in analog.

- The system supports multiples of 128 (one synapse chip) direct digital inputs. Also, direct digital outputs are provided as multiples of 128. These I/O lines can be clustered into any standard word-length format.

- On-chip full learning hardware mechanism.

- System may be configured to operate synchronously or asynchronously

- The host can monitor any part(s) of the system by reading its neural values.

- In the recall operations, pipelining is possible and it allows a throughput of one pattern per bus cycle. Whereas in training operations, pipelining is not allowed, however, training requires two bus cycles, one to recall the pattern and one to learn its desired response.

Bibliography

[1] Y. Arima and M. Murasaki. A refreshable analog vlsi neural network chip with 400 neurons and 40k synapses. *IEEE Journal of Solid-State Circuits*, vol.27(no.12):pp.1854–1861, December 1992.

[2] B. L. Barranco and E. S. Sinencio. A modular t-mode design approach for analaog neural network hardware implementations. *IEEE Journal of Solid-State Circuits*, vol.27(no.5):pp.701–713, May 1992.

[3] B. E. Boser and E. Sackinger. An analog neural network processor with programmable topology. *IEEE Journal of Solid-State Circuits*, vol.26(no.12):pp.2017–2025, December 1991.

[4] S. Ebberhardt and T. Duong. Design of parallel hardware neural network systems from custom analog vlsi 'building block' chips. *International Joint Conference on Neural Netwoks*, vol.II:pp.183–189, June 1989.

[5] P. Hasler and L. Akers. A continuous time synapse employing a refreshable multilevel memory. *International Joint Conference on Neural Netwoks*, vol.I:pp.563–568, July 1991.

[6] M. Holler and S. Tam. An electrically trainable artificial neural network (etann) with 10240 "floating gate" synapses. *International Joint Conference on Neural Netwoks*, vol.II:pp.191–196, June 1989.

[7] B. W. Lee and B. J. Sheu. General-purpose neural chips with electrically programmable synapses and gain-adjustable neurons. *IEEE Journal of Solid-State Circuits*, vol.27(no.9):pp.1299–1302, September 1992.

[8] A. J. Montalvo and P. W. Hollis. On-chip learning in the analog domain with limited precision circuits. *International Joint Conference on Neural Netwoks*, vol.I:pp.196–201, June 1992.

[9] T. Nordstorm and B. Svensson. Using and designing massively parallel computers for artificial neural networks. *Journal of Paraller and Distributed Computing*, vol.14:pp.260–285, 1992.

[10] S. Satyanarayana and Y. P. Tsividis. A reconfigurable vlsi neural network. *IEEE Journal of Solid-State Circuits*, vol.27(no.1):pp.67–81, January 1992.

[11] C. Schneider and H. Card. Cmos implementaion of analog hebbian synaptic learning circuits. *International Joint Conference on Neural Netwoks*, vol.I:pp.437–442, July 1991.

[12] T. Shima and T. Kimura. Neuro chips with on-chip back-propagation and/or hebbian learning. *IEEE Journal of Solid-State Circuits*, vol.27(no.12):pp.1868–1876, December 1992.

[13] J. V. Spiegel and P. Mueller. An analog neural computer with modular architecture for real-time dynamic computations. *IEEE Journal of Solid-State Circuits*, vol.27(no.1):pp.82–92, January 1992.

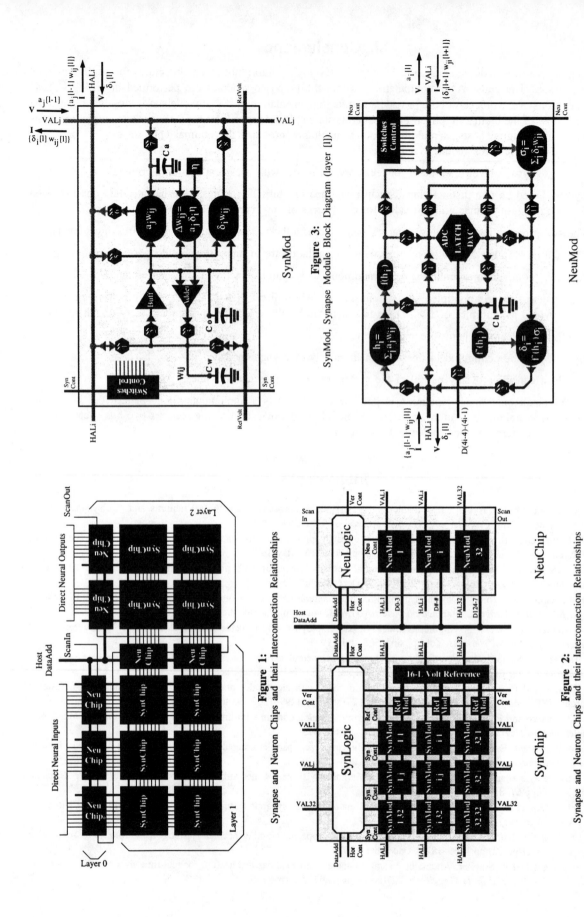

Figure 3:
SynMod, Synapse Module Block Diagram (layer [l]).

Figure 4:
NeuMod, Neuron Module Block Diagram (layer [l]).

Figure 1:
Synapse and Neuron Chips and their Interconnection Relationships

Figure 2:
Synapse and Neuron Chips and their Interconnection Relationships

A Neural Network VME-module for recognizing AC Current Demand Signatures in Space Shuttle Telemetry Data

Robert O. Shelton

Information Technology Division, Software Technology Branch (PT4)

NASA Johnson Space Center, Houston, TX, USA

Sölve Hultberg and Thomas Lindblad
Department of Physics (Frescati)
Royal Institute of Technology, Stockholm Sweden[1)]

Abstract: An implementation of an analog neural network trained to identify signatures from the AC electrical power system on the Space Shuttle Orbiter is described. This demonstration project shows that a small stand alone system in the form of a VME-module can be designed, constructed and tested within days, provided a proper set of training vectors are available.

1. Introduction

In the Mission Control Center (MCC), situated at the NASA Johnson Space Center in Houston TX [1], controllers visually monitor many critical systems on the space shuttle orbiter by means of paper strip chart displays. In some cases, such as the Electrical Generation and Integrated Loading (EGIL) system, the controllers must recognize signatures of various events by inspection of the strip chart. Events here are transient signals produced by startup of various devices such as fans, pumps, etc. Each event produces a fairly unique signal. The EGIL controllers must optimize the use of fuel for power generation. It is imperative that the state of the system, i.e., which loads are present, be known at all times.

With the introduction of the Real-Time Data System (RTDS) [2], which makes over 1400 shuttle telemetry channels available on conventional work-stations at the Johnson Space Center (JSC) as well as other NASA centers, it is now possible for researchers to tap into real-time data in order to develop advanced automation techniques. The EGIL signatures provide an ideal situation to test advanced pattern recognition methods . If successful, the method would contribute significantly to improve the efficiency in an operations environment. To this end, a UNIX-based application was created by a group in the Software Technology Branch of NASA/JSC [3].

[1)] Formerly the Manne Siegbahn Institute of Physics

Fig. 1. Photo of the Endavour shuttle.

The application [3] can read any RTDS channel and includes a screening algorithm which captures EGIL events, and several pattern recognition algorithms which process these events. The algorithms tested to date include cross correlation, a fuzzy Bayesian classifier, a back-propagation neural network classifier, a "binary" neural network and a basis function classifier. This application has run in the MCC as well as on distributed RTDS work-stations, during three shuttle flights [4]. The classification methods are evaluated post-flight by comparing results to controller logs and by consultation with EGIL controllers. Although the original purpose of the project was to construct a software pattern recognition and signature analysis tool-kit for MCC controllers, the issues related to building the MCC applications are quite general. It is easy to imagine situations where it would be useful to be able to recognize similar signatures without using a UNIX work-station, but rather to incorporate advanced neural-based pattern recognition algorithms into application specific analog circuits (ASIC). ASIC devices are considered to be the logical next step toward the creation of "smart" sensors — devices which combine measurement and low-level interpretation/ pattern recognition. The fact that it was possible to go from a data set to an operational classifier in silicon in a matter of days makes a strong case for the practicality of such an approach.

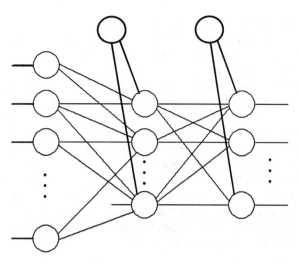

Fig. 2. Schematic drawaing of the neural network used in the present investigation. There are 60 inputs, 30 hidden neurons and 9 output neurons. Note that each active layer has a bias neuron (two top circles).

2.   Collection of Sample Signatures

The current flows in the three three-phase AC electrical busses on the shuttle orbiter are monitored at a rate of 10 Hertz and these values enter the shuttle telemetry frame that is fed to the Real-Time Data System (RTDS). The data acquired by the EGIL application consists of 9 streams (three busses by three phases) of real values, each stream arriving at 10 Hertz. To apply pattern identification, it is necessary to perform figure-ground segmentation, i.e. define events in a form suitable for processing by pattern recognition algorithms, and implement a segmentation process to extract events from the data stream. As is normally the case for such problems, the event detection scheme for the EGIL signatures is highly domain-specific. In particular, the definition of an event is driven by two opposing requirements. The window should be large enough to characterize the event, but sufficiently narrow to provide timely identification for the EGIL controllers. Initial experiments demonstrated that there is no value for which both conditions are completely satisfied. The value that was adopted (6 seconds) was chosen as the largest delay acceptable to the controllers. In practice, most events are well characterized by a relatively short — less than 2 seconds — start-up transient followed by a steady-state load. Other events, such as door activation sequences, that do not follow such a profile must be treated as series of shorter events, and the final recognition of the sequence is performed by logic that follows the window-based pattern recognition. This situation is similar to the problems with recognition of continuous speech in which phoneme-based pattern recognition is followed by logic that understands the context of phonemes in a sequential grammar. Once the window size is determined, it is only necessary to determine a condition that signals the beginning of an event. Since the events for which pattern recognition would be required are all start-up signatures of devices being turned on, a simple slope-threshold event detector was implemented. Specifically, a smoothed value of the first derivative of the current was computed and compared to an experimentally determined threshold. When the estimate of the rate of change of any phase of any bus exceeds the threshold, an event is opened on all three phases of that bus. The 180 values corresponding to 6 seconds of 10 Hertz data on three phases of one bus comprise an event. Some events, such as motor starts, are characterized by three similar patterns on each phase, while others, such as lighting events, only show demand on a single phase. In either case, it is reasonable to process events one phase at a time. Finally, to eliminate as much context sensitivity as possible, an estimate of the background (pre-event) current on each phase is subtracted from the values before they are processed by the pattern recognition algorithm. Examples of events are shown in fig. 3 and a list of events considered are given in table 1.

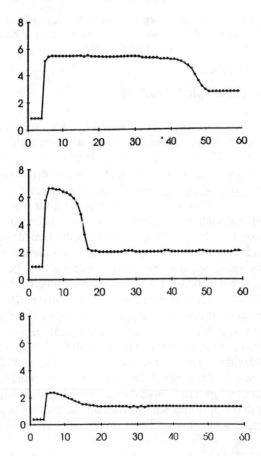

Fig. 3. Examples of three different AC current signatures sampled at 10 Hz. The horizontal axis corresponds to 60 channels equal to 6 seconds.

II-634

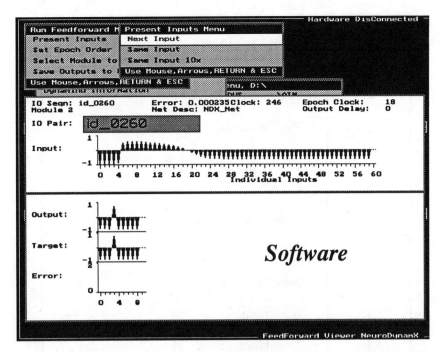

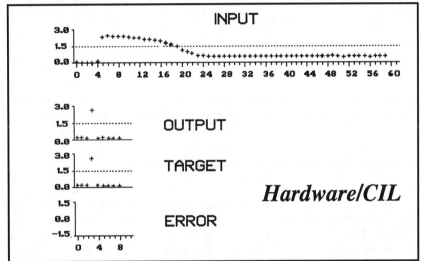

Fig. 4 .Example of a test vector during simulation using the DynaMind code (top) and during the hardware run (bottom). In the latter case an analog voltage of 0 to 3 volts is presented to each of the 60 input nodes. The 9 output nodes will have a voltage close to 3 volts on the node corresponding to the pertinent event, while all other nodes output voltages are close to zero volts.

Signal ID-no.	Signal origin, etc
0	Conventional toilet (WCS)
1	Vacuum cleaner
2	Flood lights (1 phase), Multi urine fan
3	Cabin fan
4	Gallery fan
5	CO_2 recycling system (RCRS)
6	Propellant valve
7	Water pump
8	Termal impact printer, Multi Commode fan
none	Undefined

Table 1 . The various origin of the selected AC-signals considered for identification in the present investigation. Examples of the type 1, 2 and 6 signals are shown in fig. 3

3. Neural Network Architecture and Training

Following the selection of the training vectors as described above a total set of nearly 1500 training pairs was available. Each set consisted of 69 floating-point numbers, such that 60 of these served as input values while 9 represented expected outputs. We use 80 percent of these for training and 20% for testing the neural network. This is a straightforward and quite general procedure. Since we have 60 input numbers and 9 output numbers, the network will have exactly those numbers of neurons for the input and output layers, respectively (cf. fig 2). The input numbers are normalized to the range -1 to +1 corresponding to 0.0 amps to about 8.5 amps and rearranged to the iDynamind format [5] using a short C++ program. The 9 outputs will represent the events given in table 1. During training a "-0.8" ("+0.8") value will represent a "high" ("low") bit.

The training proceeded in two steps. Firstly, we simulated the network with the iDynaMind [5] code and a fairly "classical" backpropagation. The network had 30 neurons in the hidden layer and sigmoid transfer functions (cf. fig. 4). Following some 3000 epochs of training, during which the learning rate was changed interactively from 0.20 to 0.12, all the data in the training set produced the proper answers. By this we mean that there was one and only one of the 9 outputs that yielded an output larger than "0" while the rest of the outputs remained negative. Clearly, the criteria could be chosen differently, and in the vast majority of cases we have "very binary" outputs, i.e. one output is close to "0.8" while the rest of the outputs are close to "-0.8". This is discussed in ref [8-10]. An example of a test vector (as well as the result) is shown in the top part of fig. 4. Although this is a very representative case, there are a few I/O-vectors where two events (mainly no. 4 and 6) come very close, when presented to the present network. The total average square error is, however, very small (0.1%).

The second part of the training is referred to as "chip-in-loop" or CIL training and involves presenting the ETANN 80170 chip with the actual analog input data and reading the outputs. The chip will be presented with a voltage in the range 0 - 3 volts corresponding to the "-1" and "+1" above. In a real implementation, these values correspond to currents in the range of 0.0 to 8.5 amps. The CIL training is performed using the Intel ETANN development system [4,6] . The same set of more than 1000 training vectors were used but now the training proceeds more slowly. After several hours and 300 epochs, an average error of 0.20% was achieved and the training was terminated. A subsequent test using those I/O-pairs not included in the training show that in all cases but five, the neural network will identify the proper event. Again we have some problems with events 4 and 6. Most likely these events are too few in the training set and this problem could be overcome by including more examples of both events. Generally speaking though, it is quite clear that the system behaves very well and returns the proper event in 99% of the cases. The bottom part of fig. 4 shows, as an example of the hardware test, the same vector as mentioned above.

4. Hardware implementation

After the CIL training above, the chip is placed on a double-height VME-card as shown in figs. 5 - 6. This card is based on the ELTEC SAC-8 module [7] and has been used previously [8-10] in connection with other NNW implementations. The VME-module has two parts of which the top one is a rather straighforward design of a 68070 micro-computer. This system is shown in fig. 5 and has a kernel-code in EPROM making it possible to execute a code down-loaded to the RAM or permanently residing in the EPROM. The lower half of the module contains a piggy-back card with the ETANN mounted on the VME-board on top of eight 8-fold digital to analog converters. This piggy-back card connects to the motherboard by means of two 96 pole Euro-connectors. Rows "a" and "c" of one of these connectors carry the input signals, while the outputs are available on the other connector (the control signals are available in the middle "b" row of the connector). In this way, it is possible to use a short flat cable to connect a 64 pole input front panel connector to the ETANN piggyback card (fig. 6). The discriminators and interface electronics are mounted on the VME-board in essentially the same way as in refs [8-10]. The only major difference in the present implementation is that we are using 60 inputs rather than 64 and that we use 9 outputs, representing the 9 possible classes. The analog to digital converters employed at the outputs in refs [8-10] are thus not necessary.

Instead a simple logic decoder is employed (lower right corner of fig. 5).The 60 analog inputs are also directly available from the front panel of the VME-module using a short flat-cable to the ETANN piggy-back card. This means that the card can be used with inputs either directly with analog signals in the range of 0.1 to 3.0 volts or from the VME-system following conversion of the digial data as mentioned above. The response of the neurons is determined by three voltages V_{gain}, V_{refi}, and V_{refo}, which get their values by the code via DACs (cf. fig. 4). The neuron response is approximated by a tanh function

$$f_j(x_j) = 3.0/[1.0 + \exp(x_j)] + 0.06 \text{ volts}, \tag{1}$$

where

$$x_j = \Sigma\, w_{jh}(V_h - 1.6) + \Sigma\, w_{jb}(V_b - 1.6), \tag{2}$$

and where w_{jh} and w_{jb} are weights. In eq. (2) we have used values of the three reference voltages corresponding to 3.3, 1.49 and 1.6 volts, respectively.

After signals are presented to the hidden layer (cf. fig. 2), the outputs of this layer are available at the chip output pins. These signals will, however, be the input to the output layer and this processing is controlled with several clock signals generated by the software. The processing of the hidden layer takes about 3 μs and of the output layer approximately 5 μs, i.e a total of 8 μs is required for one input.

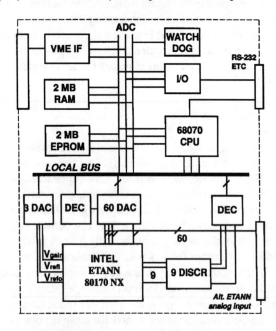

Fig. 5. Block scheme of the VME-module showing the ETANN stand-alone implementation. The top part is a commercial 68K based computer, which connects to the user-specific part (bottom). Note that inputs to the ETANN can be either from the VME-bus, the RAM memory (in the case of which 60 DACs are used) or from a front panel connector (analog inputs).

Fig. 6. Photo of the semi-custom VME-module shown as a block scheme in fig. 5. The proprietary bus is available on the connector joining the 68070 computer part and the ETANN part. The ETANN chip is mounted on a piggy-back card with analog inputs/outputs available (on rows a and c) of a Euroconnectors. The former ones are made available to a 64 pin front-panel connector through a short flat cable.

We are using a cross-assembler code and a special program to download this code in Motorola S-format. Although we download the code over the VME-bus, the "kernel" also supports downloading via the RS-232 front panel serial interface. The executable code resides from address 1000 (HEX) and is then started by typing "GO 1000" on the terminal (connected to the aforementioned front panel serial port). Depending on the code previously downloaded, the ETANN will take inputs either from the dual-ported RAM belonging to the 68070 system or from the analog inputs. When used in the latter mode, nothing but the power supply is required for the VME-module. However, if data is presented in digital form, another VME module is expected to place the input vectors in the dual-ported RAM of the present board or, alternatively, this can be included in the assembler code of the 68070 CPU. A photograph of the VME-module is shown in fig. 6

5.   Summary and conclusions

The main goal of the present investigation has been to show that it is possible to design, train and implement an analog neural network (the ETANN 80170) on a semi-ready "standard" VME-module using very few extra components and that it requires very little time for special design. Clearly the neural network in the present case is not a very complicated one. However, we feel it is a typical one and well suited for the analog ETANN chip. Furthermore, the use of a cross-assembler running on a PC/386/486 has made the software development for the target easy and conveniently located on the same "platform" as the ETANN development system (INNTS).

6. Acknowledgements

The authors would like to acknowledge the support of the Carl Trygger Foundation and the Swedish Research Council for Engineering Sciences (TFR). Comments by Clark S. Lindsey on the manuscript is appreciated.

References

1. Orignal signature clasification by Ms Lynn Fox (priv. comm); flight controller, MCC, JSC, NASA, Houston TX

2. J. Mutatore, *et al.*, "Real-Time Data Acquisition at Mission Control", Communication of the ACM, 33:12 (December 1990), pp 18-31.

3. David G. Hammen, Travis A. Moebes, Robert T. Savely and Robert O. Shelton: " A Strip Chart Pattern Recognition Tool Kit for Shuttle Operations", Proceedings of American Institute of Aeronautics and Astronautics, San Diego, October, 1993

4. 80170NX Electrically Trainable Analog Neural Network, Intel Corp, 1993 (March)

5. iDynaMind User´s Guide Version 3.0, NeuroDynamX, Boulder, CO, 1992

6. INNTS User´s Guide Version 3.0, Intel Corp., Santa Clara, CA, 1992

7. ELTEC Elektronik, GMbH, Mainz, Germany, SAC-700/800 User´s manual

8. B. Denby, Th. Lindblad, C.S. Lindsey, Géza Székely, J. Molnar, Åge Eide, S.R. Amendolia and A. Spaziani, Nucl. Instr. Meth. **A335**(1993)296-304

9. J. Molnar, G. Székely, Th. Lindblad, C.S. Lindsey, B. Denby, S.R. Amendolia and Å. Eide, to be published in ICFA Instrumentation Bulletin spring 1994.

10. Tommy, Akkila, Tom Francke, Thomas Lindblad and Åge Eide, An analog neural network hardware solution to a Cherenkov ring imaging particle identifier, Nucl. Instr. Meth. **A327**(1993)566-572

Image Restoration and Compression by Neurochips

Harold Szu and Joseph Landa

Physics Dept. , American University, Mass Ave. NW, Washington DC 20016
NSWC Dahlgren Division, Code B44, Silver Spring/White Oak MD 20903-5640

Abstract

Real time implementation of the Wiener filters for noisy TV imagery restoration is given at the pixel level employing a massive parallel neurochip. Furthermore, mimicking the human visual system, we use the Maxican hat Wavelet Transform (WT) to compress the TV imagery and then we can efficiently restore those dominant scales information for channel distortion in satellite and/or fiberoptics communications. We have coined the name Wiener-Hopfield Neurochip for such a class of LMS restoration neurochips which can solve a large class of filtering in the digital domain.

1.   Introduction

Why should we use the artificial neural network (ANN) technology for image processing in the first place?

Since ANN is a mature technology, various application neurochips are available [1-4]. Since the set of data that a high definition television (HDTV) has is about a few million pixels changing in time (with a 30 Hz frame rate), then each pixel is closely matched with the discrete nature of simple neuron processor in time, and the architecture of massively parallel ANN matches naturally with the liquid crystal projection style circuitry board. Since the input and the output relationship can not be certain in all cases (e.g. due to the propagation medium fluctuations), and since an adaptive echo cancellation may be necessary (e.g. due to the impedance mismatch discontinuity at the electrical and fiberoptical connectors), then a hardware implementation of a distributive, and fault-tolerant ANN algorithm becomes desirable. In this paper, we point out that Hopfield-like neurochip is available, that happens to be designed by input currents and output voltages. Therefore, we have mathematically mapped the image domain Wiener filter to ANN's, where the corrupted image pixels i(x,y) are proportional to the input currents and each neuron output is the voltage proportional to the restored object v(x,y).

In this paper, we have used the Fourier transform to derive the Hopfield neural network model for Wiener-like image restoration processing. Then, at the fixed-point dynamics level of Hopfield-like neurodynamics we can implement the image restoration Wiener filter in the image domain for the real time operation. This is possible because the Hopfield dynamics is a linear equation which allows us to use Fourier de-convolution theorem to transform the product of Fourier amplitudes into the correlation operation, i.e. matrix vector multiplication in the image domain.

We wish to address several technology issues for image restoration and compression tasks. Since the major impact of these tasks will be in the Broad-band Integrated System of Digital Networks (B-ISDN) for the picture phones (with on-line fax printers) for interactive telecommunication and teleconference at home/office, one would ask--
   •How inexpensive a neurochip can be designed for enhancing image display?
   •Can the modulation transfer function of HDTV display be modeled and then adaptively measured realistically ?
   •Will the TV noise--flicker, fractal 1/f, be modeled and adaptively measured in real time ?

Obviously answers to these are research beyond the scope of current report. Instead, we assume that all these answers are affirmative, and the need of neurochip designs and implementations is a critical component for real time image processing in the image pixel domain, rather than using the traditional Wiener filter in the Fourier Transform domain, for which it requires to transform the image twice----- back and forth wasting the time and resource.

2. Mathematical Definitions of Wiener Filters and Wavelet Transforms

We assume a shift-invariant and time-independent point spread function (psf) s(x,y) and an additive noise of zero mean (for modeling a noisy TV except the shift-variant and multicative noise case).

$$i(x,y,t) = s(x,y)_{**} o(x,y,t) + n(x,y,t); \quad <o(x,y,t)n(x,y,t)> = 0 \quad (1)$$

where the ensemble average is denoted by the angular brackets (when in ergodic systems it can be replaced by the time average), and the double star denotes the double convolution in the image pixel domain. Then, the least mean square (LMS) filter has been derived and known as the Wiener filter $w(x,y)$ [5] which convolves with the corrupted image $i(x,y,t)$ gives the estimated object $v(x,y,t)$

$$< || o(x,y,t) - v(x,y,t) ||^2 > = \text{min. w.r.t. } w(x,y) \quad (2).$$

We will give the derivation in the Fourier domain, so that we can implement it in the image domain by ANN. First we introduce the TV scanning coordinate on the two dimensional (2-D) domain which is one dimensional space-filling curve, say lexicographic scan line-by-line, or the Peano curve preserving the local proximity relationship [6] at point p denoted by p real numbers or integers

$$p <--> p = (x_p, y_p). \quad (3)$$

This paper's theme is that the LMS restoration Eq(2) of any linear and shift-invariant integral Eq(1) is equivalent to each other mathematically and can therefore be solved by implementing a Wiener-Hopfield (W-H) Neurochip whose design is given for the first time. In order to illustrate this point, we have chosen the image compression by the Wavelet Transform (WT) as another test problem in additional to the real time image restoration, Eq(1,2). Since the WT has been adopted by FBI for a lossless finger-print compression (having the 27/1 compression ratio record and better than the traditional JPEG DCT scheme), then with the availability of W-H neurochips the WT shall become more popular in the teleconference and video community.

A mother wavelet $\psi(x)$ that can mimic the human visual system complex cell response function is known to be the difference of Gaussian (dog) or Mexican Hat model used early by computer vision researchers, Marr, Adelson & Barr, Mallat [7]

$$\psi(x) = (1 - |x|^2) \exp(- |x|^2/2) \quad (4a)$$

$$\Psi(f) = \int dx \exp(-2\pi i f x) \psi(x) = 4\pi^2 |f|^2 \exp(-2\pi |f|^2) \quad (4b)$$

Eq(4b) indicates the Laplacian Pyramid Paradigm based on the Laplacian operator: $\Delta <--> 4\pi^2 |f|^2$ is a band pass filter under a Gaussian window that is useful for the curvature detection under a fixed resolution scale. The completeness condition that insures such an admissible mother wavelet $\Psi(f)$ is that the power spectral density (PSD) must be inversely-linear bounded [7,8]

$$\int df \, || \Psi(f) ||^2 / |f| = \text{Const.} < \infty. \quad (4c)$$

which implies no d.c. frequency component, i.e. a zero integrated area for a "little" oscillatory wavelet such that the total area vanish and decay rapidly in a compact support.

$$\Psi(f=o) = \int dx \, \psi(x) = 0. \quad (4d)$$

The daughter wavelets are the affine scaled and shifted version $\psi_{ab}(x) = \psi((x-b)/a)$ of the mother wavelet $\psi(x)$. For integers j and k, a dyadic daughter (meaning a factor of 2 in scale) is given as follows:

$$\psi_{j,k}(p) = 2^{-j/2} \psi(2^{-j} p - k) \tag{5a}$$

Additional tight frame condition is required [7] to turn the admissible mother into a complete orthonormal (CON) set written in terms of the Kronecker delta, using the Dirac notation for the dual space, bra vector $< \mid$, to the ket vector, $\mid >$. Then, the following outer product matrix is diagonal because of CON:

$$\Sigma_{jk} \mid \psi_{jk} > < \psi_{j'k'} \mid \ = \delta_{j,j'} \delta_{k,k'} \tag{5b}$$

The inverse Wavelet Transform of a p-scanned image is obtained from Eq(5)

$$\mid i(p)> = \ \Sigma'_{jk} \mid \psi_{jk}> <\psi_{j'k'} \mid i(p)> + \mid r(p)> \tag{6}$$

When a reduced set of the inner product wavelet coefficients $<\psi_{j'k'} \mid i(p)>$ indicated by the prime over the summation sign is used to keep the image up to a certain resolution scale and the remainder $i(p) - \mid i(p)> = \mid r(p)>$ is a low pass residue which is somewhat like the noise of Eq(1). Thus, WT can accomplish an image compression which is digitally equivalent to the sub-band coding method or known as Quadrature Mirror Filter (QMF) method for data compression[7]. This image wavelet compression can be embedded into the W-H neurochip because of such a mathematical isomorphism.

3. Wiener-Hopfield Neural Networks In Fourier Domain

The corresponding upper case letters denote the Fourier amplitudes in the Fourier frequency domain (f_x, f_y), Eq(1) becomes, after invoking the Fourier deconvolution theorem [11]:

$$I(f_x, f_y, t) \ = \ S(f_x, f_y) O(f_x, f_y, t) + N(f_x, f_y) \tag{7}$$

The estimated object spectrum is defined by

$$V(f_x, f_y, t) \ = \ W(f_x, f_y) I(f_x, f_y, t) \tag{8}$$

where W is the celebrated Wiener filter such that the estimated V, which will be the ANN neuron outputs, must be as closely as possible to the true object spectrum O in the LMS sense

$$E \ = (1/2) < (V - O)(V^* - O^*) > = \ \text{minimum} \tag{9}$$

Since $V^* = W^* I^*$, where the superscript * denotes the complex conjugate, one finds by the partial differentiation $\partial E / \partial W^* = 0$, the important orthogonality principle for the error correction update rule used in any stable algorithm:

$$< (V - O) I^* > \ = 0 \tag{10}$$

Eq (10) says when the data I^* used can no longer narrow down the error $(V - O)$, the filter becomes the best. Using this orthogonality principle, we can replace unknown V with O, after multiplying Eq(8) with I^*: $V I^* = W I I^*$, taking the average, $<V I^*> = W <I I^*>$, and then replacing $<V I^*>$ with $<O I^*>$, the Wiener filter is obtained:

$$W \ = \ <O \ I^* > / <I \ I*> \tag{11}$$

We wish to make a comment to other well known filters in image processing. Using Eq(7), we can rewrite the Wiener filter Eq(11) as follows:

$$W \ = \ S^*/\{\mid \mid S \mid \mid^2 + \varepsilon\} = \ S^{-1}/\{1 + \varepsilon/\mid \mid S \mid \mid^2\} \tag{12}$$

where ε is defined to be the noise to object PSD ratio:

$$\varepsilon \ = \ <\mid \mid N \mid \mid^2>/<\mid \mid O \mid \mid^2> \tag{13}$$

Clearly, the Wiener filter Eq(12) is reduced to the Vander Lugt matched filter S^* in optics in the limit of large noise $\varepsilon \gg 1$, and also to the Inverse Filter S^{-1} in the opposite limit of no noise [5]. Substituting Eq(11) into Eq(8) gives the restored object

$$V \quad = \quad \{ <O\,I^* > / <I\,I* > \}\,I \qquad\qquad (14)$$

Formally, if we denote the above Eq(14), factor-by-factor, as $a = \{b/c\}d$. Since image PSD $c = <I\,I*> \neq 0$, then for reasons of easy implementation one can remove the denominator by multiplying the resulting a with a nonzero c gives $ac = bd$, which suggests that the minimum of the scaler constant $E = (1/2)\,|\,ac - bd\,|^2$ gives the desired output a. Likewise, multiplying the image PSD through both sides of Eq(14) forms a quadratic energy function E for the restored spectrum V:

$$E(V) \quad = \quad (1/2)\,\{ <I\,I* > V - <O\,I^* > I \}^2 \qquad\qquad (15)$$

For arbitrary object spectrum, the Hopfield-like energy function is normalized

$$H(V) \equiv E(V) / <||O||^2> = \quad (1/2)\,\{ W'\,V - S*I \}^2 \qquad (16a)$$

where W' is the object-normalized image PSD, the inverse Wiener filter, see Eq(12),

$$W' \equiv (||S||^2 + \varepsilon) \qquad\qquad (16b)$$

The Hopfield-like neural dynamics is given by a local gradient descent, or fixed point dynamics. Let l be the discrete index (along the space-filling scanning curve on constant wavelet fidelity $Q = f^*/\delta f$ patches on Fourier domain f^*=center freq. and δf=r.m.s. freq. spread): $l \longleftrightarrow f_l = (f_x, f_y)$.

$$\partial U_l / \partial t = - \partial H / \partial V_l = - \Sigma_m W_{lm}\,V_m + I_l \qquad (17)$$

where synaptic interconnect weight is the square of the object-normalized image PSD

$$W_{lm} \equiv (||S_l||^2 + \varepsilon_l)^2\,\delta_{l,m} \qquad\qquad (18)$$

and the external input to the ANN is derived from the given image spectrum I_l

$$I_l \equiv (||S_l||^2 + \varepsilon_l)\,S^*_l I_l \qquad\qquad (19)$$

and neuron net input is

$$U_l = \Sigma_m W_{lm}\,V_m + \theta_l \qquad\qquad (20)$$

and the sigmoidal output is

$$V_l = \sigma\,(U_l) = 1/\{ 1 + \exp(-U_l) \} \qquad\qquad (21)$$

Convergence Theorem: Given image data I_l, such a system converges, because of the monotonic logic Eq(20) $(dV_l/dU_l) \geq 0$, and the quadratic real energy slopes $(\partial H / \partial V_l)^2$ derived by chain rules: $dH/dt = \Sigma_l\,(\partial H / \partial V_l)\,(dV_l/dU_l)\,(dU_l/dt)$ and replacing the last factor by the gradient descent Eq(17),

$$dH\,(V_1\,V_2,...V_n)/dt = - \Sigma_l\,(\partial H / \partial V_l)^2\,(dV_l/dU_l) \leq 0 \qquad (22)$$

Our convergence proof is independent of any detail of the energy function H which may vary in video.

4.   Image Domain Hopfield-like Neural Networks

Image domain dynamics is the Fourier Transformed of Eq(17), because of linear v(x,y,t).

$$v_i\,(t) = v(x,y,t) \qquad\qquad (23)$$

$$u_i\,(t) = \Sigma_j\,w_{i-j}\,v_j(t) + \theta_i \qquad\qquad (24)$$

$$\partial u_i / \partial t = - \Sigma_j\,w_{i-j}\,v_j(t) + i_i(t) \qquad\qquad (25)$$

where the index i is stepping over the Peano scanning curve $p_i = (x_i, y_i)$, and

the cyclic index in the weight matrix is the well known Toeplitz matrix w_{i-j} owing to the Fourier

convolution theorem [11].

We have mathematically mapped the image domain Wiener filter to Hopfield-like ANN's, where the synaptic weight is the square of the object-normalized image PSD, and the corrupted image pixels i(x,y, t) are proportional to the input currents and each neuron output is the voltage proportional to the restored object v(x,y, t). Such a Hopfield neurochip exists, and given in Fig. 1.

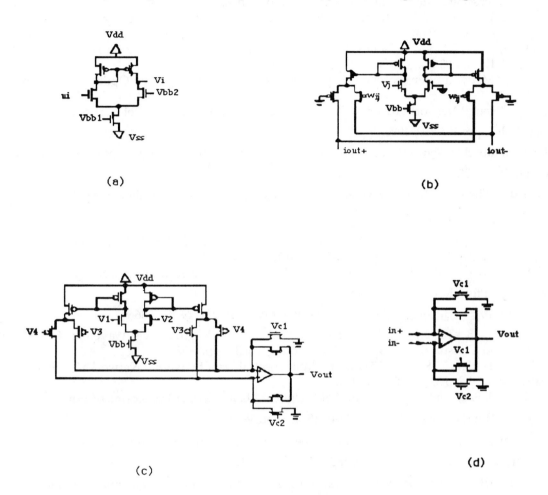

Fig 1.

Fig. 1 shows analog CMOS implementations. Fig. 1(a) shows a CMOS diff. amp. circuit at -1/+1 V power supplies which is used to generate the sigmoid nonlinearity. Fig. 1(b) and Fig.1 (c) are synaptic multiplier (c.f. Mead's Gilbert) and the wide-rage four quadrant Gilbert synaptic multipliers

respectively. These circuits are used to maintain the values of the weight matrix w_{ij}. The trans

impedance amplifier circuit shown in Fig. 1(d) is used to convert the diff. current to a single end voltage output to a neuron. Although Hopfield neurochip interconnect pattern is well known and not shown here for it requires no weight change at the lattice intersection, we expect a slow change of weights may occur at the Video rate image processing, and therefore we have adapted our circuit design from Mead and the weight change circuitry used in "back prop" [1]. Numerical and SPLICE simulations of

TV pictures have either been or will be presented [9-20].

H. Szu wishes to acknowledge the Seed and Venture Fund from NSWC Dahlgren Division.

References

1.   Yiwen Wang,(U. Minn.)"Analog CMOS Implementation of Backward Error Propagation," ICNN-1993, pp. 701-706, March 28, 1993, San Francisco (IEEE Cat. 0-7803-0999).

2.   E. Lange, E. Funatsu, K. Hara, and K. Kyuma, "Artificial Retina Devices--Fast Front Ends for Neural Image Processing Systems," IJCNN-93 Nagoya, pp.801-804, Oct. 1993.

3.   Y. Nitta, J. Ohta, S. Tai, K. Kyuma,"Optical Neurochip for image processing," IJCNN-93 Nagoya, pp. 805-808, Oct. 1993.

4.   M. Oita, S. Tai, K. Kyuma,"A novel model of two-dimensional image associative memory for optical storage," IJCNN-93 Nagoya, pp. 809-812, Oct. 1993.

5.   H. Szu, "Matched filter spectrum shaping for light efficiency," Applied Optics, Vol. 24, pp. 1426-1431, May 5, 1985.

6.   H. Szu,"Neural Networks based on Peano Curves and Hairy Neurons," Telematics and Informatics, Vol. 7, pp. 403-430, 1990.

7.   Ingrid daubechies Ten Lectures on Wavelets, Society for Industrial and Applied Mathematics. Philadelphia, Pa. 1992

8.   H. Szu, Y. Sheng, J. Chen, " Wavelet Transform as a bank of matched filters," Applied OpticsVol. 31, pp. 3267 -3277, July 1992.

9.   Y. Sheng, D. Roberge, H. Szu, "Optical Wavelet Matched Filters for Shift-Invariant Pattern Recognition,"Opt. Lett. Vol.18, No. 4, pp. 299-301, Feb 15, 1993.

10.   H. Szu, X-Y. Yang, B. Telfer, Y. Sheng, "Neural Network Wavelet Transform for Scale-Invariant Data Processing," Phys. Rev. E, Vol. 48, No. 2, pp.1497 -1501, Aug. 1993

11.   J. Goodman, Introduction to Fourier Optics, McGraw Hill, NY, N.Y., 1986

12.   H.H. Szu, B. Telfer, S. Kadambe, "Neural Network Adaptive Wavelets for Signal Representation and Classification," Optical Engineering Vol.31, pp.1907-1916, Sept. 1992.

13.   B. Telfer, H. Szu, R. Kiang, "Classifying Multispectral Data by Neural Networks," Telematics & Informatics, Vol. 10, No.3, pp. 209-222, 1993.

14.   X. Yang, H. Szu, Y. Sheng, H.J. Caulfield,"Optical Haar Wavelet transforms of Binary Images," Optical Engineering Vol. 31, pp. 1846-1851, Sept. 1992.

15.   G. Rogers, J. Solka, C. Priebe, H. Szu, "Optoelectronic Computation of Wavelet like-based Features,"Optical Engineering Vol. 31, pp. 1886-1893, Sept. 1992.

16.   H. Szu, "Why the Soliton Wavelet Transform is useful for Nonlinear Dynamic Phenomena," Proceedings of SPIE , Vol. 1705, pp. 280-288, 1992.

17.   M. Bodruzzaman, X. Li, K. Kuah, H. Szu, B. Telfer,"Speaker recognition Using Neural Network and Adaptive Wavelet Transform,"Proceedings of SPIE Vol. 1961, Orlando April, 1993

18.   B. Telfer, H. Szu, A. Dubey, N. Witherspoon, "Detecting Blobs in Multispectral Electro-Optical Imagery Using Wavelet techniques," Proceedings of SPIE Vol. 1961, Orlando April 1993.

19.   H. Szu, L. Zadeh, C. Hsu, J. Dewitte, G. Moon, D. Gobovic, M. Zaghloul, "Chaotic Neurochips for Fuzzy Computing", Proceedings of SPIE, Vol. 2037, San Diego, July, 1993.

20.   H. Szu,"Auto. Fault Reco. by Image Corr. N. N.techniques,"IEEE Trans,IE-40,197-207, 1993

VLSI Implementation of the Hippocampal Dentate Gyrus

Oscal T.-C. Chen[*,†], Theodore Berger[†], Bing J. Sheu[*]

[*]Department of Electrical Engineering, mc-0271
[†]Department of Biomedical Engineering, mc-1451
University of Southern California, Los Angeles, CA 90089.

Abstract -- The VLSI implementation of a mathematical model of the functional properties of the hippocampal formation has been developed. The hippocampal formation is a brain system which performs the cognitive functions of learning and memory. The design scheme of analog cellular neural network has been extensively applied. The architecture of the proposed hardware implementation has a topology highly similar to the anatomical structure of the hippocampus, and the dynamical properties of its components are based on experimental characterization of individual hippocampal neurons. The prototype chip with 9 neurons in a two-dimensional 3x3 mesh array occupies a silicon area of 4.6 mm x 6.8 mm and was fabricated in a 2-μm double-polysilicon CMOS technology. According to the SPICE-3 circuit simulator, the response time of each neuron is around 1 μ sec which is much faster than that of the biological neuron.

I. Introduction

Algorithms based on neural network paradigms have been demonstrated to be useful in signal processing and pattern recognition tasks. In order to effectively address complex real world problems, the neural networks must be scaled up, or modularized, and then must be efficiently implemented in hardware. In general, a neural network module consists of a large collection of simple processing elements. These simple processing elements execute mathematical algorithms to collectively carry out information processing through their responses to stimuli. There are technological constraints to the scale size and capacity of neural network hardware. In contrast, biological networks which incorporate features of real neurons and the connectivity of real neural networks have been shown to exhibit theoretical advantages in dimensional scaling and processing time. In order to develop a hardware implementation of the proposed model [1], the role of cellular and circuitry characteristics in the computational basis of hippocampal memory function have been studied.

Rapid advances in silicon fabrication and design technologies, especially the advent of very large-scale integration (VLSI) circuits, have made possible the implementation of engineering and biological neural networks. There has been much research in the area of analog neural network hardware implementations for various applications of adaptive signal processing. Lyon and Mead [2] described an analog electronic cochlea for speech recognition. Koch et al. [3] reported a real-time chip for rudimentary computer vision and robotics. Moore et al. [4] presented the VLSI implementation of an artificial neural system for color constancy. Saäckinger et al. [5] developed the analog neural processor for high-speed character recognition. Sheu et al. implemented a motion sensor chip [6] and a neuroprocessor for self-organization mapping [7]. Many cellular neural network (CNN) implementations have been reported [8,9]. In addition to CMOS technology, various design and fabrication technologies such as BiCMOS [10], field-programmable gate array (FPGA) [11], and charge-coupled device (CCD) [12] also have been used for efficient construction of neurocomputing systems.

The custom VLSI hardware for neuron network applications can be constructed by the digital or analog design approaches. In the digital approach, a higher resolution and less noise-sensitive can be achieved. However, the silicon area and power consumption is higher than those of the analog design. On the other hand, an analog design can have many properties in common with real neural tissue. Analog computation can allow many neurons to collectively perform complicated functions in real time. Due to the regular and local connections among neural cells, the architecture of analog CNN circuitry is well-structured and the

This research was partially supported by ONR under Grants N-00014-92-J-4111.

operation speed is independent of the network size. Usually, current saturation problems can occur in large-dimensional, global-connected neural networks. This effect can be alleviated by using the local-connected networks, such as CNN, or the networks with a small volume of interconnections. The analog CNN design scheme has been extensively studied for the proposed neural memory systems.

II. Nonlinear Systems Model of the Hippocampus

The dynamic properties of individual hippocampal neurons were characterized experimentally using a nonlinear systems analytic approach [13]. Experiments were conducted using *in vitro* slice preparations of the hippocampus of New Zealand white rabbits. The primary afferents to the hippocampus, perforant path axons of the entorhinal cortex, were stimulated with a random interval train of electrical impulses: a series of 4064 impulses with a Poisson distribution inter-impulse intervals. The mean inter-event interval (Δ) was 500 ms, with a range of 1-5000 ms. Throughout random train delivery, electrophysiological activity was recorded intracellularly from single granule cells of the dentate gyrus, which receive excitatory input from perforant path axons.

The nonlinear input/output properties of granule cells were defined as the kernels of a functional power series expansion:

$$y(t) = G_0 + G_1[h_1,x(t)] + G_2[h_2,x(t)] + G_3[h_3,x(t)] + ...,\tag{1}$$

where y(t) is the output of dentate granule cells, (G_i) is a set of mutually orthogonal functions, and (h_i) is a set of kernels which characterize the relationship between the input and output:

$$G_0(t) = 0,\tag{2}$$

$$G_1 = \int h_1(\tau)x(t-\tau)d\tau,\tag{3}$$

$$G_2(t) = 2\iint h_2(\tau,\tau+\Delta)x(t-\tau)x(t-\Delta-\tau)d\Delta d\tau, \text{ and}\tag{4}$$

$$G_3 = 6\iiint h_3(\tau,\tau+\Delta_1,\tau+\Delta_2)x(t-\tau)x(t-\tau-\Delta_1)x(t-\tau-\Delta_1-\Delta_2)d\Delta_1 d\Delta_2 d\tau.\tag{5}$$

The train of discrete input events defined by x(t) is a set of δ-functions. The first, second and third order kernels of the series are obtained by the process of orthogonalization using cross-correlation techniques applied to point process events [14].

The first order kernel, $h_1(\tau)$, is the average of all evoked granule cell responses occurring during train stimulation as shown in Fig. 1(a). The second order kernel, $h_2(\tau,\Delta)$ as shown in Fig. 1(b), represents the modulatory effect of a preceding stimulus occurring Δ ms earlier on the number or probability of granule cell activation by the most current stimulation impulse, where τ is the cell activation latency. The third order kernel, $h_3(\tau,\Delta_1,\Delta_2)$ as shown in Fig. 1(c) represents the modulatory effect of any two preceding stimuli occurring Δ_1 ms and Δ_2 ms earlier on the number or probability of granule cells activation by the most current stimulation impulse. In total, the kernel functions represent a complete characterization of the functional properties resulting from the interaction among whatever system of neural elements is studied, and provide a basis for predicting the activity of those elements in response to any arbitrarily selected stimulus condition.

III. Biologically-Inspired Neural Network Implementation

The proposed neural network is based on the biological neural input/output and interconnection models. All neural operations are performed asynchronously according to biological neural functions. The neural network is a dynamic system which will be trained according to the stimuli. Potential applications are in the areas of data storage, classification, and understanding. Generally, the VLSI implementation of one neuron cell includes some fundamental circuit components such as synaptic input drivers, synaptic weight memories, and a output function generator.

(a) Synaptic input driver:

A synaptic input driver buffers the input signal voltage and provides the driving capability for the neuron operation. Thus, a fast settling response of the synaptic input driver is highly desirable. In addition, the synaptic input driver should occupy a compact silicon area and consume low power because many synaptic input drivers are required in a large network.

(b) Synaptic weight memory:

The main function of the synaptic weight memory is to achieve a linear multiplication and to provide reliable storage of the weight value. Since the number of the synaptic weight memories is a dominant factor in a VLSI neural network chip, the careful design of the synaptic weight memory is crucial in achieving the compact silicon area, minimized power consumption, and large dynamic range. In some analog designs of the synaptic weight memories [15,16], the weight value is stored on the capacitor and can be modified by injecting (or extracting) some charge onto (or from) the capacitor. The electrical charge on the capacitor represents the weight value. When the signal from the synaptic input driver is "low", the output current is produced by the bias voltage (corresponding to the reference zero). When the signal from synaptic input driver is "high", the output current is dependent on the synaptic weight value. Thus, the current output is the product of the synaptic weight value and the binary input. However, the charge retention is a major design issue in analog weight storage. It needs to be carefully addressed because the weight value might be decayed due to the leakage current in the reverse-biased pn-junction. For some applications, a periodic refreshing is required.

(c) Output function generator:

The output function generator needs to accumulate all synaptic weight currents and generate a specific output result based on the summed current. Thus, the current-to-voltage converter is a major component of the output function generator. The transimpednce amplifier consisting of an operational amplifier and a feedback resistor can provide the current-to-voltage conversion. The transimpedance amplifier ought to have a sufficient capability to handle a large magnitude of current for proper linear conversion. The feedback resistor can be implemented by six active transistors for high accuracy and occupies a much smaller silicon area than a passive resistor [16]. According to the neural function, the voltage result from the converter can be appropriately transformed through another analog circuitry, or can be used as a output result for a linear neural output function.

IV. VLSI Implementation of the Nonlinear Model of the Dentate Gyrus

The response properties of the granule cells have been analyzed by using the time-series neural model. The output of a neural cell can be described with the estimated kernel functions. The hardware implementation is used to realize the Eq. (1). Figure 2 shows an architecture design of a neural cell, which is a hybrid analog/digital design. Before the operation of neuron function being performed, the signal RESET is issued to set the contents of input latch and shift registers to the V_{ss}. The input signal X is pipelined into the input latch. The previous input sequence is stored in the shift registers. The signal CLK1 is used to control the data shifting among the input latch and shift registers. The timing relationship in the neural model is mapped into the relationship of space connection in the shift registers. The signal READ is used as a enable signal for memory access. It controls the period of memory access which is determined by the response time of the analog current-sum circuitry. The AND gate functions are used to generate the memory access signal. From timing diagram shown in Fig. 3, the processing of the neural cell can be divided by three different operations: (a) shift the previous data and latch the incoming data, (b) generate memory access signals, fetch the memory data, and generate the output result, and (c) refresh the memory cell.

The h_1, h_2, and h_3 are stored dynamically in the analog memory cells which can be implemented by using the modified Gilbert multiplier. The circuit schematic of the compact and wide-range Gilbert multiplier for the neuron memory cell is shown in Fig. 4(a). By using the SPICE-3 circuit simulator, the linear characteristics between the synaptic voltage pair ($W_{j,i+}$ and $W_{j,i-}$) and output current can be achieved. The measured dc characteristics of the synaptic weight memory is shown in Fig. 4(b). Since the memory for synaptic weights is implemented by using the gate capacitances of MOS transistors, periodical refresh is required to prevent the leakage current through the diffusion-to-substrate junction from changing the stored value. From the measurement on charge retention characteristics, a refresh cycle of around 0.1 sec is sufficient to retain the 8-bit accuracy [15]. Each updating or refreshing the data is performed while the correct memory address is provided. A decoder is required to decode the memory address in order to generate the control signals for the pass transistors. The input data will be stored in the synaptic weight memory through pass transistors. The refresh operations can be overlapped with the operations of the neuron function.

The currents from the synaptic weight memory will sink to the I-to-V converter which is an operational amplifier with a linear floating active resistor feedback. Figure 5(a) shows the circuit schematic of I-to-V converter for the operation of the current summation. The measured characteristics of this I-to-V converter is also shown in Fig. 5(b). Due to the operation range of I-to-V converter, the total current from the synaptic weight memory is limited. According to Fig. 5(b), the 500 μA is the maximum total current. In the Fig. 4(b), the linear current range of memory cell is adjustable by using different voltages, V_{IN}. Empirically, the contribution of higher order kernels can result in output values that range from -100% to +400% of the magnitude of the h_1 value. Since the currents are proportional to the values of h_1, h_2, and h_3, the total current will be within four times the current from the h_1 memory cell. Therefore, the N can be a large number, if the physical layout routing and propagation delay issues can be efficiently implemented. If the 500 μA is the maximum operation current in the I-to-V converter, the h_1 memory cell can provide the 125 μA with the maximum data resolution. The total current from the h_2 and h_3 will be within -250 μA to 375 μA so that the circuitry of I-to-V converter still performs in the linear operation range.

A set of 9 neurons is arranged in a two-dimensional 3x3 mesh array. Each neuron connects with its four neighboring neurons and has a physical size 1,000 λ x 1,200 λ with the number of stored time units equaling four (N=4). Figure 6 shows a layout of a complete neuron with a decoder for refreshing address. According to the SPICE-3 circuit simulation, the functionality of a neuron with 11 synaptic weights can be correctly addressed. The total response time is approximately 1 μs. The 3x3 neuron array with some testing modules, as shown in Fig. 7, was fabricated in a 2-μm double-polysilicon CMOS technology through the MOSIS Service of USC/Information Sciences Institute at Maria del Rey, CA.

V. Conclusion

A mixed analog/digital approach is one of the good choices in the implementation of electronic neural systems. The local data computation is executed by analog circuitry to achieve full parallelism and to minimize power consumption. Interneuron communication is carried out in the digital format to achieve network scalability by using an array of neural chips. The proposed VLSI implementation of a nonlinear model of the hippocampus will not only facilitate for efficient emulation of biological systems or simulation of neural network paradigms but also produce useful knowledge and results for scientific and engineering applications.

VI. Acknowledgments

The authors would like to thank Dr. Joongho Choi for discussion on the detailed circuit design. Mr. Choi Choi provided the experimental and analytical results of the hippocampus. Mr. Tony Wu and Mr. Vincent Wang helped on the layout of some circuits.

Reference

[1]   T. W. Berger, J. L. Bassett, "System properties of the hippocampus," *Learning and Memory: The Biological Substrates,* I. Gormezano, E. A. Wasserman (Eds.), Hillsdale, New Jersey: Lawrence Erlbaum, pp. 275-320, 1992.

[2]   R. F. Lyon, C. A. Mead, "An analog electronic cochlea," *IEEE Trans. Acoustics, Speech, and Signal Processing,* vol. 26, no. 7, pp. 1119-1134, July 1988.

[3]   C. Koch, W. Bair, J. G. Harris, T. Horiuchi, A. Hsu, J. Luo, "Real-time computer vision and robotics using analog VLSI circuits," *Advances in Neural Information Processing Systems 2,* Editor: D. Touretzky, pp. 750-757, Morgan Kaufmann: San Mateo, CA, 1990.

[4]   A. Moore, J. Allman, R. M. Goodman, "A real-time neural system for color constancy," *IEEE Trans. Neural Networks,* vol. 2, no. 2, pp. 237-247, Mar. 1991.

[5]   E. Sačkinger, B. E. Boser, J. Bromley, Y. LeCun, L. D. Jackel, "Application of the ANNA neural network chip to high-speed character recognition," *IEEE Trans. Neural Networks,* vol. 3, no. 3, pp. 498-505, May 1992.

[6]   J.-C. Lee, B. J. Sheu, W.-C. Fang, R. Chellappa, "VLSI neuronprocessors for video motion detection," *IEEE Trans. on Neural Networks,* vol. 4, no. 2, pp. 178-191, Mar. 1993.

[7]   W.-C. Fang, B. J. Sheu, O. T.-C. Chen, J. Choi, "A VLSI neural processor for image data compression using self-organizing networks," *IEEE Trans. on Neural Networks,* vol. 3, no. 3, pp. 506-518, May 1992.

[8]   L. O. Chua, L. Yang, "Cellular Neural Networks: Applications," *IEEE Trans. on Circuits and Systems,* vol. 35, no. 10, pp. 1273-1290, Oct. 1988.

[9]   T. Roska, L. O. Chua, "The CNN universal machine: an analogic array computer," *IEEE Trans. on Circuits and Systems - II: Analog and Digital Signal Processing,* vol. 40. no. 3, pp. 163-173, Mar. 1993.

[10] T. Morishita and Y. Tamura and T. Otsuki, "A BiCMOS analog neural network with dynamically updated weights," *Tech. Digest IEEE Inter. Solid-State Circuits Conf.,* pp. 142-143, San Francisco, CA, Feb. 1990.

[11] E. K. F. Lee and P. G. Gulak, "A CMOS field-programmable analog array," *IEEE Jour. Solid-State Circuits,* vol. 26, no. 3, pp. 1860-1867, Dec. 1991.

[12] A. M. Chiang and M. L. Chuang, "A CCD programmable image processor and its neural network applications," *IEEE Jour. Solid-State Circuits,* vol. 26, no. 12, pp. 1894-1901, Dec. 1991.

[13] T. W. Berger, G. Barrionuevo, S. P. Levitan, D. N. Krieger, R. J. Sclabassi, "Nonlinear systems analysis of network properties of the hippocampal formation," *Neurocomputation and Learning: Foundations of Adaptive Networks,* J. W. Moore, M. Gabriel (Eds.), Cambridge, MA: MIT Press, pp. 283-352, 1991.

[14] H. Krausz, "Identification of nonlinear systems using random impulse train inputs," *Biological Cybernetics,* vol. 19, pp. 217-230, 1975.

[15] B. W. Lee, B. J. Sheu, *Hardware Annealing in Analog VLSI Neurocomputing,* Kluwer Academic Publishers, 1991.

[16] J. Choi, S. H. Bang, B. J. Sheu, "A programmable analog VLSI neural network processor for communication receivers," *IEEE Trans. on Neural Networks,* vol. 4, no. 3, pp. 484-495, May 1993.

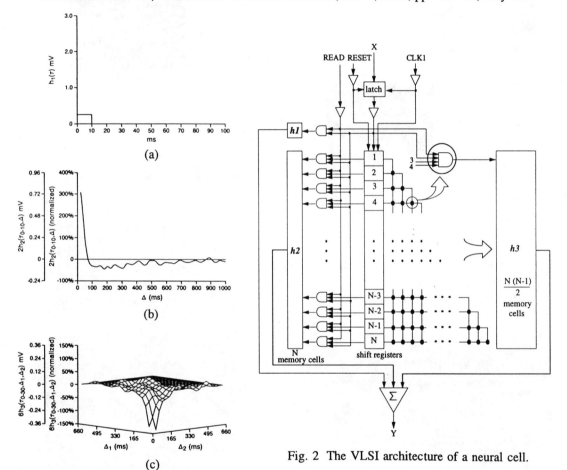

Fig. 2 The VLSI architecture of a neural cell.

Fig. 1 The kernels for dentate granule cells *in vitro*. Insets: temporal characteristics of the input represented in each order kernel.

(a) First order kernel.

(b) Second order kernel.

(c) Third order kernel.

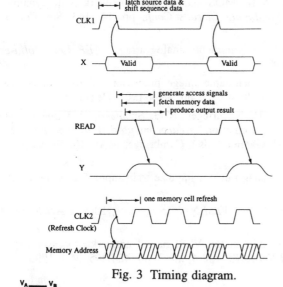

Fig. 3 Timing diagram.

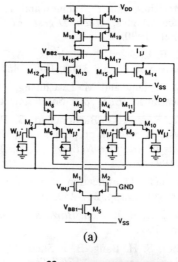

(a)

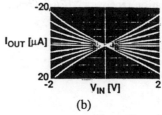

(b)

Fig. 4 Synaptic weight memory.

(a) Circuit schematic of the compact and wide-range Gilbert multiplier.

(b) Measured dc characteristics.

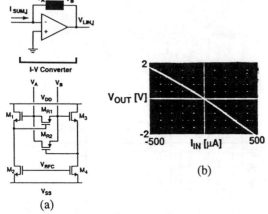

(b)

(a)

Fig. 5 Output function generator.

(a) Circuit schematic of I-to-V converter with linear floating active resistor.

(b) Measured characteristics of I-to-V converter.

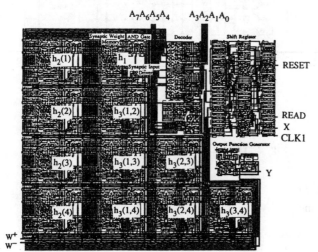

Fig. 6 Layout of a complete neuron with N equaling four.

Fig. 7 Prototype 3x3 neuron array.

Skeletonization of Arabic Characters Using a Neural Network Mapped on Maspar

Majid M. Altuwaijri, Rafic A. Ayoubi, and Magdy A. Bayoumi.
The Center for Advanced Computer Studies
University of Southwestern Louisiana
Lafayette, Louisiana 70504

ABSTRACT

In this paper, we employ a back-prop neural network for skeletonization of Arabic characters to be used in an Arabic character recognition system. The neural network is trained to learn the thinning algorithm which is a variation of the parallel algorithm proposed by Zhang and Suen. Zhang and suen's algorithm was modified so that dots are thinned into single pixels. The neural network as well as the binary image are mapped on a massively parallel machine (Maspar) in order to speed up the skeletonization process.

1. INTRODUCTION

Skeletonization (or thinning) is a procedure which transforms a pattern to a skeleton of a unit width. It permits a simpler structural analysis and more intuitive design of recognition algorithms. Skeletonization is essential in a broad range of problems in image processing, such as character recognition, inspection of printed circuit boards, chromosome shape analysis, the reduction of the required memory space for storing the essential structural information of the patterns, and the reduction of the required processing time.

Generally, for a skeletonization algorithm to be effective, it should ideally compress data, eliminate local noise, and retain significant features of the pattern. Although there is no formal definition of a skeleton, there appears to be a general agreement that a good skeletonization algorithm must meet the following requirements:

1. preserve the connectivity of skeletons.
2. converge to skeletons of unity width.
3. approximate the medial axis.
4. achieve a high data reduction efficiency.

There are two approaches for skeletonization: iterative approach and noniterative approach.

➢ Iterative thinning algorithm in which pixels on the boundary of the pattern are deleted successively until only a skeleton remains. This approach can be further classified into two classes namely: sequential and parallel.
  - In sequential algorithms, the pixels are examined for deletion sequentially in each iteration, and the deletion of a pixel depends on the result of the previous iteration as well as on the pixels already processed in the current iteration.
  - In parallel algorithms, deletion of pixels depends only on the results of the previous iteration.
➢ Noniterative algorithms produce a certain median on the center line of the pattern directly in one pass without examining all pixels individually. Most of these algorithms were designed heuristically.

The authors acknowledge the support of the National Science Foundation and State of Louisiana grant NSF/LEQSF (1992–96)-ADP-04.

Although the skeletonization has been a very active research area, few articles addressed the thinning of Arabic characters. Due to the characteristics of Arabic characters, they do not allow direct application of the techniques developed for other languages such as Latin and Chinese ; for example, applying some thinning algorithms to an Arabic character with a single dot will produce a skeleton with a small straight line for the dot. This is not allowed in Arabic since many Arabic writers represent two dots by a small straight line. Some of the characteristics of Arabic characters are the following:

1. Arabic is a cursive type language written from right to left.
2. It has 28 letters each of which has 2 to 4 representations depending on the position.
3. Characters may have a dot, two dots, three dots, or a zigzag associated with the character and can be above or below or even inside the character.

In this paper, we have modified the parallel thinning algorithm proposed by Zhang and Suen[1] so that dots are thinned into just single pixels. We have employed a neural network for skeletonization of binary images. The network is trained to learn the proposed thinning algorithm.

In order to speed up the thinning process performed by the neural network, The network is mapped on a massively parallel machine (Maspar). In section 2, we describe some preprocessing techniques. In section 3, we present the proposed thinning algorithm. In section 4, we show how the thinning algorithm can be implemented using a neural network. In section 5, a brief description of the Maspar is given. In section 6, the mapping procedure of the neural network on the Maspar is shown.

2. PREPROCESSING

The first step in skeletonization is to acquire a digitized image of the text using a suitable scanning system. Text image is then converted to a binary matrix of zeros and ones. The ones will represent the dark characters on a light background.

As in any type of data acquisition system, noise errors will occur on the input. Smoothing is needed to eliminate the noise from the text image. Each pixel is set to 1 if and only if the number of 1 pixels in the eight neighbors exceeds a given threshold as in figure 2.

3. THE THINNING ALGORITHM

In this section we will describe the proposed thinning algorithm which is based on the algorithm developed by Zhang and Suen[1]. The deletion of a pixel depends on the 8-neighbors of the pixels which are labeled as shown in fig. 3. Assuming that the pattern points have value 1 and background points have value 0, the thinning algorithm consists

IF	EF	MF	BF		IF	EF	MF	BF
ض	ض	ضـ	ضـ		ا	ـا	ـا	ا
ط	ط	ـط	ط		ب	ـب	ـبـ	بـ
ظ	ظ	ـظ	ظ		ت	ـت	ـتـ	تـ
ع	ع	ـع	عـ		ث	ـث	ـثـ	ثـ
غ	غ	ـغ	غـ		ج	ج	ـجـ	جـ
ف	ـف	ـفـ	ف		ح	ح	ـحـ	حـ
ق	ـق	ـقـ	ق		خ	خ	ـخـ	خـ
ك	ـك	ـكـ	كـ		د	ـد	ـد	د
ل	ـل	ـلـ	ل		ذ	ـذ	ـذ	ذ
م	ـم	ـمـ	مـ		ر	ـر	ـر	ر
ن	ـن	ـنـ	نـ		ز	ـز	ـز	ز
ه	ـه	ـهـ	هـ		س	ـس	ـسـ	سـ
و	ـو	ـو	و		ش	ـش	ـشـ	شـ
ي	ـي	ـيـ	يـ		ص	ـص	ـصـ	صـ

Fig 1. Arabic charactors in all its forms (end form EF, middele form MF, begnning and Isolated

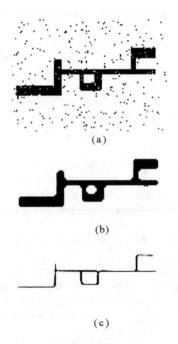

(a)

(b)

(c)

Fig.2. Arabic word with noise. (b) Result of smoothing. (c) Result of thinning.

of successive passes of four basic steps applied to the contour points of the pattern. In the first step, p is deleted if the following conditions are satisfied:

➤ **step 1**

Z_1: $2 \leq N(p) \leq 6$.
Z_2: $S(p) = 1$.
Z_3: $x_1 x_3 x_7 = 0$.
Z_4: $x_1 x_5 x_7 = 0$.

where $N(p)$ is the number of black neighbors of p and $S(p)$ is the number of 0-1 transitions when the neighbors are traversed in clockwise order. Conditions Z1 and Z2 remains the same in all the four steps. Conditions Z3 and Z4 are replaced by their 90° rotations in the second step, by their 180° rotations in the third step, and by their 270° rotations in the fourth step.

➤ **step 2**

Z_3: $x_3 x_5 x_7 = 0$.
Z_4: $x_1 x_5 x_7 = 0$.

➤ **step 3**

Z_3: $x_1 x_3 x_5 = 0$

Z_4: $x_3 x_5 x_7 = 0$.

x_4	x_3	x_2
x_5	p	x_1
x_6	x_7	x_8

Fig 3. Neighborhood arrangement used by the thinning algorithm.

➤ **step 4**

Z_3: $x_1 x_3 x_7 = 0$.
Z_4: $x_1 x_3 x_5 = 0$.

- Condition Z_1 ensures that p is not an end point and also avoids causing erosion into the pattern. Condition Z_2 ensures that the deletion of p would not break the connectedness of the pattern.
- Condition Z_3 and Z_4 of step 1 deletes pixels on the south and east boarders as well as north-west corner pixels.
- Conditions Z_3 and Z_4 of step 2 deletes pixels on the south and west boarders as well as north-east corner pixels.
- Conditions Z_3 and Z_4 of step 3 deletes pixels on the north and west boarders as well as south-east corner pixels.

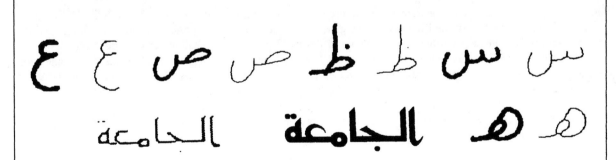

Fig. 4. Skeletons of some Arabic characters using the proposed thinning algorithm. Note that the dotsre correctly
thinned into one pixel each.

- Conditions Z_3 and Z_4 of step 4 deletes pixels on the north and east boarders as well as south-west corner pixels.

Figure 4. shows the result of applying the above algorithm to Arabic characters. Note that the dots are thinned into a pixel.

4. THINNING USING ANN

In this work, we have employed an Artificial neural network for the thinning of Arabic characters. The network is trained to learn the thinning algorithm.

We have implemented a back-prop model with one hidden layer. The 8 neighbors are used as the input of the neural network. Since the neural network has to decide whether a pixel is deletable or not (i.e., two-class problem), therefore, a single output node is needed. Four nodes in the hidden layer are found to be sufficient. The ANN used for thinning Arabic characters is shown in fig. 6. Since a pixel has eight neighbors, the total number of possible training pattern is 2^8. In the proposed algorithm, there are 4 steps in each iteration. Thus 4 different ANN's are needed, but due to symmetry, only one ANN is sufficient.

5. MASPAR ARCHITECTURE

The MASPAR MP-1 system is a massively parallel SIMD computer system. It consists of two major components: the Front-End (FE), and the Data Parallel Unit (DPU). The FE is a DECstation 5000 which runs ULTRIX operating system. The DPU consists of two components: The Array Control Unit (ACU) which controls the interaction between the FE and the Processor Element (PE) array. It also performs singular data calculations within the DPU. The PE array consists of 1024 to 16,384 arithmetic processors, together with associated registers and RAM.

The PEs are arranged in a two-dimensional mesh where each PE has eight neighbors (N, E, W, S, NE, SW, SE, SW) including those at the edges of the PE array (i.e. wraparound connections are supported). There are two types of PE communications: Communication between the PEs and the ACU, and communication between different PEs in the PE array. Communication between the PEs and the ACU takes place over a special ACU/PE bus. Communication between PEs in the PE array can be via X-net or the Global Router. In this paper, we are only interested in the X-net communication.

X-net allows communication between any one PE in the array that lies in a straight line from the sending PE in one of eight possible directions.

All PEs perform the same instruction at the same time. However, a subset of the PEs could be disabled . The set of PEs that are enabled at any given time is called the active set.

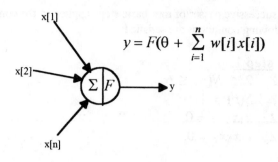

$$y = F(\theta + \sum_{i=1}^{n} w[i]x[i])$$

Fig 5. Structure and function of a neuron model.

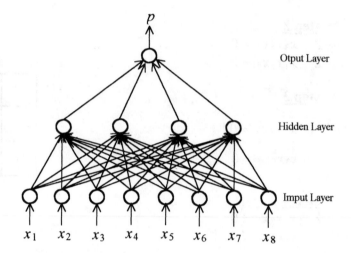

Fig 6. The network used for thinning of Arabic characters.

6. MAPPING ON MASPAR

In our method, we map each pixel of the binary image on one PE of the Maspar PE array. The mapping is based on the 2-dimensional cut-and-stack. This is to ensure that the neighboring pixels are mapped on neighboring PEs. The image is divided into blocks of size nxproc * nyproc (the size of the PE array) where each block is mapped onto the PE array (fig. 7). If we assume the size of an image is X*Y where

$$X= m * nxproc + a \text{ and}$$
$$Y= n * nyproc + b$$

then the number of blocks is determined as follows:

1. m * n if X and Y are multiple of nxproc and nyproc.
2. (m+1)*n if Y is multiple of nyproc.
3. m*(n+1) if X is multiple of nxproc.
4. (m+1)*(n+1) if neither is multiple.

Recall that the weight matrices of the neural network are 8x4 between the input and hidden layers and 4x1 between the hidden and output layers. In our approach, the same neural network will be mapped on each PE., hence each PE will contain a pixel of the image as well as the thinning neural network. This strategy allows each PE in the active set to perform a sequential recall with no inter-PE communication. Thus, we can achieve a maximum of N concurrent recall phase operations.

Since the image is binary, the eight neighboring pixels can be stored in an 8-bit vector P. Thus, the matrix-vector multiplication of W*X between the input layer and the output layer is reduced to an addition operations as shown in line 8 of the algorithm delete.

We can distinguish two cases: the first case is when the image size KxL is less than the PE array size MxP, the second case is the opposite of the first case.

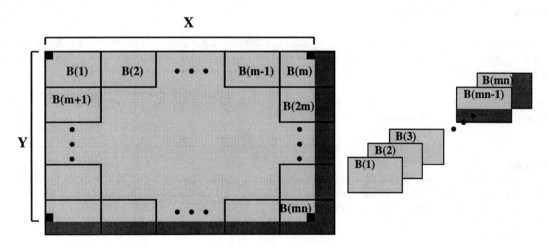

Fig 7.   2–D Cut-and-Stack layout

Case 1: In this case, each pixel is mapped onto one PE such that all the eight neighbors of each pixel are neighbors on the physical PEs. We assume that there is no wrap around along the edges of the 2-d mesh. The following algorithm performs a sequential recall phase on each PE:

```
1.   algorithm delete
2.   do while more pixels to delete
3.       for all pixels which are ON pardo
4.               get the eight neighbor pixels and store in P
5.               for j = 0, 3 do                /* no. of hidden nodes   */
6.                   for i =0, 7 do             /* no. of input nodes    */
7.                       if ( P(i) == 1 ) then
8.                           sum = sum + W1(j,i)
9.                       endif
10.                  enddo
11.                  apply sigmoid function to sum and store in out1(j)
12.              enddo
13.              for i =0, 3  do
14.                  sum = sum + out1(i) * W2(i)
15.              enddo
16.              apply sigmoid function to sum and store in out
17.              if ( out ==1 ) then            /* pixel is deleteable   */
18.                  pixel =0
19.              endif
20.      endpardo
21.  endwhile
```

Case 2 In this case, data is mapped onto PEs in layers using 2-d Cut-and-Stack as explained above. The same algorithm of case 1 is repeated for each layer.

7. CONCLUSION

The main objective of this paper is to develop a fast and accurate thinning algorithm for Arabic characters to be used in Arabic character recognition. The used thinning algorithm is a modification of the parallel algorithm proposed by Zhang and Suen[1] so that dots are thinned into single pixels. This is very important because applying the original algorithm to an Arabic character with a single dot produces a skeleton with a small straight line for the dots which is not allowed in Arabic since many Arabic writers represent two dots by a small straight line. This creates a conflict situation in the recognition phase.

We have trained a back-prop neural network to learn the thinning algorithm. The network takes the eight neighbors of a dark pixel as an input and outputs the result of the thinning algorithm. In order to speed up the thinning process, we have mapped the neural network on a massively parallel machine (Maspar).

The algorithm were tested and proven to be very fast and can be used in a real time character recognition system. Some of the results were shown in fig. 4.

REFERENCES
1. T. Y. Zhang and C. Y. Suen, "A fast algorithm for thinning digital patterns," Commu. ACM, Vol. 25, no. 3, pp. 236-239, 1984.
2. R. Krishnapuram and L. F. Chen, "Implementation of Parallel Thinning Algorithms Using Recurrent Neural Networks," IEEE Trans. Neural Network, Vol. 4, no. 1, Jan. 1993.
3. L. Lam, S. W. Lee, and C. Y. Suen, "Thinning Methodologies- A comprehensive Survey," IEEE Trans. PAMI, Vol. 14, no. 9, Sep. 1992.
4. S. A. Mahmoud, I AbuHaiba, "Skeletonization of Arabic characters Using clustering based skeletonization algorithm (CBSA)," Pattern Recognition, Vol. 24, no. 5, pp. 453-464, 1991.
5. J. Hertz, A. Krogh, and R. G. Palmer, Introduction to the theory of Neural Computation. Redwood city, CA: Adison Wesley, 1991, lecture notes, Vol. 1.
6. T. Blank, "The Maspar MP-1 Architecture," Proc. IEEE Compcon Spring 90, IEEE, pp. 20-24 , Feb. 1990.
7. R.C. Gonzalez and P. Wintz, Digital Image Processing. Reading, MA: Addison Wesley, 1987, ch. 8.
8. M. M. Altuwaijri and M. Bayoumi, "Arabic Text Recognition Using Neural Network," To be published in the ISCAS 1994 London, England, 30 MAY-2JUNE.

Biological Neural Networks

Session Chairs: Thomas McKenna
Joel Davis

ORAL PRESENTATIONS

Odor Processing in the Insect Olfactory System

Wayne M. Getz

Department of Environmental Science, Policy and Management

University of California, Berkeley, CA 94720

Abstract

The central problem in insect olfaction is to identify the quality of an odor stimulus impinging on the antennae of an individual, given that odor stimuli are often borne on highly turbulent airflows and sometimes are embedded in noisy odor backgrounds. From the literature, it is evident that the response of olfactory receptor cells of olfactory generalist insects (e.g., worker honey bees) are highly nonlinear in response to changes in odor concentration and odorant blend (synergistic and, especially, inhibitory phenomena are ubiquitous). Thus it appears beyond the capabilities of linear filters to extract general odor quality information from receptor input. The question is: what sort of neural network is required, given the spatio-temporal structure of natural odor stimuli and empirical measured response behavior of receptor neurons in the insect antenna, to successfully extract odor quality information? Here I will formalize some of the essential features of the odor perception problem, as well as review what is know about the network architecture of olfactory neurons in the antennal lobe of insects. I will contrast critical differences between pheromonal and non-pheromonal detection subsystems and identify physiological and anatomical issues that need to be resolved to gain a fuller understanding of receptor input integration and feature extraction in insects.

Introduction

Olfaction in insects has been widely studied in the context of pheromone detection (for reviews see Kaissling, 1987; Masson & Mustaparta, 1990), and less so in the context of odor detection (for review see Smith & Getz, 1994). The insect antennal lobe, the part of the insect brain receiving input from olfactory receptor afferents, has a number of underlying architectural features in common with the vertebrate olfactory bulb (Boeckh *et al.*, 1990—convergence of a large number of receptor afferents onto many fewer glomerular neuropil structures from which relay neurons project to convey olfactory information to higher processing centers of the brain). Thus some understanding of the function of these underlying architectural features may provide insight into olfactory processing in all organisms. To date, the insect antennal lobe has not been extensively modeled (but see Linster *et al.*, 1993), although the vertebrate olfactory cortex and various olfactory processes have been modeled (Baird, 1986; Bower, 1991; Freeman and Skarda, 1985; Getz, 1991, Getz and Chapman, 1987; Hopfield, 1991; Li and Hopfield, 1989; Schild and Riedel, 1992; Skarda and Freeman, 1987; Wang *et al.*, 1991).

A number of critical questions need to be addressed at all levels of olfactory information processing, before we have a clear picture of the basic elements of olfactory coding and perception. Some of these questions relate to the nature of the stimuli, to receptor transduction, and antennal lobe computations. The olfactory computations performed by the insect antennal lobe can be characterized by the relationship between the output from the antennal lobe (the firing patterns of the projection neurons) and the input stimulus impinging on olfactory sensillae located on the antenna of the insect. Generating this input-output relationships are the response characteristics of the receptor neurons embedded in these sensillae, as well as computational properties of the antennal lobe network itself.

Unlike visual or auditory stimuli, olfactory stimuli are highly noisy: they contain much less spatial information than visual stimuli, and much less temporal information than auditory stimuli. Visual and auditory stimuli are directly quantifiable in terms of amplitudes and frequencies of wave forms over time and space, and the response fields of associated receptors have natural metrics in terms of stimulus frequencies and amplitudes. In contrast, olfactory stimuli can only be characterized in terms of the concentrations of component odorants making up odor blends, while receptor responses may be ordinated with respect to odorant concentration, but (in general) have no natural ordination with respect to their response to different odorants. Further, odor stimuli are transported on air plumes that exhibit turbulent structure so that stimulation of an insect antennae, for example, may be highly variable among neighboring sensillae and with respect to time for a particular sensillum. This presents a problem that can only be effectively dealt with through various types of integration processes at different levels of neuronal processing. In fact, this spatial and temporal variation may provide a mechanism for an odor stimulus to be extracted from a noisy background (Getz, 1991).

Receptor neurons, located in special antennal hair-like (sensillae trachoidea), peg-like (sensillae basiconica), or plate-like (sensillae placoidea) structures, depending on the species of insect, can be either "specialists" or "generalists" (Schneider, 1987). The former refers to neurons responding to one or a very few odorants (typical of pheromone receptors — Kaissling, 1987; Masson and Mustaparta, 1990), the latter to neurons responding to one or more classes of odorants such as aliphatic alcohols, aldehydes, keytones, monoterpenes, etc., (Akers and Getz, 1992 & 1993; Den Otter *et al.*,1980; Fujimura *et al., 1991*; Kafka, 1987; Ma and Visser, 1978; Sass, 1978; Selzer, 1984; Vareschi, 1971). Studies of generalist receptors have typically employed suites of single compounds, often presented at single concentrations, in an effort to define reaction spectrum classes among populations of receptor neurons. The degree to which each neuron specializes with respect to a set of n specified odorants can be quantified using an appropriate breadth responsiveness measure such as (c.f. Giradot and Derby, 1988; Smith and Travers, 1979) $H = -\frac{1}{\log n} \sum_{i=1}^{n} p_i \log p_i$, where p_i is the proportional response of the neuron in question to the ith odorant (i.e., the relative levels of the responses to the odorants are normalized so that $\sum_{i=1}^{n} p_i = 1$). A number of insects, including the honey bee (Vareschi, 1971; Getz and Akers, 1993), and the cockroach (Selzer, 1984; Fujimura *et al., 1991*) have broadly tuned receptors with highly nonlinear responses as functions of concentration and odorant blend.

Very little is known about the anatomy of arborizations of olfactory receptor neuron afferents other than these afferents are uniglomerular (in both insects and vertebrates—Boeckh *et al.*, 1990). In honey bees, the antennal nerve containing these afferents splits into several fiber bundles, each of which arborize in glomeruli in different regions of the honey bee brain (Arnold *et al.*, 1985; Flanagan and Mercer, 1989a; Gascuel and Masson, 1991). Also, in male moths it has been recently demonstrated that different classes of specialized pheromonal receptors arborize in different sub-regions of the antennal lobe macroglomerulus (Hansson *et al.*, 1992). The broad spectrum response of honey bees placodes, and also cockroach trachodes (different cells in the same cockroach trachode respond to different odorants sets of odorants) suggests that different receptor neurons in the same sensillae should arborize in different glomeruli in the antennal lobe. This appears to be the case in honey bees (D. Brückner, personal communication).

The antennal lobe of an insect essential contains a neural network that receives input from the receptor neurons and produces output in neurons that project from the glomeruli of the antennal lobe to higher centers of the insect brain. In the honey bee and cockroach, for example, the typical glomerulus gives rise to one uniglomerular projection neuron, while large atypical glomeruli give rise to several uniglomerular projection neurons. In the cockroach, only the male has a large glomerulus (called the macroglomerulus—see Boeckh *et al*, 1990). It gives rise to approximately 15 projection neurons (Ernst and Boeckh, 1983). In honey bees, drones have four large glomeruli (called macroglomerular complexes), queens have one, and workers none (they have about 166 regular glomeruli—see Masson and Mustaparta, 1990). The firing patterns across these uniglomerular projection neurons provide a convenient representation of the output of the antennal computation. Odor responsive multiglomerular projection neurons also exist (Fonta *et al.,*, 1993), but they invade only the "core" not the "periphery" of the glomeruli where they can feedback information to the intrinsic neurons (Malun, 1991a & b). Thus these multiglomerular projection neurons are not an intrinsic part of the computational network, but rather appear to be passive collectors of output that may relate to the intensity of input in a multiglomerular region of the antennal lobe. Hence they do not appear to influence the uniglomerular projection neuron output and need not be considered, at least in the initial stages, in modeling this output.

Formalization of Problem

Following my earlier work (Getz and Chapman, 1987; Getz, 1991), I assume for all systems that an appropriate odor space Ω can be identified consisting of r odorants (pure compounds) O_ρ, $\rho = 1, \ldots, r$ so that the instantaneous concentration at time t of an odor stimulus at the κth odor sensillum, $\kappa = 1, \ldots, k$, is represented by the vector $c_\kappa(t) = (c_{\kappa 1}(t), \ldots, c_{\kappa r}(t))'$ (' denotes vector transpose and Ω is the positive quadrant of $\mathbb{R}^n$). The instantaneous overall concentration of the stimulus at the κth sensillum is $\bar{c}_\kappa(t) = \sum_{\rho=1}^{r} c_{\kappa r}(t)$, while the instantaneous quality of this stimulus can be characterized by the direction of the vector $c_\kappa(t)$ in Ω. Further, when odor concentrations are not extraordinarily low, it is reasonable to assume that, although $c_\kappa(t)$ may be highly variable with respect to time across the k different sensillae on the antennae of the insect in question, all receptor neurons (RNs) within the same sensillum are subject to the same instantaneous stimulus $c_\kappa(t)$. It is also useful to define an odor stimulus $C(t)$ with respect to an individual insect as the matrix $C(t) = (c_1(t), \ldots, c_k(t))$, where k is the number of olfactory sensillae on both antennae or, if necessary, over the whole body of the individual in question.

Using this notation, we can define the quality of an odor stimulus in a number of ways. For example, if for some suitably small $\epsilon > 0$ we can show that for any times t_1 and $t_2 \in [0, t_s]$ and sensillae κ_1 and κ_2 the columns of a stimulus $C(t)$ satisfy

$$\frac{c_{\kappa_1}(t_1) \cdot c_{\kappa_2}(t_2)}{\|c_{\kappa_1}(t_1)\|\|c_{\kappa_2}(t_2)\|} > 1 - \epsilon \tag{1}$$

(where $\| \cdot \|$ is the usual Euclidean sum-of-squares norm), then the elementwise average over all columns in $C(t)$, denoted by $\bar{c}(t) = (\bar{c}_1(t), \ldots, \bar{c}_r(t))'$, can be used to represent the quality and concentration of the stimulus $C(t)$ over the sampling interval $t \in [0, t_s]$. Of course, we would not want to refer to a stimulus as a having the feature of quality unless inequality (1) holds for $\epsilon > 0$ sufficiently small. (The appropriate size for ϵ depends ultimately on the resolution of the system in question. The higher the resolution, the smaller ϵ needs to be).

Every stimulus $C_i(t)$ induces a response pattern in p suitably selected output neurons projecting from the antennal lobe of higher centers of the insect brain (e.g. the set of uniglomerular PNs projecting to the mushroom bodies of the protocerebrum). We will assume that this response pattern can be represented by a time-dependent vector of firing rates $\psi_i(t) = (\psi_{1i}(t), \ldots, \psi_{pi}(t))'$. We assume that the vectors $\psi_i(t)$, $i = 1, \ldots, n$, contains an extractable feature over some sub-interval $[t_1, t_2] \subset [0, t_s]$ that is invariant for all i whenever the stimuli $C_i(t)$ $i = 1, \ldots, n$ have the same odor quality and the same concentration (i.e., the average of the stimuli $C_i(t)$ over time and space are the same to a tolerance of ϵ). A formal statement of the problem of antennal lobe function in the context of odor perception in insects is that the average quality and concentration of an input stimulus $C_i(t)$ over a natural sampling period $[0, t_s]$ (e.g., a sniff cycle—see Getz, 1991) be represented in terms of some invariant feature in the PN firing rates $\psi_i(t)$ over some sub-interval $[t_1, t_2] \subset [0, t_s]$

Nonlinearities in Receptor Neuron Input

Receptor neurons are highly nonlinear in their response to both odor concentration and odor quality. The typical response of an olfactory receptor neuron to an odorant is to be inactive or exhibit a background spiking rate below a certain threshold and to respond linearly to the logarithm of concentration over several orders of magnitude of concentration until saturation and ultimately depression (adaptation) of the spiking rate ensues. With respect to odor quality, however, the response to mixtures of odors often deviates from an interpolation of the response to the components of the mixtures when components and mixture are stochiometrically equivalent (Akers and Getz, 1993; Getz and Akers, 1993, in press).

The instantaneous spiking rate $R_\kappa(c_\kappa)$ of the κth receptor, as a function of its current input stimulus c, can be modeled using ideas from chemical kinetic theory to calculate the proportion of activated receptor proteins of different types and then to express $R_\kappa(c)$ in terms of negative exponential (to account for inhibition) and logarithmic (to account for excitation) functions to account for the response of internal cellular processes (i.e., second messenger cascades associated with ligand-gated ion channels) to receptor activation (Getz and Akers, in press). In particular, suppose each receptor neuron has the genetic potential to express p types of receptor proteins. Assume that the total density of receptor molecules on a receptor cell (and assuming the same membrane surface area for each cell so that total numbers are the same) is a constant $\bar{u}$. Further, suppose that the κth RN has its own unique partition of $\bar{u}$ into p subclasses of receptor molecules, each at density $u_{\kappa\pi}$, $\pi = 1, \ldots, p$, so at

$$\bar{u} = \sum_{\pi=1}^{p} u_{\kappa\pi}. \tag{2}$$

If the binding constant of odorant O_ρ with receptor protein of type π is $h_{\pi\rho}$ (this constant is the ratio of association to disassociation rates—see Getz and Akers, in press) and the instantaneous flux of molecules impinging on the κth RN is $c_\kappa(t) = (c_{\kappa 1}(t), \ldots, c_{\kappa r}(t))'$, then the number of bound receptors $y_{\kappa\pi}$ of type π in the κth RN is (Beidler, 1962; Getz and Akers, in press)

$$y_\pi(c_\kappa) = \frac{\sum_{\rho=1}^r c_{\kappa\rho} h_{\pi\rho}}{1 + \sum_{\rho=1}^r c_{\kappa\rho} h_{\pi\rho}} u_{\kappa\pi}. \tag{3}$$

For a set of weighting constants a_π, $\pi = 1, \ldots, p$, the variable

$$z_\kappa(c_\kappa) = \sum_{\pi=1}^p a_\pi y_\pi(c_\kappa) \tag{4}$$

can be regarded as a "membrane depolarization activity index" (e.g., if $a_1 = 2a_2 > 0$, then twice as many type 2 receptor proteins need to be activated as type 1 receptor proteins to get the same level of membrane depolarization; or if $a_1 = -a_2 > 0$, then activated type 2 receptor proteins are linked to spike inhibiting pathways and one-for-one they cancel out the effect of each activated type 1 receptor protein — see Getz and Akers, in press, for a discussion of this modeling approach and Michel *et al.*, 1991, for an example of channels inhibiting the firing of chemosensory receptor cells in lobsters). The actual firing or spiking rate $R_\kappa(c_\kappa)$ of the κth receptor can then be modeled in terms of the activity index $z_\kappa(c_\kappa)$ defined in expression (4) using the following general spiking function $s(z)$ that applies to all neurons whose "activity index" has value z (see Getz and Akers, in press, for a more general formulation of this model)

$$\begin{aligned} s(z_\kappa) &= \bar{s} e^{b_1(z_\kappa + b_2)} & z \leq -b_2 \\ s(z_\kappa) &= \bar{s} & -b_2 \leq z_\kappa \leq b_3 \\ s(z_\kappa) &= \bar{s} + b_4 \log\left(\frac{z_\kappa}{b_3}\right) & z \geq b_3 \end{aligned} \tag{5}$$

where b_2 and b_3 are threshold values for the onset of inhibition and excitation respectively with respect to the background firing rate $\bar{s}$ and the constants b_1 and b_4 are "shape" functions relating to how steeply the background rate respectively falls or rises per unit change in the activity index z_κ. The instantaneous spiking rate of the κth neuron to stimulus $c_\kappa(t)$) is now given by

$$R(c_\kappa(t)) = s(z_\kappa(c_\kappa(t))). \tag{6}$$

Hence equations (3)–(6) provide a method for generating input activity in the k RNs in terms of the κth RN stimulation profiles $c_\kappa(t)$, $\kappa = 1, \ldots, k$, if the parameters in these equations can be estimated from data such as that reported in Akers and Getz (1993).

Structure of the Antennal Lobe

The olfactory receptor axonal inputs to the antennal lobe arborize in the glomeruli (Figure 1A), which are grape-like neuropil structures enclosed by a sheath of glial cell process (Masson and Mustaparta, 1990; Homberg *et al.*, 1989; Gascuel and Masson, 1991; Boeckh *et al.*, 1990). These arborizations synapse almost exclusively with neurons that interconnected several glomeruli, but remain intrinsic to the antennal lobe. All intrinsic neurons (INs—also referred to as local interneurons) identified thus far appear to be inhibitory (they are GABA-ergic—but see Michelson and Wong, 1991), although it is thought that excitatory intrinsic neurons may exist (Linster *et al.*, 1993; in the honey bee brain, for example, only 5% of the almost 10,000 intrinsic neurons are GABA-ergic—Gerd Bicker, personal communication). The intrinsic neurons synapse with the dendrites of neurons that project in tracts (lateral and medial AGTs, etc.) from the antennal lobe to higher centers of the insect brain. These projection or relay neuron dendrites, in turn, synapse back onto the intrinsic neurons before they exit a glomerulus (Figure 1B) (Malun, 1991 a & b), thereby forming excitatory-inhibitory feedback loops that could well parallel aspects of the mitral-granule cell interactions in the vertebrate olfactory bulb (e.g., see Li and Hopfield, 1989).

Besides providing the backbone to the glomerular network, a network of intrinsic neurons informationally link all the glomeruli (Figure 1C). At this point, it is not know if some or all intrinsic neurons have input regions in one glomerulus and output regions in several others, or are bi-directional in terms of current flow. Some of these intrinsic neurons are symmetric in the sense of arborizing with the same intensity in all the glomeruli they invade, while others have the asymmetry of arborizing intensely in only one of the glomeruli and less intensely in others (Mercer and Flanagan, 1989; Fonta *et al.*, 1993). It is not clear which are the input and output regions of these sensory neurons or even whether bi-directional current flow occurs. Further, it is not know exactly what parts of the intrinsic neuronal membranes are active or passive, although the glomerular interconnection segments are known to spike (Flanagan and Mercer, 1989).

Network Equations

A standard approach to modeling a feedback network of the type described in the previous section is to regard the voltage changes v_η in the ηth neuron as space-clamped and write down the electrical circuit equations (Hopfield and Tank, 1986; Simpson, 1991)

$$\frac{dv_\eta(t)}{dt} = -\alpha_\eta v_\eta(t) + \sum_\xi w_{\eta\xi} f^\xi(v_\xi(t - \tau_{\eta\xi})) + v_\eta^0(t) \tag{7}$$

over appropriate ranges for the indices η and ξ. The parameters α_η are the reciprocals of the product of the appropriate implicit membrane capacitances and resistances, the parameters $w_{\eta\xi}$ are a measure of the synaptic strength between the ηth neuron and all neurons presynaptic to it, and $f^\xi : \mathbb{R}^+ \to \mathbb{R}^+$ are sigmoidal response functions that relate post-synaptic voltage changes to current flow across the synapses as a function of the voltage gradient across the synapse. The terms v_η^0 in equation (7) allow us to account for a background or spontaneous levels of activity (e.g., in some of the PNs and INs) that is not due to network inputs, while the time delays $\tau_{\eta\xi}$ allow us to account to some extent for finite transmission times in neurons and across synapses.

The intrinsic interneurons (IN) (Fig. 1C) require special treatment because of their unusual spatial structure. In particular, if we assume that current can flow in either direction along the interconnecting segments then, for a particular IN arborizing in g glomeruli, and letting $\gamma = 1, \ldots, g$ denote the g segments of this neuron that arborize in the g glomeruli and $\gamma = g + 1, \ldots, 2g$ represent the g "spoke" elements that connect the g glomerular elements to a central point (just below the soma of the neuron in question — Fig. 1C), then the voltage v_γ of the space clamped element in the γth glomerulus is

$$\frac{dv_\gamma(t)}{dt} = -\alpha_\gamma v_\gamma(t) - \beta_\gamma(v_{g+\gamma}(t) - v_\gamma(t)) + \sum_\xi w_{\gamma\xi} f_\xi(v_\xi(t - \tau_{\gamma\xi})) + v_\gamma^0(t) \qquad \gamma = 1, \ldots, g, \tag{8}$$

where the index ξ ranges over all the neurons synapsing with the segment of the neuron in question, $v_{g+\gamma}(t)$ is the voltage in the segment contiguous to the γth glomerulus, and the term $\beta_\gamma(v_{g+\gamma}(t) - v_\gamma(t))$ relates to voltage changes due to the current flow induced by the voltage gradient between the two segments in question. In keeping with the convention that the direction of current flow is from the positive to the negative, it follows that current flows out of the γth glomerulus whenever $v_\gamma(t) < v_{g+\gamma}(t)$ and vice versa. Since the element $g + \gamma$ is connected only to the element γ and the central hub (just below the soma) of the neuron in question (Fig. 1C), its dynamics are governed by the simpler equation

$$\frac{dv_{g+\gamma}(t)}{dt} = -\alpha_{g+\gamma} v_{g+\gamma}(t) - \beta_{g+\gamma}(v_h(t) - v_{g+\gamma}(t)) + v_{g+\gamma}^0(t) \qquad \gamma = 1, \ldots, g, \tag{9}$$

where v_h is the voltage at the hub of the neuron in question, and the term $\beta_{g+\gamma}(v_h(t) - v_\gamma(t))$ relates to voltage changes due to the current flow induced by the voltage gradient $v_h(t) - v_\gamma(t)$.

The voltage at the hub, $v_h(t)$, is easily expressed in terms of the voltages $v_{g+\gamma}(t)$, $\gamma = 1, \ldots, g$, using Kirchoff's circuit law that currents entering and leaving a point must sum to zero; viz.,

$$v_{g+\gamma}(t) = \frac{\sum_{\xi=1}^g \beta_\gamma^* v_{g+\gamma}}{\sum_{\xi=1}^g \beta_\gamma^*} \qquad \gamma = 1, \ldots, g, \tag{10}$$

where the parameters β_γ^* are the parameters $\beta_{g+\gamma}$ multiplied by the appropriate conductance values required to convert voltages in each of the elements into current flows.

Analysis

With the inputs characterized by equations (2) to (10), and the network dynamics modeled by equations (7) to (10), we can investigate the computational properties of the antennal lobe model presented here based on architectural features (i.e., which of the synapse parameters $w_{\xi\eta}$ are negative, zero, or positive) and system parameter values. Supervised and unsupervised learning procedures (Simpson, 1990) can be used to select values for the synapse parameters $w_{\xi\eta}$, the former requiring that we define some performance measure relating to the invariance among projection neuron firing patterns $\psi_i(t)$ over some sub-interval $[t_1, t_2] \subset [0, t_s]$ in response to stimuli $C_i(t)$ $i = 1, \ldots, n$ that have the same odor quality and concentration. Other system parameters can be obtained either from biological data (Linster *et al.*, 1993) or optimization of network performance.

References

Akers, R. P. and W. M. Getz, 1992. A test of identified response classes among olfactory receptors in the honeybee worker. Chemical Senses 17:191–209.

Akers, R. P. and W. M. Getz, 1993. Response of Olfactory Sensory Neurons in Honey Bees to Odorants and their Binary Mixtures. J. Comp. Physiol. 173:169–185.

Arnold, G, C. Masson, and S. Budharugsa, 1985. Comparative study of the antennal lobes and their afferent pathway in the worker bee and the drone (*Apis mellifera*). Cell and Tissue Res. 242:593–605.

Baird, B., 1986. Nonlinear dynamics of pattern formation and pattern recognition in the rabbit olfactory bulb. Physica D. 22:150–175.

Beidler, LM, 1962. Taste receptor stimulation. Prog. Biophys. Biophys. Chem. 12:107-151.

Boeckh, J., P. Distler, K. D. Ernst, M. Hösl, and D. Malun, 1990. Olfactory bulb and antennal lobe. In: D. Schild (ed.), Chemosensory Information Processing. Springer-Verlag, Berlin, pp. 201–227.

Bower, J. M., 1991. Piriform cortex and olfactory object recognition. In: J. L. Davis and H. Eichenbaum (eds.), Olfaction: A Model System for Computational Neuroscience, The MIT Press, Cambridge, Massachusetts, pp. 265–85.

Den Otter, C. J., M. Behan, and F. W. Maes, 1980. Single cell responses in female *Pieris brassicae* (Lepidoptera: Pieridae) to plant volatiles and conspecific egg odours. J. Insect Physiol. 26:465-472.

Ernst, K. D. and J. Boeckh, 1983. A neuroanatomical study on the organization of the central antennal pathways in insects: III. Neuroanatomical characterization of physiologically identified response types of deutocerebral neurons in *Periplaneta americana*. Cell Tissue Res. 229:1–22.

Flanagan, D. and A. R. Mercer, 1989. Morphology and response characterstics of neurones in the deuto-cerebrum of the brain in the honeybee *Apis mellifera*. J. Comp. Physiol. A 164:483–494.

Fonta, C., X.-J. Sun, and C. Masson, 1993. Morphology and spatial distribution of bee antennal lobe interneurones responsive to odours. Chem. Senses 18:101–119.

Freeman, W. J. and C. A. Skarda 1985. Spatial EEG patterns, non–linear dynamics and perception: the neo–Sherringtonian view. Brain Research Reviews 10:147–175.

Fujimura, K., F. Yokohari, and H. Tateda, 1991. Classification of antennal olfactory receptors of the cockroach, *Periplaneta americana* L. Zool. Sci. 8:243-255.

Gascuel, J. and C. Masson, 1991. A quantitative unltrastructural study of the honeybee antennal lobe. Tissue and Cell 23:341–355.

Getz, W. M., 1991. A neural network for processing olfactory-like stimuli. Bull. Math. Biol. 53:805–823.

Getz, W. M. and R. P. Akers, 1993. Olfactory Response Characteristics and Tuning Structure of Placodes in the Honey Bee *Apis mellifera*. Apidologie (to appear).

Getz, W. M. and R. P. Akers, in press. Partitioning nonlinearities in the response of honey bee olfactory receptor neurons to binary odors. Biosystems.

Getz, W. M. and R. F. Chapman, 1987. An odor discrimination model with application to kin recognition in social insects. International J. Neuroscience 32:963–967.

Giradot, M.-N. and C. D. Derby, 1988. Neural coding of quality of complex olfactory stimuli in lobsters. J. Neurophysiol. 60:303–324.

Hansson, B. S., H. Ljungberg, E. Hallberg, and C. Löfstedt, 1992. Functional specialization of olfactory glomeruli in a moth. Science 256:1313–1315.

Homberg, U., T. A Christiansen, and J. G. Hildebrand,1989. Structure and function of the deutocerebrum in insects. Annu. Rev. Entomol. 34:477–501.

Hopfield, J. J., 1991. Olfactory computation and object perception. Proc. Natl. Acad. Sci. USA 88:36462–36466.

Hopfield, J. J. and D. W. Tank, 1986. Computing with neural circuits: a model. Science 233:625–633.

Kafka, W. A., 1987. Similarity of reaction spectra and odor discrimination: Single receptor cell recordings in *Antheraea polyphemus* (Saturniidae). J. Comp. Physiol. A. 161:867-880.

Kaissling, K. E., 1987. R. H. Wright Lectures on Insect Olfaction. Edited by Konrad Colbow, Simon Fraser University, Burnaby, British Columbia, Canada.

Li, Z. and J. J. Hopfield, 1989. Modeling the olfactory bulb and its neural oscillatory processings. Biol. Cybern. 61:379–392.

Linster, C., C. Masson, M. Kerszberg, L. Personnaz, and G. Dreyfus, 1993. Computational diversity in a formal model of the insect olfactory macroglomerulus. Neural Computation 5:228–241.

Ma, W. C. and J. H. Visser, 1978. Single unit analysis of odour quality coding by the olfactory antennal receptor system of the Colorado beetle. Entomol. Exp. Appl. 25:520–533.

Malun, D., 1991a. Synaptic relationships between GABA-immunoreactive neurons and an identified uniglomerular projection neuron in the antennal lobe of *Periplaneta americana*: a double-labeling electron microscope study. Histochemistry 96:197–207.

Malun, D., 1991b. Inventory and distribution of synapses of identified uniglomerular projection neurons in the antennal lobe of *Periplaneta americana*. J. comp. Neurology 305:348–360.

Masson, C. and H. Mustaparta, 1990. Chemical information processing in the olfactory system of insects. Physiological Reviews 70:199–245.

Michel, W. C., T. S. McClintock, and B. W. Ache, 1991 Inhibition of lobster olfactory receptor cells by an odor-activated potassium conductance. J. Neurophysiol. 65:446–453.

Michelson H. B. and R. K. S. Wong, 1991. Excitatory synaptic response mediated by $GABA_A$ receptors in the hippocampus. Science 253:1420–1423.

Sass, H., 1978. Olfactory receptors on the antenna of *Periplaneta*: response constellations that incode food odors. J. Comp Physiol. 128:227–233.

Schild, D. and H. Riedel, 1992. Significance of glomerular compartmentalization for olfactory coding. Biophys. J., 61:704–715.

Schneider, D., 1987. Plant recognition by insects: a challenge to neuroethological research. In: V. Labeyrie, G. Fabres, and D. Lachaise (eds.), Insects–Plants, Funk, Dordrechts, Netherlands, pp. 117–123.

Selzer, R., 1984. On the specificities of antennal olfactory receptor cells of *Periplaneta americana*. Chemical Senses 8:375–395.

Simpson, P. K., 1990. Artificial Neural Systems: Foundations, Paradigms, Applications, and Implementations. Pergamon Press, Elmsford, New York, p. 210.

Skarda, C. A. and W. J. Freeman 1987. How brains make chaos in order to make sense of the world. Behavioral and Brain Sciences 10:161–195.

Smith, B. H. and W. M. Getz. 1994. Non-pheromomal olfactory processing in insects. Annu. Rev. Entomol. (to appear).

Smith, D. B. and J. B. Travers, 1979. A metric for the breadth of tuning of gustatory neurons. Chemical Senses 4:215–229.

Vareschi, E. 1971. Duftunterscheidung bei der Honigbiene — Einzelzell–Ableitungen und Verhaltensreaktionen. Z. vergl. Physiol. 75:143–173.

Wang, D., L. Buhmann, and C. von der Malsburg, 1991. Pattern segmentation in associative memory. In: J. L. Davis and H. Eichenbaum (eds.), Olfaction: A Model System for Computational Neuroscience, The MIT Press, Cambridge, Massachusetts, pp. 213–224.

Caption to Figure 1

The basic organization of the multiglomeruli model of the antennal lobe is illustrated in terms of the receptor neuron (RN) inputs, the glomeruli (G) connected together by intrinsic neurons (IN, also know as local interneurons), and the projection neuron (PN) outputs. **B:** Details of the architecture of the neural network within each glomerulus and the flow of information, as indicated by the arrows. **C:** A representation of the $2g$-segmental of an IN which arborizes in g glomeruli

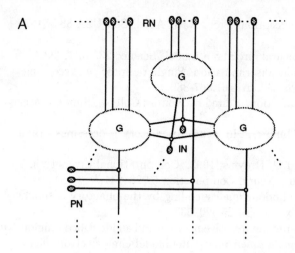

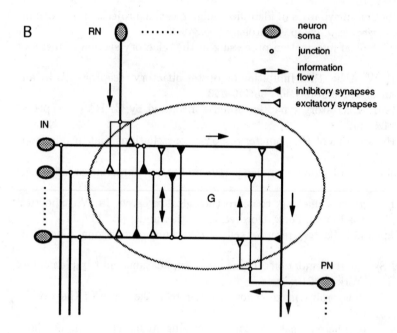

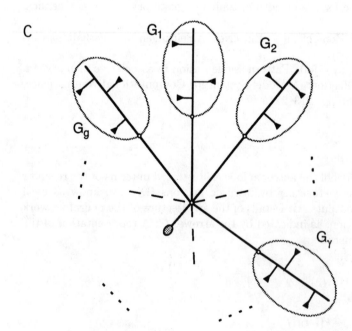

A Class of Functions for the Adaptive Control of the Cerebellar Cortex

P. Chauvet[*], G.A. Chauvet[*,**]

[*]Institut de Biologie Théorique, Université d'Angers, 49100 Angers (France)
[**]Department of Biomedical Engineering and Program for Neuroscience,
University of Southern California, Los Angeles, CA 90089 (USA)

Abstract.
    A class of functions is proposed, which could describe the adaptive control of the closed loop involving the cerebellar cortex. The mathematical model of the cerebellar cortex is a basic biologically constrained neural network regarding the connectivity around the Purkinje cell. The output of a neuron is the transformation, by a linear or non-linear firing function, of the summation of weighted inputs. Covariance learning rules are used for synaptic weights. It is assumed that only synapses between parallel fibers and Purkinje cell are modifiable, and that the climbing fiber transports an error signal, closing the loop between the output and the inputs of a unit. Asymptotic stability is then shown for an isolated linear unit and the same results are given with conditions on several parameters for a non-linear unit.

1. Introduction

    It is now well admitted that the cerebellum, and specifically the cerebellar cortex, plays an important role in the adaptive control of movements. This control is achieved through a closed loop that involves on one hand, climbing fibres and mossy fibres as inputs, and on the other hand, the Purkinje cell axon as an output. The last decade has also shown the importance of the cerebellar cortex in the learning and memorization of space trajectories (see Chapeau-Blondeau and Chauvet, 1991). Although different authors have proposed models to describe the cerebellar function (see Tyrrel and Willshaw, 1992), adaptive control is not yet quantitatively well understood, nor is the implication of its neuro-anatomical structure in the capacity to learn motor coordination. In previous papers, we introduced a basic local circuit of the cerebellar neural network called a *Purkinje unit* (Chauvet G.A., 1986; Chauvet P. and Chauvet G.A., 1993). This basic local circuit was an open-loop neural network biologically constrained, i.e. having: (i) a real connectivity, (ii) specific activating or inhibiting synaptic properties, (iii) an anatomical hierarchical structure.

    The aim of this paper is to mathematically prove the existence of a class of functions that could describe the adaptive control of the closed loop involving the cerebellar cortex, in which the climbing fibre, as is widely admitted, propagates the error signal.

2. Model of the Purkinje unit

    Let us recall the definition of the local circuit called "*Purkinje unit*" (Chauvet G.A.,1986). A Purkinje unit consists of one Purkinje cell, the single output system of the cerebellar cortex, with some of the neurons connected to it in the cerebellar cortex, and with the closest Golgi cell. A granule cell denoted gc is in a specific unit numbered k if: gc has synapses with the Purkinje cell k of the unit k, the distance between gc and the Purkinje cell k is the smallest distance between gc and any Purkinje cell it contacts, and gc has synapses with the Golgi cell k. The basket and stellar cells included in the unit k are those which are contacted by the granule cells of the unit k and which are connected to the Purkinje cell k. It is possible to separate this unit into two subsystems: the granule subsystem and the Purkinje subsystem. Figures 1 and 2 show the two components of a Purkinje unit.

    The output S of a neuron is considered to be equal to a short-term mean frequency. This is given as a function of its inputs by:

$$S = F\left[s_0 + {'\underline{w}}.\underline{E}\right]$$

The real(${'\underline{w}}.\underline{E}$) is the scalar product between $\underline{w}$ and $\underline{E}$, where $\underline{w}$ is the vector of n synaptic weights w_i and $\underline{E}$ is the vector of n inputs E_i . s_0 is a basic activity. We consider for F two kinds of function: a "linear" function, where F is the identity on positive real values and zero on negative real values; a non-linear but continuous function defined by a sigmoïd: $F(s) = (1 + e^{-qs})^{-1}$ with $q > 0$. Then, the output $\underline{S}$ of a layer is $\underline{F}[\underline{s}_0 + W\underline{E}]$ where W is the matrix of the synaptic weights.

2.1 The granule subsystem

The granule subsystem includes a layer of g granule cells and the Golgi cell. The subsystem's inputs are: a pattern $\underline{U}$ of m elements 1 or 0 that represent information propagated along the m mossy fibers; the external context X_e representing activities propagated along the parallel fibers connected with the Golgi cell but that do not issue from this unit; the activity V on the climbing fiber. The output of the granule subsystem before the transformation by F is the vector $\underline{x}$ and after the transformation it is the vector $\underline{X}$ of g activities X_i along the parallel fibers, which are the outputs of the granule layer.

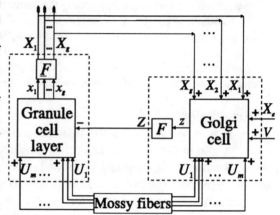

Equations that give $\underline{x}$ and $\underline{X}$ as a function of time, inputs and parameters are now established. All the synaptics weights are positive because the excitatory or inhibitory effects of synapses are included in signs between the elements of the following equations. The Golgi cell is excited by parallel fibers $\underline{X}$ via the synaptic vector $\underline{\eta}_p$, by X_e, by mossy fibers $\underline{U}$ via the synaptic vector $\underline{\eta}_m$ and by climbing fiber. Then, denoting as z its output before transformation by F, and Z its output after transformation by F:

Figure 1 : The granule subsystem.

$$Z(t) = F[z(t)] = F[z_0 + {}^t\underline{\eta}_p.\underline{X}(t) + {}^t\underline{\eta}_m.\underline{U} + \eta_e X_e(t) + \eta_c V(t)] \qquad (1.a)$$

The granule cell layer receives excitatory impulses from mossy fibers $\underline{U}$ by the way of synaptic matrix S_m and inhibitory impulses from the Golgi cell by synaptic vector $\underline{\sigma}_G$:

$$\underline{X}(t) = \underline{F}[\underline{x}(t)] = \underline{F}[\underline{\sigma}_0 + S_m\underline{U} - \underline{\sigma}_G Z(t)] \qquad (1.b)$$

We then obtain in the linear case, when F is taken to be equal to the identity, the expressions of Z and $\underline{X}$:

$$Z(t) = z(t) = z_0 + {}^t\underline{\eta}_p.\underline{X}(t) + {}^t\underline{\eta}_m.\underline{U} + H_0(t) \quad,$$

$$(Id + G)\underline{X}(t) = \underline{X}_0 + S\underline{U} - H_0(t)\underline{\sigma}_G \qquad (2)$$

where
$G = \underline{\sigma}_G.{}^t\underline{\eta}_p$, $\underline{X}_0 = \underline{\sigma}_0 - \underline{\sigma}_G z_0$, $S = S_m - \underline{\sigma}_G.{}^t\underline{\eta}_m$,
and $H_0(t) = \eta_e X_e(t) + \eta_c V(t)$.

2.2 The Purkinje subsystem

The Purkinje subsystem includes a layer of b basket or stellate cells, and one Purkinje cell. It receives as inputs: the vector $\underline{X}$ of activities X_i , which is the output of the granule subsystem; the external context X_e, and X_d , which are activities propagated along parallel fibers connected,

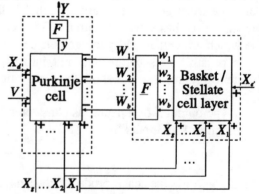

Figure 2 : The Purkinje subsystem.

respectively, with the basket cells by sysnapses γ_e, and with the Purkinje cell by the synapses μ_d; and the climbing fiber V. The output activity along the Purkinje cell axon is the main output of the unit, and it is denoted as Y. y is the output of the Purkinje cell before transformation by F.

Equations that give y and Y as a function of time, inputs and parameters are now established. The basket cell layer, denoting as $\underline{w}$ its output before transformation by F and $\underline{W}$ after transformation, is excited by parallel fibers via the synaptic matrix G_p:

$$\underline{W}(t) = \underline{F}[\underline{w}(t)] = \underline{F}[\underline{\gamma}_0 + G_p\underline{X}(t) + \underline{\gamma}_e X_e(t)] \tag{3.a}$$

The Purkinje cell is inhibited by b basket cells via synaptic vector $\underline{\mu}_b$, excited by the g parallel fibers of the granule subsystem via synaptic vector $\underline{\mu}_p$, and by the climbing fiber:

$$Y(t) = F[y(t)] = F[\mu_0 + {}^t\underline{\mu}_p(t)\,.\underline{X}(t) - {}^t\underline{\mu}_b\,.\underline{W}(t) + \mu_c V(t) + \mu_d X_d(t)] \tag{3.b}$$

We then obtain in the linear case:

$$Y(t) = y(t) = Y_0 + {}^t\underline{\mu}(t)\,.\underline{X}(t) + H(t) \tag{4}$$

where $Y_0 = \mu_0 - {}^t\underline{\mu}_b\,.\underline{\gamma}_0$, ${}^t\underline{\mu}(t) = {}^t\underline{\mu}_p(t) - {}^t\underline{\mu}_b\,.G_p$,

and $H(t) = \mu_d(t)X_d(t) - {}^t\underline{\mu}_b\,.\underline{\gamma}_e X_e(t) + \mu_c V(t)$.

We assumed that only the synaptic weights between the parallel fibers and the Purkinje cells, called μ_p^i, are modifiable in the cerebellar cortex. The long-term variation of synaptic efficacy μ_p^i for the synapse in the Purkinje cell that receives the input X_i is assumed to depend on the difference between the signal and its long-term mean value, which itself depends on the molecular calcium concentration in the presynaptic terminal. Then, it is shown (Chauvet G., 1986) that:

$$\frac{d\mu_p^i}{dt}(t) = \alpha_i(X_i(t) - \overline{X}_i(t))(Y(t) - \overline{Y}(t)) \tag{5}$$

for $1 \le i \le g$, where α_i is a plasticity coefficient, $\overline{X}_i$ and $\overline{Y}$ are the long-term weighted means of X_i and Y which take into account a memory effect (Sejnowski, 1977). We choose the continuous mean, for a given function S of time:

$$\overline{S}(t) = \frac{1}{M}\int_0^T S(t-\tau)\,e^{-\frac{\tau}{T}}\,d\tau \quad \text{with} \quad M = \frac{T(e-1)}{e}, \ T>0.$$

This average satisfies the following properties: (i) if $S \equiv 1$ then $\overline{S} \equiv 1$; (ii) $\overline{aS_1 + bS_2} = a\overline{S}_1 + b\overline{S}_2$, with real a and b; (iii) $c_1\frac{dS}{dt}(t) \le S(t) - \overline{S}(t) \le c_2\frac{dS}{dt}(t)$, with positive real c_1 and c_2. This third property is of great importance in the following.

Since $\underline{\mu}_b$ and G_p do not depend on time, we can write:

$$\frac{d\mu_i}{dt}(t) = \alpha_i(X_i(t) - \overline{X}_i(t))(Y(t) - \overline{Y}(t)) \tag{5}$$

where μ_i is the i-th component of $\underline{\mu}$.

2.3 The climbing fiber loop

The Purkinje unit presented here is not only included in a network of Purkinje units but also in a global sensory-motor loop. This loop connects the outputs Y of Purkinje units to the signals V via various deep nuclei and sensory systems. It is supposed (Ito, 1984) that V transports error signals. Then, for one Purkinje unit we write:

$$V(t) = \frac{1}{a(t)}\left[Y(t) - Y^* - \frac{1}{b(t)}\frac{dY}{dt}(t)\right] \tag{6}$$

where a and b are functions of time, $Y(t)$ is the output of the Purkinje unit at time t, Y^* the target that the cerebral cortex has to reach for a given input $\underline{U}$.

3. Conditions for adaptive control during the learning phase

3.1 Study of the linear case

We study the stability of an isolated linear Purkinje unit: then, we consider that the transfer function F is the identity, and that inputs X_e, $X_{e'}$ and X_d are constant. We introduce two new variables called $\underline{\breve{X}}$ and $\breve{Y}$, defined by:

$$\underline{\breve{X}} = (Id + G)^{-1}\underline{X}_0 + (Id + G)^{-1}S\underline{U} - \eta_e X_e (Id + G)^{-1}\underline{\sigma}_G \tag{7.a}$$

$$\breve{Y}(t) = Y(t) - \mu_c V(t) + \eta_c \sum_{i=1}^{8} s_i \mu_i(t) V(t) \tag{7.b}$$

where s_i is the i-th element of the vector $[Id + G]^{-1}\underline{\sigma}_G$. $\breve{Y}$ is the output of the Purkinje unit when V is not taken into account in the model. Then:

$$\breve{Y}(t) = Y_0 + {}^t\underline{\mu}(t).\underline{\breve{X}} - \gamma_e X_{e'} + \mu_d X_d$$

We now seek to calculate the derivative of V with respect to time as a function of $\breve{Y}$. We rewrite equation (6), adding four terms, under the form:

$$\frac{dV}{dt}(t) = \frac{1}{a(t)}\left[\left(Y(t) - a(t)V(t)\right) - Y^* - \left(\frac{1}{b(t)}\frac{dY}{dt}(t) - a(t)\frac{dV}{dt}(t) + \eta_c \sum_{i=1}^{8} s_i \frac{d\mu_i}{dt}(t) V(t)\right) + \eta_c \sum_{i=1}^{8} s_i \frac{d\mu_i}{dt}(t) V(t)\right] \tag{8}$$

If we put:

$$a(t) = \mu_c - \eta_c \sum_{i=1}^{8} s_i \mu_i(t) \ , \quad b(t) = 1 \ , \tag{9}$$

then we have

$$\breve{Y}(t) = Y(t) - a(t)V(t) \tag{10.a}$$

$$\frac{d\breve{Y}}{dt}(t) = \frac{dY}{dt}(y) - a(t)\frac{dV}{dt}(t) + \eta_c \sum_{i=1}^{8} s_i \mu_i(t) \frac{dV}{dt}(t) \tag{10.b}$$

Finally, we obtain from (8):

$$\frac{dV}{dt}(t) = \frac{1}{a(t)}\left[\breve{Y}(t) - Y^* - \frac{d\breve{Y}}{dt}(t) + \eta_c \sum_{i=1}^{8} s_i \frac{d\mu_i}{dt}(t) V(t)\right] \tag{11}$$

We come back to equation (5). Using the property (iii) for the weighted average, we have:

$$c_1 \alpha_i (X_i(t) - \overline{X}_i(t))\frac{dY}{dt}(t) \leq \frac{d\mu_i}{dt}(t) \leq c_2 \alpha_i (X_i(t) - \overline{X}_i(t))\frac{dY}{dt}(t) \tag{12}$$

But, using equality (10.b) and replacing the derivative of V by (11):

$$\alpha_i\left(X_i(t) - \overline{X}_i(t)\right)\frac{dY}{dt}(t) = \alpha_i\left(X_i(t) - \overline{X}_i(t)\right)\left(\tilde{Y}(t) - Y^*\right) \tag{13}$$

We introduce an energy function called E, given by:

$$E(\underline{\mu},t) = \frac{1}{2}\left|\tilde{Y}(\underline{\mu},t) - Y^*\right|^2 + \rho^2 \tag{14}$$

The derivative of E with respect to $\underline{\mu}$ is:

$$\frac{\partial E}{\partial \underline{\mu}}(\underline{\mu},t) = \left(\tilde{Y}(\underline{\mu},t) - Y^*\right)\underline{\tilde{X}} \tag{15}$$

then, replacing the derivative in (13):

$$\alpha_i\left(X_i(t) - \overline{X}_i(t)\right)\frac{dY}{dt}(t) = \alpha_i\frac{X_i(t) - \overline{X}_i(t)}{\tilde{X}_i}\frac{\partial E}{\partial \mu_i}(\underline{\mu},t) \tag{16}$$

Noting that:

$$X_i(t) - \overline{X}_i(t) = -\eta_c s_i\left(V(t) - \overline{V}(t)\right)$$

and from inequalities (12) we obtain:

$$-c_1\rho_i(t)\frac{\partial E}{\partial \mu_i}(\underline{\mu},t) \leq \frac{d\mu_i}{dt}(t) \leq -c_2\rho_i(t)\frac{\partial E}{\partial \mu_i}(\underline{\mu},t) \tag{17}$$

with: $\rho_i(t) = -|\alpha_i|\eta_c s_i\dfrac{V(t) - \overline{V}(t)}{\tilde{X}_i}$. When the error V decreases, the difference between V and $\overline{V}$ goes toward zero and is negative, because of the third property of the weighted mean. Then ρ_i is positive and goes toward zero: the two values framing the derivative of μ_i with respect to time follow the gradient method and the vector $\underline{\mu}$ converges toward a vector which minimizes the energy function E.

3.2 Study of the non-linear case

We give here only an outline of the proof of stability for an isolated non-linear Purkinje unit, then with the transfer function F equal to a sigmoïd. First, the vector $\underline{X}$ appears in the two members of equations (1). Then this equation admits one and only one solution $\underline{X}$ if the function which associates with $\underline{X}$ the right member of (1) is a contraction, by application of the fixed-point theorem. After some calculus, we find that the output of the granule cell subsystem, and then the output Y of the Purkinje subsystem, is well defined if and only if:

$$q^2\left|\underline{\sigma}_G\,\underline{\eta}_P\right| < 16 \tag{18}$$

where the matrix norm has to be chosen, knowing that all the matrix norms on the real values are equivalent.

Second, with this condition (18), it is possible to show that if $a(t)$ and $b(t)$ in V are defined by:

$$a(t) = F'[\tilde{y}(t)]\left(\mu_c - \eta_c\sum_{i=1}^{g}\mu_i s_i\right) \quad \text{with} \quad \mu_i = \mu_p^i - F'[\tilde{z}]\sum_{j=1}^{b}\mu_b^j\gamma_P^{ji}$$

$$b(t) = F'[\tilde{y}(t)]$$

then the loop is asymptotically stable and the energy function E defined by (14) reaches a minimum. To demonstrate this result, it is necessary to linearize the system of equations (1) and (3). It is easy to verify that we retrieve functions a and b of the linear case if F is equal to the identity, replacing F' by unity.

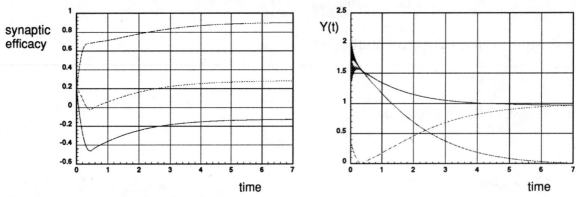

Figure 3: Effect of adaptive control $V(t)$

Fig. 3 shows a numerical simulation of the model presented in this paper, in the linear case. Conditions are those resulting from the mathematical analysis, and the goal Y^* is taken to be equal to one. We see on the graphics (right) V passing from 2.0 to 0.0, Y passing from approximatively 1.5 to 1.0 and $\tilde{Y}$ from 0.35 to 1.0 . Then, the error goes toward zero when Y goes toward Y^*. The evolution of the variables μ_i is shown on the left graphics.

4. Conclusion

A Purkinje unit has been defined using the real connectivity around a Purkinje cell. Each neuron is formal and its transfer function is a sigmoïd or the identity. A function measuring the error between the output of a unit and a goal provided by the cerebral cortex and the sensory-motor system is proposed for the climbing fiber V. Mathematical conditions of stability have been stated in linear and non-linear cases during the learning phase, the closed-loop system performing a minimization of an energy function E by adaptation of synaptic weights between the parallel fibers and the Purkinje cell.

Necessary conditions of convergence for a network of Purkinje units without delays between units have been determined (Chauvet P., 1993). In a network with delays between units, the same condition of stability has been found for one unit plus a set of sufficient conditions on those parameters that are included in the global connectivity. The study of the global net, using this hierarchical approach, allows us to demonstrate and to anticipate certain aspects of behaviour at the higher level from the study of the lower levels, specifically from interactions between Purkinje circuits and their own individual properties.

References

Chapeau-Blondeau, F., Chauvet, G.A. (1991). A neural network model of the cerebellar cortex performing dynamic associations, *Biological Cybernetics*, **65** 267-279.

Chauvet, G.A. (1986). Habituation rules for a theory of the cerebellar cortex, *Biological Cybernetics*, **55** 1-9.

Chauvet, P., Chauvet, G.A. (1993). On the ability of cerebellar Purkinje units to constitute a neural network, *Proceedings of the World Congress on Neural Networks, Portland, July 11-15, 1993, WCNN'93*.

Chauvet P. (1993). Etude d'un réseau de neurones hiérarchique à propos de la coordination du mouvement, *PhD Thesis, Université d'Angers*.

Ito, M. (1984). The cerebellum and neural control, *Raven press, New York*.

Sejnowski, T.J. (1977). Storing covariance with nonlinearly interacting neurons, *J. Math. Biol.*, **4**, 303-321.

Tyrrell, T., Willshaw, D. (1992). Cerebellar cortex: its simulation and the relevance of Marr's theory, *Phil. Trans. R. Soc. Lond.*, **B 336** 239-257.

Distribution of Gamma and Beta Oscillations in Olfactory and Limbic Structures during Olfactory Perception in Rats: Evidence for Reafference

Leslie Kay

Graduate Group in Biophysics, University of California, Berkeley
129 LSA, UCB, Berkeley, Calif. 94720
Email: lmk2@garnet.berkeley.edu

Keywords: gamma, beta, oscillations, reafference, olfaction, entorhinal cortex, dentate gyrus, olfactory bulb

This report presents preliminary evidence of a physiological candidate for reafference in olfactory perception. In this case reafference is the directed "tuning" of a primary sensory area in the brain to receive an expected stimulus. Local field potential recordings from some of the structures in the olfactory and limbic processing areas -- olfactory bulb (OB), prepyriform cortex (PPC), entorhinal cortex (EC), and dentate gyrus (DG) -- show three related phenomena. The first is the transmission of the "primary" olfactory bulb burst (60-100 Hz) through these structures. The second is the apparent handshaking burst (at a lower frequency than the primary burst frequency) transmitted from the EC back to the PPC and OB and forward from the EC to the DG. The third is a brief period of activity in the beta range (12-25 Hz) just before and possibly assisting in the state transition of these structures into the primary burst, which occurs at the end of an inhalation. The beta activity described here seems to arise in the EC and is transmitted along the same temporal path as the handshaking burst. This activity may be a mechanism for pushing forward the state change of the dynamical system, while the handshaking burst may provide either a reinforcement or fine tuning to the primary olfactory bulb burst.

INTRODUCTION

The mammalian olfactory system is a complex dynamical system, which exhibits chaotic activity and self-organization (1,2,3). Freeman and Viana Di Prisco (4,5) have shown that in response to a meaningful stimulus the olfactory bulb (OB) produces a distinguishable spatial pattern of amplitude of a common wave form during the olfactory burst (gamma range, 40-100 Hz) when an animal identifies the stimulus. Recently these findings have been extended to other primary sensory cortices (6): prepyriform cortex (PPC), visual cortex, auditory cortex, and somatosensory cortex. This report presents preliminary findings describing a possible central mechanism controlling the perceptual state of the system.

In the olfactory tract many structures interact in the initial processing of sensory information during perception [Fig. 1]. The olfactory bulb (OB) receives input from the olfactory nerve and projects, via the lateral olfactory tract, to the anterior olfactory nucleus (AON), the olfactory tubercle, the prepyriform cortex (PPC), and the entorhinal cortex (EC). The PPC also projects directly to the EC and back to the OB via the medial olfactory tract (MOT). From the caudal portion of the EC arises the perforant path through the subiculum and into the dentate gyrus (DG) of the hippocampus (HPC), and the HPC projects back to the deep and superficial layers of the EC. The EC then projects back to the PPC and AON (7). Boeijinga and Lopes da Silva previously showed that the EC is involved in odor sampling in cats (8,9).

The EC is a prime candidate for controlling recognition in sensory cortical areas. It receives input from all sensory areas, provides the major input to the limbic system, receives the major output from the limbic system (via the subiculum), and projects back to all the sensory areas. It is most implicated in olfaction, especially in lower mammals where there is a monosynaptic connection from the OB to the EC, but it is connected to other sensory areas through higher level cortices.

The controlling mechanism, termed here "reafference," is a mechanism by which a higher brain structure "tunes" the primary sensory cortex to receive and recognize an expected stimulus, thus referring to the historical use of the term (10). This phenomenon in a dynamical system may consist of a rise in the gain of a neuronal population, enabling a specific state change, or even a transmission back to alter an already existing pattern of activity.

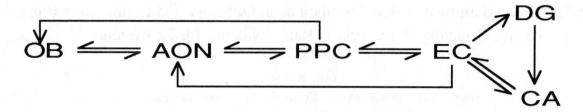

Figure 1. Schematic of connections in olfactory processing. Transmission away from the OB is along the lateral olfactory tract (LOT). Transmission towards the OB is along the medial olfactory tract (MOT). Abbreviations: OB-olfactory bulb, AON- anterior olfactory nucleus, PPC- prepyriform cortex, EC-entorhinal cortex, DG-dentate gyrus of hippocampus, CA-Ammon's horn of hippocampus.

MATERIALS AND METHODS

Surgery
Adult male Sprague-Dawley rats (450 gm) were anesthetized with pentobarbital intravenously and surgically implanted stereotaxically with bipolar electrodes in the OB, PPC, EC, and DG. A pair of stimulating electrodes was placed in the LOT to assist in placing recording electrodes. All electrodes were on the left side of the brain. Reference and ground leads were attached to stainless steel screws implanted in the right side of the dorsal surface of the skull. Surgical techniques and animal handling were in accordance with the NIH guidelines for the care and use of laboratory animals.

Recording
After recovery (2 days) initial recordings were made to determine that good bipolar recordings were possible. The animals were then trained in a classical conditioning odor identification task. (Animals were deprived of water for 24 hours prior to conditioning experiments.) Two odors were delivered: with odor A (peppermint) water was given after 2 sec; with odor B (banana) no water was given. Trials were interspersed with delivery of plain air to the odor chamber. Simultaneous recordings (1 msec sampling, band pass 1-300 Hz) were made from all four recording electrodes and odor delivery was timed to begin at 3 seconds after initiation of each 6 second record. Water delivery (when appropriate) began at 5 seconds. Records were digitized, stored, and analyzed on a Macintosh II fx computer. The experiment has been successful so far with two animals, and all data presented here are from one animal.

Analysis
    Record Selection. Records were divided into three groups: Those where the rat correctly identified the odor, those recorded at the beginning or end of a conditioning session without odor delivery (motivated controls), and those recorded when the rat was in an unmotivated state (unmotivated controls).
    Processing. Data were filtered at two different pass bands, 35-160 Hz and 5-35 Hz and prestimulus (1.5-3.0 sec) and odor delivery (3.5-5.0 sec) segments.
    Power Spectra. Estimates of auto and cross spectra were performed using the fast fourier transform (FFT) of the auto and cross correlation estimates, respectively, with application of a 512 point Hamming window. Averages were then taken of the spectra over seven records.

RESULTS

Qualitative description of field potentials
Figure 2 shows four samples of data each 1 second long: 1) a record where the rat was resting; 2) a control record where the rat had been deprived of water, but no stimulus was presented (motivated control); 3) a prestimulus segment of an odor delivery record (motivated prestimulus); 4) a segment of the same record during odor delivery but before the reward period (odor A). Motivated prestimulus and odor delivery records look similar, but the number of OB bursts is higher during odor delivery, because the rat is sniffing at a higher rate.

Identification of possible reafference signals
Data were filtered at two different pass bands to assess the characteristics of both high frequency (35-160 Hz) and low frequency (5-35 Hz) activity. Figure 3 shows an example of one

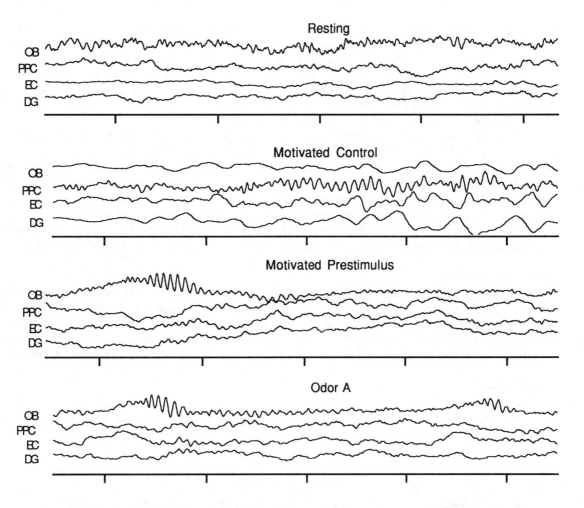

Figure 2. Sample data from four different behavioral states. The top four traces are from the resting rat. The next four are from a control period at the beginning of a conditioning session where the rat had been deprived of water for 24 hours. The third set is from the prestimulus period of an odor delivery and reward record. The fourth set is from the same record during odor A delivery but before the water reward.

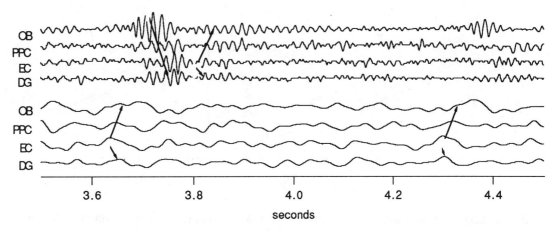

Figure 3. Top four traces are same data as Odor A above filtered at band pass 35-160 Hz. Bottom four are the same data filtered at 5-35 Hz. Arrows indicated temporal dispersion of activity along the pathways.

record during odor presentation. The raw data are compared with the same data filtered at the two pass bands. While the high frequency burst is evident in the raw data, arising at the crest of the respiratory wave at the end of inhalation, it is only after filtering out lower frequencies that transmission of the burst through successive olfactory and limbic processing structures becomes evident. In addition, there is a second burst after the first, which appears to be passed back from the EC to the PPC and OB and also forward to the DG. The frequency of the second burst is lower than that of the first, often 2/3 to 3/4 the original frequency.

The low frequency pass band shows a different phenomenon. Before each of the two bursts coincident with the crest of the respiratory wave in the raw data the low band shows a brief period of activity (one cycle, approximately 20 Hz in this record) passed along from the EC to the PPC and OB and also to the DG. This momentary rise in amplitude of the background activity of the OB just before a burst may serve the purpose of *pushing* the OB into a state change whereby it can create the burst of activity coherently over the OB, indicating a perceptual state (1).

These phenomena occur often during the presumed odor recognition period and occasionally during prestimulus control periods. In unmotivated animals they occur extremely rarely.

Spectral analysis

Averaged auto and cross spectra are shown in figure 4 for the OB with the other structures. These show that the sharing of both the high and low frequency components is prominent, deviating from the 1/f slope of the log-log power spectrum, which is characteristic of the background activity of these structures (1). The only apparent difference between these spectra and those estimated from the prestimulus period is a slight narrowing in the burst frequency peak.

DISCUSSION

Freeman described bursting in the gamma range (30-70 Hz in rabbits and cats, 50-100 Hz in rats) in the OB (10) and Bressler showed that this high frequency activity is correlated with

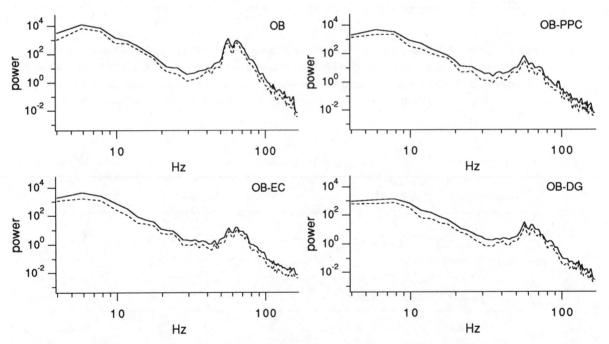

Figure 4. Log-log plots of averaged auto spectrum of OB and cross spectra of OB with PPC, EC, and DG. High frequency peak corresponds to burst frequency, low frequency peaks from interburst activity. Averaged spectra from 7 1.5 sec segments recorded during odor delivery (odor A). Data band pass filtered at 5-160 Hz. Power spectra estimated using a 512 pt Hamming window. Dashed lines are standard deviation.

episodes of like activity in the PPC (12,13). Recently Bragin, et al (14) reported seeing gamma frequency in the HPC (in the CA1 area) and DG, which seemed to be driven by or to originate in the EC.

I show here that some of the high frequency activity seen in all four structures is tied and apparently driven by the burst in the OB. Other high frequency activity may be initiated in the EC at a lower frequency than the OB burst and transmitted in both directions along the olfactory and limbic processing tracts. This may be either a "handshaking" arrangement or an adjustment to or reinforcement of the first burst in the OB. The transmission of the lower frequency cycle of activity in the beta range before production of the high frequency burst may be seen as a state change facilitator, similar to what has been postulated for the lower frequency (1-4 Hz) activity of the respiratory driving force (1).

Auto and cross spectra show a strong coherence of both high and low frequency components between the OB and all the structures studied. However, the low frequency activity described here may not be present ina spectral analysis as it is a transient and sporadic phenomenon, and these spectra are estimated from time segments much longer than the period of interest. Other work in progress (15) suggests that coherent theta activity (5-10 Hz) is increased significantly among all four structures during the odor delivery periods, so this too may play a role in odor recognition.

CONCLUSION

Viewing sensory processing in the mammalian brain as a dynamical system requires some suspension of the notion of compartmentalization of function. One must also question the idea of packets of information representing sensory objects being passed, compared, and processed by each structure. However this report shows that some passing of activity does seem to exist in this system. High frequency bursts (50-100 Hz) are passed from the OB all the way into the DG, and a putative handshaking burst is transmitted back, beginning in this subset of structures with the EC. The EC also sends a lower frequency (12-20 Hz), short duration "stimulus" through the system back to the OB. Rather than passing information, these signals can be viewed in the dynamical sense as tuning mechanisms, which enable the OB and other structures to enter a perceptual state.

Experiments are currently underway to further verify these results and to explicated their functional and behavioral significance.

Acknowledgments. The author thanks Walter J. Freeman for guidance and Theoden Netoff for invaluable assistance in surgical procedure. This work was supported by NIMH grant MH06686, Office of Naval Research grant ONR-N63373 (Nonlinear Neurodynamics of Biological Pattern Recognition), and USPHS grant GM07379 (Systems and Integrative Biology Training Grant).

REFERENCES

1   Freeman, W.J., Tutorial on neurobiology: from single neurons to brain chaos, *International Journal of Bifurcation and Chaos*, 2 (1992) 451-482.
2   Freeman, W.J., Strange attractors that govern mammalian brain dynamics shown by trajectories of electroencephalographic (EEG) potential, *IEEE Transactions on Circuits & Systems*, 35 (1988) 781-783.
3   Skarda, C.A. and Freeman, W.J., How brains make chaos in order to make sense of the world, *Behavioral and Brain Sciences*, 10 (1987) 161-195.
4   Viana Di Prisco, G., and Freeman, W.J., Odor-related bulbar EEG spatial pattern analysis during appetitive conditioning in rabbits, *Behav. Neurosci.* 99 (1985) 964-978.
5   Freeman, W.J. and Viana Di Prisco, G., EEG spatial pattern differences with discriminated odors manifest chaotic and limit cycle attractors in olfactory bulb of rabbits, *Brain Theory*, Ed. G. Palm and A. Aertsen, Springer-Verlag, Berlin (1986) 99-119.
6   Freeman, W.J. and Barrie, J., Spatio-temporal patterns of visual, auditory, and somesthetic EEGs in perception by trained rabbits, *Society for Neuroscience Annual Meeting Abstracts 1993*.
7   De Olmos, J., Hardy, H., Heimer, L. The afferent connections of the main and the accessory olfactory bulb formations in the rat: an experimental HRP study, *J. Comp. Neurol.*, 181 (1978) 213-244.
8   Boeijinga, P.H. and Lopes de Silva, F.H., Differential distribution of beta and theta EEG activity in the entorhinal cortex of the cat, *Brain Research*, 448 (1988) 272-286.

9   Boeijinga, P.H. and Lopes de Silva, F.H., Modulations of EEG activity in the entorhinal cortex and forebrain olfactory areas during odour sampling, *Brain Research*, 478 (1989) 257-268.

10 Grüsser, O.-J., Historical remarks on the ideas involved in the reafference principle, *Society for Neuroscience Annual Meeting Abstracts 1993*.

11 Freeman, W.J., *Mass Action in the Nervous System*, New York, Academic Press, 1975.

12 Bressler, S.L., Relation of olfactory bulb and cortex. I. Spatial variation of bulbocortical interdependence, *Brain Research*, 409 (1987) 285-293.

13 Bressler, S.L., Relation of olfactory bulb and cortex. II. Model for driving of cortex by bulb, *Brain Research*, 409 (1987) 294-301.

14 Bragin, A., Jando, G., Nadasdy, Z., Hetke, J., Wise, K., and Buzsaki, G., Beta frequency (40-100 Hz) patterns in the hippocampus: modulation by theta activity, *Society for Neuroscience Annual Meeting Abstracts 1993*.

15 Kay, L., unpublished results

James S. Schwaber
E.I. duPont Company
Wilimington, Delaware

Title: COMBINING CELLULAR DYNAMICS, SYSTEMS DESCRIPTIONS AND COMPUTATIONAL METHODS FOR REVEALING SENSORY INTEGRATION FUNCTIONS IN CARDIO-RESPIRATORY BRAINSTEM CIRCUITS

Abstract: System's level function must be shaped by the neuronal dynamics which arise from fundamental nonlinearities in cellular properties. Computational modeling is a natural, even necessary, handmaiden to understanding these processes. The cardiorespiratory nucleus of the solitary tract provides a useful model system to combine cellular, systems, and computational methods to understand sensory processing and integration. This approach is proving useful, for example in understanding the apparently non-additive response of second-order baroreceptor neurons. However, it also has highlighted unresolved issues of the function of the cardiorespiratory control systems. In addition, use of membrane channels in neuron models has pointed up important issues for the interpretation of the significance of conductances to neuronal behavior. Neuronal behavior does not appear to arise from unique, specific parameter values. Consequences for experimental design, data interpretation, and more broadly for understanding neural systems (!) will be discussed.

Modeling the Baroreceptor Reflex Neural Network Performing Blood Pressure Control in Mammals

I.A. Rybak, J.S. Schwaber, and R.F. Rogers

Neural Computation Group, The Experimental Station, E.I.DuPont de Nemours & Co, Wilmington, DE 19880-0323
Department of Neuroscience, University of Pennsylvania, Philadelphia, PA 19104

Abstract. A model of the baroreceptor reflex is considered. The model includes first-order neurons (baroreceptors) and second-order NTS neurons, and is incorporated into a generalized model of blood pressure control. The developed model is based on some known physiological data and on the hypothesis of barotopical organization of the baroreflex neural network. The results of modeling are discussed.

Introduction

The baroreceptor vagal reflex is an important part of the cardiovascular control system. It may be defined as the biological neural control system responsible for the short-term blood pressure regulation. A simplified scheme of the baroreceptor vagal reflex circuit is the following. Baroreceptors, typical mechanoreceptors located in the great arteries (i.e. the aortic arch and the carotid sinuses), provide the sensory information to the system by transducing arterial pressure into action potential trains. Baroreceptors provide input to second-order neurons in the nucleus tractus solitarii (NTS) located in the lower brainstem [8]. Via a network of interneurons, the second-order neurons affect motor neurons which in turn control heart rate and total peripheral resistance and thus blood pressure [6]. The responses of the first-order neurons (baroreceptors) are well described as highly sensitive, adapting neurons that encode each pressure pulse with a frequency-adapting train of spikes on the rising phase of pressure [1,10]. One of the mysteries of the identified baroreflex related second-order neurons in NTS is that in spite of receiving direct monosynaptic inputs from the first-order neurons, they do not show any pulse-rhythmic activity that contains the frequency component corresponding to cardiac frequency. They do not respond to each heart beat and probably perform a low pass filtration of their input signals [9]. Inhibitory interactions in the NTS network of second-order neurons probably play the important role in this process, as well as in the functioning of the baroreflex neural network in general. This is confirmed by the findings of inhibitory postsynaptic potentials (IPSP) in the barosensitive NTS neurons [8] and by the experiments in which the behavior of these neurons was investigated in the conditions of blocking GABAergic synaptic inhibition [11]. Recent investigation [9] revealed two groups of barosensitive presumed second-order NTS neurons called "silent" and "active" neurons. A typical response of a neuron from the second group to induced blood pressure challenges is shown in Fig. 1. Analysis of neuronal responses in this group allows us to assume and underline some behavioral properties of these neurons, that were employed in the development of a neural model of early stages of the baroreflex:

(i) These barosensitive second-order NTS neurons respond to blood pressure changes with an expressed burst of activity whose frequency is much lower than the frequency of cardiac cycle.

(ii) The character of their responses allows to assume that they are inhibited just before and after the bursts.

(iii) The bursts of these neurons are the sources of regulatory signals to the object of regulation (the heart), which in turn provide compensatory changes of blood pressure by changing cardiac output.

(iv) Possibly, each of these neurons responds to pressure changes and provides the above regulation in a definite static and dynamic range of these changes.

Model

The developed baroreflex model was based on two main hypotheses. The first hypothesis, one of "barotopic" organization, has been offered earlier [12]. It consists in the supposition that individual baroreceptors' pressure thresholds (below which they are silent) are topically distributed in a working area of the pressure space, and that each second-order barosensitive neuron receives inputs from the first-order ones, whose thresholds lie in a definite small area of pressure. There are some anatomical [2, 3] and physiological [9] data which support this supposition. The second hypothesis assumes that projections of the first-order neurons onto second-order ones are organized like ON-center-OFF-surround receptive fields in the visual and other sensory systems. It means that each group of the second-order neurons gets "lateral" inhibition from neighboring neural structures tuned to higher and lower levels of blood pressure. This assumption id derived from the above statement (ii) and corresponds to general principles of organization of sensory systems.

The scheme of the considered neural network model of early stages of the baroreflex consisting of the first- and second-order neurons is shown in Fig. 2. The network is incorporated into a generalized model of the system for blood pressure control. The first order neurons get the excitatory input signal that is proportional to the blood pressure. These neurons are arranged sequentially with respect to increasing pressure threshold. The second-order neurons get synaptic excitation and inhibition from the first-order ones as it is shown in the Fig. 2. In the considered network, the lateral inhibition between the second order neurons was organized by the direct synaptic inhibition from "the periphery of the receptive field". A more biologically realistic version is the lateral inhibition via inhibitory interneurons. It also would be interesting to consider a reciprocal inhibition between the second order neurons. We left the investigation of the above versions of inhibition for future study and have considered the simplest version shown in the Fig. 2. Parallel outputs of the second-order neurons are integrated, and via an intermediate subsystem (INT), provide negative feedback to a subsystem for blood pressure generation. This subsystem simulates the heart and vessels. It operates under the influence of an uncontrolled input signal that causes a deviation of the mean pressure from the setpoint.

Simulation of single first- and second-order neurons considering the membrane currents and conductance dynamics has been performed earlier [12]. Here, for the purpose of network modeling, we employed a simpler spiking neuron model that describes the dynamics of neuron spike frequency well without taking into account biophysical details. The developed single neuron is a modification of some models described earlier [4, 5, 7].

The dynamics of the neuron membrane potential V have been described by the following differential equation:

$$c*\frac{d}{dt}V = g_o*(V_r - V) + g_{esyn}*(E_{esyn} - V) + g_{isyn}*(E_{isyn} - V) + g_{AHP}*(E_K - V) + I. \qquad (1)$$

where c is the membrane capacity; V_r is the rest membrane potential; E_{isyn} and E_{isyn} are correspondingly the reversal potentials for the excitatory and inhibitory synaptic currents; E_K is the potassium reversal potential; g_{esyn} and g_{isyn} are the conductances for excitatory and inhibitory synaptic currents, which are opened by action potentials (AP) coming from synaptically connected neurons; g_{AHP} conductance for potassium current, that is opened by AP generating in the neuron itself; g_o is the generalized rest conductance; I is the input signal defined by blood pressure. For first-order baroreflex neurons, which do not get synaptic inputs, we considered that g_{esyn} and g_{isyn} equal to zero. For the second-order neurons, $I = 0$.

In models of the considered type [4, 5, 7] it is usually accepted that g_o is constant, and g_{esyn}, g_{isyn} and g_{AHP} depend on time, but do not depend on the membrane potential. It is considered that the neuron generates AP at the moments of time when its membrane potential reaches or exceeds a threshold. Dynamics of the threshold H in our model have been described as follows:

$$\tau_{Ho}*\frac{d}{dt}H_o = -H_o + H_r + Ad*(V - V_r); \qquad (2)$$

$$H = H_o + (H_m - H_o)*\exp(\frac{t - t_o}{\tau_H}). \qquad (3)$$

Equation (3) describes fast changes of the threshold just after the AP that is generated in the neuron at a moment t_o. Other words, it describes the dynamics of refraction. In accordance with this equation the threshold H jumps from the current level H_o to the very high constant level H_m at the moment t_o, and then decays with the time constant τ_H. Equation (2) describes the slow adaptive dynamics of the current threshold level, H_o. The degree of adaptation is defined by the coefficient Ad. H_r is the rest level of the threshold. τ_{Ho} is the time constant of adaptation.

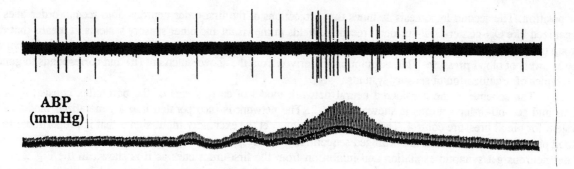

Fig. 1. Typical response of an "active" second-order neuron to increasing mean arterial blood pressure (ABP).

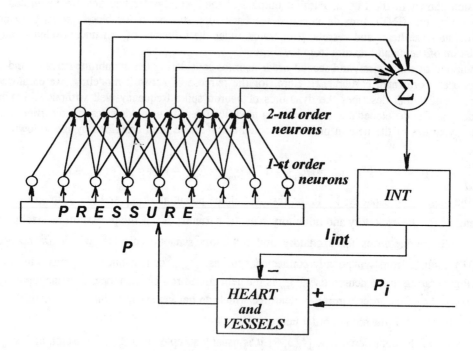

Fig. 2. Scheme of the model.

The dynamics of g_{AHP} conductance are described as follows:

$$g_{AHP} = g_{mAHP} * \exp(\frac{t - t_o}{\tau_{AHP}}). \tag{4}$$

It increases by the constant value g_{mAHP} at the moments t_o and then decays with time constant τ_{AHP}. The changes in g_{AHP} result in a short-time hyperpolarization after each AP. The equations (2) and (3)/(4) define correspondingly slow and fast interspike dynamics of the neuron excitability and slow and fast dynamics of AP frequency.

The output activity of the neuron Y is defined as follows:

$$Y = V + (Am - V) * f(t - t_o), \tag{5}$$

where Am is the AP amplitude, and $f = 1$, if $t = t_o$ and 0 otherwise.

Synaptic potentials in the target neuron, that recall its excitation or inhibition, result in the model from **changes of** correspondingly g_{esyn} and g_{isyn} of that neuron.. These changes are defined by the output variable of the **source neuron** y.

$$y = y_m * \exp(\frac{t - t_o}{\tau_y}),\qquad(6)$$

were y_m and τ_y are the parameters that define the normalized amplitude and decay time constant synaptic conductances changes of the target neuron.

Incoming synaptic signals are integrated at the neuron in accordance with synaptic weights and types of synapses.

$$g_{esyn} = k_e * \sum_j a_{ej} * y_j;$$

$$g_{isyn} = k_i * \sum_j a_{ij} * y_j.\qquad(7)$$

where a_{ej} and a_{ij} are correspondingly the weights of excitatory and inhibitory synaptic inputs from the neuron j; k_e and k_i are coefficients.

The rest levels of thresholds H_r of the first-order neurons in Fig. 2 increase from one neuron to another with some threshold step ΔH_r. The input signal to all first-order neurons depends on the pressure P, $I = f_p(P)$. In the first approximation we have considered that $f_p(P) = k_p * P$, where k_p is a coefficient. The synaptic inputs from the first-order neurons to the second-order ones correspond to Fig. 2. The outputs of the second-order neurons are summarized at the input of the intermediate subsystem, the dynamics of which are described by the differential equation

$$\tau_{int} * \frac{d}{dt} I_{int} = -I_{int} + k_{int} \sum_j y_j.\qquad(8)$$

Dynamics of blood pressure are described by the following equations:

$$P = P_o + P_m * \exp(-\frac{t - t_1}{\tau_p});$$

$$T_p * \frac{d}{dt} P_{min} = -P_{min} + P_{mino} + P_t - k_{fb} * I_{int}\qquad(9)$$

The pressure decays from a current level P to the level P_o with the time constant τ_p. At each moment t_1, when P reaches P_{min} ($P_{min} > P_o$) it jumps up on P_m (that simulates the pressure changes resulted from the heart bits) and then again decays. P_{min} changes with the time constant T_P. The rest level for P_{min} is P_{mino} (setpoint). The changes made by an uncontrolled influence, P_t, and compensate by the feedback from the intermediate subsystem. k_{fb} is the coefficient of the feedback.

Modeling Results

The modeling was carried out with IBM PC computer. Differential equations were numerically solved using the MacGregor's method [7]. Fig. 3 shows the responses of four first-order neurons (baroreceptors) with different blood pressure thresholds (the four upper rows; thresholds increase from the bottom to the top) to the increasing mead blood pressure (the bottom row). These neurons demonstrate the adaptive type of responses and respond with the spike to each pulse of the pressure. Fig. 4 and Fig. 5 show the responses of four first-order neurons (the 2nd-5th rows) and one second-order one (the upper row) to the pressure dynamics (the bottom row). Because of barotopical distribution of thresholds the first-order neurons start to respond to increasing mean blood pressure sequentially. In these figures the central two first-order neurons (3rd and 4th rows) excite the second-order neuron, but the other two inhibit it in accordance with the scheme in Fig. 2. In Fig. 4 the feedback control loop is broken off (k_{fb}=0), and mean pressure increases during the time of P_t action. In the Fig. 5 the feedback

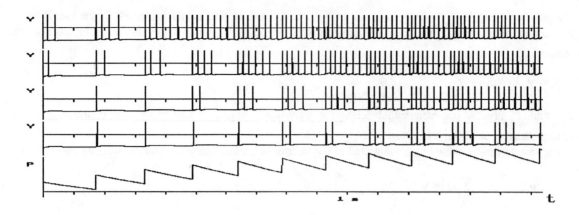

Fig. 3. Responses of four first-order neurons with different pressure thresholds to the increasing mead blood pressure

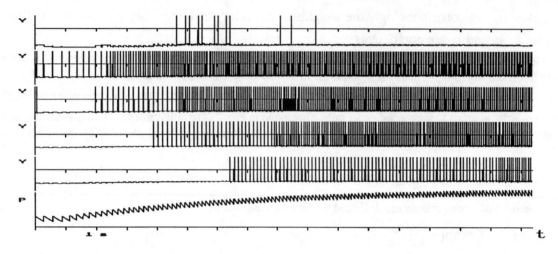

Fig. 4. Responses of four first-order and one second-order (at the top) neurons (the feedback control loop is broken).

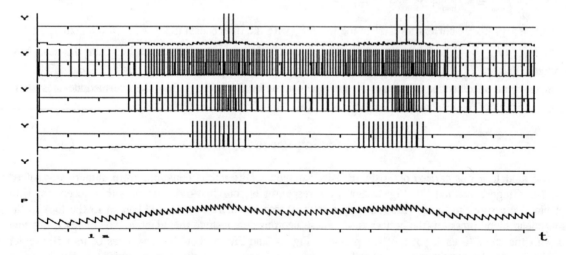

Fig. 5. Responses of four first-order and one second-order (at the top) neurons (the feedback control loop is closed).

control loop is closed , and the second-order neuron performs the regulation of the pressure. The second-order neuron demonstrates low frequency spike bursts like its real prototype (Fig. 1). The behavior of the second-order neuron in the model corresponds in the first approximation to the behavior of real neurons and answers to the above statements (i)-(iv). It supports the hypotheses which the described model is based on. Future experimental and model investigation of structural and functional organization of the network of the first- and second-order neurons will allow to evaluate and revise this model and to understand the role the second-order neurons in the baroreflex.

One of the most interesting features of the considered model is that each second-order neuron responds to changes of the mean blood pressure and provides its response only in a definite static and dynamic range of these changes. The set of the second-order neurons controls the pressure via some sequence of control actions of individual second-order neurons that is formed automatically and adaptive to dynamics of pressure changes. Thus, the set of second-order neurons may be considered to be a set of interacting controllers. Each of these controllers dominates and provides control in a definite range of changes of the controlled parameter. Together they perform some kind of adaptive schedule control. This type of adaptive control is interesting from the control theory point of view, and may be applied for the control of some complex nonlinear processes.

References

1. Abboud, F.M., and Chapleau, M.W. Effects of pulse frequency on single-unit baroreceptor activity during single-wave and natural pulses in dogs. *J. Physiol.*, 1988, 401, 295-308.

2. Bradd, J., Dubin, J., Due, B., Miselis, R.R., Monitor, S., Rogers, W.T., Spyer, K.M., and Schwaber, J.S. Mapping of carotid sinus inputs and vagal cardiac outputs in the rat. *Neurosci. Abstr.*, 1989, 15, 593.

3. Donoghue, S., Garcia, M., Jordan, D., and Spyer, K.M. Identification and brainstem projections of aortic baroreceptor afferent neurons in nodose ganglia of cats and rabbits. *J. Physiol.*, 1982, 322, 337-352.

4. Getting, P.A. Reconstruction of small neural networks. In Methods in Neuronal Modeling (C. Koch and I. Segev, eds.), MIT Press, 1989, 171-194.

5. Hill, A.V. Excitation and accommodation in nerve. *Proc. R. Soc. London*, 1936, B119, 305-355.

6.Karemaker, J.M., Neurophysiology of the baroreceptor reflex. In *The Beat-By-Beat Investigation of Cardiovascular Function* (R.I.Kitney and C. Rompelman, Eds.) Claredon Press, Oxford, 1987, 27-49.

7. MacGregor, R.J. Neural and Brain Modeling. Acad. Press, Inc., 1987.

8. Miffin, S.W., and Felder, R.B. Synaptic mechanisms regulating cardio-vascular afferent inputs to solitary tract nucleus. *Am. J. Physiol.*, 1990, 259, H653-H661.

9. Rogers, R.F., Paton, J.F.R., and Schwaber, J.S. NTS neuronal responses to arterial pressure and pressure changes in the rat. *Am. J. Physiol.* (in press).

10. Seagard, J.L., Brederode, F.M.van, Dean, C., Hopp, F.A., Gallenberg, L.A., and Kampine, J.P. Firing characteristics of single-fiber carotid sinus baroreceptors. *Circ. Res.*, 1990, 66, 1499-1509.

11. Suzuki, M., Kuramochi, T., and Suga, T. GABA receptor subtypes involved in the neuronal mechanisms of baroreceptor reflex in the nucleus tractus solitarii of rabbits. *J. Aut. Nervous Syst.*, 1993, 43, 27-35.

12. Schwaber, J.S., Paton , J.F.R., Rogers, R.F., Spyer, K.M., and Graves E.B., Neuronal model dynamics predicts responses in the rat baroreflex. In Computation and Neural Systems (F. Eekman and J. Bower, eds.) Kluwer Academic Publications, 1993, pp. 89-96.

Circuit Model of Neuronal Inhibition and Sustained Excitation

Michael D. Levine, D.Sc.

ONR-ASEE Postdoctoral Fellowship Program
Naval Research Laboratory
Washington, DC 20035

Abstract

A circuit model of the postsynaptic membrane of a neuron is developed for simulation of inhibition and sustained excitation. The model is simulated using SPICE (Simulation Program with Integrated Circuit Emphasis). The circuit uses MOSFETs (metal-oxide-semiconductor field-effect transistors) as an analog of the conductance of receptor-gated ion channels in the postsynaptic membrane. Transmitter-receptor binding activity serves as the input to the system and is simulated by an electrical signal. In the model, sustained excitation is a result of biochemical feedback from the postsynaptic to presynaptic neuron. This feedback can maintain the release of excitatory neurotransmitter. Postsynaptic inhibition is then demonstrated as a plausible mechanism for limiting the duration of sustained excitation in the nervous system within individual neurons.

1. Introduction

Long-term potentiation (LTP) is a sustained postsynaptic excitatory response to presynaptic stimulation. During LTP a neuron may undergo physical changes that promote neural growth and new connections between neurons, which are essential in learning and memory. Under pathological conditions, such as in epilepsy and stroke, prolonged excitation can lead to degradation of neurons [1]. Inhibition is an important mechanism for preventing toxic effects of prolonged excitation [2].

In-vitro electrophysiological experimentation suggests that sustained excitation occurs in hippocampal neurons [3]. A hypothetical model of sustained excitation, based on an adaptation of a more complex neurobiological description [1], is shown in Figure 1. The model does not

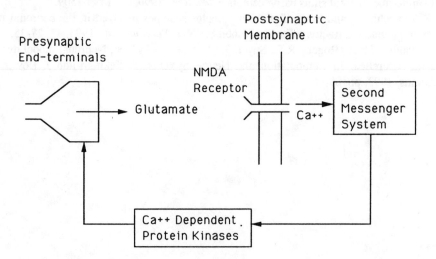

Figure 1. Model of a synapse with NMDA receptors, showing feedback mechanism for sustained excitation.

include the voltage-gating mechanism of NMDA receptors, which has been well characterized in other studies [4-8].

In this model, the neurotransmitter glutamate binds with NMDA receptors. The binding causes the opening of ion channels and a subsequent influx of calcium into the postsynaptic neuron. The increase of intracellular calcium activates a second messenger system, which is characterized as a series of biochemical reactions. These reactions result in the synthesis and release of calcium-dependent kinases by the postsynaptic neuron. The protein kinases diffuse from the postsynaptic cell to the presynaptic neuron, and activate the release of glutamate at the presynaptic end-terminals. This biochemical feedback-activated release of glutamate sustains the transmitter-receptor binding activity and excitable state of the postsynaptic neuron.

2. Circuit Model of Sustained Excitation

The circuit model of the postsynaptic membrane consists of the membrane capacitance, ionic conductances, and Nernst potentials [9] with a component representing the biochemical feedback. A schematic of the circuit is shown in Figure 2.

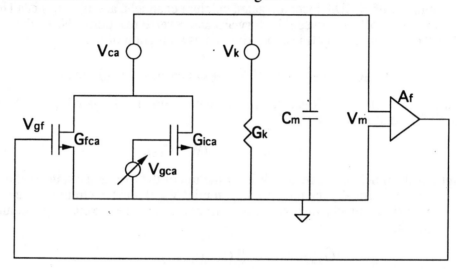

Figure 2. Circuit model of postsynaptic membrane with feedback. NMDA receptor-gated calcium channels are represented by MOSFETs. Conductance G_{ica} is a function of the initial transmitter-receptor binding activity, which is represented by V_{gca}. Conductance G_{fca} is function of feedback component A_f.

An important parameter in this model is the calcium conductance. The calcium conductance is described by two variables G_{ica} and G_{fca}, which are respectively associated with the initiating and sustaining periods of excitation. In the initiating stage, G_{ica} is a function of the glutamate-NMDA receptor binding activity. During sustained excitation, G_{fca} is primarily controlled by the biochemical feedback.

In the circuit, the variable conductances are physically represented with MOSFETs (Metal-Oxide-Semiconductor Field-Effect Transistor), in contrast to using a mathematical model [10]. The MOSFET is a suitable analog, because it functions as a voltage-controlled variable conductance in the linear operating region, where

$$G_{ds} = W \, u \, C_{ox} \, (V_g - V_t) \, / \, L. \qquad (1)$$

G_{ds} is the drain-to-source conductance, W the channel width, L the channel length, u the carrier mobility, C_{ox} the oxide capacitance, V_g the variable input gate voltage, and V_t the threshold voltage. In simulation, V_g is the variable input and $V_t = 0$.

The transmitter-receptor binding activity is the synaptic input to the system that controls calcium conductance G_{ica}. Binding activity is a chemical reaction represented by the gate voltage. Modeling of the binding activity entails transformation from a chemical to an electrical description, as elucidated in the following steps.

First, the binding activity is characterized by the chemical reaction of glutamate and NMDA receptors, where

$$\text{Glutamate} + \text{NMDA} \underset{k_2}{\overset{k_1}{\rightleftharpoons}} \text{Glutamate-NMDA}.$$

k_1 is the rate constant for the forward reaction and k_2 the rate constant for the reverse reaction. During the initial binding activity the number of open calcium channels N_{oca} is approximated as a function of the rate constants, where

$$N_{oca} = N_{ca} (1 - \exp(-k_1 t) + \exp(-k_2 t) \, u(t - t_m)). \tag{2}$$

N_{ca} is the total number of NMDA receptor-gated calcium channels, and $u(t - t_m)$ is a Heaviside function representing an offset between the forward and reverse reactions. Next, the conductance of the calcium channels is approximated as a function of the rate constants, where

$$G_{ica}(t) = N_{ca} (1 - \exp(-k_1 t) + \exp(-k_2 t) \, u(t - t_m)) \, G_{oca}. \tag{3}$$

G_{oca} is the conductance of a single open calcium channel. Finally, the gate input voltage applied to elicit a MOSFET conductance of G_{ica} is

$$V_{gca}(t) = G_{ica}(t) \, L / (W \, u \, C_{ox}). \tag{4}$$

The strength of the biochemical feedback is a function of the excitatory state of the postsynaptic neuron, specifically the membrane potential $V_m(t)$ and the strength of the feedback gain A_f. In this model, the biochemical feedback drives the sustained excitatory calcium conductance G_{fca}, where

$$G_{fca} = W \, u \, C_{ox} \, (V_m(t) \, A_f) / L. \tag{5}$$

3. Circuit Simulation

The circuit in Figure 2 is simulated using SPICE (Simulation Program with Integrated Circuit Emphasis). Strong, moderate and weak excitations are modeled as a function of the feedback component A_f. Wherever possible, the parameters in the simulation are based on biologically feasible values. In the case of a hypothetical parameter such as the feedback gain, values are chosen for demonstration of the biological effect.

In simulation, weak excitation is obtained with $A_f = 10$, moderate excitation with $A_f = 100$ and 160, and sustained excitation with $A_f = 170$ and 270. The simulation parameters for input binding activity are $k_1 = 1$ kHz, $k_2 = 1$ kHz, $t_m = 800$ usec and $G_{oca} = 50$ pS. The membrane capacitance is $C_m = 1$ nF and the potassium conductance is $G_k = 2.5$ uS. The Nernst potentials are $V_{ca} = 50$ mv and $V_k = -90$ mv. The physical and design parameters for the n-channel MOSFET are $L = 15$ um, $W = 2$ um, $u_n = 600$ cm^2/V-sec, and oxide thickness $t_{ox} = 100$ nm. The forcing function applied to the input gate is 5 volts.

The simulation input $V_{gca}(t)$ applied in all cases is shown in Figure 3 (a). The membrane potentials associated with weak, moderate and strong sustained excitation are shown in Figure 3 (b). SPICE simulation illustrates the sustained excitation of the membrane potentials as a function of the feedback gain. For the cases of moderate and strong sustained excitation, the membrane potential is characteristic of transient and long-term memory storage respectively.

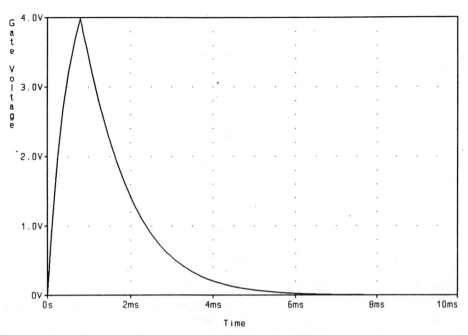

Figure 3 (a). SPICE simulation waveform representing the initial synaptic input of transmitter-receptor binding activity. The input is applied as V_{gca} to the circuit in Figure 2.

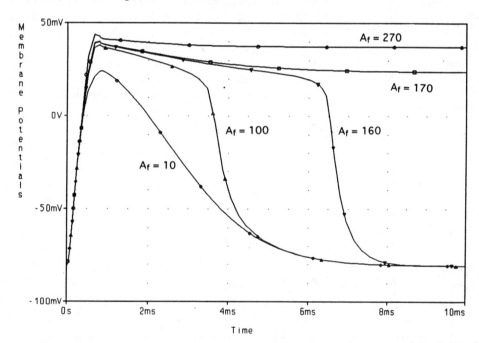

Figure 3 (b). SPICE simulation waveforms representing the postsynaptic membrane potentials elicited for different strengths (A_f) of feedback. Sustained excitation is shown for A_f = 170 and 270. Transient or short-term changes in membrane potential are shown for A_f = 10, 100, 160.

4. Sustained Excitation and Inhibition

Inhibition in the central nervous system limits excessive excitation that can lead to excitotoxicity [1]. Excitotoxicity can arise from excessive influx of calcium and prolonged membrane depolarization. This condition causes metabolic changes in the neuron leading to cell injury and death.

GABA (gamma amino butyric acid) is the primary inhibitory neurotransmitter in the central nervous system. The binding of GABA with GABA receptors causes the opening of chloride channels, followed by an inhibitory postsynaptic potential. The binding reaction is

$$\text{GABA} + \text{GABA receptor} \; \underset{k_4}{\overset{k_3}{\rightleftharpoons}} \; \text{GABA-GABA receptor.}$$

k_3 is the rate constant for the forward reaction and k_4 the rate constant for the reverse reaction. The conductance of the chloride channels is approximated as a function of the rate constants, where

$$G_{cl}(t) = N_{cl} \left(1 - \exp(-k_3 t) + \exp(-k_4 t)\, u(t - t_m) \right) G_{ocl}. \tag{6}$$

G_{ocl} is the conductance of a single open chloride channel and N_{cl} is total number of transmitter-gated chloride channels.

The inhibitory effects of GABA limit excessive excitation. GABA receptors have been colocated in some of the same neurons as NMDA receptors [2]. The implication is that inhibition of sustained excitation occurs in certain neurons.

A circuit model composed of excitatory and inhibitory components is shown in Figure 4. The simulation parameters for the inhibitory channels in this model are $k_3 = 2$ kHz, $k_4 = 1$ kHz, $t_m = 800$ usec, $G_{ocl} = 30$ pS, and Nernst chloride potential $V_{cl} = -100$ mv. The physical and design parameters for the p-channel MOSFET are L = 15 um, W = 2 um, $u_p = 600$ cm²/V-sec and $t_{ox} = 100$ nm. The forcing function applied to the gate is -5 V. All other simulation parameters have been defined in the preceding section.

The excitatory and inhibitory inputs for simulation are shown in Figure 5 (a). The onset of the inhibitory input is 30 msec after the initiation of the excitatory input. The output membrane potentials are shown in Figure 5 (b). Simulation illustrates how inhibition limits the duration of sustained excitation.

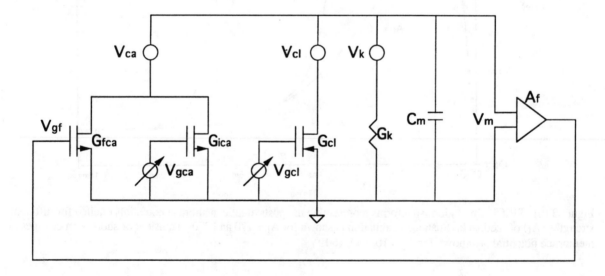

Figure 4. Circuit model of postsynaptic membrane with glutamate and GABA receptors for simulating inhibition and sustained excitation. Inhibitory transmitter-gated chloride conductance is represented by MOSFET G_{cl}.

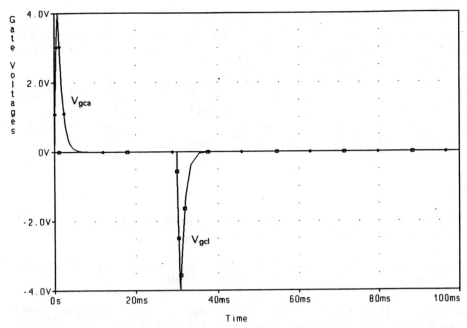

Figure 5 (a). SPICE simulation waveforms representing excitatory and inhibitory inputs applied respectively as V_{gca} and V_{gcl} to the circuit in Figure 4.

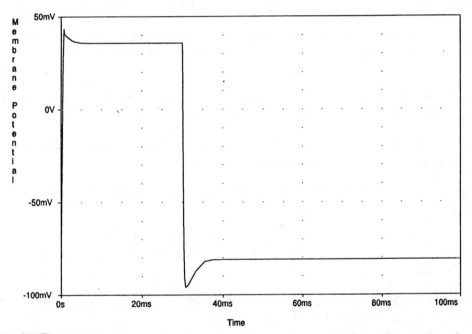

Figure 5 (b). SPICE simulation representing the postsynaptic membrane potential, which consists of sustained excitation limited by inhibition.

5. Discussion

Individual neurons possess intrinsic physical mechanisms for preventing pathological effects on the nervous system. The circuit model of sustained excitation and inhibition provides a framework for interpreting and understanding these mechanisms. A challenge in developing this framework is selection of appropriate circuit elements as analogs to specific neural parameters.

In the model, the MOSFET serves a suitable circuit analog to the variable conductance of a group of ion channels. The input gate voltage is shown to describe the activity that controls the variable calcium conductance. The circuit simulates the effects of sustained excitation and inhibition on the postsynaptic membrane potential.

From a computational perspective, most artificial neural networks utilize nodes based on an over-simplified model of the neuron, consisting of a summation and threshold. The non-linear characteristics of sustained excitation and inhibition could serve as a model for a more versatile element in the next generation of neural networks. The implementation of the model in SPICE provides an important step towards realization of neuronal functions in hardware.

References

[1] Kandel E., J. Schwartz, and T. Jessel, *Principles of Neural Science,* Third Edition, Elsevier, New York , 657-658 and 1019-1024, (1991) .

[2] Collinridge G., and R. Lester, "Excitatory Amino Acids in the Vertebrate Central Nervous System", *Pharmacological Reviews,* 42, 143-209, (1989).

[3] Gustafsson B., and H. Wigstrom, "Physiological Mechanisms Underlying Long-Term Potentiation", *Trends in Neuroscience* , 11, 156-162 (1988).

[4] Jahr C., and C. Stevens, "A Quantitative Description of NMDA Receptor Channel Kinetic Behavior", *Journal of Neuroscience,* 10, 1830-1837 (1990).

[5] Jahr C., and C. Stevens,, "Voltage Dependence of NMDA-Activated Macroscopic Conductances Predicted by Single Channel Kinetics", *Journal of Neuroscience,* 10, 3176-3182 (1990).

[6] Kitajima T., and K. Hara, "A Model of the Mechanisms of Long-Term Potentiation in the Hippocampus", *Biological Cybernetics.*, 64, 33-39 (1990).

[7] Mel B., "NMDA-Based Pattern Discrimination in a Modeled Cortical Neuron", *Neural Computation,* 4, 502-517 (1992).

[8] Zador A., C. Koch, and T. Brown, "Biophysical Model of a Hebbian Synapse", *Proc. Natl. Acad. Sci. USA.,* 87, 6718-6722 (1990).

[9] Hodgkin A., and A. Huxley, "A Quantitative Description of Membrane Current and Its Application to Conduction and Excitation in Nerve", *Journal of Physiology (London).*, 117, 500-544 (1952).

[10] Koch C., and I. Segev (editors), Methods in Neuronal Modeling : From Synapses to Networks, Chapter 3, MIT Press, Boston, (1989).

Acknowledgments

The work of the author is supported by Joel Davis, Ph.D. of the Office of Naval Research and Tomos ap Rhys, Ph.D. and Charles Bachmann, Ph.D. of the Naval Research Laboratory in Washington, DC.

Steady-State and Transient Properties of a Neural Network for Hexapod Leg Control

D. Micci Barreca and H. Öğmen

Department of Electrical Engineering
University of Houston
Houston, Texas, 77204-4793 USA

Abstract. *We present a neural network model inspired from the cockroach* Periplaneta Americana *for leg control. The model consists of a central rhythmic pattern generator and a sensory-motor network. We show that it exhibits various behavioral properties observed in cockroaches: It produces a continuum of stable gaits ranging from metachronal to tripod. The changes in the duration of protraction retraction phases for various walking speeds follow closely the behavioral data. It is shown that the network is insensitive to the initial position of the legs, in that it can achieve rapidly a coherent phase relationship regardless of the initial conditions. In addition, this transient property also extends to situations where rapid changes occur in the walking speed: The network can reorganize its phase rapidly during fast accelerations as well as fast decelerations.*

1 Introduction

Experimental studies on deafferented insects (where leg receptors are severed) support the theory that gait patterns are centrally generated, but modulated by sensory feedback. Therefore, it is assumed that a *central pattern generation* system, probably located in the thoracic ganglion, is responsible for the production of rhythmic commands which drive the stepping of each leg. This central system also provides coordination among the legs, which results in stereotyped walking patterns. Sensory feedback from leg receptors, although not essential for the production of gaits, allows the animal to adapt its walking patterns to the environmental conditions (e.g., during walking on irregular surfaces).

In this article we propose a neural network model for leg coordination and sensory-motor integration for a six-legged structure. The model is inspired by the neurophysiological and behavioral findings from the cockroach *Periplaneta Americana* [Pea72],[PFW73],[Pea76].

2 Model Description

2.1 The Central Rhythmic Pattern Generator (CRPG)

· *The oscillator for each leg:* During walking, each leg follows a rhythmic pattern of activity consisting of stepping (protraction) and stance (retraction) phases. In order to model the central control of the rhythmic activity of each leg, we used the nonlinear oscillator network proposed by Ellias and Grossberg [EG75] (see also [MCP93]). This model takes the form of a simple neural network consisting of two nodes, called the *excitatory* node (EN) and the *inhibitory* node (IN). The dynamics of the system is described by the following two shunting equations:

$$\dot{x} = -Ax + (B - x)(I + f(x)) - (C + x)g(y), \tag{1}$$
$$\dot{y} = E((D - y)[x]^+ - y), \tag{2}$$

with $[x]^+ = max(x, 0)$, where x denotes the activity of the EN and y denotes the activity of the IN. The excitatory input node EN receives an external signal I. It has been shown that within a range of values of this external input, the network exhibits stable oscillations whose frequency depends on I [EG75]. Accordingly, I will be called the *command signal* and will represent the signal that controls the walking speed. The activity of EN within a single period of oscillation consists of an active (depolarization) and a passive (hyperpolarization) phase. In order to map these complementary phases to the complementary protraction and retraction motor activities, the following behavioral observation will be taken into consideration: In insects, the ratio between the duration of the protraction and the retraction phases is frequency dependent [Wil66]. In particular, when the stepping frequency increases the duration of the retraction phase decreases, while the protraction phase maintains an approximately constant duration [Wil66]. Such a property can emerge from the oscillator network by using the positive phase oscillation in the EN to drive the stepping phase (protraction) of the leg movement. During the negative phase of the oscillation, the stance phase (retraction) is assumed to take place. A stereotyped positive elongation, independent of the overall frequency, can be obtained by strengthening the self-excitatory connection in the oscillator. In fact, if the self-excitation signal function $f()$ is selected so that $f(x) >> I$ within the range of values of I that generates rhythmic activity, the positive elongation of the oscillator will be determined mainly by the feedback signal and therefore will be fairly independent of the driving input I.

Coupling between the oscillators: In order to generate a structurally stable coordinated walking pattern, the oscillators should be coupled to achieve a global phase relationship. The coupling will be guided by behavioral data on the general properties of the phase relationship among the legs in the cockroach: It has been reported that *(i)* adjacent legs never step simultaneously; *(ii)* during slow walking speeds the order of stepping proceeds from back to front [Hug52],[Wil66]. To incorporate the first property, inhibitory interactions between the EN nodes, controlling adjacent legs, are introduced as shown in Figure 1. Such inhibitory connections prevent adjacent legs to step simultaneously. The IN node of an oscillator makes an

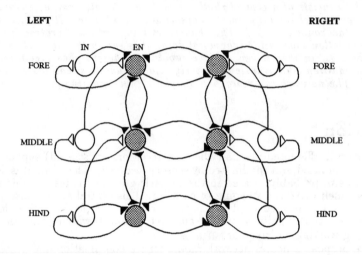

Figure 1: the Central Rhythmic Pattern Generator. Open and solid synaptic symbols represent excitatory and inhibitory connections respectively.

excitatory connection with the EN node of the oscillator controlling the ipsilateral leg positioned "in-front" to incorporate the second property. Since the activity of the IN is a delayed version of that of the EN, a *delayed excitation* is established from one oscillator to the successive one.

Comparison with other models: The proposed model differs from Graham's model [Gra77] and its more recent variations [Bee90], in both the type of oscillator used and in its coupling scheme. In particular, we use direct inhibitory and excitatory connections that enable our model to achieve a rapid phase reorganization in response to sudden changes in walking speed. The proposed model uses the same type of oscillator as the model proposed by [MCP93] for gait control in cats. A main difference between their model and ours is that the [MCP93] model uses a switch between coupling connectivities controlling different gaits. In our model, different gaits emerge from a *single* coupling scheme. As a result our model is capable of producing a *continuum* of stable gaits as exhibited by cockroaches [Wil66]. On the other hand, the model proposed by the same authors for human gait [PCG93] control uses a fixed connectivity scheme as in our model. However, our model uses both excitatory and inhibitory connections while their model is based on inhibitory connections between the oscillators. The excitatory connections in our model produce an entrainment in the oscillators.

2.2   Sensory-Motor Network (SMN)

The second part of the model consists of the circuit that transforms the centrally generated motor command signals into motor activities. This circuit also integrates sensory feedback and therefore is called the sensory-motor network (SMN). Two fundamental aspects characterize the motor behavior observed in freely walking cockroaches. First, the levator and depressor motoneurons, driving respectively the protraction and retraction phases, exhibit complementary activity [Pea72],[PFW73],[PI73]. Second, sensory feedback from two groups of receptors, the *hair plate* and the *campaniform sensilla*, modulates the motor activity [Pea72],[PFW73],[PI73],[Pea76]. In order to generate two complementary activities from the EN node of the oscillator, the EN output of the oscillator feeds into a *gated dipole* circuit [Gro72] as shown

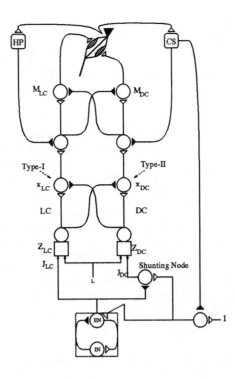

Figure 2: The sensory-motor network. Open and solid synaptic symbols represent excitatory and inhibitory connections respectively.

in the bottom of Figure 2. The gated-dipole consists of two opponent channels, referred to as the levator channel (LC) and the depressor channel (DC). The inverse-U shaped positive phase of the EN's activity is used as a *velocity command* signal and fed into the levator channel of the gated dipole. Since the duration of this phase is designed to be approximately constant, the duration of protraction will also be approximately constant. The duration of the retraction, however, varies with the walking speed. Since the walking speed is controlled by the external input I, a signal proportional to I is fed to the depressor channel of the gated dipole. As one can see from Figure 2, this signal is conveyed by a "shunting node" which receives an inhibitory signal from EN. This signal turns off the input to the depressor channel during the protraction phase. The output neurons of the gated dipole, denoted by x_{LC} and x_{DC}, are analogous to the non-spiking interneurons Type-I and Type-II found in the third thoracic ganglion [Pea72]. They provide the complementary velocity command signals to the motoneurons. The layer following the output of the gated dipole consists of neurons that integrate sensory feedback with these velocity command signals.

The hair plate receptors are modeled by a sensory neuron (HP) which is sensitive to the forward angle position. In particular, the HP will be gradually activated while the leg approaches the maximum forward position. The HP has projections to the motoneuron cells, inhibiting the levator motoneuron and exciting the depressor. This sensory loop controls the final part of the protraction phase, preventing overstrokes of the leg. Pearson found that deafferention produced an uncontrolled protraction resulting in exaggerated stepping movements [Pea72].

The campaniform sensilla (CS) sensors are mainly excited during the retraction phase. The activity of these receptors is correlated with the intensity of the load supported by the leg. Since the CS excites the depressor motoneuron which drives the retraction movement, a *positive* feedback loop is produced during the first part of the retraction phase. However, since the movement of the body will reduce the amount of load carried by the leg, this positive loop will not cause instability.

The motoneuron cells model the actuators of the motor system controlling each leg. Levator and depressor motoneuron cells receive input from the output cells of the gated dipole and directly project to the corresponding muscles. The Type-I cell excites the levator motoneuron and inhibits the depressor motoneuron. The Type-II cell has opposite projections. Since levator and depressor bursts represent velocity commands, motoneurons are described as non-leaky shunting integrators of the incoming signals to generate position commands. The mutual inhibition between the motoneuron cells ensures that the total activity is normalized (reciprocal innervation principle).

Another important effect elicited by the CS is the inhibition of the central pattern generator system.

This particular reflex can explain why walking patterns are also load dependent. For example, when the insect is climbing a hill or drags a small weight, the stepping rate decreases. When the insect is walking on rough surfaces, the stepping rate of each leg depends on its load and the stepping pattern becomes irregular. In our system, this modulation effect of the CS receptor has been modeled with an inhibitory pathway from the CS back to the EN of the corresponding oscillator in the CRPG.

3 Simulation Results

The model consists of a system of nonlinear ordinary differential equations. The equations can be found in [Bar93]. For the simulations, we used the Runge-Kutta-Fehlberg algorithm to solve the system numerically.

In a first set of simulations we studied whether the model could reproduce the empirically observed relation between the durations of protraction and retraction. The result is illustrated in Figure 3. The plot in Figure 3 shows the duration of the protraction and retraction phases as a function of the external input I. Since the walking speed is approximately an increasing linear function of the control signal I, the curves can also be interpreted as the protraction and retraction durations as a function of walking speed. For low values of the external input, the duration of the positive phase of the oscillation (protraction) is substantially shorter that that of the negative oscillation (retraction). When the value of the external input is increased, the frequency of the oscillation increases. The decrease in the period of the oscillation mainly results from the shortening of the duration of the negative elongation, for the positive oscillation maintains almost a constant duration. The plot in Figure 3 shows the duration of the protraction and retraction phases for increasing values of the external input. These curves strongly resemble those obtained from experimental measurements during insect walking [Pea76],[Cha82].

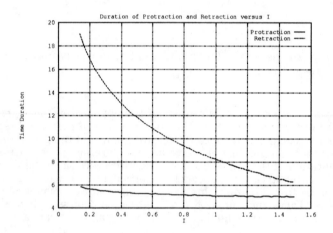

Figure 3: Duration of protraction and retraction as a function of I

In a second set of simulations, we studied the the steady-state phase relationship between coupled oscillators. We found that the model is capable of generating a continuum of phase relations ranging from the wave (metachronal) gait at low speeds to tripod gait at high speeds. Three of the gaits are shown in Figure 4. The plots in the left column of the Figure show the activities of the velocity command neurons (EN) of the CRPG. Simulations of the CRPG network were conducted on a three-oscillator system, representing the three ipsilateral legs. In this case, contralateral inhibition is not taken into consideration. The behavior of the total (six-oscillator) network is shown in the right column. In these plots, a bar represents the duration and timing of the protraction of a leg. The six legs are denoted by LH, LM, LF, RH, RM, RF for left-hind, left-middle, left-fore, right-hind, right-middle, and right-fore respectively. The first row in the Figure shows the metachronal gait produced by the model. During this gait, the rear oscillator is triggering a *wave* of protractions going from back to front. Increasing the value of the external input, the time interval between the end of one wave and the starting of the next one decreases. This is because the duration of the retraction part of the oscillation decreases more rapidly than the duration of the protraction part. Consequently, the next stepping of the hind leg tends to be anticipated, and eventually overlaps in time with the stepping of the fore leg. When the overlap occurs, one obtains the tripod gait as shown in the third row of the Figure. The middle row shows an intermediate gate within the continuum from metachronal to tripod. Overall, these results show that the network can generate and maintain a continuum of stable gaits ranging from metachronal to tripod gaits.

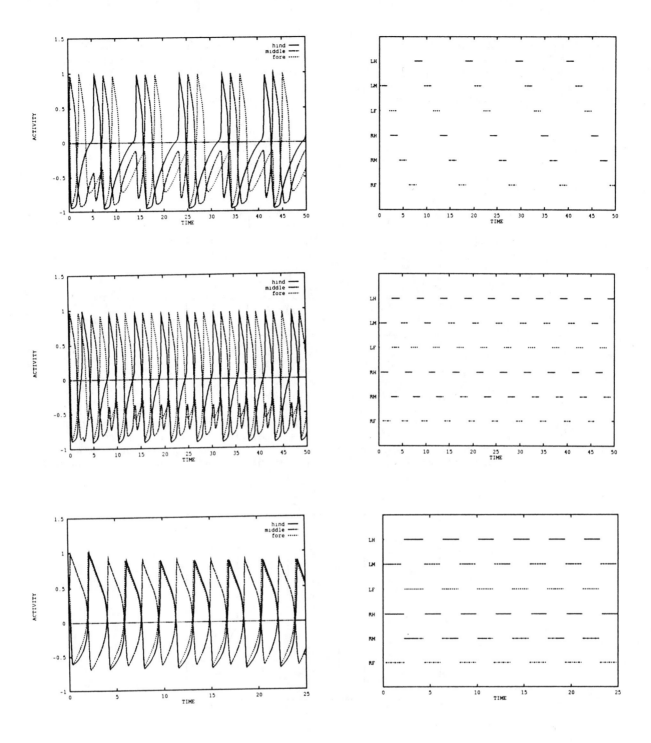

Figure 4: Metachronal gait (up), Tripod gait (bottom) and an intermediate gait (middle) produced by the model

In the next set of simulations, we studied the transient behavior of the network. First, we examined the ability of the network to establish a stable phase relationship from arbitrary initial conditions. We found that the CRPG is able to induce a stable phase relation independently from the initial state of the system. A three-oscillator system was simulated with initial conditions such that the stepping was initially out of order. Figure 5 shows that, after a small number of steps, the oscillatory pattern converges to the correct phase relation. Similar behavior has been found for the six oscillator network.

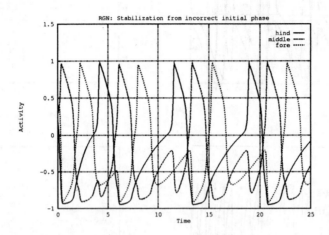

Figure 5: Insensitivity to initial conditions

We then analyzed the transients of the network in response to rapid changes in the control input, i.e. rapid acceleration and rapid decelerations. To simulate a fast acceleration, we varied the external input by a step increase and found that the system immediately reorganizes the stepping pattern from metachronal to tripod without any apparent loss of synchronization (Figure 6). A rapid deceleration is simulated by

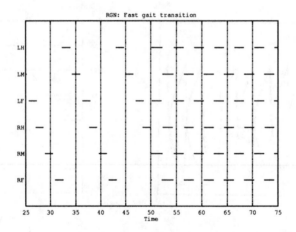

Figure 6: Fast gait transition for the six-oscillator CRPG

a step decrease in the control signal. In the model proposed by Graham [Gra77], and later adopted by Beer [Bee90], a fast decrease in frequency can cause a loss of synchronization among the oscillators. The proposed CRPG system does not suffer from this problem. The reason for the loss of synchronization in Graham's model is that oscillators are not continuously coupled. Moreover, the coupling is not mutual. In the CRPG the oscillators are continuously mutually coupled, thus a rapid variation of the activity of one oscillator directly influences its neighboring oscillators. Figure 7 shows a rapid deceleration occurring without any loss of coordination; the stepping pattern rapidly shifts from tripod to metachronal gait.

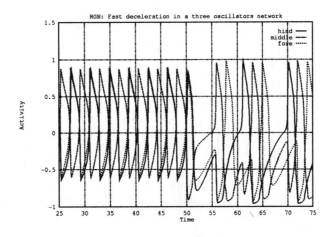

Figure 7: Rapid deceleration in the CRPG

In all the previuos simulations, the behavior of the network has been illustrated directly from the output of the CRPG. This is because when the animal is walking on a flat surface, sensory feedback does not play a strong role and the SMN closely follows the command signals from CRPG. Figure 8 shows the activities of a levator burst neuron and the corresponding levator and depressor motoneurons in the SMN. Figure 9 shows the activities of CS and HP neurons during the walk. As one can see from this Figure, since the animal is walking on a flat surface, the sensory signals maintain their morphology in time.

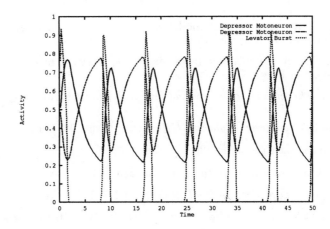

Figure 8: Activities of the levator motoneuron and depressor motoneuron cells during walking on a flat surface

4 Concluding Remarks

We have shown that the proposed neural network is capable of generating a continuum of stable gaits ranging from metachronal to tripod. In addition, the transient behavior of the network shows that it is capable of achieving a stable phase relationship among the legs irrespective of the initial position of the legs as well as undergo rapid phase reorganization in rapid accelerations and decelerations.

An important aspect of the model, which remains to be explored, is its ability to cope with complex terrains. This will require either a hardware implementation of the system or a sophisticated simulation environment capable of emulating complex terrains.

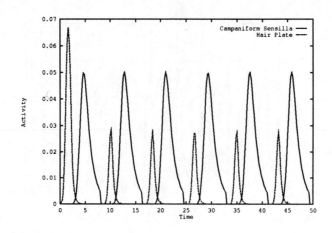

Figure 9: Activities of the HP and CS receptor cells during walking on a flat surface

Our future work will also include the integration of this network with sensory (visual) and sensory-motor gate networks [OM92]. Such an integration will enable to control the command signals directly from visual inputs and thereby achieve a closed environment-sensory-motor feedback loop.

Acknowledgements

H. Öğmen is supported in part by grant R29-MH49892 from the National Institute of Mental Health and a grant from NASA-JSC.

References

[Bar93]   D. Micci Barreca. A neural network model for leg coordination and sensory-motor control. Master's thesis, University of Houston, 1993.

[Bee90]   R.D. Beer. *Intelligence as Adaptive Behavior: An Experiment in Computational Neuroethology.* Academic Press, San Diego, CA, 1990.

[Cha82]   R.F. Chapman. *The Insects: structure and function.* Harvard University Press, Cambridge, MA, 1982.

[EG75]   S.A. Ellias and S. Grossberg. *Biological Cybernetics,* 20:69–98, 1975.

[Gra77]   D. Graham. *Biological Cybernetics,* 26:187–198, 1977.

[Gro72]   S. Grossberg. *Mathematical Biosciences,* 15:253–285, 1972.

[Hug52]   G.M. Hughes. *Journal of Experimental Biology,* 29:267–284, 1952.

[MCP93]   S. Grossberg M. Cohen and C. Pribe. In *Proc. of the World Conf. on Neural Networks [WCNN'93],* 1993.

[OM]   H. Ogmen and M. Moussa. *Biological Cybernetics,* 68.

[PCG93]   C. Pribe, M. Cohen, and S. Grossberg. In *Proc. of the World Conf. on Neural Networks [WCNN'93],* 1993.

[Pea72]   K.G. Pearson. *Journal of Exppermental Biology,* 56:172–193, 1972.

[Pea76]   K.G. Pearson. *Scientific American,* 235:72–86, 1976.

[PFW73]   K.G. Pearson, C.R. Fourtner, and R.K. Wong. In Smith S. Stein R.B, Pearson K.G. and Redford J.B., editors, *Control of Posture and Locomotion,* pages 495–514. Plenum, New York, 1973.

[PI73]   K.G. Pearson and J.F. Iles. *Journal of Experimental Biology,* 58:725–744, 1973.

[Wil66]   D.M. Wilson. *Annual review of Entomology,* 11:103–122, 1966.

Flexible Motor Control by Forebrain, Cerebellar, and Spinal Circuits

Daniel Bullock[1]
Cognitive and Neural Systems Department, Boston University
111 Cummington Street, Boston, MA 02215
danb@cns.bu.edu

Abstract: This paper reviews the theoretical picture that has emerged from a series of studies by which my colleagues and I have attempted to understand the interacting neural networks that may account for several dimensions of flexibility in primate sensory-motor control, especially voluntary arm control. These modeling studies have been guided by both psychophysical data and detailed information on biological neural networks. Many aspects of known anatomy (connectivity) and physiology (membrane and other transduction properties, excitatory or inhibitory sign of action) have now been incorporated into a comprehensive model. The model is built up from several distinct network modules, which correspond to forebrain, cerebellar, and spinal circuits. The behavioral range of the theory now includes key aspects of the following competencies: variable speed trajectory generation, size and speed scaleable handwriting production, independent control of joint angle and joint stiffness, automatic gain control of stretch (error) feedback, automatic force-pulse generation for velocity command tracking, self-organization of timing and gain of context-conditioned feedforward movement commands, self-organization of a 3-D egocentric coordinate system for representing external target locations, and self-organization of a direction-to-rotation mapping that allows efficient use of redundant degrees of freedom during visually-directed reaches.

1. A framework for understanding sensory-motor control: Generation and realization of desired trajectories.

Figure 1 presents an abstract scheme for a sensory-motor control system modeled on primate data. In the upper left section, labeled VITE or DIRECT, is a desired trajectory generator. There is abundant evidence that such a generator exists in distributed form in the primate forebrain (Bullock & Grossberg, 1991). As abstracted here, this generator takes a speed scalar and two vectors as inputs. One vector is a representation of a target position and the other is a representation of current arm position. Given such inputs, the generator continuously computes a difference vector and uses it to dynamically create a trajectory sufficient to gradually update arm position in the direction of the target position. The overall rate of position command updating is controlled by the speed scalar, and the desired velocity profile is smooth and bell shaped. In the VITE model (Bullock and Grossberg, 1988, 1991) updating can proceed wholly in joint coordinates. In the DIRECT model (Bullock, Grossberg and Guenther, 1993), the target's position is initially compared with the end-effector's position in 3-D spatial coordinates. This comparison yields a desired direction of movement, which is combined with information about current limb configuration to compute joint rotations adequate to move the end-effector in the desired direction. In either case, the output of the modeled generator is a series of desired joint positions and velocities, i.e. desired joint-space kinematics.

---

[1] Supported by the Office of Naval Research (ONR N00014-92-J-1309).

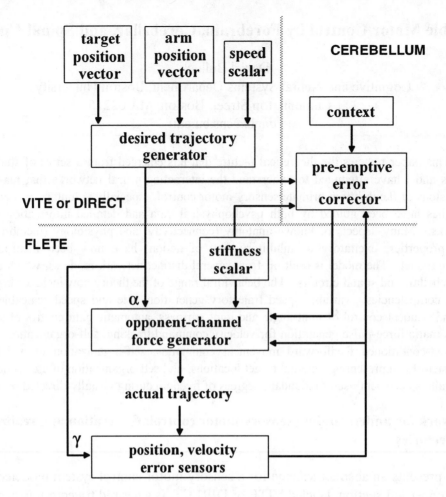

Figure 1. A scheme to explain primate data on sensory-motor control.

The remainder of Figure 1 depicts elements that work to realize the desired joint-space kinematics. In the lower section, labeled FLETE, is an opponent-channel force generator. This force generator consists of opponently organized pairs of muscles, sensors embedded in muscles and joints, and neural circuitry specially designed to regulate the balance of forces created by opponent muscles. The FLETE model began (Bullock & Grossberg, 1989) with an explanation of how known spinal circuitry might function to assure Factorization of muscle LEngth and muscle TEnsion, which is necessary for independent control of joint angles and joint stiffness. Figure 1 shows four kinds of inputs to the FLETE model: desired joint-space position and velocity signals carried by the descending pathways labeled alpha and gamma, a stiffness scalar, feedbacks of position and velocity errors, and learned error-preempting inputs based on past experience with similar contexts. The stiffness scalar (Humphrey and Reed, 1983) allows the system to exhibit a variable neuro-mechanical resistance to perturbations of the trajectory, whereas the position and velocity feedbacks work largely to compensate for the inertial properties of the arm itself.

Unfortunately, long feedback lags render high gain position and velocity feedbacks incompatible with stability. The performance cost associated with low gain feedback can be largely avoided without sacrificing stability if the system is augmented with a high gain feedforward controller that is slowly adapted by error feedback over a series of performance trials (Grossberg & Kuperstein, 1986; Kawato, Furukawa and Suzuki, 1987). This second key element for realization of desired trajectories is shown on the upper right of Figure 1. In our model this adaptive, preemptive error-corrector consists of cerebellar and epi-cerebellar circuitry. The cerebellum and closely related nuclei such as the inferior olive are known to be recipients of many kinds of descending and ascending motor-system signals, and Figure 1 shows this nexus receiving four kinds of inputs: the desired joint-space trajectory, the stiffness control scalar, context-specifying signals, and joint-space feedbacks of position and velocity errors. In pertinent modeling studies (Bullock, Contreras-Vidal and Grossberg, 1993a, b; Bullock, Fiala and Grossberg, 1994; Contreras-Vidal, 1994), this module learns to reduce its error-feedback inputs by conditionalizing its outputs (to the force-generator) on predictive context signals that include desired kinematics signals.

In summary, Figure 1 schematizes a set of interrelated hypotheses about the design of the generators of voluntary movement. Forebrain circuits are responsible for generating desired trajectories and translating them into kinematic commands in joint-space coordinates. These circuits allow effective parallel control of many muscular degrees of freedom, and allow voluntary speed adjustments that leave spatial properties of the trajectory invariant. Joint-space error feedbacks generated in the muscles are used reactively at the spinal level to improve the arm's tracking of the desired trajectory. The cerebellum uses preprocessed versions of the same error-feedback signals to gradually learn how to augment the net descending command so that errors are progressively reduced for similar movements in similar contexts. Such cerebellar learning is one of the processes constitutive of skill development. Thus in skill development there is a gradual shift in the balance between reactive and predictive control and a corresponding redistribution of signal flows within the system. The ability of an internally differentiated system to undergo such a gradual shift during on-line performance was referred to as autonomous supercession of control in Bullock and Grossberg (1991). I will now summarize the body of results that have accumulated within the broad framework defined by Figure 1. The forebrain-relevant results will be discussed with respect to data on the basal ganglia and motor cortex, because the points of contact between model and neurobiological data are clearest for these areas. The cerebellar and spinal modeling results will be used to indicate the kinds of detailed hypotheses that can be advanced within a comprehensive model that makes dense contact with neurobiological data on specialized brain circuits.

2. Some heuristics of forebrain trajectory generation.

To allow time to assess expected consequences internally -- a hallmark of deliberative voluntary movement -- or to optimally coordinate the movement with external events, it is critical to separate central response activation from response execution. Thus it is important that any model of voluntary movement allow response priming.

To minimize reaction time once the primed response is to be executed, it is necessary to pre-compute the dimensions of the response in motor coordinates. In the VITE model, precomputation of the dimensions of a response can occur at the difference vector stage. Vector cells in motor cortex are primable, and can be interpreted to code response dimensions in motor coordinates (Caminiti, Johnson and Urbano, 1990).

To release a primed motor response for execution, it is then necessary to send a gating signal that gives the primed response access to the effector apparatus. In the VITE model this gating signal is called the GO signal. Progressive damage to an *in vivo* GO pathway would produce movement slowing and ultimately an inability to execute planned movements. Parkinson's disease shows a similar progression, and because it is known to result from basal ganglia lesions in the substantia nigra pars compacta (Jankovic and Tolosa, 1993), we propose that a gating signal is generated *in vivo* by a circuit consisting of the basal ganglia and perhaps its thalamic targets.

To modulate movement speed (and duration) without affecting direction, it is sufficient to use a variable-magnitude, multiplicative gating signal. In VITE, this variable-magnitude GO signal acts by multiplying the difference vector. Evidence indicates that some motor cortex cells may carry a desired velocity corresponding to such a product.

To avoid both ballistic movement onsets and slow exponential homing, it suffices to give the movement gating signal a slow onset and gradual buildup. In the VITE model, this is accomplished by making the GO signal grow gradually during movement. *In vivo*, lesions to the subthalamic nucleus of the basal ganglia produce hemi-ballism (Jankovic and Tolosa, 1993).

Finally, to maximize across-speed generalization of learned torque-generating commands, Newtonian considerations (Atkeson & Hollerbach, 1985) indicate that steady-state, gravity-compensating torques must be learned separately from dynamic, inertia-compensating, torques, and that normalized desired velocity profiles should be approximately invariant. Such approximate invariance is characteristic of VITE profiles, and the desired position signals and desired velocity signals generated within VITE provide a basis for separate learning of static and dynamic torques.

These heuristics of the original VITE model have been carried forward in two recent papers devoted to variable-size, variable-speed handwriting production. The first paper (Bullock, Grossberg and Mannes, 1993) presented the VITEWRITE model of cursive handwriting production, and showed that it was capable of generating a full cursive alphabet from a very highly compressed code. The model also exhibits various well-known psychophysical characteristics such as a velocity-curvature tradeoff and isochrony. The second paper (Contreras-Vidal, Stelmach and Teulings, 1993) showed that the VITEWRITE model could be applied to explain the progressive micrographia characteristic of the handwriting of patients with Parkinson's disease.

The DIRECT model (Bullock, Grossberg and Guenther, 1993) also respects VITE heuristics, but introduces a design that allows enormous flexibility in the way that mechanical degrees of freedom are recruited to realize a desired trajectory specified in 3-D spatial coordinates. As such, it represents a neurally plausible solution to the problem of computing rapid solutions to the inverse kinematics problem when there are redundant degrees of freedom and variable constraints on those DOFs. The same network also solves the motor equivalence problem, and explains how primates can use tools as end effectors without relearning inverse kinematic mappings. The key insight of the DIRECT model is that the learned mapping from spatial to motor coordinates is a (spatial) DIrection to (joint) Rotation Effector Control Transform, rather than a (spatial) position to (joint) configuration transform. A second paper on DIRECT models (Fiala, 1993) demonstrates one biologically plausible way of ensuring that DIRECT-generated velocity profiles

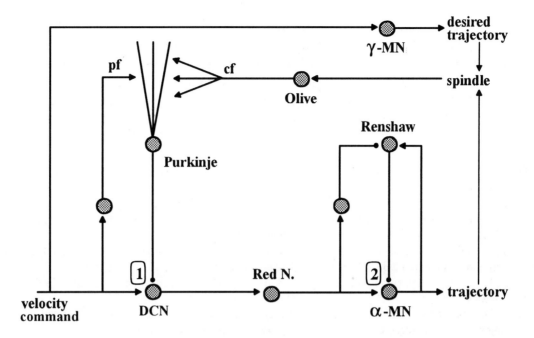

Figure 2: Two sites for gain control by release from inhibition in a model of cerebello-spinal interactions. pf = parallel fibers in cerebellar cortex; cf = climbing fibers in cerebellar cortex; DCN = deep cerebellar nuclear cell in nucleus interpositus; Red N. = Red Nucleus.

have the same bell-like shape seen in VITE trajectories and in human movements (Nagasaki, 1989).

These recent extensions respecting the original VITE heuristics suggest a number of strong hypotheses regarding the organization and self-organizational tuning of forebrain circuits, but much work remains to be done to test these hypotheses and to elaborate improved versions of the models that incorporate more detailed aspects of forebrain cell types, physiology and anatomy. I now turn to recent developments in the domain of cerebello-spinal interactions. In this case, much greater anatomical and physiological detail have already been incorporated into the model.

3. Speed scaling and adaptive cerebellar control of Renshaw cell and motoneuron gains.

Figure 2 illustrates a hypothesis recently elaborated in Bullock, Contreras-Vidal, and Grossberg (1993b). Namely, that for purposes of stability and economy of effort, the path for velocity commands through the cerebellum is "normally closed" by Purkinje inhibition of nucleus interpositus cells (site 1 in the figure), while the gain of excitatory signals through the motoneuron stage (site 2 in the figure) is low due to Renshaw cell inhibition of alpha-motoneurons. To enable fast and forceful movements, these conditions must be transiently reversed. Spindle receptor signals representing trajectory errors are preprocessed in the inferior olive and guide long term depression (LTD) of active parallel fiber to Purkinje synapses. Such LTD opens the gate on the trans-cerebellar sidepath, and allows velocity commands to simultaneously excite motoneurons and inhibit Renshaw cells. This learned feedforward control hypothesis significantly extends the proposal by Hultborn, Lindstrom and Wigstrom (1979) that descending inhibition of Renshaw cells could control the gain of motoneuron response to excitatory inputs. The hypothesis is also consistent with research showing that nucleus interpositus influenced areas of the Red Nucleus (site Red N. in the figure) often show velocity-like responses during limb movements in well-trained subjects (Martin & Ghez, 1991) and that stimulation of Red Nucleus can facilitate motoneurons while simultaneously inhibiting Renshaw cells (Henatsch, Meyer-Lohmann, Windhorst, & Schmidt, 1986). Computer simulations have confirmed that learning by this circuit greatly enhances the arm's ability to dynamically track the desired velocity command.

References

1. Atkeson, C. and Hollerbach, J. (1985). Kinematic features of unrestrained vertical arm movements. *Journal of Neuroscience*, 5:2318-2330.

2. Bullock, D., Contreras-Vidal, J.L., and Grossberg, S. (1993a). Cerebellar learning in an opponent motor controller for adaptive load compensation and synergy formation. *Proceedings of the World Congress on Neural Networks* (Portland), **IV**, 481-486. Hillsdale, NJ: Erlbaum Associates.

3. Bullock, D., Contreras-Vidal, J.L., and Grossberg, S. (1993b). Speed scaling and adaptive cerebellar control of Renshaw cell and motoneuron gain. *Abstracts of the Society for Neuroscience,* **19**(2): 1594.

4. Bullock, D., Fiala, J., and Grossberg, S. (1994). A neural model of timed response learning in the cerebellum. *Neural Networks*, in press.

5. Bullock, D., and Grossberg, S. (1988). Neural dynamics of planned arm movements: Emergent invariants and speed-accuracy properties during trajectory formation. *Psychological Review*, **95**: 49-50.

6. Bullock, D., and Grossberg, S. (1989). VITE and FLETE: Neural modules for trajectory formation and postural control. In W.A. Hershberger (Ed.), **Volitional action**. Amsterdam: North-Holland/Elsevier, pp. 253-298.

7. Bullock, D., and Grossberg, S. (1991). Adaptive neural networks for control of movement trajectories invariant under speed and force rescaling. *Human Movement Science*, **10**: 3-53.

8. Bullock, D., Grossberg, S., and Guenther, F. (1993). A self-organizing neural model of motor equivalent reaching and tool use by a multi-joint arm. *Journal of Cognitive Neuroscience,* **5**: 408-435.

9. Bullock, D., Grossberg, S., and Mannes, C. (1993). A neural network model for cursive script production. *Biological Cybernetics*, **70**: 15-28.

10. Contreras-Vidal, J.L. (1994). **Neural networks for motor learning and regulation of posture and movement**. Doctoral Dissertation, Boston University.

11. Contreras-Vidal, J.L., Stelmach, G.E., and Teulings, H-L. (1993). Neural network control of handwriting: Application to Parkinson's mocrographia. IFAC Symposium on Biomedical Engineering.

12. Fiala, J. (1993). A network for learning kinematics with application to human reaching models. Boston University Technical Report CAS/CNS-93-055.

13. Grossberg, S. and Kuperstein, M. (1986). **Neural dynamics of adaptive sensory-motor control: Ballistic eye movements**. Amsterdam: Elsevier.

14. Henatsch, H.D., Meyer-Lohmann, J., Windhorst, U., and Schmidt, J. (1986). Differential effects of stimulation of the cat's red nucleus on lumbar alpha motoneurones and their Renshaw cells. *Experimental Brain Research*, **62**: 161-174.

15. Hultborn, H.M., Lindstrom, S., and Wigstrom, H. (1979). On the function of recurrent inhibition in the spinal cord. *Experimental Brain Research*, 37:399-403.

16. Humphrey, D.R., and Reed, D.J. (1983). Separate cortical systems for control of joint movement and joint stiffness: Reciprocal activation and coactivation of antagonist muscles. In J. Desmedt (Ed.), **Motor control mechanisms in health and disease**. New York: Raven Press, pp. 347-372.

17. Jankovic, J. and Tolosa, E. (1993). **Parkinson's disease and movement disorders**, 2ed. Baltimore: Williams and Wilkins.

18. Kawato, M., Furukawa, K., and Suzuki, R. (1987). A hierarchical neural-network model for control and learning of voluntary movement. *Biological Cybernetics*, **57**: 169-185.

19. Martin, J.H. and Ghez, C. (1991). Task-related coding of stimulus and response in cat red nucleus. *Experimental Brain Research*, **85**: 373-388.

20. Nagasaki, H. (1989). Asymmetric velocity and acceleration profiles of human arm movements. *Experimental Brain Research,* **74**: 319-326.

UNDERSTANDING HANDWRITING MOTOR IMPAIRMENTS IN PARKINSON DISEASE THROUGH NEURAL NETWORKS

José L. Contreras-Vidal[1], Hans-Leo Teulings, and George E. Stelmach

Department of Exercise Science and Physical Education

Arizona State University

Tempe, AZ 85287-0404 USA

Abstract

A neural network model of handwriting generation is used to explain Parkinson's micrographia, a motor impairment characterized by a progressive decrease in letter size, handwriting baseline, and a general slowness of movement. The goal is to understand the neurophysiological and neuropharmacological bases of this disease, and its effects on movement production. Simulations support the view that the basal ganglia are responsible for (1) defining the degrees of freedom used during a movement task, (2) controlling the build-up of signals that modulate global movement speed and size, (3) rapid resetting of these signals upon movement completion, and (4) spatiotemporal modulation of these gating signals. Parkinson's disease is simulated in terms of these gating signals, and the results correspond with the clinical observations demonstrating the predictive value of the model.

1 Introduction

During the past 10 years, the study of handwriting has become a substantial part of motor control research [21], [23]. The emergence of handwriting in studying motor control is due not only to the advances in movement recording techniques, but also to the realization that handwriting is a highly practiced skill that exhibits complex control strategies that can be precisely analized. Handwriting constitutes a motor task that is very well suited for studying the neuromuscular control system as it has limited contribution from factors such as visual and propioceptive feedback, friction, visco-elasticity, gravity, inertia, speed, or movement amplitude.

Furthermore by studying motor impairments associated with handwriting, it is possible to gain insights about how the motor load is distributed across brain structures, and how these structures cooperate in specifying and generating handwriting movements. A well known handwriting impairment is micrographia, a motor impairment associated with Parkinson's disease (PD) [16].

Figure 1 shows a handwriting sample from a PD subject at different times during the intake cycle of medication. Although motor variability in Parkinsonian handwriting can be large across subjects, this example illustrates the main characteristics of this motor impairment. In particular, PD subjects show a progressive decrease in letter size, an increase in movement time, and a change in handwriting baseline. The magnitude of these effects may depend on the stage of the disease and the medication cycle.

At the level of the spinal cord, in normal handwriting, the electromyogram (EMG) is essentially unimodal and restricted to a small portion of the total movement time near or just before the beginning of the movement. EMG activity in the antagonist group is not observed until the time there is a reversal in the direction of the same component of the movement. On the other hand, in PD patients, the data suggest an impairment in force amplitude and the rate of force development (dF/dt) [22], [29]. Teulings and Stelmach (1991) have suggested that this force-amplitude impairment is caused by impaired discharges of motor units [24]. Wierzbicka et al., (1991) propose that prolongued contraction times, segmentation of force profiles, and the failure to generate adequate initial bursts in the agonist EMG may be due to delays in motoneuron recruitment, abnormally low discharge frequency of motoneuron, or lapses in firing rates [29]. Furthermore, these investigators show that PD patients are capable of increasing the EMG and dF/dt with target amplitude like normal subjects, but the increased agonist EMG and dF/dt are less at any target level than needed to produce a fast response during isometric elbow flexor muscle contractions. In particular, these data suggest that this motor impairment is due to an improper scaling of motoneuron output. It has also been suggested that micrographia is caused by a slow build-up and release of force in PD subjects [31]. A slow dF/dt in PD subjects prevents them from reaching appropiate force amplitudes within the short duration of a stroke.

[1]Supported by a Flinn Foundation Grant. On leave from Monterrey Institute of Technology, México.

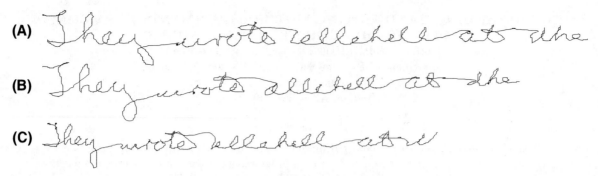

Figure 1: Handwriting examples of Parkinsonian handwriting at different times during the intake cycle of medication. The subject writes: *"They wrote ellehell at the"*. (A) Full effect of medication; (B) few minutes after medication intake; and (C) before medication intake. Each line represents approximatelly 20 seconds of writing, except in (A) where the subject took 12 sec. Note the changes in writing baseline and the progressive decrease in letter size, and slowness of handwriting generation. Due to the medication the loss of writing speed and size are recovered. The movements of the pen above the paper are also shown.

The aim of this paper is to define more precisely the neurophysiological locus of this movement impairment through a comprehensive neural network model of handwriting generation. In the next section, the biomechanics of handwriting will be presented. Next, the neural network model of handwriting generation first proposed by Bullock et al. will be reviewed and expanded to account for micrographia [6]. Finally, simulations will be presented in the case of normal and Parkinsonian handwriting that support the hypotheses that basal ganglia impairment prevents 1) build-up of gating signals that control the degrees of freedom needed during handwriting, 2) rescalability of these signals to control variable movement speeds and sizes, 3) rapid resetting of these signals upon movement completion, and 4) on-line amplitude and time modulation.

2   Biomechanics of handwriting

Although in handwriting the output is a graphic 2D pattern, the trajectory is not generated by a two degrees-of-freedom (DOF) system. The number of DOFs involved in handwriting is much larger, involving every joint from the shoulder to the fingers. Even restricting the biomechanical model of the handwriting apparatus to the hand, seven DOFs remain (three DOFs for the wrist and lower arm, and four DOFs for the index finger; thumb and other fingers merely help holding the pen). For the sake of simplicity, a three DOFs system is used to model the three main groups of synergies: vertical wrist rotation (supination/pronation), responsible for movements in the X (longitudinal) axis; finger extension/retraction, responsible for movements in the Y (transversal) axis; and horizontal wrist rotation, responsible for the left-to-right progression within words [30]. In fact, the geometrical model of the hand is simplified by assuming that the X-Y axes form an orthogonal system (Figure 2A). Larger movements of the pen across the page or in a blackboard are achieved mainly by movement of the upper arm but they are neglected here.

During normal handwriting, each successive movement within a letter unfolds ballistically and the actual trajectory is strongly determined by physical factors rather than under active control. For this reason it is important to include in any handwriting model the biomechanics and dynamics of the hand and the writing device (e.g., pen). The biomechanics can be simplified by decomposing the dynamics of the plant along the transversal and longitudinal axes of movement as follows (Adapted from [30]):

Longitudinal axis of movement

$$\frac{d^2}{dt^2}x = \frac{1}{m_1}[F_x - (k(t) + b_1)\frac{d}{dt}x - f[((\frac{d}{dt}x)^2 + (\frac{d}{dt}y)^2)^{0.5}] - c_1 x] \tag{1}$$

Transversal axis of movement

$$\frac{d^2}{dt^2}y = \frac{1}{m_1 + m_2}[F_y - ((k(t) + b_1 + b_2)\frac{d}{dt}y - f[((\frac{d}{dt}x)^2 + (\frac{d}{dt}y)^2)^{0.5}] - (c_1 + c_2)y] \tag{2}$$

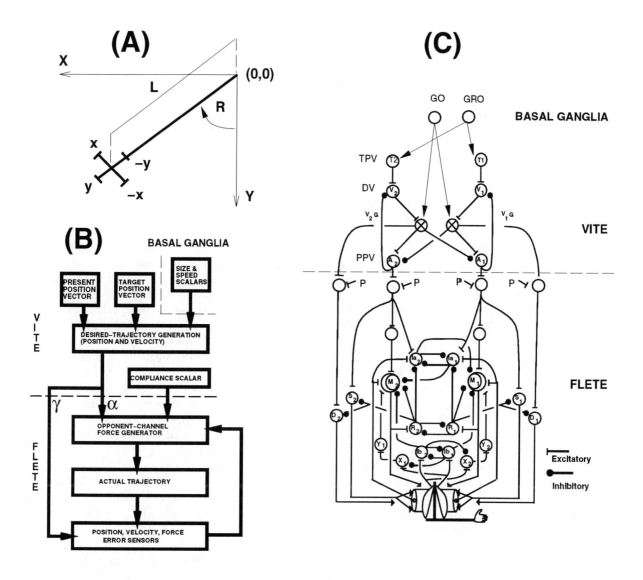

Figure 2: Neural network of movement control as applied to handwriting. (A) The geometric model of the three DOFs hand: finger extension or retraction, which moves the pen along the transversal axis (Y), vertical wrist rotation (supination/pronation), which moves the pen along longitudinal axis (X); and horizontal wrist rotation (R), which provides the left-to-right progression within words along the longitudinal axis (X). (B) Neuromuscular control system of handwriting for each DOF. A stage associated with the basal ganglia specifies the degrees of freedom, in terms of parallel GO (speed) and GRO (size) scalar signals according to the demands of the task. A stage associated with motor cortex (VITE) specifies the desired kinematics of the movement in terms of position and velocity [7]. The outflow signals from VITE are processed by a neural network of the spinal cord (FLETE) that rotates the joints by changing the balance of muscle forces across the joints [5]. (C) Neural network representation of the neuromuscular control system depicted in (B) showing an opponently organized, spino-muscular circuit (lower part) receiving descending signals of two types from a trajectory generator (upper part) and other sites presumed to be located in the higher brain. In the theory, the balance between signals emerging from neuron pools A_1 and A_2 sets desired joint angle, while the signal P sets desired joint stiffness. Signals V_1G and V_2G set desired shortening/lengthening velocities for the opponent muscles during movements. The lower circuit's structure is based on anatomical and physiological studies of the spinal cord circuitry [5].

where (x, y), $(\frac{d}{dt}x, \frac{d}{dt}y)$, and $(\frac{d^2}{dt^2}x, \frac{d^2}{dt^2}y)$ represent the position, velocity, and acceleration of the hand and pen along the longitudinal and transversal axes respectively; m_1 and m_2 are the inertial loads of the hand and fingers respectively, including the mass properties of the pen; $k(t)$ is a time-varying friction coefficient; $f()$ represents a static friction function to account for reaction forces that oppose movement onset; $(b_1\frac{d}{dt}x, (b_1 + b_2)\frac{d}{dt}y)$ and $(c_1 x, (c_1 + c_2)y)$ represents the muscle viscosity and muscle stiffness along the longitudinal and transversal axes respectively; and F_x and F_y represent the muscle forces (or torques) that act to move the hand. A further simplification can be made if the friction and muscle viscosity and stiffness are neglected. In this case, the acceleration of the pen along the longitudinal and transversal axes of movement are proportional to the muscle forces generated.

3 Neural network model of handwriting generation

Empirical and neural network evidence suggests a multi-module model of handwriting movement control [6], [25], [28]. In the simplified model, the highest-level module is the (1) motor memory, containing the abstract description of the handwriting letters (e.g. relative stroke sizes). Before execution, the appropiate letter descriptions are extracted from motor memory by the (2) retrieval module. The extracted sequence of movement descriptors forms the motor program, where the movement parameters still have to be specified. The muscle-independent scale parameters (e.g. overall speed, size, and force) are specified in the (3) parameter-setting module. The muscle-dependent parameters (e.g. limb, orientation, and degrees of freedom) are specified in the lowest level module, which forms the (4) muscle-initiation module. This symbolic model of movement control can be formally specified in terms of neural networks of the basal ganglia, motor cortex, and spinal cord schematized in Figure 2C.

In the neural network of Figure 2C, a subcortical structure associated with the basal ganglia provides multiple gating signals that specify the degrees of freedom used during movement execution. These signals are known as GO signals that code movement onset and movement speed. Another type of signal (GRO) specifies the size of the movement [6]. Experimental evidence supports the existence of these gating signals. It has been found that neurons in the putamen tend to have a linear relation to the amplitude (a GRO signal) and speed (a GO signal) of movement [9]. Alexander and DeLong (1985) found that amplitude, velocity, and acceleration of movement increase monotonically in microstimulation-evoked movements in the putamen [2].

These gating signals are part of the global parameter-setting stage in the model. The motor program contains normalized directional commands that code individual strokes' direction and amplitude. It has been suggested that stroke-length ratios are most likely parameters to be stored in the handwriting motor program [27]. This conclusion is based upon the observation that the vertical stroke size is highly invariant across replications in comparison to stroke duration or peak acceleration. The spatial character of the motor program is also supported by the observation that if a stroke has a greater size than planned, the subsequent stroke, which is in the opposite direction, will automatically have a greater size than planned, so that the disturbing effect of the previous stroke is corrected [27]. These corrections have not been found for stroke durations.

In the model, a graphic motor-pattern store prescribes the sequence of strokes and also the relative sizes required to perform the allograph. This code is stored in a graphic motor-pattern buffer awaiting movement initiation. This buffered movement code needs to be completed with the expected scale and speed scalars before it can be released by a sequential controller in a first-in, first-out fashion. This completion takes place in the parameter setting stage in a central trajectory formation module. This module known as Vector-Integration To-Endpoint (VITE) takes spatio-temporal disjoint commands from a sequential controller at times when a velocity peak in a given synergy is obtained. The VITE module receives information about the target position vector for the pen (TPV) from the sequential controller. The TPV can be rescaled by a GRO signal to specify a smaller or larger than usual letter size. The difference between the TPV and the PPV is computed continuously in the difference vector stage (DV) that provides information about the direction and magnitude of the movement. The output of the DV is gated multiplicatively by the GO signal. Improper onset and amplitude scaling of the GO signal would result in a delay and slowness of movement as seen in Parkinsonian subjects. The product DV*GO is the desired velocity to launch the sequential motor commands. Note that the inhibitory feedback from the PPV to the DV stage drives the DV towards zero as the PPV approaches the TPV (Figure 2C).

To generated smooth curvilinear strokes, the VITE model processes new motor commands at discrete times, e.g. at times when one or more velocity traces reach a maximum [6]. Detection of one or more peak velocities trigger read-in of a new movement command from the buffered graphic motor-pattern code containing the directional commands for each degree of freedom used by the handwriting apparatus. The order and timing of the motor commands determine the curvature of the movement.

Each degree of freedom is controlled by its own VITE circuit, each with an independent GO signal. Bullock and Grossberg have hypothesized that the basal ganglia is the source of this signal [7]. Recent experimental data of the basal ganglia indeed support the existence of parallel motor channels through the basal ganglia [1], [18]; e.g. through neurochemical compartmentalization in the striatum, pallidum, and substantia nigra that could allow finely individuated control under normal physiological conditions [14]. Furthermore, the data suggest that these pathways are somatotopically organized in a parallel fashion [11].

Basal ganglia has been implicated in the selection or gating of the DOFs or joints involved in multijoint movements [13]. This task would involve learning or adaptation of the motor program. This adaptability could provide a basis for explaining the strategy of PD patients who stiffen the wrist joint (leaving it outside from the programmed movement) in order to reduce tremor. The adaptive preference to use mainly fingers for handwriting by PD subjects is supported by that fact that the pyramidal system controlling the fingers is not affected by PD, whereas the extrapyramidal system that controls the wrist is affected by PD [8].

In the model, each synergetic group of muscles acting to rotate a joint forms a DOF. The VITE modules provide the outflow motor commands to the spinal motoneurons that innervate the opponent muscles crossing the joint. Rotation of the joint is performed by changing the balance of muscle forces across the underlying joints. In [5] a neural network of the spinal cord has been analized. The model follows closely the anatomy, neurophysiology, and neural components of the spinal circuitry. The model known as the FLETE circuit stands for Factorization of LEngth and Tension, and has advanced the hypothesis that the spinal cord has evolved to achieve position-code invariance, or the ability of the system to mantain a given position, while varying joint stiffness. The FLETE model provides access to variables that can be readily associated with experimental measurements such as joint stiffness (P), muscle forces, joint position, velocity, and acceleration, and motoneuron activities. In this paper, we focus in the kinematics of normal and Parkinsonian handwriting.

4 Simulations

Neural network simulations were performed to study normal and Parkinsonian handwriting. Figure 3 shows simulations of the sentence " *They wrote ellehell*" for (A) normal and (B) a motor system where PD impairments have been implemented. The buffered graphic-motor pattern consisted of a sequence of 109 motor commands that fully specify the production of the 17 connected letters in the handwriting sample (Table 1). This buffer was completed by specifying the global movement speed (GO) and handwriting size (GRO) scalars.

The simulation of the Parkinsonian handwriting was performed as follows. The sigmoidal GO signal that specifies the global speed of the movement was decreased in amplitude to simulate a slowdown of the movement as seen in Parkinsonian subjects. Also the scalar factor given by the GRO signal was recursively decreased during the execution of the movement (e.g. negative feedback). The effects of these signal manipulations were to decrease the letter size progressively, to change the handwriting baseline, and to increase movement time.

Figure 3 also depicts the velocities for each degree of freedom illustrated in the geometric model of the handwriting apparatus shown in Figure 2A. The velocity along the longitudinal plane from the horizontal wrist rotation (V_R) is responsible for the left-to-right progression (within words), and for some of the horizontal displacement of the pen within a single character.

Figure 4 shows an analysis of the simulated handwriting in terms of longitudinal and transversal velocities, tangential velocity, and accelerations of the pen. By assuming small dynamic effects of the system during handwriting production (e.g. friction, viscosity, and inertia), it is possible to associate the acceleration of the pen to the muscle forces generated by the spinal circuitry during the production process. From the simulation by the Parkinsonian neural network, we see that the peak forces (e.g. accelerations) are smaller than in the normal case. Also a progressive decrease in peak force is observed.

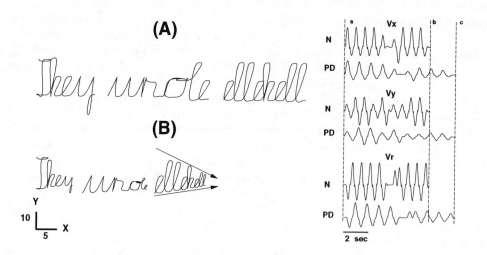

Figure 3: Neural network simulation of handwriting. (A) Normal handwriting of the sentence " *They wrote ellehell*". (B) Parkinsonian handwriting. Note the progressive decrease in letter size, and the change in writing baseline. The velocities for each DOF (Vx, Vy, and Vr) are shown for the world *ellehell*. Movement time in the Parkinsonian simulation (PD) is increased with respect to the intact system (N). Keys: *a*, movement onset; *b* and *c* represent end of movement for the normal and Parkinsonian cases respectively.

References

[1] Alexander, G.I.M., & Crutcher, M.D. (1990). Functional architecture of basal ganglia circuits: Neural substrates of parallel processing. *Trends in Neuroscience*, **13**:266-271.

[2] Alexander, G.E., and DeLong, M.R. (1985a). Microstimulation of the primate neostriatum. I. Physiological properties if striatal microexcitable zones. *Journal of Neurophysiology*, **53**:1401-1416.

[5] Bullock, D. and Contreras-Vidal, J.L. (1993). How spinal neural networks reduce discrepancies between motor intention and motor realization. In K. Newell and D. Corcos (Eds.), **Variability and Motor Control**, Champaign, Illinois: Human Kinetics Press, pp. 183-221.

[6] Bullock, D., Grossberg, S., and Mannes, C. (1993b). A neural network model for cursive script production. *Biological Cybernetics*. In Press.

[7] Bullock, D. and Grossberg, S. (1988). Neural dynamics of planned arm movements: Emergent invariants and speed-accuracy properties during trajectory formation. *Psychological Review*, **95**:49-90.

[8] Côte, L., & Crutcher, M.D. (1985). Motor functions of the basal ganglia and diseases. In E.R. Kandell and J.H. Schwartz (Eds.), **Principles of Neural Science**, (pp. 523-535). Amsterdam: North Holland.

[9] Cruther, M.D. and DeLong, M.R. (1984b). Single cell studies of the primate putamen. II Relations to Direction of movement and pattern of muscular activity. *Experimental Brain Research*, **53**:244-258.

[11] Flaherty, A.W., and Graybiel, A.M. (1991). Corticostriatal transformations in the primate somatosensory system. Projections from physiologically mapped body-part representations. *J Neurophysiol*, **66**, 1249-1263.

[13] Golani, I. (1992). A mobility gradient in the organization of vertebrate movement: The perception of movement through symbolic language. *Behavioral and Brain Sciences*, **15**, 249-308.

[14] Graybiel, A.M. (1984). Neurochemically specified subsystems in the basal ganglia. In Evered, D., and O'Connor, M. (Eds.), **Functions of the Basal Ganglia**, London:Pitman, pp. 114-144.

[16] Margolin, D.I. and Wing, A.M. (1983). Agraphia and micrographia: Clinical manifestations of motor programming and performance disorders. *Acta Psychologica*, **54**, 263-283.

| They | | | wrote | | | ellehell | | |
X	Y	R	X	Y	R	X	Y	R
4	-10	0	20	100	0	25	100	0
0	0	5	0	0	0	0	0	-4
4	10	0	-5	-100	0	-10	-100	0
0	0	0	0	0	4	0	0	6
0	0	-5	20	100	0	25	200	0
4	-200	0	0	0	0	0	0	-4
0	0	-4	-5	-100	0	-10	-200	0
0	0	0	0	0	4	0	0	6
0	0	8	20	100	0	25	200	0
15	200	0	0	0	0	0	0	-4
0	0	-4	-5	-100	0	-10	-200	0
2	-200	0	0	0	0	0	0	6
0	0	0	10	100	0	25	100	0
10	100	0	0	0	0	0	0	-4
0	0	4	2	-20	0	-10	-100	0
-20	-100	0	0	0	6	0	0	6
0	0	5	-10	-80	0	15	200	0
2	100	0	0	0	5	0	0	-4
0	0	-4	0	0	0	2	-200	0
-10	-100	0	0	0	2	0	0	0
0	0	6	10	100	0	10	100	0
20	100	0	0	0	10	0	0	4
0	0	0	0	0	0	-20	-100	0
-5	-100	0	0	0	-10	0	0	5
0	0	4	-10	-100	0	25	100	0
20	100	0	0	0	10	0	0	-4
0	0	0	10	100	0	-10	-100	0
-5	-200	0	0	0	0	0	0	6
0	0	-2	0	0	5	25	200	0
5	100	0	-5	-10	0	0	0	-4
0	0	6	0	0	8	-10	-200	0
0	0	0	25	100	0	0	0	6
			0	0	-4	25	200	0
			10	-200	0	0	0	-4
			0	0	6	-10	-200	0
			25	100	0	0	0	6
			0	0	-4	0	0	0
			-10	-100	0			
			0	0	6			
			0	0	0			

Table I: Motor code for the production of the sentence *They wrote ellehell*. X,Y, and R define the 3 DOFs for the hand.

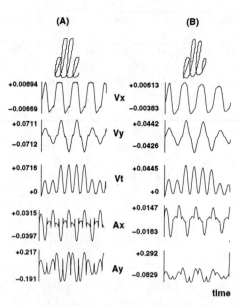

Figure 4: Analysis of the simulated handwriting showing longitudinal (Vx) and transversal (Vy) velocities; tangential velocity (Vt) of the end-point (pen); and accelerations (Ax,Ay). The acceleration are proportional to the net muscle forces generated by the synergies moving the hand and pen in the longitudinal and transversal axes. Note the smaller peak amplitudes for the Parkinsonian (B) than for the normal handwriting (A). Also note the progressive decay in amplitude in the acceleration profiles in the Parkinsonian handwriting.

[18] Parent, A. (1990). Extrinsic connections of the basal ganglia. *Trends in Neurosciences*, **13**:254-258.

[21] Rosenbaum, D.A. (1991). **Human Motor Control**. New York: Academic Press.

[22] Stelmach, G.E., & Worringham, C.J. (1988). The preparation and production of isometric force in Parkinson disease. *Neuropsychology*, **26**, 93-103.

[23] Teulings, H.L. (in press). Handwriting movement control. In S.W. Keele and H. Heuer (Eds.), **Handbook of Perception and Action**. Vol. 3: Motor Skills. London: Academic Press.

[24] Teulings, H.L., and Stelmach, G.E. (1991). Control of stroke size, peak acceleration, and stroke duration in Parkinsonian handwriting. *Hum Mov Sci*, **10**, 315-333.

[25] Teulings, H.L., Thomassen, A.J.W.M., & Van Galen, G.P. (1983). Preparation of partly precued handwriting movements: The size of movement units in writing. *Acta Psychologica*, **54**:165-177.

[27] Teulings, H.L., & Schomaker, L.R.B. (1993). Invariant properties between stroke features in handwriting. *Acta Psychologica*, **82**:69-88.

[28] Van Galen, G.P. (1991). Handwriting: Issues for a psychomotor theory. *Human Movement Science*, **10**:165-191.

[29] Wierzbicka, M.M., Wiegner, A.W., Logigian, E.L., and Young, R.R. (1991). Abnormal most-rapid isometric contractions in patients with Parkinson's disease. *J Neurol, Neurosurg, and Psychiatry*, **54**, 210-216.

[30] Wing, A.M. (1978). Response timing in handwriting. In G.E. Stelmach (Ed.), **Information Processing in Motor Control and Learning**, (pp.153-172). New York: Academic Press.

[31] Wing, A.M. (1988). A comparison of the rate of pinch grip force increases and decreases in Parkinsonian bradykinesia. *Neuropsychology*, **26**, 479-482.

A Neurocomputational Theory of Hippocampal Region Function in Associative Learning

Catherine E. Myers & Mark A. Gluck
Center for Molecular and Behavioral Neuroscience
Rutgers University, Newark, NJ 07102

Abstract

Brain function can be elucidated both by top-down connectionist models, which attempt to account for behavior, and bottom-up models which are constrained by the anatomy and physiology of brain regions. We have previously presented a top-down model of hippocampal-region processing in associative learning which accounts for a range of conditioned behaviors in the intact and hippocampal-lesioned animal. In turn, this top-down model can be instantiated by smaller, bottom-up modules which each represent processing in one specific structure. A bottom-up model has been developed for the parahippocampal region, and suggests the way in which that subregion might contribute to the overall processing of the hippocampal region. The resulting model combines both top-down and bottom-up constraints, addressing both behavioral data and physiological observations.

Introduction

Connectionist network models are becoming increasingly useful as tools for the understanding of the neural bases of learning and memory. Such models can operate at many different levels. At one extreme are the top-down, behaviorally-motivated models which seek to reproduce learning phenomena without any particular attention to how such functions might be implemented in the brain; at the other extreme lie bottom-up, physiologically-driven models which closely mimic the anatomical and physiological structure of brain regions, in an attempt to quantify how they might process information. Often, these two paths are pursued independently; we believe however that there is much to be gained by attempting to combine the top-down and bottom-up approaches, resulting in models which characterize overt behavior but are implementable via processes known to exist in the brain (c.f., Gluck & Granger, 1993).

A great deal of empirical and theoretical study has centered on the hippocampal region, a series of structures in the brain which are implicated in learning and memory in humans (Scoville & Millner, 1957; Squire, 1987) and animals (Misking, 1982; Squire & Zola-Morgan, 1983). Hippocampal-dependent memories are especially marked by their accessibility to conscious recollection while the hippocampal region appears not to be critical for the formation of skills or habits which are formed incrementally over time (c.f., Squire, 1987). Lesions of the hippocampal region have been shown to disrupt performance in a wide range of tasks ranging from spatial learning to intermediate-term memory to contextual processing and more. What is lacking, however, has been a computational description of the functional role of the hippocampal region, such that lesion to the region would result in the observed impairments.

We have presented a top-down theory of hippocampal-region function which can be implemented via a connectionist network model and which successfully accounts for a wide range of conditioned behaviors in the intact and hippocampal-lesioned animal and human (Gluck & Myers, 1993). More recently, we have considered a bottom-up, physiologically-motivated model which can instantiate some of the processes implicit in the top-down model (Myers, et al., 1994/submitted). The convergence of these two models provides strong support for this account of hippocampal-region function and shows how the top-down and bottom-up approaches can interact and inform each other.

A Top-Down Connectionist Model of Hippocampal-Region Function

We have recently presented a computational theory of hippocampal-region function in associative learning which emphasizes an information processing role in the representation of stimulus information (Gluck & Myers, 1993). Central to this account of hippocampal-region function is the idea of a stimulus representation, the pattern of activity evoked by a stimulus input. This representation is presumed to be distributed over many elements, which could be neurons in a brain or nodes in a connectionist network. Within this conceptual framework, learning about various stimuli is equivalent to associating the representations they activate with the appropriate behavioral outputs. This conceptualization can be illustrated in terms of learning in a standard multi-layer connectionist network: inputs are mapped to a representation in the hidden layer nodes; associations are then formed between these representations and an appropriate output.

In this way, learning about one stimulus will generalize to other stimuli as a function of how similar (or overlapping) their representations are. If the representations of two stimuli are very similar, then associations which have accrued to one stimulus will tend to generalize to the other. If the representations are very dissimilar, then associations will generalize only minimally. From this perspective, we can see how learning will be facilitated if the representations are biased by two constraints. First, stimuli which are to be associated with maximally different output should have minimally overlapping representations, to lessen generalization between them. We have called this constraint representational differentiation. Second, stimuli which co-occur and therefore should have maximal generalization, should have similar representations. We have called this a bias to compress the representations of co-occurring, mutually redundant information.

The core of our proposal is that the hippocampal region has the ability to construct new stimulus representations which are biased by these two constrains of differentiation and compression (Gluck & Myers, 1993). Other regions in the cerebral and cerebellar cortices, which are presumed to be the sites of long-term memory, may not be able to form these new representations themselves; these other regions can, however, adopt the new representations formed in the hippocampal region.

This theory can be instantiated, and tested, with a simple connectionist network model (Gluck & Myers, 1993). A "hippocampal" network, on the right in Figure 1a, learns to map from inputs representing the stimulus to outputs which reproduce that stimulus, plus a prediction of future reinforcement. This network contains a narrow hidden layer, and therefore is forced to form representations in that layer which compress redundant information while preserving (or differentiating) information which predicts the desired outputs (c.f., Hinton, 1989). A second "cortical" network, on the left in Figure 1a, represents a highly-simplified model of some aspects of long-term memory in cerebral and cerebellar cortices (Gluck, et al., 1994/in press). This network is assumed to be trained only by applications of some correlative learning rule such as LMS (Widrow & Hoff, 1960), which is related to known mechanisms of biological plasticity (c.f., Gluck & Granger, 1993; Donegan, et al., 1989). Therefore, on its own, the cortical network cannot form new stimulus representations in its hidden layer (see Rumelhart, et al., 1986). However, we assume that it can acquire the representations formed in the hippocampal network and then, independently, learn to map from these representations to an output which is interpreted as the system's behavioral response.

A hippocampal lesion is simulated in this model by disabling the hippocampal network (Figure 1b). The cortical network remains intact, but can no longer acquire new representations in its hidden layer. It can still form new associations, by training its upper layer of weights, which map from existing hidden layer representations to the output. Together, the intact model of Figure 1a and the lesioned model of Figure 1b have been shown to accurately predict a wide range of learning and generalization behaviors in the intact and lesioned animal (Gluck & Myers, 1993). For example, it explains why intact but not lesioned animals should show such effects as latent inhibition, sensory preconditioning and reversal facilitation, and why

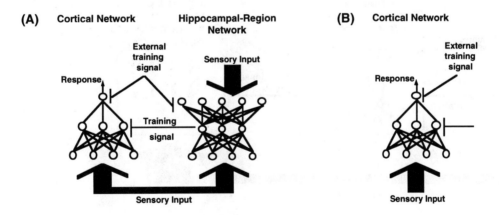

Figure 1. *The top-down hippocampal-region model. (A) In the intact model, a "hippocampal" network forms new stimulus representations in its hidden layer which are biased to compress redundant information and differentiate predictive information. These new representations are provided to a "cortical" network which is assumed to be the site of long term storage, and which learns to map from the representations to an appropriate behavioral response. (B) In the lesioned model, the cortical network can still learn new responses based on existing representations, but can form no new representations (After Gluck & Myers, 1993).*

electrical disruption of hippocampal processing should impair simple learning more than outright removal of the hippocampus (Gluck & Myers, 1993). This model also suggests that new stimulus representations in the hippocampal region should incorporate information about the context of learning, and therefore correctly predicts that intact animals might often be more sensitive than lesioned animals to a sudden change of context (Myers & Gluck, 1994/submitted).

The top-down model described above manifests many of the behaviors of intact and hippocampal-lesioned animals, and provides a computational interpretation of hippocampal-region function. It does not, however, address how this function might arise from the biological substrate. In the next section, we discuss a bottom-up model of processing in one component of the hippocampal region, and show that it instantiates one of the core components of the top-down model.

A Bottom-Up Model of the Parahippocampal Region

The top-down hippocampal-region model described above suggests that the hippocampal region is responsible for forming new stimulus representations which are biased to compress redundant information while differentiating predictive information. These two biases can be dissociated and performed serially: so that the hippocampal network shown in Figure 1a can be recast as a pair of networks, one each to implement representational compression and differentiation. These two networks could then operate serially to re-code stimulus representations. The resulting model retains many of the behaviors of the original intact model of Figure 1a.

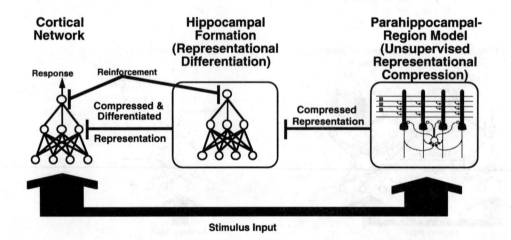

Figure 2. Integrating the top-down model of Figure 1a with a bottom-up model of parahippocampal region processing results in a new hypothesis about distribution of function among structures of the hippocampal region (Myers, et al., 1994/submitted). Inputs are first processed in an unsupervised clustering network, based on the physiology of the parahippocampal region. The resulting compressed representation is next processed by structures (probably the hippocampal formation) which differentiate predictive information. The resulting representation is provided to the cortical network as in the original top-down model of Figure 1a.

Might these two representational processes likewise be localized in different anatomic substrates of the hippocampal region? One possible mapping is proposed by a bottom-up model of the parahippocampal region, which forms a primary input (and output) for the hippocampus itself. This bottom-up model takes into account many of the anatomical and physiological properties of the parahippocampal region, specifically superficial entorhinal cortex, and is derived from an earlier model of the highly similar superficial olfactory cortex (Ambros-Ingerson, et al., 1990). An emergent property of this bottom-up model is the ability to perform unsupervised clustering on its inputs, based on similarity and co-occurrence. As a result, we have extrapolated from this bottom-up model to hypothesize that the entorhinal cortex (or, more broadly, the parahippocampal region) performs representational compression. Other structures, such as the hippocampus proper, could then perform differentiation on the resulting representation. The final output, biased by both compression and differentiation, could then be provided back to cortical structures for long-term storage.

This hypothesis, illustrated in Figure 2, has several implications for interpreting recent empirical studies. In particular, it predicts that while lesions of the complete hippocampal region should fully eliminate the ability to form new stimulus representations, more restricted lesions may result in more selective representational deficits -- to the extent that these restricted lesions do not disrupt input and output pathways to other hippocampal-region structures. Some experimental evidence shows that such a circumscribed lesion of the hippocampus does not destroy parahippocampal processing (e.g., Jarrard & Davidson, 1991; Zola-Morgan, et al., 1992). And where appropriate data is available, behaviors which are expected to depend on representational compression in the parahippocampal region are in fact not disrupted by hippocampal lesion which leaves the parahippocampal region intact (Myers, et al., 1994/submitted).

Conclusions

This hypothesis about division of function in the hippocampal region was suggested by an integration and comparison between two types of model: one which incorporates physiological and anatomical detail of a brain structure, and another which inferred an information-processing function for a more diffuse brain region based on a wide range of behavioral studies comparing intact and lesioned animals. The most important conclusion to be drawn from this analysis is that there is great potential for the integration of these two modelling approaches. In this case, the top-down and bottom-up models combine to provide an account of hippocampal-region function which is stronger and more convincing than either model individually. This convergence of top-down and bottom-up methodologies is, we feel, a promising development, and suggests that both approaches -- along with further empirical studies -- can contribute to the development of a unified understanding of hippocampal-region function in learning and memory.

Acknowledgements

This research was supported by NIMH National Service Award 1-F32-MH10351-01 to CEM and by the Office of Naval Research through the Young Investigator Program and grant N00014-88-K-0112 to MAG.

References

Ambros-Ingerson, J., Granger, R., Lynch, G. (1990)   Simulation of paleocortex performs hierarchical clustering. Science, 247, 1344-1348.

Donegan, N., Gluck, M. & Thompson, R. (1989) Integrating behavioral and biological models of classical conditioning. In: Computational models of learning in simple neural systems. Vol. 22. Psychology of Learning and Motivation (Hawkins, R.D., Bower, G.H., eds.) New York: Academic Press, pp. 109-159.

Eichenbaum, H. & Buckingham, J. (1991) Studies of hippocampal processing: Experiment, theory and model. In: Neurocomputation and Learning: Foundations of Adaptive Networks (Gabriel, M. & Moore, J., eds.) Cambridge, MA: MIT Press.

Gluck, M.A., Goren, O., Myers, C. & Thompson, R. (1994/in press) A hierher-order recurrent network model of the cerebellar substrates of response timing in motor-reflex conditioning.

Gluck, M., & Granger, R. (1993) Computational models of the neural bases of learning and memory. Annual Review of Neuroscience, 16, 667-706.

Gluck, M. & Myers, C. (1993) Hippocampal mediation of stimulus representations: A computational theory. Hippocampus, 3(4), 491-516.

Hinton, G. (1989) Connectionist learning procedures. Artificial Intelligence, 40, 185-234.

Jarrard, L., & Davidson, T. (1991). On the hippocampus and learned conditional responding: Effects of aspiration versus ibotenate lesions. Hippocampus, 1, 107-117.

Mishkin, M. (1982) A memory system in the monkey. Philos. Royal Society of London (Biol.), 298, 85-92.

Myers, C. & Gluck, M. (1994/submitted) Context, conditioning and hippocampal re-representation.

Myers, C., Gluck, M. & Granger, R. (1994/submitted) Dissociation of hippocampal and entorhinal function in associtive learning: A computational approach.

Rumelhart, D., Hinton, G. & Williams, R. (1986) Learning internal representations by error propagation. In: Parallel Distributed Processing: Explorations in the Microstructure of Cognition, vol 1 (Rumelhart, D. & McClelland, J., eds.) Cambridge, MA: MIT Press, pp. 318-362.

Scoville, W. & Milner, B. (1957) Loss of recent memory after bilateral hippocampal lesions. Journal of Neurology, Neurosurgery & Psychiatry, 20, 11-21.

Squire, L. (1987) Memory and Brain. New York: Oxford University Press.

Squire, L. & Zola-Morgan, S. (1983) The neurology of memory: The case for correspondence between the findings for man and non-human primate. In: The Physiological Basis of Memory (Deutsch, J., ed.) New York: Academic Press.

Widrow, B. & Hoff, M. (1960) Adaptive switching circuits. Institute of Radio Engineers, Western Electronic Show and Convention, Convention Record, 4, 96-194.

Zola-Morgan, S., Squire, L., Rempel, N., Clower, R., & Amaral, D. (1992). Enduring memory impairment in monkeys after ischemic damage to the hippocampus. Journal of Neuroscience, 12(7), 2582-2596.

STIMULUS CONFIGURATION, CLASSICAL CONDITIONING, AND SPATIAL LEARNING: ROLE OF THE HIPPOCAMPUS

Nestor A. Schmajuk
Department of Psychology: Experimental
Duke University, Durham, NC 27706, U.S.A.

Abstract

Schmajuk and DiCarlo (1992) presented a neural network model that describes complex classical conditioning paradigms as well as spatial learning. In the context of the network, the hippocampus is assumed to control (a) stimulus configuration in cortical regions, and (b) stimulus selection in subcortical areas. According to the model, whereas aspiration or colchicine-kainic acid lesions of the hippocampus eliminate both cortical configuration and subcortical stimulus selection, ibotenic acid lesions of the hippocampus abolish only cortical configuration. The model correctly describes most of the effects of hippocampal aspiration and ibotenic acid lesions in both classical conditioning and spatial learning paradigms.

The S-D model

Schmajuk and DiCarlo (1992) proposed a neural network (the S-D model) that describes classical conditioning and spatial learning. In the framework of the S-D model, the hippocampus modulates (a) stimulus configuration in neocortex, and (b) competition in subcortical regions. Configuration refers to the combination of simple stimuli into a complex stimulus, which represents a pattern of stimuli that better predicts the future than its individual constituents. Competition refers to the selection of the stimulus best predicting the future from among different simple and complex stimuli.

The S-D model (Figure 1) is a multilayer network that (a) incorporates a layer of "hidden" units positioned between input and output units that internally codes configural stimuli, (b) includes inputs that are connected to the output directly and indirectly through the hidden-unit layer, and (c) employs a biologically plausible backpropagation procedure to train its hidden-unit layer (see Rumelhart, Hinton, and Williams, 1986). In contrast to models of classical conditioning that describe behavior on a trial-to-trial basis, the S-D network describes behavior in real time. This description is formalized by a set of differential equations that depict changes in the values of neural activities and connectivities as a function of time (see Schmajuk and Blair, 1993; Schmajuk and DiCarlo, 1992).

Figure 1 shows a network with one input layer, one hidden-unit layer, and two output layers. Each input unit's activation represents a temporal trace of a conditioned stimulus (CS_1 and CS_2) or the context (CS_3) in the case of classical conditioning, or the visual angle of a spatial landmark in the case of place learning. Input units form direct associations, VS_1, VS_2, VS_3, with the first output layer. In addition, input units form associations, VH_{ij}, with the hidden-unit layer. In turn, hidden units form associations, VN_1, VN_2, VN_3 with the first output layer. The output activities of the hidden-unit layer are assumed to code configural stimuli denoted by CN_1, CN_2, CN_3. Unit activity in the first output layer is summed in the second output layer to generate the output of the system, given by $\Sigma_i CS_i VS_i + \Sigma_j CN_j VN_j$. The output of the network represents the prediction of the unconditioned stimulus (US) in time and space. In the case of classical conditioning, the temporal course of this prediction is reflected in the topography of conditioned response (CR). In the case of spatial learning, the output represents the spatial distribution of the prediction of the location of the US.

Figure 1 shows that a CS_i accrues a direct association VS_i with the output units, and becomes configured with other CSs in hidden units, which are assumed to reside in cortical areas. Stimulus configuration is achieved by adjusting CS-hidden unit associations VH_{ij}, and hidden units become associated with the output through modifiable weights VN_j. Figure 1 also shows an "error network", assumed to reside in the hippocampal formation, which performs two different functions. First, it regulates the associations VH_{ij} of simple stimuli with the hidden units, by computing hidden unit error signals EH_j. This is accomplished using a biologically plausible backpropagation procedure (Schmajuk and DiCarlo, 1992). Second, it regulates connections VS_i and VN_j by computing the aggregate prediction of the US, $B = \Sigma_i CS_i VS_i + \Sigma_j CN_j VN_j$. VS_i and VN_j associations are controlled by a delta rule that reduces the output error, $EO = US - B$, between the aggregate prediction and the actual value of the US.

Hippocampal Lesions. Schmajuk and Blair (1993) suggested that the effect of (a) aspiration, or (b) colchicine-kainic acid lesions of the hippocampal formation (HF, comprising the dentate gyrus, CA1 and CA3 regions, subiculum, and entorhinal cortex) can be simulated by removing or disconnecting the "Hippocampal Formation" block in Figure 1. This manipulation produces important changes in the performance of the model. First, the aggregate prediction of the US, $B = \Sigma_i CS_i VS_i + \Sigma_j CN_j VN_j$, is no longer computed. B controls competition among CSs and CNs to gain association with the US. In the absence of B, CS_i-US and CN_j-US associations are independent of one another, yielding impairment in paradigms such as blocking, conditioned inhibition, and negative patterning. Second, removal of the hippocampal formation block prevents the computation of hidden unit error signals, EH_j, and therefore no new configurations are formed in association cortex. However, previously stored configurations are not modified.

The effect of lesioning the hippocampus proper (HP, comprising CA1 and CA3 regions) with ibotenic acid can be described by removing or disconnecting the block labelled "Hippocampus Proper" in Figure 1 (Schmajuk and Blair, 1993). Removal of this block prevents the computation of hidden unit error signals, EH_j, so that no new stimulus configurations are formed in association cortex. It is important to notice that, since previously stored configurations are not disrupted following lesions of the hippocampus proper, these lesions should not impair tasks which do not require changes in cortical unit configurations. By contrast, tasks which require retraining of cortical hidden units should be impaired.

<u>Cortical Lesions.</u> The effect of extensive cortical lesions (CL) can be described by removing the block labelled "Cortex" in Figure 1. Removal of this block eliminates all hidden units, preventing the formation of new configurations and disrupting previously stored configurations. Cortical lesions impair tasks which require configuration, but preserve tasks which only require competition among stimuli.

Computer Simulations

Figures 2 to 10 show simulated results of the effects of HF, HP, and CL lesions in many classical conditioning paradigms as well as in place learning in a Morris water maze. Brief descriptions of each simulated protocol are provided in the figure captions.

Table 1 compares simulations obtained with the S-D model with different experimental results. References to the experimental data listed in Table 1, as well as a detailed explanation of the simulated results, can be found in Schmajuk and DiCarlo (1992) and Schmajuk and Blair (1993).

Table 1. Simulations obtained with the S-D model compared with different experimental results.

Paradigm	HF Data	HF Model	HP Data	HP Model	CL Data	CL Model
Delay Conditioning	+, 0	+	?	+	0	0
Trace Conditioning	+, 0, -	+	?	0	0	0
Extinction	0, -	-	?	-	0	0
Explicitly Unpaired Extinction	0	- *	?	-	?	-
Acquisition Series	-	-	?	-	?	-
Extinction Series	-	-	?	-	?	-
Blocking	0, -	-	?	0	0	0
Overshadowing	0, -	-	?	0	?	0
Discrimination						
Acquisition	0	0	0	0	0	0
Reversal	-	-	?	0	+	0 *
Conditioned Inhibition	0	- *	?	0	0	0
Feature-positive Discrimination						
Acquisition	-	-	0	0	0	0
Retention	-	-	0	0	0	0
Conditional Discrimination	-	-	0	0	?	-
Differential Conditioning	-	-	?	0	?	0
Negative Patterning						
Acquisition	-	-	0	0	?	-
Retention	-	-	?	0	?	-
Positive Patterning						
Acquisition	?	-	0	0	?	-
Retention	?	-	?	0	?	-
Context Switching	-	-	?	0	?	-
Place Learning						
Acquisition	-	-	-	-	0, -	-
Retention	-	-	0	0	-	-

Note. - = Deficit, + = Facilitation, 0 = No effect, ? = no available data, * = fails to describe the data.

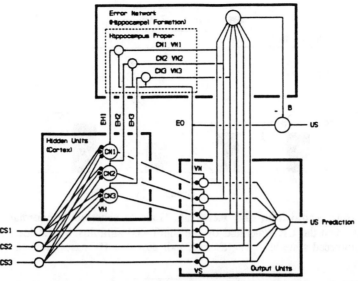

Figure 1. Diagram of the S-D model. Stimuli: Unconditioned (US), Conditioned (CS), Configural (CN). Associations: CS-US (VS), CN-US (VN), CS-CN (VH). B: aggregate prediction. Error signals: for hidden units (EH), for output units (EO). Arrows represent fixed synapses. Solid circles represent variable synapses.

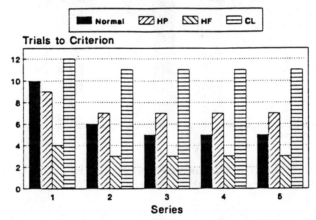

Figure 2. Acquisition Series. Simulated trials to acquisition criterion (.18) for normal, HP, HF, and CL cases.

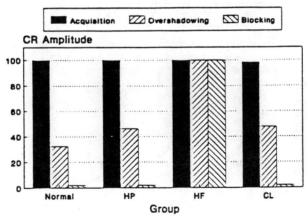

Figure 3. Blocking and Overshadowing. Peak CR amplitude for normal, HP, HF, and CL HL cases evoked by CS_2 after 10 reinforced CS_1-CS_2 trials following 10 reinforced CS_1 trials in the case of blocking, and 10 CS1-CS2 reinforced trials in the case of overshadowing.

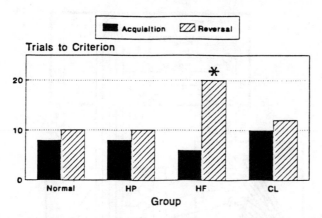

Figure 4. Discrimination Acquisition and Reversal. Trials to criterion for normal, HP, HF, and CL cases. Criterion was reached when the CR generated by the reinforced stimulus was at least twice as large as the CR generated by the unreinforced stimulus. The asterisk indicates that HF case failed to achieve reversal within 20 trials.

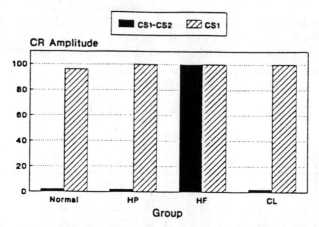

Figure 5. Conditioned Inhibition. Peak CR amplitude for normal, HP, HF, and CL cases evoked by CS_1 and CS_1-CS_2 after 20 reinforced CS_1 trials alternated with 20 nonreinforced CS_1-CS_2 trials.

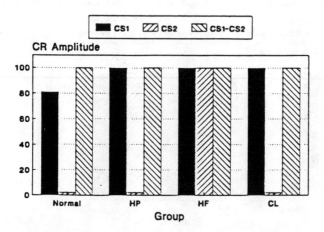

Figure 6. Feature-Positive Discrimination. Peak CR amplitude for normal, HP, HF, and CL cases evoked by CS_1, CS_2, and CS_1-CS_2 after 75 reinforced CS_1-CS_2 trials alternated with 75 nonreinforced CS_2 trials.

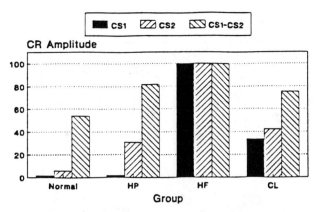

Figure 7. Conditional Discrimination. Peak CR amplitude for normal, HP, HF, and CL cases evoked by CS_1, CS_2, and serial presentation of CS_1-CS_2 after 75 reinforced serial CS_1-CS_2 trials alternated with 75 nonreinforced CS_2 trials.

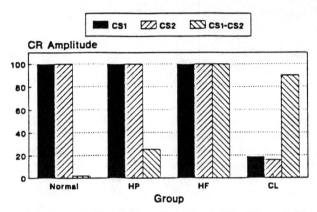

Figure 8. Negative Patterning. Peak CR amplitude for normal, HP, HF, and CL cases evoked by CS_1, CS_2, and CS_1-CS_2 after 100 reinforced CS_1 trials, alternated with 100 reinforced CS_2 trials, and 100 nonreinforced CS_1-CS_2 trials.

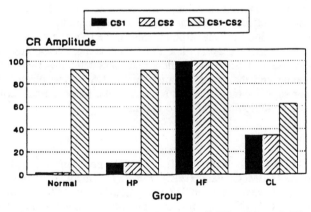

Figure 9. Positive Patterning. Peak CR amplitude for normal, HP, HF, and CL cases evoked by CS_1, CS_2, and CS_1-CS_2 after 60 nonreinforced CS_1 trials, alternated with 60 nonreinforced CS_2 trials, and 60 reinforced CS_1-CS_2 trials.

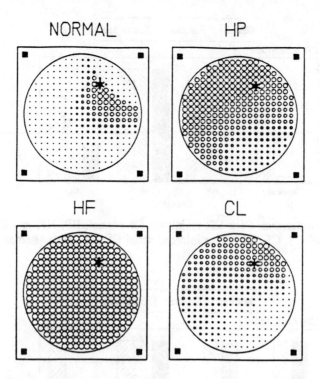

Figure 10. Place Learning Acquisition. Simulated prediction of the location of the hidden platform at different points in the Morris water maze after 20 trials, for normal, HP, HF, and CL cases. The large circle represents the boundary of the Morris tank, four spatial landmarks are represented by solid boxes, and the asterisk indicates the location of the hidden platform. The magnitude of the network's prediction of the location of the platform at each point in the pool is represented by the sizes of the small circles.

Table 1 shows that the model is able to describe the effects of HF, HP, and CL lesions on acquisition and extinction of delay and trace conditioning, acquisition and extinction series, blocking, overshadowing, discrimination acquisition and reversal, feature-positive discrimination, conditional discrimination, differential conditioning, contextual effects, acquisition and retention of positive patterning, and acquisition and retention of negative patterning. Importantly, the model describes the effect of HF, HP, and CL lesions on acquisition and retention of place learning. Table 1 indicates that the model has difficulty simulating the effect of HF lesions in explicitly unpaired extinction and conditioned inhibition. Also as indicated in Table 1, the model makes numerous novel predictions about the effects of HP on many learning paradigms.

In addition to simulating behavioral effects of brain lesions, the model also describes hippocampal activity in normal animals. Because the model suggests that the hippocampus computes aggregate predictions of environmental events in time and space, it correctly predicts that hippocampal activity reflects the topography of the CR during classical conditioning and the spatial location of the US during place learning.

In sum, the present paper suggests how different regions of the hippocampal formation and the neocortex might participate in both classical conditioning and place learning.

References
Rumelhart, D.E., Hinton, G.E., & Williams, R.J. (1986). Learning internal representations by error propagation. In D.E. Rumelhart & J.L. McClelland (Eds.), *Parallel Distributed Processing: Explorations in the Microstucture of Cognition. Vol. 1: Foundations* (pp.318-362). Cambridge, MA: Bradford Books, MIT Press.

Schmajuk, N.A., & Blair, H.T. (1993). Stimulus configuration, spatial learning, and hippocampal function. *Behavioural Brain Research, 59,* 103-117.

Schmajuk, N.A., & DiCarlo, J. (1992). Stimulus configuration, classical conditioning, & hippocampal function. *Psychological Review, 99,* 268-305.

FEEDBACK REGULATION OF CHOLINERGIC MODULATION AND HIPPOCAMPAL MEMORY FUNCTION.

Michael E. Hasselmo and Eric Schnell

Dept. of Psychology, Harvard University 33 Kirkland St.,
Cambridge, MA 02138   hasselmo@katla.harvard.edu

ABSTRACT

Acetylcholine may set the appropriate dynamics for learning within cortical structures, while removal of this modulatory influence may set the appropriate dynamics for recall. Here we use a combination of computational modeling and brain slice physiology to explore the role of cholinergic modulation in the hippocampal formation. A computational model of the feedback regulation of cholinergic modulation in hippocampal region CA1 was developed, with an emphasis on the putative heteroassociative memory function of the Schaffer collaterals projecting from region CA3 to region CA1. Feedback regulation of cholinergic modulation in the model allowed the network to respond to novel patterns with strong cholinergic modulation, allowing accurate learning, and to respond to familiar patterns with a decrease in cholinergic modulation, allowing recall. This function required differences in the suppression of synaptic transmission at CA1 synapses arising from region CA3, when compared to CA1 synapses arising from the entorhinal cortex. Experiments in brain slice preparations of the hippocampal formation confirmed this prediction of the model.

INTRODUCTION

A number of models of hippocampal function have focused on the possible autoassociative memory function of hippocampal region CA3 [Marr, 1971; McNaughton and Morris, 1987; McClelland et al., 1992; Levy, 1989; 1990] and the possible heteroassociative memory function of the Schaffer collaterals from region CA3 to region CA1 [Levy, 1989; 1990; McNaughton, 1991]. However, these models have not accounted for the fact that associative memory models require very different activation dynamics during learning versus recall. To prevent recall of previously learned associations from interfering with the learning of new associations, modifiable synapses must not be the predominant influence on post-synaptic activity during learning. In many models of associative memory function, the associations being stored in the network are clamped during learning (Kohonen, 1984; Anderson, 1983; Hopfield, 1984; Amit, 1988) to prevent the spread of activity across previously modified synapses.

Previous research in this laboratory has shown that the effects of cholinergic modulation may set the appropriate dynamics for storing new information in cortical networks (Hasselmo et al., 1992, 1993; Hasselmo, 1993a, 1993b; Hasselmo and Bower, 1993). Acetylcholine has a number of different physiological effects in cortical structures. In the piriform cortex, acetylcholine has been shown to selectively suppress synaptic transmission at intrinsic but not afferent fiber synapses [Hasselmo and Bower, 1992]. In addition, cholinergic modulation suppresses the neuronal adaptation of cortical pyramidal cells (Hasselmo et al., 1993), and enhances long-term potentiation of synaptic potentials (Barkai et al., 1993). In computational models of piriform cortex, application of the selective cholinergic suppression of synaptic transmission during learning prevents recall of previously stored information from interfering with the storage of new information (Hasselmo et al., 1992, 1993; Hasselmo, 1993a, 1993b). Simulation of the cholinergic suppression of neuronal adaptation and the cholinergic enhancement of synaptic modification enhances the rate of learning in the network (Hasselmo et al., 1993).

If the level of acetylcholine determines the appropriate dynamics for learning or recall, this requires some mechanism for feedback regulation of cholinergic modulation. Cortical regions must be able to set the appropriate level of cholinergic modulation dependent upon the novelty or familiarity of a particular input pattern. We have explored possible mechanisms for the feedback regulation of cholinergic modulation in a simulation of the interaction between the hippocampus and medial septum. Modeling results show that heteroassociative memory function can be obtained with self-regulation of learning and recall. However, this heteroassociative memory function depends upon the effects of acetylcholine within region CA1. In particular, effective heteroassociative memory function depends upon stronger cholinergic suppression of synaptic transmission in stratum radiatum than stratum lacunosum moleculare of region CA1. Experiments in brain slice preparations show that this prediction of the model holds true.

METHODS

Computational modeling: The feedback regulation of cholinergic modulation was explored in a computational simulation of hippocampal region CA1. The simulation contained representations of entorhinal cortex layer III and regions CA1 and CA3 of the hippocampus. As shown in Fig. 1, the simulation incorporated both the perforant pathway input from entorhinal cortex, terminating in stratum lacunosum-moleculare (s. l-m) of region CA1, as well as the Schaffer collateral input from region CA3, terminating in stratum radiatum (s. rad) of region CA1. These inputs influenced the activity of pyramidal cells in region CA1. The summed output of all neurons in region CA1 decreased the level of cholinergic modulation arriving from the medial septum.

Simulations evaluated how the cholinergic suppression of synaptic transmission influenced the self-regulated heteroassociative memory function of Schaffer collateral synapses. Thus, in these simulations, activity patterns were induced sequentially in the entorhinal cortex and region CA3. When the Schaffer collaterals showed effective heteroassociative memory function, they could store associations between the activity in region CA3 and the coincident activity induced in region CA1 by input from the entorhinal cortex. The recall of these associations could be tested by inducing activity in region CA3 alone and evaluating how close the activity spreading into region CA1 resembled the activity previously provided by input from the entorhinal cortex. These results are illustrated in Fig. 2.

Cholinergic modulation: The level of cholinergic modulation in the network determined a range of parameters in region CA1. In particular, different amplitudes of cholinergic suppression of synaptic transmission in s. l-m and s. rad were explored. In addition, the cholinergic modulation of neuronal adaptation was simulated as a change in the threshold of a threshold linear output function. In addition, cholinergic modulation enhanced the rate of synaptic modification and caused suppression of inhibitory synaptic transmission.

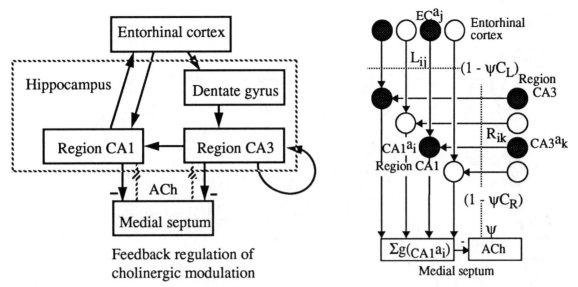

Figure 1. **A.** Schematic representation of the circuitry of the hippocampus with feedback regulation of cholinergic modulation from the medial septum. Anatomical evidence suggests that activity in region CA1 and region CA3 can inhibit activity in the medial septum, and thereby downregulate cholinergic modulation. Dotted lines represent cholinergic modulation. **B.** Basic components of the model focusing on input to region CA1. Entorhinal cortex input was represented by the identity matrix, while connections from CA3 to CA1 were modifiable and started with random initial connectivity. The summed output of region CA1 decreased the level of cholinergic modulation from the medial septum. The best heteroassociative memory function of synapses from CA3 to CA1 was obtained when cholinergic suppression was stronger on the input from CA3 than on the input from entorhinal cortex.

Brain slice experiments: Computational modeling generated a specific prediction about the relative magnitude of the cholinergic suppression of synaptic transmission in s. l-m and s. rad. This prediction was tested in brain slice preparations of rat hippocampal region CA1 by analysis of the influence of the cholinergic agonist carbachol on synaptic potentials elicited by stimulation of s. l-m and s. rad. These experiments utilized techniques developed for the comparison of s. l-m and s. rad synaptic potentials in slice preparations (Colbert and Levy, 1992).

RESULTS

In the computational model, feedback regulation of cholinergic modulation allowed the network to respond to novel patterns with appropriate dynamics for learning and to respond to familiar patterns with appropriate dynamics for recall. The function of the model is summarized in Fig. 2. When the pattern pair was novel, cholinergic modulation remained high, allowing appropriate dynamics for learning. When the pattern pair was familiar, the output of the network decreased cholinergic modulation, thereby setting appropriate dynamics for recall. Thus, the testing of heteroassociative memory function did not involve a separate stage of testing recall, but could be performed by presenting only the CA3 component of previously learned pattern pairs

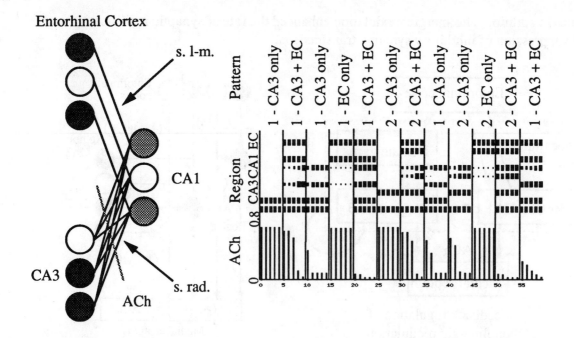

Figure 2. Left. Basic components of a simplified model with 3 neurons in each region (simulations were also performed with 30 neurons in each region). The model focused on obtaining effective heteroassociative memory function on the connections from region CA3 to region CA1. **Right.** Activity in the network during each simulation step. Size of black squares represents the activity of the 3 neurons in each region of this simple example. In the bottom row, level of cholinergic modulation (ACh) is plotted. During steps 1 to 5, input to region CA3 is presented alone. Cholinergic suppression prevents spread of activity to CA1. Steps 6-10: Presentation of activity in both CA1 and entorhinal cortex (EC) causes sufficient activity in CA1 for learning. As synapses from CA3 are strengthened, activity in CA1 increases enough to suppress cholinergic modulation. The network thereby makes a transition from learning to recall. Steps 11-15: Subsequent presentation of CA3 input alone now causes sufficient activity in region CA1 to decrease cholinergic modulation, allowing recall in response to this familiar input.

The simulation demonstrates that effective heteroassociative memory function of the connections from region CA3 to CA1 can be obtained with feedback regulation of cholinergic modulation. However, this heteroassociative memory function depended upon cholinergic suppression of synaptic transmission being stronger in s. rad (at the synapses of the Schaffer collateral input from region CA3) than in s. l-m (at the synapses of perforant path input from entorhinal cortex). This difference in magnitude of cholinergic suppression meant that during learning, entorhinal cortex activity could strongly influence the pattern of activity in region CA1, while cholinergic suppression prevented interference due to the spread of activity across previously modified synapses from CA3. Thus, the model generated an experimentally testable prediction about the relative magnitude of cholinergic suppression of synaptic transmission in s. rad and s. l-m. Extracellular recording in brain slice preparations of hippocampal region CA1 demonstrated that perfusion of the cholinergic agonist carbachol more strongly suppressed synaptic potentials recorded in s. rad than in s. l-m, as shown in Fig. 3.

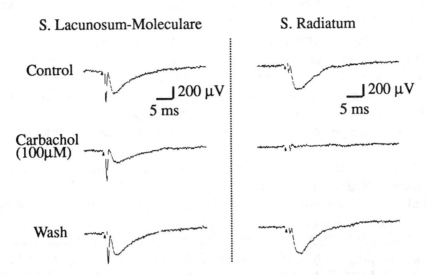

Fig. 3. Laminar differences in the cholinergic suppression of synaptic transmission in hippocampal region CA1. On the left, synaptic potentials were elicited in stratum lacunosum-moleculare (s. l-m) in control conditions and during perfusion with the cholinergic agonist carbachol. At this concentration, carbachol suppressed synaptic potentials on average by 40.1% (n=13). On the right, synaptic potentials elicited in stratum radiatum were more strongly suppressed by cholinergic modulation. Carbachol suppressed synaptic potentials in s. rad by an average of 89.1%.

DISCUSSION

Feedback regulation of cholinergic modulation in the hippocampal formation may set appropriate dynamics for learning in response to novel stimuli, and appropriate dynamics for recall in response to familiar stimuli. In simulations, effective associative memory function depends upon stronger cholinergic suppression at the synapses of the Schaffer collaterals in CA1 than at the synapses of the perforant path. Brain slice experiments demonstrate this predicted difference in magnitude of cholinergic suppression in region CA1. Thus, the interaction of the hippocampus and septum may be vital to the effective memory function of the hippocampal formation. This provides a theoretical framework for linking the considerable behavioral evidence for a role of acetylcholine in memory function (Kopelman, 1986; Hagan and Morris, 1989) to the neurophysiological evidence for the effects of acetylcholine within cortical structures (Hasselmo and Bower, 1992; 1993). The physiological mechanisms explored in these simulations concern some of the similar issues considered in adaptive resonance theory (Carpenter and Grossberg, 1993).

Amit DJ (1988) Modeling brain function: The world of attractor neural networks. Cambridge, U.K.: Cambridge Univ. Press. [1]

Anderson, JA (1983) Cognitive and psychological computation with neural models. *IEEE Trans. Systems, Man, Cybern.* SMC-13: 799-815.

Barkai E, Horwitz G, Bergman RE, Hasselmo ME (1993) Long-term potentiation and associative memory function in a biophysical simulation of piriform cortex. Soc. Neurosci. Abstr. 19:

376.3.

Carpenter GA, Grossberg S (1993) Normal and amnesic learning, recognition and memory by a neural model of cortico-hippocampal interactions. Trends Neurosci. 16:131-137.

Colbert CM, Levy WB (1992a) Electrophysiological and pharmacological characterization of perforant path synapses in CA1: mediation by glutamate receptors. J. Neurophysiol. 68:1-8.

Hagan, JJ and Morris, RGM (1989) The cholinergic hypothesis of memory: A review of animal experiments. In *Psychopharmacology of the Aging Nervous System*, L.L. Iversen, S.D. Iversen and S.H. Snyder, eds. New York: Plenum Press, p. 237-324.

Hasselmo, M.E. (1993a) Acetylcholine and learning in a cortical associative memory. *Neural Comp.* 5: 22-34.

Hasselmo ME (1993b) Runaway synaptic modification in models of cortex: Implications for Alzheimer's disease. Neural Networks in press.

Hasselmo ME, Anderson, BP and Bower, JM (1992) Cholinergic modulation of cortical associative memory function. J. Neurophysiol. 67(5): 1230-1246.

Hasselmo ME and Bower JM (1992) Cholinergic suppression specific to intrinsic not afferent fiber synapses in rat piriform (olfactory) cortex. *J. Neurophysiol.* 67(5): 1222-1229.

Hasselmo ME, Bower JM (1993) Acetylcholine and memory. Trends Neurosci 16:218-222.

Hasselmo ME, Barkai E, Horwitz G, Bergman RE (1993) Modulation of neuronal adaptation and cortical associative memory function. In: Computation and Neural Systems II (Eeckman F, Bower JM, ed). Norwell, MA: Kluwer Academic Publishers. In press.

Hopfield, J. J. (1984) Neurons with graded responses have collective computational properties like those of two-state neurons. *Proc. Natl. Acad. Sci. USA* 81: 3088-3092.

Kohonen T (1984) Self-organization and Associative Memory. Berlin: Springer-Verlag.

Kopelman, M.D (1986) The cholinergic neurotransmitter system in human memory and dementia: A review. *Quart. J. Exp. Psychol.* 38: 535-573.

Levy WB (1989) A computational approach to hippocampal function. In: Computational models of learning in simple neural systems (Hawkins RD, Bower GH, ed), pp. 243-305. Orlando, FL: Academic Press.

Levy WB, Colbert CM, Desmond NL (1990) Elemental adaptive processes of neurons and synapses: A statistical/computational perspective. In: Neuroscience and connectionist theory (Gluck MA, Rumelhart DE, ed), pp. 187-236. Hillsdale, NJ: Lawrence Erblaum Assoc.

Marr D (1971) Simple memory: A theory for archicortex. Phil. Trans. Roy. Soc. B B262:23-81

McClelland JL, McNaughton BL, OReilly R, Nadel L (1992) Complementary roles of hippocampus and neocortex in learning and memory. Soc. Neurosci. Abstr. 18: 508.7.

McNaughton BL (1991) Associative pattern completion in hippocampal circuits: New evidence and new questions. Brain Res. Rev. 16:193-220.

McNaughton BL, Morris RGM (1987) Hippocampal synaptic enhancement and information storage within a distributed memory system. Trends Neurosci. 10:408-415.

Biological Neural Networks

Session Chairs: Thomas McKenna
Joel Davis

POSTER PRESENTATIONS

LTP learning rules and categorization: effects of physiological parameters

Karl Kilborn
Center for the Neurobiology of Learning and Memory, and
Department of Information and Computer Science
University of California, Irvine
Irvine, CA 92717

Richard Granger
Center for the Neurobiology of Learning and Memory, and
Department of Information and Computer Science
University of California, Irvine
Irvine, CA 92717

Long-term potentiation (LTP), the current leading candidate biological mechanism for learning, has as physiological parameters a step size (the amount by which a single potentiation episode increases synaptic efficacy) and a ceiling (the level at which further potentiation results in no further increase). Recent findings have identified endogenous agents that modulate these two parameters of LTP[1]. A statistical model of a cortical network was used to predict the effect these parameters have on categorizing input patterns. Results show that a larger step size (i) leads to faster learning and (ii) causes the network to form narrower (more restrictive) categories. Furthermore, results show that a larger ceiling (i) leads to slower learning and (ii) causes the network to form more general (less restrictive) categories. The effects of step size and ceiling interact, and their relationship to category breadth is highly nonlinear. Settings of the ratio of step size to ceiling are identified that optimize the tradeoff between generalization and learning rate.

[1]Arai, A. and Lynch, G. (1992) Factors regulating the magnitude of long-term potentiation induced by theta pattern stimulation. *Brain Research* **598**: 173 - 84.

An Artificial Neural Network Architecture for Multiple Temporal Sequence Processing

S.L. McCabe*, M.J. Denham**

* Control Engineering Dept., Royal Naval Engineering College, Plymouth, U.K.

** School of Computing, University of Plymouth, Plymouth, U.K.

Abstract

An important feature of the auditory system is its ability to perceive acoustic temporal sequences from many simultaneous sound sources. Various characteristics of the acoustic signals trigger the formation and sequential integration of a number of 'streams'. An artificial neural network system to perform streaming and acoustic sequence recognition is outlined. The influences of attention and memory on the streaming process are also considered. It is hoped that these investigations will be a useful step towards intelligent sensory processing.

Introduction

The perception of temporal sequences is fundamental to human intelligence. Both external and internal states change continuously with time and our brains have evolved the ability to recognise relationships between current and previous events and to generate expectations of future states. Artificially intelligent machines require a similar capability. A number of artificial neural network schemes have been devised to tackle this difficult problem, but are generally quite limited in scope. The principal feature of the human auditory system is its ability to perceive acoustic sequences and to distinguish many simultaneous sound sources. The auditory system manages this even though the signals and their numerous reflections generally overlap in frequency space and time. The system has therefore to cope with multiple temporal sequence processing, and requires mechanisms for separating the various streams, and for switching attention from one stream to another. These techniques could usefully be applied to signal processing in noisy environments, for example speech recognition in a crowded room, music cognition, target tracking, failure prediction and general sensory processing.

The Auditory System

Acoustic signals enter the auditory system via the auditory sensory organ, the cochlea, which is located in the inner ear. The cochlea performs a spectral analysis of the acoustic signal by means of a coupled pair of vibrating membranes, the basilar and tectorial membranes; von Bèkèsy showed that the position of maximum vibration on the basilar membrane is a monotonic function of the frequency of the signal [Handel83]. Located on the basilar membrane in the organ of Corti are the inner and outer hair cells; the outer hair cells form an active non-linear coupling mechanism between the two membranes, the inner hair cells are the principal source of the afferent signals. The frequency components of an acoustic signal are conveyed by the positions of the active inner hair cells and by the phase locking of their responses to the appropriate frequency component; there is place and temporal coding of the signal [Dallos88]. The way in which the intensity of the various frequency components is encoded is not clear since the mean firing rate of auditory nerve fibres saturates over a 40dB range while intensity levels can be perceived over a 120dB range. However, onset firing rate and synchronisation do seem to have an adequate dynamic range, although adaptation is so rapid that this effect is usually masked. In addition, the existence of nerve fibres with staggered thresholds may mean that a group of nerve fibres could together encode the full intensity range [Smith88].

The afferent path from cochlea to auditory cortex passes through a number of relay stations, and is characterised by a large fan-out and conservative transmission [Pickles85]. The principal organising parameter of auditory processing is frequency, and tonotopic maps are found throughout the auditory system. Other important organisational features are binaural (for encoding spatial locations), and temporal (based on envelope variations or modulations). The tonotopic organisation appears to be hardwired, while binaural and temporal maps show large differences between individuals and are therefore probably learnt by experience [Brugge85], [Schreiner88]. The afferent path actually consists of two principal channels, one which is tonotopically organised, and the other which is not [Brugge88]. The tonotopic path is characterised by accurate transmission, short response latencies, sharp tuning curves, insensitivity to anaesthesia, and little or no learning. The non-tonotopic path, on the other hand, contains neurons with longer response latencies and broader tuning curves. It is modified by learning and affected by anaesthesia, and combines with other sensory modalities in the thalamus. In general, there appears to be an inverse relationship between the accuracy with which neurons encode stimuli and their plasticity [Weinberger88]. The two pathways finally come together in the cortex where they overlap to some extent. (There is also an efferent path which provides extensive feedback connections between the various auditory stages [Pickles85].)

The first relay station on the path from ear to cortex is the cochlear nucleus. The ventral cochlear nucleus performs very accurate and rapid transmission of the original signals, but also contains cells with broader tuning curves and large dynamic ranges, onto which signals from neurons with a wide range of characteristic frequencies appear to converge, and other cells which are sensitive to rapid changes in intensity. The dorsal cochlear nucleus responds mainly to the dynamic parts of the acoustic signal, and contains cells with non-monotonic rate-intensity functions, and sensitivity to modulation, onset or offset. In addition, noise suppression, response sharpening and the formation of new functions are achieved by means of inhibitory connections [Handel83]. Sound source localisation is accomplished in the superior olivary complex, where interaural time and intensity differences are decoded by means of a correlation analysis of converging signals from the contralateral and ipsilateral ears [Brugge88]. The inferior colliculus receives binaural signals from the superior olivary complex (including space localisation information), as well as complex responses (such as amplitude modulation information) from the contralateral dorsal cochlear nucleus. The central region of the inferior colliculus is both tonotopically and temporally organised, containing iso-frequency sheets with concentric rings of characteristic modulating frequencies. It is thought that this arrangement may provide the basis for residue pitch extraction [Schreiner88]. The principal thalamic nucleus involved in auditory signal processing is the medial geniculate nucleus. Tonotopic, binaural and temporal organisation are found and maintained in specific projections to tonotopically organised areas of the auditory cortex. Non-tonotopically organised sectors, particularly the medial division of the medial geniculate, integrate auditory information with that from other modalities and exhibit extensive and rapid learning [Weinberger88]. This area has widespread influence, projecting to all auditory cortical fields and can therefore generate widespread 'recruiting' responses [Herkenham85].

Clearly extensive pre-processing occurs in the auditory system. Since most discrimination tasks can be accomplished without the auditory cortex, the prime role of the auditory cortex may be in detecting similarity and in grouping sets of stimuli which have a common origin, i.e. auditory object recognition [Whitfield85]; a complex activity requiring the association and temporal integration of disparate signals. Other tasks which involve the auditory cortex include the transfer of knowledge, ordering of stimuli, prolonging the effects of short stimuli, and auditory memory and consciousness. The auditory cortex consists of a number of different fields and contains multiple representations of the acoustic information. Some areas have frequency maps, and binaural bands, but so far no maps encoding modulation information have been found in the human auditory cortex (although they have in the bat). The human auditory cortex has not been extensively mapped which is perhaps why a clearer idea of its organisation has not been established, however, it has been suggested that many more maps, particularly frequency transition combination maps, will be found [Suga88]. (Frequency transitions are important in speech processing and spatiotemporal trajectories in transition combination maps could be used to encode speech patterns.) Temporal resolution decreases towards centre in the auditory system, and sensitivity to modulation frequencies only up to about 28Hz are found in the cortex [Schreiner88], (corresponding to the range for rhythmic perception). The left and right cortices have different auditory specialisations, the left being devoted to language processing, and the right to the more prosodic aspects of speech and music [Zatorre93].

Streaming and Multiple Sequence Recognition

The auditory system is capable of processing many simultaneous signals, each of which may have complex wave patterns, overlapping frequency spectra, and numerous (delayed) reflections, depending on the environment. The system is able to distinguish the various sources, establish their locations, and interpret their informational content. The complexities of auditory scene analysis are resolved by means of 'auditory streaming'; the sequential grouping of components of the acoustic signal into a number of co-occurring subsets. Psychological tests suggest that there are automatic, preattentive as well as higher level, attentive streaming mechanisms at work [Bregman90].

Principal factors determining the assignment of sounds to different streams are pitch proximity, timbre, spatial origin and pitch trajectory; pitch proximity being the dominant one. The tendency to segregate streams increases with presentation rate, abrupt rather than smooth changes in pitch, and inconsistencies between pitch changes and previously received pitch contours. (For example, if a series of tones alternating between high and low pitch are received, i.e. H L H L ..., then at a low presentation rate the subject will perceive a single oscillating sequence, but as the rate increases the sounds will eventually be perceived in two separate streams, one consisting of H H H... and the other L L L...) An important feature of higher level auditory processing is the perceived invariance of pitch and time interval relationships; the structure of a pitch pattern is perceived to be the same if shifted along the pitch axis, as long as the ratios between the pitches remain the same; similarly for timing shifts. It is useful to visualise sound in terms of three psychological dimensions, relative pitch, loudness and time. Whenever a sequence is translated along the relative time axis, then the amount of change tolerable in the other dimensions without provoking stream segregation is dependent on the time period [Jones76].

Primitive preattentive mechanisms are automatic, unlearned and data driven [Bregman90]. They partition the sensory input, operate over short time spans and exhibit improved performance with increasing presentation rate. The extraction of pitches from the incoming frequency spectra appears to be the principal component of preattentive streaming, the basic assumption made by the organism being that frequencies which form part of the same harmonic spectrum are likely to come from the same source. The pitch or fundamental frequency of a complex tone is the frequency of repetition of the wave form. The spectral balance or timbre of a sound is affected by the relative amplitudes of the associated harmonics, but these are not normally perceived separately. Frequencies are usually interpreted as belonging to the same fundamental pitch if they are integer multiples of the fundamental (to within about 4%); even if that fundamental frequency is not contained in the signal. At a different time scale (< 20 Hz), periodicity or a regular pulse is also used as a clue to indicate a common source. If the phase and intensity changes of a number of frequencies are synchronised, then they tend to be associated with the same stream. Rhythmic or temporal integration of the incoming signals is important for good perception, and enables the listener to generate expectancies and to perform temporal 'chunking' [Jones76]. Spatial clues are also used in preattentive streaming, but these are overridden by pitch clues if they are in conflict [Bregman90].

Higher level streaming involves attention, auditory short term memory and stored knowledge, and only operates on one stream at a time. It spans longer time periods and mainly acts to sharpen the focus of a primitive stream, but performance degrades with increasing presentation rate. Sequential integration is achieved within streams and emergent properties including rhythm, melody and speech generally only occur within, and not across, streams [Bregman90]. The effect of attention on the streaming process can be easily demonstrated by the marked difference between the minimum pitch separation necessary for streaming and the maximum separation beyond which integration is impossible [Bregman90].

Intended Functionality of the Neural Network Processing System

An architecture for a system able to distinguish and track an arbitrary number of simultaneous streams contained within an acoustic input signal is proposed. The output from the system is the attended stream, where attention can be switched from one stream to another. Included in the system is the capacity for learning, recognising and reproducing the resultant temporal patterns, essential if memory is to influence the streaming process and if the system is required to detect novel or unexpected pattern progressions. Another important feature is rhythmic perception, used both for generating within stream expectancies and as a global feature linking mechanism, allowing the synchronisation of a number of streams within a global context. In accordance with psychological results, initial streaming of the signal is achieved by means of the preattentive grouping mechanisms of pitch proximity and timbre. At this stage only a monaural system is proposed and spatial localisation is not considered.

Although such a system could have widespread use, it is thought that a more tractable experimental domain may be that of music cognition. In this context the identity of the various streams is known and the role of rhythm in generating temporal expectancies and as a feature linking mechanism is clear. Novel patterns and pattern progressions and unexpected rhythmic changes can easily introduced and explored. Similarities between music and the prosodic aspects of speech, which almost certainly guide the streaming of speech signals, make this domain particularly relevant.

Processing Stages

The initial processing stage, corresponding to the cochlea, receives the incoming acoustic signals and produces a tonotopically ordered set of signals in which frequency is coded by both place and timing and is discretised in terms of equal spacing of a logarithmic frequency scale. The firing rate of each channel should be proportional to the amplitude of the corresponding frequency component, and phase locked to it. Various schemes for producing these spike trains are being investigated, including Fourier and wavelet transforms, however, it is intended at present to generate the signals by modelling the mechanical aspects of the cochlea and the inner hair cells as interacting and overlapping banks of low-pass and band-pass filters [Lyon88], and to concentrate on temporal coding methods. A noise suppression mask, generated from competitive interactions in the next stage, will be used to improve resolution and enhance or suppress various frequencies. Complications of intensity coding, such as adaptation and saturation will be ignored, unless it becomes apparent that these are necessary for onset detection and synchronisation.

The tonotopically organised set of signals will then be processed in ways suggested by the operations of the cochlear nucleus, where various dynamic aspects of the signals, such as onset, amplitude and frequency modulation coding, are extracted. The actual processing required will be determined by the

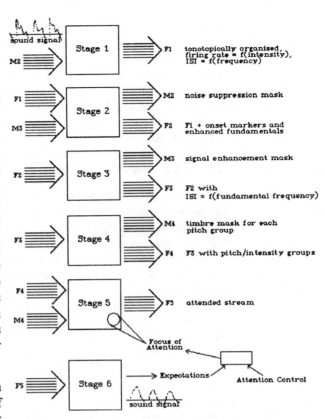

Figure 1. Outline of the processing stages involved in multiple temporal sequence processing.

information needs of later processing stages. A serious problem to be addressed when splitting the acoustic signal into a number of processing paths, some of which are intrinsically slower than others and require longer time windows for extracting the relevant information, is how to synchronise them. Therefore, as far as possible, superimposing additional information on the original signal, (e.g. enhanced onset markers), will generally be preferred. Information necessary for noise suppression can be found by lateral inhibition and competition amongst different frequency channels and used to suppress those frequencies considered spurious, to enhance significant frequency components, and to influence initial coding in the previous stage. Preparations for pitch extraction are also required, particularly the enhancement of fundamentals, (a mask, produced in the next stage, for enhancing candidate fundamental frequencies, could be useful). Amplitude modulation may be an important pitch cue, but other useful methods include the detection of periodicity in the interference firing pattern of groups of phase-locked frequency channels, or the enhancement of the subharmonics of each active frequency.

Processing analogous to that in the inferior colliculus will be used to enhance the outputs corresponding to the 'best' modulating frequencies. The arrangement of iso-frequency sheets and concentric modulating frequency sensitivity thought to underlie the pitch extraction mechanism, can be modelled as a characteristic-frequency / modulating-frequency map; competitive interactions within each iso-frequency column can be used to generate output signals modulated by the dominant modulating frequency for each frequency channel. Firing patterns, synchronised to the perceived fundamental frequency, will allow groups of associated harmonics to be identified, however, complications, caused by the simultaneous production of the same pitch from more than one source, will have to be resolved. The power of fundamental frequencies appears to be enhanced at the expense of the associated harmonics [Bregman90]; the creation of a mask to enhance fundamental frequencies in proportion to the intensities of the harmonics will have a similar effect. The resulting output signals, while still understood to be tonotopically organised will only encode carrier frequencies in terms of place and the spike trains will be modulated by the associated fundamental frequency.

The modulated frequency channels will then be processed by coincidence detectors in order to identify the pitch groups and their associated timbres and intensities; onset markers and modulation frequencies will used as the determining grouping cues. Relationships between the frequency and intensity of the various harmonics in a pitch group determine its sound quality and may therefore be used to characterise the various sound sources. This necessitates the extraction of relative pitch information and the production of pitch invariant masks. (The ratio of the interspike intervals for the channels concerned carries the information required, but since the frequencies may no longer be phase-locked to the carrier frequencies by this stage, either the relative relationships may have to be extracted sooner, or some of the carrier frequency information must be retained in the signal.) A mechanism for associating the characteristic pitch patterns with each group also has to be devised. The intensity of each pitch group is probably best encoded in terms of the mean firing rate of the fundamental.

The pitch/intensity and timbre patterns found will then be processed to form sequential associations between the various signals. Sequential associations can be formed by means a pitch/intensity map which is activated at appropriate places by incoming signals. If this activation spreads gradually with time before dying out, new inputs falling into previously sensitised areas could become associated with previous signals, (unless other clues, like timbre, distinguish them). Signals falling outside existing sequential integration regions would trigger the formation of new streams. Psychological results demonstrating the dependence of streaming on timing, pitch and loudness transitions could be accommodated by this procedure. This method can also be used to ensure that signals which satisfy expectations generate smaller responses than those which don't; the response activity resulting from signals falling into existing integration areas could be suppressed by presensitisation, while those signals falling into unsensitised areas and resulting in new streams could generate greater responses. The timbre patterns of previous and current signals falling into the same integration region should also match for sequential association to occur. In effect there may be a number of such regions which can overlap, but which are characterised by different timbre patterns. By default everything will be included in the output, but by sharpening the focus of attention onto restricted areas of the map, output could become restricted to a particular stream. The focus of attention could be manipulated externally and switched from area to area or used to scan the map for interesting or particularly high activity. It could also be increased in size to include large areas of the map in relatively inattentive states, or reduced for very sharply concentrated attention in localised areas. Connection strengths between the nodes in the map will determine the shape and trajectories of the expanding sensitised regions, and could be modified by memory-derived expectations. Alternatively the connections could remain fixed and the focus of attention could be manipulated by memory.

The attended stream will then be processed in a variety of ways in order to generate pattern and timing expectations or to signal novelties or failed expectations. In order to achieve this, storage of the temporal sequence of patterns in the attended stream will be required. To be useful, the correct timing patterns will need to be preserved by the process and disambiguation of complex sequences will also be required. Generally methods which are based on the use of dynamic neurons retain timing structures best [Reiss92], [Taylor92]. The problem of the recognition and recall of temporal sequences will also have to be solved if many patterns are to be stored in the same network and used to generate expectations. A suitable system could be based on the approach described by [Wang90], but their simulations only demonstrate recognition and recall of single sequences and it is not clear what happens when more than one sequence is stored. Rhythmic perception will be necessary to generate timing expectations, this process could also be used to adjust patterns to different presentation rates while maintaining the correct timing ratios. Another important psychological effect of rhythm is to produce variations in emphasis or significance, which could prove useful in the temporal pattern matching context. Finally, it is intended to reconstruct an acoustic signal from the components of the attended stream, providing an effective way to monitor the performance of the system.

Conclusion

An artificial neural network architecture, based on aspects of the mammalian auditory system, has been proposed. The system will be able to process complex signals and form a number of separate, temporally integrated, streams.

Attention and memory will also be used to manipulate the streaming processes. Work is in progress on implementing the structure described, using a variety of leaky integrator and pacemaker neurons. It is intended to present further details of the implementation in the near future.

References

[Bregman90] Bregman, 'Auditory Scene analysis', MIT Press, 1990

[Brugge85] Brugge, J.F., Reale, R.A, 'Auditory cortex', in Peters, A., Jones, E.G., ed.s, 'Cerebral Cortex Volume 4: Association and Auditory Cortices', Plenum Press, New York, 1985

[Brugge88] Brugge, J.F. 'Stimulus coding in the developing auditory system' in Edelman, G.M., Gall, W.E. Cowan, W.M., (eds), 'Auditory function', John Wiley & Sons, 1988

[Dallos88] Dallos, P., 'Cochlear neurobiology: some key experiments and concepts of the past two decades' in Edelman, G.M., Gall, W.E. Cowan, W.M., (eds), 'Auditory function', John Wiley & Sons, 1988

[Handel83] Handel, S., 'Listening: An introduction to the perception of auditory events', Bradford Books/MIT Press, Cambridge, MA, 1983.

[Herkenham85] Herkenham, , 'New perspectives on the organisation and evolution of nonspecific thalamocortical projections', in Peters, A., Jones, E.G., ed.s, 'Cerebral Cortex Volume 5', Plenum Press, New York, 1985

[Jones76] Jones, M.R., 'Time our lost dimension: Toward a new theory of perception, attention and memory', Psychological review, 83, pp323-355, 1976

[Lyon88] Lyon, R.F., Mead, C., 'An analog electronic cochlea', IEEE transactions on Acoustics, Speech and Signal Processing, 36, pp1119-1134, 1988

[Pickles85] Pickles, 'An introduction to the physiology of hearing', Academic Press, 1985

[Reiss92] Reiss, M., Taylor, J.G., 'Storing temporal sequences', Neural Networks, 4, pp773-787, 1992

[Schreiner88] Schreiner, C.E., Langner, G., 'Coding of temporal patterns in the central auditory nervous system' in Edelman, G.M., Gall, W.E. Cowan, W.M., (eds), 'Auditory function', John Wiley & Sons, 1988

[Smith88] Smith, R.L., 'Encoding of sound intensity by auditory neurons' in Edelman, G.M., Gall, W.E. Cowan, W.M., (eds), 'Auditory function', John Wiley & Sons, 1988

[Suga88] Suga, N. 'Auditory neuroethology and speech processing: complex-sound processing by combination sensitive neurons', in Edelman, G.M., Gall, W.E. Cowan, W.M., (eds), 'Auditory function', John Wiley & Sons, 1988

[Taylor92] Taylor, J.G., 'Temporal sequence storage', Proceedings of the 1992 International Conference on Artificial Neural Networks (ICANN92), Vol. 2, pp 841-845, 1992

[Wang90] Wang, D., Arbib, M.A., 'Complex temporal sequence learning based on short term memory', Proceedings of the IEEE, Volume 78, No 9, September 1990

[Weinberger88] Weinberger, N.M., Diamond, D.M., 'Dynamic modulation of the auditory system by associative learning' in Edelman, G.M., Gall, W.E. Cowan, W.M., (eds), 'Auditory function', John Wiley & Sons, 1988

[Whitfield85] Whitfield, I.C., 'The role of the auditory cortex in behaviour', in Peters, A., Jones, E.G., ed.s, 'Cerebral Cortex Volume 4: Association and Auditory Cortices', Plenum Press, New York, 1985

[Zatorre93][Zatorre93] Zatorre, R.J., Halpern, A.R., 'Effect of unilateral temporal-lobe excision on perception and imagery of songs', Neuropsychologia 31(3), pp221-232, 1993

Modeling of the Three-Phase Respiratory Rhythm Generation

J.S. Schwaber and I.A. Rybak

Neural Computation Group, The Experimental Station, E.I. DuPont de Nemours & Co, Wilmington, DE 19880-0323
Department of Neuroscience, University of Pennsylvania, Philadelphia, PA 19104

Abstract. In Richter's theory of the origin of the three-phase respiratory rhythm the oscillations in the respiratory network are provided by both specific interconnections and individual properties of neurons of several respiratory groups. Several versions of the neural architecture capable of autonomous generation of the respiratory rhythm and reproducing of specific activity patterns of real neurons of different groups have been developed. Results are analyzed and compared with physiological data. Some prediction are considered.

Introduction

It is known that the basic respiratory rhythm in mammals that controls and coordinates the behavior of the whole respiratory system is formed by neural networks located in a relatively small area of the medulla in the brainstem. For many years the neural mechanism of respiratory rhythmogenesis has been among the most popular subjects of experimental investigation and computational modeling. A huge amount of data has been accumulated. Nevertheless, many mysteries remain. It should be noted that most neural network models of respiratory rhythmogenesis [1,2,3,7] are based on relatively simple continuous model of a single neuron. Current intracellular data from single respiratory neurons [6,10] in concert with the development of new computational approaches to simulation of complex, more realistic neuron models [11] now provide an opportunity to develop more realistic and predictable neural models of respiratory rhythmogenesis. These models can allow investigating of the significance and contribution of both network and intrinsic neuronal properties in respiratory rhythmogenesis mechanisms.

We have based our models on the network hypothesis for origination of the respiratory rhythm using Richter's theory of a three-phase respiratory cycle [8,9]. In this theory the respiratory cycle consists of three phases: inspiration, post-inspiration and late (stage II) expiration. The oscillations in the respiratory network are provided by both specific interconnections and some individual properties of neurons of several respiratory groups. Initially, the respiratory neurons were classified into five types depending on the part of the respiratory circle in which they shows a specific burst of activity. These types (groups) of respiratory neurons were: early inspiratory (early-I), ramping inspiratory (ramp-I), late inspiratory (late-I), post-inspiratory (post-I), and stage II expiratory (E-2) neurons. The e-I neuron shows an adapting burst (with a decrease of spike frequency) during the inspiratory phase. The ramp-I neuron is also active during the inspiratory phase. It shows an unique burst pattern: a single (probably $Ca++$) spike, then a delay, and than an augmenting increase of spike frequency. The late-I neuron gives a short burst at the end of the inspiratory phase. The post-I neuron shows an adapting burst during the post-inspiratory phase. The E-2 neuron is active in the late expiratory phase and shows a pattern of augmenting activity at least in the beginning of its burst. In Richter's theory the switch between inspiration and postinspiration emerges by the following way [8,9]: (1) Because of the excitatory synapses of the ramp-I neuron onto the late-I neuron, the increasing activity of the ramp-I neuron excites the late-I neuron at the end of the inspiratory phase. (2) The latter inhibits the early-I neuron, which in turn disinhibits the post-I and E2 neurons. (3) The two latter are connected with mutual reciprocal inhibition, but the post-I neuron is excited first. Because of the postulated mechanism of this switch, the adaptation of the activity of the early-I neuron is not a key feature for the switch. The switch between postinspiration and expiration emerges as a result of the reciprocal interactions between the post-I neuron and the E2 neuron, and because of adaptation in the burst pattern of the post-I neuron. Thus, the feature of adaptation of the post-I neuron is very important for the switch. The switch between expiration and inspiration (expiratory off-switch) is most interesting but poorly understood. The only explanation of this switch in the framework of Richter's initial scheme might be based on the reciprocal interaction between the E2 and early-I neuron, and on adaptation in the burst pattern of the E2 neuron. But this does not correspond to the convention (in the theory, based on some data) that the E2 neuron should demonstrate an augmenting and not an adapting burst of activity. To overcome this contradiction we have either to assume that the E2 pattern actually shows adaptation, at least at the end of the expiratory phase, or to alter the initial five-neuron Richter's scheme by including additional neural elements and offering a different expiratory off-switch mechanism.

Modeling Results

Our goal was to investigate the contribution of both network and individual neuronal properties to respiratory rhythm generation. First, we decided to develop a simplified neuron model, with spiking and tunable dynamics, to explore directly the role of dynamics in rhythm generation. At the same time, we recognized the need to constrain the behavior of our simplified neuron model to the domain of the possible, and to be congruent with known data - a role best served by the Hodgkin-Huxley type neuron models. In order to compare the simulation results based on the different single neuron models, we developed a simulation package which allowed the incorporation of single neuron models of different (simplified and Hodgkin-Huxley) types into the same neural network architecture. The matrix of interneuronal connections and method of simulation of synaptic potentials were used the same. In developing our neural network models we have tried to find the matrix of connections that produces the required behavior with both types of single neuron models.

The Model 1 for a single neuron was developed as an extension of spiking models [4, 5]. The main differential equation for the neuron membrane potential corresponds to the Hodgkin-Huxley formalism. It has just three items on its right side which corresponds to two synaptic conductances (excitatory and inhibitory) and one AHP conductance. The synaptic conductances are opened by each action potential coming from other neurons. They form an excitatory or inhibitory postsynaptic potential, and so change the membrane potential. The AHP conductance is opened just after the spike in the same neuron. It forms an afterhyperpolarisation following each spike that decays with some time constant. The spike is generated when the membrane potential exceeds a threshold. After each spike the threshold jumps up from a resting level to some higher level. Then it decays with some time constant. This simulates the dynamics of neuronal refractivity. An additional differential equation describing the slow dynamics of the resting level of the threshold is used to provide the adaptive changes of the threshold and correspondingly the adaptive character of neuronal responses. The augmenting type of activity of some neurons (the ramp-I , sometimes the E2) is based on the increase of AHP amplitude during the inhibition preceding the neuronal burst.

The Model 2 neuron was developed in the typical Hodgkin-Huxley style. The following types of ionic channels were included in the model: fast sodium (Na); delayed potassium (K); transient potassium (A); calcium L (CaL); calcium T (CaT); calcium-dependent potassium (AHP); and passive (leak). Adaptive neuronal activity is based on the combination of CaL and AHP currents. A combination of AHP and increased CaT currents allowed us to reproduce the typical augmenting pattern of the ramp-I neuron including: Ca++ spike, delay and increase of spike frequency. Thus, in both above models the specific activity patterns of respiratory neurons, adaptive and augmenting, are based on intrinsic properties of neurons.

Four schemes of the basic respiratory network have been simulated. The mechanisms for switches between inspiration and postinspiration, and between postinspiration and late expiration are the same in all four schemes, corresponding to the above description. The differences between the schemes consist in different hypothetical mechanisms for the expiratory off-switch.

In the first scheme, the expiratory off-switch emerges as a result of the reciprocal interaction between the E2 and early-I neurons, and because of the adaptive burst pattern of the E2 neuron. This does not correspond to the idea that E2 neuron should demonstrate an augmenting but not an adaptive burst of activity. There is only a small increase of frequency at the start of E2 bursts. The dynamics of activity of neurons of this scheme is shown in Fig. 1 a,b.

The second scheme has the same structure of interneuronal connections, but differs in the weights of synaptic connections. The expiratory off-switch emerges in this scheme because of a second burst of the post-I neuron at the end of the late expiratory phase. Unfortunately, in this version we also need adapting E2 activity to provide the switch between the pattern of the E2 neuron and the second burst of the post-I neuron. The dynamics of activity of neurons of this scheme is shown in Fig. 2 a,b.

The third scheme is based on the use of an additional pre-inspiratory (pre-I) neuron. In this scheme the expiratory off-switch emerges like the switch between inspiration and postinspiration. The E2 burst has the purely augmenting character (the E2 and ramp-I are the same in this scheme). The pre-I neuron plays the role similar to that of the late-I in the switch between inspiration and postinspiration. It is excited by the increasing spike frequency of E2, and then terminates the E2 burst by strong feedback inhibition. The E2 in turn disinhibits the early-I and ramp-I neurons. The dynamics of activity of neurons of this scheme is shown in Fig. 3 a,b.

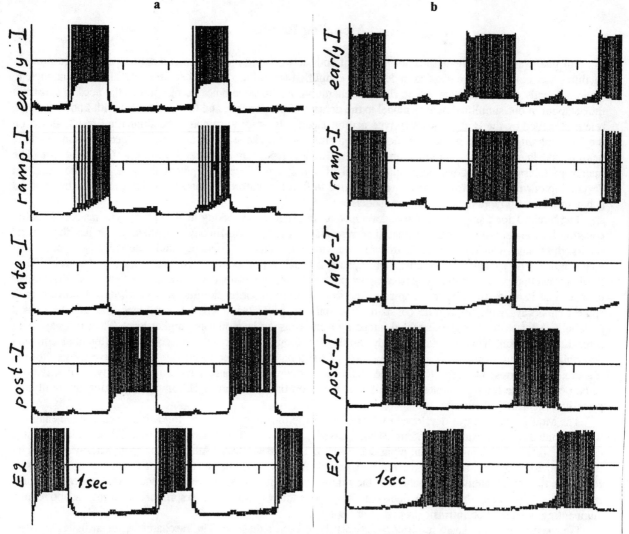

Fig. 1. The dynamics of activity of different respiratory neurons of the first network scheme in the process of generation of the three-phase respiratory rhythm:

    a corresponds to the simplified model of single neuron (Model 1);

    b corresponds to the Hodgkin-Huxley style model of single neuron (Model 2).

The fourth scheme was based on the use an additional hypothetical early-E2 neuron. The early-E2 and E2 neurons works in parallel (like the early-I and ramp-I ones). But, the E2 neuron (the same as the ramp-I neuron) shows an augmenting burst pattern and give the expiratory output to expiratory motoneurons. The early-E2 in contrast has an adapting pattern and provides the expiratory off-switch like the E2 neuron do in the first scheme. The dynamics of activity of neurons of this scheme is shown in Fig. 4 a,b.

The dynamics of the three-phase respiratory rhythm and the activity patterns of respiratory neurons in all the above models look very similar to experimental data. The various schemes give a series of explanations for the genesis of the respiratory rhythm and set the tasks for further experimental investigations.

A very interesting point in analysis of the above modeling results is the comparison models based on the 1-st and 2-nd single neuron models. This comparison shows that the models based on the simpler single neuron Model 1 gives in some cases produces more realistic dynamics of neuronal membrane potentials than the models using the Hodgkin-Huxley type Model 2. This gives us guidance on how to improve the Model 2 by emulating performance features of the Model 1.

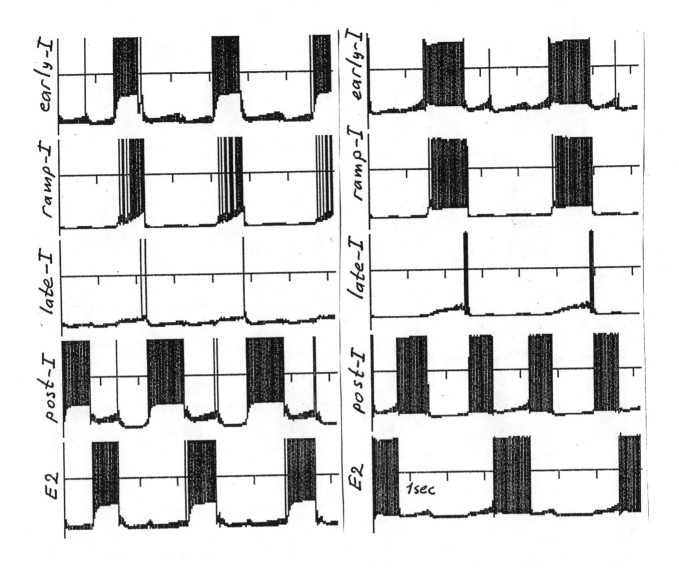

Fig. 2. The dynamics of activity of different respiratory neurons of the second network scheme in the process of generation of the three-phase respiratory rhythm:

    a corresponds to the simplified model of single neuron (fModel 1);

    b corresponds to the Hodgkin-Huxley style model of single neuron (Model 2).

Reference. **[1]** U Bassler. *Biol. Cybern.*, 1986, 370, 433-456. **[2]** SN Botros and EM Bruce. *Biol. Cybern.*, 1990, 63, 143-153. **[3]** S Geman and M Miller. *J. Appl. Physiol*, 1976, 41, 931-938. **[4]** PA Getting. In: *Methods in Neuronal Modeling* (Eds. C Koch and I Segev), Cambridge: The MIT Press, 1989, 171-194. **[5]** RJ MacGregor. *Neural and Brain Modeling*. Acad. Press, San Diego, 1987. **[6]** S Miffin et al. In: *Neurogenesis of Central Respiratory Rhythm* (Eds. A Bianchi and M Denvait-Saubie), Lancaster, UK: MTP, 1985, 179-182. **[7]** M D Oligvie et al. *Am. J. Physiol.*, 1992, 263, R962-R975. **[8]** DW Richter and D Ballantyne. In: Central Neurone Environment (Eds. M Schlafke et al.) Berlin: Springer, 1983, 164-174. **[9]** DW Richter et al. *News Physiol. Sci.*, 1986, 1, 109-112. **[10]** DW Richter et al. *J. Neurophysiol.*, 1975, 38, 1162-1171. **[11]** WM Yamada et al. In: *Methods in Neuronal Modeling* (Eds. C Koch and I Segev), Cambridge: The MIT Press, 1989, 97-133.

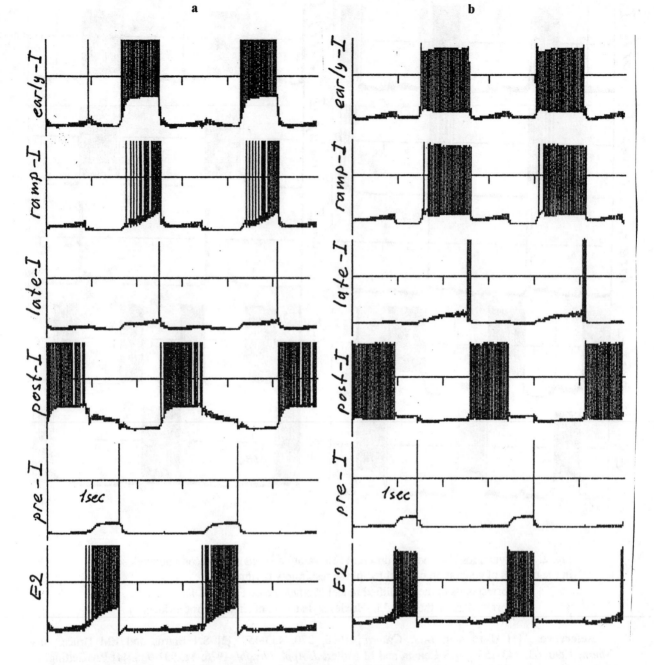

Fig. 3. The dynamics of activity of different respiratory neurons of the third network scheme
in the process of generation of the three-phase respiratory rhythm:
     a corresponds to the simplified model of single neuron (Model 1);
     b corresponds to the Hodgkin-Huxley style model of single neuron (Model 2).

a
b

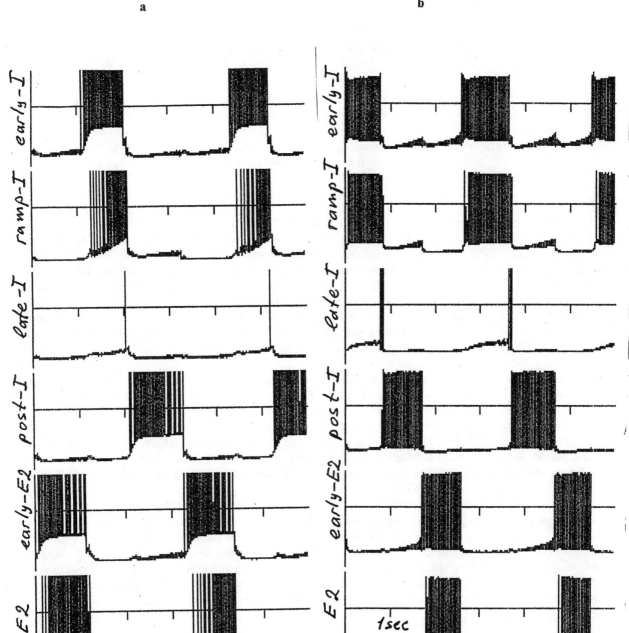

Fig. 4. The dynamics of activity of different respiratory neurons of the fourth network scheme in the process of generation of the three-phase respiratory rhythm:
a corresponds to the simplified model of single neuron (Model 1);
b corresponds to the Hodgkin-Huxley style model of single neuron (Model 2).

Phase Modulation in Oscillatory Model Neurons

F. James Eisenhart[*] and Peter F. Rowat[‡]

Group in Neurosciences[*] and Department of Biology[‡], University of
California, San Diego, La Jolla, CA 92093

Oscillations are important in many neural systems. Often these systems can be modeled by networks of simplified model neurons based on limit-cycle oscillators. Here we investigate how current pulses modulate the oscillatory phase of one kind of simplified model neuron. We describe several kinds of phase modulation observed, and we explain these phenomena mathematically using phase-plane analysis. Similar analyses may help to explain modulatory phenomena in real oscillatory neural systems.

1. Introduction

Oscillations are important in many neural systems. In the crustacean stomatogastric ganglion (STG), coordinated oscillations in a network of motor neurons control the chewing behavior of the stomach (Harris-Warrick et al. 1992). In jamming avoidance response of electric fish, phase and amplitude information from the electrosensory system modulates the oscillatory discharges of the fish's electric organ (Heiligenberg 1991). And in mammals, there is evidence suggesting that phase-locking between oscillations in different cortical areas contributes to perceptual feature binding (Engel et al. 1990). However, in none of these systems do we really understand how the physiological properties of individual cells interact to produce the behavior of the entire system. In part, this is because our experimental methods are clumsy, and we can't observe all of the properties that we would like to. But it is also because even those properties that we can observe are too complex to produce an intuitive understanding of how the systems work.

One way to deal with this complexity is to build simplified neural models. Simplified models include some physiological properties of a system and ignore others. For instance, they may assume that a cell is a single isopotential compartment, or they may lump some currents together. The hope is that a simplified model that includes the right physiological details will replicate the behavior of a system in a way that makes it easy to understand. Fitzhugh (1960, 1961) used a simplified model to analyze and explain the behavior of the Hodgkin-Huxley equations, as did Rose and Hindmarsh (1985) for bursting in thalamic neurons. On the systems level, Rowat and Selverston (1993) have recently used a network of simplified neurons to model the oscillations in the gastric mill network of the lobster STG.

In this work, we investigate phase modulation by current pulses in simplified oscillatory model neurons. Work in several systems, including the STG (Ayers and Selverston 1977), electric fish (Kawasaki and Heiligenberg 1988), and *Aplysia* (Pinsker 1977a, 1977b), has shown that current pulses can modulate the phase of oscillatory neural systems. Such modulations presumably help the system respond to sensory input representing changing environmental conditions. Here we show that the oscillatory phase of a simplified model is also modulated by current pulses. Because the model is so simple, we are able to explain many of the modulatory phenomena that we observe mathematically. If these phenomena occur in real systems, then similar explanations may hold for them as well.

2. Model Cells

Our model cells are based on those used by Rowat and Selverston (1993) to simulate slow-wave oscillations in the gastric mill network of the lobster STG. In an *in vitro* preparation, Elson and Selverston (1992) have shown that gastric mill oscillations continue with approximately unchanged phase relationships in the presence of tetrodotoxin, which suppresses action potentials. Accordingly, the oscillations must be based on graded synaptic transmission, as has been shown to occur in the pyloric network of the STG (Graubard et al. 1983). Rowat and Selverston (1993) simulated the gastric mill oscillations using a network of simplified model cells. Each cell was assumed to act as single isopotential compartment with two voltage-activated currents, an N-shaped fast current and a linear slow current. These assumptions can be used to write an equation for the membrane voltage of a model cell like that used by Hodgkin and Huxley (1952) to describe the action potential of the squid giant axon:

$$\tau_m \frac{\delta V}{\delta t} + I_{fast} + I_{slow} + I_{syn} = I_{inj},$$

(1)

where τ_m is the membrane time constant, V is the membrane potential, I_{fast} is the fast current, I_{slow} is the slow current, I_{syn} is the synaptic current, and I_{inj} is the injected current. I_{fast} is assumed to be an instantaneous function of the membrane voltage V, given by the piecewise-linear function

$$F(V) = \begin{cases} V + A_f & \text{for } V < -A_f/\sigma_f \\ V - A_f & \text{for } V > A_f/\sigma_f \\ (1-\sigma_f)V & \text{otherwise,} \end{cases} \qquad (2)$$

where A_f and σ_f are parameters that determine the shape of the function (see figure 1). The $I-V$ curve for I_{fast} has a region of negative resistance, which makes the cell electrically excitable. I_{slow} is equivalent to the state variable q, which is described by the equation

$$\tau_s \frac{\delta q}{\delta t} = -q + q_\infty(V), \qquad (3)$$

where the steady-state current $q_\infty(V)$ is given by

$$q_\infty(V) = \sigma_s V. \qquad (4)$$

σ_s is a parameter that determines the slope of the function $q_\infty(V)$ (see figure 1). The synaptic current into a postsynaptic cell is given by

$$S(V_{pre}, V_{post}) = Wf(V_{pre})(V_{post} - E_{post}), \qquad (5)$$

where W is the synaptic weight, $f(V_{pre})$ is given by the threshold function

$$f(V_{pre}) = \begin{cases} 1 & \text{for } V_{pre} > \theta \\ 0 & \text{otherwise,} \end{cases} \qquad (6)$$

and E_{post} is the synaptic reversal potential.

Each model cell can now be summarized by equations for its two state variables, V and q. Rewriting (1) yields the equation

$$\tau_m \frac{\delta V}{\delta t} + F(V) + q + S = I_{inj} \qquad (7)$$

for V. The other state variable, q, is described by (3).

Rowat and Selverston (1993) found that their model was robust for a wide range of parameter values. For each of the experiments described here, the same values were used: $\tau_m = 0.25$, $\tau_s = 5$, $A_f = 1$, $\sigma_s = 3$, $\theta = 0.2$, and $E_{rev} = -4$. Different values of σ_f and W were used for each experiment. These are noted below.

3. Phase-Plane Analysis

One way to analyze a system of differential equations is by a graphical method called *phase-plane analysis* (see Jordan and Smith 1987). A phase-plane is a two-dimensional representation of the state of a system. Figure 2a shows a phase-plane for a single oscillatory model cell. The state variables V and q are plotted on the axes, and the *state point*, which represents the current state of the system, moves through the phase-plane as a function of time. Information about the behavior of such a system can be gained by plotting the *nullclines* for the state variables. Nullclines are curves on which one of the state variables does not change. The V nullcline can be found from (7) by setting $dV/dt = 0$. Solving for q gives $q = I_{inj} - S - F(V)$, which reduces to $q = -F(V)$ for a single cell with no injected current. On this curve, V does not change, so the state point moves vertically, in the directions indicated by the arrows. Similarly, the q nullcline can be found from (3) by setting

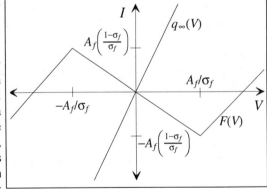

Figure 1. Steady-state I-V curves for the fast and slow currents.

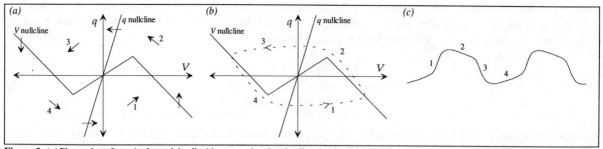

Figure 2. *(a)* Phase-plane for a single model cell with arrows showing the direction in which the state point moves along the nullclines and in regions 1-4. *(b)* Limit cycle trajectory of the state point. *(c)* V waveform as a function of time.

$dq/dt = 0$. Solving for q yields $q = q_\infty(V) = \sigma_s V$. On this line, q does not change, so the state point moves horizontally, as shown by the arrows. The point where the two nullclines intersect is a *fixed point*. Since both $dV/dt = 0$ and $dq/dt = 0$, the state point cannot move from the fixed point if it ever winds up there. However, for an oscillatory cell the fixed point is unstable, so small perturbations move the state point away from it.

When the state point is not on one of the nullclines, its behavior can still be predicted from the phase-plane diagram of the system. The V and q nullclines divide the phase-plane into four sections, numbered 1-4 in figure 2a. Since dV/dt and dq/dt change continuously, the direction in which the state point moves must change continuously as well. This means that the state point must move diagonally in sections 1-4, roughly as shown by the diagonal arrows in figure 2a. The actual steady-state trajectory that the state point follows over time is called a *limit cycle* (dotted line in figure 2b). This limit cycle is *attracting* because small perturbations move the state point back towards it. When viewed as a function of time (see figure 2c), this means that the voltage waveform of the cell oscillates in a slow wave pattern.

4. Methods

The phase modulation behavior of a single cell and pairs of cells connected by reciprocal inhibition were analyzed by injecting them with simulated EPSPs and IPSPs at various phases in their oscillatory cycles. Phases were measured relative to the upward (increasing) zero-crossing of the voltage waveform for each cell, scaled between 0 and 1. Current pulses were applied at least every 0.1 phase units, and all current pulses lasted 0.2 time units. In single cells, phase shifts were measured by comparing the upward zero-crossings of a cell's post-pulse voltage waveform to its anticipated upward zero-crossings (based on the pre-pulse average period) without a pulse. The difference between these signals was then scaled to produce a phase shift between 0.5 (a half cycle phase advance) and -0.5 (a half cycle phase delay). In pairs of cells, current pulses were applied to one cell, and both cells were allowed to settle into a steady phase shift, which was measured as before. In all cases, both cells settled to the same phase shift because reciprocal inhibition tends to make them oscillate 180° out of phase with one another. This steady state phase shift was then taken as the phase shift for the two cell pair.

Computational results were generated with a neural simulation system called "The Preparation" (Rowat and Selverston 1993) which represents model cells using systems of differential equations. The Preparation continuously integrates a model, displays on-line graphical output, and allows parameters to be changed without restarting the model. Integration is done by the LSODA package (Petzold and Hindmarsh 1987), which uses automatic method switching when equations become stiff.

5. Results

5.1 Regions of Phase Advance and Phase Delay

Single cells and pairs of cells both showed broad regions of phase advance and phase delay. Figure 3a shows the phase response of a single oscillatory cell ($\sigma_f = 1.8$, $W = 0$) for various size EPSPs ($I_{inj} = 5, 3,$ and 1). For stimulus phases less than about 0.2 or greater than about 0.7, EPSPs produced phase advances. Figure 3b illustrates why this happens. At these stimulus phases, the state point lies in the bottom half of the phase plane ($q < 0$). The equation for the V nullcline is $q = I_{inj} - F(V)$, so an EPSP shifts the V nullcline upward from its original position (solid line) to a new position (dashed line) further from the state point. Since the state point moves faster when it is further from the V nullcline, it moves more during the course of an EPSP than it would have if the V nullcline were in its original position (dotted arrow). This additional movement produces a phase advance.

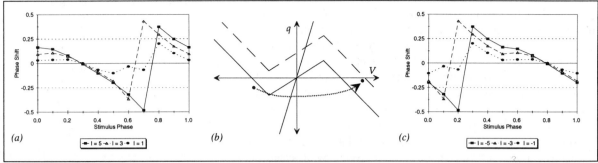

Figure 3. Phase response curves for single cells perturbed by simulated EPSPs *(a)* and IPSPs *(c)*. *(b)* gives a phase-plane explanation for the phase advances seen in *(a)*.

For stimulus phases between about 0.2 and 0.7, EPSPs produced phase delays. This happens for reasons analogous to those for phase advances. At these intermediate stimulus phases, the state point lies in the upper half of the phase plane ($q > 0$). When the EPSP shifts the fast nullcline up, it moves closer to the state point or even past it for large EPSPs. This causes the state point to slow down or reverse directions, producing a phase delay.

Similar results were obtained for IPSPs. Figure 3c shows the phase response of the same cell for $I_{inj} = -5$, -3, and -1. The phase space for a single cell is symmetrical for rotations of 180°, so IPSPs produce the same phase shifts as EPSPs, except that the stimulus phase is shifted by 0.5 phase units. This shift corresponds to a rotation of 180° in phase space. The effect of IPSPs on the V nullcline and state point is analogous to that of EPSPs.

5.2 Type 0 and Type 1 Phase Response Curves

Winfree (1980) describes two types of phase response curves that occur in oscillatory systems, both of which were seen here. Type 1 phase response curves have a topological winding number of 1. This commonly occurs when a stimulus produces a small phase shift, so the new phase remains close to the original stimulus phase. In phase response graphs like those above, type 1 curves are represented by continuous responses, like those for $I_{inj} = 1$ (figure 3a) and $I_{inj} = -1$ (figure 3c). These responses occur with moderate EPSPs and IPSPs, where the magnitude of the pulse is too small to move the V nullcline very far. As shown in figure 4a, this means that the state point only moves a short distance before it runs into the V nullcline again. Thus, small pulses produce small movements of the state point and, accordingly, small phase shifts.

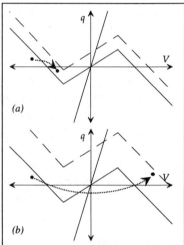

Type 0 phase response curves have a topological winding number of 0. This usually happens when a stimulus produces a large phase shift, so that the new phase is relatively independent of the original stimulus phase. In phase response graphs like those above, type 1 curves are represented by discontinuous responses, like those for $I_{inj} = 3$ and 5 (figure 3a, near a stimulus phase of 0.7) and $I_{inj} = -3$ and -5 (figure 3c, near a stimulus phase of 0.2). These responses occur with large EPSPs and IPSPs that move the V

Figure 4. EPSPs generating *(a)* type 1 and *(b)* type 0 phase response curves.

nullcline far from the state point. As shown for an EPSP in figure 4b, this allows the state point to move all the way from the left arm of the V nullcline to the right arm during the duration of a pulse. This produces a large phase shift, and the state point winds up in almost the same place no matter where it started from.

5.3 Effects of Reciprocal Inhibition

Pairs of cells connected by reciprocal inhibition do not produce phase response graphs exactly like those for single cells. In order to study how reciprocal inhibition affects pairs of cells, we tested endogenously oscillating cells ($\sigma_f = 1.8$) with various size synaptic weights. Figure 5a summarizes the results for moderately sized EPSPs ($I_{inj} = 3$). With a synaptic weight of 0, the two cells operate independently, so the results are the same as for a single cell. With larger synaptic weights, two trends become apparent. First, the responses are relatively unchanged at stimulus phases of 0.4 or less. This happens because the unstimulated cell has $V < 0$ at these stimulus phases, so it is below the synaptic threshold from equations (5) and (6). Consequently, it exerts no synaptic influence on the stimulated cell. Second, the responses are dampened at stimulus phases of 0.5 or greater. In part, this is because the unstimulated cell is active for these stimulus phases, so synaptic inhibition from it opposes the effect of the EPSP. However, for small synaptic weights, this opposition probably has little effect. Instead, the dampening is likely due to the cells' tendency to "split the difference" for any sudden phase shift. A sudden phase shift in one cell breaks the 180° separation between the phases of the two cells. Because they are connected by reciprocal inhibition, the cells reestablish this 180° separation cooperatively, with each one pushing the other. As a result, they split the difference in any sudden phase shift. This effect is strong enough that, even for synaptic weights as small as 0.01, reciprocally inhibitory cells have type 1 (continuous) rather than type 0 (discontinuous) phase response curves. Similar results were seen with IPSPs (see figure 5b, $I_{inj} = -3$).

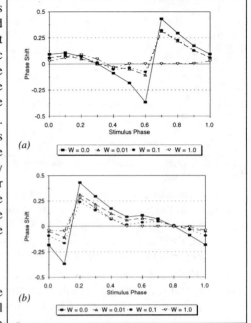

(a)

(b)

Figure 5. Effects of synaptic inhibition of phase modulation for *(a)* EPSPs and *(b)* IPSPs.

5.4 Phase Modulation in Non-Oscillatory Cells

A central pattern generator like the gastric mill network of the lobster STG can produce oscillations even though its individual cells are not endogenous oscillators (Elson and Selverston 1992). In order to study how the oscillatory properties of individual cells affected phase modulation, we tested reciprocally inhibitory pairs of cells with a fixed synaptic weight ($W = 0.5$), a fixed sized IPSP ($I_{inj} = 3$), and various sizes of σ_f (from 0.0 to 3.0). When $\sigma_f > 1$, cells are endogenous oscillators, and the state point approaches the oscillatory limit cycle more quickly as σ_f gets larger. When $\sigma_f \leq 1$, cells are not endogenous oscillators, and the state point approaches the fixed point at the origin faster as σ_f gets smaller (see Rowat and Selverston 1993). As is shown in figure 6, a pair of cells produced qualitatively similar phase response curves for all values of σ_f. One curious phenomenon is that both strong oscillators ($\sigma_f = 3.0$) and strong non-oscillators ($\sigma_f = 0.0$) show large phase advances at a stimulus phase of 0.7, while cells with intermediate values of σ_f do not. More work is needed to explain these responses.

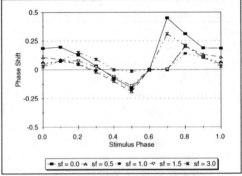

Figure 6. Phase response curves for endogenously non-oscillating (sf ≤ 1) and oscillating (sf > 1) cells. "sf" stands for "sigma sub f".

6. Conclusions

This work has shown how four kinds of modulatory phenomena can occur in simplified model neurons stimulated by current pulses: (1) regions of phase advance and phase delay, (2) type 1 and type 0 phase responses, (3) effects of reciprocal inhibition, and (4) phase modulation in non-oscillatory cells. Two questions are now important. First, do real oscillatory neural systems exhibit these phenomena? If so, then simplified models designed to mimic their individual connectivities and dynamics may be able to make quantitative predictions about their phase response characteristics. Second, do the explanations for these phenomena in simplified neural models hold for real systems as well? If so, then the simplified models would seem to be good approximations of the real systems. More work is needed to address these issues experimentally.

Acknowledgements. PFR was supported by the Office of Naval Research #N0014-91-5-1720, the National Institute of Mental Health #NH-46899, and the National Science Foundation #IBN-9122712.

References

Ayers, J. L. and A. I. Selverston (1977). Synaptic control of an endogenous pacemaker network. *J. Physiol., Paris* 73:453-461.

Elson, R. C. and A. I. Selverston (1992). Mechanisms of gastric rhythm generation in the isolated stomatogastric ganglion of spiny lobsters: Bursting pacemaker potentials. *J. Neurophysiol.* 68:890-907.

Engel, A. K., P. König, A. K. Kreiter, C. M. Gray, and W. Singer (1990). Temporal coding by coherent oscillations as a potential solution to the binding problem: Physiological evidence. Preprint from *Nonlinear dynamics and neural networks*, eds. H. G. Schuster and W. Singer.

Fitzhugh, R. (1960). Thresholds and plateaus in the Hodgkin-Huxley nerve equations. *J. Gen. Physiol.* 43:867-896.

Fitzhugh, R. (1961). Impulses and physiological states in theoretical models of nerve membrane. *Biophysical J.* 1:445-466.

Graubard, K., J. A. Raper, and D. K. Hartline (1983). Graded synaptic transmission between identified spiking neurons. *J. Neurophysiol.* 50:508-521.

Harris-Warrick, R. M., E. Marder, A. I. Selverston, and M. Moulins (1992). *Dynamic biological networks: The stomatogastric nervous system.* Cambridge: MIT Press.

Heiligenberg, W. (1991). *Neural nets in electric fish.* Cambridge: MIT Press.

Hodgkin, A. L. and A. F. Huxley (1952). A quantitative description of membrane current and its application to conduction and excitation in nerve. *J. Physiol.* 117:500-544.

Jordan, D. W. and P. Smith (1987). *Nonlinear ordinary differential equations.* Oxford: Oxford Press.

Kawasaki, M. and W. Heiligenberg (1988). Individual prepacemaker neurons can modulate the pacemaker cycle of the gymnotiform electric fish, *Eigenmannia. J. Comp. Physiol.* 162:13-21.

Petzold, L. R. and A. C. Hindmarsh (1987). LSODA: Livermore solver for ordinary differential equations, with automatic method switching for stiff and nonstiff problems. Lawrence Livermore National Laboratory, Computing and Mathematics division, 1-316. Livermore, CA.

Pinsker, H. M. (1977a). *Aplysia* bursting neurons as endogenous oscillators: I. Phase-response curves for pulsed inhibitory synaptic input. *J. Neurophysiol.* 40:527-543.

Pinsker, H. M. (1977b). *Aplysia* bursting neurons as endogenous oscillators: II. Synchronization and entrainment by pulsed inhibitory synaptic input. *J. Neurophysiol.* 40:544-556.

Rose, R. M., and J. L. Hindmarsh (1985). A model of a thalamic neuron. *Proc. R. Soc. Lond.* 225:161-193.

Rowat, P. F. and A. I. Selverston (1993). Modeling the gastric mill central pattern generator of the lobster with a relaxation oscillator network. *J. Neurophys.* 70:1030-1053.

Winfree, A. T. (1980). *The geometry of biological time.* New York: Springer-Verlag.

Neurosolver: A Neural Network Based on a Cortical Column

ANDRZEJ BIESZCZAD

Systems and Computer Engineering, Carleton University, Ottawa, Canada K1S 5B6

Abstract: *In this paper, a neural network based on a model of a biological cortical column is presented. The cortical column has been found to play the fundamental role in information processing in the cerebral cortex. The model of the column presented in this work displays similar functionality. The stress is laid on the cooperative behavior of many artificial columns interconnected in a network. The network is capable of recording trajectories of time related events. Those recorded trajectories let the network use time dependencies to perform breadth-first searches. The device can solve stimulus-response type problems in a given domain and because of that is called Neurosolver. The Neurosolver can use a context update mechanism to perform dynamic searches.*

1.0 Introduction

The cortical column, the "module-concept", has been proposed as an anatomical entity by Szentagothai [1]. Later, Mountcastle [2] and Zeki and Shipp [3] enriched the hypothesis by describing the functional context of the cortical column. Ballard in [4] was the first to propose the model that clearly identifies three distinct parts of the column: the upper, the intermediate and the lower divisions. Burnod in [5] proposed the concepts of a columnar call and action tree and the use of the trees to explain the functionality of the cortex.

A modified version of the Burnod's model of the cortical column has been used as a processing element of a neural network architecture that we call the Neurosolver. The Neurosolver is capable of computing solutions to problems in a given, well defined domain through traversing trajectories that encode temporal relationships between the objects in the domain. The recollection mechanism produces solutions to presented problems in a form of sequences of patterns of network activity. The topographical relationships of the objects of the domain are used explicitly, because the problem of creating such maps has been settled by others, for example Kohonen [6].

Cho, Rosenbloom and Dolan in [7] have reported their work on Neuro-Soar that has similar to the Neurosolver objectives. Their approach is, however, completely different from the one presented in this paper.

2.0 Architecture of an artificial column

2.1 Connectivity

The column and its connectivity, as illustrated in Figure 1, are inspired by the neurobiological data. The column has two divisions: upper and lower. The Upper-Upper connections carry signals between the upper divisions of two columns. The Lower-Upper connections, in turn, carry signals from the lower division of the sender to the upper division of the receiver. In addition to the external connections, there are two internal connections. The Upper-Lower connection transmits the activity from the upper division to the lower division. The internal Lower-Upper connection is used to inhibit the upper division by high activity in the lower division. The activity of the lower division constitutes the output of the column.

In spite of many similarities, there are important simplifications made in comparison to the biological cortical column.

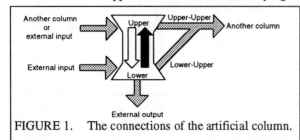

FIGURE 1.   The connections of the artificial column.

2.2 Functionality

The artificial column is a three-state device. If there is no input activity and no sustained internal activity from the past, the column is inactive. The interpretation of the inactive state from the information processing perspective is that the concept represented by the column is not present in the current computing context. There is no output activity whatsoever from a column in that state.

The upper division of the column can be activated by action potentials from other columns, incoming through the connections from both, upper and lower, divisions, and from the external, cortical, afferents. The input activity of the upper division is calculated according to the following formula:

$$inputActivity \ = \ \sum_{activeConnections} actionPotential \ * \ connectionStrength$$

where activeConnections are those from the columns that have not been recently activated directly by this column.

That rule prevents creation of self-exciting pairs of columns.

After the input activity is integrated in the upper division, action potentials are sent to other columns. The pattern with which the activity diffuses throughout the network depends on the strengths of the connections. The activity in the upper division is also transmitted to the lower division. The Upper-Lower channel does not have any resistance, so the lower division gets exactly same level of activity as the upper one. The activity of the lower division is not transmitted anywhere until the threshold level is reached. If that happens, it is said that the column fired. Then, the activity is distributed by the means of action potentials to the receiving columns. The strength of a specific connection determines how big influence on the receiver the firing of the column will have.

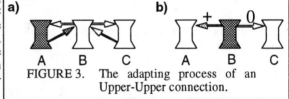

FIGURE 2. Setting the goal (a) and its satisfaction (b).

Both the lower and upper divisions receive external afferents. These afferents play an important role as the inputs to the system. The cortical afferents are incoming to the upper division, and the thalamic afferents are incoming to the lower division. The cortical input can be used to express goals by activating the upper division of the column that represents a specific, desirable state, feature or concept. The persistence of that activity denotes the goal to achieve – the desire to satisfy. The goal is reached when the activity is suppressed. That will happen when the column fires. The firing of the column can also trigger some external action. Figure 2 illustrates that process.

The upper division of the column is a vehicle for processing abstract data through the changes to the activity patterns depicting concepts or sequences of concepts. On other hand, the lower division is in touch with the physical world as represented by the activity of the sensors.

The upper division is the integrating part of the column, since it correlates signals from other columns. The lower division is the decisive component of the column. It determines whether the concept is perceived and controls the output that may, in turn, alter the environment. Ultimately, the lower division is a vehicle that drives the behavior of the column toward the goal satisfaction.

After firing, the column becomes insensitive for some time. No input activity, neither thalamic nor cortical, is accepted. That prevents two mutually connected columns from firing in an oscillating manner.

2.3 Adaptivity

There are two rules of how the connections are modified depending on the patterns of changes in the activity of a column and the columns that transmit signals to and receive signals from that column. The first rule (*the feedback rule*) states that if a specific column fires, the strengths of all of the Upper-Upper connections to the columns that fired directly before are increased. That process is illustrated in Figure 3. Column B is the focus of our attention in the example. Columns A and C are connected to B. At a certain point in time, let us say *t*, column A fires; columns B and C do not. In the next tick, *t*+1, column B fires. According to the adaptation rule, column A fired directly before column B, the connection to the upper division of column A from the upper division of column B is strengthened. The connection to column C stays the same or is, at least relatively, weakened.

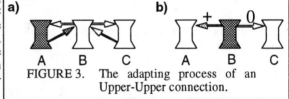

FIGURE 3. The adapting process of an Upper-Upper connection.

It is important to note that after the connection strengths are modified, it will be more likely that activity in the upper division of column B will cause changes in the activity of column A rather than in column C.

The second adaptation rule (*the feed forward rule*) says that the strengths of all Lower-Upper connections are increased between the columns that fire now and those that fired just before. Figure 4 illustrates that process. In the

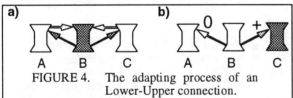

FIGURE 4. The adapting process of an Lower-Upper connection.

figure, there are again three columns: A, B and C. Column B fires at the time *t* and sends the action potentials to columns A and C. At the time *t*+1, column C fires. The adaptation process increases the strength of the connection between the lower division of column B and the upper division of column C.

The implications of the feed forward rule of adaptation are similar to those stated for the feedback rule: after the modification, firing of column B will have bigger impact on the activity in column C than in column A.

Both adaptation rules work at the same time. For the clarity of the description they were separated in the examples.

The ability of a column to adapt the strengths of the connections with other modules depending on the patterns of network activity will be analyzed from the network's perspective later on.

2.4 Connection strength

One of the premises of this work was to design a formula for the strength of a connection that would allow an input pattern to be recorded fast. A probabilistic approach was proposed for the column by Burnod [5], but the learning rules presented in this paper are different.

To determine the strengths of the connections, certain statistical parameters are recorded for every division of each column, let us say C, and every connection, C_iC_j. When the activity of a division increases from low to high, then the counter C_{up} is increased. Another counter, C_{in}, is increased for each column that has sent action potential to the inputs of the column in question, so it counts the global influences on the column. The third statistical parameter, C_{out}, counts all receivers that fired as a consequence of receiving action potentials after this column fired. A counter of influences, C_iC_{jcons}, is maintained for each connection. It is increased each time the connection carries an action potential from the presynaptic column, the transmitter, that has fired to the postsynaptic column, the receiver, that fires as a consequence. These statistical data are used to calculate the strength of both, the incoming and outgoing, connections.

There are several probabilities calculated for the purpose of computing the strength of a given connection. In the following formulas, A and B are presynaptic and postsynaptic, with respect to the connection in question, cortical divisions respectively.

• The probability indicating how likely the change of the activity of the presynaptic division from low to high is to generate a successful action potential (i.e., such that it will take part in influencing the postsynaptic division):

$$P_{cons} = \frac{AB_{cons}}{A_{up}}$$

• The probability of how inclined the action potential carried through the connection is to increase the activity of the postsynaptic division:

$$P_{in} = \frac{AB_{cons}}{B_{in}}$$

• The probability of how prone the postsynaptic division is to change its activity from low to high upon reception of any action potential from any input:

$$P_{up} = \frac{B_{up}}{B_{in}}$$

• The probability of how likely is the action potential that is carried over the connection after the presynaptic division's activity moves from low to high to change the state of the postsynaptic division:

$$P_{out} = \frac{AB_{cons}}{B_{out}}$$

• The probability of how prone the post-synaptic division is to influence other columns after changing its state from low to high:

$$P_{up_2} = \frac{B_{up}}{B_{out}}$$

The strength of the Lower-Upper connection is calculated using the first three coefficients:

$$\sigma_{AB} = P_{cons}*P_{in}*P_{up}$$

The strength of the Upper-Upper connection may be computed using the same formula but with the first and two last coefficients instead:

$$\rho_{AB} = P_{cons}*P_{out}*P_{up2}$$

There is a number of alternate ways to combine P_{cons}, P_{in}, P_{up}, P_{out} and P_{up2} in the formulas for the strength of the connection. For example, for the Upper-Upper connection it might be advantageous to just use $\rho_{AB} = P_{cons}$.

The strength of the connection between the upper and lower division is fixed and its value is 1. Consequently, any activity in the upper division is transmitted to the lower division. The strength of the connection in the opposite direction is also fixed to -1. If the activity in the lower division exceeds the threshold, the activity in the upper division is suppressed.

2.5 Thresholds

Each division of a column has a number of activity thresholds:
• a low activity threshold defines the inactive state,
• a high activity threshold defines the active state and
• an output threshold indicates the minimum activity that can be transmitted in the form of an action potential to the receivers through the output connections.

All activity thresholds in the model have been fixed; i.e., they are not adaptive. The output threshold of the upper division is 0. The output threshold of the lower division is the same as the high activity threshold. The latter determines when the column fires, because the lower division is the output component of the column.

3.0 Neurosolver - a network of cortical columns

The Neurosolver is a device that is capable of recording the behavior of any physical system or object. The object can be observed by the system of sensors that detect its state. The states and, more importantly, the patterns of their changes are input to the neurosolver. The neurosolver modifies its inter-columnar connections according to the adaptation rules. On the other end, each column has a determined meaning and may output signals that afflict the manipulators ready to alter some aspect or aspects of the observed object. The recorded information may be used to activate required actions of the manipulators as presented by the goal. It is a certain state of the object, a point in the space of all possible states. The Neurosolver is capable of activating the path in that space that leads from the current state to the goal state through a number of intermediate states. In the course of that activation, some of the columns involved fire and control the manipulators in the same way as it was observed and recorded in the past. Through the sequence of the manipulations, the required state of the object is achieved. The goal has been satisfied, the problem - solved: that is the origin of the name of the device: neuro-solver.

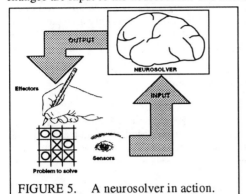

FIGURE 5.   A neurosolver in action.

The Neurosolver starts to interact with the subject system as a *tabula rasa*. It gains all its experience, and problem solving capabilities, through the interchange of the sensory and manipulation control data with the system through the inputs and outputs. There is no separate learning cycle - the Neurosolver learns while servicing the system, though at the beginning there is not much it can do.

There is evident similarity of the behavior of the Neurosolver to that of classical problem solvers that use problem space representation like GPS [8] and its successor SOAR [9].

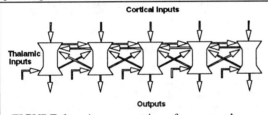

FIGURE 6.   A cross-section of a neurosolver.

In the further parts of this section of the paper, the mechanics of the problem solving capabilities of the neurosolver are explained. To better visualize the behavior of the network, all considerations involve a simplification that each goal is initially given as an activation of a single column. Usually, any complex problem requires a distributed representation.

3.1 Architecture

The inter-columnar connectivity follows the scheme described for a single column. Figure 6 illustrates the connectivity for a number of columns that are shown in a cross-section of the neurosolver. The neurosolver has a matrix architecture, as illustrated in Figure 7. Each node is connected, through lower-upper and upper-upper connections, to its neighbors in eight directions on the plane: vertical, horizontal and diagonal.

The behavior of such regular architecture is easier to illustrate than more complex variants.

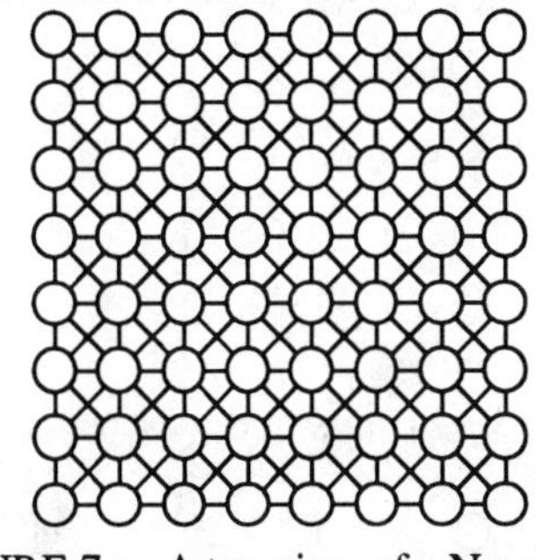

3.2 Learning

The initial strength of the connections in the neurosolver is zero, that is no activity can be propagated from one column to others. When the sensors start to communicate the sequences of events occurring in the observed system, the connections between firing columns are adjusted according to the adaptation rules. That process is illustrated in Figure 8. In the cross-section of a part of a neurosolver there are

FIGURE 7.   A top view of a Neurosolver

four columns: A, B, C and D. The initial strengths of the connections between all of the columns are zero. However, when, for example, column A fires and that is followed by the firing of column B, then the upper-upper connection between B and A is strengthened using the feedback rule. Additionally, the value of the strength of the lower-upper connection between A and B is increased as well using the feed forward rule. If column C fires next in the sequence, than the connections between B and C are modified in the same way as between A and B. Column D is the next to fire in the illustration. Again, the connections between C and D are modified appropriately. After some time depending on the learning schema used, two chains are recorded as shown in Figure 9. When using the probabilistic learning rules, the chains are formed just after one presentation of the sequence. The hebbian schema usually require more time to form the associations.

The first chain links the upper divisions of the columns through the upper-upper connections. It is created in the reverse direction to that of the firing columns. If the firing of column B is treated as a consequence of the firing of column A, than spreading a low level activity from B to A may be understood as a call, or a search, for the reason of B firing. The same reasoning applies to all columns in the chain. Therefore, if **D** is activated at a low level and that activity is propagated to **C** to **B** to **A**, than that is a search for the reasons of **D** firing. If **D** represents a desired state of the observed system, than **ABCD** is one of the possible paths to satisfy that goal. The chain that is generated between the upper divisions is, therefore, called a call chain.

The increasing strength in the lower-upper connections between **A**, **B**, **C** and **D**, constitutes another chain. That is called an action chain, because if any of the column of the chain gets highly activated, it will cause the next column in the chain to fire as well. That type of chain requires many more repetitive presentations of the input sequence than the call chain.

3.3 Call trees - a breadth-first search

3.3.1 A call tree

When a goal node is activated, like node **G** in Figure 10, its activity spreads along all chains that were recorded. It is not a single call chain created anymore; it is a call tree. The activity will spread in

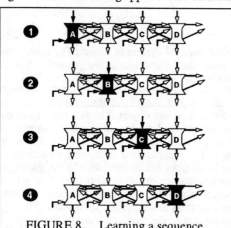

FIGURE 8.   Learning a sequence.

steps into all directions that may be the solution to the problem. The nodes that are already in the active call tree are shadowed. The arrows that are outlined indicate the recorded direction of the call - the connections that were strengthened in the past due to the columns firing in the opposite direction. One of the chains, or paths, of the tree has been labeled. Column **G** is the goal, that is the root of the call tree. Each of the subsequently activated columns, **A**, **B** and **C**, becomes a subgoal to achieve the main goal **G**. In Figure 10, column **D** is activated as the next subgoal and added, in that way, to the chain GABCD. In the same step, many other new leaves are added in the same way to the tree.

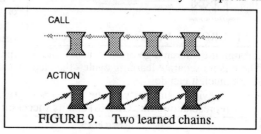

FIGURE 9.   Two learned chains.

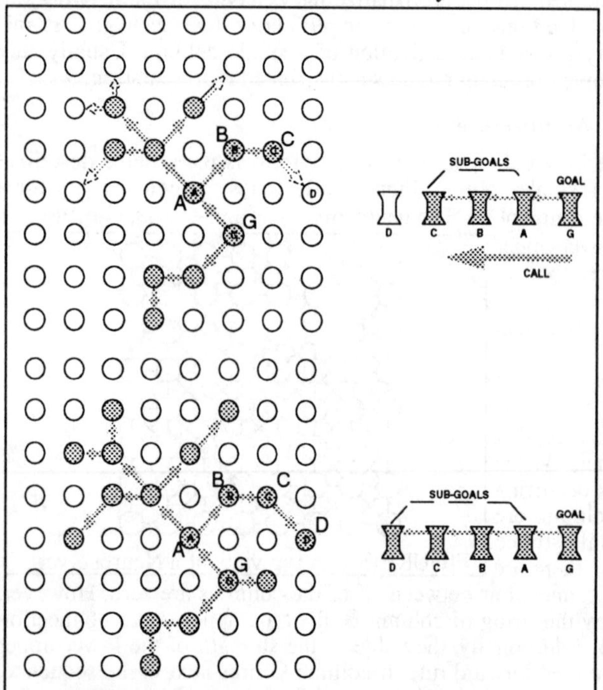

3.3.2 Triggering the resolution

The activity initiated by the goal column spreads throughout the network until one of the columns in the tree fires. That may happen due to the sensory input, as illustrated in Figure 11, or through the accumulation of sufficiently high activity in the upper division caused by action potentials arriving through several cortical inputs. Although the activity may continue to spread out along other branches of the tree, the propagation in this particular chain is terminated. The external input to the firing column means that there is an observation made now or a clue, or an axiom, set a priori, that indicates that this path may lead to achieving the goal. The firing column, column **D** in Figure 11, is called the trigger of the solution to the posed problem.

Note that the use of an eye and a hand in the figures is only a means to better visualize the processes occurring in the neurosolver. The reader should consider those symbols to be representations of any type of sensations and actions. For example, the trigger can be just a state of mind that is sufficient to trigger an action along the path toward the solution of the problem. The effector that is represented by the hand can range from a robot arm to a voice synthesizer explaining the solution to the user applying pre-built rules associated with each node.

FIGURE 10.   The construction of a call tree.

3.3.3 The resolution path

The trigger of the problem resolution, the column that fires first in the search path, is, subsequently, shut down. The firing and shutting down of column **D** means that the subgoal represented by that column has been satisfied. If the Lower-Upper connection to the next node in the tree in the direction toward the root, from **D** to **C** in Figure 12, is strong enough, the action potential that it carries to the recipient sums up with the sustained expectation activity in the receiver and may cause the next column to fire. That is shown in the figure: column **C** fires. Similar processes occur now in column **C**. There might be a connection from the firing column to the effectors, so in addition to perhaps triggering the firing of the next column in the search tree, the firing of that column might have some impact on the observed system because of the changes to the activity patterns of the output of the neurosolver that impact the effectors. In that way, a part of the overall task has been carried out.

3.3.4 Sensory-guided resolution

It may happen, that the Lower-Upper connection between the firing column and the target columns in the call tree are weak. None of them can fire. In that case, the system cannot decide what the next step in the resolution of the problem should be. The resolution is suspended waiting for further clues. The activity can again be spread throughout the network in an attempt to search for the clues. The explorations may lead to partial resolutions being found in other parts

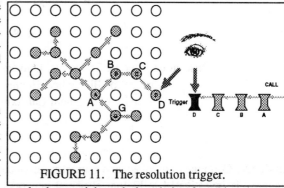

FIGURE 11. The resolution trigger.

of the call tree. That may affect the system. For example, one of the columns in the original path that was not getting sufficiently high signals might suddenly receive a thalamic input and finally fire. The implication is that the clue the neurosolver has been waiting for has been found. The resolution may proceed further in this branch.

If the Neurosolver is unable to solve a task or has some doubts about the next step in the solution, the activity patterns may be interpreted as requests to update the context with a new or more detailed data. That may be considered as one of the external actions controlled by the Neurosolver. That action may include explorations in search for new data.

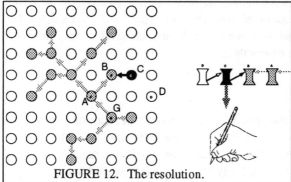

FIGURE 12. The resolution.

3.3.5 The goal satisfaction

When a column fires, and is shut down by the inhibition action described before, the activity in its upper division, of course, disappears. Subsequently, all columns that have been activated by the firing column in the call tree will also shut down as the result, unless they receive input signals from other sources. Actually, the whole sub-tree of the call tree with the inhibited column as its root is shut down.

3.4 Action trees

Sometimes, certain sequences of events occurring in the system and corresponding changes to the patterns of columnar activity happen very often. As a consequence, the strength of the connections from lower to upper divisions of the columns involved grow considerably in the direction of the firing sequence. The connections become so strong that they are able to induce a high level of activity in the recipients in the chain even without any expectation activity. Each of the columns involved realizes a part of a certain action by outputting action potentials to the effectors, so the chain generated in that way is called an action tree.

4.0 BIBLIOGRAPHY

[1] Szentagothai, J., *"The module concept in cerebral cortex architecture"*, Brain Research, 1979.
[2] Mountcastle, V. B., *"An organization principle for cerebral function: the unit module and the distributed system"*. In "The Mindful Brain", Schmitt, F. O., MIT Press, Cambridge, 1978.
[3] Zeki, S. and Shipp, S., *"The functional logic of cortical connections"*, Nature, Vol.335, pp. 311-317.
[4] Ballard, D. H., *"Cortical connections and parallel processing: structure and function"*, Behavioral and Brain Sciences, 1986.
[5] Burnod, Y., *"An adaptive neural network: the cerebral cortex"*, Masson, Paris, 1988.
[6] Kohonen, T., *"Self-organization and associative memory"*, Springer-Verlag, Berlin, 2nd edition, 1988.
[7] Cho, B., Rosenbloom, P. S. and Dolan, C. P., *"Neuro-Soar: A neural network architecture for goal-oriented behavior"*, Proceedings of Thirteenth Annual Conference of the Cognitive Science Society, Chicago, Lawrence Erlbaum Associates, 1991.
[8] Newell, A. and Simon, H. A., *"GPS: A program that simulates human thought"*, in Feigenbaum, E. A. and Feldman, J. (Eds.), *"Computer and thought"*, McGrawHill, New York, 1963.
Laird, J. E., Newell, A. and Rosenbloom, P. S., *"SOAR: An architecture for general intelligence"*, Artificial Intelligence, Vol. 33, pp. 1-64, 1987

On the Relation between Topology and Geometry in Biological Neural Networks

G. A. Chauvet

Institut de Biologie Théorique, Université d'Angers, 49100 Angers (France), and
Department of Biomedical Engineering and Program for Neuroscience
University of Southern California, Los Angeles, CA 90089 (USA)

———

Abstract: Coupling of topology and geometry, i.e. of connectivity between structures of the nervous tissue and their anatomy, is investigated in biological neural networks. It is shown that a function called the *synaptic density-connectivity function* plays a central role in the description of the dynamical processes. The topology of the neural network, i.e. the functional organization, is described in terms of non-symmetric functional interactions. The continuous geometry imposes non-local dynamics described in terms of fields at each level of the functional organization. Learning rules are discussed in the framework of this theory.

Introduction

Most studies of biological neural networks involve learning in a network of neurons assumed to be automata for a given connectivity [15-17]. A major reason for using automata theory is the ease of implementing the learning algorithms on digital computers. These "formal" or "artificial" neural networks, are based on two specific nervous properties, synaptic modifiability and non-linear spatial summation of inputs. However, biological constraints are now commonly introduced in neural networks [1,2,5]. We discuss a basic aspect of a new approach published elsewhere in more mathematical terms [6,7].

The Hierarchical Organization of Biological Neural Networks

Functional organization

From receptor-channel complexes to groups of neurons, the structure of the nervous tissue is hierarchically organized: each group contains neurons, each neuron contains synapses, each synapse contains receptor-channel complexes (RCC). However, the reality is sometimes more difficult to describe. For example, the cerebellar cortex contains groups of neurons corresponding to microzones, and composed of a certain number of Purkinje units defined by several cell types, such as granule, basket, star and Golgi cells. Each of these cells have synapses, and each of these synapses have receptor-channel complexes.

Thus, it is clear that the simple structural hierarchy presented above does not correspond to the actual functional hierarchy: some synapses are modifiable and result in learning rules, others are not modifiable; some neurons have specific electric properties, others have different properties due to the different values of the parameters in the Hodgkin-Huxley equation for ionic transport; moreover, the extracellular space is not necessarily homogeneous. It is therefore more convenient to bring together the structures (groups, neurons, synapses, RCC) that are involved in a given physiological function. Such a classification of nervous structures (called structural units) gives rise to the functional organization [8] of the biological system.

One problem is to define properly the *physiological function*. Because it corresponds to the dynamics of the corresponding structural units, the time scale of the process plays an important role. The level of organization is defined by the time scale in such a way that the global dynamics result from the partial dynamics decoupled in time at each level. For example, there are at least two time scales for the synaptic efficacy μ: the short-term modifiability μ_T in the long-term time scale {T} of the activity, called "instantaneous", and the long-term modifiability μ_t in the long time scale {t}, e.g., the Long-Term Potentiation (LTP). Thus, there are two levels of functional organization, one for the activity and the synaptic efficacy μ_T, the other for the synaptic efficacy μ_t [9]. To each of them corresponds a collective behaviour of structural units described by the dynamics at this level. We have called E^{AP} these lower-level structures, the physiological function being the long-term synaptic modifiability. They involve all the structures that participate in this time variation of μ_t, e.g., extra- and intra-synaptic channels and receptors, chemical pathways incorporating cAMP, cytoskeleton. We have proposed to call these structures "*synapsons*". At the higher level, denoted as E^{NN}, we find all the structures that participate in the emission of an action potential, i.e. the synapses with short-term modifiability μ_T, and the extra-synaptic channels and possible receptors in this short time scale. This level E^{NN} is the neural network. Of course there exists the lowest level, the molecular level, called E^{MP}, which is constitutes a structural unit in E^{AP}, and which is possibly defined by another time scale. The proposed functional organization of the neural network is described in Fig.1.

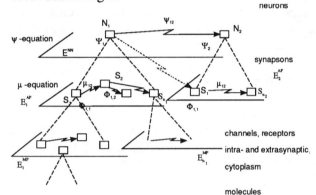

Figure 1: Functional hierarchy for the neural network

Since the structural organization differs from the functional organization, it is important to determine the levels of functional hierarchy which are related to the dynamics through the time scales.

Non-symmetric functional interactions

An analysis of the functional organization shows that it can be decomposed into a set of *non-symmetric* interactions between the structural units, *sources* and *sinks*, at each of the levels in the hierarchy [8]. In E^{NN}, a neuron acts on another through the synapses in the same time scale. More specifically, in the framework of the present formalized description, the set $E_1^{AP} \equiv \{s_\alpha^1, \alpha=1,n_1\}$ of n_1 synapsons s_α^1 constitutes the 1-neuron. The collective behavior of E_1^{AP}, the source, is to produce an action potential Ψ_1 that acts upon another set $E_2^{AP} \equiv \{s_\alpha^2, \alpha=1,n_2\}$ of n_2 synapsons, the sink, i.e. a 2-neuron set, that produces an action potential Ψ_2 (Fig.1). Therefore, the set of neurons E^{NN}, which is a real neural network localized in a space denoted the r-space, constitutes a third level of organization. In other words, a structural unit of the neural network (the neuron) is composed, at the lower level, of the structural units that are represented by one set of synapsons, with *non-symmetric functional interactions* between them due to their connectivity. These interactions couple the two levels of organization, because one neuron is connected to other neurons via their synaptic connections, i.e. the units of the second level directly connect (regarding their topology and not their possible distance) the units of the first level. The transport of the signal membrane potential between two neurons 1 and 2 can be expressed by:

(1)
$$\Psi_2 = \psi_{12}(\Psi_1)$$

Due to the construction of the functional organization, the same schema applies to the lower level: a structural unit of the synaptic network (the synapson) is composed, at the lower level, of the structural units that are represented by one set of intra- and extrasynaptic channels and cytoplasmic chemical parthways, with functional interactions between them due to their connectivity. The transport of the signal between two synapsons s_1 and s_2 is described according to the equation:

(2)

where Φ_1 is the postsynaptic potential that $\Phi_2(s_2) = \mu_{12}(\Phi_1; s_1)$ results from a sequence of phenomena such as transmitter release in the synaptic cleft, binding with postsynaptic receptors, and ion channel activation. The couplings between the two levels of organization E^{NN} and E^{AP} is described by the following equation deduced from (1) and (2):

(3)
$$\Psi_2 = F[(\Phi_\alpha)_1, (\Phi_\alpha)_2; \mu_{12}, \Gamma_2]$$

where Γ_2 represents transformations in the 2-neuron, and $(\Phi_\alpha)_i$ is the postsynaptic potential at the synapson α in the i-neuron.

In conclusion: (i) the description of the dynamics in the framework of the functional organization leads to introducing dynamics at each level of the hierarchy defined by the *time scale* of the processes; (ii) This abstract formulation, in terms of *non-symmetric functional interactions*, leads to the determination of equations (2) and (3); (iii) the functional organization is described by a *directed graph* in which the nodes are the structratal units and the oriented edges are the non-symmetric functional interactions. *This graph, called the (O-FBS, Organization of the Formal Biological System) , represents the topology of the neural network.*

The Continuous Geometry of Biological Neural Networks

Interpretation in terms of fields

In the previous section, equations (2) and (3) formally described the transport of the interaction from a structural 1-unit to another 2-unit in each level of the functional organization. Only the topological data were concerned, i.e. the fact that the interaction is emitted by the 1-unit and acts upon the 2-unit.

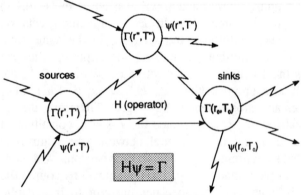

Figure 2: Representation of the fields ψ

Obviously, structural 1- and 2-units of the neural network E^{NN} are located in physical space, at some points r_1 and r_2 respectively, and structural 1- and 2-units of the synaptic network E^{AP} are located in physical space, at some points s_1 and s_2 respectively. Therefore, equations (2) and (3) become:

(4)
$$\Phi_2(s_2) = \mu_{12}(\Phi_1(s_1))$$

(5)
$$\Psi_2(r_2) = \psi_{12}[\Psi_1(r_1); \mu_{12}, \Gamma_2]$$

This equation expresses the membrane potential at r_2 as the result of the transport of the membrane potential Ψ_1 at r_1, under the influence of some transformations Γ_2 in the 2-neuron, and μ_{12} in the synapses.

The geometry of the nervous tissue is thus included in the formulation. However, the finiteness of the velocity of the signal propagation has an influence on the dynamics whenever structural units are at definite locations in physical space. This involves delays which are related to the time scales at each level of organization.

Now, equations (4) and (5) may be interpreted as follows. For example, taking equation (5), because the action potential Ψ_1 at r_1 is unidirectionnaly transformed into another action potential Ψ_2 at r_2 (under certain physiological conditions), we can say that some variable ψ at a point r and at time t is transported to another point at a later time (due to the finiteness of the velocity) under the effect of a non-symmetric operator H, depending on a source Γ. The same interpretation for equation (4) is valid. Thus, we have the same formulation at each i-level of the functional organization:

(6) $$H^{(i)} \, \psi^{(i)}(r, t) \; = \; \Gamma^{(i)}(r, t)$$

In terms of field theory, the field $\psi(r,t)$ is propagated from one point to another in physical space under the effect of H (Fig.2). Therefore, what is observed at point (r_2,t) results from what was emitted at point (r_1,t) where $t_2 = t_1 + |r_2 - r_1| / v$ and v is the velocity of the interaction. Since the space of synapsons is structurally included in the space of neurons, and since two time scales are functionally attached to these spaces, a hierarchical functional system is defined by the two field variables $\psi^{(2)}(r,t)$, *soma membrane potential*, and $\psi^{(1)}(r,t)$, *synaptic efficacy*. This formalism generalizes to n levels the descriptions already offered for one level [3,12-14,20].

Consequence of the continuous geometry: non-locality

However, a basic difficulty appears in this continuous formulation: what is the field variable at a point r ? As discussed in (7), because of the functional hierarchy, a point such as r does not exist. The point r is a *volume* in physical space, where the phenomena involved in the emission of the field variable $\psi(r,t)$ occur. The schema of the propagation from one point to another (Fig.2) is, in reality, an interaction between two volumes (Fig.3).

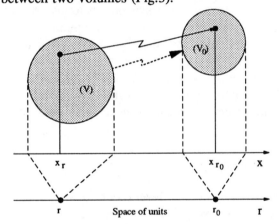

Figure 3: Non-locality: interaction between volumes in the physical space, NOT between points

In physical space, the location of a structural unit at r is denoted by x_r (Fig.3) and the location of units at the lower level by x_s. Since the structural unit is not reducible to a point from which the interaction originates, it is difficult to locate x_r and x_s. This fundamental incertitude raises conceptual and technical difficulties in the use of a field theory in biology. We have chosen to represent the biological structure in *"spaces of units"*, i.e. r-space and s-space with the above notations, which are the abstract spaces where the functional process occurs. The field variable "soma membrane potential" evolves from r to $r+dr$ in the continuous r-space, i.e. between two infinitesimally close neurons, considered to be points. But, the structural unit "neuron" is not reducible to a point because other different structural units "synapsons" exist in the neuron.

This fact is crucial, because *it imposes that H be a non-local operator*. The existence of non-locality appears to be a general fact in biology, due to the hierarchy and the geometry of the biological system. The non-local term can be determined by writing the balance equation at each of the levels [7]: it represents all the inputs from the sub-levels, i.e. the transport of the field variable in the physical space from x_r to x_r+dx_r. The action potential resulting at level 2 from membrane potential is propagated from one axon hillock to another, which means that x_r is its coordinate. In the same way, the synaptic efficacy is propagated from one synapson to another, which means that x_s is its coordinate.

In conclusion, taking into account of both the continuous geometry and the functional hierarchy of the nervous tissue leads to considering *non-local dynamics* for a description of the processes. We call the corresponding dynamical system (*D-FBS for Dynamics of the Formal Biological System*).

Relation Topology-Geometry in Biological Neural Networks: Density-connectivity

Let us use the following notations: r_0 denotes the present point in the r-space; r_i denotes the points where presynaptic neurons are located. Subscript i is used to represent the rank of the synapse relatively to r_0. For example, neurons at r_1 are connected to neurons at r_0 via a monosynaptic pathway, neurons at r_2 are connected to neurons at r_0 via a disynaptic pathway, i.e. with neurons at r_1 via a monosynaptic pathway. Points r_1', r_1'' are points such as r_1 in r-space, r_2', r_2'' are points such as r_2, etc (Fig. 4). When the subscript for an afferent neuron points is not specified, a monosynaptic pathway is assumed.

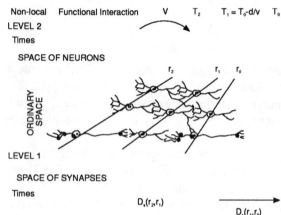

Figure 4: Notations for a polysynaptic pathway

The "local postsynaptic membrane potential" is denoted as $\Phi(s,t)$ at a point (s,t) in the space of one neuron at (r_0,T_0) and corresponds to a presynaptic neuron at (r,T). The "local somatic depolarization" is denoted as $\psi(r_0,T_0)$ at the axon hillock at (r_0,T_0) in the space of neurons. With these definitions, a general definition of synaptic efficacy between presynaptic neurons in r and postsynaptic neurons in r_0 at synapses in $s(r,r_0)$ is $\mu(s,t)$. This expression for μ depends implicitly on the mechanisms for pre-synaptic efficacy with $<\psi>(t)$, and on the mechanisms for post-synaptic efficacy with Φ. The "instantaneous local somatic activity" $X(r_0,T_0)$ in the time scale $\{T\}$ is deduced from ψ by a non-linear, generally sigmoïd input-output function F :

$$(7) \qquad X(r_0,T_0) \equiv X(<\psi(r_0,T_0)>) = F(<\psi(r_0,T_0)>(T_0))$$

Therefore, the passage from one level of organization (synapse) to a higher level (neuron) with ψ and μ as local somatic depolarization and local synaptic efficacy respectively, leads us to our considering the ψ-field and the μ-field as varying in two different spaces whose points are denoted by (r,T) and (s,t) respectively. A *given space at one point of a given level is a point for the next higher level*. This is the hierarchical structure due to the continuous geometry.

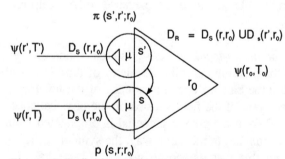

Figure 5: Definition of the spaces of units: spaces of neurons (axon hillocks) and synapsons.

The role of topology, i.e., the connectivity, may be seen as follows. Non-local potentials depend on membrane receptors and neurotransmitters: the postsynaptic potential at s in the neuron localized at r_0, which is connected with neurons at r, results from other synapses localized at s' on the same dendritic tree, due to the activation of neurons localized in r' (Fig. 5). These heterosynaptic effects depend on two anatomical functions: (i) the *synaptic density-connectivity* $\pi(s',r';r_0)$ which is defined in a space $D_s(r',r_0)$ and constituted by the density of synapses localized at $s(r',r_0)$ in the neurons at r_0, which are connected with a certain probability to the neurons at r'. (ii) the *density of neurons* $\rho(r')$ at r' which is defined in space $D_R(r_0)$, the recombination of subspaces $D_s(r',r_0)$ when r' varies. It is possible to describe this field effect as a distance effect with a mathematical potential kernel function $U_\Phi(s,t,s',t';\xi,\eta)$ where the variables: presynaptic efficacy ξ and postsynaptic efficacy η are considered as parameters that are defined at the lower level. The interaction operator is:

$$(8) \qquad H_I^\Phi = \int_{D_R(r_0)} \rho(r') \int_{D_s(r'r_0)} U_\Phi(s,t,s',t';\xi,\eta)\ \pi(s',r';r_0)\ ds'dr'$$

where

$$s \equiv s(r,r_0)$$
$$D_R(r_0) = \bigcup_{r'} D(r',r_0)$$

Thus, U_Φ is a function which has to include the set of phenomena which occur at s' and act upon s (Figs.5). For example, the passive conduction implies an attenuation of potential between these two points [18]. The potential Φ is modified ($\delta\Phi$) due to a variation in the number of activated receptors that occurs as a consequence of biochemical dynamics. The derivation of non-local expressions for ψ and μ results from the expression of non-local interaction operators such as (8) [6].

In conclusion, coupling between topology and geometry in the nervous tissue is made up by the synaptic density-connectivity function that plays a crucial role in the non-local dynamics. Specifically, the learning rules are involved in the non-local interaction operator, i.e. the source of the field, because they are produced by the dynamics at the lower levels. The present formulation provides means of deducing the learning rules from the molecular level.

Discussion and Conclusion: On the Structure of Learning Rules

Neural field equations: We have shown [6] that the neural field equations at each level of the functional organization may be written:

$$(9\text{-}1) \qquad \frac{\partial\mu(s,t)}{\partial t} = \nabla_s(D^s\nabla_s\mu(s,t)) + \int_{D_R(r_0)} \rho(r') \int_{D_s(r'r_0)} \mu_0(s',t')\pi(s',r';r_0)A(s,s')ds'dr' + \Gamma_\mu(s,t)$$

$$(9\text{-}2) \qquad \frac{\partial\psi(r_0,T_0)}{\partial t} = \nabla_r(D^r\nabla_r\psi(r_0,T_0)) + \int_{D_R(r_0)} \rho(r)\psi(r,T) \int_{D_s(rr_0)} \mu(s,t)\pi(s,r;r_0)B(r_0,T_0,r,T)dsdr + \Gamma_\psi(r,T)$$

where D^s and D^r are the diffusion coefficients, A and B are the "propagators", i.e. the space and time functions that describe the non-local transport. Thus, in these equations: the first terms represent the *diffusion* transport through the *extra-unit space*, extracellular space for neurons, and membrane and cytoplasm for synapsons; the second terms are the *non-local sources* of the fields, i.e. represent the *propagation* through the *intra-units space*; the third terms represent the *local sources*. Learning rules are expressed in Eq. (9.1) through the sources, local and non-local, which involve the dynamics at the lower, molecular level.

Suppression of the geometry: connectionnist neural network. The geometry can be suppressed by choosing the density of neurons and the density-connectivity of synapses as Dirac functions that concentrate all the neurons at one point, and by suppressing the delays between neurons, i.e. an infinite velocity of propagation: $\rho(r') = \delta(r'-r)$ and $\pi(s',r';r_0) = \delta(s'-s)$ which implies: $A(s,s') = 1$ and $B(r_0,T_0,r,T) = 1$. Assuming an appropriate non-local interaction operator, i.e. certain dynamics in the sources, we can retrieve the classical continuous equations that describe the neural network [10,11]. Thus, we have here the means to define new learning rules, or at least interpreting the form of Hebbian learning rules [4,19].

Acknowledgments: The author is very grateful to the Conseil Général de Maine-et-Loire and to the DRED (France) for having supported this research, and to Pr. T.W. Berger for very helpful discussions.

References

1. Ambros-Ingerson, J., Granger, R., and Lynch, G. (1990): Simulation of paleocortex performs hierarchical clustering.. *Science*, 247:1344-1348.

2. Berger, T.W., Harty, T.P., Barrionuevo, G., and Sclabassi, R.J. (1989): Modeling of Neuronal Networks Through Experimental Decomposition. In: *Advanced Methods of Physiological System Modeling*, edited by V.Z. Marmarelis, pp. 113-128. Publishing Corporation,

3. Beurle, R.L. (1956): Properties of a mass of cells capable of regenerating pulses. *Philos.Trans.R.Soc.Lond.*, 668,240:8-94.

4. Brown, T.H., Kairiss, E.W., and Keenan, C.L. (1990): Hebbian synapses: Biophysical mechanisms and algorithms. *Annu.Rev.Neurosci.*, 13:475-511.

5. Chapeau-Blondeau, F. and Chauvet, G.A. (1991): A neural network model of the cerebellar cortex performing dynamic associations. *Biol.Cybern.*, 65:267-279.

6. Chauvet, G.A. (1993): An n-Level field theory of biological neural network. *J.Math.Biol.*, 31:

7. Chauvet, G.A. (1993): Non-locality in biological systems results from hierarchy: Application to the nervous system. *J.Math.Biol.*, 31:475-486.

8. Chauvet, G.A. (1993): Hierarchical functional organization of formal biological systems: a dynamical approach I. An increase of complexity by self-association increases the domain of stability of a biological system. *Phil.Trans.R.Soc.Lond.B*, 339:425-444.

9. Chauvet, G.A. (1993): Hierarchical functional organization of formal biological systems: a dynamical approach. II. The concept of non-symmetry leads to a criterion of evolution deduced from an optimum principle of the (O-FBS) sub-system. *Phil.Trans.R.Soc.Lond.B*, 339:445-461.

10. Cooper, L.N. and Scofield, C.L. (1988): Mean-field theory of a neural network. *Proc.Natl.Acad.Sci., USA*, 85:1973-1977.

11. Easton, P. and Gordon, P. (1984): Stabilization of hebbian neural nets by inhibitory learning. *Biol.Cybern.*, 51:1-9.

12. Griffith, J. (1963): A field theory of neural nets. I-. *Bull.Math.Biophys.*, 25:111-120.

13. Griffith, J. (1965): A field theory of neural nets. II-. *Bull.Math.Biophys.*, 27:187-195.

14. Grossberg, S. (1969): Some network that can learn, remember, and reproduce any number of complicated space-time patterns, I. *J.Math.Mech.*, 19,1:53-91.

15. Hopfield, J.J. (1982): Neural networks and physical systems with emergent collective computational abilities. *Proc.Natl.Acad.Sci., USA*, 2554-2558.

16. Hopfield, J.J. (1984): Neurons with graded response have collective computational properties like those of two-state neurons. *Proc.Natl.Acad.Sci., USA*, 3088-2092.

17. Peretto, P. (1984): Collective properties of neural networks: a statistical physics approach. *Biol.Cybern.*, 50:51-62.

18. Rall, W. (1962): Electrophysiology of a dendritic neuron model. *Biophys.J.*, 2:145-167.

19. Sejnovski, T.J. (1977): Storing covariance with non-linearly interacting neurons. *J.Math.Biol.*, 4:303-321.

20. Wilson, H.R. and Cowan, J.D. (1972): Excitatory and inhibitory interactions in localized populations of model neurons. *Biophys.J.*, 12:1-24.

Average firing-rate of a compartmental model network with randomly distributed synaptic background activity.

Paul C. Bressloff

Department of Mathematical Sciences, Loughborough University of Technology, Loughborough, Leicestershire LE11 3TU

Abstract. The ensemble-averaged response function of a compartmental model neuron with randomly distributed synaptic background activity is calculated using a *coherent potential approximation*. This is used to determine the steady-state firing-rate of a recurrent neural network. The firing-rate is found to decrease as the mean level of background activity across the network is increased; a uniform background (zero variance) leads to a greater reduction than a randomly distributed one (non-zero variance).

1. Compartmental model neuron .

Consider a compartmental model neuron [1] that consists of a chain of $2M+1$ dendritic compartments labelled $m = 0, \pm 1,...,\pm M$ together with a single somatic compartment. The passive membrane properties of each compartment m may be represented electrically in terms of an equivalent circuit consisting of a membrane leakage resistor R_m in parallel with a capacitor C_m, with the ground representing the extracellular medium (assumed to be an isopotential). The electrical potential V_m across the membrane is measured with respect to the resting potential, i.e. the potential when there is no current flowing across the membrane. The compartment is joined to its immediate neighbours in the chain by the junctional resistors $R_{m,m-1}$ and $R_{m,m+1}$. We shall also assume that each compartment contains two groups of identical synapses, one excitatory and the other inhibitory. The time evolution of the membrane potential is then given by

$$C_m \frac{dV_m}{dt} = -\frac{V_m}{R_m} + \sum_{<n;m>} \frac{V_n - V_m}{R_{mn}} + E_m(t)\left[S^{(e)} - V_m(t)\right] + I_m(t)\left[S^{(i)} - V_m(t)\right] \quad (1)$$

where E_m and I_m are respectively the net rates of excitation and inhibition of the mth compartment, and $S^{(e)}, S^{(i)}$ are the corresponding membrane reversal potentials with $S^{(e)} > 0$ and $S^{(i)} \leq 0$. Here $<n;m>$ indicates that the summation over n is restricted to immediate neighbours of m. Note that more complex dendritic geometries can be modelled by taking the compartments to lie on the nodes of a tree. However, for the purposes of this paper it will be sufficient to consider the simpler one-dimensional lattice. A major simplification of the model is to view the soma as a point processor that is isopotential with the dendritic compartment nearest to it. The latter is chosen to be at the centre of the chain so that the membrane potential of the soma satisfies $V \equiv V_0$. (This choice allows us to ignore end effects in the large chain limit). If $V(t)$ is slowly varying, then one can approximate the instantaneous firing-rate $f(t)$ of the neuron by a sigmoid function $f(t) = F(V(t)) = f_{max}/(1+\exp(-g(V(t)-\kappa))$ for some gain g and threshold κ. The maximum firing-rate f_{max} is determined by the absolute refractory period.

It is convenient to rewrite equation (1) in the form

$$\frac{dV_m}{dt} = \sum_n Q_{mn} V_n(t) - A_m(t) V_m(t) + B_m(t), \tag{2}$$

where $A_m(t) = E_m(t) + I_m(t)$, $B_m(t) = S^{(e)} E_m(t) + S^{(i)} I_m(t)$, and

$$Q_{mn} = -\left(\frac{1}{\tau_m} + \sum_{<m';m>} \frac{1}{\tau_{m'm}}\right) \delta_{mn} + \sum_{<m';m>} \frac{\delta_{m'n}}{\tau_{mm'}}, \quad \tau_m = R_m C_m, \quad \tau_{mm'} = R_{mm'} C_m \tag{3}$$

We shall refer to $A_m(t)V_m(t)$ as a shunting term since it arises from the voltage-dependent contribution to the synaptic input of equation (1). It is clear from equations (2) and (3) that one can interpret the shunting term as an input-dependent modification of the membrane time constant τ_m, i.e., $1/\tau_m \to 1/\tau_m + A_m(t)$. Integrating equation (1) with respect to t leads to the Volterra integral equation (cf. Poggio and Torre [2])

$$V_m(t) = \sum_n G_{mn}(t) V_n(0) + \int_0^t dt' \sum_n G_{mn}(t-t')[B_n(t') - A_n(t') V_n(t')], \quad t \geq 0 \tag{4}$$

where $G_{mn}(t) = [e^{t\mathbf{Q}}]_{mn}$. We identify $G_{mn}(t)$ as the membrane potential response function or Green's function of the dendritic chain in the absence of shunting. That is $G_{mn}(t')$ determines the membrane potential of compartment m at time t in response to a voltage-independent input current stimulation of compartment n at time t-t'. A simple analytical expression can be derived for the Green's function of an infinite uniform chain. The uniformity condition is imposed by setting $R_m = R$, $C_m = C$, $R_{m,m+1} = R_{m+1,m} = R'$, $\tau = RC$, $\tau' = R'C$. Then expanding the matrix $e^{t\mathbf{Q}}$ in powers of t, and using results from the theory of random walks on a lattice one finds that [3]

$$G_{mn}(t) \equiv \left[e^{t\mathbf{Q}}\right]_{mn} = \int_{-\pi}^{\pi} \frac{dk}{2\pi} e^{ik(m-n)} e^{-t\varepsilon(k)} \qquad \varepsilon(k) = \frac{1}{\tau} + \frac{2}{\tau'}(1 - \cos k) \tag{5}$$

Note that this expression can be generalized to the case of more complex dendritic topologies [4]. Equation (4) has the formal solution

$$V_m(t) = \sum_n \hat{G}_{mn}(t,0) V_n(0) + \int_0^t dt' \sum_n \hat{G}_{mn}(t,t') B_n(t') \tag{6}$$

where $\hat{G}_{mn}$ is the so called renormalized response function defined by the Dyson equation

$$\hat{G}_{mn}(t,t') = G_{mn}(t-t') - \int_0^t dt'' \sum_k G_{mk}(t-t'') A_k(t'') \hat{G}_{kn}(t'',t') \tag{7}$$

Note that $\hat{G}_{mn}$ reduces to G_{mn} when the shunting terms $A_n(t)V_n(t)$ are absent from equation (4). The right-hand side of equation (7) may be expanded as a Neumann series in $A_k(t)$ and $G_{mn}(t)$, which is convergent for bounded continuous functions $A_k(t)$ [2].

2. Low-firing rates in a recurrent compartmental model network

In the presence of shunting the membrane potential V_m satisfying equation (6) is a nonlinear function of the excitatory and inhibitory inputs E_m and I_m. As pointed out previously [5,3], this feature is important since a recurrent network of such neurons can operate in a regime of self-sustained firing in which the neurons are firing well below their maximum rate f_{max}; this is consistent with what is observed in real cortical systems. (Standard associative networks, on the other hand, consist of neurons whose membrane potential or activation state is linear in inputs so that they tend to fire at their maximum rate [6]).

To illustrate this point in more detail, we shall follow the discussion of Ref. [3] and determine the steady-state value V^∞ of the membrane potential at the soma in the case of the infinite uniform dendritic chain with time-independent inputs. We shall take the pattern of input stimulation to be in the form of *non-recurrent lateral inhibition*. That is, an input that excites the mth compartment also inhibits all other compartments in the chain so that $I_n = \Sigma_{n \neq m} E_n$. We also choose a pattern of excitatory stimulation for which (i) $E_0 = 0$ (no direct stimulation of the soma), and (ii) $E_n = a_n E$, for $n \neq 0$ with $\Sigma_{n \neq 0} a_n = 1$ (fixed relative distribution of excitation across chain). Finally, we restrict our discussion to the case of *shunting inhibition*, $S^{(i)} = 0$. In other words, the inhibitory inputs only contribute to the modification of the time constant A_m and not the effective external input B_m. Under these assumptions we see that $A_m = E$ and $B_m = S^{(e)} a_m E$. Since A_m is time-independent, we have $\hat{G}_{mn}(t,t') = \hat{G}_{mn}(t-t')$

Taking the limit $t \to \infty$ in equation (6), leads to the result that the steady-state potential V^∞ at the soma (m = 0) is

$$V^\infty(E) = S^{(e)} E \sum_{n \neq 0} a_n \hat{\mathcal{G}}_{0n}(0;E) \qquad (8)$$

where $\hat{\mathcal{G}}_{mn}(s;E)$ is the Laplace transform of $\hat{G}_{mn}(t)$, and we have indicated that $\hat{\mathcal{g}}$ depends explicitly on E. To determine $\hat{\mathcal{G}}_{mn}(s;E)$ we Laplace transform equation (7) to obtain (in matrix form)

$$\hat{\mathcal{G}}(s;E) = \frac{\mathcal{G}(s)}{\mathbf{I} + \mathcal{G}(s)E} = \frac{1}{(s+E)\mathbf{I} - \mathbf{Q}} = \mathcal{G}(s+E) \qquad (9)$$

where $\mathbf{I}$ is the unit matrix and $\mathcal{G}(s)$ is the Laplace transform of $\mathbf{G}(t)$, equation (5). In deriving equation (9) we have used the fact that $\mathcal{G}(s)$, is equal to the inverse matrix $(s\mathbf{I}-\mathbf{Q})^{-1}$. Moreover, it can be shown using equation (5) that for a uniform, infinite dendritic chain

$$\mathcal{G}_{0n}(E) = \tau' \frac{(\lambda_-(E))^n}{\lambda_+(E) - \lambda_-(E)}, \quad \lambda_\pm(E) = 1 + \frac{\tau'(E + \tau^{-1})}{2} \pm \sqrt{\left(1 + \frac{\tau'(E + \tau^{-1})}{2}\right)^2 - 1} \qquad (10)$$

It follows from equations (9) and (10) that $\hat{\mathcal{G}}(0;E) = \mathcal{G}(E)$, and hence that the steady-state is a nonlinear function of the input rate of excitation E. For low levels of excitation E, V^∞ is approximately a linear function of E. However, as E increases, the contribution of shunting inhibition to the effective time constant becomes more and more significant and V^∞ eventually begins to decrease with $V^\infty(E) \to 0$ as $E \to \infty$.

Now consider a population of excitatory neurons each of which has the pattern of stimulation as described above with the net excitatory rate E impinging on an individual neuron being determined by the average firing-rate $<f>$ of the population. For a large population, a reasonable approximation is to take $\beta E = <f>$ for some constant β. Within a mean field approach the steady-state behaviour is given by the self-consistency condition $\beta E = F(V^\infty(E))$, where F is the sigmoidal function and $V^\infty(E)$ satisfies equation (8). Using graphical methods [5,3], it can be shown that there are two stable solutions, one corresponding to the silent state $E = 0$ and the other to a state with a firing-rate well below f_{max}. On the other-hand, in the absence of shunting $V^\infty(E)$ is a linear function of E and the second stable state has a firing-rate close to f_{max}. Since the network settles into a state of a low firing-rate in the presence of shunting one can take the output function F to be approximately linear. Such a linearization will greatly simplify our subsequent analysis.

3. Synaptic background activity.

Suppose that a given neuron in the population has the same pattern of input stimulation as before except that there is now an additional random background contribution to the inhibitory rate $I_m \to I_m + \xi_m$, with the ξ_m distributed randomly across the population of neurons according to the probability density $\rho(\xi)$ where ρ is site-independent. (For simplicity, any correlations between ξ's at different sites are discounted, $<\xi_m\xi_n> = 0$ for $m \neq n$). The steady-state membrane potential at the soma of an arbitrary neuron in the population is now given by equation (8) with $\hat{G}(s;E)$ determined by Laplace transforming equation (7) and performing a series expansion,

$$\hat{G}_{mn} = G_{mn} - \sum_k G_{mk}(E+\xi_k)G_{kn} + \sum_{k,k'} G_{mk}(E+\xi_k)G_{kk'}(E+\xi_{k'})G_{k'n} - \ldots \tag{11}$$

Note that here $A_m = E + \xi_m$ is site-dependent so that there is nolonger a simple relationship between $\hat{G}$ and G. We wish to calculate the average firing-rate of the network. Using mean-field arguments we have $<f> = \beta E$ for some β where E satisfies the self-consistency condition $\beta E = <F(V^\infty(E))>_\xi$. The evaluation of the ensemble average over ξ is a non-trivial problem for a nonlinear function F such as a sigmoidal. However, progress can be made if we assume that the firing-rate is a linear function of V^∞ (see previous comments) such that $\beta E = \alpha<(V^\infty(E))>_\xi + \varphi$. for constants α, φ. As we shall show below, approximate expressions for the ensemble average of $\hat{G}$ can be obtained using Green's function techniques familiar from the theory of disordered crystalline solids [7].

At first sight it would appear that one could determine $<\hat{G}>$ by performing an ensemble average of the right-hand side of equation (11) term by term. However, the resulting series cannot be resummed exactly. The simplest and crudest approximation is to replace each factor ξ_m by the site-independent average $\bar{\xi}$. This leads to the so called *virtual crystal approximation* (VCA) where $\hat{G}(0;E) = G(E+\bar{\xi})$. In other words, statistical fluctuations associated with the random synaptic inputs are ignored so that the ensemble averaged Green's function is equivalent to the Green's function of a uniform dendritic chain with a modified membrane time constant, $1/\tau \to 1/\tau + E + \bar{\xi}$. When we attempt to take into account statistical fluctuations we run into the difficulty that there are no restrictions imposed on the summation over site indices so that an element ξ_m may appear several times in the same product. For example, if a particular term in the series expansion of equation (11) involves ξ_m^2 then ensemble averaging will lead to a contribution $\Delta = \langle \xi^2 \rangle$, and in general the variance of ξ will be non-zero implying $\Delta \neq \bar{\xi}^2$. Thus the ensemble average of the series will lead to successively more complex contributions from successive terms whose sum cannot be calculated exactly. Hence, various approximation schemes have been developed to improve upon the VCA formulation.

The most effective single-site approximation scheme in the study of disordered lattices is the so called *coherent potential approximation* (CPA). In the context of our neural network model, this scheme involves taking each dendritic compartment to have an effective (site-independent) background synaptic input $\hat{\Sigma}(E)$ for which the associated Green's function is $\hat{\mathcal{G}}(0;E) = \mathcal{G}(E + \hat{\Sigma}(E))$. The self-energy term $\hat{\Sigma}(E)$ is assumed to take account of any statistical fluctuations (at least at the single-site level), which leads to a self-consistency condition for $\hat{\Sigma}(E)$ of the form [7]

$$\int \frac{(\xi_m - \hat{\Sigma}(E))}{1 + (\xi_m - \hat{\Sigma}(E))\mathcal{G}_{00}(E + \hat{\Sigma}(E))} \rho(\xi)d\xi = 0 \tag{12}$$

This is an implicit equation for that can be solved numerically to obtain $\hat{\Sigma}(E)$ as a function of E. A particularly simple choice for the distribution of the random background activity is to assume that each dendritic compartment receives either an input ξ_A with probability p_A or an input ξ_B with probability $p_B = 1 - p_A$. (cf. the tight-binding alloy model of disordered solids [7]). Then equation (12) reduces to the algebraic equation

$$\hat{\Sigma}(E) = \frac{\bar{\xi} + \xi_A \xi_B \mathcal{G}_{00}(E + \hat{\Sigma}(E))}{1 + (\xi_A + \xi_B - \hat{\Sigma}(E))\mathcal{G}_{00}(E + \hat{\Sigma}(E))}, \tag{13}$$

which can be evaluated by iterative substitution in the denominator.

Once the self-energy $\hat{\Sigma}(E)$ has been determined from equation (13), the average firing-rate of the network can then be found by numerically solving the mean field equation $\beta E = \alpha S^{(e)} E \sum_n a_n \mathcal{G}_{0n}(E + \hat{\Sigma}(E)) + \varphi$. The required non-trivial solution is denoted by E^*. The results are displayed in figure 1 where the steady-state firing-rate f, $f = \beta E^*$, is plotted for a range of $\xi_{A,B}$ values and $a_n = \delta_{n,1}$. The firing-rate and the inputs E^*, $\xi_{A,B}$ are all measured in units of $1/\tau$, and the constant φ is set to zero for simplicity. Two particular cases are considered. The first is the variation of f with the mean $\bar{\xi} = p_A \xi_A + p_B \xi_B$ for fixed variance $\sigma^2 = p_A p_B (\xi_A - \xi_B)^2$, as shown in figure 1a for $\beta' = 0.01$ and $\beta' = 0.015$, where $\beta' = \beta/\alpha S^{(e)}$. It can be seen that the firing-rate decreases as the mean activity across the network increases. The second case is the variation of f as a function of σ^2 for fixed $\bar{\xi}$. Here the firing-rate increases as the variance in the distribution of activity across the network increases, see figure 1b.

4. Discussion.

We conclude from the above results that (i) synaptic background activity can influence the behaviour of a neural network and, in particular, leads to a reduction in a network's steady-state firing-rate, and (ii) a uniform background reduces the firing-rate more than a randomly distributed background. The main underlying mechanism of these effects is shunting, which leads to an input-dependent modification of the effective membrane time constant of a neuron.

This feature has recently been observed experimentally [8,9], where variations in background synaptic activity were found to produce a range of values for the time constant between 5-80ms. The possible consequences of this from the viewpoint of temporal pattern processing have been explored elsewhere [10, 3].

One simplification of our analysis was to take the firing-rate to be a linear function of the membrane potential at the soma. A partial justification of this is that, in the absence of background activity, the network settles into a state that has a relatively low firing-rate corresponding to the linear regime of the sigmoid function. A fuller treatment would need to evaluate ensemble averages of the form $<F(V^\infty)>_\xi$. One approach is to perform a perturbation expansion in powers of the gain g leading to higher order terms such as $<\hat{g}\,\hat{g}>$; these can then be evaluated using an extension of the CPA formalism presented here. Another possible application of the CPA formalism is analysing the response to sinusoidal inputs. One is now concerned with Fourier rather than Laplace transforms so that E is replaced by $i\omega$ where ω is the frequency of response. Consequently, the self-energy contribution becomes complex leading to a non-trivial modification in both the phase and amplitude of response.

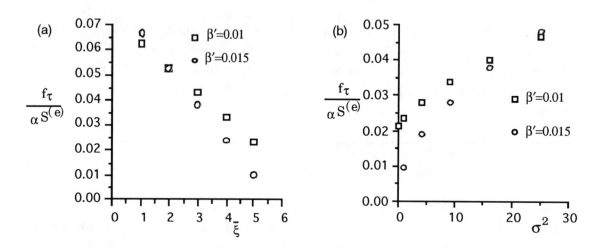

Figure 1. Firing-rate f (in units of τ^{-1}) as a function of (a) the mean level of background activity for fixed variance ($\Delta = 1$), and (b) the background variance at a fixed level of mean activity ($\bar{\xi}=1$).

References.

[1] W. Rall, In *Neural Theory and Modeling*, ed. R. F. Reiss. (Stanford: Stanford University Press) pp. 73-97 (1964).

[2] T. Poggio and V. Torre. In: *Lecture Notes in Biomathematics*, **21**, 89 (1977).

[3] P. C. Bressloff and J. G. Taylor. *Phys. Rev. E*. **47**, 2899 (1993).

[4] P. C. Bressloff and J. G. Taylor. *Biol. Cybern.* **69** (1993).

[5] L. F. Abbott. *Network* **2**, 245-258 (1991).

[6] D. J. Amit, *Modelling Brain Function*, (Cambridge: Cambridge University Press, 1989).

[7] J. M. Ziman, *Models of Disorder* (Cambridge: Cambridge University press, 1979).

[8] O. Bernander, R. J. Douglas, A. C. Martin, and C. Koch. *Proc. Natl. Acad. Sci. U. S. A.* **88**, 11569-11573 (1991).

[9] M. Rapp, Y. Yarom, and I. Segev. *Neural Computation* **4**, 518-533 (1992).

[10] P. C. Bressloff. *Network*, **4**, 155 (1993).

Cumulative Learning in a Scaffolded Neural Network

Rose Paradis and Eric Dietrich
Program in Philosophy and Computers and Systems Science(PACSS)
Binghamton University
Binghamton, New York 13902-6000

Abstract

The scaffolded network is a network of neural networks whose objective is to test the hypothesis that the learning of complex concepts requires both a developmental progression and multiple perspectives of input data. The scaffolded network model incorporates three kinds of basic neural network architectures: a recurrent cascade net, a Kohonen net, and a recurrent Elman network and is motivated by physiological and psychological models. It is tested by teaching it simple mathematical concepts and functions and then comparing output and intermediate results with studies from developmental psychology. This design attempts to extend neural network capabilities to a more robust approximation of the cognitive phenomenon of cumulative learning.

Introduction

We define *cumulative learning* as the process of learning new concepts based on a foundation of concepts and categories either previously acquired or innate. Cumulative learning is an inherently developmental process: it occurs as the organism or system develops from an infant to an adult. An example of cumulative learning is the elaboration of the concept of number that a child acquires as she begins to learn basic arithmetic.

Cumulative learning contrasts with one-shot learning in which the system learns a single concept or non-hierarchical group of concepts used for discriminating a limited set of inputs. One-shot learning has commanded far more attention in AI and cognitive science than cumulative learning (see Bates and Elman, 1993). But one-shot learning takes for granted background and conceptual information that should have been learned first to serve as a basis for further learning. Using one-shot learning, machines will *not* be able to learn complex concepts because such concepts are combinations of simpler concepts arranged in intricate hierarchies. We believe more attention should be paid to cumulative learning if we are ever to have robust theories of learning and development in humans and other animals, and if we hope to build machines that learn any of the complexities of the world that we come to know.

In this paper, we describe an architecture we call the scaffolded neural network that appears to learn cumulatively. Our working domain is early arithmetic, i.e. the numerical competencies learned by young children.

The Scaffolded Network Architecture

The *scaffolded network* comprises three neural networks: a recurrent cascaded correlation network (based on Fahlman and Lebiere, 1990), a Kohonen network (based on Kohonen,1984) and a recurrent network (based on Elman, 1990). The network is called 'scaffolded' because though it is hierarchically structured, information does *not* flow linearly through the system from the bottom input layer to the top output layer. In a standard linear format, the output of layer N is input to layer N+1, and the layers share information only in this way. In our scaffolded network, the layers do indeed share input-output information in the standard way, but they also share information from their hidden layers, which represents learning and calculation in progress. Furthermore, the information flow is not always from layer N to layer N+1: layer N also gets feedback from layer N+1 as well as from more distant non-consecutive layers (see figure 1).

The scaffolded network's architecture is based on a physiological, functional model of the brain developed by Paul MacLean (1991). MacLean's model, called the *triune brain model* claims that there are three major assemblies of mammalian brains called the "Reptilian" system, the "Limbic" (or Paleomammalian) system, and the "Neocortical" (or neomammalian) system (the R, L, and C complexes). MacLean's model is evolutionary and functional; the R, L and C complexes are not anatomically precise. Devotion to implementing the exact neuroanatomy of the brain is misguided at this stage of modeling high-level cognitive processes such as cumulative learning. First, making an anatomically correct model is beyond the capabilities of current computers. Secondly, definitions of systems based on anatomy only *appear* more precise than those based on functionality: we don't know the precise anatomy of the brain nor the precise roles of many known components. A strict, bottom-up perspective, therefore, is not warranted at this time. A functional approach provides the best level for formulating theories of high-level cognitive processes.

On MacLean's model, the three major divisions of mammalian brains have evolved and expanded from the ancestral structures found in reptiles, early mammals, and recent mammals. The R complex acts as an initial basic processor, performing learning tasks that are associative and autonomic, and then passing this data onto the other complexes. The L complex plays a different role than the R complex in that it is a regulator of function in the R and C complexes, acting as controller at some times (clamping or activating regions of the R and C complexes) and an assistant at other times (enhancing the computational power of the R and C complexes). The C complex provides a higher level of learning capacity than the R complex, gathering data from the other two complexes and using the information to do more sophisticated functions such as problem solving.

The scaffolded architecture mimics the relationships of the triune brain, having three identifiable networks that perform functionally like the R, L and C complexes: the recurrent cascade network, the Kohonen network and the recurrent network (see Figure 1). Each network in the scaffolded model has different input, hidden and output nodes, and acts on different aspects of the information presented. The recurrent cascade network is analogous to the R complex. It takes all the training data as input and constructs associations between them. Output from this network is passed to the Kohonen network; hidden layer information is passed back to itself and intermittently to the recurrent and the Kohonen nets. Because this network compresses input information necessary for progressive learning sequences, the information that is sent to the other networks is not sent on every cycle of its processing.

The recurrent cascade network is in a class of ontogenic neural networks that develop their architecture as they learn instead of requiring the user to specify the architecture before training. Hidden units are added to the network during training one at a time and then do not change. This architecture is also fairly fast, and corresponds to properties of the R-complex where simple associative learning takes place fairly rapidly and is relatively resistant to change. Lavond, McCormick, Clark, Holmes, and Thompson (1991) have demonstrated the importance of the R complex structures in simple learning and memory.

The Kohonen network is the director of information, acting like a switchboard to send information to the appropriate network, and corresponds to the L complex. This network uses an unsupervised learning algorithm and assigns information to the other two networks in a way that echoes the L complex. Input to this network is from the hidden layer output of the cascade network, hidden layer information from the recurrent network and affect input. Because the L complex is, among other things, the emotional modulator of the other complexes, vastly simplified affect input to the Kohonen network is also included in order to simulate the interest-driven aspect of learning.

The recurrent Elman network is the high-level component that can process sequentially ordered information with a memory of previous experience. It is based on a network architecture similar to that of Elman (1990), and corresponds to the C complex in the triune brain model. This network gathers information about what is being done in the other two networks, and uses this along with its own historical data to determine the output for the entire system. This is the network where actual calculations or strategy determination takes place. The input to this network consists of hidden unit data from the cascade network, data from its own hidden layer, and output data from the Kohonen network. Together, this input gives the recurrent network a broad picture of all the activity that is occurring in the entire scaffold, corresponding to the neocortical ability to estimate actions based on environmental effects and to anticipate future events based on past experience. The hidden layer input from the cascade network provides inhibitory information and noise to the input layer of the recurrent Elman network. The inhibitory information allows the Kohonen network fine level control of the Elman network. (This corresponds with the nature of cortical information, in which most of the data is inhibitory(Kandel and Schwartz, 1991).) The noise keeps the Elman network from settling into false minima.

The scaffolded network is based on the triune brain functional model because this model most closely captures our intuition that learning complex concepts requires viewing input data from many different perspectives. Also, from a developmental perspective, specific connectivity in an organism may be determined by a competition for resources that leads to a specialization in a particular area. Each network included in the scaffolded network attempts to approximate this developmental aspect, learning by a series of incremental and recurrent changes. The scaffolded network is not meant to just be a variation of other artificial neural networks that can learn some numerical concepts. The network is a vehicle through which we are arguing that complex concepts must be learned in a developmental, multi-perspective approach.

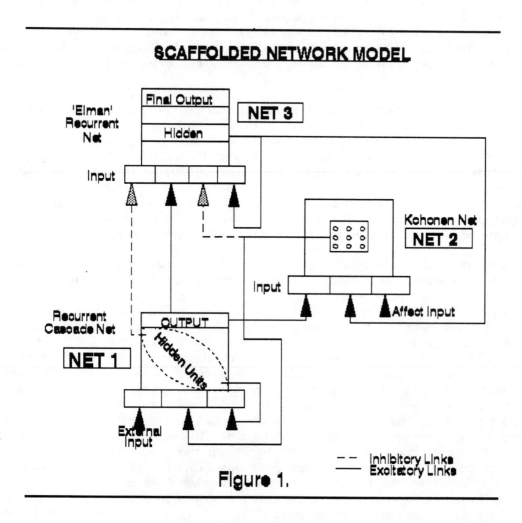

Figure 1.

Training the network: learning early arithmetic

Our domain for the scaffolded network is early arithmetical development, primarily based on the work of Robert Siegler (1982, 1991, in press). Additionally, background numerical competency information has been taken from Ashcraft(1993), Gelman and Gallistel (1986), McCloskey (1993) and Piaget (1952). The scaffolded network will be trained following the progression of developmental steps that Siegler and others have found that children go through on their journey to arithmetic competence. According to Gelman and Gallistel (1986), a child obtains representations of *numerosity* (a measurable numerical quantity) by counting, which requires certain counting principles. The counting principles are the one-one principle, the stable-order principle, the cardinal principle, the abstraction principle and the order-irrelevant principle. The concept of number is taught to the scaffolded network, following this developmental progression of numerical competency that has been found in animals and children. It appears crucial for children to go through such a sequence for learning these concepts: this may also be the case for machine models of this ability.

The individual networks are not trained separately; rather, the entire scaffold is trained as a single network. If the networks were to be trained individually, then the hidden layer information, along with inhibitory and excitatory information from the output layers would not be available as additional information for the networks during training. This would preclude the individual networks from having access to the incremental representations and recycled information while the network is learning. Training the network as a whole allows the scaffold network to use earlier information by re-describing it internally. Karmiloff-Smith has presented this as *representation redescription*: the 'process by which information implicit in an organism's special purpose responses to an environment is repeatedly recoded and made available to serve a wide variety of ends' (Karmiloff-Smith, 1992). All networks in the scaffolded network are involved in its learning and development, and each step redescribes incoming information in this developmental process.

Conclusion

The scaffolded network is an experiment in cumulative learning: the kind of learning in which complex concepts develop by building on simple concepts and categories that are learned first. It is fairly uncontroversial that cumulative learning is the primary way complex concepts are learned. What's been missing is a way to model cumulative learning. Our contribution to this enterprise is the architecture and learning algorithm of the scaffolded network, which is based on our hypothesis that concept learning requires both a developmental progression and multiple perspectives of input data.

Finally, the scaffolded network incorporates insights, data, and hypotheses from neuroscience, developmental psychology, and connectionism. Such interdisciplinary endeavors are probably essential if we are ever to have robust theories of learning and robust learning machines.

REFERENCES

Ashcraft, M.H. (1993). "Cognitive Arithmetic: A Review of Data and Theory". In S. Dehaene (ed.), *Numerical Cognition*. Cambridge,MA:Blackwell Press.

Bates,E.A. and Elman,J.L. (1993). "Connectionism and the Study of Change". In M.H. Johnson,(Ed.). *Brain Development and Cognition*. Cambridge,MA:Blackwell Press.

Elman, J.L.(1990). "Finding Structure in Time". *Cognitive Science*, 14, 170-211.

Elman, J. (1991). "Incremental learning, or The Importance of starting small", *Technical Report 9101*, Center for Research in Language, University of California, San Diego. March,1991.

Fahlman, S.E. and Lebiere,C. (1990). "The Cascade-Correlation Learning Architecture". In D.S. Touretzky,(Ed.). *Advances in Neural Information Processing Systems 2*. San Mateo, CA:Morgan Kaufmann.

Gelman,R. and Gallistel,C.R. (1986). *The Child's Understanding of Number*. Cambridge,MA:Harvard University Press.

Kandel,E.R., Schwartz,J.H., and Jessell,T.M. (1991). *Principles of Neural Science, Third Edition*. New York, NY:Elsevier.

Karmeloff-Smith, A. (1992). *Beyond Modularity: A Developmental Perspective on Cognitive Science*. Cambridge,MA:MIT Press/Bradford Books.

Kohonen, T. (1984). *Self-organization and Associative Memory*. Berlin:Springer-Verlag.

Lavond,D.G., McCormick,D.A., Clark,G.A., Holmes,G.T. and Thompson,R.F.(1991). "Effects of ipsilateral rostral pontine reticular formation lesions on retention of classically conditioned nictitating membrane and eyelid responses". *Physiological Psychology*, 9,335-339.

MacLean, P.(1991). *The Triune Brain in Evolution*. New York, NY:Plenum Press.

McCloskey, M. (1993). "Cognitive Mechanisms in Numerical Processing". In S. Dehaene (ed.), *Numerical Cognition*. Cambridge,MA:Blackwell Press.

Piaget, J. (1952). *The Child's Conception of Number*. New York, NY:Norton Press.

Rummelhart,D.E. and McClelland,J.L.(Eds.) (1986). *Parallel Distributed Processing. Volume 1: Foundations*. Cambridge,MA:MIT Press.

Siegler, R.S. In Press. "Variation, Selection, and Cognitive Change". In G. Halford and T. Simon (Eds.), *Developing Cognitive Competence: New Approaches to Process Modeling.*. Erlbaum Press.

Siegler, R.S. (1991). *Children's Thinking*. Prentice-Hall, Inc.

Siegler, R.S. and Robinson, M. (1982). "The development of numerical understandings". In H.W. Reese and L.P. Lipsitt (Eds.), *Advances in child development and behavior*, 16, 242-307. New York, NY:Academic Press.

Endoneurology:
virtual imaging of neural ensemble signals
by quantum - neurodynamics

Gustav Bernroider
Institute for Zoology, University of Salzburg
A-5020 Salzburg, Austria

Higher level brain functions can be composed from the most basic or quantum-level, provided by the train of action-potentials. Here, I propose an 'insight-out' view of endogenous brain function in close analogy to the concepts of quantum-electro-dynamics. 'Images' are created in concert with progressive modifications of an emerging neural population code and become causally associated with functional issues.

Attempts to understand how the brain models the world roughly divide into two main streams: correlation of physio-anatomical findings with behaviour (e.g. event-related imaging, Grinvald, et al., 1991; Rose, 1991) and relating the structure of self-organizing models to the brains anatomy and function (e.g. ART networks for learning, Carpenter & Grossberg, 1993). Because of the inventive fascination behind recent progress, visualization techniques emerging from both approaches are presently at the center of attention. Despite this prevailing enthusiasm, one key problem has been largely overseen: functional imaging, ranging from reconstructive tomography to optophysiology, at its best highlights the spatially selective distribution of neural activities. The artificial construction of simulation models leaves behind pure suggestions on how the brain might accomplish given tasks. To this point there is no causal explanation on how and why neuroimages, as those observed for isomorphic or functionally segregated representations of visual space, (Bonhoeffer & Grinvald, 1993) relate to an orchestrated spread of the neural code residing within the spike train of functionally engaged cells. This is also true for "seeing the mind" approaches, seeking individual differences of component mental operations in terms of PET or MRI localizations (Posner, 1993).

A conceptually plausible explanation for the mentioned constraints may be found within at least two natural restrictions in the study of brain function: 'Outside-in views' of the brain typically expose the result of (unknown) coded equivalents of external circumstances. Coding involves early functional segregation, together with higher order, topical and confluent convergence (e.g. Zeki, 1990 for visual systems), and , at progressive stages, cooperative neural ensembles distributing the code "non-topographically" (e.g. Eichenbaum, 1993 comments Wilson and McNaughton, 1993). Causal relevance of outside-in views therefore critically depends on the interpretation of unknown design principles in order to pertain imaging information to cells that causally control cerebral action. A goal far beyond reach at this moment. The second restrictive issue relates to the chronic absence of a coherent neurotheory that composes higher level phenomena from the only mechanistic microfactor provided, the train of action potentials.

Here I propose an 'insight-out', virtual view, synthesizing higher level brain functions from unit or 'quantum' signals provided by the spatio-temporal changes of voltage pulses or action-potentials. I argue that the suggested quantum-neurodynamcal model coherently uncovers neural computation underlaying the formation of spatially construed neural activities. Further, the model rationalizes most empirical evidence available for issues such as sensory representation, perceptual learning and recognition. Importantly, images, in this approach, are being created in concert with progressive operational modifications of the neural population code. Thus 'images' become causally associated with neural computation and finally reflect the neural equivalent of the 'external problem'.

Dissociated brain levels- the endo-perspective:

A strong line of evidence supports the view, that in the brain operational modifications usually 'overlay' sensory and motory representations. For example, experience dependent perceptual improvement gradually 'overlays' place coded representations at the level of maps during perceptual learning (Karni & Sagi, 1993). These configurations may become dissociated by unfolding the underlaying transformational configuration. Supportive empirical evidence for this idea has also come from the dissociation of visual processing domains in the primate prefrontal cortex (F.A.W. Wilson, et al., 1993).

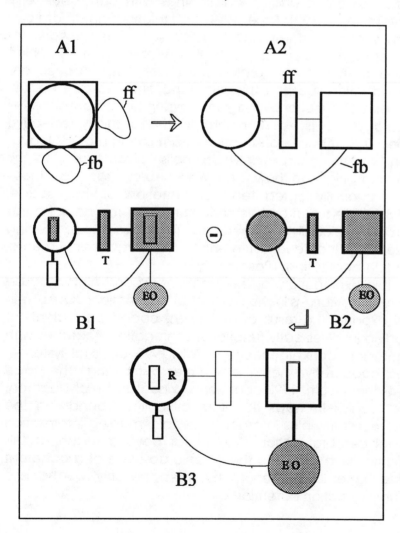

Figure 1

Dissociation of operational modifications from underlaying sensory representations.
An initially overlayed topography (A1) is unfolded, preserving intrinsic feedforward (ff) and feedback (fb) connections, into the situation A2.
External observes (EO) have access to the transformed images (square symbol).
In B1 the unfolded module is exposed to an external object. Immediate transformation by the operator (T) changes its representation, whereas a sensory deprived module (B2) images intrinsic transformation only.
Here, operational changes are assumed to change any pattern from white to grey. Notice, the set difference for B1 and B2, as outlined in B3, uncovers those neural activities that relate isomorphically to the external situation.

Operational levels and implementation:

The present strategy revolves around signal propagation and exchange between the dissociated levels O and □, that is intrinsic and observed levels (I-O levels). Both levels remain bidirectionally interconnected with continuous adjustment taking place in terms of bottom up and top down modifications of signals (this formally resembles the two level topology of Artificial Resonance Theories (ART, reviewed by Carpenter & Grossberg, 1993). In a simplified version, the basic assumptions of the model involve the following steps with constructive dependence among the various levels of realization:

i-3:   signal propagation and coupling
i-2:   representational principles at the level of maps (signal segregation and
        integration)
i-1:   systems or circuit level, extending over multiple anatomical 'compartments'
i: behavioural (level of motoric expression)

i-3: Confined to single cells, the neural code resides in space-time changes of essentially identical signals provided by the train of action-potentials (APs). Disregarding possible contraints imposed by higher level issues and external observers (a set point for the present approach), every AP can possibly be connected to everything else. Thus probabilistic propagation permeates the quantum level, awating macroscopically construed appearance only during higher level compositions.

We associate probabilities to the propagation of APs between two locations A,B by

$$P(A \rightarrow B) := |z|^2$$

with $z = r. \exp(i.\alpha)$ and r denoting the modulus of the complex number z. It is relevant to see this probability being attributed to the spatial spread of APs, rather than to operative mechansim associated with input-output relations of neurons (which will be denoted as 'coupling'). Coupling probability reflects a transition between different states of neurons,

$$P(B_1 \rightarrow B_2) := C_B(\Delta t; \Delta\alpha; R; S/N)$$

depending on several pre- and postsynaptic parameters such as spike frequency (Δt) and timing ($\Delta\alpha$) characteristics of synaptic input, together with signal/noise (S/N) conditions of the involved response threshold (R). This part of the model relates to previous studies on the probabilistic response of neurons at activated input sites (Katz, 1969; Taylor, 1972 and more recently Otmakhov, et al, 1993). Reflecting on the (i-3) level, there are no connective constraints imposed on the spread of signals. Every signal has an amplitude to go anywhere. However, as coding principles emerge from multiple stage compositions of many signals, $P(A \rightarrow B)$ becomes related to C_B and higher level issues. Inherent to the lowest (i-3) level, there is an intrinsic susceptibility of $P(A \rightarrow B)$ to higher level modifications provided by its dependence on the signals 'interval', $[(A-B)^2 - (t2-t1)^2]$ in space-time. That is, for a given discharge rate Δt-, the distance the signals travels to the next coupling event, heaviliy determines $(r. e^{i\alpha})$ in terms of a rotation of z (Figure 2). Naturally, this affects timing characteristics of presynaptic coupling parameters in the above sense.

(i-2) level modifications become consistently available from a stepwise expansion of P(A→B) into a series of terms, such as

$$\sum_j \sum_t r\, m_j \cdot e^{-i(2.\sum \alpha j + 2.\varphi)}$$

where φ denotes a 'coupling constant' attributed to local transmission (it also reflects Δt and α(max)) and expansion extends for j=1, ..,m 'states' (or cells) and total time t (as measured by the codes own timing φ / 2.Δt). Note that whenever the expansion increases (with m), non-direct paths contribute more to the final (population) vector z_{A-B}. In essence the above equation totally accounts for all transformational changes involved in the cooperative transmission of signals among several populations of neurons, albeit the following levels are essential to 'construct' a nervous system.

Figure 2 demonstrates the basic operations involved at the (i-2) level (for a very simplified, 1-dim activity map, propagating signals (3 spikes) along 3 different path-lengths and one 'coupling' unit. The example only gives a 'first order- bottom up population vector', with no feedback modifications.

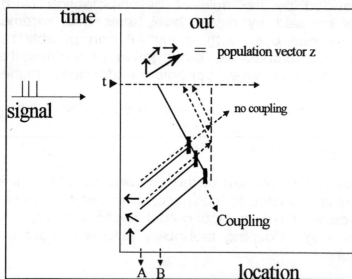

Figure 2

The propagation of 3 spikes along locations (A,B) and time t. Coupling compensates for time differences of the emitted signals (virtually by adjusting the pathlength). During propagation, the vector -z- representing the spike, rotates clockwise as time progresses. In addition to rotation, any type of coupling (postsynaptic activation) also shortens the signals amplitude. The coupling effect 'focuses' signals to one point in space-time. There, a population vector is built up by the sum of 3 complex numbers, representing the spikes. The modulus of these numbers is reduced by the succession of events and coupling (multiplication of z). It is assumed that the coupling effect is limited by the plasticity of the transforming cell layer. Thus, signals that take a longer spatial path (dotted lines) may remain partially or completely uncoupled. For a given time of observation (t) these signals are spread at different locations. Thus, the main contribution to the population or ensemble signal -z- is made by the more direct paths. In optical analogy, the signal is 'mirrored' between A and B, but the signals spatio-temporal attributes leave behind traces at the mirrors-level. Note, as time passes during spike emission, the signals change by a counterclockwise rotation of z. This is where temporal issues of the neural code (intervals between successive spikes) exert their dramatic effect on forming spatial activity maps. The 'traces' left behind by the 'most probable' paths at the coupling layers, start to exert strong propagating effects after repetition (i.e. top-down transformation of the input image A). For example, only parts of the code need to enter the path after prolonged exposure to become efficiently 'mirrored' to identical space-time locations after prolonged exposure. This phenomenon is basically self-organized and relates to learning and memory. The example in Figure 2 leaves out multiple sources for simplicity (signals happening concomitantly, e.g. from arrays of neurons forming a map, would be multiplied during their spread). In 'real nervous systems' all possible paths for signal spread become spatially confined by the connective topology among neurons. However, the basic principles remain the same.

i-1) level introduces connective organization to the spatial spread of signals. This level imposes connective topology to smaller neuronal ensembles, emerging from lower level operations. To complete the view at this level, the processing architecture of functionally defined systems (such as vision) determine the exponential expansion of the population code at the (i-2) level. In particular, late stage reconvergence for ascending, perceptual systems as those established for the primate cortical visual system (Young, 1992) essentially contribute to final modelistic coherence. Present realizations involve the anatomic repertoire available for the birds visual system.

i-level issues deal with motoric responses to environmental changes (behaviour). Rather than simulating neural responses, the endo-perspective will, consequently, create respones to changes, that is, synthetize all previous levels into artifical devices that respond to 'exo-states'. Along this line, the construction of robots completes the excursion. One additional aspect, concerning the dissociation paradigm outlined in Figure 1 at the behavioural level, should be mentioned. If, for perceptually guided motoric responses, the stimulus deprived module (Fig.1, B2) becomes subtracted from the stimulus exposed situation (Fig.1, B1), we can register those motoric expressions that are related to sensory representation. For example, the results of McLennan and Horn on the role of the IMHV in early learning responses of the chick (McLennan & Horn, 1992) reveal stimulus specific changes after subtracting naive from trained responses, indicating that only novel stimuli induce 'representative activities' in the left IMHV. These effects become only appearant from the 'dissociative or endo-perspective'.

Taken together, this short outline demonstrates the basic ideas behind a new theory of 'quantum-neurodynamics' that coherently composes high-level brain functions, such as perceptual presentations, learning and memory, from the most basic or quantum level, provided by the train of action potentials. In a beautiful analogy to quantum-electro-dynamics (Feynman, 1961), 'real-macroscopic' issues emerge from organizational constraints provided by the brains anatomy. The stepwise composition of basic operations consistently discerns those issues of brain function that have received most attention - timing and plasticity, perceptual exposure learning and memory. Some aspects of the proposed model parallel issues found in self-organizing and resonance theories, e.g. the relevance of time with respect to plasticity. However, as opposed to previous efforts, this attempt does not require any 'external assumptions' , but exposes 'internal processing characteristics' that naturally link to those behavioural impressions that emerge from hitherto 'outside-in' views. The more extensive version of this paper should allow a coherent communication of the basic principles, together with imaging demonstrations from the 'endo-perspective'.

References
Bonhoeffer, T. & A. Grinvald (1993) J. Neurosci 13(10) 4157-4180
Carpenter, G.A. & St. Grossberg (1993) TINS, 16(4) 131-137
Eichenbaum, H. (1993) Science, 261, 993-994
Grinvald, A. Frostig, R.D.; Siegel, R.M., Bartfeld, E. (1991)
        Proc. Natl Acad Sci USA 88, 11559-11563
Katz, B. (1969) Liverpool Univ. Press
Karni, A, & D. Sagi (1993)   Nature, 365, 250-252
Otmakhov, N., A.M. Shirke & R. Malinow (1993) Neuron, 10, 1101-1111
Posner, M.I. (1993) Science, 262, 673-674
Taylor, J.G. (1972) J. Theor. Biol. 36, 513-528
Wilson, F.A.W., S.P. O. Scalaidhe, P.S. Goldman-Rakic, (1993) Science, 260, 1955-1958
Wilson, M.A. & B.L. Naughton (1993) Science, 261, 1055-1058
Young, M.P. (1992) Nature, 358, 152-155
Zeki, S. & S. Shipp (1988) Nature, 335, 311-317

Pre-Conditional Correlation between Neurons in Cultured Networks

Guenter W. Gross and David C. Tam

Center for Network Neuroscience
Department of Biological Sciences
University of North Texas
Denton, TX 76203

E-mail: gross@nervous.cnns.unt.edu
          dtam@brain.cns.unt.edu

Abstract

Multi-channel spike train analysis is applied to extract dynamical interactions of firing activity in spontaneously active monolayer neuronal network in cell culture. A pre-conditional correlational analysis is used to determine the conditional probability of firing of these neurons based on the preceding firing of another neuron in the network. Using this pre-conditional interspike interval analysis, we are able to determine the excitation coupling between the firing of neurons in this network and the timing relationship between the firing of spikes in various neurons of the network. The analysis also reveals which neurons in the network are not coupled.

1. Introduction

Networks of biological neurons cultured on multi-microelectrode plates (MMEP) are routinely obtained to study the dynamics of the interactions among neurons (Gross, 1994; Gross and Kowalski, 1991, Gross *et al*, 1993; Tam and Gross, 1994b). In this paper, we will study the conditional coupling between neurons in a biological neuronal network. Other spike train analytical techniques were recently developed: (1) detection of specific conditional interactions among neurons (Tam *et al*, 1988; Tam and Gross, 1994a); (2) logical conditional correlation among neurons (Tam, 1993a); (3) spatio-temporal correlation among neurons (Tam, 1993b, c; 1992a, b); (4) time-delayed neural network equivalence of cross-correlation computation (Tam, 1993d); and (5) artificial neural network implementation of enhanced cross-correlation computation (Tam, 1993e). In this paper, we will specifically address how the firing probability in neurons is dependent on preceding action potentials from other neurons in the same network. With this analysis, we are able to detect the probabilistic conditions under which the firing of one neuron is coupled to the prior firing of spikes in another neuron. We anticipate that the dynamical interactions of neuronal activity patterns in these networks can be revealed with this analysis. The accompanying paper (Tam and Gross, 1994b) will address the interactions between neurons based on the conditions subsequent to the firing of a neuron to deduce the inhibitory coupling between them (Tam, 1993f) which would otherwise not be revealed with conventional pre-conditional correlation analyses.

2. Methods
2.1. Cultured Monolayer Neuronal Networks

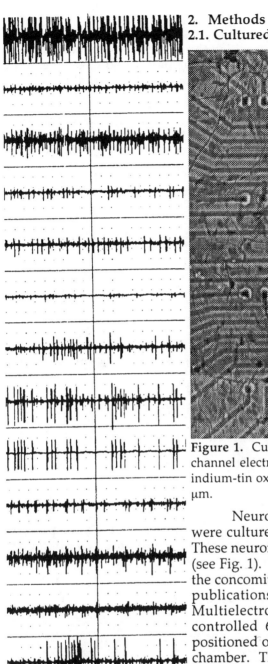

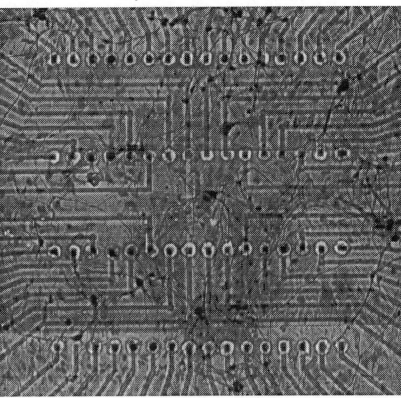

Figure 1. Cultured network of mouse spinal neurons grown on a 64-channel electrode plate. Conductor width: 8 μm; conductor material: indium-tin oxide; spacing between craters – rows: 200 μm, columns: 40 μm.

Neurons obtained from the spinal cord of embryonic mice were cultured on the multimicroelectrode plate (MMEP) surface. These neurons formed a network on the 64-channel electrode plate (see Fig. 1). The steps involved in the preparation of MMEPs and the concomitant culture methods have been described in previous publications (Gross and Kowalski, 1991; Gross et al, 1993). Multielectrode recording was performed with a computer-controlled 64 channel amplifier system. Preamplifiers were positioned on the microscope stage to either side of the recording chamber. The amplifier bandwidth was usually set at 500 Hz to 6 KHz. Activity was displayed on oscilloscopes and recorded on a 14 channel analog tape recorder. Spike data from active channels were also integrated (rectification followed by RC integration with a resulting time constant of 300ms) and displayed on a 12 channel strip chart recorder. Simultaneous action potential data was sampled at 40 kHz. Individual action potentials generated by neurons were isolated and discriminated based on the spike profiles. Once discriminated, the spikes generated from individual neurons were recorded in the computer as spike train signals. These spike trains were used to investigate the dynamical coupling between neurons in the network. A 160 msec sample of 13 channels simultaneously digitized electrical activity from the network is displayed in Fig. 2.

Figure 2. Display of 13 channels of simultaneous electrical activity recorded from neurons in the cultured network (before spike discrimination).

2.2. Pre-Conditional Correlation

To determine the various pre-conditions under which the firing of one neuron may be influenced by the firing of another neuron in the same network, we performed cross-interspike interval analyses (Tam *et al*, 1988), which allowed us to determine conditional probabilities of firing for a reference neuron based on the firing of other neurons.

The conditional cross-interspike interval (CISI) statistic estimates the conditional probability of spike firing at a particular interspike interval (ISI) after a spike has occurred in a reference neuron given that another neuron has fired at a specific time prior to the firing of the reference neuron (Tam *et al*, 1988).

Let spike trains A with a total of N_A spikes and B with a total of N_B spikes be represented by:

$$f_A(t) = \sum_{a=1}^{N_A} \delta(t - t_a)$$ (1)

and

$$f_B(t) = \sum_{b=1}^{N_B} \delta(t - t_b)$$ (2)

where t_a and t_b are the times of occurrence of spikes in spike train A and B, respectively and $\delta(t)$ is a delta function representing the time of occurrence of spikes.

Let us select spike train A as the reference and spike train B as the conditional spike train, then CISI statistics can be constructed by:

$$C(\tau_x, \tau_y) = \sum_{a=1}^{N_A-1} \delta(t_{a+1} - t_a - \tau_x)\delta(t_a - t_b - \tau_y)$$ (3)

for all t_a and t_b that satisfy $t_b \le t_a < t_{a+1}$.

The relationships of the pertinent spike intervals used in the CISI scatter plot are illustrated in Fig. 2. The pre-cross interval between two neurons is represented as y in the xy-scatter plot, and the post-interspike interval of the reference neuron is represented as x.

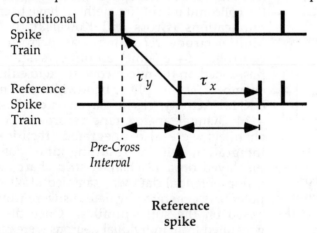

Figure 3. Schematic diagram illustrating the relationships of the cross interval and interspike interval in the spike trains being analyzed.

3. Results

Multi-channel spike trains (Fig. 2) recorded from the network shown in Fig. 1 were used for this analysis. Although 64 independent electrodes were available for the monitoring of network activity, we only stored 14 simultaneous channels on analog magnetic tape. We will limit our discussion to four neurons. Figure 4 shows the CISI scatter plots of the firings of neuron #7 used as the reference neuron, relative to the preceding firing of neurons #3, #5 and #6 respectively. The vertical bands of points in the CISI scatter plot show that the next spike firing probability of the reference neuron #7 is independent of the firing of spikes in the conditional neurons #5 and #6 (see Fig. 4B and C). But the next spike firing probability of the reference neuron #7 is dependent on the preceding firing of neuron #3, as revealed by the horizontal band of points in the Fig. 4A. Specifically, the firing of neuron #3 at a 3 msec interval before the firing of neuron #7 (horizontal band) is more likely than any other time interval. In other words, the firing of neuron #7 is coupled with neuron #3, when the latter fires 3 msec before neuron #7. Such coupling is not revealed for neurons #5 or #6.

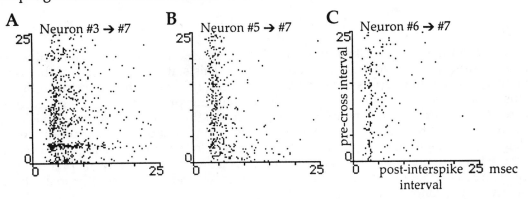

Figure 4. Pre-conditional interspike interval scatter plots of reference neuron # 7 relative to the firing of neurons #3, #5 and #6.

To identify whether such coupling between neurons #3 and #7 was reciprocal, we used neuron #3 as the reference neuron in the next analysis. The CISI plots (Fig. 5) show that the firing of spikes between neurons #3 and #6 is independent, as indicated by the vertical bands of points (see Fig. 5B). The density gradient of points in the vertical band of Fig. 5A suggests that the subsequent firing of spikes in reference neuron #3 is somewhat dependent on the firing of neuron #5, with higher probability of firing when these two neurons are firing within short time intervals. The coupling relationship decreases as the firing intervals between them (i.e., the cross-intervals) increases. Finally, the relationship between firing of spikes for neurons #3 and #7 is not as strongly coupled as the reciprocal case seen before. That is, the probability of firing in neuron #7 does not increase when neuron #3 fired 3 msec before #7 as in the previous case (i.e., there is no horizontal band of points at 3 msec pre-cross interval). But the CISI scatter plot reveals a dense cluster of points at the 1 msec pre-cross interval. This suggests that when neuron #7 fired 1 msec before the firing in neuron #3, neuron #3 was much more likely to fire again at 3 msec (i.e., with a 3 msec interspike interval). This phenomenon reveals that when neuron #7 fires 1 msec before neuron #3, neuron #3 will tend to fire another spike (consecutive firing) at 3 msec interspike interval. Thus, this analysis reveals that the coupling between neurons #3 and #7 is not symmetrical, but reciprocal with different firing probabilities.

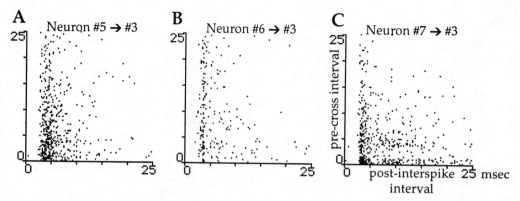

Figure 5. Pre-conditional interspike interval scatter plots of reference neuron # 3 relative to the firing of neurons #5, #6 and #7.

4. Summary

Pre-conditional interspike interval analysis was used to extract the dynamical coupling between neurons in a network of cultured neurons. This statistical analysis of the conditional probability of firing in neurons based on the preceding firing of other neurons in the network demonstrated the existence of some interesting coupling phenomena among neurons in the network. (1) It revealed which neurons were coupled in their spike firings and which were not. (2) When the firings between neurons were coupled, it revealed under what conditions they are coupled. (3) The analysis also showed which timing relationships of firings between neurons were more likely to fire than other time intervals. (4) It also revealed how the preceding firing of one neuron was related to the firing of the first and second spike firing probability (i.e., the consecutive firing conditions).

Acknowledgments

This research was supported in part by the Hillcrest Foundation and the Texas Advanced Technology Program (to Dr. Gross) and ONR grant number N00014-93-1-0135 (to Dr. Tam).

References

Gross, G. W. (1994) Internal dynamics of randomized mammalian neuronal networks in culture. In: *Enabling Technologies for Cultured Neural Networks.* (T. McKenna & D. A. Stenger, eds.) Academic Press, San Diego. (in press)

Gross, G.W., and Kowalski, J.M. (1991). Experimental and theoretical analysis of random nerve cell network dynamics. In: *Neural Networks: Concepts, Applications, and Implementations*, Vol 4, (P Antognetti and V Milutinovic, eds), Prentice Hall, Englewood, New Jersey, pp. 47-110.

Gross, G.W., Rhoades, B.K., and Kowalski, J.M. (1993). Dynamics of burst patterns generated by monolayer networks in culture. In: *Neurobionics* (H.W. Bothe, M. Samii and R. Eckmiller, eds). Elsevier Press, Amsterdam, pp. 89-121.

Tam, D. C. (1993a) A new conditional correlation statistics for detecting spatio-temporally correlated firing patterns in a biological neuronal network. Proceedings of the World Congress on Neural Networks, July 1993. Vol. 2. pp. 606-609.

Tam, D. C. (1993b) Novel cross-interval maps for identifying attractors from multi-unit neural firing patterns. In: Nonlinear Dynamical Analysis of the EEG.. (B. H. Jansen and M. E. Brandt, eds.) World Scientific Publishing Co., River Edge, NJ. pp. 65-77.

Tam, D. C. (1993c) A multi-neuronal vectorial phase-space analysis for detecting dynamical interactions in firing patterns of biological neural networks. In: Computational Neural Systems. (F. H. Eeckman and J. M. Bower, eds.) Kluwer Academic Publishers, Norwell, MA. pp. 49-53.

Tam, D. C. (1993d) Computation of cross-correlation function by a time-delayed neural network. In: Intelligent Engineering Systems through Artificial Neural Networks, Vol. 3. (Cihan H. Dagli, Laura I. Burke, Benito R. Fernández, Joydeep Ghosh, eds.), American Society of Mechanical Engineers Press, New York, NY. Vol. 3. pp. 51-55.

Tam, D. C. (1993e) A hybrid time-shifted neural network for analyzing biological neuronal spike trains. Progress in Neural Networks (O. Omidvar, ed.) Vol. 2, Ablex Publishing Corporation: Norwood, New Jersey. (in press)

Tam, D. C. (1993f) A new post-conditional correlation method for extracting excitation-inhibition coupling between neurons. Society for Neuroscience Abstract. Vol. 19, p. 1598.

Tam, D. C. (1992a) Vectorial phase-space analysis for detecting dynamical interactions in firing patterns of biological neural networks. Proceedings of the International Joint Conference on Neural Networks, June 1992. Vol.3 pp. 97-102.

Tam, D. C. (1992b) A novel vectorial phase-space analysis of spatio-temporal firing patterns in biological neural networks. Proceedings of the Simulation Technology Conference. Nov., 1992, pp. 556-564.

Tam, D. C., Ebner, T. J., and Knox, C. K. (1988) Cross-interval histogram and cross-interspike interval histogram correlation analysis of simultaneously recorded multiple spike train data. Journal of Neuroscience Methods, Vol. 23, pp. 23-33.

Tam, D. C. and Gross G. W. (1994a) Dynamical changes in neuronal network circuitries using multi-unit spike train analysis. In: Enabling Technologies for Cultured Neural Networks. (T. McKenna and D. A. Stenger, eds.) Academic Press, San Diego, CA. (in press)

Tam, D. C. and Gross G. W. (1994b) Post-conditional correlation between neurons in cultured neuronal networks. Proceedings of the World Congress on Neural Networks (this volume).

Post-Conditional Correlation between Neurons in Cultured Neuronal Networks

David C. Tam and Guenter W. Gross

Center for Network Neuroscience
Department of Biological Sciences
University of North Texas
Denton, TX 76203

E-mail: dtam@brain.cns.unt.edu
gross@nervous.cnns.unt.edu

Abstract

A new conditional spike train analytical method is developed to estimate the post-conditional probability of firing of spikes in neurons to reveal both excitation and inhibition coupling between firing times. This method allows us to determine how the spike firing probability density function is related to the conditional probability of firing of another neuron in the network subsequent to the firing of a reference neuron. When this analysis is applied to the firing patterns of neurons in a cultured network, it revealed that some of the neurons have excitatory coupling whereas other neurons display inhibitory coupling. The coupling between these neurons is also found not to be reciprocal.

1. Introduction

The accompanying paper (Gross and Tam, 1994) revealed the excitation coupling relationships between the firing of spikes in neurons in a network of biological neurons cultured on multi-microelectrode plates (MMEPs). These cultured networks are now routinely used to study the dynamics of the interactions among neurons (Gross, 1994; Gross and Kowalski, 1991, Gross *et al*, 1993; Tam and Gross, 1994b).

In this paper, we present a new post-conditional probability spike train analysis technique to extract the inhibition coupling between neurons in a network (Tam, 1993f). Conventional spike train analysis methods have been frequently used to demonstrate excitation coupling (or positive correlation) among neurons. These analytical techniques include the cross-correlation analysis (Perkel *et al*, 1967) for detection of specific conditional interactions among neurons (Tam *et al*, 1988; Tam and Gross, 1994a), logical conditional correlation among neurons (Tam, 1993a), spatio-temporal correlation among neurons (Tam, 1993b, c; 1992a, b), time-delayed neural network equivalence of cross-correlation computation (Tam, 1993d), and artificial neural network implementation of enhanced cross-correlation computation (Tam, 1993e).

We will address how the firing probability of a spike immediately following a reference spike is dependent on the conditions of firing in other neurons after the reference spike. This post-conditional statistical analysis will be able to detect the conditions under which spiking may be suppressed by the intervening spike in another (conditional) neuron. Thus both the excitatory and inhibitory dynamical interactions of activity patterns in these networks can be revealed with this analysis. The accompanying paper has addressed the interactions between neurons based on the conditions prior to the firing of a neuron to deduce the excitatory coupling between them.

2. Methods
2.1. Cultured Neuronal Networks

Spike train data for this analysis was obtained from neuronal networks growing on multimicroelectrode plates (MMEPs). As in the accompanying paper (Gross and Tam, 1994), the tissues were obtained from the spinal cords of embryonic mice. The electrical signals generated by the neurons were amplified and discriminated to obtain the spike trains as described earlier.

2.2. Post-Conditional Correlation

The firing of spikes usually implies that the neurons are excited enough to reach threshold and generate action potentials. But if a neuron is inhibited, the membrane potential of the neuron may not reach threshold. The conditional suppression of spike firing cannot be easily demonstrated with conventional spike train analyses.

The post-conditional probability spike train analysis provides a new way to extract the conditional probability of firing if firing generation in a neuron is reduced relative to the firing of another neuron in the same network. Thus, it will provide correlational statistics that will allow us to detect subtle inhibitory coupling between neurons.

The post-conditional cross-interspike interval (PCISI) statistic estimates the conditional probability of spike firing at a particular interspike interval (ISI) after a spike has occurred in a reference neuron given that another neuron has fired at a specific time *after* the firing the reference spike in the reference neuron (Tam, 1993f).

Let spike trains A with a total of N_A spikes and B with a total of N_B spikes be represented by:

$$f_A(t) = \sum_{a=1}^{N_A} \delta(t - t_a) \tag{1}$$

and

$$f_B(t) = \sum_{b=1}^{N_B} \delta(t - t_b) \tag{2}$$

where t_a and t_b are the times of occurrence of spikes in spike train A and B, respectively and $\delta(t)$ is a delta function denoting the occurrence of spikes.

Let us select spike train A as the reference and spike train B as the conditional spike train. CISI statistics can be then constructed by:

$$C(\tau_x, \tau_y) = \sum_{a=1}^{N_A-1} \delta(t_{a+1} - t_a - \tau_x)\delta(t_a - t_b - \tau_y) \tag{3}$$

for all t_a and t_b such that $t_a \leq t_b$ and $t_a < t_{a+1}$.

The construction of the PCISI scatter plot is illustrated in Fig. 1. The post-cross interval between two neurons is represented as y in the xy-scatter plot, and the post-interspike interval of the reference neuron is represented as x.

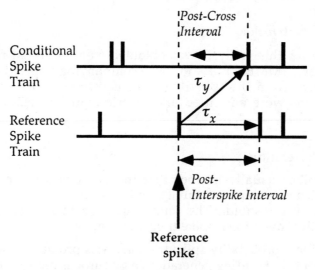

Figure 1. Schematic diagram illustrating the relationships of the post-cross interval and interspike interval in the spike trains being analyzed.

3. Results

Figure 2 shows the post-conditional cross-interspike interval scatter plots of the firings of neuron #7 (the reference neuron) conditioned on the succeeding firing of spikes in neurons #3, #5 and #6 respectively. The prominent bands of points parallel to the diagonal line indicate synchronized firing between these neurons.

The 45 degree diagonal line is the coincidence line, indicating that a pair of neurons is firing in synchrony. Lines parallel to the diagonal line indicate the firing between the neuron pair is offset by a specific finite time interval. Parallel lines above the diagonal indicate the conditional neuron fires a spike after the second spike firing in the reference neuron. In that case, the reference neuron will fire two consecutive spikes before the conditional neuron fires the next spike, and the consecutive firing of spikes are not affected by the intervening firing of another neuron. Parallel lines below the diagonal line indicate the conditional neuron fires an intervening spike between the first and second spike of the reference neuron. The diagonal line of points in Fig. 2B indicates that neurons #7 and #5 tend to fire in synchrony occasionally.

The vertical band of points in the PCISI scatter plot indicates the independence of firing of spikes between the neuron pair, since the probability of firing of the consecutive spike in the reference neuron does not vary with the firing times in the other conditional neuron. When the independence of firing intervals between these neuron pairs is compared with the pre-conditional probability statistics discussed in the accompanying paper (Gross and Tam, 1994), both techniques show the independence of firing between neurons #7 and #5, and neurons #7 and #6. The previous method showed that the prior firing history of the conditioning neurons #5 and #6 does not have any effect on the probability of firing of another spike for the reference neuron #7. The current method also shows that subsequent firing of the conditional neurons #5 and #6 firing within the interspike interval period of the reference neuron #7, does not have any effect on the probability of firing of the second spike, except for occasional synchronous firing between neurons #7 and #5 as indicated by the diagonal line of points in Fig. 2B.

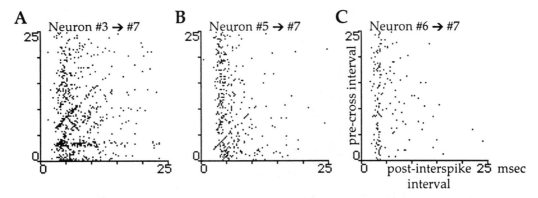

Figure 2. Post-conditional interspike interval scatter plots of reference neuron # 7 conditioned on the firing of neurons #3, #5 and #6.

When neuron #3 is used as the reference neuron for the post-conditional cross-interspike interval analysis, the dependence relationship between these neurons is revealed to be congruent with those revealed from the previous analysis, i.e., for those pairs of neurons that are found to be coupled in their firing times using the pre-conditional correlation analysis are also found to be coupled using the post-conditional correlation analysis. That is, proximity in firing times between conditional neuron #5 and reference neuron #3 occurs more often than longer duration intervals (denser gradient of points with shorter cross-intervals in Fig. 3A). The firing intervals between neurons #6 and #3 are relatively independent as indicated by the vertical band of points (Fig. 3B). Dense clusters of points are found in Fig. 3C, suggesting a coupling relationship between the firing times of these two neurons (#3 and #7). Specifically, the probability of firing 3 msec interspike interval for the reference neuron #3 is higher when neuron #7 fires 1 msec after the reference spike or 4 msec after it. This suggests that neuron #3 tends to lead the firing of neuron #7 by 1 msec.

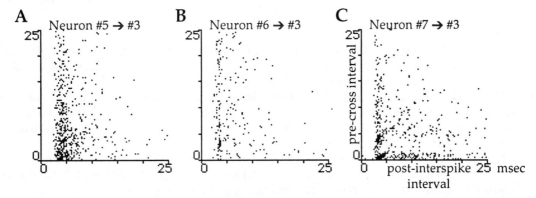

Figure 3. Post-conditional interspike interval scatter plots of reference neuron # 3 conditioned on the firing of neurons #5, #6 and #7.

We will look at the relationship of another pair of neuron to reveal inhibitory coupling between them. Figure 4 shows the PCISI scatter plot for neuron #11 as the reference conditioned on neuron #10. A diagonal band of points slightly above the 45 degree diagonal can be seen. Furthermore, most of the points lie above the diagonal line with only a few points lying below the diagonal. This suggests that the firing of the next spike for the reference neuron #11 is less likely if neuron #10 fired before this next spike, implying suppression of firing probability (or inhibition). In other words, the firing of another spike in neuron #11 occurs only when neuron #10 fired after the second spike, but not between them. This strongly suggests that there is an inhibitory coupling relationship between the firing of spikes in these two neurons.

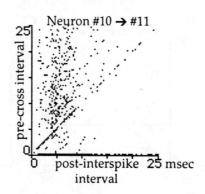

Figure 4. Post-conditional interspike interval scatter plots of reference neuron # 11 conditioned on the firing of neurons #10.

Summary

A new post-conditional spike train analysis is introduced to detect both excitatory and inhibitory coupling of firing times between neurons. This method allows us to reveal how the probability of the next firing in a reference neuron is dependent on the timing of firing in another (conditional) neuron after the current spike in the reference neuron. When the analysis was applied to the spike trains recorded from a network of cultured neurons, it revealed the excitation and inhibitory coupling between specific pairs of neurons as well as those neurons that are not coupled in the network.

Acknowledgments

This research was supported in part by ONR grant number N00014-93-1-0135 (to Dr. Tam) and the Hillcrest Foundation and the Texas Advanced Technology Program (to Dr. Gross).

References

Gross, G. W. (1994) Internal dynamics of randomized mammalian neuronal networks in culture. In: *Enabling Technologies for Cultured Neural Networks*. (T. McKenna & D. A. Stenger, eds.) Academic Press, San Diego. (in press)

Gross, G.W., and Kowalski, J.M. (1991). Experimental and theoretical analysis of random nerve cell network dynamics. In: *Neural Networks: Concepts, Applications, and Implementations*, Vol 4, (P Antognetti and V Milutinovic, eds), Prentice Hall, Englewood, New Jersey, pp. 47-110.

Gross, G.W., Rhoades, B.K., and Kowalski, J.M. (1993). Dynamics of burst patterns generated by monolayer networks in culture. In: *Neurobionics* (H.W. Bothe, M. Samii and R. Eckmiller, eds). Elsevier Press, Amsterdam, pp. 89-121.

Perkel, D. H., Gerstein, G. L. and Moore, G. P. (1967) Neuronal Spike Trains and Stochastic Point Process. II. Simultaneous Spike Trains. *Biophysical Journal*, **7**: 419-440.

Tam, D. C. (1993a) A new conditional correlation statistics for detecting spatio-temporally correlated firing patterns in a biological neuronal network. Proceedings of the World Congress on Neural Networks, July 1993. Vol. 2. pp. 606-609.

Tam, D. C. (1993b) Novel cross-interval maps for identifying attractors from multi-unit neural firing patterns. In: Nonlinear Dynamical Analysis of the EEG.. (B. H. Jansen and M. E. Brandt, eds.) World Scientific Publishing Co., River Edge, NJ. pp. 65-77.

Tam, D. C. (1993c) A multi-neuronal vectorial phase-space analysis for detecting dynamical interactions in firing patterns of biological neural networks. In: Computational Neural Systems. (F. H. Eeckman and J. M. Bower, eds.) Kluwer Academic Publishers, Norwell, MA. pp. 49-53.

Tam, D. C. (1993d) Computation of cross-correlation function by a time-delayed neural network. In: Intelligent Engineering Systems through Artificial Neural Networks, Vol. 3. (Cihan H. Dagli, Laura I. Burke, Benito R. Fernández, Joydeep Ghosh, eds.), American Society of Mechanical Engineers Press, New York, NY. Vol. 3. pp. 51-55.

Tam, D. C. (1993e) A hybrid time-shifted neural network for analyzing biological neuronal spike trains. Progress in Neural Networks (O. Omidvar, ed.) Vol. 2, Ablex Publishing Corporation: Norwood, New Jersey. (in press)

Tam, D. C. (1993f) A new post-conditional correlation method for extracting excitation-inhibition coupling between neurons. Society for Neuroscience Abstract. Vol. 19, p. 1598.

Tam, D. C. (1992a) Vectorial phase-space analysis for detecting dynamical interactions in firing patterns of biological neural networks. Proceedings of the International Joint Conference on Neural Networks, June 1992. Vol.3 pp. 97-102.

Tam, D. C. (1992b) A novel vectorial phase-space analysis of spatio-temporal firing patterns in biological neural networks. Proceedings of the Simulation Technology Conference. Nov., 1992, pp. 556-564.

Tam, D. C., Ebner, T. J., and Knox, C. K. (1988) Cross-interval histogram and cross-interspike interval histogram correlation analysis of simultaneously recorded multiple spike train data. Journal of Neuroscience Methods, Vol. 23, pp. 23-33.

Tam, D. C. and Gross G. W. (1994a) Dynamical changes in neuronal network circuitries using multi-unit spike train analysis. In: Enabling Technologies for Cultured Neural Networks. (T. McKenna and D. A. Stenger, eds.) Academic Press, San Diego, CA. (in press)

Tam, D. C. and Gross G. W. (1994b) Post-conditional correlation between neurons in cultured neuronal networks. Proceedings of the World Congress on Neural Networks (in press).

NEURAL NETWORK TRAINING
VIA A PRIMAL-DUAL INTERIOR POINT METHOD
FOR LINEAR PROGRAMMING

Theodore B. Trafalis and Nicolas P. Couellan
School of Industrial Engineering
University of Oklahoma
Norman, OK 73019

Abstract : We propose a new training algorithm for feedforward supervised neural networks based on the primal-dual interior point method for linear programming. Specifically we consider single layer networks where the error function is defined by the L_1-norm and the activation function of the output layer is linear. Because of the special structure of the problem, our problem is equivalent to solving a block-structured linear system of equations.

1. INTRODUCTION:

The training phase of a supervised feedforward Artificial Neural Network (ANN) can be defined as an optimization problem. ANN are often complex, involving many nodes and even more connection weights. This results in a large scale optimization problem. The purpose of this paper is to propose a new method of training for large scale ANN using the most recent techniques of optimization. There are various non-linear optimization methods that can be used for training of ANN [Hertz, Krogh and Palmer (1991)]. One of those is the gradient descent method on which the backpropagation method is based [Werbos (1974), Rumelhart, Hinton and Williams (1986)]. A major drawback of the current learning algorithms is the long training (learning time) for large scale problems [Shepanski (1988)]. Recent breakthroughs of interior point methods (IPM) for solving large scale constrained optimization problems [Lustig et al. (1992), Gonzaga (1991, 1992), Anstreicher et al. (1990)] suggest that IPM can be used to develop new fast learning laws in ANN which can enlarge the set of problems which can be solved successfully. Some new ideas along these lines have already been studied such as Training of ANN by a Logarithmic Barrier Function Adaptation Scheme [Trafalis and Sieger (1993)] .

This paper will explain an interior point primal-dual approach of training an ANN. In order to convey the idea, we will deal with a single layer neural network where the activation function of the output nodes is linear. The use of the L_1-norm will allow us to transform the original minimization problem into a linear programming problem having a block-matrix structure. Then we apply the algorithm of the Primal-Dual interior point method for linear programming to update the weights. Since our linear programming problem has a special structure, we simplify the updating equation of the weights to improve the Primal-Dual algorithm.

This paper is organized as follows : Section 2 discusses the optimization problem, Section 3 discusses a primal-dual interior point method training approach, Section 4 gives computational results and Section 5 is the conclusion.

2. STATEMENT OF THE PROBLEM :

Consider a single layer artificial neural network (See Fig. 1).
Let :
x be the input vector $x = (x_1, x_2, ..., x_n)$
b be the desired output vector $b = (b_1, b_2, ..., b_m)$
w_{ij} be the connection weight from the ith input component to the jth neuron

Assumptions :

1- In our case we do not introduce the threshold inputs.

2- We are studying the case of supervised training where we know the desired output vector b for each input vector x. The objective is to minimize the sum of the errors between the current and desired output with respect to the weights w_{ij}.

3- The weights are not constrained.

4- We use the L_1-norm to define the error function.

5- The function f is the activation function for all the neurons of the layer. In the following, we will consider a linear activation function.

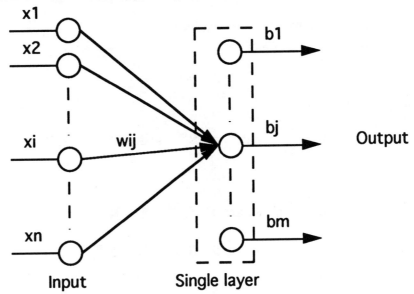

Figure 1.

The minimization problem is as follows :

$$\min \sum_{j=1}^{m} \left| b_j - f\left(\sum_{i=1}^{n} w_{ij}x_i \right) \right|$$

Note : The values x_i and b_j are known and the variables are the weights w_{ij}.

3. A PRIMAL-DUAL INTERIOR POINT METHOD TRAINING APPROACH :

In order to convey the idea of our approach we consider the one-layer case where the activation function is linear.

For simplicity we consider the identity function as the activation function. Then the problem becomes :

$$\min \sum_{j=1}^{m} \left| b_j - \sum_{i=1}^{n} w_{ij}x_i \right|$$

By defining $e_j = \left| b_j - \sum_{i=1}^{n} w_{ij}x_i \right|$, it is easy to show that the problem is equivalent to the following :

$$\min \sum_{j=1}^{m} e_j$$

subject to

$$e_j \geq b_j - \sum_{i=1}^{n} w_{ij} x_i \qquad \text{for } j = 1, \ldots, m$$

$$e_j \geq -b_j + \sum_{i=1}^{n} w_{ij} x_i \qquad \text{for } j = 1, \ldots, m \qquad \text{(O)}$$

This linear problem has the following form :

(D)
$$\max -d^T z$$
$$\text{st}$$
$$A^T z + s = f$$
$$s \geq 0$$

Where :

$$z = \begin{pmatrix} e \\ w \end{pmatrix} \quad \text{with} \quad e \in R^m, \ w \in R^{mn} \Rightarrow z \in R^{m(n+1)}$$

$$d = \begin{pmatrix} 1 \\ 0 \end{pmatrix} \quad \text{where} \quad \mathbf{1} = (1,1,\ldots,1) \in R^m$$

$$\mathbf{0} = (0,0,\ldots,0) \in R^{mn}$$

$$f = \begin{pmatrix} b \\ -b \end{pmatrix} \quad \text{with } b \in R^m$$

$s \in R^{2m}$ slack variables

$$A^T = \begin{bmatrix} 1 & & x_1 & \cdots & x_n & & & & & \\ & \ddots & & & & & \cdots & \cdots & \cdots & \\ & & 1 & & & & & x_1 & \cdots & x_n \\ 1 & & -x_1 & \cdots & -x_n & & & & & \\ & \ddots & & & & & \cdots & \cdots & \cdots & \\ & & 1 & & & & & -x_1 & \cdots & -x_n \end{bmatrix}$$

It is easy to see that (D) is the dual problem of (P) defined as :

(P)
$$\min f^T y$$
$$\text{st}$$
$$A y = -d$$
$$y \geq 0 \qquad y \in R^{2m}$$

Next we are going to find the optimal solution of (O) by using the following iterative procedure : $z^{k+1} = z^k + \alpha \, d_z^k$ where d_z^k is the search direction of the primal-dual algorithm [Lustig, Marsten and Shanno (1991)]. Specifically d_z^k is given by :

(*) $\qquad (A Y_k S_k^{-1} A^T) \, d_z^k = - A S_k^{-1}(\mu^k e - Y_k S_k e)$

where : $\qquad e = (1, 1, \ldots, 1)$

$$Y_k = \text{diag}\{y_{k1}, y_{k2}, ..., y_{k2m}\}$$
$$S_k = \text{diag}\{s_{k1}, s_{k2}, ..., s_{k2m}\}$$

and μ^k is the barrier parameter at the kth iteration.

The equation (*) defines a linear system of equations which depends mostly on the matrix $AY_kS_k^{-1}A^T$. Next we are going to study the structure of the matrix $AY_kS_k^{-1}A^T$.

After some calculations (matrice multiplications), we can show that $AY_kS_k^{-1}A^T$ has the following form :

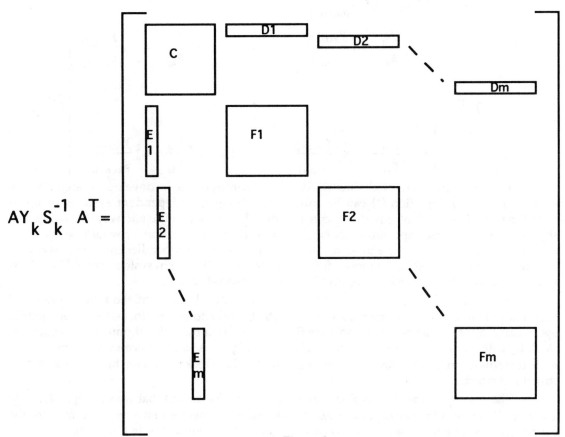

Figure 2

This matrix has a block-structure. The blocks are defined as follows :

$$C = \begin{bmatrix} \dfrac{y_{k1}}{s_{k1}} + \dfrac{y_{k(m+1)}}{s_{k(m+1)}} & & 0 \\ & \ddots & \\ 0 & & \dfrac{y_{km}}{s_{km}} + \dfrac{y_{k2m}}{s_{k2m}} \end{bmatrix}$$

$$D_j = \begin{bmatrix} x_1\dfrac{y_{kj}}{s_{kj}} - x_1\dfrac{y_{k(m+j)}}{s_{k(m+j)}} & \cdots & x_n\dfrac{y_{kj}}{s_{kj}} - x_n\dfrac{y_{k(m+j)}}{s_{k(m+j)}} \end{bmatrix} \quad j=1,...,m$$

$$E_j = \begin{bmatrix} x_1 \dfrac{y_{kj}}{s_{kj}} + x_1 \dfrac{y_{k(m+j)}}{s_{k(m+j)}} \\ \cdot \\ \cdot \\ \cdot \\ x_n \dfrac{y_{kj}}{s_{kj}} + x_n \dfrac{y_{k(m+j)}}{s_{k(m+j)}} \end{bmatrix} \quad j=1,...,m$$

$$F_j = \begin{bmatrix} x_1^2 \dfrac{y_{kj}}{s_{kj}} - x_1^2 \dfrac{y_{k(m+j)}}{s_{k(m+j)}} & \cdots & x_1 x_n \dfrac{y_{kj}}{s_{kj}} - x_1 x_n \dfrac{y_{k(m+j)}}{s_{k(m+j)}} \\ \cdot & \cdot & \cdot \\ \cdot & \cdot & \cdot \\ \cdot & \cdot & \cdot \\ x_n x_1 \dfrac{y_{kj}}{s_{kj}} - x_n x_1 \dfrac{y_{k(m+j)}}{s_{k(m+j)}} & \cdots & x_n^2 \dfrac{y_{kj}}{s_{kj}} - x_n^2 \dfrac{y_{k(m+j)}}{s_{k(m+j)}} \end{bmatrix} \quad j=1,...,m$$

The block-structure of the matrix is very useful in order to develop an algorithm to solve equation (*). Equation (*) can be solved by solving m independent systems of linear equations. Each system of equations can be solved in a very efficient way by using fast algorithms like LU-decomposition, QR factorization. Then the equation (*) would be solved in a time m.T where T is the time to solve each system. The use of a parallel computer having at least m processors would be the most efficient way to solve (*) . The m systems would be solved simultaneously and then the time required would be T instead of m.T.

The matrix $AY_kS_k^{-1}A^T$ is not really a block-matrix because of the first m rows and columns but by a simple transformation it would be easy to get a block-structured matrix. Specifically, if we exchange for example the first column with the mth column, we can combine block E_1 with the block F_1 to form a bigger block (See Fig. 2). A similar permutation can be done with the rows. Proceeding in the same way for all the blocks, we can have a real block-structured matrix.

The matrix $AY_kS_k^{-1}A^T$ is also a sparse matrix which means that we can represent it in a very efficient way in memory. In order to minimize the memory size required to store the matrix, we can store only the non-zero components and their coordinates in the matrix.

4. COMPUTATIONAL RESULTS :

In this part we will show some results obtained by running the Primal-Dual algorithm (code OB1 [Lustig, Marsten and Shanno (1991)]). The algorithm used does not contain the improvement that we have introduced in the previous part related to the special structure of our problem. Next we present three simple examples to illustrate the use of a primal-dual interior point algorithm for the training of a single layer ANN. The computational results give the behavior of our method when the ANN has to recognize only one pattern.

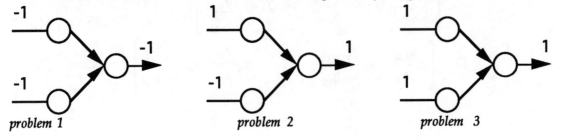

problem 1   problem 2   problem 3

	problem 1:	problem 2:	problem 3:
	min e_1	min e_1	min e_1
	st	st	st
	$w_{11} + w_{12} - e_1 \leq 1$	$-w_{11} + w_{12} - e_1 \leq -1$	$-w_{11} - w_{12} - e_1 \leq -1$
	$-w_{11} - w_{12} - e_1 \leq 1$	$w_{11} - w_{12} - e_1 \leq -1$	$w_{11} + w_{12} - e_1 \leq -1$

Table 1 gives the results of the running of the code OB1 with the above problems :

	e_1	w_{11}	w_{12}	# iterations
Problem 1	0.62538580 E -10	0.13199070 E +03	0.44076848 E +02	10
Problem 2	0.62538580 E -10	0.73359710 E +02	0.73359710 E +02	10
Problem 3	0.62538580 E -10	0.43663567 E +02	0.13123054 E +03	10

Table 1

The interior point method gives very accurate results in a short time. The value of the error is very small (order 1E-10) which means that we could use the interior point method for problems that are not classification problems and even for problems which require good accuracy. Since the interior point methods have the advantage to converge in polynomial time, we plan to extend our approach for the multi-layer case and for large scale problems. This is important for ANN training because the number of neurons can be very large (for example a small problem of pattern recognition using a matrix 10x10 may have hundreds of weigths). The results that we have achieved by running the previous examples do not have a lot of practical significance but they show us that the use of interior point method could be promising for the extension of this algorithm to a multi-layer ANN scheme.

5. CONCLUSIONS AND FUTURE RESEARCH :

In this paper we have developed a primal-dual interior point approach to train a one layer ANN by transforming the optimization learning problem into a linear programming problem. We are currently investigating the extension of our approach in a multi-layer ANN. Our method would be applied to ANN having a linear activation function at the output layer and the sigmoid function for example at the hidden layers. We could use ideas from the backpropagation algorithm to backpropagate the error from the output layer.

ACKNOWLEDGEMENT :
The present work has been supported by the NSF grant ECS-9212003. Research Initiation Award.
We thank Paul Werbos for his encouragement and for posing the problem.

REFERENCES :

Anstreicher K. M., D. Den Hertog, Roos C. and Terkaly T., (1990) "A long Step Barrier Method for Convex Quadratic Programming", *Technical Report* 90-53, Delft University of Technology, Delft, Netherlands.

Gonzaga, C. C. (1991), "Large Step Path-following Methods for Linear Programming, Parts 1 & 2", *SIAM Journal of Optimization* 1, 268-280.

Gonzaga, C. C. (1992), "Path-following Methods for Linear Programming", *SIAM REVIEW*, 34, No. 2, 167-224.

Hertz J., Krogh A., and Palmer R. G., (1991) *Introduction to the Theory of Neural Computation*, Redwood City, CA: Addison-Wesley.

Lustig, I. J., Marsten R. E., and Shanno D. F., (1991) "Computational Experience with a Primal-Dual Interior Point Method for Linear Programming", *Linear Algebra and Its Applications*, 152, 191-222.

Lustig, I. J., Marsten R. E., and Shanno D. F., (1992) "Interior Point Methods for Linear Programming : Computational State of the Art", *Technical Report* SOR 92-17, Program in Statistics and Operations Research Department of Civil Engineering and Operation Research, Princeton University, Princeton, NJ 08544.

Rumelhart D. E., Hinton G. E., and Williams R., (1986) "Learning Internal Representations by Error Propagation", in D.E. Rumelhart and J.L. McClelland (Eds), *Parallel Distributed Processing : Explorations in the Microstruture of Cognition*, 1, Foundations, MIT Press.

Shepanski J., (1988) "Fast learning in artificial neural networks : Multilayer perceptron training using optimal estimation", *Proceedings of the IEEE International Conference on Neural Networks*, 1, 465-472, San Diego : IEEE.

Trafalis T. B., and Sieger D. B., (1993) "Training of Multilayer Feedforward Artificial Neural Networks by a logarithmic Barrier Function Adaptation Scheme", *Intelligent Engineering Systems Through Artificial Neural Networks*, Vol. 3, Editors : C.H. Dagli, L.I. Burke, B.R. Fernandez and J. Ghosh, 167-173.

Werbos P., (1974) "Beyond regression : New tools for prediction and analysis in the behavioral sciences" PhD. Thesis, *Committee on Applied Mathematics*, Harvard University, Cambridge, MA.

STORAGE CAPACITY OF QUANTUM NEURAL NETWORKS

Alexei Samsonovich

University of Arizona
Applied Math. Program
Mathematics bldg. #89
Tucson, AZ 85721, USA

Quantum mechanical counterparts of traditional
neuronet models together with new retrieval
paradigms are defined and studied analytically
and numerically for their ability to recognize
patterns. Depending on the values of
parameters, storage capacity of QNNs can vary
from zero up to the classical limit. Parallel
processing of a quantum superposition of
patterns is possible.

Introduction

As dimensions of computing elements become smaller and smaller,
quantum effects inevitably come into play. For arrays of quantum
dots or molecular-level elements quantum corrections may be so
significant that it makes sense to think in terms of quantum
mechanical (QM) computer models (Feynman, 1986; Lloyd, 1994)
rather than in terms of errors or quantum corrections to
classical models. This remark primarily concerns such parallel
architectures as neural networks.

On the other hand, models of quantum neural networks (QNNs)
may be related to information processing in living organisms at
the molecular level (Samsonovich et al., 1992; Hameroff et al.,
1992).

The class of the QM models that we are going to introduce
have not been investigated at all or at least in the aspect of
neuro-like behavior. However, the number of mathematical models
that have been tested for ability to retrieve or to classify
patterns is huge, and it seems strange that none of them was
purely quantum (quantum spin glass and related models usually are
considered prom physical point of view without respect to
information processing: see for example Goldschmidt, 1990; Ray et
al., 1989). Combination of words "quantum" and "neural" rarely
occurs in literature (Lewenstein & Olko, 1992; Pribram, 1993),
and never in connection with an exact solution of a
quantum-mechanical problem.

Models and retrieval paradigms

We define a QNN model in general as a network of n nonlinear oscillators (or localization centers) at each node, that can be physically connected to any other oscillator. The Hamiltonian is a nonlinear Hermitean function of creation and annihilation operators of all nodes, it is independent of time and preserves the number of quanta. Some modifications can be applied further.

QUANTUM HOPFIELD. Quantum mechanical counterpart of the traditional Hopfield model (Hopfield, 1982) can be defined by the Hamiltonian

$$H = \Omega_o \Sigma_i^n a_i^+ a_i - \epsilon \Sigma_{i=j} a_i^+ a_j - \gamma \Sigma_{ij} W_{ij} a_i^+ a_j^+ a_i a_j \tag{1}$$

where a^+, a are boson creation and annihilation operators; ϵ and γ are some positive constants - parameters of the model; diagonal elements of W are supposed to be negative and large in absolute value in order to neglect multiple occupations, and the off-diagonal elements are computed according to a simplified Hebbian rule:

$$W_{ij} = \Sigma_\mu^P x_i^\mu x_j^\mu , \quad \Sigma_i x_i^\mu = m, \quad x_i^\mu \in \{0,1\}. \tag{2}$$

A weak interaction with a thermostat, another set of oscillators, that preserves the number of quanta in the network, can be added to the model.
The recognition paradigm consists in:
i) formation of the initial psi-function of the network containing m quanta - the input pattern;
ii) it's quantum evolution and relaxation to a local minimum;
iii) measurement of resultant occupation numbers - the output pattern.
We will be interested in the limiting case of n tending to infinity with m/n << 1, fixed. The first question is the multiplicity of the ground state of the model (1), (2) in this limit (see also Ray et al., 1989; Goldschmidt, 1990).
First, in the case of just one stored pattern the ground state problem can be solved analytically. Hamiltonian (1) can be reduced to the Hamiltonian of a linear chain, where index k corresponds to half-Hamming distance from the stored pattern:

$$H_{kk'} = w_k \delta_{kk'} - \alpha_k \delta_{k-1,k'} - \alpha_{k+1} \delta_{k+1,k'} \tag{3}$$

$$\alpha_k = \epsilon k \sqrt{m-k+1} \sqrt{n-m-k+1} \tag{4}$$

$$w_k = \gamma [\binom{m}{2} - \binom{m-k}{2}] - \epsilon k (n-2k) \tag{5}$$

The continuous limit solution at small k is the exponent:

$$Psi^o = æ^{-1} \exp(-k/æ), \quad æ = æ(\gamma, \epsilon), \tag{6}$$

$$\gamma/\epsilon > 2 \sqrt{n/m-1}. \tag{7}$$

The last inequality (which is actually more complicated in it's precise form) is the condition for existence of a localized state near the stored pattern. Therefore, the existence of the localized states (localized in the Hilbert space of states with number states taken as the basis) depends on behavior of the parameters γ, ϵ when n goes to infinity. If ϵ is negligibly small as compared to γ, we have the classical limit. In the quantum case patterns can be stored until the smallest Hamming distance between patterns becomes of the order of the localization radius æ.

QUANTUM BOOLEAN NET. Another interesting example of a purely quantum system that is capable of pattern recognition is quantum Boolean net: each node is connected to k<<N other nodes. The interaction part of the Hamiltonian is constructed in such manner that it takes one quanta from the preceding node and sends it to the current node only if the occupation numbers of the k neighbors match one of the stored patterns. Otherwise it does not work. Note that links in this model are not symmetric, however, this is a Hamiltonian model.

As numerical modeling shows, if the number of quanta in the system is not big enough and the input pattern is far from stored patterns, then nothing will happen, that means, the input state will remain localized, or there will be few local transitions back and forth. But if the input pattern is close to the stored pattern, and if the number of quanta exceeds a certain limit, then some quanta will jump, continuously changing the pattern around the "attractor", which is the stored pattern. In this case recognition means delocalization instead of localization, and it can be detected as appearance of quasicontinuous spectrum of states in the system, or as global conductivity. If now interaction with thermostat is added, then Bose condensation at the "attractor" is possible.

QUANTUM PERCEPTRON. The last model that we briefly discuss here is a quantum analog of a layered feed-forward neural network. Now the Hamiltonian is time-dependent, so that each link in the network is directed and interactions occur at given moments of time only. Roughly speaking the model can be viewed as a four dimensional Feynman graph with fixed topology and geometry, possessing some internal freedoms that are be computed under given boundary conditions. Some other fixed internal variables as well as the structure of the graph itself serve as memory of this network.

Thus, quantum perceptron is a QM model on a Feynman graph. By the way, it would be interesting to consider a nonlinear field theory model where these graphs appear in perturbation series, thus making one more connection between continuous nonlinear field models and neural networks with discrete subunits. However, this is beyond the scope of this paper.

Quantum perceptron seems to be an interesting model because: i) it does not require dissipation or pumping for information processing; ii) it can be truly quantum, i.e., it can process a quantum superposition of patterns at once.

The last circumstance allows to utilize advantages of the quantum way of computations that can lead to qualitatively different computer characteristics (Feynman, 1982; Rujan, 1988; Samsonovich, 1991).

Final remarks

Apart from their possible implementations, QNN models may be related to information processing that occurs in the cytoskeleton (Hameroff et al., 1992; Samsonovich et al., 1992). This will be the subject of another paper.

Acknowledgements

I am grateful to Alwyn Scott, Stuart Hameroff, Thom Kennedy, Judith Dayhoff, Stephen Grossberg, Thom McKenna for valuable discusions.

References

Feynman R.P. (1982) "Simulating physics with computers", Int.J.Theor.Phys. 21.467.

Feynman R.P. (1986) "Quantum mechanical computers", Found.Phys.16.6.507.

Goldschmidt Y.Y. (1990) "Solvable model of the quantum spin glass in a transverse field", Phys.Rev.B 41.7.4858.

Hameroff S.R., Dayhoff J.E., Lahoz-Beltra R., Samsonovich A.V., Rasmussen S. (Nov.1992) "conforomational automata in the cytoskeleton", Computer, p.30.

Hopfield J.J. (1982) Neural networks and physical systems with emergent collective computational abilities. PNAS 79.2554.

Lewenstein M., Olko M. (1992) "Storage capacity of "quantum" neural networks", Phys.Rev.A 45.12.8938.

Lloyd S. (Jan.1994) "A potentially realizable quantum computer", CNLS Newsletter, Los Alamos Natl.Lab., 97.1.

Pribram K.H., editor (1993) "Rethinking neural networks: quantum fields and biological data", Lawrence Erebaum Assoc. Pub., Chapter 2.

Ray P., Chakrabarti B.K., Chakrabarti A. (1989) "Sherrington-Kirkpatrick model in a transverse field: Absence of replica symmetry breaking due to quantum fluctuations", Phys.Rev.B 39.11828

Rujan P. (1988) "Searching for optimal configurations by simulated tunneling", Z.Phys.B 73.391.

Samsonovich A., Scott A., Hameroff S. (1992) "Acousto-conformational transitions in cytoskeletal microtubules: implications for intracellular information processing", Nanobiology 1.457.

Samsonovich A.V. (1991) "Molecular-level neuroelectronics", in: Lazarev P.I. (ed.), "Molecular electronics", Kluwer, p.241.

Weisbuch G., Stauffer D. (1987) "Phase transitions in cellular random Boolean nets", J.Physique 48.11.

Motion Interpretation of Trochoidal Paths*

Irwin K. King
king@cu.cuhk.hk

Michael A. Arbib
arbib@pollux.usc.edu

Department of Computer Science
The Chinese University of Hong Kong
Shatin, New Territories, Hong Kong

Center for Neural Engineering
University of Southern California
Los Angeles, CA 90089-2520

Abstract

This paper presents a simulation of neural networks for motion interpretation of trochoidal paths generated by points placed on a rotating disc translating in the frontoparallel plane of the visual field. We posit this motion interpretation process involves two mechanisms: first the extraction of *relative* rotational motion with respect to a moving point and second the presence of an attention mechanism that tracks the *common* motion. Specifically, the paper demonstrates simulation results for rotational motion extraction from trochoidal paths. We construct our neural network according to the directional and speed sensitivity profiles observed in neurophysiological data in the first stage of the network. The layer of neural network which is sensitive to the intermeditate spatiotemporal pattern of rotational motion is then assembled. Lastly, we show that without an attention mechanism the perception is insufficient to elicit a translating wheel perception. However, with an attention mechanism to track the center of the rotation, the rotating wheel is perceived readily.

1 Introduction

An object in motion produces different families of absolute motion trajectories with different points on it surface; however, often it could have a simple relative motion interpretation.[1] This phenomenon is demonstrated in Duncker's original experiment [5]. By placing light sources on a rotation and translating wheel in the frontoparallel plane, different trochoidal paths are formed with different points on the rotating disc despite that they are all rotating and translating at the same time with respect to the center of the wheel.

Several trochoids are possible with this type of configuration for motion interpretation (see Fig. 1). When only a single point is placed at the rim of the wheel, a cycloidal trajectory is observed. Its absolute motion generates no percept of a rotating wheel as shown in the solid line **C**. However, when the center point, e.g., the translatory line **A**, of the wheel is shown superimposed on the same cycloidal path generated by the point on the rim of the wheel, an impression of a rotation wheel is immediately available despite the fact the the point on the rim continues to trace out a cycloidal path.

---

*The research described in this paper was supported in part by a grant from the Center for Neural Engineering at USC, Los Angeles, CA (M. A. Arbib, principal investigator).

[1]The statement goes against the approach of motion interpretation based on measuring the absolute motion of moving objects. In biological organisms, it seems that relative motion interpretation is more important, relevant, and effective for the interpretation of moving objects than the absolute motion measurement.

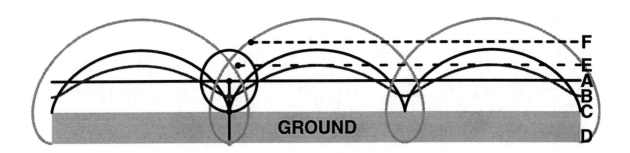

Figure 1: Trochoidal paths generated by different points on a disc which is rolling along on a straight line along the frontoparallel plane. The disc in this case is moving from left to right. The line **A** is the path traces out by the center (hub) of the rotating wheel, line **B** traces out a curtate cycloidal trajectory by a point between the center and the rim, line **C** traces out a perfectly cycloidal path, and line **D** etches a prolate cycloidal path by a point which lies outside of the rim of the wheel. Dashed lines **E** and **F** are two lines that are also translating lines superimposed with the cycloidal line **C**. However, they both are off-center points undergoing translatory motion.

Nonetheless, when the translatory point at the center of the wheel is moved to some external points off-center or outside of the rotating wheel, e.g., the dashed lines of **E** and **F**, subjects will only observe two independent motion paths with the same common motion.[2] The result indicates that it is necessary but insufficient to use the common motion of the object to interpret its movement. More importantly, it is far more crucial to fixate the attention mechanism at the *correct* point, i.e., the center of the rotation for a coherent interpretation than other off-center points in order to extract the underlying motion structure.

To explain the above observation, we hypothesize that two mechanisms must cooperate in order to produce the coherent translating rotational motion interpretation. First, an independent mechanism to detect in-place rotational motion is needed. This is backed by neurophysiological finding reported in [11, 10] where neuronal cells sensitive to intermediate motion such as contraction, expansion, and rotation were found in the MST area of macaque monkeys.

The other mechanism needed involves the tracking of the common motion in a meaningful way in order to obtain the relative motion within the common motion framework. Attention mechanism is natural for the visual system to locate meaningful moving points for the interpretation of the relative motion. Neurophysiological and psychophysical findings were reported in [4, 9, 8] to suggest that attention mechanisms can be used to extract relative motion for invariant motion interpretation.

2 Model Defined

To mimic plausible biological circuitries, our model is constructed in several stages. The first stage of the neural network is composed of motion detection cells as shown in Fig. 2 (a). The basic motion detection circuit follows the convention of the Elementary Movement Detector (EMD) proposed in [1, 2]. The information from the motion detection layer is then segregated and fed into the next layer to form a slab of a uniform motion selective layer shown in Fig. 2 (b). These layers are directional and speed sensitive with the sensitivity profiles shown in Fig. 2 (c) and (d). The connection masks in these layers are statically hard-wired in order to produce the profiles.

---

[2] When the point is within in the perimeter of the rotating wheel but not at the center, the perception of a rotating wheel seems to decrease gradually according to the distant away from the center. The interplay between common, absolute, and relative motions is discussed in [3].

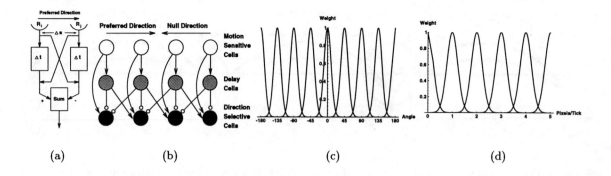

(a)   (b)   (c)   (d)

Figure 2: (a) A simple EMD network based on the spatiotemporal integration of two receptors R_i and R_j. (b) a slab of EMDs which assemble into a row of directional selective cells. (c) and (d) are the angle and speed profile of the neural network respectively.

Each layer has a specific orientation of preferred motion direction and its unique temporal delay constant to control the range of speed selectivity. The maximum neural activities in one specific layer corresponds to a stimulus moving in the preferred direction and also within the range of the preferred speeds. This is set by adjusting the size and the weight of the masks. The larger the mask, the larger the range of speed the layer can accommodate.

Previously, the author and colleagues have presented a plausible neural network for rotational motion extraction [6]. Moreover, neural networks for visual reversal and invariant motion perception was also dealt in [7]. The basic construction of the rotational circuit integrates the output activities of the distributed coding when perceiving a rotational motion from different layers in a sequential manner (see [10] for the plausible biological circuitries). The output of the rotational sensitive network contains excited neural activities at the center of the rotation motion.

Currently, we do not have a formal model for the attention mechanism. Instead, we simulate the effect of the attention mechanism via software through tracking a moving point. The functional property is performed by updating the position of the point undergoing the translatory motion whether it is the center or some points off-center of the rotational motion. A rotational sensitive mask is then dynamically coupled and shifted in time for the interpretation.

3   Simulation Results

The simulation was conducted on Unix workstations using the Neural Simulation Language (NSL)[12]. The size of the input is an array of size 15×60. Two trials are performed in 50 time steps (0 to 5.0 second in 0.1 second increment) for the wheel to make about two and a half rotation across the visual field.[3] The input to the neural network contains both the cycloidal motion with an external point either with or without the attention mechanism being activated. Figure 3 shows that without the attention mechanism, the activities in the rotational sensitive layer is unaffected by the stimulus since the network *sees* no rotational motion when the attention mechanism is solely focused on the point itself so the integration for rotation motion does not exist. However, when the center point which is translating horizontally with the common motion is presented along with the attention

---

[3]A typical run of a single trial takes about 4 to 5 minutes on a SPARC Classic workstation.

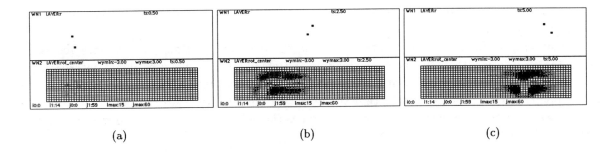

(a)   (b)   (c)

Figure 3: Simulation results for a rotational sensitive layer without the attention mechanism. The layer shows difficulties in integrating a consistent interpretation with different regions of the network activated in an incoherent manner.

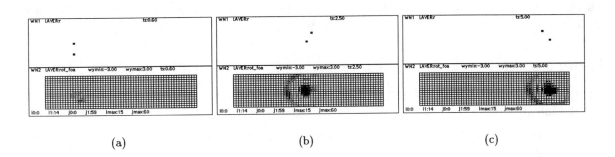

(a)   (b)   (c)

Figure 4: Simulation results for a rotational sensitive layer with the attention mechanism. The result shows that the rotational network with the attention mechanism proffers a coherent integration which renders a consistent motion interpretation of the rotational motion.

mechanism focused on the translating point, the neural activities in the rotational sensitive layer contains high activities indicating the presence of a rotational motion as shown in Fig. 4.

In the figures, there are two layers indicating the output. For the cycloidal path in Fig. 3, we only show the **rot_center** layer. The **rot_foa** layer as shown in the bottom of Fig. 4 is omitted for the first case since it does not have any activity at all when the attention mechanism is switched off.

Figure 3 shows that no integration is apparent. The neural activities are distributed without a coherent activation. However, Figure 4 illustrates that once a full revolution is made, a distinct activation at the center of the rotation, in this case is also equivalent to the point of focus, is apparent.

4   Discussions

The software implementation of the attention mechanism is very similar to a shift circuit that dynamically displaces the rotational sensitive network to the focal point which is the center of the rotating wheel for the proper interpretation of relative motions [8]. This also explains why the perception of the rotation decreases when the external translatory point is placed to locations that are off-center since the rotational sensitive layers will receive less integration when the focus is off-center.

The simulation further demonstrates that it is the invariant motion features with respect to the center of rotation that are most meaningful and should guide the subsequent interpretation process. However, we have not deal the problem of how the attention mechanism attends to the *correct* point. Although we speculate that the attention mechanism takes the point with the most simple trajectory that matches the common motion as the point of interpretation of relative motion, further studies will be needed to verify the above conjuncture.

5   Conclusion

From the simulation result, we conclude that two mechanisms must cooperate to elicit the percept of a rotating wheel when presented with trochoidal paths. First, a neural connection mask capable of extracting rotational motion path is needed. Second, an attentional mechanism must cooperate with the rotational motion sensitive network to dynamically track and integrate the relative motion path into a consistent motion perception of the movement.

References

[1] H. B. Barlow and Richard M. Hill. Selective sensitivity to direction of movement in ganglion cells of the rabbit retina. *Science*, 139:412–414, 1963.

[2] H. B. Barlow and W. R. Levick. The mechanism of directionally selective units in rabbit's retina. *Journal of Physiology*, 178:477–504, 1965.

[3] James E. Cutting and Dennis R. Proffitt. The minimum principle and the perception of absolute, common, and relative motions. *Cognitive Psychology*, 14:211–246, 1982.

[4] R. M. Davidson and D. B. Bender. Selectivity for relative motion in the monkey superior colliculus. *Journal Of Neurophysiology*, 65(5):1115–33, 1991.

[5] K. Duncker. Uber induzierte bewegung. *Psychol. Forsch.*, 12:180–259, 1929.

[6] I. King, J. Liaw, and M. A. Arbib. A neural network for the detection of rotational motion. In *International Joint Conference on Neural Networks*, volume 1, pages 707–712, Seattle, WA, 1991. IEEE Computer Society.

[7] I. King and M. A. Arbib. A neural network model for extracting visual motion reversal invariant events. In *International Joint Conference on Neural Networks*, Beijing, 1992. IEEE Computer Society.

[8] B. A. Olshausen and D. C. Anderson, C. H.; Van Essen. A neurobiological model of visual-attention and invariant pattern-recognition based on dynamic routing of information. *JOURNAL OF NEURO-SCIENCE*, 13(11):4700–4719, 1993.

[9] D. Regan. Visual processing of four kinds of relative motion. *Vision Res.*, 26(1):127–45, 1986.

[10] K. Tanaka, Y. Fukada, and H. A. Saito. Underlying mechanisms of the response specificity of expansion/contraction and rotation cells in the dorsal part of the medial superior temporal area of the macaque monkey. *J. Neurophysiol.*, 62(3):642–56, 1989.

[11] K. Tanaka and H. Saito. Analysis of motion of the visual field by direction, expansion/contraction, and rotation cells clustered in the dorsal part of the medial superior temporal area of the macaque monkey. *J. Neurophysiol.*, 62(3):626–41, 1989.

[12] Alfredo Weitzenfeld. NSL - Neural Simulation Language version 2.1. Technical report, University of Southern California, 1991.

Principles of Neural Computation
from the Evolution of Neural-like Systems

Alan M. Horowitz
Department of Mathematics
Thackeray Hall
University of Pittsburgh
Pittsburgh, PA 15260
horowitz@neurocog.lrdc.pitt.edu

Abstract: Biologically realistic, neural-like systems were evolved in computer simulations to solve a variety of life-like dynamical problems. Problem-independent properties of the networks were found which suprisingly also prevail in real nervous systems. These include inequalities between inhibitory and excitatory parameters, and the tendency of neurons to cluster into feed-forward inhibitory and other biologically common circuits. A simple scheme for connecting the neurons, based on idealized axons and dendrites was found to have advantages over full connectivity, because of its relative sparcity in connections and parameters and superior scaling behavior with network size.

While an enormous wealth of detail has accumulated from research in neurophysiology, general principles are scarce. One way to look for them, which bypasses the complexity of real nervous systems, is to evolve idealized neural-like systems in computer simulations. While the feasibility of developing control systems by this approach has recently been demonstrated [1,2], no attempt was made to make detailed links to neurobiology. The results from the simulations reported below (or in greater detail in ref. 3) suggest that biological features, beyond the minimal features commonly incorporated till now, can be useful in man-made networks, and conversely that evolved properties of artificial networks may shed light on neurophysiology. That this two-way exchange between real and artificial networks can be more fruitfully exploited is the main thrust of this paper.

The dynamics of the networks, given by the following equations, are generalizations of those popularized by Hopfield [4], Grossberg [5] and others:

$$\dot{V}_i + \lambda_V(V_i - V_r) = J_{syn,i} + J_{sensory,i} \, , \tag{1a}$$

$$J_{syn,i} = \bar{g}_{EE}(V_E - V_i)\sum_{j \in E} w_{ji} m_{E,j} + \bar{g}_{IE}(V_I - V_i)\sum_{k \in I} w_{ki} m_{I,k} \tag{1b}$$

$$\dot{m}_{E,i}(t) = \sigma_E(V(t)) - \lambda_E m_E. \tag{1c}$$

Neurons are exclusively excitatory (E) or inhibitory (I). In eq. 1 neuron i is E. If it were I, replace $(\bar{g}_{EE}, \bar{g}_{IE})$ by $(\bar{g}_{EI}, \bar{g}_{II})$ and in eq. 1c, E by I. In eq. 1, V corresponds to membrane potential, J_{syn} to incoming synaptic current, and $J_{sensory}$ to external input, while V_r and $1/\lambda_V$ correspond to the membrane resting potential and relaxation time, respectively. Units are defined such that $V_r = -1$ and $\lambda_V = 1$, while V_E and V_I were fixed to 0 and -1.3, respectively. The function, $\sigma(V)$, corresponding in biology to firing frequency, is a threshold-type function of V as depicted in Fig. 1a. Biological motivation for this form can be found in ref. 6. The synaptic weights w_{ij}, restricted to the interval [0,1], are time-independent: there is no synaptic plasticity. The nets acquire their problem-solving abilities through evolution of parameters between generations.

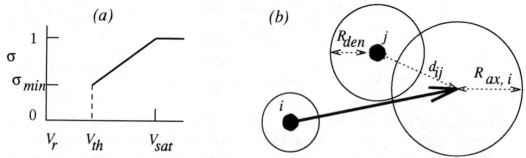

FIGURE 1. (a) The neuron output function; (b) The Axden scheme for w_{ij}.

In networks used by Hopfield [4] and Grossberg [5], synaptic transmission is instantaneous: $m(t) = \sigma(t)$, instead of dynamical as in eq. 1c. I found that, except for problems requiring very fast processing, the evolution procedure was more efficient on networks with dynamical transmission, apparently due to the presence of the 2 extra time scales ($1/\lambda_E$ and $1/\lambda_I$), enabling more versatile temporal behaviors with less fine-tuning of parameters.

To remain of practical interest, the parametrization and evolution procedure must scale well as the network size and problem complexity is increased. The parameters scaling with network size specify the w_{ij}. Full or naive connectivity, with an independent w_{ij} for each pair of neurons, entails N^2 parameters and connections for N neurons. In real nervous systems the number of connections scales more like N, since the number of connections a neuron makes is usually independent of the total number of neurons. I empirically compared the naive scheme to a scheme abstracted from neurobiology, which I call the Axden scheme.

In the Axden scheme the neurons sit on the nodes of an N_x by N_y rectangular lattice, ($N = N_x \times N_y$). When the axon field of neuron i intersects the dendritic field of j as shown in Fig. 1b, the weight is defined as

$$w_{ij} = 1 - \frac{d_{ij}}{R_{ax}(i) + R_{den}(j)}, \tag{2}$$

For each neuron there are 4 real-valued architecture parameters: x, y, R_{ax}, and R_{den}. That makes $4N$ in total. The number of connections is also linear in N assuming the optimal values of R_{ax} and R_{den} are independent of N, or at least approximately so. The linearity in N of the number of parameters and connections gives the Axden scheme two strong, practical advantages over the naive scheme. For one, optimization schemes converge faster with fewer parameters. Secondly, in a simulation, the computer time required to integrate the equations of the network is proportional to the number of connections.

The task of the evolution procedure is to maximize the fitness F, a functional of the network output, by varying both the dynamics parameters ($V_{th,E(I)}$, $V_{sat,E(I)}$, $\sigma_{min,E(I)}$, $\lambda_{E(I)}$, $\bar{g}_{EE}$, $\bar{g}_{IE}$, $\bar{g}_{EI}$, $\bar{g}_{II}$), and the architectural parameters (x_i, y_i, $R_{ax,i}$, $R_{den,i}$ for the Axden scheme, or w_{ij} for full connectivity). This was done with a simulated annealing algorithm, based on small stochastic variations of the parameters (correlated with previously successful variations), augmented with sporadic "mutations" of the architectural parameters. The neuron-type (I or E) of the interneurons (non-I/O neurons) also evolves. Between each generation, there is a small probability to flip the neuron-type at any given interneuron site.

A typical run consists of a few thousand generations (i.e. evaluations of F), beginning with random architecture. Usually multiple runs, with different random number seeds, were required in order to find, and be confident of having found, the global maximum.

An application

The application presented here is a life-like variational problem in one space dimension. A point-like bug is free to move along a line. "He" begins at $x = 0$. Food sits to the right, at $x = 4.8$. The bug loses energy (E) due to his motion and gains energy when he eats. He must stop to eat. The problem is to evolve bugs to maximize the fitness $F = \Delta E / \Delta t - \beta u_f^2$, where ΔE is the net change in energy from $t = 0$ until Δt when the food is eaten, and u_f is the final velocity when food is reached: $u_f = 0$ is achieved in the limit $\beta \to \infty$. The results below are with $\beta = 1$. To maximize F the bug must adjust his velocity u as a function of time to get to the food quickly, but without expending too much energy.

Newton's law for the bug's motion is $\dot{u} = 2(\sigma_R - \sigma_L)$, where σ_R and σ_L are the output functions of the right- and left-propelling motor neurons, M_R and M_L. The rate of energy loss due to motion is defined as $\dot{E} = -10(\sigma_R^2 + \sigma_L^2)$. The food supplies $\Delta E = 5$.

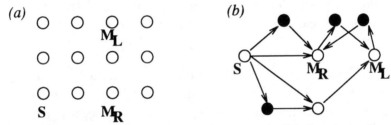

FIGURE 2. (a) Architecture used for the application; (b) Statistically significant connections found. Filled circles are inhibitory.

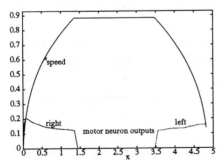

FIGURE 3. Speed and outputs of M_R and M_L vs. distance for the fittest bug found.

The net predominantly used on this problem had 12 neurons, as shown in Fig. 2a. The geometrical properties of this network are of course only relevant for the Axden scheme. To emulate olfactory input, the input to the sensory neuron S increases as the distance d to the food decreases: $J_{sensory} \equiv 3/(d + 1)$.

Fig. 3 shows $u(x)$, $\sigma_R(x)$, and $\sigma_L(x)$ for the best network-produced solution to this problem ($F_c = .449$). Note the approximate left-right symmetry of the plots, coming from the time-reversal symmetry of the problem. That the network found a solution with this symmetry strengthens the case for this being the optimal solution.

Par.	Init.	a. $V_I = -1.3$		b. $V_I = -2.0$	
		Av.	St. dev.	Av.	St. dev.
$V_{th,E}$	-.99f				
$V_{th,I}$	-.95f				
$V_{sat,E}$	-.20	-.08	.23	-.05	.22
$V_{sat,I}$	-.20	-.06	.23	-.10	.22
$\sigma_{min,E}$	.10f				
$\sigma_{min,I}$	.10	.48	.22	.38	.21
λ_E	.70	.99	.65	.71	.42
λ_I	.70	.44	.32	.50	.29
$\bar{g}_{EE}$	.80	.74	.34	.81	.37
$\bar{g}_{IE}$	.80	1.21	.50	1.10	.52
$\bar{g}_{EI}$	.80	1.06	.45	.98	.31
$\bar{g}_{II}$	.80	.88	.55	.91	.45

TABLE 1. *Averages, standard deviations and initial values of evolved dynamics parameters for 2 values of V_I. An 'f' means 'held fixed'. The data comprises 52 and 39 parameter sets for $V_I = -1.3$ and -2.0, respectively. Assuming normal distributions, the statistical uncertainties in the averages can be obtained from the standard deviations by dividing by $\sqrt{52}$ or $\sqrt{39}$.*

Networks with neurons connected with the Axden scheme gave comparable results to fully connected networks. Also, the results depended little on network size, based on simulations with 8, 12 and 20 neurons. The evolution procedure converged slower on average with fully connected nets, by tens of percent, which is not much considering the relatively large number of connection parameters (144 on a 12 neuron net, compared with 48 with the Axden scheme). The CPU time for a 12 neuron net was about a factor of 2 higher with full connectivity.

Different sets of parameter values can produce nearly optimal fitness values. It is important to know what the important parameters are, and what trends can be discerned in the values. Table 1 gives the averages and standard deviations of the final parameters of successful runs - $F_c > .4$ for all of them - differing only by random number seeds (and thus initial architectures). The values of $V_{th,E}$, $V_{th,I}$, and $\sigma_{min,E}$ were fixed to values gleaned from previous runs. In all 6 applications, $V_{th,E}$ and $\sigma_{min,E}$, and in this application $V_{th,I}$ as well, were the most sensitive parameters: they had the smallest standard deviations. Fixing them improved the probability of a run being successful, in this case by a factor of 3 or so. The contents of Table 1 will be discussed further below.

The connectivity

The connectivity of 125 successful Axden-connected nets with $F_c > .4$ was examined. On average, each neuron synapsed to 4.8 others. Of the interneurons, 55% were inhibitory.

In 124 of the nets the sensory neuron S directly excited the right-propelling motor neuron M_R, and in 123 also inhibited it via at least one I neuron, as shown in Fig. 2b. This so-called feedforward inhibitory circuit is ubiquitous in biological nervous systems. The statistical significance of these and other connections were assessed by comparing their frequency with that in the same 125 nets but with randomized axon endpoints and randomly permuted interneurons. For more details see ref. 3. Fig. 2b summarizes the results for the most commonly occuring and statistically significant connections found in the 125 nets. Note that: 1) input to E interneurons from S also preferred to be in the form of feedforward inhibition; 2) the antagonistic motor neurons M_R and M_L preferred to mutually inhibit each other via pathways with one I interneuron; 3) the preferred path from S to M_L went through a single E interneuron, which served to delay the excitation to M_L.

Other applications

I now list the other 5 applications on which extensive simulations were made:
1) a one-dimensional food-finding task, the same as above, except there is drag on the bug, and u_f is unconstrained. This is a simpler problem. The optimal $u(t)$ was produced by a network with only 4 neurons.
2) a two-dimensional food-finding task. The bug, confined by a circular wall, was evolved to track 3 pieces of food in random configurations. This was the most elaborate and lifelike application. Because of the variability of the environment (i.e. the food configuration), the fitness had to be averaged over several environments. The bug had right and left retinal neurons and a visual field 34° wide, received sensory input when against the wall, and had motor neurons for forward motion and rotation. The most highly evolved bug had 20 neurons.
3) balancing an inverted pendulum by applying forces to the cart on which it is hinged. This is a popular test problem for control methodologies. The fitness is defined as $-\int dt \, \theta^2(t)$, where θ is the deviation from vertical. Networks were evolved to balance poles of any length, as well as to simultaneously balance two poles on the same cart.
4) differential equation solving. The fitness is a functional F of the output σ_{out} of a chosen neuron, as well as of $\dot\sigma_{out}$. The condition that F be extremal is equivalent to the condition that σ_{out} satisfies a second order differential equation. To gauge the accuracy of the method, I made simulations only for a quadratic functional, where F_{max} and σ_{out} could be computed analytically. Within 5000 generations the network attained attained 5 and 4 significant digit accuracy in F_{max} and σ_{out}, respectively.
5) oscillatory function-fitting. As is well known, a 2 neuron system, an E and I neuron coupled together (with self-connections allowed), can oscillate. The system was evolved so that the output of the E neuron fit various waveforms (sinusoid, sawtooth and square wave).

Network properties and neurobiology

Table 1 reveals statistically significant inequalities between averages of corresponding E and I parameters. These inequalities also occurred in the other applications even though the initial E and I parameters in each run were set equal. Comparing Tables 1a and 1b one sees that one contribution to the E-I asymmetry comes from the asymmetric positioning of reversal potentials: in 1a, V_I is closer to V_r than is V_E, the consequences of which can be understood from the factors of $(V - V_{I(E)})$ in eq. 1b. However even with symmetric positioning as used in Table 1b, the inequalities remain. It is intriguing that the inequalities also hold widely in biological nervous systems, especially those which, like the artificial systems, have both a clean division between E and I neurons, and E input and output. The inequalities are now listed, along with biological support, mostly from the mammalian nervous system (neurobiological facts not cited can be found in ref. 7 or 8):

1) $\lambda_E > \lambda_I$: the time scale $(1/\lambda_I)$ for the action of I transmitter is longer than for E. This was observed in all applications except for the 2-neuron oscillatory system, where $\lambda_E \approx \lambda_I$. In the brain, the predominant I transmitter is GABA, the effects of which are longer lasting (through receptor channels A or B) than the most common mediating (as opposed to modulating) E transmitter, glutamate. In the spinal cord, the synaptic action of the glycine-emitting Ia inhibitory interneurons is likewise longer than, though sometimes comparable to that of E neurons [9].

2) $\bar{g}_{IE} > \bar{g}_{EE}$: synaptic coupling to E neurons is stronger from I than from E neurons. This was observed in all applications except the pole-balancing problem, where $\bar{g}_{IE} \approx \bar{g}_{EE}$. The inequality is manifested in real nervous systems by the tendency of I synapses to land closer to the cell bodies and axon hillocks of E neurons than E synapses [10]. This E-I asymmetry was observed in the simulations, not only in terms of the $\bar{g}$s, but also directly in terms of the w_{ij} within the Axden scheme, where the asymmetry is topological as in biology.

3) $\bar{g}_{EI} > \bar{g}_{EE}$: synaptic coupling from E neurons is stronger to I than to E neurons. This was observed in all applications except the pole-balancing problem, where $\bar{g}_{EI} \approx \bar{g}_{EE}$. In cortex, for example, most of the E synapses on E neurons (pyramidal and stellate cells) are on dendritic spines, whereas on I neurons they are directly on dendritic shafts. Presumably synapses on shafts have higher efficacy. Also, E synapses can land directly on the soma of I but not E neurons [10].

4) $\sigma_{min,I} > \sigma_{min,E}$: the output level at and near threshold is higher for I neurons. This was observed in all applications. In reflex circuits in the spinal cord, for example, the fastest spiking cells, the Renshaw cells, are inhibitory. The same is true in the cortex: the smooth (I) cells spike faster than pyramidal (E) cells [11].

5) $V_{th,E} < V_{th,I}$: E neurons are easier to excite than I neurons. This was observed in all applications. It is not suprising, since if the inequality were reversed, it might be hard for the network to generate any activity; there could be too much inhibition. In some applications $V_{th,E} < V_r$, meaning that E neurons were active even when $V = V_r$. In guinea pig cortex *in vitro* [12] and in anesthetized cat cortex [13], the frequency of spontaneous E postsynaptic potentials (EPSPs) was observed to exceed that of spontaneous IPSPs by a large factor (10 in the cats), providing some indirect corroboration of inequality 5, at least in effect. More direct evidence, reported in the same papers, comes from experiments with injected current. As the current was increased, the level of EPSP activity increased until the onset of a long duration, strong hyperpolarizing IPSP, presumably via GABA$_B$ channels.

While inequality 5 may be realized in the cortex it is not a general rule of neurobiology. For example, the circuit which controls saccadic eye movements, contains tonically active I cells (the Pause cells). However this circuit also violates the condition under which the inequality was observed, namely that sensory input is excitatory. The fact that information from input to output is carried by E signals almost certainly contributes to the above inequalities, as does the need for I input to a neuron to follow E input.

Another network feature, besides parameter inequalities, common to all applications, was the tendency of the input neurons to feedforward inhibit (i.e. simultaneously excite and, via one interneuron, inhibit) E neurons, including the output neuron, as shown in Fig. 2b. Feedforward inhibition is ubiquitous in real nervous systems, especially in sensory pathways. It ensures that E signals are followed by proportional I signals.

Besides feedforward inhibition, other biologically familiar connections were found to be statistically significant, such as reciprocal inhibition between antagonistic motor neurons, as in Fig. 2b. In the differential-equation solving problem, a so-called synaptic triad - feedforward inhibition, but with feedback to the I neuron - was found.

The Axden scheme performed comparably to full connectivity on all problems, except on the most difficult problem, the 2-dimensional food-finding problem, where it was superior - in 40 runs with fully connected networks starting from random architecture, no good solutions were found, whereas in 10 runs with the Axden scheme, 3 produced bugs able to efficiently track the food. It is reassuring that a scheme for connecting the neurons based on axons and dendrites is at least as computationally effective as full connectivity. The latter is cumbersome and unnecessary.

In conclusion, evolving biologically realistic networks appears to be a promising way to get insights into real nervous systems, and at the same time may lead to useful devices.

References

1. Beer, R.D. and Gallagher, J.C. *Adaptive Behavior* 1, 91-122 (1992).
2. Husbands, P., Harvey, I. and Cliff, D. in: *Proc. third IEEE Int. Conf. on Artificial Neural Nets* (IEEE press, 1993).
3. Horowitz, A.M. Technical Report MTH-93-9/25.
4. Hopfield, J.J. *Proc. Natn. Acad. Sci.* 81, 3088-3092 (1984).
5. Grossberg, S. *Neural Networks and Natural Intelligence* (MIT Press, Cambridge, 1988).
6. Kleinfeld, D., Raccuia-Behling, F. and Chiel, H.J. *Biophys. J.* 57, 697-715 (1990).
7. Kandel, E., Schwarz, J. and Jessel, T. *Principle of Neural Science* (Elsevier Press, New York, 1991).
8. Shepherd, G. *The Synaptic Organization of the Brain* (Oxford University Press, New York, 1990).
9. Burke, R.E., and Rudomin, P. In: *Handbook of Physiology, Section 1: The Nervous System, Vol. 1.* (ed. E.R. Kandel). pp 877-944 (American Physiological Society, Bethesda, 1977).
10. White, E.L. *Cortical Circuits* (Birkhäuser Press, Boston, 1989).
11. Connors, B.W. and Kriegstein, A.R. *J. Neurosci.* 6, 164-177 (1986).
12. Connors, B.W., Gutnick, M.J. and Prince, D.A. *J. Neurophysiol.* 48, 1302-1320 (1982).
13. Creutzenfeldt, O.D., Lux, H.D. and Wantabe, S. in: *The Thalamus* (eds. D.P. Purpura and M. Yahr). pp 209-235 (Columbia University Press, New York, 1966).